Poland

THE ROUGH GUIDE

There are more than one hundred Rough Guide titles
covering destinations from Amsterdam to Zimbabwe

Forthcoming titles include
Jamaica • New Zealand • South Africa • Southwest USA

Rough Guide Reference Series
Classical Music • The Internet • Jazz • Rock Music • World Music • Opera

Rough Guide Phrasebooks
Czech • French • German • Greek • Hindi & Urdu • Indonesian •Italian
Mandarin Chinese • Mexican Spanish • Polish • Portuguese
Russian • Spanish • Thai • Turkish • Vietnamese

Rough Guides on the Internet
http://www.roughguides.com/
http://www.hotwired.com/rough

Rough Guide Credits

Text Editor:	Jo Mead
Series Editor:	Mark Ellingham
Editorial:	Martin Dunford, Jonathan Buckley, Samantha Cook, Alison Cowan, Amanda Tomlin, Annie Shaw, Paul Gray, Vivienne Heller, Sarah Dallas, Chris Schüler, Helena Smith, Kirk Marlowe, Julia Kelly
Online:	Alan Spicer (UK), Andrew Rosenberg (US)
Production:	Susanne Hillen, Andy Hilliard, Melissa Flack, Judy Pang, Link Hall, Nicola Williamson, David Callier, Helen Ostick
Marketing & Publicity:	Richard Trillo, Simon Carloss, Niki Smith (UK), Jean-Marie Kelly (US)
Finance:	John Fisher, Celia Crowley, Catherine Gillespie
Administration:	Tania Hummel, Mark Rogers

Acknowledgements

Mark Salter would like to thank Chris for his hard work on Silesia, Pomerania and Wielkopolska; Simon Broughton for infectious enthusiasm for the music and *cerkwi* updates; Stanisław Cydzik of the Polish National Tourist Office; Jacek Grzelak and staff at *Orbis*, Stockholm for their invaluable practical assistance; Tatiana Tobolewicz in Kraków; Andrzej Nowodworski in Lublin; (as ever) Adam, Anya and family in Gdańsk; Mia and Hannah for their support; and last but not least, 'nuff respect to Jo at the Rough Guides office for her thorough and discerning editing of this edition.

Thanks also to Narrell Leffman and Jeanne Muchnick for "Getting There" updates; Jane Bainbridge for proofreading; Sam Kirby for map production; and Ronan Gallagher at Irish Academic Press and Emma Sinclair-Webb at I.B. Tauris for extracts permissions; and all the readers who have written in, see p.xii.

The publishers and authors have done their best to ensure the accuracy and currency of all information in *The Rough Guide to Poland*; however, they can accept no responsibility for any loss, injury, or inconvenience sustained by any traveller as a result of information or advice contained in the guide.

This third edition published May 1996 by Rough Guides Ltd, 1 Mercer Street, London WC2H 9QJ.
Reprinted in June 1997.

Distributed by the Penguin Group:

Penguin Books Ltd, 27 Wrights Lane, London W8 5TZ
Penguin Books USA Inc., 375 Hudson Street, New York 10014, USA
Penguin Books Australia Ltd, 487 Maroondah Highway, PO Box 257, Ringwood, Victoria 3134, Australia
Penguin Books Canada Ltd, 10 Alcorn Avenue, Toronto, Ontario, Canada M4V 1E4
Penguin Books (NZ) Ltd, 182–190 Wairau Road, Auckland 10, New Zealand

Typeset in Linotron Univers and Century Old Style to an original design by Andrew Oliver.
Printed in the United Kingdom by Cox and Wyman Ltd (Reading).
Illustrations in Part One and Part Three by Edward Briant; illustrations on p.1 and p.605 by Henry Iles.

704p. Includes index.

A catalogue record for this book is available from the British Library.

ISBN 1-85828-168-7

Poland

THE ROUGH GUIDE

Written and researched by
Mark Salter and Gordon McLachlan

Additional updates by
Chris Scott

THE ROUGH GUIDES

LIST OF MAPS

MAP SYMBOLS

GENERAL SYMBOLS

———	Main road
———	Road
———	Minor road
- - - - -	Path
+—+—+—	Railway
— —	Ferry route
▪▪▬▪▬▪	National border
▬▬ ▬▬	Chapter division boundary
✈	Airport
⌂	Campsite
⌂	Hostel
⌧	Border crossing
◆	Point of interest
+	Church
⚞	Concentration camp

⌃⌃	Mountain range
▲	Mountain peak

TOWN MAP SYMBOLS

═══	Road
▨▨▨	Pedestrianized road
———	Railway
▪▪▪▪	Wall
(i)	Tourist office
⌧	Post office
◼	Building
⊞	Church
+++	Christian cemetery
✿✿	Jewish cemetery
▨▨▨	Park

CONTENTS

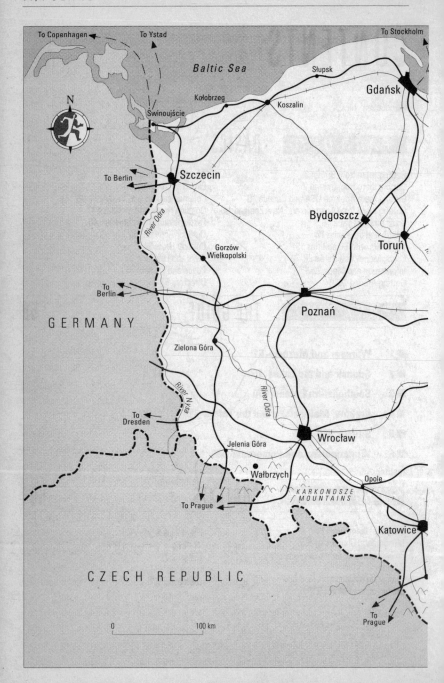

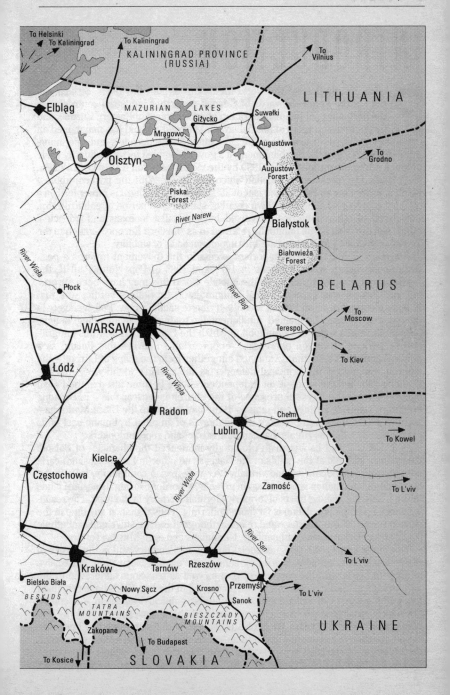

INTRODUCTION

Polish images flooded the world media throughout the 1980s. Strikes and riots at the Lenin shipyards of Gdańsk and other industrial centres were the harbingers of the disintegration of communism in Eastern Europe, and throughout the years of martial law and beyond, Poland has maintained an exemplary momentum towards political change. At the decade's end, the annus mirabilis of 1989 saw the establishment of a government led by the Solidarity trade union, a development followed in 1990 by the victory of union leader Lech Wałęsa in Poland's first presidential election since the 1920s. With the post-communist political order now an established fact of life, the media spotlight is rather less on a country enjoying what is, by its own peculiar standards, a period of political calm. Compared to other countries convulsed by nationalist tensions and fratricidal ethnic wars in what is still habitually referred to as "Eastern Europe" – much to the locals' annoyance – Poland can at times appear an oasis of stability.

For many Poles, the most important events in the movement towards a post-communist society were the visits in 1979 and 1983 of Pope John Paul II, the former archbishop of Kraków. To the outside world this may have been surprising, but Poland was never a typical communist state: Stalin's verdict was that imposing communism on Poland was like trying to saddle a cow. Polish society in the postwar decades remained fundamentally traditional, maintaining beliefs, peasant life and a sense of nationhood to which the Catholic Church was integral. During periods of foreign oppression – oppression so severe that Poland as a political entity has sometimes vanished altogether from the maps of Europe – the Church was always the principal defender of the nation's identity, so that the Catholic faith and the struggle for independence have become fused in the Polish consciousness. The physical presence of the church is inescapable – in Baroque buildings, roadside shrines and images of the national icon, the Black Madonna – and the determination to preserve the memories of an often traumatic past finds expression in religious rituals that can both attract and repel onlookers.

World War II and its aftermath profoundly influenced the character of Poland: the country suffered at the hands of the Nazis as no other in Europe, losing nearly one quarter of its population and virtually its entire Jewish community. In 1945 the Soviet-dominated nation was once again given new borders, losing its eastern lands to the USSR and gaining tracts of formerly German territory in the west. The resulting make-up of the population is far more uniformly "Polish" than at any time in the past, in terms of both language and religion, though there are still significant ethnic minorities of Belarussians, Lithuanians, Ukrainians and even Muslim Tartars.

To a great extent, the sense of social fluidity, of a country still in the throes of major transitions, remains a primary source of Poland's fascination. A decisive attempt to break with the communist past as well as tenacious adherence to the path of radical market economic reforms adopted in the late 1980s have remained the guiding tenets of Poland's post-communist political leadership – a course seemingly unaltered by the election in 1993 of a government led by ex-communists, nor two years later, of a president of the same political hue. Few would question the economic and human toll reaped by Poland's attempt to reach the eldorado of capitalist prosperity. Despite this, the Polish people, as so often before, continue to demonstrate what to the visitor may appear an extraordinary resilience and patience. Hope springs eternal in the minds of Poles, it seems, and for all the hardships involved in establishing a new economic order – an order to which the majority of Poles retain a remarkable, if grumbling, political commitment – individual initiative and enterprise of every conceivable kind is flourishing as almost nowhere else in the region. By 1993 the first tentative signs of the much hoped for economic recovery were beginning to make themselves apparent. By 1996, many aspects – not least a projected annual growth in GDP of six percent and upwards for the foreseeable future – pointed to an overall economic upturn strong enough to earn the country a place among the world's Top Ten "boom economies" in official financial ratings. Tourism is proving no exception to the general "all change" rule, but despite the continuing state of flux in the country's tourist infrastructure, it is now easier – if not, given the continuing alarming rise in crime, always safer – to explore Poland than anyone could have imagined only a few years back. This sea change is reflected in continuing and significant increases in the numbers of people visiting the country.

Encounters with the people are at the core of any experience of the country. On trains and buses, on the streets or in the village bar, you'll never be stuck for opportunities for contact: Polish hospitality is legendary, and there's a natural progression from a chance meeting to an introduction to the extended family. Even the most casual visitor might be served a prodigious meal at any hour of the day, usually with a bottle or two of local vodka brought out from the freezer.

Where to go

Poles delineate their country's attractions as "the mountains, the sea and the lakes", their emphasis firmly slanted to the traditional, rural heartlands. To get the most out of your time, it's perhaps best to follow their preferences. The **mountains** – above all the Carpathian range of the Tatras – are a delight, with a well-established network of hiking trails; the **lakes** provide opportunities for canoeing and a host of other outdoor pursuits; and the dozen or so **national parks** retain areas of Europe's last primeval forests, inhabited still by bisons, elks, wolves, bears and eagles. Yet you will not want to miss the best of the **cities** – Kraków, especially – nor a ramble down rivers like the Wisła for visits to Teutonic **castles**, ancient waterside towns and grand, Polish **country mansions**, redolent of a vanished aristocratic order. The **ethnic regions** offer insights into cultures quite distinct from the Catholicism of the majority, while the former centres of the **Jewish** community, and the concentration camps in which the Nazis carried out their extermination, are the most moving testimony to the complexity and tragedy of the nation's past.

Unless you're driving to Poland, you're likely to begin your travels with one of the three major **cities**: Warsaw, Kraków or Gdańsk. Each provides an immediate immersion in the fast-paced changes of the 1990s and a backdrop of monuments that reveal the complexities of the nation's history.

Warsaw, the capital, had to be rebuilt from scratch after the war, and much of the city conforms to the stereotype of Eastern European greyness, but the reconstructed Baroque palaces, churches and public buildings of the historic centre, the burgeoning street markets and the bright shopfronts of Poland's new enterprise culture are diverting enough. **Kraków**, however, the ancient royal capital, is the real crowd puller for Poles and foreign visitors alike, rivalling the Central European elegance of Prague and Vienna. This is the city where history hits you most powerfully, in the royal Wawel complex, in the fabulous open space of the Rynek, in the one-time Jewish quarter of Kazimierz, and in the chilling necropolis of nearby Auschwitz-Birkenau, the bloodiest killing field of the Third Reich. **Gdańsk**, formerly Danzig, the largest of the Baltic ports and home of the legendary shipyards, presents a dynamic brew of politics and commerce against a townscape reminiscent of mercantile towns in the Netherlands.

German and Prussian influences abound in the **north** of the country, most notably in the austere castles and fortified settlements constructed by the Teutonic Knights at **Malbork**, **Chełmno**, and other strategic points along the **River Wisła** – as the Vistula is known in Poland. **Toruń** is one of the most atmospheric and beautiful of the old Hanseatic towns here.

Over in the **east**, numerous minority communities embody the complexities of national boundaries in Central Europe. The one-time Jewish centre of **Białystok**, with its Belarussian minority, is a springboard for the eastern borderlands, where onion-domed Orthodox churches stand close to Tartar mosques. Further south, beyond **Lublin**, a famous centre of Hasidic Jewry, and **Zamość**, with its magnificent Renaissance centre, lie the homelands of Ukrainians, Lemks and Boyks – and a chance to see some of Poland's extraordinary wooden churches.

In the **west**, ethnic Germans populated regions of the divided province of **Silesia**, where **Wrocław** sustains the dual cultures of the former German city of Breslau and the Ukrainian city of L'viv, whose displaced citizens were moved here at the war's end. The other main city in western Poland is the quintessentially Polish **Poznań**, revered as the cradle of the nation, and today a vibrant and increasingly prosperous university town.

Despite its much-publicized pollution problems, Poland has many regions of unspoilt natural beauty, of which none is more pristine than the **Białowieża forest**, straddling the Belarussian border; the last virgin forest of the European mainland, it is the habitat of the largest surviving herd of European bison. Along the southern borders of the country lie the wild **Bieszczady** mountains and the alpine **Tatras** and further west, the bleak **Karkonosze** mountains – all of them excellent walking country, interspersed with less demanding terrain. North of the central Polish plain, the wooded lakelands of **Mazury** and **Pomerania** are as tranquil as any lowland region on the continent, while the Baltic coast can boast not just the domesticated pleasures of its beach resorts, but also the extraordinary desert-like dunes of the **Słowinski Park** – one of a dozen National Parks.

When to go

Spring is arguably the ideal season for some serious hiking in Poland's mountainous border regions, as the days tend to be bright – if showery – and the distinctive flowers are at their most profuse. **Summer**, the tourist high season, sees plenty of sun, particularly on the Baltic coast, where the resorts are crowded from June to August and temperatures consistently around 24°C. The major cities can get pretty stifling at these times, with the effects of the heat compounded by the influx of visitors; accommodation can be tricky in the really busy spots, but a good network of summer hostels provides a low-budget fall-back.

Autumn is the best time to come if you're planning to sample the whole spread of the country's attractions: in the cities the cultural seasons are beginning at this time, and the pressure on hotel rooms is lifting; in the countryside, the golden "Polish October" is especially memorable, the rich colours of the forests heightened by brilliantly crisp sunshine that's often warm enough for T-shirts.

In **winter** the temperatures drop rapidly, icy Siberian winds blanketing many parts of the country with snow for anything from one to three months. Though

AVERAGE DAILY TEMPERATURES °C (°F) & MONTHLY RAIN mm

		Kraków	Gdynia	Poznań	Przemśyl	Warsaw
January	Max	0 (32)	2 (3)5	1 (33)	0 (32)	0 (32)
	Min	-5 (22)	-3 (27)	-4 (24)	-7 (20)	-5 (22)
	Rain	28	33	24	27	27
February	Max	1 (34)	2 (35)	1 (34)	1 (34)	0 (32)
	Min	-5 (22)	-4 (25)	-5 (22)	-6 (21)	-6 (21)
	Rain	28	31	29	24	32
March	Max	7 (45)	4 (40)	7 (44)	6 (43)	5 (42)
	Min	-1 (30)	-1 (30)	-1 (30)	-2 (29)	-2 (28)
	Rain	35	27	26	25	27
April	Max	12 (55)	9 (48)	12 (54)	12 (55)	11 (53)
	Min	3 (38)	2 (36)	3 (37)	3 (37)	3 (37)
	Rain	46	36	41	43	37
May	Max	19 (67)	15 (59)	19 (67)	19 (67)	19 (67)
	Min	9 (48)	7 (45)	8 (47)	8 (46)	9 (48)
	Rain	46	42	47	57	46
June	Max	22 (72)	19 (66)	22 (72)	23 (73)	23 (73)
	Min	12 (54)	11 (52)	11 (52)	11 (53)	12 (54)
	Rain	94	71	54	88	69
July	Max	24 (76)	21 (70)	24 (76)	24 (75)	24 (75)
	Min	14 (58)	14 (58)	14 (57)	14 (57)	14 (58)
	Rain	111	84	82	105	96
August	Max	23 (73)	21 (70)	23 (73)	23 (73)	23 (73)
	Min	13 (56)	14 (57)	13 (55)	12 (55)	13 (56)
	Rain	91	75	66	93	65
September	Max	19 (66)	18 (64)	19 (67)	19 (67)	19 (66)
	Min	9 (49)	10 (51)	9 (48)	9 (48)	9 (49)
	Rain	62	59	45	58	43
October	Max	13 (56)	12 (55)	13 (56)	14 (57)	12 (55)
	Min	5 (42)	7 (44)	5 (41)	4 (40)	5 (41)
	Rain	49	61	38	50	38
November	Max	7 (44)	7 (44)	6 (43)	6 (43)	5 (42)
	Min	1 (33)	2 (36)	1 (33)	1 (33)	1 (33)
	Rain	37	29	23	43	31
December	Max	3 (37)	3 (38)	3 (37)	3 (38)	2 (35)
	Min	-2 (28)	0 (31)	-2 (28)	-2 (28)	-2 (28)
	Rain	36	46	39	43	44

the central Polish plain is bleak and unappealing at the end of the year, in the south of the country skiers and other winter-sports enthusiasts will find themselves in their element. By mid-December the slopes of the Tatras and the other border ranges are thronged with holidaymakers, straining the established facilities to the limit.

HELP US UPDATE

A lot of effort has gone in to ensure that this edition of *The Rough Guide to Poland* is up-to-date and accurate. However, things are changing fast in Poland: new restaurants, hotels and businesses appear all the time, and prices and opening hours alter. Any suggestions, comments, corrections or updates towards the next edition would be much appreciated. All contributions will be credited, and the best letters will be rewarded with a copy of the new book (or any other *Rough Guide*, if you prefer). Please mark all letters "Rough Guide Poland Update" and send to:

Rough Guides, 1 Mercer Street, London WC2H 9QJ
  or
Rough Guides, 375 Hudson Street, 9th Floor, New York NY10014
  or
Poland@roughtravl.co.uk

THANK YOU

Thanks to the readers of the last edition who wrote in with helpful comments and suggestions. Apologies for any names we were unable to read clearly:

G.A. Hughes, J.A.H. Braidwood, David Page, Andrez Nowodworski, Richard Hoggart, Graham Williams and Larrie Lanes, Thomas T. Shingler, Sheila Hill, Kay Rand, Rowan Collier-Wright, Melanie Brantan, Rachel Hyde, S. Leeming, M.K. Stockhill, Margaret Healy & Graeme Brock, Simon Martin, Chris Hunter, D. Thatcher, David Waters, Simon Thompson, Kathryn Chinn, Sheena Kinmond, Ian Mihell, Ivor R. Hosgood, P.W. Peacock, Richard Caddel, Mrs. E. L. Williamson, Andrew Melvin, Susan Tamlyn, Michelle Senior, Peggy N. Westerman, Peter Brewitt, Mathilde van der Kooij, Ros and Meg Powell, Jonathan Weiniger, H. Jane Shute, Paula Sullivan, Victoria L. White, Pat & Geoff Dodd, Colin Wilkinson, Joan D. Chapman, Caroline F. Birks, Ben Bergonzi, David Cook, Paul Myszor, Kevin Jackson, Gavin Gibb, M. McDonough, Joe Champion-MacPherson, Mark Farmer, Maciej, Tom, Iza, Karen, Ola, Anka, Demon, Kate and Justine, Sarah Jackson, Jenny McNeil, Isabel Willey, Gary Spinks, Helen Absalom, Phil Green, Robert M. Olesnevich, Stephen Barnard, Mrs H. Giejgo, Jim Carman, Michael Bowen, David Key.

PART ONE

THE
BASICS

GETTING THERE FROM BRITAIN

There are regular services from Britain to Poland by air, train and bus. Daily direct flights (2hr 30min) link London and Warsaw, with connections to other major Polish cities; return tickets average out at £200–250, depending on the season. Trains (24–36hr) are only marginally cheaper, unless you're under 26, in which case you can buy a discount *BIJ* ticket or an *Inter-Rail* pass. At around £100, return buses – run mainly for the benefit of Polish émigrés – are an overlooked bargain. Taking around 27 hours, they are sometimes quicker than the train. An option worth considering if money is tight, is to get a cheap flight to Berlin and continue from there by train. By car, it's an all-motorway 1000-kilometre run to the Polish border from the Channel tunnel or ferry ports, via Belgium, Holland and Germany – a surprisingly fast haul, but best covered over two days.

BY PLANE

From London Heathrow both *LOT* (Polish Airlines) and, more expensively, **British Airways** operate daily **scheduled flights** (more at peak periods) to **Warsaw**, with connections on to all major cities throughout the country. In most cases, you'll arrive in Warsaw in time to catch the onward domestic flight, but you'll need to check this – for some cities you may end up having to spend the night in the capital. In addi-

tion, there are two direct weekly flights from London Heathrow to **Kraków** and **Gdańsk**. If you're travelling from a regional British airport, add on around £60 for the connecting flight.

Early booking is always advisable, with flights filling up weeks in advance at peak times, particularly at Christmas when émigré Poles return home in force.

BUYING A TICKET

The cheapest way to travel on a scheduled flight is with an **Apex** (Advance Purchase Excursion) ticket which carries certain restrictions. These tickets must be reserved fourteen days in advance and your stay must include a Saturday night. Your return date must be fixed when purchasing and no further changes are allowed. Tickets are valid for three months and can be booked from either airline or most travel agents. Currently, the London–Warsaw Apex fare with *LOT* is £225 in low season (Jan 16–May 31 & Oct 1–Dec 15) and £255 during the rest of the year. *BA* further divide their low-season fares into midweek and weekend; midweek is £307, rising to £322 at the weekend. All high-season fares are £354. For **under-24s**, there's a year-round return youth fare from *BA* of £318, only bookable the day before, subject to availability and only economically viable in the high season.

However, if you shop around, you should be able to come up with a cheaper **discounted fare**. The best specialist **agents** to try are *Polorbis*, the official tourist office, *Fregata* and the *Polish Travel Centre*, two established Polish-run travel outfits (see box below). From these operators, one-month returns cost £166–180 low season, £206–232 at peak periods; none offer additional student reductions. Although Poland is hardly a major discount destination, you'll find other discount agents in the classified travel sections of the national Sunday papers, London's *Evening Standard* newspaper or *Time Out* magazine, and in major regional newspapers and listings magazines. If you are a **student or under-26**, you may be able to get further discounts on flight prices through agents such as *Campus Travel* or *STA Travel* (see box below).

As a cheaper alternative, you might consider flying **to Berlin** (discounted return fares can

AIRLINES

British Airways, 156 Regent St, London W1R 6LB; 146 New St, Birmingham B2 4HN; 19–21 St Mary's Gate, Market St, Manchester M1 1PU; 32 Frederick St, Edinburgh EH2 2JR; 64 Gordon St, Glasgow G1 3RS (all enquiries ☎0345/222111).

LOT Polish Airlines, 313 Regent St, London W1R 7PE (☎0171/580 5037).

DISCOUNT AGENTS

Campus Travel, 52 Grosvenor Gardens, London SW1W 0AG (☎0171/730 3402); 541 Bristol Rd, Selly Oak, Birmingham B29 6AU (☎0121/414 1848); 166 Deansgate, Manchester M3 3FE (☎0161/833 2046); 53 Forest Rd, Edinburgh EH1 2QP (☎0131/668 3303). *Student/youth travel specialists, with branches also in YHA shops and on university campuses all over Britain.*

Fregata Travel, 13 Regent St, London SW1Y 4LR (☎0171/734 5101); 117 Withington Rd, Manchester M16 8EE (☎0161/226 7227). *Established specialists in discounted travel and tours to Poland.*

German Travel Centre, 403–409 Rayners Lane, Pinner, Middx HA5 5ER (☎0181/429 2900). *Discounted flights to Berlin.*

Polish Travel Centre, 246 King St, London W6 0RF (☎0181/741 5541). *Specialist in discounted flights and buses to Poland.*

Polorbis, 82 Mortimer St, London W1N 8HN (☎0171/636 2217). *UK office of the Polish tourist bureau.*

STA Travel, 86 Old Brompton Rd, London SW7 3LH, 117 Euston Rd, London NW1 2SX , 38 Store St, London WC1 (☎0171/361 6161); 75 Deansgate, Manchester M3 2BW (☎0161/834 0668); 88 Vicar Lane, Leeds LS1 7JH (☎0113/244 9212); and branches throughout the country. *Worldwide specialists in low-cost flights and tours for students and under-26s.*

Trailfinders, 42–50 Earls Court Rd, London W8 6FT (☎0171/937 5400); 194 Kensington High St, London, W8 7RG (☎0171/938 3939); 22–24 The Priory, Queensway, Birmingham B4 6BS (☎0121/236 1234); 58 Deansgate, Manchester M3 2FF (☎0161/839 6969); 254–284 Sauchiehall St, Glasgow G2 3EH (☎0141/353 2224). *One of the best informed and most efficient agents.*

Travel Bug, 597 Cheetham Hill Rd, Manchester M8 5EJ (☎0161/721 4000). *Large range of discounted tickets.*

cost as little as £89), and continuing to Warsaw by train, an inexpensive eight-hour journey. In addition to the general discount agents listed in the box, it's worth contacting specialists such as the *German Travel Centre* for competitive fares to Germany.

BY TRAIN

Travelling **by train** to Poland can be an enjoyable way of getting there if you're intending to **stop off** along the way, but you'll only really save money over the cost of a flight if you're under 26, and some of the complex routings will end up taking longer than a direct bus.

The **ordinary return fare** in high season is £288 for London–Warsaw via the Channel tunnel and Berlin (24hrs), or £218 via Ostend with three changes and a journey time of around 36 hours. Low-season prices on these routes are £226 and £169 respectively. Trains leave London's

Waterloo terminal for the Channel tunnel, and Liverpool Street station for the Ostend route. Couchettes cost £15, but are theoretically reserved for people going all the way to Moscow and can be difficult to book. Tickets, which you can buy from any *British Rail* ticket office and most travel agents, are valid for two months and allow any number of stopovers.

Cheaper rates are available from **specialist operators** such as *Fregata* and the *Polish Travel Centre* (see Discount Agents box): *Polish Travel Centre* quote £189 for the return trip to Warsaw via Ostend in high season.

Eurotrain offers **under-26s** a return *BIJ* **fare** on the same route for £160; again tickets are valid for two months, with unlimited stops en

For details on how to take your **bike** to Poland, see p.32.

RAIL TICKET AGENTS

British Rail, European information and reservations line (☎0171/834 2345).

Eurostar, EPS House, Waterloo Station, London SE1 8SE (☎0345/881881).

Eurotrain, 52 Grosvenor Gardens, London SW1W 0AG (☎0171/730 3402).

Wasteels, Victoria Station (by platform 2), London SW1V 1JY (☎0171/834 7066).

route. Another option for under-26s is the *Inter-Rail* pass, allowing the holder free travel on most European rail lines, including Poland, plus around a third off rail travel in Britain and discounts on some ferries, including cross-Channel services. The pass operates on a zonal system, costing £185 for fifteen days' travel in eastern Europe alone, or £245 for a month's travel from the Channel ports into eastern Europe, excluding the Mediterranean and Scandinavian countries. A month's travel in all seven European zones costs £275. *Inter-Rail* passes for those **over 26** cost £215 for fifteen days and £275 for one month and are not valid for France or Belgium en route from the UK. **Senior citizens** with a *Rail Europe Senior Card* can travel to Poland for £155 return. See "Getting Around" for details of passes for rail travel within Poland only.

One **warning** about rail travel, however. There have been reports of numerous robberies on international night services into Poland, especially from Berlin and Prague. Some bizarre heists have involved entire compartments being stripped while their occupants are put to sleep by gas fed through the ventilation system. Always sleep with your valuables close to you.

BY BUS

Bus travel is an inexpensive and straightforward way to get to Poland, much favoured by Poles during the holiday seasons and, with Polish drivers taking frequent cigarette breaks, not as gruelling as you might expect.

The most reliable services are operated by *Eurolines*, a division of the *National Express* bus company, in conjunction with *Fregata*. They run a regular service **from London to Warsaw** (via Ostend, Brussels, Frankfurt an der Oder and Poznań) and **to Kraków** (same route to Poznań,

then via Wrocław, Opole and Katowice). These run daily in summer and twice a week throughout the rest of the year. Return tickets for both destinations start at £96, with £5 off for under-26s and further reductions for senior citizens and children. Tickets can be bought at any *National Express* office in the UK, and will include connecting fares from anywhere outside London.

In addition, a number of other **Polish émigré-run companies** run "buses", which can mean anything from a double-decker Mercedes to a minibus. The best established of these is the *Polish Travel Centre*, which runs buses from London to Warsaw via Amsterdam and Poznań, and to Kraków via Amsterdam, Wrocław and Katowice. Prices are from £85 return from London. On all services there's a £5 discount for under-26s and senior citizens, and a £20–30 discount for children. *Tazab* operates similar services at similar prices, again aimed primarily at the Polish community in this country, as do *Bogdan Travel*, who also offer a service from London to Gdańsk via Szczecin. Some of these companies also do pick-ups from major northern English cities which adds betwen £10–20 to the price of the ticket.

BUS OPERATORS

Bogdan Travel, 5, The Broadway, Gunnersbury Lane, London W3 8HR (☎0181/992 8866).

Eurolines, *National Express* all enquiries ☎0990/808080.

Fregata Travel, *see Discount Agents box opposite*.

New Millennium, 20 High St, Solihull, Birmingham B91 3TB (☎0121/711 2232).

Tazab Travel, 273 Old Brompton Rd, London SW5 9JB (☎0171/373 1186).

Polish Travel Centre *see Discount Agents box opposite*.

BY CAR

Driving to Poland means a long haul of 1000km from Calais or Ostend to the Polish border – and another 450–500km from there to Warsaw or Kraków. Flat out, and using the Channel tunnel, you could do the journey to the border in eighteen hours, but it makes more sense to allow longer, breaking the journey in central Germany.

The most convenient Channel crossings are the *P&O* services from Dover/Folkestone to

Calais, *Sally Line* to **Ostend** (around £180 return for 2 adults and a car depending on season), or the *Le Shuttle* Channel tunnel option from Folkestone to Calais (£150–220 for 2 adults and a car depending on season, although there are frequent special offers). From either of these ports, the most popular and direct route is on toll-free motorways all the way, bypassing Brussels, Düsseldorf, Hanover and Berlin.

A more relaxing alternative, which halves the driving distance, is to catch the thrice-weekly *Scandinavian Seaways* ferry **from Harwich to Hamburg** (20hr) and then drive east past Berlin, getting to the Polish border queues in another six hours. This costs £226 per passenger (including a comfortable cabin with shower and toilet) and £128 for a car, although special *Seapex* fares booked 21 days in advance and leaving on Sundays to Thursdays offer around 25 percent discount on these prices. Better value still is the *All-in-a-Car* deal which operates from April to September where up to four adults can travel for £519 weekdays or £629 on weekends. The most convenient ferry route from the north of England is the daily *North Sea Ferries* service **from Hull to Rotterdam** (14hr), costing £116 return for the car (half price midweek) with return passenger fares from £94 for a seat, £116 for a basic cabin and £136 for a plusher berth, whatever the season.

CROSS-CHANNEL TICKETS

Hoverspeed, Reservations ☎01304/240241. *To Boulogne and Calais.*

Le Shuttle, Customer Services Centre (☎0990/353535). *To Calais.*

North Sea Ferries, King George Dock, Hedon Road, Hull HU9 5QA (☎01482/377 177). *To Rotterdam and Zeebrugge.*

P&O European Ferries, Reservations ☎0990/980980. *To Calais.*

Sally Line, Ramsgate (☎01843/595522); London (☎0181/858 1127). *To Dunkerque and Ostend.*

Scandinavian Seaways, Parkeston Quay, Harwich, Essex CO2 4QG (☎01255/243456), or 15 Hanover St, London W1 (☎0171/409 6060). *To Hamburg, Ejsberg, Gothenburg.*

Stena Sealink Line, Ashford (☎01233/647047). *To Calais and Dieppe.*

HITCHING

The safest way to hitch to Poland, is to contact one of the specialist organizations which match drivers and passengers. **Freewheelers**, 25 Low Friar St, Newcastle-upon-Tyne NE1 5UE (☎0191/222 0090) sets up contacts for lifts across the UK and to Europe. Membership fee is £10 for one year; £22 for three years. The German *Mitfahrzentralen* organizations, might also be worth trying. They charge a small fee for linking up hitchers and drivers, and passengers are expected to contribute towards fuel costs. They probably won't get you to Poland, but for around £40 you should be able to make it to Berlin, a big chunk of the journey. Try *Mitfahrzentrale*, Kurfürstendamm Eck 27, 1000 Berlin 15 (☎30/882 7604).

BY BOAT

For anyone happy with a slow journey by sea, there's the option of travelling on the *MS Inowrocław* to the port of **Gdynia**. The Polish freighter leaves **Felixstowe** in Suffolk every Monday at 6am, calling at **Hull** and arriving in **Gdynia** early on Friday morning.

Accommodation (12 places in all) is in two-berth cabins. The fares are £143 from Felixstowe, £110 from Hull, plus £12 port tax per person. Cars cost a further £100–£138 depending on size, and motorbikes cost £55; all prices are one-way and there's an additional £10 vehicle tax. For more details contact *Gdynia-American Lines*, 238 City Rd, London EC1V 2QL (☎0171/251 3389).

PACKAGES AND ORGANIZED TOURS

The number of foreign visitors on **package tours** continues to outweigh independent travellers. During the communist era, *Orbis*, the state tourist company (possibly soon to be privatized), had unquestioned dominance of this market, with a couple of Polish émigré-run operators coming a distant second. However, in recent years, small travel operations have mushroomed in Poland – a recent estimate was over 2500 – and a growing number of British and other western European travel companies have set up their own programmes, often in co-operation with local private operators.

ORBIS/POLORBIS

Orbis now operates a somewhat reduced range of mainstream tours, which are retailed overseas through *Polorbis* agencies. The bulk of the tours

BORDER CROSSINGS

Following the breakup of the Soviet Union – and the split of neighbouring Czechoslovakia – Poland now shares **land borders** with seven countries: **Germany**, the **Czech Republic**, **Slovakia**, **Ukraine**, **Belarus**, **Lithuania** and the **Russian Federation** (Kaliningrad region). Recent political changes have made the formalities of entering Poland from Germany, the Czech Republic or Slovakia pretty straightforward, though in summer long delays often build up at the busiest customs points, as the pitifully understaffed Polish customs force search for smuggled goods – a major and growing problem, owing to bigtime cigarette, alcohol and drug operations run by post-Soviet mafias.

Theoretically at least, entering or leaving Poland from **the east** via the former Soviet republics ought to be less difficult now than in the past. Despite the easing of travel restrictions, though, the actual state of affairs is pretty uneven: the mentality of many post-Soviet guards is very much "business as usual", and this, combined with the lack of properly functioning crossing points, means that the delays (by car especially) can be considerable, a day being about average.

To keep locals up to date during the summer holiday season, Polish radio broadcasts "border reports" after the weather news, giving details of the length of the queues (anything up to 10km on a bad day) and expected waiting time (up to 60 hours). The opening of more border crossings features prominently in high-level discussions between politicians on all sides – indeed in some instances (Lithuania, for example) it can be taken as a litmus test of the state of relations between the two countries. To date, however, little substantial progress has been made, the number of new or expanded crossing points being more than matched by the volume of people wanting to travel.

Current border crossings (open 24 hours unless specified) are:

Germany–Poland (north to south)

Ahlbeck–Świnoujście (Baltic coast).

Linken–Lubieszyn.

Pomellen–Kołbaskowo (Berlin–Gdańsk route).

Schwedt– Krajnik Dolny.

Bad Freienwalde–Osinów (Berlin– Gorzów Wielopolski route).

Seelow–Kostrzyn (Berlin– Gorzów Wielopolski route).

Frankfurt an der Oder–Słobice (Berlin–Warsaw route).

Frankfurt an der Oder–Świecko (Berlin–Warsaw route).

Guben–Gubin.

Forst–Olszyna (Berlin–Wrocław/Kraków route).

Bad Muskau–Łeknica.

Görlitz–Zgorzelec (Dresden–Wrocław route).

The Czech Republic–Poland (listed from west to east)

Habartice–Zawidów (Prague–Gorlitz).

Harachow–Jakuszyce (Prague–Wrocław route, via Jelenia Góra).

Pomezni Boudy–Przełęcz Okraj (Prague–Wrocław route, via Wałbrzych).

Kralovec–Lubawka (Prague–Wrocław route, via Wałbrzych).

Nachod/Slone–Kudowa (Prague–Wrocław route, via Kłodzko).

Dolni Lipka–Boboszów (Prague–Wrocław route, via Kłodzko).

Mikulovice–Głuchołazy (Brno–Opole route).

Krnov–Pietraszyn (Brno–Opole route).

Bohumin–Chałupki (Ostrava–Katowice route).

Česky Tesin–Cieszyn (Brno/Ostrava–Kraków route).

Slovakia–Poland (west to east)

Oravská Polkora–Korbielów.

Trstena–Chyżne (Ruźomberok–Kraków route; 8am–6pm; currently only Poles, Czechs and Slovaks can cross here, but this is expected to change soon.

Javorina–Łysa Polana (Poprad–Nowy Targ route, via Tatra mountains; currently only Poles, Czechs and Slovaks can cross here, but this is expected to change soon.

Mnisek–Piwniczna (Poprad–Nowy Sącz route, via Beskid Sądecki).

Vysny Komarnik–Barwinek (Presov–Rzeszów, via Dukla).

Poland–Ukraine (north to south)

Dorohusk–Lubomi (Lublin–Kowiel route).

Hrebenne–Raba Russkaja (Lublin–L'viv route).

Medyka –Sudowaja Wisznia (Kraków–L'viv route).

Poland–Belarus (north to south)

Brzugi–Kuźnica (Białystok–Grodno route).

are one- or two-week packages, their busy schedules taking in Warsaw and Kraków plus a combination of places such as Poznań, Wrocław, Częstochowa, Gdańsk, Lublin and the Tatras. At around £500 for one week, £1000 for two weeks, these are pricey ways of seeing the country.

More interesting, although still not cheap, are some of their **specialist ventures**, such as **Warsaw Opera weekends**, a long-weekend package starting at £305, or **Easter** in Zakopane, Kraków and Warsaw; eight days for £545. Their Jewish tours (see p.24) are run rather infrequently, depending on the number of enquiries. *Polorbis* also offers hiking in the Tatras, horse-riding and cycling tours (from £250), but these do not include flights.

OTHER SPECIALISTS

Few of the larger general operators feature Poland in their brochures. *Shearings* does a fourteen-day "Polish Highland" tour around Zakopane, with a day in Prague, for £537. *Fregata Travel* offers a range of packages along similar lines to *Orbis*: historic cities, theme tours such as "Chopin's country" and skiing, hiking and biking holidays. Prices too are similar to *Orbis*. They also operate a number of all-in **city breaks** to Warsaw, Kraków and Gdańsk throughout the year (2 or 3 nights), starting from £194. *Polish Travel Centre*, *Tazab* and *Bogdan Travel*, which, like *Fregata*, are run in Britain by Polish émigrés, also offer this kind of tour.

New Millennium, one of the most popular operators in Britain, offers packages to the Tatras base of Zakopane, for £129–199 per person, depending on season, comprising a return bus trip plus a week's accommodation in a pension. The same deal in Sopot on the Baltic coast costs £139–209 and in Kraków, £149–219. *Silesian Villas* has well-equipped chalets and villas in Warsaw, Zakopane and the Beskid Śląski – prices start at

£180 per week for four people, not including transport. *Travel Guide Holidays* does a twelve-day bus trip to Zakopane and the Tatras, with day trips to Kraków and Auschwitz from £199.

Other UK-based specialists include *Inter-Church Travel*, which runs ten-day trips at Easter, Corpus Christi and the Feast of the Assumption, taking in Warsaw, Częstochowa, Zakopane, Kraków, Kalwaria and Wadowice for around £699. *Exodus Expeditions* offers a fifteen-day tour, flying to Kraków and incorporating an eleven-day trek through the Tatras and Pieniny for £745 plus a £70 local payment in złoty for food.

GETTING THERE FROM IRELAND

There are no direct flights from Ireland to Poland, so you will need to fly via London. With through fares costing around IR£250, there's little to be saved by getting a cheap flight to London and shopping around there, unless you are really looking for rock-bottom prices or are considering taking the budget route via Berlin (see p.3-4).

Students and anyone under 26, should contact *USIT*, which generally has the best discount deals on flights and train tickets. It's always worth trying the airlines direct, especially if you are over 26, as they often have special deals. For *Inter-Rail* details see "Getting There From Britain", p.5.

If you're considering **driving**, the main ferry contacts are given in the box below (see p.5 for routes).

AIRLINES, FERRY COMPANIES AND TRAVEL AGENTS

AIRLINES

Aer Lingus, 46 Castle St, Belfast (☎01232/245151); 40 O'Connell St, Dublin 1 (☎01/844 4777); 2 Academy St, Cork (021/327155); 136 O'Connell St, Limerick (☎061/474239).

Air UK Reservations ☎0345/666777.

British Airways, 9 Fountain Centre, College St, Belfast BT1 6ET (☎0345/222111); Dublin reservations (☎1800/626747).

British Midland, Belfast reservations ☎0345/676676; Nutley, Merrion Rd, Dublin 4 (☎01/283 8833).

Ryanair, 3 Dawson St, Dublin 2 (☎01/677 4422).

FERRY COMPANIES

Irish Ferries (*B&I*), 16 Westmoreland St, Dublin 2 (☎01/661 0511); 2–4 Merrion Row, Dublin 2 (☎01/661 0511); St Patrick's Bldgs, Cork (☎021/504333); 24-hour information service (☎01/661 0715). *Dublin–Holyhead; Rosslare–Pembroke.*

Also hooks up ("landbridge") with P&O, to serve Dover–Calais and Felixstowe–Zeebrugge, and with Le Shuttle, Scandinavian Seaways, North Sea Ferries and Condor.

P&O European Ferries, Rosslare, Co. Wexford (☎053/33115); c/o Tourist Office, Grand Parade,

Cork (☎021/272 965); Terminal Building, Larne Harbour, Co. Antrim, N. Ireland (☎01574/274321; ☎1800/409049). *Larne–Cairnryan (onward tickets at an inclusive fare for Hull to Zeebrugge or Rotterdam, and Newcastle to Ejsburg, Hamburg or Gothenburg).*

Stena Sealink Line, Adelaide House, Haddington Terrace, Dun Laoghaire, Co. Dublin (☎01/280 7777); Sea Terminal, Larne Harbour, Co. Antrim (☎01574/273616). *Dun Laoghaire–Holyhead; Rosslare–Fishguard; Larne–Stranraer.*

DISCOUNT AGENTS

Discount Travel, 4 South Great Georges St, Dublin 2 (☎01/679 5888).

Flight Finders International, 13 Baggot St Lower, Dublin 2 (☎01/676 8326).

Inflight Travel, 92–94 York Rd, Belfast 15 (☎01232/740187 or 743341).

JWT Holidays, 34 Grafton St, Dublin 2 (☎01/671 8751); 69 Upper O'Connell St , Dublin 2 (☎01/872 2555).

Joe Walsh Tours, 8–11 Baggot St, Dublin (☎01/676 3053).

Specialised Travel Services, 32 Bachelor's Walk, Dublin 1 (☎01/873 1066).

Student & Group Travel, 71 Dame St, Dublin 2 (☎01/677 7834).

Travel Shop, 35 Belmont Rd, Belfast 4 (☎01232/471717).

USIT, Fountain Centre, Belfast BT1 6ET (☎01232/324073); 10–11 Market Parade, Patrick St, Cork (☎021/270900); 33 Ferryquay St, Derry (☎01504/371888); Aston Quay, Dublin 2 (☎01/679 8833).

GETTING THERE FROM THE USA AND CANADA

The easiest way to get to Poland from the US and Canada is to fly direct to Warsaw. Once in Warsaw, *LOT* connects with most of the major Polish cities. Alternatively, if expense is a main consideration, you might consider flying to London, Frankfurt or another good-value western European destination, and continuing by a combination of bus, train and ferry.

SHOPPING FOR TICKETS

Barring special offers, the cheapest of the airlines' published fares is usually an **Apex** ticket, although this will carry certain restrictions: you have to book – and pay – at least 21 days before departure, spend at least seven days abroad (maximum stay three months), and you tend to get penalized if you change your schedule. There are also winter **Super Apex** tickets, sometimes known as "Eurosavers" – slightly cheaper than an ordinary Apex, but limiting your stay to between 7 and 21 days. Some airlines also issue **Special Apex** tickets to people younger than 24, often extending the maximum stay to a year. Many airlines offer youth or student fares to **under 25s**; a passport or driving licence are sufficient proof of age, though these tickets are subject to availability and can have eccentric booking conditions. It's worth remembering that most cheap return fares involve spending at least one Saturday night away and that many will only give a percentage refund if you need to cancel or alter your journey, so make sure you check the restrictions carefully before buying a ticket.

You can normally cut costs further by going through a **specialist flight agent** – either a **consolidator**, who buys up blocks of tickets from the airlines and sells them at a discount, or a **discount agent**, who in addition to dealing with discounted flights, may also offer special student and youth fares and a range of other travel-related services such as travel insurance, rail passes, car rentals, tours and the like (see box opposite). Bear in mind, though, that penalties for changing your plans can be stiff. Remember too that these companies make their money by dealing in bulk – don't expect them to answer lots of questions. Some agents specialize in **charter flights**, which may be cheaper than anything available on a scheduled flight, but again departure dates are fixed and withdrawal penalties are high (check the refund policy). If you travel a lot, **discount travel clubs** are another option – the annual membership fee may be worth it for benefits such as cut-price air tickets and car rental.

Regardless of where you buy your ticket, **fares** will depend on the season, and are highest from around June to September, when the weather is best. They drop during the "shoulder" seasons — April to May and October to November — and you'll get the best prices during the low season, December to March (excluding Christmas and New Year when prices are hiked up and seats are at a premium). Note also that flying on weekends ordinarily adds $20–60 to the round-trip fare; price ranges quoted below assume midweek travel.

FLIGHTS FROM THE US

LOT (Polish Airlines) flies **direct to Warsaw** from New York's JFK five times a week, four times a week from Chicago's O'Hare Airport and twice a week from Newark and New Jersey. As a rule, tickets are not cheap — a low-season, round-trip Apex fare from New York or New Jersey will set you back $750, rising to $975 in the summer high period (from Chicago expect to pay $800 in low season, $1100 during high season). Connecting from the East Coast, you'll be looking at $850 low season and $1160 high season. *LOT* does occasionally make special offers, arranged though the formerly official travel agency **Polorbis** (see box below), and you could find fares reduced to as little as $530.

Several other carriers, including *BA*, *Delta*, *KLM*, *Swissair*, *Lufthansa* and *Sabena* offer more reasonable fares to Warsaw **via other European cities**. *Sabena*, for instance, flies via

---

DISCOUNT FLIGHT AGENTS AND CONSOLIDATORS

American Travel Abroad Inc, 250 W 57th St, New York, NY 10107 (☎212/586 5230). *Essentially a charter firm but one which also sells individual flights on the major airlines.*

Council Travel, 205 E 42nd St, New York, NY 10017 (☎1-800/226 8624 or 212/661 1450), and branches in many other US cities. *Student/budget travel agency. A sister company, Council Charter (☎1-800/223 7402), specializes in charter flights.*

International Student Exchange Flights, 5010 E Shea Blvd, Suite 104A, Scottsdale, AZ 85254 (☎602/951 1177). *Student/youth fares; student IDs required.*

Interworld Travel, 800 Douglass Rd, Miami, FL 33134 (☎305/443 4929). *Consolidator specializing in European destinations.*

Moment's Notice, 7301 New Utrecht Ave, Brooklyn, NY 11204 (☎718/234 6295). *Discount travel club.*

New Frontiers/Nouvelles Frontières, 12 E 33rd St, New York, NY 10016 (☎1-800/366 638); 1001 Sherbrook East, Suite 720, Montréal, H2L 1L3 (☎514/526 8444); and other branches in LA, San Francisco and Québec City. *French discount travel firm.*

Now Voyager, 74 Varick St, Suite 307, New York, NY 10013 (☎212/431 1616). *Courier flight broker and consolidator.*

Pekao International Travel and Tours, *see Specialist Operators box, p.13.*

Polorbis, 342 Madison Ave, New York, NY 10173; (☎212/867 5011). *No longer nationalized, but*

retains a special agreement with LOT to sell discounted tickets on most flights.

STA Travel, 10 Downing St, New York, NY 10014 (☎1-800/777 0112 or 212/627 3111), and other branches in the Los Angeles, San Francisco and Boston areas. *Worldwide discount travel firm specializing in student/youth fares; also student IDs, travel insurance, car rental, rail passes.*

TFI Tours International, 34 W 32nd St, New York, NY 10001 (☎1-800/745 8000 or 212/736 1140), and other offices in Las Vegas and Miami. *Consolidator.*

Travac, 989 6th Ave, New York NY 10018 (☎1-800/872 8800 or 212/563 3303). *Consolidator and charter broker.*

Travel Avenue, 10 S Riverside, Suite 1404, Chicago, IL 60606 (☎1-800/333 3335 or 312/876 6866). *Full-service travel agent offering discounts in the form of rebates.*

Travel CUTS, 187 College St, Toronto, ON M5T 1P7 (☎416/979 2406), and other branches all over Canada. *Organization specializing in student fares, IDs and other travel services.*

Travelers Advantage, 3033 S Parker Rd, Suite 900, Aurora, CO 80014 (☎1-800/548 1116). *Full-service travel club.*

UniTravel, 1177 N Warson Rd, St Louis, MO 63132 (☎1-800/325 2222 or 314/569 2501). *Consolidator.*

Worldtek Travel, 111 Water St, New Haven, CT 06511 (☎1-800/243 1723 or 203/772 0470). *Discount travel agency.*

Brussels and can run as low as $599 in low season, $748 in high. *Delta* flies via Frankfurt for broadly similar fares.

FLIGHTS FROM CANADA

LOT flies **direct to Warsaw** from Toronto and Vancouver. The cheapest fare they offer from Toronto is CDN$950 in low season, CDN$1280 in high. *LOT* also runs charters from Toronto; contact *Pekao*, their travel agency there (see box).

To give you more flexibility, it's worth checking out the other major airlines, who all fly to Warsaw as well, but require a change of plane in New York or western Europe – *British Airways* flies to Warsaw via London, *Lufthansa* via Frankfurt or Dusseldorf and *Swissair* via Zurich. Savings are not dramatic, but you will usually get a cheaper fare.

TRAVELLING VIA EUROPE

If you have the time, travelling to another European capital and **continuing your journey overland** can be an excellent and economical way to reach Poland, allowing stopovers en route and enabling you to see much more of Europe along the way. See "Getting There From Britain" for details of the options from London. Discounted flights to London from New York start at around $350, and to Frankfurt from $570.

There are a variety of **rail passes** available which must be purchased before you arrive in Europe. A *Eurail Pass* is only likely to pay for itself if you're planning to travel widely around Europe en route to Poland. Allowing unlimited free train travel in seventeen countries, not including Poland, it will get you there from other European destinations, but not allow travel within Poland itself. The *Eurail Youthpass* (for under-26s) costs US$398 for fifteen days, $578 for one month or $768 for two months; if you're 26 or over you'll have to buy a first-class pass, available in 15-day ($498), 21-day ($648), one-month ($798), two-month ($1098) and three-month ($1398) increments.

The new *Central Europe Pass*, covering Poland, Germany, the Czech Republic and Slovakia, has no age restrictions, allowing five days first-class travel during a one-month period for $296. The *Polrail Pass* is valid for travel solely within Poland (see "Getting Around" p.27 for details).

For passes contact *Rail Europe*, 226 Westchester Ave, White Plains, NY 10604 (☎1-800/438 7245), the official *Eurail Pass* agent in North America; *Polorbis*; or in Canada, *Canadian Reservations Centre*, 2987 Dundas East, Suite 105, Mississauga, ON L4X 1M2 (☎1-800/361 7245).

PACKAGES AND ORGANIZED TOURS

With the opening up of Poland, independent travel is gradually becoming easier, but the **organized package tour** still remains the most popular method of seeing the country. Despite a recent growth in the number of small travel operators, most packages from the States are still booked through *Polorbis*, the state tourist company. They have an extensive selection, ranging from 6 to 21 days, including flights, accommodation, and most meals, but they're not especially cheap. A fifteen-day planned excursion called "Panorama of Poland", which takes in the main sights of the country, will cost around $2000, if travelling from New York; from Chicago and Los Angeles you'll need to add on extra for the airfare. "Southern Delight" is a ten-day tour of the country's southern provinces, starting in Warsaw and visiting Kraków, Zakopane, Częstochowa, Wadowice (birthplace of the pope) and Wola, before returning to Warsaw. From New York, this will cost you between $1600 and $1800, depending on the time of year.

Their "Jewish Heritage" tour ($1470–1800) is based mainly around Warsaw exploring the sights of the old Ghetto area, although they can also arrange visits to Kraków, Lublin, Auschwitz and Treblinka.

In addition, *Polorbis* arranges tours with a wider scope, taking in other countries. Their "Eastern Europe Highlights Circle" tour, visiting Warsaw, Kraków, Budapest, Vienna, Prague and Wrocław in fourteen days, costs around $3000 flying from New York or Chicago. This tour runs from the end of May through mid-September.

Another major operator to Poland is *PAT (Polish American Tours)*. Their packages include the "Best of Poland", a twelve-day ten-night tour of Warsaw, Kraków, Auschwitz, Częstochowa, Zakopane, Toruń, Gdynia and Mrągowo. This costs between $1700 and $2000, depending on city of departure and time of year. *PAT* also features several other themed packages, including "Historic Poland" and "Southern Adventure" that offer good value for money.

In addition, *Polorbis* also runs a separate tour company, called *Orbis Independent Travel*, for those wanting a bit more freedom. This arranges the minimum necessary and leaves exploring up to the individual, although there are organized day excursions, for instance to Polish castles and cathedrals, for those who want them. If you're considering this form of travel, bear in mind that rail tickets for journeys within Poland should, wherever possible, be purchased inside the country, as prices for tickets reserved abroad can be up to fifty percent higher. See "Getting Around" p.26.

SPECIALIST OPERATORS

AD International Inc, 136 Lawrenceville-Penn Rd, Lawrenceville, NJ 08648 (☎1-800/288 3242). *Warsaw, Kraków, Gdansk, Rzeszow, Zakopane and Częstochowa, including religious and Polish heritage tours, and specialized music, choir and band tours.*

Air Tours Poland, 500 Fifth Ave, Suite 408, New York, NY 10110 (☎1-800/223 0593 or 212/852 0243). *A division of LOT Polish Airlines, offering general interest escorted tours as well as folk art and Jewish heritage tours.*

Best Catholic Pilgrimages, 640 N. La Salle St, Chicago, IL 60610 (☎1-800/908 BEST). *"Catholic shrines and sights of Poland" tour.*

Canadian Travel Abroad, 80 Richmond St W, Suite 804, Toronto ON M5H 2A4 (☎1-800/387 1876 or 416/364 2738). *General interest and Jewish-oriented tours to Poland.*

Cedok Tours, 10 E 40th St, New York, NY 10016 (☎1-800/800 889 or 212/689 8891). *Comprehensive tours of Kraków.*

Eastern European Travel Centre Ltd, 1324 E 15 St, Brooklyn, NY 11230 (☎1-800/304 3050 or 718/339 1100). *City packages to Warsaw and Kraków.*

Exotik Tours, 1117 Ste Catherine St W, Suite 806, Montréal, Québec H3B 1H9 (☎1-800/361 6164 or 514/284 3324). *Motorcoach tours of Warsaw, Kraków and most other cities.*

General Tours, 139 Main St, Cambridge, Mass 02142 (☎1-800/221 2216 or 617/621 0977). *Warsaw city packages and fully hosted tours of Eastern Europe.*

Isram World of Travel, 630 Third Ave, New York, NY 10017 (☎1-800/223 7460 or 212/661 1193). *Escorted tours of Warsaw and Kraków plus Jewish heritage tour.*

ITS Tours, 1055 Texas Ave, Suite 104, College Station, TX 77840 (☎1-800/533 8688 or 409/764 9400). *Overview of Poland's most popular cities as well as comprehensive tours of Poland's historic regions. Independent and escorted options.*

Kentours, 294 Queen Street West, Toronto, Ontario, M5V 2A1 (☎416/593 0837). *Offers a variety of city packages and Polish heritage tours.*

Kompas, 2826 E Commercial Blvd, Fort Lauderdale, FLA 33308 (☎1-800/233 6422). *Warsaw and Kraków city packages.*

Orbis Independent Travel, *Same address as Polorbis.*

PAT Tours, 1053 Riverdale Rd, West Springfield, MA 01089; (☎1-800/388 0988 or 413/747 7702). *Services the large Polish-American tourist market, organizing tours and courses, often in liaison with local emigracja organizations.*

Pekao International Travel and Tours, 1610 Bloor St West, Toronto, Ontario M6P 1A7 (☎1-800/387 0325 or 416/588 1988). *Emigré flight agent and tour company operating direct deals from Toronto to Poland.*

Polorbis, *see Discount Flight Agents box.*

Rahim Tours, 12 South Dixie Highway, 2nd Floor, Lake Worth, FLA 33460 (☎407/585 5305). *Historic splendours of Warsaw.*

Travcoa, PO Box 2630, Newport Beach, CA 92658-2630 (☎1-800/992 2003 or 714/476 2800). *City tours of Warsaw and Kraków and trips to Zakopane.*

Unique World Travel/Pilgrimage Tours and Travel, 39 Beechwood Ave, Manhasset, NY 11030 (☎1- 800/669 0757 or 516/627 2636). *Fully escorted tours of Warsaw, Kraków and Częstochowa.*

Weigel Tours/World Convention Services (WCS), 1985 Main St, Springfield, MA 01103 (☎1-800/333 307). *Offers a Catholic Religious Tour as well as basic city highlights. Also a Jewish tour "From Warsaw Ghetto to Israel's Independence" which travels from Warsaw to Jerusalem.*

GETTING THERE FROM AUSTRALIA & NEW ZEALAND

There are no direct flights to Poland from Australia or New Zealand, however, the Polish national carrier, *LOT*, in combination with *Air New Zealand, Qantas* and *BA*, has scheduled flights to Warsaw via a stopover in Bangkok with free onward flights to other destinations in Poland. *Aeroflot, Alitalia, BA* and *KLM* also fly to Warsaw via a transfer in their respective national capitals. Alternatively, you can pick up a cheap fare on an Asian carrier to their European hub (usually Frankfurt), and then continue on to Poland by train. Many Round-The-World tickets also include Poland. There are no advance purchase rail passes available in Australia and New Zealand for travel within Poland. See "Getting Around", p.27 for details of Polish rail passes.

It is always worth checking the current lowest fares and latest information with a **travel agent** (see box), as changes are made constantly throughout the year. Low season is usually mid-January to the end of February and October to November, with high season from the middle of May to the end of August, and December through to the middle of January. The rest of the year is shoulder season.

FROM AUSTRALIA

The cheapest connecting fares to Warsaw **via Europe** are with *KLM* and *Aeroflot* starting at A$1700 in the low season and rising to A$2400 in high season. With *Alitalia* and *BA* expect to pay around A$2300/2900. **Via Bangkok**, *LOT* is also highly competitive flying twice weekly from Sydney, Melbourne, Adelaide, once weekly from Brisbane and once weekly from Perth for around A$1800/2150. The cheapest option is to fly to Frankfurt with *Garuda* (A$1550/2030) and pick up a train to Poland; worth considering if the lower-priced flights are fully booked.

FROM NEW ZEALAND

From New Zealand, the best fare is with *Air New Zealand-LOT*, which fly twice weekly to Warsaw from Auckland via Bangkok for NZ$2250 low season, NZ$2650 high season. *Alitalia* flies via Sydney and Rome, and *BA* via LA and London, both NZ$2605 in low season, NZ$3250 in high season. As from Australia, if you're looking for the cheapest option, *Garuda* to Frankfurt, via a stopover in Denpasar or Jakarta, for NZ$2110/2420, then overland to Poland, is worth considering.

ROUND-THE-WORLD TICKETS

Poland is included in both *ANZ-KLM-Northwest*'s "World Navigator" and *BA-Qantas-USAir*'s "Global Explorer" tickets. Expect to pay around A$2350/NZ$2650 low season; A$2900/NZ$3300 high season.

PACKAGES AND ORGANIZED TOURS

The *Eastern European Travel Bureau* is the main agent for **Orbis**, the Polish tourist office, and offers a variety of accommodation packages and tours for independent travellers, excluding flights. These include two-night Warsaw and Kraków **city breaks** (twin share) with breakfast and airport transfers from A$200/NZ$225 and A$160/NZ$180 respectively, and a seven-day **bus tour** Warsaw–Kraków return visiting Zakopane and Auschwitz from A$900/NZ$1000.

Trekking tours are on offer from *Exodus Expeditions*, 15-day small group tours from Kraków to the High Tatras (A$1200/NZ$1470), including hotel and hut accommodation and local transport.

AIRLINES

Aeroflot, 388 George St, Sydney (☎02/9233 7911). *No NZ office.*

Air New Zealand, 5 Elizabeth St, Sydney (☎02/9223 4666); Quay St, Auckland (☎09/357 3000).

Alitalia, Orient Overseas Building, 32 Bridge St, Sydney (☎02/9247 1308); 6th Floor, Trustbank Building, 229 Queen St, Auckland (☎09/379 4457).

British Airways, 64 Castlereagh St, Sydney (☎02/9258 3300); 154 Queen St, Auckland (☎09/356 8690).

Garuda, 175 Clarence St, Sydney (☎02/334 9900); 120 Albert St, Auckland (☎09/366 1855).

KLM, 5 Elizabeth St, Sydney (☎02/9231 6333; toll-free 1800/505 747). *No NZ office.*

LOT Polish Airlines, 388 George St, Sydney (☎02/9232 8430). *No NZ office.*

Qantas, Chifley Square, cnr Hunter and Phillip streets, Sydney (☎02/957 0111); Qantas House, 154 Queen St, Auckland (☎09/357 8900).

DISCOUNT AND SPECIALIST AGENTS

Accent on Travel, 545 Queen St, Brisbane (☎07/3832 1777).

Anywhere Travel, 345 Anzac Parade, Kingsford, Sydney (☎02/663 0411).

Brisbane Discount Travel, 360 Queen St, Brisbane (☎07/3229 9211).

Budget Travel, 16 Fort St, Auckland; other branches around the city (☎09/309 4313; toll-free 0800/ 808 040).

Destinations Unlimited, 3 Milford Rd, Milford, Auckland (☎09/486 1303).

Eastern European Travel Bureau, 75 King St, Sydney (☎02/9262 1144); 343 Little Collins St, Melbourne (☎03/9600 0299); 131 Elizabeth St, Brisbane (☎07/3229 9716).

Exodus Expeditions, Suite 5, Level 5, 1 York St, Sydney (☎02/9251 5430; toll-free 1800/800 724).

Flight Centres, Australia: Circular Quay, Sydney (☎02/9241 2422); Bourke St, Melbourne (☎03/650 2899); plus other branches nationwide. New Zealand: National Bank Towers, 205–225 Queen St, Auckland (☎09/309 6171); Shop 1M, National Mutual Arcade, 152 Hereford St, Christchurch (☎09/379 7145); 50–52 Willis St, Wellington (☎04/472 8101); other branches countrywide.

Northern Gateway, 22 Cavenagh St, Darwin (☎08/8941 1394).

Harvey World Travel, Princess Highway, Kogarah, Sydney (☎02/567 099); branches nationwide.

Passport Travel, 320b Glenferrie Rd, Malvern, Melbourne, (☎03/9824 7183).

STA Travel, Australia: 732 Harris St, Ultimo, Sydney (☎02/9212 1255; toll-free 1800/637 444); 256 Flinders St, Melbourne (☎03/9347 4711); other offices in Townsville, state capitals and major universities. New Zealand: Travellers' Centre, 10 High St, Auckland (☎09/366 6673); 233 Cuba St, Wellington (☎04/385 0561); 223 High St, Christchurch (☎03/379 9098); other offices in Dunedin, Palmerston North, Hamilton and major universities.

Topdeck Travel, 45 Glenfell St, Adelaide (☎08/8232 7222).

Tymtro Travel, 428 George St, Sydney (☎02/9223 2211).

UTAG Travel, 122 Walker St, North Sydney (☎02/956 8399); branches throughout Australia.

VISAS AND RED TAPE

Citizens of the UK, USA, Ireland and most EU nations require only a passport, which must be valid for at least six months, in order to enter Poland: they no longer require a visa of any type. However, nationals of many other countries – including Australia, New Zealand and Canada – still require a visa, which should be obtained prior to arriving in Poland.

Visas are valid for ninety days and must be used within six months of the date of issue. To qualify for a visa, you must have a **full** passport, valid for at least nine months beyond the date of your application and with at least one clear page for the authorization stamp. The visa **application form** can be obtained (in person or by post) either from *Orbis*, *Polorbis* or from a Polish consulate. *Polorbis* can also handle the whole transaction on your behalf on payment of a handling charge. You should allow two to three weeks for delivery by post, two to three days if you lodge your application in person. Currently the **fee** is CDN$55 in Canada, A$60 in Australia and NZ$70 in New Zealand.

POLISH EMBASSIES AND CONSULATES ABROAD

Australia 7 Turran St, Yaralumla (☎06/273 1211).

Canada 2603 Lakeshore Blvd W, Toronto, Ontario MAV 1GS (☎416/252 5471); 1500 Pine Ave O, Montréal, Québec H3G1B4 (514/937 9481); 443 Daly Ave, Ottowa, Ontario K1N 6H3 (☎613/789 0468); 1177 West Hastings St, Suite 1600, Vancouver BC V6E 2K3 (☎604/688 3530).

Denmark Richlieu Alle 12, Hellerup, Copenhagen (☎627244).

Ireland *Use UK office.*

Netherlands Alexanderstraat 25, Den Haag (☎70/602806).

New Zealand *Use Australian office.*

Norway Olaf Kyrres Plass 1, Oslo 2 (☎02/550208).

Sweden Karlavägen 35, Stockholm (☎08/114132).

UK 19 Weymouth St, London W1N 3AG (☎0171/580 0476); 2 Kinnear Rd, Edinburgh EH3 5PE (☎0131/552 0301).

USA 2224 Wyoming Ave NW, Washington, DC 20008 (☎202/234 3800); 223 Madison Ave, New York, NY 10016 (☎212/889 8360); 1530 N. Lake Shore Drive, Chicago, IL 60610 (☎312/337 8166); 12400 Wilshire Blvd, Suite 555, Los Angeles, CA 90025 (☎310/442 8500).

POLORBIS OFFICES ABROAD

Netherlands Leidsestraat 64, Amsterdam 1017 PD (☎20/253570).

Norway 1 Biugata 0186, Oslo 1 (☎02/419140).

Sweden Birger Jarlsgatan 71, Stockholm 10432 (☎08/235345).

UK 82 Mortimer St, London W1N 7DE (☎0171/637 4971).

USA 342 Madison Ave, New York, NY 10173 (☎212/867 5011).

HEALTH AND INSURANCE

Reciprocal arrangements between Poland and Britain mean British travellers are entitled to free basic medical care in the country; there is, however, a charge for certain imported drugs and for some specialized treatments. It's important to carry your NHS card as proof of your entitlement to free treatment; without it you will probably end up paying the full cost. However, these arrangements do not cover everything, and it is advisable for everyone to have adequate private health insurance. North Americans, Canadians, Australians and New Zealanders must arrange full insurance before leaving home.

Inoculations are not required for a trip to Poland. Tap water is officially classified as safe, but in the cities no one drinks it without boiling it first; bottled mineral water (*woda mineralna*) is readily available.

PHARMACIES AND HOSPITALS

Simple complaints can normally be dealt with at a regular **pharmacy** (*apteka*), where basic medicines are dispensed by qualified pharmacists. In the cities, many of the staff will speak at least some English or German. Even in places where the staff speak only Polish, it should be easy enough to obtain repeat prescriptions, if you bring along the empty container or remaining pills. In every town there's always one *apteka* open 24 hours; addresses are printed in local newspapers.

For more serious problems, or anything the pharmacist can't work out, you'll be directed to a public hospital (*szpital*), where conditions will probably be pretty bad, with more patients than beds, a lack of medicines and occasionally insanitary conditions. Doctors are heavily overworked and scandalously underpaid. If you are required to pay for any medical treatment or medication, remember to keep the receipts for your insurance claim when you get home. At least among the wealthier sections of the population, **private health care** – including privately run hospitals – is establishing itself and many of the places Westerners now get directed to belong in this category.

An alternative is provided by the larger Western embassies, who run **health clinics** which nationals can attend for a fee. See the relevant city listings for Warsaw, Kraków and Gdańsk.

INSURANCE

Most people will find it essential to take out a good travel insurance policy. Bank and credit cards (particularly *American Express*) often give certain levels of medical or other insurance to their customers, and travel insurance may also be included if you use a major credit or charge card to pay for your trip. This can be quite comprehensive, anticipating anything from lost or stolen baggage and missed connections to charter companies going bankrupt; however certain policies (notably in North America) only cover medical costs.

If you plan to participate in risky outdoor activities such as **skiing or mountaineering**, you'll probably have to pay an extra premium; check carefully that any insurance policy you are considering will cover you in case of an accident. Note also that very few insurers will arrange on-the-spot payments in the event of a major expense or loss; you will usually be reimbursed only after going home.

In all cases of loss or theft of goods, you will have to contact the local police to have a **report** made out so that your insurer can process the claim. This can be a tricky business in Poland since many officials outside the big cities may not be accustomed to this and making yourself understood can be a problem, but be persistent.

EUROPEAN COVER

In Britain and Ireland, travel insurance schemes (from around £20 a month) are sold by almost every travel agent or bank, and by specialist insurance firms. Policies issued by *Campus Travel* (see p.4 for address), *Endsleigh Insurance* (97–107 Southampton Row, London WC1; ☎0171/436 4451), *Snowcard Insurance Services* (Freepost 4135, Lower Boddington, Daventry, Northants NN11 6BR; ☎01327/62805), *Frizzell Insurance* (Frizzell House, County Gates, Bournemouth, Dorset BH1 2NF; ☎01202/292 333) and *Columbus Travel Insurance* (17 Devonshire Square, London EC2; ☎0171/375 0011) are all good value. In Ireland, *USIT* (see p.9) offers a full range, with discounts offered to students of any age and anyone under 26.

NORTH AMERICAN COVER

In the US and Canada, insurance tends to be much more expensive, and may include medical cover only. Before buying a policy, check that you're not already covered by existing insurance plans. **Canadian provincial health plans** typically provide some overseas medical coverage, although they are unlikely to pick up the full tab in the event of a mishap. Holders of official **student/teacher/youth cards** are entitled to accident coverage and hospital in-patient benefits – the annual membership is far less than the cost of comparable insurance. **Students** may also find that their student health coverage extends during the vacations and for one term beyond the date of last enrolment.

Homeowners' or renters' insurance often covers theft or loss of documents, money and valuables while overseas.

Only after exhausting the possibilities above might you want to contact a **specialist travel insurance company**; your travel agent can usually recommend one. *Isis* (through travel agencies) charges $50 for fifteen days, $80 for a month, $150 for three months. Also worth trying are *Access America* (☎1-800/284 8300); *Carefree Travel Insurance* (☎1-800323 3149); and *Travel Guard* (☎1-800/826-1300).

None of these policies insure against **theft** of anything while overseas. North American travel policies apply only to items **lost** from, or **damaged** in, the custody of an identifiable, responsible third party – hotel porter, airline or luggage consignment.

AUSTRALASIAN COVER

Travel insurance is put together by the airlines and travel agent groups in conjunction with insurance companies. They are all comparable in premium and coverage. Most adventure sports are covered – except mountaineering with ropes – but always check the policy. Expect to pay around A$150/NZ$170 for one month, A$280/NZ$320 for 3 months.

Try *UTAG*, 347 Kent St, Sydney (☎02/9819 6855 or 1800/809 462); *Cover More*, Level 9, 32 Walker St, North Sydney (☎02/9202 8000 or 1800/251 881); and *Ready Plan*, 141–147 Walker St, Dandenong, Victoria (☎1800/337 462); 10th Floor, 63 Albert St, Auckland (☎09/379 3208).

TRAVELLERS WITH DISABILITIES

In the past, very little attention was paid to the needs of the disabled in Poland. Attitudes are slowly changing, but there is still a long way to go and there is not a lot of money available for improvements.

Elevators and escalators are gradually becoming more common in public places and an increasing number of **hotels**, mainly in Warsaw and Kraków have access and rooms designed for the disabled. *Orbis* offers special facilities in its hotels in over fifteen cities in Poland including Poznań, Częstochowa and Zakopane. A handful of **youth hostels** also offer facilities suitable for wheelchair users; contact the Polish Youth Hostel Federation (*PTSM*) for further details.

Transport is a major problem, since buses and trams are virtually impossible for wheelchairs, and although Polish Railways claims that seats in each carriage are designated for disabled passengers, this can't be relied on. Taxi drivers in eastern Europe in general are also very reluctant to lift passengers to and from their wheelchairs.

A shortlist of organizations which should be able to provide some help and advice are listed in the box below.

CONTACTS FOR DISABLED TRAVELLERS

AUSTRALIA AND NEW ZEALAND

ACROD (Australian Council for Rehabilitation of the Disabled), PO Box 60, Curtin ACT 2605 (☎06/682 4333); 55 Charles St, Ryde (☎02/9809 4488).

Disabled Persons Assembly, PO Box 10, 138 The Terrace, Wellington (☎04/472 2626).

BRITAIN AND EUROPE

Catholic Association of the Disabled, Grojecka 118, PL-02-367 Warsaw (☎022/22 80 26).

Holiday Care Service, 2nd floor, Imperial Building, Victoria Rd, Horley, Surrey RH6 9HW (☎01293/774535). *Information on all aspects of travel.*

Mobility International, 25 rue de Manchester, 1070 Brussels, Belgium (☎032/2410 6297 or 2410 6874).

Polish Society for Rehabilitation of the Disabled, ul. Oleandrow 4m 10, 00-629 Warsaw (☎022/25 98 39, fax 25 70 50).

RADAR, 12 City Forum, 250 City Rd, London EC1V 8AS (☎0171/250 3222; Minicom ☎0171/250 4119). *A good source of advice on holidays and travel abroad. Their guide European Holidays and Travel Abroad will tell you everything you need to know.*

Tripscope, The Courtyard, Evelyn Rd, London W4 5JL (☎0181/994 9294). *A national telephone information service offerig free transport and travel advice.*

USA AND CANADA

Directions Unlimited, 720 N Bedford Rd, Bedford Hills, NY 10507 (☎1-800/533 5343). *Tour operator specializing in custom tours for people with disabilities.*

Jewish Rehabilitation Hospital, 3205 Place Alton Goldbloom, Montréal, PQ H7V 1R2 (☎514/688 9550). *Guidebooks and travel information.*

Mobility International USA, PO Box 10767, Eugene, OR 97440 (Voice and TDD: ☎503/343 1284). *Information and referral services, access guides, tours and exchange programs.*

Society for the Advancement of Travel for the Handicapped (SATH), 347 5th Ave, New York, NY 10016 (☎212/447 7284). *Non-profit travel-industry referral service that passes queries on to its members as appropriate; allow plenty of time for a response.*

Travel Information Service, Moss Rehabilitation Hospital, 1200 West Tabor Rd, Philadelphia, PA 19141 (☎215/456 9600). *Telephone information and referral service.*

Twin Peaks Press, Box 129, Vancouver, WA 98666; ☎206/694 2462 or 1-800/637 2256). *Publisher of the Directory of Travel Agencies for the Disabled, listing more than 370 agencies worldwide; Travel for the Disabled; the Directory of Accessible Van Rentals and Wheelchair Vagabond , loaded with personal tips.*

COSTS, MONEY AND BANKS

Poland is currently one of the great travel bargains. Though the long-term trend is clearly towards greater convergence with EU price levels, many of the essentials of travel, such as food and drink, public transport and entrance fees remain relatively cheap for the average Western visitor. Accommodation is priced on a different scale, but is still inexpensive as a rule. Note that prices are often much higher in Warsaw than in the rest of the country, and are similarly increased in places which see a lot of foreign visitors, such as Kraków and Poznań.

AVERAGE COSTS

The rampant inflation and lifting of subsidies resulting from the reforms of the first post-communist governments in the early 1990s, put severe economic pressures on Poles. However, for Western visitors, prices for most goods remain low. You can **eat** and **drink** well for £5/ $7.50 or less even at some of the country's best restaurants, though it's becoming increasingly easy to spend £10/$15 or more for a meal. In a more basic restaurant, a meal can be had for not much more than £2/$3, and substantial hot meals are available at milk and snack bars for much less than this – 40p/60¢ will often buy a main course. Coffee or tea with cakes in a café costs a similarly nominal amount.

Prices for **public transport** are little more than pocket money – even travelling across half the length of the country by train or bus only costs around £7/$10. Similarly, you never have to fork out much more than £1/$1.50 to visit even the most popular **tourist sights**, with 25–50p/ 40–75¢ the normal asking price. Consequently, entrance fees are not given in the text, unless they are unusually high.

Only if you go for expensive **accommodation** will your costs start to rise. Here at least there's plenty of opportunity to spend money, with international hotels in the main cities charging up to £180/$270 per night. On the other hand, if you stick to campsites, youth and tourist hostels or sports hotels, you'll seldom spend much more than £5/$7.50 on a bed. Budget on about twice as much for a room in a private house or in the cheapest hotels. In the most popular resort areas, full-board terms in pensions and holiday homes can generally be found for £7–10/$10–15.

CURRENCY

The Polish unit of currency is the **złoty** (abbreviated as zł). As a result of a major **currency reform** initiated in January 1995, the złoty currently operates simultaneously in two parallel versions. The **new złoty**, a conscious return to prewar denominations, and widely seen as a symbol of the country's new-found economic self-confidence, comes in notes of 10zł, 20zł, 50zł, 100zł and 200zł; and coins in 1, 2 and 5zł denominations, subdivided into groszy (1, 2, 5, 10, 20 and 50). Currently the exchange rate is 3.8zł to the pound sterling and 2.48zł to the US dollar. The old currency, which will remain legal tender until 1998, comes in notes of 1000, 2000, 5000, 10,000, 50,000, 100,000, 500,000, 1 million and 2 million denominations.

TRAVELLERS' CHEQUES, CREDIT CARDS AND EXCHANGE

Although **travellers' cheques** are the safest way of carrying your money, in Poland only **main banks**, *Orbis* **offices** and **hotels** will accept them. *American Express*, who now have offices in Warsaw, are a useful alternative and will cash most brands of travellers' cheques, in addition to their own. The number of places providing a travellers' cheque exchange service is actually decreasing, and transactions can often be a lengthy process. This is not a particular problem in major cities and tourist areas, but cashiers in provincial towns are often so unfamiliar with the procedure that you can be kept waiting for hours. If you're travelling in such areas, you really do need a supply of cash as a backup. Hotels usually charge a hefty commission of five percent, banks around one percent, while *American Express* will cash cheques free of charge (into local currency only).

Credit and charge cards are more established than you might expect. *Access/ Mastercard, American Express, Diners Club, Eurocard, JCB* and *Visa* are accepted by *Orbis* in payment for accommodation, meals, telephone and telex bills, transportation tickets, car rental and tourist services; you can also arrange a cash advance on most of these cards at big hotels and main *Orbis* offices, though, with the latter, you have to wait for an authorization call to Warsaw. An increasing number of shops, particularly branches of multinational companies, will also take your plastic. Europeans also have the option of using **Eurocheques**, accepted in banks throughout the country.

ATMs are slowly beginning to appear in Poland. In Warsaw there are currently two 24-hour machines dispensing cash (złotys) on *American Express* cards – one at the *American Express* office and the other at the *Marriot Hotel*. The latter should also take *Visa, Plus* and *Electron* cards in the near future. More machines are planned in Warsaw during 1996, and at over 1000 sites throughout the country over the next three years.

EXCHANGE

Poland's appetite for foreign currency is reflected in the ease with which it's possible to **change cash**. In general, Poles tend to use the **US dollar** as their yardstick and this is the currency they're keenest to acquire; the **Deutschmark**, staple of Central European trading these days, is only marginally less in demand, the **pound** less so, though it should still be accepted quite readily. Bear in mind, however, that notes with any kind of pen mark on them, a common feature of British bank notes, may well be refused by many exchange offices. It therefore makes sense to take a supply of dollars, if only for contingency purposes.

As a rule, the most competitive **exchange rates** are offered by the **banks** (usually open Mon–Fri 7.30am–5pm, Sat 7.30am–2pm), though you'll almost certainly be kept waiting at the desk. A flat commission of around 3zł per transaction is normally deducted.

Orbis **hotels** also have exchange desks, which are usually open round the clock; they tend to offer poor rates (especially at the airports) and charge hefty commissions, though these are not uniformly applied. The main *Orbis* **office** in each town is supposed to offer a full travellers' cheque and currency exchange service; this is usually quick and efficient, with a better rate than you'll get in their hotels. However, most offices now seem to be prepared to change cash only.

A whole host of **private banks**, designated by the names *kantor* or *walut*, have sprung up in all the cities. These range from little more than kiosks run in tandem with another retail business to flashy offices, and all are usually open till late at night. They change **cash only**, and some may only take dollars and Deutschmarks.

The effective legalization of the **black market** rate means that illicit currency transactions are definitely no longer worth the risk; the likelihood is that you'll be given counterfeit notes or swindled in some other way.

INFORMATION AND MAPS

Poland has now finally established a National Tourist Office (see box) with branches in a number of European countries and the US. Within the country, however, the provision of information remains diffuse, to say the least. Warsaw, for example, has no central tourist office, and tourist information is disseminated by a host of offices, shops and hotels bearing the sign *Informator Turystyczny* (IT). What follows is a guide to the country's various tourist organizations and the services they provide. As yet, they're still mainly geared to organized group visits, though the importance of independent travel is increasingly being recognized.

ORBIS

By far the largest tourist outfit in Poland is *Orbis*, usually known outside the country as *Polorbis*. Founded in the 1920s, it was turned by the communists into a vast organization with an unusually wide range of functions. Presumably it will at some time be broken up into several parts, but despite talk of imminent privatization, there's no sign of anything concrete happening as yet. However, some offices have been franchised off to the former management, while there's increasing competition from the new private agencies.

In Poland, *Orbis* at present runs 55 international-type hotels and 160 offices. These offices sell air, rail, bus and ferry tickets, change money, arrange guided tours, car rental and special inter-

est activities, make hotel reservations, organize bookings for sports and cultural events, and process visa extensions. Their responsibility for promoting tourism in their own region is rather nebulous, though special offices for foreign visitors do exist in the largest cities, and many other branches are well clued-up on the tourist facilities in their area. Others, however, seem to have brochures and up-to-date information on anywhere in the world except their own region. The addresses of the most important *Orbis* offices are listed in the appropriate sections of the *Guide*.

Abroad, the company acts both as the main agent for holidays in Poland and as a state tourist office (see p.4,11 and 14 for addresses). Even if you're intending to visit Poland under your own steam, it's well worth writing to or going along to one of their offices to pick up free **promotional material** in English, which is often difficult to come by in Poland itself. In addition to a series of six glossy brochures covering the whole country, there are also a few booklets on specialist interests (music, architecture, folklore, activity holidays) and an excellent road map.

OTHER TOURIST ORGANIZATIONS

PTTK – which translates literally as "The Polish Country Lovers' Association" – has a rather more direct responsibility for internal Polish tourism

---

NATIONAL TOURIST OFFICE ADDRESSES

Belgium 18/24 Kolonienstraat, 1000 Brussels (☎ 02/ 511 8169; fax 02/502 1261).

Germany Waidmarkt, 50676 Cologne (☎221/23 05 45; fax 221/23 89 90).

Netherlands Leidsestraat 64, 1017 PD Amsterdam (☎20/625 35 70; fax 20/623 09 29).

Sweden Kungsgatan 66, Box 449 1012 Stockholm (☎08/21 60 75 or 21 81 45; fax 21 04 65).

UK 310–312 Regent St, London W1R 5AJ (☎ 0171/580 8811; fax 0171/580 8866).

USA 333 N. Michigan Ave, Suite 224, Chicago, IL 60601 (☎312/236 9013 or 236 1125); 275 Madison Ave, Suite 1711, New York NY 10016 (☎212/338 9412; fax 212/338 9283).

than *Orbis*, administering information offices throughout Poland, a particularly good source of local maps. In addition, it runs hostels in both city and holiday areas, and rents bungalows for family holidays in the lake regions. Its main foreign service department is at ul. Świętokrzyska 36, Warsaw (☎022/20 82 41).

Almatur is a student and youth travel bureau – and the obvious contact point for getting to meet young Poles. It arranges international work camps, special study, activity and hobby programmes, educational exchanges and, during the summer, accommodation in international student hotels, holiday centres and camps (*Baza Studentowa*). These are open to anyone under 35 on production of *Almatur* vouchers, which are available from their offices; rates are reduced if you have an *ISIC* card. *Almatur*'s head office is at ul. Ordynacka 9, Warsaw (☎022/26 23 56); other addresses can be found in the *Guide* under the appropriate section.

Elsewhere, a number of **city- or municipal-based tourist offices** dispense information and run tours and excursions for their particular patch. Among the best established of these are *Syrena* in Warsaw and *Wawel Tourist* in Kraków. A host of **local, private tourist agencies** have set up over the past year or two, as well, running a variety of trips and providing accommodation, and these are all detailed in the *Guide*.

THE POLISH EMIGRACJA

Over the last two centuries Poland's economic problems and turbulent political history have produced one of Europe's largest streams of **emigrants**, known in Polish as the *emigracja*.

Today's worldwide *emigracja* population is estimated as around fifteen million, encompassing both actual Polish citizens and people of Polish origin. Of these, by far the largest group are **Polish Americans**, thought to number anywhere from seven to ten million, with a particularly strong base in Chicago, still said to have the largest Polish population in the world after Warsaw. Publicly the community's most prominent representative is the Polish American Congress, a thriving national organization that has lobbied the US Congress to some effect on issues such as support for Solidarity and according Poland NATO ally status.

In Europe, the largest populations are in Germany and France (around one million each). Despite its smaller size, the Polish community in **Britain** (around 200,000), the majority of whom originally came during World War II as refugees or with the Polish armed forces, held a symbolically significant position as the home of the **Polish Government-in-Exile** which moved to London in 1939.

Since the dawn of the post-communist era in 1989, growing numbers of original emigrants, as well as second and third generation descendants,

POLISH CULTURAL ORGANIZATIONS

AUSTRALIA AND NEW ZEALAND
Federal Council of Australian Polish Association, GPO Box 1246 L, Melbourne VIC 3001.

Polish Association in New Zealand, 257 Riddiford St, GPO Box 853, Wellington.

NORTH AMERICA
Canadian-Polish Congress, 288 Roncesvalles Ave, Toronto, Ontario M6R 2M4 (☎416/532 2876 or 532 7197).

Kościuszko Foundation, 15 E 65th St, New York NY 10021 (☎212/734 2130). *Prominent Polish American foundation established in the 1920s. Organizes Polish cultural heritage tours and summer study programs at several of the major Polish universities.*

Polish American Congress, 5711N Milwaukee Ave, Chicago, IL 60646-6215 (☎312/ 763 9944). *Also has branches in many other cities including Washington, New York, Miami, Boston and Pittsburgh.*

POLAND
Wspólnota Polska, Krakowskie Przedmieście 64, Warsaw (☎022/635 04 40, fax 26 87 40 or 26 71 14). *Polish headquarters of one of the key civic emigracja organizations. Currently focused on developing links with Poles throughout the former Soviet Union.*

UK
Union of Poles in Great Britain, 238–246 King St, London W6 0RF (☎0181/741 1606, fax 746 3798). *Lively centre of Polish cultural life in London, with two libraries, two restaurants and a useful bookshop.*

are now returning to Poland, most to visit relatives or as **"roots" tourists**. All the major English-speaking countries have cultural and other Polish organizations which are worth contacting if you have Polish heritage and are interested in specialist tours or courses in Poland.

JEWISH TOURISM

Jews and **Jewish heritage** loom large in the history of Poland. Prior to the outbreak of World War II, Jews comprised roughly ten percent (three million) of the country's population, the largest Jewish community in Europe and the second largest in the world at the time. Of a current world population of fifteen million Jews, more than half are reckoned to have historical connections to Polish Jewry.

Up until the mid-1980s, **Jewish tourism** in Poland was a small-scale affair. Historically rooted fears of anti-Semitism, combined with generalized Western apprehension over travel to the communist East, limited the numbers prepared to make the trip to the land of their own or ancestor's birth. The re-establishment of diplomatic relations with Israel in 1987 and the ending of the communist era in 1989 altered the situation radically. By the mid-1990s **organized tour groups**, principally (though by no means exclusively) from Israel and the USA, have become an established feature in many parts of the country, particularly cities such as Warsaw, Kraków and Lublin which had the largest pre-Holocaust Jewish populations and which constituted the traditional focal points of Polish Jewish life and culture.

Many Jewish groups come with their own pre-arranged schedules and guides, normally focusing on surviving Jewish monuments alongside Holocaust memorials such as Auschwitz-Birkenau and the other concentration camps. To help meet the growing level of Jewish tourism, *Orbis* offers special tours, complete with travel, accommodation, guides and (on request) kosher catering. Lasting around ten days, the usual itineraries take in some or all of the following: Warsaw, Treblinka, Tykocin, Lublin, Białystok, Majdanek, Kraków, Auschwitz-Birkenau, Częstochowa, Łódz, Zamość, Łańcut and Rzeszów (see relevant entries for all these in the *Guide*), as well as visits to some of the country's sixteen functioning Jewish congregations.

For people travelling independently, an effort has been made in the *Guide* to cover sites of interest to Jews. If you find yourself hunting

---

POLISH/JEWISH ORGANIZATIONS

Jewish Historical Institute, ul. Tlomackie 3/5, Warsaw (☎022/27 18 43). *Archives, exhibitions, library and irregularly open bookstore.*

Jewish Communities Federation (Związek Religijny Wyznania Mojzeszowego), ul. Twarda 6, Warsaw (☎022/20 43 24). *Headquarters of religious congregations throughout Poland.*

Jewish Cultural Centre, ul. Meiselsa 17, Kraków (☎012/22 55 87 or 22 55 95). *Ambitious new cultural centre in the heart of the Kazimierz district.*

Our Roots, ul. Twarda 6, Warsaw (☎/fax 022/20 05 66). *Jewish travel agency that provides general information, local guides, produces guide books and helps with tracing family ancestry in Poland.*

Ronald Lauder Foundation, ul. Twarda 6 (☎022/20 07 93). *US-based foundation supporting Jewish cultural and religious initiatives within Poland.*

---

around the backstreets of a town in search of Jewish buildings and monuments – a common experience in the further flung reaches of the country – the basic words and phrases to know when asking for directions are *bożnica* or *synagoga* (synagogue) and *cmentarz żydowski* (Jewish cemetery). However, you can't bank on everyone knowing where to find to what you're looking for: generally speaking, the older the person the more likely they are to be able to point you in the right direction. Although the *Guide* will help you locate many Jewish sites and buildings, bear in mind that, for example, many former synagogues are now used for something totally different, and all too often, don't have any signs indicating their original use.

For anyone interested in following up on further aspects of Jewish history and culture in Poland consult the "Books" section in *Contexts*. On a practical level there are a number of organizations in Poland worth contacting (see box).

MAPS

The most detailed **road map** of the country is *Bartholomew's Europmap: Poland* (1:800,000), which is especially clear on rail lines. The *Orbis Poland: Roadmap* (1:750,000) is useful, too, and widely available in Poland; it's available through *Polorbis* or in map shops, in a modified form, as

MAP OUTLETS IN THE UK AND IRELAND

London:
Daunt Books, 83 Marylebone High St, W1 (☎0171/224 2295).

National Map Centre, 22–24 Caxton St, SW1 (☎0171/222 4945).

Stanfords, 12–14 Long Acre, WC2 (☎0171/836 1321); 52 Grosvenor Gardens, SW1W 0AG; 156 Regent St, W1R 5TA.

The Travel Bookshop, 13–15 Blenheim Crescent, W11 2EE (☎0171/229 5260).

The Travellers' Bookshop, 25 Cecil Court, WC2 (☎0171/836 9132).

Belfast:
Waterstone's, Queens Bldg, 8 Royal Ave, BT1 1DA (☎01232/247355).

Dublin:
Easons Bookshop, 40 O'Connell St, Dublin 1 (☎01/873 3811).

Hodges Figgis Bookshop, 56–58 Dawson St, Dublin 2 (☎01/677 4754).

Glasgow:
John Smith and Sons, 57–61 St Vincent St ,G2 5TB (☎0141/221 7472).

Maps are available by **mail or phone order** from *Stanfords* ☎0171/836 1321.

MAP OUTLETS IN NORTH AMERICA

Chicago:
Rand McNally, 444 N Michigan Ave, IL 60611 (☎312/321 1751).

Montréal:
Ulysses Travel Bookshop, 4176 St-Denis (☎514/289 0993).

New York:
The Complete Traveler Bookstore, 199 Madison Ave, NY 10016 (☎212/685 9007).

Rand McNally, 150 East 52nd St, NY 10022, (☎212/758 7488).

Traveler's Bookstore, 22 West 52nd St, NY 10019 (☎212/664 0995).

San Francisco:
The Complete Traveler Bookstore, 3207 Fillmore St, CA 92123 (☎415/923 1511).

Rand McNally, 595 Market St, CA 94105 (☎415/777 3131).

Sierra Club Bookstore, 730 Polk St, CA 94109 (☎415/923 5500).

Santa Barbara:
Map Link, Inc, 25 E Mason St, CA 93101 (☎805/965 4402).

Toronto:
Open Air Books and Maps, 25 Toronto St, ON M5R 2C1 (☎416/363 0719).

Vancouver:
World Wide Books and Maps, 1247 Granville St, BC V6Z 1E4 (☎604/687 3320).

Washington DC:
Rand McNally, 1201 Connecticut Ave NW, Washington DC 20003 (☎202/223 6751).

Note: *Rand McNally* has an extensive network of stores across the US: call ☎1-800/333 0136 (ext 2111) for the address of your nearest store, or for **direct mail** maps.

MAP OUTLETS IN AUSTRALIA AND NEW ZEALAND

Adelaide:
The Map Shop, 16a Peel St, SA 5000 (☎08/8231 2033).

Auckland:
Specialty Maps, 58 Albert St (☎09/307 2217).

Melbourne:
Bowyangs, 372 Little Burke St, VIC 3000 (☎03/9670 4383).

Sydney:
Travel Bookshop, 20 Bridge St, NSW 2000 (☎02/9241 3554).

Perth:
Perth Map Centre, 891 Hay St, WA 6000 (☎09/322 5733).

Hildebrand: Poland. PPWK, the state map company, produces an extremely good, though not always easily available, *Atlas Samochodowa* (1:300,000), divided into regions, with supplementary schematic town plans. *PPWK* also produces the atlas as a series of sixteen individual regional maps.

Should you need more detailed **city maps**, try to get hold of the appropriate *plan miasta*, available cheaply at local tourist offices, kiosks, street sellers and bookstores. These list all streets in A–Z format, and give exhaustive listings on bus and tram routes, places of entertainment, restaurants and cafés, often in several languages, including English. In the past, they have often been out of print for long periods; the situation has improved enormously lately, but remains unpredictable and patchy. Most bookstores keep a reasonable national selection. Useful words to look out for are *ulica*, often abbreviated to ul. (street); *alejela* or al. (avenue); *plac* or pl. (square) and *rynek* (old town

square). Bus routes are generally shown in blue, tram lines in red.

Even more essential, if you intend doing any serious walking, are the **hiking maps** of the National Parks and other tourist areas. Known as *Mapa Turystyczna*, these cost only a nominal amount and are very clear and simple to use: although the texts are usually only in Polish, the keys to the symbols are in several languages, including English. They can be even harder to come by than the city plans, though again things have been better recently: if you see a map you'll need later on in your travels, snap it up rather than risk not being able to get it in the region itself.

Finally for **campers**, there's the *Camping in Poland* (*Camping w Polsce*) map of the whole country, available in many tourist offices and bookstores. The map shows most of the official sites, though locations tend to be a bit inaccurate – the *Atlas Samochodowa* (see above) is more reliable in this respect.

GETTING AROUND

Poland has comprehensive and cheap public transport services, though they can often be overcrowded and excruciatingly slow. As a general rule, trains are the best means of moving across the country, as even the most rural areas are still crisscrossed by passenger lines. Rail buffs, in addition, will find Poland the most fascinating country in Europe: more than two dozen narrow-gauge lines are still in operation (identified in timetables by the word *wąsk*), and steam is used on some of these, as well as on a few mainline routes. For infor-

mation on the major train connections, consult the "Travel Details" section at the end of each chapter. The text of the *Guide* points out those places where it's preferable to take buses – which are usually better for short journeys or in the more remote areas.

Driving is also covered in the following section. You'll find car rental prices surprisingly high, but taxis are cheap enough to be considered for the occasional inter-town journey, especially if you can split costs three or four ways.

TRAINS

Polish State Railways (**PKP**) is a reasonably efficient organization, though its services, particularly on rural routes, have been heavily cut since the fall of communism and continue to be reduced at frequent intervals. *PKP* runs three main types of train (*pociąg*):

Inter-city or **express** services (*ekspresowy*) are the ones to go for if you're travelling long distances, as they stop at the main cities only (although they are still slow by western European standards, with the exception of a few recently introduced "named" trains). Seat reservations, involving a small supplementary charge, are compulsory; if you haven't understood the reservations system the ticket inspector can sell you one, albeit at a heavy supplement. Expresses are marked in red on timetables, with an R in a box alongside.

Fast trains (*pośpieszne*), again marked in red, have far more stops than express trains, and reservations are optional.

The **normal** services (*normalne* or *osobowe*) are shown in black and should be avoided whenever possible: in rural areas they stop at every haystack, while even on inter-urban routes it usually takes about an hour to cover 20km.

Fares won't burn a hole in the pocket of even the most impoverished Westerner. Even a long cross-country haul such as Warsaw to Wrocław, Kraków or Gdańsk will set you back little more than £10/$15. At these prices, it's well worth paying the fifty percent extra to travel **first-class** or make a **reservation** (*miejscówka*) even when this is not compulsory, as sardine-like conditions are fairly common. Reservations can be made up to sixty days in advance, or ninety days for return trips.

Most long inter-city journeys are best done overnight; they're often conveniently timed so that you leave around 10 or 11pm and arrive between 6 and 9am. For these, it's best to book either a **sleeper** (*sypialny*) or **couchette** (*kaszet*) at the "Polres" offices at main junctions or *Orbis* offices; the total cost will probably be little more than a room in a cheap hotel; the second-class sleepers are around £10/$15 per head; first class is £14/$21. Second class sleeps three to a compartment offering comfortable bunks along with a washbasin, towels, sheets and blankets; first class has just two bunks. Although preferable to sitting up, the couchettes (about £6/$9) are rather cramped, with six to a cabin. Mid-week, an alternative is to buy a regular first-class ticket, as there's a good chance of the compartment being empty, allowing you to sleep on the seats. Finally, a reminder about theft on trains: overnight sleepers on the principal lines are prime targets for robberies. One major hazard to watch out for is night-time stops at Warsaw's Central station en route to elsewhere – thieves regularly hop on, steal what they can, and hop off again. The best

advice is to keep your compartment locked and your valuables well hidden at all times.

TICKETS AND PASSES

Buying tickets is no problem in small places, but in the main city train stations it can be a major hassle, due to the bewildering array of counters, each almost invariably with a long snaking queue. Make sure you join the line long before your train is due to leave; in the worst cases (such as Warsaw and Poznań), you may have to wait for several hours.

Tickets come in all shapes and sizes, but you won't need to think too much about them unless you have an **undated ticket**, which you must validate in a machine on the platform before departure. If you're booking a sleeper or couchette, major stations have special counters. Since most officials don't speak any English, a good way to get the precise ticket you want is to write all the details down and show them at the counter; include destination, time of departure, class (first is *pierwsza*, second is *druga*) and whether you want a seat reservation (*miejscówka*).

As an alternative to the station queues, you can buy tickets for journeys of over 100km at *Orbis* offices. The main branches of these are also the best places to book for **international journeys**.

Discounts (*ugtowy*) are available for pensioners and for children aged between four and ten years; those under four travel free, though they're not supposed to occupy a seat. For students, *ISIC* cards no longer entitle you to discounted travel within Poland. However, on local trains you can often get away with only paying half price as many conductors are still not aware that the rules have changed.

British citizens under 26 can buy a *Polish Explorer Pass* giving unlimited second-class travel in Poland (£21 for 7 days up to £49 for 21 days) – worth doing if you plan any rail travel just to save on the queues, although not all conductors in Poland may be familiar with this type of pass. A first-class ticket option is also available, and some over-26s are also eligible for the pass (check before you leave home, see p.5 for agents). North Americans are eligible for the *Polrail Pass*, available from *Polorbis* before leaving home (see p.11). This covers any period from eight days up to a month and gives free travel on the entire rail network, although you'd have to take an awful lot of trains to justify the outlay. An eight-day pass starts at $60 for second-class, or $80 for first-class travel, rising to $100/$140 for one month. *Inter-Rail* passes are valid in Poland, but not *Eurail*.

STATION PRACTICALITIES

In train stations, the **departures** are normally listed on yellow posters marked *odjazdy*, with **arrivals** on white posters headed *przyjazdy*. Due to the recent spate of cutbacks, some stations may only have makeshift arrival and departure boards listing the services currently in operation. Unfortunately, these give no indication of journey time. "Ex" indicates express trains, fast trains are marked in red and normal services in black. An "R" in a square means that seat reservations are obligatory. Additionally, there may be figures at the bottom indicating the dates between which a particular train does (*kursuje*) or doesn't run (*nie kursuje*). Platform (*peron*) is also indicated.

If you're intending to do a lot of travelling in Poland, it makes sense to invest in the six-monthly network **timetable** (*rozkład*) which can be bought at all main stations. Otherwise, you may find yourself having to queue regularly at the information counters, which often have the longest lines of all.

Each **platform** has two tracks, so take care that you board the right train; usually only the long-distance services have boards stating their route, so you'll need to ask. To make matters worse, it's fairly common practice for trains to be re-routed to a different platform at the last minute: if you don't understand Polish you should always keep a sharp look out for the sudden movement of people from one platform to another. Electronic departure boards are increasingly common, though as yet are confined to major cities.

The **main station** in a city is identified by the name *Główny* or *Centralna*. These are open round the clock and usually have such facilities as waiting rooms, toilets, kiosks, restaurants, snack bars, cafés, a left luggage counter and a 24-hour post office. Outside the main cities, they can be the only place where you'll be able to get something to eat after about 9pm. The Poles operate an eccentric system for **checking in luggage**. You have to declare its value to the attendant at the left luggage office (*przwerza bagażu*) and pay one-hundredth of this sum as insurance on top of the basic storage charge. In practice, it's pointless offering a realistic estimate as chances of theft are slight. Payment is made when you retrieve your luggage not when depositing it. Only a couple of stations in the country have individual lockers.

Facilities **on the trains** are much poorer, though all inter-city trains, and occasionally others, have a buffet car (check on the departure board) and light refreshments are available on all overnight journeys. **Ticket control** is rather haphazard, particularly on crowded services, but it does happen more often than not. If you've boarded a train without the proper ticket, you should seek out the conductor, who will issue the right one on payment of a small supplement.

BUSES

The extent to which you'll need to make use of the services of *PKS*, the Polish national **bus company**, depends very much on the nature of your trip. If you're concentrating on cities, then the trains are definitely the better bet: **inter-city** buses (*autobusy pospieszne*) are often over-crowded and slow, and services less frequent and marginally more expensive, though in a few instances, such as in Mazuria, they travel on more direct and faster routes than the trains. There are only a few long-haul routes and even fewer overnight journeys. However, in **rural areas**, notably the mountain regions, local buses (*zwykłe*) are usually the best means of getting around, scoring in the choice and greater convenience of pick-up points and frequency of service.

TICKETS

In towns and cities, the main **bus station** (*dworzec autobusowy*) is usually alongside the train station. **Tickets** can be bought in the terminal building; in larger places there are several counters, each dealing with clearly displayed destinations. In a few places the terminal is shared with the train station, so make sure you go to the right counter. Booking the departure terminal ensures a seat, as a number will be allocated to you on your ticket. However, the lack of computerized systems means that many stations cannot allocate seats for services starting out from another town. In such cases, you have to wait until the bus arrives and buy a ticket – which may be for standing room only – from the driver.

The same procedure can also be followed, provided the bus isn't already full to overflowing, if you arrive too late to buy a ticket at the counter. With a few exceptions, it isn't possible to buy tickets for return journeys on board. Note too that a few routes are now run by private companies; these generally leave from outside the bus station. As with the trains, *Orbis* offices are the best place to go if you want to book on an **international** route. There are no student discounts on either buses or trams.

TIMETABLES

Noticeboards show **departures** and **arrivals** not only in the bus stations, but on all official stopping places along the route. "Fast" buses (which carry a small supplement) are marked in red, slow in black. The towns served are listed in alphabetical order, with the relevant times set against each, and mention made of the principal places passed on the way. This can be extremely confusing, as the normal practice is to list only services which terminate in that particular town, and not those which continue onwards. Thus you'll have to check down the "via" (*przez*) column to find additional departure times to your destination.

If in doubt, ask at the information counter, which will be equipped with the multi-volume set of timetables listing all *PKS* routes. It's usually best to write your destination down to avoid any confusion.

CITY TRANSPORT

Trams (usually antiquated boneshakers) are the basis of the public transport system in nearly all Polish cities. They usually run from about 5am to midnight, and departure times are clearly posted at the stops. **Tickets**, which cost around 80 grosz (about 18p/27¢), must be bought from a *Ruch* kiosk; nearly all use an overstamp, meaning they can only be used in the city where they were bought. On boarding, you should immediately **cancel your ticket** in one of the machines; checks by inspectors are rare, but they do happen from time to time. Note that some tickets have to be cancelled at both ends (arrows will indicate if this is so): this is for the benefit of children and pensioners, who travel half-price and thus have to cancel only one end per journey. If you transfer from one tram to another you'll need a second ticket.

The same tickets are valid on the municipal **buses** (which are usually red, in contrast to the yellow favoured by *PKS*) and the same system for validating the tickets applies – but note that **night services** require two tickets. The routes of the municipal buses go beyond the city boundaries into the outlying countryside, so many nearby villages have several connections during peak times of the day.

The price of **taxis** is cheap enough to make them a viable proposition for regular use during your visit. In the new free-market economy, plenty of people have turned to taxi driving, and outside hotels, stations and major tourist attractions you often have to run the gauntlet of cabbies. Be wary of unmetered taxis (unless you agree firmly the price in advance) and of drivers who demand payment in hard currency, and always ensure that the driver switches on the meter when you begin your journey. Because of the riproaring inflation of the past few years, what you actually pay is often the meter fare times a multiplier, the current figure for the latter being displayed on a little sign; prices are fifty percent higher after 11pm.

Prices are also raised by fifty percent for journeys outside the city limits. However, costs are always negotiable for longer journeys, between towns, for example, and can work out very reasonable if split among a group.

PLANES

The domestic network of **LOT**, the Polish national airline, operates regular **flights from Warsaw** to Gdańsk, Katowice, Kraków, Poznań, Rzeszów, Szczecin, Słupsk and Wrocław – all of which take about an hour. Some routes are covered several times a day, but services are sharply reduced on Sundays and during the winter months. Most of the cities mentioned are also linked directly to some of the others, but Warsaw is very much the lynchpin of the system. As a general rule, airports are located just outside the cities, and can be reached either by a special *LOT* bus or by a municipal service.

Tickets can be purchased at the airport itself or from *LOT* and *Orbis* offices, where you can also pick up free **timetables**. Prices are currently in the region of £40–45/$60–70 one-way (there are no savings on returns). Children up to the age of two travel for ten percent of the adult fare, provided they do not occupy a separate seat; under-12s go for half price. Private competitors also operate on some routes.

BOATS

In summer, ferries and hydrofoils serve towns along the **Baltic coast**, notably around Szczecin and in the Gdańsk area where they connect the Tri-City of Gdańsk, Sopot and Gdynia with each other and with the Hel Peninsula. The main companies are: *The Szczecin Shipping Company*, Marine Terminal, ul. Jana z Kolna 7, Szczecin (☎091/22 59 18), and *The Gdańsk Shipping Company*, ul. Wartka 4, Gdańsk (☎058/31 19 75). If you're in Poland and want to book tickets for international services, such as to Scandinavia, contact the *Polish Baltic Shipping Co.* head office: ul. Morska 2, 78–100 Kołobrzeg (☎0965/25211). The company also has offices in Świnoujście and Gdańsk.

Inland, excursion boats also run along certain stretches of the country's extensive system of **canals** – most enjoyably from Augustów near Białystok and along the ingeniously constructed Elbląg Canal – and short sections of the main **rivers**, such as the Wisła. Additionally, a curious and somewhat antiquated system of chain-haul car/passenger ferries serves the upper reaches of the Wisła and coastal surroundings.

DRIVING

Access to a **car** will save you a lot of time in exploring rural areas, and driving is relatively easy going anywhere in the country. Poles are not – as yet – routine car owners, although with car ownership currently increasing in leaps and bounds, notably in the cities, traffic is much more of an issue than it has ever been.

CAR RENTAL

Car rental in Poland is expensive: costs vary but you should reckon on spending around £60/$90 a day, £400/$600 a week for a Fiat Uno or Peugeot 205 with unlimited mileage – prices are often quoted and calculated in Deutschmarks. Cars can be booked through the usual agents in the West (see box) or in Poland itself: all the four major operators now have their own agents in all or most of the major Polish cities. Alternatively you can rent through the main *Orbis* offices (Gdańsk, Katowice, Kraków, Łódź, Poznań, Szczecin, Warsaw and Wrocław: see the relevant sections for addresses). Payment can be made with cash or any major credit card, and you can drop a car at a different office from the one where you rented it.

Cars will only be rented to people **over 21** who have held a full licence for more than a year. If you're planning on **renting a car outside Poland** and bringing it into the country you should be aware that rising levels of **car theft** (see box opposite) have led several of the major rental companies to slap severe restrictions on taking their cars east.

Check the conditions carefully before renting anything – if you do take a rental car into Poland without permission it means you effectively accept the financial risk for the car's full value if it's damaged in an accident or stolen. Of the major companies, *Hertz* currently seems to operate the least restrictive policies, but since they (like the other majors) have agents in Poland, you're better off renting inside the country.

If you're bringing your **own car**, you'll need to carry your vehicle's registration document. If the car is not in your name, you must have a letter of permission signed by the owner and authorized by your national motoring organization. You'll also need your driving licence (international driving licences aren't officially required, though they can be a help in tricky situations), and an international insurance green card to extend your insurance cover – check with your insurers to see whether you're covered or not. You're also required to carry a red warning triangle, a first-aid kit, a set of replacement bulbs and display a national identification sticker.

RULES OF THE ROAD

The main **rules of the road** are pretty clear, though there are some particularly Polish twists liable to catch out the unwary. The basic rules are: traffic drives on the right; it is compulsory to wear seat belts outside built-up areas; children under twelve years of age must sit in the back; right of way must be given to public transport vehicles (including trams). Drinking and driving is strictly prohibited – anyone with a foreign number plate driving around after 11pm, however innocently, has a strong chance of being stopped and breathalyzed.

Speed limits are 60kph in built-up areas (white signs with the place name mark the start of a built-up area, the same sign with a diagonal red line through it marks the end), 90kph on country roads, 110kph on motorways, and 70kph if you're pulling a caravan or trailer. **Fines**, administered on the spot, range from the negligible up to around £10/$15, although there is currently discussion of increasing these substantially up to £200/$300. Speed traps are common, particularly on major trunk roads, such as the Gdańsk–Warsaw route, so caution is strongly advised, especially on the approach to, and travelling through, small towns and villages. Also, be aware that a major overhaul of the traffic codes is being discussed by the Ministry of Transport. If enacted it will, among other things, further reduce speed limits in urban areas (50kph is proposed) and oblige you to have your headlights on all year round, Scandinavian style.

Other problems occur chiefly at night, especially on country roads, where potential disasters include horses and carts, mopeds without lights and staggering inebriated peasants. In cities, beware of a casual attitude towards traffic lights and road signs by local drivers and pedestrians.

Road conditions are generally pretty good, though in the east of the country especially, things can get a bit bumpy once you start veering off the beaten track. Motorways are still confined to a couple of stretches in the southwest,

although, with **major new projects** such as the proposed "Via Baltica", linking the whole southern Baltic coastline, the subject of ongoing discussion, and the country's road infrastructure benefiting from some far-reaching EU investments, the picture could well change significantly by the end of the decade. Prime examples include the proposed **A1** (Gdańsk–Łodz–Katowice–Gorzyce) motorway link with the Czech Republic; the **A2** (Świecko–Warsaw–Terespol route) on the Berlin–Moscow axis; and the **A4** (Zgorzelec–Kraków–Mędyke route) running on into Ukraine; 2600km of new motorway in total.

FUEL

With car ownership increasing rapidly, and operators of all kinds waking up to the economic potential of the Polish market, the old problems with finding **fuel** are fading away fast. An increasing number of small-scale operators, privatized *CPN* fuel depots and brand new multinational outlets have added substantially to the number of service stations around. Many stations in cities and along the main routes are open 24 hours a day, others from around 6am to 10pm; almost all out-of-town stations close on Sunday. Fuel is often **colour coded** at the pumps: red – 98 octane; yellow – 94 octane; green – 86 octane. As a rule always go for the highest octane available: 86 octane is much too low for most Western cars. While **diesel** is usually available (the pumps

---

CAR CRIME

With **car-related crime** – both simple break-ins and outright theft – one of the biggest criminal growth areas in Poland today, and foreign-registered vehicles one of the major targets, it pays to take note of the following simple precautions: especially in big towns, always park your vehicle in a guarded parking lot (*parking strzeżony*), never in an open street – even daylight break-ins occur with depressing frequency. Never leave anything of importance, including vehicle documents, in the car. Guarded lots cost little (rarely more than £2/$3 a day) and in most towns and cities you can usually find one located centrally – the major hotels almost always have their own nearby. If you have a break-in, report it to the police immediately. They'll probably shrug their shoulders over the prospects of getting anything back, but you'll need their signed report for insurance claim purposes back home.

have an ON sign), getting hold of **lead-free fuel** (*benzyna bezołowiowa*) is more problematic. Though the number of stations selling unleaded (either 91 octane or, for Western vehicles perilously low, 82.5 octane) is gradually increasing, especially in the big towns, tourist resorts and along the major routes, finding the stuff can still occasionally be a headache – a **Pb** sign with a diagonal red line through the middle indicates a station which has unleaded petrol.

Carrying at least one fuel can permanently topped up is thus advisable, especially in rural areas where lead-free can still be hard to obtain. If you can find it at a major station, there's a brochure listing unleaded filling stations throughout the country.

BREAKDOWNS AND SPARES

The Polish motoring association *PZMot* runs a 24-hour **car breakdown** service: for addresses and phone numbers, see the "Listings" section at the end of each main city account. The national HQ, which can provide some English-language pamphlets on their services, is at ul. Krucza 6/14, Warsaw (☎022/29 06 47 or 29 35 41). Anywhere else dial ☎954 or 981 at the nearest phone and wait for assistance. Though still dominant, the traditional national vehicle, a 1960s Fiat design, popularly known as the "Polski" Fiat, has now been joined by a welter of luxury and foreign imports. As a consequence, finding spares for major Western makes like Volvo, Renault and Volkswagen is much less of a headache than it used to be, at least in the cities: driving in through the suburbs you'll now see a host of dealers' adverts pointing you to the nearest supplier. If it's simply a case of a flat tyre, head for the nearest sizeable garage.

HITCHING

A by-product of the previous scarcity of private vehicles in Poland is that **hitchhiking** is positively encouraged. *PTTK* has institutionalized the practice through their *Społeczny Komitet Autostop* (Social Autostop Committee), which sells a package comprising a book of vouchers for 2000km of travel, an ID card, maps and an insurance policy. The relevant number of vouchers should be given to the driver, who then qualifies for various prizes and is indemnified for any compensation claims. The *Autostop* packages are valid from May to September (nominal charge), and available to anyone over seventeen from larger *PTTK* offices

and some youth hostels; the head *Autostop* office is ul. Narbutta 27a, Warsaw (☎022/49 62 08).

Finally, note that the Polish convention is to stick out your whole arm – not just your thumb.

CYCLING

Cycling is often regarded as an ideal way to see a predominantly rural country like Poland. Even on the back roads, surfaces are generally in good shape, and there isn't much traffic around – anyone used to cycling in Western traffic is in for a treat. An additional plus is the mercifully flat nature of much of the terrain, which allows you to cycle quite long distances without great effort. You'll need to bring your own machine and a supply of spare parts: except in a few major cities like Warsaw and Kraków, and a number of southern mountain areas like the Bieszczady, bike rental and spare part facilities are still a rarity. In rural areas, though, bikes are fairly common, and with a bit of ingenuity you can pick up basic spares like inner tubes and puncture repair kits.

Taking your bike on **the train** won't present any problems: there's a nominal charge, and your bike normally goes in the luggage compartment. The same goes for hotels, which usually put your machine either in a locked luggage room or guarded parking lot. You need to exercise at least as much caution concerning **security** as you would in any city at home: strong locks and chaining your bike to immobile objects are the order of the day, and always try and take your bike indoors at night.

TAKING YOUR BIKE TO POLAND

At the time of writing, it's not possible to send an unaccompanied bicycle to Poland **by train** from Britain: the ferry companies have decided they won't carry riderless bikes, so *British Rail* will refuse your machine unless you are travelling with it. Once on the continent you're free to send the bike off alone: it takes about a week from France or Holland, and can be done from almost any station for a small fee, although be warned that thefts from Polish baggage stations are now a regular occurrence. One safer (and quicker) option is to send your bike to Frankfurt an der Oder on the German/Polish border, collect it there and take it across the border by road. Should the regulations change, the **British Rail European Travel Centre**, Victoria Station, London SW1 (☎0171/834 2345) will have the details.

ACCOMMODATION

Accommodation will probably account for most of your essential expenditure in Poland, though you're by no means confined to the international hotels so heavily touted in most promotional material: almost everywhere, there are now plenty of cheap alternatives. Listings in the *Guide* have been made as wide-ranging as possible to reflect the immense diversity on offer: privately run hotels, pensions, hostels, workers' hostels, youth hostels, rooms in private houses and a good range of campsites.

HOTELS

Orbis runs some 55 **international hotels** throughout Poland, which can be booked with a minimum of fuss before your departure. A few of these are famous old prewar haunts, but the vast majority date from the last twenty years and are in the anonymous concrete style favoured for business purposes the world over. This stock is now being supplemented in the big cities by a mass of even more luxurious establishments, often as joint ventures with well-known Western hotel chains. Double room prices start at £80/$120, with singles from £50/$75, although you may well find good reductions at weekends (often up to fifty percent), but you must stay at least two nights to qualify for these.

Even if they are way beyond your budget, it's still worth knowing about these hotels, as you're more likely to find helpful staff speaking English and other foreign languages here than you are in any tourist office. Non-guests are also able to make use of their very Westernized **facilities**. Particularly useful are the 24-hour currency exchange, the telex and telephone services – often the easiest, though expensive, means of making an international call. In addition, these hotels have restaurants, cafés and bars, and may have other facilities such as a swimming pool, solarium, sauna, tennis court, hairdresser, night-club and disco.

Orbis also runs a number of **motels** on the outskirts of major cities; these are usually a bit cheaper than their more central counterparts, but generally only practical if you've got your own transport.

Most other hotels have far more rudimentary facilities. They're graded on a **star system** (officially abolished but informally retained by the establishments themselves), but these are generously awarded: most four-star Polish hotels would be lucky to be graded as two-star anywhere else. One of the biggest deficits in the accommodation field remains the lack of small competitively priced **mid-range hotels** – small-scale tourist-oriented initiatives were never a strong point of communist-era economic policy. Prices and quality vary considerably in this category (see Accommodation Price Codes box), but for a standard double medium-range room expect to pay £15–20/$23–30 a night. **Breakfast** is sometimes included in the room price, but more often is not. Always ask for prices with and without bath – there may be a substantial difference.

The cheapest of all hotel rooms are provided by **sports hotels** (*Dom Sportowy*), under £10/$15 a night. These, however, exist mainly for the use of visiting sporting teams, which means they're likely to be fully booked for at least part of the weekend, and at other times deserted. They're also usually located in a park way out from the centre. They don't serve meals and you may be asked to share a room with a stranger.

PENSIONS AND HOLIDAY HOMES

Some of Poland's best accommodation deals can be found in the growing stock of **pensions** (*pensjonaty*) situated in the resort towns of major holiday areas such as the Tatras, the Karkonosze and the Kłodzko region. These are a particularly attractive option if you're travelling in a group, as triples and quadruples offer substantial savings over doubles; singles, however, are extremely scarce. Half-board terms range between £8–16/$12–24 per head; it's sometimes possible to get bed and breakfast only, but it would be a pity to

ACCOMMODATION PRICE CODES

All accommodation listed in the guide (apart from youth hostels) is **price graded** according to the scale below. Unless specified otherwise, prices given are for the cheapest double room. In some *PTTK* and workers' hostels, which often do not have private rooms, the price code represents the price for two beds in a dorm.

In the cheapest places (**categories ①–②**), rooms generally come without their own private bath/ shower, breakfast is often not included, and in some instances (specified in the text) beds are in dorms only. Even in **categories ③–⑤**, the range of facilities is extremely uneven: you'll probably have your own washing sink, but private bathroom and/or toilet, for example, are unpredictable accessories. Overall, room quality in the middle ranges is affected by the age of the building (generally speaking the newer the place, especially post-1990, the better) and its geographical location – the more popular tourist centres are improving room quality faster than the rest, and the east of the country is lagging noticeably behind western regions. Into the top bracket hotels (**categories ⑧–⑨**) it's another story, high prices are generally matched by consistently high standards. From minimum rates of around £80/$120 per double room, prices rise up to £180/$270 in the most exclusive addresses in Warsaw.

To help you, price equivalents are expressed in (new) złotys, along with pound sterling and US dollars. The majority of places will expect you to pay in złoty, though the really upmarket hotels generally show prices in dollars/Deutschmarks and will accept payment in Western currencies, major credit cards included.

① under 20zł (under £5/$7.5)   ② 20–38zł (£5–10/$7.5–15)   ③ 38–58zł (£10–15/$15–23)

④ 58–75zł (£15–20/$23–30)   ⑤ 75–95zł (£20–25/$30–38)   ⑥ 95–135zł (£25–35/$38–53)

⑦ 135–210zł (£35–55/$53–83)   ⑧ 210–300zł (£55–80/$83–120)   ⑨ over 300zł (over £80/$120)

miss out on the excellent regional cuisine that's usually provided. For reservations and further details, contact an *Orbis* office in the appropriate area.

Another possibility is to rent a **summer cottage**. Available between mid-May and the end of September, these are roughly analogous to the French *gîtes*. Intended for quiet breaks, with opportunities for cycling, rambling, angling and water sports, they are mostly located in secluded rural areas, notably the Mazurian Lakes, the Lubuska region and Western Pomerania, though there are also some along the Baltic coast. All have a living room with dining area, a bathroom with hot and cold running water, a fully equipped kitchen, a fire-place, and a patio or balcony. They have between one and five bedrooms, sleeping from three to eight people, and are priced accordingly. These cottages must be booked in advance: for full details, contact any *Polorbis* or *Orbis* office, or a specialist tour operator (see "Getting There", p.8 and p.13).

Since the beginning of the 1990s, there has been a new addition to the holiday lodging scene – **workers' holiday homes** (often designated *FWP*). These were formerly run by unions and factories for their own employees, but are increasingly being privatized and opened to general trade. Cheap, often attractively located in traditional holiday areas, they are generally desperate for custom. The bigger places have a range of extra facilities, including tennis courts, swimming pools, and are an option well worth exploring. Expect to pay £10–15/$15–30 per person per night.

PRIVATE ROOMS

You can get a **room in a private house** (*kwatery prywatny*) almost anywhere in the country. It's an ideal way to find out how the Poles themselves live, but be prepared for some shabby flats, which may be situated on the outskirts of town.

All major cities have an office providing a room-finding service, usually known as the *Biuro Zakwaterowańia*. Expect to pay around £6–10/$9–15 per person per night, and at least half as much again in Warsaw. You should be given a choice of location and category (from 1 down to 3); you register and pay for as many nights as you wish, then are given directions to the house where you'll be staying. You must arrive there before 10pm; there will probably also be a restriction on how early you check in (perhaps 1pm). In case you don't like the place you're sent to, it makes sense not to register for too many nights ahead, as it's easy enough to extend your stay by going back to the *Biuro*, or paying your host directly. Note that there's no scope under this setup for negotiating special rates: the host is obliged to inform the *Biuro* if you're staying on, or else is liable to have someone else sent by them to occupy your room.

Some **Orbis offices** also act as agents for householders with rooms available to let. These are often a little more expensive and may be subject to a minimum stay of three nights (or else a hefty surcharge). However, the administration is far less tight than with a *Biuro Zakwaterowańa* and you can subsequently extend the length of your stay by negotiation with your host, who'll no doubt be happy to pass on in the form of a price reduction some of the substantial share of your payment that would otherwise go to *Orbis*.

At the unofficial level, many houses in the main holiday areas hang out **signs** saying *Noclegi* (lodging) or *Pokoje* (rooms). It's up to you to bargain over the price; £3/$4.50 is the least you can expect to pay. In the cities, you won't see any signs advertising rooms, but you may well be approached outside stations and other obvious places. Before accepting, establish the price and check that the location is suitable.

TOURIST AND STUDENT HOSTELS

One reason the youth hostels maintain the accent on youth is that there's a network of adult **tourist hostels**, often run by **PTTK** and usually called **Dom Turysty**. Found in both cities and rural locations, these are generally cheaper than any hotel, but are often a poor bargain at around £5/$7.50 for a bed in a small dorm with basic shared facilities. Double rooms are also sometimes available The price codes given in the text represent the total cost for two people per night whether in a private room or in a dorm.

In July, August and early September **Almatur** also organizes accommodation in **student hostels** in the main university towns. Rooms have two, three or four beds; the charges including breakfast are around £4/$6 for students (proof will be required), £6.50/$10 for others under 35, which is the age limit. You can eat cheaply at the cafeteria on the premises, and there are often discos in the evenings. The location of these hostels can vary from year to year: contact an *Almatur* office (relevant addresses are given in the text) or *Polorbis* before you go.

In mountain areas, a reasonably generous number of **refuges** (*schroniska*), which are clearly marked on hiking maps, enable you to make long-distance treks without having to make

---

ECO-HOLIDAYS IN POLAND

Into the mid-1990s the traditional image of Poland as fearsome environmental blackspot is changing (Greenpeace has christened the country the Green Tiger of Europe). One of the factors behind this reassessment is a growing appreciation of the relatively unspoiled condition of much of the **rural Polish environment**. Uniquely among the former communist states of Eastern Europe, agriculture in Poland remained relatively unaffected by Stalinist-era collectivization, and a large proportion of the country is dominated by **small-scale privately run holdings**. Increasing numbers of these land holders are adopting organically based farming practices, and to help supplement their incomes are turning towards small-scale tourism, mostly in the form of rural **bed and breakfast.**

Many are now linked to the network established by the **European Centre for Eco-Agro Tourism** (*ECEAT*), a Dutch-based foundation dedicated to supporting practical initiatives in the field of eco-friendly tourism. *ECEAT* produces a yearly handbook of farms throughout Poland offering holiday stays. The accommodation on offer is cheap and (usually) fairly basic, but includes easy access to some of the most beautiful parts of the Polish countryside, plenty of scope for outdoor activities (for example, many farms keep horses that guests are welcome to use) and the knowledge that you're doing something to support the local rural economy. The range of accommodation is growing and also includes facilities connected with national parks, environmental organizations, and village community projects.

To order a copy of the *ECEAT Poland* handbook, which has listings from all over the country, contact:

Netherlands *ECEAT*, Postbox 10899, 1001 EW Amsterdam (☎20/668 1030; fax: 20/665 0166).

Poland Glebock 24, 58 835 Milkow (☎/fax 075/53346; Tues & Thurs 10am–1pm).

UK *Eco Tourism Ltd*, 161 Camp Rd, St. Albans, AL1 5LZ (☎01727/760854; fax: 01727/760855).

detours down into the villages for the night. Accommodation is in very basic dormitories, but costs are nominal and you can often get cheap and filling hot meals; in summer the more popular refuges can be very crowded indeed, as they are obliged to accept all-comers. As a rule, the refuges are open all year round but it's always worth checking for closures or renovations in progress before setting out.

YOUTH HOSTELS

Scattered throughout Poland are some 200 **official youth hostels** (*Schroniska Młodzieżowe*), identified by a green triangle on a white background. However, a large percentage of these are only open for a few weeks at the height of the summer holiday period, usually in converted school buildings, and are liable to be booked solid, especially mid-May to mid-June by school groups. Most of the permanent year-round hostels are still very much in line with the hairshirt ideals of the movement's founders. Children under ten years old are not allowed in, and preference is supposedly given to those under 26, though there's no upper age restriction. Make sure you bring a sheet or sleeping bag. Cooking facilities are usually available.

Two plus points are the **prices** (rarely more than £2.50/$4 a head, with £1.50/$2.50 a likely average) and the **locations**, with many hostels placed close to town centres. Against that, there's the fact that dormitories are closed between 10am and 5pm, you must check in by 9pm, and a 10pm curfew is usually enforced.

The most useful hostel **addresses** are given in the *Guide*, but if you need a complete list,

either buy the official International Handbook or contact the head office of the Polish Youth Hostel Federation (*PTSM*) at ul. Chocimska 28, Warsaw (Mon–Fri 8am–3.30pm; ☎022/49 83 54 or 49 81 28) for their own comprehensive handbook (*Informator*). It's best to buy an **IYHF** membership card before you go (see box below for addresses).

CAMPSITES

There are some 500 **campsites** throughout the country classified in three categories: category 1 sites usually have amenities such as a restaurant and showers; while category 3 sites amount to little more than poorly lit, run-down expanses of grass. The most useful are listed in the text; for a complete list, get hold of the *Camping w Polsce* **map**, available from bookstores, some travel bureaux or the motoring organization *PZMot*. Apart from a predictably dense concentration in the main holiday areas, sites can also be found in most cities: the ones on the outskirts are almost invariably linked by bus to the centre and often have the benefit of a peaceful location and swimming pool. The major drawback is that most are open May–September only, though a few do operate all year round. **Charges** usually work out at less than £2/$3 per head, a bit more if you come by car.

One specifically Polish feature is that you don't necessarily have to bring a tent to stay at many campgrounds, as there are often **chalets** for rent, generally complete with toilet and shower. Though decidedly spartan in appearance, these are good value at around £3.50/$5 per head. In summer, however, they are invariably booked long in advance.

YOUTH HOSTEL ASSOCIATIONS

Australia *Australian Youth Hostels Association*, Level 3, 10 Mallet St, Camperdown, Sydney (☎02/565 1325).

Canada *Hostelling International/Canadian Youth Hostels*, Room 400, 205 Catherine St, Ottawa, ON K2P 1C3 (☎613/237 7884 or ☎1-800/663 5777).

England and Wales *Youth Hostel Association* (*YHA*), Trevelyan House, 8 St Stephen's Hill, St Alban's, Herts AL1 2DY (☎01727/855215). London information office: 14 Southampton St, London WC2 7HY (☎0171/836 1036).

Ireland *Youth Hostel Association of Northern Ireland*, 22 Donegall Rd, Belfast BT12 5JN (☎01232/324 733); *An Oige*, 61 Mountjoy St, Dublin 7 (☎01/830 4555).

New Zealand PO Box 436, Christchurch (☎03/379 9970).

Scotland *Scottish Youth Hostel Association*, 7 Glebe Crescent, Stirling, FK8 2JA (☎01786/451181).

USA *Hostelling International/American Youth Hostels (HI-AYH)*, 733 15th St NW, Suite 840, PO Box 37613, Washington, DC 20005 (☎1-800/444 6111).

Camping wild, outside of the National Parks, is acceptable so long as you're reasonably discreet.

If you're planning to do a lot of camping, an **international camping carnet** is a good investment, available from home motoring organizations, or from the following: in Britain, the *Camping and Caravan Club*, Greenfields House, Westwood Way, Coventry, CV4 8JH (☎01203/694995); in the US, *Family Campers and RVers* (*FCRV*), 4804 Transit Rd, Building 2, Depew, NY 14043 (☎1-800/245 9755); and in Canada, 51 W 22nd St, Hamilton, Ontario LC9 4N5 (☎1-800/245 9755). The carnet serves as useful identification and covers you for third-party insurance when camping.

EATING AND DRINKING

Poles take their food seriously, providing snacks of feast-like proportions for the most casual visitors, and maintaining networks of country relatives or local shops for especially treasured ingredients – smoked meats and sausages, cheeses, fruits and vegetables. The cuisine itself is a complex mix of influences: Turkish, Russian, Lithuanian, Ukrainian, German and Jewish traditions all leaving their mark. To go with the food, there is excellent beer and a score of wonderful vodkas.

The best meals you'll have in Poland are likely to be in people's homes, if you get the invitation. However, with the moves towards a market economy, the country's growing number of **restaurants** – most of which specialized in ungarnished slabs of meat during the communist era – have been looking up. At their best, in fact, they are as good as any in central Europe, dishing out a spoonful of caviar for starters before moving on through traditional soups to beef, pork or duck dishes. And, like much else, they are generally cheap for Western tourists.

Drinking habits are changing. Poles for years drank mainly at home, while visitors stuck to the hotels, with such other **bars** as existed being alcoholic-frequented dives. Over the last couple of years, though, something of a bar culture has been emerging in the cities, supplementing the largely non-alcohol-serving cafés. Elsewhere, drinking is still best done at the local hotel or restaurant.

FOOD

Like their central and eastern European neighbours, Poles are insatiable **meat** eaters: throughout the austerities of the past decade, meat consumption here remained among the highest in Europe. Beef and pork in different guises are the mainstays of most meals, while hams and sausages are consumed at all times of the day, as snacks and sandwich-fillers. In the coastal and mountain regions, you can also expect **fish** to feature prominently on the menus, with carp and trout being particularly good.

Although a meal without meat is a contradiction in terms for most Poles, **vegetarians** will find cheap refuge in the rapidly diminishing stock of milk bars (see below), whose dairy-based menus exclude meat almost entirely (continuing Jewish traditions). They have a very mixed reputation, popular on the whole with the young and with students, but often scorned by their elders. At the opposite end of the economic scale, the plusher restaurants normally carry a selection of vegetarian dishes (*potrawy jarskie*); if the menu has no such section, the key phrase to use is *bez mięsne* (without meat).

BREAKFASTS, SNACKS AND FAST FOODS

For most Poles, the first meal of the day, eaten at home at around 7am, is little more than a sandwich with a glass of tea or cup of coffee. A more leisurely **breakfast** might include fried eggs with ham, mild frankfurters, a selection of cold meats and cheese, rolls and jam, but for most people this full spread is more likely to be taken as a second breakfast (*drugie śniadanie*) at around midday. This is often eaten in the workplace, but a common alternative for younger, city Poles is to stop at a milk bar or self-service snack bar (*samoobsługa*).

Open from early morning till 5 or 6pm (later in the city centres), **snack bars** are soup-kitchen-type places, serving very cheap but generally uninspiring food: small plates of salted herring in oil (*śledź w oleju*), sandwiches, tired-looking meat or cheese, sometimes enlivened by some Russian salad (*sałatka jarzynowa*).

Milk bars (*bar mleczny*) are even cheaper options, offering a selection of solid, non-meat meals with the emphasis on quantity. Milk bars and snack bars both operate as self-service cafeterias: the menu is displayed over the counter, but if you don't recognize the names of the dishes, you can just point. Unfortunately, the milk bar seems to be becoming something of a threatened institution; many have closed down in recent years.

TAKEAWAY AND FAST FOOD

Traditional Polish **takeaway stands** usually sell *zapiekanki*, baguette-like pieces of bread topped with melted cheese; a less common but enjoyable version of the same thing comes with fried mushrooms. You'll also find **hotdog stal's**, doling out sub-Frankfurter sausages in white rolls, and stalls and shops selling **French fries**; the latter are generally fat and oily, sold by weight, and accompanied by sausage or chicken in the tourist resorts and some city stands, or by fish in the northern seaside resorts and lakeland areas.

Western-style **fast food**, the totemic symbol of transformation towards a market economy all over Eastern Europe, has been seized on with eager enthusiasm in Poland. Many of the major international burger/pizza chains – *McDonalds*, *Burger King*, *KFC* and *Pizza Hut* – are now established in the big cities, generally no better or worse than their counterparts elsewhere. Local

initiatives have also proliferated, and no self-respecting Polish town is now without at least one burger joint gracing the main street.

DO-IT-YOURSELF SNACKS

If the snacks on offer fail to appeal, you can always stock up on your own provisions.

Most people buy their **bread** in supermarkets (*samoobsługowe*) or from market traders; bakeries (*piekarnia*) are mostly small private shops and still something of a rarity, but when you do find them they tend to be very good, as the queues indicate. The standard loaf (*chleb zakopiański*) is a long piece of dense rye bread, often flavoured with caraway seeds. Also common is *razowy*, a solid brown bread sometimes flavoured with honey, and *mazowiecki*, a white, sour rye bread. Rolls come in two basic varieties: the more common is the plain, light white roll called a *kajzerka*, the other is the *grahamka*, a round roll of rougher and denser brown bread.

Supermarkets are again a useful source for **fillers**, with basic delicatessen counters for cooked meats and sausages, and fridge units holding a standard array of hard and soft cheeses. Street markets often reveal rather more choice – certainly for **fruit and vegetables**. Few market stalls supply bags, so bring your own.

COFFEE, TEA AND SWEETS

Poles are inveterate tea and coffee drinkers, their daily round punctuated by endless cups or glasses, generally with heaps of sugar.

Tea, which is cheaper and so marginally more popular, is drunk Russian-style in the glass, without milk and often with lemon. Cafés and restaurants will give you hot water and a tea bag (Chinese tea as a rule), but in bars it's more likely to be *naturalna* style – a spoonful of tea leaves with the water poured on top.

Coffee is served black unless you ask otherwise, in which case specify with milk (*z mlekiem*) or with cream (*ze śmietaną*). Most **cafés** (*kawarnia*) offer only *kawa naturalna*, which is a strong brew made by simply dumping the coffee grounds in a cup or glass and pouring water over them. *Espresso* and *capuccino*, usually passable imitations of the Italian originals, are confined to the better cafés or restaurants. In cafés and bars alike a shot or two of vodka or *winiak* (locally produced cheap brandy) with the morning cup of coffee is still frequent practice.

FOOD AND DRINK GLOSSARY

The *Rough Guide to Polish* phrasebook has a more detailed selection of useful food and drink terms.

Basic Foods

Bułka	Bread rolls	*Kołduny*	Dumplings	*Pieprz*	Pepper
Chleb	Bread	*Kotlet*	Cutlet	*Potrawy*	Vegetarian
Chrzan	Horseradish	*Makaron*	Macaroni	*jarskie*	dishes
Cukier	Sugar	*Masło*	Butter	*Ryby*	Fish
Drób	Poultry	*Mięso*	Meat	*Ryż*	Rice
Frytki	Chips/French fries	*Ocet*	Vinegar	*Śmietana*	Cream
Jajko	Egg	*Olej*	Oil	*Sól*	Salt
Jarzyny/	Vegetables	*Owoce*	Fruit	*Surówka*	Salad
warzywa		*Pieczeń*	Roast meat	*Zupa*	Soup
Kanapka	Sandwich	*Pieczyste*	Steak		

Common Terms

Antrykot/wołowy	Mixed	*Mielone*	Minced	*Surowy*	Raw
Filiżanka	Cup	*Na zdrowie!*	Cheers!	*Świeży*	Fresh
Gotowany	Boiled	*Nadziewany*	Stuffed	*Szaszłyk*	Grilled
Grill/z rusztu	Grilled	*Nóż*	Knife	*Szklanka*	Glass
Jadłospis	Menu	*Obiad*	Lunch	*Sznycel*	Escalope/
Kolacja	Dinner	*Słodki*	Sweet		schnitzel
Kwaśny	Sour	*Smacznego!*	Bon appetit!	*Talerz*	Plate
Łyżka	Spoon	*Śniadanie*	Breakfast	*Widelec*	Fork
Marynowany	Pickled				

Soups

Barszcz czerwony –	Beetroot soup (borsch)	*(zupa) Cebulowa*	Onion soup
z paszetcikem	– with pastry	*(zupa) Fasolowa*	Bean soup
Barszcz ukraiński	White borsch	*(zupa) Grochowa*	Pea soup
Bulion/rosół	Bouillon	*(zupa) Grzybowa*	Mushroom soup
Chłodnik	Sour milk and	*(zupa) Jarzynowa*	Vegetable soup
	vegetable cold soup	*(zupa) Ogórkowa*	Cucumber soup
Kapuśniak	Cabbage soup	*(zupa) Owocowa*	Cold fruit soup
Kartoflanka	Potato soup	*(zupa) Pomidorowa*	Tomato soup
Krupnik	Barley soup	*Żurek*	Sour cream soup

Fish and Poultry

Bażant	Pheasant	*Kaczka*	Duck	*Łosoś*	Salmon	*Sardynka*	Sardine
Dziczyzna	Game	*Karp*	Carp	*Makrela*	Mackerel	*Śledź*	Herring
Gęś	Geese	*Kurczak*	Chicken	*Pstrąg*	Trout	*Węgorz*	Eel
Indyk	Turkey						

Meat

Baranina	Mutton	*Golonka*	Leg of pork	*Wątróbka*	Liver with onion
Befsztyk	Steak	*Kiełbasa*	Sausage	*Wieprzowe*	Pork
Bekon boczek	Bacon	*Kotlet schabowy*	Pork cutlet	*Wołowe*	Beef
Cielęcina	Veal	*Salami*	Salami		
Dzik	Wild boar	*Sarnina*	Elk		

FOOD AND DRINK GLOSSARY (cont...)

Vegetables

Cebula	Onion	*Kalafior*	Cauliflower	*Papryka*	Paprika
Ćwikła/buraczki	Beetroot	*Kapusta*	Cabbage	*Pomidor*	Tomato
Czosnek	Garlic	*Kapusta kiszona*	Sauerkraut	*Szparagi*	Asparagus
Fasola	Beans	*Marchewka*	Carrots	*Szpinak*	Spinach
Groch	Peas	*Ogórek*	Cucumber	*Ziemniaki*	Potatoes
Grzyby/pieczarki	Mushrooms	*Ogórki*	Gherkins		

Fruits and Nuts

Ananas	Pineapple	*Czereśnie*	Cherries	*Morele*	Apricots
Banan	Banana	*Gruszka*	Pears	*Orzechy włoskie*	Walnuts
Cytryna	Lemon	*Jabłko*	Apple	*Pomarańcze*	Orange
Czarne jagody	Blackberries	*Kompot*	Stewed fruit	*Śliwka*	Plum
borówki		*Laskowe/orzechy*	Almonds	*Truskawki*	Strawberries
Czarne porzeczki	Blackcurrant	*Maliny*	Raspberries	*Winogrona*	Grapes

Cheese

Bryndza	Sheep's cheese	*(ser) Myśliwski*	Smoked cheese	*Twaróg*	Cottage cheese
Oscypek	Smoked goats' cheese	*(ser) Tylżycki*	Cheddar cheese		

Cakes and Desserts

Ciastko	Cake	*Galaretka*	Jellied fruits	*Pączki*	Doughnuts
Ciasto drożdżowe	Yeast cake	*Lody*	Ice cream	*Sernik*	Cheesecake
	with fruit	*Makowiec*	Poppyseed cake	*Tort*	Tart
Czekolada	Chocolate	*Mazurek*	Shortcake		

Drinks

Cocktail mleczny	Milk shake	*Sok pomarańczowy*	Orange juice
Gorąca czekolada	Drinking chocolate	*Sok pomidorowy*	Tomato juice
Herbata	Tea	*Spirytus*	Spirits
Kawa	Coffee	*Winiak*	Polish brandy
Koniak	Cognac/brandy (imported)	*Wino*	Wine
Miód pitny	Mead	*Wino wytrawne*	Dry wine
Mleko	Milk	*Wino słodkie*	Sweet wine
Napój	Bottled fruit drink	*Wódka*	Vodka
Piwo	Beer	*Woda*	Water
Sok	Juice	*Woda mineralna*	Mineral water

CAKES AND ICE CREAM

Cakes, pastries and other sweets are an integral ingredient of most Poles' daily consumption, and the cake shops (*cukiernia*) – which you'll find even in small villages – are as good as any in central Europe. Cheesecake is a national favourite, as are poppyseed cake, *drożdówka* (a sponge cake, often topped with plums), and *babka piaskowa* (marble cake). In the larger places you can also expect to find *torcik wiedeński*, an Austrian-style *schlagtort* with coffee and chocolate filling, as well as *keks* (fruitcake) and a selection of eclairs, profiteroles and cupcakes. Wherever you are, go early in the day, as many cake shops sell out quickly, as do the cafés with their more limited selections.

Poles eat **ice cream** at all times of the year, queueing up for cones at street-side kiosks or in *cukiernia*. The standard kiosk cone is watery and pretty tasteless, but elsewhere the selection is better: decent cafés, and in particular the misleadingly named alcohol-free **cocktail bars**, offer a mouthwatering selection of ices.

RESTAURANT MEALS

The average **restaurant** (*restauracja*, sometimes *jadłodajnia*) is open from late morning through to mid-evening: all but the smartest close early, though, winding down around 9pm in cities, earlier in the country. Some don't open till 1pm due to the ban on the sale of alcohol before that time. Relatively late-night standbys include *Orbis* hotel restaurants and, at the other end of the scale, train station snack bars. Bear in mind too, that the total shutdown principle, applied around religious festivals and public holidays, often applies to restaurants. In smaller towns, the big hotels may be the only place open.

Officially restaurants are **graded** from *kat 1* (luxury) down to *kat 4* (cheap), categories which are displayed at the top of the menu; unless your funds are very limited, stick to the top two ratings only – *kat 3* and *4* places can be dirty and dire. Many of the newer private places seem to have eluded this system, however, and categories may well be entirely redefined over the next year or two.

Except in the big hotels and poshest restaurants, **menus** are usually in Polish only; the language section opposite should provide most of the cues you'll need. While the list of dishes apparently on offer may be long, in reality only things with a price marked next to them will be available, which will normally reduce the choice by fifty percent or more. If you arrive near closing time or late lunchtime, the waiter may inform you there's only one thing left.

There are no hard and fast rules about **tipping**, but a common practice is to round the bill up to the nearest złoty, except in upmarket places, where leaving ten percent is the established practice.

READING THE MENU

Menus are broken up into courses with separate headings:

Zupy	Soups
Przekąski	Starters/Hors d'oeuvres
Dania drugie	Main course
Dodatki	Side dishes
Desery	Desserts
Napoje	Drinks

SOUPS AND STARTERS

First on the menu in most places are **soups**, definitely one of Polish cuisine's strongest points, varying from light and delicate dishes to concoctions that are virtually meals in themselves.

Best known is *barszcz*, a spicy beetroot broth that's ideally accompanied by a small pastry. Other soups worth looking out for are *żurek*, a creamy white soup with sausage and potato; *botwinka*, a seasonal soup made from the leaves of baby beetroots; *krupnik*, a thick barley and potato soup with chunks of meat, carrots and celeriac; and *chłodnik*, a cold Lithuanian beetroot soup with sour milk and vegetable greens, served in summer.

In less expensive establishments, you'll be lucky to have more than a couple of soups and a plate of cold meats, or herring with cream or oil to choose from as a starter.

In better restaurants, though, the **hors d'oeuvres** selection might include Jewish-style gefilte fish, jellied ham (*szynka w galarecie*), steak tartare (*stek tatarski*), wild rabbit paté (*pasztet z zająca*), or hard-boiled eggs in mayonnaise, which sometimes come stuffed with vegetables (*jajka faszerowane*).

MAIN COURSES

The basis of most main courses is a fried or grilled cut of **meat** in a thick sauce, commonest of which is the *kotlet schwabowy*, a fried pork cutlet. However, Poland's stock of wild animals means that in better restaurants you may find wild boar and elk on the menu. Two national specialities you'll find everywhere are *bigos* (cabbage stewed with meat and spices) and *pierogi*, dumplings stuffed with meat and mushrooms – or with cottage cheese, onion and spices in the non-meat variation (*pierogi ruskie*). Another favourite is *flaczki*, tripe cooked in a spiced bouillon stock with vegetables; also worth trying are *gołabki* (cabbage leaves stuffed with meat, rice and occasionally mushrooms) and *golonka* (pig's leg with horseradish and pease pudding). Duck is usually the most satisfying poultry, particularly with apples, while carp, eel and trout are generally reliable **fish** dishes, usually grilled or sautéed, occasionally poached. **Pancakes** (*naleśniki*) often come as a main course, too, stuffed with cottage cheese (*z serem*).

Main dishes come with some sort of **vegetable**, normally boiled or mashed potatoes and/or cabbage, either boiled or as sauerkraut. Fried potato pancakes (*placki ziemniaczane*) are particularly good, either in sour cream or in a spicy paprika sauce. Wild forest mushrooms (*grzyby*), another Polish favourite, are served in any number of forms, the commonest being fried or sautéed. **Salads** are generally a regulation issue plate of lettuce, cucumber and tomato in a watery dressing. If available, it's better to go for an individual salad dish like *mizeria* (cucumber in cream), *buraczki* (grated beetroot) or the rarer *ćwikła* (beetroot with horseradish).

DESSERTS

Desserts are usually meagre, except in the big hotels and plush restaurants, where a selection of cakes and ice creams will probably be on offer. If it's available try *kompot*, fruit compote in a glass – in season you may chance upon fresh strawberries, raspberries or blueberries. Pancakes are also served as a **dessert**, with jam and sugar or with *powidła*, a delicious plum spread.

DRINKS

Poles' capacity for alcohol has never been in doubt, and drinking is a national pursuit. Much of the drinking goes on in **restaurants**, which in smaller towns or villages are often the only outlets selling alcohol.

In the cities and larger towns, you'll come upon **hotel bars** (frequented mainly by Westerners or wealthier Poles), a growing number of **privately run bars** (*bary*), which mimic Western models, and the very different and traditional **drink bars**. The latter, basic and functional, are almost exclusively male terrain and generally best avoided: the haunt of wideboys and hardened alcoholics, they reflect the country's serious alcohol problems, caused in part by a preference for spirits rather than beer or wine.

BEER

The Poles can't compete with their Czech neighbours in the production and consumption of **beer**, but there are nevertheless a number of highly drinkable, and in a few cases really excellent, Polish brands.

The best and most famous **bottled beers** are all from the south of the country. Żywiec produces two varieties: the strong, tangy *Tatra Pils* and *Piwo Żywiecki*, a lighter, smoother brew, ideal for mealtime drinking. Other nationally popular beers include *Okocim*, the largest

national brewery, based in the southwest, *Leżajsk*, a strongish brew from the town of the same name near Rzeszów and *EB*, from the recently revived Elbląg brewery, a big seller throughout the country. There's also an assortment of regional beers you'll only find in the locality, *Gdańskie* and *Wrocławskie* being two of the most highly rated.

Draught beer (*ciemne*) is still the exception rather than the rule, though wooden barrels of local beer do occasionally crop up in the most unlikely places, particularly villages in the south.

VODKA AND OTHER SPIRITS

It's with **vodka** that Poles really get into their stride. Such is its place in the national culture that for years the black market value of the dollar was supposed to be directly pegged to the price of a bottle. If you thought vodka was just a cocktail mixer you're in for some surprises: clear, peppered, honeyed – reams could be written about the varieties on offer. Ideally vodka is served neat, well chilled, in measures of 25 or 50 grammes (a *czysta* – 100 grammes – is common, too) and knocked back in one go, with a mineral water chaser. A couple of these will be enough to put most people well on the way, though the capacities of seasoned Polish drinkers are prodigious – a half-litre bottle between two or three over lunch is nothing unusual.

Best of the **clear vodkas** are *Żytnia*, *Krakus* and *Wyborowa*, valuable export earners often more easily available abroad than at home. A perfectly acceptable everyday substitute is *Zwykla* or ordinary vodka, such as *Polonez*, one of the most popular brands and the one you're most likely to encounter in people's houses and in the average restaurant. Of late there's been a revival of **kosher** vodkas – whether their rabbinic stamps of approval are all entirely authentic is a matter of some debate

Of the **flavoured varieties**, first on most people's list is *Żubrówka*, a legendary vodka infused with the taste of bison grass from the eastern Białowieza forest – there's a stem in every bottle. *Tatrazańska*, the Tatra mountain equivalent, flavoured with mountain herbs is harder to find, but excellent. *Pieprzówka*, by contrast, has a sharp, peppery flavour, and is supposed to be good at warding off colds. The juniper-flavoured *Myśliwska* tastes a bit like gin, while the whisky-coloured *Jarzębiak* is flavoured with rowanberries. Others to look out for are *Wiśniówka*, a sweetish, strong wild cherry concoction; *Krupnik*, which is akin to whisky liqueur; *Lytrynówka*, a lemon vodka; and *Miodówka*, a rare honey vodka. Last but by no means least on any basic list comes *Pejsachówka*, which, at 75 percent proof, is by far the strongest vodka on the market and is rivalled in strength only by home-produced *bimber*, the Polish version of moonshine.

Other popular **digestifs** are *śliwowica*, the powerful plum brandy which is mostly produced in the south of the country, and *miód pitny*, a heady mead-like wine. Commonest of all in this category however is *winiak*, a fiery Polish brandy you'll find in many cafés and restaurants.

SOFT DRINKS

The commonest **soft drink** is *napój*, a bottled blend of fruit juice and mineral water, the most popular varieties being strawberry (*truskawkowy*) and apple (*jabłkowe*). They are tasty and refreshing, and always preferable to the sickly varieties of *oranzada* and *lemonada*. There are plenty of sweet Polish-style Pepsis and Cokes on sale, too, as well as the much higher priced originals, which are consumed with gusto by Poles keen to identify with the symbols of Western consumerism.

Western-style bottled water is becoming increasingly common. Poland's own sparkling **mineral water** from the spas of the south is highly palatable and available throughout the country; the commonest brand name is *Kryniczanka*. Considerably less recommended is *syfon*, the stringent carbonated water you get on train platforms and in some of the cheaper restaurants.

COMMUNICATIONS AND THE MEDIA

POST OFFICES AND THE MAIL

Post offices in Poland are identified by the name *Urząd Pocztowy* (*Poczta* for short) or by the acronym *PTT* (*Poczta, Telegraf, Telefon*). Each bears a number, with the head office in each city being no. 1. Theoretically, each head office has a **poste restante** facility: make sure, therefore, that anyone addressing mail to you includes the no. 1 after the city's name. This service works reasonably well, but don't expect complete reliability. **Mail** to the UK currently takes up to a week, to the US a fortnight, but seems to move twice as fast in the other direction. Always mark your letters "Par avion", or better still "*Lotnicza*", or pick up the blue stickers with both on from post offices; if you don't, they will almost certainly go surface – taking up to six weeks to the UK, several months to the US – even if you have paid the correct airmail postage. **Post boxes** are green, blue or red; these are respectively for local mail, airmail, and all types of mail.

Opening hours of the head offices are usually Mon–Sat 7 or 8am–8pm; other branches usually close at 6pm, often earlier in rural areas. A restricted range of services is available 24 hours a day, seven days a week, from post offices in or outside the main train stations of major cities.

TELEPHONES

The antiquated **telephone system** bequeathed by the communist system is one of the biggest obstacles to Poland's economic development. Frantic efforts, with a great deal of foreign help, have been made at modernization, with significant progress in digitalizing the main city networks, but the system is likely to be in transition for some time to come.

MAKING CALLS

Currently, three types of public **pay phones** are in existence. The old grey machines with dials are still common. They're very unreliable and can only really be used for making local calls. Gradually, these are being replaced by yellow and by large blue rectangular push-button phones, which work much more efficiently. Finally, there are the brand-new **cardphones** (also blue) which are best of all and becoming increasingly widespread. These are operated by a card (*karta telefoniczna*), bought at post offices and *Ruch* kiosks. Cards come in 50 units (8.03zł) and 100 units (16.05zł). The grey, yellow and rectangular blue phones require **tokens** (*żetony*), which can also be bought at kiosks. These come in two types: the small **A** tokens (currently costing 0.16 grosz) are for **local calls** lasting three minutes; the larger **C** tokens (currently 1.6zł) for **long distance calls**. When dialling, place the

token on the slide, but do not insert it until someone answers at the other end – otherwise you'll lose it and be cut off.

Local calls, and dialling from one city to another, should present few problems. However, countrywide area codes are pretty patchy for all but the biggest towns (see box below) and it's always best to ask at the post office before dialling. Different codes can apply for the same place depending on where you are calling from within Poland. Some of the furthest flung places, especially in southeast Poland, do not even have codes and you will have to place your call through the operator.

Making **international calls**, at least within Europe, is far less of a problem these days than it was. Be sure to stock up with a good supply of tokens, as each lasts for less than a minute. For calls **outside Europe**, you'll probably have to rely on the services of the operator (☎900), and

---

PHONING POLAND FROM ABROAD

Dial the international access code (given below) + 48 (country code) + area code (minus initial 0) + number

Australia ☎0011   Canada☎011   Ireland ☎010   New Zealand ☎00   UK☎00   USA ☎011

PHONING ABROAD FROM POLAND

Dial the country code (given below) + area code (minus initial 0) + number

Australia ☎0061   Canada☎001   Ireland ☎00353   New Zealand ☎0064   UK☎0044   USA ☎001

CHARGECARD ACCESS NUMBERS

AT&T ☎01 04 80 01 11   BT ☎044 00 99 48   Canada Direct ☎01 04 80 01 18

MCI ☎01 04 80 022   Sprint ☎01 04 80 01 15

POLISH PHONE CODES

Białystok ☎085	Katowice	Nowy Sącz 018	Tarnów ☎014
Bielsko-Biała ☎030	6 digit nos ☎032	Olsztyn ☎089	Toruń ☎056
Bydgoszcz ☎052	7 digit nos ☎03	Opole ☎077	Warsaw:
Częstochowa ☎034	Kielce ☎041	Poznań ☎061	6 digit nos ☎022
Elbląg ☎050	Kraków ☎012	Rzeszów ☎017	7 digit nos ☎02
Gdańsk/Gdynia/Sopot ☎058	Łódź ☎042	Szczecin ☎091	Wrocław ☎071
	Lublin ☎081		Zakopane ☎0165

TIME

Poland is one hour ahead of GMT, nine hours ahead of US Pacific Standard Time and six hours ahead of Eastern Standard Time. Clocks go forward one hour at the end of March and an hour back at the end of September.

be prepared to wait. To speed up the process, ask for the call to be put through fast (*szybko*), but note that this will double the price.

Emergency calls (police ☎997, fire ☎998, ambulance ☎999) are free. To make a **collect call**, go to a post office, write down the number you want and "*Rozmonta R*" and show it to the clerk – persistence, and above all, patience will eventually pay off. Remember, too, that **calls from hotels** are far more expensive, usually at least double the normal rate.

AT&T, MCI, Sprint, BT and other long-distance phone companies all enable their customers to make **credit-card calls** while overseas. Most provide service from Poland (see box below for toll-free access codes). When calling from outside Warsaw, remember to dial zero and wait for a tone first.

THE MEDIA

With the collapse of communist rule, the Polish **media** were transformed, leaving the party line and *samizdat* traditions behind in a sudden rush of legal, free expression. The free press that has flourished in the wake of communism's demise in Poland is arguably the most dynamic in the region: an indication of this is provided by a 1995 state press index, which listed over 3000 registered publications, including 124 newspapers and over 200 weeklies.

Things have moved rather slower in **television and radio**: it took until March 1, 1993 for the authorities to approve legislation dismantling the state monopoly on radio and TV. The country's two state-run TV channels, one private national channel (Polsat), four national radio stations, three private radio stations, including Warsaw's Radio Zet, now licensed to broadcast nationally, and a growing network of local TV and radio stations are technically regulated by the powerful State Radio and Television Council (*KRRT*), whose head is directly appointed by the prime minister. Up until his defeat in the November 1995 presidential elections, the council was the focus of consistent interventions by Lech Wałęsa, notably after its decision to grant a licence to *Polsat*, a private company, allowing national TV broadcasting. Using his presidential veto, Wałęsa dismissed the *KRRT* chairmen in March 1994 and engineered his replacement with someone seen as more favourable to the president.

NEWSPAPERS AND MAGAZINES

The Polish *samizdat* press of the 1980s was the most sophisticated and widely read in eastern Europe, forcing a degree of liberalization on the official press through the necessity to compete for readers. The **transition** from an underground medium has been difficult, and articles are still often long on argument and short on reporting; design and style have some way to go to match Western equivalents, with poor-quality paper, monotonous slabs of text, and poorly reproduced photographs still the norm.

The difficulties of the transition have been further compounded by the ex-communist party members' struggle to retain control over part of the media, as well as the protracted period of domestic political infighting and instability that continued throughout the early 1990s and which has only recently begun to show signs of abating.

Arguments about **ownership** continue to rattle on: one of the first things the country's first post-communist government did in 1989–90 was to liquidate the old party publishing company *RSW*. The problem was that the way the process was handled left the door open for smarter elements of the *nomenklatura* to retain effective control over significant parts of the existing press network, which they have duly done – an example of the so-called "enfranchisement of the *nomenklatura*" which has embittered ordinary Polish people. Further complicating matters is the issue of foreign ownership. Despite the overall welcome now extended to outside investors wanting to buy into the Polish media, foreign investment is still viewed equivocally in some quarters. Hostility towards the French Robert Hersant group, now majority shareholders in *Rzeczpospolita* (see below) and Bavarian publisher Passauer Neue Presse, who've invested heavily in a range of national and local titles, is a case in point.

Among **Polish-language daily newspapers**, most popular is the tabloid *Gazeta Wyborcza*, eastern Europe's first independent daily, set up in 1989. Forced to abandon the Solidarity logo from its masthead following a bitter dispute between its editor, veteran dissident and intellectual Adam Michnik, and Lech Wałęsa, the paper has gone from strength to strength, with a daily circulation (450,000, rising to 750,000 at weekends) that puts it among the top ten selling European dailies. *Gazeta* is strong on investigative journalism, has a mildly left-of-centre political stance and, in a bid to further enhance its popularity, now comes with regional supplements. For the last few years it has broadly supported the Freedom Union (UW) and most recently Jacek Kuroń's 1995 presidential bid.

Other national daily papers include *Rzeczpospolita*, originally the official voice of the communist government, now a highbrow independent paper with a strong following among businesspeople and government officials. *Zycie Warszawy* is a centrist Warsaw-based daily with a strong nationwide circulation: recent investments in state-of-the-art hi-tech printing equipment have given it the most Western appearance of all the dailies. *Trybuna*, once the official newspaper of the communist party, is still pursuing a leftist agenda and supporting the current post-communist-led government. As in many countries, **local** rather than national papers are what most of the population read, a fact partly explicable by the delays in getting Warsaw-based dailies out to the country until the following day: though generally pretty unexciting, they're often useful for current events.

Weekly papers comprise a colourful mix of the specialist (women's magazines are the nation's best-sellers), the political and the sensationalist. Top sellers in the latter category include *Skandale*, which features the usual diet of sex, violence and pure invention; and *Nie*, edited by the flamboyant and outspoken Jerzy Urban, spokesman for the communist government throughout most of the 1980s.

Of the **political organs**, the theoretically inclined *Polityka* is another former communist mouthpiece (in this case for the liberal wing of the party), while the recently set up *Wprost* explicitly aims itself at Poland's new breed of yuppies. *Tygodnik Solidarność*, the original union weekly established in the heydays of the early 1980s and then banned until 1989, is now firmly in the hands of a faction within the currently reviving Solidarity movement. Circulation of the once hugely popular *Tygodnik Powszechny*, a liberally minded Catholic weekly that used to be the country's only officially published independent newspaper, has declined rapidly following some rather misjudged forays into the political domain during the Mazowiecki government era.

There's only one **English-language newspaper**, the *Warsaw Voice*, a Warsaw-based weekly that's widely available throughout the country. Highly readable and informative, though noticeably slanted towards the business community of late, it's also a useful source for listings in the capital.

Western newspapers and magazines are now available the same day in the big cities. Most common are the *Guardian* International Edition, *Financial Times*, *Times* and *Herald Tribune*, plus magazines like *Newsweek*, *Time* and *The Economist*.

Ruch **kiosks** are the main outlets for papers and magazines. You can also find foreign newspapers in hotel lobbies, foreign-language bookstores and foreign press clubs (KMPiK) in the major cities.

TV AND RADIO

In addition to the Polish **TV channels**, anyone living in the east of the country can get Russian, Belarussian and Ukrainian stations, anyone in the south Czech or Slovak, and in the west, German. Many Poles consider these a useful supplement to the national network, whose standards (pedestrian news programmes, makeshift sets, lots of dubbed imports, shameful football coverage) are very slowly becoming more sophisticated. As political infighting within and between successive government administrations diminishes, some of the instabilities affecting domestic TV are levelling off, with attendant beneficial effects on the quality of programming. For increasing numbers of Poles **satellite** and, in the big cities, **cable TV** are popular additions to the range of TV viewing options: the *Orbis* chain of hotels and a number of others now carry a selection of international cable/satellite channels, including CNN International, BBC World Service TV, MTV and Sky (in German).

The state **radio stations** also present a strange interim picture, broadcasting programmes imported from the BBC (in English and Polish) plus German- and French-language programmes amid the mix of local bulletins and shows. If you want to pick up the complete **BBC World Service** in English, you'll need a short-wave radio tuned to 12.095 MHZ (24.80 metres) or 9.410 MHZ (31.88 metres).

The Polish Radio 1 programme broadcasts news and weather reports in English on the hour from 9am–noon in summer. Wavelengths vary around the country – check the local press for details. In the major cities, such as Warsaw, Kraków and Gdańsk, privately run **local radio stations** are worth tracking down for their dynamic music programming and English-language news bulletins during the summer months.

OPENING HOURS AND HOLIDAYS

Most shops are open on weekdays from approximately 10am to 6pm. Exceptions are grocers and food stores, which may open as early as 6am and close by mid-afternoon – something to watch out for in rural areas in particular. Many shops are closed altogether on Saturdays, with others opening for just a few hours.

Other idiosyncrasies include *Ruch* kiosks, where you can buy newspapers and municipal transport tickets, which generally open from about 6am; some shut up around 5pm, but others remain open for several hours longer. Increasing numbers of **street traders** and makeshift kiosks also do business well into the evening, while you can usually find the odd shop in most towns offering late-night opening throughout the week (in the cities this is no problem). Additionally, in the cities, there are increasing numbers of **night shops** (*sklepy nocne*), generally all-purpose stores, many of which really do stay open throughout the night; the most useful are listed in the *Guide*.

As a rule, ***Orbis* offices** are open from 9 or 10am until 5pm (later in major cities) during the week; hours are shorter on Saturdays, sometimes with closure on alternate weeks. Other **tourist information offices** are normally open Monday to Friday 9am to 4pm.

TOURIST SITES

Visiting **churches** seldom presents any problems: the ones you're most likely to want to see are open from early morning until mid-evening without interruption. However, a large number of less famous churches are fenced off beyond the entrance porch by a grille or glass window for

PUBLIC HOLIDAYS

The following are **national public holidays**, on which you can expect most shops and sights to be closed, and often for as much as a couple of days either side. It's welll worth checking if your visit is going to coincide with one of these to avoid frustrations and disappointments:

January 1 New Year's Day

March/April Easter Monday

May 1 Labour Day

May 3 Constitution Day

May/June Corpus Christi

August 15 Feast of the Assumption

November 1 All Saints' Day

November 11 National Independence Day

December 25 & 26 Christmas

much of the day; to see them properly, you'll need to turn up around the times for Mass – first thing in the morning and between 6 and 8pm. Otherwise it's a case of seeking out the local priest (*ksiąz*) and persuading him to let you in.

The current visiting times for **museums** and **historic monuments** are listed in the text of the *Guide*. They are almost invariably closed one day per week (usually Monday) and many are closed two days. When they are open, many open for only about five hours, often closing at 3pm. Some of the museums in the major cities have managed to extend their opening times recently, but this has often been at the expense of having only one section open to the public at any particular time. **Entrance charges** are generally nominal.

FESTIVALS AND ENTERTAINMENT

One manifestation of Poland's intense commitment to Roman Catholicism is that all the great feast days of the Church calendar are celebrated with wholehearted devotion, many of the participants donning the colourful traditional costumes for which the country is celebrated. This is most notable in the mountain areas in the south of the country, where the annual festivities play a key role in maintaining a vital sense of community. As a supplement to these, Poland has many more recently established cultural festivals, particularly in the fields of music and drama. As well as a strong ethnic/folk music scene, contemporary music in Poland is intriguing, if a little inaccessible to outsiders.

RELIGIOUS AND TRADITIONAL FESTIVALS

The highlight of the Catholic year is **Holy Week** (*Wielki Tydzień*), heralded by a glut of spring fairs, offering the best of the early livestock and agricultural produce. Religious celebrations begin in earnest on **Palm Sunday** (*Niedziela Palmowa*), when palms are brought to church and paraded in processions. Often the painted and decorated "palms" are handmade, sometimes with competitions for the largest or most beautiful. The most famous procession takes place at Kalwaria Zebrzydowska near Kraków, inaugurating a spectacular week-long series of mystery plays, re-enacting Christ's Passion.

On **Maundy Thursday** (*Wielka Czwartek*) many communities take symbolic revenge on Judas Iscariot: his effigy is hanged, dragged outside the village, flogged, burned or thrown into a river. **Good Friday** (*Wielka Piątek*) sees visits to mock-ups of the Holy Sepulchre – whether permanent structures such as at Kalwaria Zebrzydowska and Wambierzyce in Silesia, or *ad hoc* creations, as is traditional in Warsaw.

In some places, notably the Rzeszów region, this is fused with a celebration of King Jan Sobieski's victory in the Siege of Vienna, with "Turks" placed in charge of the tomb. **Holy Saturday** (*Wielka Sobota*) is when baskets of painted eggs, sausages, bread and salt are taken along to church to be blessed and sprinkled with holy water. The consecrated food is eaten at breakfast on **Easter Day** (*Niedziela Wielkanocna*), when the most solemn Masses of the year are celebrated. On **Easter Monday** (*Lany Poniedziałek*), it's the people themselves who are doused, usually by gangs of children armed with buckets and sprays.

Seven weeks later, at **Pentecost**, irises are traditionally laid out on the floors of the house, while in the Kraków region bonfires are lit on hilltop sites. A further eleven days on comes the most Catholic of festivals, **Corpus Christi** (*Boże Ciało*), marked by colourful processions everywhere and elaborate floral displays, notably in Łowicz. Exactly a week later, the story of the Tartar siege is re-enacted as the starting point of one of the country's few notable festivals of secular folklore, the **Days of Kraków**.

St John's Day on June 24 is celebrated with particular gusto in Warsaw, Kraków and Poznań; at night wreaths with burning candles are cast into the river, and there are also boat parades, dancing and fireworks. July 26, **St Anne's Day**, is the time of the main annual pilgrimage to Góra Świętej Anny in Silesia.

The first of two major Marian festivals on consecutive weeks comes with the **Feast of the Holy Virgin of Sowing** on August 8 in farming areas, particularly in the southeast of the country. By then, many of the great pilgrimages to the Jasna Góra shrine in Częstochowa have already set out, arriving for the **Feast of the Assumption** (*Święto Wniebowzięcia NMP*) on

ARTS FESTIVALS

January
WARSAW Traditional jazz
WROCŁAW Solo plays

February
POZNAŃ Boys' choirs
WROCŁAW Polish contemporary music

March
CZĘSTOCHOWA Violin music
ŁÓDŹ Opera; student theatre
WROCŁAW Jazz on the Odra

April
KRAKÓW Organ music
KRAKÓW Student song
SEJNY Borderlands culture

May
BIELSKO-BIAŁA International puppet theatre (every even-numbered year – 1996, 1998, 2000)
GDAŃSK "Neptunalia" (student festival)
HAJÓNWKA Orthodox choirs
KRAKÓW "Juvenalia" (student festival)
ŁĄCKO (near Nowy Sącz) Regional folk festival
ŁANCUT Chamber music
WROCŁAW Contemporary Polish plays (May/June)
WROCŁAW Jazz on the Odra

June
BRZEG Classical music
KAMIEŃ POMORSKI Organ and chamber music
KAZIMIERZ DOLNY Folk bands and singers (June/July)
KODOWA-ZDRÓJ Moniuszko Music Festival
KRAKÓW Short feature films; Jewish culture
KRYNICA Arias and songs
OPOLE Polish songs
PŁOCK Folk ensembles

July
GDAŃSK-OLIWA Organ music
JAROCIN Rock festival
KOSZALIN World Polonia Festival of Polish Songs (every 5 years – next 1996)

KUDOWA-ZDRÓJ Music of Stanisław Moniuszko
MIĘDZYZDROJE Choral music
MRĄGROWO Country and Western festival and country picnic
RZESZÓW World Festival of Polonia Folklore Groups (every 3 years – next 1998)
STARY SĄCZ Old music
ŚWINOUJSCIE Fama Student Artistic Festival

August
DUSZNIKI-ZDRÓJ Music of Frédéric Chopin
GDAŃSK Dominican fair
JELENIA GÓRA Street theatre
KRAKÓW Classical music
SOPOT International songs
ZAKOPANE Highland folklore
ŻYWIEC Beskid culture

September
BYDGOSZCZ Classical music
GDAŃSK Polish feature films
SŁUPSK Polish Piano Competition
TORUŃ International Old Music Festival
WARSAW Contemporary music
WROCŁAW "Wratislavia Cantans" (choral music)
ZAKOPANE Festival of Highland Folklore
ZIELONA GÓRA International song and dance troupes

October
KRAKÓW Jazz music
WARSAW Film Week
WARSAW International Chopin Piano Competition (every 5 years – next 2000)
WARSAW Jazz Jamboree

November
GYDNIA Film festival
POZNAŃ International Violin Competition (every 5 years – next 1996)
WARSAW "Theatrical Encounters"

December
WARSAW Theatre festival
WROCŁAW Old music

August 15. This is also the occasion for the enactment of a mystery play at Kalwaria Pacławska near Przemyśl.

All Saints' Day (*Dzień Wszystkich Świętych*), November 1, is the day of national remembrance, with flowers, wreaths and candles laid on tombstones. In contrast, **St Andrew's Day**, November 30, is a time for fortune-telling, with dancing to accompany superstitious practices such as the pouring of melted wax or lead on paper. **St Barbara's Day**, December 4, is the traditional holiday of the miners, with special Masses held for their safety as a counterweight to the jollity of their galas.

During **Advent** (*Adwent*), the nation's handicraft tradition comes to the fore, with the making of cribs to adorn every church. In Kraków, a competition is held on a Sunday between December 3 and 10, the winning entries being displayed in the city's Historical Museum. On **Christmas Eve** (*Wigilia*) families gather for an evening banquet, traditionally of twelve courses; this is also the time when children receive their gifts. **Christmas Day** (*Boże Narodzenie*) begins with the midnight mass; later, small round breads decorated with the silhouettes of domestic animals are consumed. **New Year's Eve** (*Sylwester*) is the time for magnificent formal balls, particularly in Warsaw, while in country areas of southern Poland it's the day for practical jokes – which must go unpunished.

MUSIC

Though less dynamic than some of its eastern European neighbours, Polish **folk music** nevertheless plays a noteworthy role in national cultural life. Traditional folk comes in (at least) two varieties: a bland, sanitized version promoted by successive communist governments and still peddled, with varying degrees of success, principally for foreign consumption: and a rootsier, rural vein of genuine and vibrant folk culture, which you chiefly find among the country's minorities and in the southern and eastern parts of the country. Thanks in part to Chopin, who was profoundly influenced by the music of his native **Mazovia** (*Mazowsze*), Mazovian folk music is probably the best known in the country, traditional forms like the mazurka and polonaise offering a rich vein of tuneful melodies and vibrant dance rhythms. Other regions with strong traditional folk musical cultures include Silesia, the **Tatras**, whose music-loving *górale* have developed a rousing

polyphonically inclined song tradition over the centuries, and the **Lemks** of the Beskid Niski, whose music bears a tangled imprint of Ukrainian, Slovak and Hungarian influences. Among the notable showcases for Polish folk music of all descriptions are the triennial **Festival of Polonia Music and Dance** in Rzeszów which draws a welter of *emigracja* ensembles from the worldwide Polish diaspora, and the annual summer folk festival bash in **Kazimierz Dolny**.

The nation's wealth of folk tunes have found their way into some of the best of the country's **classical music**, of which Poles are justifiably proud, the roster of Polish composers containing a number of world-ranking figures, including Chopin, Moniuszko, Szymanowski, Penderecki, Panufnik, Lutoslawski and the 1990s runaway best-seller Henryk Górecki. The country has also produced a wealth of classical musicians, mostly in the first half of the twentieth century when pianists Artur Rubinstein and musician-premier Ignacy Paderewski gained worldwide prominence. A cluster of Polish orchestras, notably the Polish Chamber Orchestra, the Warsaw and Kraków Philharmonics, and the Katowice-based Radio and TV Symphony Orchestra, have made it into the world league and are regularly in demand on the international touring circuit.

All the big cities have **music festivals** of one sort or another, which generally give plenty of space to national composers, the international **Chopin Piano Festival in Warsaw** (held every five years) being the best known and most prestigious of the events. Throughout the year it's easy to catch works by Polish composers since the repertoires of many regional companies tend to be oriented towards national music.

Jazz has a well-established pedigree in Poland: ever since the 1950s when bebop broke through in the country there's been a wealth of local talent, and a number of home-grown musicians, notably tenorist Zbigniew Namysłowski, singer Urszula Dudziak, violinist Michał Urbaniak and trumpeter Tomas Stanko, have made it into the international big league. The annual Warsaw *Jazz Jamboree* in October is well established as a major international event that always attracts a roster of big names. Jazz **club life** is still largely confined to a scattering of venues in the big cities, principally Warsaw, and until the economic situation improves significantly it's unlikely this will change much, though there are hopeful signs in a number of more out of the way towns like Zamość.

More than any of its eastern European counterparts Polish **rock and pop music** has always been open to and influenced by the latest Western trends. In the 1970s psychedelia and experimental rock held sway while in the 1980s punk and reggae came to the fore, the popularity of both due in part to their latent espousal of political protest – anything gobbing at authority or chanting down Babylon went down particularly well in post-martial-law Poland, and every Pole understood exactly which incarnation of apocalyptic evil was being referred to. For every band like cult stars Dezerter that made it at the popular level (though not with the communist authorities, who remained suspicious of anything that smacked of cultural subversion) there were a hundred inventively named and obscure outfits such as the The Dead Pork Cutlets, and Millions of Bulgarians who enjoyed their brief moment of counter-cultural musical glory.

Into the 1990s a Polish **rap/house** scene has begun to develop, with hard-hitting artists like Tadzik gaining a strong following among Polish youth disaffected with the new-found joys of capitalism. From the wealth of Polish rock and pop only some of the music ever makes it onto disc, but especially in university areas and the youth-oriented city bars and clubs check out the fly-posters for up-and-coming gigs, which cover the whole spectrum from acid jazz combos to frenzied death metal outfits. The annual **Jarocin** Festival (July) which started life in the mid-1980s as an explicitly alternative event has since broadened its base to include a range of more "respectable" acts, though you'll still find the defiantly prickly Polish chapter of "Crass" anarchists out in force among the more sober-jeaned characters that dominate the audience.

Coming out of the rich heritage of traditional Polish *górale* music (see above), the Trebunia-Tutko family have recently combined with Jamaican combo the Twinkle Brothers – longstanding favourites in Poland – to produce an improbable, quirkily enjoyable folk-reggae fusion. The pair of albums produced to date, *Twinkle Inna Polish Stylee – Higher Heights* and *Come Back Twinkle 2 Trebunia*, have both sold well, and garnered a fair bit of international attention in "world music" circles, suggesting that there is a rich vein of musical and cultural cross-fertilization to be further explored.

For a detailed account of Polish folk music see *Contexts*, p.649.

CINEMA

Cinemas (*kino*) are cheap and generally rudimentary – Dolby sound systems are just beginning to filter through to the cities – and can be found in almost every town in Poland, however small, showing major international films (especially anything American) as well as the home-produced ones. Many foreign films are dubbed into Polish, though of late a welcome trend towards using subtitles has begun to develop. This month's listings are usually fly-posted up around town or outside each cinema with the titles translated into Polish. (The film's country of origin is usually shown – WB means British, USA American, N German.)

Based around the famous **Łódź film school**, postwar Polish cinema has produced a string of important directors, the best known being **Andrzej Wajda**, whose powerful *Człowiek z Żelaza* ("Man of Iron") did much to popularize the cause of Solidarity abroad in the early 1980s. As in all the ex-communist countries the key issue for Polish film-makers used to be getting their work past the censors: for years they responded to the task of "saying without saying" with an imaginative blend of satire, metaphor and historically based parallelism whose subtle twists tend to leave even the informed Western viewer feeling a little perplexed. In the case of Wajda and other notables like **Agnieszka Holland**, **Krzysztof Zanussi** and **Krzysztof Kieślowski**, though, a combination of strong scripting, characterization and a subtle dramatic sense carries the day, and all these directors enjoy high prestige in international film circles.

Into the 1990s, the picture looks a little different, concerns over the censor now replaced by the more conventional film-maker's headache of securing funding (whatever else the communists did wrong, they did, as some directors ruefully recall now, guarantee a level of film financing) and responding to a profoundly changed political and social reality. Post-communist efforts like Kieślowski's award-winning *Veronica's Double Life*, his masterful *Red*, *White* and *Blue* trilogy, and Wajda's *Korczak* suggest an artistically productive future for Polish cinema.

THEATRE

Theatre in Poland is popular and still cheap (though less so than it used to be), and most towns with a decent-sized population have at least one permanent venue with the month's programme pinned up outside and elsewhere in the town. The serious stuff tends to go on in the often sumptuous *fin-de-siècle* creations established by the country's trio of Partition-era rulers – Habsburg opulence if you're in Kraków, Russian-tolerated classicism in Warsaw, Prussian austerity in Gdańsk. Aside from the odd British or US touring company, there's little in English, though the generally high quality of Polish acting combined with the interest of the venues themselves – Poles go as much for the interval promenade as the show itself – usually makes for an enjoyable experience.

Theatre's special role in Polish cultural life dates from the Partition-era, when it played a significant role in the maintenance of both the language and national consciousness. In recent decades **Jerzy Grotowski**'s experimental **Laboratory Theatre** in Wrocław (disbanded in 1982 when he emigrated to Italy) gained an international reputation as one of the most exciting and innovative trends in theatrical theory and practice

to emerge since Stanislavsky's work in Moscow in the early part of this century. Theatre companies like the excellent **Teatr Ósmego Dnia** ("Theatre of the Eighth Day") from Poznań, who also moved to Italy subsequently, carried the torch through the trials of martial law in the early 1980s, developing a probing, politically engaged theatre that closely reflected the struggles of the period. Till his death in 1992 **Tadeusz Kantor**, an experimental director of international stature and long based in Kraków, was another figure at the creative forefront of contemporary Polish theatre. Among a handful of companies currently in demand internationally is **Gardziennice**, a consistently innovative experimental group based in a village near Lublin of the same name who specialize in field trips to villages throughout eastern Europe where oral cultural traditions are kept alive. The resulting productions, led by the company's founder and director Włodzimierz Staniewski, a close collaborator with Grotowski in the 1970s, are inspirational part-improvised, part-scripted happenings drawing on a wealth of dramatic resources.

OUTDOOR ACTIVITIES

For a growing number of visitors, it's the wide range of outdoor pursuits Poland has to offer, as well as its better known cultural and architectural attractions, that constitute the country's chief lure. Most obvious of these are the hiking opportunities provided by the extensive national (and regional) parks, several of which incorporate areas of Europe's most authentic surviving wilderness. Equally attractive for skiers are the slopes of the Tatra mountains – long the country's most developed, but by no means its only, ski resort area. Riding enthusiasts will find plenty of scope for pursuing a pastime that remains a favourite among wealthier Poles, while anglers can sample Poland's significant collection of pristine fishing areas, notably in the the outlying eastern regions of the country.

WALKING

Poland has some of the best **hiking** country in Europe, specifically in the fifteen areas designated as **National Parks** and in the mountain-

ous regions on the country's southern and western borders. There's a full network of **marked trails**, the best of which are detailed in the *Guide*. Many of these take several days, passing through remote areas served by refuge huts (see "Accommodation" p.35). However, much of the best scenery can be seen by covering sections of these routes on one-day walks.

Few of the trails are too strenuous and, although specialist footwear is recommended, well worn-in sturdy shoes are usually enough. For more on hiking in the mountains, and some important tips, see p.462.

An account of hiking in the Tatras is included in *Contexts* on p.654.

SKIING

Poland's mountainous southern rim provides some good **skiing** opportunities, seized on, in season, by what can often seem like the country's entire population. The best and not surprisingly, most popular ski slopes are in the **Tatras**, the highest section of the Polish Carpathians,

associated with the dashing cavalry regiments for which the country was long famous. Even today, equestrian prowess is regarded as one of the higher art forms. Long established horse-breeding traditions, particularly at the stud farms begun in the nineteenth century, continue unabated, with internationally known centres such as **Janów Podlaska** rearing what connoisseurs view as some of the world's finest fullbloods, in particular classical Arabian purebreds. The annual autumn auctions at Janów are pretty big news in the horse world, with visiting celebrities including Jane Fonda and Rolling Stones' drummer Charlie Watts bidding for the best mounts.

Equestrian holidays in Poland are becoming a real draw. There's a wide and growing selection of state-owned stud farms, horse farms and other horse-riding and equestrian centres to choose from, encompassing easy-going family-oriented packages through to more strenuous holidays for the serious enthusiast. All the holiday deals are reasonably priced, and generally include meals, accommodation and the availability of riding instruction.

Orbis has a good range of stud farms and riding centres detailed in their brochure "Horse-riding Holidays". If you're staying in Warsaw and simply fancy a day or two's riding nearby, the riding centre at Żaborów, 24km west of the city, offers the prospect of some fabulous riding in the Kampinoski Forest National Park. Contact Dom Dziennikarza, 05-083 Żaborów (☎058/55 42 63).

FISHING

Especially in the more outlying regions of the country, where the rivers are generally less polluted, **fishing** is a popular pastime. The season effectively runs all year in one form or another, with winter fishing through holes in the ice and on the major Mazurian lakes, and fishing for lavaret with artificial spinners in summer.

The best fishing areas include the **Mazurian Lakes** (pike and perch), the **Bieszczady Mountains**, notably the River San and its tributaries (trout), and the **southeast** in general. Several of the standard *Orbis* brochures provide a fair bit of angling-related information, as does a more detailed one produced by the National Tourist Board. For really comprehensive advice, including details on how to purchase compulsory fishing licences, contact: *The Polish Fishing Association*, ul. Twarda 42, Warsaw (☎022/20 50 83), the National Tourist Board or *Orbis*.

where the skiing season runs from December through into March.

Although still in the shadow of of the Alps and other well-known European resorts, **Zakopane**, the resort centre of the Tatras, has acquired a strong and growing international following, not least in the UK, where a variety of travel operators specialize in cheap, popular skiing packages (see p.8). Though the skiing facilities in and around Zakopane may still leave a little to be desired, both in volume and quality, the cash-strapped local authorities are working hard to improve matters, particularly the provision of ski-lifts. Certainly, you shouldn't have any problems renting skiing gear in Zakopane itself.

Less dramatic alternatives to the Tatras include: the **Beskid Sudety**, notably the resorts at Karpacz, Szklarska Poreba and Duszniki; the **Beskid Zywiecki** and the **Bieszczady Mountains** (a favourite with cross-country skiers). One great advantage with all these is that they are relatively unknown outside Poland, although, consequently, facilities are fairly undeveloped. Both *Orbis* and the National Tourist Board are very keen to promote skiing as an integral part of the country's tourist profile, and have plenty of brochures and information.

RIDING

Horses and **riding** have a special place in the affections of many Poles. In a country that takes great pride in its military traditions, horses are

CULTURAL HINTS

In a country in which rural life continues to play a major role (over thirty percent of the population still lives in the countryside), mainstream Polish culture remains fundamentally conservative in outlook. The divide between city and country is pronounced: while the major cities such as Warsaw, Kraków, Wrocław and Gdańsk increasingly tune in to urban Western lifestyles and habits, the picture is very different in rural areas, particularly the further east you travel, where traditional peasant-based lifestyles remain the norm. Despite the inroads of the communist era in relation to work practices, traditional gender roles are still dominant, with women shouldering responsibility for the home and rearing children, and men generally occupying the main breadwinner role.

Anybody dressing conspicuously in Western **clothes** will be stared at in the villages, and modest attire is definitely a must if you don't want to offend when visiting churches. Nude or topless **sunbathing** will attract attention and sometimes direct protest on the beaches of the Baltic coast or Mazurian lakesides. While men tend to stick to fairly routine shirt and trousers, in the cities many women put a lot of effort and attention into their appearance, with traditional femininity the chief emphasis. While this doesn't necessarily mean women visitors will feel out of place in jeans and T-shirts, you will be marking yourself out if you don informal garb for concerts, the theatre or more upmarket restaurants.

Polish **hospitality** is proverbial. "A guest is God in the house" runs the traditional saying, and if your visit involves any kind of home-based encounter with Poles you're more than likely to experience this at first hand. Home is the important word here. One of the more corrosive social effects of the communist era was to heighten the **division between public and private life**. Straitened economic circumstances resulted in the descent of the public sphere into a grinding, often ruthless struggle to secure the basic necessities of life for one's family, with public interactions a necessary but despised aspect of life. By contrast, the private, meaning the home, friends and family, became the place where Poles really came into their own. The economic and political circumstances may have changed but the public/private division persists. If your encounters with Poles are restricted to waiters, shop assistants and hotel receptionists, you'll have a very different experience of the country than if you manage to establish some more personalized contacts. The good news for those who don't have friends or family awaiting them is that it isn't difficult to establish contact, especially among people of younger Western-oriented generations.

Social conventions are important to get a grip on. Poles are inveterate handshakers, even the most casual street encounter with second cousins three times removed is prefaced and ended by a short, firm handshake. If you're invited to somebody's home, a bouquet of flowers for your hostess (size is not important) is an indispensable item of traditional etiquette.

Polish attitudes to **time** are fairly relaxed: lateness for social appointments is fairly standard, at least within a half-hour margin, but not turning up at all definitely constitutes a sin of the first order, particularly if you've been invited to someone's house: in true Polish style, people will have made an effort for you, and will be offended if this is not at least minimally reciprocated.

GAYS AND LESBIANS

Although there are few telltale signs of a dynamic sub-culture emerging in post-communist Poland, life for Polish gays and lesbians is not as bleak as the featureless gay landscape might suggest.

Unlike the grim juridical situation prevailing in much of the former Soviet Union, homosexuality is not proscribed under the provisions of Poland's 1963 criminal code. The statutory age of consent is 15, irrespective of the sexual orientation of the partners. Indeed, in this regard Polish **laws** governing sexual behaviour actually are relatively more liberal than those in Britain, not to mention those in nearly half of the states in the USA whose statutes continue to outlaw gay sexual relations altogether. Polish gays and lesbians also are legally free to establish clubs and newspapers and all of the other paraphernalia sexual minorities seeking a voice in, say, New York or London employ.

For the gay and especially the lesbian visitor accustomed to the energetic sub-cultures flourishing in cities in the United States, Britain and other western European countries, the **Polish gay scene** may seem a bit of a disappointment. A few soft-porn magazines (catering mostly to men) and other gay-oriented publications have begun to appear for sale in some shops and kiosks in recent years, but there are otherwise few visible traces of an active gay urban insurgency. The "scene" as such still remains largely subterranean (in some cases quite literally), and tends to be limited to clandestine cruising activities in such traditional locales as train stations, parks and public toilets. Visitors to the **major Polish cities** should not expect to find a thriving gay nightlife oriented around discos and watering holes; one way into making contact with local gays and lesbians though, is to head for bars and cafés with reputations for attracting a mixed clientele or in a very few instances, with an explicitly gay profile (see "Listings" in the relevant city sections), though even here you should bear in mind that tracking down gay haunts in Poland is still most reliably accomplished on a word-of-mouth basis.

Perhaps it's not surprising that there's a worryingly low prevailing level of "safe sex" and AIDS awareness in Polish society. Though the exact figures are not known, Poland has the highest incidence of AIDS in eastern Europe. The Church's influence is something of a hindrance in combating the disease, but AIDS helplines are becoming established in the major cities. (See also "Contraceptives" in "Directory", p.57). As in other homophobically-inclined cultures, too, caution is generally the watchword – **gay-bashings** do occur outside places known to be frequented by homosexuals.

GAY ORGANIZATIONS

Two organizations worth contacting before or during a visit to Poland are the Warsaw-based **Pink Service**, the country's only established agency for gays and lesbians, at Waryńskiego 6 m. 89 (Mon–Fri 11am–4pm; ☎022/25 39 11), which also welcomes foreign visitors. The *Pink Service's* activities include acting as an information resource for and about the Polish lesbian and gay scene, running an annual Gay Pride Day, publishing their own magazines – *Men* (for gays), *Arabella* (for lesbians) and an occasional English-language gay newsletter – as well as distributing international gay publications. The Poznań-based ***Inaczej*** agency (PO Box 84, 61-255 Poznań 59; ☎048/77 50 89) publishes an annual *Gay Guide to Eastern Europe*: though the listings can be a bit hard to decode it's nevertheless a useful source of gay contacts and addresses in Poland and other countries in the region. *Lambda* is a national network of gay and lesbian organizations, with branches in several major cities; they can be contacted through the Warsaw branch (see p.117).

For an inside perspective on the Polish **gay and lesbian scene** see *Contexts*, p.634. For more on the **Polish Women's Movement**, see "Directory" overleaf.

USEFUL PUBLICATIONS

Ferrari Publications, PO Box 37887, Phoenix, AZ 85069 (☎602/863 2408). Publishes *Ferrari Travel Planner*, a worldwide gay and lesbian guide; *Inn Places: USA and Worldwide Gay Accommodations*; the pocket guides *Ferrari for Men* and *Ferrari for Women*, and the quarterly *Ferrari Travel Report*.

Spartacus International Gay Guide In the US available from gay bookstores or through *Damron Company*, PO Box 422458, San Francisco CA 94142 (☎1-800/462 6654 or 415/255 0404); in Europe at all good gay bookstores or direct from the publisher, *Bruno Gmünder Verlag*, PO Box 110729, 10837 Berlin (☎30/261 1646).

POLICE AND TROUBLE

Nothing epitomizes recent political change in Poland better than what's happened to the police. Gone now is the secret police structure and the *ZOMO*, the hated riot squads responsible for quelling the big demonstrations from martial law onwards. What's left is the *milicja*, or, as they've been diplomatically renamed now, the *policja*, who are responsible for everyday law enforcement.

Transforming the ethos of a force accustomed to operating outside the bounds of public control is a difficult task, and all in all the *policja* seem to be in a pretty demoralized state, with the entire force supposedly being put through retraining programmes. In common with other east European countries, Poland has experienced a huge increase in crime in recent years, the police seemingly unable or unwilling to do much about it. Sales of alarms, small firearms and other security paraphernalia are on the increase, and residents of Warsaw's high-rise blocks have resorted to organizing their own night watches to stem the flood of car break-ins.

For Westerners, the biggest potential hassles are **hotel room thefts**, **pickpocketing** in the markets and **car break-ins**. There has also been a marked increase in thefts on international trains, especially at night, with accounts of organized multiple robberies emerging with worrying frequency. Sensible precautions should include avoiding leaving cars unattended overnight anywhere in the city centres (larger hotels have guarded parking lots: *parking strzeżony*); keeping valuables on you at all times; trying not to look conspicuously affluent; and, on trains, keeping compartments firmly locked at all times at night. Your best and only protection ultimately is to take out travel insurance before you go, as the chances of getting your gear back are virtually zero.

On a bureaucratic level, Poles are still supposed to carry some form of **ID** with them: you should always keep your passport with you, even though you're unlikely to get stopped unless you're in a car; Western number plates provide the excuse for occasional unprovoked spot checks – particularly late at night, when the police tend to think you'll turn out to be a Pole travelling in a stolen vehicle.

SEXUAL HARASSMENT

Sexual harassment is less obviously present than in the West, but lack of familiarity with the cultural norms means it's easier to misinterpret situations, and rural Poland is still extremely conservative culturally: the further out you go, the more likely it is that **women travelling alone** will attract bemused stares.

Polish women tend to claim that men leave off as soon as you tell them to leave you alone, but this isn't always the case, particularly with anyone who's had a few drinks. However, if you do encounter problems, you'll invariably find other Poles stepping in to help – the Polish people are renowned for their hospitality to strangers and will do much to make you feel welcome. The only particular places to avoid are the drinking haunts and hotel nightclubs, where plenty of men will assume you're a prostitute.

DIRECTORY

ADDRESSES The street name is always written before the number. The word for street (*ulica*, abbreviated to *ul.*) or avenue (*aleja*, abbreviated *al.*) is often missed out – for example ulica Senatorska is simply known as Senatorska. The other frequent abbreviation is *pl.*, short for *plac* (square). In towns and villages across the country, street names taking the stars and dates of Polish and international communism have almost all been replaced. Where a prewar name existed, that name is being reinstated, but with new streets there's been much controversy over whether to use prewar names or to adopt new heroes (the pope – Jan Paweł II – being a chief contender). Figures on the way out include General Swierczewski, Nowotko, Marchlewski, Dzierżyński and the once-ubiquitous Lenin. See *Contexts* for details on the most common street names.

BOTTLES All nationally produced drinks come in bottles which have a deposit on them. Shops will accept bottles from other outfits providing they stock the type you're trying to fob off on them.

CIGARETTES Most Polish brands are pretty gruesome unless you've a strong liking for cheap tobacco. *Extra Mocne* are the cheapest – bonfire-smoky, highly damaging and popular; *Klubowe*, *Giewont* and *Popularne* are similar; *Carmen* and *Caro* are more upmarket. Among imported brands, *Marlboro* and *Camel* lead the way. Matches are *zapałki*. Smoking is banned in all public buildings and on most public transport within towns.

CONTRACEPTIVES Polish-produced condoms (*prezerwatywa*) of uncertain quality are available from most kiosks and some chemists, though with Catholic mores in operation, many pharmacies are reticent to stock them. It's wisest to bring your own.

DRUGS Hard drug abuse – principally amphetamines, *kompot*, a locally produced opium derivative, and heroin – is on the rise. Marijuana and hashish are fairly common, and possession of small quantities of soft drugs is currently legal.

ELECTRICITY is the standard continental 220 volts. Round two-pin plugs are used so you'll need to bring an adaptor.

EMBASSIES AND CONSULATES All foreign embassies are in Warsaw, though a number of countries maintain consulates in Gdańsk and Kraków. See respective listings for addresses.

EMERGENCIES Police ☎997; fire ☎998; ambulance ☎999.

FILM Domestic colour films are poor quality (and you may have problems getting them developed at home), but imported ones are reasonably priced and widely available at the Western-style shops you can now find in many towns.

FOOTBALL Franz Beckenbauer described the Polish national side as "the best team in the world" in 1974, and in that year's World Cup – and the following two tournaments – Polish players such as Lato, Denya and Boniek became household names. After a dismal early 1990s – failure to qualify for the 1990 and 1994 World Cups and a string of disappointing European Championship performances – Polish football is currently in the doldrums, though rejuvenated Legia Warsawa, currently making waves in Europe are helping to revive spirits nationally, even leading some to predict a late 1990s renaissance for Polish football. Most of the top teams are still worth a look, producing football that is up to the standard of middle-order Premier Division stuff in Britain. The top teams are Legia Warszawa, Górnik Zabrze (14-times league champions), followed by GKS Katowice, Ruch Chorzów and the two Łódź sides. The season lasts from August to November, then resumes in March until June. You shouldn't have trouble buying tickets ($2/$3) on the gate for most games.

JAYWALKING is illegal and if caught you'll be fined on the spot.

LANGUAGE COURSES Summer Polish language schools are run by the universities of Kraków, Poznań, Lublin (KUL) and Łódź. Courses last from two to six weeks, covering all levels from beginners to advanced; a six-week course with full board and lodging will cost in the region of £350/$525. Information on these courses can be obtained from the Polish Cultural Institute, 34 Portland Place, London W1N 4HQ (☎071/636 6032) or Polish consulates abroad. One of the better private schools is in Sopot: *Sopocka Szkoła Języka Polskiego*, al. Niepodległości 763, 81-838 Sopot (☎058/51 41 31, fax 51 15 26). A four-week course costs around £240/$360 (longer courses also available), and the school arranges cheap accommodation.

LAUNDRY Laundries (*pralnia*) exist in the major cities, but are very scarce, and will do service washes only. Elsewhere you can get things service-washed in the more upmarket hotels. Dry cleaners – also *pralnia* – are far more numerous.

STUDENT CARDS Carrying an *ISIC* card will only save you a few pence in admission fees to museums. Reductions on domestic trains have recently been scrapped.

TAMPONS Sanitary towels (*podpaski higieniczne*) are cheap and available from some pharmacies; tampons (*tampony*) similarly suffer from supply problems and, though improving, are mostly poor quality – it's best to bring your own.

TIME Poland is one hour ahead of GMT, nine hours ahead of US Pacific Standard Time and six hours ahead of Eastern Standard Time. Clocks go forward one hour at the end of March and an hour back at the end of September – the exact date changes from year to year.

TOILETS Public toilets (*toalety*, *ubikacja* or *WC*) are few and far between (except in the biggest cities) and would win few design awards; restaurants or hotels are a better bet. Once in, you can buy toilet paper (by the sheet) and ask for use of the towel from the attendant, whom you also have to tip (signs usually indicate the amount).

Only in the top-class hotels does toilet paper come free. Gents are marked ▼ or ▲, ladies ●.

VOLUNTARY WORK *Global Volunteers*, a US-based international organization founded in the mid-1980s, organizes a range of voluntary work programmes in Poland, lasting anything from a couple of weeks to longer-term stays. Contact them at 3758 Little Canada Rd, St Paul, MN 55117-1628 (☎612/482 1074). The *US Peace Corps*, 1990 K St NW, Washington, DC 20526 (☎1-800/525 4621) has a strong programme in Poland working in everything from environmental projects to local business development. It's also worth contacting the *Association for International Practical Training*, 10400 Little Patuxent Pkwy, Suite 250, Columbia, MD 21044 (☎410/997 2200); and *Volunteers for Peace*, 43 Tiffany Rd, Belmont, VT 05730 (☎802/259 2759).

WOMEN'S MOVEMENT Following the demise of communism and concurrent with the growing ascendancy of Catholic mores in the country's social and political life, the status of **women** is on the political agenda – in particular, what many see as their treatment as second-class citizens. The biggest single cause of this is the heated debate about **abortion** sparked by government moves to criminalize abortion in all but the most exceptional circumstances, moves (softened by the Sejm in 1994) that put Poland on a par with Eire in the regressive abortion legislation league. A feminist **women's movement** is weak at the popular level, ironically part of the reason being a widespread adverse reaction to campaigns for sexual equality as a relic of communist-era sloganeering. Women's groups currently campaigning on issues such as reproductive rights and abortion include the *Polish Feminist Association*, which has active chapters in Warsaw (Mokstowska 55; ☎/fax 022/29 48 47), Kraków, Poznań and Łódź, the *Federation for Women and Family Planning* (ul. Barcicka 35, Warsaw 01 839; ☎/fax 022/35 47 91) and the *Polish Women's League* (*Liga Kobiet Polskich*; ul. Karowa 31, Warsaw 00 324; ☎022/26 88 25). For a perspective on women's situation in post-communist Poland see the piece by Małgorzata Tarasiewicz in *Contexts*, p.631.

PART TWO

THE

GUIDE

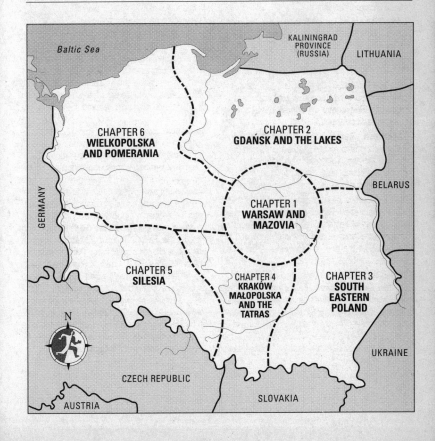

CHAPTER ONE

WARSAW AND MAZOVIA

Warsaw has two enduring points of definition: the Wisła River, running south to north across the Mazovian plains, and the Moscow–Berlin road, stretching across this terrain – and through the city – east to west. Such a location, and four hundred years of capital status, have ensured a history writ large with occupations and uprisings, intrigues and heroism. Warsaw's sufferings, its near-total obliteration in World War II and subsequent resurrection from the ashes, has lodged the city in the national consciousness and explains why an often ugly city is held in such affection. In the latest era of political struggle – the fall of communism, the emergence of Solidarity and the current democratic experiment – Warsaw has at times seemed overshadowed by events in Gdańsk and the industrial centres of the south, but its role has been a key one nonetheless, as a focus of popular and intellectual opposition to communism, the site of past and future power and, increasingly, as the centre of the country's rapid economic transformation.

Likely to be most visitors' first experience of Poland, Warsaw makes an initial impression which is all too often negative. The years of communist rule have left no great aesthetic glories, and there's sometimes a hollowness to the faithful reconstructions of earlier eras. However, as throughout Poland, the pace of social change is tangible and fascinating, as the openings provided by the post-communist order turn the streets into a continuous market place. Many of the once grey and tawdry state shopfronts of the city centre have given way to a host of colourful new private initiatives, while the postwar dearth of nightlife and entertainments is gradually becoming a complaint of the past, as a mass of new bars, restaurants and clubs establish themselves.

Though the villages of **Mazovia** – *Mazowsze* in Polish – are the favoured summer abodes of wealthier Varsovians, these surrounding plains are historically one of the poorer regions of Poland, their peasant population eking a precarious existence from the notoriously infertile sandy soil. It is not the most arresting of landscapes, but contains a half-dozen rewarding day trips to ease your passage into the rural Polish experience. The **Kampinoski National Park**, spreading northwest of Warsaw, is the remnant of the primeval forests that once covered this region, with tranquil villages dotted along its southern rim. A little further west is **Żelazowa Wola**, the much-visited birthplace of Chopin, and on the opposite side of the river, the historic church complex at **Czerwińsk nad Wisła**. **Łowicz** is well known as a centre of Mazovian folk culture, while the Radziwiłł palace at **Nieborów** is one of the finest and best-preserved aristocratic mansions in the country. Southwest of the capital lies industrial **Łódź**, the country's second city and an important cultural centre, while to the north, there are historic old Mazovian centres, notably the market town of **Pułtusk**. Finally, fans of Secessionist art won't want to miss the outstanding museum at **Płock**, west along the river.

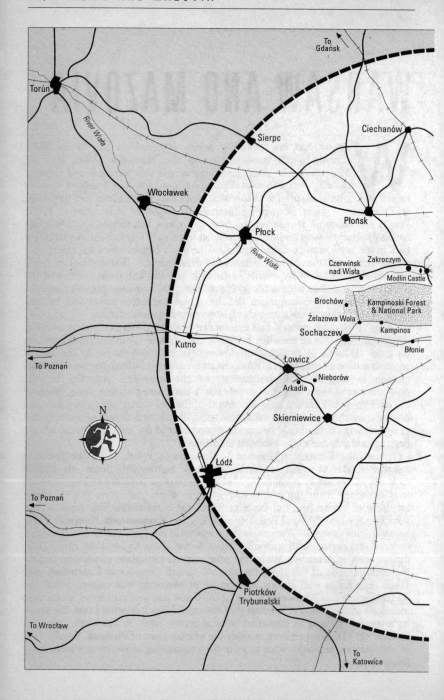

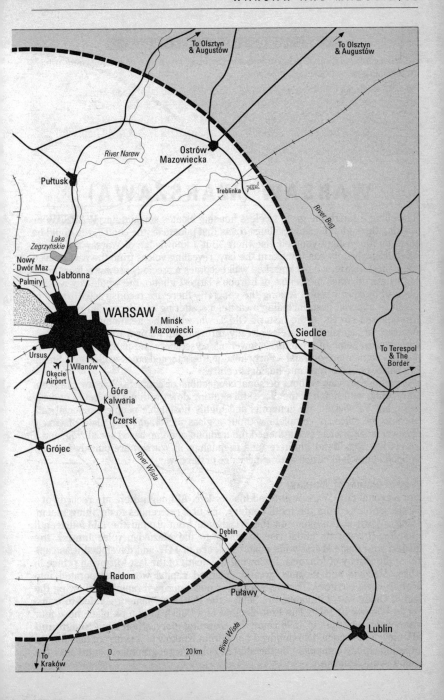

WARSAW (WARSZAWA)

Travelling through the grey, faceless housing estates surrounding **WARSAW** or walking through the grimy Stalinist tracts that punctuate the centre, you could be forgiven for wishing yourself elsewhere. But a knowledge of Warsaw's rich and often tragic history can transform the city, revealing voices from the past in even the ugliest quarters: a pockmarked wall becomes a precious prewar relic, a housing estate the one-time centre of Europe's largest ghetto, the whole city a living book of modern history. Among the concrete, there are reconstructed traces of Poland's imperial past, including a castle, a scattering of palaces and parks, and the restored streets of the historic Old Town, while the headlong rush into the embrace of capitalist culture is already throwing up its own particular architectural legacy, some of it familiar – towering skyscrapers and plush Western shopfronts – some more original – Party headquarters turned stock exchanges, Stalinera palaces transformed into business centres.

For those arriving without personal connections or contacts, Warsaw can seem forbidding, with much of the place still shutting down within a few hours of darkness, but Varsovians are generous and highly hospitable people: no social call, even to an office, is complete without a glass of *herbata* and plate of cakes. Postwar austerity has strengthened the tradition of home-based socializing, and if you strike up a friendship here (and friendships in Warsaw are quickly formed) you'll find much to enrich your experience of the city.

A brief history of Warsaw

For a capital city, Warsaw entered history late. Although there are records of a settlement here from the tenth century, the first references to anything resembling a town at this point on the Wisła date from around the mid-fourteenth century. It owes its initial rise to power to the Mazovian ruler **Janusz the Elder**, who made Warsaw his main residence in 1413 and developed it as capital of the Duchy of Mazovia. Following the death of the last Mazovian prince in 1526, Mazovia and its now greatly enlarged capital were incorporated into **Polish** royal territory. The city's fortunes now improved rapidly. Following the Act of Union with Lithuania, the Sejm – the Polish parliament – voted to transfer to Warsaw in 1569. The first election of a Polish king took place here four years later, and then in 1596 came the crowning glory, when **King Sigismund III** moved his capital two hundred miles from Kraków to its current location – a decision chiefly compelled by the shift in Poland's geographical centre after the union with Lithuania.

Capital status inevitably brought prosperity, but along with new wealth came new perils. The city was badly damaged by the **Swedes** during the invasion of 1655 – the first of several assaults – and was then extensively reconstructed by the **Saxon kings** in the late seventeenth century. The lovely Saxon Gardens (Ogród Saski), in the centre, date from this period, for example. Poles tend to remember the eighteenth century in a nostalgic haze as the **golden age** of Warsaw, when its concert halls, theatres and salons were prominent in European cultural life.

The **Partitions** abruptly terminated this era, as Warsaw was absorbed into Prussia in 1795. Napoleon's arrival in 1806 gave Varsovians brief hopes of liberation, but the collapse of his Moscow campaign spelled the end of those hopes, and, following the 1815 Congress of Vienna, Warsaw was integrated into the Russian-controlled **Congress Kingdom of Poland**. The failure of the **1830 Uprising** brought severe reprisals: Warsaw was relegated to the status of "provincial town" and all Polish institutes and places of learning were closed. It was only with the outbreak of **World War I** that Russian control began to crumble, and late in 1914 the **Germans** occupied the city, remaining until the end of the war.

Following the return of Polish independence, Warsaw reverted to its position as capital; but then, with the outbreak of **World War II**, came the progressive annihilation of the city. The Nazi assault in September 1939 was followed by round-ups, executions and deportations – savagery directed above all at the Jewish community, who were crammed into a tiny ghetto area and forced to live on a near-starvation diet. It was the Jews who instigated the first open revolt, the **Ghetto Uprising** of April 1943, which resulted in the wholesale destruction of the ancient Warsaw Jewry.

As the war progressed and the wave of German defeats on the eastern front provoked a tightening of the Nazi grip on Warsaw, **resistance** stiffened in the city. In August 1944, virtually the whole civilian population participated in the **Warsaw Uprising**, an attempt both to liberate the city and ensure the emergence of an independent Poland. It failed on both counts. Hitler, infuriated by the resistance, ordered the total elimination of Warsaw and, with the surviving populace driven out of the city, the SS systematically destroyed the remaining buildings. In one of his final speeches to the Reichstag, Hitler was able to claim with satisfaction that Warsaw was now no more than a name on the map of Europe. By the end of the war, 850,000 Varsovians – two-thirds of the city's 1939 population – were dead or missing. Photographs taken immediately after the **liberation** in January 1945 show a scene not unlike Hiroshima: General Eisenhower described Warsaw as the most tragic thing he'd ever seen.

The momentous task of **rebuilding** the city took ten years. Aesthetically the results were mixed, with acres of socialist functionalism spread between the Baroque palaces, but it was a tremendous feat of national reconstruction nonetheless. The recovery that has brought the population up to over one and a half million, exceeding its prewar level, is, however, marred by a silence: that of the exterminated Jewish community.

Arrival, information and getting around

The wide open expanse of the Wisła River is the most obvious aid to **orientation**. The heart of Warsaw, the **Śródmieście** district, sits on the left bank; above it is the **Old Town** (Stare Miasto) area, with **plac Zamkowy** a useful central

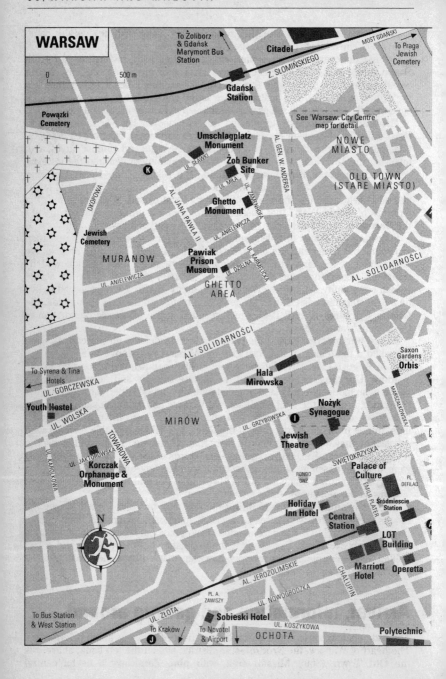

WARSAW

0   500 m

To Żoliborz & Gdańsk Marymont Bus Station

Citadel

MOST GDAŃSKI

To Praga Jewish Cemetery

Z. SŁOMIŃSKIEGO

Gdańsk Station

Powązki Cemetery

See 'Warsaw: City Centre' map for detail

Umschlagplatz Monument

UL. SŁAWKI

Żob Bunker Site

UL. MIŁA

NOWE MIASTO

AL. GEN. W. ANDERSA

OKOPOWA

AL. JANA PAWŁA II

OLD TOWN (STARE MIASTO)

Ghetto Monument

UL. ZAMENHOFA

Jewish Cemetery

UL. ANIELEWICZA

MURANÓW

Pawiak Prison Museum

UL. KARMELICKA

UL. DZIELNA

UL. ANIELEWICZA

GHETTO AREA

AL. SOLIDARNOŚCI

AL. SOLIDARNOŚCI

To Syrena & Tina Hotels

UL. GORCZEWSKA

Saxon Gardens

Orbis

Hala Mirowska

MARSZAŁKOWSKA

Youth Hostel

UL. WOLSKA

MIRÓW

UL. GRZYBOWSKA

Nożyk Synagogue

TOWAROWA

UL. KAROLKOWA

UL. JAKTOROWSKA

Korczak Orphanage & Monument

Jewish Theatre

ŚWIĘTOKRZYSKA

Palace of Culture

PL. DEFILAD

RONDO ONZ

EMILII PLATER

Śródmieście Station

N

Holiday Inn Hotel

Central Station

LOT Building

CHAŁUBIN

Marriott Hotel

Operetta

AL. JEROZOLIMSKIE

UL. NOWOGRODZKA

PL. A. ZAWISZY

To Bus Station & West Station

UL. ZŁOTA

Sobieski Hotel

UL. KOSZYKOWA

Polytechnic

To Kraków

To Novotel & Airport

OCHOTA

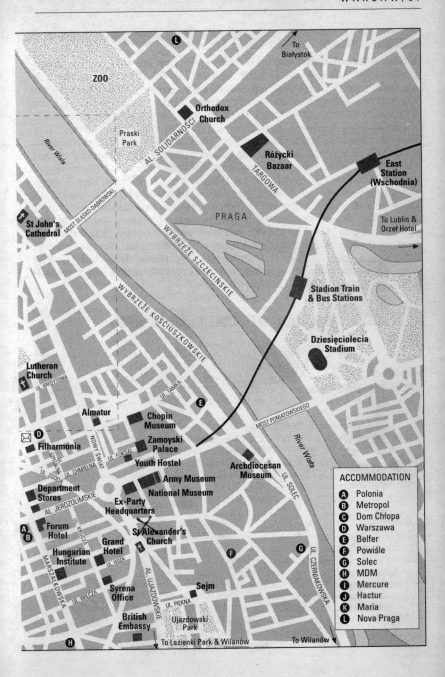

ZOO

Praski Park

River Wisła

L

Orthodox Church

Różycki Bazaar

TARGOWA

To Białystok

AL. SOLIDARNOŚCI

MOST ŚLĄSKO-DĄBROWSKI

St John's Cathedral

WYBRZEŻE SZCZECIŃSKIE

P R A G A

East Station (Wschodnia)

To Lublin & Orzeł Hotel

WYBRZEŻE KOŚCIUSZKOWSKIE

Stadion Train & Bus Stations

Dziesięciolecia Stadium

Lutheran Church

UL. KREDYTOWA

UL. TAMKA

E

MOST PONIATOWSKIEGO

River Wisła

Almatur

Chopin Museum

SPRA… NOWY ŚWIAT UL. FOKSAL

D

Filharmonia

UL. 2GODA

UL. CHMIELNA

Zamoyski Palace

Youth Hostel

Archdiocesan Museum

UL. SOLEC

Department Stores

AL. JEROZOLIMSKIE

Army Museum

National Museum

UL. KRÓZA

A
B

Forum Hotel

Ex-Party Headquarters

St Alexander's Church

F

G

UL. CZERNIAKOWSKA

Hungarian Institute

Grand Hotel

UL. HOŻA

MARSZAŁKOWSKA

AL. UJAZDOWSKIE

UL. WILCZA

Syrena Office

Sejm

British Embassy

UL. PIĘKNA

Ujazdowski Park

H

To Łazienki Park & Wilanów

To Wilanów

ACCOMMODATION

A Polonia
B Metropol
C Dom Chłopa
D Warszawa
E Belfer
F Powiśle
G Solec
H MDM
I Mercure
J Hactur
K Maria
L Nova Praga

reference, while over on the east bank lies the **Praga** suburb. The main **points of arrival** are all within easy reach of the city centre.

• **Okęcie international airport** (Lotnisko Międzynarodowe) is a thirty-minute journey from the city centre on public buses #175, #188 and #488 (buy your tickets inside the terminal building). Additionally, swifter yellow "Airport City" buses (every twenty minutes weekdays, every thirty minutes weekends), will take you into town, main hotels included for 8zł; journey time twenty minutes, departing from the lower arrivals level. **LOT** also runs a bus service (12zł, departing from the same place) to their new terminal on al. Jerozolimskie, which will drop people off at the major central hotels. The **domestic airport** (Lotnisko Krajowe) is ten minutes closer to the centre; the only bus serving this airport is route #114. Watch out for pickpockets on all these lines – newly arrived visitors often prove easy prey for the professional gangs working the buses to and from the airport. The city's notorious **taxi drivers** are at their worst at the airport – even the officially registered ones may well try to sting you for upwards of 40zł for the ride into town. Settle the price (which shouldn't be more than around 25zł at current rates) before setting off. The cheapest way of getting a taxi into town is to order one from **Radio Taxi** (☎919) – they usually turn up within ten minutes, and also currently charge a fare multiple below the usual rate (see "Taxis", p.70).

INTERNATIONAL CONNECTIONS

Trains

The central train station serves all international routes and the major national ones – Poznań, Kraków, Gdańsk, Lublin. Northbound trains also stop at Warszawa Gdańska (ul. Buczka 4), west- and southbound at Dworzec Zachodni (ul. Towarowa 1), eastbound at Dworzec Wschodnia (ul. Lubelska 1). Śródmiescie station, just east of the central station, handles local traffic to Łowicz, Pruszkow and Skierniewice.

For **international tickets**, booking at least 24 hours in advance is highly advisable, not least because of the long queues. An alternative to queuing at the central station's *kasa międzynarodowa* (international counters), which are upstairs on the second floor, is to book at *Orbis* offices; the offices at ul. Bracka 16, pl. Konstytucji 4, ul. Świętojańska 23/25 and upstairs in the *Metropol* hotel on Marszałkowska, all sell international and domestic tickets. The *Wagon Lits Tourisme* office, Nowy Świat, sells tickets for west European destinations.

Buses

The main **bus station**, Dworzec Centralny Warszawa Zachodni, out west on al. Jerozolimskie, is for all international departures and for major national destinations to the south and west. Dworzec Stadion, next to the Praga train station on the line from Dw. Sródmiescie, is for northern and eastern destinations.

International and advance **bus tickets** to all destinations are available from the main station, from the *Orbis* office at ul. Puławska 43 (Mon–Fri 9am–4pm) and from the *PKS* bureau at ul. Żurawia 26 (☎21 34 69) and ul. Świętokrzyska 30 (☎20 49 48). National bus tickets are available at the appropriate station or from the *Syrena* office at ul. Krucza 16/22, PKS (☎23 63 94 or 23 63 95) or the private *Polski Express* (☎630 29 30).

• **Warszawa Centralna**, the main **train station**, is just west of the central shopping area, a ten-minute bus ride (#160, #174 or #175) from the Old Town. This is definitely not a place to hang around at night: robbery of unsuspecting passengers is an everyday occurrence, so keep a close eye on your luggage at all times and never leave it unattended. Queues are lengthy at the **left-luggage** offices, particularly in summer; if you're lucky you may be able to get a more convenient locker downstairs. Another option is the left-luggage counter in the *Marriott* across the road. Most trains run straight through to Centralna, but it's possible that you'll stop (or even need to change trains) at **Dworzec Wschodnia** (East) station, out in the Praga suburb, or **Dworzec Zachodni** (West), in the Ochota district. Both stations have regular connections to Centralna.

• **Dworzec Centralny PKS**, the main **bus station**, is across the road from Dworzec Zachodni in Ochota, a ten-minute bus ride (#127) into the city centre. **Arriving by car** isn't too problematic. Potholes aside, Warsaw's road system is easy to navigate, with all the major routes – from Gdańsk, Poznań, Kraków or the Belarus border – leading to the centre.

Information

Remarkably for a capital city, Warsaw still lacks a properly organized – and funded – tourist information centre. For general practical **information**, the best place is the *Informator Turystyczny* (IT) office on plac Zamkowy (daily 8am–6pm; ☎635 18 81), a privately run office operating on a threadbare budget, though you can't always count on staff being multilingual. There are rudimentary information desks in the airport arrivals lounge and at the central station. The *Orbis* office at the corner of Królewska and Marszałkowska has an information desk (often crowded), and most of the big hotels have IT points too.

The growing influx of Western tourists has resulted in a couple of free English-language **publications** directly aimed at visitors: *Welcome to Warsaw* and *Warsaw: What Where When?* (the latter also in German) are both glossy, advertising-based magazines with a useful set of current listings and general information. You can pick them up at the airport and in the lobbies of the more upmarket hotels. Equally informative and less obviously commercially biased is the weekly English-language newspaper *Warsaw Voice* (see *Basics*, p.46), which you can buy at hotels and many kiosks around town. *WIK*, the weekly city listings magazine, is a useful Polish-language compliment (most *Ruch* kiosks stock it), while for really comprehensive listings, you can't beat the local weekend editions of *Gazeta Wyborcza* and *Zycie Warszawy*, particularly useful for a stop-press on films and concerts around town.

Anyone staying for a long period should consider getting hold of a detailed **city map**. Tourist offices hand out town plans of varying quality, but the thing to look out for is the book-format *Warszawa – plan miasta*, which as well as having clear maps is a mine of useful addresses for everything from restaurants to embassies. It's generally available from tourist offices, bookstores and street sellers. The *Ruch* kiosk on the lower level of the central train station keeps a stock of just about everything that's currently available, as does the IT on plac Zamkowy and the *Atlas* bookstore at al. Jan Pawłka II. In addition, there's a specialist travellers' bookstore at ul. Grójecka 46 (Mon–Fri 11am–7pm, Sat 10am–3pm; ☎22 44 56).

Getting around

Bus and **tram** are the main forms of city transport, and even after the big price rises of the early 1990s, both are still very cheap for foreigners. They get very crowded at peak hours, but services are remarkably punctual. Trams are best for short hops around the centre. Regular bus and tram routes close down about midnight; from 11pm to 5am **night buses** leave from behind the Palace of Culture on ul. Emilii Plater at 17 and 47 minutes past the hour; tickets can be bought from the driver. Throughout central Warsaw, the shabby open stops are being replaced by sprawling new covered halts, the only drawback being the relentless piped music courtesy of the local ZET radio station.

Tickets

Tickets (*bilety*) for both trams and buses are bought from *Ruch* counters (not from drivers) displaying the MZK logo, or from street sellers, normally in batches of ten or twenty, and currently cost 80 grosz each – prices will certainly continue to go up. For buses or trams numbered #1–199 you need one ticket, for those numbered #400–599 and for *pospieszne* (speed) buses, marked A–U, you need two, and for night buses (#600 and up), you need three.

Punch your tickets on both ends in the machines on board – pleas of ignorance don't cut much ice with inspectors, who'll fine you at least 30zł on the spot if they catch you without a validated ticket. Remember too, that you're supposed to stamp an extra ticket for any large items of luggage – backpacks included – that you carry on board. Failure to do so will land you a 50zł fine if you're caught, and checks are visited on foreigners with increasing frequency. Tickets can be much harder to get hold of at weekends when kiosks have unpredictable opening hours, so it's worth stocking up on Fridays. Alternatively, you can purchase day (2zł) or week (14zł) passes from the MZK at plac Bankowy or ul. Sentorska 37.

Taxis

For Poles, recurrent price increases have made **taxis** a luxury, though for Westerners they're still reasonable, and easy to get. In a reversal of twenty years' established practice, taxis now queue for customers at the main taxi stops. That said, you need to be aware that an alarming proportion of the post-communist brand of Warsaw cab driver are little more than licensed bandits, who'll take every opportunity to rip off anyone they sense doesn't know the ropes – and even many that do.

Make sure the **meter** has been turned on when you set off. The fare is currently the price displayed multiplied by 600–1000; there should be a little sign giving the present multiple. Some taxis operate a different **multiple system** – 10 on the meter equals 1 złoty is a common one now. An increasing number of taxis, however, have responded to the introduction of the "new złoty" by showing the fare in new money – in other words, what you see displayed is what you pay.

Especially at night, or from hotels, the airport and the train station you should be prepared for drivers who will try to charge you well above the going rate: knowing what you ought to be paying – hotel reception desks, IT points or friendly locals can usually help out – is always a good starter, but in the worst cases you may have to resign to paying up.

Radio taxis (☎919), now joined by the privately run *Supertaxi* (☎9622), *Top Taxi* (☎966), *Korpo Taxi* (☎9624) and *Express Taxi* (☎9626), are pretty reliable, though sometimes hard to get hold of at night. If you really need to be sure of getting a taxi you can usually order cabs a day in advance.

The Metro

After many years of delay, the city's public transport network has finally been augmented by a swish new **metro** system opened in early 1995 – over a decade after construction work began. The metro currently consists of one eleven-stop line running from **Politechnika**, south of plac Konstitucji, to **Kebaty**, 11km out in the southern suburbs. Planned expansion (due to be completed in 1997) will take the line up through the city centre, including stations at the Palace of Culture and plac Bankowy, to **Młociny** in the northern outskirts of town. Trains run daily from 4.30am to 11.30pm. Tickets are the same as for buses and trams and the same standard fares apply

> The **telephone code** for Warsaw is
> ☎022 for five- and six-digit numbers, ☎02 for seven digits

Accommodation

The listings below give a comprehensive guide to the **accommodation** available in the city area including hotels, hostels, private rooms and even a couple of campsites. The lack of cheap, decent-quality hotel accommodation makes renting a private room a particularly attractive option in Warsaw.

Finding an office or information point in town to help you make a **reservation** is hard work – the queues, at the airport and train station information desks especially, can be forbidding. The best bets for hotel bookings are the reception of the *Grand* hotel, ul. Krucza 28 (☎29 40 51), which can help with *Orbis* places, the *Syrena* office, ul. Krucza 16/22 (☎21 7 864 or 628 75 40), which handles *Syrena*-run hotels, as well as private room bookings (see overleaf), and the IT office on plac Zamkowy. Otherwise it's a case of phoning or calling in person – staff in larger hotels usually speak English or German.

Hotels

In summer even the biggest hotels can be completely booked out for weeks at a time. The only way to ensure a **hotel** room in high season is to book well in advance. Places at the bottom end of the scale (①–④) vary a lot in quality and accessibility. These are about the only places, apart from hostels, that most Poles can afford, so there is plenty of competition for beds. Be aware, also, that a number of the cheaper places are a long way out of the centre. Rooms in the moderate-to-expensive categories (⑤–⑦) will have a bathroom, and normally include breakfast in the price. Upmarket hotels are quite a growth sector in Warsaw, a by-product of the government's drive to attract Western capital. Prices of £100/$150 and upwards for double rooms are now standard for the top-bracket international hotels. Prices have stabilized recently, but inflation means they're still rising noticeably each year.

City centre

Belfer, Wybrzeże Kościuszki 33 (☎/fax 625 05 71). Near the waterfront, this is a good budget option a short walk down from Nowy Świat. A former teachers' hotel, it's big enough to ensure there are generally rooms available. ⑤.

Bristol, Krakowskie Przedmieście 42/44 (☎625 25 25, fax 625 25 77). Legendary prewar hotel reopened under the Forte hotel chain after a complete overhaul. As swish as they come; all rooms over $300 a night. ⑨.

Dom Chłopa, pl. Powstancόw Warszawy 2 (☎27 92 51, fax 26 14 54). Used by a wider clientele than its name (Farmers' House) suggests, the old-style rooms here are gradually being modernized. ⑥.

Dom Literatury, Krakowskie Przedmieście 67/69 (☎635 04 04, fax 26 05 89). Double rooms only in a new arrival on the city centre hotel market. Biggest plus is the central location. ⑥.

Europejski, Krakowskie Przedmieście 13 (☎26 50 51, fax 26 11 11). Across from the *Victoria*, the shabbiness of this nineteenth-century building makes it one of the more appealing upper-bracket hotels. Rooms start at $300 per night. ⑨.

Forum, ul. Nowogrodzka 24/26 (☎621 02 71, fax 625 04 76). Skyscraper haunt of *Orbis* package tours, on the corner of busy Marszałkowska and al. Jerozolimskie. Good views over the city. ⑨.

Garnizonowy, ul. Mazowiecka 10 (☎682 25 69, fax 27 23 65). Centrally located former soldiers' overnighter. Shared bathrooms. ③.

Grand, ul. Krucza 28 (☎29 40 51, 21 97 24). One of a string of drab *Orbis* places – the advantage of this one being its relatively central location. Lively bar and billiards room upstairs. ⑦

Harctur, ul. Niemcewicza 17 (☎659 00 11, fax 658-1507). West of the central station off Puławska. Dingy hotel, popular with students; tram #7, #8, #9 or #25. ④.

Harenda, Krakowskie Przedmieście 4/6 (☎26 00 71, fax 26 26 25). Located centrally just below the university campus. Revamped recently, with a good bar downstairs, see p.113. ⑥.

Jan Sobieski, pl. Artura Zawiszy (☎22 12 65 or 65 84 44, fax 659 88 28). Glamorous Austrian-backed hotel in Ochota, west of the Central station – the wacky exterior colour remains a local source of contention. ⑨.

Maria, al. Jana Pawla II 71 (☎38 40 62, fax 38 38 40). Small, private well-run hotel on the northern side of the city. Deservedly popular in summer, so booking ahead is a good idea. Tram #16, 17, 19 and bus #148, 170 and 500 pass by. ⑦.

Marriot, al. Jerozolimskie 65/79 (☎630 63 06, fax 630 52 39). One of the city's top hotels; with a casino for the jet set too. Rooms from $250 a night. ⑨.

MDM, pl. Konstytucji 1 (☎621 62 11, fax 621 41 73). Rooms here are quieter and pleasanter than the hotel's location and external appearance might suggest. ⑦.

Mercure, ul. Jana Pawła 11 (☎20 02 01, fax 20 87 79). Plush new addition to the city's growing coterie of top class hotels, and part of the French chain of the same name. The excellent *Stanislaus* and *Balzac* restaurants (see p.110) are many people's main reason for coming here. Rooms start at $185. ⑨.

Metropol, Marszałkowska 99a (☎29 40 01, fax 635 30 14). Sited within easy walking distance of the Central station, which means this is often full. Book ahead if possible. ⑦.

Polonia, al. Jerozolimskie 45 (☎628 72 41, fax 628 66 22). Just round the corner from the similar *Metropol*, but noisier. ⑥.

Powiśle, ul. Szara 10a (☎621 03 41, fax 621 66 57). Reasonable quality overnighter on the edge of Łazienki Park, close to the river bank. Swimming pool in nearby sports facilities, free for residents. ④.

Riviera-Remont, ul. Waryńskiego 12 (☎25 74 97). Cheap student hotel off the southern end of Marszałkowska. Triple rooms only. ②.

Saski, pl. Bankowy 1 (☎620 46 15). The cheapest and nicest of the group of hotels located just off Saski Park. Decent rooms and plenty of character – it's worth paying the little bit extra for a quieter, larger room. The only drawback is the occasional legions of dubious-looking mafia types. ④.

Solec, ul. Zagórna 1 (☎25 92 41, fax 25 92 42). One of the better *Orbis* hotels, located just south of the centre, near the river. ⑦.

Trojan, ul. Wybrzeże Kościuszkowskie (☎628 05 26). Boat hotel moored under the Poniatowski bridge – good views of the Old Town. Small selection of basic rooms, mostly shared. Popular with students. May–Sept only. ②.

Vera, Boh. Bitwy Warszawskiej 1920r 16 (☎22 74 21, fax 23 62 56). Another good *Orbis* hotel, just down from the bus station. ⑦.

Victoria, ul. Królewska 11 (☎27 92 71, fax 27 98 56). Traditional favourite with businesspeople, journalists and upmarket tourist groups; overlooking plac Piłsudskiego. Rooms start at $225. ⑨.

Warszawa, pl. Powstańców Warszawy 9 (☎26 94 21, fax 27 18 73). Just off Swiętokrzyska; popular with East European tour groups. Expensive and the least value for money of the soon-to-be-privatized *Syrena* group of hotels. ⑥.

Praga, Żoliborz, Wola and Muranów

Albert, ul. Wały Miedzeszyński 394 (☎10 71 24). Reasonably priced hotel in the Praga Południe district. ⑤.

Arkadia, ul. Radzymińska 182 (☎678 48 54 or 678 65 50, fax 578 56 06). Decent quality hotel on the edge of the Praga Północ district. Acceptable restaurant, but dubious live music. ⑤.

Bursa, ul. Targowiecka 55 (☎610 25 35). Another cheap teachers' hostel, this time well out in the eastern Praga district. ②.

Elżbieta, ul. Gdańska 25. (☎33 73 42). Smallish new hotel out in the Żoliborz district. ⑥.

Felix, ul. Omulewska 24 (☎10 97 72 or 10 97 73). Highly touted new government-run hotel east of the centre on the Lublin road. ⑥.

Kampol, ul. Białołęcka 127 (☎11 09 26). New hotel about 3km north of the centre on the edge of Praga Północ district. Buses #120, 145 pass close by. ④.

Marco, ul. Półczyńska 55 (☎664 63 52 or 36 79 82, fax 13 02 55). Small, quiet private place in the Wola district. No restaurant. ④.

Na Wodzie, ul. Zamoyskiego 2 (☎19 40 12 ext. 59). Converted river boat moored on the Wisła parallel to the East station (Dworzec Wschodnią). Doubles and triples, plus a small breakfast restaurant. ④.

Novotel, ul. 1 Sierpnia 1 (☎46 40 51, fax 46 36 86). Motel with swimming pool, close to the airport. ⑦.

Nowa Praga, ul. Brechta 7 (☎19 50 51). Humdrum place at the cheaper end of the scale – out to the east in Praga; any bus going over the Sląsko-Dąbrowski bridge takes you nearby. ④.

Orzeł, ul. Podskarbińska 11/15 (☎10 50 60). Smallish sports hotel (30 rooms) in southern Praga; bus #102 or #115. Restaurant and bar. ④.

Pod Grotem, ul. Modlińska 15 (☎11 14 51, fax 11 26 44). New place well north of the centre on the Jabłonna road. ④.

Syrena, ul. Syreny 23 (☎32 82 97). Well out to the west of town in Wola; there's generally a good chance of a room here if all else fails. ③.

Tina, ul. Górczewska 212 (☎36 64 79, fax 26 43 86). Friendly new place in the Wola district. Reasonable quality rooms, and decent restaurant too. ④.

Zajazd Napoleoński, ul. Płowiecka 83 (☎15 30 68, fax 15 22 16). Small luxury inn reputedly frequented by Napoleon, well out of the centre in the Praga district. ⑧.

Wilanów and the southern suburbs

Boss, ul. Żwanowiecka 20 (☎12 99 53, fax 12 96 92). Cosy, quietly situated hotel on the rural southeastern outskirts of the city. Bus #C passes close by. Nice restaurant too. ③.

Gwardia, ul. Racławicka 132 (☎44 62 74). Cheap sports hotel, in the southern Rakowiec district. ②.

Ikar, Nowoursynowska 161 (☎47 29 08). Cheapish, comfortable student hotel well south of the centre in Wilanów – Wilanów buses pass close by. ④.

Pensjonat Stegny, ul. Inspektowa 1 (☎/fax 42 27 68). A sports-stadium hotel, on the way to Wilanów. Three-bedded rooms and camping nearby. Bus #116, #195. ②.

Skra, ul. Wawelska 5 (☎25 51 00). Sited next to the Skra stadium in Ochota; bus #167, #187 or #188. ②.

Hostels and student hotels

Warsaw has only two **IYHF hostels**, monstrous underprovision for a city of its size. At both, you have to be out of the building from 10am to 5pm and reception is from 5 to 9pm. During July and August, the *Almatur*-run **international student hotels** are another inexpensive possibility. The *Almatur* office at ul. Kopernika 15 (☎26 23 56) has current location details. Reservations for the two–four person rooms aren't needed as long as you get there before 2pm.

Youth hostels

Ul. Karolkowa 53a (☎32 88 29). Out in the western Wola district – take tram #13, 26 or 34 north from the central station towards the Mirów district and get off on al. Solidarności, near the *Wola* department store. ②.

Ul. Międzyparkowa 46 (☎23 62 42). Smallish summer-only hostel, not far from the Gdańsk train station, on the edge of the northern Żoliborz district (April 15–Sept 15). ①.

Ul. Smolna 30 (☎27 89 52). On the fourth floor of a grey concrete building just a five-minute bus ride along al. Jerozolimskie from the central station – any bus heading towards Nowy Świat will drop you at the corner of the street. Predictably, the central location means it gets very crowded in summer. ②.

Ul. Wały Międzeszyński (☎617 18 85). Summer-only, and located a long way out in Praga Potudnie. ①.

Private rooms

The main source of information for **private rooms** is *Syrena*'s often grumpy *biuro kwatery prywatnych* office, ul. Krucza 16/22 (☎628 75 40 or 621 78 64), a fifteen-minute walk east from the train station, just down from the *Grand* hotel. It's open Monday to Saturday from 8am to 7.30pm, but get there as early as possible – finding anything after 4pm is pushing your luck. Check locations carefully, as you may well be offered something on the far edge of the city: showers are included in each room.

Until recently the only alternative to the *Syrena* office was to trust one of the eager individuals touting rooms at the train station and other tourist haunts. All this has changed and a number of privately run bureaux are now functioning: English-speaking Mrs. Teresa Batko, ul. Złota 69 m.40 (☎24 33 55) has a good range of rooms on offer (③ breakfast 5zł extra). Open regular office hours, longer in summer.

Campsites

Even in Warsaw, **camping** is extremely cheap and popular with Poles and foreigners alike. On the whole, site facilities are reasonable and several offer bungalows (around 16zł per person per night).

Camping Gromada, ul. Zwirki i Wigury 32 (☎25 43 91). Best and most popular of the Warsaw campsites, on the way out to the airport – bus #128, #136 or #175 will get you there. As well as tent space the site has a number of cheap bungalows – though these are often all spoken for.

Wisła, Boh. Bitwy Warszawskiej 1920r. 15/17 (☎23 37 48). Just south of the bus station – take bus #154. Less crowded than the *Gromada* site. Some bungalows too.

PTTK Camping, ul. Połczyńska 6a. (☎664 67 36). Out in the Wola district on the Poznań road. Cabins available. Bus #129, #149, #506 or tram #10 or #26.

Turysta, ul. Grochowska 87 (☎37 25 48). An alternative site in Wola district.

Turysta, ul. Grochowska 1. (☎610 63 64). Quite a distance out of town on the road to Terespol (Praga Potudnie district). Plenty of cabins and useful if you're making an early morning start for the border. Bus #145, #188 or tram #3, #6 or #9.

Stegny, Next to the *Pensjonat Stegny*; see p.74 for details.

The City

Wending its way north towards Gdańsk and the Baltic Sea, the **Wisła** River divides Warsaw neatly in half: the main sights are located on the western bank, the eastern consists predominantly of residential and business districts. To the north of the centre, the busy **Old Town (Stare Miasto)** provides the historic focal point. Rebuilt from scratch after the war, like most of Warsaw, the magnificent **Royal Castle**, ancient **St John's Cathedral** and the **Old Town Square** are the most striking examples of the capital's reconstruction. Baroque churches and the former palaces of the aristocracy line the streets, west of the ring of defensive walls, and to the north, in the quietly atmospheric **New Town (Nowe Miasto)**.

West of the Old Town, in the **Muranów** and **Mirów** districts, is the former **ghetto** area, where the Nożyck Synagogue and the ul. Okopowa cemetery bear poignant testimony to the lost Jewish population. South from the Old Town lies **Śródmieście**, the city's commercial centre, its skyline dominated by the Palace of Culture, Stalin's permanent legacy to the citizens of Warsaw. Linking the Old Town and Sródmieście, **Krakowskie Przedmieście** is dotted with palaces and Baroque spires, and forms the first leg of the **Royal Way**, a procession of open boulevards stretching all the way from plac Zamkowy to the stately king's residence at **Wilanów** on the southern outskirts of the city. Along the way is **Łazienki Park**, one of Warsaw's many delightful green spaces and the setting for the charming **Łazienki Palace**, the so-called "palace on the water".

Further out, the city becomes a welter of high-rise developments, but among them, historic suburbs like **Żoliborz** and **Praga** – on the east side of the river – give a flavour of the authentic life of contemporary Warsaw.

The Old Town (Stare Miasto)

The Old Town (Stare Miasto) is in some respects a misnomer for the historic nucleus of Warsaw. Fifty years ago, this compact network of streets and alleyways lay in rubble – even the cobblestones are meticulously assembled replacements. Yet surveying the tiered houses of the main square, for example, it's hard to believe they've been here only decades. Some older residents even claim that the restored version is in some respects an improvement.

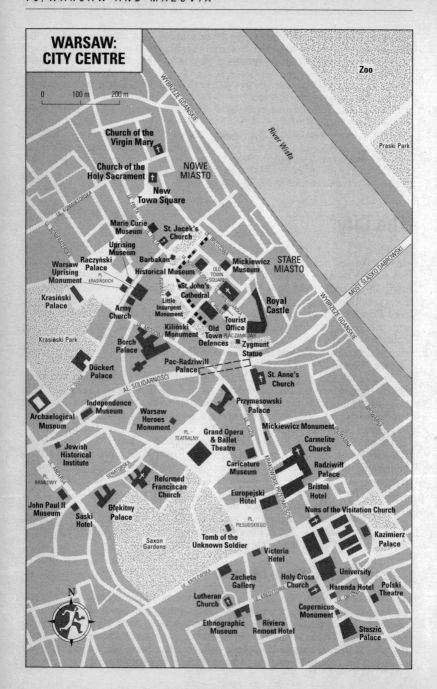

WARSAW: CITY CENTRE

0   100 m   200 m

Zoo

WYBRZEŻE GDAŃSKIE

River Wisła

Praski Park

Church of the Virgin Mary

Church of the Holy Sacrament

NOWE MIASTO

New Town Square

UL. FRETA

UL. KONWIKTORSKA

UL. BONIFRATERSKA

Marie Curie Museum

St. Jacek's Church

Uprising Museum

Raczyński Palace

Barbakan

Mickiewicz Museum

STARE MIASTO

Warsaw Uprising Monument

PL. KRASIŃSKICH

Historical Museum

OLD TOWN SQUARE

Krasiński Palace

St. John's Cathedral

Little Insurgent Monument

Army Church

Royal Castle

Krasiński Park

Kiliński Monument

Old Town Defences

Tourist Office

MOST ŚLĄSKO DĄBROWSKI

WYBRZEŻE GDAŃSKIE

Borch Palace

PLAC ZAMKOWY

Zygmunt Statue

Dückert Palace

Pac-Radziwiłł Palace

AL. SOLIDARNOŚCI

St. Anne's Church

Independence Museum

Warsaw Heroes Monument

Przymasowski Palace

Archaelogical Museum

PL. TEATRALNY

Grand Opera & Ballet Theatre

Mickiewicz Monument

BRACKA

Carmelite Church

Jewish Historical Institute

SENATORSKA

Caricature Museum

Radziwiłł Palace

KRAKOWSKIE PRZEDMIEŚCIE

PL. BANKOWY

Reformed Franciscan Church

Europejski Hotel

Bristol Hotel

John Paul II Museum

PL. ANDERSA

Błękitny Palace

Nuns of the Visitation Church

Saski Hotel

Saxon Gardens

PL. PIŁSUDSKIEGO

Kazimierz Palace

Tomb of the Unknown Soldier

Victoria Hotel

University

UL. KRÓLEWSKA

Zachęta Gallery

Holy Cross Church

Harenda Hotel

Polski Theatre

Lutheran Church

UL. KREDYTOWA

Copernicus Monument

Ethnographic Museum

Riviera Remont Hotel

Staszic Palace

N

Plac Zamkowy (Castle Square), on the south side of the Old Town, is the obvious place to start a tour. Here the first thing to catch your eye is the bronze **statue** of Sigismund III, the king who made Warsaw his capital. Installed on his column in 1640, Sigismund suffered a direct hit from a tank in September 1944, but has now been replaced on his lookout; the base is a popular and convenient rendezvous point.

The Royal Castle

On the east side of the square is the former **Royal Castle** (Zamek Królewski), once home of the royal family and seat of the Polish parliament, now the **Castle Museum** (guided tours Tues–Sat 10am–4pm, Sun 10am–6pm; last admission 3pm). Confusingly, tickets (one each for the bulk of the castle and for the Royal Apartments – specify if you want both) are sold round the corner from the main entrance at ul. Świętojańska 2. Sunday is the only day you are allowed to wander around by yourself. During the summer months, the obligatory guided tours are often heavily booked up, so buy your tickets in advance if possible. Failing that, get here well before opening time.

Dynamited by German troops in the aftermath of the Warsaw Uprising, the seventeenth-century castle was rebuilt as recently as the 1970s. In July 1974 a huge crowd gathered to witness the clock of the domed Sigismund Tower being started up again – the hands set exactly where they were stopped by the first Luftwaffe attack. Attachment to a crucial symbol of independent nationhood explains the resurrected magnificence of the castle: the rebuilding was almost entirely financed by private donations from Poles worldwide, and hundreds of volunteers helped with the labour. Though the structure is a replica, many of its furnishings are originals, scooted into hiding by percipient employees during the first bombing raids. Parallel with its tourist role these days, the castle regularly serves as a glorified reception hall for myriad dignitaries visiting the country. Less frequently it hosts exhibitions and concerts, notably during the annual Ancient Music and Mozart festivals.

Entry is through the Senatorial Gate and a vaulted hallway that's always bustling with tourist groups. The first part of the set tour takes you through the **Jagiellonian Rooms**, overlooking the river from the northeast wing. Originally part of the residence of Sigismund August, they are adorned with portraits of the Jagiellonian royal families and some outstanding Flemish tapestries, including the ominously titled *Tragedy of the Jewish People*.

Next are the chambers where the Sejm (parliament) used to meet. Beyond the chancellery, which features more tapestries and portraits of the last dukes of Mazovia, comes the **Old Chamber of Deputies**, formerly the debating chamber. During parliamentary sessions, the deputies sat on benches on the left side of the chamber, with the Speaker in the centre of the room, while members of the public could stand and listen on the right-hand side. Democracy as practised here was something of a mixed blessing. On the one hand, the founding decree of the Polish Commonwealth, hammered out here in 1573, demonstrated an exceptionally tolerant attitude to religious differences; on the other, it was also here that the principle of *liberum veto* – unanimity as a prerequisite for the passing of new laws – was established in 1652, often seen as the beginning of the end of effective government in Poland. Arguably the Sejm's finest hour, however, came precisely at the moment when political developments threatened it and the country's very existence: the famous **Third of May**

Constitution, passed here in 1791, being one of the radical highpoints of European constitutional history (see *Contexts*, p.612). The painted pillars and heraldic emblems adorning the chamber are recently completed reconstructions of the original decorations by Baptista Quadro (of Poznań Town Hall fame) in the Italianate style typical of much Polish architecture of the period.

The seventeenth-century **Grand Staircase** leads to the most lavish section of the castle, the **Royal Apartments of King Stanisław August**. Amid all the pomp and circumstance, it can be hard to remember that this is all a reconstruction of the eighteenth-century original – in this case, postwar architects had to rely on archival sources from Dresden to rebuild the rooms from scratch. Through two smaller rooms you come eventually to the magnificent **Canaletto Room**, with its views of Warsaw by Bernardo Bellotto, a nephew of the famous Canaletto – whose name he appropriated to make his pictures sell better. Marvellous in their detail, these cityscapes provided important information for the architects involved in rebuilding the city after the war. Next door is the richly decorated **Royal Chapel**, designed and decorated by Domenico Merlini in the 1770s, where an urn contains the heart – sacred to many Poles – of Tadeusz Kościuszko, swashbuckling leader of the 1794 insurrection, and hero of the American War of Independence (see box on p.402). Like many other rooms on this floor, the **Audience Chamber** has a beautiful parquet floor as well as several original furnishings. The four pictures on display here are by Bacciarelli, court painter to Stanisław August, and symbolize the cardinal virtues of Courage, Wisdom, Piety and Justice, while the room itself was again designed by Merlini, a good example of solid Polish Neoclassicism.

The **King's Bedroom**, another lavishly decorated set-up, is followed by the **Study Room**, decorated with paintings by the last Polish king's court artists, where Napoleon is supposed to have slept during his short stay – apparently he had Stanisław's bed moved in here, not wishing to sleep in the bedroom occupied so recently by a deposed ruler. In these rooms, as well as in the nearby Yellow and Green rooms, some of the paintings recently donated to the country by the last surviving member of the Lanchorońshi family are destined to go on display, the most noteworthy items being Rembrandt's *The Jewish Bride* and accompanying *Father of the Bride*.

From here you proceed through to the reception rooms, where the sumptuous **Marble Room** is dominated by portraits of the twenty-two Polish monarchs, including a much-reproduced portrait of Stanisław August in his coronation robes. Highlight of the parade of royal splendour is the **Ball Room**, the largest room in the castle, with its aptly titled ceiling allegory by Bacciarelli, *The Dissolution of Chaos*. Napoleon met the elite of Warsaw society here in 1806, the occasion on which he made his comments (legendary in Poland) about the beauty of Polish women – his mistress-to-be Countess Maria Walewska included, presumably.

The final leg of the tour – which for the less than obsessionally interested can, by this stage, feel something of an endurance test – is a climb to the upper part of the **north wing**, where paintings by Matejko invest key moments of Polish history with romantic fervour. *Rejtan* shows a bare-breasted deputy blocking the path of a group of deputies preparing to accept the First Partition, imploring them to kill him rather than Poland, while *The Third of May Constitution* celebrates an enlightened moment – the declaration of one of the first democratic constitutions in Europe – in a similarly intense vein (see above).

North of the castle

Shops, bars, restaurants and impromptu pavement stalls line **Piwna** and **Świętojańska**, the two narrow cobbled streets leading northwards from plac Zamkowy. There's a lot of junk about, but occasional nuggets too, especially in the record and book shops. Each street has a church worth a stop-off as well. On Piwna there's **St Martin's** (Św. Martina), a fourteenth-century structure whose Baroque interior was carefully restored after the war. Among those buried here is Adam Jarzębski, king's musician and author of the first guide to Warsaw – written in verse.

On Świętojańska, is the entrance to **St John's Cathedral** (Archikatedra Św. Jana), the main city church, an early fourteenth-century structure built on the site of an earlier wooden shrine, and subsequently remodelled in the local Mazovian Gothic style. Some of the bitterest fighting of the 1944 Warsaw Uprising took place around here. German tanks entered the church after destroying its southern side, and you can still see sections of their caterpillar tracks built into the wall along ul. Dziekania. After the war, a lot of money was invested in rebuilding the cathedral in its original brick Gothic style.

For all the hard work, though, the cathedral's a bare, rather cold sort of place, interest mainly provided by the tombstones of the dukes of Mazovia, a sixteenth-century crucifix from Nürnberg with real hair on the head, and a number of famous Poles lodged in the crypt. Notable among these are Nobel Prize-winning writer **Henryk Sienkiewicz**, former primate of Poland **Cardinal Wyszyński** and, the most recent addition, former pianist and prime minister **Ignacy Paderewski**, whose remains were installed here with much ceremony in July 1992 in the presence of presidents Lech Wałesa and George Bush, a fulfilment of the exile Paderewski's last wish that his body only be returned to a free Poland. The Catholic-dominated governments of the post-communist era have seen to it that the church's old official functions are revived, so, especially at weekends, there's a fair chance of your visit being cut short by the arrival of a visiting foreign dignitary.

Next to the cathedral is the **Sanctuary of Our Lady of Charity**, a Jesuit-run shrine to the city's patron saint, its high belfry, the tallest in the Old Town area, standing out for miles around.

The Old Town Square and around

The compact Old Town Square, **Rynek Starego Miasto**, is one of the most remarkable bits of postwar reconstruction anywhere in Europe. Flattened during the Warsaw Uprising, the three-storey merchants' houses surrounding the square have been scrupulously rebuilt to their seventeenth- and eighteenth-century designs, multicoloured facades included. By day the buzzing Rynek teems with visitors, who are catered for by buskers, artists, cafés, moneychangers and *doroski*, the traditional horse-drawn carts that clatter tourists round the Old Town for a sizeable fee. Plumb in the centre is a nineteenth-century **water pump**; for years the only creatures capable of stomaching its offerings were the *doroski* horses, but now following the installation of a filter system, it's a good alternative to the overpriced drinks in the square's cafés.

The **Warsaw Historical Museum** (May–Sept Tues & Thurs 11am–6pm, Wed & Fri 10am–3.30pm, Sat & Sun 10.30am–4.30pm; Oct–April closes 4pm Tues & Thurs) takes up a large part of Strona Dekerta, the north side of the square. Entrance is through a house known as the Pod Murzynkiem, where a sculpted

ADAM MICKIEWICZ (1789–1855)

If one person can be said to personify the Polish literary Romantic tradition it is **Adam Mickiewicz**. A passionate, mystically inclined writer, Mickiewicz's unabashedly patriotic writings have long served as a central literary (and sometimes, in times of crisis, political) reference point for generations of Poles. Quotations from and references to Mickiewicz's considerable volume of writings litter subsequent Polish literature and politics – even the avowedly unacademic Lech Wałesa has been known to cite a line or two from the hugely popular epic poem, *Pan Tadeusz* – and performances of his plays are still numbered among the most popular in the country. More controversially, there's an increasing (though muted) discussion of the man's "ethnic" origins, with several scholars now claiming that at least one of Mickiewicz's parents was **Jewish**, a view that might go some way, it is argued, to accounting for the sympathetic portrayal of Jews – notably the musical inn-keeper, Jankiel – in a work like *Pan Tadeusz:* aired publicly to the average Pole, this view provokes plenty of controversy. Despite the fact that the best of Mickiewicz's writings rank among the finest outpourings of nineteenth-century Romanticism, he's still relatively unknown in the West, a situation not helped by the general lack of decent, readily available translations of his works.

Born in Lithuania of an impoverished Polish *szlachta* (gentry) family, Mickiewicz studied at **Vilnius University** where he, like many of his generation, was rapidly drawn into conspiratorial anti-Russian plotting. Already a budding writer (*Poezye*, his first collection of ballads and romances based on Lithuanian folklore, appeared in 1822), Mickiewicz was arrested along with fellow members of a secret student organization on suspicion of "spreading Polish nationalism" and was deported to Russia in 1823, where he remained, mostly in **Moscow**, for the rest of the decade, befriending a number of Russian writers, Pushkin included. Notable works of this period include *Dziady* ("Forefather's Eve"), the innovative patriotic drama whose Warsaw performance in spring 1968 sparked subsequent student protests, and *Konrad Wallenrod*, a popular epic poem depicting the medieval struggle between Teutonic Knights and Lithuanians, in reality a thinly disguised allegory of the age-old Polish–German conflict.

black head on the facade symbolizes the first owner's overseas trading concerns. Exhibitions here cover every aspect of Warsaw's life from its beginnings to the present day, with a particularly moving chronicle of everyday resistance to the Nazis – an uplifting complement to the wartime horrors documented in the film shown every hour from 10.30am (11.30am Tues & Thurs) to 3.30pm.

On the square's east side, Strona Barssa, the **Mickiewicz Museum** (Mon, Tues & Fri 10am–3pm, Wed & Thurs 11am–6pm, Sun 11am–5pm) is a temple to the national Romantic poet. Among a stack of first editions, contemporary news-papers and family memorabilia, there's actually a shrine room, with portrait and crucifix enveloped in church-like gloom.

If the crowds in the open-air cafés are too much for you, the *Manekin*, in the southeast corner, is a nice little coffee dive with a bar at the back. The south side of the square, Strona Zakrzewskiego, is also mainly concerned with eating and drinking, the exclusive *Bazyliszek* restaurant being the most famous attraction. If you're happy with something a little less grand, the *Hortex Jezuicka* café is an acceptable alternative, and there are a couple of popular café-restaurants and wine cellars on the west side too (see "Eating and drinking", p.107), plus a good poster shop at no. 23.

Following the failure of the **November 1830 Uprising**, Mickiewicz moved to exile in **Paris**, like many Polish intellectuals, and quickly immersed himself in émigré politics. It was here too that Mickiewicz wrote *Pan Tadeusz* (1834), his greatest epic poem; modelled on the novels of Walter Scott, it is a masterful, richly lyrical depiction of traditional gentry life in his native Polish–Lithuanian homeland, a region dear to many Polish writers – Miłosz and Konwicki are two contemporary examples – both for its outstanding natural beauty and powerful historical Polish associations.

The remaining years of Mickiewicz's life read like a litany of personal and political disappointments. Appointed to a professorship in Lausanne in 1839, Mickiewicz resigned in the following year to teach Slavonic literature at the Collège de France. Increasingly drawn to mystical and theosophical doctrines, the uncompromising Mickiewicz was suspended from his post in 1844. With the outbreak of the **1848 revolutions** in central Europe, the "Springtime of the Nations" that briefly appeared to herald a new dawn for the oppressed nations of the region, Mickiewicz travelled to Rome to try and persuade the new pope Pius IX to come out in support of the cause of Polish independence. Later the impassioned Mickiewicz also organized a small Polish military unit to fight with Garibaldi's forces – the nucleus, he hoped, of a future Polish national liberation army – and assumed editorship of the radical agitprop newspaper *Tribune des Peuples* ("Tribune of the Peoples"), a move which led to dismissal from his tenure at the Collège de France by Napoleon III.

The writer's life came abruptly to an end in 1855 when Prince Adam Czartoryski, a leader of the Paris exile community, sent Mickiewicz on a mission to Turkey to try and resolve the factional quarrels bedevilling the Polish military forces that had volunteered to fight against Russia in the approaching Crimean War: having contracted typhus soon after his arrival, Mickiewicz died in November 1855 in **Istanbul**, and is commemorated in a museum there. He was already a national hero of almost mythic proportions, and his remains were eventually brought back to Poland and placed, along with other Polish "greats", in the crypt of Kraków's Wawel Cathedral.

The west side of the Rynek, Strona Hugo-Kołłątaja, named after the co-author of the 1791 Constitution, features a number of fine reconstructed residences, notably the **Fukier House** (no. 27), longtime home of one of the city's best-known *winiarnia* and still going strong, and the **Klucznikowska Mansion** (no. 21), which includes a carefully reconstructed Gothic doorway among its features.

The Old Town may be liveliest by day, but at night it's at its most atmospheric. Backstreets like ul. Brzozowa, between the Rynek and the river, are particularly handsome, the slanting tiled roofs, silent courtyards and tight passageways seemingly untouched by time.

West of the Rynek, the narrow cobbled streets and alleyways bring you out to a long section the old **city walls**, split-level fortifications with ramparts, rebuilt watchtowers and apple trees lining their grassy approaches. Along Podwale, the open path surrounding the walls and a favourite with evening strollers, an array of plaques commemorates foreigners who supported the Polish cause, notably the French poet Alfred de Vigny. Here, as in many places around the city, the fresh flowers laid on the ground mark places where the Nazis carried out wartime executions. The most poignant of the memorials, however, is the recently raised **Monument to the Little Insurgent**, a bronze figure of a small boy with an oversized helmet carrying an automatic rifle – a solitary figure commemorating the children and young people killed fighting in the Warsaw Uprising, personifying all that was heroic, yet so singularly tragic, in the city's resistance to the Nazis (see box, p.84-5).

From the Rynek, ul. Nowomiejska runs north to the edge of the Old Town, passing the city archives (no. 12; entrance by appointment) and an excellent postcard shop (no. 19). The street ends at the sixteenth-century **Barbakan**, which formerly guarded the Nowomiejska Gate, the northern entrance to the city. The fortress is part of the Old Town defences, running all the way round from plac Zamkowy to the northeastern edge of the district. In summer, the Barbakan attracts street artists, buskers and hawkers of kitsch souvenir jewellery – credit cards accepted. Walk east along the walls to the Marshal's Tower, and you have a good view over the river to the Praga district (see p.106). Conversely, some of the best views of the Old Town itself are from the **Praga waterfront**: take any tram over the bridge, Most Śląsko-Dąbrowski, immediately south of the Old Town, get off at the first stop and cross into **Praski Park** then down to the river bank.

The New Town (Nowe Miasto)

Across the ramparts from the Barbakan is the **New Town** district, which despite its name dates from the early fifteenth century, but was formally joined to Warsaw only at the end of the eighteenth. At that time, the wooden buildings of the artisan settlement were replaced by brick houses, and it's in this style that the area has been rebuilt.

Up to the Market Square

Over the rampart bridge and down ul. Długa (the first street on the left), you'll find the eighteenth-century **Raczyński Palace**, used as one of several field hospitals in the city centre during the Warsaw Uprising. A tablet on the corner with ul. Kilińskiego commemorates over 400 wounded insurrectionists murdered in their beds when the Nazis marched into the Old Town. It's now an archive.

Ul. **Freta** – the continuation of Nowomiejska – runs north through the heart of the New Town. To the east, **St Jacek's Church** (Św Jacka), a Dominican foundation, is an effective blend of Gothic and early Baroque. The adjoining monastery, the largest in Warsaw, was another field hospital and was heavily bombed as a consequence; hundreds died here when the Nazis regained control

---

SQUARES IN CENTRAL WARSAW

The severe wartime destruction meted on central Warsaw during the Warsaw Uprising left the city with a number of gaping open spaces that no one really knew what to do with, especially in places where there were no plans (or money) to reconstruct buildings that had stood there before the war. Notable examples include: **plac Teatralny** (north of the theatre), **plac Defilad** (surrounding the Palace of Culture) and **plac Bankowy**. As the drive to develop the city centre as a modern "European" metropolis hots up, and money from foreign investors keeps coming in, several of these areas look set for major redevelopments. Once the problematic issue of land ownership is cleared up, work is likely to proceed – not exactly a Berlin-scale rebuilding programme, but a significant development nonetheless.

---

in October 1944. The *Pod Samsonen* gallery at ul. Freta 3 (Tues–Sun noon–5pm) holds occasional exhibitions of Asian and Pacific art, shown alongside a small permanent collection. For a time, the German Romantic writer E.T.A. Hoffmann lived at ul. Freta no. 5, and no. 16 was the birthplace of one of Poland's most famous women, **Marie Skłodowska-Curie**, the double Nobel Prize-winning discoverer of radium (see box, p.95). Inside there's a small **museum** dedicated to her life and work (Tues–Sat 10am–4.30pm, Sun 10am–2pm).

Ul. Freta leads to the New Town Market Square – **Rynek Nowego Miasto** – once the commercial hub of the district. Surrounded by elegantly reconstructed eighteenth-century facades, this pleasant square makes a soothing change from the bustle of the Old Town. Tucked into the eastern corner is the **Church of the Holy Sacrament**, commissioned by Queen Maria Sobieska in memory of her husband Jan's victory over the Turks at Vienna in 1683 (see "History" in *Contexts*); as you might expect, highlight of the remarkably sober interior is the Sobieski funeral chapel. The architect of the church, Tylman of Gameren, was the most important figure in the rebuilding of Warsaw after the destruction of the Swedish wars in the 1660s. Invited to Poland from Utrecht by Count Jerzy Lubomirski, he went on to redesign what seems like half the city in his distinctive, rather austere Palladian style.

Just off the northern edge of the square, the early fifteenth-century **Church of the Virgin Mary**, one of the oldest churches in Warsaw and once the New Town parish church, has retained something of its Gothic character despite later remodellings. The adjoining belfry is a New Town landmark, easily identifiable from the other side of the river.

The Uprising Monument and Krasiński Palace

The streets northwest of the square lead across ul. Bonifraterska to ul. Gen. W. Andersa, a main thoroughfare which marks the boundaries of Muranów (see p.87). South, ul. Bonifraterska leads to the large plac Krasińskich, now augmented by the **Warsaw Uprising Monument**, a controversial piece commissioned by the communist authorities and viewed with mixed feelings by many Varsovians. Built on the spot where Home Army (AK) battalions launched their assault on the Nazis on August 1, 1944, it's a memorably dramatic piece, the large metal sculpture depicting AK insurgents surfacing from streetside manholes to begin their attack on the Germans, as well as their final forlorn retreat into the sewers of the city. Just beyond the monument, on the corner of ul. Miodowa, is the **Museum of the Warsaw Uprising** currently housed in the

THE 1944 WARSAW UPRISING

Of the many acts of resistance to the savage Nazi occupation of Poland, the **1944 Warsaw Uprising** was the biggest. Half a century on, the heroic, yet ultimately tragic, events of the autumn of 1944 remain firmly lodged in the national memory, at once a piece of history whose interpretation remains controversial and a potent source of national self-definition.

The immediate circumstances of the Uprising were dramatic. With Nazi forces reeling under the impact of the determined push west launched by the Red Army in mid-1944, a German withdrawal from Warsaw began to seem a possibility. The **Polish Home Army** (Armia Krajowa) or AK as they were commonly known, the largest of the Polish resistance forces (indeed, with over 400,000 soldiers, the largest resistance force anywhere in Europe) were thereby confronted by an agonizing dilemma. On one side, they were being strongly urged by the Allies to co-operate actively with advancing Soviet forces in driving back the Nazis. On the other, news of the treatment being meted out to AK units in areas of Eastern Poland already liberated by the Red Army served to confirm the long-held suspicion that there was little, if any room for the AK and its political backing, the Polish government-in-exile in London, in the Soviet scheme of things to come, a fact chillingly symbolized in news of the Soviet detention of AK units in the ex-Nazi concentration camp at Majdanek.

Throughout the second half of July, AK Commander **Tadeusz Komorowski**, known as **Bór**, hesitated over which course of action to take. With the arrival of the first Soviet tanks in the eastern suburbs of the city (Praga), the decision to launch a single-handed attack on the Germans was taken and on August 1, the main Warsaw AK corps of around 50,000 poorly armed troops sprang an assault on the city centre. For the first few days the element of surprise meant AK forces were able to capture large tracts of the city centre. By August 5, however, the tide was already beginning to turn against them. Supported by dive bombers and hastily drafted reinforcements, Nazi troops under the command of ruthless General von dem Bach-Zelewski began the task of clearing out the insurgents. Partisans and civilians alike were treated as legitimate targets for reprisals by the fearsome collection of SS and Wehrmacht units – including three battalions of half-starved Soviet POWs, an "anti-partisan" brigade made up of pardoned criminals and the notorious RONA Red Army deserters brigade – assembled for the task. The Nazi recapture of the **Wola district,** the first to be retaken on August 11, was followed by the massacre of over 8000 civilians. Even worse followed in **Ochota**, where over 40,000 civilians were murdered. Hospitals were burned to the ground with all their staff and patients; during the initial attack, women and children were tied to the front of German tanks to deter ambushes, and rows of civilians were marched in front of infantry units to ward off AK snipers.

With German troops and tanks systematically driving the beleaguered partisans into an ever diminishing pocket of the city centre, the decision was made to abandon the by now devastated Old Town. On September 2, around 1500 of the surviving AK troops, along with over 500 other wounded, headed down into the city sewers through a single manhole near pl. Krasiński – an event imprinted firmly on the national consciousness as much thanks to Wajda's legendary film *Kanał*, a stirring

office of the Union of Warsaw Insurgents, the surviving combatants from the Uprising. The small exhibition details the course of the 63-day assault in different parts of the city, showing, among other things, how the AK used old aerial maps of the city to plan their initial attacks on German positions. There's an English-

1950s rendition of the Uprising, as to its symbolic depiction in the contemporary Warsaw Uprising monument. Fighting continued for another month in the suburbs and pockets of the city centre until October 2, when General Bór and his troops finally surrendered to the Germans, 63 days after fighting had begun. Heavy AK casualties – around 20,000 dead – were overshadowed by the huge losses sustained by the city's civilian population, with over 225,000 killed during the fighting.

With the AK and eventually almost the entire population of Warsaw out of the way, Nazi demolition squads set about the task of fulfilling an enraged Hitler's order to wipe the city off the face of the map, dynamiting and razing building after building until the city centre had to all intents and purposes ceased to exist, as confirmed in the desolation-filled photos taken when the Soviets liberated Warsaw in January 1945.

Of the many controversial aspects of the Uprising, the most explosive, in Polish eyes at least, remains that of the **Soviet role**. Could the Red Army have intervened decisively to assist or save the Uprising from defeat? Throughout the postwar years, the official Soviet line combined the (arguably accurate) claim that the Uprising was a mistimed and strategically flawed diversion from the goal of driving the Germans west in 1944, with absurd ideological denigrations of the AK as reactionary, anti-Soviet nationalists whose actions were a betrayal of the anti-Nazi cause. Certainly Soviet action, or lack of it, during August 1994 was fertile ground for subsequent Polish misgivings about Stalin's real intentions. The Soviet tanks that had reached Praga, for example, sat idly by throughout September 1944 as the Germans pounded the city across the river. Equally significantly, on several occasions the Soviet authorities refused Allied access to Soviet airbases for airlifts of supplies to the beleaguered insurgents, and the secret telegram correspondence between Stalin, Roosevelt and Churchill at the time reveals a Stalin deeply scornful of the whole operation, arguing on one occasion that sooner or later "the truth about the handful of criminals who started the Warsaw disturbance to take over power, will become known to all."

Crudely stated, a common Polish interpretation of all this was that Stalin had simply allowed the Germans to do what his future plans for Poland would have anyway necessitated – the systematic annihilation of the sections of Polish society that formed the core of the AK forces with their uncompromising commitment to a free, independent postwar Poland. With sentiments like these around, it's not surprising that the Warsaw Uprising has remained, if no longer a "blank spot" then certainly a continuing sore in Polish-Russian relations.

Tensions surfaced visibly during the solemn **fiftieth anniversary commemorations** of the start of the Uprising, held in the city throughout August 1994. In a move widely criticized in Poland, particularly among older sections of Polish society, President Wałesa invited his Russian and German counterparts to participate at the opening ceremony held in Warsaw on August 1. While the German President **Roman Herzog** accepted the invitation (reportedly under the mistaken impression that the 1943 Ghetto Uprising was being commemorated) and made a speech asking Polish forgiveness for the country's treatment at the hands of the Nazis, Russian President **Boris Yeltsin** declined the invitation, sending a lower-level aide instead, giving rise to the wry popular quip that the Russians had accepted the invitation but decided to stay in Praga instead.

language brochure you can borrow to take round the displays to fill you in on the details. Additionally, a short but sobering film chronicling the events of the Uprising is shown downstairs regularly throughout the day. Following the fiftieth anniversary of the Warsaw Uprising in August 1994, plans were announced for a permanent, fully fledged Uprising museum in a new complex on nearby ul. Bielańska, built on the site of the prewar Bank Polski, a key insurgents' stronghold. Work on the site, temporarily halted by lack of money, is supposed to continue in the near future.

Immediately opposite the Uprising monument is the **Garrison Church** (Kościół Garnizonowy), the main soldiers' place of worship, with the key Uprising symbol, a large anchor and a streetside tablet with a roll call of World War II battles in which Polish units participated. Overlooking the west side of the square is the huge and majestic **Krasiński Palace**, built for regional governor Jan Krasiński by the tireless Tylman of Gameren, its facade bearing fine sculptures by Andreas Schlüter. Most of the palace's collection of documents – forty thousand items in all – was destroyed in the war, so today's collection comes from a whole host of sources. Theoretically, the building is only open to official visitors, but enquiries at the door should get you in to see at least some of the library. The inside of the palace is splendid, the Neoclassical decorations being restored versions of the designs executed by Merlini in the 1780s. Behind the palace are the **gardens**, now a public park, and beyond that the ghetto area. If you've got the stomach for it, the **Pawiak Prison Museum**, to the west at ul. Dzielna 24/26 (Tues–Sat 9am–4pm, Sun 9am–3pm), tells the grim story of Warsaw's most notorious prison from tsarist times to the Nazi occupation.

On and around ulica Długa

Further down ul. Bonifraterska, at the corner of ul. Długa and ul. Miodowa, is a small streetside **plaque**, one of the least conspicuous yet most poignant memorials in the city. It commemorates the thousands of half-starved Varsovians who attempted to escape from the besieged Old Town through the sewer network during the Warsaw Uprising. Many drowned in the filthy passageways, were killed by grenades thrown into the tunnels, or were shot upon emerging, but a hundred or so did make it to freedom. The bitter saga was the subject of Andrzej Wajda's film *Kanał*, the second in his brilliant war trilogy.

A number of old patrician residences can be seen west along ul. Długa, which leads to the **Warsaw Archeological Museum** (Tues–Fri 9am–4pm, Sat & Sun 10am–5pm), housed in the seventeenth-century arsenal. Starting with Neolithic, Palaeolithic and Bronze Age sites, the museum continues through to early medieval Polish settlements, the highlight being a reconstruction of the early Slav settlements in Wielkopolska and records of forty other excavations from around the country, notably the Jacwingian burial site at Jegleniec near Suwałki (see p.244).

A little way east from the museum, along al. Solidarności, on the traffic island, is the newly established **Museum of Independence** (Tues–Fri 10am–5pm, Sat & Sun 10am–4pm), a dowdy old building featuring changing displays on the theme of the national struggle for independence. The absence of concessions to the faint-hearted (or the non-Polish speaker, for that matter) make this a museum one for the dedicated, as demonstrated in the above average quotient of elderly Poles among the visitors.

Palaces on Miodowa

South from plac Krasińskich, along ul. Miodowa, you find yourself in the heart of aristocratic old Warsaw. The palaces lining Miodowa mainly date from the prosperous pre-Partition era, when this section of the city hummed with the life of European high society. Next door to the **Przymasowski Palace** – now the residence of the Catholic Primate, Cardinal Glemp – stands the **Radziwiłł Palace**, designed by Tylman of Gameren, and adjoined by the later Pac Palace, with its distinctive frieze-topped entrance, while across the street is the Basilan Church and Monastery, the city's only Greek Catholic (Uniate) church, designed with an octagonal interior by Merlini in the 1780s.

Close by is the late seventeenth-century **Capuchin Church**, repository of the heart of Jan Sobieski, while off to the left, on ul. Podwale, the **Jan Kiliński Monument** commemorates another stirring figure in the country's history. During the 1794 Insurrection, it was the shoemaker Kiliński who led the citizens of Warsaw in their assault on the tsarist ambassador's residence on this street. His special place in local consciousness was amply demonstrated during World War II after the Nazi governor took down the uncomfortably defiant-looking monument and locked it up in the National Museum – the next day this message was scrawled on the museum wall: "People of Warsaw, here I am! Jan Kiliński."

Muranów and Mirów: Jewish Warsaw

Like Łódź, Białystok and Kraków, Warsaw was for centuries one of the great Jewish centres of Poland. In 1939 there were an estimated 380,000 Jews living in and around the city – one-third of the city's total population. By May 1945, around three hundred were left. Most of Jewish Warsaw was destroyed after the Ghetto Uprising (see box p.89), to be replaced by the sprawling housing estates and tree-lined thoroughfares of the **Muranów** and **Mirów** districts, a little to the west of the city centre. However, a few traces of the Jewish presence in Warsaw do remain, along with a growing number of newly erected monuments to the notable personalities of the city's historic Jewish community. Equally important, there's a small but increasingly visible Jewish community here – well supported by its exiled diaspora.

Virtually all the Jewish monuments and memorials you will find today are enclosed within the confines of the wartime ghetto area, sealed off from the city's "Aryan" population by the Nazis in November 1940. Warsaw Jews actually lived in a considerably larger part of the city before World War II. The wholesale obliteration of the area both during and after the 1943 Ghetto Uprising meant that several of the streets changed their name, course or simply disappeared altogether after the war, which can make deciphering maps hard going.

"OUR ROOTS" FOUNDATION

To cater for the increasing number of Jews from around the world now visiting Poland, a specialist agency-cum-foundation, **Our Roots**, was set up in 1987. Located close to the Nożyk Synagogue at ul. Twarda 6 (9am–5pm; ☎/fax 620 05 56), the agency stocks a range of detailed guides to Jewish monuments in various parts of the country, offers guided tours of Warsaw and elsewhere, by arrangement, and helps visitors trace their Jewish ancestry in Poland. The staff, young Polish Jews, generally speak English.

Nożyk Synagogue

First stop on any itinerary of Jewish Warsaw is the **Nożyk Synagogue** on ul. Twarda, the only one of the ghetto's three synagogues still standing. (The majestic Great Synagogue on ul. Tłomackie – which held up to three thousand people – was blown up by the Nazis, and in a gesture of crass insensitivity, the Polish authorities decided to build a flashy skyscraper on the site.)

The Nożyk, a more modest affair built in the early 1900s, was used as a stable, a food store and then gutted during the war, reopening in 1983 after a complete restoration. The refined interior is officially only open to tourists from 10am to 3pm on Thursdays, but in practice it's possible to get in at other times with a little diplomacy. The **Jewish Theatre**, rehoused just south of the synagogue on plac Grzybowski, continues the theatrical traditions of the ghetto.

The Ghetto Heroes Monument and Path of Remembrance

Some way north of the synagogue is the **Ghetto Heroes Monument** on the eponymously named plac Bohaterów Getta. Made from granite blocks ordered from Sweden by Hitler in 1942 to construct a monument to the Third Reich's anticipated victory, and unveiled in 1948 on the fifth anniversary of the Ghetto Uprising, the stark monument recalls both the immense courage of the Jewish resistance and the helplessness of the deportees to moving effect. If you're keen to strike up a conversation, the enterprising character selling books, guides and other wartime Jewish memorabilia from a stall in front of the monument is more than happy to fill you in on further details. Once at the heart of the ghetto area, the **square** itself is a wide-open green expanse surrounded by drab apartment buildings, with, as in much of the ghetto area, only the occasional rubble-filled bump disturbing the surface to remind you of what used to be there. Plans to build a major new museum complex dedicated to the history of Polish Jewry in the nearby district were announced in spring 1995, though it's too early as yet to say when (and whether) this will actually happen.

Beginning in the late 1980s, a series of memorial plaques, known as the **Path of Remembrance** was laid out. Starting from plac Bohaterów Getta, the route stretches north along ul. Zamenhofa, ending up at the Umschlagplatz (see below) on ul. Stawki. The plaques, nineteen simple granite blocks engraved in Polish and Hebrew, honour important individuals and events of the ghetto. Those commemorated by name include ghetto historian **Emmanuel Ringenblum** (stone 5; see "Books" in *Contexts*); **Szmul Zygielbojm** (stone 8), Jewish Bund representative of the wartime Polish government-in-exile in London, who committed suicide in May 1943 in protest at Allied passivity over the destruction of Warsaw Jewry during the Ghetto Uprising; **Mordechai Anielewicz** (stone 10), legendary commander of the Jewish Combat Organization (ŻOB) and leader of the Ghetto Uprising (see below); and Janusz Goldszmidt, better known as **Janusz Korczak** (stone 15), the writer-doctor who voluntarily went with the children of his famous Warsaw orphanage to the Treblinka gas chambers in 1942.

Along the way, the route takes you past the grass-covered memorial mound covering the site of the **ŻOB Bunker** at ul. Miła 18. (see box below) – the mound's height representing the level of rubble left after the destruction of the ghetto area. In many of the surrounding streets you'll find houses built on a similar level, as the postwar communist authorities simply went ahead and constructed new housing blocks on the flattened remains of the ghetto. Continuing on up ul. Zamenhofa soon brings you to the junction with ul. Stawki.

A short way west, on the edge of a housing estate is the **Umschlagplatz**, where Jews were loaded onto cattle wagons bound for Treblinka and the other death camps. The simple white marble **monument** standing here, raised in the late 1980s and designed to resemble the cattle trucks used in the transportations, is covered inside with a list of four hundred Jewish first names, the chosen way of symbolizing the estimated 300,000 Jews deported from here to the death camps. A stone stands at the exact point from which the trains departed, while across the road, one of the few surviving prewar buildings (no. 5/7) was the house of the SS commander supervising operations at the Umschlagplatz.

The Jewish Cemetery and Korczak's Orphanage

West along ul. Stawki and down ul. Okopowa, the large **Jewish Cemetery** (10am–3pm, closed Fri & Sat), established in 1806, contains the graves of more than 250,000 people, and is one of the very few Jewish cemeteries still in use in Poland today. The tombs range from colossal Gothic follies to simple engraved stones. This site was left almost untouched during the war, the reason being that, unlike in smaller Polish towns, the Nazis didn't need the materials for building new roads.

Scattered among the plots are the **graves** of eminent Polish Jews like Ludwig Zamenhof, the inventor of Esperanto (see p.259), early socialist activist Stanisław Mendelson and writer D.H. Nomberg. Also worth seeking out is a powerful sculpted monument to **Janusz Korczak**, erected in his honour in the 1980s. The caretaker at the entrance lodge has detailed guidebooks to the tombstones for anyone wanting to know more (information is also available from the Jewish Historical Institute and the Our Roots Foundation offices).

THE WARSAW GHETTO AND THE GHETTO UPRISING

In 1940, on the order of Ludwig Fisher, the governor of the Warsaw district, 450,000 Jews from Warsaw and the surrounding area were sealed behind the walls of the Nazi-designated ghetto area, creating the largest ghetto in Nazi-occupied Europe. By 1941, nearly one and a half million Jews from all over Poland had been crammed into this insanitary zone, with starvation and epidemics the predictable and intended consequence. By mid-1942, nearly a quarter of the ghetto population had died from disease and hunger, a plight communicated to the Allied command by a series of seeringly forthright reports from the budding Polish underground.

Deportations to the death camps from Umschlagplatz began in summer 1942, with 300,000 taken to Treblinka in that summer alone. After further mass round-ups, the Nazis moved in to "clean out" the ghetto in January 1943, by which time there were only 60,000 people left. Sporadic resistance forced them to retreat, but only until April, when a full-scale Nazi assault provoked the **Ghetto Uprising** under the leadership of the Jewish Combat Organization (ŻOB). For nearly a month, Jewish partisans battled against overwhelming Nazi firepower, before ŻOB's bunker headquarters on the corner of ul. Miła and Zamenhofa were finally surrounded and breached on May 9, following the suicide of the legendary Mordechai Anieliewicz and his entire staff. A few combatants survived and escaped to join up with the Polish resistance in the "Aryan" sector of the city. Of those remaining in the ghetto, 7000 were shot immediately, the rest dispatched to the camps. On May 15, Jürgen Stroop, commander-in-chief of the German forces, reported to Himmler, "The Jewish quarter in Warsaw no longer exists".

The Ghetto Uprising has remained a potent symbol both of the plight of Jews under Nazi tyranny and – contrary to the dominant received images – of the absolute will to resist under conditions of systematic terror manifested by a small but significant minority of the Jewish community. The dual nature of the Uprising's legacy was amply attested to in the fiftieth anniversary commemorations held in Warsaw in May 1993, attended by a broad assembly of Jewish and Gentile dignitaries from around the world including a handful of survivors of the Uprising, notably Marek Edelman, the only ŻOB commander still alive today.

From the cemetery entrance, a ten-minute walk south down ul. Towarowa and west along ul. Jaktorowska brings you to the site of the prewar **orphanage** set up by **Janusz Korczak**, the focus of Andrzej Wajda's film *Korczak*. Set back from the road, and still functioning as an orphanage, the original building, which survived the war, has a Korczak memorial plaque on the outside and a monument to him in the main hall. The caretaker will let you have a look inside, and there's also a small selection of souvenirs on sale at the reception. Most powerful of all, though, is the simple statue of Korczak in front of the building – here at least, the city's Jewish past has been done justice.

The Jewish Historical Institute and Ghetto Wall

The **Jewish Historical Institute**, next to the former Great Synagogue at ul. Tłomackie 3/5, stands on the site of the prewar Judaic Library, and is part museum (Mon–Fri 9am–3pm), part library and research archive (Mon–Fri 8am–4pm). The museum details life in the wartime ghetto, a fascinating and moving corrective to the familiar images of passive victims. The international section of the library includes English-language books and journals about Polish Jewry and related issues, as well as a large collection of books rescued from Lublin at the outset of World War II. The archival section contains documents of Jewish life in Poland going back to the seventeenth century, along with an extensive collection of over thirty thousand photos. To meet an increasing demand, the Institute also stocks the indispensible *Guide to Jewish Warsaw* (15zł).

Finally, anyone with a sense of historical symbolism should make their way downtown to ul. Złota, at the southern edge of the wartime ghetto area. Wedged between ul. Sienna 55/59 and ul. Złota 64 is one of the very few surviving fragments of the three-metre-high wartime **Ghetto Wall**. Tucked away in a backyard, in between modern tenement buildings, the short section of brick wall stands as a poignant testimony to the rude separation of the ghetto – so close, and yet so far from life (and death) on the other side of the wall. The isolation was never absolute – post and phone communication with the Aryan sector continued long into the Nazi occupation, and food was continually smuggled into the starving ghetto, despite the threat of instant execution for anyone, Pole or Jew, caught doing so. A small commemorative plaque records the removal of two bricks from the wall to the Holocaust Museum in New York.

Śródmieście

Śródmieście, the large area which stretches from the Old Town down towards Łazienki Park, is the increasingly fast-paced heart of Warsaw. However, in keeping with the Polish spirit of reverence for the past, the sector immediately below the Old Town contains an impressive number of reconstructed palaces, parks, churches and museums, all contributing to a distinctive atmosphere of slightly grubby grandeur. Further south, below ul. Świętokrzyska and east of the Palace of Culture, the brash shopfronts, office blocks and fast-food stands of the main commercial zone epitomize the changing face of Warsaw city life.

Plac Teatralny and around

Running west from plac Zamkowy is ul. Senatorska, once one of Warsaw's smartest shopping streets, now studded with wall plaques recording the civilian victims of Nazi street executions. The pseudo-classical giant dominating the nearby plac

Teatralny is the **Grand Opera and Ballet Theatre**, a monster playhouse designed by Corazzi in the 1820s, with a fine classicist facade decorated with Greek sculptures. Rebuilt and enlarged after wartime destruction, the main theatre now holds almost two thousand people, though even then it regularly sells out in summer. Inside, the elegant entrance hall has a sumptuous rotunda overhead and an intricate parquet floor, worth a look even if you're not planning to attend one of the lavish operas, theatre or ballet productions which are staged here throughout the year (see "Nightlife", p.113).

The north side of plac Teatralny is one of the city areas currently in line for a major facelift. Once the site of the city's town hall, reduced to rubble during the war, the whole area became subject to an officially sponsored campaign for innovative redesign ideas in the early 1990s. After a succession of bids and legal hassles surrounding land ownership, it was announced in May 1995 that construction work on a new shopping and office complex, designed by a French company, would begin by the end of the year. There are strong suggestions that the facade will at least mimic the Old Town Hall building. The redoubtable sword-waving goddess rising from the stone plinth on the other side of the square is Nike, otherwise known as the **Warsaw Heroes Monument**, the state's tribute to the war dead. Like most Warsaw monuments, it could do with a clean-up, which it will hopefully get when it is eventually moved to its (probable) new site on nearby plac Lubomirski to make way for the new complex.

Continuing west along Senatorska, the Baroque **Reformed Franciscan Church** – a quiet place with restful cloisters – is followed by the **Mniszech Palace** and the **Błękitny Palace**, where Chopin gave one of his earliest concerts at the age of six. Tragically, the palace's destruction in 1944 engulfed the fabulous Zamoyski library of over 250,000 books and manuscripts.

Plac Bankowy

Senatorska ends at **plac Bankowy**, formerly plac Dzierżyńskiego: the giant statue of its former namesake, the unloved Russian revolutionary, was removed in 1990 to public rejoicing. On the northeast corner of the square is a tall, silver-looking skyscraper that's long been a city talking point: built on the former site of the Great Synagogue (see p.87) – and cursed, according to local legend, as a consequence – it's taken over twenty years to complete this lumbering Yugoslav-financed giant of a project. The west edge of the increasingly smart-looking square is taken up by a palatial early nineteenth-century complex designed by Antoni Corazzi, and originally housing Congress Kingdom-era government offices (see p.613). This grand building has been the seat of the city's administrative authorities since the destruction of the original town hall in 1944. On the southwest corner of the square is the old **National Bank** building, until recently the official Museum of the Workers' Movement but now taken over by the John Paul II Museum.

The John Paul II Museum

The **John Paul II Museum** (Tues–Thurs, Sat & Sun 10am–4pm, Fri 9.30am–5pm) comprises a large art collection (some 400 paintings in all) assembled by the wealthy émigré Carroll-Porczyński family in the early 1980s and donated to the Polish Catholic church a few years later, with works ranging from the fourteenth to the twentieth centuries, and a heavy emphasis on religious subjects. Already the museum has proved controversial: sections of the academic art world are proving reticent about the value of the collection, and the Porczyńskis went to great – and ultimately unsuccessful – lengths to try to block the publication of an article by a leading Polish art expert claiming that several of the more famous paintings, in particular the early Italian works, are actually fakes. Alongside the museum's unquestionably high artistic aspiration, there's an unabashedly cata-chestic tone to the place, the portraits of the Pope and current Catholic Primate Cardinal Glemp placed at the entrance reminding you who the collection is supposed to be in honour of. Most of the collections, too, are arranged according to themes drawn from the Catholic theological canon – the Bible and Saints, the Life of Mary, Myth and Allegory, Motherhood and the like – the rest being set up on the basis of national "schools" of art.

ITALIAN AND GERMAN WORKS

Once into the museum, tour groups make straight for the main ground-floor room, a large domed auditorium once occupied by the Warsaw Bourse that now doubles as a concert recital hall – hence the chairs filling the body of the building. The large collection of portraits lining the walls is divided into national "schools", as are most of the ground-floor collections. The **Italian school** features a fine *Death of Lucretia* from the Titian school, as well as a notable *Sacrifice of the Dead Abraham* from the Caravaggio workshop, probably a replica of a smaller painting of the same title housed in the Uffizi in Florence. Highlights of the **German** collection include portraits of Luther and his wife Catherine by Cranach the elder, and one of the oldest known versions of the lost *St Anne* by Albrecht Dürer, dated 1523.

FLEMISH AND DUTCH WORKS

The big guns of **Flemish and Dutch** Baroque provide some of the museum's leading works, with self-portraits of Rubens and Rembrandt, the latter placed alongside the thoughtful *Portrait of a Nobleman* by van Dyck beneath the impassive bust of patron John Paul peering out over the auditorium. Additionally there are a couple of works by Jordaens, while *Farm in Hoogeveen*, a typically brooding early Van Gogh, is one of several works in the "Still Lifes and Landscapes" section housed in an adjoining room, which also features a Constable still life and an evocative pair of landscapes by the French-born English painter Alfred Sisley: here as elsewhere in the collection, enjoyment is somewhat marred by the neck-wrenching height at which the pictures have been hung.

FRENCH, ENGLISH AND SPANISH WORKS

The **French** collection is particularly strong on portraiture, featuring a wealth of courtly eighteenth-century aristocracy, a fine portrait of Henry IV, a Renoir picture of his son, Pierre, and a plaster mould head of John the Baptist by Rodin. The same goes for the **English** section: notable works here include Sir Joshua Reynolds' penetrating *Portrait of Miss Nelly O'Brien* – one of three he painted of the Irish woman – and a noble-looking self-portrait. **Spanish** artists provide some of the most powerful works in the auditorium, particularly the self-portraits by Murillo and Velásquez, Ribera's hauntingly intense *Portrait of a Philosopher,* and *Woman Carrying Water*, a powerful later Goya work.

THE UPPER FLOORS

The upper floors of the building house the theologically oriented "theme" rooms, including the art-crammed "mother and child" section populated by the inevitable welter of fleshy-looking Baroque cherubs. The upper sections contain plenty of notable works too, with **Italian** artists providing the earliest (and most controversial) works, especially a fine *Jesus' Offertory in the Temple* from the circle of Jacopo Bellini, a mid-fourteenth-century *Virgin and Child* from the Marches school (the oldest painting in the collection), a *Madonna and Child* by Carucci, Titian's *Child from the Medici Family*, and a *Last Supper* by Tintoretto. Works from other countries include another *Last Supper* by Brueghel the Younger, a dreamy *Ecstasy of St Francis* by David Teniers, and an outstanding Mannerist *Crucifixion* by Cornelis van Haarlem housed in the "crucifixion room" whose centrepiece is a huge, dramatic depiction of Calvary by the Polish nineteenth-century artist Wojciech Gerson.

Plac Piłsudskiego and the Saxon Gardens

Returning to plac Teatralny, the way south leads onto an even larger square, **plac Piłsudskiego**, where a huge flower cross lay for some time after martial law was imposed. After the authorities had cleared the cross away, the whole area was closed off for public works for years, presumably to prevent embarrassing demonstrations happening in full view of the tourists staying in the *Victoria* and *Europejski* hotels. These days the military guard in front of the **Tomb of the Unknown Soldier** is the only permanent security presence. Here, as with neighbouring squares, plans are afoot to give the area a major facelift, the temptation to go for plush new office complexes currently looking the likeliest bet, although there is talk of reconstructing at least part of the royal palace (see below).

Beyond the tomb, stretch the handsome and well-used promenades of the **Saxon Gardens** (Ogród Saski), laid out for August II by Tylman of Gameren in the early 1700s, and landscaped as a public garden in the following century. The **royal palace** built in the gardens by August II was blown up by the Nazis in 1944 and never rebuilt; the Tomb of the Unknown Soldier is the only surviving part of the building. Other sections of the park were luckier, notably the scattering of Baroque sculptures, symbolizing the Virtues, Sciences and Elements, an elegant nineteenth-century fountain pool above the main pathway, the old **water tower** (Warsaw's first) built by Marconi in the 1850s and the park's fine crop of **trees**, over a hundred species in all. Long one of Warsaw's most popular green areas, the gardens are benefiting from a concerted attempt to spruce the place up.

Immediately south of the gardens on plac Małachowskiego, to the west of the plush *Victoria* hotel, is the **Zachęta Gallery** (Tues–Sun 10am–6pm), built at the turn of the century as the headquarters of the Warsaw Fine Arts Society, and one of the few buildings in central Warsaw left standing at the end of World War II. The stucco decoration in the entrance gives a taste of the building's original qualities. The gallery's considerable original art collection (Matejko's *Battle of Grunwald* included) was packed off into hiding in the National Museum at the start of the war, subsequently forming part of that museum's permanent collection. The Zachęta is now a contemporary art gallery operating under the patronage of the recently reformed Fine Arts Society, which stages a wealth of generally high-quality exhibitions. Along with the Ujazdowskie Castle Contemporary Art Centre, it has quietly established itself as the city's leading contemporary art gallery.

Along Krakowskie Przedmieście

Of all the long thoroughfares bisecting central Warsaw from north to south, the most important is the one often known as the Royal Way, which runs almost uninterrupted from plac Zamkowy to the palace of Wilanów. **Krakowskie Przedmieście**, the first part of the Royal Way, is lined with historic buildings. **St Anne's** (Św. Anna), directly below plac Zamkowy, is where Polish princes used to swear homage to the king; founded in 1454, the church was destroyed in 1656 by the besieging Swedes, then rebuilt in Baroque style in the following century. All that remains of the original church is the Gothic brick presbytery adjacent to the nave and Baroque chapel dome. There's a fine view over the Wisła from the courtyard next to the church, though your enjoyment of it is somewhat marred by the traffic thundering through the tunnel below. By 1983, the second year of martial law, resourceful oppositionists had moved their flower cross to this courtyard after the authorities removed the huge one from plac Piłsudskiego, previously Zwycięstwa. These days, the courtyard is filled with a busy outdoor café that's at least as popular with Polish sightseers as the cross used to be. For an even better view, you can climb the belfry tower on the northern side of the courtyard for a small fee.

South of St Anne's the bus-congested street broadens to incorporate a small green. The **Mickiewicz Monument** stuck in the middle of it is the first of many you'll see if you travel round the country – he's a hero with whom everyone seems comfortable, communist governments included (see p.80-81). Unveiled on the centenary of the poet's birth, before a twelve-thousand-strong crowd (the Russians were enforcing a ban on rallies and speeches at the time), it's one of the monuments the cleaners clearly haven't got round to brushing up yet.

Just south of the statue stands the seventeenth-century **Carmelite Church** (Karmelitów) whose finely wrought facade, complete with a distinctive globe of the world, is one of the first examples of genuine classicism in Poland. Next door in the **Radziwiłł Palace** is where the Warsaw Pact was formally created in 1955, at the height of the Cold War. Thirty-four years later, it hosted another equally momentous event in the spring 1989 "Round Table" talks between the country's communist authorities and the Solidarity-led opposition. In front of the palace's large courtyard is a statue of another national favourite, Józef Poniatowski, nephew of the last king of Poland and a die-hard patriot who fought in the 1794 Insurrection.

West of the main street on ul. Kozia, a quiet, atmospheric cobbled backstreet, is the **Museum of Caricatures** (Tues–Sun 11am–5pm), a quirky but enjoyable set-up featuring exhibitions of work by Polish cartoonists. The main feature for some time to come is likely to be a large display of work by the late Eryk Lipiński, a veteran cartoonist whose satirical portraits seem to cover just about every famous Pole you're likely to have heard of, and many more besides. The overall tone of his pictures is hearteningly irreverent – no-one is sacrosanct, not even the Pope or other national icons past and present.

Back on Krakowskie Przedmieście, two grand old hotels face each other a little further down the street: the *Europejski*, Warsaw's oldest hotel, and the *Bristol*. Begun in the 1850s, the **Europejski**, was badly hit in World War II, but it's been restored well enough to preserve at least a hint of *fin-de-siècle* grandeur. After years out of action, the *Bristol*, a neo-Renaissance pile completed in 1899, is now back in business. Once owned by musician–premier Ignacy Paderewski and a legendary prewar journalist's hangout, it's been transformed into a super-luxury hotel by the English Forte group, its new owners.

Even in a city not lacking in Baroque churches, the triple-naved **Church of the Nuns of the Visitation** (Siostr Wizytek) stands out, with its columned, statue-topped facade; it's also one of the very few buildings in central Warsaw to have come through World War II unscathed. The church's main claim to fame, in

Polish eyes, is that Chopin used to play the church organ here, mainly during services for schoolchildren.

THE UNIVERSITY
Most of the rest of Krakowskie Przedmieście is taken up by **Warsaw University**. Established in 1818, it was closed by the Tsar in 1832 as part of the punishment for the 1831 Insurrection, and remained closed till 1915. During the Nazi occupation, educational activity of any sort was made a capital offence, and

MARIE CURIE (1867–1934)

Nobel Prize-winning scientist **Marie Curie** is a good example of the "famous person/ anonymous Pole" syndrome – Joseph Conrad being the other obvious one. To anyone brought up on a conventional diet of school science it comes as something of a surprise to discover that unlike her French husband, Pierre, and despite her adoptive country, France, Curie (née **Manya Skłodowska**) was a Pole through and through, and a strongly patriotic one at that. Born into a scientifically oriented Warsaw family (her father was a physics teacher), the young Manya showed academic promise from the start. After completing her secondary education at the city's Russian lyceum – also engaging in the clandestine "free university" organized by fellow Polish patriots, see "History" in *Contexts* – Curie travelled to Paris in early 1890 to follow the lectures of the prominent French physicists of the day at the Sorbonne.

The intellectually voracious Curie threw herself into the Parisian scientific *milieu*, landing a job in the laboratory of the noted physicist Gabriel Lipmann and meeting fellow researcher Pierre Curie, whom she married in 1895. Thus began a partnership that was to result in a number of spectacular scientific achievements, most famously the discovery of **polonium** – so named in honour of her native country – in summer 1898, and soon afterwards, **radium**. Following her colleague Henri Becquerel's discovery of the phenomenon she eventually dubbed "radioactivity", Curie set to work on systematic research into the revolutionary new wonder, work which eventually gained worldwide recognition in the **Nobel Prize for Physics** which she, Pierre Curie and Becquerel were awarded jointly in 1903. Pierre's sudden death in 1906 was a heavy emotional blow, but one which led to Curie's appointment to the professorship her husband vacated, making her the first woman ever to teach at the Sorbonne. A **second Nobel Prize**, this time in chemistry, came in 1911 for the isolation of pure radium.

Despite the upheavals of World War I, with the assistance of one of her two daughters, Curie worked on developing the use of **X-rays** and was a prime mover in the founding of the famous **Institut de Radium** in 1918, which rapidly developed into a worldwide centre for chemistry and nuclear physics. By now a figure of world renown, and deeply committed to developing the medical applications of the new radiological science, Curie and her daughters visited the US in 1921, receiving a symbolic gram of prized radium from the president, Warren G. Harding, in the course of the visit. During the rest of the 1920s Curie travelled and lectured widely, founding her own **Curie Foundation** in Paris and eventually realizing a long-standing ambition, the setting up of a Radium Institute in her native Warsaw in 1932, of which her sister Bronia was appointed director. Constant exposure to radiation began to have its effect, however, and in early 1934 it was discovered that Curie had **leukaemia**, of which she died only a few months later, in July 1934. The scientific community in particular mourned the loss of one of its outstanding figures, a woman whose research into the effects of radioactivity pioneered both its medical and research-oriented application, simultaneously paving the way for the major subsequent developments in nuclear physics.

thousands of academics and students were murdered. However, clandestine university courses continued throughout the war – a tradition revived in the 1970s with the "Flying University", when opposition figures travelled around the city giving open lectures on politically controversial issues. Today the university's reputation remains as much political as academic, and even the new political order doesn't seem to have extinguished its traditional radicalism. During term time, you'll find groups hustling books and leaflets on the streets outside the main entrance, and if they can speak English, a political discussion won't be hard to initiate either – like many Poles, the students love a good argument. The cafés, restaurants and milk bars just down the street and round the corner on ul. Oboźna are established student hangouts.

On the main campus courtyard, the **Library** stands in front of the seventeenth-century **Kazimierz Palace**, once a royal summer residence, while across the street from the gates is the former **Czapski Palace**, now home of the Academy of Fine Arts. Just south is the twin-towered Baroque **Holy Cross Church** (Kóściół Świętego Krzyża), which was ruined by a two-week battle inside the building during the Warsaw Uprising. Photographs of the distinctive stone figure of Christ left standing among the ruins became poignant emblems of Warsaw's suffering. Another factor increases local affection for this church – an urn containing Chopin's heart stands on a pillar on the left side of the nave.

Biggest among Warsaw's consistently big palaces is the early nineteenth-century **Staszic Palace**, which virtually blocks the end of Krakowskie Przedmieście. Once a Russian boys' grammar school, it's now the headquarters of the Polish Academy of Sciences. In front of the palace is the august **Copernicus Monument**, designed by the Danish sculptor Bertel Thorvaldsen in the 1830s and showing the great astronomer holding one of his revolutionary heliocentric models. Past the monument down the narrow ul. Oboźna is the **Polish Theatre** (Teatr Polski) building.

Downtown Warsaw

The area below the Saxon Gardens and west of Krakowskie Przedmieście is the city's busiest commercial zone. **Marszałkowska**, the main road running south from the western tip of the park, is lined with department stores and privately run clothes shops and workshops, selling everything from jewellery to car spares. South of ul. Swiętokrzyska, in the long narrow streets surrounding Chmielna and Zgoda, it's worth scouting around for good-quality items like heavy winter coats and hand-crafted leather goods.

North of ul. Swiętokrzyska, on ul. Kreditowa, the eighteenth-century **Lutheran Church** is topped with Warsaw's largest dome. The building's excellent acoustics have long made it popular with musicians – Chopin played a concert here at the age of fourteen, and the church still holds regular choral and chamber concerts (see "Nightlife", p.113). Opposite, stands the **Ethnographic Museum** (Tues, Thurs & Fri 9am–4pm, Wed 11am–6pm, Sat & Sun 10am–5pm), whose collection of over 30,000 items was virtually destroyed in the war. They've done pretty well to revive the place since then, restocking with African tribal artefacts, Latin American outfits and local folk items. Polish objects take up much of the second floor, a highlight being an absorbing collection of traditional costumes from all over the country. Folklore enthusiasts will enjoy the section devoted to straw men, winter processions and a host of other arcane rural customs.

Towering over everything in this part of the city is the **Palace of Culture**, a gift from Stalin to the Polish people, and not one that could be refused. Officially dubbed "an unshakeable monument to Polish-Soviet friendship" during the communist era, but popularly known as "the Russian cake", this neo-Byzantine leviathan provokes both intense revulsion and admiration for its sheer audacity. Slick marketing slogans have replaced the admonitions from Marx and Lenin on the banners over the giant entrance, up the steps from the expansive plac Defilad – recently the subject of an international design competition. The winning proposal – to fill the area with small-scale buildings and a pedestrian boulevard, but leave the palace essentially untouched – has angered many Varsovians, a good few of whom support the idea of demolishing the whole thing. The debate still rages, and it's unlikely that work of any sort will begin before the late 1990s. Apart from a vast conference hall, the cavernous interior contains offices, cinemas, swimming pools, some good foreign-language bookstores, and, the ultimate capitalistic revenge, a casino. City residents maintain that the best view of Warsaw is from the top floor – the only viewpoint from which one can't see the palace. A lift whisks visitors up to the thirtieth-floor platform from where, on a good day, you can see out into the plains of Mazovia.

While the planners debate the future, the area immediately in front of the palace is now filled with a series of huge covered **markets**. The piped muzak, sense of institutionalization and well-organized stalls are a definite step further along the capitalist path from the scramble of open-air vendors that previously occupied the square. A small section of open-air stalls still functions around the covered markets, though it's likely that this will be permanently moved before too long. In the meantime, work continues in front of the palace on the new metro station, due to open in 1997.

Al. Jerozolimskie, the major highway south of the palace, is dominated by the gleaming chrome and marble of the new *LOT* building and Warsaw's feted Western marvel, the luxury **Marriot Hotel**. (The opening of the *Holiday Inn* just north of the nearby central station confirmed this region as Warsaw's top-bracket tourist quarter.) The department stores continue south down tramlined Marszałkowska towards plac Konstytucji, interspersed with tourist offices, glitzy shops and the cultural institutes of other erstwhile communist countries. Cross-streets such as Hoża and Wilcza comprise a residental area whose discreetly well-heeled inhabitants are served by increasing numbers of chic little stores.

West of plac Konstytucji, on Nowowiejska, is the turn-of-the-century **Warsaw Polytechnic** building, where political groups often hold meetings. If you happen to be here at the right time, there's nothing to stop you sitting in on these impassioned mini-parliaments, sometimes attended by government ministers and other political luminaries.

The Nowy Świat district

South from the Staszic Palace, the main street becomes **Nowy Świat** (New World), an area first settled in the mid-seventeenth century. This wide boulevard, is currently being redeveloped giving way to shops and cafés. The *Nowy Świat* café, on the corner with Świętokrzyska, is a popular coffee shop, while the *Blikle* further down still produces the cakes for which it's been famed since 1869.

Numerous cultural luminaries have inhabited this street, the most famous being Joseph Conrad, who once lived at no. 45. A left turn down ul. Ordynacka brings you to the **Chopin Museum** (Mon, Wed, Fri & Sat 10am–2pm, Thurs noon–6pm), housed in the late seventeenth-century Ostrogski Palace on ul. Okólnik, which also forms the headquarters of the Chopin Society. Memorabilia on display includes the last piano he played, now used for occasional concerts. Monday evening concerts are held here throughout the summer months (May–Sept) and there are also regular performances in Łazienki Park (see p.100) and at Żelazowa Wola (see p.126). The Society organizes the International Chopin Piano Competition held every five years.

The neo-Renaissance **Zamoyski Palace**, off to the left of Nowy Świat at the end of ul. Foksal, is one of the few Warsaw palaces you can actually see inside. In 1863, an abortive attempt to assassinate the tsarist governor was made here; as a consequence the palace was confiscated and ransacked by Cossacks, who hurled a grand piano used by Chopin out of the window of his sister's flat in the palace. These days it's a suitably elegant setting for an architectural institute, with a restaurant and a nice quiet café open to the public.

Further down Nowy Świat, the concrete monster on the southern side of the junction with al. Jerozolimskie, was for decades the headquarters of the now defunct **Polish Communist Party**. After protracted wrangling over who should take it over, it was finally decided (with pleasing irony) to turn the building into the new Warsaw Stock Exchange – hence the parade of chauffeur-driven top-range BMWs and Mercedes outside. Due to the expansion of the Exchange's operations it is expected to relocate to a new purpose-built complex soon to be constructed on ul. Książęca in the western Koło district.

THE NATIONAL MUSEUM

Immediately east along al. Jerozolimskie is the **National Museum** (Tues & Sun 10am–5pm, Wed, Fri & Sat 10am–4pm, Thurs noon–6pm), an equally ugly and daunting 1930s building, and one of the few central Warsaw buildings to survive World War II intact. Its collections comprise an impressive compendium of art and archeology, but the museum is currently undergoing major renovation, and this, coupled with a continuous lack of staff, means that some galleries are likely to be shut.

The displays begin to the right of the entrance with the department of **ancient art** – assorted Egyptian, Greek, Roman and Etruscan finds. These, however, are completely overshadowed by the stunning array in the corresponding wing to the left of **art from Faras**, a town in Nubia (the present-day Sudan), excavated by Polish archeologists in the early 1960s. There are capitals, friezes, columns and other architectural fragments, together with 69 murals dating from between the eighth and thirteenth centuries. The earliest paintings – notably *St Anne, The Archangels Michael and Gabriel* and *SS Peter and John Enthroned* – are direct and powerful images comparable in quality with the much later productions of the European Romanesque, and prove the vibrancy of African culture at this period. No less striking are the later portraits such as the tenth-century *Bishop Petros with St Peter* and the eleventh-century *Bishop Marianos*.

In the rooms off the central hall, in which stand notable sculptures by Adrian de Vries, Bernini and Canova, is the museum's other star collection, that of **medieval art**, which is dominated by a kaleidoscopic array of carved and painted altarpieces. Although all the objects come from within the modern borders of Poland, the predominance of works from Silesia and the Gdańsk area suggests that most were created by German or Bohemian craftsmen, whose style was closely imitated elsewhere. Highlights include a lovely late fourteenth-century "Soft Style" polyptych from the castle chapel in Grudziądz; the monumental fifteenth-century canopied altar from St Mary in Gdańsk; and the altar from Pławno depicting the life of Saint Stanisław, painted by Hans Süss von Kulmbach, a pupil of Dürer who spent part of his career in Poland.

Much of the first floor is given over to **Polish painting**, beginning with a number of examples of what is a quintessential national art form, the coffin portrait. There's a comprehensive collection of works by nineteenth-century and modern artists, many of them relatively little known; an important section is the group of works from the turn-of-the-century *Młoda Polska* school. Stanisław Wyspiański's intense self-portraits stand out, as do Jacek Malczewski's haunting images of Death disguised as an angel. Matejko is represented by some of his most heroic efforts, notably the huge *Battle of Grunwald*, which depicts one of the most momentous clashes of the Middle Ages, the defeat of the Teutonic Knights by combined Polish–Lithuanian forces.

The left wing of the first floor, plus all of the second floor, are given over to the extensive but patchy department of **foreign paintings**. In the Italian section, look out for some notable Renaissance panels, such as the tondo of *The Madonna and Child with St John* from the workshop of Botticelli, *Portrait of a Venetian Admiral* by Tintoretto and *Christ among the Doctors* by Cima da Conegliano. Among the French paintings in the following rooms are a badly damaged little canvas called *The Polish Woman* attributed to Watteau and Ingres' sensual *Academic Study*. Upstairs, the German Renaissance is represented by a fine group of works – including *Adam and Eve*, *The Massacre of the Innocents* and *Portrait of a Princess* – by Cranach, and *Hercules and Anteus* by Baldung. From the same period in the Low Countries are an impressive *Ecce Homo* triptych by van Heemskerk and the satirical *Money Changers* by van Reymerswaele. Later Dutch works include *Queen Sylvia*, a brilliant Mannerist composition by Goltizius and a couple of striking examples of Tenebrism: *King David Playing the Harp* by Terbrugghen and *Boy Blowing Charcoal* by Rembrandt's collaborator, Jan Lievens.

THE ARMY MUSEUM

The **Army Museum** next door (Tues–Sun 10am–4pm), established in the 1920s, is devoted to an institution that has long played a pivotal role in national consciousness, as much, many Poles would argue, for its role in preserving national identity during periods of foreign occupation as for militaristic self-glorification. Greeting you outside the museum is an intimidating collection of heavy combat equipment, from sixteenth-century cannons through to modern tanks and planes. A unique item is *Kubuś*, as it's affectionately known, an improvised truck-cum-armoured car cobbled together by Home Army forces and used to notable effect during the Warsaw Uprising. Inside there's a wide array of guns, swords and armour from over the centuries. Exhibits include an eleventh-century Piast-era helmet (the oldest exhibit); early cannon prototypes produced by the Teutonic Knights; fearsome Hussar "whistling" feather headgear; and scythes of the type used in combat by Polish peasants during the Partition-era struggles. All in all the museum is a must for avid amateur military historians (and there are plenty of them in Poland), though the appeal of the insistently militarist ambience wears a little thin by the end of the exhibits. Newspaper reports have hinted that the museum will be moving to a new location in the Citadel (see p.105) before long.

THE PARLIAMENT AND SENATE
South of the museum, plac Trzech Krżyzy (Three Crosses), with the Pantheon-style **St Alexander's church** in the centre, leads to the tree-lined pavements and magisterial embassy buildings of al. Ujazdowskie. Past the unattractive US embassy and off to the left down ul. Jana Matejki, is the squat 1920s **Parliament** (Sejm) and **Senate** building. Hardly worth a mention a few years ago, these days it's where veteran Solidarity-era oppositionists jostle for power as much among themselves as with their former communist (now dubbed post-communist) political opponents – and the perennial national tendency towards factional political intriguing on show in the first years of post-communist rule is doing little to endear the new breed of politicians to the wider public.

A short way east across the parkland behind the parliament buildings, on ul. Solec, is the **Archdiocesan Museum** (Tues–Fri 11am–4pm, Sat 11am–3pm), an important centre ever since the martial law years of the early 1980s when it served as a focal point for independent cultural activity. The permanent collection comprises a wide range of religious art from the fifteenth century to the present day, including a lovely set of 48 woodcuts by Dürer and an intriguing collection of early clock-calendars. Alongside the permanent exhibits, the museum continues its tradition of supporting contemporary work, playing host to an ongoing series of imaginative exhibitions of work by noted contemporary Polish artists such as Zbigniew Beksiński, Feliks Czapski and Jerzy Topolski, as well as the occasional visiting show from abroad. It's always worth checking the city's listings magazines for what's currently showing at the museum.

South along al. Ujazdowskie and over the junction with al. Armii Ludswej is the grim **Museum of Struggle and Martyrdom**, al. Armii Wojska Polskiego 25 (Wed–Sun 9am–4pm). Housed in the former Gestapo headquarters, now occupied by government ministries, the basement museum commemorates the thousands tortured and murdered here during World War II.

Łazienki Park and Palace

Parks are one of Warsaw's distinctive and most attractive features. South of the commercial district, on the east side of al. Ujazdowskie, is one of the best, the **Łazienki Park** (open daily till sunset). Once a hunting ground on the periphery of town, the area was bought by King Stanisław August in the 1760s and turned into an English-style park with formal gardens. A few years later the slender Neoclassical **Łazienki Palace** was built across the park lake. Designed for the king by the Italian architect Domenico Merlini, in collaboration with teams of sculptors and other architects, it's the best memorial to the country's last and most cultured monarch. Before this summer residence was commissioned, a bathhouse built by Tylman of Gameren for Prince Stanisław Lubomirski stood here – hence the name "Łazienki", meaning simply "baths".

The oak-lined promenades and pathways leading from the park entrance to the palace are a favourite with both Varsovians and tourists. On summer Sunday lunchtimes and afternoons, concerts and other events take place under the watchful eye of the ponderous **Chopin Monument**, just beyond the entrance. These are an enjoyable introduction to Polish culture in populist form – stirring performances of Chopin études or mazurkas, declamatory readings from Mickiewicz and other Romantics, and so on. On the way down to the lake you'll pass a couple of the many buildings designed for King Stanisław by Merlini: the **New Guardhouse**, just before the palace, is now a pleasant terrace café.

The Palace

The only way to see the **palace interior** (Tues–Sun 9.30am–4pm; last entrance 3.20pm) is on a group tour, and these get booked early in the day – so get there by 9.30am in summer or be prepared for a long wait. Nazi damage to the rooms themselves was not irreparable, and most of the lavish furnishings, paintings and sculptures survived the war intact, having been hidden during the occupation.

On the ground floor are rooms incorporated from the earlier bathhouse; the baths themselves are long gone, but the bas-reliefs decorating the walls serve as a reminder of their original waterbound function. In the main section of the palace, the stuccoed **ballroom**, the largest ground-floor room, is a fine example of Stanisław's classicist predilections, lined with a tasteful collection of busts and sculptures. As the adjoining **picture galleries** demonstrate, Stanisław was a discerning art collector. The Nazis got hold of some of the best pieces – three Rembrandts included – but a large collection drawn from all over Europe remains, with an accent on Dutch and Flemish artists.

Upstairs are the **king's private apartments**, most of them entirely reconstructed since the war. Again, period art and furniture dominate these handsome chambers: a stately and uncomfortable-looking four-poster bed fills the royal bedroom, while in the study a Bellotto canvas accurately depicts the original Łazienki bathhouse. An exhibition devoted to the history of Łazienki completes the tour.

The Park

The buildings scattered round the park are all in some way connected with King Stanisław. Across the lake, and north along the water's edge, is the **Old Guardhouse,** built in the 1780s in a style matching the north facade of the main palace, which features regular exhibitions of contemporary art. Immediately next to it is the so-called **Great Outbuilding** (Wielka Oficyna), another Merlini construction, the former officer's training school where young cadets hatched the anti-tsarist conspiracy that resulted in the November 1830 Uprising. The building now houses the **Paderewski Museum** (Tues–Sun 10am–3pm) inaugurated during the summer 1992 celebrations surrounding the return of the composer's body to Warsaw from the US. Much of the museum's collection consists of items bequeathed to the country by the exile Paderewski in his will. Pride of place goes to the grand piano he used at his longtime home on the shores of Lake Geneva. Standing on it, as during the man's lifetime, are the improbably paired autographed photos of fellow composer Saint-Saëns and Queen Victoria, while the walls are decorated with Paderewski's personal art collection. Adjoining rooms contain the dazzling array of prizes, medals and other honours awarded to him during his distinguished musical and political career, as well as his fine personal collection of assorted Chinese porcelain and enamel ware. To finish off there's a section devoted to mementoes of the Polish *emigracja*.

Immediately next to the museum is the **Myślewicki Palace**, a present from the king to his nephew Prince Józef Poniatowski, which imitates the studied decorum of the main palace. In summer the Greek-inspired **amphitheatre**, constructed for the king on an islet just along from the palace, still stages the occasional open-air performance; rustling trees and the background duck chorus can make it hard to hear the proceedings on occasion.

Back up towards the park entrance, past the guardhouse, is the **White House** (Biały Dom), built in the 1770s by Merlini for King Stanisław August to live in while the main palace was being finished. It retains the majority of its original eighteenth-century interiors, including a **dining room** decorated with a wealth of grotesque animal frescoes, and an octagonal-shaped **study** which features enjoyable *trompe l'oeil* floral decoration.

Just beyond it, the main **Orangery** houses a well-preserved wooden theatre (one of the few in Europe to retain its original eighteenth-century decor), with room for over two hundred people, royal boxes not included. To complete the classical pose, pieces from King Stanisław's extensive sculpture collection fill the long galleries behind the auditorium.

Back out on al. Ujazdowskie, south from the Chopin monument, stands the **Belvedere Palace**, another eighteenth-century royal residence redesigned in the 1820s for the governor of Warsaw, the Tsar's brother Konstantine. Official residence of Polish heads of state since the end of World War I (with a brief interlude as home of the Nazi governor Hans Frank), it was used for ten years by General Jaruzelski, in turn supplanted by Lech Wałęsa, the country's first freely elected president in over fifty years. In 1995, Wałęsa announced that he was moving the presidential residence to the Namiestnikowski Palace on Krakowskie Przedmieście, so paving the way for the opening of a new museum dedicated to **Józef Piłsudski**, the country's venerated president for much of the interwar period, and a former resident. The museum is due to open in 1996.

The Royal Way slopes gently down from here towards the Mokotów district, passing the huge **Russian embassy** building – its security looking a lot more relaxed these days – and the *Universus*, one of Warsaw's largest bookstores, at the bottom of the hill. The Royal Way then continues a few kilometres south to Wilanów, its ultimate destination.

Wilanów

The grandest of Warsaw's palaces, **Wilanów** is tucked away in almost rural surroundings on the outskirts of Warsaw, and makes an easy excursion from the city centre: buses #B, #122, #130, #180, #193 and #422 run to the station just over the road from the palace entrance. Sometimes called the Polish Versailles, it was originally the brainchild of King Jan Sobieski, who purchased the existing manor house and estate in 1677. He spent nearly twenty years turning it into his ideal country residence, which was later extended by a succession of monarchs and aristocratic families. Predictably, Wilanów was badly damaged during World War II, when the Nazis stole the cream of the art collection and tore up the park and surrounding buildings. In 1945, the palace became state property, and for eleven years was extensively renovated and its art collection refurbished. It's now a tourist favourite, and at the height of summer the welter of coach parties can make it almost impossible for individual visitors to get in. Your best bets for ensuring easy entry are either to get here early (as always), to go on a Sunday (theoretically the non-group visitors' day), or to swallow your pride and sign up for an *Orbis* tour.

The approach to the palace takes you past former outhouses, including the smithy, the butcher's and an **inn**, now an exclusive restaurant (see "Eating and drinking", p.107). Also close at hand are some decent **cafés**, welcome refuges after the palace tour. The domed eighteenth-century **St Anne's Church** and ornate neo-Gothic Potocki mausoleum across the road lead to the gates, where you buy your tickets – if the crowds are big you'll be given a wooden token telling you what time your designated group is going to be let in.

The Palace

Laid out in a horseshoe plan with a central core flanked by a pair of projecting wings, the classical grandeur of the **facade**, complete with Corinthian columns, Roman statuary above the pavilions and intermingled Latin inscriptions, reflects Sobieski's original conception. The centrepeice of the main facade – a golden sun with rays reflecting from decorated shields bearing the Sobieski coat of arms – clarifies the essential idea of the palace; the glorification of Sobieski himself.

Despite extensive wartime damage, the essentials of the interior design have remained largely unchanged. Among the sixty or so rooms of Wilanów's **interior** (Mon & Wed–Sun 9.30am–2.30pm; park open till sunset) you'll find styles ranging from the lavish early Baroque of the apartments of Jan Sobieski and John III, to the classical grace of the nineteenth-century Potocki museum rooms. Some might find the cumulative effect of all this pomp and glory rather deadening – even the official guides seem to recognize this, easing off with the facts and figures in the last part of the guided tour.

Several flights of stairs lead to the **portrait galleries**. After the opening set of rooms, which are among the oldest, outlining the history of the palace, the galleries contain a number of casket images, intended to be interred with the subject, but sometimes removed from the coffin before burial. They are part of a total collection of over 250 portraits, most of which are hung in long corridor galleries – an intriguing introduction to the development of Polish Samartian fashion, with its peculiar synthesis of Western *haute couture* and Eastern influences such as shaved heads and wide sashes. If you've already visited other museums, the portrait of Jan Sobieski in the **Sobieski Family Room** will probably look familiar – the portly military hero most often crops up charging Lone Ranger-like towards a smouldering Vienna, trampling a few Turks on the way. Here as in the later galleries, the presence of portraits of the (aristocratic) great and good of Polish history provides the opportunity for the impromptu history lessons administered to local tour groups by the guides – naturally enough with an emphasis on insurgents, uncompromising oppositionists and other heroes of the struggle for independence over the centuries. One of the undoubted highlights of the collection is the great masterpiece of Neoclassical portraiture, *Stanisław Kostka Potocki on Horseback* by Jacques-Louis David.

After Sobieski's **Library**, with its beautiful marble-tiled floor and allegorical ceiling paintings, you come to the **Faience Room**, clad in blue with white Delft tiles and topped by an elegant copper-domed cupola surrounded by delicate period stucco mouldings, the centrepeice an eagle raising aloft the ubiquitous Sobieski coat of arms. The **August Locci Room**, named after Sobieski's chief architect, who designed most of the early interiors is one of several where the fine original seventeenth-century wooden beams have been uncovered. Many of the rooms on this floor offer excellent views over the palace gardens. The **Painted Cabinet Room**, next door, features recently uncovered eighteenth-century frescoes, notably a turbaned black man carrying a parrot in a cage. In contrast, restoration work in the **Quiet Room** has uncovered seventeenth-century frescoes of preening Greek goddesses.

Next comes another series of long **portrait galleries**, mostly from the Enlightenment era, including Kościuszko (see box p.402), the architects of the Third May Constitution (see p.612), and a benign looking Stanisław Poniatowski, Poland's last king, and family. Another flight of stairs takes you up into the nine-teenth-century portrait galleries, much used by the guides-cum-teacher with tour groups, with a suitably demure Maria Walewska, Napoleon's mistress, next to a bust of the general himself.

Downstairs again brings you to the other main set of apartment rooms. First comes the grand **Great Crimson Room,** as colourful as its name suggests, replete with a fabulously ornate ceiling filled with decorative cherubs and medallions and lashings of period art and furniture, including a massive dining table big enough to seat at least fifty people. Continuing on, you pass through the **Etruscan Study,** filled with third- and fourth-century BC vases from the Naples region, collected by nineteenth-century palace owner Stanisław Potocki during his regular architectural excursions. The **Lower North Gallery** further on, links the two wings to the main building. Converted into a mini-museum of antiquities by Potocki in the 1820s to show off his archeological finds, it's now been restored to its original early-eighteenth state, murals included, though the classical sculptures have remained.

The end of the gallery brings you into the **Queen's Apartments** originally used by Maria Kazimierza, Sobieski's wife, the most impressive of which are the **Antechamber**, containing two cabinets of fine late seventeenth-century porcelain, an inevitably sumptuous bedchamber, and the **Great Vestibule**, a three-storied affair of marble pillars and classicist mouldings connecting the royal apartments. The **King's Bedchamber** sports a great four-poster bed surrounded by period military trappings – precisely the kind of things the indefatigably warfaring Sobieski probably dreamed about. Past the **Chapel**, a simple shrine built by Potocki to commemorate his royal predecessor, you pass through further galleries containing more of Potocki's collection of classical sculpture, including some Roman sarcophagi, and a prize plaster **Sobieski Monument** of the corpulent king striking his customary pose charging a horse over the hapless Turks on his way to lifting the Siege of Vienna.

Last, but by no means least, comes the **Grand Hall of August II**, also known as the **White Hall**. Designed in the 1730s for King August II and thoroughly renovated after 1945, the mirrors on the walls combine to create a feeling of immense space. Box galleries, with balconies for the royal musicians, stand above the fireplaces at both ends, though the hall is more often used for piano recitals these days.

The Gardens

If your energy hasn't flagged after the palace tour, there are a couple of other places of interest within the grounds. The gate on the left side beyond the main entrance opens onto the stately **palace gardens** (Mon & Wed–Sun 10am till sunset). Overlooking the garden terrace, the graceful well-proportioned rear palace facade is again topped by statuary featuring a golden sundial on the southern side. Designed by Gdańsk astonomer Jan Hevelius, whose relief sits on the opposite side of the facade, the dial has Saturn, god of time, holding out the mantle of the heavens, on which both the time and the season's astrological sign are displayed. The fresco sequence punctuating the facade shows scenes from classical Greek literature, notably the *Aeneid* and *Odyssey*. Strolling along the back terrace, it's easy to appreciate the fine synthesis between regal residence and country mansion achieved by the palace.

The gardens reach down to the waterside, continuing rather less tidily along the lakeside to the north and south; in autumn this is a fine place for a Sunday afternoon scuffle through the falling oak leaves. Beyond the Orangery is the so-called **English Park**, whose main feature is a Chinese pavilion. Just down from the main gates, the **Poster Museum** (10am–4pm), has a mish-mash of the inspired and the bizarre, from an art form which has long had major currency in Poland.

The Suburbs

For most visitors anything outside the city centre and Royal Way remains an unknown quantity. While not visually attractive, some of the Warsaw **suburbs** are worth visiting both for their atmosphere and for their historic resonance, while at its furthest limits, the city merges into the villages of the Mazovian countryside, with head-scarved peasants and horse-drawn carriages replacing the bustle of city life.

Żoliborz

Until the last century, the **Żoliborz** district (whose name comes from a corruption of the French "joli bord"), due north of the centre, was an extension of the Kampinoski forest (the Bielany reserve in the northern reaches of the city today is a remnant), but then evolved into a working-class stronghold. The district's heart is the large square near the top of **ul. Mickiewicza** – the northern extension of Marszałkowska and Gen. Andersa. Officially restored to its prewar name, **plac Wilsona** has a gritty, down-to-earth feeling that contrasts strongly with the gentrified airs of the city centre. Politics are gritty here too: the tough campaign fought by local resident and veteran oppositionist-turned-government-minister Jacek Kuroń in the 1989 elections, led to several sizzling confrontations with his political opponents before packed audiences at the old *Wisła* cinema on the square. The district remains a touchstone of political feeling in the city.

  St Stanisław Kostka's Church, off to the west side of plac Wilsona, was Solidarity priest Jerzy Popiełuszko's parish church until he was murdered by militant security police in 1984 – a major event in Polish political life of the 1980s that ensured his popular canonization. After Popiełuszko's funeral, attended by over half a million people, his church developed into a major Solidarity sanctuary and focus for popular opposition. Although Western politicians no longer troop here, the custom of newlyweds dropping by to pay their respects at Father Jerzy's shrine continues. The basement houses a poignant **memorial to Jerzy Popiełuszko** (open erratically; ask in the church for current times). In the grounds there's a Via Dolorosa – a path marking the Stations of the Cross – taking you through the major landmarks of modern Polish history.

  South of plac Wilsona, bordering on the New Town, is an altogether more sinister place, the fearsome **Citadel** (Cytadela). These decaying fortifications are the remains of the massive fortress built here by Tsar Nicholas I in the wake of the 1831 Uprising. Houses were demolished to make way for it, and Varsovians even had to pay the costs of the intended instrument of their punishment, whose function was to control and terrorize the city as opposed to guarding it. For the next eighty years or so, suspected activists were brought here for interrogation and eventual imprisonment, execution or exile. Those held here, included the later president, Józef Pitsudski.

  The large steps up the hill lead to the grim **Gate of Executions**, where partisans were shot and hanged, with particular regularity after the 1863 Uprising. Uneasy with so obvious a symbol of Russian oppression and Polish nationalist aspirations, the postwar Communist Party attempted to present the Citadel as a "mausoleum of the Polish revolutionary, socialist and workers' movement": thus, alongside the plaque commemorating the leaders of 1863, there are memorials to the tsarist-era Socialist Party, the Polish Communist Party and "the proletariat". Part of the prison is now a **Historical Museum** (Tues–Sun 9am–3.30pm), with a few preserved cells and some harrowing pictures by former inmates depicting the agonies of Siberia. The wagon in the courtyard is a reconstruction of the vehicles used to transport the condemned to their bleak exile.

Praga

Across the river from the Old Town, the large **Praga** suburb was the main residential area for the legions of tsarist bureaucrats throughout the nineteenth century – particularly the Saska Kempa district, south of al. Waszyngtona. Out of range of the main World War II battles and destruction, the area still has some of its prewar architecture and atmosphere. Immediately across from the Old Town is the **Warsaw Zoo** (daily 9am–sunset), whose rundown yet attractive park-like expanses house a varied collection of animals including elephants, hippos and bears.

The **Russian Orthodox Church** (closed except during services) just beyond, on al. Solidarności, is one remaining sign of the former Russian presence. A large neo-Byzantine structure topped by a succession of onion domes, its original mid-nineteenth-century interior decoration remains intact. Pretty much the only way to get to see inside is to turn up during services, (Wed 9am, Sun 10am), when you can hear the excellent choir in action.

Praga's most notorious connection with Russia stems from the time of the Warsaw Uprising (see box on p.84–5). At the beginning of September 1944, Soviet forces reached the outer reaches of Praga. Insurrectionists from the besieged town centre were dispatched to plead with them to intervene against the Nazis – to no avail. Throughout the Warsaw Uprising, Soviet tanks sat and waited on the edges, moving in to flush out the Nazis only when the city had been virtually eradicated. For the next forty years, the official account gave "insufficient Soviet forces" as the reason for the non-intervention; as with the Katyn massacre, every Pole knew otherwise.

On a lighter note, Warsaw's best-known and longest-running **flea market** – the Różyckiego Bazar – is five minutes' walk south from the Orthodox Church on ul. Ząbkowska. The claim that you can buy almost anything here if the price is right still holds, though with perhaps less drama than in the mid-1980s, when you could reputedly pick up the odd contraband Kalashnikov from Afghanistan. If you do go, keep all valuables well in hand – pickpockets are numerous and skilful. Further south along the river, close to the Poniatowski bridge, is the **Dziesięciolecia stadium**, the city's largest sports stadium, now taken over by a sprawling outdoor market (see "Markets and bazaars" p.119).

Praga was once home to a significant proportion of the city's Jewish population. Directly over the Stąśko-Dąbrowski bridge, south of the leafy Park Praski, there are a number of streets, notably ul. Ks. Kłopołowckiego and ul. Sierakowskiego where you can still see some typical old Jewish residences. A little further out, in the Brodno district, is the **Praga Jewish Cemetery** (entrance at the corner of ul. Odrozona and ul. Wincentego; buses #135 and #162 from the centre pass nearby), founded in the 1780s. It was badly damaged by the Nazis, who used many of the stones for paving. Restoration work is in progress on the thousand or so graves remaining.

For motorists, the main pull of Praga may turn out to be the garages and spare-parts shops scattered round its eastern stretches. The high incidence of break-ins on unattended cars nowadays makes a hunt for side-windows a common exercise for foreigners and Varsovians alike.

Eating and drinking

It doesn't seem that long ago since Warsaw enjoyed the reputation of gastronome's nightmare, the majority of eating places marred by dingy surroundings, unimaginative menus and a lack of interest in the concept of service. One of the definite plusses of the post-communist era, therefore, has been a gradual but marked turnaround in the city's **restaurant** culture. Though the emphasis often tends to be on imitating Western habits – fast food included – the main thrust of change is towards diversity rather than uniformity. Alongside a good smattering of places specializing in traditional Polish cuisine, there's a welcome trend towards culinary variety – a collection of **ethnic restaurants** being the most obvious expression – giving Varsovians the chance to savour genuine Indian, Japanese and other ethnic cuisines on their home patch for the first time. Sadly, **prices** – increasingly comparable to Western ones – by and large ensure it's only the more wealthy city inhabitants who get to enjoy the best of the city's new food culture.

In the **café** scene also, a wealth of new or renovated places has sprung up in the past few years, offering everything from the most calorific haunts to down-to-earth student hangouts. Cakes and pastries, worthy of the best of central Europe, are no longer hard to come by, and if you follow the traditional local example, you'll doubtless find yourself passing many hours musing over the edge of a cup of coffee, or Russian-style, a glass of tea.

Bars, long something of a low spot of Warsaw nightlife, are improving in leaps and bounds. Alongside the ubiquitous traditional "drink-bars" serving hard spirits to hard-drinking locals, there's now a wide choice of newer, Western-influenced places, serving big-name German beers and other European brands alongside an increasing range of local brews, aimed partly at the tourists, partly at the city's young and upwardly mobile.

> The **telephone code** for Warsaw is ☎022 for five- and six-digit numbers, ☎02 for seven digits

Restaurants and snack bars

Though many **restaurants**, especially cheaper places, still follow the traditional communist-era practice of closing relatively early (9–10pm), a positive result of the transformation of the city's eating culture is the increasing number of places that stay open late. If you're really stuck late at night, you'll always get something in and around the central station. Foreign-language menus are available in the hotels and pricier restaurants, but don't count on it; refer to the food glossary in *Basics* for help with vocabulary. Remember the basic rule, that only things with prices next to them are likely to be available – even then, *niema* (there is none) is a word you'll soon get used to.

Nowhere in Warsaw, apart from the really top-category places, is going to make a serious dent in your finances. The restaurants below have been categorized as "moderate" (around £5–10/$7.50–15 a head) and "expensive" (£10–20/£15–$30). Of the restaurants listed under the "**ethnic**" category – mostly newer places – the majority are on the expensive side, though several offer cheaper set-menu lunches. The rapid demise of the **milk bar** means there's precious few of these traditional low-cost haunts left in the city. **Fast-food** joints, mostly, but not exclusively, in their standard American incarnation are now firmly established all over the city, while for a more traditional Polish alternative, it's worth trying the numerous **kiosks** and **snack bars** lining the pavements of the main city streets.

Fast food

Western-style **fast food** has finally hit the streets of the capital in a big way. Alongside the real thing – *McDonalds, Burger King* and the *Pizza Hut/Taco Bell/ KFC* triumvirate – you'll find plenty of Polish imitations. In addition to the hamburger joints and hot-dog stalls springing up on every street corner, **pizza** is a well-established favourite, either in Italian form or in the tasty traditional Polish variant of the *zapiekanki*, a half-baguette type morsel with liberal sprinklings of cheese on top. The **central station** has now been invaded by a variety of fast-food stands; several are open round the clock, meaning you're guaranteed a burger at almost any time of day – providing you're prepared to brave the generally dubious late-night company.

Milk bars and snack bars

Arrosto, ul. Poznańska 4. Small, cheap and central with good, fast lunchtime service.

Bambino, ul. Krucza 21. Budget place near the *Grand* hotel, with a good range of Polish dishes.

Bambola, ul. Wspólna 27. Nice pizzeria, serving seventeen kinds of pizza to eat in or take away. Other branches on Puławska and al. Jerozolimskie. All open till 10pm.

Boston Port, ul. Okolska. Small, good-quality lunchtime joint offering US East Coast-style dishes, including New England Fish Chowder. Closes early.

Delhi Dabar, Nowogrodzka 22. Tiny Indian takeaway (standing table only) opposite the Forum. Biryanis are worth a try.

Dziekanka, Krakowskie Przedmieście 56. Popular student hangout with an emphasis on fast food – though there are tables and chairs. Open till midnight.

Economistów, Nowy Świat 49. Basic student cafeteria that's as economical as its name suggests. The *barszcz* and chicken dishes are both recommended.

Expres, ul. Bracka 20. A tiny, private operation in the city centre, offering an efficient lunch service – gets very full around midday.

Expresso, ul. Bracka 18. Cheap, central joint offering Polish-style basics. Open for breakfast.

Familijny, Nowy Świat 30. Solid traditional-style milk bar, serving mostly vegetarian dishes.

Fuks, ul. Madalińskiego 38/40. One of the few avowedly vegetarian restaurants in town and already a firm favourite with many for its imaginative creations. Open late.

Grill Bar, ul. Zgoda 4. Ex-milk bar turned budget diner. Good for late breakfasts.

Krokiecik, ul. Zgody 1. Fast service, in a useful downtown shoppers' location.

Max, ul. Poznańska 38. Small private bar serving Arab food, particularly kebabs and shashlik; close to the Central station.

Mesa, pl. Zbawiciela. Small downtown restaurant with a line in Polish-style fish dishes.

Murżynem, ul. Nowomeijska 13. A good basic spaghetti and pizza house just north of the Old Town square.

Pod Barbakanem, ul. Mostowa 27/29. Deservedly popular milk bar-turned-restaurant near the Barbakan where you can sit outside and watch the crowds.

Pod Gołebami, ul. Piwna. Slightly upmarket Old Town bistro, popular with tourists.

Pod Samsonem, ul. Freta 3/5. Popular New Town restaurant offering a cheap, good-quality Polish menu with a sprinkling of Jewish dishes.

Salad Bar, ul. Tamka 17 and ul. Chmielna 13. Excellent, cheapish salad bars in the city centre, but so tiny you're best off with a takeaway.

Sneakers, ul. Paca 48. Warsaw's first experiment with original US diner culture, recently established by a Polish-American family, and featuring pancakes, hash browns and barbecue ribs. Flawless Middle America decor includes salad bar in an old Chevy.

Stylandia, ul. Marszałkowska 18. Cheap central snack bar with a good line in Chinese snacks.

Uniwersytecki, Krakowskie Przedmieście 20. Classic milk bar much frequented by students; just up from the university gates.

Wygodna, ul. Chmielna 23. Another unpretentious lunchtime restaurant in a useful central shopping location.

Zapiecek, ul. Piwna 34/36. Old Town student haunt, good for a breakfast fill-up: opens 9am.

Zodiak, ul. Widok 26. Basic town-centre cafeteria to fill yourself up at lunchtime. Just across from the *Forum* hotel.

Moderate restaurants

Bistro Corner, ul. Marszałkowska 82. Reasonably priced restaurant close to the *Forum* hotel. A centre-of-town shopper's lunchtime favourite.

Bong Sen, ul. Poznańska 12 (☎21 27 13). Vietnamese restaurant on a quiet central back-street. It's sister restaurant at ul. Długa 29 (☎635 38 88), south of the Central station serves similar dishes. Both open 11am–10pm. Booking recommended.

Capri, ul. Smolna 14. Straightforward pizzeria opposite the National Museum, useful for museum-goers.

Da Elio, ul. Żurawia 20a. Popular new pizzeria with excellent adjacent salad bar. Open till midnight.

Delfin, ul. Twarda 42. Straightforward little place widely regarded as the best fish restaurant in town.

Don Giovanni, Krakowskie Przedmieście 37 (☎26 27 88). Serviceable pizzeria, popular with Westerners – take-away and local deliveries too. Open till 11pm.

Flik, ul. Puławska 43. (☎49 44 34 or 49 44 06). Highly popular with Varsovians for its high quality/low cost formula. Solid traditional Polish food with an excellent inexpensive buffet. Booking generally advisable.

Galleria, Marszałkowska 34. Reasonably priced and good-quality place upstairs in a shopping centre, popular with Warsaw intellectuals and dedicated card-players.

Kahlenberg, ul. Koszykowa 56 (☎630 88 50). Good-quality Polish/Austrian venture near the Polytechnic; a popular lunchtime venue.

Kamienne Schodki, Rynek Starego Miasta 26. Duck with apples is the house speciality in this simple but popular Old Town hangout.

Kuchnia Artystów, al. Ujazdowski 6 (☎625 76 27). Good, cheap vegetarian-oriented restaurant servicing the Ujazdowski modern art centre. Quirky post-modernist decor heightens the culinary experience.

Kuźnia, Wiertnicza 24. Wilanów's second-string restaurant. Pork dishes are a good bet, as are the peach and pear desserts. Open 10am–11pm.

Le Petit Trianon, ul. Piwna 40/42 (☎31 73 13). Good traditional Polish cuisine in small Old Town tourist trap that's beginning to nudge up into the expensive bracket. Tiny, so reservations are recommended in season. Open till midnight.

London Steak House, al. Jerozolimskie 42. The name says it all – roast beef and Yorkshire pudding, across from the central station. Open till midnight.

Nowe Miasto, corner of New Town square. Trendy, self-styled "ecological" restaurant (ignore the rainforest furniture) with good, mostly vegetarian menu. Highly popular.

Opus One, pl. E. Młynarskiego. Newly refurbished Austrian-run restaurant housed in the Philharmonic building. Good quality Austro-Polish food with an imaginative menu that changes every other day. Popular with Warsaw yuppies, a far cry from its former student/Russian champagne-swilling profile.

Pod Krokodylem Gessler, Rynek Starego Miasta 21. Low ceilings and decent Polish cuisine in an Old Town basement venue that's a favourite with provincial Poles on a weekend in the capital. However, service and food standards have slipped of late, coupled with an increasingly pricey menu. Open 1pm–3am.

Pod Retmanem, ul. Bednarska 9. Gdańsk is the theme of the decor in this central and popular fish-oriented restaurant. Try the unusual house drink, *napój rajeów Gdański*. Open Mon–Sat 11am–10pm.

Pod Samsonem, ul. Freta 3/5. Unassuming New Town locale favoured by Warsaw intellectuals. Solid Polish home cooking including a selection of Jewish dishes. Recommended.

Staropolska, ul. Krakowskie Przedmieście 8. Newly spruced-up decor and reasonable service, with a good, inevitably pork-based menu. A handy place if you're in the university area. Open late.

Szanghaj, ul. Marszałkowska 55/57. An ugly building houses Warsaw's best-known but hardly its best Chinese restaurant. The humdrum menu is backed by dubious music most evenings. Open 11am–11pm.

Ti Amo, ul. Świętokrzyska 34. Decent no frills pizza joint, with friendly, efficient service.

Expensive restaurants

Ambassador, al. Ujazdowskie 8 (☎25 99 61). Luxurious establishment over the road from the US embassy. Good *zurek*, pork dishes and Georgian mineral water – reputedly Stalin's favourite. Open 11am–11pm.

Balzac, ul. Jana Pawła 11 (☎20 02 01). *Hotel Mercure's* flagship restaurant, offering classic French cuisine at higher than average prices. Closes at 8.30pm. The hotel's other restaurant, *Stanislaus*, offers a markedly cheaper version of the same: the lunchtime buffets are definitely worth a try.

Bazyliszek, Rynek Starego Miasta (☎31 18 41). Traditional Polish cuisine, with an emphasis on fish (eels and carp) and game (boar and wild pig) in glamorous old-world surroundings. Open weekdays 10am–midnight, weekends 10am–1am; reservations essential.

Belvedere, in Łazienki Park. Classy new restaurant inside the elegant park orangery. Ideal for a summer evening binge – it's worth going for the traditional Polish menu instead of the more touted (and expensive) French one. Reservations advisable in summer and at weekends (☎41 48 06). Open till midnight.

Cristal Budapeszt, ul. Marszałkowska 21 (☎25 34 33). Decent Hungarian food and wine with a sprinkling of Polish dishes. There's a folk band and dancing in the evenings. Open 11am–1am, later at weekends.

Europeijski Hotel, ul. Krakowskie Przedmieście 13 (☎26 50 51). The smaller hotel restaurant is open 11am–9pm, the main restaurant 1pm–midnight, with a dance show and obligatory ticket purchase after 7pm. Dependable if unexceptional *Orbis* fare.

Foksal, ul. Foksal 3/5 (☎27 72 25). One of the best of the top-bracket restaurants, premium French-based cuisine that'll leave a sizeable hole in your wallet. Located a couple of blocks north of the National Museum. Reservations advised. Open till 3am.

Forum Hotel, ul. Nowogrodzka 24/26 (☎21 02 71). Two decent restaurants catering mainly for tourists – very useful if you arrive in town late and famished, though they like to keep you waiting, however empty they are. Reservations are a good idea for larger groups. Open 7am–11am & 1pm–midnight.

Fukier, Rynek Starego Miasta 27 (☎31 10 13). Top notch Old Town restaurant with a strong line in imaginatively reinterpreted traditional Polish cuisine – expect your wallet to feel the difference though, £30/$45 and over per head. Get a table on the back patio if you can in summer. Reservations virtually essential. Open 12am until the last people leave.

Gessler, ul. Senatorska 37 (☎27 06 33). Serving gourmet European cuisine in demure surroundings, overlooking the Saxon Gardens. Prices are among the highest in town. Open 10am till late. Reservations definitely advisable.

Montmartre, Nowy Świat 7 (☎628 63 15). Spacious, chic centre-of-town French restaurant – bring your credit card along for this one (£33/$50 a head). Open till midnight.

Rycerska, ul. Szeroki Dunaj 9/11 (☎31 36 88). Popular, but pricey, Old Town venue swamped in boar's heads and suits of armour. If they're available, the lamb dishes are worth a try. Reservations are a good idea. Open 10am–11pm.

Świętoszek, ul. Jezuicka 2 (☎31 56 34). High-class Old Town haunt housed in brick Gothic cellars – strictly suit and tie – serving some excellent Polish specialities. Usually a high percentage of journalists and diplomats among the diners. Reservations essential.

Victoria Hotel, ul. Królewska (☎27 80 11). Contains two well-established luxury restaurants, the *Canaletto* and the *Hetmańska*. The former is one of the best *Orbis* places in town, with a good line in traditional fowl and game dishes. Reservations essential at weekends. Open 1pm–midnight.

Wilanów, Wiertnicza 27 (☎42 13 63). Right outside Wilanów Palace. Exclusive but not overly expensive joint frequented by diplomats – many of whom live nearby – and visiting dignitaries. The "old Polish" spread is good, the waiters among the most obsequious you'll ever encounter. Reservations essential.

Zajazd Napoleoński, ul. Płowiecka 83 (☎15 30 68). Small, exclusive Praga restaurant, housed in an inn where Napoleon is supposed to have stayed en route to Moscow. Popular with the smart set. Reservations essential. Open late.

Ethnic restaurants

Dong Nam, ul. Marszałkowska 45/49 (☎21 32 34). Good quality Vietnamese joint. Open till 11pm.

El Popo, ul. Senatorska 27 (☎27 23 40). Deservedly popular, authentic Mexican restaurant, with the *salsa* toned down just enough to suit the local palate. The *gaspacho* is excellent.

Hoang Kim, ul. Freta 18. Decent Chinese/Vietnamese restaurant in the New Town.

Maharajah, ul. Ostrzycka 2/4 (☎13 48 74). Commendable new Praga district Indian venture with a Nepalese chef and curries as hot as you want them. Reservations advisable at weekends. Open till midnight.

Maharaja-Thai, ul. Szeroki Dunaj 13 (☎635 25 01). Indian-Thai spinoff from the success of the *Maharajah* restaurant. Commendable mix of Asian dishes in an enjoyable Old Town location.

Mekong, ul. Wspólna 35 (☎21 18 81). Excellent small central restaurant, owned by a Vietnamese student who stayed on. Vietnamese and some Chinese food; the fish dishes are definitely worth the extra twenty-minute wait. Open 10am–10pm. Booking recommended.

Menora, pl. Grzybowski 2. Genuine kosher restaurant across from the synagogue – the gefilte fish is worth trying.

Parnas, ul. Krakowskie Przedmieście 4/6 (☎26 00 71). Upmarket town-centre Greek restaurant and coffee house: cheaper food upstairs.

Pekin, ul. Senatorska 27 (☎27 48 04). Well regarded new Chinese restaurant with a good line in Northern Chinese specialities. Reasonably priced too. Open till 11pm.

Szecherezada, ul. Zajązkowska 11 (☎41 02 69). Syrian-run place, giving Warsaw its first taste of Middle Eastern cuisine: kitsch Arabian Nights decor, good *szaslik* dishes, but erratic service.

Tokio, ul. Dobra 17. Japanese restaurant with a high-quality *sushi* bar. Open till 10pm (bar 8pm).

Tsumbame, ul. Folksal 16 (☎26 51 27). Excellent Japanese restaurant and accompanying *sushi* bar off Nowy Świat. Cheap lunchtime menus. Open till midnight.

Valencia. ul. Smocza 27 (☎38 32 17). Upmarket Spanish place complete with arty decor and (variable quality) live flamenco. The seafood specialities are the priciest on the menu. Open till midnight.

Cafés and bars

Cafés are usually enjoyable in Warsaw, though interest is as much social as gastronomic. In the better-stocked places, the things to ask for are *ciastka* (cakes) and *cukiernia* (sweets); when available, they tend to be excellent. The

Hortex cocktail bars (nothing to do with alcohol) are known for some of the best ice creams in town – besides the *Jezuicka* (see below), there's also one at ul. Świętokrzyska 35 and on plac Konstytucji.

Most of the **bars** are of the archetypal Polish "drink bar" variety. If you don't fancy their atmosphere, hotel bars are always an option; for a good general choice try the places along Krakowskie Przedmieście, the main street south from the Old Town. If seedy drinking bars really do appeal, you'll find a number of them at the top end of ul. Freta, in the New Town.

Cafés

Aleje, al. Jerozolimskie. Decent, if smoky, cafe with a basic selection of pizzas and Polish food. Drinks served all day, plus there's the obligatory pavement terrace in summer. Ideal place to sit and watch the world go by.

Amatorska, Nowy Świat 21. Trendy, popular and in a classic location.

Blikle's, Nowy Świat 25. The oldest cake shop in the city: you won't get coffee here, just some of the most mouth-watering pastries anywhere in Warsaw.

Bowta, ul. Freta. A very pleasant café with outside seating on the New Town square.

Bristol, Krakowskie Przedmieście 42/44. Main café of the hotel of the same name. An upmarket clientele understandably tempted by the mouth-watering selection of cakes and desserts.

Danusia, al. Jerozolimskie 57. A cosy little morning-coffee shop, next door to the British Institute, close to the Central station.

Eljat, al. Ujazdowskie 47. Coffee house run by the Polish–Israeli Friendship Society. Some Jewish food too.

Europejski, corner of Krakowskie Przedmieście. Delicious pastries and ices, in the hotel coffee shop.

Jezuicka, Rynek Starego Miasto 15, below the *Bazyliszek* restaurant. A busy Old Town rendezvous. The creamy *ciastka* desserts and ice creams are good, the service unpredictable.

Manekin, Rynek Starego Miasto 27. An enjoyable basement coffee dive on the Old Town square, with a bar at the back.

Nowa Oranżeria. Enjoyable indoor café in the grounds of Łazienki Park. Next to the smart *Belvedere* restaurant. The *Amfiteatr* café by the lake is equally good. Both are pricey.

Nowy Świat, ul. Nowy Świat 63. Classic downtown hangout – Allen Ginsberg wrote a poem about it. Good breakfast stopoff.

Pasieka, ul. Freta. Small intimate pizzeria in the New Town more noted for its delicious house drink – hot honey with cinnamon or crunched cardamom.

Pod Krokodyl, Rynek Starego Miasto 19. Popular Old Town café-cum-restaurant.

Polonia, al. Jerozolimskie 45. The hotel's *cukiernia* is a congenial central stopoff with a good selection of cakes, ice creams and desserts.

U Pana Michała, ul. Freta. Small, rather sedate coffee shop in the New Town.

U Szczepka i Tońka, ul. Jan Pawła 36. Café-bar run by local Lwów (L'viv) Friendship Foundation, re-creating the prewar atmosphere of the former eastern Polish "capital".

Wedel's, corner of ul. Szpitalna. Next to *Wedel* shop. Excellent rich hot chocolate and chocolate waffles.

Bars

Drinking out has become a lot easier than it used to be – there's more choice and places are open later. In the city centre, especially, you can find numerous Western-style watering holes, many of them open into the early hours of the morning. **Pubs** (both English and Irish) have quickly established themselves as a trendy city favourite, though with the price of a pint matching (and in some cases exceeding) those in the West, it's a mystery how anyone but foreigners and the most wealthy Poles can afford them. Watch spirit prices – anything beyond a Polish-produced vodka or *winiak* tends to add significantly to the bill.

Amsterdam, ul. Traugutta 4. Highly popular student hangout with plenty of nooks and crannies and a garden in summer.

The Blues Bar, ul. Agrykola. Small, student-oriented bar with rock music cranked up loud.

Der Elefant, ul. Mickiewicza 20. Popular bar near the *Sobieski* hotel.

Elefant Pub, pl. Bankowy 1. One of the best of the new breed of Warsaw pubs. Lively atmosphere, Guinness and other international beers on tap, plus a decent line in filling snacks.

Europejski, Krakowskie Przedmieście 13. In summer, the hotel's terrace is one of the nicest places in town to sit out and enjoy an early evening drink.

Fugazi, ul. Leszno 5. Determinedly alternative hangout that's popular with the city's punks and other black-clad types. Enjoy your beer sitting in half a bus – live gigs too.

Harenda, ul. Obozna 4. Hip student café-bar in the university area serving draught Guinness. Nice outdoor bar area in summer, but it's not cheap.

Hookie Pookie Pub, ul. Kopernika. Close to the *Skarga* cinema. Reasonably priced beer, convivial background music and a couple of pool tables. Open late.

Irish Pub, ul. Miodowa 3. Deservedly popular Irish joint with plenty of atmosphere; despite above average prices, the place is regularly filled to overflowing. Live music (cajun, c&w and Polish–Irish mix) every night of the week. The Guinness is especially pricey – you're better off with the cheaper draught *Żywiec* instead. Get here early if you want a seat. Also see "Clubs and gigs" below.

John Bull Pub, ul. Jezuicka 4. Old Town attempt at the genuine British article – polished wooden bar, back copies of *The Times* and draught keg bitter at over £2/$3 a pint is the result. Live jazz Thursday evenings. Open till 11pm.

Lapidarium, ul. Nowomiejska 4. Upmarket bar-restaurant inside scenic ivy-decked Old Town courtyard. Entrance fee includes a drink. Live music most evenings in in summer.

Maria, Podwale 19. Cheap studenty hangout in the Old Town area.

Marywil, ul. Senatorska 27. Old-style *winiarnia* near the opera – as you'd expect, a wide selection of wines on offer.

Na Trakcie, Krakowskie Przedmieście 47. Popular bar with ritzy background muzak, open late. Serves food, too.

Okrąglak, Emilii Plater. On the square below the Palace of Culture. Popular local drinking spot housed in an ex-public toilet: a local vodka-swillers' favourite.

Pod Baryłka, ul. Garbarska 7. Small Old Town bar with a wide selection of Polish beers.

Pod Herbami, ul. Piwna 21/23. An archetypal "drink bar" – but one that hip young Varsovians now like to be seen in.

Smocza Jama, ul. Nowa Lipki 5. Basic local dive with draught beer, a billiards table and little else. Good stopping-off spot if you're touring the former ghetto area.

Studio M, Krakowskie Przedmieście 27. Trendy, expensive designer bar frequented by arty types – there's even a small art gallery. Open till 1am.

That's it Pub, Marszałkowska 55. Anodyne town-centre pub run by *Quick* burgers downstairs; the ambience is rescued by some solid occasional live blues and rock performances.

U Hopfera, Krakowskie Przedmieście 55. Winebar and restaurant that's a favourite with students, but closes at 10pm.

U Szwejka, pl. Konstucji 1. Lively, enjoyable Czech-oriented pub downstairs in the *MDM* hotel. Czech Budweiser on draught, and a full range of meals available until late.

Nightlife

If Chopin concerts and intense avant-garde dramas are your idea of a good night out, you're unlikely to be disappointed by Warsaw **nightlife**. In summer especially, high-quality theatre productions, operas and recitals abound, many of them as popular with tourists as with Varsovians themselves. At the other end of the scale, there's the schmaltzy nightclub/cabaret scene centred on the big hotels, a bigger pull for businesstypes and prostitutes than for the average visitor.

Finding something in between still isn't that easy. The centre-of-town student clubs are still the most reliable places for dancing – equally as accessible to non-students – and it's always worth checking out what's going on in and around the university area. Additionally, there's a slowly increasing selection of bars and cafés that regularly feature live music at night (usually free).

For up-to-date **information** about what's on, check the current listings sections of the *Warsaw Voice*, *Welcome to Warsaw* or *Warsaw: What Where When* (see p.69). Regular Warsaw **festivals** include the excellent annual **Jazz Jamboree** in October (Miles Davis, Michael Brecker, John McLaughlin are among recent headline artists), the biennial **Warsaw Film Festival** (next in 1996), the **Festival of Contemporary Music** held every September, and the five-yearly **Chopin Piano Competition** – always a launch-pad for a major international career and next to be held in the year 2000. The **October Film Week**, organized by the *Hybrydy* club, is a vaguely alternative arts event.

Clubs and gigs

Warsaw's few decent clubs have been feeling the economic pinch in recent years, and the same goes for the music scene generally – appearances by major Western bands are still a rarity. When artists with the pulling power of Carlos Santana or Aerosmith do turn up, they generally play outdoors at the **Gwardia stadium** in the southern Rakowiec district, on the way to the airport.

Except for the big names, the touring circuit for **Polish bands** is confined to student clubs and occasional one-off festivals. **Jazz clubs** are scarce, a pity in view of the number of excellent local jazz musicians, some of them international figures, such as Zbigniew Namysłowski (tenor sax) and Tomas Stanko (trumpet). As a rule, **discos** are tacky, Europop affairs, frequented by a combination of young reticents and inveterate drunkards. Most of the clubs listed below are known as student venues, though students aren't the only customers. With nearly all of them, it's worth calling in advance – or checking listings – for the current programme.

Akwarium, ul. Emilii Plater 49 (☎20 50 72). Situated just behind the Palace of Culture, and the only genuine jazz club in town, with at least one good Polish or foreign act a week. The MTV screen in the café downstairs attracts the Warsaw trendies. Unfortunately, it's still plagued by early closing restrictions.

Alcatraz, pl. Bankowy 1. Smallish centre-town joint in the basement of the *Al Capone* pub. Free admission Thurs.

Centrum, Marszałkowska. Upstairs in the shopping centre immediately north of the *Forum* hotel. A taste of the archetypal Polish-style disco – if you can get past the bouncer.

Europa Voltaire, ul. Szkolna 2/4. Favoured haunt of local rock musicians. Regular live gigs with the odd "happening" or mini–fest to cheer things up. City centre, just south of the Saxon Gardens.

Filtry, ul. Krzywickiego. Styled as "futurist industrial" – meaning lots of pipes everywhere – the music is staple chart-oriented techno; a no-nonsense partytime vibe. Open till late.

Fiolka, ul. Puławska 257 (☎43 98 22). Lively café-cum-disco (normally runs late) with regular hip-hop/rap dance sessions and a weekly gay disco. Also does food. Call for current details as it's a long way south of the centre.

Fugazi, ul. Leszno 5. Premier alternative live venue, and always worth checking for current action. (Also see "Bars", p.113).

Giovanni, ul. Krakowskié Przedmieście 26/28. Central student club favoured by art students. Occasional live bands, mostly discos.

Ground Zero, ul. Wspólna 62. (☎625 52 80). Ultra-hip nightclub in a converted downtown bomb shelter. Dress is smart and the poseur count high. Members only on Sat, student night on Wed.

Hybrydy, ul. Złota 7/9 (☎27 37 63). Behind the *Centrum* department store on Marszałkowska. Weekend discos with a decent beat, a "Rap-Club" and occasional live gigs. Photo exhibitions too.

Irish Pub, ul. Miodowa 3. Live music every night of the week: unpredictable mix of traditional Irish, cajun and c&w. (See "Bars", p.113).

Na Barce, near the Śląsko-Dąbrowski bridge. Waterside barge turned into an imaginative bar/club in summer. Entrance fee includes a drink. Alternative-oriented music, occasional raves and acid house. Excellent fun.

Ochota, Cultural Centre ul. Grójecka 75. Regular live gigs, especially reggae.

Park, al. Niepodległości 196 (☎25 71 99). In the Piłsudski Park, southwest of the town centre. Regular late-night dancing; some live bands, too.

Remont, ul. Waryńskiego 12 (☎25 74 97). Best of the student clubs, with regular rock, folk and jazz concerts, discos – and weekly Hare Krishna meditation sessions.

Stodoła, ul. Batorego 10 (☎25 60 31). Ten minutes' walk from the *Park*. Lively spot at weekends, with a late disco. Large dance floor.

Van Beethoven, al. Krakowska 17 (☎46 09 94). Well out of the centre, but worth seeking out for the eclectic rave-oriented music mix, high-class lighting rig and fun atmosphere. Fridays are generally a good bet.

Opera and concerts

Opera is a big favourite in Warsaw, and classical concerts – especially anything with a piano in it (preferably Chopin) – tend to attract big audiences, so it's always advisable to book. **Tickets** for many concerts are available from the theatre ticket office (Kasa Teatralny) at al. Jerozolimskie 25, just along from the *Forum* hotel (Mon–Fri 11am–6pm, Sat 11am–2pm; ☎621 94 54 or 621 93 83). Other useful ticket sources are the *Estrada* offices at ul. Szpitalna 8 (Mon–Fri 9am–7pm; ☎27 17 47) and *Mazurka Travel* in the *Forum* hotel lobby (Mon–Sat 8am–6pm; ☎29 12 49), the latter specializing in tickets for Teatr Wielki and Opera Kameralna (particularly useful during the annual summer Mozart Festival).

Akademia Muzyczna, ul. Okólnik 2 (☎27 83 08). Regular concerts by talented students. Free entry.

Chopin Museum, ul. Okólnik 1. Summer piano recitals and other occasional performances.

Evangelical Church, pl. Małachowskiego. Focuses on organ and choral music, often with visiting choirs. Excellent acoustics.

Filharmonia, ul. Jasna 5 (☎26 72 81 or 26 57 13). Regular performances by the excellent National Philharmonic Orchestra and visiting ensembles. This is the venue for the International Chopin Piano Competition held every five years. Tickets from the box office at ul. Sienkiewicza 12 (daily 12–6pm) or just before the performance.

Łazienki Park, al. Ujazdowskie. Varied summer programme of orchestral, choral and chamber concerts, often held in the Orangery and also in the Contemporary Art Centre at Ujazdowski Castle, al. Ujazdowskie 6, on the northern edge of the park.

Opera Kameralna, al. Solidarności 76b (☎628 30 96). Chamber opera performances in a magnificent white and gold stucco auditorium. Also a key venue during the Mozart Festival.

Operetka Warszawska, ul Nowogrodzka 49 (☎628 03 60). Operetta and occasional chamber music performances.

Teatr Wielki Operyi Balet, pl. Teatralny (☎26 32 87 or 26 32 88). The big opera, ballet and musical performances – everything from Mozart to contemporary Polish composers, such as Moniuszko and Penderecki – are performed here in suitably grandiose surroundings. Tickets bookable by phone up to fourteen days in advance or in person from the box office (Mon–Fri 9am–7pm, Sun 10am–2pm & 5–7pm).

Theatre and cinema

Theatre is one of the most popular and artistically strong forms of entertainment in Warsaw, served by a wide, and growing, range of theatres, seemingly unaffected by cuts in state arts subsidies. Not speaking Polish is, of course, an obstacle, but for the acting style alone, it's worth considering a performance at one of the major theatres including *Teatr Narodowy*, plac Piłsudskiego (under reconstruction following a fire and due to reopen in late 1996), the *Atenaeum*, ul. Jaracza 2, the venerable old *Polski*, ul. Karasia 2, the *Studio* (inside the Palace of Culture), the *Powszechny*, ul. Zamoyskiego 20, or the *Teatr Żydowski*, plac Grzybowski. In addition, the Centre for Contemporary Art in Ujazdowski Castle plays host to many international thatre and dance groups. There is usually quite a range of productions on offer – translations of Shakespeare, adaptations of classical European drama, Polish musicals and some remarkable home-grown avant-garde. For children, the *Lalka Puppet Theatre* (☎20 02 11), inside the Palace of Culture, is a popular source of entertainment. Tickets, both advance and on the day, as well as details of current productions, are available from the Kasa Teatralny (see "Opera and concerts" above).

The traditional mixture in Warsaw's **cinemas** of "safe" Western pictures, eastern European art movies and home-grown hits is gradually broadening towards a more varied selection, including soft porn – much to the Church's horror. As on television, subtitling rather than dubbing is the rule. Again, newspaper listings, *WLK* and the *Warsaw Voice* are your best source of information about what's showing currently. Places with regular showings of **foreign films** include the *Atlantic* (one of the few cinemas with wheelchair access) and *Non-Stop*, both at ul. Chmielna 33, the *Relax*, ul. Złota 8, the *Polonia* at Marszałkowska 56 and the *Iluzjon*, ul. Wspólna 5, which has a regular schedule of classics and art films. The *Kultura*, Krakowskie Przedmieście 21/23, close to the Old Town, is one of the few cinemas in the country equipped with a fully up-to-date Dolby sound system, though others are supposed to be following suit in the near future.

If you have a car, you might consider an evening at Grupa Adyton's summertime **drive-in cinema** in the Żerań district, the only one in Warsaw. Late-night movie addicts are served by the *Cinema Nocne*, ul. Bednarska 2/4, run by the same people as the drive-in.

Gay Warsaw

Despite the difficulties of operating in the current Catholic-dominated political climate, the city has now developed a small network of **gay nightlife**. The organizational lynchpin of Warsaw's gay community is the **Pink Service**, the country's only agency for gays and lesbians – their office is at ul. Waryńskiego 6/89 (Mon–Fri 11am–4pm; ☎25 39 11). The *Pink Service*'s principal activities include acting as an information resource for and about the Polish lesbian and gay scene, running an annual Gay Pride Day, publishing their own magazines – *Men* (for gays), *Arabella* (for lesbians) and an occasional English-language gay newsletter

– as well as distributing international gay publications. Their office, which welcomes foreign visitors, is without doubt your best source of information for local gay events and happenings, new bars and clubs included. They also run an Information Line (Wed & Fri 6–9pm; ☎628 52 22) in English and Polish.

The gay **student group**, *Słowarzyszenie Grup Lambda*, Uniwersytet Warszawski, ul. Krakowskie Przedmieście 24, also welcomes contact and runs a semi-underground club (Fri 4–6pm; ☎628 03 26). Listed below are a selection of the most popular current gay haunts.

Café Rudawka, ul. Elbląska 53. North of the centre café with gay and lesbian disco on Friday nights.

Casablanca, ul. Foksal 21. Popular gay club/bar off Nowy Świat. Mon–Sat open till 3am.

Corner, ul. Żurawia. Gay café haunt near the *Grand* hotel.

Ewa, ul. Konopnickiej 9. Café just off pl. Trzech Krzyży that's become a regular gay haunt of late.

Polonia, al. Jerozolimskie 25. Small central bar near Nowy Świat favoured by city gays.

U Nowocina, ul. Stołeczna 11. Restaurant with gay disco Fri & Sat.

Shopping

Shopping in Warsaw has changed dramatically in the last few years. The old state-owned shops were one of the first things to go at the end of the communist era, replaced in the majority of cases by a wide array of private concerns, both Polish and Western-owned shops, that now adorn the streets of the capital. While it's not exactly Paris or Frankfurt yet, there are enough chic boutiques and other upmarket places around the commercially bustling central areas of Warsaw, to have you thinking twice about where you've landed. There's no shortage of goods either, with specialist stores catering to most consumer whims, alongside the regular general stores: bananas and exotic fruits, for instance, virtually unobtainable only a few years back, can now be picked up almost anywhere (at Western prices). A specific touch of Polishness is provided by the welter of markets, bazaars and street traders that you'll find around the capital, these increasingly organized gatherings adding a characteristic element of energy – and occasionally, uneasy hustle – to the commercial proceedings.

On a broader note, the general trend back towards Polish products, now that the initial post-communist lure of all things Western has worn off, is reflected in the increasing range of professionally packaged domestically produced consumer goods on sale in stores and shops.

Books, cards and records

For **books**, the *antykwariaty* scattered around the Old Town and central shopping area sometimes produce gems, especially in the art field. Several contemporary bookstores, like the huge *Universus* store at ul. Belwederska 20/22 or the ones in the Palace of Culture, are also worth checking out. Other bookstores to look out for include *Omega*, ul. Piekna 8, and *Lexicon*, Nowy Świat 9. *Im. B Prusa*, the large main university bookstore also on Nowy Świat, is one also of the best around. If you're desperate for an English-language paperback the *Bookland* bookstore at al. Jerozolimskie 61, next to the British Institute, has all the latest Penguin titles. Other major English-language outlets include the sprawling new

American Bookstore, Krakowskie Przedmieście 45, which stocks a wide range of US book and magazines; *Co-Liber*, plac Bankowy 4; and *Logor*, al.Ujazdowskie 16, good for second-hand books. The best selection of art **postcards**, old and new, is in the shop at ul. Nowomiejska 17, near the Barbakan.

Records and **cassettes** are more unpredictable. Really good buys like Chopin boxed sets on the state labels are hard to get hold of, precisely because they are so good. Selections in the bigger stores, like those on Nowy Świat, still tend to be a bit limited, though for rock music they're rivalled by the ranks of street entrepreneurs trading in the latest Western sounds, particularly pirated cassettes of varying quality. About the best selection of **CDs** around is at the *Salon Muzyczny*, ul. Mazowiecka 9 (near the *Warszawa* hotel), particularly worth checking for Polish-label classical selections. Also worth checking out is the *Polskie Negramie* store at the corner of Nowy Świat and ul. Świętokrzyska. For everything but Polish-produced releases, **prices** for records, tapes and CDs aren't much different from what you'd pay at home. Cheap pirate cassettes are much in evidence, but the virtual boycott of live gigs by major rock and pop bands they have caused might make you think twice about buying them.

Clothes, crafts and hard-currency shops

The shops at the northern end of Marszałkowska, and the streets east of the Palace of Culture, are the places to hunt for **clothes**, shoes and general finery, with the shops evenly divided between Polish- and Western-owned boutiques, stocking the latest French and Italian fashions. It's also worth looking in at the big department stores on Marszałkowska for clothes, and the *Moda Polska* department store on ul. Swiętokrzyska which stocks women's winter coats and hats. Other bargains are handmade shoes, made to high quality by cobblers like the one just below plac Trzech Krzyzy on al. Ujazdowskie.

Quality and taste is variable at the *Cepelia* **handicraft shops** scattered around town – the best buys are wooden boxes and occasional pieces of attractive jewellery. The biggest of the shops is at Marszałkowska 99/101, with others at plac Konstytucji 5 and ul. Krucza 23. *Polski Len* shops, like the one on ul. Targowa, are worth checking for linen (always 100 percent pure). For wooden crafts, *Arex Społkazoo* at ul. Chopina 5B, just down from the US embassy, has a wide selection of items from all over Poland

The old **hard-currency** *Baltona* and *Pewex* shops aren't as important as they used to be, given the widespread availability of Western goods, but they're still useful for alcohol, tobacco, confectionery and luxury goods, as well as basic items like toothpaste and toothbrushes. You'll find them in the big hotels and at other locations all over town, such as in the *LOT/Marriot* building on al. Jerozolimskie (Mon–Fri 8am–8pm, Sat 8am–4pm).

Galleries and antiques

The commercial **galleries** scattered around the city centre range from the arty to the downright tacky, with the biggest concentrations on Marszałkowska and Krakowskie Przedmieście. *Piotr Nowicki's*, on Nowy Świat, has a good range of modern jewellery, but ignore the paintings. The art at *Zapiecek* in the Old Town on ul. Zapiecek is worth checking out, and *Dziekanka* and *Kordegarda* galleries on Krakowskie Przedmieście often have interesting exhibitions, as does the

Folksal gallery in the regal-looking building on the corner of ul. Folksal and Nowy Świat. Another particularly well-known gallery is the *Zachęta* at plac Malachowskiego 3, just below the Saxon Gardens (see p.93), while the *ZPAF* gallery, plac Zamkowy 8, run by the city photographer's club, has regular exhibitions by both Polish and foreign photographers. *Gallery SPAM*, the artists' and musicians' union centre at ul. Krucza 14, is a trendy hangout with the art crowd – as well as exhibitions they also have occasional live music performances.

The **Centre for Contemporary Art**, al. Ujazdowskie 6 (Tues–Sun 11am–5pm, Fri till 9pm; ☎628 76 83 or 628 12 71), housed in the Ujazdowski Castle on the northern edge of Łazienki Park, is rapidly becoming one of the city's premier galleries, with a good range of exhibitions, concerts and a decent restaurant (see p.109). Its permanent collection features the work of over eighty Polish and international artists and recent exhibitions have included Ron Arad, John Cage, Yoko Ono and Frank Gehry.

Antiques enthusiasts looking for bargains should try the Sunday **Koło bazaar** (see "Markets" below). Of the established antique dealers, the formerly state-owned *Desa* chain of shops are worth checking out. They have four city-centre outlets: al. Andersa 20, Marszałkowska 34, Nowy Świat 48 and plac Zamkowy 4/6. Other dealers include *Rempex,* Krakowskie Przedmieście 4/6, *Optimus* (graphics, coins), Mokotowska 45, and *Kolekcjoner* (maps, graphics), ul. Targowa 19. For old cameras and lenses, especially Soviet models, there's a special market every Sunday at the *Stodoła* student club on ul. Batorego (see "Clubs and gigs", p.115).

Supermarkets and food stalls

With queues, low-quality products and scarce supplies now a thing of the past, buying food from **supermarkets** is a more feasible prospect than anyone could have dreamed of a few years ago, especially if you're on a tight budget. Though many places stock a reasonably comprehensive range of Western products, it pays to look out for the generally cheaper Polish version, particularly if you're after meats, cheeses and other dairy products. For alcohol to wash down an *al fresco* meal, you'll save money buying Polish beer (bottled or canned) or Hungarian and Bulgarian wine, widely available, as opposed to the pricier German or Dutch lagers that status-conscious Poles favour. Fresh fruit and vegetables are generally better bought from **street stalls and vendors** than the supermarkets.

A popular modern supermarket chain with a number of stores round the central city area is *WW*, at ul. Przechodnia 2, ul. Złota 9 and Lazurowa 8. They stock a full range of Polish and imported products. (Mon–Sat 7am–10pm, Sun 9am–3pm). Also good is the *Marco Polo* supermarket in front of the Palace of Culture, plac Defilad. Out of the centre, chainstores are rapidly establishing themselves, notably *Hit*, *Macro Cash* and *Carry and Billa*.

Markets and bazaars

At weekends, traditional market areas like the **Hala Mirowska**, on pl. Mirowski, west of the Saxon Gardens, are packed with stalls and worth visiting for the atmosphere alone. There are also a few established specialist **markets** worth exploring:

Centrum, in front of the Palace of Culture. Large array of stalls, mostly clothes, hi-fi and bric-a-brac. Now joined by two large covered market areas for the more established shops.

Ciuchy bazaar, Rembertów, in the south of the Praga district. Clothes bargains.

Dziesięciolecia stadium, Praga district, near Poniatowski bridge. Biggest of the outdoor city markets and reckoned to be Europe's largest. It's held in a sports stadium, where many street vendors moved when the city authorities cleared them out of the city centre. Everything you could imagine anyone thinking of selling – Soviet bric-a-brac, cars, rifles, fur coats and all things in between. The best bargains tend to be on the higher levels, as opposed to the more organized lower section.

Food market, ul. Polna. If you want avocados or papayas and can't find them on street stalls, this is where the affluent stock up, diplomats included.

Koło bazaar, ul. Obozowa, in the Wola district (near the end of tram lines #1, #13, #20 and #24, or bus #159, #167 and #359). Held on Sundays, this is the main antiques and bric-a-brac market, with everything from sofas and old Russian samovars to genuine Iron Crosses on offer. On Monday mornings, there's a pets market selling everything from hamsters to carnivorous turtles and beyond.

Różycki market, Praga (see p.106). The ranks of Polish and gypsy traders here are swelled these days by increasing numbers of Romanians and Russians – a Warsaw experience not to be missed, though hold on to your wallet. All day, every day.

Late-night shopping

For anyone caught short of a bottle of vodka for an impromptu party, or just desperate for a late-night snack, the following shops might be useful.

Michel Badre, Puławska 53, in Mokotów. French establishment, open round the clock, selling baguettes, beer, champagne and Western newspapers at French prices.

German shop, corner of al. Niepodległości and Wawelska. All things German.

Sklepy Nocne (Night Shops), Grójecka 47 & 79 (8am–1pm); *Max*, ul. Puławska at the corner of ul. Dolna (8pm–2am); *ala Człuchowska,* al. Soldiarności 72 and ul. Targowa 26/30 (8pm–2am); *Przy Agorze 22* (8pm–3am); *Kijowanka* ul. Targowa, (8pm–6am).

Listings

AIDS helpline ☎628 03 06.

Airlines The *LOT* building at al. Jerozolimskie 65/79 (☎630 50 07/9; 3 lines) makes bookings for domestic and foreign flights, as do all the major *Orbis* offices. All the big international airlines have offices in the city, mainly on ul. Krucza, ul. Szpitalna and ul. Marszałkowska, as well as booking desks at Okęcie airport. *PC Express* (☎637 24 61) is an English-speaking agent for leading IATA airlines. *Aeroflot*, al. Jerozolimskie 29 (☎628 25 57); *Air Canada*, ul. Marszałkowska 99A (☎25 99 15); *American Airlines*, al. Ujazdowskie 20 (☎625 30 02); *British Airways*, ul. Krucza 49 (☎628 94 31, 625 57 88 or 628 39 91); *Delta, Victoria Hotel*, ul. Królewska 11 (☎26 02 57 or 26 02 58); *KLM*, pl. Konstytucji 1 (☎621 70 41 or 628 47 86); *Lufthansa*, ul. Królewska 11 (☎630 25 55 or 27 54 36); *United*, ul. Koszykowa 54 (☎630 85 20 or 630 85 21).

Airport information International flights ☎46 17 00; domestic flights ☎650 19 53.

American Express Krakowskie Przedmieście 11 (☎635 20 02; 24hr phone service ☎625 40 30; Mon–Fri 9am–5pm). Express cash machine service available and at the *Marriot* hotel.

Banks *Amerbank*, Marszathowska 115 (☎24 85 02); *Barclays*, ul. Stawki 2 (☎635 05 65); *Citibank*, ul. Senatorska 12 (☎657 72 00); *Narodowy Bank Polski:*, ul. Świętokrzyska 11/12 & pl. Pow. Warszawy 4; *PKO*, ul. Trauguta 7/9. The *National Bank* at ul. Świętokrzyska 11/21 can help with transferring money from abroad, though this (like all other transactions) can take a long time.

Billiards Join the latest national craze at one of the number of newly established pool halls such as *Valdi*, ul. Piękna 7/9, *Bilard Amerykanski* (in the *Metropol* hotel), *U Docenta*, ul. Banacha 2.

Boat trips Along the Wisła to the Zegrze Bay and back. Daily May–Oct 9am–5pm departing from Most Poniatowskiego (☎628 05 26 or 19 40 11 ext. 50).

Buses *Polski Express* (☎650 44 21) runs buses to all major cities throughout Poland departing from ul. Jan Pawła II, near the Central train station, and from Okęcie airport.

Camera repairs, *Vino Service*, ul. Jan Pawła II 43a paw. 31 (Mon–Fri 10am–6pm).

Car repairs The main office of *PZMot*, the Polish motorists' association, is at al. Jerozolimskie 63. A 24hr breakdown service, run by *PZMot*, is at ul. Kaszubska 2b (☎981 or ☎41 66 21 or 41 04 23) and ul. Krucza 6/14 (☎29 35 41). The *Polmozbyt* breakdown service at ul. Omulewska 27 in southern Praga is open 6am–10pm (☎954). Both should be able to track down mechanics for most Western makes of car. For spare parts, the *Baltona* shop at ul. Radzymińska 78 in Praga is a good starting point (Mon–Sat 10am–6pm; ☎19 55 54).

Car rental *Avis*: Okęcie airport (daily 7am–10pm; ☎650 48 72) and at the *Marriot* hotel (daily 8am–6pm; ☎630 73 16); *Budget*: airport (daily 8am–8pm; ☎650 40 62) and the *Marriot* hotel (daily 7am–10pm; ☎630 72 80); *Orbis* rental service, ul. Nowogrodzka 27 (Mon–Sat 8am–8pm; ☎621 1 3 60).

Dentist 24hr service at ul. Ludna 10 (☎635 01 02).

Embassies *Australia*, ul. Estońska 3/5 (☎617 60 81/6; 6 lines); *Austria*, ul. Gagarina 34 (☎41 00 81/5; 5 lines); *Belgium*, ul. Senatorska 34 (☎27 02 33/5; 3 lines); *Bulgaria*, al. Ujazdowskie 33/35 (☎29 40 71); *Canada*, ul. J. Matejki 1/5 (☎29 80 51); *Czech Republic*, ul. Koszykowa 18 (☎628 72 21); *Denmark*, ul. Starościńska 5 (☎49 00 56 or 49 00 79); *Finland*, ul. Chopina 4/8 (☎29 40 91); *France*, ul. Piękna 1 (☎628 84 01); *Germany*, ul. Dąbrowiecka 30 (☎617 30 11); *Italy*, pl. Dąbrowskiego 6 (☎26 34 71); *Netherlands*, ul. Rakowiecka 19 (☎49 23 51); *Norway*, ul. Chopina 2a (☎621 42 31); *Romania*, ul. Chopina 10 (☎628 31 56); *Russia*, ul. Belwederska 49 (☎621 34 53 or 621 34 75); *Sweden*, ul. Bagatela 3 (☎49 33 51); *UK*, al. Roż 1 (☎628 10 01/5; 5 lines); *USA*, al. Ujazdowskie 29 (☎628 30 41/9; 9 lines).

Exchange Any of the *kantors*, tourist offices or hotels can change money. *Orbis* accepts travellers' cheques, but they may try to extract a ten percent commission, so a hotel (or *American Express*) is often a better bet.

Fax *Komertel* communications centre, ul. Nowogrodzka 45. Fax and satellite telecommunications service 24hr a day.

Ferries *Polish Baltic Steamship Company*, ul. Chałubińskiego 8. Ferry information ☎30 29 63 or ☎30 09 30.

Football The stadium of Legia Warszawa, the city team, is at Lazienkowska to the southeast of the city centre.

Foreign cultural institutes *Britain,* al. Jerozolimskie 59 (Mon–Fri 8.30am–5.30pm; ☎628 74 01); *Goethe Institute* (German), pl. Defilad 1 (Palace of Culture); *France*, ul. Senatorska 38; *Italy*, ul. Foksal 11; *Russia*, ul. Foksal 10; *US*, ul. Senatorska 13/15.

Health food shops *Bios*, ul. Folksal 8, *Corcot*, Marszałkowska 56, *Kabanos*, ul. Puławska 52, *U Stańczyków*, ul. Wilcza 23.

Hitchhiking The *Biuro Autostop*, ul. Narbutta 27a (Mon–Fri 9am–4pm), has English-language information about the ins and outs of hitching in Poland, and sells maps and autostop coupons. *PTTK*, on the Old Town square at no. 23, sells hitchhikers' guides.

Horse-racing In a country famous for producing Arabian thoroughbreds, it's not surprising to discover that a day out at the races is a popular pastime among Varsovians. The main race track is in the southern Służewiec district of town, ul. Wyścigowa 1 (trams #14, #19, #33, or #36 from the centre). The big annual events (such as the Warsaw Derby, held on the first Sunday of July, and the Great Warsaw races) draw crowds of 40,000 and up. The season runs from April to November. Races are on Wed, Sat & Sun. Check local listings for the current details.

Internet cafés You can now log on at: the centrum *EMPik* store on Marszałkowska (Mon–Thurs 9am–10pm, Fri & Sat 9am–11pm, Sun 10am–4pm); *Hector*, ul. Gwiaździsta 19 in Żoliborz (9am–7pm); and *Ruch*, pl. Unii Lubelskiej (Mon–Fri 9am–7pm, Sat & Sun 9am–3pm). Cost is 5–10zł per hour. For latest details contact *Internet Technologies* (☎ 640 03 10).

Laundry Ul. Mordechaja Anielewicza, on corner of the ghetto monument square (Mon–Fi 9am–7pm, Sat 9am–4pm); bus #180 passes right by. Also *Luxomat*, ul. Broniewskiego 89 (Mon–Fri 7.30am–7.30pm, Sat 7.30am–5pm; ☎633 28 79), self-service laundry plus dry-cleaning service; English spoken.

Left luggage At the Central train station (24hr) and *Marriott* hotel.

Lost property On city transport, ul. Słowackiego 45. Otherwise try the offices at ul. Floriańska 10 and ul. Wery Kostrzewy 11.

Medical services *Central Medical Centre*, ul. Hoża 56. Emergency service *SOS* (☎635 54 59; 24hr; or, ☎628 24 24). Some of the bigger hotels such as the *Marriott* have their own medical facilities too. Private clinics include *Capricorn*, ul. Podwale 11 (☎31 89 69); *Inspol*, Marszatkowska 85 (☎28 66 09); and *Unitas*, Marszatkowska 66 (☎21 66 59).

Newspapers You can now find yesterday's, and occasionally, the same day's editions of Western newspapers like *The Herald Tribune*, *Le Monde*, *The Financial Times* and *The European*, as well as mainstream magazines like *Time* and *Newsweek*, in major hotel lobbies as well as in the *Kodak* "Fast Film" photo shops in the *Centrum Shopping Centre* on Marszałkowska and in the Old Town, and in the *Fuji* shops on ul. Bagatela and in the Old Town. For Polish news, the English-language weekly *The Warsaw Voice* is indispensable.

Opticians Contact lens specialists include: ul. Belwederska 4, ul. Bracka 22, ul. Złota 11 and Nowy Świat 50.

Parking Hotel car parks aside, the multi-storey car park on the appropriately named ul. Parkingowa, behind the *Forum* hotel, is the safest place in the centre. Other guarded parking lots in the centre are on ul. Sentorska, ul. Boleść, ul. Ossolińskich, ul. Górskiego, ul. Ludna and ul. Żelazna.

Pharmacies All-night *apteka* at ul. Zielna 45, ul. Freta 13, ul. Leszno 38, ul. Żeromskiego 13 and ul. Puławska 39. There's also *Grabowski* inside the Central station. For homeopathic treatments try ul. Miła 33 and Marszałkowska 11a.

Police Theft is a depressingly common experience. Report crimes to the police office at ul. Wilcza 21, including a full list of stolen items and their value.

Post offices Main offices are at ul. Świętokrzyska 31/33 and in the Central train station; both open 24hr for telephones, 8am–8pm for post. Both provide poste restante: (Warsaw 1 is the code number for the former, Warsaw 120 for the latter).

Radio English-language news and views on *Radio Wawa* (91FM) on the hour 6–10am & at 10pm. *Kolor* (103FM) broadcasts "Central Europe Today" every weekday morning at 7.05am.

Skating Winter ice rink at *Torwar*, ul. Łazienkowska 6; open-air rink at ul. Idzikowskiego 4, in Stegny.

Student office *Almatur*, ul. Kopernika 23 (☎26 35 12). Open 9am–3pm.

Swimming pools In summer there are a number of crowded and over-chlorinated open-air pools at: ul. Gorczewska 69/73, Namysłowska 8 (children's pool), ul. Puławska 101, ul. Racławicka 132, ul. Wawelska 5, the Gwardia stadium and ul. Wat Miedzeszyński 407 (children's pool). Indoor pools at the *Victoria*, *Novotel* and *Solec* hotels generally open to non-residents, for a fee.

Telephones Always to be found in main post offices, as well as phone boxes on the street. Phone boxes with their own specific numbers enabling you to be called back: corner of Marszałkowska and Puławska; and Koszykowa and Żurawia.

Tours Apart from the obvious *Orbis* choices, there are a wealth of small private agencies around town. *Mazurka* (☎29 12 49), based inside the *Forum* and *Novotel*, offers tours round the city and bus trips to Żelazowa Wola. *Trakt*, the Warsaw Guides Association, ul. Kredytowa 6 (☎27 80 68 or 27 80 69), offers individual guides, bus tours and a ticket-booking service.

Travel information Bus schedules ☎23 63 94, train schedules: ☎620 03 61 (domestic), ☎620 45 12 (international), though you'll be lucky to get someone who speaks English.

Youth hostels The central office of *PTSM*, the Polish Youth Hostel Federation, is at ul. Chocimska 28, fourth floor, room 427 (Mon–Fri 9am–3pm; ☎49 83 54); they produce a book listing hostels all over Poland.

MAZOVIA

The attractions of **Mazovia** – the plain surrounding Warsaw – are outlined briefly in the introduction to this chapter. If time is limited, then at least take a break outside the city in the beautiful forest of the **Kampinoski National Park**, or to Chopin's birthplace at **Żelazowa Wola**. Southwest of the capital, the great manu-facturing city of **Łódź** offers a major dose of culture. Other towns south of Warsaw are less inviting, and industrial centres such as **Skierniewice** and **Radom** are likely to be low on most people's priorities. **Płock**, under two hours by train west of the city, is altogether more enticing, with an historic old town complex and a couple of notable museums. The northern stretches of Mazovia offer some good day excursions, chiefly the palace at **Jabłonna** and the market town of **Pułtusk**.

Just about everywhere covered in the following section can be reached from Warsaw on **local buses and trains**, though prospective day-trippers to the forest will need to watch out for erratic evening bus services back to the city. Łódź is particularly well served by regular express trains, making a day's outing from Warsaw an easy option.

The Kampinoski National Park

With its boundaries touching the edge of Warsaw's Żoliborz suburb, the Puszcza Kampinoska – or **Kampinoski National Park** – stretches some 30km west of the capital, a rare example of an extensive forest area coexisting with a major urban complex. An ideal retreat, this open forest harbours the summer houses of numerous Varsovians, and in autumn is a favoured week-end haunt for legions of mushroom-pickers. As with all national parks, the forest's nature reserves are carefully controlled to help preserve the rich plant and animal life – elks, wild boars, beavers (recently reintroduced here from the northeast of the country) and lynx (also reintroduced in the early 1990s) are sighted from time to time – but access for walkers and cross-country skiers is pretty much unrestricted. Beware that it's all too easy to get lost in the woods, so stick to marked routes: signposts at the edge of the forest show clearly the main paths.

Originally submerged under the waters of the Wisła, which now flows north of the forest, the picturesque park landscape intersperses dense tracts of woodland – pines, hornbeams, birch and oaks are the most common trees – with a patchwork terrain of swamp-like marshes and belts of sand dune. Though most of the forest is now under local forestry commission management, a few parts of the area still retain the wildness that long made them a favourite hunting spot with the Polish monarchy.

Truskaw and Palmiry

Bus #708 from the Marymont bus station in northern Żoliborz takes you 10km out to **TRUSKAW**, a small village on the eastern edge of the forest. It's a rapidly developing place, home to the headquarters of the park authorities. The small museum here details the often bloody history of the forest (see below) as well as a section devoted to the local flora and fauna. From Truskaw, it's a pleasant five-kilometre walk to the hamlet of **PALMIRY**, along sandy paths that seem a world removed from the bustle of the city. People in the scattered older houses will give you well-water if you ask, and may have jars of the excellent local honey for sale.

The forest's proximity to town made it a centre of resistance activity – notably during the 1863 Uprising and World War II – and also made it an obvious killing ground for the Nazis. The war cemetery that you pass on the Truskaw–Palmiry walk contains the bodies of about 2000 prisoners and civilians, herded out to the forest, shot and hurled into pits. To get back into Warsaw, walk the one-kilometre track north from Palmiry to the main road bus stop and take any bus to Marymont station.

If you're not in a hurry to get back, it's worth crossing the main road by the bus stop and continuing on a couple of kilometres east to the village of **DZIEKANÓW POLSKI** on the banks of the Wisła. The area round the village is one of several

---

FRÉDÉRIC CHOPIN (1810–49)

Of all the major Polish artists, **Frédéric Chopin** – Fryderyk Szopen as he was baptized in Polish – is the one whose work has achieved the greatest international recognition. He is, to all intents and purposes, the national composer, a fact attested to in the wealth of festivals, concerts and, most importantly, the famous international piano competition held in his name. Like other Polish creative spirits of the nineteenth century, the life of this brilliantly talented composer and performer reflects the political upheavals of Partition-era Poland. Born of mixed Polish–French parentage in the Mazovian village of **Żelazowa Wola**, where his father was a tutor to a local aristocratic family, Frédéric spent his early years in and around Warsaw, holidays in the surrounding countryside giving him an early introduction to the Mazovian folk tunes that permeate his compositions. Musical talent began to show from an early age: at six Chopin was already making up tunes, a year later he started to play the piano, and his first concert performance came at the age of eight. After a couple of years' schooling at the Warsaw lyceum, the budding composer – his first polonaises and mazurkas had already been written and performed – was enrolled at the newly created Warsaw Music Conservatory.

Chopin's first journey abroad was in August 1829, to Vienna, where he gave a couple of concert performances to finance the publication of some recent compositions, a set of Mozart variations. Returning to Warsaw soon afterwards, Chopin made his official **public debut**, performing the virtuoso Second Piano Concerto (F Minor), its melancholic slow movement inspired, as he himself admitted, by an (unrequited) love affair with a fellow Conservatory student and aspiring opera singer. In the autumn of 1830 he travelled to Vienna, only to hear news of the **November Uprising** against the Russians at home. Already set upon moving to Paris, the heartbroken Chopin was inspired by the stirring yet tragic events in Poland to write the famous *Revolutionary Étude*, among a string of other works. As it turned out, he was never to return to Poland, a fate shared by many of the fellow exiles whose Parisian enclave he entered in 1831. He rapidly befriended them and the host of young composers (including Berlioz, Bellini, Liszt and Mendelssohn) who lived in the city. The elegantly dressed, artistically sensitive Chopin soon became a Parisian high society favourite, earning his living teaching and giving the occasional recital. Some relatively problem-free years followed, during which he produced a welter of new compositions, notably the rhapsodic *Fantaisie-*

noted birdwatchers' haunts in and around the national park, a fact explained by the forest's location along one of the country's main bird migration routes. Among the birds regularly sighted here is the **white stork**, whose nests are common in and around the village, some of the telegraph poles sporting special platforms to which the storks return each year to raise their young. Further into the fields and dense undergrowth closer to the river, you may be able to catch the call of the **lapwing**, while on the water, you can spot brilliantly coloured **kingfishers** and **bluethroats** as well as a variety of gulls, terns and ducks.

Leszno and Kampinos

On the southern side of the park, you can head further into the forest from the villages of **ZABORÓW**, **LESZNO** or **KAMPINOS**, all of which are sited along the main road to Żelazowa Wola (see below). To get to the villages, take a blue regional bus from the Central bus station (Centralny Dworzec PKS).

Impromptu, a book of études and a stream of nationalistically inspired polonaises and mazurkas.

Chopin's life changed dramatically in 1836 following his encounter with the radical novelist **George Sand**, who promptly fell in love with him and suggested she become his mistress. After over a year spent hesitating over the proposal in the winter of 1838, Chopin – by now ill – travelled with her and her two children to Majorca. Though musically productive – the B Flat Minor Sonata and its famous funeral march date from this period – the stay was not a success, Chopin's rapidly deteriorating health forcing a return to France to seek the help of a doctor in Marseilles. Thereafter Chopin was forced to give up composing for a while, earning his living giving piano lessons to rich Parisians and spending the summers with an increasingly maternal Sand at her country house at **Nohant**, south of Paris. The rural environment temporarily did wonders for Chopin's health, and it was in Nohant that he produced some of his most powerful music, including the sublime *Polonaise Fantasie*, the Third Sonata and several of the major ballades. Increasingly strained relations with Sand, however, finally snapped when she broke with him in 1847. Miserable and almost penniless, Chopin accepted an invitation from an admiring Scottish pupil Jane Stirling to visit **Britain**. Despite mounting illness, Chopin gave numerous concerts and recitals in London, also making friends with Carlyle, Dickens and other luminaries of English artistic life. Increasingly weak, and unable either to compose or return Stirling's devoted affections, a depressed Chopin returned to Paris in November 1848.

Just a few months later, he finally succumbed to the tuberculosis that had dogged him for years, and died in his apartment on place de Vendôme in central Paris: in accordance with his deathbed wish Mozart's *Requiem* was sung at Chopin's funeral, and his body was buried in the **Père-Lachaise Cemetery**, the grave topped, a year later, with a monument of a weeping muse sprinkled with earth from his native Mazovia. Admired by his friends yet also criticized by many of his peers, the music Chopin created during his short life achieved a synthesis only few fellow Polish artists have matched – a distinctive Polishness combined with a universality of emotional and aesthetic appeal. For fellow Poles, as well as for many foreigners, the emotive Polish content is particularly significant: many, indeed, feel his music expresses the essence of the national psyche, alternating wistful romanticism with storms of turbulent, restless protest – "guns hidden in flowerbeds", in fellow composer Schumann's memorable description.

There are a number of walking options. One of the best is to get off at Leszno and take the marked forest path to Kampinos, a good twelve-kilometre walk in all. The *PTTK* hostel and the *toś pensjonat* at ul. Chopina 19, in Kampinos both have basic **restaurants** where you can fortify yourself. Walking north through the village on the marked path, you soon reach the swampy edges of the forest. In summer you'll need to watch out for the particularly bloodthirsty mosquitoes, but the forest itself is a treat, with acres of undisturbed woodland and only very occasional human company. Unless you plan to stay overnight in Kampinos, start out early from Warsaw, as return buses stop at about 6pm, after which the only option is a taxi, charging double for journeys outside the city.

Żelazowa Wola

Fifty kilometres west of Warsaw, just beyond the western edge of the Kampinoski National Park, is the little village of **ŻELAZOWA WOLA**, the birthplace of composer and national hero, **Frédéric Chopin**. The journey through the rolling Mazovian countryside makes an enjoyable day out from the city: unless you've got a car, you'll need to take a bus from the main bus station (direction Sochaczew; 1hr) or book up on an *Orbis* excursion.

The house where Chopin was born is now a **Museum** (May–Sept Tues–Sun 10am–5.30pm; Oct–April Tues–Sun 10am–4pm) surrounded by a large, tranquil garden. The Chopin family lived here for only a year after their son's birth in 1810, but young Frédéric returned frequently to what was long his favourite place, and one which gave him contact with the Polish countryside and, most importantly, the folk musical traditions of Mazovia. Bought by public subscription in 1929, the Chopin family residence was subsequently restored and turned into a museum to the composer run by the Warsaw-based Chopin Society. The piano recitals held here every Saturday and Sunday at 11am and 3pm (occasionally Wed & Thurs too) from the beginning of May to the end of September – check Warsaw listings sources for the current programme details – are a popular tourist attraction, and are included in the *Orbis* and other organized tours.

The house itself is a typical *dwór*, the traditional country residence of the *szlacta* (gentlefolk) class, numerous examples of which can be found all over rural Poland – Mazovia and Małopolska in particular. All the rooms have been restored to period perfection and contain a collection of family portraits and other Chopin memorabilia. Through the main entrance way the old **kitchen**, the first room on your right, has an attractively painted characteristic nineteenth-century Mazovian ceiling.

Next along is the **music room**; the exhibits here including a caseful of manuscripts of early Chopin piano works as well as a plaster cast of the virtuoso pianist's left hand. If you've come for the popular weekend **piano recitals** – often by noted international performers who consider it an honour to play at the house – this is where they're held, performed on a luxury Steinway grand donated by wealthy Polish-Americans. On fine days, the audience sits outside, the music wafting through the open windows – an eminently uplifting and pleasurable experience.

The **dining room** walls sport some original Canaletto copper-worked views of Warsaw, while upstairs is the **bedroom** where the infant Frédéric was born, now something of a Chopin shrine. Back outside it's worth taking a leisurely stroll through the magnificent house grounds, turned into a sort of botanical **park** (open till 7pm) following the place's conversion into a museum. In spring or autumn you'll catch the scented blossoms of the rich variety of trees and bushes donated from botanical gardens around the world. The *Pod Wierzbami*, on the corner of the main road, provides reasonable food, mainly for visiting tour groups.

If you're travelling by car (although many of the bus tours also stop here), you could consider making a brief detour 11km north into the countryside to the village of **BROCHÓW**. The imposing brick **Parish Church**, a fortified sixteenth-century structure (currently undergoing a complete interior overhaul), became the Chopin family place of Sunday worship following the parents' marriage here in the early 1800s. The original of young Frédéric's birth certificate is proudly displayed in the sacristy, along with assorted other Chopin family records.

Łowicz and around

At first sight **ŁOWICZ**, 30km southwest of Żelazowa Wola, looks just like any other small, concrete-ridden central Polish town, but this apparently drab place is, in fact, a well-established centre of folk art and craft. Locally produced handicrafts, handwoven materials, carved wood ornaments and *wycinanki* – coloured paper cut-outs – are popular throughout the country, the brilliantly coloured local Mazowsze costumes (*pasiaki*) being the town's best-known product. Historically Łowicz has not been without importance, for several centuries providing the main residence of the archbishops of Gniezno, normally the Catholic primates of all Poland, who endowed Łowicz with its scattering of historic building – chiefly churches. Łowicz is a ninety-minute train journey from Warsaw and there's a regular local service from Śródmieście station (see p.90).

The ideal time to come here is at **Corpus Christi** (late May/early June) – or, failing that, during one of the other major **church festivals** – when many of the women turn out in beautiful handmade traditional costumes for the two-hour procession to the Collegiate Church. Wearing full skirts, embroidered cotton blouses and colourful headscarves, they are followed by neat lines of young girls preparing for their first Communion. The crowds gathered in the main square may well contain a sizeable contingent of camera-clicking foreigners, but they are never numerous enough to ruin the event's character and sense of tradition.

The old **Rynek**, ten minutes from the train station, is the pivot of the town, along with the vast **Collegiate Church**, a brick fifteenth-century construction, remodelled to its present form in the mid-seventeenth century. Size apart, its most striking features are the richly decorated tombstones of the archbishops of Gniezno and former Polish primates, and the ornate series of Baroque chapels.

The other attraction is the **Local Museum** across the square (Tues–Sun 10am–4pm), housed in a missionary college designed by Tylman of Gameren and rebuilt following wartime destruction. The upstairs floor contains an extensive and carefully presented collection of regional folk artefacts, including furniture, pottery, tools and costumes whose basic styles are the same as those still worn on feast days. Downstairs, as well as a section devoted to local history and archeology, the former seminary **chapel** houses a notable collection of Baroque art from all over the country, the vault of the chapel itself adorned with frescoes by Michelangelo Palloni, court painter to King Jan Sobieski. Many houses around the square contain examples of the distinctive coloured cut-out decorations on display in the museum too. The back of the museum is a kind of mini-*skansen*, containing two old cottages complete with their original furnishings. If you're intrigued by the local craftwork, there's a generally reasonable selection on sale at the *Cepelia* shop on the main square. Of the clutch of historic buildings dotted around the town centre, the most notable are the Baroque former **Piarist Church**, with some enjoyable ceiling paintings, and the remains of the **castle** on ul. Zamkowa, originally the bishop's residence until it was razed to the ground by marauding Swedes in the mid-seventeeth century.

For an overnight stay, the only real options are the down-at-heel *Turystyczny* **hotel** at ul. Sienkiewicza 1 (☎04037/6960; ②), south of the main square; the better quality *Łowicki*, ul. Blich 36 (☎04037/4164; ②) on the Poznań road on the western side of town; and the **youth hostel** at ul. Poznańska 30 (June–July only). The *Turystyczny* has a passable **restaurant**; otherwise try the *Polonia* in the main square – but don't expect too much.

Arkadia and Nieborów

A short distance east of Łowicz are a couple of sights redolent of the bygone Polish aristocracy. They combine for an easy and enjoyable day trip from Warsaw; get off the Warsaw–Łowicz train at **Mysłaków**, 1km west of Arkadia, and pick up a bus. From Łowicz, buses run fairly regularly – anything going in the direction of Bolimów or Skierniewice will get you to the palace at Nieborów, while for Arkadia Park, the service is even more frequent, though you might be forced to hitch the five kilometres between the two places.

Arkadia Park

The eighteenth-century **Arkadia Park** is as wistfully romantic a spot as you could wish for an afternoon stroll. Conceived by Princess Helen Radziwiłł as an "ancient monument to beautiful Greece", the classical park is dotted with lakes and walkways, a jumble of reproduction classical temples and pavilions, a sphinx and a mock-Gothic house that wouldn't look out of place in a Hammer House film production. Many of the pieces were collected by the princess on her exhaustive foreign travels, and the air of decay – the place hasn't been touched since World War II – only adds to the evocation of times long past, consciously created by the princess, who was caught up in the cult of the Classical that swept through the Polish aristocracy in the latter half of the eighteenth century.

Nieborów

The Arkadia bus continues on for 5km to the village of **NIEBORÓW**, whose country **Palace** was designed by the ever-present Tylman of Gameren and owned for most of its history, like the park, by the powerful Radziwiłł clan – just one of dozens this family possessed right up until World War II. Now part of the National Museum, the Nieborów Palace is one of the handsomest and best-maintained in the country, surrounded by outbuildings and a manicured **park and gardens**.

The palace **interior** (Tues–Sun 10am–3.30pm), restored after the war, is furnished on the basis of the original eighteenth- and nineteenth-century contents of the main rooms – a lavish restoration that makes you wonder whether Polish communists suffered from a kind of ideological schizophrenia. Roman tomb-stones and sculptural fragments fill a lot of space downstairs, gathered about the palace's prize exhibit, the **Nieborów Apollo**. The grandest apartments (including a library with a fine collection of globes) are on the first floor, reached by a staircase clad in finely decorated Delft tiles. It all has an air, these days, of studied aristocratic respectability, somewhat belying Radziwiłł history. Karol Radziwiłł, for example, head of the dynasty in the late eighteenth century, used to hold vast banquets in the course of which he'd drink himself into a stupor, and, as often as not, kill someone in a brawl. He would then, as historian Adam Zamoyski puts it in his book *The Polish Way*, "stumble into his private chapel and bawl himself back to sobriety by singing hymns". A far cry from today's genteel environment, which, in the spring, is host to a much publicized series of **classical concerts** by international artists.

There's a **café/restaurant** in the palace itself, while Nieborów village offers the small regional-style *Jagusia* restaurant, a seasonal **youth hostel** (May–Sept) and a *PTTK* **campsite**.

Łódź

Mention **ŁÓDŹ** (pronounced "Woodge") to many Poles and all you'll get is a grimace. Poland's second city, 110km southwest of Warsaw, is certainly no beauty, but it does have a significant place in the country's development, and a unique atmosphere that grows on you the longer you stay. Essentially a creation of the Industrial Revolution, and appropriately nicknamed the "Polish Manchester", Łódź is still an important manufacturing centre. Much of it survives unchanged – the tall, smoking chimneys of the castellated red-brick factories; the grand historicist and Secessionist villas of the industrialists; the theatres, art galleries and philanthropic societies; and the slum quarters, all caked in a century-and-a-half of soot and grime. It served as the ready-made location for Andrzej Wajda's film *The Promised Land*, based on the novel by Nobel Prize-winning author Władysław Reymont, depicting life in Industrial Revolution era Poland.

International business and trade fairs account for most of Łódź's visitors, but its cultural scene is pretty lively as well. The **orchestra** is one of the best in the country, and there's an impressive array of cinemas, theatres, museums, opera houses and art galleries here. The Łódź **film school** is also internationally renowned, attracting aspiring movie-makers aiming to follow in the footsteps of alumni such as Wajda, Polański, Kieślowski and Zanussi.

A brief history

Missionaries came to the site of Łódź in the twelfth century, but the first permanent settlement does not seem to have taken root until a couple of hundred years later, and at the end of the 1700s it was still an obscure village of fewer than two hundred inhabitants. Impulse towards its development, strangely enough, only came during the Partition period, with the **1820 edict** of the Russian-ruled Congress Kingdom of Poland, which officially designated Łódź as a new industrial centre and encouraged foreign weavers and manufacturers to come and settle.

People poured in by the thousand each year, and within twenty years Łódź had become the nation's second largest city, a position it has maintained ever since. Despite being the imperial rulers, the Russians played little more than an

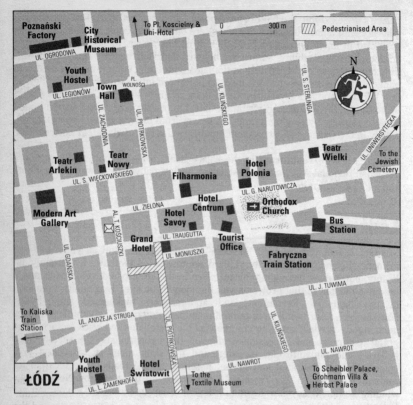

administrative role, though they adopted a higher profile following the failed nationalist insurrection of 1863. The true political elite consisted in the main of **German entrepreneurs**, most of them Protestant, who founded large textile factories which made vast fortunes within a very short period of time. These were operated principally by **Polish peasants** enticed by the prospect of a better standard of living than they could claw from their meagre patches of land. By the end of the century, the urban proletariat had swelled to over 300,000. Industrialization brought politicization, and Łódź, like other new cities such as Białystok, had become a centre for working-class and anti-tsarist agitation.

The **Jews** were another highly significant community. When they first arrived, they functioned mainly as artisans and traders, but a number managed to rise to the status of great industrial magnates, notably the Poznańskis, whose luxurious homes now house many of the city's institutions. The Jewish contribution to the cultural life of Łódź was immense, two of the city's most famous sons being the pianist Artur Rubinstein and the poet Julian Tùwim.

Łódź's reputation as a melting-pot of four great peoples and religions was only marginally affected by the fall of the tsarist empire, but was dealt a terminal blow by **World War II**. At first, the Nazis aimed to make it the capital of the rump Polish protectorate, the so-called General Government, but, incensed by the largely hostile stance adopted by the powerful local German community, incorporated it into the Reich. In the process, they renamed it "Litzmannstadt" in honour of a somewhat obscure general who had made a breakthrough against the nearby Russian line in 1914, and established the first and longest-lasting of their notorious urban ghettos (see box overleaf).

For all the visual similarities, postwar Łódź has been, in an important sense, a spectre of its former self; nearly all the Jews were wiped out, while most of the German expatriates fled west, leaving only a tiny minority behind.

> The **telephone code** for Łódź is ☎042

Arrival, information and accommodation

The main **train station**, Łódź Fabryczna, and the **bus station** are right next to each other in the heart of the city. Note that the former is a dead-end terminus of the line from Warsaw; through trains (especially from the west and north) tend not to make the long detour, stopping instead at the Kaliska station, 2km west of the city centre and connected by tram #12. It's also possible you could arrive at the Chojny station, 4km southeast of the centre: from here, take tram #5 from the left of the entrance, or tram #7 from the right.

The municipal **tourist office**, across from the main station, at ul. Traugutta 18 (Mon–Fri 9am–5pm, Sat 10am–1pm; ☎33 71 69), has a good supply of maps and information and is generally helpful. **Orbis** is at ul. Piotrkowska 68 (☎36 97 98) and **LOT** at ul. Piotrkowska 122 (☎33 48 59).

Łódź's top-ranked **hotel** is the *Orbis*-run *Grand*, ul. Piotrowska 72 (☎33 99 20 or 32 19 95; ⑥–⑦), a *bel époque* establishment which for once really does live up to its name. Its four-star rating is shared by two modern alternatives – the less impressive but aptly-named *Centrum*, ul. Kilińskiego 59/63 (☎32 86 40; ⑦), and the similar *Światowit*, al. Kościuszki 68 (☎36 36 37; ⑥–⑦). Best of the medium-priced options include the classy *Savoy*, ul. Traugutta 6 (☎32 93 60; ⑤), and the recently refurbished *Polonia* at ul. Gabriela Narutowicza 38 (☎32 87 73; ⑤). Of the cheaper possibilities try the *Uni-Hotel*, ul. Łagiewnicka 54 (☎55 34 94; ③), north of the centre, served by trams #8 and #16.

Both **youth hostels**, at ul. Zamenhofa 13 (☎36 65 99) and ul. Obrońców Stalingradu 27 (named ul. Legionów on the latest maps; ☎33 03 65), are just ten minutes' walk from the central area and are open all year. The **campsite** is nearly 2km south of the Chojny station at ul. Rzgowska 247 (☎81 25 51), the main road leading south out of town, and a few minutes' walk beyond the terminus of trams #2, #4 and #18. If, as is probable, the tourist office can't help with **private rooms**, try the *Centrum Usług Turystycznych*, plac Wolności 10 (☎36 10 46).

The City

The first sight for visitors arriving at Łódź Fabryczna – the Central train station – is the **Orthodox Church** across the road. Once used by the city's Russian rulers, it's a compact example of nineteenth-century Orthodox architecture, which is something of a rarity in central Poland; unfortunately, it's generally kept locked. A couple of blocks west of here is **ul. Piotrkowska**, which bisects the city from

THE ŁÓDŹ GHETTTO

The fate of the **Jews** of Łódź, who numbered over a quarter of a million in 1939, is undoubtedly one of the most poignant and tragic episodes of World War II, particularly as a pivotal role was played by one of their own number, **Chaim Rumkowski**. He has become the most controversial figure in modern Jewish history, widely denounced as the worst sort of collaborator, yet seen by others as a man who worked heroically to save at least some vestiges of the doomed community to which he belonged.

Within two days of the Nazi occupation of the city on September 8, the first definite anti-Semitic measures were taken, with Jews hauled at random off the streets and forced to undertake seemingly pointless manual tasks. The following month, Rumkowski, a former velvet manufacturer who had made and lost fortunes in both Łódź and Russia before turning his attentions towards charitable activities, was selected by the Nazis as the "elder" of the Jews, giving him absolute power over the internal affairs of his community and the sole right to be their spokesman and negotiator. Plans were made to turn the entire Jewish community into a vast pool of slave labour for the Nazi war machine, and the run-down suburb of **Baluty** to the north of the centre was earmarked for this **ghetto**, partly because this was where the bulk of the Jews lived. Those who resided elsewhere were rounded up into barracks or else chosen for the first transportations to the death camps. By the following spring, the ghetto area had been sealed off from the rest of the city, and anyone who dared come near either side of its perimeter fences was shot dead.

Rumkowski soon made the ghetto a self-sufficient and highly profitable enterprise, which pleased his Nazi masters no end, even though this conclusively disproved a key tenet of their racist ideology, namely that Jews were inherently lazy and parasitical. He ruled his domain as a ruthless **petty despot**, attended by a court of sycophants and protected by his own police force and network of informers; his vanity extended to the minting of coins and manufacturing of stamps bearing his own image. Anyone who crossed him did so at their peril, as his omnipotent powers extended to the distribution of the meagre food supplies and to selecting those who had to make up the regular quotas demanded by the Nazis for deportation to the concentration camps. He cultivated a variation on the oratorical style of Hitler for

north to south. Its pedestrianization and cleaning up have seen the city begin to tackle the task of improving its image, and most of Łódź's sights are located on or around this avenue. All around this area you'll come across the grubby, peeling mansions and tenements of the city's former *haute bourgeoisie*, which will hopefully receive attention as funds permit.

The northern area

Plac Koscielny, the old market square way up at the top of ul. Piotrkowska, is dominated by the twin brick towers of the neo-Gothic **Church of the Ascension**. On the other side is the rather forlorn Stary Rynek, which soon lost its original function as the hub of everyday life when the city rapidly expanded southwards.

From here, walk one block south and another west to the junction of ul. Zachodnia and ul. Ogrodowa, where you'll find one of the most complete complexes to have survived from the Industrial Revolution anywhere in Europe. On the corner itself is the haughty stone bulk of the **Poznański Palace**, formerly the main residence of the celebrated Jewish manufacturing family. Right

his frequent addresses to the community. The most notorious and shocking of these was his "Give me your children" speech of 1942, in which he made an emotional appeal to his subjects to send their children off to the camps, in order that able-bodied adults could be spared.

Whether or not Rumkowski knew that he was sending people to their deaths is unclear. There is no doubt that he saw the ghetto as at least the **embryonic fulfilment of the Zionist ideal** and believed that, after the Nazis had won the war, they would establish a Jewish protectorate in central Europe, with himself as its head. He also seems to have had few qualms about his role, insisting he would be prepared to submit himself for trial to a Jewish court of law once the war was over. It seems that his repeated claims to have cut the numbers demanded for each quota were true, and it's also the case that the ghetto was far from being a place with no hope. On the contrary, there was a rich communal life of schooling, concerts and theatre, and many inhabitants were inspired to make detailed diaries recording its history.

The Łódź ghetto was **liquidated** in the autumn of 1944, following a virulent dispute at the top of the Nazi hierarchy between Speer, who was keen to preserve it as a valuable contributor to the war effort, and Himmler, who was determined to enforce the "Final Solution". Some one thousand Jews were allowed to remain in Łódź to dismantle the valuable plants and machinery; Rumkowski voluntarily chose to go with the others to Auschwitz, albeit armed with an official letter confirming his special status. He died there soon afterwards, though there are three versions of how he met his end: that he was lynched by his incensed fellow Jews; that he was immediately selected for the gas chambers on account of his age; and that he was taken on a tour of the camp as a supposedly honoured guest, and thrown into the ovens without being gassed first. Had he remained in Łódź, he would have been among those who were **liberated** by the Red Army soon afterwards. Perhaps not surprisingly, the staunchest apologists for Rumkowski's policies have come from this group of survivors.

A large and fascinating collection of extracts from diaries kept by members of the ghetto, along with transcriptions of Rumkowski's speeches and many photographs, including some in colour, can be found in *The Łódź Ghetto*, edited by Alan Adelson and Robert Lapides (see "Books" in *Contexts*).

alongside is their still-functioning **factory**, behind whose monumental mock-Gothic brickwork facade are weaving and spinning mills, plus a number of warehouses, while across the street are the tenement flats of the workforce.

The palace, now designated the **City Historical Museum** (Tues & Thurs–Sun 10am–2pm, Wed 2–6pm), is an excellent example of the way Łódź's *nouveaux riches* aped the tastes of the aristocracy, transferring, both inside and out, the chief elements of a Baroque stately home to an urban setting. Downstairs are temporary exhibitions of modern art and photography, while up the heavily grand staircase are the showpiece chambers, the dining room and the ballroom, along with others of more modest size which are now devoted to displays on different aspects of the city's history. Archive photographs show the appearance of prewar Łódź, including the now-demolished synagogues, while there's an extensive collection of memorabilia of **Artur Rubinstein**, one of the greatest pianists of this century. He was particularly celebrated for his performances of Chopin, and his recordings remain the interpretative touchstone for this composer. A quintessential hedonist, he was reputed to have played more music, loved more women and drunk more champagne than any other man – yet he was able to keep up the itinerant lifestyle of the modern concert virtuoso almost to the end of his ninety years.

One block southwest of the museum is the circular plac Wolności, with the Neoclassical town hall, regulation Kościuszko statue, and the domed Greek cross-plan Uniate church. At no. 14 on the square, the **Archeology and Ethnography Museum** (Tues, Thurs & Fri 10am–5pm, Wed 9am–4pm, Sat 9am–3pm, Sun 10am–3pm) has a wide-ranging collection of local artefacts, costumes and archeological finds.

The Modern Art Gallery

A couple of blocks further south is the **Modern Art Gallery** or Galeria Sztuki, at ul. Więckowskiego 36 (Tues 10am–5pm, Wed & Fri 11am–5pm, Thurs noon–7pm, Sat & Sun 10am–4pm), installed in a mock-Renaissance palace with lovely stained glass windows, which once belonged to the Poznański clan. Founded in 1925, when it was one of the world's first museums devoted to the avant-garde, it is the finest modern art collection in the country (though it also contains some earlier pieces). Major artists represented include Chagall, Mondrian, Max Ernst and Ferdinand Léger, but there's also an excellent selection of work by modern Polish painters such as Strzeminski (quite a revelation if you've not come upon his work before), Wojciechowski, Witkowski, Witkiewicz and the Jewish artist Jakiel Adler. From a memorable collection of Stalinist-era socialist realism, the lower-floor displays move on to the 1960s and 1970s, where, for some reason, British artists are strongly represented. The ground floor includes an assortment of "events" by contemporary artists – colour effects, bricks, rotating boxes and other everyday objects – guaranteed to raise a laugh and infuriate traditionalists. Be warned, however, that there are occasions when the permanent collection is packed away completely and replaced by a temporary loan exhibition.

Down ul. Piotrkowska

Back on ul. Piotrkowska, behind the *Grand* hotel, it's worth taking a detour along **ul. Moniuszki**, an uninterrupted row of plush neo-Renaissance family houses. Some six blocks south, on the east side of ul. Piotrkowska, is the large *Olympia* factory, followed by several more villas of the old industrial tycoons, often set in spacious grounds and showing an eclectic mix of architectural styles.

Across from them are two of the city's most important churches. The neo-Gothic **Cathedral**, dedicated to St Stanisław Kosta, looks rather unprepossessing from the outside, mainly because of the cheap yellow bricks used in its construction. The interior, with its spacious feel and bright stained glass windows, is altogether more impressive.

A little further south is the Lutheran church of **St Matthew**, a ponderous mid-nineteenth-century temple used by the descendants of the old German oligarchy. Frequent recitals are given on its Romantic-style organ, the finest instrument of its kind in Poland.

Towards the end of ul. Piotrkowska, around a thirty-minute walk from the centre, the huge **White Factory**, at no. 282, is the oldest mechanically operated mill in the city. Part of it is now given over to the **Textile Museum** (Tues & Sat 10am–4pm, Wed & Fri 9am–5pm, Thurs 10am–5pm, Sun 10am–3pm), which features a large number of historic looms, documentary material on the history of the industry in Łódź and an impressive exhibition of contemporary examples of the weaver's art.

The eastern area

Łódź's newest museum, the **Herbst Palace** or Księży Młyn (Tues 10am–5pm, Wed & Fri noon–5pm, Thurs noon–7pm, Sat & Sun 11am–4pm), is situated in the eastern part of the city at ul. Prędzalniana 72. To get here from the White Factory, it's a fifteen-minute walk along ul. Przbyszewskiego, followed by a left turn once you reach its junction with ul. Prędzalniana; from the centre, take tram #9 and alight when you reach the palace's lakeside park. The building, which belonged to one of the leading German families, outwardly resembles the Renaissance villas built by Palladio in northern Italy. Its interiors – with the grand public rooms downstairs, the intimate family ones above – are evidence of decidedly catholic tastes, with influences ranging from ancient Rome via the Orient to Art Nouveau. The ballroom, which was added as an afterthought, is an effective pastiche of the English Tudor style.

A few minutes' walk west of here on ul. Tylna, and likewise at the corner of a park, is the **Grohmann Villa**, which is now an informally run **Artists' Museum** and studio (daily 10am–5pm), with a motley collection of local works and occasional exhibitions. Due north from here is the vast plac Zwycięstwa, which spans both sides of the busy al. Piłsudskiego. Its southern side is almost entirely occupied by the fortress-like **Scheibler Palace**, the former home of the most powerful of the German textile families. Part of it now houses the **Cinematography Museum** (Wed–Fri 10am–2pm, Sat & Sun 11am–5pm, currently closed for renovation), which celebrates Łódź's status as one of Europe's major training grounds for film makers.

The cemeteries

Perhaps appropriately, the most potent reminders of the cultural diversity of Łódź's past are its **cemeteries**. The two most worthwhile are some way from the centre of town, but are worth the effort of getting there. Of these, the Christian **Necropolis** is the more accessible in every sense: it's kept open throughout the day, and is a ten-minute walk west from the Poznański factory along ul. Ogrodowa. Of it's three interconnected plots, by far the largest is the Catholic cemetery, whose monuments, with rare exceptions, are fairly simple. Even less ostentatious is its Orthodox counterpart, containing the graves of civil servants, soldiers and policemen from the tsarist period. In contrast, the Protestant cemetery is full of appropriately grandiose memorials to deceased captains of industry. Towering over all the other graves, though now crumbling and boarded up, is the **Scheibler family mausoleum**, a miniaturized Gothic cathedral with a soaring Germanic openwork spire.

The **Jewish Cemetery**, the largest in Europe with some 180,000 tombstones (and twice as many graves), including many of great beauty, is situated on ul. Bracka, right beside the terminus of trams #1, #15 and #19. Unfortunately, it's nearly always kept locked; it's best to ask for the key at the city centre synagogue and prayer house at ul. Zachodnia 78 before setting out.

Eating, drinking and entertainment

Things are slowly improving on Łódź's **restaurant** scene, but as is often the case in Poland, many places appear desperately gloomy from the outside. The hotels all have their own restaurants, of which the *Malinowka* at the *Grand* is the best and priciest. Elsewhere in town, *Europa*, al. Kościuszki 116/118, does a good range of Polish dishes, *Troll Old Rock Café-Bar*, ul. Moniuszki 1, tries to imitate *Hard Rock Café*s the world over, while the *Smakosz*, ul. 6 Serpnia 2, offers a better than average setting for sampling local cuisine. There's also a decent Chinese restaurant, *Złota Kaczka*, on ul. Piotrkowska, across from and just south of the *Grand*. A string of old and new style **snack bars** line the top end of ul. Piotrkowska, and you'll find plenty of Italian places here: *La Dolce Vita* is at no. 91, with the *Frutti di Mare* at no. 90, specializing in seafood. Vegetarians will have to make do with the new *Restauracja Wegetanańska*, on the corner of ul. Kościuszki and ul. Mickiewicza, where the mellow New Age ambience makes up for the lacklustre menu.

Bars and **clubs** are also opening up quicker than they're shutting down in Łódź. No emerging Polish city would be complete without its Irish-style, Guinness-serving "pub"; in Łódź it's the *Irish Pub 77* set in a courtyard off ul. Piotrkowska 77, an occasional venue for live bands. Other good bars to try are the arty *Baghdad Café*, situated behind the pharmacies between ul. Nanitowicza and ul. Naracza, near the Teatr Wielki (see below) and *Wall Street* on ul. Sięnkiewicza. Though hard to find, the uncluttered futurist interior of the *Klub Fabryka*, in an alleyway between ul. Piotrkowska 80 and ul. Sienkiewicza, is also very popular with Łódź's trendsetters.

As for the cultural scene, the *Teatr Wielki* on plac Dąbrowskiego (☎33 99 60) presents both **drama and opera**; visiting foreign companies regularly perform both here and at the *Teatr Nowy*, ul. Więckowskiego 15 (☎33 44 94). For children, there are **puppet shows** at *Arlekin*, ul. Wólczańska 5 (☎32 58 99), and *Pinokio*, ul. Kopernika 16 (☎36 59 88), a couple of streets east of the southern youth hostel. The **concert** programmes of the *Państwowa Filharmonia*, ul. Gabriela Narutowicza 20 (☎37 26 53), feature soloists of international renown, while the *Teatr Muzyczny*, ul. Połnocna 47/51 (☎78 35 11), is the main venue for operetta and musicals. Among regular special events are the **opera festival** (March), a **ballet festival** (May–June every other year), and a **student theatre festival** (March). Check at the box office at ul. Moniuszki 5 for current details of what's happening in town, or pick up the monthly *Kalejdoskop* from the tourist office.

For mainstream films, you'll find the multiscreen *Bałtyk* **cinema** on ul. Gabriela Narutowicza 20, opposite the *Hotel Centrum*; the *Capital* on ul. Zachodnia; and *Przedwiosnie* on ul. Żeromskiego 74–76. Arthouse and retrospectives are regularly shown at the tiny, twin-screen *Tatry* at ul. Sienkiewicza 40, a lovely old cinema brimming with character. Of the two **football** teams, Widzew Łódź play at the stadium at al. Piłsudskiego 138, just before the eastern terminus of trams #10 and #25, while the ŁKS ground is at al. Unii 2, north of the Kaliska station, on the route of tram #17.

West along the Wisła

Northwest of Warsaw, the Mazovian countryside is dominated by the meandering expanse of the Wisła as it continues its trek towards the Baltic Sea. Many of the towns ranged along its banks still bear the imprint of the river-bound trade they once thrived on. Of these, the most important is **Płock**, one-time capital of Mazovia, and a thriving industrial centre, that's recently been attracting some of the biggest new Western investments in Poland. With a major museum and an enjoyable historic complex, it makes an eminently worthwhile outing from

Warsaw. Closer to the capital, is the ancient church complex at **Czerwińsk nad Wisłą,** serviced by occasional **boat trips** along the Wisła.

Modlin Castle

Some 36km northwest of Warsaw, at the intersection of the Wisła and the Narew rivers, stand the eerie ruins of **Modlin Castle** – you can see them from the north-bound E77 road to Gdańsk. A huge earth and brick fortress raised in the early nineteenth century on Napoleon's orders, the already large complex was restored and extended by Russian forces in the 1830s and 1840s; at its height, the huge complex accommodated a garrison of some 26,000 people. It was devastated during the early part of World War II, but you can still wander through the atmospheric ruins of the castle, which offer a pleasant view over the river below.

Czerwińsk nad Wisłą

CZERWIŃSK NAD WISŁĄ, around 70km from Warsaw along the main Płock turnoff just beyond Modlin, is a placid riverside village overlooking the banks of the Wisła. What pulls the crowds (and there can be plenty of them in summer) to this idyllic, out of the way setting, is the Romanesque **Church and Monastery Complex**, one of the oldest, and finest, historic ensembles in the Mazovia region. If you're not travelling by boat or on a bus tour, local buses (blue line) to Czerwińsk run from Dworzec Centralny Warsaw via Nowy Dwór (8 daily), a journey of an hour and a half approximately each way.

Sitting atop the hill above the village, the ancient **church complex**, founded by the monks who were brought here in the early twelfth century by the dukes of Mazovia to hasten along the conversion of the region, retains much of its original Romanesque structure, still visible amid the later Gothic and Baroque additions. The entrance, flanked by high twin towers, is through a delicately carved, brick Romanesque **portal** inside the brick facade added onto the building in the seventeenth century, its original ceiling decorated with some delightful geometrically patterned frescoes, featuring plant motifs and representations of the Virgin Mary. Inside the building, a couple of fine Romanesque stone columns have survived, as has a remarkable selection of early polychromy, notably in the **chapel** off the east aisle – its luminous Romanesque frescoes were uncovered in the 1950s during renovation work on the building. The late Gothic **belltower** near the church, whose powerful bells are among the oldest in the country, was once the gateway to the town. If you're here during the summer season, you should be able to climb this, or one of the church towers, for a panoramic view over the flat pastoral surroundings. Round the back of the church is the **monastery complex**, now occupied by a Salesian Fathers seminary, some of whose members act as guides in summer – if you ask, you should be able to get hold of someone who speaks English to take you round. It's also worth asking to see round the **cloisters**, which contain a fine Gothic refectory and a small **museum** of local ethnography and church art, the quiet toing and froing of the seminarists blending in with the restful, contemplative feel of the whole place.

If you haven't climbed one of the towers, there's a nice view over the river from the terrace in front of the church. With time to spare, it's also worth taking a stroll down the hill into the tumbledown **village**, which has a notable predominance of wooden houses, and on down to the river bank, as peaceful a rural setting as you could wish for. In summer the village is a stopoff point for weekly **boat trips** down the Wisła – the tourist information office in Warsaw will have the current details. Despite the summer tourist crowds, curiously no one in the village has thought to start up a restaurant or snack bar yet, so unless the seminary invites you in for a meal, the village shop is the only place you'll find anything to eat.

Płock

Initial impressions of **PŁOCK**, the major town of western Mazovia located some 115km west of Warsaw, suggest there aren't going to be many reasons to hang around for very long. First appearances can be deceiving, though, for in the midst of the sprawling industrial connurbation spread along the banks of the Wisła, is the oldest urban settlement in Mazovia. The first kings of Poland later took up residence here, in the eleventh century, where they remained for nearly a hundred years. An important bishopric, and one of the number of strategically located riverside towns that grew fat on the medieval Wisła-bound commercial boom, Płock felt the full weight of mid-seventeenth-century Swedish invasions – the Płock bishopric's valuable library was purloined and taken to Uppsala, where it remains. A modern industrial centre, whose huge petrochemical works and oil refinery located just north of the town centre add a definite tang to the

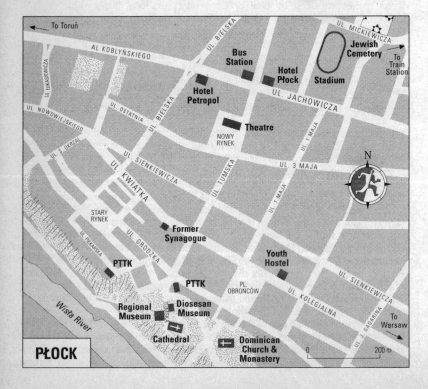

local air, Płock's strategic location and large workforce have made both the town and surrounding region a prime target for foreign investment, multinational jeans giants Levis among those who've established major new plants in the area.

The Old Town

Nestling on a clifftop overlooking the wide expanses of the Wisła, the **Old Town area**, a small central part of modern-day Płock, provides the town's main point of interest. Known locally as "little Kraków", because the important buildings are grouped together at the top of a hill, the old town area has undergone recent excavations which have unearthed an ancient (c.400 BC) stone altar and pillar, indicating the early presence of pagan cults here. Walking down to the old town from either the bus or train station takes you along **ul. Tumska**, a busy pedestrianized thoroughfare and the town's main shopping area. Crossing ul. Kollegialna, Tumska leads directly into the ancient core of the town.

THE CATHEDRAL

First stop is the medieval **Cathedral**, a magnificent Romanesque building begun after the installation of the Płock bishopric in 1075 and completed in the following century. A monumental basilical structure with an imposing cupola almost worthy of St Paul's in London, the cathedral was clearly intended to dominate the surroundings, an effect it definitely achieves. Successive rebuildings, the most significant of them being the classicist remodelling undertaken by Italian architect Merlini in the mid-eighteenth century, mean there are few traces left of the building's original character. The sumptuous interior decoration, however, including some ornate choir stalls and a magnificently carved pulpit, all indicate that the oldtime bishops of Płock were a wealthy bunch.

Other notable features of the building are the **royal chapel** containing the Romanesque sarcophagi of Polish princes **Władysław Herman** (1040–1102) and his son, **Bolesław the Wrymouth** (Krzywousty; 1086–1138), and the Secessionist frescoes decorating parts of the building. The sculptured **bronze doors**, probably the cathedral's most famous feature, were the subject of a major piece of architectural detective work. The Romanesque originals commissioned by the bishop of Płock from the Magdeburg artist Riquin in the mid-twelfth century went missing for over six centuries, when Władysław King Jagiełło gave them to his Russian counterpart as a present, around the time his own brother became Prince of Novgorod. Subsequently hung in the entrance to the Orthodox church of Saint Sophia in Novgorod, and adorned with fake Cyrillic inscriptions identifying them as booty from a twelfth-century Russian expedition to Sweden, the doors were located in 1970 by a Polish academic. He had noticed the Latin inscriptions mentioning Płock on a late nineteenth-century gypsum copy of the doors hanging in the Historical Museum in Moscow. A further bronze copy of the originals (still in Novgorod) was made for the cathedral after the discovery, and it's these you see today, two dozen **panels** filled with a magnificent series of **reliefs** depicting scenes from the Old Testament and the Gospels as well as a number of allegorical pieces. Back from the building, the skyline is dominated by the twin brick Gothic **Zegarowa** and **Szlachecka towers** beside the cathedral – the former the cathedral belfry – the best-preserved fragments of the fourteenth-century castle that once stood here.

THE REGIONAL AND DIOCESAN MUSEUMS

A short way from the cathedral is Płock's other major monument, the Gothic former **Mazovian dukes' castle**, home of the **Regional Museum** (June–Sept Tues–Sun 10am–3pm, Fri 10am–5pm; closed rest of the year), one of the oldest such exhibitions in Europe, established here by the local Historical Society in 1820. The main reason for traipsing round this museum is the superb selection of turn-of-the-century **Secessionist** work. Art Nouveau in all its various artistic forms is represented here, with a wide array of paintings, ceramics, sculpture, glass and metalware both from the Polish "Młoda Polska" movement and from other countries – Austria and Germany included – where the style gained a strong following. Anyone drawn to the sensuous curves, intricate colouring and flowing figures of *fin-de-siècle* central European art will have a field day wandering around the rich collection of objects assembled here. The really outstanding feature, however, is the **re-creation** of several rooms furnished and decorated as they would have been when Art Deco was in vogue. For anyone whose principal acquaintance with the style is via the *Jugendstil* architecture of Vienna and other central European cities, it will come as a revelation to see how the style was applied to the ordinary everyday business of living. Additionally, the collection of Młoda Polski era art is hugely impressive, featuring works by Wyspiański, Witkiewicz, Mehoffer, Malczewski and Tetmajer, a veritable gallery of turn-of-the-century Polish artists.

Directly across from the castle entrance is the **Diocesan Museum** (Wed–Sat 10am–3pm, Sun 11am–4pm), very much the Old Town's "other" collection, but housing a worthy exhibition of sacral art both Polish and foreign, local archeological finds and wooden folk art, nonetheless. Back up along ul. Tumska and west past the former bishop's palace, halfway down ul. Małachowskiego, is the **Płock Lyceum**, the oldest school in the country, founded in the 1180s and still going strong 800 years later. Next to it is a gallery sitting on the foundations of two recently uncovered Romanesque pillars located in the west wing of the school.

ALONG THE WATERFRONT

As you turn back towards the cathedral you'll see the high **platform** to the left of the building, overlooking the Wisła waterfront. An open, blustery spot on a fine day, it offers huge panoramas over the wide expanse of the river below, at its widest around Płock. A wooded path leads off in both directions along the clifftop, the Wisła spread below you along with the sandy promontories running out into the main stream of the river. Walking north, refreshments will once again be available at the *PTTK* **café-restaurant** when it reopens after current renovation (check with the *PTTK* office). The dramatic views from the terrace still make a stroll up here worthwhile. Directly below the terrace, close to the river bank, is an open-air amphitheatre much in use in the summer for folk dance festivals and other musical spectaculars. Walking south from the cathedral terrace and down through the park, brings you to the **Dominican Church and Monastery,** a thirteenth-century edifice originally built for Duke Konrad of Mazovia, later given a predictably ornate classicist treatment. A Protestant church up until 1945, it sits isolated from the town in the middle of a park, part of the rolling woodland that covers much of the waterfront below the Old Town.

Finally, there are reminders of the city's vanished Jewish population in the former **Synagogue** at ul. Kwiatka 7, west of ul. Tumska, built in 1810 and now used as a shop, and the relatively well-maintained **Jewish Cemetery** on ul.

Mickiewicza, ten minutes' walk northeast of the bus station, which contains a monument honouring local Jews who perished in the concentration camps.

Practicalities

The **bus and train stations**, a little way apart, are both on the northern side of town, some fifteen minutes' walk from the Old Town centre. For **information**, the most useful of the various tourist bureaux is the *PTTK* office, at ul. Tumska 4 (Mon–Sat 8am–4pm; ☎024/62 94 97) close to the Old Town complex.

There's nothing very exciting on offer as far as **accommodation** goes, the main options being the humdrum *Płock*, al. S. Jachowicza 38 (☎024/62 34 56; ④) in a noisy but central location; the *Petropol*, just down the road at no. 49 (☎024/62 44 51; ⑤), a faded-looking *Orbis* joint with a passable restaurant; and the offputtingly named *Petrochemia*, ul. 3 Maja 33 (☎024/62 40 33; ③). If you don't mind the marked step-down in quality, the *PTTK* hostel, Piekarska 1, close to the cathedral, makes up for lack of comfort by its excellent scenic location (currently closed for renovation, check with the *PTTK* office). Finally, there's a year-round **youth hostel** at ul. Kolegialna 19 (☎024/62 38 17), also centrally located.

For **restaurants**, *Mr. Smarty's*, ul. Tumska 14, Płock's own McDonald's look-alike, is now the town's most popular venue, part of the chain of hamburger joints set up around the country by a Swedish-Polish joint venture. As well as the *Petropol*, the other options include *Pizzeria Roma*, ul. Grodzka, a short way up from the Old Town complex; the *Hollywood*, ul. Tumska 8, a café-restaurant; and the popular *Wezoś*, in the town theatre, just off the Nowy Rynek.

South of Warsaw

South of the city, the Wisła again provides the enduring point of definition to the flat, agricultural landscape that rapidly opens up as you leave the outer suburbs. Of the towns of the area, the legendary Hassidic centre of **Góra Kalwaria**, and the nearby Gothic castle at **Czersk**, offer the prospect of an enjoyable and eminently manageable day trip from Warsaw.

Góra Kalwaria

Thirty-four kilometres south of Warsaw (1hr by bus from the *PKS* Mokotów station, close to Racław Icka metro station) is **GÓRA KALWARIA**, a dusty provincial Mazovian town with a forlorn end-of-the-world feel to it, and on first impressions, little to recommend the place. As often, awareness of the place's history is what gives the place its primary interest.

The Bishop of Poznań, Stefan Wierzbowski, purchased the original village in the 1660s, and set about developing the site as a pilgrimage centre, building a town on the layout of a Latin crucifix, with a long central Way of the Cross modelled on Jerusalem's Mount Calvary. This was a popular innovation at the time, examples of which can be found dotted around the country, notably at Kalwaria Zebrzydowska (see p.423). Legions of chapels and devotional shrines were erected on and around the two principal town axes, today's ul. Kalwarijska and Dominikańska, the majority of which were destroyed during World War II, though the basic plan visibly remains. Devotional buildings that survived the Nazis include **Pilate's Chapel** (Kaplica Pilata) on ul. Dominikańska, a relatively

IN THE COURT OF THE REBBE OF GÓRA KALWARIA

The German writer Alfred Döblin visited Góra Kalwaria in the 1920s. The following excerpts from his account of the visit in *Journey to Poland* (see *Contexts*, "Books") gives a glimpse of the powerful atmosphere of Hasidic fervour that once enveloped the town:

One morning before seven o'clock, I set out from Warsaw with my companion; we are traveling to see the great rebbe of Gura Kalwarja. The church portals are open, beggars huddle outside, people sing inside. In the cool gray morning, we drive through the silent Sunday city; the car fills up with men in long black coats and black skullcaps. They all carry and lift packages, pouches, whole sacks, crates. We don't know where the railroad station is, but all we have to do is follow the black procession of men, the young, old, black-bearded, red-bearded Jews, whole scores of whom are now trotting along the street.

The trolley passengers gaped at the Jews, whispered, smiled: "Gura!" Now, coarse, sturdy Poles sit in the railroad carriage, with dogs and hunting rifles. At a few stations, they joke around, yell: "Gura!" but the Jews ignore them. People curiously eye me and my companion, we are both wearing European clothes; he addresses them in Yiddish, and the Jews become friendly. But will I, I get to see the rebbe: their heads sway, they whisper, they're very skeptical. These people come from far away; one of them – with a fine intelligent face – wears a round black velvet hat. He's from East Galicia; the rebbe of Gura has a large following there.

When the little train has swum along for two hours, it stops in Gura, emptying out completely. And, once again, we don't have to ask the way to the village. As we turn into the broad main street, a fantastic unsettling tableau heaves into view. This swarm of pilgrims in black – those who came with us and others – with bag and baggage, teeming along the lengthy street. These black skullcaps bobbing up and down. The yellow trees stand on either side, the sky above is pale gray, the soil tawny – between them, an almost frightening, bustling black throng moves along, hundreds of heads, shoulders serried together, an army of ants plods along, inches along. And from the other side, people trudge toward them, look down from the windows of the cottages, wave.

But the men and boys who await the travelers and come to meet them are a very special breed. They have long hair, their curls shake; the curls, twisted as tight as corkscrews, drop sideways from under the skullcaps and dangle in front of their ears, next to their cheeks, on their throats. I get a picture of what earlocks are; what a proud adornment. How proudly these men, youths, boys stride along in clean black caftans, in high shiny black caps; they look romantic, rapturous, medieval. Their faces have an extraordinary look, an earnest stillness. Some of them boast free, proud expressions. The handsome boys are festive in white stockings and beautiful slippers.

"Where is the rebbe's court?" At every step we take, we are surrounded by men (no woman walks here) who gape at us, talk among themselves. Their eyes are distrustful, chilly. It doesn't help that my companion speaks Yiddish to them nonstop. New ones keep sizing us up. I feel as if I've come upon an exotic tribe; they do not want me, me or my companion, they regard us as intruders. At the left, amid the small houses, a huge wooden gate is open. We go over there with the others, find ourselves in a vast crowded rectangular courtyard. It is closed off by a clean, simple, sprawling wooden house, one floor.

We are in the vestibule of the house. Men with raised arms emerge from the left-hand door; some men swirl towels: beyond the door lies a room for prayer and assembly.

More and more keep pouring into the room. We are the butt of universal attention. People keep coming over to me. Since I cautiously hold my tongue, my companion instantly steps in. This doesn't go on for long. Because soon we are completely wedged in, and it's every man for himself. A dreadful, incredible mobbing has begun at the door. Silently, they push, squeeze. Silently, they all press against the narrow door, which opens from time to time and closes again. This is much worse, much worse than any urban crowd that I have ever experienced. I can say nothing. I keep wishing they'd let me out. But when I see the way they cling to one another, this fierce mute doggedness, I give up. I do not jam along, I hang between the others, who pant into the back of my neck, into my ears. I let my feet hang loose, I draw up my knees, and I am carried.

Slowly – I'm almost done for – I see the crack in the door coming nearer. The door now remains open; the man inside, the doorman, is no longer able to shut it. The big bearded men in skullcaps have reached over the heads of the other, and their hairy hands have grabbed the door hinges, the door jambs; with red faces, they wordlessly pull themselves over to the door. And no one complains, no one curses. They moan.

A long arm strikes out at the men ahead of me. I see the big doorman pushing against the mass. With his left shoulder, he pushes the first few back, his long right arm beats, bangs on the fingers thrust into the door hinges, on the shoulders, on the black skullcaps. The hands let go. I cringe, he's about to reach me. But instead, he punches the chest of the man next to me, reaches out, grabs my arm. He yanks me inside. I'm at the head of the line, I see my companion standing inside, he waves me over. Another step, I'm inside the room.

An enormous, completely empty room, wooden floor, wooden walls. My companion stands in front of me with an elderly man, who points toward the window, at the right. I look there, walk over. There is a table at the window. And at the table, with his back to the light, sits a stocky, pudgy man. He keeps rocking to and fro, incessantly, now less, now more. A round black skullcap perches on the crown of his head. His head is completely wreathed in a tremendous mass of curls, dark brown, with touches of gray. Thick sheaves of curls tumble over his ears, over his cheeks, along the sides of his face all the way down to the shoulders. A full fleshy face surges out from the curls. I can't see his eyes; he doesn't look at me, doesn't look at my companion, as we stand next to the plain wooden table. The rabbi's thick hands burrow through a heap of small papers lying in front of him: slips of paper; with writing on them. He and my companion are conversing. The rabbi stops rocking, he keeps rummaging throught the papers. His expression is ungracious, he never looks up for even an instant. He shakes his head. All at once, my companion says: "He says you can ask him something." I think to myself: Impossible, that's not what I'm after; I want to speak to him, not question him. But the rebbe is already speaking again, softly; I can't understand a single word of this very special Yiddish. Then, suddenly, I have his hand, a small slack fleshy hand, on mine. I am astonished. No pressure from his hand; it moves over to mine. I hear a quiet *"Sholem,"* my companion says: "We're leaving." And slowly, we leave. Someone else has already come in, he puts down a slip of paper, says a few words, goes out, backward, facing the small rocking figure at the window.

Reprinted by permission of I.B Tauris.

restrained Baroque ensemble with a characteristic period cycle of Passion paintings and the late Baroque **Bernardine Church**, now the parish church, which retains most of its original ornamentation.

However, it's the town's **Jewish connections** that really set the imagination –and at one stage, arguably, the European world – alight. Following the decision to allow Jews to settle here in 1745, Góra went on to become the seat of the famous **Hasidic dynasty** founded in the early nineteenth century by **Tzaddik (Rebbe) Meir Alter**. The fame of the Rebbe spread fast among the growing ranks of the Hasidim, and by the 1850s, they were flocking to his court in Góra (known popularly as "New Jerusalem" or "Gura") from all over the western regions of the Russian Empire. The dynasty continued into this century, culminating in the leadership of **Tzaddik Abraham Mordechai Alter**, grandson of Meir Alter and founder of the deeply conservative *Agudas Israel* party who promoted the court at Góra as a rallying point for Orthodox Jews of all persuasions, committed to the goal of preserving traditional Orthodox Judaism from modernizing influences, Zionism included. Rebbe Alter narrowly managed to escape to Palestine before hostilities broke out in 1939: the dynasty has continued up to the present time, directed from Jerusalem.

Armed with this knowledge, a visit to Góra becomes both a fascinating, though in many ways also depressing, experience. Both the **Ger Synagogue** and many of the buildings of the Hasidic court are still here today, though you certainly won't find any signs informing you where to look. The once proud squat brick synagogue is now a dilapidated old furniture workshop tucked away at the back of a filthy courtyard off ul. Pijarska (entry through the gate to no. 10). If the less than friendly local contingent of local dogs let you stay long enough, you'll be able to make out the frame of a Star of David up in one of the windows and a small commemorative tablet on the wall. If you're brave enough to persevere, the caretaker of the adjoining building, formerly part of the Hasidic court complex, may let you in to have a look around, though there really isn't a lot to see now. Wandering through the dusty courtyards of the surrounding streets under the inquiring gaze of local residents, it requires an effort of the imagination to picture what things must have been like here when Hassidim filled the streets and houses.

If you have your own transport, or feel up for a reasonable stroll, the well-fenced and irregularly open **Jewish Cemetery**, out of town past the Catholic graveyard at the end of al. Kalwarija, provides the only other tangible reminder of Jewish presence in the town – a monument to Kalwaria Jews murdered by the Nazis is visible from the roadside.

The only **accommodation** to speak of in town is a youth hostel at ul. Wyzwolena 1, while the **eating** options are confined to a couple of snack bars located round the main square.

Czersk

Three kilometres east of Góra stands the village of **CZERSK**, set back from the river. From Góra, there's a picturesque six-kilometre route leading east of town down to the riverside, and south through the orchards along the banks of the River Wisła to the village. If ever there were a case of having seen better days, this is it. An important medieval commercial centre straddling the vital river-bound trade route, and noted for its cloth production, Czersk was one of the principal towns of the then independent principality of Mazovia. Decline set in from the mid-fifteenth century, when changes in the course of the Wisła eventually left the town stranded a few kilometres from the river bank and, hence, adrift from its main source of commercial opportunity. Things went from bad to worse, culminating in the devastation wreaked on the town in the course of the Swedish invasions of the mid-seventeenth century, when much of Czersk was razed to the ground. By this stage, Warsaw was on the ascent as the newly established capital of the country, and the chance of ever again aspiring to regional dominance had disappeared for good. By the early 1800s, Czersk had been reduced to a village, and to crown the humiliation, its municipal status was revoked in 1869. Aside from some brief action and destruction during World War II, things have been pretty quiet since then.

The Castle

The most potent symbol of Czersk's once lofty status are the splendid ruins of its medieval **Castle** (Tues–Sun 8am–8pm), located on the edge of the town, up the road from the market square. A towering Gothic brick structure, reached by a solid bridge built in the 1760s to replace a medieval drawbridge, a considerable portion of the original fortifications are intact. Chief among these are the eight-metre-thick walls surrounding the castle and a formidable looking set of bastions, originally somewhat lower and raised to their current towering height in the mid-1500s, when the **northeast tower** was redesigned as a gate watch. This tower, the best preserved of the three, serves as venue for **exhibitions** of regional painting, tapestry and sculpture organized by the local culture centre in Góra Kalwaria (☎ 0531/58 21 93), which also plans to establish a permanent exhibition of local archeological finds here in the near future. Moving round the inner castle area, the western tower is the only one that be reached directly from the courtyard. It's worth climbing the staircase leading up to the very top of the **eastern tower**, for the grandstand view over the surrounding countryside. Formerly the castle prison, Prince Konrad of Mazovia kept his brother Henryk the Bearded, prince of Silesia, and nephew Bolesław the Chaste, locked up in the tower's dungeons. Back in the castle courtyard, you can see the foundations of the twelfth-century castle chapel, recently uncovered by archeologists. The concerts held here on weekends in the summer are a favourite with local visitors, while for the adventurous, there's the chance to hold your own castle bonfire – for 30 zł the Góra Cultural Centre (see above) will provide you with the necessary firewood, but you need to book in advance. Recently, there are have also been summer medieval theme fairs in the castle courtyard, complete with crossbow competitions and jousting, arranged by the mysterious sounding Warsaw Sword and Crossbow Brotherhood.

If you feel like **staying overnight** in Czersk, basic campbed sleeping space is available at the privately-run *pensjonat* at ul. Warszawska 1 (☎0531/57 34 38), with the option of higher grade accommodation if you call in advance. A basic restaurant- cum-coffee shop on the main square is virtually the only place to get a bite **to eat** in the village.

North of Warsaw

North of Warsaw, the main routes whisk you through the suburbs and out into the flat Mazovian countryside, its scattered farmland bisected by the Wisła from the west and by the smaller, and less polluted, River Narew to the east. Close to Warsaw, and popular with the increasing number of city commuters, the towns and villages are beginning to show signs of benefiting from the country's economic transformation – small industrial units, new villas and advertising boards are appearing. Slightly further afield, but still in striking distance of Warsaw, are a number of older centres, notably **Pułtusk** and **Ciechanów**, which retain the rustic feel of a traditional Mazovian market town. Other attractions include the palace at **Jabłonna**, close enough to the city for a leisurely afternoon outing. **Transport links** are pretty straightforward this close to the capital, a well-serviced network of **local buses** providing the most convenient way of getting around.

Jabłonna

Sixteen kilometres north of the city – a thirty-minute bus journey (#133, #723 or #801 from Dworzec Marymont, in the northern suburb of Żoliborz) – is **JABŁONNA**, a small commuter-belt town that's clearly benefiting from its location close to the main roads into Warsaw. The town itself is nondescript, the main attraction being the fine Neoclassical **Palace** built on the edge of town in the 1770s by architect Domenico Merlini (of Warsaw's Łazienki Park fame), for Prince Józef Poniatowski. Now owned and run by the Polish Academy of Sciences, it's a popular venue for international academic meetings and conferences. Following the palace's recent restoration, there are currently no official **opening hours**, but you can just turn up and ask to look around – you're generally in with a good chance of seeing at least the ground floors and garden.

The Palace

The palace gates front on to the main road from Warsaw (the bus stop is just across the road), with the elegant bestatued facade of the main **palace building** standing some way back from the entrance, in the middle of a large park. Formerly owned by the Potocki family, the palace was badly damaged during the war, and has recently undergone a complete overhaul. Inside the building, the ground floor follows a conventional pattern with ornate reception rooms, including a glamorous **ballroom** complete with graceful high cupola, still used for the occasional concert, the **Rococo room**, with a portrait of a victorious Prince Poniatowski after the battle of Raszyn, and an elaborate **Moorish room**. Some of the palace's original eighteenth-century frescoes were uncovered downstairs in the basement during postwar reconstruction work. It's all a bit gloomy down there at the moment, but visitors will soon be able to enjoy the frescoes while relaxing in the planned upmarket restaurant.

Back out of the main entrance, the recently completed **hotel** (☎022 21 57 37 or 74 48 62; ⑥), in the palace building to the left, has a wonderful location, surrounded by the ramshackle thirty-hectare palace **park**, clearly once a grand affair. The park is ideal for a Sunday walk, with broody, overgrown woods stretching all the way down to the nearby banks of the Wisła. Several of the old palace outbuildings survive: an orangery, a pagoda, and, most impressively, a classical triumphal arch erected to commemorate the death of the dashing Prince Poniatowski at the battle of Leipzig in 1813.

An additional curio is the **tunnel** that runs underneath part of the palace grounds, formerly used by members of the diplomats' club that used to function here to get members from the river bank – the Wisła used to run much closer to the palace – to the palace in secret. Later used as a World War II hideout by

Polish resistance fighters, the tunnel is now locked up, though you can still see the ruins of the small fortified stronghold where the boats of publicity-shunning diplomats used to alight.

Pułtusk

Sixty kilometres north of Warsaw along the west bank of the River Narew stands **PUŁTUSK**, a lively provincial Mazovian market town that's a popular day-tripper's outing from Warsaw. One of the earliest towns founded in the region, and established on the site of an earlier trading settlement, for many years Pułtusk was a leading grain-trading centre on the river route to Gdańsk, the town's political influence stemming from the presence of the powerful bishops of Płock, whose seat the town was for several centuries. Pułtusk twice hit the headlines in the nineteenth century, first in 1806 when Napoleonic and Russian forces fought a major battle here – a French victory recorded alongside Bonaparte's other notable triumphs on the walls of the Arc de Triomphe – and later, in 1868, when a huge meteorite, known, unsurprisingly, as the Pułtusk meteorite, fell near the town. Badly damaged, like much of northern Mazovia, during the Soviet advance of winter 1944–45 when eighty percent of the buildings were destroyed, the town has nevertheless managed to retain its oldtime market town atmosphere, thanks, in part, to a major postwar reconstruction programme.

The Town

As often, the **market square** provides the main focus of the town. In the large cobbled area – at nearly 400m long, the square is claimed to be one of the biggest in Europe – a number of the original eighteenth- and nineteenth-century burghers' houses are still in evidence. These apart, the square mostly consists of surpassingly tasteful postwar reconstruction, with the main excitement currently being provided by the Russian number-plated cars lined up in the centre, their owners enthusiastically peddling their wares to the slightly cautious-looking locals.

The imposing high Gothic **brick tower** tacked on to the town hall, in the middle of the square, houses the enjoyable **Regional Museum** (Tues–Sat 10am–4pm, Sun 10–2pm). Erected in the 1400s, the tower was originally part of the town's defences, subsequently serving as a craftsman's storehouse, Jesuit boarding-school house and local prison. Inside, the first-floor exhibitions cover the wealth of archeological finds uncovered when the square and surroundings were systematically excavated in the 1970s. The mostly medieval objects on display include reconstructed early wooden sailing vessels, military paraphernalia, silver and metal work, and some fine decorated tiles from the castle area. The collection of folk art and craft on other floors comes mostly from the forested **Kurpie region** to the east of the town, an area noted for its strong folk artistic traditions. It's worth climbing the full six floors of the tower for the panoramic view over the town and surroundings from the top of the building – you can borrow binoculars from the woman at the entrance.

The monumental **Collegiate Church** at the north end of the square is a Gothic brick basilica, remodelled in the sixteenth century by the Venetian architect Giovanni Battista. A striking feature is the arched vault of the nave, the design motif of circles connected by belts being a characteristic ornamental element of Renaissance-era churches in the Mazovia and Podlasie regions. The Renaissance

Noskowski Chapel, modelled on the Wawel Sigismund Chapel, is a beauty, featuring a Renaissance copy of Michelangelo's famous *Pietà*, and some delicate original polychromy. More eccentric is the main rear chapel, stuffed with local Catholic standards for use on Holy Day processions and lined from floor to ceiling with blue Dordrecht tiles.

Off the southern end of the square is the town **Castle,** one-time residence of the bishops of Płock, an oft-rebuilt semi-circular brick structure straddled across an artificial raised mound, overlooking the banks of the Narew. A wooden fortification was in place here by the early 1300s, destroyed soon after (along with the rest of the town) by marauding Lithuanians. Rebuilt from scratch in the 1520s, the arcaded bridge leading up to the brick castle was added a century later, only to be pummelled by the Swedes in the 1650s. The castle's claim to historical fame is as the site of the first public theatre in Poland, opened here by the Jesuits in 1565. As with many towns in Mazovia, there's a Napoleonic connection too: Bonaparte stayed here with his brother Jerome in 1806, prior to the nearby battle against Russian forces, and again in 1812 during the disastrous retreat from Moscow. It's also one of several places where he is supposed to have first met his lover-to-be, Maria Walewska.

In the 1970s, the castle was taken over by *Polonia*, the state-sponsored organization dedicated to maintaining links between émigré Poles and their home country. As a result the **Dom Polonii,** as it's known, has now been converted into a luxury hotel (see below) and holiday/conference centre for the huge Polish diaspora, with émigré Poles young and old from all over the world – the USA and Germany in particular – taking part in events here throughout the year.

The **gardens,** laid out when the moat was drained and covered in the sixteenth century, lead down to the water's edge – a pleasant, tranquil place for a stroll, with sailing and other aquatic activities much in evidence during the summer season. In summer there's also a café open by the water. Back out towards the main square is the old castle **chapel**, a Renaissance structure largely rebuilt after wartime destruction.

Practicalities

The **bus station**, on the Nowy Rynek, is a ten-minute walk from the Rynek. For **information** you can try the *PTTK* office, Rynek 5 (Mon–Fri 9am–4pm), on the main square, or the reception desk at the **Dom Polonii** (see above).

For anyone tempted by a stay out in the country, the swish castle **hotel** (☎0238/2031 or 4081, fax 0238/4524; ⑦) can't be bettered for its quiet location close to Warsaw. The alternative is the much more basic *Zawimex*, ul. Kolejowa 19 (☎0238/2523; ③). The castle **restaurant**, housed in a magisterial dining room, is also reasonably pricey, but again worth trying, especially for the traditionally prepared duck dishes. Alternative places to eat are the *Arkadia* on the Rynek or the *Słoneczna* on the Nowy Rynek, while the *Magdalenka* is a down-to-earth café at the castle end of the main square.

Ciechanów

Continuing northwest for 40km brings you to **CIECHANÓW**, a largish, dowdy-looking Mazovian town on the main rail line to Gdańsk, where life passes slowly – someone forgot to give the place a centre too. There's nothing here to get the crowds stampeding in, but if you happen to be passing through, it's worth stopping off to see the remains of the imposing fourteenth-century **Mazovian Dukes' Castle** stuck out on a limb on the eastern edge of town, one of the scattering of fortifications around the region originally occupied by the medieval rulers of Mazovia. A redoubtably solid-looking brick structure (the walls are over 55m high), the interior houses a minor **museum** (Tues–Sun 10–4pm), the main point of going in being for the chance to look around the castle itself. Totally unlike the Teutonic castles of the Gdańsk region, the castle has only two towers of the original building still standing. Back into town, over the river and past the solemn neo-Gothic Town Hall, the local **museum**, on central ul. Sienkiewicza (Tues–Sun 10am–4pm), is a rather unimaginatively presented display of nevertheless colourful local crafts and folk items.

The parish **Church of St Joseph,** off what passes for the main town square, is a good example of Mazovian Gothic, a high brick structure with a tiered facade arranged in thin pointed layers. The vaulted interior boasts some solid chunky-looking Gothic pillars – locally it's known as the church that writer **Ignacy Krasiński** attended regularly. Next door to the church you'll find something of a Polish rarity, a local Catholic teetotallers' club. Immediately north of town, the countryside is scattered with **military cemeteries**, a reminder of the major battle fought here in September 1939, where German forces attempting to push straight to Warsaw encountered some stiff resistance from the retreating Polish Army.

If you need **accommodation**, the options, both hotels, are the central *Zacisze* hotel, ul. Mikotaczyka 8A (☎2046; ②) or *Polonia*, ul. Warszawska 40 (☎3459; ②). For **restaurants**, try the *Zacisze* hotel, the *Jagienka*, ul. Strazacka 5, or *U Bony*, ul. Sienkiewicza 81.

travel details

Trains

Łódź to: Bydgoszcz (10 daily; 3–4hr); Częstochowa (9 daily; 2hr 30min–3hr 30min); Gdańsk (6 daily; 6hr); Katowice (7 daily; 4hr); Kraków (6 daily; 5–6hr); Lublin (5 daily; 5–6hr); Poznań (7 daily; 4–5hr); Warsaw (20 daily; 2–3hr); Wrocław (15 daily; 4–5hr).

Warsaw to: Białystok (14 daily; 3–4hr); Bydgoszcz (6 daily; 3hr 30min–5hr); Częstochowa (13 daily; 3–5hr); Gdańsk/Gdynia (19 daily; 3hr 30min–5hr; expresses at 6am & 5pm); Jelenia Góra (4 daily; 10hr; couchettes); Katowice (17 daily; 3–5hr); Kielce (12 daily; 3–4hr); Kraków (18 daily; 3–6hr; expresses at 6am, 9am, 4.25pm & 5.45pm); Krynica (2 daily; 10–13hr; couchettes); Lublin (11 daily; 2hr 30min–3hr); Łódź (7 daily; 2–2hr 30min); Olsztyn (8 daily; 3–5hr); Poznań (19 daily; 4hr); Przemyśl (4 daily; 6–8hr); Rzeszów (4 daily; 5–6hr); Suwałki (6 daily; 4–6hr); Świnoujście (3 daily; 10 hr; couchettes); Szczecin (5 daily; 6–8hr); Toruń (6 daily; 3–4hr); Wrocław (16 daily; 5–6hr; couchettes); Zagórz, for Sanok (2 daily; 11hr); Zakopane (6 daily; 6–10hr; expresses at 6.15 & 6.35am; couchettes).

Buses

Warsaw (Dworzec Stadion) to: Lublin (2 daily; 4hr), Przemyśl (1 daily; 8hr), Zamość (3 daily; 7hr).

Warsaw (Dworzec Zachodni) to: Krosno (1 daily; 7hr), Mikołajki (1 daily; 5hr), Olsztyn (3 daily; 5hr), Rzeszów (1 daily; 8hr), Toruń (1 daily; 3hr 30min), Zakopane (1 daily; 7hr).

Planes

Warsaw to: Gdańsk (2–6 daily; 1hr); Katowice (1 daily, May–Oct only; 1hr); Koszalin (1–3 daily; 1hr); Kraków (2–6 daily; 1hr); Szczecin (1–2 daily; 1hr); Wrocław (2–6 daily; 1hr).

International trains

Warsaw to: Berlin (12 daily; 6hr 30min); Budapest (3 daily; 10hr); Kiev (3 daily; 10hr); Leipzig (2 daily; 12hr); Moscow (7 daily; 26hr); Ostend (2 daily; 19hr); Prague (3 daily; 8hr); Riga (2 daily; 22hr); Vilnius (4 daily; 14hr).

CHAPTER TWO

GDAŃSK AND THE LAKES

E ven in a country accustomed to shifts in its borders, northeastern Poland presents an unusually tortuous historical puzzle. Successively the domain of a Germanic crusading order, of the Hansa merchants and of the Prussians, it's only in the last forty years that the region has really become Polish. Right up until the end of World War II, large parts of the area belonged to the territories of East Prussia, and although you won't see the old place names displayed any more, even the most patriotic Pole would have to acknowledge that Gdańsk, Olsztyn and Toruń have made their mark on history under the German names of Danzig, Allenstein and Thorn. Twentieth-century Germany has left terrible scars: it was here that the first shots of World War II were fired, and the bitter fighting during the Nazi retreat in 1945 left many historic towns as sad shadows of their former selves.

Gdańsk, Sopot and Gdynia – the Tri-City as they are collectively known – dominate the area from their coastal vantage point. Like Warsaw, historic Gdańsk was obliterated in World War II but now offers some reconstructed quarters, in addition to a booming economic life and its contemporary political interest as the birthplace of Solidarity. It makes an enjoyable base for exploring neighbouring Kashubia, to the west, with its rolling hills, lakeside forests and distinctive communities of Prussianized Slavs. While waters round the Tri-City are a dubious though ever-improving proposition, the Hel Peninsula and the coast further west make a pleasant seaside option. On the other side of the Tri-City, Frombork, chief of many towns in the region associated with the astronomer Nicolaus Copernicus, is an attractive and historic lagoon-side town across the water from the Wiślana Peninsula, a beachside holidaymakers' favourite.

South from Gdańsk, a collection of Teutonic castles and Hanseatic centres dot the banks of the Wisła and its tributaries. Highlights include the huge medieval fortress at Malbork, long the headquarters of the Teutonic Knights, and Toruń, with its spectacular medieval ensemble. Eastwards stretches Mazury, Poland's biggest lakeland district, long popular with Polish holidaymakers and, increasingly, with the Germans. Canoe and yacht rental are the main attractions of its resorts, but for anyone wanting to get away from the crowds, there are

ACCOMMODATION PRICE CODES

The accommodation listed in this book has been given one of the following price codes. For more details see p.34.

① under 20zł (under £5/$7.5)	⑤ 75–95zł (£20–25/$30–38)
② 20–38zł (£5–10/$7.5–15)	⑥ 95–135zł (£25–35/$38–53)
③ 38–58zł (£10–15/$15–23)	⑦ 135–210zł (£35–55/$53–83)
④ 58–75zł (£15–20/$23–30)	⑧ 210–300zł (£55–80/$83–120)
⑨ over 300zł (over £80/$120)	

much less frequented patches of water and nature to explore, both in Mazury and, above all, in the neighbouring **Suwalszczyna** and **Augustów** region.

South again, lakes give way to the forests, open plains and Orthodox villages of **Podlasie**, the border region with Belarus, centred on the city of **Białystok**. Both city and region maintain one of Poland's most fascinating ethnic mixes, with a significant **Belarussian** population and smaller communities of **Tartars**. The Nazis wiped out the **Jewish** population, but their history is important in these parts too, with one of Poland's finest synagogues, well restored at **Tykocin**.

GDAŃSK AND AROUND

For outsiders, **GDAŃSK** is perhaps the most familiar city in Poland. The home of Lech Wałęsa, Solidarity and the former Lenin Shipyards, its images flashed across a decade of news bulletins during the 1980s. Expectations formed from the newsreels are fulfilled by the industrial landscape, and suggestions of latent discontent, radicalism and future strikes are all tangible. What is more surprising, at least for those with no great knowledge of Polish history, is the cultural complexity of the place. Prewar Gdańsk – or **Danzig** as it then was – was forged by years of Prussian and Hanseatic domination, and the reconstructed city centre looks not unlike Amsterdam, making an elegant and bourgeois backdrop. What has changed entirely, however, is the city's demography. At the outbreak of the last war, nearly all of the 400,000 citizens were German-speaking, with fewer than 16,000 Poles. The postwar years marked a radical shift from all that went before, as the ethnic Germans were expelled and Gdańsk became Polish for the first time since 1308. Germans are returning in numbers now, chiefly as tourists and business people, making an important contribution to the city's rapid emergence as one of the economic powerhouses of the country's post-communist development.

With a population of around 750,000, the **Tri-City** (Trojmiasto) conurbation comprising **Gdańsk**, **Gdynia** and **Sopot**, ranks as one of the largest in the country. It's an enjoyable area to explore, with ferries tripping between the three centres and up to the **Hel Peninsula**, and offering a good mix of Poland's northern attractions: politics and monuments in Gdańsk, seaside chic in Sopot, gritty port life in Gdynia and sandy beaches and clean water up at the Hel Peninsula. The lakes and forests of **Kashubia** are just an hour or two from Gdańsk by bus, and **Frombork**, too, makes an easy day trip, as do Elbląg and the Wiślana Peninsula. As you'd expect, Gdańsk also has excellent **transport connections** with the rest of Poland, with a host of buses, trains and flights.

Some history

The city's position at the meeting point of the Wisła and the Baltic has long made Danzig/Gdańsk an immense strategic asset: in the words of Frederick the Great, whoever controlled it could be considered "more master of Poland than any king ruling there". First settled in the tenth century, the city assumed prominence when the **Teutonic Knights** arrived in 1308, at the invitation of a population constantly threatened from the west by the Margraves of Brandenburg. The Knights established themselves in their accustomed style, massacring the locals and installing a colony of German settlers in their place.

The city's economy flourished, however, and with the ending of the Knights' rule in 1454 – acompanied by the brick-by-brick dismantlement of their castle by

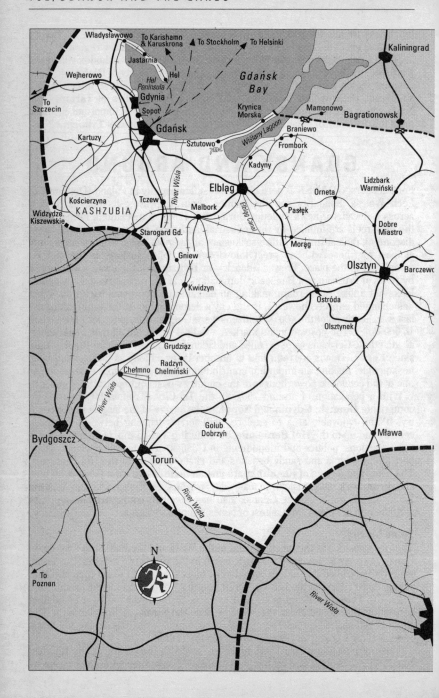

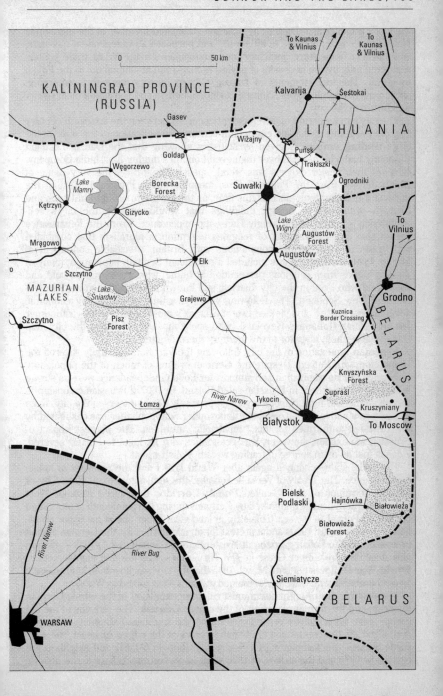

0   50 km

To Kaunas & Vilnius

To Kaunas & Vilnius

KALININGRAD PROVINCE (RUSSIA)

Gasev

Kalvarija

Šeštokai

LITHUANIA

Wiżajny

Puńsk

Goldap

Trakiszki

Węgorzewo

Suwałki

Ogrodniki

Lake Mamry

Borecka Forest

Kętrzyn

Gizycko

Lake Wigry

To Vilnius

Mrągowo

Augustów Forest

Augustów

Szczytno

Ełk

MAZURIAN LAKES

Lake Śniardwy

Grodno

Szczytno

Grajewo

Pisz Forest

Kuznica Border Crossing

BELARUS

Knyszyńska Forest

Supraśl

Łomza

River Narew

Tykocin

Kruszyniany

To Moscow

Białystok

Bielsk Podlaski

Hajnówka

Białowieża

Białowieża Forest

River Narew

River Bug

Siemiatycze

BELARUS

WARSAW

the city's inhabitants – Danzig, by now an established member of the mercantile Hanseatic League, became to all intents and purposes an independent city-state, with its own legislature, judiciary and monopolies on the Wisła trade routes, restricted only by the necessity of paying homage and an annual tax to the Polish monarch. The key elements of Danzig/Gdańsk history were thus emerging: autonomy, economic power, cultural cosmopolitanism and German–Polish rivalry for control of the city.

The city's main period of development occurred between the sixteenth century and the Partitions of the late eighteenth century. An indication of the scale of the city's **trading empire** is given by statistics showing that the Danzig Eastland Company had a bigger turnover than even London's mighty East India Company. (One of their major exports was wood, specifically spruce, the very name of which derives from the Polish *Z Prus*, meaning "from Prussia".) Most of the important building took place at this time, as the burghers brought in Dutch and Flemish architects to design buildings that would express the city's self-confidence – hence the strikingly Hanseatic appearance. From the Renaissance period also dates a tradition of religious toleration, a pluralism that combined with trade to forge strong connections with Britain: a sizeable contingent of foreign Protestant merchants included a significant Scottish population, many of them refugees from religious persecution at home, who were granted land and rights and who lived in the city districts still known as Stare and Nowe Szkoty – Old and New Scotland. The following century, a time of continuing economic development for the city, yielded two of Gdańsk's most famous sons – astonomer Jan Heweliusz (Johannes Hevelius), who spent most of his life in the city, and Daniel Fahrenheit, inventor of the mercury thermometer

Prussian annexation of the city, following the Partitions, abruptly severed the connection with Poland. Despite the German origins of much of the population, resistance to Prussianization and support for Polish independence were as strong in Danzig as elsewhere in Prussian-ruled Poland. In 1807, a Prussian campaign to recruit soldiers to fight Napoleon yielded precisely 47 volunteers in the city. Even as German a native of Danzig as the philosopher Schopenhauer was castigated by the Prussian authorities for his "unpatriotic" attitudes. The biggest impact of Prussian annexation, however, was economic: with its links to Poland severed, Gdańsk lost its main source of trading wealth, Polish wheat.

Territorial status changed again after World War I and the recovery of Polish independence. The Treaty of Versailles created the semi-autonomous **Free City of Danzig**, terminus of the so-called **Polish Corridor** that sliced through West Prussia (an area heavily dominated by Germans during the nineteenth century) and connected Poland to the sea. This strip of land gave Hitler one of his major propaganda themes in the 1930s and a pretext for attacking the city: the German assault unleashed on the Polish garrison at Westerplatte on September 1, 1939 – memorably described by Günter Grass in *The Tin Drum* – was the first engagement of **World War II**. It was not until March 1945 that the city was liberated, after massive Soviet bombardment; what little remained was almost as ruined as Warsaw.

The postwar era brought communist rule, the expulsion of the ethnic German majority, and the formal renaming of the city as **Gdańsk**. The remains of the old centre were meticulously reconstructed and the traditional shipping industries revitalized. As the communist era began to crack at the edges, however, the shipyards became the harbingers of a new reality. Riots in Gdańsk and neighbouring Gdynia in 1970 and the strikes of 1976 were important precursors to the historic

1980 **Lenin Shipyards** strike, which led to the creation of **Solidarity**. The shipyards remained at the centre of resistance to General Jaruzelski's government, the last major strike wave in January 1989 precipitating the Round Table negotiations that heralded the end of communist rule. Following the traumas of "shock therapy", the reform programme pursued with vigour in the early 1990s, the city and its surroundings are showing signs of rapid economic development, ranking second only to Warsaw in terms of foreign investment.

The **telephone code** for the Tri-City is ☎ 058

Arrival, information and getting around

The main **train station** (Gdańsk Główny) is a ten-minute walk west of the core of the old city. The traffic speeding along Wały Jagiellońskie, the wide main road running immediately in front of the station is lethal, so be sure to take the pedestrian underpass on your way into the centre and to get to the island tram stops in the middle of the same road. The **bus station** (Dworzec PKS) is located right behind the train station across ul. 3 Maja.

The city **airport** is at Rębiechowa, about 15km west of town, a thirty-minute bus journey (#110, B) from Targ Węglowy on the east side of Wały Jagiellońskie. *LOT* also runs special faster buses to and from the airport to the centre – ask at the airport counter for departure details.

Coming **by car**, signposting into the city centre is reasonably clear, although the last leg of the journey in from Warsaw takes you along a rather tortuous approach road which gets heavy with lorries and buses.

If you're arriving **by boat** from Scandinavia, you'll find yourself disembarking at the Nowy Port ferry terminal, 6km north of the city centre; ignore the unscrupulous taxi drivers congregating outside and head for the Nowy Port ferry terminal train station, 500m walk south and take one of the regular local trains into town.

Orientation is fairly straightforward, the main sites of interest being located in three historic districts: Główne Miasto, Stare Miasto and Stare Przedmieście. **Główne Miasto** (Main Town), the central area, is in easy walking distance of the main station. The main pedestrianized avenues, ul. Długa and its continuation Długi Targ, form the heart of the district, which backs east onto the attractive waterfront of the Motława Canal and the island of Spichlerze. To the north is the **Stare Miasto** (Old Town), bounded by the towering cranes of the shipyards, beyond which the suburbs of Wrzeszcz, Zaspa and Oliwa sprawl towards Sopot. South of the centre stands the quieter **Stare Przedmieście** (Old Suburb).

Information

The **tourist information centre**, at ul. Heweliusza 27 (Mon–Fri 9am–4pm; ☎31 43 55), a five-minute walk from the train station, is one of the best in the country, with extremely helpful and knowledgeable staff. Although their resources get stretched in the summer, they generally have a good supply of maps, timetables and local tips. **Orbis**, ul. Heweliusza 22 (Mon–Fri 10am–5pm, Sat 10am–2pm; ☎31 44 25), in the ground floor of the *Heweliusz* hotel, mainly caters for the hotel's welter of German tourist groups, though they're good for bus and train ticket bookings. The **PTTK** office at ul. Długa 45 (☎31 30 08) in the city centre stocks a useful supply of maps and brochures. **Almatur**, in the centre of town at Długi Targ 11 (Mon–Fri 9am–5pm; ☎31 29 31), is also friendly, and employs several English-speakers; unlike most offices they've adapted their style to accommodate the strange requirements – in Polish terms – of Western travellers. In summer they'll help you sort out accommodation in student hotels.

The English-language monthly *Welcome to Gdańsk,* available in the *Orbis* hotels, provides plenty of practical information, including details of current events, as does the *Gdańsk Airport* magazine. More comprehensively – but only in Polish – the local edition of *Gazeta Wyborcza* has in-depth listings, and can be bought in kiosks and some bookstores.

Getting around

Travelling within the city area is pretty straightforward. A regular local **train** service, Szybka Kolej Miejska (SKM), between Gdańsk's local station (immediately north of the main station), Sopot and Gdynia, with plenty of stops in between, runs roughly every ten minutes until 1am; tickets, which must be validated before you get on the train, can be bought in the passage beneath the main station or at any local station (most have ticket machines). Total journey time from Gdańsk to Gydnia is 35 minutes.

Trams run within all districts of Gdańsk, and **trolley buses** in Sopot and Gdynia, but services do not connect between the districts. **Buses**, however, operate right across the conurbation. The large-scale map of Gdańsk available from kiosks and some bookstores gives all bus and tram routes. Tickets for both trams and buses can be bought from any kiosk, street vendor or from the driver and must be validated upon entry. You can change buses as often as you like during the period your ticket is valid, on all buses, trams and trolley buses. Current tarifs are 0.4zł for ten minutes; 0.8zł for thirty minutes and 1.2zł for an hour. An all-day ticket up until midnight is 2.4zł, and an all-night ticket, 2.1zł.

Ferry services, chiefly aimed at visitors, operate between Gdańsk and a number of local destinations, notably Westerplatte, Sopot, Gdynia and further out to Hel and Jastarnia (see p.182). The Gdańsk landing stage is on the main waterfront (Długie Pobrzeże) close to the Green Gate; in Sopot and Gydnia, it's on the pier. Current timetables (adjusted seasonally) are posted at all landing stages. The main season is from mid-May to the beginning of September, though some services, for example to Westerplatte, usually continue into the autumn. **Tickets** are sold at the landing stages or, occasionally on the boat itself. The boat tour to Westerplatte and back via the port currently costs 7zł; one-way tickets to Hel, Gydnia and Sopot are 11zł, 9zł and 7zł respectively.

Accommodation

As in the other big tourist cities, **accommodation** in Gdańsk ranges from the ultra-plush to the ultra-basic – and rooms in the centre are at a premium in summer. At the top end of the scale, *Orbis* runs a string of **hotels** aimed very firmly at Western tourists and businesspeople. Lower down the price scale, hotels are still surprisingly thin on the ground, but if you're prepared to stay a little further out, the range of options increases considerably.

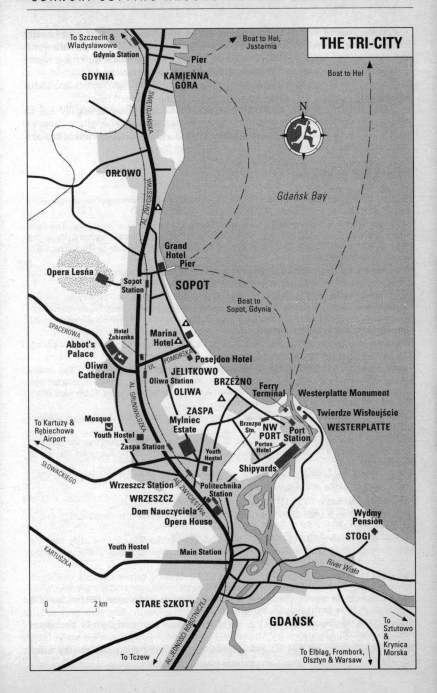

THE TRI-CITY

To Szczecin &
Wladyslawowo
Gdynia Station

Boat to Hel,
Jastarnia

Pier

Boat to Hel

GDYNIA

KAMIENNA
GÓRA

N

ORŁOWO

Gdańsk Bay

Grand
Hotel
Pier

Opera Leśna

Sopot
Station

SOPOT

Boat to
Sopot, Gdynia

SPACEROWA

Hotel
Żabianka

Marina
Hotel

Abbot's
Palace

Posejdon Hotel

UL. POMORSKA

Oliwa
Cathedral

JELITKOWO

Oliwa Station

BRZEŹNO

AL. GRUNWALDZKA

OLIWA

Ferry
Terminal

Westerplatte Monument

To Kartuzy &
Rębiechowa
Airport

Mosque

Youth Hostel

ZASPA

Mylniec
Estate

Zaspa Station

Brzezno
Stn.

NW
PORT

Youth
Hostel

Portos
Hotel

Twierdze Wisłoujście

Port
Station

WESTERPLATTE

SŁOWACKIEGO

Shipyards

Wrzeszcz Station

Politechnika
Station

AL. ZWYCIĘSTWA

WRZESZCZ

Dom Nauczyciela

Opera House

Wydmy
Pension

STOGI

KARTUSZKA

Youth Hostel

Main Station

River Wisła

0   2 km

STARE SZKOTY

GDAŃSK

To
Sztutowo
& Krynica
Morska

AL. JEDNOŚCI ROBOTNICZEJ

To Tczew

To Elbląg, Frombork,
Olsztyn & Warsaw

SWIĘTOJAŃSKA

AL. WŁADYSŁAWA IV

Private rooms (②) can be arranged either with the efficient, if occasionally frosty, **Biuro Zakwaterowań** at ul. Heweliusza 8 (daily May–Sept 8am–7pm; Oct–April closes 5pm; ☎31 93 71 or 31 26 34), or with the locals who hang about outside the *Biuro* and at the main train station. Be prepared to haggle over prices with the latter, though, and remember to check location before accepting any offers.

There are four **youth hostels** open year-round, all of them usually full in season; the student hotel is worth trying for its functional rooms, as are *Almatur* (☎31 44 03) who provide rooms in student hostels. All of the city's **campsites** are open from June to September.

Hotels and pensjonat

Bartan, ul. Turystyczna 99 (☎/fax 38 07 79). Holidaymakers' *pensjonat* in an attractive seaside location, but it's well east of the centre in the Sobieszewo. ④.

Centrum Edukacji Nauczycielki, ul. Gen J Hallera 14 (☎41 93 73 or 41 07 63). Teachers' centre based in Wrzesecz, although they don't insist on professional eligiblity. Basic but clean double rooms. Trams #2, 33 and 38 pass the door or take the train to the Politechnika station (10min walk). ③.

Dom Aktora, ul. Straganiarska 55/56 (☎41 55 87, fax 31 97 38). Pleasant, quiet *pensjonat* in a useful central location, with its own restaurant. ④.

Dom Nauczyciela, ul. Upenhaga 28 (☎41 91 16). Nice location out in Wrzeszcz – five minutes' walk north of Gdańsk-Politechnika station – in a quiet side street. Some rooms have private bathrooms and there are also basic singles, three-person and four-person rooms available. Restaurant and guarded car park. ③.

Hewelius, ul. Heweliusza 22 (☎31 56 31, fax 31 19 22). The big *Orbis* showpiece – pretentious and a bit too overt a contrast with regular Gdańsk life. ⑦.

Jantar, Długi Targ 19 (☎31 62 41). Its excellent location in the heart of the Old Town makes it very difficult to get into this one. The view from the top-floor rooms is magnificent, although the place could do with a lick of paint. Avoid the first-floor rooms if you want peace and quiet, as there is live music right below. ④.

Lechia, ul. Traugutta 29 (☎47 77 88). Former workers' hotel near the football stadium (Gdańsk-Politechnika station). ③.

Marina, ul. Jelitkowska 30 (☎53 20 79, fax 53 04 60). A "luxury" *Orbis* hotel on the seafront, complete with tennis court and swimming pool. However, there are no balconies and lots of concrete. ⑦.

Mesa, ul. Wały Jagiellońskie 36 (☎31 80 52 or 37 65 03, fax 31 80 52). Relatively upmarket new hotel close to the city centre. ⑥.

Novotel, ul. Pszenna (☎31 56 11). A typical and quite friendly motel. ⑦.

Orle, ul. Lazurowa 8 (☎38 07 91, fax 38 07 97). Good seaside resort accommodation east of the centre. ④.

Portos, ul. Wyzwolenia 48 (☎43 92 92). Seamen's hotel in the Nowy Port district, near the main ferry terminal, offering basic rooms with shared bathroom facilities. Well out of the centre, take tram #10 or a train to Nowy Port. ②.

Posejdon, ul. Kapliczna 30 (☎53 18 03, fax 53 02 28). Halfway between Gdańsk and Sopot, this is arguably the nicest *Orbis* hotel in town. Balconied rooms, some with a sea view, while others look onto the woods. There's also a popular nightclub. Easily accessible by tram (#26 to Jetlikowo), 200m from the Jetlikowo terminus. ⑦.

Srebry Młyn, ul. Słowackiego (☎41 83 37). Basic no-frills overnighter out on the airport road. ③.

Wydmy, ul. Wydmy 1 (☎38 31 51). Seaside pension in the Stogi resort east of the city. Good if you want the beach. ③.

Żabianka, ul. Dickmana 15 (☎52 27 72). Small, decent-quality place, the disadvantages being its off-centre location – halfway between Oliwa and Zabianka streets – and a fair bit of noise from passing trains. ③.

Zaulek, ul Ogarna 107/108 (☎31 41 69). Plain, decent-quality former workers' hostel bang in the Old Town centre and very popular. ②.

Hostels, student hotel and campsites

Al. Grunwaldzka 238/40 (☎41 16 60). Near Oliwa in the northern Wrzeszcz suburb. A decent-quality hostel inside a sports centre; to get here take a local train to Gdańsk-Zaspa or tram #8, #12 or #15.

Al. Legionów 11 (☎41 41 08). A lower-quality hostel, once again in Wrzeszcz. Take trams #2, #4, #7, #8 or #14 or walk from the Gdańsk-Wrzeszcz station.

Student hotel, ul. Wyspańskiego 7 (☎414-414). Cheap rooms in student lodgings.

Ul. Morska 108c (☎27 00 55). Summer-only hostel near the seaside. Close to the *Poseidon* up in Jetlikowo.

Ul. Smoluchowskiego 11 (☎32 38 20). Also in Wrzeszcz; take tram #2, #6, #8, #12, #13 or #14.

Ul. Wałowa 21 (☎31 34 61). The most central hostel – a sizeable red-brick building ten minutes' walk from the main station.

Campsites

Ul. Hallera 234 (☎56 65 31). In the suburb of Brzeżno, due north of the town centre; trams #7, #13 and #15, and buses #124 and #148 pass nearby.

Ul. Jelitkowska 23 (☎53 27 31). Near the beach at Jetlikowo. Regular camping facilities plus bungalows – at around 20zł a bed, a bargain if you can get one. It's a short walk from the terminus of trams #2, #4 and #15.

Ul. Lazurowa 6 (☎38 07 96). Even further out in Orle, east of the city along the Martwa Wisła; bus #112 passes it.

The City

The **Główne Miasto**, the largest of the historic quarters, is the obvious starting point for an exploration of the city; the **Stare Miasto**, across the thin ribbon of the Raduna Canal, is the natural progression. The third, southern quarter, **Stare Przedmieście**, cut off by the Podwale Przedmieskie, has its main focus for visitors in the National Museum. Moving north, out towards Sopot, is the **Oliwa** suburb with its cathedral – one of the city's most distinctive landmarks – and botanical gardens.

North along the canal, **Westerplatte** – and its monument commemorating the outbreak of World War II – can be reached by **boat** from the central waterfront (as can Gdynia, Sopot and the Hel Peninsula), a trip that allows good views of the famous **shipyards**.

The Main Town (Główne Miasto)

Entering the **Main Town** is like walking straight into a Hansa merchants' settlement. The layout, typical of a medieval port, comprises a tight network of streets, bounded on four sides by water and main roads – the Raduna and Motława canals to the north and east, Podwale Przedmieskie and Wały Jagiellońskie to the south

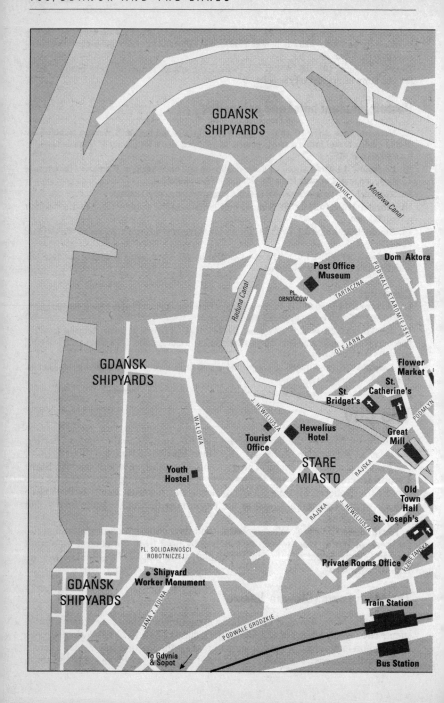

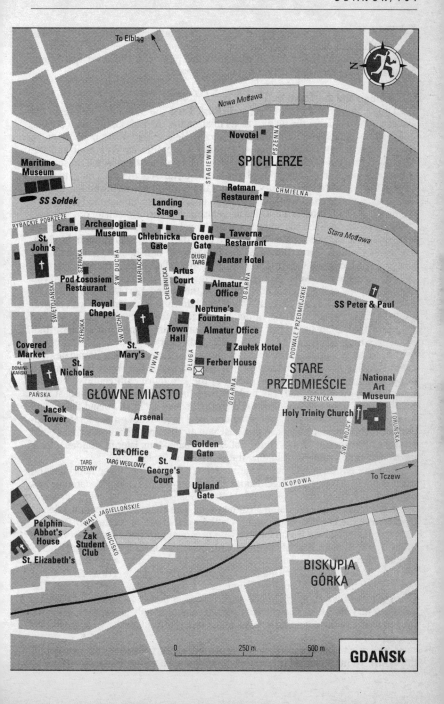

To Elbląg

Nowa Motława

Novotel

SPICHLERZE

Maritime
Museum

SS Sołdek

Retman
Restaurant

STAGIEWNA

PSZENNA

CHMIELNA

RYBACKIE POBRZEŻE

Stara Motława

Landing
Stage

Crane

Archeological
Museum

Chlebnicka
Gate

Green
Gate

Tawerna
Restaurant

St.
John's

SZEROKA

ŚW DUCHA

MARIACKA

CHLEBNICKA

DŁUGI
TARG

Jantar Hotel

Pod Łososiem
Restaurant

Artus
Court

Almatur
Office

OGARNA

SS Peter & Paul

Royal
Chapel

ŚW DUCHA

SZEROKA

Neptune's
Fountain

Town
Hall

Almatur Office

PODWALE PRZEDMIEJSKIE

Covered
Market

St.
Mary's

PIWNA

DŁUGA

Zaułek Hotel

Ferber House

STARE
PRZEDMIEŚCIE

National
Art
Museum

PL
DOMINI-
KAŃSKI

St.
Nicholas

GŁÓWNE MIASTO

OGARNA

RZEŹNICKA

PAŃSKA

Jacek
Tower

Arsenal

Holy Trinity Church

ŚW. TRÓJCY

TORUŃSKA

Lot Office

TARG
DRZEWNY

TARG WĘGLOWY

St.
George's
Court

Golden
Gate

Upland
Gate

OKOPOWA

To Tczew

WAŁY JAGIELLOŃSKIE

HUCISKO

Pelphin
Abbot's
House

Żak
Student
Club

St. Elizabeth's

BISKUPIA
GÓRKA

0   250 m   500 m

GDAŃSK

and west. The ancient appearance of this quarter's buildings is deceptive: by May 1945 the fighting between German and Russian forces had reduced the core of Gdańsk to smouldering ruins. A glance at the photos in the town hall brings home the scale of the destruction and of its reversal.

Ulica Długa and the Town Hall

Ul. Długa, the main thoroughfare, and **Długi Targ**, the wide open square on the eastern part of it, form the natural focus of attention. As with all the main streets, huge stone gateways guard both entrances. Before the western entrance to Długa, take a look round the outer **Upland Gate** (Brama Wyżynna) and the recently renovated Gothic **Prison Tower** which contains a gruesome museum of prison exhibits, some of them displayed in the torture chambers. The gate itself, built in the late sixteenth century as part of the town's outer fortifications, used to be the main entrance to Gdańsk. The three coats of arms emblazoned across the archway – Poland, Prussia and Gdańsk – encapsulate the city's history.

This gate was also the starting point of the "royal route" used by Polish monarchs on their annual state visits. After the Upland Gate they had to pass through the richly decorated **Golden Gate** (Brama Złota), reminiscent of a Roman triumphal arch, alongside **St George's Court** (Dwór Św. Jerzego), a fine Gothic mansion appropriately housing the architects' society, with a statuette of St George and the Dragon on its roof – a copy of the original now housed in the National Art Museum in the Old Suburb (see p.168). From here, ul. Długa leads down to the town hall, with several gabled facades worth studying in detail – such as the sixteenth-century **Ferber mansion** (no. 28), usually open to the public, or the imposing **Lion's Castle** (no. 35), where King Władysław IV entertained local dignitaries.

Topped by a golden statue of King Sigismund August which dominates the central skyline, the huge and well-proportioned tower of the **Town Hall** makes a powerful impact. Originally constructed in the late fourteenth century, with the tower and spire added later, the building was totally ruined during the last war, but the restoration was so skilful you'd hardly believe it. "In all Poland there is no other, so Polish a town hall" observed one local writer, though the foreign influences on the interior rooms might lead you to disagree. They now house the **Historical Museum** (Tues–Thurs, Sat & Sun 10am–4pm, later in summer), their lavish decorations almost upstaging the exhibits on display.

From the entrance hall an ornate staircase leads to the upper floor and the main council chamber, the **Red Room** (Sala Czerwona). Interior decoration was obviously one thing that seventeenth-century Gdańsk councillors could agree on: the colour red completely dominates the room. The chamber's sumptuous decor, mostly from the late sixteenth century, is the work of various craftsmen: its furniture was designed by a Dutch fugitive who became municipal architect of Gdańsk in the 1590s; Willem Bart of Ghent carved the ornate fireplace – note the Polish-looking Neptunes in the supports; while most of the ceiling and wall paintings were produced by another Dutchman, Johan Verberman de Vries. The central oval ceiling painting, by another Dutchman, Isaac van den Block, is titled *The Glorification of the Unity of Gdańsk with Poland*, a period panorama of the city, stressing its Polish ties. The council used this chamber only in summer; in winter they moved into the adjoining smaller room, entered through the wooden door to the right of the fireplace.

As well as another reconstructed seventeenth-century fireplace, the next room, the **court room,** contains a haunting photomontage of the ruins of Gdańsk in

1945. One floor up, the **archive rooms** now house permanent exhibitions including a display of prewar Gdańsk photographs, plus temporary shows such as the display of engravings by the city's best known writer, Günter Grass. The old municipal finance office contains a pair of paintings by van den Block, one a forbidding representation of the Flood, and a statue of King Jagiełło taken from the neighbouring Arthur's Court.

Arthur's Court

Immediately south of the town hall is the **Arthur's Court** (Dwór Artusa; Tues–Sun 10am–4pm, though often closed for functions): even in a street lined with many fine mansions, this one is impressive. Recently opened to the public following extensive (and continuing) renovation work, the building encapsulates some fascinating aspects of the history of the city. Its origins date back to the early fourteenth century, a period marked by a widespread awakening of interest in British Arthurian legends among the European mercantile class. Attracted by the ideals of King Arthur's fabled court at Camelot, merchants began establishing their own latter-day courts, where they could entertain in the chivalrous and egalitarian spirit of their knightly forebears. Founded in 1350, the Gdańsk Court grew rapidly to become one of the most fabulous and wealthy in Europe. Initially occupied by the Brotherhood of St George, by the 1500s it had become a focal point of the city, with a growing array of guild- and trade-based brotherhoods establishing their own meeting benches in the main hall. The court's development was encouraged (and financed) by the city authorities, creating what was effectively northern Europe's first non-sectarian, non-political meeting place, combining the functions of guild house, civic hall, judicial court and reception centre for foreign guests.

Reconstructed in the 1480s, with the main facade reworked by the ever-present Abraham van den Block in the early seventeenth century, the building was almost completely destroyed during the Nazi retreat in spring 1945. Mercifully, however, much of the court's rich interior was spirited away in advance of the Soviet bombardment and thus saved. Today it forms the highlight of the cavernous, reconstructed main hall and adjoining chamber, notably sections of the original ceiling decoration in the main hall including the starred vaulting, supported on a brace of graceful granite columns, and the Renaissance ceramic heating oven used to keep the assembled burghers of Gdańsk from freezing during the winter.

Continuing just to the south, you'll come to the **Golden House** at Złota Kamienieza 41, an impressive Renaissance mansion named after the luminous gilding that covers its elegant four-storeyed facade.

The waterfront and Maritime Museum

The archways of the **Green Gate** (Most Zielona), a former royal residence for the annual visit, open directly onto the **waterfront**. From the bridge over the Motława Canal you get a good view of the old granaries on **Spichlerze Island** to the right (there used to be over 300 of them), and to the left of the old harbour quay, now a tourist hang-out and local promenade.

Halfway down is the massive and largely original fifteenth-century **Gdańsk Crane** (Żuraw Gdański), the biggest in medieval Europe; it and a number of buildings make up the **Maritime Museum** (Tues–Fri 10am–4pm, Sat–Sun 10am–4pm, extended opening hours in summer, last tickets 1hr before closing), one of the best-organized and most interesting in the country. Only the ticket system remains a bit of a trial: tickets can be bought at the *kasa* inside the crane, and as there are different stubs for each part of the museum, you'll end up carrying round a bundle of them. To visit all sections of the museum, you'll need at least three hours.

The crane itself houses a colourful and, for once, well laid-out collection of **marine-life** specimens from around the world, a selection of sea birds, swordfish, dried starfish, delicate coral, sea shells and some huge lobsters greeting you from the corners. Like their countryman Joseph Conrad, Poles have long been avid sea-farers and explorers: mementoes of some of their travels around the world have been gathered together, the exhibition animated by some rollicking recordings of Polish sea shanties playing in the background. An additional bonus is the bird's-eye view of the inner workings of the massive crane from the museum rooms.

Across the street, another building houses an anthropological collection of **boats** from around the world: again, well thought out and presented. There's an enjoyable selection of vessels here, many of them painted canoes, catamarans, barques and other fishing vessels from Africa, Asia and Polynesia.

The main part of the museum is housed in three recently renovated Renaissance granaries across the water on Spichlerze Island. To get across you can take a short boat trip in the vessel moored at the waterside beneath the crane. The boat leaves as soon as it's full, which in summer means it travels pretty well non-stop between the two sides of the water: last boat over is at 4pm October–April (extended service May–Sept), the journey offering you a good view back onto the houses along the city waterfront. The stout-looking granaries, known as "*Panna*" (The Virgin Mary), "*Miedz*" (Copper) and "*Oliwski*" (Oliwa), respectively recall the days when the bustling, international Gdańsk port reached right into the city centre.

Entitled "Poland and the Baltic Sea", the **exhibition in the granaries** comprises a rich array of items connected in some way to the city's maritime past. Everything the maritime enthusiast could want is here: model ships, paintings on stirring sea themes, ship fittings, instruments, old binoculars and compasses, and an extensive display devoted to the various stages of the traditional ship-building process. The biggest room houses a fearsome display of cannons mounted on their wooden rollers, a good proportion seemingly Swedish weapons dating from the mammoth assaults on the city of the 1650s and 1660s. Colourful mastheads recovered from ships, including the decorative Polish *Artus* figurehead, decorate the walls, and a series of maps illustrates the struggle for control of the Baltic over the centuries. Appropriately enough, the exhibition concludes with a display devoted to the modern struggles of the Gdańsk shipyards, the birth of Solidarity in particular.

Back out of the granaries, there's the chance to clamber around the solid-looking *Sołdek*, the first **steamship** built in Gdańsk after World War II, moored in front of the granaries. The trek through the ship's holds, crew cabins, engine and boiler rooms culminates in a display devoted to the 1980 strikes in the Gdańsk shipyards and the advent of Solidarity.

All the streets back into the town from the waterfront are worth exploring. Next up from the Green Gate is **ul. Chlebnicka**, reached through the fifteenth-century **Chlebnicka Gate**, built during the era of Teutonic rule. The **English House** (Dom Angielski) at no. 16, built in 1569 and the largest house in the city at the time, is a reminder of the strong Reformation-era trading connections with

Britain. Close by, the **Schlieff House** (no. 16), a graceful early sixteenth-century Gothic mansion is minus its original facade, which was spirited off to Potsdam by the Prussian ruler, Wilhelm III, where it remains. Several of the best bars are on Chlebnicka, as is the headquarters of the local police – they're the lads sitting around in the carelessly parked cars.

St Mary's Church

Both ul. Chlebnicka and neighbouring ul. Mariacka, a charmingly atmospheric and meticulously reconstructed street, with gabled terraced houses and expensive clothes shops, end at the gigantic **St Mary's Church** (Kościół Mariacka), reputedly the biggest brick church in the world. Estimates that it could fit 20,000 people inside were substantiated during the early days of martial law, when huge crowds crammed the cold whitewashed interior. Overall, the building is beginning to lose some of it austerity thanks to the gradual return of elements of original decoration removed to the National Museum in Warsaw after the war, such as the strikingly beautiful Madonna figure in the south aisle.The **high altar**, totally reconstructed after the war, is a powerful sixteenth-century triptych featuring a *Coronation of the Virgin*. Of the chapels scattered round the church, two of the most striking are the **Chapel of 11,000 Virgins**, which has a tortured Gothic crucifix for which the artist apparently nailed his son-in-law to a cross as a model, and the **St Anne's Chapel**, containing the wooden *Beautiful Madonna of Gdańsk* from around 1415. A curiosity is the reconstructed fifteenth-century **astronomical clock**, which tells not only the day, month and year but the whole saints' calendar and the phases of the moon; when completed in 1470 it was the world's tallest clock.

If you're feeling fit, make sure you climb up St Mary's **tower** (daily mid-May to mid-Oct 9am–5.30pm) – on a good day the view over Gdańsk and the plains is excellent; for a few złotys the old man who sits up there all day will let you look around with his binoculars. After the bareness of the church, the Baroque exuberance of the domed late seventeenth-century **Royal Chapel**, directly opposite on ul. Św. Ducha, and designed by Tylman of Gameren for use by the city's then minority Catholic population, makes a refreshing change, though it's often shut. The **Archeological Museum** (Tues–Sun 10am–5pm), at the east end of ul. Mariacka, is a bit of a disappointment, perhaps unavoidably after the maritime museum: the exhibitions are dry and lifeless, with only the Peruvian finds lightening the tone.

From the Arsenal to the Flower Market

Ul. Piwna, another street of high terraced houses west of the church entrance, ends at the monumental **Great Arsenal** (Wielka Zbrojownia), an early seventeenth-century armoury facing the **Coal Market** (Targ Węglowy), whose appearance underscores its Flemish ancestry. Now a busy shopping centre, the coal market leads north to the **Wood Market** (Targ Drzewny), and on to the Old Town over the other side of the canal. Ul. Szeroka, first off to the right, is another charming old street with a nice view of St Mary's from the corner with ul. Furty Groba.

The Dominican-run **St Nicholas' Church** (Św. Mikołaja) on ul. Świętojańska is another fourteenth-century brick structure, the only city centre church to come through the war relatively unscathed. The interior houses a rich array of furnishings, in particular some panelled early Baroque choir stalls, a massive high altar and a fine Gothic *Pietà* in one of the nave bays, while **St John's** (Św. Jana), further down the same street, is a reputedly beautiful Gothic church badly damaged during World War II and still closed for restoration. Continuing north towards the canal, at the edge of pl. Obrończów, stands the old **Post Office Museum** building immortalized by Günter Grass in *The Tin Drum*. Rebuilt after the war, it's here that a small contingent of employees of the Free City's *Poczta Polska* (Polish Post Office) battled it out with German forces in September 1939. As at Westerplatte the Germans clearly weren't anticipating such spirited resistance; despite the overwhelmingly superior firepower ranged against them the Poles held out for nine hours, finally surrendering when the Nazis sent in flamethrowers. Official postwar accounts maintained that the survivors were taken to the nearby Zaspa cemetery and summarily shot. At least two appear to have survived, in fact, surfacing in recent years to tell their own story.

The spiky-looking monument on the square in front of the building commemorates the event that has played an important role in the city's postwar communist mythology, the Poles' heroic resistance presented as a further vindication of the claimed "Polishness" of the city. Inside the post office there's a small **museum** (Tues–Sat 10am–4pm) mainly devoted to the events of 1939, including copies of Nazi photos of the attack on the building. Additionally there's an exhibition of local postal history underscoring the importance of postal communications to the city ever since its early trading days.

The terraced houses and shops tail off as you approach the outer limits of the main town, marked by several towers and other remnants of the **town wall**. **Baszta Jacek**, the tower nearest the canal, stands guard over the Pod Myślinksa, the main route over the canal into the Old Town. The area around the tower provides the focus of the annual Dominican fair (Jarmark) in August (see "Listings", p.176). The **Flower Market** opposite is a fine example of the Polish attachment to the finer things of life – even when there was nothing in the food shops, you still found roses or carnations in one of the stalls here. The appeal has been somewhat diminished by the spate of stark new brick buildings erected in place of the old stalls, though nothing has yet conspired to stop the group of withered-looking traders that cluster round the market hall selling their farm produce.

The Old Town (Stare Miasto) and the Shipyards

Crossing the canal bridge brings you into the **Old Town** (Stare Miasto), altogether a patchier and less reconstructed part of town characterized by a jumbled mix of old and new buildings. Dominating the waterside is the seven-storey **Great Mill** (Wielki Mlyn), built in the mid-fourteenth century by the Teutonic Knights and another Gdańsk "largest" – in this case the biggest mill in medieval Europe. Its eighteen races milled corn for 600 years; even in the 1930s it was still grinding out 200 tons of flour a day, and local enthusiasts see no reason why it couldn't be doing the same again. The building has recently been converted into an upmarket shopping centre complete with glass lifts. Traces of the original building are still in evidence, notably the old foundations.

St Catherine's Church (Katarzynka), the former parish church of the Old Town, to the right of the crossway, is one of the nicest in the city. Fourteenth century – and built in brick like almost all churches in the region – it has a well-preserved and luminous interior. The astronomer, Jan Hevelius, and his family are buried here in a tomb in the choir. If you're keen to catch a glimpse of **Lech Wałęsa**, there's a good chance of seeing him at his local church, **St Bridget's**

(Św. Brigida), next to St Catherine's, on Sundays, when (as is the case rather more often these days) he happens to be in Gdańsk. Under the charismatic guidance of Father Jankowski, still a close confidant of Wałęsa, though seriously compromised of late by some highly publicized anti-Semitic outpourings, the church became a local Solidarity stronghold in the 1980s. The oil painting of the Black Madonna in a T-shirt sporting the *Solidarność* logo accurately captures the aura of what now seems like a bygone era. Although the political importance of the church is diminishing in tandem with the new political configurations of the post-communist order, it's still worth visiting places like this – ideally on a Sunday – to experience the specifically Polish mixture of religion and politics that is personified in the man whose statue watches over the church, Karol Wojtyła, aka John Paul II.

Moving further into the Old Town, the merchants' mansions give way to postwar housing, the tattier bits looking like something off the set of *1984*. The most interesting part of the district is just west along the canal from the mill, centred on the **Old Town Hall** (Ratusz Staromiejski), on the corner of ul. Bielanska and Korzenna. Built by the architect of the main town hall, this delicate Renaissance construction, until recently occupied by four local government offices, has now been smartened up and converted into the new **Baltic Cultural Centre** (daily 9am–11pm). The main ground-floor room houses a lively changing series of exhibitions, devoted to local and regional cultural and historical themes. There's also a pleasant café and bookstore, again with a historical bent. When it's not being used for receptions and other events, the place is fully open to the public – all in all, an inspired venue fully deserving of the support it has already garnered. The bronze figure in the entrance hall is of Jan Hevelius, the Polish astronomer after whom *Orbis* has named its nearby skyscraper hotel. Like the better-known Mr Fahrenheit, he was a Gdańsk boy.

Continuing west from the town hall, Gothic **St Joseph's** (Św. Jożefa) and **St Elizabeth's** (Św. Elżbiety) – facing each other across ul. Elzbietańska – and the Renaissance **House of the Abbots of Pelplin** (Dom Opatów Pelplińskich) make a fine historic entourage. From here you're only a short walk through the tunnels under the main road (Podwale Grodzkie) from the train station.

The ex-Lenin Shipyards

Looming large in the distance are the cranes of the famous **Gdańsk Shipyards** (Stocznia Gdańska) – Lenin's name was dropped in the late 1980s. With the Nowa Huta steelworks outside Kraków, this was the crucible of the political struggles of the 1980s.

Ten minutes' walk or one tram stop north along the main road brings you to the shipyard gates on plac Solidarności Robotniczej. In front of them stands an ugly set of steel crosses, a **monument** to workers killed during the **1970 shipyard riots**; it was inaugurated in 1980 in the presence of Party, Church and opposition leaders. A precursor to the organized strikes of the 1980s, the 1970 riots erupted when workers took to the streets in protest at price rises, setting fire to the Party headquarters after police opened fire. Riots erupted again in 1976, once more in protest at price rises on basic foodstuffs, and in **August 1980** Gdańsk came to the forefront of world attention when a protest at the sacking of workers rapidly developed into a national strike.

The formation of **Solidarity**, the first independent trade union in the Soviet bloc, was a direct result of the Gdańsk strike, instigated by the Lenin Shipyards workers and their charismatic leader **Lech Wałęsa**. Throughout the 1980s the Gdańsk workers remained in the vanguard of political protest. Strikes here in

1988 and 1989 led to the **Round Table Talks** which forced the Communist Party into power-sharing and, ultimately, democratic elections.

Standing at the gates today, you may find it hard to experience this as the place where, in a sense, contemporary Poland began to take shape. Yet ironically the shipyards remain at the leading edge of political developments: for several years, successive governments attempted (unsuccessfully) to sell them off to Western investors. Despite wavering on the brink of bankruptcy on several occasions, by 1995 the yards appeared to have got the worst behind them, the considerably reduced workforce gradually carving out a niche for itself in the competitive international shipbuilding market. Though they haven't gone the whole way in exploiting the yards' tourist-pulling potential, it is possible to visit the yards in **tour groups** organized by *Almatur* (see p.156). They need time to organize this, so book several days in advance. If you don't make it into the yards, you can pick up your Solidarność badge or T-shirt from the stalls near the main gates.

The Old Suburb (Stare Przedmieście)

Stare Przedmieście – the lower part of old Gdańsk – was the limit of the original town, as testified by the ring of seventeenth-century bastions running east from plac Wałowy over the Motława.

The main attraction today is the **National Art Museum** (Tues–Thurs, Sat & Sun 10am–3pm), housed in a former Franciscan monastery at ul. Toruńska 1. Currently, it's the subject of an arcane property dispute with the building's one-time monastic occupants lodging an official claim on the premises they haven't occupied for over four centuries. There's enough local Gothic art and sculpture here to keep enthusiasts going all day, as well as a varied collection of fabrics, chests, gold and silverware – all redolent of the town's former wealth. The range of Dutch and Flemish art in the "foreign galleries" – Memling, the younger Brueghel, Cuyp and van Dyck are the best-known names – attests to the city's strong links with the Netherlands.

The museum's most famous work is Hans Memling's colossal *Last Judgement* (1473), the painter's earliest known work – though he was already in his thirties and a mature artist. The painting has had a more than usually chequered past, having been commissioned by the Medici in Florence, then diverted to Gdańsk, looted by Napoleon, moved to Berlin, returned to Gdańsk, stolen by the Nazis and finally, after being discovered by the Red Army, hidden in the Thuringian hills, to be returned to Gdańsk by the Russians in 1956.

Adjoining the museum is the old monastery, **Holy Trinity Church** (Kościół Św. Trójcy), a towering brick Gothic structure with characteristic period net vaulting. One of the best preserved Gothic churches in the city, the interior features a fine high altar, an assemblage of triptych pieces cobbled together following the wartime destruction of Isaac van Blocke's original, a delicately carved pulpit (the only Gothic original left in the city) and an array of other period furnishings, notably a pair of winged altar pieces.

Twierdze Wisłoujwcie

A half-hour bus journey from the city centre out along the Westerplatte peninsula is the old **Gdańsk Fortress** (Twierdze Wisłoujście), from which the local *kaper* defence force (see below) used to guard the city port. Long neglected, it's now been substantially renovated and turned into a section of the city **Historical Museum** (May–Sept Tues 11am–5pm, Wed–Sun, 9am–5pm, otherwise by appointment – the tourist office has the current details).

Designed by Dutch architects using the octagonal zigzag defence plan popular at the time, the first fortifications for the two-storey fortress were put up in the 1480s, with additions built on throughout the following century. Doubling as the main port lighthouse, the whole construction was enlarged to its current size in the mid-eighteenth century, and reinforced by Napoleon's forces in the early nineteenth. (Napoleon himself visited the place on his way to Moscow.) The city's Partition-era Prussian masters used the fortress as a jail, notably for Polish political prisoners – Josef Piłsudski included – which probably explains why they didn't dismantle it along with all the other port fortifications in the 1870s.

Despite years of modern neglect the fortress still looks formidable: through the heavily fortified entrance you enter the main courtyard, with the high former lighthouse tower – as featured on the local *Kaper* beer label – in the centre. Clamber up to the top of the tower, the walls of which are lined with prints of the old Prussian plans of the fortress, for an excellent view out over the city, with the shipyards to the south and Westerplatte and beyond it the Hel Peninsula out to the north.

Back down to ground level you can wander around the ramparts, stopping now and then to peer out through the menacing-looking cannon holes looking

THE KAPER OF GDAŃSK

In a city with a tradition of cosmopolitan and independent-minded attitudes the story of Gdańsk's one-time mercenary naval defence force is instructive. Right from the city's early days, the citizen merchants of Gdańsk appreciated the need for some form of sea-based protection to keep potential invaders out. The first Polish king to try and establish a proper navy was Kazimierz Jagiellończyk (1444–92), during his thirteen-year-long war with the Teutonic Knights. A significant portion of his navy actually consisted of local mercenaries – **kaper** as they came to be known, after *kaap*, the Old Dutch for "ship" – who agreed to work on contract for the king, but not officially as his representatives.

The crews on the *kaper* vessels were a mixed bunch, the contingent of locals from the Gdańsk and Elbląg regions supplemented by an assortment of Swedish, Flemish, Scottish and Kashubian adventurers. Skilled sailors keen on risk, the *kaper* were ostensibly employed to guard the Gdańsk merchant fleet, which by the late fifteenth century was already nearly 100 vessels strong. In 1482 the newly constructed fortress at Wisłoujście became the base of their operations. Protecting the harbour aside, the *kaper* clearly weren't averse to a bit of adventuring-cum-piracy. Under the designation "the king's maritime military", King Sigismund Stary employed a *kaper* force for his assault on Moscow in 1517; their main interest, however, was actually in the Baltic port of Memling, which the *kaper* captured single-handedly under the leadership of one Adrian Flint, an English adventurer.

By the mid-sixteenth century, with their own base, ships and uniforms, the increasingly ill-disciplined *kaper* appear to have developed into a fully fledged para-military naval outfit capturing twenty vessels in one year (1568) alone. Recognizing that the Gdańsk *kaper* were flourishing in the vacuum left by the absence of a proper navy, King Sigismund Wasa set about creating a standing force and in 1600 asked *kaper* to work for him. It was left to King Jan Sobieski, however, to reign the *kaper* in fully, and finally to integrate them into an official Polish navy.

out onto the waters of the harbour approach – not a pretty sight for a passing assailant.

If you're with the guide he'll show you the dank, old, sixteenth-century kitchens as well as the former commandant's room, currently being refurbished (like much of the building), and due to be converted into a tourist café/restaurant. Finally you can wander through the cavernous fortress cellars reaching down to, and in some places below, the water's edge. Big enough to hold supplies to keep the *kaper* going for a whole year, these days the smoke-blackened cellars are piled high with barrels of strawberries for jam-making, a commercial revival, apparently, of an old mercenary pastime.

There are a number of ways of getting to the fortress: after passing the huge local sulphur factory, bus #106 from outside the main station stops close by, continuing on to Westerplatte; a more attractive alternative is to take a tram or bus to Nowy Port, then a ferry (every half-hour in summer) across to the fortress.

Westerplatte

It was at **Westerplatte**, the promontory guarding the harbour entrance, that the German battleship *Schleswig-Holstein* fired the first salvo of World War II, on September 1, 1939. For a full week the garrison of 170 badly equipped Poles held off the combined assault of aircraft, heavy guns and over 3000 German troops, setting the tone for the Poles' response to the subsequent Nazi–Soviet invasion. The ruined army guard-house and barracks are still there, one of the surviving buildings housing a small **Museum** (Tues–Sun 10am–4pm) chronicling the momentous events of September 1939. Beyond the museum it's a fifteen-minute walk to the main **Westerplatte Monument,** a grim, ugly-looking 1960s slab in the best socialist-realist traditions, whose symbolism conveys a tangible sense of history. The green surroundings of the exposed peninsula make a nice, if generally blustery, walk to the coast, with good views out onto the Baltic.

You can get to Westerplatte by bus #106 or #158 from the centre, but a much better way is to take one of the tourist **boats** from the main city waterfront, just north of the Brama Zielona. (There are boats to several destinations – Gdynia, Sopot and Hel included – so make sure you're on the right one.) Taking about thirty minutes each way, the trip provides an excellent view of the **shipyards** and the array of international vessels anchored there.

Wrzeszcz

Moving north from the centre, the **Wrzeszcz** district is a leafy, quietly affluent suburb. Wrzeszcz, or Langfuhr as it was known in the days of the Free City, was Günter Grass' childhood stamping ground in the years immediately before and during World War II: it's in the streets round the family flat near Wrzeszcz station, for example, that the central action of *The Tin Drum* takes place. Though much of Wrzeszcz was destroyed in 1945, one building Grass would certainly still recognize is the old **Gdańsk Brewery** on ul. Wajdeloty, just behind the train station, as well as the fine old mansions backing onto Jaśkowa Dolina, the hills here offering good walking at any time of year.

```
THE GDAŃSK BREWERY
```

Built in the 1870s, the **Gdańsk Brewery** – *Kleinhammer Brauerei* as it was originally called – is currently undergoing something of a revival following its purchase
by an Australian company. For the first time in many decades decent, locally
brewed beer is now plentifully available in bars, restaurants and shops around the
Tri-City, though it's having to put up with some stiff competition from the Western
(particularly German) brews that have flooded the Polish market.

The brewery itself makes an enjoyable visit. You need to book in advance (☎41
52 15) for the **guided tours**, which include the chance to do a bit of beer-tasting at
the end of the visit. To get to the brewery take the local train to Wrzeszcz station,
and from there it's two minutes' walk to the brewery gates. Much of the building
(and brewing equipment) is pretty old-fashioned, but things are changing fast as a
result of the new owner's ambitious modernization plans. In among the mixture of
1950s equipment and 1990s hi-tech apparatus, you can still see several bits of the
original brewery, including the attractive stained glass windows, carthorses'
entrance and solid *Danziger* walls. Five beers, mostly bottled but some on draught,
are currently produced:

Artus Popular prewar brand revived ten years ago. A strong, full-bodied lager beer.

Gdańskie A light, full-flavoured lunchtime beer. May have to be renamed soon due
to extortionate rates demanded by the local authorities for use of the city name.

Hewelius Named after the seventeenth-century Gdańsk-born astronomer who also
kept his own private brewery. An excellent, hoppy pilsner worthy of the great
astronomer-brewer's name.

Kaper Loosely translated as "Pirate's brew", this is a strong, dark and heavy porter-
type ale popular among the heavy drinkers.

Remus Named after local Kashubian hero, a lighter beer aimed at the large
Kashubian market .

Oliwa

The modern Oliwa suburb, the northernmost area of Gdańsk, has one of the best-
known buildings in the city, **Oliwa Cathedral**. To get here, take the local train to
Gdańsk-Oliwa station, and walk across the park west of the main Sopot road.

Originally part of the monastery founded by the Danish Cistercians who
settled here in the mid-twelfth century at the invitation of a local Pomeranian
prince, the cathedral has seen its fair share of action over the years. First in a
long line of plunderers were the Teutonic Knights, who repeatedly ransacked the
place in the 1240s and 1250s. A fire in the 1350s led to a major Gothic-style overhaul, the structural essence of which remains to this day. The wars of the seventeenth century had a marked impact on Oliwa, the Swedish army carrying off
much of the cathedral's sumptuous collection of furnishings as booty in 1626, the
church bells and main altarpiece included. The second major Swedish assault of
1655–60 eventually led to the Oliwa Peace Treaty (1660), signed in the abbey hall:
the following century brought lavish refurbishment of the building, (notably the
organ, begun in 1755), most of which you can still see today. The Prussian
Partition-era takeover of Gdańsk spelled the end of the fabulously wealthy
abbey's glory days, the monastery finally being officially abolished in 1831.
Unlike most of its surroundings, the cathedral miraculously came through the

end of World War II largely unscathed, though the retreating Nazis torched the abbey complex. Today the complex is a remarkable sight, both the cathedral and the abbey having been thoroughly renovated and restored.

The cathedral complex

Approached from the square in front of the building, the towering main **facade** combines twin Gothic brick towers peaked with Renaissance spires and dazzling white Rococo stuccowork to unusually striking effect. The fine, late seventeenth-century portal brings you into the lofty central **nave**, a dazzlingly exuberant structure topped by a star-spangled vaulted ceiling supported on arched pillars. Past the side chapels filling the two side aisles, the eye is immediately drawn to the **high altar**, a sumptuous Baroque piece from the 1680s containing several pictures from the Gdańsk workshops of the period, including one ascribed to Andreas Schlüter the Younger. Above the altar rises a deliciously over-the-top decorative ensemble, a swirling mass of beatific-looking cherubs being sucked into a heavenly whirlpool, surrounded by angels and with gilded sun rays breaking out in all directions, the whole thing leading towards a central stained glass window.

Apart from some fine Baroque choir stalls and the old Renaissance high altar-piece, now in the northern transept, the building's finest – and most famous – feature is the exuberantly decorated eighteenth-century **organ** which completely fills the back of the nave. In its day the largest instrument in Europe – seven men were needed to operate the bellows – the dark heavy oak of the organ is ornamented with a mass of sumptuous Rococo wood carving, the whole instrument framing a stained glass window of Mary and Child, a mass of supporting angels and cherubs again filling out the picture. It's a beautiful instrument with a rich, sonorous tone and a wealth of moving parts, trumpet-blowing angels included. In summer (May–Sept) there are organ recitals daily at 10am, noon, 1pm, 3pm and 4pm, although more are being added all the time to cope with demand.

Passing through the gateway round the edge of the cathedral brings you into the old **Bishop's Palace complex,** originally the abbey buildings. The stately main palace building now houses a **Modern Art Museum** (Tues–Sat 9am–3pm, Sun 9.30am–3pm). Past the upmarket shop at the entrance flogging "modern art" to the tourists, the ground-floor rooms contain changing graphic exhibitions by local artists. Upstairs is an enjoyable gallery of twentieth-century Polish art, the centrepiece being a large selection of 1960s pop art, artistic "events" and other weird and wonderful sculpted constructions. Several better-known modern artists are represented, most notably Jan Łodiński, as well as a whole room of works by Henryk Staszewski (1894–1988). The palace rooms themselves are pretty grand too, notably the old bishop's dining room, now also used for concerts.

Across the courtyard from the palace the old bishop's granary contains an **Ethnographic Museum** (same opening times), a smallish collection of local exhibits taking you through the district's complicated historical heritage, including a section of Kashubian folk art.

Surrounding the complex is the old **Palace Park,** a pleasant, shaded spot verging on a botanical gardens with an enjoyable collection of exotic trees, hanging willows and a stream meandering through the middle – a pleasant place for an afternoon stroll. Unfortunately the one tree you won't find here is the olive whose branches the Cistercians adopted as their symbol and after which they named the monastery they founded here. Olive motifs do crop up in the cathedral decorations around, however, most notably on the back of the high south window.

If you happen to be here on **All Souls' Day** (November 1), the large **Cemetery** over the road is an amazing sight, illuminated by thousands of candles placed on the gravestones. Whole families come to visit the individual graves and communal memorials to the unknown dead, in a powerful display of remembrance which says much about the intertwining of Catholicism and the collective memory of national sufferings.

Around the cathedral

Another national monument lives just down the road. **Lech Wałęsa**, having vacated the people's paradise of the Młyniec housing estate in the late 1980s, has his home in the wealthier zone west of the rail track.

Like several Polish cities, Gdańsk has a small, low-profile **Tartar** community (see also "Białystok", p.254). They've recently put the finishing touches to a new **mosque** not far from Wałęsa's house; already in use by local Muslims, including the Arab student population, the mosque is at the south end of ul. Polanki, on the corner with ul. Abrahama (nearest station Gdańsk-Zaspa; trams #6, #12 and #15 also run nearby). Further up the same road, the attractive, late eighteenth-century mansion at number 122 is where Arthur **Schopenhauer** (1788–1860), the Danzig-born philosopher, grew up.

Eating, drinking and entertainment

In a city accustomed to tourism, finding a place to eat is relatively straightforward: there's a good range of **cafés and snack bars**, McDonalds and Pizza Hut with an increasing number of local Western **fast-food** lookalikes, as well as some genuinely recommendable **restaurants**. On the down side, heavy demand in summer makes queueing an occasional ordeal, with the best places it's quite common to turn up only to find them reserved for tourist groups. As for local specialities, fish dishes are generally worth sampling, especially now that fears of the effects of local Baltic pollution are diminishing. As throughout Poland, it can be difficult to find a restaurant open after 9pm, except in *Orbis* hotels, which are more adapted to tourist habits.

Drinking in the city centres on a number of bars and cafés on ul. Długa and parallel streets to the north. In summer the attractive terrace cafés of ul. Chlebnicka and Mariacka make the ideal place to sit out and enjoy the sun – and more often than not a decent *espresso*.

Fast food

Baryłka, Długie Pobrzeże 24. Bistro-type hang-out on the main waterfront. Open till 10pm.

Gyros, Pańska 9/11. Vaguely Greek-style fast food – kebabs and the like.

Itaka, ul. Długa 18. One of the first genuine Polish fast-food joints, with hamburgers, fries and all the rest. Poles love it, as much for the novelty of fast (that is, normal) service as anything else.

Mleczny, ul. Długa 33/34. Business as usual in one of the few old-style milk bars in town to survive privatization.

Neptuny, ul. Długa 32. One of the city's classic milk bars – try the specialities of the day.

Uniwersalny, Korzenna 1. Another traditional milk bar: offers basic Polish cuisine at ultra-low prices.

Restaurants

Athena, ul. Długa. Regular-quality Greek restaurant. Good value.

Birland, ul. Chlebnicka 26. Beery former ZOMO (security police) hang-out: basic Polish cuisine plus a casino.

Czardasz, ul. Śląska 66. Wholesome Hungarian food in Oliwa, but watch out for unpredictable early closing times.

La Famiglia, ul. Szeroka 31/32. Solid, Italian-owned and -run restaurant in the Old Town. Good no-nonsense pasta and pizza, also takeaways.

Ha Long, ul. Szeroka 37. One of the better places among the new central Chinese restaurants. Open till 10pm.

Hewelius, ul. Heweliusza 22 (☎31 56 31). If you don't mind paying for it, this *Orbis* hotel restaurant offers dishes you won't find in many other places. The smooth-talking waiters are a bit of a trial, though.

Karczma Michał, ul. Jana Z. Kolna 8. Cosy little place close to the shipyards, where the world's media used to hang out during the strikes. Solid local food produced on the owner's farm outside town.

Kubicki, ul. Wartka 5. Good food in slightly murky maritime-influenced surroundings. Popular with foreign sailors, hence the multilingual menus.

Major, ul. Długa 18. Upmarket new venture on the main city thoroughfare with a line in traditional Gdańsk dishes.

Milano, ul. Chlebnicka 4. Quiet pizzeria in the town centre with a nice line in lasagne. Open till midnight.

Pizza Bella, ul. Pilotów 9a. One of the best of the new pizza joints in town. Open till 10pm.

Pod Basztami, ul. Latamiana 2. Traditional Polish food in historic city buildings.

Pod Łososiem, ul. Szeroka 54 (☎31 7 652). The most luxurious and expensive restaurant in town. Specializes in seafood; also known locally as originator of *Goldwasser* liqueur, a thick yellow concoction with flakes of real gold that's as Prussian as its name suggests.

Pod Wieżą, ul. Piwna 51. A favourite stopoff with tourists trekking round the Old Town, though rather lacking in atmosphere.

Pod Zieloną Bramą, Długi Targ 17/18. Good fish dishes, friendly service. Open till 10pm.

Pod Żurawiem, ul. Warzywnicza 10. Right on the waterfront, this is one of the few places where you can eat outside. Solid Polish food.

Retman, ul. Stągiewna 1 (☎31 92 48). Situated by the waterfront, serving good fish dishes with salmon a speciality. Increasingly oriented towards German tourists, with prices to match. Open till around midnight.

Stara Karczma Gdańska, ul. Sienna 9. Off the beaten track east of the centre, with surprisingly good Lithuanian-influenced cuisine. Closes early.

Tan-Viet, ul. Podmłyńska 1/5. Presentable new Vietnamese restaurant close to the town centre. Open till 10pm. Also takeaway.

Tawerna, ul. Powrźnicza 19–20. Especially good steak and duck – but only serves food till 8.30pm; drinks till about 10pm.

Trakia, Gospody 3. Well north of centre, excellent value Polish food in pleasant surroundings. Open late.

Wielki Shanghai, al. Grunwaldzka 82. Passable new Asian restaurant in Wrzeszcz with Chinese-based menu. Open till 11pm.

Zołty Kur, ul. Długa 4. A decent cheap restaurant in a central location, with Delft tiles for decoration. Chicken specialities.

Cafés

Artus, Długi Targ 1/7. Centrally located, this a prime tourist spot. Open late in summer.

C14, Barbary 3. Avant-garde artists' haunt in dynamic new gallery.

Café de Columbia, ul. Długa 77/78. Passable centre-of-town café-bar (bar closes earlier).

Café Lord, ul. Gen. Hallera 241. Café-bar, the Tri-City's most popular local gay and lesbian haunt. Discos (gay and lesbian) Wed, Fri and Sat.

Istra, ul. Piwna 64/65. Pleasant, French-style café in useful location, the disadvantage being its early closing hours.

LOT, Wały Jagiellońskie 2/4. Airline café that serves a decent cup of coffee in upmarket surroundings, adorned with paintings by art students.

Marysieńka, ul. Szeroka 37/39. Enjoyable Old Town café.

Nad Motławą, Długie Pobrzeże 5. Waterfront café – a good place to sit out in summer.

Palowa, ul. Długa 47, underneath the Town Hall. An ideal rendezvous point which often has a good selection of cakes too. Service is what Poles would call "relaxed".

Pod Holendrem, ul. Mariacka 37/39. Terrace café with good local cakes and pastries.

Pod Zagłobą, Pod Staromiejskie 62. Popular Old Town bar, stays open a bit later than many.

Rudy Kot, ul. Gamcarska 18/20. Out-of-centre haunt popular with local student crowd.

Trops, ul. Czyżewskiego 29. Café with live music, with lots going on, especially at weekends.

Bars and clubs

Alex, ul. Grunwaldzka 87/91. Trendy night-club/restaurant in the Wrzeszcz district.

Architects' Club, just off Targ Węglowy. A great spot. Talk your way in with a Polish friend and soak up an excellent atmosphere with the architecture students.

Big Johnny, Targ Rybny. Raunchy newcomer to the city pub scene. Also serves food.

Coton Club, Złotników 25/29. Fashionable bar/nightclub frequented by local Solidarity politicians and Gdańsk yuppies. Irish music a couple of nights a week.

Flisak, ul. Chlebnicka 9/10. Smoky dive for serious drinkers only. Open till 2am.

GTPS Artists' Bar, ul. Piwna. Late-night hang-out of arty types..

Klub Aktora, ul. Mariacka 1/3. Quiet, relaxed Western-style bar – too expensive for the vodka-swillers, so there's no hassle from local drunks. Also serves food.

Pierot, Węglarska 5. Basic beer-drinkers' haunt in the town centre. Closes early.

Punkt, ul. Chlebnicka 2. Pub-type joint aimed at locals as much as tourists. Open till 1pm.

Staromiejska, Korzenna 33/35. Cellar wine bar with a good line in beef *stroganoff*. Open till 10pm.

U Szkota, ul. Chlebnicka 10. Popular, enjoyable Scottish-theme bar, small and often difficult to get a table – but you can normally sit at the bar downstairs.

Unnamed club, Wały Piastowskie. Open every evening with some live bands (rock, jazz) and a rousing disco at weekends.

Vinifera, Wodopój 7. A nice canal-side bar-cum-café in a doll-size house, with seats outside. A good place to relax in the city; open till midnight.

Yellow Jazz Club. A boat moored off Targ Rybny in the summer months, with live jazz and a good bar.

Żak, ul. Wały Jagiellońskie. Best of a lively bunch of student clubs, just down from the main station. Live bands (rock and jazz), art film club, and plenty more going on. The building was formerly the seat of the interwar League of Nations' High Commissioner.

Entertainment

The National Philharmonic and Opera House, al. Zwycięstwa 15 (nearest station Gdańsk Politechnika) is one of the best **classical venues** in the country, with a varied programme of classical performances and occasional ballet productions. Information and ticket reservations from the box office (41 05 63). The *Wybrzeże* theatre, ul. Św. Ducha 2, just behind the Armoury, is the main city-centre **theatre**.

In a recessionary economic climate, the *Żak* club (see "Bars and clubs", above) is about the only place seriously geared towards **youth culture**. *Café C14* (see "Cafés", opposite) has musical and literary events one or two evenings a week.

Check listings section in the regional edition of *Gazeta Wyborcza* for a comprehensive guide to what's going on each week.

The Tri-City boasts a variety of **festivals** and other major cultural get-togethers. The Dominican Fair (Jarmark Dominikański) held annually in the first three weeks of August is an important local event, with artistes and craftspeople setting up shop in the centre of town, accompanied by street theatre and a wealth of other cultural events. St Nicola's Fair (Jarmark Mikołaja) in the first three weeks of December is a pre-Christmas variation on the same theme. Musically there's the annual international Chamber Music Festival timed to coincide with the Dominican Fair, an International Choral Festival, held in the Town Hall (June–Aug) and the Festival of Organ Music in Oliwa Cathedral during July and August. For film buffs, the Gdańsk Film Festival takes place in late September. Alongside the regular festivals, there's an increasing number of lively one-offs. Earmarked as the city's **millennium year, 1997** promises to yield a bumper crop of cultural festivals and events – watch listings and promotional literature for details.

Listings

Airline offices *LOT*, ul. Wały Jagiellońskie 2/4 (☎31 28 21 or 31 11 61).

Airport information ☎41 51 10, 41 51 62 or 41 51 31. Reservations ☎41 52 51 or 41 23 35.

American Express Located in the *Orbis* office, *Hewelius* hotel, ul. Heweliusza 22 (Mon–Fri 10am–5pm, Sat 10am–2pm; ☎31 44 25).

Banks *Narodowy Bank Polski*, Okopowa 1, *Bank Gdański*, Targ Drzewny 1 and Długi Targ 14/16 for international transactions. *Kantor* shops are fine for regular foreign exchange.

Billiards In Gdańsk as elsewhere the latest craze to hit the country. If you fancy a frame or two of *bilardy* the *Klub Bilardy*, ul. Wajdeloty 12/13 in the town centre, is currently the most popular haunt. Open till midnight.

Car rental At the *Hevelius* hotel (☎31 40 45) and at the airport.

Car repairs Repairs: ul. Dąbrowszczaków 14 (☎53 16 52), al. Grunwaldzka 339 (☎52 28 12). Breakdown service: in Gdańsk, Kartuska 187 (☎32 35 55) & al. Hallera (☎41 16 93); in Sopot, ul. 3 Maja 51 (☎51 80 30); in Gdynia, ul. Olsztyńska 35 (☎20 25 41) & ul. 3 Maja 20 (☎21 05 22). Emergency assistance: in Gdańsk (☎56 64 98 or 52 29 87 24hr); in Gydnia (☎21 63 71 24hr).

Children There are a number of worthwhile diversions and entertainments for kids in town. The open-air *Cricoland* amusement park just north of the main train station has all the usual fairground attractions: stalls, roller-coasters, ghost trains, and a hall of mirrors. You pay for the rides with tokens. Open all year. The *Lazurkowa* centre in Gdynia has a children's paddling pool, with open-air terraces surrounding it for parents to keep an eye on things from. The *Miniatura* puppet theatre, ul. Grunwaldzka 16 (☎41 23 86), is excellent: performances every Saturday and Sunday with weekday morning performances for schools. Buy tickets one hour in advance. Nice theatre interior, and children love the performances. Cinemas often have matinees. Check the local paper for details of performances. Finally there's the zoo in Oliwa at Karwińska 3, set in enjoyably forested, hilly surroundings.

Cinemas The latest Western – in particular US – movies make their way to Gdańsk pretty speedily. The main centre-of-town cinema complex is at ul. Długa 57. The *Żak* cinema club, ul. Wały Jagiełłońskie, is art-oriented.

Consulates *Belgium*, ul. Świętojańska 32 (☎20 15 61); *Finland*, Grunwaldzka 132a (☎41 60 90); *France*, Waty Piastowskie 1 (☎31 44 44); *Germany*, al Zwycięstwa 23 (☎41 43 66); *Italy*, ul. Świętojańska 32 (☎20 15 61); *Netherlands*, Wały Jagiellońskie 36 (☎46 63 52); *Sweden*, *Norway* & *Denmark*, ul. Jana z Kolna 25 (☎21 62 16); UK ☎46 15 58. No US consulate – the embassy in Warsaw is the nearest.

Ferry tickets ul. Wartka 4: ☎31 49 26. Information: ☎31 72 31; advance booking: ☎31 19 75; in Sopot, ☎51 12 93, in Gdynia, ☎20 26 42. International ferries depart for Travemunde (Germany), Ystad and Oxelösund (Sweden) and Helsinki from Nowy Port, opposite Westerplatte, see p.170. *PolFerries* tickets can be booked through *Orbis* or the ferry office at ul. Świętojańska 132 (☎43 18 87).

Football The aptly named Lechia Gdańsk are a solid First Division side – despite a purple and white strip that makes Aston Villa's outfit look like an Armani job. They play at the BKS Lechia stadium on ul. Traugutta; nearest station is Gdańsk-Politechnika.

Fuel stations The following are open 24hr a day: in Gdańsk, ul. Dąbrowskiego 4 & ul. Elbląską; in Oliwa, ul. Grunwaldzka & ul. Dąbrowszczaków; in Sopot, ul. 3 Maja 51; in Gdynia, ul. ślaską and ul. Chylońska. New stations are opening up all the time, so you shouldn't have trouble finding somewhere to fill up.

Galleries Of the wealth of galleries in the city many are fairly upmarket places with Western tourists very much in mind. The local art scene is pretty lively too – alongside Kraków the Tri-City is one of the main student art centres. A couple of the more interesting galleries in town are *Malarze Kobiet*, ul. Św. Barbary 3/4, a women's art centre with regular artistic happenings; *Gdańska Galeria Fotografii*, ul. Grobla 11; *ZPAP*, Długi Targ 35/38; and *FOS*, ul. Długie Pobrzeże 29.

Gays and lesbians Local contact: *Lambda Gdańsk*, PO Box 265, 81-806 Sopot 6. Also *Café Lord* (see "Cafés", p.175).

Hospitals Wrzeszcz, al. Zwycięstwa 49 (☎41 10 00 or 32 29 29); Zaspa, al. Jan Pawła 11 50 (☎56 45 15).

Medical assistance Ul. Podbielanska 17 (Mon–Fri 7am–5pm; ☎31 51 68); 24-hour emergency facilities and English spoken at al. Zwycięstwa 49 (☎32 39 29 or 32 39 24).

Newspapers Dailies *Głos Wybrzeże* and *Gazeta Wyborcza* both give detailed listings for local events and a host of other useful local information, as does the Friday edition of *Dziennik Bałtycki*.

Parking (guarded) Jaśkowa Dolina 101, Pilotów 18, pl. Gorkiego 1 and Startowa 23 plus all the *Orbis* hotels.

Pharmacy In Main Town: Długa 54/56, Chmielna 47/52 and Grobla III 1/6. There are always a few all-night chemists on duty on a rotating basis; check local papers for details.

Police City headquarters, ul. Okopowa 15 (☎31 62 21).

Post office Main office (for *poste restante*) is at ul. Długa 22; open 24hr for telephones, 8am–8pm for postal business.

Radio The local Radio Gdańsk (67.85FM) is a decent-quality FM station with an emphasis on rock music and phone-ins.

Radio taxi ☎9192 or 31 49 49, ☎31 55 17 or *Tele-Taxi* ☎20 25 00; in Sopot ☎51 12 13; in Gdynia ☎20 50 72.

Shopping The *Hala Targowa* on ul. Pańska has vegetables and fresh chickens outside, loads of small stalls inside, selling anything from caviar to condoms – price often negotiable. There's a good **bookstore** in the shopping arcade on ul. Heveliusza opposite the *Hewelius*. **Ul. Mariacka**, east from St Mary's, is a lovely shopping street that somehow retains its peaceful atmosphere even at the height of the summer tourist onslaught. The street-level shops sell jewellery, amber products (the city's most popular souvenirs) and quality leather at Western prices. *Danziger Bowke*, Długie Pobrzeże 21, is a newly acquired city curiosity, a shop specializing in *alt Danzig* memorabilia and aimed squarely at the older generation of German tourists.

Sports equipment Sailing boats and canoes for rent from *MOSiR*, ul. Ogarna 29.

Swimming pools Indoor pools at the *Marina* and *Poseidon* hotels; in Sopot, ul. Haffnera 55; and in the *Gydnia Hotel* in Gdynia.

Tennis courts At the Hotel *Marina*, ul. Wiejska 1 and ul. Ks. Sychty 23. In Sopot, *Sopocki Klub Tenisowy*, ul. Ceynowy 5/7; in Gdynia, *Klub Arka*, ul. Ejsmonda 1.

Train tickets International rail tickets from the *PKS* office (☎32 15 32), *Orbis* and from main stations in Gdańsk and Gdynia.

Sopot

One-time stamping ground for the rich and famous, who came from all over the world to sample the casinos and the high life in the 1920s and 1930s, **SOPOT** is still a beach resort popular with landlocked Poles, and is increasingly attractive to Westerners – Germans and Swedes in particular. It has an altogether different atmosphere from its neighbour: the fashionable clothes shops and bars scattered round ul. Bohaterów Monte Cassino – the main avenue down to the pier – seem light years away from both historic central Gdańsk and the industrial grimness of the shipyards. If you're tired of tramping the streets of Gdańsk, Sopot's an excellent place for a seaside change of air.

The **pier**, constructed in 1928 but later rebuilt, is the longest in the whole Baltic area. Long sandy beaches stretch away on both sides; on the northern section you'll find ranks of bathing huts, some with marvellous 1920s wicker beach chairs for rent. For years, the levels of untreated filth pouring into the Gdańsk Bay from the Wisła meant the beaches here were considered a no-go zone. Considerable efforts have gone into cleaning up the area in recent years, however, including reducing pollution emissions at source. As a result, for the first time in 1995, a number of Sopot beaches were officially declared safe for swimming. In summer, the beaches are now tested daily for toxic levels – anything close to dangerous and they are closed. Further north from the pier, there's a beach restaurant, a sauna and, right at the end, some very cheap tennis courts.

Upper Sopot, as the western part of town is known, is a wealthy suburb of entrepreneurs, architects and artists. Here and in other residential areas of Sopot, many of the houses have a touch of Art Nouveau style to them – look out for the turrets built for sunrise viewing. The **park** in upper Sopot offers lovely walks in the wooded hills around Łysa Góra, where there's a ski track in winter.

> The **telephone code** for the Tri-City is ☎ 058

Practicalities

The simplest way to get to Sopot is by commuter **train** from Gdańsk, a twenty-minute journey. Other options are the ferry service from Gdańsk or city bus (see p.156). The **tourist office**, which can help with accommodation is at ul. Dworcowa 3 (daily 10am–6pm; ☎51 26 17) opposite the train station. For an alternative source of information, including travel details and tickets, the **Orbis** office at ul. Boh. Monte Cassino 49 (daily 10am–5pm; ☎51 41 42) is your best bet.

Accommodation

Sopot's holiday popularity means that rooms can be scarce, and during July and August, prices are often considerably increased. As well as the places listed below, there are several seasonal hostels and hotels, details of which are given out by the tourist office. Private rooms are a plausible alternative which the tourist office can also help you with, although you're more than likely to be offered something if you stand around outside long enough. In addition, a number of former state workers' holiday hotels are in line for privatization – the tourist office will have the latest details. **Campers** have two options, both reasonable: the *PTTK* site at Kamienica Potok (train to Kamienny Potok) next to the *Miramar*, and *Sopot Camping*, close to the beach at Bitwy Pod Plowcami 79, about a kilometre south from the pier (June–Aug).

The best of the **hotels** is the *Grand Hotel*, near the sea on ul. Powstańców Warszawy (☎51 00 41; ⑦), which for once more than lives up to its name. Built in the 1920s in regal period style, the *Grand* was a favourite with President de Gaulle, Giscard d'Estaing and the Shah of Iran, and after a long interval it has recently reopened its casino. Tarted up to suit the demands of an increasingly prominent local *nouveau riche* clientele, it retains some of its former magnificence, with huge old rooms making this an enjoyable indulgence. Of the other options, the *Miramar*, ul. Zamkowa Góra 21/25 (☎51 80 11; ⑤), well north of the town centre near Kamieny Potok station, is cheaper but usually full in summer; unfortunately the same generally goes for the nearby *Pensjonat Maryła*, ul. Sepia 22 (☎51 00 34; ④), the better-quality *Hotel Sopot*, ul. Haffnera 81 (☎51 32 95; ④) and the *Plagnolia* in the same street at no. 100 (☎51 32 96; ③). The *Irena*, ul. Chopina 36 (☎51 20 73; ④), is a large, reasonably priced and well kept *pensjonat* a short way down the hill from Sopot station. A cheap option is the *Jeżdziecki*, ul. Polna 1 (☎51 20 11; ②), a basic, old state holiday hotel.

Eating and drinking

The *Grand Hotel* **restaurant** is a treat, serving excellent salmon, trout and smoked eel; the hotel café is great for afternoon coffee – and men shouldn't miss the luxurious old *pissoirs*. The *Pod Strechą*, further up the promenade at ul. Bohaterów Monte Cassino 42, is a trendy eating place, while the *Albatros*, opposite the station at pl. Konstytutcji 3 Maja 2, is more down-to-earth. Further up ul. Monte Cassino the trendy haunts continue, notably *Złoty Ul* at no. 37, with some nice, recently rediscovered Art Deco interior decoration; the *Teatralna*, at no. 50; and, chicest of the lot, *Bazaar* at no. 5, at the far end of the street, a designer café-restaurant favoured by youthful arty types – occasional live bands too. The *Saj-Gon*, Grunwaldzka 8, is a popular Vietnamese restaurant, while the self-consciously old-fashioned *Staropolska*, ul. 3 Maja 7, emphasizes traditional Polish cuisine. Up in the hills of west Sopot, the old *Parkowy* motel restaurant (the motel part has now disappeared) is a quiet, relaxing spot. Also out of the way but worthwhile, is the *Belfer*, ul. Kościuszki 64, a popular bar serving down-to-earth traditional food.

In summer especially, the **pier area** is full of bars, coffee shops and pleasant old milk bars, with Western-style fast-food joints making noticeable inroads of late. The *Fantom* near the pier entrance is the **café** from which to watch the promenaders and skateborders. On ul. Haffnera, just off the promenade, the *Miramar* has lousy service but great cakes, which you may be forced to buy in absurdly large portions. *Spatif*, the artists' club upstairs at no. 54 on the promenade, has an eccentrically decadent cabaret tradition – look artistic to get in. The *Rotunda*, overlooking the pier and with good views across the bay, is another popular artists' club, frequented by just about everyone except artists.

The lower part of the promenade is the place to be seen in Sopot: the *Niki* and *Alga* **clubs**, near the pier, are popular evening hang-outs, especially with Arab students and Syrians from Berlin. Billiards fans should head for the *Snooker Pub* ul. Wejherowska 35 – open till 3am.

Entertainment

The open-air **Opera Leśna**, in the peaceful hilly park in the west of Sopot, hosts large-scale productions including an **International Song Festival** in August which includes big names from the Western rock scene alongside homegrown performers; local hotels are filled to bursting point during the days it's on. For tickets and current details of what's on, check with the *Orbis* office. The "Friends of Sopot" hold **chamber music** concerts every Thursday at ul. Czyzewskiego 12 (off al. Bohaterów), in a room where Chopin is said to have played.

The *Sopot* hotel has a **swimming pool** and good **tennis courts** – Davis Cup matches are sometimes played here. In upper Sopot there's a racecourse hosting showjumping and horse races every June.

Gdynia

Half an hour's train journey from central Gdańsk (trains every 5–10min), **GDYNIA** is the northernmost section of the Tri-City. Originally a small Kashubian village, it was the property of the Cistercian monks of Oliwa from the fourteenth to the eighteenth centuries. Boom time came after World War I, when Gdynia, unlike Gdańsk, returned to Polish jurisdiction. The limited coastline ceded to the new Poland – a thirty-two-kilometre strip of land stretching north from Gdynia and know as the "Polish Corridor" – left the country strapped for coastal outlets, so the Polish authorities embarked on a massive port-building programme, which by the mid-1930s had transformed Gdynia from a small village into a bustling harbour, which by 1937 boasted the largest volume of naval traffic in the Baltic region. The injustice of the Corridor's existence provided Hitler with one of his major propaganda themes, and following Gdynia's capture in 1939, the Germans deported most of the Polish population, established a naval base and, to add insult to injury, renamed the town Gotenhafen. Their retreat in 1945 was accompanied by wholesale destruction of the harbour installations, which were subsequently rebuilt from scratch by the postwar authorities. The endearingly run-down, almost seedy atmosphere of today's port makes an interesting contrast to the more cultured Gdańsk. Into the 1990s, Gdynia has undergone something of a transformation too: rapid privatization of state-owned shops – thanks to Gdynia's historical position within Polish territory a much easier business than in the old Free City, where establishing retroactive property rights is proving a tricky business – has given centre-of-town shopping streets like ul. Starowiejska a brash facelift, helping to develop Gdynia's position at the forefront of the country's burgeoning economic transformation and development.

Betraying its 1930s origins, sections of the city centre are pure Bauhaus, with curved balconies and huge window fronts, many now on the receiving end of a much-needed facelift: the contrast with the faceless postwar concrete jungle that envelops much of the rest of the centre couldn't be more striking. The place to head for is the **port area**, directly east across town from the main station. From the station walk down bustling ul. Starowiejska past the *Lark* hotel and fountains and you'll find yourself at the foot of the large southern-most **pier**. Moored on its northern side is the *Błyskawica*, a World War II destroyer now a miniature **Maritime Museum** (May–Sept Tues–Sun 10am–4pm though subject to sudden unexplained closures); the sailors manning the ship are quick to point out to British visitors the decktop plaque commemorating the vessel's year-long wartime sojourn in Cowes on the Isle of Wight, where it helped to defend the port against a major German attack in May 1942. Often anchored in the yacht basin beyond the ferry embarkation point is another proudly Polish vessel, the three-masted frigate *Dar Pomorża*, built in

Hamburg in 1909 and now a training ship; guided tours are given when it's in dock (Tues–Sun 10am–4pm). At the very end of the pier, a hamfisted monument to Polish seafarer and novelist Joseph Conrad stands near the **aquarium**, home to piranhas, barracudas and sharks. A walk along the north side of the pier takes you past the welter of yachts kept here by the growing number of seriously wealthy Poles.

If you want more local maritime history, the **Naval Museum** on Bulwar Nadmorski, south of the pier (Tues–Sun 10am–4pm), fills in the details of Polish seafaring from early Slav times to World War II, though its value to foreigners is limited by the minimal, Polish-only captioning. To complete the tour there's a nice view over the harbour from the hilltop of Kamienna Góra, a short walk south of the town centre.

Information and accommodation

Gdynia's **tourist information office** (Mon–Fri 9am–6pm, Sat & Sun 9am–4pm; ☎28 53 78) is located in the main station. The town has a reasonable range of **hotels**, headed by the *Gdynia*, ul. Armii Krajowej 22 (☎20 66 61; ⑦), a flashy modern *Orbis* joint for the rich sailing contingent who hang out here in the summer. The rooms are nothing much to talk about, and prices are the same as *Orbis* hotels in Gdańsk. The *Lark* (☎21 80 46; ③), on ul. Starowiejska in the town centre, is a sensibly priced alternative. Other options are the reasonably upmarket *Bałtyk*, ul. Kielecka 2a (☎21 06 49; ④); the cheaper *Antracyt*, ul. Korzenowskiego 19d (☎20 68 11; ③); the *Dom Rybacka*, ul. Jana Z Kolna 27 (☎20 87 23; ②); *Dom Marynarza*, ul. Piłsudskiego 1 (☎22 00 25; ③); and the *Garnizonowy*, ul. Jana Z Kolna 6 (☎26 64 72; ③).

Private rooms are organized by the *biuro zakwaterowań* at ul. Starowiejska 47 (daily 8am–6pm; ☎21 82 65). The main **youth hostel**, open all year, is at ul. Morska 108C (☎27 00 05); take the local train to Gdynia-Grabowek, or bus #109, #125, #141, or tram #22, #25, #26 or #30. There's also a summer **hostel** at ul. Wiczlińska 93. South Gdynia has two **campsites**: at ul. Świętopełka 19/23 right by the sea, and at Spacerowa 7; for both, take the train to Gdynia-Orłowo station.

Eating and drinking

The *Gdynia* has a restaurant considered by some to be one of the best in the region; fine if you like an expensive Westernized menu and can put up with the jet set. The *George* pizza joint at ul. 3 Maja 21, *Ermitage* at Świętojańska 39, *Mysliwśka* at ul. Abrahama 18 and *Róza Wiatrow*, ul. Zjednoczenia 2 on the pier, are all better priced and more Polish alternatives. Two Asian places worth checking out are the Chinese *Chiński Mur*, ul. Dworcowa, and the Vietnamese *Song Lam*, ul. Zgoda 10, while *La Gondala* at ul. Portowa 8 is a good but pricey Italian restaurant.

The *Lark* hotel has a restaurant and adjoining beer bar serving the enjoyable *Elbląg* special brew that's a popular spot with the locals. There's also a host of assorted milk bars and cafés dotted around the town centre. For a coffee break, the *Ambrozja*, at ul. Starowiejska 14, has a good selection of *sernik* and other home-baked cakes, while the *Checz Kaszubska* further down at no. 32 offers local Kashubian specialities.

Entertainment

The **Musical Theatre** (*Teatr Muszyczny*), pl. Grunwaldzki 1, near the Gdynia hotel, is a favourite venue with Poles and tourists alike, featuring quality Polish musicals, as well as all-too-frequent productions of the Andrew Lloyd Webber oeuvre. Tickets (hard to find in the summer season) are available from the box office (☎21 60 24 or 21 60 25) or the *Orbis* bureau in the *Gdynia*. Emphasizing the naval connection there's also an annual Sea Shanty Festival held here in August.

The new money coming into town has brought a splash of **nightclubs** in its wake: obvious places like the *Gdynia* aside, enthusiasts of ritzy Polish nightlife can check out the *Bodega*, Chylońska 341, the *Ermitage*, Swiętojańska 39, *Mayor*, ul. Mickiewicza 3 or *Vega*, Sędzkiego 19, all open to the small hours at weekends.

The Hel Peninsula

If the prospect of escaping from the rigours of the city appeals, head for the **Hel Peninsula**, a long thin strip of land sticking out into the Baltic Sea 20km above Gdańsk. As in several places along the Polish section of the Baltic coast, the peninsula was formed over the centuries by the combined action of current and wind. The sandy beaches dotted along the north side of the peninsula are well away from the poisonous Wisła outlet, making the water around here as clean as you'll get on the Baltic coast; what's more, they are easily accessible and, away from the main resorts, never overcrowded, providing one of the Tri-City's increasing number of holiday spots popular with foreigners.

> The **telephone code** for the Tri-City is ☎ 058

Hel

HEL, the small fishing port at the tip of the peninsula, is the main destination and a day-trippers' favourite. It's an enjoyable two-and-a-half-hour trip from Gdańsk in an open boat from the Motława waterfront (first departure 8am in summer), giving you the chance to see the shipyard complex on the way out to sea. Boats also run from Sopot pier and Gdynia – check with the tourist office for current details. The train from Gdynia is the fastest route, with trains and more frequent buses also running from Gdańsk (2hr).

Despite heavy fighting – a German army of 100,000 men was rounded up on the peninsula in 1945 – the main street retains some nineteenth-century wooden fishermen's cottages. For the locals the main attraction seems to be the bar/restaurants on ul. Wiejske, several of which serve strong draught beer in apparently limitless quantities.

Hel's **Maritime Museum** (Tues–Sun 9am–4pm), housed in the village's Gothic former church, has plenty of model ships and fishing tackle as well as some local folk art. As on the adjoining mainland, the people of the peninsula are predominantly Kashubian, as evidenced in the local dialect and the distinctive embroidery styles on show in the museum.

The only **tourist office** in town, the *PTTK* at ul. Wiejska 78 (Mon–Fri 10am–2pm), can help you find private accommodation if you decide to make a night of it. The village's only **hotel** is the presentable *Hel Riviera* at the far end of ul. Wiejska (☎75 05 28; ④). For a bite **to eat**, the choice is widening. You'll find a number of snack bars on ul. Wiejska, with the most substantial place being *U Macka* at no. 82.

The rest of the peninsula and beyond

If you're not in a hurry to get back to town, you could take one of the regular trains along the wooded, sandy shoreline for an afternoon swim; the really energetic could do the thirty kilometres of the peninsula in a solid day's walking, beach stops included. Whichever way you do it, two worthwhile stopping-off places are the small harbour at **JASTARNIA**, a few kilometres to the west of Hel with a large lighthouse nearby, and **KUŹNICA**, a short way further still.

Jastarnia has two decent **hotels**, the upmarket *Jurata* (☎75 23 29; ⑤) and the *Jastarnia* (☎75 21 83; ③), as well as a number of *pensjonat* – notably the *Albin*, ul. Mickiewicza 54 (③), and *U Franka*, ul. Stelmaszczyka 6 (☎75 52 55; ④)– as well as a **PTTK hostel** at ul. Baltycka 5, a campsite and one or two basic eating places. Kuźnica, like nearby Chalupy, is basically a good beach with camping space nearby, the latter with a reasonable *pensjonat*, the *Polaris* (☎74 16 47; ③).

The peninsula joins the mainland at **WŁADYSŁAWOWO**, a small but busy fishing port. The old fish hall, the **Dom Rybacka**, has a restaurant on the second floor where the local fish dishes are excellent, but some customers might be deterred by the pollution hazards. For local **information** try the tourist office at Gen. Hallera, just up from the hall. **Accommodation** options include the hotel on the upper floor of the Dom Rybacka itself (☎74 00 66; ③), and a range of *pensjonat* including the *Janina*, ul. Żwirowa 9 (☎74 12 46; ③), *Kesztel*, ul. Żeromskiego 48 (☎74 03 76; ③), *Agnieszka*, ul. Rybacka 10 (☎74 05 12; ④), *U Alków*, ul. Manoperli (☎74 02 56; ③) the summer-only *Altona*, ul. Młyńska 36 (☎74 03 21; ③), and the *Perełka*, al. Zeromskiego 1 (☎74 07 91; ④), open all year. There's also a summer **campsite** on ul. Helska. Regular local trains run from here to Gdynia and Gdańsk, taking between an hour and ninety minutes.

A ten-kilometre bus journey further along the coast is **JASTRZĘBIA GÓRA**, a popular holiday resort, once the playground of the interwar Polish elite, Józef Piłsudski included. The buildings are perched somewhat precariously on a cliff, suffering from severe erosion by storm waves, but there's a quaint 1930s air to it and some good nearby beaches. Wholesale privatization in what used to be one of the main workers' holiday resorts on the Polish Baltic coast has left the place with a fair selection of nicely situated seaside accommodation. The local tourist industry knows it's on to a good thing, and you're as likely to find yourself rubbing shoulders on the beach with British tour groups as Polish holidaymakers, many of whom can no longer afford to come here.

The **tourist office** at ul. Królewska 5, the western part of the main drag through town, has all the local details. Of a wealth of **accommodation** options the *Europa* hotel, ul. Topolowa 9 (☎74 95 52; ⑤), is the swankiest, while the *Pod Zagłem*, on ul. Rozewska (☎74 91 53; ④) in the resort centre, is a passable enough motel. *Pensjonat* include the *Leśna Perła*, ul. Leśna 2 (☎74 97 18; ④), the *Atlantyda*, ul. Zygmunt 111 Waza 9 (☎74 96 29; ③), the *Astore*, ul. Wesoła 10 (☎74 90 92; ④), the *Gwarek*, ul. Jantarowa 3 (☎74 90 13; ④) – one of the few open all year round – and the *Barbara*, ul. Topolowa 22 (☎74 92 63; ④). The nearest **campsite** is at Lisi Jar, just east of the main resort. Hotels and boarding houses aside, the *Faleza*, ul. Klifowa 5, in Lisi Jar is about the best **restaurant** around.

Kashubia

The large area of lakes and hills to the west of Gdańsk – **Kashubia** – is the homeland of one of Poland's lesser-known ethnic minorities, the **Kashubians**. "Not German enough for the Germans, nor Polish enough for the Poles" – Grandma Koljiaczek's wry observation in *The Tin Drum* – sums up the historic predicament of this group.

Originally a western Slav people linked ethnically to Poles, and historically spared the ravages of invasion and war, thanks to their relative geographical isolation, the Kashubians were subjected to a German cultural onslaught during the Partition period, when the area was incorporated into Prussia. The process was resisted fiercely: in the 1910 regional census, only six out of the 455 inhabitants of one typical village gave their nationality as German, a pattern of resistance continued during World War II.

However, the Kashubians' treatment by the Poles has not always been better, and it's often argued that Gdańsk's domination of the region has kept the development of a Kashubian national identity in check. Certainly the local museums are sometimes guilty of consigning the Kashubians to the realm of quaint historical phenomena, denying the reality of what is still a living culture. You can hear the distinctive Kashubian language (supposedly derived from the original Pomeranian tongue) spoken all over the region, particularly by older people, and many villages still produce such Kashubian handicrafts as embroidered cloths and tapestries.

Żukowo and Kartuzy

The old capital of the region, Kartuzy, is tucked away among the lakes and woods 30km west of Gdańsk. From the main Gdańsk station a bus climbs up through ŻUKOWO, the first Kashubian village. The fourteenth-century **Norbertine Church and Convent** here has a rich Baroque interior and organ, resembling a country version of St Nicholas in Gdańsk. The arrangement of buildings – church, convent, vicarage and adjoining barns – has a distinctly feudal feel. Leaving Żukowo, on the Kartuzy road, gourmets should keep an eye out for the excellent Swiss **restaurant** signposted off to the right.

Though it can be reached in just an hour, the dusty, rather run-down market town of **KARTUZY** feels a long way from Gdańsk. The **Kashubian Regional Museum** at ul. Ludowa Polskiego 1 (March–Sept Tues–Fri 8am–4pm, Sat 8am–3pm, Sun 10am–2pm; Oct–April closed Sun) will introduce you to some of the intricacies of Kashubian domestic, cultural and religious traditions. Highlight of the curator's guided tour is his performance of a Kashubian folk song complete with dramatic accompaniment – introducing the musical and theatrical delights of such instruments as the *bazuna*, *burchybas* and *skrzypce diabelskie*. The Gothic **Church**, part of a group of buildings erected in 1380 on the northern edge of town by Carthusian monks from Bohemia, is a sombre sort of place. The building itself is coffin-shaped – the original monks actually used to sleep in coffins – while the pendulum of the church clock hanging below the organ sports a skull-like angel swinging the Grim Reaper's scythe and bears the cheery inscription "Each passing second brings you closer to death". Apart from the church, nothing much remains of the original monastery. More appealing are the paths leading through the beech groves which surround nearby **Lake Klasztorne**, a nice place to cool off on a hot summer's day.

If you decide to make a night of it, you can try either the *Rugan*, ul. 3 Maja 39 (☎81 16 35; ③), or find out about **private rooms** by asking at the **tourist office** at ul. Dworcowa 4/8 (☎81 18 19). Otherwise, there's the summer **youth hostel** at ul. Piłsudskiego 10. With the exception of a few *kawiarnia*, the only **restaurants** in Kartuzy worth mentioning are at the *Rugan* hotel and the *Kaszubska* at ul. Parkowa 4, but you shouldn't expect too much. The only alternatives are a couple of snack bars around the station area.

The strawberry festival

In the postwar years, Kashubia has gathered some wealth through the development of strawberry production: if you want to sample the crop, the June **strawberry festival** held on a hill 2km out of Kartuzy (anyone will direct you) provides an ideal opportunity. The occasion is part market, part fair – a little like a German *Jahrmarkt* – with the local farmers bringing baskets of strawberries to the church at nearby Wygoda.

Around Kashubia

Behind Kartuzy the heartland of Kashubia opens out into a high plateau of **lakes**, low hills and tranquil woodland dotted with villages and the occasional small town. Running round the whole area is the **Ostrzydkie Circle**, an Ice Age hill formation that has a winter ski slope at **Wieżyca**, some 10km south of Kartuzy on the road to Kościerzyna. Being an intensely religious region, Kashubia is especially worth visiting during any of the major **Catholic festivals** – Corpus Christi for example, or Marian festivals such as the Dormition of the Virgin (August 15).

Buses and a couple of local **train lines** service the region, but a car is a definite bonus. In summer, bus excursions are usually on offer from Gdańsk to Wdzydze Kiszewski and elsewhere; ask at *Orbis* or the Gdańsk tourist offices for details of current offers.

Round the Ostrzydkie Circle

With its rolling hills and quiet backwater villages the **Ostrzydkie Circle** – known locally as "Kashubian Switzerland" – makes a good introduction to the region. Alpine hyperbole aside, there's undeniably a special charm to the area, the tranquil lakes, green meadows and thickly wooded slopes providing an ideal holiday spot, a fact evidenced in the welter of old workers' resorts scattered around the bigger lakes within the Circle. If you've got your own transport it's worth considering doing the round trip. Travelling from Kartuzy you approach the Circle from Brodnica Górna, from where the road begins the climb upwards. Instead of heading directly west, however, it's better to take the longer route south via **WIEŻYCA**, where you can find a 320-metre-high winter ski slope (the uppermost point in the region) complete with ski-lift.

Predictably the ski slope has generated something of a mini winter tourist centre: a good place to **stay** is the nearby *Jezorianka* (☎84 17 83; ④) at the edge of Lake Patulskie, although the best views are from the *Hubertówka* (☎8438; ③), a holiday hotel signposted off the road high up overlooking the lake. If these are full, there are plenty of other *pensjonat* and privatized workers' holiday centres to choose from in and around Wieżyca. New places are springing up all the time round here, so watch roadside signs for details.

Continuing south from Wieżyca there's a beautiful drive round the lake through some wonderful hilly countryside, a sort of mini Polish version of the Lake District without the in-season crowds.

Chmielno and Sierakowice

Of several holiday centres around the area, **CHMIELNO**, at the western edge of the **Ostrzydkie Circle**, is the most idyllic. Set in tranquil, beautiful surroundings overlooking the shores of Lake Kłodno, the waterside nearest the village is dotted with workers' rest centres, many of them looking a little derelict these days. Despite the village's holidaytime popularity, you shouldn't have any trouble finding a hut or bungalow to rent. A centre of traditional Kashubian ceramics, the village has a pottery run by the Nelc family, with an attractive range of pots and plates on sale – you can also have a look round the pottery. South of the village lies **Lake Radunia**, a long, thin, fjord-like strip of water firmly established as one of the region's most popular sailing and canoeing spots. Ask around at one of the former workers' holiday centres in and around Chmielno and you'll be able to secure yourself a canoe or yacht for the day. For a lakeside stay, the *Wodnik* (☎84 21 26; ③), a *pensjonat* 2km out of the village on the road south, is the obvious venue. Other options in the village include the *U Lusi* (☎84 22 37; ③) and *Olenka* (☎84 21 34; ③), the *pensjonat* at ul. Grzedzinskiego 10 and 14 (②), and the (summer only) youth hostel at ul. Gryfa Pomorskiego.

Moving west, the town of **SIERAKOWICE**, 15km further on, borders on a large expanse of rolling forestland, some of the prettiest in the region, and deservedly popular hiking country. **MIRACHOWO**, a ten-kilometre bus journey northeast across the forest, is a good base for walkers. The village has several traditional half-timbered Kashubian houses similar to those featured at the *skansen* at Wdzydze Kiszewskie (see below). The same holds for **ŁEBNO**, some 15km north, and many of the surrounding villages, a firm indication that you're in the heart of traditional Kashubian territory.

Kościerzyna and Wdzydze Kiszewskie

Continuing south through the region, **KOŚCIERZYNA**, the other main regional centre, some 40km south of Kartuzy, is an undistinguished market town – bus change or a bite to eat on the way to Wdzydze aside, there's no reason for stopping over here. A look at the tarted-up shops on the main town square suggests money is starting to come in, and down below the Baroque parish church, a smattering of Russian "trade tourists" have established an impromptu bazaar in the car park. The central *Pomorski*, ul. Gdańska 15 (☎86 22 90; ③), and the *Bazuny* on ul. Kaszubska (☎86 37 18; ④), 2km out of town, are the only **places to stay** in town worth mentioning, while the newish-looking *Pizza Mamorosa* on the main square provides a decent bite to eat.

Sixteen kilometres on through the sandy forests south of Kościerzyna brings you to **WDZYDZE KISZEWSKIE**: if your tongue has trouble getting round this tongue-twister of a name, simple "*skansen*" will probably do the trick when asking for the right bus. Feasible as a day trip from Gdańsk (72km) – in summer buses travel direct, at other times you have to change in Kościerzyna – the *skansen* here (Tues–Sun 9am–4pm, last tickets 3.30pm) is one of the best of its kind, bringing together a large and carefully preserved set of **traditional Kashubian wooden**

buildings collected from around the region. Established at the beginning of the twentieth century, it was the first such museum in Poland. Spread out in a field overlooking the nearby Lake Goluń, the *skansen*'s location couldn't be more peaceful. After the real towns and villages of the region there's a slightly artificial "reservation" feel to the place, however – buildings without the people. That said the *skansen* is clearly a labour of love, an expression of local determination to preserve and popularize traditional Kashubian folk culture. Most people join the hourly **guided tours** round the site (English- and German-speaking guides are available in summer) since most of the buildings are kept locked when a guide's not present.

The panoply of buildings, most culled from local farms, ranges from old wind-mills and peasant cottages to barns, wells, furnaces, a pigsty and a sawmill with a frame saw so big that it was originally driven by a steam engine. The early eight-eenth-century **wooden church** from the village of Swornegacie in the south of the region, renovated on the *skansen* grounds, is a treat: topped by a traditional wood-shingled roof, the interior is covered with regional folk-baroque designs and biblical motifs, with the patron Saint Barbara and a ubiquitous all-seeing Eye of God peering down from the centre of the ceiling. The thatched cottage interi-ors are immaculately restored with original beds and furniture to reflect the typi-cal domestic set-up of the mostly extremely poor Kashubian peasantry of a century ago. Even the old-style front gardens have been laid out exactly as they used to be. Finances permitting, there are plans to expand the collection of build-ings to reflect a broader selection of regional architectural styles.

Skansen aside, lakeside Wdzydze Kiszewskie is another popular local holiday spot. In summer, **private room**s are on offer in the houses by the lake, and there's a seasonal youth hostel and a number of camping sites. The rather run-down *Pod Niedzwiadzkiem* **motel** (☎86 12 85; ④), 1.5km down the road from the *skansen* is the only place open all year. If you feel like joining the welter of water-sports enthusiasts you can rent canoes and small boats from the hotel.

ALONG THE WISŁA

Following the **Wisła** south from Gdańsk takes you into the heart of the territory once ruled by the **Teutonic Knights**. From a string of fortresses overlooking the river this religio-militaristic order controlled the lucrative medieval grain trade, and it was under their protection that merchant colonists from the northern Hanseatic League cities established themselves down the Wisła as far south as Toruń. The Knights' architectural legacies are distinctive redbrick constructions: tower-churches, sturdy granaries and solid burghers' mansions surrounded by rings of defensive walls and protected by castles. **Malbork**, the Knights' head-quarters, is the prime example – a town settled within and below one of the larg-est fortresses of medieval Europe. Continuing downriver a string of lesser fortified towns – **Kwidzyn**, **Gniew**, **Grudziądz** and **Chełmno** – lead to the ancient city of **Toruń**.

During the Partition era – from the late eighteenth century up until World War I – this upper stretch of the Wisła was **Prussian** territory, an ownership that has left its own mark on the neat towns and cities. After 1918, part of the territory returned to Poland, while part remained in East Prussia. During World War II, as throughout this region, much was destroyed during the German retreat.

Physically, the **river delta** is a flat plain of isolated villages, narrow roads and drained farmland, with the towns an occasional and imposing presence. The river itself is wide, slow-moving and dirty, the landscape all open vistas under frequently sullen skies. **Travel connections** aren't too bad, with buses and trains between the main towns (and cross-river ferries at several points along the Wisła), all of which are within reasonable striking distance of Gdańsk.

Malbork

For Poles brought up on the novels of Henryk Sienkiewicz, the massive river-side fortress of **MALBORK** conjures up the epic medieval struggles between Poles and Germans that he so vividly described in *The Teutonic Knights*. Approached from any angle, the intimidating stronghold dominates the town, imparting the threatening atmosphere of an ancient military headquarters to an otherwise quiet, undistinguished and, following war damage, predominantly modern town.

The history of the town and castle is intimately connected with that of the **Teutonic Knights** (see box opposite), who established themselves here in the late thirteenth century and proceeded to turn a modest fortress into the labyrinthine monster whose remains you can see today. After two centuries of Teutonic domination, the town returned to Polish control in 1457, and the Knights, in dire financial difficulties, were forced to sell the castle to the Czechs, who in turn sold it to the Polish Crown. For the next three hundred years the castle was a royal residence, used by Polish monarchs as a stopover en route between Warsaw and Gdańsk. Following the Partitions, the **Prussians** turned the castle into a barracks and set about dismantling large sections of the masonry – a process halted only by public outcry in Berlin. The eastern wings aside, the castle came through World War II (when it was used as a POW camp) largely unharmed. The sections destroyed during the Soviet assault in 1945, when much of the old town was unnecessarily smashed, have been painstakingly restored to something resembling their original state.

The Fortress

The approach to the main **Fortress** (May–Sept Tues–Sun 8.30am–5pm; Oct–April 9am–2.30pm) is through the old outer castle, a zone of utility buildings which was never rebuilt after the war. Officially you have to join one of the regular guided tours to get into the castles – arduous affairs lasting up to two hours, but you should be able to detach yourself from the group and look round by yourself without too much difficulty.

Passing over the moat and through the daunting main gate, you come to the **Middle Castle**, built following the Knights' decision to move their headquarters to Malbork in 1309. Spread out around an open courtyard, this part of the complex contains the Grand Master's palace, of which the **main refectory** is the highlight. Begun in 1330, this huge vaulted chamber is one of the few rooms still preserved in pretty much its original condition; the elegant palm vaulting, supported on slender granite pillars, shows the growing influence of the Gothic cathedral architecture developed elsewhere in Europe. Displays of weaponry are arranged round the refectory, but more interesting is the painting that fills one of the walls: *The Battle of Grunwald* is archetypal Matejko romanticism, a heroic, action-packed interpretation of a key moment in Polish history.

Leading off from the **courtyard** are a host of dark, cavernous chambers. The largest ones contain collections of ceramics, glass, sculpture, paintings and, most importantly, a large display of Baltic **amber**, the trade which formed the

THE TEUTONIC KNIGHTS

The Templars, the Hospitallers and the **Teutonic Knights** were the three major military-religious orders to emerge from the Crusades. Founded in 1190 as a fraternity serving the sick, the order combined the ascetic ideals of monasticism with the military training of a knight. Eclipsed by their rivals in the Holy Land, the Knights – the Teutonic Order of the Hospital of St Mary, to give them their full title – established their first base in Poland at Chełmno in 1225, following an appeal from Duke Konrad of Mazovia for protection against the pagan Lithuanians, Jacwingians and Prussians. The Knights proceeded to annihilate the Prussian population, establishing German colonies in their place. It's ironic that the people known as Prussians in modern European history are not descendants of these original Slavic populations, but the Germanic settlers who annihilated them.

With the loss of their last base in Palestine in 1271, the Teutonic Knights started looking around for a European site for their headquarters. Three years later they began the construction of Malbork Castle – **Marienburg**, "the fortress of Mary", as they named it – and in 1309 the Grand Master transferred here from Venice.

Economically the Knights' chief targets were control of the **Hanseatic cities** and the trade in Baltic amber, over which they gained a virtual monopoly. Politically their main aim was territorial conquest, especially to the east – which, with their religious zealotry established in Palestine, they saw as a crusade to set up a theocratic political order. Although the Polish kings soon began to realize the mistake of inviting the Knights in, until the start of the fifteenth century most European monarchs were still convinced by the order's religious ideology; their cause was aided by the fact that the Lithuanians, Europe's last pagan population, remained unconverted until well into the fourteenth century.

The showdown with Poland came in 1410 at the **Battle of Grunwald**, one of the most momentous clashes of medieval Europe. Recognizing a common enemy, an allied force of Poles and Lithuanians inflicted the first really decisive defeat on the Knights, yet failed to follow up the victory, and allowed them to retreat to Malbork unchallenged. It wasn't until 1457 that they were driven out of their Malbork stronghold by King Kazimierz Jagiełło. The Grand Master of the Order fled eastward to Königsberg.

In 1525, the Grand Master, Albrecht von Hohenzollern, having converted to Lutheranism, decided to dissolve the order and transform its holdings into a secular duchy, with himself as its head. Initially, political considerations meant he was obliged to accept the Polish king as his overlord, and thus he paid homage before King Sigismund in the marketplace at Kraków in 1525. But the duchy had full jurisdiction over its internal affairs, which allowed for the adoption of Protestantism as its religion. This turned out to be a crucially important step in the history of Europe, as it gave the ambitious Hohenzollern family a power base outside the structures of the Holy Roman Empire, an autonomy that was later to be of vital importance to them in their ultimately successful drive to weld the German nation into a united state.

backbone of the order's fabulous wealth. Innumerable amber pieces of all shapes and sizes are on show here – everything from beautiful miniature altars and exotic jewellery pieces to an assembly of plants and million-year-old-flies encased in the precious resin. If you're visiting in summer, the main courtyard provides the spectacular backdrop for the castle's *son et lumière* shows.

From the Middle Castle a passage rises to the smaller courtyard of the **High Castle**, the oldest section of the fortress, which dates from the late thirteenth century. Climbing up from the courtyard you enter a maze of passages leading to turrets whose slit windows scan the approaches to Malbork. The religious focus of the Knights' austere monasticism was the vast **Castle Church**, complete with seven-pillared refectory and cloisters; features from the church's delicately sculptured **Golden Gate** are mirrored in the portals of the **Chapel of St Anne**, a later extension of the main structure. The Knights' spartan sleeping quarters are nearby, down the passageway running to the Gdanisko Tower – the castle toilet.

For a small extra sum, you can now also climb the main square tower in the centre of the castle – the view both of the castle complex and the flat surrounding countryside is excellent. On the way up you can also peer into the castle chapel, currently under restoration which probably won't be completed until the next century. When you've finished looking round inside, head over the newly built wooden **footbridge** leading from the castle to the other side of the river (technically the Nogat – a tributary of the Wisła), where the view allows you to appreciate what a Babylonian project the fortress must have seemed to medieval visitors and the people of the surrounding country.·

The castle aside, there is little to say about Malbork, whose Old Town was virtually razed in World War II. Evidence of the intense fighting which took place in these parts can be seen in the **Commonwealth War Graves** on the edge of the town.

Practicalities

The **train station** and **bus station** are sited next to each other about ten minutes' walk south of the castle; Malbork is on the main Warsaw line, so there are plenty of trains from Gdańsk (1hr) as well as a regular bus service. Tourist **information** is available from the **PTTK office** located inside the castle area at ul. Hibnera 4, or from the *Hotel Zbyszko*, between the stations and the castle.

Of the three **hotels**, the best and priciest by far is the *Zamek* (☎055/2738 or 2989; ⑧), inside the lower castle grounds, with a swanky restaurant housed in the Gothic refectory. The hotel is already an established tourist favourite, so it's best to book ahead. Of the other places in town, the run-down, though reputedly soon to be renovated, *Zbyszko*, ul. Kościuszki 43 (☎055/3394; ②), is marginally preferable to the dingy *Sportowy* (☎055/2413; ②) east of the castle at ul. Portowa 3, or the *Dom Wycieczkowy* (☎055/3311; ②) at ul. Mickiewicza 26. **Private rooms** should be available through the reception at the *Zbyszko*. The **youth hostel** is at ul. Żeromskiego 45 (055/2511; July & Aug), about 2km south of the station along al. W. Polskiego. There's a decent **campsite** at ul. Portowa 1 (June–Sept), next to the *Sportowy*.

For a **meal** try either the *Zamek* restaurant, the pizzeria at ul. Kościuszki or *Nad Nogatem* on pl. Słowianski, just west of the castle complex. Otherwise, there's an array of milk bars and takeaway joints in and around the town centre.

Kwidzyn and around

Set in the loop of a tributary a few kilometres east of the Wisła, **KWIDZYN** is a smallish fortified town amid a sprawling, dirty industrial belt. The first stronghold established by the Teutonic Knights – in the 1230s, some forty years before the move to Malbork – its original fortress was rapidly joined by a bishop's residence and cathedral. Three hundred years on, the castle was pulled down and rebuilt, but the cathedral and bishop's chapter house were left untouched: unlike the rest of the Old Town area, the entire complex survived the fierce fighting in 1945 unscathed, after which it was the subject of some careful restoration work.

Most of the **Castle** is poised on a hilltop over the River Liwa, but the immediately striking feature is the tower stranded out in what used to be the river bed; connected to the main building by means of a precarious roofed walkway – it looks more like the remains of a bridge-builder's folly than a solid defensive structure. Originally the castle toilet, the best views of it and the castle as a whole are from the other side of the river.

Ranged around a large open courtyard, the castle houses a rather run-down local **Museum** (Tues–Sun 10am–4pm; last tickets 3.30pm), charting the early development of human settlements along the length of the Wisła basin, with additional sections on folklore, natural history and the tangled ethnography of the region. Despite later reconstructions the large, moody **Cathedral**, adjoining the castle, retains several original Gothic features, the most noteworthy being a beautiful late fourteenth-century mosaic in the southern vestibule.

There's no particularly good reason to stop over in what – cathedral and castle apart – is a pretty undistinguished sort of place. However, **accommodation** is provided by the **hotels** *Saga*, ul. Chopina 42 (☎0555/3731; ③), the *Miejski*, ul. Braterstwa Narodów 42 (☎0555/3433; ②), the *Pensjonat Miłosna* on ul. Miłosna (☎0555/4052; ③), and the **youth hostel** on ul. Braterstwa Narodów 58 (☎0555/3876; June & July). There's also a **campsite** on ul. Sportowa, 2km south of town.

For **eating**, the *Piastowska*, in the *Miejski* hotel, and the *Kaskada* on ul. Chopina are the main options; other than this, the hotels are your best bet. Tourist **information** is handled by the *Saga*. The town has regular **bus** services to Tczew, Malbork and Grudziądz. **Trains** run to Gdańsk twice daily (1hr 30min).

Across the river

If you're travelling by car, it's worth continuing west from Kwidzyn some 20km through the lush farmland of the Wisła delta to the river banks just beyond the village of Janowo and the **ferry crossing** over to Gniew (see below). "Ferry" *(rzeka)* in this case means an amazingly dilapidated old contraption operated by an extraordinary mechanical chain system. It's one of three similarly archaic-looking vessels in operation along the northern stretches of the Wisła. All run from early morning till around sunset (seasonally adjusted). The trip costs nothing, since by law the local authorities are obliged to provide free transportation wherever a river "breaks" a road. The boats aren't large – the maximum car load at Janowo is four at a time – so especially in summer car passengers may face a bit of a wait for the blustery ten-minute boat trip. It's an experience not to be missed though, giving you probably your only chance to see the river – and the sadly polluted state of it – from close up.

The other two ferry-crossing points are at **Korzeniewo**, west of Kwidzyn, and **Swibno** right up by the coast. Further east on the River Nogat, two crossing points operate northwest of Elbląg (**Kępiny** and **Kępki**), with a further one on the River Elbląg at **Nowakowo**, close to the coast just north of the city.

Gniew

Sixty-five kilometres south of Gdańsk, the little town of **GNIEW** is one of the most attractive and least known of the former Teutonic strongholds studding the northern shores of the Wisła, an out-of-the-way place that's worth a stopover. Clearly visible from the ferry, thanks to the Wisła's changing course, the town has been left stranded on the top of a hill a kilometre back from the river. Gniew's original strategic location overlooking the river led the Teutonic Knights to set themselves up here in the 1280s, taking the place over from the Cistercian Order and completing the requisite castle within a few years. Untouched by wars, it's a quiet and, by Polish standards, remarkably well-preserved country town, one of those places modern history seems simply to have passed by. It's also a curiously unknown spot – the standard tourist literature barely mentions the town – so you're unlikely to encounter many other visitors, the odd German tour group excepted. However, the place's popularity is gradually increasing thanks to the activities of the enthusiastic group of locals who have now started organizing medieval jousting tournaments and costume battle re-enactments during the summer months – check with the Gdańsk tourist offices for current details.

At the centre of the Old Town the solid-looking brick **Town Hall** provides the focus of such action as the deserted surrounding square sees – mostly kids kicking their footballs against the building. The atmosphere is enhanced, however, by the many original sixteenth- and eighteenth-century dwellings lining the square. West of here, the Gothic **Parish Church** is a typically dark, moody building filled, as often, with wizened old characters reciting their rosaries. A short walk east of the square brings you to the battered remains of the **Castle**, a huge deserted ruin of a place that would make an ideal Gothic horror movie set, its cavernous heights dimly hinting at the past glories of the place. Ask at the **tourist office** – more accurately, makeshift shed – (10am–4pm) in front of the castle for details of a guided tour round what was clearly once an impressive fortress. A little way behind the castle perched on the spur overlooking the river, the **Marysieńki Palace,** added on by King Jan Sobieski in the late seventeenth century for his wife, is a real find: a reasonably priced and scenically situated **hotel**, the *Pałac Marysieńki* (☎35 26 25; ④), an excellent restaurant and a view over the Wisła from the hotel balcony that's one of the best in the region. There's also a summer-only **hostel**, the *Dormitorium*, in the town centre.

Reasonably regular **buses** to and from Gdańsk (1hr 20min), Tczew and Grudziądz stop off at Gniew from the shelter on the western edge of the town centre.

Grudziądz and Radzyń Chełmiński

The garrison town of **GRUDZIĄDZ**, 35km downriver of Kwidzyn, was another early Teutonic stronghold and is again flanked by unprepossessing industrial development, with a huge power station dominating the town centre. **Bus** and **train** terminals are right in the centre: a short walk west towards the river and you're inside the more attractive confines of the **Old Town**.

The Old Town

Grudziądz has changed hands several times. The Teutonic Knights took control of an early Polish settlement on this site, then were forced to hand it back in 1454. Included in territory annexed by Prussia during the Partitions period, it became part of the interwar Polish corridor, was taken by the Germans in 1939 and finally returned to Poland in 1945. Those years of Prussian control explain the Germanic feel of the town, which despite the damage of the war, retains several old buildings.

For all the faded shopfronts and crumbling houses, the orderly arrangement of the charming **Rynek** bespeaks Prussian orderliness and sense of proportion. As the cars and buses parked below the Old Town indicate, slowly but surely Germans are coming back to old haunts like these, to visit the homes of their ancestors or the scenes of their own childhoods. Most of the sights are a few minutes' walk from the Rynek. The Gothic **Parish Church**, to the north, is a typically Teutonic high brick construction, with an equally typical Baroque overlay applied to the interior. The most striking feature is a finely carved Romanesque font in the sacristy. A short way south on ul. Ratoszowa, are the fomer **Jesuit Church and College**, founded in 1622, the former an aisleless Baroque structure with lavish chinoiserie decoration adorning the interior. To the south, the **Benedictine Monastery** houses a **museum** (Tues–Sun 10am–4pm, Wed 10am–3pm) that's as interesting for the exhibitions by local artists as for the established displays recounting the town's history.

Above the river, the **granaries** built into the hillside fortifications are a reminder of the importance once attached to the grain trade. Together with the **mansions** topping the walls they form the centrepoint of the famous view of the town from the other side of the river; one of the best vantage points is from the train to or from Bydgoszcz and Gdańsk. The hill north from the Rynek – **Góra Zamkowa** – is the former castle site, now scattered with just a few foundations (the remains of the fourteenth-century Teutonic Knights' building), and an obelisk modelled on an ancient pagan statue of Światowid, a Slav deity.

As with Malbork, the area surrounding Grudziądz is peppered with **war memorials**. A particularly moving one, in the forest near the village of **Grupa**, 3km out of town on the west bank of the river, commemorates more than 10,000 local Poles, most of them civilians, who were murdered here by the Nazis between 1939 and 1945.

Practicalities

For an overnight stay in the town, the *U Karola*, a short walk south of the Old Town at ul. Toruńska 28 (☎051/36137; ④), is definitely the **hotel** to go for; as well as an IT point selling local maps, it's got the best **restaurant** in town. Other options are the *Pomorzanin*, ul. Kwiatowa 28 (☎051/26141; ③), the *Garnizonowy*, ul. Legionów 53 (☎051/26446; ③), and the all-year **youth hostel** at ul. Chełmińska 102 (☎051/20821), a bus ride south from the centre.

Trains run frequently to Bydgoszcz and Toruń (both 1hr) and twice daily to Gdańsk (2hr). There are **bus** connections with Kwidzyn, Chełmno and Toruń.

Radzyń Chełmiński

For every well-known Teutonic castle in the region there's at least one other one that's a neglected ruin. The fortress at **RADZYŃ CHEŁMIŃSKI** 20km south of Grudziądz is a particularly memorable example of the phenomenon. Stuck out at the edge of a nondescript little town, in its time the castle here was the largest Teutonic stronghold after Malbork. Surrounded by a large dry moat, the walls of the ruins, which you can wander around the edge of, have a lost but rather epic feel to them. The "keep out" sign stuck up on the gateway claiming that the castle will open as soon as reconstruction is completed has obviously been there for years.

Chełmno

The hilltop town of **CHEŁMNO**, another important old Prussian centre, escaped World War II undamaged and has remained untouched by postwar industrial development. Perhaps the most memorable thing about the place is its atmosphere – an archetypal quiet rural town, steeped in the powerful mixture of the Polish and Prussian that characterizes the region as a whole.

Although a Polish stronghold is known to have existed here as early as the eleventh century, Chełmno really came to life in 1225 with the arrival of the Teutonic Knights. They made the town their first political and administrative centre, which led to rapid and impressive development. An academy was founded in 1386 on the model of the famed University of Bologna, and despite the damage inflicted by the Swedes in the 1650s, the town continued to thrive right up to the time of the Partitions, when it lapsed into provincial Prussian obscurity.

The Old Town

To enter the Old Town area pedestrians pass through the **Grudziądz Gate**, a well-proportioned fourteenth-century Gothic construction topped by fine Renaissance gables; cars have to park outside. Continue along ul. Grudziądzka and you're soon amid the Prussian ensemble of the **Rynek**, a grand open space at the heart of the grid-like network of streets. Gracing the centre of the square is the brilliant white **Town Hall**, its facade exuding a real hat-in-the-air exuberance. Rebuilt in the 1560s on the basis of an earlier Gothic hall, its elegant facade, decorated attic and soaring tower are one of the great examples of Polish Renaissance architecture.

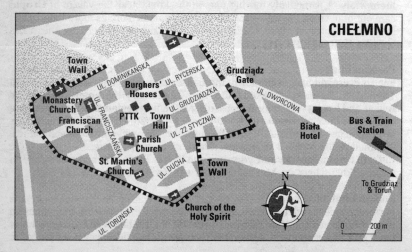

Inside there's a fine old courtroom and an appealing local **Museum** (Tues–Sun 10am–4pm), whose exhibits include an intriguing section devoted to brick production – traditionally the main building material in this part of Poland – with examples of how each individual brick was painstakingly smoothed down to the required size by hand. At the back of the Town Hall is the old Chełmno measure, the **pręt**, used up until the nineteenth century. Employed in the original building of the town, it explains why all the streets are the same width. Clearly a town of individual predisposition, it also used to have its own unique system of weights.

Most of Chełmno's seven churches are Gothic, their red-brick towers and facades punctuating the streets of the Old Town at regular intervals. Best of the lot is the **Parish Church** standing just off the Rynek to the west, an imposing thirteenth-century building with a fine carved doorway. The interior retains sculpted pillars, a Romanesque stone font and fragmentary frescoes. Further west, past St James' Church, is an early fourteenth-century **Monastery**, former home to a succession of Cistercian and Benedictine orders, and now to Catholic sisters who run a handicapped children's hostel here. Its church, whose Baroque altar is reputed to be the tallest in the country, features some original Gothic painting and a curious twin-level nave. The church backs onto the western corner of the town walls, crumbling but complete and walkable for excellent views over the Wisła and low-lying plains.

Practicalities

For a town with some potential commercial pull, there are precious few tourist facilities here. Even the train station has recently been closed to passenger services, leaving buses as the only form of public transport. The **bus station** is on ul. Dworcowa, a fifteen-minute walk to the west of the Old Town.

There's no real **information** office to speak of, but it might be worth trying the *PTTK* on the main square at no. 12. The *Biała*, ul. Dworcowa 23 (☎056/86 02 12; ③), just up from the station, is the only decent **hotel** and the only **restaurant** worthy of the name. A seasonal **youth hostel** operates at ul. Klasztorna 12 (☎056/ 86 24 70; June & July), on the western edge of the Old Town, or there's the extremely basic *Pilawa*, just south of the station at Harcerska 1 (☎056/86 27 50; ②).

Toruń and around

Poles are apt to wax lyrical on the glories of their ancient cities, and with **TORUŃ** – the biggest and most important of the Hanseatic trading centres along the Wisła – it's more than justified. Miraculously surviving the recurrent wars afflicting the region, the historic centre remains one of the country's most evocative, bringing together a rich assembly of architectural styles. The city's main claim to fame is as the birthplace of Nicolaus Copernicus (see p.210), whose house still stands. Today, it is a university city: large, reasonably prosperous and – once you're through the standard postwar suburbs – one with a definitely cultured air.

Some history

The pattern of Toruń's early history is similar to that of other towns along the northern Wisła. Starting out as a Polish settlement, it was overrun by Prussian tribes from the east towards the end of the twelfth century, and soon afterwards the **Teutonic Knights** moved in. The Knights rapidly developed the town,

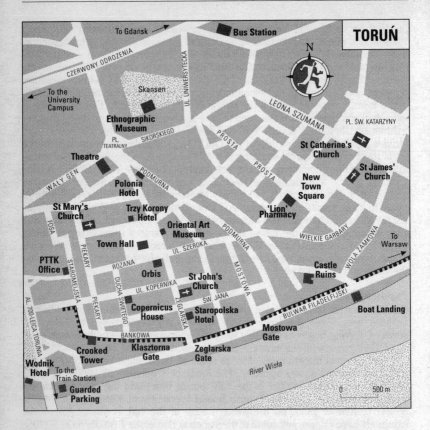

thanks to its access to the burgeoning river-borne grain trade, a position further consolidated with its entry to the Hanseatic League. As in rival Gdańsk, economic prosperity was expressed in a mass of building projects through the following century; together these make up the majority of the historic sites in the city.

Growing disenchantment with the Teutonic Knights' rule and heavy taxation, especially among the merchants, led to the formation of the Prussian Union in 1440, based in Toruń. In 1454, as war broke out between the Knights and Poland, the townspeople destroyed the castle in Toruń and chased the Order out of town. The 1466 **Treaty of Toruń** finally terminated the Knights' control of the area.

The next two centuries brought even greater wealth as the town thrived on extensive royal privileges and increased access to goods from all over Poland. The Swedish invasion of the 1650s was the first significant setback, but the really decisive blow to the city's fortunes came a century later with the Partitions, when Toruń was annexed to Prussia and thus severed from its hinterlands, which by now were under Russian control. Like much of the region, Toruń was subjected to systematic Germanization, but as in many other cities a strongly Polish identity remained, clearly manifested in the cultural associations that flourished in the latter part of the nineteenth century. Toruń returned to Poland under the terms of the 1919 Versailles Treaty as part of the "Polish Corridor" that was so to enrage Hitler, and was liberated from the Nazis in 1945.

Arrival, information and accommodation

The main **stations** are on opposite sides of the Old Town. Toruń Główny, the main **train station**, is south of the river: leave the station by the subway on the north (left) of the entrance, emerging a short way from the bus stop for the centre; buses #12 and #22 run over the bridge to pl. Rapackiego, on the west of the Old Town. From the **bus station** on ul. Dąbrowskiego it is a short walk north to the centre.

The well-organized main **tourist office**, in the Town Hall (Mon & Sat 9am–4pm, Tues–Fri 9am–6pm; May–Aug also Sun 9am–1pm; ☎056/23746), doles out free brochures and maps and is a useful source of information for the whole region. *Orbis*, on the corner of the Rynek at ul. Żeglarska 31, issues travel tickets, while *Almatur*, near the university at ul. Gagarina 21, sorts out beds in student hotels.

Accommodation

There's a reasonable choice of **accommodation** on offer in Toruń. *Orbis* has two hotels aimed at foreign tourist groups: the *Kosmos*, ul. ks. Popiełuszki 2 (☎056/ 28900; ⑦), west near the river, and the inferior *Helios*, ul. Kraszewskiego 1/3 (☎056/25 03 18, fax 23565; ⑧), northwest of the centre. Slightly cheaper and a lot more attractive is the *Zajazd Staropolski*, ul. Żeglarska 10/14 (☎056/26061 or 26063, fax 25384; ⑤), well situated just down from the Rynek; it's very popular in summer though, so you'll be lucky to get a room without booking. A step down in quality are the *Polonia*, pl. Teatralny 5 (☎056/23028, fax 27837; ③), and the *Zajazd Wileski*, ul. Mostowa 7 (☎056/25024; ③), though both are in easy walking distance of the Rynek.

The recently renovated *Pod Trzema Koronami*, Rynek Staromiejski 21 (☎056/ 26031; ③), has a good location on the edge of the main square, overlooking the town hall, although the late-night downstairs bar can be noisy. Other options include the good quality *Wodnik*, ul. Bulwar Filadelfijski 12 (☎056/26049, fax 25114; ④), overlooking the waterfront and the public swimming pool (free entry for hotel residents); the *Garnizonowy*, ul. Wola Zamkowa 16 (☎056/16 28 83; ②), an old army hotel in the New Town area; and the extremely basic *Statek Kilinski*, ul. Turystycznia 135 (☎056/48 69 27; ②), well east of the centre in the Klaszczorek district. Consider the *PTTK* hostel, well north of the centre at ul. Legionów 24 (☎056/23855), only as a last resort – it's a long way out.

The only all-year **youth hostel** is over the river some way to the east of the train station at ul. Rudacka 15 (☎056/27242); bus #13 runs nearby. However, during the summer months the university runs **international student hotels** – details of which are available from the *Almatur* office (see above). The *Tramp* **campsite** at ul. Kujawska 14 (☎056/24187), a short walk west of the train station, has some bungalows for rent as well as tent space – and it's not a bad setting.

The City

The historic core of Toruń is divided into Old Town and New Town areas, both established in the early years of Teutonic rule. Traditional economic divisions are apparent here, the Old Town quarter being home for the merchants, the other for the artisans; each had its own square, market area and town hall.

Overlooking the river from a gentle rise, the medieval centre constitutes a relatively small section of the modern city and is clearly separated from it by a ring of signs pointing to the centre: ask for the way to the Stare Miasto. For motorists, the Old Town centre's impenetrable one-way system is pretty much a case of "abandon hope all ye who enter here" – you're better off walking.

The Old Town (Stare Miasto)

The Old Town area is the obvious place to start looking around – and as usual it's the **Rynek**, in particular the **Town Hall**, that provides the focal point. Town halls don't come much bigger or more striking than this: raised in the late fourteenth century on the site of earlier cloth halls and trading stalls, this elegant work is one of the finest Gothic buildings in northern Europe. A three-storey brick structure topped by a sturdy tower, its outer walls are punctuated by indented windows, framed by a rhythmic succession of high arches peaking just beneath the roof, and complemented by graceful Renaissance turrets and high gables.

The south side entrance leads to an inner courtyard surrounded by fine brick doorways, the main one leading to the **Town Museum** (Tues–Sun 10am–4pm), which now occupies much of the building. Over the centuries Toruń's wealth attracted artists and craftsmen of every type, and it's their work that features strongest here. Most of the ground floor – once the wine cellar – is devoted to medieval artefacts, with a gorgeous collection of the **stained glass** for which the city was famed and some fine **sculptures**, especially the celebrated "Beautiful Madonnas". Also housed on this floor is an extensive archeological section, bringing together highlights of a vast array of Neolithic and early Bronze Age relics uncovered in this region. On the first floor, painting takes over, with rooms covered in portraits of Polish kings and wealthy Toruń citizens. A small portrait of the most famous city burgher, Copernicus, basks in the limelight of a Baroque gallery. Before leaving, it's worth climbing the **tower** for the view of the city and the course of the Wisła, stretching into the plain on the southern horizon.

Lining the square itself are the stately mansions of the Hansa merchants, many of whose high parapets and decorated facades are preserved intact. The finest houses flank the east side of the square. Number 35, next to one of the Copernicus family houses, is the fifteenth-century **Pod Gwiazdą**, with a finely modelled late Baroque facade; inside, a superbly carved wooden staircase ends with a statue of Minerva, spear in hand. The house is now a small **Oriental Museum** (Tues–Sun 10am–4pm), based on a private collection of art from China, India and other Far Eastern countries.

Off to the west of the square stands **St Mary's Church**, a large fourteenth-century building with elements of its early decoration retained in the sombre interior. There's no tower to the building, supposedly because the church's Franciscan founders didn't permit such things; monastic modesty may also help to explain the high wall separating the church from the street. Back across the square, on the other side of the town hall, a blackened but noble **statue of Copernicus** watches over the crowds scurrying round the building.

South of the square, on the dusty, narrow and atmospheric ul. Żeglarska, is **St John's Church**, another large, magnificent Gothic structure, whose clockface served as a reference point for loggers piloting their way downstream. The presbytery, the oldest part of the building, dates from the 1260s, but the main nave and aisles were not completed till the mid-fifteenth century. Entering from the heat of the summer sun, you're immediately enveloped in an ancient calm, heightened by the damp, chilly air rising from the flagstones and by the imposing rose window. The tower, completed late in the church's life, houses a magnificent fifteenth-century bell, the *Tuba Dei*, which can be heard all over town. Opening hours for the church are a little unpredictable; your best bet is turn up when a service is being held. Check the noticeboard outside for current details.

West from St John's runs ul. Kopernika, halfway down which you'll find the **Copernicus Museum** (Tues–Sat 10am–4pm), installed in the high brick house where the great man was born. Restored in recent decades to something resembling its original layout, this Gothic mansion contains a studiously assembled collection of Copernicus artefacts: priceless first editions of the momentous *De Revolutionibus*, models of gyroscopes and other astronomical instruments, original household furniture, early portraits. Authenticity is abandoned on the upper floors, which are given over to products of the modern Copernicus industry: Copernicus coins, badges, stamps, even honey pots and tea labels.

Ul. Kopernika and its dingy side streets, lined with crumbling Gothic mansions and granaries, blend past glory and shabbier contemporary reality. Further down towards the river, the high, narrow streets meet the old defensive **walls**, now separating the Old Town from the main road. These fortifications survived virtually intact right up to the late nineteenth century, only for some enterprising Prussian town planners to knock them down, sparing only a small section near the river's edge. This short fragment remains today, the walls interspersed by the old gates and towers at the ends of the streets.

To the west, at the bottom of ul. Pod Krzywa Wieża, stands the mid-fourteenth-century **Crooked Tower** (Krzywa Wieża), followed in quick succession by the **Monastery Gate** (Brama Klasztorna) and **Sailors' Gate** (Brama Żeglarska), all from the same period, the last originally leading to the main harbour.

Heading east, past the large **Bridge Gate** (Brama Mostowa), brings you to the ruins of the **Teutonic Knights' Castle**, sandwiched between the two halves of the medieval city. While not in the same league as the later Malbork fortress, the scale of the ruins here is enough to leave you impressed by the Toruń citizenry's efforts in laying it waste. In the vaults, a small **museum** (May–Sept Tues–Sun 10am–4pm) recounts the history of this redoubtable building. The castle grounds are the location for occasional summertime concerts (folk and classical) – check with the tourist offices for details.

A little further east along the river bank is a **landing stage**, from which in summer you can take a ninety-minute **boat trip** downriver and back. One glance at the state of the water will be enough to wipe out any thoughts of a quick dip.

The New Town (Nowe Miasto)

Following ul. Przedzamcze north from the castle brings you onto ul. Szeroka, the main thoroughfare linking the Old and New Town districts. Less grand than its mercantile neighbour, the **New Town** still boasts a number of illustrious commercial residences, most of them grouped around the **Rynek Nowomiejski**. On the west side of this square, the fifteenth-century **Pod Modrym Faruchem** inn (no. 8) and the Gothic **pharmacy** at no. 13 are particularly striking, while the old **Murarska** inn at no. 17, on the east side, currently houses an art gallery displaying children's work from all over the country.

The fourteenth-century **St James' Church**, south of the market area of the Rynek, completes the city's collection of Gothic churches. Unusual features of this brick basilica are its flying buttresses – a common enough sight in western

Europe but extremely rare in Poland. Inside, mainly Baroque decoration is
relieved by occasional Gothic frescoes, panel paintings and sculpture – most notably a large fourteenth-century crucifix.

North of the square, ul. Prosta leads onto Wały Sikorskego, a ring road which
more or less marks the line of the old fortifications. Across it there's a small
park, in the middle of which stands the former arsenal, now the **Ethnographic
Museum** (Tues–Sat 10am–4pm) dealing with the customs and crafts of northern Poland. The displays covering historical traditions are enhanced by imaginative attention to contemporary folk artists, musicians and writers, whose
work is actively collected and promoted by the museum. The surrounding park
houses an enchanting *skansen* containing an enjoyable and expanding collection
of traditional wooden buildings from nearby regions, including a blacksmith's
shop, windmill, watermill and two complete sets of farm buildings from
Kashubia.

The park and Bielany

If you're feeling the need for a bit of tranquillity, there's a pleasant **park** along the
water's edge west of the city centre, reached by tram #3 or #4 from pl.
Rapackiego. On weekends you'll be joined at the waterside by picnickers and the
odd group of horse-riders.

North of the park, the **Bielany** district houses the main section of the university campus, largely unmemorable in itself, but it's the location of the main
student hotels (see "Accommodation", p.197), and of several of the really lively
student clubs and discos (see below). To get here, take bus # 11 or 15.

Eating, drinking and entertainment

The hotels provide some of the better places to **eat**. Gothic brickwork, stone
floors and high wooden ceilings are the decor in *Zajazd Staropolski* restaurant,
which offers a considerably better-than-average menu. The *Helios* and *Kosmos*
have the usual uninspiring *Orbis* decor but decent, if predictable, *Orbis* food. The
noisier *Polonia* is reasonable, but *Pod Trzema Koronami*'s restaurant is probably
best avoided, as drunken brawls are a regular sight.

A number of places aimed specifically at tourists have opened recently. The
renovated *Staromiejska*, ul. Szcztyna 2/4, is now a fairly good pizza place – and
the Gothic brick decor is a treat too. *Zamek*, ul. Przedzamcze 5, is a respectable
Chinese joint, open late; the *Lotos*, ul. Strumykowa 16, has a passable mixed
Asian menu; the *Palomino*, ul. Wielkie Garbary 18, offers standard Western fare,
and the *Bella Italia* on the main square serves straightforward pizza.

Western-style **fast food** has moved in in a big way too, with the (Swedish) *Mr Smarty's* hamburger chain leading the way. Finally, *Kombinat*, ul. Reya 25, is a cheap no-nonsense place popular with students.

Cafés are in good supply, with terrace places on streets such as ul. Szeroka providing an opportunity to enjoy the atmosphere of the Old Town. The regal *Pod Atlantem* in ul. Św. Ducha stays open late, while at the nearby *Flisaka*, an old loggers' haunt, you can sit outside and enjoy the view over the river. The *Pod Kryża Wieża* on the same street is an enjoyable haunt, while the terrace at the *Pod Gotembia*, ul. Szerska, provides a good vantage point over the main square.

Bar life is picking up too: the *Czarna Obraza*, ul. Rasiańska 9, on the eastern edge of the Rynek, serves draught Guinness and DAB; the *Piwarnia* on the northeast corner of the square is more basic, but ultimately more enjoyable. The "pub" in the Old Brewery (Stary Browar), on ul. Browarna in the New Town has live music, mostly blues and country, several times a week. The curiously named *Political Club* on ul. Bankowa is a tiny trendy bar, crammed inside an old-style Toruń burgher's house. Ul. Kopernika and the surrounding streets are developing their own slightly ritzy tourist-oriented bar and nightclub culture. Try places like the *Kaitachino* or the *Azyl*, a bar and billiards haunt, if you're feeling like joining in.

Some of the best **nightlife** in town happens in the university district, clustered on and around ul. Gagarina. The main campus clubs/bars are the *Imperial*, ul. Gagarina 17, and *Odnowa*, ul. Gagarina 37, located close to one of the main student hotels. The *Olimp* at ul. Gagarina 33 is a noisy and popular basement club running well into the night on weekends. Non-students welcome.

Entertainment

The grand old **Toruń Theatre** on pl. Teatralny, is home of one of the country's most highly regarded repertory companies. It's also worth checking the listings in the local newspaper for occasional classical **concerts** in the town hall and regular ones given by the Town Chamber Orchestra in the Dwór Artusa at Rynek Staromiejska 6.

The city has a number of regular **festivals**, notably the International Theatre Festival (May), held in the theatre, a Folk Festival (also May) and an International Early Music Festival (September).

Golub-Dobrzyń

About 35km east of Toruń, the elegant facades of the castle at **GOLUB-DOBRZYŃ** are a traditional *Orbis* poster favourite. While the town itself is nothing to write home about, the Renaissance **Castle**, located high up on a hill overlooking the town, is an impressive sight. Coming in on the long, straight approach road from Toruń, the castle is signposted off to the right just before you enter the town – if you're coming by bus ask the driver to drop you off near the castle (*zamek*). **Bus** services run to Toruń and, less frequently, to Grudziąz.

A Teutonic stronghold raised in the early 1300s on the site of an early Slav settlement overlooking the River Drwęca, the original castle was built on the square ground plan with arcaded central courtyard that survives today. Following the conclusion of the Treaty of Toruń (1460) the place fell into Polish hands; the real changes to the building came in the early 1600s, when Anna Waza, sister of King Sigismund III, acquired the castle. The king's redoubtable sister, a polyglot and botanical enthusiast reputed to have imported the first tobacco to Poland and planted it on the hills near the castle, had the whole place remodelled in Polish Renaissance style, adding the elegantly sculptured facades and Italianate courtyard you see today. After taking a severe battering during the Swedish wars of the 1650s the abandoned castle was left to crumble away, restoration work beginning following the town's final return to Polish territory in the postwar era.

The castle buildings

Past the large cannons greeting you at the entrance the **Castle Museum** (Tues–Sun, 9am–3pm, hourly guided tours only) begins unpromisingly, with a small regional museum housed in one of the ground-floor rooms containing a routine collection of straw shoes, local costumes and assorted wooden objects, many of them related to the river economy.

Up the stairs to the second floor things get more interesting. The classy main **banqueting hall** sports the coats of arms of all the major old Polish aristocratic families – the Jaruzelski clan included – as well as the emblem of the castle's last eighteenth-century owners, the Dutch Van Doren family. In recent years the castle has begun hosting invitation-only New Year medieval banquets with everyone turning up dressed in period costume. There are now plans to set up a "period" medieval restaurant here on a commercial basis.

The former castle **chapel** next door is anything but religious in atmosphere, being filled to the brim with replicas of Polish battle standards from the battle of Grunwald as well as an amazing array of old cannon, including tiny fourteenth-century pieces to monster seventeenth-century contraptions – and just about everything in between. The original Gothic structure built by the Teutonic Knights underwent substantial alterations in Anna Waza's time, her strict Protestant convictions possibly accounting for the severe feel of the place. The rest of the rooms on this floor once comprised the Knights' living quarters: apparently everyone used to ride their horses straight up the stairs to their rooms, the resulting local legend holding that anyone who merely walks up the stairs is liable to break out in unexpected public fits of neighing – you have been warned.

The upper rooms of the castle are now a fairly basic **hotel** (☎056/05683 or 2455; ④). Irritatingly there's no restaurant, just a daytime **café**, the *Rycerska* on the ground floor. Out of the castle it's worth strolling out to the viewpoint at the edge of the field next to the building for the view over the surroundings. Every July (usually around the middle of the month) the field here is the scene of a major international **chivalry tournament**, with national teams of jousters battling it out on horseback: a spectacular event by all accounts, it's worth trying to catch the event if you're in the area at the time.

East of Gdańsk

East from Gdańsk a short stretch of Baltic coastline leads up to the Russian border and, beyond, to Kaliningrad. An attractive and largely unspoilt region, the beaches of the **Wiślana Peninsula** and its approaches are deservedly popular seaside holiday country with Poles and, increasingly, returnee Germans. Inland the lush rural terrain, well watered by countless little tributaries of the Wisła, boasts a host of quiet, sturdy-looking old Prussian villages, and more ominously, the Nazi concentration camp at **Sztutowo (Stutthof)**. This is the region most closely associated with astronomer Nicholas Copernicus, and several towns, notably the medieval coastal centre of **Frombork**, bear his imprint. Of the other urban sites, **Elbląg** is a major old Prussian centre now finally regaining something of its old character. As for **transport**, cross-country **bus links** are generally good in this part of the country, with the additional option of a scenic coastal **train** route along the southern shore of the **Wiślany Lagoon** and short-hop **ferry services** in several places.

The Wiślany Lagoon and around

Through the flatlands of the former Wisła basin, the coast road east passes the popular local seaside resort of **STOGI**, the only place in the immediate vicinity of Gdańsk where the water has always been clean enough to swim in: additionally there's a nudist beach 2km east of the main resort. Continuing east, there's a ferry crossing over one of the small Wisła tributaries at **Świbno**. Over the other side, with your own tranpsort, it's worth making a short detour 6km south to **DREWNICA**, where there's a fine example of the old wooden windmills that used to cover the area. If you happen to be heading south along the main Elbląg–Warsaw road instead, the *Złota Podkowa* restaurant in the village of **PRZEJAZDOWO**, 8km out of town, is well worth a stopoff; the house speciality is excellently prepared local duck.

Back on the main coastal road 15km further east you come to **STEGNA,** an attractive spot with a charming, half-timbered brick church that wouldn't look out of place in a Bavarian village, the ornate Baroque frescoes decorating the interior enhancing the feel of an archetypal German country church. Elsewhere in the village the smattering of *"Zimmer frei"* signs in the windows tell you you've hit what's now become a popular German holiday centre.

Stutthof (Sztutowo) concentration camp

May our fate be a warning to you – not a legend. Should man grow silent, the very stones will scream.

Franciszek Fenikowski, Requiem Mass, quoted in camp guidebook.

Two kilometres further east on the main coastal road, the sense of rural idyll is rudely shattered by the signs pointing north to the gates of the Nazi **concentration camp site** at **Stutthof (Sztutowo).** The first camp to be built inside what is now Poland (construction began in August 1939, before the German invasion), it started as an internment camp for local Poles but eventually became a Nazi extermination centre for the whole of northern Europe. The first Polish prisoners arrived at Stutthof early in September 1939, their numbers rapidly swelled by legions of other locals deemed "undesirables" by the Nazis. The decision to transform Stutthof into an international camp came in 1942, and eventually, in June 1944, the camp was incorporated into the Nazi scheme for the "Final Solution", the whole place being considerably enlarged and the gas ovens installed. Although not on the same scale as other death camps, the toll in human lives speaks for itself: by the time the Red Army liberated the camp under a year later, in May 1945, an estimated 65,000 to 85,000 people had disappeared here.

The Camp

In a large forest clearing surrounded by a wire fence and watchtowers, the peaceful, completely isolated setting of the **camp** (May–Sept 8am–6pm, Oct–April 8am–3pm, children under 13 not allowed) makes the whole idea seem unreal at first. In through the entrance gate, though, like all the Nazi concentration camps, it's a depressing and shocking place to visit. Rows of stark wooden barrack blocks are interspersed with empty sites with nothing but the bare foundations left. Much of the camp was torn down in 1945 and used as firewood; the narrow-gauge rail line still criss-crossing the site reminds you of the methodical planning that went into the policy of mass murder carried out here.

A **Museum** housed in the barracks details life and death in the camp, the crude wooden bunks and threadbare mats indicating the "living" conditions the inmates had to endure. A harrowing gallery of photographs of gaunt-looking inmates brings home the human reality of what happened here: name, date of birth, country of origin and "offence" are listed below each of the faces staring down from the walls, the 25 nationalities present including a significant contingent of political prisoners, communists and gays. Over in the far corner of the camp stand the gas ovens and crematoria, flowers at the foot of the ovens, as well a large monument to the murdered close by. "Offer them a rose from the warmth of your heart and leave – here lies infamy": the words from Polish poet Jan Górec-Rosiński's elegy on visiting the camp, quoted in the official guidebook, seem an appropriate response.

By **bus**, the Stutthof camp is a 75-minute journey from Gdańsk (buses travel here from Elbląg too): get off at the Sztutowo-Museum stop, and walk up from the main road.

The Wiślana Peninsula

East from Stutthof, the coast road leads onto the **Wiślana Peninsula** (Mierzeja Wiślana), a long, thin promontory dividing the sea from the **Wiślana Lagoon** (Zalew Wiślany) – a land-locked tract of water known as the "Frische Haff" in Prussian times that continues some 60km up towards Kaliningrad. On the northern side of the peninsula a dense covering of mixed beech and birch forest suddenly gives way to the sea, while to the south, the marshy shore beyond the road looks out over the tranquil lagoon – 15km across at its widest – and beyond that to **Frombork** and the mainland. A naturalist's paradise, the peninsula forest is idyllic walking country, while the northern coastline offers some of the best and most unspoilt beaches on the Baltic coast. A couple of resorts aside, the camping sites dotted along the peninsula provide the main source of local accommodation.

Four kilometres along the peninsula is **KĄTY RYBACKIE**, an attractive little resort town and fishing port with long sandy beaches stretching out as far as the eye can see along the coast up by the harbour. Several houses in the village offer **rooms** in season, so you shouldn't have trouble finding a place to stay, though the place does get pretty crowded in high season. The scenically situated camping site on ul. Plażowa (☎0507/8705), is the only other alternative.

Just east of the village off the main road is another natural wonder, Europe's largest **cormorant sanctuary**. Beautifully situated in the middle of some thick forestland, the sanctuary is a bird-watchers' delight, with every chance of spotting the large flocks of cormorants. Twenty-five kilometres on, the road brings you to **KRYNICA MORSKA**, a few kilometres short of the Russian border and the main holiday resort on the peninsula. The *Gabriella*, ul. Gdańska 87 (☎/fax 050/76122; ③) is a pleasant *pensjonat* overlooking the harbour. For **campers** the site at ul. Marynarzy 1 (☎050/76126) near the beach is an attractive option, otherwise the best thing to do is check at the *biuro zakwaterowańia* on ul Gdańska (☎050/76155) for private rooms (②). The wonderful beaches continue further up at **PIASKI**, 2km from the border. In summer a **ferry** crosses the lagoon from Krynica Morska to Elbląg and, less frequently, to Frombork.

Elbląg

The ancient settlement of **ELBLĄG**, after Gdańsk the region's most important town, was severely damaged at the end of World War II: its Old Town centre, reputed to have been Gdańsk's equal in beauty, was totally flattened in the bitter fighting that followed the Nazi retreat in 1945. After languishing for decades in a postwar architectural limbo, Elbląg is now finally getting the regenerative pick-me-up it badly needs. The Old Town area is being completely rebuilt, the deal being that investors – of whom there are apparently plenty – copy the feel, if not necessarily the precise architectural details, of the city's prewar architecture. Since its inception in 1991 the project has already proved a real success: several half-timbered brick houses have already gone up with more clearly in the pipeline. Ironically the revived popularity of the town in Poland these days has more to do with the runaway nationwide success of the revitalized town brewery's flagship beer, EB, than its spirited attempt at urban renewal. It's an avowedly ambitious project, but if things carry on the way they've started, by the end of the decade Elbląg should once again have the handsome Old Town centre it deserves.

The Old Town

Surrounded by an undistinguished postwar urban sprawl, the **Old Town** is a small section at the heart of modern Elbląg. Some parts of the old city walls remain, mostly notably around the old **Brama Targowa** (Market Gate) at the northern entrance to the area. Elbląg played an important role in Hitler's wartime plans, specifically as a centre of U-boat production – the city's easy access to the sea, via the Wiślana Lagoon, made it a perfect spot. The empty area between the Brama Targowa and the cathedral hides the ruins of the dry docks where scores of newly produced submarines were launched into wartime action – no wonder the Soviets hammered the place.

Standing out rather incongruously, the **Cathedral**, rebuilt after the war, is another massive brick Gothic structure, its huge tower the biggest in the region. Despite the restorers' efforts to give the building back some of its former character, the job was clearly a bit of an uphill struggle. A couple of fine original Gothic triptychs and statues, and some traces of the original ornamentation aside, the interior is mostly rather vapid postwar decoration, leaving the place with a sad, empty feel to it. The area immediately surrounding the cathedral is busy with reconstruction work: Alongside the old Prussian-style mansions, a few restaurants, bars and cafés have already sprung up, with more in the pipeline, mostly catering for the busloads of (principally German) day-trippers piling in throughout the summer season.

KALININGRAD

Kaliningrad – formerly Königsberg – the longtime capital of East Prussia, annexed by the Soviet Union at the end of World War II, was left geographically stranded outside the Russian Federation following the collapse of the Soviet Union. How long it will technically remain within the Federation is unclear, and a number of countries are taking a keen interest in discussions about the region's future, Poland and Lithuania, its immediate neighbours, included.

A heavily militarized area often referred to as Russia's "western aircraft-carrier", Kaliningrad occupied an important place in Soviet strategic military thinking. A key air defence centre, the region also houses the main base of the former Soviet, now Russian Baltic Fleet at Baltysk, as well as a number of infantry divisions. A drive through the Kaliningrad *oblast* confirms the weight of local military presence: in between the crumbling Prussian villages you can easily spot a welter of air defence installations, some camouflaged, some not. Estimates of current force levels vary widely, but it's likely that at least 150,000 troops remain in the region. The picture's still pretty tangled: while the units being transferred from Germany continue to trundle in, the Russian military are also pulling out some others. Additionally, they're now being physically prevented from bringing new conscripts into the area by the determined blocking of entry points by the Baltic states.

The former threat of military confrontation may have subsided, but while agreeing that troop levels should be reduced to "reasonable" levels, the Russian authorities have so far stopped short of accepting Polish and Lithuanian calls to demilitarize the region completely. As with earlier negotiations on troop withdrawals in eastern Europe, behind this stance lurks the genuine and difficult issue of what to do with returning soldiers in a country already deep in the throes of a serious economic crisis, not least suffering from a chronic lack of employment and housing opportunities.

Predictably enough, a key player in the Kaliningrad saga is **Germany**. As with all of former East Prussia there still remain strong emotional bonds linking many older-generation Germans to their former *Heimat*. Since the border of this formerly closed area reopened in 1989 it's they who have been pouring over to visit the city. Informal opinion surveys carried out among Kaliningrad residents suggest they welcome reviving German interest – and in particular German investment – in the region. In deference, perhaps, to the historical sensitivities of neighbouring countries, German officials have been taking a cautious line on Kaliningrad, with both the former foreign minister Hans-Dietrich Genscher and his successor Klaus Kinkel consistently rejecting the notion of any German claim on the city.

Though clearly nervous about anything that smacks of a German reoccupation of its former eastern possessions, the main **Polish interest** in Kaliningrad (Królewiec) nevertheless seems to be in developing business links and rebuilding the local cross-border infrastructure as part of an overall strategy of economic regeneration for the northern Baltic region.

In this sense the Polish authorities appear to have no objection to German involvement in the Kaliningrad region – especially if it means financial investment – and have reacted to various proposals for a definite German stake in the region with a noticeable lack of alarm. As regards Russia, Polish officials have already had a number of direct talks with their Moscow counterparts over Kaliningrad, most significantly during Lech Wałęsa's visit to Moscow in May 1992, when the Polish president signed an agreement with Russian officials over the development of cross-border cooperation in the region. Commercial interest already seems to be bearing fruit: the Olsztyn region has signed a reciprocal trade agreement with

Kaliningrad, and eighty percent of the joint ventures already established in the region involve Polish trading concerns.

To date the **Lithuanian position** on Kaliningrad has been a bit more obscure. Citing the region's medieval positioning within Lithuanian territory, at least one senior official has suggested that Kaliningrad – *Karaliaucius* as it's called in Lithuanian – ought really to be "returned" to their control. Quite how seriously such statements are supposed to be taken is unclear: what is evident, however, is Lithuanian concern over the Russian military presence in the region, in particular the vexed issue of troop transits. The country's infrastructure has already been badly damaged by recent troop withdrawals – ploughed-up roads, damaged rail track and so on – and the prospect of more of the same following a Russian pull-out from Kaliningrad is viewed with understandable alarm. Whichever way things go, however, Lithuania will certainly press for recognition of its interests in what was at one time known as "lesser Lithuania".

One serious proposal recently floated is to turn the region into a (joint) **Russian-German-Polish condominium**. Alternatively, it may remain as an autonomous republic within the Russian Federation, but strongly linked to a putative new Baltic "Euroregion" or "Hanseatic region". A new fourth independent Baltic state has also been suggested, though the experience of becoming a **special economic zone**, as the region has officially been designated since January 1992, suggests that Kaliningrad would have a tough time going it alone economically.

Most importantly, perhaps, official sensitivities in Moscow over the prospect of decoupling the region from Russia remain a crucial factor. Into the mid-1990s, moves to encourage foreign investment are still regularly balanced by official statements warning against creeping foreign expansionism and the fostering of **separatism** in the region. Significantly, in 1993, a new language law was passed prohibiting the use of foreign language signs unless accompanied by a Russian translation, three times larger. Coming at a time when the ethnic makeup of the region's population – actually a complex mix of ethnic Russians, minorities from within the Russian Federation, Ukrainians, Belarussians, Lithuanians, Poles and Germans – was beginning to emerge as a focal point of discussion, it confirmed the fact in the post-Soviet political configuration, that latent Russian nationalism should not be underestimated.

VISITING KALININGRAD

For all the recent tourist influx there's actually not a great deal worth seeing in Kaliningrad, since most of the city was first flattened by Allied bombing raids, then by the fighting around the city in 1945, and afterwards rebuilt in what seems like the crassest and ugliest way the Soviets could come up with. In the old city only the ruins of the medieval **Cathedral** survive, with a special stone marking the **grave of Immanuel Kant**, the city's most famous philosopher and about the only one deemed acceptable by the postwar Soviet authorities. Moving out into the suburbs, however, the uniform concrete blocks begin to give way to sections of characteristic old Prussian houses which can be found throughout former East Prussia.

How to get there

Special **buses** now run from Warsaw, Gdańsk and Olsztyn to Kaliningrad crossing the border at Bezledy–Bagrationovsk, about 40km north of Lidzbark Warmiński. Only open during daytime, the crossing is still theoretically closed to non-Poles or Russians, though bus passengers do seem to get through providing they have a visa. The new border crossing at Gronowo–Mamonowo, due to open for international

Contd. overleaf

KALININGRAD (cont...)

traffic in 1996 will provide an alternative route into the region for anyone travelling by car, and there is, in addition, a recently opened crossing at Goldap–Gasev.

By train, there are now some direct connections from Berlin that cross the border at Gronowo–Mamonowo just north of Braniewo. From within Poland, there are a couple of trains daily from Braniewo, as well as plans for a regular service from Gdańsk, due to be up and running in 1996.

However, the best way of getting to Kaliningrad from within Poland, is by **boat**. In summer, there's a daily hydrofoil service from Elbląg – a two-hour trip leaving early in the morning and returning in the evening – visas are sorted out on board. The service connects with a bus from Gdańsk, organized by the *Lewer* agency, ul. Piwna 31/33 (☎058/31 16 19), a friendly efficient bunch who charge DM140 for the road trip including visa costs (you will need three passport-sized photos).

Finally, an **air service** has recently started between Gdańsk (Rebięchowo) and Khrabov, near Kaliningrad by *Sky-Pol*, a new private company specializing in domestic flights within Poland – check with the airport for details. The flight takes an hour each way.

Not far from the cathedral is the Gothic **St Mary's Church**: no longer consecrated, the building houses a small rather downbeat **Modern Art Gallery** (Mon–Fri 10am–5pm, Sat–Sun 10am–4pm) in the cloisters. More interesting than the pictures on display are the old gravestones and tablets lining the walls, notably that of Samuel Butler, one of the many English merchants who settled here as a result of the city's strong Reformation-era Anglo-Polish commercial links, symbolized in the establishment of the Eastland Company's headquarters here in 1579.

South along the river, the former town grammar school on ul. Wigiligna, now houses the local **Museum** (Tues–Sat 8am–4pm, Sun 10am–4pm) which features the usual displays dedicated to local history and archeology, as well as an absorbing collection of photos of the German city from the prewar era and beyond.

Practicalities

Elbląg's **bus** and **train stations** are close to each other, a fifteen-minute walk east of the Old Town centre. The **hydrofoil to Kaliningrad** departs from the wharf on the northern edge of the Old Town. Tickets are available from the *Orbis* office or on board. For **information**, try the tourist office at ul. 1 Maja 30 or the *Orbis* bureau, ul. Hetmanska 24.

The best **hotel** in town is the swish *Elzam*, al. Słowiański 2 (☎050/34 81 11, fax 32 40 88; ⑦), an old Party hotel close to the cathedral and clearly aimed at German tourists. Alternatives are the *Żuławy*, ul. Królewicka 126 (☎050/34 57 11, fax 34 83 38; ⑤), a decent-quality place with a good restaurant; the cheap and basic *Dworczowy*, ul. Grunwaldzka 49 (☎050/27011; ④), across the road from the stations; the centrally located *PTTK*, ul. Krótka 5 (☎050/24808; ③); and two similarly basic *Dom Wyciezkowy*, the *Atletikon*, ul. Agrikola 8 (☎050/33 54 05; ②), buses #8 and 17 from the stations pass by; and the *Modrzewie*, ul. Mazurska 6 (☎050/34 51 41; ②) on the eastern side of town. The main **camping site**, which also has a few cabins, is at ul. Panieńska 14 (June–Sept), on the river close to the Old Town.

While you're here you'll be hard pressed to avoid the local **Elbląg Special** (*EB*), a decent brew produced in the recently revived town brewery (there's also a branch in Braniewo): you'll find it on tap at most places, notably the *Aliva* bar, on the square just down from the cathedral.

East of Elbląg

Continuing east towards the Russian border, the high morainic inclines of the Elbląg plateau (Wzniesienie Elbląskie) stretch east along the high ridge overlooking the coast. Beyond this stirring piece of terrain scarred by deep ravines and craggy rock, lies the cathedral town of **Frombork**, below it Kaiser Wilhelm's old stables at **Kadyny**, and a little further east, the Russian border. The closer you get to the Russian frontier the more deserted things become, with few cars in evidence near the border crossing just north of Braniewo. The **main road** east of Elbląg, the old **prewar motorway** from Berlin to Königsberg via Elbląg (Elbling), will be familiar to anyone who has driven on the Autobahn of the former GDR, a Hitler-era construction that doesn't look – or drive – as if it's been touched since. Just short of the border, the road ends abruptly at an enormous wartime crater left slap bang in the middle – the map simply indicates that beyond this it's "forbidden to cars". All this is soon set to change dramatically, however. As part of the drive to improve overall regional infrastructure, reconstruction of the motorway is now high on the agenda. A joint Polish-German-Russian consortium has now been formed to carry out the major overhaul required, and if things go according to plan, a brand new road (and border crossing) should be open to traffic by late 1996/early 1997.

Kadyny

Twenty kilometres northeast of Elbląg along the coastal road, through some stunningly beautiful scenery, the village of **KADYNY** (Cadinen) conceals one of the region's real surprises: German Kaiser Wilhelm II's personal **Stables and Stud Farm**. Established in 1898 as part of the Kaiser's summer residence here, the stables are still going strong, with 170 high-quality horses kept in trim for use by a predominantly German tourist clientele. Along with the stables the half-timbered buildings of the Kaiser's **Palace** have recently been bought up by a US company, restored to their former Prussian opulence and converted into a luxury **hotel** (☎050/31 61 20 or 31 61 74, fax 31 62 00; ⑧). The rooms are small, though equipped with all the usual Western accessories. The excellent but pricey hotel **restaurant**, housed inside the old stable brewery, still has its old cast-iron staircases and large windows. The hotel's already proving very popular, with plenty of group bookings in summer, so if you want to stay you'd be well advised to reserve well in advance. Up behind the palace it's worth wandering up to see the Kaiser's private **chapel**: it's kept locked, but ask at reception and they'll organize entry.

The magnificent **stables** are mostly for use by hotel guests, but turn up early enough and you could probably negotiate for a day's riding, with or without escort. The main riding routes are along the coast and up along the plateau: reports from riding enthusiasts indicate that the plateau routes in particular make for some exhilarating riding.

To **get to Kadyny**, take the **bus** from Elbląg (25min) or the local **train** on the coastal line between Elbląg and Braniewo, via Frombork.

Frombork

A little seaside town 90km east along the Baltic coast from Gdańsk, **FROMBORK** was the home of **Nicolaus Copernicus**, the Renaissance astronomer whose ideas overturned Church-approved scientific notions, specifically the earth-centred model of the universe. Most of the research for his famous *De Revolutionibus* (see below) was carried out around this town, and it was here that he died and was buried in 1543. Just over a century later, Frombork was badly mauled by marauding Swedes, who carted off most of Copernicus' belongings, including his library. The town was wrecked in World War II, after which virtually none of the Old Town was left standing. Today it's an out-of-the-way place, as peaceful as it probably was in Copernicus' time, though of late the town has been rocked over land ownership – the Church, which owned much of the town centre before World War II, is now claiming the whole place back.

Around the Cathedral

The only part of Frombork to escape unscathed from the last war was the **Cathedral Hill**, up from the old market square in the centre of town. A compact unit surrounded by high defensive walls, its main element is the dramatic fourteenth-century Gothic **Cathedral**, with its huge red-tiled and turreted roof. Inside, the lofty expanses of brick rise above a series of lavish Baroque altars – the High Altar is a copy of the Wawel altarpiece in Kraków. The wealth of tombstones, many lavishly decorated, provide a snapshot of Warmian life in past centuries; Copernicus himself is also buried here. The seventeenth-century Baroque **organ** towering over the nave is one of the best in the country, and the Sunday afternoon and occasional weekday recitals in summer are an established feature: check the concert programme at the tourist office in Gdańsk. If you like organ music but can't make it to a concert, Frombork organ records are available from

---

NICOLAUS COPERNICUS

Nicolaus Copernicus – Mikołaj Kopernik as he's known to Poles — was born in Toruń in 1473. The son of a wealthy merchant family with strong church connections, he entered Kraków's Jagiellonian University in 1491 and subsequently joined the priesthood. Like most educated Poles of his time, he travelled abroad to continue his studies, spending time at the famous Renaissance universities of Bologna and Padua.

On his return home in 1497 he became administrator for the northern bishopric of Warmia, developing a wide field of interests, working as a doctor, lawyer, architect and soldier (he supervised the defence of nearby Olsztyn against the Teutonic Knights) – the archetypal Renaissance man. He lived for some fifteen years as canon of the Frombork chapter house and here constructed an **observatory**, where he undertook the research that provided the empirical substance for the *De Revolutionibus Orbium Caelestium*, whose revolutionary contention was that the sun, not the earth, was at the centre of the planetary system. The work was published by the Church authorities in Nuremberg in the year of Copernicus' death in 1543; it was later banned by the papacy.

the unofficial guide who hangs around outside the cathedral; he is also an authority on the intricacies of local ethnic history.

To the west of the cathedral, the **Copernicus Tower**, the oldest part of the complex, is supposed to have been the great man's workshop and observatory. Doubting that the local authorities would have let him make use of a part of the town defences, some maintain that he's more likely to have studied at his home, just north of the cathedral complex. The **Radziejowski Tower**, in the southwest corner of the walls, houses an assortment of Copernicus-related astronomical instruments and has an excellent view of the Wiślana Lagoon stretching 70km north towards Kaliningrad from the top (same opening times as the museum). Further equipment and memorabilia of the astronomer are to be found in the **Copernicus Museum** in the Warmia Bishops' Palace, across the tree-lined cathedral courtyard (Tues–Sun 9am–4.30pm). Among the exhibits are early editions of Copernicus' astronomical treatises, along with a number of his lesser-known works on medical, political and economic questions, a collection of astrolabes, sextants and other instruments, plus pictures and portraits.

Practicalities

Frombork's **bus and train stations** are located next to each other not far from the seafront; you're likely to use the PKP only if you're making your way towards Elbląg. The bus journey from Gdańsk Central station takes between two and three hours – for a day trip take the earlier of the two morning buses, returning late afternoon: if there's no direct bus back, take one to Elbląg and change there. **Information** is provided by the summertime IT booth across from the station (8am–8pm) and the main sister office at ul. Elbląska 2. These offices can sort out most things from private accommodation to local guides and boat trips.

For an overnight stay the best of a limited choice of **rooms** is a decent-quality *PTTK* hostel at ul. Krasickiego 3 (☎0506/7251; ②), in the park west of the Cathedral Hill. The other options are the *Kopernik*, a more upmarket hotel near the cathedral at ul. Koscielna 2 (☎0506/7285; ⑤), or the summer *Copernicus* youth hostel at ul. Elbląska 11 (☎0506/7453). The **PTTK camping** on ul. Braniewska (May 15–Sept 15) is some way from the centre on the Braniewo road.

Apart from some summer takeaway bars and hotel restaurants (*Kopernik* and *PTTK*), the only places **to eat** worth mentioning are the *Pod Wzgorzem* on ul. Rynek and the *Akcent*, ul. Rybecka 4, which stays open late.

Braniewo

Another old Copernicus hang-out, and onetime Hansa League member, the little Prussian town of **BRANIEWO** really got it in the neck in 1945, when some 85 percent of the buildings were destroyed: German resistance was stiff, as evidenced by more than 30,000 Soviet soldiers buried in the local cemetery. As the last stop before the border the town is assuming greater prominence, and if the plethora of satellite dishes dotted around the roofs in town are anything to go by, Braniewo is already doing very nicely out of the growing cross-border traffic. An additional source of income is the large army barracks on the edge of town, hence the droves of (Polish) soldiers milling around the centre. That said there's not much to see here, the journey on to the border being most visitors' reason for coming here, though the place does have a curiously genteel atmosphere to it.

As usual the few sites in town are grouped round the **Old Town centre**. The ruins of the town fortifications are clearly visible around **Holy Cross Church** (Św. Krzyża). Another fine Gothic brick structure badly mauled in the war, reconstruction was only finished in 1980s, but they've done a good job of it – so good in fact it's hard to believe the photos from 1945 stuck up in the porch of a desolate wreck of a building. Inside, the bareness of the high brick nave is offset at points by traces of the original structure and accompanying decoration. Round the back of the cathedral the park gives onto a brick tower that formed part of the fortifications: the tower now houses an enjoyable new bar, the *Pod Baszta*, serving cocktails and respectable cappucino with a nice view over the surroundings from the top floor.

The main **stations**, right by each other, are both near the town centre. The hotel *Warmia*, ul. Kościuszki 70 (☎0506/2029; ③), which has a decent restaurant, the *Astra*, ul. Żeromskiego 14 (☎0506/2465; ④) and the *Kopernik* (☎0506/7285; ③), are the main **accommodation** options. As in Elbląg, a pint of the locally-brewed EB is firmly recommended.

Buses run here from Elbląg (1hr), Frombork, and Gdańsk via Elbląg (2hrs 30mins), trains on the scenic coastal line to Frombork, Kadyny and Elbląg. Additionally there's a daily **train** to Kaliningrad (see box on p.206).

South from Elbląg

Travelling south from Elbląg, the main approach route to the Mazurian Lakes runs through some characteristic and attractive rural terrain, the historic towns of **Pasłęk** and **Morąg** providing the main points of architectural interest. If you're travelling by car, it's worth leaving the main road to check out some of the backwoods villages of the area, many of them hiding atmospheric and sometimes beautifully decorated old Prussian country churches.

Pasłęk

Twenty-five kilometres south of Elbląg just off the main road into Mazury, lies the charming old town of **PASŁĘK** – Preussisch Holland (Holąd Pruski), as it used to be known, a name commemorating the Dutch Mennonites who settled here in the seventeenth century to escape persecution at home, their descendants helping to build the Elbląg canal (see p.214) two centuries later. An early Baltic Prussian settlement seized and colonized by the Teutonic Knights in the late thirteenth century, Pasłęk had a pretty quiet time of it until 1945, when much of the town was suddenly reduced to ruins. Still a peaceful out-of-the-way spot, the town's tranquil provinciality encapsulates the combination of bygone rural Prussia and contemporary Polishness that characterizes the surrounding region.

The Old Town

From the bus and train station, a ten-minute walk north through the New Town area – undistinguished blocks in the main – brings you to plac Tysiąclecia, the town hub, and beyond it the walls of the Old Town. Up through the renovated Gothic **Wysoka Brama** (High Gate), you enter the Old Town area, a characteristic mix of old Prussian dwellings interspersed with the unimaginative slabs of concrete that passed for modern apartments in Polish postwar architecture. Predictably, the **Parish Church of St Bartholomew** is brick Gothic: unusually, though, the interior – generally locked, but you can ask for the key from the priest's house just north of the main entrance – has classical arched pillars rather than the usual brick supports, a result of nineteenth-century Protestant renovation of the building, making the whole building lighter than usual. With the exception of some luminous early Gothic polychromy in the presbytery, it's pretty much all basic Baroque otherwise.

The **modern history** of this church says a lot about the region's tortuous ethnic and religious development. As a result of the church being taken over by the town's minority Protestant population in the early 1800s, Pasłęk's Catholic majority was forced to build itself a small **chapel** east of the Old Town, which remained their main place of worship until the end of World War II. With the tables turned after 1945, the Catholics reoccupied St Bartholomew's: in a laudably conciliatory gesture, however, the Catholic authorities have now given the town's dwindling Protestant population – a few of the older ones are Autochtones (see the box on East Prussia, p.218) – use of the selfsame chapel. They share it with another minority, the local Ukrainian-origin **Uniate population**, on alternating weeks – hence the icons inside and Cyrillic-language signs you'll see posted on the noticeboard in the porch. To get to the chapel go through the Gothic **Brama Młynska** just east of the church and walk up the hill through the main cemetery.

At the northern edge of the area overlooking the approach to the town the former **Teutonic Knights' Castle**, rebuilt after wartime destruction, is now nothing more threatening than local government offices and the public library. A scattering of Partition-era burghers' houses apart, the only other significant survivor of the prewar ensemble is the **Town Hall**, a typical Gothic-Renaissance arcaded brick structure close by the church.

Practicalities

For an overnight stop the run-down looking *Kormoran*, ul. Bohaterów Westerplatte 8 (☎050/3119; ③), on the way up from the station, is about your only option. It also claims to double as the main tourist information point. The hotel restaurant aside, the *Ratuszowa* up by the town hall is the only presentable culinary refuge.

Pasłęk is on the main Gdańsk–Elbląg **train** line, so services in both directions are reasonably frequent. **Bus** services run to Elbląg (30 min), Morąg (40min) Gdańsk (2hr 30min) and Olsztyn (1hr 30min).

Morąg

Twenty-five kilometres further south, **MORĄG** is another notable old Prussian settlement. Travelling by car from Pasłęk you can either take the main route via Małdyty or the charming cross-country backroad signposted as you leave Pasłęk: on this route you pass through **Kwitajny**, where there's a large World War I monument to the German soldiers of Kwittin – its Prussian name – killed in Flanders.

Historically Morąg's chief claim to fame is as birthplace of the German Enlightenment poet and philosopher **Johann Gottfried Herder** (1744–1803), a thinker known for his generally pro-Slav sympathies, a fact which explains German President Richard von Weizsäcker's decision to stop off at the town during his first state visit to Poland, specifically to inspect the great man's birthplace.

The Old Town

As usual the **Old Town centre**, in slightly better shape than many neighbouring places, provides the focus of interest of an otherwise unmemorable postwar sprawl: the entrance to the empty-looking Gothic **Town Hall** in the middle of the main square sports a pair of French cannon captured by German forces during the 1870 Franco–Prussian War. The brick-vaulted Gothic **Parish Church** nearby received the usual heavy-duty Rococo-Baroque treatment, though overall there's a distinctly Protestant feel to the building – which is what it was until 1945. Later additions aside, some sections of Renaissance polychromy are still visible in the presbytery, and there's a memorial tablet to Herder at the back. Behind the church the ruins of the **Teutonic Knights' Castle**, embedded in the Old Town walls, afford a fine view over the surrounding countryside, nearby Lake Skiertąg included. Close by a newish-looking **statue** of Herder – it hasn't always been exactly kosher to commemorate famous Germans born inside the borders of modern Poland – stands opposite the house where he was born.

Continuing the Herder theme, the elegant seventeenth-century **Dohna Palace** off the other side of the square, destroyed during the war and rebuilt to the original design, is now a branch of the Warmia and Mazury **Regional Museum** (Tues–Sun 9am–4pm). The first room contains an exhibition of the **life of Herder**: first editions of his work, manuscripts, paintings, busts and other contemporary memorabilia place the man firmly in his historical context, emphasizing Herder's extensive network of contacts with other Enlightenment thinkers around Europe – a testament to the eminent sanity and level-headedness of an internationalist-minded philosopher. A large chunk of the rest of the museum is devoted to some impressive and well-displayed collections of art, furniture and handicrafts including porcelain, glass and metal work culled from four artistic schools – Baroque, Biedermeier, Secessionist and Second Empire style. If you like lamps, teasets and other period household paraphernalia you're in for a treat. Last but by no means least comes the museum's artistic showpiece, a large collection of Dutch seventeenth-century portraits and landscapes by, among others, the Honthorst brothers, Pieter Nason and Caspar Netscher. The historical connection with Warmia is underlined by the portraits of the Dohna family, a branch of which moved to Warmia in the seventeenth century and built the palace here. The current exhibition, it turns out, substantially reassembles the palace's own prewar family portrait collection, carefully restored in the 1970s and 1980s at the castle museum in Olsztyn.

Practicalities

There's little in the way of **accommodation** or **restaurants** in the town, the *Morąg*, ul. Żeromskiego 36 (☎08985/4212, fax 2668; ③), close to the picturesque Lake Narwie, being the only obvious choice. The town has regular **bus** connections to Pasłęk, Gdańsk and Olsztyn, while by **train** it's on the main Malbork–Olsztyn line.

The Elbląg Canal

Part of the network of canals stretching east to Augustow and over the Belarus border, the 81-kilometre-long **Elbląg Canal** was constructed in the mid-nineteenth century as part of the Prussian scheme to improve the region's economic infrastructure. Building the canal presented significant technical difficulties (it took over 30 years to complete the project), in particular the large difference in water level (over 100m) between the beginning and end points. To deal with this problem, Prussian engineers devised an intricate and often ingenious system of locks, choke-points and slipways: the slipways, the canal's best-known feature, are serviced by large rail-bound carriages that haul the boats overland along the sections of rail tracks that cover the sections of the route where there's no water. Five of these amazing Fitzcarraldo-like constructions operate over a ten-kilometre stretch of the northern section of the canal, located roughly halfway between Elbląg and the village of Małdyty.

If you feel like travelling on the canal, day trips along the whole stretch of the route operate daily from mid-May to the end of September, though these are sometimes cancelled if too few people turn up (20 is the minimum required). In high summer you should have no problem, but it's probably still best to check with the Elbląg *PTTK* (see p.208) or the main *Orbis* office in Olsztyn (who organize round trips from the city, p.219) before setting out. Bear in mind, too, that you'll need to bring your own food – only drinks are served on board. **Boats** start at 8am from Elbląg, arriving in **OSTRÓDA**, at the southern tip of the canal, in the early evening (a total journey time of 11–12 hours): alternatively you can travel in the other direction on the boat leaving Ostróda at the same time and finishing up in Elbląg in the evening. If you don't feel like trekking the whole distance, you can at least follow a section of the canal from **MAŁDYTY**, an attractive village just east of the main Elbląg–Ostróda road, some 40km south of Elbląg. If you're travelling by car and want to glance at the **slipways**, turn west off the main road at **Marzewo**, a few kilometres north of Małdyty, and you'll meet the canal 5km down the road.

THE LAKES

The woodlands that open up to the east of Morąg signal the advent of **Mazury or Mazuria**, the "land of a thousand lakes" that occupies the northeast corner of the country, stretching for some 300km towards the Lithuanian border. Geologically, the region's current form was determined by the last Ice Age, the myriad lakes a product of the retreat of the last great Scandinavian glacier. A sparsely populated area of thick forests and innumerable lakes and rivers, Mazury is one of the country's main holiday districts – and rightfully so. It's a wonderful haunt for walkers, campers, watersports enthusiasts or just for taking it easy.

Coming from Gdańsk, **Olsztyn** is the first major town and provides a good base for exploring the lesser-known western parts of Mazury, a landscape of rolling woodland interspersed with farming villages. Enjoyable as this area is, though, most holidaymakers head east to the area around lakes **Mamry** and **Śniardwy** – the two largest of the region – and to more developed tourist towns like **Giżycko**, **Mrągowo** and **Mikołajki**. Further east still, up beyond **Ełk**, is the **Suwalszczyzna**, tucked away by the border, in many ways the most enchanting part of the region. As with other border areas there is a minority population, in this case Lithuanians.

Transport links within the region are reasonably well developed if slow. Local trains and/or buses run between all the main destinations: further afield, notably in the Suwalszczyzna, the bus service becomes more unpredictable, so you may have to rely on hitching – which is not too much of a problem in the holiday season. Approaching Mazury from the south can be tricky, however, as the lakelands were in a different country until 45 years ago. Olsztyn and Augustów are on main rail lines from Warsaw; anything in between may involve a couple of changes, so the bus from Warsaw to Mikołajki may be a better idea if you're heading direct to the central lakes.

For **trekking** or **canoeing**, a tent, a sleeping roll, food supplies and the right clothing are essential – don't count on being able to buy equipment in Poland. Canoe rental can usually be organized by *Almatur* or *PTTK*, and sometimes by *Orbis*, though all three should be contacted well in advance (see *Basics* for addresses). As tourism develops, however, there's a fair chance that you may find facilities on offer from new local operators, or established workers' holiday homes which are now having to make their own way.

Olsztyn

Of several possible stepping-off points for the lakes, **OLSZTYN** is the biggest and the easiest to reach, and owing to the summertime tourist influx it's well kitted-out to deal with visitors, most of whom stop here en route for points further east. The town itself is located in pleasant woodland, but owing to wartime destruction – Soviet troops burnt the place down in 1945 after the fighting had ceased – much of the old centre is the usual residential postwar greyness. Nestled among the concrete blocks and dusty main thoroughfares, though, quiet streets of neat brick houses built by the city's former German inhabitants remain, their durability and calm orderliness forming a strong contrast with the often shabby modern constructions. While there's not really enough to justify a special detour, you can easily while away half a day here if you're passing.

Olsztyn was something of a latecomer, gaining municipal status in 1353, twenty years after its castle was begun. Following the 1466 Toruń Treaty, the town was reintegrated into Polish territory, finally escaping the clutches of the Teutonic Knights. Half a century later Nicolaus Copernicus took up residence as an administrator of the province of Warmia, and in 1521 helped organize the defence of the town against the Knights.

Coming under **Prussian control** after the First Partition, it remained part of East Prussia until 1945. Resistance to Germanization during this period was symbolized by the establishment here, in 1921, of the Association of Poles in Germany, an organization dedicated to keeping Polish culture alive within the Reich. With Hitler's accession, the Association became a target for Nazi terror, and most of its members perished in the concentration camps. The town also suffered, roughly forty percent being demolished by 1945.

Nonetheless, postwar development has established Olsztyn as the region's major industrial centre, with a population of 160,000. Ethnically they are quite a mixed bunch: the majority of the German-speaking population, expelled from the town after World War II, was replaced by settlers from all over Poland, particularly the eastern provinces annexed by the Soviet Union, and from even further afield – such as a small community of Latvians.

The Town

The main places to see are concentrated in the **Old Town**, fifteen minutes' walk to the west of the **bus and train stations**, and you won't need more than a couple of hours to take in the main sights. As an alternative to walking, just about any bus heading down al. Partyzantów will drop you at **plac Wolności**, the

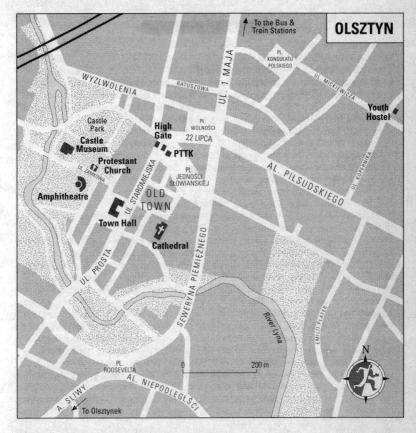

town's main square, with the Gothic **High Gate** (Brama Wysoka) – the entrance
to the Old Town – a short walk away at the end of ul. 22 Lipca.

Once through the gate, ul. Staromiejska brings you to the **Rynek**, which
retains a few of its old buildings, most notably the Prussian-looking Town Hall,
appearing rather stranded in its centre.

Over to the west is the **Castle**, fourteenth-century but extensively rebuilt,
surveying the steep little valley of the River Lyna. Its **Museum** (Tues–Sun 10am–
4pm) is an institution with an ideological mission: defining the region's historical
record from an unashamedly Polish perspective. The ethnography section
contains a good selection of folk costumes, art and furniture, while the historical
section stresses the Warmians' general resistance to all things German. There's
also a large archeological collection, including objects from ancient burial
grounds – look out for the mysterious granite figure in the castle courtyard, a
relic of the original Slavic Prussians. **Copernicus' living quarters**, on the first
floor of the southwest wing, are the castle's other main feature: along with a wistful portrait by Matejko and several of the astronomer's instruments, the rooms
contain a sundial supposed to have been designed by Copernicus himself. It's

EAST PRUSSIA

Present-day Warmia and Mazuria make up the heartlands of what until forty years ago was called **East Prussia** (Ostpreussen). Essentially the domains ruled by the Teutonic Knights at the height of their power, the whole area was originally populated by pagan Baltic and Borussian (later known as Prussian) tribes, most of whom were wiped out by the Teutonic colonizers. **Warmia** (Royal Prussia), the main part of the territory, whose name derives from the Prussian tribe of the Warms that once lived here, passed into Polish control following the Treaty of Toruń (1466), after which Polish settlers began moving into the area in numbers. It remained part of Poland until the First Partition (1772) when it was annexed by Prussia.

Mazuria proper, the eastern part of the territory – Ducal Prussia as it eventually became known – has been **German-ruled** for most of its modern history. Following the secularization of the Teutonic Knights' lands in 1525, the Brandenberg Hohenzollern family acquired the region as a hereditary duchy, though they were still obliged to pay homage to the Polish king.

This was not the end of the original "**German question**", however, for in 1657, under the pressure of the Swedish wars, King Jan Kazimierz released the branch of the powerful Hohenzollern family ruling Ducal Prussia from any form of Polish jurisdiction, allowing them to merge the province with their own German territories. By 1701 Elector Frederick III was able to proclaim himself king of an independent Ducal Prussia, and impose limits on Polish settlement in the region: the way was now cleared – from the Polish point of view – for the disastrous slide to Frederick the Great and Partition-era Prussia.

From the German point of view Prussia's first real setback in centuries came at the end of **World War I**, when the region was reduced to the status of a *Land* within the Weimar Republic and subjected to a series of plebiscites to determine whether Germany or Poland should have control of several parts of the territory. As it turned out, both the Warmian and Mazurian provinces voted to remain in Germany, with the easternmost area around Suwałki going to Poland. Heavily militarized during the course of **World War II**, in 1945 East Prussia was sliced across the middle, the northern half, including the capital Königsberg, designated a new province of the Russian Federation (though separated from it by Lithuania), the southern half becoming part of Poland.

Prusso-German culture had a strong impact on the character of the area, as evidenced by the many Protestant churches and German-looking towns dotted around – Olsztyn was once known as Allenstein, Elbląg as Elbling, Ełk as Lyck. Today the most obvious sign of Prussian influence is the influx of Germans who flock to the major lakeside holiday resorts in the summer. The Mercedes and BMW bikes look out of place in tatty Polish tourist towns, but many of the older visitors had family roots here until 1945, when – as in other areas of newly liberated Poland – everybody of German origin was ordered to leave. Most fled to West Germany, joining the millions of other displaced or uprooted peoples moving across Europe in the immediate postwar period.

A particularly sad example of the Polish government's rigid displacement policy occurred with the **Autochtones**, a peasant minority from the villages around Olsztyn. Like the other historic peoples of Warmia, the Autochtones were of Baltic origin, but unlike the original Baltic Prussians they survived the onslaughts of the Teutonic Knights, only to be strongly Germanized then Polonized during the Polish rule of Ducal Prussia. Yet after centuries of tending the forests, they were pressurized into leaving the Olsztyn area for good on account of the German taint in their history.

also worth making the climb up the **castle tower** (same opening hours) for the view over the town and surroundings. Directly below the castle is a large open-air **amphitheatre**, used for theatre and concert performances in summertime, nestled on the leafy banks of the River Łyna. Coming out of the back of the castle you can stroll across the bridge over the gently coursing river to the park on the other side – an atmospheric spot, particularly at sunset.

Back towards the centre, up from the castle entrance there's a stern neo-Gothic **Protestant Church**, formerly used by the predominantly non-Catholic German population. To get to the early fifteenth-century – and Catholic – **Cathedral**, whose high brick tower dominates the surroundings, walk back across the Rynek. Originally a grand parish church, including an intricately patterned brick ceiling that's among the most beautiful in the region and a powerful crucifixion triptych hanging over the high altar, this retains some of its original Gothic features: despite extensive renovations it's still a moodily atmospheric place.

Practicalities

The well-organized **COIT office**, part of a tourist office complex just down from the High Gate on pl. Jedności Słowiańskiej (☎089/27 27 38), will give you all the information you need, probably in English, both for the town itself and journeys on into the lakes – several of the staff speak English too. At the time of writing, however, the office has had to close down temporarily due to financial problems. If it is still shut, try the *PTTK* bureau next door, the tourist office at ul. Grunwaldzka 15, south of the Old Town complex, or *Orbis*, al. Dąbrowszczakow 1.

Olsztyn has a excellent range of **accommodation**. **Hotels** include the upmarket *Kormoran*, near the station at pl. Konstytucji 3 Maya 4 (☎089/33 58 64, fax 33 61 95; ⑤), popular with German tourists; the *Relax*, ul. Zołnierska 13a (☎089/27 75 34; ③); the central *Nad Łyną*, ul. Wojska Polskiego 14 (☎089/26 71 66; ②); and the *Garnizonowy*, Gietkowska 1 (☎089/26 93 81; ③). The *Warmiński*, ul. Głowackiego 8 (☎089/33 53 53; ③), recently renovated, has one of the best restaurants in town. Among the budget options, the best bet is the central **PTTK hostel** (☎089/27 36 75; ②); housed in the gate itself, it's a nice, unpretentious overnighter, with shared bathrooms.There's also the *Jantar*, ul. Kętrynskiego 5 (☎089/33 54 52; ②), a former workers' hotel near the train station, and the *Lotnisko*, ul. Sielska 43 (☎089/27 52 40; ②), well west of the centre in the Dajti district – buses #7 and 13 from the train station pass by. Also out of the centre, the *Orbis Novotel* motel is on the western edge of town, at ul. Sielska 4a (☎089/27 40 81, fax 27 54 03; ⑥). Finally the *Park*, ul. Warszawska 119 (☎089/23 66 04, fax 27 60 77; ⑧), 2km south of town on the Warsaw road, part of the international *Park* chain, is the classiest – and most expensive – addition to the town's accommodation stock.

For **private rooms**, ask at the *COIT* office. The main **youth hostel** is at ul. Kopernika 45 (☎089/27 66 50; open all year). In summer, cheap beds are also available in the **student hotels** at the Agricultural College in the southern suburb of Kortowo; check with the *Almatur* office at ul. Kopernika 20 (☎089/33 05 00) for what's currently on offer. Finally, there's a good, large *PTTK* **campsite** (May–Sept) by Lake Krzywe, near the *Novotel* (May–Sept); bus #7 passes the entrance.

Restaurants in Olsztyn seem to be on the up. Aside from the *Warmiński*, there is a good French place, the *Francuska* at ul. Dąbrowszczakow 39, and a heartily recommended Syrian restaurant, the *Eridu* at ul. Prosta 3–4 in the Old

Town. Other options include the *Kasztelanka*, ul. Mieszka 1 in the old town centre with a nice bar, the *Andromeda*, ul. Piłsudskiego, and the *Kolorowa*, al. Wojska Polskiego 74. The *Staromiejska*, on the main square, is a lively bar-café with live music a couple of nights a week, and the *ZPAF* gallery, inside the castle grounds, has a popular bar that fills with tourists in summer. The enjoyable *Sarp* café at ul. Kołtataja 14, housed in a restored granary, is the local Architects' Society hang-out, while the *Yogurcik*, ul. 22 Lipca 5, does a good line in ice cream and cakes.

North of Olsztyn

If you're not eager to press straight on to the lakes, it's worth considering a day trip – feasible by bus – through the attractive countryside north of Olsztyn to the town of **Lidzbark Warmiński**.

The forty-kilometre journey takes you through the open woodlands and undulating farmland characteristic of western Mazury, and if you've caught an early bus there's enough time for a stopoff en route at **DOBRE MIASTO**, a small town with a vast Gothic **church** – the largest in the region after Frombork cathedral – rising majestically from the edge of the main road. Baroque ornamentation overlays much of the interior, and there's a florid late-Gothic replica of Kraków's Mariacki altar; the collegiate buildings round the back house a minor local museum.

Lidzbark Warmiński

Set amid open pastureland watered by the River Łyna, **LIDZBARK WARMIŃSKI** started out as one of the numerous outposts of the Teutonic Knights. When they'd finished conquering the region, they handed the town over to the bishops of Warmia, who used it as their main residence from 1350 until the late eighteenth century. Following the Toruń Treaty, Lidzbark came under Polish rule, becoming an important centre of culture and learning – Copernicus lived here, just one member of a community of artists and scientists. A later luminary of the intellectual scene in Lidzbark was **Ignacy Krasicki** (1735–1801), a staunch defender of all things Polish; after Prussian rule had done him out of his job as archbishop, he turned his attention to writing, producing a string of translations, social satires and one of the first Polish novels.

The Castle

Sadly, much of the old town centre was wiped out in 1945, only the parish church, town gate and a few sections of the fortifications managing to survive the fighting. Lidzbark's impressive Teutonic **Castle**, however, came through unscathed, a stylish, well-preserved, riverside fortress which ranks as one of the architectural gems of the region. Used as a fortified residence for the Warmian bishops, it has the familiar regional period look to it: the square brick structure echoes Frombork cathedral in its tiled roof, Malbork in the turreted towers rising from the corners.

Moving through the main gate you find yourself in a courtyard, with arcaded galleries rising dreamily above, while at ground level there are Gothic cellars with delicate ribbed vaulting. Inside the main structure, fragments of fifteenth-century frescoes are visible in places, and the **chapel** retains its sumptuous Rococo decorations. But the chief interest comes from the exhibits in the

Regional Museum (June–Sept Tues–Sun 9am–5pm, Oct–May 9am–4pm) that now occupies much of the building. The displays begin with excellent Gothic sculpture in the **Great Refectory**, featuring the tombstones of several Warmian bishops, whose heraldic devices still cover the walls. On the second floor are a collection of modern Polish art, not very riveting, and an exquisite exhibition of **icons**. These come from the convent at Wojnowo (see p.238), where the nuns are members of the strongly traditionalist Starowiercy (Old Believers) sect, a grouping which broke away from official Orthodoxy in protest at the religious reforms instigated by Peter the Great.

The east wing of the castle was demolished in the mid-eighteenth century to make way for a bishop's palace and gardens. The **winter garden** opposite the approach to the castle is the most attractive bit left, with a Neoclassical orangery that wouldn't be out of place in a royal residence. Into the town centre the tall **Parish Church** is another Gothic brick hall structure, similar in style to Dobre Miasto: the aisles off the vaulted nave reveal some fine Renaissance side altars and old tombstones. The old **Protestant Church** in town is now an Orthodox *cerkiew* used by the Eastern settlers who moved here following the postwar border shifts.

Practicalities

The High Gate, now the local **PTTK hostel** (☎08983/2521; ②), is a good place for an overnight stay, closely followed by the much more upmarket *Pod Kłobukiem*, ul. Olsztyńska 4 (☎08983/3291 or 3292; ⑥), 2km out of town on the Olsztyn road, which also has a restaurant. The other options are the **youth hostel** at ul. Piłsudskiej 3 (July & Aug only; ☎08983/3147), not far from the station, and the summer **campsite** next to the *Pod Kłobukiem*.

Orneta

Just under 50km northwest of Olsztyn lies **ORNETA**, a small market town that boasts one of the finest of the many Gothic brick churches scattered around Warmia. Arriving in town by bus brings you almost immediately into the attractive old market square, at one end of which stands the Gothic brick **Town Hall**, with a snazzy new *kawiarnia* and billiard hall tucked away in its dimly lit medieval cellars.

Off the other end of the square stands the magnificent, robust-looking Gothic **St John's Church** (Kosciol Sw. Jana). Here for once the austere brick facade customary in the Gothic churches of northern Poland is transformed by some imaginative and exuberant decoration. A welter of tall slender parapets rises up on all sides of the building, while close inspection of the carved walls reveals sequences of grotesquely contorted faces leering out at the world – the masons obviously retained their sense of humour. Above them a set of five menacing-looking dragon heads jut out from the roof edge, jaws agape and spitting fire down on the onlooker. Surmounting the church is a characteristic high brick tower, thicker and stockier than usual, lending solidity to the ensemble.

After the fabulous exterior the interior lives up to expectations, the highlight being the complex geometrically patterned decorations on the brick vault soaring above the high nave. An even more than usually ornate high altarpiece and pulpit are matched by the large, solid-looking Baroque organ astride the entrance portal. A fine Gothic triptych stands in the right-hand aisle and Gothic and

Renaissance murals decorate several of the side chapels, one sporting a colourful portrait of Renaissance-era Warmian cardinal Stanislaus Hosius. One of the most satisfying Gothic buildings in the region, it's well worth the detour to get here.

By **bus** the town's a one-and-a-half-hour journey from Olsztyn, making it another feasible day trip. Like Dobre Miasto, it's also on the main Olsztyn–Braniewo **rail** line, with services running a couple of times a day in each direction. The only real place to stay in town is the basic *EWA* at ul. 1 Maja 8 (☎284; ②).

South from Olsztyn

South of Olsztyn takes you into more of the attractive rolling countryside for which the approaches to Mazuria are known. For most people, however, the main reason for heading this way is the battlefield at **Grunwald**, the well-kept *skansen* at **Olsztynek** providing an additional worthwhile stopoff.

Olsztynek and around

OLSZTYNEK, 26km south of Olsztyn, is home to an excellent **skansen** (June–Aug Tues–Sun 9am–5pm; May, Sept–Oct Tues–Sun 9am–4pm; Nov–April Tues–Sun 9am–3pm). Located on the northern edge of the small town, the park is devoted to eighteenth- and nineteenth-century folk architecture from Warmia, Mazuria and, surprisingly, Lithuania as well. Many fine examples of sturdy regional architecture have been gathered here: take a close look at the joints on some of the half-timbered cottages and you'll appreciate the superb workmanship that went into these buildings. Alongside the assorted farm buildings, barns, workshops, and a watermill, there's a fine, early eighteenth-century wooden Protestant church with a thatched roof. The highlight of the lot, though, is undoubtedly the group of old windmills, two of them over two hundred years old. With its huge coloured blades and sturdy plank frame, the **Lithuanian mill** at the edge of the park, known as "Paltrak", is a picture-postcard favourite.

For an **overnight stay** in Olsztynek – the town makes a good base if you're going onto Grunwald – the *Mazurski*, ul. Gdańska 15 (☎089/19 28 85; ②), is the obvious venue: there's also a good **restaurant** here, with the excellent local fish dishes a house speciality.

The Hindenburg Mausoleum

About a kilometre west of the *skansen* close to the village of Sudwa lie the ruins of the notorious **Hindenburg Mausoleum**. The original monument was built here by the German army after World War I to commemorate victory under the command of Field Marshal Paul von Hindenburg over Russian forces at the battle of Tannenberg in August 1914. Following Hindenburg's death in 1934, Hitler ordered a huge mausoleum to be built for one of his favourite Prussian military figures. With defeat in sight the retreating Nazis moved his remains to Worms Cathedral in Germany in 1945. The mausoleum was obliterated by Soviet forces soon afterwards, the stones eventually being used for a Soviet war monument near Olsztyn. The site isn't marked on the road, but you'll find it in the forest behind the village, a large enclosure marking the site of what was by all accounts a massive structure.

Grunwald

If there's one historical event every Polish schoolchild can give you a date for it's the battle of **Grunwald** (1410). One of the most important European battles of the medieval era, the victory at Grunwald came to assume the mythological status of a symbol of the nation's resistance to – and on this occasion triumph over – German militarism. Predictably, the reality of the battle was rather more complicated. Commanded by King Władysław Jagiełło, the combined Polish-Lithuanian army opposing Grand Master Ulrich von Jungingen and his Knights included plenty of other nationalities among its ranks – Czechs, Hungarians, Ruthenians, Russians and Tartars. In an era when the modern concept of the nation-state was far from established the straight Polish-German struggle proposed in latterday nationalist interpretations of the event seems something of an oversimplification. What is certain is the fact that Grunwald was one of the biggest – over 30,000 men on each side – and bloodiest of medieval battles. The eventual rout of the Knights left the Grand Master and 11,000 of his men dead, with another 14,000 taken prisoner. The defeat at Grunwald finally broke the back of the Knights' hitherto boundless expansionist ambitions and paved the way for the first of a succession of peace treaties (1411) with Poland-Lithuania that decisively weakened their control over the northern and eastern territories.

The battlefield

The **battle site** lies 20km southwest of Olsztynek. It's not easy to get here without your own vehicle – by public transport local buses run from Olsztynek and, less frequently, Olsztyn. Stuck out in the middle of the pleasant, tranquil Warmian countryside, it's hard to square the surroundings with your idea of a major battle site. The odd modern farmhouse apart, though, the battlefield probably doesn't look that different today from the site that greeted the opposing armies 580-odd years ago. Walking up from the bus stop past the souvenir kiosk brings you to the centrepiece of the site, an imposing thirty-metre-high steel monument that looks uncannily like the Gdańsk Shipyard memorial, set on a hilltop overlooking the battlefield. To help you visualize the whole thing in context, just beyond the monument there's a large stone diagram set out on the gound illustrating the battle positions of the two armies and their movements throughout the fighting.

Back behind the monument the Grunwald **Museum** (May–Sept Mon–Sun 9am–6pm Oct–April 10am–4pm) contains a heavyweight display of armour, weapons, standards and other military paraphernalia from the battle, some original, most later copies. The shield inscribed "Grunwald 1410, Berlin 1945" says much about the postwar Polish state's appropriation of Grunwald for its own specific ideological ends.

Barczewo

Seventeen kilometres east of Olsztyn, set back from the main E16 road into Mazuria, is **BARCZEWO**, another dusty old provincial town where nothing much seems to be changing: the main reason most Poles have heard of the place is the fact that the notorious former Nazi Gauleiter of Mazuria, **Jozef Koch**, was imprisoned here until his death, aged 92, in the early 1980s.

Surprisingly, for a town of this size, Barczewo boasts two attractive Gothic churches. Altar triptych apart, the austere interior of the **Parish Church of St**

Annes', a chunky brick edifice overlooking the river, looks as though it was given a thorough Prussian Protestant reworking. By contrast **St Andrew's Church**, a fourteenth-century Franciscan foundation off the square, is basic Gothic with a strongly Baroque overlay, the main feature being a delicately sculptured marble Renaissance memorial to Warmian bishop Andreas Batory and his brother Balthazar, designed by Dutch architect Wilhelm van den Blocke of Gdańsk fame. Batory's actual remains aren't here, however, but lost in the Moldavian countryside, where he died in the early 1600s fighting for the independence of his Transylvanian homeland.

Mazuria's not a region usually associated with **Jewish culture**, though until the Nazi era there were in fact plenty of Jews living in the region. South of the square on ul. Kościuszki stands the mid-nineteenth-century former **Synagogue**, one of the very few in the region to survive the war. A wartime Nazi ammunition dump, the synagogue was converted into a *Dom Kultury* after 1945.

In 1980 it also became the workshop of local textile artist **Barbara Hulanicka**, who lives next door at no. 13 – call at her place to get into the synagogue. A skilled weaver with an impressive track record of international exhibitions, Hulanicka has devoted herself to reviving and promoting the folk weaving traditions of Warmia and Mazuria. Using some wonderful old nineteenth-century looms she's rescued from surrounding villages, Hulanicka produces unusual tapestries, often with themes drawn from different world religions, and several of which you'll find adorning the walls of the building. A mine of information about the region, she's always pleased to show visitors round the workshop, fellow artists in particular.

If you decide to **stay over**, your only option is the old workers' hotel just down from the square at ul. Wojska Polskiego 48 (☎584; ②).

The Mazurian Lakes

East of Olsztyn, the central Mazury lakeland opens out amid thickening forests. In summer the biggest lakes – **Mamry** and **Śniardwy** – are real crowd-pullers, with all the advantages and disadvantages that brings. On the plus side, tourist facilities are well developed in many places, and you can rent sailing and canoeing equipment in all the major resorts. On the other hand, the crush can be intolerable, and the primitive sewage facilities of the bigger towns has led to severe pollution. If solitude and clean water are what you're after, the best advice is to get a detailed map and head for the smaller lakes: as a general principle, tranquillity increases as you travel east.

Among highlights, **Mrągowo**, the most westerly of the major holiday resorts, is now at least as well known for its Country and Western Festival. Perched on the southern edge of Lake Mamry, **Giżycko** attracts yachters and canoeists and is a useful base for exploring the lakes, while **Mikołajki** to the east is arguably the most pleasant and most attractively located of the major-league lakeside resorts. Alongside the holiday centres, Mazury also boasts a wealth of historic churches and castles, including the famous monastery complex at **Święta Lipka** and the Gothic ensembles at **Reszel**. A detour into the region's tangled ethnic history is provided by the Orthodox nunnery at **Wojnowo** and, in addition, Mazury hides one of the strangest and most chilling of all World War II relics, Hitler's wartime base at **Gierłoz**.

On the whole, **transport** around the lakes isn't too problematic. While a car is a definite advantage for venturing into the further-flung reaches, bus and train connections between the main centres are more than adequate.

Mrągowo

MRĄGOWO, situated on the main Olsztyn–Augustów road, is one of the principal centres of the district, and if you're anywhere near in late July it would be folly to miss its acclaimed **Country Picnic Festival**, held in an amphitheatre adjoining the *Orbis Hotel Mrągowia*. In Poland, as elsewhere in eastern Europe, C&W is big news, decried even more than jazz during the communist era as imperialist culture, and loved by the Poles as a consequence. The festival, which has been running since 1983, is an opportunity for aspiring Slav Hank Williamses and Dolly Partons to croon their hearts out in front of large, appreciative audiences; over 15,000 people attended the 1995 festival. Alongside the local bands, there's always at least a couple of big-name stars from the US.

Festival aside, Mrągowo is a pleasant enough resort town, with a decidedly German feel to its architecture – hardly surprising when you consider it was a Prussian possession for almost seven centuries. Focus of the town is the central square, just up from the edge of Lake Czos, a small expanse of water that sees plenty of activity in season. The **Local Museum** (Tues–Sun 10am–3pm), housed in the old town hall, features an extensive collection of local wooden chests and cabinets alongside some elegant eighteenth-century furniture pieces from around Prussia. A display centring on **Krzystof Mrongoviusz** fills you in on the locally born priest and nineteenth-century champion of Polish culture after whom the town – originally Sensburg – was renamed in 1945. East of the square near the main Catholic church is the town's brick nineteenth-century Protestant temple, now used by the local Russian Orthodox community

Practicalities

Scenically positioned on the lakeside facing the town (a two-kilometre drive), the *Mrongovia*, ul Giżycka 6 (☎08984/3221 or 3229, fax 3220; ⑧), a much-hyped *Orbis* joint, is where most of the foreign tourists stay. It's also your best source of tourist **information**. As well as canoes and kayaks on the lake in summer the hotel also offers (fairly pricey) **byplane trips** over the area; ask at the hotel reception for details. Cheaper accommodation alternatives are the central *Polonia* at ul. Warszawska 10 (☎08984/3572; ③), the *Krajan*, ul. Kolejowa 9 (☎08984/2275; ②), opposite the train station, and the welter of small *pensjonaty* and former workers' hotels scattered around the town, especially on the road up behind the *Mrongovia*. The *Camp Park*, Wilamówek 1 (☎08984/8750 or 8770), in **Borowski Las**, 9km southwest of town is a well-organized and popular site, complete with shop and restaurant – there are also rooms on offer. Of the **restaurants** in town, the *Mrongovia* offers decent enough, if pricey, *Orbis* fare. Otherwise there are plenty of smaller places, many of the fast-food variety, in the town centre.

Trains from the station on the western outskirts of town, run three times a day (more in summer) to Mikołajki and Olsztyn. In July and August, there are also a couple of daily trains to Warsaw. By **bus** from the central bus station, there are frequent services to Kętrzyn, Mikołajki and Olsztyn, and two express bus departures to Warsaw.

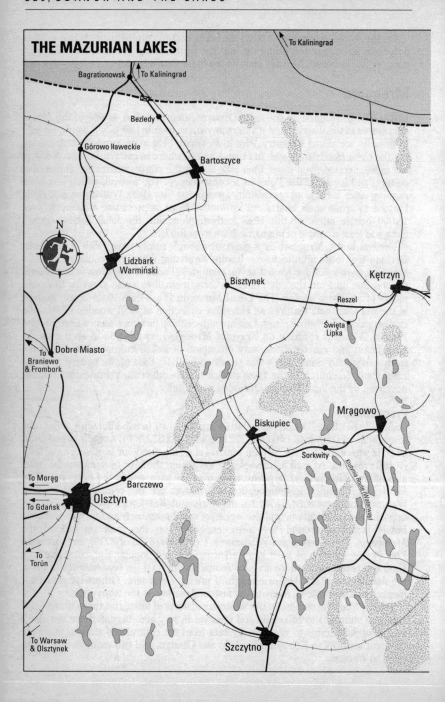

THE MAZURIAN LAKES

To Kaliningrad

To Kaliningrad

Bagrationowsk

Bezledy

Górowo Iławeckie

Bartoszyce

N

Lidzbark
Warmiński

Bisztynek

Kętrzyn

Reszel

Święta
Lipka

To
Braniewo
& Frombork

Dobre Miasto

Mrągowo

Biskupiec

Sorkwity

Krutynia Route (Waterway)

To Morąg

Barczewo

Olsztyn

To Gdańsk

To
Toruń

To Warsaw
& Olsztynek

Szczytno

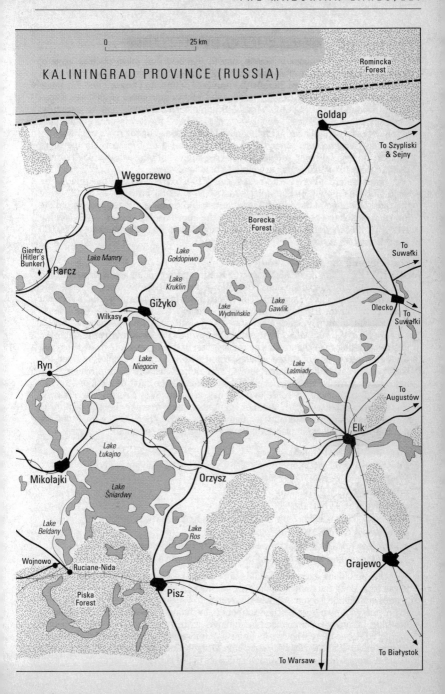

CANOEING IN THE LAKES

If you like messing about in **boats**, one of the best and most exciting ways of exploring the region is from the water. The vast complex of lakes, rivers and waterways means there are literally thousands of options to choose from. For those who haven't lugged their canoes, kayaks and yachts on trailers all the way across Poland – and increasing numbers of Scandinavians, French and in particular Germans are joining Poles in doing so every summer – the key issue is getting hold of the necessary equipment. With the tourist trade opened up to private operators it's becoming easier to turn up and rent yourself a canoe on the spot. On the more popular routes, however, demand is increasingly high in season, so it would definitely pay to try and organize yourself a boat in advance.

A good resource here is the network of **PTTK offices** around the region, the main office in Olsztyn, ul. Staromiejska 1 (☎089/27 51 58/5015, fax 27 34 42) being the most useful point of contact. Plenty of detailed **maps** of the region appropriate for canoeists have come on the market; the most useful general ones are the 1:120,000 *Wielkie Jezioro Mazurskie* and a new Polish/English language 1: 300,000 *Warmia and Masuria*.

Sorkwity and the Krutynia route

SORKWITY, 12km west of Mrągowo, is the starting point for a beautiful and popular canoeing run which ends 90km downstream at Lake Bełdany, adjoining the western edge of Lake Sniardwy. The *Orbis* hotel in Mrągowo can help sort out canoe rental for the trip, but in summer advance notice is virtually essential.

Canoeists generally start from the *PTTK* waterside hostel (*stanica wodna*; May–Sept) at the edge of Sorkwity village. Known as the **Krutynia route**, after the narrow, winding river that makes up the last part of the journey, the route takes you through a succession of eighteen lakes, connected by narrow stretches of river, the banks often covered with dense forest. The journey usually takes anything from nine days upwards, with Ruciane-Nida or Mikołajki the final destination, though you can also shorten the route to a five-day trip ending at Krutyń. The Krutynia route is very popular in high summer, so the best time to make the trip is either in spring (April–May) or late summer (late August–September). Overnight stops are generally in the following places (in *stanice wodne* unless specified):

- **day one** BIEŃKI (15km)
- **day two** BABIITA (12km), there's also a youth hostel (July-Aug) here
- **day three** SPYCHOWO (12.5km)
- **day four** ZGONIE (10.5km)
- **day five** KRUTYŃ (14km)
- **day six** UTKA (18.5km), the first stop on the Krutynia river itself
- **day seven** NOWY MOST (6.5km)
- **day eight** KAMIEŃ (10.5km) on the beautiful **Lake Bełdany**, the final
- **day nine** ending up at RUCIANE-NIDA (13.5km; see p.236).

If this ambitious excursion sounds appealing, the **Olsztyn PTTK** offers ten-day kayak trips along the route including overnight stops for under $150. In summer, only groups are eligible, so you may have to arrange to tag along with others. You will need to provide your own gear for the trip though, including a sleeping bag. For **advance booking** (strongly recommended in summer) write or even call – if you do there's usually someone there who speaks English or, more likely, German. Alternatively, for shorter excursions the *Hotel Mrongowia* in Mrągowo may be able to sort you out with a canoe, though here again, in summer advance notice is virtually essential.

Święta Lipka

Twenty kilometres north and a forty-minute bus ride from Mrągowo is the **church** at ŚWIĘTA LIPKA, probably the country's most famous Baroque shrine. Lodged on a thin strip of land in between two lakes, the magnificent church is stuck out in the middle of nowhere. As an approach area stuffed with souvenir stalls and locals peddling "folk art" at inflated prices suggests, the out-of-the-way location doesn't stop the tourists turning up in droves. As often in Poland, the draw of the church isn't purely its architectural qualities; Święta Lipka is also an important centre of pilgrimage and Marian devotion, and during religious festivals the church is absolutely jammed with pilgrims, creating an intense atmosphere of fervent Catholic devotion.

The name Święta Lipka – literally "holy linden tree" – derives from a local medieval legend according to which a Prussian tribal leader, released from imprisonment by the Teutonic Knights, is supposed to have placed a statue of the Virgin in a linden tree as a token of thanks. Within a few years healing miracles were being reported at the place, and a chapel was eventually built on the site by the Knights in 1320. The fame and supposed curative powers of the shrine increased by leaps and bounds, to such an extent that by the end of the fifteenth century it had become an important centre of pilgrimage. Following their conversion to Lutheranism, the Teutonic Knights destroyed the chapel in 1526, in characteristically brutal fashion placing gallows in front of the site in a bid to deter pilgrims. In 1620 Poles managed to purchase the ruins, and another chapel was constructed under the direction of Stefan Sadorski, King Sigismund II's private secretary, and handed over to Jesuits from the Lithuanian section of the Order in the 1630s. With pilgrims turning up in ever-increasing numbers the Jesuits decided to build a new and more ambitious sanctuary. Work on the Baroque edifice you see today was begun in 1687 under the direction of Jerzy Ertly, an architect from Vilnius, so to anyone familiar with the churches of the Lithuanian capital and its surroundings, the "eastern" Baroque of Święta Lipka will come as no surprise.

The Church

In a country with a major predilection for Baroque richness the Święta Lipka complex is unquestionably one of the most exuberant of them all. Approached from a country road, the low cloisters, tapering twin towers of the **church facade** and plain yellow and white stucco covering the exterior are quintessential eastern Polish Baroque. Entrance to the complex (Mon–Sat 8am–6pm, Sundays in between Masses) is through a magnificent early eighteenth-century wrought-iron gate designed by Johann Schwartz, a local from Reszel, the surrounding cloisters topped by 44 stone statues representing the genealogy of Christ.

Through the main door you enter the body of the building, a rectangular structure with a long central nave, side aisles divided from the nave on each side by four sets of pillars supporting overhanging galleries and a presbytery. The first thing to catch the eye is the superb **fresco work** covering every inch of the ceiling, the work of one Maciej Meyer from nearby Lidzbark Warmiński, which draws on a wide range of themes ranging from the lives of Christ and Mary and Old Testament stories, to depictions of Jesuit missions and the Marian cult of Święta Lipka itself. Young Meyer was sent off to Rome in the early 1700s to improve his craft, in particular the execution of three-dimensional and *trompe* *l'oeil* effects. He clearly learned a thing or two: particularly in the central nave's vaulted ceiling the polychromy is a triumph, several of the frescoes employing the newly acquired *trompe l'oeil* techniques to powerful effect.

Towering above the nave the lofty main **altarpiece**, an imposing wooden structure completed in 1714, has three levels; the upper two contain pictures on biblical themes, the lowest a seventeenth-century icon of the Madonna and Child – the Holy Mother of God of Święta Lipka as it's known locally – based on an original kept at Santa Maria Maggiore in Rome. Much revered by Polish pilgrims, the Madonna figure was adorned with its crown in the 1960s by the then Polish Catholic primate Cardinal Wyszyński, with a certain Karol Wojtyła in attendance. Imitating the original medieval shrine, a rather grubby-looking eighteenth-century **linden tree** stands to the left of the altar, topped by a silver statue of the Virgin and Child, the base smothered in pennants pinned there by virtuous pilgrims.

Filling virtually the entire west end of the building is the church's famous Baroque **organ**. Built in 1720 by Johann Mozengel, a Jew from Königsberg – many of the church artists and sculptors came from the old East Prussian capital – it's a huge, fantastically ornate creation, decked with two layers of blue gilded turrets topped by figures of the saints. Renovated by one of the Jesuit brothers during the 1960s, the instrument is in fine shape, producing a marvellously rich sound. When enough people are around, short concerts are given by one of the brothers, the real show-stopper being the exhibition pieces when the instrument's celestial assortment of moving parts are brought into action: the whole organ appears to come alive, gyrating angels blowing their horns, cherubs waving, stars jingling and cymbals crashing – Bach fugues with a heavenly back-up group in accompaniment.

It's certainly an extraordinary sight and sound, worth capturing on one of the tapes or CDs you can pick up from the kiosk outside the church. Additionally there are special evening organ concerts every second and fourth Friday of the month from June to August, the second Friday of the month only in September.

Back out of the main building, the **cloisters** are a nice calm spot to recuperate in after the exertions of the church, the ceilings featuring more sumptuous polychromy by Meyer, most notably in the domed cupolas ornamenting the four corners of the structure.

Practicalities

If you plan **to stay** overnight, the *Dom Pielgrzyma* in the monastery is where pilgrims usually lodge. Accommodation is cheap, but around the time of any major festivals – and for much of the summer– its generally full. The basic *Zalesie* restaurant on the road facing the cloisters provides refreshment after a stint in the church. As well as the regular local services to Mrągowo and Kętrzyn, **buses** run to Olsztyn (via Reszel), Gdańsk and Suwałki.

Reszel

Four kilometres west of Święta Lipka is the historic Warmian centre of **RESZEL**. Seat of the bishops of Warmia for over five centuries, from the establishment of Christianity in the region (1254) until the First Partition (1772), Reszel is also one of Copernicus' many old regional haunts. These days the town is another quiet end-of-the-world provincial hang-out, the main attraction being the small old town area that sits atop a plateau overlooking the surroundings.

Of the many Gothic country churches in Warmia, Reszel's **Church of St Peter and Paul** is one of the most immediately striking. Hardly the most elegant of buildings from the exterior, what the church lacks in delicacy it certainly makes up for in sheer size – perhaps that's how those bishops preferred things on their home patch. The monster **church tower** is visible for miles around, and from close up you feel almost as dwarfed as in St Mary's in Gdańsk. The altarpiece is a fine piece of Neoclassical elegance, the nave vaulting displaying some of the intricate geometric brick patternwork common throughout the region. On a more delicate note, early Renaissance polychromy using enjoyable plant and animal motifs is still in evidence on the pillars and arches of the nave.

Bulk is also the name of the game in the fourteenth-century **Bishop's Castle**, just up from the church, an impressive hulk surrounded by the ruins of the old town walls. The castle now houses a rather superior **Art Gallery** (Tues–Sun 10am–4pm) featuring regular exhibitions – generally of the "disturbed and alienated" variety – by well-known contemporary artists, both Polish and foreign. In fact painters and sculptors are regularly invited to live and work in the castle for a few months, so in summer particularly the place is a mine of creative activity. For those mere mortals who aren't offered a castle bedroom of their own, there's the possibility of climbing up the castle tower (same hours as the gallery) for the view over the surroundings. The chic café inside the castle courtyard is exactly what you'd expect of an artists' centre – more *Quartier Latin* than back-of-the-woods Warmia.

The other **places to stay** in town are the basic *Majper*, ul. Krasickiego 6 (☎273; ②) and the summer-only youth hostel at ul. Chrobrego, both close to the bus station, a short walk north of the Old Town. **Buses** run regularly to Kętrzyn (via Święta Lipka), Mrągowo and Olsztyn, with two daily to Gdańsk.

Kętrzyn and the Wolf's Lair

Known as Rastenburg until its return to Polish rule in 1945, **KĘTRZYN**, 15km east of Święta Lipka, is a quiet, unexceptional town whose main interest lies in its proximity to Gierłoz – Hitler's "Wolf's Lair" (see below).

A short walk up the hill from the train station stands the old Teutonic town complex, itself built on the site of an earlier Prussian settlement. Badly destroyed in 1945, the well-restored Gothic **Teutonic Knights' Castle** houses a **Regional Museum** (Tues–Thurs, Sat–Sun 10am–4pm, Fri 10am–5pm) housing an exhibition combining local archeology and wildlife. If you don't get to see boars, beavers or badgers in the Mazurian wild you'll find plenty of stuffed ones here, alongside a selection of similarly preserved birds, eagles, owls and cormorants. If the officious attendants let you get that far, the second floor is largely devoted to **Wojtech Ketrzyn**, a nineteenth-century local historian and patriot, the epitome of the sort of characters after whom the postwar Polish authorities renamed the Mazurian towns.

Across from the castle the Gothic **St George's Church**, also rebuilt after 1945, is a rather barren, sorry-looking place, a couple of old Prussian memorial tablets all that's left of the original interior decoration. The small fourteenth-century chapel next door, rebuilt in the seventeenth century, and a small house down the hill are both Protestant chapels, while on the other side of town, on ul. Mickiewicza, there's an early nineteenth-century freemasons' lodge, now a *Dom Kultury*.

THE JULY BOMB

In the summer of 1944, the Wolf's Lair was the scene of the assassination attempt on Adolf Hitler that came closest to success – the **July Bomb Plot**. Its leader, **Count Claus Schenk von Stauffenberg**, an aristocratic officer and member of the General Staff, had gained the support of several high-ranking members of the German army. Sickened by atrocities on the eastern front, and rapidly realizing that the Wehrmacht was fighting a war that could not possibly be won, von Stauffenberg and his fellow conspirators decided to kill the Führer, seize control of army headquarters in Berlin and sue for peace with the Allies. Germany was on the precipice of total destruction by the Allies and the Soviet Army: only such a desperate act, reasoned the plotters, could save the Fatherland.

On July 20, Stauffenberg was summoned to the Wolf's Lair to brief Hitler on troop movements on the eastern front. In his briefcase was a small bomb, packed with high explosive: once triggered, it would explode in under ten minutes. As Stauffenberg approached the specially built conference hut, he triggered the device. Taking his place a few feet from Hitler, Stauffenberg positioned the briefcase under the table, leaning it against one of the table's stout legs no more than six feet away from the Führer. Five minutes before the bomb exploded, Stauffenberg quietly slipped from the room unnoticed by the generals and advisers, who were listening to a report on the central Russian front. One of the officers moved closer to the table to get a better look at the campaign maps and, finding the briefcase in the way of his feet under the table, picked it up and moved it to the other side of the table leg. Now, the very solid support of the table leg lay between the briefcase and Hitler.

At 12.42 the bomb went off. Stauffenberg, watching the hut from a few hundred yards away, was shocked by the force of the explosion. It was, he said, as if the hut had been hit by a 155mm shell; there was no doubt that the Führer, along with everyone else in the room, was dead.

Stauffenberg hurried off to a waiting plane and made his way to Berlin to join the other conspirators. Meanwhile, back in the wreckage of the hut, Hitler and the survivors staggered out into the daylight: four people had been killed or were dying of their wounds, including Colonel Brandt, who had moved Stauffenberg's briefcase and thus unwittingly saved the Führer's life. Hitler himself, despite being badly shaken, suffered no more than a perforated eardrum and minor injuries. After being attended to, he prepared himself for a meeting with Mussolini later that afternoon.

It was quickly realized what had happened, and the hunt for Stauffenberg was on. Hitler issued orders to the SS in Berlin to summarily execute anyone who was

For local **information**, the *Orbis* office is at ul. Westerplatte 1 and the *PTTK* is at ul. Poczkowa 6, just west of the station. If you're planning on **staying over**, the *Agros*, ul. Kasztanowa 1 (☎0886/5240; ④), a *pensjonat* on the western side of town, is your best bet – it has a decent restaurant and the staff here can also organize rooms in private houses. Other options are the *Pod Zamkiem*, ul. Stuga 3 (③), just below the castle, the *Garnizonowy*, ul. Sikorskiego 71 (☎0886/2134; ③) and a summer-only youth hostel at ul. Kopernika 12 in the town centre. For a bite to eat, hotels aside, try the *Aria* at ul. Daszyńskiego 6.

Gierłoz

GIERŁOZ lies 8km east of Kętrzyn and can be reached from there by a regular local bus service (#5), *PKS* buses to Węgorzewo or the steam train to Węgorzewo, which stops at **Parcz**, a kilometre from the site (be careful to check

slightly suspect, and dispatched Himmler to the city to quell the rebellion. Back in the military Supreme Command headquarters in Berlin, the conspiracy was in chaos. Word reached Stauffenberg and the two main army conspirators, generals Beck and Witzleben, that the Führer was still alive: they had already lost hours of essential time by failing to issue the carefully planned order to mobilize their sympathizers in the city and elsewhere, and had even failed to carry out the obvious precaution of severing all communications out of the city. After a few hours of tragicomic scenes as the conspirators tried to persuade high-ranking officials to join them, the Supreme Command HQ was surrounded by SS troops, and it was announced that the Führer would broadcast to the nation later that evening. The coup was over.

The conspirators were gathered together, given paper to write farewell messages to their wives, taken to the courtyard of the HQ and, under the orders of one General Fromm, shot by firing squad. Stauffenberg's last words were "Long live our sacred Germany!"

Fromm had known about the plot almost from the beginning, but had refused to join it. By executing the leaders he hoped to save his own skin – and, it must be added, knowingly saved them from the torturers of the SS.

Hitler's ruthless revenge on the conspirators was without parallel even in the bloody annals of the Third Reich. All the colleagues, friends and immediate relatives of Stauffenberg and the other conspirators were rounded up, tortured and taken before the "People's Court", where they were humiliated and given more-or-less automatic death sentences. Many of those executed knew nothing of the plot and were found guilty merely by association. As the blood lust grew, the Nazi Party used the plot as a pretext for settling old scores, and eradicated anyone who had the slightest hint of anything less than total dedication to the Führer. General Fromm, who had ordered the execution of the conspirators, was among those tried, found guilty of cowardice and shot by firing squad. Those whose names were blurted under torture were quickly arrested, the most notable being Field Marshal Rommel, who, because of his popularity, was given the choice of a trial in the People's Court – or suicide and a state funeral.

The July Bomb Plot caused the deaths of at least five thousand people, including some of Germany's most brilliant military thinkers and almost all of those who would have been best qualified to run the postwar German government. Within six months the country lay in ruins as the Allies and Soviet Army advanced; had events at Rastenburg been only a little different, the entire course of the war – and European history – would have been altered incalculably.

return times). If you're driving here from Kętrzyn, watch carefully for signposts – the route is badly marked.

Here, deep in the Mazurian forests, Hitler established his military headquarters in the so-called **Wolf's Lair** (Wilczy Szaniec; Tues–Sun 8am–6pm), a huge underground complex from which the Germans' eastward advance was conducted. Other satellite bunker complexes were built for the army and Luftwaffe and are spread out in a forty-kilometre radius round the site, mostly now overgrown ruins.

Encased in several metres of concrete were private bunkers for Göring, Bormann, Himmler and Hitler himself, alongside offices, SS quarters and operations rooms. The 27-acre complex was camouflaged by a suspended screen of vegetation that was altered to match the changing seasons, and was permanently mined "in case of necessity". In 1945 the retreating army fired the detonator, but it merely cracked the bunkers, throwing out flailing tentacles of metal reinforcements. Most of today's visitors come in tourist groups – an English-speaking guide is generally on hand to take you round. A flashlight is handy for scouting around the underground bunkers, although the large signs outside indicate that this is officially frowned upon.

Peering into these cavernous monsters today is an eerie experience. You can see the place, for example, where the assassination attempt on Hitler failed in July 1944 (see box on previous page), the SS living quarters, the staff cinema and other ancillaries of domestic Nazi life. Gruesome photographs and films remind visitors of the scale of German atrocities, but as so often with official anti-fascist material, there's a tendency to resort to horrifying images at the expense of information and critical understanding.

The **airstrip** from which Stauffenberg departed after his abortive assassination attempt is a couple of kilometres east from the main site, a lone runway in the middle of some heathland – you'll need a guide to show you the way.

For anybody wanting to stay, there's a basic **hostel** (☎0886/4429; ④), summer **campsite** and **restaurant** at the bunker site. If you're interested in the nuts and bolts of the site there's a special edition of the UK magazine *After the Battle* available from one of the guides, devoted to a meticulously researched account of a postwar attempt to identify every building on the site.

Mikołajki

Hyped in the brochures as the "Mazurian Venice", **MIKOŁAJKI** is unquestionably the most attractive of the top Mazurian resorts. Straddled across the meeting point of two attractive small lakes – the Tałty and Mikołajskie – the small town has long provided a base for yachting enthusiasts on popular nearby Lake Śniardwy. Legend associates the town's name with a monster creature, known as the King of the Whitefish, that terrorized the local fisherman and destroyed their nets. The beast finally met its match in a young local called Mikołajek who caught the huge fish in a steel fishing net. Cobbled streets, half-timbered houses and the old fishing boats lined up on the lake shore give the town a pleasing feeling of authenticity – something that is lacking in the other big lakeside tourist centres. Despite a relative abundance of decent accommodation, it can still be hard work finding a place to stay in high summer.

The Town

If you walk around the town centre you'll see a couple of buildings to remind you of the town's historic Protestant roots. Unusually for modern Poland, the main church in town is the Protestant **Church of the Holy Trinity,** overlooking the shores of Lake Tałty. Designed by German architect Franz Schinki, this solid-looking early nineteenth-century structure is the centre of worship for the region's Protestant community. Portraits of two early pastors apart, it's a fairly spartan place, light years away in feel from the usual Catholic churches. Talk to the minister, a jovial character and mine of local information who lives just across from the church, and he'll probably offer to show you the newly completed parish building, a German-financed setup used for international conferences.

For more insights into the Protestant life of the country check out the **Museum of the Polish Reformation** (Tues–Sun 10am–4pm) in the large *Dom Kultury* just up the road. Set up by the retired former town pastor, it features a collection of old Protestant hymnals, Bibles and prayerbooks from around the country: as well as describing each object in minute detail, the pastor's likely to try and collar you for a sizeable donation towards the museum.

Down by the lakeside there are plenty of centres for **yachting and watersports**. You can also take **boat trips** on the lakes, the embarkation point and ticket office (*przystań żeglugi pasażerski*) is just down from market square. Most of the lakeside hotels also have their own stock of canoes and watersports equipment for use by guests, some also extending to bicycles, handy if you want to visit the nature reserve round **Lake Łukajno**, 4km east of town, the home of one of Europe's largest remaining colonies of wild swans. The best viewing point is the **tower** (Wieża Widokowa), signposted off the main road and located at the lake's edge, though even here, it's very much a hit-and-miss issue whether you get to see the birds.

Practicalities

The **train station**, on the main Olsztyn–Ełk line, is some way out northeast of the town centre. The **bus station** is closer in, over the road from the Protestant church. Mikołajki's *Wigry* tourist office, ul. Kolejowa 9 near the bus station, is the best source of **tourist information**, a useful alternative being the *Sagit* office, pl. Wolnosci 3, which organizes specialist sport activities (horse riding, yachting, water-skiing) and can usually rent you a kayak or rowing boat at reasonable hourly rates (book in advance in the summer). They can also find you a room in one of the local *pensjonat*.

There's a fair range of **accommodation** to choose from: at the top end of the scale you'll find the luxury *Gołębiewski*, ul. Mrągowska 34 (☎0878/16517, fax 16010; ⑥), on the northern edge of town, and the *Król Sielaw*, ul. Kajki 9 (☎0878/ 18323; ④), a new and already highly rated place aimed at Westerners and bang in the centre. Other options are the *Złoty Widok* guest house, ul. Leśna 7 (☎0878/ 16164; ④), and the *pensjonat Mikołajki*, ul. Kajki 18 (☎0878/16437; ⑤), another new, good-quality place close to the centre. Moving further out, the *Na Skarpie*, ul. Kajki 130 (☎0878/16418; ④), and *Wodnik* (☎0878/16141; ④), 2km east of town, are both good bets; the latter in particular has a beautiful quiet waterside location, canoeing equipment to hand and is run by a helpful and extremely accommodating couple. Other *pensjonaty* out of town include the *Złote Wrota*, Stare Sady 3 (☎0878/16520; ④), at the edge of Lake Tałty 3km north of town, and the *Tałty* (☎0878/16398; ④), 2km further out on the other side of the same lake. Finally there's a good **camping site**, *Camping Wagabunda* at ul. Leśna 2 (☎0878/16018) 2km west of town, with four-person bungalows also on the site, and a (summer only) **youth hostel** in town (☎0878/18293). With the exception of the *Golębski* and *Król Sielaw*, most places are only open from June to mid-October, so it's probably best to phone ahead if you're planning to come at any other time of year.

Many of the hotels and *pensjonaty* also have decent **restaurants**, especially the *Król Sielaw*. Predictably, fish – eel in particular – is the local speciality, most of it fresh out of the surrounding lakes. If you want to fry your own, the *Centralna Rybna* fish market just off the square at 3 ul.1-go Maja has a good selection of the day's catch on offer.

South from Mikołajki

Travelling south from Mikołajki you're soon into the depths of the Puszcza Piska, a characteristic Mazurian mix of woodlands and water. A huge tangle of crystal-clear lakes, lazy winding rivers and dense forest thickets, it's the largest *puszcza* in the region, one of the surviving remnants of the primeval forest that once covered much of northeastern Europe. The forest is mainly pine, many of the trees reaching thirty to forty metres in height, with some magnificent pockets of mixed oak, beech and spruce in between. A favourite with both canoers – the Krutynia River (see p.228) runs south through the middle of the forest – and walkers, who use the area's developed network of hiking trails, the Puszcza Piska is a delightful area well worth exploring, with the forest lakeside resort of **Ruciane-Nida** providing the obvious base.

Ruciane-Nida

Twenty-five kilometres south of Mikołajki along a scenic forest road is the lakeside resort of **Ruciane-Nida**. Actually two towns connected by a short stretch of road, it's an understandably popular holiday centre, offering a combination of forest and lakeland.

Arriving by train or bus **RUCIANE** is the first stopoff point. Walk just south of the mainline station and you're at the water's edge, in this case the narrow canal connecting the two lakes nearest the town: the jetty with the sign marked *Żegluga Mazurska* is the boarding point for excursion boats on the Giżyck–

THE OLD BELIEVERS

In a country characterized by a proliferation of historic religious groups, the Orthodox sect of **Old Believers** – *Starowiercy* or *Staroobrzędowcy* as they are known in Polish – are among the smallest and most archaic. The origins of the group lie in the **liturgical reforms** introduced into the Russian Orthodox Church by **Nikon**, the mid-seventeeth-century patriarch of Moscow. Faced with the task of systematizing the divergent liturgical texts and practices by then in use in the national church, Nikon opted to comply with the dominant contemporary Greek practices of the time, such as the use of three fingers instead of two when making the sign of the cross and the use of Greek ecclesiastical dress.

Widespread **opposition to the reforms** focused around a group of Muscovite priests led by archpriest Avvakum Petrovich, for which he and a number of others were eventually executed. In many instance, opponents of the reforms were motivated not so much by opposition to the substance of the changes as by the underlying assumption that the contemporary Greek church represented the "correct" mode of liturgical practice.

The stern attitude of the church authorities, who swiftly moved to endorse Nikon's reforms, anathemize dissenters and pronounce acceptance of the changes "necessary for salvation", ensured that compromise was out the question, and for the next two centuries, dissenters, appropriately dubbed "Old Believers" were subjected to often rigorous persecution by the tsarist authorities. Initially strongest in the northern and eastern regions of the Russian empire (they also eventually gained a significant following in Moscow itself), the dissenters or **Raskolniki**, already divided into numerous, often opposing sects, strenuously opposed all attempts at change. This included the **Westernizing reforms** introduced in the early 1700s by Peter the Great, whom they regarded as the Antichrist. Under constant pressure from the authorities, groups of Old Believers began to move west, establishing themselves in the Suwałki region around Sejny (then on the borders of the Russian empire) around the time of the late eighteenth-century **Polish Partitions** – as far as possible from Moscow's reach. A few of these early

Mikołajki–Ruciane line, the boats travelling through the connecting series of lakes culminating in Lake Nidzkie running south from the town. If you're staying in town, there are also daily summertime excursions round the lake itself.

A kilometre further down the lakeside road, **NIDA** is the main centre of activity, with plenty of canoeists and other sporty-looking types in evidence in season. The town's beautiful location makes a mockery of the unimaginative grey blocks of much of the centre, though it gets better the nearer the waterside you go. Ulica Gałczynskiego, the main drag, is showing signs of picking up Western habits, with its slick-looking *Café Rebecca* and the *Dab Pub*. If you're planning on **staying**, the lakeside *Perła Jezior* camping/holiday bungalow site, off the road halfway between the two towns, is an ideal location, the other obvious options being the *PTTK Dom Wycieczkowy*, ul. Mazurska 16 (☎0117/31006; ②), north of the train station in Ruciane, the *pensjonat Bełdan* (☎0117/31094; ③) further north beyond the lock, and the basic *Guzianka* hostel, ul. Guzianka 6 (☎0117/31057; ②) by the lakeside.

Despite its forest location, the town is actually fairly accessible, with regular **trains** west to Olsztyn, east on to Ełk and, less frequently, **buses** (45min) to Mikołajki.

settlements, including their original *molenna* (places of worship) survive in the region, notably in Suwałki, Wodziłki, Pogorzelec and Gabowe Grądy.

In the 1820s, a new wave of emigration saw the Old Believers moving further west into Prussian-ruled Mazuria, establishing the convent at Wojnowo (see above) that became the spiritual focal point of the Old Believers in the surrounding regions. Life became easier for members of the sect following the Tsar's **April 1905 Edict of Toleration**, and they were able to continue their religious practices relatively undisturbed in both the Soviet Union, newly independent Poland and Prussia. The advent of World War II, however, dealt a severe blow to the Polish Old Believer community within Poland. Prior to the Nazi occupation of the USSR in 1941, which from 1939 incorporated the Suwałki district, many Old Believers moved east into Russia. Under the pressure of **Nazi persecution** – the habitually long-bearded male members of the sect were often mistakenly identified as rabbis, for example, and subjected to all sorts of humiliations as a consequence – most of the rest fled to Lithuania, where they remain to this day in the Klaipeda region. Following the end of World War II, a few returned to their old settlements, but the soul had effectively been ripped out of the community. Today, it's estimated that no more than 2000 remain in Poland, a number that continues to diminish year by year, and at this rate the long-term future of the community definitely looks to be in doubt.

Despite the numerical decline, the rudiments of Old Beliver faith and practice remain as they have long been. In liturgical matters, the sect is egalitarian, even Protestant, rejecting the ecclesiastical hierarchy of conventional Orthodoxy, electing their clergy and sticking firmly to the use of Old Church Slavonic for services. Strict social rules are also (at least theoretically) applied – no alcohol, tobacco, tea or coffee – many families still live in unmodernized wooden rural houses, the older people speak a curious mixture of Polish and old-fashioned Russian, and the community as a whole tends towards the shy and retiring. Outwardly, at least, the one place where they really come into their own is during their services, characterized by the use of distinctive and hauntingly beautiful trance-like hymns and chants.

The Wojnowo Nunnery

For much of the last two centuries the area round Ruciane-Nida has been populated by communities of Orthodox **Old Believers**. The quiet seclusion of the forests and the proximity to water made the area an obvious choice for a habitually shy and retiring people. Slowly but surely the local Old Believers are dwindling in numbers, but you'll still find some of them living in the villages north of the town.

Some 6km west of Ruciane, however, is the best-known monument to their presence in the region, the **Nunnery** at **WOJNOWO**. Established in the mid-nineteenth century as a centre for promoting and preserving the old-style Orthodox faith in Mazuria, the nunnery has had its ups and downs. Decline forced it to close down in 1884, after which an energetic young nun was sent from the community in Moscow to revive the place. Her efforts led to a revival which continued until World War I, after which, decline set in again. Today this once-thriving community is down to two nuns, both well over eighty, who are cared for by a local fellow-believer. Coming up the track leading off from the Ruciane–Babięta road the first impression is that you must have entered a local farm by mistake. Through the gateway it turns out to be the nunnery after all, the main building set between farmyard barns and stables on one side and a plain white church on the other.

At their age, the nuns are past showing anyone round, but knock at the main door and you should find the caretaker who'll be able to take you up to the church. If you have to wait while she finishes off in the kitchens, you could take a short stroll up to the community's **cemetery**, a small rather melancholy enclosure of Cyrillic-inscribed gravestones which overlooks the banks of the Krutynia. The setting is wonderful though, the swaying trees, tall waterside rushes and graceful contours of the river making this a peaceful and memorable spot.

The **church interior** is laid out on the conventional Orthodox pattern, with a notable iconostasis and accompanying collection of old icons. It's actually only a small part of the community's icon collection, the rest having been moved some years ago to the castle museum at Lidzbark Warmiński (see p.220) once the dwindling community of nuns no longer felt able to look after them. You're not allowed to take pictures, but if you ask, the caretaker will sell you a postcard.

Giżycko and around

Squeezed between Lake Niegocin and the marshy backwaters of Lake Mamry, **GIŻYCKO** is one of the main lakeland centres. It was flattened in 1945, however, and the rebuilding didn't create a lot of character: if greyish holiday-resort architecture lowers your spirits, don't plan to stay for long before heading out for the lakes. Wilkasy (see below) is a much more pleasant base.

Incongruously, the **Orbis** office at ul. Dąbrowskiego 3 has glossy brochures and ticket-booking facilities for anywhere on the other side of the globe, but absolutely nothing about Giżycko or its surroundings. In high summer, **accommodation** of any kind can be hard to find. In the bigger tourist places, however, prices go down from mid-September through to mid-May, the official low season. As indicated by the ranks of German vehicles parked outside, the central *Wodnik* hotel, ul. 3 Maja 2 (✆0878/3872, fax 3958; ⑧), is the hub of foreign tourist activity, but it's expensive and difficult to get a room. More likely to have space is the *Zamek*, a large motel in the ruins of the Teutonic castle at ul. Moniuszki 1 (☎0878/2419, fax 3958; ⑤), which also has a **campsite** close by (☎0878/3410). Other relatively upmarket options are the *Giżycko*, ul. Moniuszki 22 (☎0878/2335 or 2337; ④) and the *Mazury*, ul. Wojska Polskiego 56 (☎0878/5956; ⑥), well out of the centre on Lake Kisajno. With privatization opening up an increasing number of former workers' holiday homes to tourists, there are also the *Dom Wycieczkowy*, ul. Nadbrezeżbna 11 (③), right in the centre by the side of the lake, and the nearby *Garnizonowy*, ul. Olsztynska 10a (④). Within walking distance of the train station you]ll find two **youth hostels**, at ul. Mickiewicza 27 (☎0878/2987) and ul. Wiejska 50 (☎0878/2135); both of these are open from July to September only. **Private rooms** are another option – ask at the reception desk at the *Wodnik* or try the *Gromada* office, ul. Warszawska 21.

Lakes near Giżycko

East of Giżycko, the tourists thin out and the lakes get quieter and cleaner. There's little accommodation, though, so you'll need to come equipped with a tent or a car, allowing you to venture out for day trips along the picturesque country roads.

Ten kilometres northeast from Giżycko are the adjoining **Gołdopiwo** and **Kruklin lakes**, located a couple of kilometres from the edge of the **Borecka forest**. A bus from Giżycko will take you to the village of **Kruklanki** on the southern edge of Lake Gołdopiwo, and from there you're pretty much on your own. Twenty kilometres to the southeast of Giżycko there's another enchanting string of lakes – **Wydmińskie**, **Jedzelewo** and **Łaśmiady**, the latter surrounded by a good supply of scenically located homebased accommodation – linked by the River Gawlik: they're all easily reached, being close to stations on the Giżycko–Ełk rail line.

Wilkasy

WILKASY is a five-kilometre bus ride southwest of Giżycko; the train from Kętrzyn stops here too, at the Niegocin station. If you want to experience how Poles (who overrun the place in summer) take their Mazurian holidays, this is the place to head for, with its assortment of lakeside rest homes, holiday cabins and hostels. Apart from some nice enclosed swimming areas by the lake, the other attraction of Wilkasy is that it's much easier to **rent canoes or kayaks** here. Before they are allowed to set oar to water, Poles have to produce an official card proving they can swim, but you should be able to persuade the attendants to let you aboard. It makes for a pleasant day, paddling round the lake, hiving off into reed beds or canals as the fancy takes you – even though the pollution becomes more obvious the nearer you get to Giżycko.

A good place to stay is the **PTTK hostel** (May–Sept; ☎0878/3078; ②) situated near the bus stop just up from the water; the hostel or one of the neighbouring houses will also allow camping in the garden for a small fee. There's also the *Yaga*, ul. Szkolna 25 (☎0878/2879; ③), a decent *pensjonat* close to the lake's edge, and the *Silnowa*, ul. Niegocińska 7 (☎0878/5594; ⑤), a plusher holiday centre on a hill overlooking the lake, with its own restaurant. The **restaurant** over the road from the *Yaga* is mainly patronized by groups of holidaymakers eating their set meals in rotas; it isn't exactly a gastronomic paradise but is, without doubt, very Polish, and as in all major tourist resorts you won't have any trouble getting a beer or ten.

BOAT TRIPS ON THE MAIN LAKES

Throughout the summer – in most cases this means from May to September – regular tourist **boat services** run on the main lakes on the following routes:

Giżycko–Mikołajki (4hr)

Mikołajki–Ruciane–Nida (3hr)

Giżycko–Węgorzewo (25km; June–Aug only)

At peak season (June–July) boats depart daily; otherwise, depending on demand, it's likely to be weekends and national holidays only. Often packed, the boats are mostly large, open-deck steamers with a basic snack bar on board for refreshments. **Timetables** (*rozkłady*) for departures are posted by the main jetties at all the major lakeside stopoff points. For enquiries contact the *Mazur Tourist* offices in Olsztyn, ul. Staromiejksa 6 (☎089/27 41 25), Giżycko, ul. 3-go Maja 2 (☎0878/3872) or the harbour office in Mikołajki (☎0878/16102).

Węgorzewo

Twenty-five kilometres north of Giżycko on the furthest edge of Lake Mamry is **WĘGORZEWO**, another former Teutonic stronghold established on the site of an earlier Prussian settlement, and one of the major holiday centres for the central Mazurian lakelands. Despite the enjoyable rural setting, however, like its bigger cousin Giżycko, the town itself is a formless, unprepossessing sort of place, the only real reason to come here being the access it offers to Lake Mamry, the second largest in the region. The ruins of the Teutonic Knights' castle, destroyed in 1945, and the old Protestant (now Catholic) church apart, there's nothing to detain you.

For **tourist information** the *Orbis* office (Mon–Fri 8am–4pm) on pl. Wolności, the main town square, is the place to head for. **Accommodation** is provided by a number of *pensjonat* including the one at ul. Sienkiewicza 13 (☎0117/2049; ④), the *Skarpa*, ul Turystyczna 13 (☎0117/2842; ④) and a basic *PTTK* hostel, ul. Nabrzeżna 10 (☎0117/2443). For campers there's the *Rusałka* (May–Sept), a good site with restaurant nicely situated on the shores of Lake Święcajty, 4km south of the town. Best of a basically undistinguished selection of **restaurants** are the *DAAB*, on ul. Jasna, and the *Szkwał*, pl. Wolności 13.

Ełk

EŁK, the easternmost main town of Mazury, is the area's major bus and train interchange. Established by the Teutonic Knights as a base from which to "protect" the locals and keep an eye on the heathen Lithuanian hordes, the town was colonized by Poles in the sixteenth century, before becoming an East Prussian border post during the Partitions.

It remained an important East Prussian centre until 1945 – German novelist Siegfried Lenz, whose work touches on the history and traditions of the region, was born here – and suffered comprehensive damage during the war. The main street, ul.Wojska Polskiego, running along the edge of the town lake, leads to the **Parish Church**, originally a Gothic construction rebuilt from scratch in the nineteenth century. Beyond it, on an island, stand the ruins of the old **Teutonic Castle**, built in the early 1400s.

However, many visitors don't get much further than the shabby square below the train station; there really isn't much to detain you in the sprawling, tatty town centre. If you're forced to spend the night here, head for the **hotel** *Mazurski*, at ul. Słowackiego 28 (☎087/10 41 15; ④), or failing that the *Dom Turystyczny* at ul. Armii Krajowej 32 (☎087/10249; ③), or *Zodiak*, ul. Kajkil (☎087/10 24 91; ④). The *Dom Turystyczny* has a basic **restaurant** and the *Mała*, ul. Wojska Polskiego 72, is worth trying for traditional Polish dishes. The **Orbis office** at ul. Mickiewicza 15 is not far from the train and bus stations, both of which are close to the centre.

Augustów and the Suwalszczyna

The region around the towns of **Augustów** and **Suwałki** is one of the least visited parts of Poland: even for Poles, anything beyond Mazury is still pretty much *terra incognita*. An area of peasant farmers and tortuous ethnic and religious loyalties, as with most parts of eastern Poland, the region north of Suwałki – the **Suwalszczyna** – is little developed economically. Like the Bieszczady Mountains (see p.333), its counterpart in obscurity, the Suwalszczyna is also one of the most beautiful, unspoilt territories in Europe. Once a part of the tsarist empire, much of the region's older architecture – most notably in the regional capital, **Suwałki** – has a decidedly Russian feel to it. **Jews** were long a major element of the region's fluid ethnic mix, almost the only surviving sign of this being the **cemeteries** you find rotting away at the edge of numerous towns and villages throughout the area. The region's proximity to Lithuania is reflected, too, in the sizeable **Lithuanian minority** concentrated in the northeast corner of the region.

Visually the striking feature of the northern part of the Suwalszczyna is a pleasing landscape of rolling hills and fields interspersed with crystal-clear lakes – often small, but extremely deep – the end product of the final retreat of the Scandinavian glacier that once covered the area. Much of the southern stretch of this region is covered by the **Puszcza Augustówska**, the remains of the vast forest that once extended well into Lithuania. In the north, by contrast, wonderfully open countryside is interspersed with villages and lakes – some reasonably well known, like **Lake Hańcza** (the deepest in Poland), others, often the most beautiful, rarely visited. Wandering through the fields and woodland thickets you'll find storks, swallows, brilliantly coloured butterflies and wild flowers in abundance, while in the villages the twentieth century often seems to have made only modest incursions, leaving plenty of time to sit on the porch and talk.

Getting around isn't exactly straightforward: buses operate in most of the region, but frequency declines the closer you get to the Lithuanian border. Suwałki and Augustów both have mainline train connections to Warsaw, and, slowly but surely, a fledgling network of rail, bus and air connections on into Lithuania is developing.

Augustów and around

The region around **AUGUSTÓW** was settled at some indistinct time in the early Middle Ages by Jacwingians, a pagan Baltic Slav tribe. The evidence suggests that the Jacwingians had a fairly advanced social structure; what's sure is that they posed a major threat to the early Mazovian rulers, persistently harrying at the edges of Mazovia from their northern domain. By the end of the thirteenth century, however, they had been effectively wiped out by the colonizing Teutonic Knights, leaving as testimony only a few sites such as the burial mound near Suwałki (see p.244) and a scattering of place names. The area remained almost deserted for the next two centuries or so, until the town's establishment in 1557 by King Sigismund August (hence the name) as a supply stopoff on the eastern trade routes from Gdańsk. It only really developed after the construction of the **Augustów Canal** in the nineteenth century. A hundred-kilometre network of rivers, lakes and artificial channels, this waterway was cut to connect the town to the River Niemen in the east, providing a transport route for the region's most important natural commodity, wood. Still in use today, the canal offers the most convenient approach to the heart of the forest (see below).

Thanks to its location on the edge of the *puszcza* and the surrounding abundance of water, Augustów has carved out a growing niche for itself as a holiday centre. As a town, though, it's no great shakes. Caught on the frontline of the Soviet assault in late 1944, it has few prewar buildings, save a handful of nineteenth-century tenements, an old sawmill, and a 1920s *PTTK* hostel on the edge of Lake Necko. Its appeal is as a base for countryside exploration.

Practicalities

Augustów's **bus station** is right in the middle of town on plac Zymunta Augusta; the nearest **train** stop, Augustów Port, is a couple of kilometres' bus ride from the centre. The **tourist information centre** on pl. Augusta (Mon–Sat 9am–5pm; ☎0119/2319) is reasonably well organized, though they may not be able to offer much help with accommodation in high season. *Orbis*, also on the square at no. 12, can provide tickets and travel information. For **kayak and canoe rental**, try the main tourist office or the desk at the *Hetman* (a *PTTK* establishment that organizes trips down the Czarna Hańcza river, see below).

The best places to stay are the *Dom Nauczyciela* at ul. 29 Listopada 9 (☎0119/ 2021; ③), next to the port, the *Hetman* (☎0119/45345; ④) and its **campsite** at ul. Sportowa 1 in Augustów Port, or – less enticingly – the *Polmozbytu* motel at ul. Mazurska 4 (☎0119/2867; ④) on the southern edge of town. From July to September there's a **youth hostel** at ul. Konopnickiej 9. The town also has an increasing number of **private rooms** available, and the information office will give you details. They can also point you in the direction of a number of old workers' holiday homes by the lake, now open for private business. In high season you may well find everything fully booked, in which case, if you have a sleeping bag, make for the *Almatur baza studentowa* (student base) by the lakeside at **STUDZIENICZNA**, a six-kilometre bus journey east; there's no food, so bring your own.

In town, the only **restaurants** worth mentioning are the one in the *Hetman* hotel, the *Albatros* at ul. Mostowa 5, in the centre, the *Pizzeria Best*, ul. Creptowicza 17 and the restaurant at the motel. **Cafés and bars** are the big current growth area – worth trying are the *Marco* and the *Delikatesy*, both on the main square, as well as the *Żagielek*, ul. 29 Listopada 7, a ritzier night-time haunt down by the boat embarkation point on the canal.

The forest and the canal

The combination of wild forest, lakes, and narrow winding rivers around Augustów has made the *puszcza* a favourite with canoeists, walkers and naturalists alike. Following in the footsteps of their partisan ancestors, whose anti-tsarist forces found shelter here during the nineteenth-century insurrections, adventurous Poles spend days and sometimes weeks paddling or trekking through the forest. Such expeditions require substantial preparation, so for most people the practical way to sample the mysteries of the forest is to take a **day trip** from Augustów along the **canal system**. Boats leave from the embarkation point at ul. 29 Listopada 7, fifteen minutes' walk from the town centre – *żegług* (boat) is the key word when asking the way. First departure is at 8.30am, and you should get there early to queue for tickets. It's also a good idea to take some food: most boats don't carry any, and restaurant stops on the way are unpredictable.

The shortest trips – a couple of hours – go east through the **Necko**, **Białe** and **Studzieniczne** lakes to **Swoboda** or **Sucha Rzeczka**, giving at least a taste of the beauty of the forest. Other boats go onward to **Plaska** and the lock at **Perkuc**, returning in the evening. Beyond this point, the canal is for canoeists only, and even they can only go another twenty or so kilometres to the Soviet border.

The **forest** is mainly coniferous, but with impressive sections of elm, larch, hornbeam and ancient oak creating a slightly sombre atmosphere, particularly along the alley-like section of the canal between Swoboda and Sucha Rzeczka – the tallest trees blot out the sun, billowing reeds brush the boat, and the silence is suddenly broken by echoing bird calls. Among the varied wildlife of the forest, cranes, grey herons and even the occasional beaver can be spotted on the banks of the canal, while deeper into the *puszcza* you might glimpse wild boars or elks.

Gabowe Grądy

Six kilometres south of Augustów down a track through the woods (the nearest bus stop is about a kilometre east), the village of **GABOWE GRĄDY** is populated by a sizeable number of Russian Orthodox **"Old Believer"** or *Starowierców* families (see box on p.236). The wizened old characters with flowing white beards sitting by their front gates indicate you've arrived in the right place. People apart, the main interest here is the church (*molenna*) at the north end of the village, one of three remaining places of Orthodox worship in the region. The Gabowe Grądy *molenna* boasts a superb all-women **choir**, the only such group in the country: you can usually hear them at the Sunday morning service, the only time you're guaranteed to be able to get into the place anyway. For anyone interested in Orthodox music this is a must, the sonorous harmonies of the old liturgical chants intermeshing with the joyous, full-throated exuberance of the women's melodizing.

Suwałki and around

Founded as late as the 1720s, **SUWAŁKI** is another slow-paced provincial town with a decidedly eastern ambience. Perhaps feeling the need to keep the intellectuals in touch with life out in the sticks (or vice versa), Solidarity nominated the medieval historian Bronisław Geremek and the film director Andrzej Wajda as candidates for the Suwałki region in the landmark 1989 elections. Accounts of their campaign encounters with local farmers suggest it wasn't all plain sailing, scepticism about the men from Warsaw's capacity to represent regional concerns being a key issue. Thanks in part to the increasing cross-border traffic with Lithuania – Lithuanian number plates are an everyday sight here – Suwałki has been picking up recently, the town centre acquiring the typical trappings of the new consumer's Poland – stores selling smart clothes, hi-fi and the like.

A rambling, unfocused sort of place, Suwałki presents a mix of fine Neoclassical architecture and Russian-looking nineteenth-century buildings, with the usual postwar buildings around the outskirts. Religion is a mixed business here as well: the majority Catholic population uses the stately Neoclassical Parish Church of St Alexandra on pl. Wolnosci, but there's also an Evangelical church, further down on the main ul. Kosciuszki, and the **molenna**, a small wooden building serving the town's Old Believer population and retaining some fine original icons. It is tucked away on a side street off al. Sejneńska close to the station; the only reliable time to gain entry is during the Sunday morning service.

The jumbled ethnic mix that characterized Suwałki up until the outbreak of World War II is clearly illustrated in the town **Cemetery** on the west side of town, on the corner of ul. Bakałarzewska and ul. Zarzecze, overlooking the Czarna Hańcza. As in Lublin and other eastern Polish towns, the cemetery is divided up into religious sections – Catholic, Orthodox, Protestant, Tartar and Jewish, the Orthodox housing a special section for Old Believers. The Tartar gravestones have almost disappeared with the passage of time, while the Jewish cemetery was predictably devastated by the Nazis – a lone memorial tablet now standing in the middle of the area.

Back in the town centre, the somewhat humdrum local **Museum** (Tues–Fri 9am–4pm, Sat & Sun 10am–5pm) contains a number of archeological finds relating to the Jacwingians.

Practicalities

The **train station**, terminus of the line from Warsaw, lies east of the centre – take bus #1, #8 or #12 into town. The **bus station**, on ul. Utrata, is also on the east side of town, but closer to the centre. Information is available from the regional **tourist office** at ul. Wojska Polskiego, next to the *Hańcza* hotel.

Suwałki doesn't go overboard on **hotels**. The *Hańcza* at ul. Wojska Polskiego 2 (☎087/66 66 33; ③), near the river in the south of town, is reasonably comfortable, reasonably priced and also has a restaurant. The revamped *Dom Nouczyciela*, ul. Kościuszki 120 (☎087/66 62 70; ④), is better and more expensive – the restaurant is pretty good too. That's it, apart from **private rooms**, available from the tourist office, and a summer **youth hostel** at ul. Klonowa 51 (☎087/5140), 2km northeast of the town centre. The only real **restaurant**, apart from the hotels, is the *Pod Temidą*, ul, Kościuszki 82, in the central area, a distinctly ordinary place.

The Jacwingian burial site and Soviet War Cemetery

The ancient Jacwingian burial ground, 4km north of Suwałki, dated between the third and fifth centuries AD, is one of the few sites left by these ancient people, and a must for lovers of mystic sites. To reach it take bus #7 to Szwacjaria, or the Jeleniewo road by car: in both cases you'll see a sign at the roadside pointing you to the **Cementarzysko Jaćwingów**. A short walk through the fields and over an overgrown ridge brings you to the round, variably sized burial mounds (the largest is 20m wide), discernible through a tangled mass of trees and undergrowth, just beyond the large Soviet war cemetery on the right-hand side of the road. Excavations around the sites have revealed a little about the Jacwingians – burying horses with their masters seems to have been a common practice. In general, though, little is known of this pagan people, but stay long enough in this beautiful and peaceful spot and you conjure up your own images of how they might once have lived.

The **Soviet War Cemetery**, established close to the site of the POW camp, Stalag 68, set up by the Nazis in 1941, contains the graves of over 45,000 inmates who died here in appalling conditions, as well as several thousand Soviet troops killed in the fighting that raged around Suwałki in the latter stages of World War II. The shoddy, unkempt state of the place says much about the enduring tension between Poland and its erstwhile Soviet/Russian neighbour.

Lake Wigry and the National Park

Lake Wigry, the district's largest lake, lies 11km southeast of Suwałki. The lake and a large part of the surrounding area were designated a **national park** in 1989, an unspoilt area of nearly 15,000 hectares comprising a mixture of lake, river, forest land and agricultural territory. The lake in particular is a stunningly beautiful spot, a peaceful haven of creeks, marshes and lakeside woods with the occasional village in between. A wealth of wildlife shelters largely undisturbed in and around its waters, the lake itself harbouring over twenty species of fish – lavaret, whitefish, smelt and river trout included – while in the shoreland woods you

---

CANOEING DOWN THE CZARNA HAŃCZA RIVER

Along with the Krutynia (see p.228) the **Czarna Hańcza River** is one of the most beautiful – and popular – canoeing routes in the northeast Polish lakelands, and part of the five percent of Polish rivers still designated as grade 1 ("clean") water. If you've ever had a hankering for a backwater canoeing expedition this is as good a chance as any to satisfy it.

Rising in Belarus, the 140-kilometre long river, a tributary of the Niemen, flows into the Puszcza Augustowska, winding its way through the Wigry National Park up to **Lake Hańcza**, 15km northwest of Suwałki. On the usual canoe route, the first leg of the journey starts from **Augustów**, following the Augustów Canal (see p.242) east to the point where it meeets the Czarna Hańcza, a few kilometres short of the Belarussian border: from there the route continues on up the river to **Suwałki** and, stamina allowing, beyond to Lake Hańcza. The local **PTTK offices** in both Suwałki and Augustów offer organized trips following this route, with the option of a detour into Lake Wigry and the surrounding national park another equally enticing alternative.

These trips start from Augustów, heading east along the canal, turning north at **Swoboda** and continuing 12km into **Lake Serwy**, an attractive forest-bound tributary. From here the canoes are transported across land to the village of **Bryzgiel**, on the southern shores of Lake Wigry.

Three days are given over to exploring the peaceful and unspoilt lake and its protected surroundings. Overnight camps are on the island of **Kamien**, one of several on the lake, and by the lakeside at **Stary Folwark** (see p.246) with a trip up to the monastery included. Leaving Wigry near the **Klasztorny peninsula**, the canoes re-enter the Czarna Hańcza, heading south through a spectacular forest-bound section of the river before rejoining the Augustów Canal and making their way back to Augustów. Both the *PTTK* canoe trips take ten or eleven days, with accommodation – mostly in *stanice wodne* (waterside hostels) – and meals provided throughout: you'll need to provide your own sleeping bag, rubber boots (ideally) and appropriate clothing. The current cost for both trips is around $105/£70 – a real bargain. Contact the *PTTK* offices at **Suwałki**, ul. Kościuszki 37 (☎087/5981), or **Augustów**, ul. Sportowa 1 (☎0119/3455 or 3456).

can find stag, wild boar, elk, martens and badgers. Wigry's most characteristic animal, however, is the **beaver**, and particularly round the lake's southern and western shores you'll find plenty of evidence of their presence in the reservations set aside for the creatures. For access to the park from Suwałki, take a local bus to the holiday centre of **STARY FOLWARK**, where there's a **PTTK hostel** (☎087/63223 or 63237; ②) and **campsite** near the water. You may be able to **rent canoes** or other boats here in which to explore the lake.

If you do get hold of a boat, head across the lake from Stary Folwark to **Wigry Church**, part of a Camaldolese monastery (see p.404) founded here by King Władysław IV Waza in the 1660s, on what was originally an island later linked to the shore. The monks were thrown out by the Prussians following the Third Partition and their sizeable possessions – 300 square kilometres of land and several dozen villages – sequestered. The church is a typical piece of Polish Baroque, with exuberant frescoes in the main church and monks' skeletons in the catacombs (guided visits only), standard practice for the death-fixated Camaldolese. The monastery itself has been turned into a popular conference-centre-cum-**hotel** (☎087/63218; ③), with a good **restaurant**. In demand by domestic politicians, church dignitaries and for local cultural events, it's worth considering for a comfortable stop in peaceful surroundings.

The Suwalszczyna

North of Suwałki the forests give way to the lush, rolling hills of the **Suwalszczyna**. Two roads take you through the heart of the region, towards the Lithuanian border: the first heads due north then veers west through sporadic villages to **Wiżajny**; the other – along with a highly recommended steam rail line – runs some way to the east, covering the 30km to **Puńsk**.

Suwałki to Wiżajny

The great appeal of this route lies in getting right off the beaten track – and tracks don't get much less beaten than that to **WODZIŁKI**, tucked away in a quiet wooded valley, around 10km north of Suwałki. The hamlet is home to a small community of Orthodox **Old Believers**, whose original wooden *molenna* is still in use, along with a nearby *bania* (sauna).

Life in this rural settlement seems to have changed little since the first settlers moved here in the 1750s: the houses are simple, earth-floored buildings with few concessions to modernity, the old men grow long white beards, the women don't appear to cut their hair, the children run barefoot. If you're lucky enough to get invited into one of their homes, you'll see amazing collections of icons, rosaries, Bibles and other precious relics. The easiest way to get to the hamlet is to take the bus through Jeleniewo. If possible, take one that's turning off to Turtul Rutka, from where it's thirty minutes' walk north to Wodziłki; otherwise get off at Sidorówka, the next stop after Jeleniewo, which leaves five kilometres' walk west, skirting **Lake Szurpiły**. The lake itself is great for swimming, and an ideal camping spot, provided the mosquitoes aren't out in force.

The next bus stop after Sidorówka is **GULBIENISKI**, the point of access for the hill called **Cisowa Góra** (258m), known as "The Polish Fujiyama". It was the site of pre-Christian religious rituals, and it's rumoured that rites connected with Perkun, the Lithuanian firegod, are still observed here. Bear in mind that the Lithuanians, who still make up a small percentage of the population of this region,

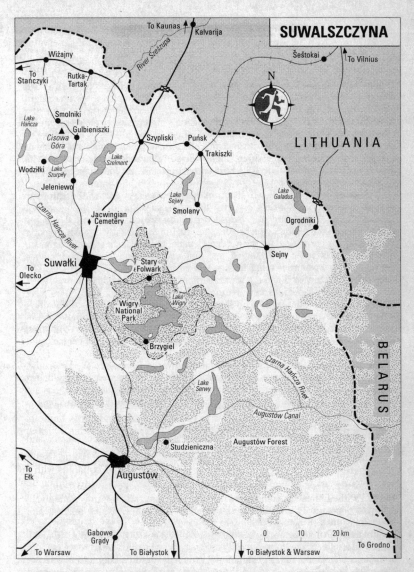

were the last Europeans to be converted to Christianity, in the late fourteenth century – Czesław Miłosz's semi-autobiographical novel *The Issa Valley*, set in neighbouring Lithuania, bears witness to the durability of pre-Christian beliefs right into the present century. Whatever the historical reality of the hill, it's a powerful place.

North of Gulbieniski the road divides: Wiżajny to the left, Rutka Tarta to the right. Continuing along the Wiżajny route, the next village is **SMOLNIKI**, just

POLES AND LITHUANIANS

Into the post-communist era, Poland's relations with Lithuania have until recently been worse than with any of the other neighbouring countries. Historically speaking, on both sides the picture is dominated by the experience of the **Polish–Lithuanian Commonwealth**, when for almost four centuries the two countries were formally united into the largest European empire of the time. Here already though, differences began to surface: while Poles tend to view the Commonwealth as the "golden age" of the nation's history, an era characterized by tolerance, co-operation and benign political influence and power, in Lithuania the picture is a little different. As with Poland's other eastern neighbours, the image of Poland as a dominant, imperial big sibling whose ruling aristocratic class built its wealth on harsh exploitation of its vast eastern estates – in Lithuania included – runs deep in the national psyche.

Tensions between the two countries surfaced clearly during the **interwar period**, following Piłsudski's eastern military campaign of 1919–20 against Trotsky's Red Army and the subsequent **annexation of Vilnius** and its surroundings, a region which, despite its predominantly Polish-speaking population, was earmarked for the newly independent Lithuanian state. Antagonism over Vilnius was never really settled, and diplomatic relations – and the border – between the two countries remained severed for most of the 1920s and 1930s. The outbreak of World War II and the wartime traumas suffered by both countries put a lid on mutual Polish–Lithuanian recriminations, though even here Poles have tended to see the Lithuanians as willing collaborators with the Nazis. Lithuania's forced incorporation into the Soviet Union in 1940 and the postwar imposition of communism in Poland enforced a new type of isolation between the two countries, with official Party-based relations about the only sanctioned source of contact right up into the mid-1980s.

The *glasnost* era, the collapse of communist power in Poland and the Lithuanian achievement of independence in 1991 opened the way for a new, and many hoped better, era in relations between the countries. To date, however, the record has not been good. The key source of conflict remains the **national minorities** residing in both countries.

Mostly located in the border area between Sejny and Puńsk, Poland's 40,000-strong **Lithuanian minority** continues to demand better educational and cultural resources for the community, in particular increased provision for native-tongue teachers, books and classes in primary and secondary schools in the region. With the notable exception of the 1989–91 struggle for Lithuanian independence, when local demonstrations in Puńsk were a regular news-feature on Polish TV, the Lithuanian community tends to be a quiet, rather introverted bunch, happy to remain in Poland as long as there's no problem in visiting relatives and maintaining contacts across the border.

Lithuania's **Polish minority** is altogether a different story. Numbering around a quarter of a million, the Poles are a significant national force – some seven percent of the total population, the largest minority grouping after Russians. The majority of them live in the eastern part of the country, in particular in the Vilnius and Salcininkai districts, where they comprise sixty and eighty percent of the populations, respectively. The biggest recent source of controversy has been the Lithuanian authorities' decision to suspend and subsequently dissolve local Polish-controlled government authorities in the Vilnius and Salcininkai districts and to transfer them to Lithuanian administrative control. Prompted by evidence that local Polish officials had actively collaborated with the organizers of the August

1991 Moscow coup attempt led by Gennady Yanayev, the Lithuanian move, officially announced in September 1991, unleashed a torrent of mutual recrimination and caused a significant setback in the (until then) steady development of diplomatic and political relations between the two countries.

Poles both inside and outside Lithuania argue that the main issue is democracy and the defence of minority rights. Furious at the local Polish officials' support for their former Soviet oppressors, Lithuanian officials have described external Polish pressure on the issue as direct interference in the country's internal affairs, a throwback to the arrogant imperial habits of the past. At the popular level, the row has reinforced the Lithuanian tendency to view Poles as "Fifth Columnists", whose primary loyalty is to the Polish state.

Despite Polish pressure, and only two months after the countries' foreign ministers signed an official friendship declaration, in March 1992 the Lithuanian Supreme Council postponed discussions of new local government elections until the autumn – an issue that has still not been wholly resolved. New laws making it harder for non-Lithuanian speakers to qualify automatically for Lithuanian citizenship didn't improve the political atmosphere either – many ethnic Poles remain legal "non-citizens", having elected not to apply for Lithuanian nationality under the new rules.

Viewed from a broader East European perspective it may be that resurfacing of long-buried ethnic tensions and rivalries is an almost unavoidable element of the transition to democratic rule, a transition in which minorities become a symbolic focal point for other anxieties and tensions. Faced with the reality of **Lithuanian independence** the country's Polish population, like its Russian counterpart, is fearful for its own identity: the often hysterical reaction of organizations such as the Lithuanian Union of Poles, the main community body, suggests it isn't finding this easy.

Compared to other regional ethnic tensions and conflicts – the Balts' "Russian question" included – Polish–Lithuanian difficulties have, however, largely been a fairly tame affair: As so often, overcoming, or at least sidestepping, historical prejudices and suspicions has been a key element of the process. The official-level breakthrough in relations finally came in 1994. After protracted negotiations, the text of a new **Friendship and Co-operation Treaty** was agreed in March, and signed by Lech Wałesa and his Lithuanian counterpart, Algirdas Brazauskas, amid much fanfare in Vilnius in April. Predictably, perhaps, even here history continued to niggle, with the Lithuanians demanding that the treaty contain an explicit condemnation of the Polish occupation of Lithuania in 1920 – the issue that initially stymied agreement. Resolved by a compromise that the text make no reference to past events, the demand was nonetheless implicitly restated by Brazauskas during the signing ceremony. Addressing the *Seimas* (parliament) in the company of Wałesa, Brazauskas stressed the Lithuanian character of Vilnius and reiterated the claim that the city and surrounding region belonged to the interwar Polish state "in fact if not in law". Though clearly irritated, the Polish delegation resisted the temptation to get drawn into further arguments and the treaty was duly ratified by both countries in October 1994.

In practical terms, the signing of the treaty presages hope for the resolution of several issues, notably the situation of the Polish minority in Lithuania, whose legal and administrative status is now explicitly "normalized" for the first time. Equally important, it finally paved the way for the long overdue construction of a **new border crossing** between the two countries at Budzisko-Kalvarija – the most modern on Poland's eastern border to date – which opened to passenger traffice during a Lithuanian state visit to Poland in September 1995.

before which there's a wonderful panorama of the surrounding lakes: if you're on the bus ask the driver to let you off at the *punkt wyściowy* (viewpoint). If you happen to have a compass with you, don't be surprised if it starts to go haywire around here – the area has large deposits of iron-rich ore, as discovered by disoriented German pilots based here during World War II at Luftwaffe installations. Despite the obvious commercial potential, the seams haven't been exploited to date owing to the high levels of uranium in the ore and the risks from direct exposure to it.

A couple of kilometres west of Smolniki, along a bumpy track through woods, is **Lake Hańcza**, the deepest in Poland at 108m, quiet, clean and unspoilt. The Czarna Hańcza River joins the lake on its southern shore. There's a **youth hostel** on the southeast edge at Błaskowizna. To get to the hostel take the Wiżajny bus from Suwałki and get off at Bachanowo, a kilometre past Turtul Rutka; it's a short walk from here. Note that camping isn't allowed in the Suwałki Park, of which this area is part.

The Stańczyki Viaduct

If you're travelling by car, the viaduct at **Stańczyki,** west of Lake Hańcza close up by the Russian border on the edge of the Puszcza Romincka, is a must for lovers of the bizarre. (Follow the main route west of Wiżajny, turning left off the road about 4km past Zytkejmy.) The reason for coming is to admire the huge deserted twin **Viaduct** straddling the Błędzianka River valley, seemingly lost out in the middle of nowhere. Before World War II this hamlet was right on the East Prussian–Polish border: in 1910 the Germans built a mammoth double viaduct here as part of a new rail line, one side scheduled to carry timber trains leaving Prussia, the other, trains entering the country from Poland. The viaduct was duly completed, the only problem being that the promised rail track never materialized. The crumbling viaducts have stood ever since, a towering monument to an architects' and engineers' folly, no-one apparently having the heart – or cash – to pull them down. These days the viaducts are a favourite Sunday outing with local people. With a bit of effort you can join them climbing up onto the viaducts to savour the view and the madness of the scheme.

For an overnight stay, there's a small **hotel** in the village (often full in summer) with its own snack bar. Camping is the most popular option here, with no restrictions on sites – the most prized spot being right under the arches of the viaduct.

From Suwałki to Puńsk and Sejny

Lithuanians are one of Poland's minorities, most of the 40,000-odd community living in a little enclave of towns and villages north and east of Suwałki. The further you go into the countryside the more common it becomes to catch the lilt of their strange-sounding tongue in bars and at bus stops.

The village of **Puńsk**, close to the border, has the highest proportion of Lithuanians in the area and is surrounded by some of the loveliest countryside. There are two ways of covering the 30km from Suwałki. The first is to take the twice-daily **train** to **TRAKISZKI** (departs at 4.30am and 4.30pm) and walk the last two kilometres. The attraction of this is that the line is still run partly by old **steam trains**, which enhance the time-slip quality of a journey that takes you through ancient meadows – their hedgerows a brilliant mass of flora – and fields tilled by horse-drawn ploughs. Keep your passport handy as the border police are sometimes in Trakiszki to check what you're up to. If you feel like a swim first, **Lake Sejwy**, 3km down the road, is an excellent spot. To get here, follow the path parallel to the rail line, turn right where the path forks and left by the first field. The other option is to travel by **bus**, changing at **SZYPLISZKI**. The bar opposite Szypliszki's bus stop serves a decent local beer, or if you fancy a more salubrious pastime you could walk the couple of kilometres west through the fields to **Lake Szelment**, another untouched corner of the region and a popular horse riding area – ask at the tourist office in Suwałki for details.

Puńsk

Tucked away a few kilometres from the Lithuanian border, **PUŃSK** used to be sunk in complete obscurity, but since 1989 has been the object of unprecedented attention. The reason is the village's **Lithuanians** – some seventy percent of the population – who, despite their small numbers, maintain a Lithuanian cultural centre, choir and weekly newspaper, giving the place a decidedly un-Polish feel. In the summer of 1989 Lithuanian flags and the symbol of Sajudis (the Lithuanian Popular Front) became common sights here, and when the Soviet blockade of Lithuania began in March 1990, the response in Puńsk was immediate: it became the collection point for supplies to Lithuania from all over Poland, and demonstrations in support of Lithuanian independence were held after Mass every Sunday. Now that independence has been achieved, things have quietened down. Locals still gripe at the logistical restraints on crossing the border to visit relatives, though the recent opening of the nearby border at Budzisko will undoubtedly ease the situation, as well as bring more economic activity and money into the village.

The neo-Gothic **Parish Church** might look nothing special as a building, but turn up on a Sunday at 11am and you'll find the place packed for Mass in Lithuanian. If it's a major feast day, you may also see a procession afterwards, for which the women, especially, don the curiously Inca-like national costume. Enquiries in the bar or shops should track down Juozas Vaina, who set up the local **Lithuanian Museum**, ul. Szklona, on the edge of the village. Inside there's an interesting collection of local ethnography, including some wonderful decorative fabrics and crafts, bizarre-looking farm implements, and prewar Lithuanian books and magazines, as well as maps that illuminate the tangled question of the Polish–Lithuanian border. There's also recent Sajudis and Lithuanian independence-related material, a section that will doubtless grow over the next few years.

Although there is no regular **accommodation** in the village, Lithuanians are immensely hospitable people, so it's worthwhile asking at the *Rutka* restaurant-bar about the possibility of a bed for the night. The *Rutka* isn't the best you'll ever visit, but a couple of beers into a chat with locals and you'll probably get some insights into local Polish–Lithuanian relations. Despite their support for Lithuanian independence and general lack of enthusiasm for things Polish, most Lithuanians seem content to stay in Poland, at least for the moment. As with other Polish minorities, however, there's a strong desire for more cultural rights, including more provision for Lithuanian language-teaching in local schools. It remains to be seen how far overwhelmingly Polish post-communist governments are prepared to go on this issue.

As well as Lithuanians, Puńsk was for centuries home to another minority – Jews. Almost every Jew from this region was either slaughtered or uprooted, but a few signs of the past – predictably ignored in the official Polish guides and maps – are still left. The *Dom Handlowy* on the main street in Puńsk used to be the rabbi's house, and the older locals can point you in the direction of the abandoned **Jewish cemetery**, on the northern edge of the village, where a few Hebrew inscriptions are still visible among the grass and trees.

Sejny

Instead of returning directly to Suwałki, you might try the bus trip via the market town of **SEJNY**, 25km south of Puńsk, a cross-country journey that's a treat in itself. Sejny is dominated by a Dominican **Monastery Complex** at the top of the town, which contains a grandiose late-Renaissance church refurbished in Rococo style in the mid-eighteenth century. The surrounding monastic buildings are currently under restoration, and likely to remain so for some time.

The main square just down the main street now hosts a regular **bazaar**, with Lithuanian traders from across the border much in evidence – the locals don't like it much, and the atmosphere can get a little tense for comfort. At the other end of town is the former **Synagogue**, its size indicating the importance of the former Jewish

---

ON TO LITHUANIA

With cross-border **travel between Poland and Lithuania** easier than at any time in the postwar period, a trip over the border to the Lithuanian capital, Vilnius, is now a genuinely feasible option.

Situated around 160km east of Suwałki, along with Ukrainian L'viv, **VILNIUS** (in Polish, Wilno) is *the* great former Polish city of the east – not a point to emphasize when you're there, incidentally – with a large Old Town complex that despite postwar neglect still ranks among the finest in Europe. Anyone expecting an orderly Protestant Hansa-town on the lines of Baltic neighbours Riga, Tallinn or even Helsinki, though, will be disappointed. Vilnius is unmistakably Catholic – and Polish – in feel and atmosphere, a jumbled mix of cobbled alleyways, high spires, Catholic shrines, *cerkwi* and old Jewish monuments. Largely unscarred by World War II, Vilnius's best-known monuments include the **Ostra Brama Gate**, a street gallery shrine housing Eastern Catholicism's most venerated icon of the Madonna, and the fabulous **St Anne's Church**, an extraordinarily exuberant Gothic masterpiece which Napoleon is supposed to have contemplated dismantling and moving to Paris.

The city's **tourist infrastructure** still has some way to go: decent restaurants are thin on the ground and accommodation is an unpredictable business. *Vilnius in Your Pocket*, available from hotels, kiosks and bookstores, provides you with all the basic tourist information. Lithuanians are a friendly and hospitable lot on the whole, and anyone tempted by the prospect of making the journey east will find it's well worth the effort.

Practicalities

British, Irish and Danish citizens excepted, foreign nationals need a **visa** to enter the country, technically valid for all three Baltic republics. In theory at least, visas are obtainable at the Lithuanian border, though it's probably better to secure your visa in advance, either at Lithuanian (as well as Latvian and Estonian) embassies and consulates established in several countries, including the USA, Britain, Germany, France, Belgium, Sweden, Canada, Australia and Norway, or at the Lithuanian embassy in Warsaw, al. Ujazdowskie 13-12 (☎02/694 24 87).

There are several options for **travel** to Vilnius. With the opening of the new border crossing at Budzisko–Kalwarija, travelling **by car** is set to become a lot

population here. Built in the 1860s and devastated by the Nazis who turned it into a fire station, it has since been carefully restored and turned into a **Museum** and cultural centre (Mon–Fri 10.30am–4.30pm). If your Polish is up to it, the curator can fill you in on local history, particularly the Lithuanian, Jewish and Old Believer minorities. Every April, the synagogue plays host to an **International Culture Festival**, organized by the local *Funacja Podgranicze* ("The Borderland Foundation") and dedicated to promoting the culture, music and art between what it calls "the borderland nations". Started in the early 1990s, the festival attracts an increasing range of theatre groups, artists and musicians from all over Europe, though the emphasis remains on "local" cross-border groups – Lithuanians, Belarussians, Ukrainians and Russians. For details of the festival and the foundation's other activities, contact the office at ul. J. Piłsudskiego 37, 16500 Sejny (☎189/200).

Despite signs in the town centre, the information office does not exist any more, while the only chance of a room is at the **hotel** *Na Skarpie* at ul. Armii Krajowej 15 (☎189/65; ②), the main street, which also has a basic restaurant, or

easier. Passport control is still slow, especially in summer, so be prepared for tailbacks at the border. There's now a daily early-morning **train** (6.50am) from Suwałki to Seštokai, just over the border, with a connecting service on to Vilnius. Since tickets are still handwritten at the station on the Lithuanian side you'll probably have to buy one from the conductor, who'll charge you around $3 for the privilege.

As well as the local service, a daily train runs from Warsaw to Vilnius travelling via Grodno in Belarus, with transit visas ($30) supposedly now available on the spot. Especially at weekends these trains are often full to the brim with local daytrippers, plus the usual consignment of "trade tourists", so be prepared to share your corridor space with the odd TV or computer and keep a careful eye on your valuables.

As with other cross-border journeys east, going **by bus** is currently the best option: the special priority accorded *PKS* buses at the border means you're through any queues and document formalities fairly speedily. Journey time from Suwałki to Vilnius is around three hours: in addition buses run from Gdańsk (8hrs), Olsztyn (6hrs) and Warsaw (9hrs). Again the demand, particularly in summer, is high, so advance purchase of tickets from the Suwałki bus station is strongly advisable. Like the trains, the buses are generally filled with the requisite contingent of trade tourists and smugglers (Armenians are currently much in evidence), so be prepared for a squash. If you're returning to Poland by bus, the journey back is with one of the privately run **minibus services** operating from the Vilnius bus station. The drivers only accept payment in **US dollars** – even Deutschmarks won't necessarily do the trick – so make sure you bring some with you; otherwise you'll be forced into lastminute street trading. At around $7.50 to Suwałki, the current price, for Westerners at least, is pretty reasonable. Two further things to bear in mind are that timetable information is much easier to get hold of in Suwałki than in Vilnius, and that Lithuania is two hours ahead of GMT.

The final option is by **plane**. A local company now operates daily flights from Suwałki to Vilnius: departure is at around 8am, with a return plane in the evening, making the notion of a day trip to Vilnius a feasible, if expensive, option. Cost for the return trip is currently around $90. For details ask at the Suwałki tourist office (see p.244) or phone the airport, actually the local aviation club southwest of town, *Aeroklub Suwalski*, at ul. Wojczyńskiego (☎087/5279).

at the summer **youth hostel** on the outskirts at ul. Łąkowa. Don't be surprised, incidentally, to see Russian and Lithuanian registration cars and trucks rumbling through Sejny. Ogrodniki, until recently the only border crossing into Lithuania, is just 20km to the east.

BIAŁYSTOK AND THE BELARUSSIAN BORDERLANDS

As you head south from the lakes or east from Warsaw, you find yourself in a region of complex ethnicity, situated right up against the borders of Belarus. The Poles call the area **Podlasie** – literally "Under the Trees" – which gives little hint of its landscape of wide, open plains, tracts of primeval forest, and dark skies. Even without the increasing presence of onion-domed Orthodox churches, it would feel Eastern, more like Russia than Poland. The whole area also feels extremely poor, and is one of the most neglected regions of the country, with an overwhelmingly peasant population. On the long potholed country roads you see as many horse-carts as cars, in the fields as many horse-drawn ploughs as tractors. In the **Białowieża Forest** the isolation has ensured the survival of continental Europe's last belt of virgin forest – the haunt of bison, elk and hundreds of varieties of flora and fauna, and home, too, of the wondrous *Żybrówka* "bison grass" vodka.

Belarussians are the principal ethnic minority, numbering some 200,000 in all. Before the war, Polish territory stretched far across the current Belarussian border, and today communities on either side are scarcely distinguishable, save that those on the eastern side are, if anything, poorer still. Another historic, but declining, minority are the **Tartars**, who settled here centuries ago and whose wooden mosques at **Bohoniki** and **Kruszyniamy** are one of the sights of the Polish east. (There are several more over the border.) Long a melting-pot of cultures, **Białystok** and the surrounding region were also one of the main areas of **Jewish settlement** in Poland. Before the war almost every town in the region boasted at least one synagogue, often more: many of these were wooden structures, whose exuberant design clearly reflected the influence of the indigenous folk architecture. Sadly all the wooden synagogues – pictures suggest many of them were spectacular – were burned down by the Nazis. A wealth of brick and stone **Jewish monuments** survive, though, and on any journey through the outlying towns and villages, you'll encounter former synagogue buildings and crumbling Jewish cemeteries. Of these the restored synagogue complex at **Tykocin** is one of the most evocative Jewish monuments in the country – as in the rest of the region, the community itself was wiped out by the Nazis.

Once again, local **transport** consists mainly of buses, with services diminishing the nearer the border you get.

Białystok

Even the habitually enthusiastic official Polish guidebooks are mute on the glories of **BIAŁYSTOK**, industrial centre of northeast Poland; it's not a beautiful place and its main development occurred during the industrialization of the nineteenth century. Uniquely among major Polish cities today, however, it has kept the healthy ethnic and religious mix – Poles, Belarussians and Ukrainians, Catholic and Orthodox – characteristic of the country before the war, though the Jews, of course, are absent. And for all the industry, it's curiously one of the country's least polluted cities.

Some history

According to legend, Białystok was founded in 1320 by Gedymin, the Grand Duke of Lithuania, but its emergence really began in the 1740s when local aristocrat Jan Branicki built a palace in the town centre. Partitioned off to Prussia and then to Russia, Białystok rapidly developed as a textile city, in competition with Prussian-dominated Łódź. In both cities, industrialization fostered the growth of a sizeable urban proletariat and a large and influential **Jewish community**. Factory strikes in the 1880s demonstrated the potency of working-class protest, as did the anti-tsarist demonstrations which broke out here in 1905. Echoing protests in other parts of the Russian empire, they elicited a similar response – an officially insti-gated pogrom, during which many Białystok Jews lost their lives. Fifteen years later, anticipating a victory that never came against Piłsudski's apparently demoral-ized forces, Lenin's troops installed a provisional government in Białystok led by Felix Dzierżyński, the notorious Polish commander of the secret police.

World War II brought destruction and slaughter to Białystok. Hitler seized the town in 1939, then handed it over to Stalin before reoccupying it in 1941 – which

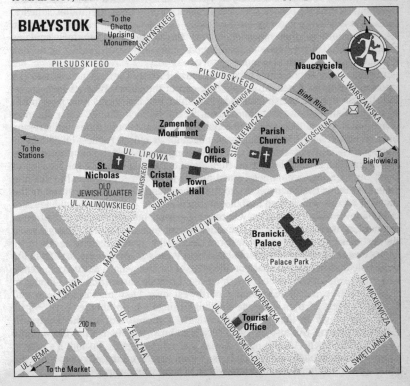

is when the Jewish population was herded into a ghetto area and deported to the death camps. The heroic Białystok **Ghetto Uprising** of August 1943 (the first within the Reich) presaged the extinction of the city's Jewry. Nor was the killing confined to Jews. By 1945, over half the city's population was dead, with three-quarters of the town centre destroyed.

Following the end of the war, the authorities set about rebuilding the town and its industrial base. From a strictly utilitarian point of view they succeeded: today Białystok is a developed economic centre for textiles, metals and timber, with a population of over 250,000. The aesthetic cost has been high, though – the usual billowing smokestacks, ugly tower blocks and faceless open streets of postwar development. But Białystok has its share of historic sights – mostly associated with its Orthodox Belarussian community – and it makes an ideal base for exploring the border region to the east.

The Town

Białystok's historic centrepoint is the **Rynek**, an unusual triangular-shaped space with a large Baroque town hall in the middle. The main sights are situated on and around **ul. Lipowa**, the main thoroughfare cutting from east to west across the city centre. The **Church of St Nicholas** here was built in the 1840s to serve the swelling ranks of Russian settlers. A typically dark, icon-filled place of Orthodox devotion, its ornate frescoes are careful copies of those in the Orthodox cathedral in Kiev. It is filled to capacity for the Sunday services – worth coinciding with to hear the choir. Further down ul. Lipowa the **Orthodox Cemetery** contains another enchanting *cerkiew* – though your only chance of getting in to look around is during the Sunday morning service.

Catholic competition comes from the huge **Parish Church** nearby and the imposing 1920s **St Roch**, at the western end of the street. With its high space-ship-like towers, the parish church is something of a historical curio: next to it is a small seventeenth-century church built by the Branicki family, while the main structure is a vast 1900 neo-Gothic building, almost twenty times the size and only permitted by the tsarist authorities because its official request billed it as an "addition". The streets south of ul. Lipowa comprise part of the old **ghetto area**. A tablet in Polish and Hebrew on the side of a building opposite the local court house on ul. Suraska commemorates the one thousand Jews burned to death in June 1941 when the Nazis set fire to the **Great Synagogue**, reputedly one of the finest in Poland, which used to stand on this site.

For a town whose population was roughly seventy percent Jewish at the turn of the century there are precious few other Jewish monuments left. Though you'd hardly guess so from today's uniform blocks, the streets leading north of ul. Lipowa were all mainly Jewish-inhabited before the war. Across the road from the town hall, in the leafy little park on the edge of ul. Malmeda, a **statue** commemorates the town's most famous Jewish citizen, **Ludwik Zamenhof,** the founder of Esperanto (see p.259). Continuing northwest over busy ul. Piłsudskiego and through streets of high concrete buildings brings you to another park, off ul. Zabia. Seemingly in the middle of nowhere, a **monument to the Białystok Ghetto Uprising** (August 16, 1943) recalls an important moment in the wartime history of the town. As with many Jewish war monuments in Poland, it's easy to miss – there's no sign and the place isn't even named on the city map – but the older local inhabitants usually know where to point you if you ask.

The most striking building in the town centre is the **Branicki Palace**, destroyed by the Nazis in 1944 but rebuilt on the lines of the eighteenth-century building commissioned by Jan Branicki – itself a reconstruction of an earlier palace. It's difficult to get inside, as the main building is now a medical academy, but you can stroll unhindered through the park and admire its classical grandeur from a distance. Look out, too, for the main front balcony, the so-called **Dzierżyński Balcony**, from which Felix Dzierzyński and associates proclaimed the creation of the Polish Soviet Socialist Republic in 1920.

Despite the heavy wartime destruction a number of characteristic examples of the regional **wooden architecture** have survived in parts of the city, most notably in the houses along streets like ul. Grunwaldzka, Żelazna and Mazowiecka down from the train station in the southern section of the centre.

Stranded on a small island at the eastern end of ul. Lipowa the **Town Hall**, a small, squat eighteenth-century building, was reconstructed from scratch after the war: these days it houses a local **Art Museum** (Tues–Sun 10am–5pm). A good selection of works by some of the better-known nineteenth- and twentieth-century artists – Malczewski, Witkiewicz, Krzyzanowski and the like – is complemented by an enjoyable collection of local art, the portraits and landscapes displaying a strong feeling for the distinctive character of the region. In addition, the museum has regular temporary thematic exhibitions of works culled from other national museums, the imagination with which they're presented suggesting a serious attempt to get on the national art map.

Białystok's proximity to the Belarussian border ensures it a key place among the growing number of Polish towns heavily involved in "trade tourism". On Sunday mornings the open-air **market** – located on ul. Kavaliejska– is thronged with Belarussians, Ukrainians and others from across the border plying a strange assortment of consumer goods: gold, clothes, hi-fis, antiques, cosmetics, anything that Poles are prepared to buy. If you want **caviar**, this is the place to buy it, as the nearer the border you get, the lower the price: Gdańsk is fifty percent higher, Warsaw seventy-five. Pay in dollars only if you have to, be prepared to haggle, buy glass containers (not metal), and bear in mind that taking caviar out of Poland is illegal. Keep in mind, too, that the crowds are a haven for pickpockets.

Perhaps the saddest reminder of the city's onetime Jewish population is the **Jewish Cemetery**, off ul. Wschodnia on the northeast edge of the city. Starting from Rynek Kościuszki in the centre of town bus #3 drops you close by just west of the cemetery – get off at the junction of ul. Władysława Wysockiego and ul. Władysława Raginisa, a 10–15-minute journey. With Catholic cemeteries on both sides, an Orthodox church under construction at the back, and children playing along the walls, the large and badly neglected cemetery looks and feels a beleaguered place. The few surviving gravestones are scattered around in the undergrowth, some of them still legible, but if things carry on this way there may not be any left in the not-too-distant future.

Practicalities

The main **train station**, a dingy pink building that wouldn't look out of place in Moscow, is a five-minute bus ride (#2, #4 or #21) west of the city centre – supposedly it was built outside the centre as a punishment for anti-tsarist protests in the city. Close by, on ul. Bohaterów Monte Cassino, is the **bus station**.

Irritatingly, the **tourist information office** (8am–5pm; ☎085/26956) is well south of the town centre at the bottom of an apartment building at ul. Skłodowskiej 13. However, it's worth the effort as it has a plentiful supply of maps and brochures and can make useful suggestions about places to stay. **Orbis**, Rynek Kościuszki 13, is a less useful but more central alternative. **Almatur**, at ul. Zwierzyniecka 12 (Mon–Fri 9am–4pm; ☎085/22041), on the southern side of the centre (bus #10 from the train station), runs a lot of youth and student camps in the area, as well as arranging boat and canoe rental. They may also be able to tell you the current locations of **student hotels** (open June–Aug), whose venues change year by year. **PTTK**, at ul. Lipowa 8 (☎085/51 71 73), specializes in local guides and trips to Białowieża (see below).

Of the **hotels**, most handy is the *Cristal*, ul. Lipowa 3/5 (☎085/42 50 61, fax 42 58 00; ④), a serviceable place popular with visiting Russians that's bang in the town centre. Other options are the *Turkus*, ul. Zwycięstwa 54 (☎085/51 32 78, fax 51 12 11; ④), west of the train station; the *Leśny*, ul. Zwycięstwa 77 (☎085/51 16 41, fax 51 17 01; ⑤), considerably further west along the same road, the main route to Warsaw; and the *Zwierzyniec,* ul. 11 Listopada 28 (☎085/22629; ③), a cheaper, lower-quality alternative. The **youth hostel**, al. Piłsudskiego 7b (☎085/52 4250), is not far east of the train station, while **campers** should head for the *Gromada* site next to the *Leśny* hotel.

All the main hotels have **restaurants**, of which the *Cristal* and *Leśny* are the more enticing. The *Grodno* at ul. Sienkiewicza 28 offers its version of Belarussian cuisine, while the *Kaunas*, ul. Wesola 18, has Lithuanian specialities like *chłodnik*. Other reasonable options are the *Karczma Słupska* on ul. Św. Rocha 29, *Hubertówka* at ul. Broniewskiego 28, the *Astoria*, ul. Sienkiewicza 4, and the *Avanti* next door, a self-styled Italian joint. A number of new bars are scattered along ul. Lipowa, each serving bottled German and, increasingly, draught Polish beers. The *Ratuszowa*, by the Town Hall on Rynek Kościuszki, is a good place to sit out in the summer and has occasional live bands. For local **nightlife** try *Casablanca*, Św. Rocha 15, a popular music club that's open late and features local blues bands.

Around Białystok

A handful of trips into the city's immediate surroundings are worth considering, notably the fine icon museum in **Supraśl**, north of the city, the Branicki palace at **Choroszcz** and the synagogue of **Tykocin**. The countryside offers some decent walking country too, chiefly the tranquil **Puszcza Knyszyńska** stretching east of the town, a popular weekend haunt with city folk. All of these are accessible using local bus connections.

Supraśl and the Puszcza Knyszyńska

A sixteen-kilometre bus journey northeast of Białystok is **SUPRAŚL**, a sleepy provincial eastern hang-out on the edge of the Puszcza Knyszyńska. The chief attraction here is the **Bishop's Palace**, a grand, crumbling seventeenth-century structure now used as a school. Slap in the middle of the palace courtyard is a large early sixteenth-century brick Orthodox *cerkiew*, built by Grand Hetman of Lithuania Aleksander Chodkiewicz for the Orthodox Order of St Basil, which

LUDWIK ZAMENHOF AND THE ESPERANTO MOVEMENT

Białystok's most famous son is probably **Ludwik Zamenhof** (1859–1917), the creator of **Esperanto**, the artificial language invented as an instrument of international communication. Born in what was then a colonial outpost of the tsarist empire, Zamenhof grew up in an environment coloured by the continuing struggle between the indigenous Polish population and its Russian rulers – both of whom were apt to turn on the Jews as and when the occasion suited them.

Perhaps because of this experience, from an early stage Zamenhof, an eye doctor by training, dedicated himself to the cause of racial tolerance and understanding. Zamenhof's attention focused on the fruits of the mythical Tower of Babel, the profusion of human languages: if a new, **easily learnable international language** could be devised it would, he believed, remove a key obstacle not only to people's ability to communicate directly with each other, but also to their ability to live together peaceably. On the basis of extensive studies of the major Western classical and modern languages, Zamenhof – Doktoro Esperanto or "Doctor Hopeful" as he came to be known – set himself the task of inventing just such a language, the key source being root words common to European, and in particular Romance, languages.

The first primer, *Dr. Esperanto's International Language,* was published in 1887, but Zamenhof continued to develop his language by translating a whole range of major literary works, *Hamlet,* Goethe's and Molière's plays and the entire Old Testament included. The new language rapidly gained international attention, and the **first world Esperanto congress** was held in France in 1905. In the same year Zamenhof completed *Fundamento de Esperanto* (1905), his main work, which soon became the basic Esperanto textbook and the one still most commonly in use today.

Even if it has never quite realized Zamenhof's dreams of universal acceptance, Esperanto – *Linguo Internacia* as it calls itself – has proved considerably more successful than any other "invented" language. With a worldwide membership of over 100,000 and national associations in around fifty countries, the *Universala Esperanto Associo* represents a significant international movement of people attracted to the universalist ideals as much as the linguistic practice of Esperanto. In Białystok itself there's a thriving **Esperanto-speaking community** that welcomes visitors at its main office at ul. Lipowa 14 (regular office hours).

became one of the spiritual centres of Orthodoxy in the Polish–Lithuanian Commonwealth. Said to have boasted a fine interior combining Gothic and Byzantine styles – the Nazis mauled the place during the war – the whole building is currently being completely renovated.

Improbably for such an out-of-the-way place, the former palace chapel contains a small but stunning **Orthodox Museum** (theoretically, Tues–Sun 10am–4pm though the lone caretaker has a habit of closing an hour or so earlier), housing some of the original frescoes and icons taken from the main *cerkiew*.

The works gathered here encompass a range of themes and images: scenes from the lives of Mary and Jesus, benign-looking early church fathers and saints, ethereal archangels and cherubim, a wonderful panorama of Orthodox art and spirituality and one in which, particularly in the frescoes, the art historians detect a strong Serbian Orthodox influence.

The Puszcza Knyszyńska

If you've come by bus from Białystok you could consider hiking back through the **Puszcza Knyszyńska**, a popular walking area with Białystok residents. The sandy local terrain is pretty easy-going underfoot, but the lack of signs once you get into the forest makes a local map, such as *Okolice Białegostoku* 1:150,000, readily available in Białystok, essential.

On a good day it's attractive and enjoyable walking country, the silence of the forest broken at intervals by cackling crows overhead or startled deer breaking for cover. Starting from the southern edge of Supraśl, a marked path takes you south through the lofty expanses of forest to the village of **Ciasne**, ending up by the bus stop near **Grabówka** at the edge of the main road back in to Białystok – a twelve-kilometre hike in total.

Choroszcz

The highways and byways of eastern Poland hide a wealth of neglected old aristocratic piles, most of them relics of a not-so-distant period when a small group of fabulously wealthy families owned most of the eastern part of the country.

The eighteenth-century **Branicki Summer Palace** at **CHOROSZCZ,** located 10km west of Białystok off the main Warsaw road, is a fine example of this phenomenon, the key difference being that the palace here has been completely renovated and converted into a **museum** (Tues–Sun 10am–3pm). To get here, catch a local **bus** from Białystok; the palace is on the west side of town, just a short walk from the main stop.

The Palace
After Białystok, you'll find that the elegant statue-topped **Palace** facade makes quite a contrast to the architectural rigours of the city, with the tranquil country location on the edge of the grounds of the local hospital another agreeable feature. Few of the building's original furnishings remain, most of them having been replaced by period replicas of the kind of things the Branickis are supposed to have liked. The main ground-floor room is the **salon**, its sedate parquet floor complemented by a choice collection of period furniture. Along with a number of family portraits, one of the original master of the house, Jan Branicki, hangs in the hallway, the finely wrought iron balustrades of the staircase illuminated by a lamp held aloft by a rather tortured-looking classical figure. The **second floor** is equally ornate, featuring a number of meticulously decorated apartment rooms, a dining room with a fine set of mid-eighteenth-century Meissen porcelain and a **Chippendale room**.

Back out of the building it's worth taking a stroll along the canal running from beneath the salon windows at the back of the palace, the overgrown **palace grounds** stretching out in all directions. From the bridge over the canal you have a good view of the whole feudal-like palace ensemble, the old lodge house and manor farm included.

Tykocin

Forty kilometres west of Białystok, north of the main Warsaw road (E18), is the quaint, sleepy little town of **TYKOCIN**, set in the open vistas of the Podlasie countryside. Tykocin's size belies its historical significance: as well as the former site of the national arsenal, it also has one of the best-restored **synagogues** in Poland today, much visited by Jewish tourist groups, a reminder that this was

POLES AND BELARUSSIANS

Poles and Belarussians have a long history of living together, but also one of long-suppressed cultural and political antagonisms, which have recently begun to surface. In the communist era, minorities were actively recruited into the party and state security apparatus, and their religion given active state backing – so long as the community kept its separatist or nationalist impulses in check. Use of the Belarussian language was forbidden in public, and there were no concessions to the culture in schools or cultural institutions. Despite this, a handful of Belarussian *samizdat* publications circulated during the communist years.

The result of these years of active state co-option, inevitably, was to reinforce Catholic Polish suspicion of their neighbours, which, with the state controls off, is surfacing in occasional bouts of openly expressed hostility. Meanwhile, for Belarussians, the new Polish political climate and freedoms, the disintegration of the Soviet empire and ever-burgeoning Polish nationalism have reawakened their own search for a meaningful national identity. In Białystok, nationalist Belarussian candidates ran against Solidarity in the 1989 elections, and the community is taking steps to re-establish its language and culture.

The radical changes of the early 1990s – most importantly, of course, the emergence of Belarus as an independent state – added a whole new dimension to the situation faced by the **Polish–Belarussian community**, whose size is currently estimated to be 250,000–300,000 (under one percent of the population), one of the largest minority groups after the Germans and Ukrainians. The cautious line previously adopted by many community leaders has given way to a much more self-confident, assertive attitude. Cultural, political and religious associations are flourishing, Belarussian newspapers, magazines and books are published in abundance, while the local radio station established in central Białystok in the early 1990s, with Orthodox church backing, has finally given Belarussians their own independent access to the media. Belarussians are also part of the joint working group established in 1992 under the auspices of the Polish Helsinki Committee by representatives of the various ethnic minority groups to defend and extend the rights of all minorities in the country. Inevitably, a key concern for the Belarussians is the question of cross-border ties with the Belarus "homeland" itself.

At the official political level, relations were long complicated by Belarussian demands that Białystok and its surroundings be declared an ethnic Belarussian region – a demand rejected by the Polish side on the grounds that its acceptance would undermine the territorial cohesion of the country. Relations improved visibly in the wake of the breakup of the USSR and the emergence of an independent Belarus in 1991. Since then, things seem to have been progressing reasonably smoothly especially following the signing of an economic and trade agreement in October 1991, followed by a further official Friendship and Co-operation Treaty in June 1992. Additional wide-ranging trade agreements and a number of **new border-crossing points** are either already established or in the pipeline – the most important being the crossing at Sławatycze–Damachava, an old military bridge now opened to civilian traffic.

As in other borderlands, the key underlying issue is whether the post-communist government policy on minorities will go further than declarations and lead to active support for their development. On the political level, Belarus' decision to enter a new customs union with the Russian Federation in 1995 and generally revive ties with Moscow – at a price, some argue of genuine independence – could have repercussions for future inter-state relations.

once home to an important Jewish community. It's a one-hour journey from the main bus station in Białystok; buses leave regularly throughout the day.

The Town

The bus deposits you in the enchanting **town square**, bordered by well-preserved nineteenth-century wooden houses. The **statue** of Stefan Czarnecki in the centre of the square was put up by his grandson Jan Branicki in 1770, while he was busy rebuilding the town and his adopted home of Białystok.

The Baroque **Parish Church**, commissioned by the energetic Branicki in 1741 and recently restored, has a beautiful polychrome ceiling, a finely ornamented side chapel of the Virgin and a functioning Baroque organ. The portraits of Branicki and his wife, Izabella Poniatowska, are by Silvester de Mirys, a Scot who became the resident artist at the Branicki palace in Białystok. Also founded by Branicki was the nearby **Bernardine Convent**, now a Catholic seminary. Next to the church looking onto the river bridge is the **Alumnat**, a hospice for war veterans founded in 1633 – a world first. Continue out of town over the River Narew and you'll come to the ruins of the sixteenth-century **Radziwiłł Palace**, where the national arsenal was once kept; it was destroyed by the Swedes in 1657.

Jews first came to Tykocin in 1522, and by the early nineteenth century seventy percent of the population was Jewish, the figure declining to around fifty percent by 1900. The original wooden **Synagogue** in the town centre was replaced in 1642 by the Baroque building still standing today. Carefully restored in the 1970s, it now houses an excellent **Jewish Museum** (Tues–Sun 10am–5pm), where background recordings of Jewish music and prayers add to a mournfully evocative atmosphere. Information sheets in English and German give detailed background on both the building and the history of Tykocin Jewry. Beautifully illustrated Hebrew inscriptions, mostly prayers, adorn sections of the interior walls, as do some lively colourful frescoes. Most striking of all is the Baroque bima, the four-pillared central podium from which the cantor led the services. Valuable religious artefacts are on display, as well as historical documents relating to the now-lost community. Over the square in the old **Talmud house** there's a well-kept **Local History Museum**, featuring an intact apothecary's shop. The **Jewish cemetery** on the edge of town is gradually blending into the surrounding meadow – as so often, there's no-one able or willing to take care of it. Among the eroded, weather-beaten gravestones, however, a few preserve their fine original carvings.

Practicalities

The *PTTK* hostel is closed at the moment, so the only official **accommodation** is a youth hostel on ul. Kochanowskiego (June & July; ☎0902/13685). Tykocin's only **restaurant**, the *Narnianka*, just off the square on ul. Bernardyńska, is pretty squalid: wait to get back to Białystok before eating.

Kruszyniamy and Bohoniki

Hard up near the Belarussian frontier, the old Tartar villages of **Kruszyniamy** and **Bohoniki** are an intriguing ethnic component of Poland's eastern borderlands, with their wooden mosques and Muslim graveyards. The story of how these people came to be here is fascinating in itself (see box), and a visit to the villages is an instructive and impressive experience.

THE TARTARS

Early in the thirteenth century, the nomadic Mongol people of central Asia were welded into a confederation of tribes under the rule of Genghis Khan. In 1241 the most ferocious of these tribes, the **Tartars**, came charging out of the steppes and divided into two armies, one of which swept towards Poland, the other through Hungary. Lightly armoured, these natural horsemen moved with a speed that no European soldiery could match, and fought in a fashion as savage as the diet that sustained them – raw meat and horse's milk mixed with blood. On Easter Day they destroyed Kraków, and in April came up against the forces of the Silesian ruler, Duke Henryk the Pious, at Legnica. Henryk's troops were annihilated, and a contemporary journal records that "terror and doubt took hold of every mind" throughout the Christian West. Before the eventual withdrawal of the Tartar hordes, all of southern Poland was ravaged repeatedly – Kraków, for example, was devastated in 1259 and again in 1287.

By the fourteenth century, however, the greatest threat to Poland was presented by the Teutonic Knights (see, p.189), and the participation of a contingent of Tartars in the Polish defeat of the Knights at Grunwald in 1410 signalled a new kind of connection. Communities of Tartars were now living close to the borders of the country (the Cossacks, for instance, were an offshoot of a Tartar tribe) and were steadily encroaching west. It was in the late seventeenth century that Poland received its first peaceable Tartar settlers, when King Jan Sobieski granted land in eastern Poland to those who had taken part in his military campaigns.

Today some six thousand descendants of these first Muslim citizens of Poland are spread all over the country, particularly in the Szczecin, Gdańsk and Białystok areas. Though thoroughly integrated into Polish society, they are distinctive both for their Asiatic appearance and their faith – the Tartars of Gdańsk, for example, have recently completed a mosque. Apart from the mosques and graveyards at Bohoniki and Kruszyniamy, little is left of the old settlements in the region east of Białystok, but there are a number of mosques still standing over the border in Belarus.

Getting to them is no mean feat. Direct **buses to Kruszyniamy** from Białystok are scarce: the alternative is to take the bus to **Krynki** (about 40km) and wait for a connection to Kruszyniamy. If there aren't any of these, the only thing left to do is hitch. The only **buses to Bohoniki** are from **Sokołka**, an hour's train journey north of Białystok. If you're trying to visit both villages in the same day, the best advice is to go to Kruszyniamy first, return to Krynki (probably by hitching) then take a bus towards Sokołka. Ask the driver to let you off at **Stara Kamionka**, and walk the remaining 4km east along the final stretch of the "Tartar Way" (Szlak Tartarski Duży), which runs between the two villages. To get back to Białystok, take the late afternoon bus to Sokołka, then a train back to the city – they depart regularly up until around 10pm.

The villages

Walking through **KRUSZYNIAMY** is like moving back a century or two: the painted wooden houses, cobbled road and wizened old peasants staring at you from their front porches are like something out of Tolstoy. Surrounded by trees and set back from the road is the eighteenth-century **Mosque**, recognizable by the Islamic crescent hanging over the entrance gate, though the architecture is strongly reminiscent of the wooden churches of eastern Poland. Despite initial protests and general grumpiness, the caretaker will let you in if you're properly dressed, which means no bare legs or revealing tops. Though the Tartar population is dwindling, the mosque's predominantly wooden interior is well maintained – a glance at the list of Arab diplomats in the visitor's book explains where the money comes from, and the imam won't refuse a donation from you either. The building is divided into two sections, the smaller section is for women, the larger and carpeted one for men, containing the *Mihrabo*, the customary recess pointing in the direction of Mecca, and a *mimber* (pulpit) from which the prayers are directed by the imam.

The **Muslim Cemetery**, five minutes' walk beyond the mosque, contains a mixture of well-tended modern gravestones and, in the wood behind, old stones from the tsarist era. Despite the Tartar presence, the population of the village is predominantly Belarussian, a fact reflected in the presence of an Orthodox church, an inspiring concrete structure that replaced the wooden original, destroyed by fire. The grimy looking **bar** in the village is the only place you'll get anything to eat in either of the villages and there's no accommodation.

The mosque in remoter **BOHONIKI** is a similar, though smaller, building, looked after by a woman who is a direct descendant of the settlers who established themselves here in 1697. She lives at no. 26 (there's only one road), and she or one of her family will open up the mosque, and the village *Ruch* kiosk if you want postcards.

In the **Tartar Cemetery**, hidden in a copse half a kilometre south of the village, gravestones are inscribed in both Polish and Arabic with characteristic Tartar names like Ibrahimowicz and Bohdanowicz – in other words, Muslim names with a Polish ending tacked on. Search through the undergrowth right at the back of the cemetery and you'll find older, tumbled-down gravestones inscribed in Russian, from the days when Bohoniki was an outpost of the tsarist empire. Tartars from all over Poland are still buried here, as they have been since Sobieski's time.

South from Białystok

Moving south of Białystok you're soon into the villages and fields of **Podlasie**, the heartland of the country's Belarussian population – you'll see the Cyrillic figures of their language on posters (though not as yet on street signs) throughout the area. It's a poor, predominantly rural region that retains a distinctively Eastern feel, and for visitors the best-known attraction is the ancient **Białowieża Forest** straddling the border with neighbouring Belarus. **Bielsk Podlaski**, the regional capital, and **Siemiatycze** are both worth investigating, the latter being near the extraordinary convent at **Grabarka**, focal point of Orthodox pilgrimage in Poland.

The Białowieża Forest

For a country with a reputation as an environmental disaster zone, Poland has an amazing number of beauty spots. One hundred kilometres southeast of

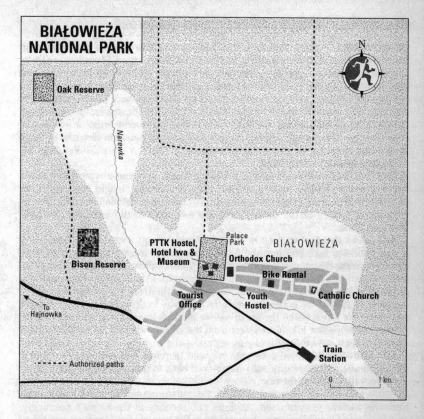

BIAŁOWIEŻA
NATIONAL PARK

Oak Reserve

Narewka

Bison Reserve

PTTK Hostel,
Hotel Iwa &
Museum

Palace
Park

BIAŁOWIEŻA

Orthodox Church

Bike Rental

Tourist
Office

Youth
Hostel

Catholic Church

To
Hajnówka

Train
Station

Authorized paths

0   1 km.

Białystok is one of the best-known of these, the **Białowieża Forest** (Puszcza
Białowieska). Covering 126,000 hectares and spreading way over the border into
Belarus, Białowieża is the last primeval forest in Europe, but its fame and popularity rest as much on the forest's large population of **European bison** as on its
antiquity and beauty.

For centuries Białowieża was a private hunting ground for a succession of
Lithuanian and Belarussian princes, Polish kings, Russian tsars and other poten-
tates – patronage which ensured the forest survived largely intact. Recognizing
its environmental importance, the Polish government turned large sections of the
puszcza into a **national park** in the 1920s, not least to protect its bison herds,
which had been eaten almost to extinction by famished soldiers during World
War I. Like most *puszcza*, Białowieża has hidden its fair share of partisan armies,
most notably during the 1863 Uprising and World War II: monuments scatter the
area, as no doubt do the bones of countless unknown dead.

Twenty-five percent of the entire forest is now a strictly controlled **nature
reserve** (*rezervat ścisty*) which can only be visited accompanied by a guide, but
the rest is open for **visits** (with or without guides). The unique atmosphere of
the place makes even a day trip an experience not to be missed.

Białowieża village and access to the forest

BIAŁOWIEŻA, a mere 2km from the border, is a **bus** journey of a couple of hours from Białystok; for a day trip there and back, take the 6.30am bus – and in summer, get there early, as tickets sell out quickly. (There are trains too, but they involve changes at Bielsk Podlaski and Hajnówka and take much longer.) On the way through the flat, wooded greenery of the Podlasie countryside you'll probably see more Orthodox onion domes than Catholic spires; the spanking new *cerkiew* in **Hajnówka**, the last town before the forest area, is a spiritual centre of the Belarussian revival; there's also a small museum devoted to local Belarussian culture in the village. Białowieża hosts a notable **Festival of Orthodox Music** in early May.

The bus stops at the gates of the **Palace Park**, opposite a typical late nine-teenth-century *cerkiew*, with a unique tiled iconostasis. Inside the park, the Białowieża **Museum** (Tues–Sun 8am–4pm) provides a detailed introduction to the natural history of the forest, including examples of the amazingly diverse flora and fauna.

Access to the forest itself is controlled: unless you want to negotiate for a private guide to take you into the forest reserve, the most popular way in is to charter a horse-drawn cart from the nearby tourist office. The other option is to rent a bike from the office at ul. Waszkiewicza 79. Prices for renting carts are reasonable, but you may have to wait some time if there are a lot of people around – a good argument for getting there early. The two- to three-hour cart tour takes you along the forest paths (green or yellow marked trails) to the **bison reserve** (open all year), a few kilometres west from the village, where some of the forest's 250 specimens can be seen lounging around – the rest are out in the wilds. The horses also kept in the reserve area are wild **tarpans**, relations of the original steppe horses which are gradually being bred back to their original genetic stock after centuries of interbreeding.

Interesting though these animals are, the main impressions of the forest stem from the ancient *puszcza* itself. At times the serenity of the forest's seemingly endless depths is exhilarating, then suddenly the trunks of oak, spruce and horn-beam swell threateningly to a dense canopy, momentarily pierced by shafts of sunlight that sparkle briefly before subsiding into gloom. One memorable thicket, known as the **Royal Oaks Way** (Szlak Dębów Królewskich) which the guide will take you to, consists of a group of forty-metre-high oaks, each named after a Polish monarch, the oldest being over four hundred years old.

Apart from the rarer animals such as elk and beaver, the forest supports an astounding profusion of **flora and fauna**: over 20 species of tree, 20 of rodents, 13 varieties of bat, 228 of birds – all told over 3000 species, not counting around 8000 different insect species.

Practicalities

The *Iwa* **hotel** in the park grounds (☎0835/12260 or 12384; ③) is geared to Western tourist requirements, but reasonably priced. The nearby **PTTK hostel** (☎0835/12505; ②), in the former palace stable, is a perfectly comfortable, cheaper alternative. In season both places get very busy, so reserving in advance is a good idea – they'll probably understand English or German at reception. The decent-sized **youth hostel** in the village at ul. Waszkiewicza 6 (☎0835/12560) is open all year.

For meals, head for the *Iwa* hotel **restaurant**, especially if you need a good breakfast after the early-morning bus journey.

Bielsk Podlaski

Fifty-five kilometres south of Białystok lies **BIELSK PODLASKI**, a dusty old market town imbued with the old-world peasant feel of the surrounding country-side. By car or train the route from Białystok takes you through the attractive open Podlasie landscape, with opportunities for stopping off at the often beautiful Orthodox *cerkwi* you'll find in villages along the way. The town itself has a couple of places of interest, but it's the atmosphere, as much as buildings, that lend the place a certain down-at-heel charm.

The Town

The sights worth seeing are scattered round the rather diffuse town centre inter-sected from north to south by ul. Mickiewicza, the main shopping street. At the north end of Mickiewicza is the Old Town **Rynek**, with some attractive examples of the local wooden architecture in evidence among the older houses ringing the square. The chunky-looking Baroque **Town Hall** at the centre of the square houses a small **museum** (Tues–Sun 10am–5pm) featuring local craft work and occasional art exhibitions. Just west of the square stands the Neoclassical **Catholic Parish Church**, built in the 1780s at Izabella Branicki's behest, while north of the Rynek is a good example of a local speciality, the impromptu **open-air market**. This one's a muddy patch generally swarming with Belarussians and other "trade tourists" from across the border camped around their cars, flogging motley assortments of clothes, jewellery, hi-fis and other knick-knacks to the locals. Just beyond the market is the seventeenth-century **Carmelite Church and Monastery**: a characteristic Polish Baroque structure, the interior is currently being totally renovated, leaving you to wander through the hollow shell of the building and wooden scaffolding surrounding it.

South along ul. Mickiewicza brings you to the ornate **Church of St Michael**, a large, bulbous blue *cerkiew* and the main centre of Orthodox worship in town. As often, the building's nearly always closed, except during services, so you'll have to ask next door at the parish house to get in and see the fine iconstasis. When he's not dealing with parishioners the local priest, a beatific-looking char-acter with a beard worthy of Mount Athos, will open up the building and take you through the details of Orthodox church architecture. If you want to pursue the subject further, there are a couple more Orthodox churches in town, most notably the small yellow wooden *cerkiew* on ul. Jagiellońska east of ul. Mickiewicza.

Practicalities

The **bus and train station** is ten minutes' walk south of the town centre. For local **information** try the *Orbis* office, ul. Mickiewicza 62, in the centre.

There's not much in the way of decent **accommodation**, the best bet being the hotel *Unibud*, ul. Widowska 4 (☎0834/2841; ③), on the northeast edge of town, with the *Dworek Smólskich*, ul. Hołowieska 7 (☎0834/3610; ②), a lesser alternative. For a meal the *Podlasianka*, ul. Mickiewicza 37, complete with regular evening dance-band, is about the best on offer, while the *Hajduczek*, ul. Mickieicza 25, is a presentable enough *kawiarnia* for an afternoon coffee.

Siemiatycze and around

Fifty kilometres south on through the quiet Podlasie countryside brings you to **SIEMIATYCZE,** a scruffy-looking place with all the hallmarks of a town suffering from the severe depression currently afflicting the rural Polish economy. As usual the main square forms the focal point of the town. The **Catholic Parish Church** is ornate early Baroque with a triumphal-looking altarpiece and the characteristic yellow and white stucco decoration. Following the Soviet invasion of eastern Poland at the outbreak of World War II, the people of Siemiatycze found themselves inside Soviet territory, a fact recalled in the recently erected plaque inside the church commemorating the many local people deported to Siberia, most of them never to return. Just down the hill is the main local **Orthodox Church**, currently undergoing a complete overhaul.

Orthodox aside, the other main religious community here used to be **Jews**: typically for the region, before the war Jews comprised some forty percent of the town's population. South of the square off ul. Pałacowa is the former town **Synagogue**, an eighteenth-century brick building that somehow survived the depredations of the Nazis. Following wartime use as an arsenal, the synagogue was restored in the 1960s and turned into the local *Dom Kultury*. If you ask, the staff can point out surviving features of the building's original architecture. As often, the **Jewish Cemetery,** east past the bus station on ul. Polna, is run down and wildly overgrown. Back in town the local **Museum** on ul. 11 Listopada (Tues–Sun 10am–4pm), south of the centre, has a presentable collection of local exhibits enhanced by some displays devoted to local Jewish themes.

For a place **to stay**, the *U Kmicica* (☎55 24 32; ②), well south of the centre at ul. 11 Listopada 139, is about the only option, with the *Ratuszowa* and *Oleńka*, both on the main square, the available **restaurants**.

The Grabarka Convent

Hidden away in the woods round Siemiatycze, the **Convent** near the village of **GRABARKA**, 10km east of town, is the spiritual centre of contemporary Polish Orthodoxy: primarily a place of pilgrimage, it occupies a place in Polish Orthodox devotions similar to that of Częstochowa for Catholics. The contrast between the two religious centres couldn't be more striking, however: where the Jasna Góra monastery is all urban pomp and majesty, the Grabarka site is steeped in a powerful aura of time-honoured rural mystery. If you've become accustomed to processions of Catholic sisters on the streets of Polish cities, the sight of the twenty or so Orthodox-robed nuns making their way to the church in Grabarka comes as quite a surprise.

Approached by a sandy forest track, the hill up to the small convent leads to the community buildings next to the main **church**: whether by accident or design – local opinion is divided on the issue – the church was burnt to the ground in 1991, a cause of great sadness among the Belarussian and Orthodox communities for whom it's long been a treasured shrine. Workmen have been hard at work rebuilding it – judging by the brass plating being used on the onion-domed roof, no expense is being spared either – and the church is now functional again. The place's best-known and certainly most striking feature, however, is the thicket of **wooden crosses**, the oldest dating back to the early eighteenth century, when pilgrims drawn by stories of local miracles first began coming here, packing the slopes below the church. A traditional gesture of piety carried by pilgrims and placed here on completing their journey, the literally thousands of characteristic Orthodox crucifixes clustered together in all shapes and sizes are an extraordinarily powerful sight: with all this wood around, the "no lighting-up" signs sprinkled among the crosses come as no surprise.

Despite the convent's backwoods location, groups of devotees can be found visiting the place at most times of the year. The biggest pilgrimages, however, centre round major Orthodox feast and holy days, notably August 19, the **Przemienienia Panskiego (Spasa)** or "Feast of the Transfiguration of the Saviour" – when thousands of Orthodox faithful from around the country flock to Grabarka, many by foot, for several days of celebrations beginning with an all-night vigil the day before the main feast day. As much celebrations of cultural identity as their Catholic counterparts are for Poles, the festivals at Grabarka offer a powerful insight into the roots of traditional, predominantly peasant Orthodox devotion.

If you don't have your own transport, **buses** run to the Grabarka village – roughly half a kilometre from the convent – two or three times a day from Siemiatycze, more often in summer.

travel details

Trains

Białystok to: Gdańsk (2 daily; 9hr; couchettes); Kraków (1 daily; 9hr; couchettes); Lublin (1 daily; 9hr); Olsztyn (5–6 daily; 6hr); Poznań (1 daily; 10hr; couchettes); Suwałki via Augustów (4–5 daily; 2hr 30min–3hr); Warsaw (8 daily; 3hr); Vilnius (2 daily; 8hr).

Gdańsk to: Białystok (2 daily; 8–9hr); Bydgoszcz (hourly; 2–3hr); Częstochowa (5 daily; 7–8hr); Elbląg (11 daily; 1–2hr); Hel (6–9 daily; 2–2hr 30min); Katowice (8 daily; 7–8hr; couchettes); Kołobrzeg (4 daily; 4–5hr); Koszalin (13 daily; 3–4hr); Kraków (5 daily; 6–10hr); Lublin (2 daily; 7hr 30min); Łódź (6 daily; 5hr 30min–7hr); Olsztyn (6 daily; 3hr 30min); Poznań (7 daily; 4hr); Przemyśl (1 daily; 13hr); Rzeszów (1–2 daily; 11–14hr; couchettes); Szczecin (8 daily; 4hr 30min–6hr); Toruń (5 daily; 3–4hr); Warsaw (6 daily, July–Aug 15 daily; 3hr 30min–5hr); Wrocław (7 daily; 7–8hr; couchettes); Zakopane (1 daily; 13hr; couchettes).

Olsztyn to: Białystok (4 daily; 5–7 hr); Elbląg (10 daily; 1hr 30min–2hr); Gdańsk (6 daily; 3–4hr); Kraków (2 daily; 7–12hr); Poznań (4 daily; 5–7hr); Suwałki (2 daily; 5–6hr); Szczecin (5 daily; 8–10hr); Toruń (8 daily; 3–4hr); Warsaw (8 daily; 3hr–5hr); Wrocław (2 daily; 7–8hr); Zakopane (1 daily; 16hr).

Suwałki to: Białystok (4 daily; 2hr 30min–3hr 30min); Kraków (1 daily June–Sept; 12hr); Olsztyn (2 daily; 6–8hr); Warsaw (4–6 daily; 4–8hr; couchettes June–Sept).

Toruń to: Bydgoszcz (30min–1hr); Gdańsk (5 daily; 3–4hr); Kraków (3 daily; 7–8hr); Łódź (11–14 daily; 2–4hr); Olsztyn (7–9 daily; 2–3hr); Poznań (5 daily; 2–3hr); Rzeszów & Przemyśl; (1 daily June–Sept; 10hr 30min; couchettes); Warsaw (6 daily; 3–5hr); Wrocław (2 daily; 5–6hr).

Useful bus routes

Augustów to Białystok; Ełk; Giżycko; Olsztyn; Sejny; Suwałki; Warsaw.

Białystok to Augustów; Lublin; Minsk; Olsztyn; Vilnius.

Chełmno to Bydgoszcz; Grudządz; Toruń.

Gdańsk to Chełmno; Grudziądz; Kartuzy; Kwidzyn; Toruń; Vilnius.

Olsztyn to Augustów; Białystok; Ełk; Gdańsk; Lidzbark Warmiński; Mrągowo; Warsaw; Vilnius.

Suwałki to Bydgoszcz; Gdańsk; Grudziądz; Kwidzyn; Olsztyn; Warsaw; Vilnius.

Toruń to Bydgoszcz; Gdańsk; Olsztyn; Warsaw.

CHAPTER THREE

SOUTHEASTERN POLAND

The southeast is the least populated and least known part of Poland: a great swathe of border country, its agricultural plains punctuated by remote, backwoods villages and a few market towns. It is peasant land, the remnants of the great European *latifundia* – the feudal grain estates – whose legacy was massive emigration, from the late 1800s until World War II, to France, Germany and, above all, the USA.

Borders have played an equally disruptive role in recent history. Today's **eastern Polish frontier**, established after the last war, sliced through the middle of what was long the heartland of the Polish **Ukraine**, leaving towns like Lublin (and L'viv, inside the Ukraine) deprived of their historic links. As border restrictions ease, the prewar links are reasserting themselves in the flood of ex-Soviet "trade tourists" – smalltime merchants – who give an international touch to the street markets of towns like Przemyśl and Rzeszów. On the Polish side, potatoes are now a major peasant crop of the southeast, for private sale to Ukrainians. In the genuine wilderness of the **highland areas** you come upon a more extreme political repercussion of the war, with the minority **Lemks** and **Boyks** just beginning to re-establish themselves, having been expelled in the wake of the civil war that raged here from 1945 to 1947. In addition, this area's ethnic diversity is further complicated by divisions between Catholic, Uniate and Orthodox communities.

None of this may inspire a visit, yet aspects of the east can be among the highlights of any Polish trip. The **mountains**, though not as high nor as dramatic as the Tatras to the west, are totally unexploited. A week or so hiking in the **Bieszczady** is time well spent, the pleasures of the landscapes reinforced by easy contact with the locals – a welcoming bunch, and drinkers to match any in the country. The **Beskid Niski**, to the west, has some great rewards too: in particular its amazing **wooden churches** or *cerkwi*, whose pagoda-like domes and canopies are among the most spectacular folk architecture of central-eastern Europe.

The undeniable historic appeal of **Lublin**, the region's major city and for centuries the home of a famous Jewish community, is overshadowed in part by the sombre sight of the Majdanek death camp on its outskirts. However, the smaller towns, like the old trading centres of **Kazimierz Dolny** and **Sandomierz** along the Wisła River, are among the country's most beautiful, long favoured by artists and retaining majestic historic centres – though again the absence of the Jews casts a pall. Over to the east, **Zamość** has a superb Renaissance centre, miraculously preserved from the war and well worth a detour, while in the south there's the stately **Łancut Castle**, an extraordinary reminder of prewar, aristocratic Poland. Each summer the castle hosts a chamber music festival, one of the most prestigious Polish music events. The most intriguing festival, however, takes place at nearby **Rzeszów** in June and July every third year, when folklore groups from *emigracja* communities get together for a riot of singing, dancing and nostalgia.

ACCOMMODATION PRICE CODES	
The accommodation listed in this book has been given one of the following price codes. For more details see p.34.	

① under 20zł (under £5/$7.5)   ⑤ 75–95zł (£20–25/$30–38)
② 20–38zł (£5–10/$7.5–15)   ⑥ 95–135zł (£25–35/$38–53)
③ 38–58zł (£10–15/$15–23)   ⑦ 135–210zł (£35–55/$53–83)
④ 58–75zł (£15–20/$23–30)   ⑧ 210–300zł (£55–80/$83–120)
⑨ over 300zł (over £80/$120)

Other towns of note in the region include **Tarnów**, much of its medieval centre intact, **Jarosław**, another of the procession of formerly Jewish-dominated towns situated along the old East–West trading routes. Beer-lovers will probably want to make a bee-line for **Leżajsk**, whose honeyed local brew is at least as popular with visitors as the annual pilgrimages to its renowned church.

Lublin

In the shops, oil lamps and candles were lit. Bearded Jews dressed in long cloaks and wearing wide boots moved through the streets on the way to evening prayers. The world beyond was in turmoil. Jews everywhere were being driven from their villages. But here in Lublin one felt only the stability of a long established community.

Isaac Bashevis Singer, *The Magician of Lublin.*

The city of **LUBLIN**, the largest in eastern Poland, presents an all too familiar ambivalence, with sprawling high-rise buildings and Stalinist smokestacks surrounding a historic centre. Once you're in the heart of the place, however, it's all cobbled streets and dilapidated mansions – a wistful reminder of the city's past glories. The fabric of this old quarter came through World War II relatively undamaged, and although years of postwar neglect left it in a pretty shambolic state, a slow-moving reconstruction programme is now under way.

In among the numerous churches you'll find reminders that for centuries Lublin was home to a large and vibrant **Jewish community**, a population exterminated in the Nazi concentration camp at **Majdanek**, just 3km from the city centre.

Some history

Like many eastern towns, Lublin started as a medieval trade settlement and guard post, in this case on the trade route linking the Baltic ports with Kiev and the Black Sea. Somehow managing to survive numerous depredations and invasions – the fearsome Tartar onslaughts in particular – Lublin was well established by the sixteenth century as a commercial and cultural centre.

The city's finest hour came in 1569 when the Polish and Lithuanian kings met here to set a seal on the formal union of the two countries, initiated two centuries earlier by the marriage of Lithuanian grand duke Jagiełło and Polish queen Jadwiga (see "History" p.609). This so-called **Lublin Union** created the largest mainland empire in Europe, stretching from the Baltic to the Black Sea. Over a

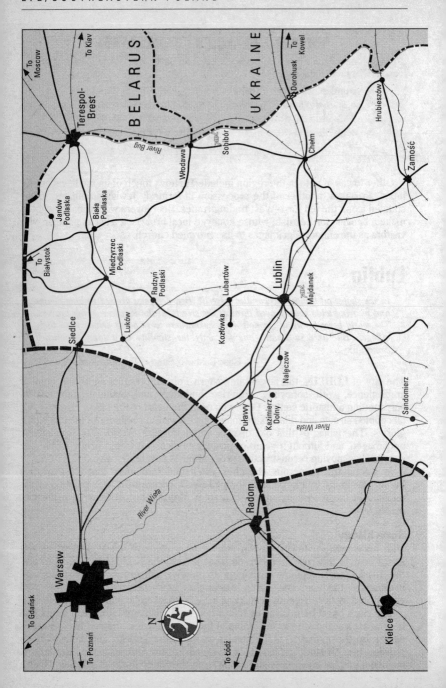

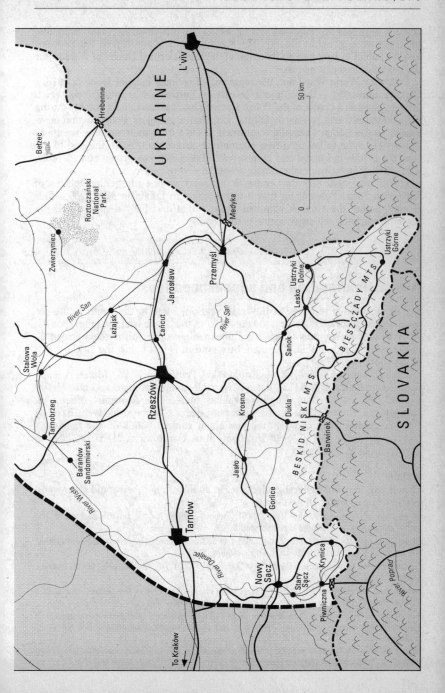

century of prosperity followed, during which the arts flourished and many fine buildings were added to the city. The Partitions rudely interrupted this process, leaving Lublin to languish on the edge of the Russian-ruled Duchy of Warsaw for the next hundred years or so.

Following World War I and the regaining of national independence in 1918, a Catholic university – the only one in eastern Europe – was established, which grew to become a cradle of the Polish Catholic intelligentsia, most notably during the communist era. It was to Lublin, too, that a group of Polish communists known as the Lublin Committee returned in 1944 from their wartime refuge in the Soviet Union to set up a new communist government. Since the end of the war, the town's industrial and commercial importance has grown considerably, with a belt of factories mushrooming around the town centre.

Lublin may also one day come to be seen as one of the birthplaces of Solidarity. Some Poles claim that it was a strike in Lublin in May 1980 – four months before the Gdańsk shipyard sit-ins – that decisively demonstrated the power of workers' self-organization to the country.

> The **telephone code** for Lublin is ☎081

Arrival, information and accommodation

You're most likely to arrive at the **train station**, 24km to the south of the old town centre; from here it's best to take a taxi (if the queue isn't too long), bus #1, #3 or #13, or trolley bus #150 – it's a fifteen-minute ride to the main street, ul. Krakowskie Przedmieście. The main **bus station** is just below the castle, north of the Old Town.

Lublin's **tourist office**, at ul. Krakowskie Przedmieście 78 (Mon–Fri 9am–5pm, Sat 10am–2pm; ☎24412), has a reasonable amount of maps and other information, but rarely has English-speaking staff. The **Almatur office**, ul. Langiewicza 10 (☎33238), in the university district, is more likely to have an English-speaker; they can also tell you about student hotels on the university campus (available July 15–Sept 15). *Orbis* at ul. Narutowicza 31/33 (☎22256) is useful for ticket bookings.

Hotels

Hotels are few, but generally adequate. In addition a number of old state workers' hotels are now open for tourists

Bystrzyce, al. Zygmuntowskie 4 (☎23003). Decent-enough rooms, but it's located in the rather unsavoury area around the train station. ③.

Dom Nauczyciela (NZP), ul. Academicka 4 (☎38235). A cheap, basic teachers' hotel near the university; take bus #150 from the train station. ②.

Garnizonowy, ul. Spadachroniarzy 7 (☎30536 or 72 30 70). Reasonably priced former soldiers' hotel, often full. ③.

Jubilat, ul. Mełgiewska 7/9 (☎76 20 71). A large cheap hotel east of the centre, near Lublin Północ station. A good budget bet if all else fails in the centre. ③.

Lublinianka, Krakowskie Przedmieście 56 (☎24261). Revamped tsarist-era extravaganza in easy walking distance of the Old Town, with reasonable rooms, a separate coffee shop and restaurant. ⑤.

Motel PZMot, ul. Prusa 8 (☎34232). North of the centre this is a good choice for motorists, with plenty of (guarded) parking space. ④.

Piast, ul. Pocztowa 2 (☎21646). A cheap former state employees' hotel directly across from the main train station. ②.
Unia, al. Raclawickie 12 (☎32061, fax 33021). *Orbis* hotel, recently modernized, with a decent restaurant. Popular with upper bracket tour groups. ⑧.
Victoria, ul. Narutowicza 56/58 (☎27011, fax 29026). A step up from the *Lublinianka* and further from the centre. ⑥.

Youth hostels and campsites

The **youth hostel** is at ul. Długosza 4a (☎30628; bus #13 or tram #150 from the train station), 1.5km west of the city centre and hard to find since there's no sign on the street – the entrance is round the back of the building. The all-year **student hotel**, ul. Sowinskiego 17 (☎551081; ①) in the university area, is another cheap alternative.

Lublin's **campsite** is west of the city at ul. Sławinkowska 46 (June–Sept), beyond the Botanical Gardens, and has bungalows as well as tent places, but you'll be lucky to get one; take bus #18 from the city centre, #20 from the station. Further out are another couple of **campsites**, at the edge of Lake Zemborzyck, 3km south of the centre. The best of these is the *Marina*, ul. Krężnicka 6 (☎41070), reached by local train to Lublin Zalew, one stop from the main station.

The City

The busy plac Łokietka forms the main approach to the Stare Miasto (Old Town), with an imposing nineteenth-century **New Town Hall** on one side. Straight across the square is the fourteenth-century **Brama Krakowska** (Kraków Gate), one of three gateways to the Old Town. Originally a key point in the city's defences against Tartar invaders, this now houses the **Historical Museum** (Wed–Sun 9am–4pm); the contents aren't greatly inspiring, but the view from the top floor makes it worth a visit to orient yourself.

Into the Stare Miasto

A short walk round to the right along ul. Królewska brings you to the **Wieża Trinitarska** (Trinity Tower), and opposite it the **Cathedral**, a large sixteenth-century basilica with an entrance framed by ornate classical-looking pillars. The interior decoration features a notable series of Baroque *trompe l'oeil* frescoes by the Moravian artist Joseph Majer, and the so-called Whispering Hall, part of the former sacristy, whose peculiar acoustic properties allow you to hear even the quietest voices perfectly on the other side of the chapel. Through the tower, a gate opens onto the Rynek, dominated by the outsize **Old Town Hall**. Built in 1389, it later became the seat of a royal tribunal, and was given a Neoclassical remodelling in 1781 by Merlini, the man who designed Warsaw's Łazienki Palace. The well-restored cellars underneath the building house the **Crown Tribunal Museum** (Tues–Sat 9am–4pm, Sun 9am–5pm), devoted to the history of the city, including a selection of ceramics and decorative objects unearthed in the course of the continuing renovation of the houses around the Rynek.

Getting round the square is tortuous, as a lot of the buildings are under reconstruction – judging by recent progress, a state of affairs that's likely to remain for years to come. Of the surrounding burghers' houses, the **Konopnica House** (no. 12) – where Charles XII of Sweden and Peter the Great were both once guests – has Renaissance sculptures and medallions of the original owners decorating its facade, while the **Lubomelski House** (no. 8) hides some racy four-

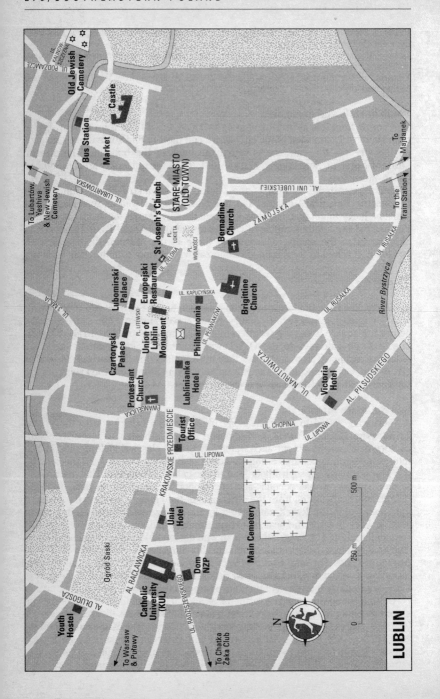

LUBLIN

teenth-century frescoes in its large triple-tiered wine cellars, which the workmen might be persuaded to show you. The **Cholewiński House** (no. 9), on the southeast corner of the square, features further lively Renaissance decoration on the facade, with a particularly fierce-looking pair of lions – it'll be even better when the builders have finished.

East of the square, down the narrow ul. Złota, lies the fine **Dominican Church and Monastery**, founded in the fourteenth century and reconstructed in the seventeenth. The church suffers from the familiar Baroque additions, but don't let that deflect you from the Renaissance **Firlej family chapel** at the end of the southern aisle, built for one of Lublin's leading aristocratic families, nor from the eighteenth-century panorama of the city just inside the entrance. Round the back of the monastery is a popular playhouse, the **Teatr im. Andersen**, one of the oldest theatres in the country, offering a good view over the town from the square in front.

The Old Town's other theatre, **Studio Teatralne**, near the centre at ul. Grodzka 32, has a gallery featuring local artists. Grodzka was part of the **Jewish quarter** and several of the buildings on the street bear memorials in Polish and Yiddish to the former inhabitants. Lublin was one of the main centres of Hasidic Jewry and its **Yeshiva** – now a medical academy – was the world's largest Talmudic school right up to the war (see box p.282).

The castle complex

On a hill just east of the Old Town is the **Castle**, an offbeat 1820s neo-Gothic edifice built on the site of Kazimierz the Great's fourteenth-century fortress, and linked by a raised pathway from the Brama Grodzka (Castle Gate) at the end of ul. Grodzka.

The castle houses a sizeable **Museum** (May–Sept daily 9am–4pm; Oct–April Wed–Sun only), the high points of which are the **ethnography** section, including a good selection of local costumes, religious art and woodcarving, and the **art gallery**, where moody nineteenth-century landscapes and scenes of peasant life mingle with portraits and historical pieces. Among the latter, look out for two famous and characteristically operatic works by Matejko: the massive *Lublin Union* portrays Polish and Lithuanian noblemen debating the union of the two countries in 1569; the equally huge *Admission of the Jews to Poland* depicts the Jews' arrival in Poland in the early Middle Ages, the two sides eyeing each other suspiciously. Another upstairs room contains an excellent collection of eighteenth- and nineteenth-century **Orthodox icons** from the Brest (formerly Brześć) area, now just over the other side of the Belarussian border. The section of the museum devoted to World War II recalls the castle's use by the Nazis as a prison and interrogation centre. Civilian prisoners were shot in the courtyard and thousands more, including many Jews, were detained here before being sent to Majdanek or other concentration camps.

The **Church of the Holy Trinity**, behind one of the two remaining towers (one of them thirteenth-century Romanesque) in the corner of the courtyard, is currently closed for restoration: officially the building is open on the last Sunday of the month only, from 10am to 3pm, though with a bit of cajoling you may be able to persuade the main castle office to let you in at other times. Behind rickety scaffolding is a glorious set of frescoes. Uncovered in the last century, they were painted by a group of Ruthenian artists from the Ukraine – exceptionally for the time, the main artist, Master Andrew, signed his name and the date, 1418.

On the way back to the Old Town, check out the **market** just below the castle: you may find something interesting among the mixture of junk and contraband. As in many Eastern towns, the squat peasants with stand-out accents selling caviar, gold and radios for dollars are from just over the border. They're what are euphemistically known as "trade tourists", an enduring Eastern European practice whereby itinerant traders buy and sell products cheaper, or products which are unobtainable in neighbouring countries.

West of the Old Town

West of pl. Łokietka stretches **Krakowskie Przedmieście**, a busy shop-lined thoroughfare with a number of sites worth taking in on and around its vicinity. Immediately west of the New Town Hall is **Holy Ghost Church** (Św. Ducha), a small, early fifteenth-century structure with the familiar Baroque overlay and a quiet, restful feel to it.

Immediately opposite the church, a turn to the south takes you onto pl. Wolności, a car-jammed square surrounded by building activity. The fifteenth-century **Bernardine Church** on the south side of the square, a large Gothic construction with a sumptuously ornate Baroque interior, has a good view over the southern rim of the city from the platform at the back of the building. On the eastern edge of another square, southwest along ul. Narutowicza, the **Brigittine Church**, raised in the 1410s by King Władysław Jagiełło as a gesture of thanks for victory at the battle of Grunwald, is another Gothic structure with the customary high brick period facade. Opposite the church stands the **Juliusz Osterwa Theatre** (see "Nightlife" p.284), an enjoyable *fin-de-siècle* playhouse with an august old stage.

Back onto Krakowskie Przedmieście, north of the main street on ul. Zielona, a narrow side passage contains the tiny **St Joseph's Church**, founded by Greek Catholic merchants in the 1790s and used by the local Uniates into this century, though there's nothing now there to inform you of this. Just beyond, on the corner of ul. St Staszica, is the crumbling eighteenth-century **Potocki Palace**, one of several patrician mansions in this part of the city.

Krakowskie Przedmieście soon brings you to **plac Litewski**, a large open square with lots of people milling about and, in summer, a host of chess games in progress. The monuments ranged along the edge of the square include the cast-iron **Union of Lublin Monument**, marking the Polish–Lithuanian concordat established here in 1569, and the **Third of May Constitution (1791) Monument**, marking another significant event in the country's history. The north side of the square features two of the city's old aristocratic palaces, both currently used by the university: first is the former **Czartoryski Palace**, in the northeast corner, a smallish building occupied by the Lublin Scholarly Society. Next is the fading seventeenth-century **Lubomirski Palace**, with a Neoclassicist facade designed by Marconi in the 1830s. The imperial-looking building to its left is just that, the old tsarist-era city governor's residence built in the 1850s.

If it's open, the eighteenth-century **Protestant Church** on ul. Ewangelicka, further along to the north of Krakowskie Przedmieście, is worth a brief look in. An austere, Huguenot-style temple with classicist stylings, it has memorial tablets ranged around the walls, mostly to the church's former German-speaking congregation.

Continuing west along Krakowskie Przedmieście turn south on ul. Lipowa, by the tourist information office, and a five-minute walk brings you to the gates of the **main cemetery**. A stroll round this peaceful, wooded graveyard provides an absorbing insight into local history. The cemetery is separated into confessional sections; to the north the predictably large **Catholic** section, with a group of "unknown soldier" graves from both world wars, is flanked by the **Protestant** and **Orthodox** cemeteries. The Orthodox section, with its own mock-Byzantine chapel, contains more wartime graves – Russian soldiers this time – as well as a sprinkling of older, tsarist-era Cyrillic tablets, including many of the city's one-time imperial administrators and rulers. The graves in the **Protestant** section reveal many German-sounding names, and many of the stones date from before and during World War I, when the city was occupied for several years by the Kaiser's forces. Finally, inspection of the group of plain tombstones without crucifixes in the western section of the graveyard reveals them to belong to those local Party members committed enough to the atheist cause to refuse Catholic burial.

Back up onto Krakowskie Przedmiescie and a short distance west along its continuation, al. Racławickie, stands the **Catholic University** (KUL), a compact campus housed on the site of an old Dominican monastery. One of the KUL's more famous professors was Karol Wojtyła, who taught part time here from the 1950s up until his election as pope in 1978. He is commemorated in a bronze statue in the main courtyard, accompanied by his predecessor as primate of Poland, Cardinal Wyszyński.

Around Jewish Lublin

For anyone interested in **Lublin's Jewish history**, a scattering of monuments around the city's former Jewish quarters are worth visiting, most of them marked by tablets in Hebrew and Polish, although these are rather hard to spot.

The Old Town
Starting in the **Old Town** – much of it long Jewish-inhabited – are a couple of buildings with wartime Jewish connections: on the corner of ul. Noworybna, east of the square, is the small house where the first **Committee of Jewish War Survivors** was set up in November 1944. Continuing on down to ul. Grodzka, at no. 11 is another plaque, commemorating the **Jewish orphanage** in operation here from 1862 until March 1942, when the Nazis removed about two hundred staff and children and shot them in the fields behind the Majdanek camp.

Continuing along Grodzka and down to pl. Zamkowy, a plaque on a raised pedestal, at the foot of the stairs up to the castle, shows a detailed **plan** of the surrounding **Podzamcze district**, the main Jewish quarter destroyed by the Nazis in 1942 (see box, p.282). The Nazi devastation was so thorough that it's hard to visualize the densely packed network of houses, shops and synagogues that used to exist in the streets around what's now a noisy main road (al. Tysiąlecia), a tatty square, the adjoining main bus station and an **Orthodox Church** – the only one remaining in town, originally a Uniate building – immediately east of it.

THE OLD JEWISH CEMETERY
Continue east along al. Tysiąlecia and opposite the bus station, on the approaches to the castle, you'll find another plaque marking the prewar site of the main **Maharszal and Maharam Synagogue**, originally constructed in the 1560s and razed, along with all the surrounding buildings, in 1942.

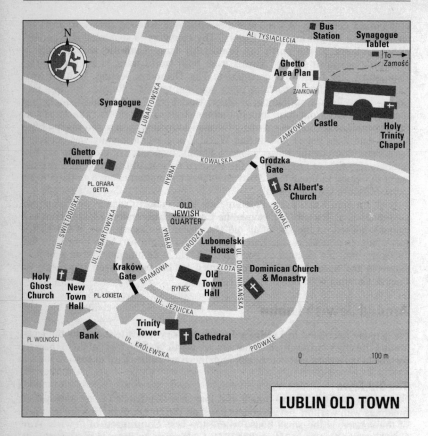

LUBLIN OLD TOWN

Cross the main road and walk along cobbled ul. Kalinowszczyzna, take the first right off ul. Lwowska and you find yourself at the **Old Jewish Cemetery**, a small walled area which covers a ramshackle, overgrown hill, set in almost rural surroundings.

Unless a group happens to be there at the time, you'll have to contact the caretaker, Pan Józef Honig, at ul. Dembowskiego 4, apt. #17 (☎77 86 76), across from the main cemetery entrance, to get in. Despite the Nazis' best efforts to destroy the oldest-known Jewish cemetery in the country – literally thousands of the gravestones were used for wartime building purposes – the surviving tombstones display the full stylistic variety of Jewish monumental art.

Alongside the oldest, dating from 1541, is a fine range of Renaissance, Baroque and Neoclassical ornamental tombstones. The oldest section of the cemetery houses the graves of many famous Jews, among them the legendary Hasidic leader **Yaakov Yitzchak Horovitz**, one of several here regularly covered with pilgrims' candles, and **Shalom Shachna**, the renowned sixteenth-century master of the Lublin *yeshiva*. Climbing to the top of the cemetery hill gives you a fine view back over the Old Town and the old Jewish quarter.

THE NEW CEMETERY AND MAUSOLEUM

Leaving the cemetery and heading north along ul. Lwowska and into ul. Walecznych brings you to the entrance of the **New Cemetery**. Established in 1829 in what was then the outskirts of town, the cemetery was predictably plundered and destroyed by the Nazis, who also used it for mass executions. The cemetery you see today covers a fragment of the original plot, the northern section having been cleared and levelled in the 1970s to make way for a trunk road (ul. Somorawińskiego).

There are precious few graves left inside, most of them dating from the late nineteenth century and the postwar years, as well as a number of collective graves for Nazi wartime victims. The whole cemetery has been renovated in the past few years with financial support from the Frenkel family, whose relatives died in Majdanek.

The domed **mausoleum** (Tues–Sun 10am–4pm), recently erected behind the cemetery entrance, houses a small exhibition detailing the history of the Lublin Jewry. To get in you'll have to negotiate your way past the menacing-looking guard dog protecting the premises: in daylight hours a ring of the bell will do the trick – wandering in is not recommended.

THE YESHIVA AND JEWISH HOSPITAL

Out of the cemetery and west along ul. Unicka brings you to the corner of ul. Lubartowska, a long, straight thoroughfare running through the heart of the prewar Jewish quarter. The large classical-looking yellow building at the top corner of Lubartowska is the site of the prewar **yeshiva** – "The School of the Sages of Lublin" as it was known – a palatial structure now occupied by the local Medical Academy. Built in the late 1920s using funds collected from Jewish communities around the world, the Lublin *yeshiva* was set up as an international Talmudic school to train rabbis and other senior community functionaries. It functioned for just over nine years until 1939, when the Nazis closed it down and eventually plundered and destroyed the huge library. To any but the trained eye there's precious little evidence of the building's former use, a simple plaque on the outside wall briefly stating the historical facts.

Next building down on the same side of Lubartowska (no. 81) is another fine palatial-looking building, erected in 1886 – the former **Jewish hospital**, still an obstetric clinic. A plaque outside commemorates the hospital staff and patients murdered in March 1942 in the course of a Nazi liquidation *Aktion*.

The old ghetto district

Continuing south along Lubartowska takes you through the heart of the old **ghetto district**; a grubby, lively area of shops and tenement houses. While there are no Jews left to speak of, wandering through the arched entrance ways into the back courtyards or scanning the small shops you can imagine what it must have been like here half a century ago. Right up towards the top of the street – a 1.5-kilometre walk – a backroom at no. 10 houses the city's only functioning **Synagogue** (the entrance is through the gateway round the side of no. 8, and up the stairs). It's officially open Sunday 1pm to 3pm, but the moody old caretaker pops in and out, so you could either try your luck or telephone him in advance – see phone number under "The Old Jewish Cemetery"). Alternatively, a local guide specializing in Jewish Lublin, Pan A. Nowodworski (☎40459), can arrange a visit for you.

THE JEWS OF LUBLIN

Along with Kraków and L'viv, Lublin ranked as one of the major – if not the most important – of the Jewish centres in Poland: at its peak the **Lublin Jewry** exerted a Europe-wide influence, dispatching locally trained rabbis to serve communities as far away as Spain and Portugal.

The **first recorded account** of Jews in Lublin dates from 1316, though it's quite possible that merchants had established themselves here considerably earlier. King Kazimierz's extension of the **Statute of Privilege** for Jews to the whole territory of Poland in the mid-fourteenth century paved the way for the development of the first major Jewish settlement in the **Podzamcze** district, located below the castle walls. Originally a marshy river delta, the area was bought up by Jewish merchants, who drained the waters and established a community there. The first brick **Synagogue** and *yeshiva* (Talmudic school) were built in the mid-sixteenth century: from then on synagogues and other religious buildings proliferated – by the 1930s there were more than a hundred synagogues in operation inside the city area. Lublin's increasingly important position on trade routes resulted in its choice as one of two locations (Jarosław was the other) for meetings of the **Council of the Four Lands**, traditionally the main consultative body of Polish Jewry, a position it retained up to the 1760s.

Occasional outbreaks of Church-inspired **"ritual murder" accusations** apart, local Jewish-Christian relations seem to have been fairly tolerant at this stage, the main blows coming in the form of outside assaults, notably the **Chmielnicki Insurrection** (1648), when Cossacks slaughtered thousands of Jews throughout eastern Poland, and the Russian siege of the city in 1655, when much of the Podzamcze district was razed. The whole area was subsequently rebuilt, this time with an emphasis on solid, brick buildings.

In the 1790s Lublin emerged as an important centre of **Hasidism**, the ecstatic revivalist movement that swept through Eastern Jewry in the latter part of the eighteenth century. The charismatic Hasidic leader, **Yaakov Yitzchak Horovitz**, settled in town in the 1790s, drawing crowds of followers from all over Poland – by all accounts, the Hassids were no respecters of Poland's Partitions-era borders – to his "court" in the Podzamcze district. Always a controversial figure – contemporary opponents, for example, claimed that Horovitz died of "excessive alcohol consumption" – Jews from all over the world continue to make the pilgrimage to his grave in the old Jewish Cemetery.

In the mid-nineteenth century, with the town's Jewish population increasing rapidly, Jews began moving into the Old Town area, also occupying much of the

Established in 1920 by the local undertakers' guild, it became the principal synagogue for the city's surviving Jews after World War II. It is still in use today and visiting Jewish tourist groups regularly hold services here. An informative collection of photos and other archival materials relating to the Lublin Jewry lines the walls, along with a small collection of ritual religious objects and some plaques dedicated to local Poles who protected Jews during World War II.

Finally, at the top of Lubartowska, on the approach to the old city, is pl. Ofiar Getta ("Ghetto Victims"), a bustling square that used to be one of the main Jewish marketplaces. A simple **monument to the ghetto victims** stands in the square centre, engraved with the legend "Honour to the Polish citizens of Jewish nationality from the Lublin region, whose lives were bestially cut short by the Nazi fascists during World War II. The people of Lublin."

new district that developed around ul. Lubartowska, to the north of the Old Town. At the close of the century Jews numbered around 24,000 – a little over fifty percent of the town's expanding population.

Following the trials of **World War I**, during which many Lublin Jews died fighting in both the Russian and Austro-Hungarian armies, Lublin Jewry flourished in the **interwar years**, developing an active web of religious and cultural associations, publishing houses, newspapers (notably the daily *Lubliner Sztyme* – "Lublin Voice"), trade unions and political organizations.

Following their capture of the town in September 1939, the **Nazis** quickly set about the business of confining and eventually murdering the nearly 40,000-strong Lublin Jewry. By December 1939 transports of Jews were being brought into the city from other parts of Europe, and in early 1940 Lublin was chosen as the co-ordinating centre for the Nazis' efforts to liquidate the Jewish population of the *Général Gouvernement*. With the Old Town area already filled to bursting with destitute Jews, an official **ghetto area** was established in March 1941 by Governor Hans Frank.

Work on constructing the **Majdanek death camp** in a southern suburb of the city began in July 1941, and in spring 1942 the hideous business of **liquidating the ghetto population** began in earnest. After initial expulsions at the end of March 1942, Jews were driven to the ghetto square (next to the modern main bus station): the old and sick were shot on the spot, the rest taken to waiting rail wagons and transported to the death camp at **Bełzec**, as the first victims of the notorious camp commander, Christian Wirth. Over the next few months, the remaining population was either taken and shot in the **Krępiecki Forest** on the outskirts of the city or moved to a new ghetto area established close to Majdanek. The effective end of over six hundred years of traditional Jewish life in Lublin came on November 3, 1943, when the remaining 18,000 ghetto inhabitants were shot at Majdanek in an extermination *Aktion* codenamed *Erntfest* – "Harvest Festival". Following the *Aktion's* "successful" conclusion the Nazis systematically demolished the buildings of Wieniawa, an outlying Jewish settlement, and the Podzamcze district.

The city was liberated by Soviet troops in July 1944, after which **Jewish partisan groups** began using Lublin as their operational base. At the end of the war several thousand Jewish refugees resettled in Lublin: as a result of **anti-Semitic outbreaks** around Poland in 1945–46, however, many of them emigrated, others following in the wake of the anti-Semitic purges of 1968, as in Kraków and Warsaw. The tiny remaining Jewish population keeps a low profile, many now too old to take an active role in the revival of local Jewish life encouraged by the increasing number of Western Jews visiting the city.

Majdanek

The proximity of **Majdanek concentration camp** is a shock in itself. Established on Himmler's orders in October 1941, this was no semi-hidden location that local people could claim or strive to remain in ignorance of – a plea that is more debatable at Auschwitz and Treblinka. Marked from the main road by a large monument erected in the 1950s in memory of its liberation by the Red Army, the huge camp compound is more shocking inside. Wandering among the barbed wire and watchtowers, staring at crematoria and rows of shabby wooden barracks, it's hard to take in the brutal fact that over 200,000 people of more than fifty nations were murdered here, a significant number of them Jews. Between November 3 and 5, 1943, the Nazis concluded their extermination of local Jewry by machine–gunning over 43,000 inhabitants of the nearby ghetto district; 18,000 were killed in a single day. The **camp museum** (May–Sept Tues–Sun 8am–6pm; closes 3pm Oct–April) in a former barracks tells the terrible story in detail. At the back of the site, a domed mausoleum contains the ashes of many of those murdered here.

Buses #14, #23, #28 and #153 run to Majdanek from pl. Wolności (30min). For more on the concentration camps in postwar Poland, see p.418.

Eating, drinking and entertainment

For a city of its size, Lublin offers remarkably little in the way of diversion. Decent **restaurants** in particular are thin on the ground, with the trend towards private ownership taking its time to penetrate east. The *Unia* hotel, an old Party dignitaries' haunt, has the best and most expensive food in town – fine if you're prepared for obsequious waiters and the occasional old time "dancing" band blasting away in the corner. The restaurant of the *Lublinianka* hotel stays open later than most, does a good *zurek* soup, and attracts a contingent of hardened local drinkers. The gloomy *Europa* at Krakowskie Przedmieście 29 has revamped itself up to "credit card" status; the *Karczma Lubelska* at pl. Litewski 2 is acceptable but nothing more; while the *Karczma Słupska*, al. Racławickie 22, well west of the centre specializes in traditional regional cuisine. The nearby *Wisła* (no. 59) is a step up in price, but not always in quality. *Jazz Pizza*, opposite the tourist office on Krakowskie Przedmieście, offers just what its name suggests: live jazz with pizza. On the same street, *Ludowa*, is a good small restaurant offering local specialities.

As in other eastern towns, **milk bars** are still hanging in here: the local options include the *Staromeijski*, just inside the Old Town at ul. Trybunalska 1, and the *Turystyczny* at Krakowskie Przedmieście 29. For **breakfast**, the *kawiarnia* in the *Lublinianka* does scrambled eggs and coffee till quite late. Of the Old Town **cafés**, the *Czarcia Łapa* on ul. Bramowa has a good cheesecake, the *Mieszczka*, ul. Grodzka 7, a decent *café au lait*, while the upbeat *Przy Bramie*, next to the Brama Krakowska, is a good place to sit outside and enjoy an ice cream in summer. In addition, the *Bauhaus*, ul. Swiętoduska 20, is a trendy local artists' hang-out.

Nightlife

Despite its student population, the city doesn't exactly bristle with **nightlife** either, though **bar life** is showing tentative signs of picking up: the *Pod Papugami*, Krakowskie Przedmieście 30, is a trendy student haunt; *Chmielewski*, further down the street at no. 8, is a popular bar and local cultural centre that includes live gigs among its activities; and you can catch the occasional band at nearby *Chata Zaka* as well (see below). In the Old Town, *U Bisów*, Rynek 18, is a nice enough beer-drinker's haunt. Typically the locals are proudest of the *Old Pub*, at ul. Grodzka 8 just east of the Old Town square, where you can pick up draught German lager or a pint of Guinness – anything as long as it isn't Polish, in fact. The *Hacienda*, ul. Grodzka 12, is a cheaper and perfectly acceptable alternative.

The *Hades*, ul. Peowiaków 12, a *Dom Kultury* just round the corner from the *Philharmonia*, has a restaurant, bar, pool hall and also hosts regular gigs with an emphasis on experimental rock and Polish rap bands – recommended. During term time the *Chata Zaka* club, behind the Catholic University (KUL) at ul. Radziszewskiego 16, is a popular student dive where you can also catch the occasional live band. The same holds for the *Graffiti* club on ul. Lipowa, part of the

Victoria hotel, which stays open late and has a student disco, often with live bands, on Saturdays. There are a number of other **student clubs** dotted around the university campuses and halls of residence. The best bet is to check out the information boards at *Chata Zaka* (see above) or wander into either the Catholic University (KUL) or the nearby state university area and ask what's going on; many students speak English, and there's an even chance of getting invited to some or other event, usually of a heavy-drinking nature.

On a more cultural front, the *Philharmonia*, ul. Osterwy 7, has a regular programme of high-quality **classical concerts** (the ticket office is at ul. Kapuczyńska), and the *Teatr im. J. Osterwy*, ul. Narutowicza 17, offers an imaginative and varied programme of modern and classical Polish **drama** – worth seeing even if you don't speak the language.

North from Lublin

North of the city takes you into the **Biała Podlaska** region, a pleasant agricultural farming area of ramshackle old market towns and sparsely populated villages that still retains a markedly old-world Eastern feel. Like most of eastern Poland, this region has its share of grand old **palaces**, many of them showing the effects of decades of neglect. The palaces at **Lubartów, Kozłówka, Radzyń Podlaski** and **Biała Podlaska**, the regional capital, all offer striking examples of the phenomenon, well worth checking out if you like rural aristocratic piles. A range of Catholic, Orthodox, Jewish and occasional Tartar monuments provide the region's mixed ethnic and religious profile. In a country of traditional horse-lovers, the breeding stables at **Janów Podlaski**, hard up by the Belarus border, are perhaps the area's best-known attraction.

As in many of the country's further-flung regions, local **buses** are the main form of transport. For motorists heading east, the main route from Warsaw to Moscow runs across the region, reaching the border at **Terespol**, east of Biała Podlaska.

Lubartów

Twenty-five kilometres from Lublin – a half-hour bus journey along the main road north of the city – the market town of **LUBARTÓW** is a historical curio worth a brief stopoff on your way elsewhere. A small, undistinguished market centre facing the banks of the Wieprz River to the east, Lubartów is a good example of an eastern town effectively created by a big-league local magnate, in this case the Firlej family who moved here in the 1540s. The place was originally known as Lewartów after the family's coat of arms the "Lewart".

The fine sixteenth-century **Firlej Palace** in the town centre is the most tangible reminder of the local grandees. A large white-stuccoed building currently occupied by local government offices, the fading facade boasts four elegant sets of double pillars surmounted by a large classical frieze. The palace **park** behind the building is a pleasant spot with some traces of its former grandeur, the orangery included, in evidence. The **Parish Church** next to the palace is classic Polish Baroque (a Renaissance doorway excepted), with numerous funeral tablets – in this case, mainly of the Sanguszko family, who took over the palace in the eighteenth century – covering the interior. The local **Museum** (Tues–Sun

10am–3pm) down to the right of the church on ul. Kościuszki is also worth a brief look, the locally based exhibits changing on a regular basis.

As in all the Lublin region, **Jews** were long a feature of the town: first mentioned in 1567, they comprised some 45 percent of the local population at the start of World War II. The entire **Jewish population** was deported to the death camps at Bełzec and Sobibór in October 1942, and most of the community buildings, including two synagogues on ul. Lubelska, were destroyed. A memorial built out of tombstone fragments and thirty or so extant tombstones are all that remains of the **Jewish Cemetery** at the corner of ul. Cicha and ul. 1 Maja, on the southern side of town.

For an **overnight stay**, the *Unitra*, ul. Lubelska 104a (☎0836/3610; ③) on the main through-town drag, is the only real option, with the *Ariańska*, further down the same road at ul. Lubelska 52, a solid if basic restaurant.

Kozłówka

Nine kilometres west of Lubartów – 35km if you're coming direct by bus from Lublin – the **Zamoyski Palace** at **KOZŁÓWKA** is among the grandest in the region. With recent restoration work on the building virtually complete, the palace is getting a fair amount of tourist hype – hence the processions of day-tripper buses already lining up outside the entrance gates. All in all it's a good example of the nostalgia for the "good old days" of the prewar era that's in vogue in Poland now. With admiration of and aesthetic preference for all things grand and aristo-cratic back at the forefront of officially sanctioned culture, it's hardly surprising to find emphasis being placed on places like this: whether you're taken with this kind of opulent aristocratic overload is very much a question of personal taste.

The Palace

Built in the 1740s by the Bieliński family, after they inherited the local estate, the original two-storey Baroque **palace complex**, surrounded by a courtyard to the front and gardens at the back, was reconstructed and expanded in the early 1900s by its longtime owner, Count Konstanty Zamoyski, whose family took over the property in 1799 and kept it up to the beginning of World War II. Zamoyski's remodelling retained the essentials of the original Baroque design, adding a number of fine outbuildings, the iron gateway, chapel and elegant porticoed terrace leading up to the entrance to the building.

Getting into the palace can actually be a bit of a performance. The opening times (March 1–Nov 30 Tues, Thurs–Fri 10am–4pm, Wed 10am–5pm, Sat–Sun 9am–5pm; guided tours only, last tickets 1 hr before closing) are subject to vari-ations, so you'd be well advised to check at the Lublin tourist office before setting out. Theoretically at least, on weekdays you can only tour the palace if you're part of a pre-booked party, though in practice you'll be fine tagging along with any group that happens to be there, which can mean anything from German tourist buses to school kids or the local works outing.

THE INTERIOR

Once **inside the palace** you're immediately enveloped in a riot of artistic elegance. The whole place is positively dripping in pictures, mostly family portraits and copies of Rubens, Canaletto and the like, along with a profusion of sculptures and period furniture, every corner of the richly decorated building crammed with something decorative. First port of call is the **hallway**, the gloom partially lightened by sumptuous lamps and the delicate stucco work of the ceiling. Past the huge Meissner stoves and up the portrait-lined **marble staircase** brings you to the main palace rooms. On through **Count Konstanty's private rooms** the procession of family portraits and superior repro art continues relentlessly, the elaborate Czech porcelain toilet set in the bedroom suggesting a man of fastidious personal hygiene. After the countess' bedroom and its handsome selection of Empire furniture, the tour takes you into the voluminous **Red Salon**, an impressive ensemble with embroidered canopies enveloping the doors and a mass of heavy red velvet curtains. The portraits are at their thickest here, the emphasis being on kings, hetmans and other national figures collected by Count Konstanty during the Partition years as a personal gesture of patriotic remembrance.

The rest of the palace is pretty much more of the same; the **Exotic Room** houses a fine selection of chinoiserie, while the **dining room** is sumptuous, heavy Baroque with a mixture of Gdańsk and Venetian furniture and enough period trinkets to keep a horde of collectors happy. As you'd expect, the **library** contains endless shelves full of books ranged around a classic old billiard table lit by a kerosene lamp in the middle. The **chapel**, out round the side of the palace, is a fine though rather cold place partly modelled on the royal chapel in Versailles and built in the early 1900s.

THE MUSEUM

After overdosing on opulence, the **museum** (same opening hours) housed in the one-time palace theatre makes for a real surprise. Entitled "Art and Struggle in Socialism", the exhibition brings together a large collection of postwar Polish socialist realist art and sculpture, most of it culled from museums around the region and kept here out of harm's way once its subjects had become politically unacceptable. The whole pantheon of international Stalinist iconography is here: Bolesław Bierut, Mao, Ho Chi Minh, Kim Il Sung and a beaming Stalin himself. Alongside the leaders, there's a gallery of sturdy proletarian and peasant types building factories, heroically swathing corn, implementing the Five Year Plan, joining the Party and other everyday communist activities. Highlight of the statues is black American singer Paul Robeson declaiming in full voice, a particularly effective piece of agitprop sculpture. If you need a walk after all the viewing, the elegantly contoured **palace gardens** stretching out behind the back of the building, provide the necessary space. Refreshments are available at the palace **café** back out near the entrance gate.

Radzyń Podlaski

Forty kilometres north of Lubartów on the main Lublin–Białystok road is **RADZYŃ PODLASKI**, another sleepy provincial market town marked by its historic association with Polish aristocracy, in this case the powerful Potocki family, who descended on the town in the early eighteenth century and built one of their many eastern palaces here on the site of an earlier castle belonging to the Mniszek family. Badly damaged in 1944, the **Potocki Palace**, dubbed the "Podlasian Versailles" in direct competition with the Branicki Palace in Białystok (see p.257), was said in its heyday to be one of the finest Rococo residences of the East. Despite the fact that it was never fully repaired after the war – much of the palace is local administrative offices now – walking round the large inner courtyard you can still sense something of the building's former grandeur. Although pretty overgrown the **palace gardens**, also designed in the 1750s by royal architect Jacob Fontana, in the course of his thorough transformation of the palace, are now the town park, a soothing spot to cool off in on a summer's day. These days the orangery is a *Dom Kultury* and Video Club, which probably accounts for the graffiti scrawled all over its walls. Across the road from the palace, the eighteenth-century **Parish Church** is a fine Mannerist building whose architecture echoes the Collegiate churches in Zamość and Kazimierz Dolny.

If you're stopping off for a **meal**, the *Polonia* on ul. Ostrowiecka, east of the bus station, will do the honours. **Buses** continue on to Białystok (3hr 30min), Biała Podlaska (1hr) and south to Lublin (1hr 30 min).

Biała Podlaska

The provincial capital, **BIAŁA PODLASKA**, offers a curious mixture of both the old and the new Poland. Weighing heavily on the town today is its strategic position along the main high road from Warsaw to the eastern border (the train station is similarly placed on the main Warsaw–Moscow line). Day and night, transit lorries thunder along the road to and from the border crossing at Terespol, forty-odd kilometres east, and local rumour has it that the Russian mafia has gained a firm foothold in the town.

Judging by some of the menacing-looking characters to be seen hanging round the town square at night, it's not a proposition the visitor should discount, either, especially when it comes to parking cars in the centre. That said, there are a number of things worth seeing, many of them associated with the powerful Radziwiłł family, the town's fifteenth-century founders and longtime aristocratic benefactors.

The Town

Inevitably for a town established by aristocracy, the former **Radziwiłł Castle complex** west of the main square, provides the town's main focus of historic interest. Left, like most other such complexes, to go to seed in the postwar era, much of the damage was actually done earlier, the main palace section of the original seventeenth-century complex having been destroyed by the tsarist authorities in the 1870s. The main building, currently being renovated, is a combined school and music academy, while the old **Tower House** contains a well-organized **Regional Museum** (June–Aug Tues–Sun 10am–5pm; Sept–May Tues–Sun 9am–4pm). Judging by the illustrations displayed here, the original castle complex was a very grand affair. The exhibitions on the upper floor feature an interesting display of local ethnography, including textiles, folk tapestries and examples of the pagan-influenced "sun" crucifixes typical of the Lithuanian part of the old Commonwealth. The artwork housed in the next room reflects traditional regional themes – hunting, horses, soldiers and the old Jewish marketplace.

Of a number of churches in town, the basilica-shaped **St Anne's Parish Church**, just up from the palace, is the most striking, an exuberant late sixteenth-century structure with twin cupolas and a richly decorated side chapel devoted to the Radziwiłłs, as well as one curiously Celtic-looking tombstone in the graveyard outside, a contrast to the kitschy electric Marian shrine standing nearby.

The statue across the road, standing on the corner of ul. Brzeska, is of the popular writer **Józef Ignacy Kraszewski** (1821–87), who attended the 350-year old local school, the old *Akademia Bialskia* (Biała Academy), which was originally affiliated with the Kraków Academy and later with the Academy in Wilno (Vilnius).

Practicalities

The **train station** is on the southern side of the town, a five-minute bus ride from the centre, with the **bus station** on pl. Wojska Polskiego, a little to the east of the main square along ul. Brzeska. For **tourist information**, the *Orbis* office located on pl. Wolności, the central square, is your best bet.

Accommodation options are pretty limited. The *PTTK* hotel, ul. Pokoju 14 (☎057/43 56 46; ②), is really very basic, and some way to the west of the centre – although buses #17, #18 or #19 will drop you reasonably close by. The *Sportowy*, ul. Piłsudskiego 38 (☎057/43 45 50; ②) next to the local stadium, is a similarly basic sports hotel, but closer to the centre. The *U Radziwiłła*, ul. Powstanców 4 (☎057/43 53 40; ④), is the best-quality place around, though the hotel's location 2km west of town means you'll have to take a taxi if you don't have your own transport. As the hotel is popular both with local lads and cross-border travellers of the shadier variety, anyone with a room on the first floor may find themselves having to contend with riotous all-night Russian parties being held just along the corridor. Finally there's a (summer only) **youth hostel** at ul. Sidorska 30, not far from the train station.

Of the **restaurants**, the dining room in the *U Radziwiłła* is serviceable enough, though you'll probably have to put up with a "dance" (read "muzak") band. In the town centre, the *Stylowa*, ul. Brezska 16, and the *Adria*, on pl. Wolności, are the main options.

Janów Podlaski

Twenty kilometres north of Biała Podlaska close up by the Belarus border, formed from here southwards by the River Bug, the town of **JANÓW PODLASKI** is home to the country's most famous **stud farm**, specializing in the rearing of thoroughbred Arab horses. Located 2km east of the town centre, luminaries of the world horse scene are regular visitors, principally during the annual international **auctions** which are held every September.

Established by Tsar Alexander 1 in 1817, the stud was intended to produce top-quality horses for his personal use. The farm has gone through its ups and downs: the stock was badly decimated by German soldiers in the latter stages of World War I, and again taken over by the Nazis during World War II, when the horses were transported to Germany, many dying in the notorious Allied bombing of Dresden in February 1944. The elegant stable complex you see today is essentially that designed by the Warsaw architect Marconi in the 1830s and 1840s. Janów horses are highly prized in the equestrian world, and with price tags reaching hundreds of thousands of zlotys it's very much a rich person's pursuit. For the less affluent, however, there's always the option of having a look around the stables: turning up without an appointment (preferably made in the *Orbis* office in Biała Podlaska) is not wildly popular, though generally the staff will let you in if you are persuasive.

CROSSING THE EASTERN BORDER

Despite the rapidly increasing volume of traffic, travel across Poland's **eastern borders** in any form – car especially – is still liable to be a major hassle. Behind the socialist unity rhetoric of the postwar era, up until the early 1990s the reality was a strictly controlled border, at least as strongly policed at major crossing points as the former East–West Germany border. The political climate may have changed radically, but in practical terms getting into (or out of) Belarus and Ukraine from Poland remains fraught with practical complications, and is likely to remain so for the foreseeable future.

Crossing points

For motorists the key problem is lack of **crossing points**, a problem compounded by the ponderous Soviet-style customs set up on the eastern side of the border and the sheer volume of traffic attempting to get across. Two major border crossings – **Terespol** near Biała Podlaska and **Medyka** near Przemyśl – were adequate as long as few people were able to travel. With the recent explosion of travel facilitated by the new political situation it's now absurd, as everyone recognizes. The response to date has been sluggish to say the least: two new crossing points, at **Dorohusk**, east of Chełm, and at **Hrebenne**, near Tomaszów Lubelski, 70km northeast of L'viv. Amazing stories of border incidents abound: one legendary story that did the rounds in Poland in the early 1990s was of a car stopped at customs on account of the peculiar smell emanating from the vehicle. Close examination of a back-seat passenger revealed that he had died (from a stroke) during the long wait: not wanting to lose their precious place in the queue, the other passengers had decided to keep the body in the car until they crossed the border.

By car

Motorists can still expect waits of anything from two to four days at either of the major crossings in the several-kilometre-long queues backed up round the clock on both sides of the border. In summer particularly, conditions at Terespol verge on the nightmarish – there are no roadside toilet or washing facilities to speak of, with food and other supplies coming from the vendors in vans parked up on the side of the road. Thousands of stationary cars – especially those with Western number-plates – are a sitting target for robbers, so you're well advised to keep a close watch on your vehicle at all times. At the time of writing, protracted negotiations between the Polish and Ukrainian authorities are due to result in the opening up of at least a couple of new purpose-built border crossings by the end of the decade. If this actually happens, the situation will undoubtedly improve for motorists.

By bus

Crossing the border **by bus** is a different story: all *PKS* buses get special treatment, so unless there's trouble with customs as a result of some of the passengers' "baggage" – a not infrequent occurrence – you should be through the border in a matter of hours as opposed to days. For any cross-border bus journey, it's a good idea to buy your ticket in advance.

By train

By train you probably won't face such a long wait – though even here a caveat is needed since if you've arrived without a visa, purchasing one from the conductor can be a long and drawn-out affair. To date, Ukrainian officials are proving better in this respect than the Belarussians, though it's important to stress that everything remains in a state of flux – there's still no final decision, for example, on whether people in transit to Lithuania via Belarus are required to have a visa, though for the moment the rule continues to be enforced. In the final analysis, apart from a few sensible precautions, it's very much a case of turning up and seeing what happens.

From its founding in the 1420s the town itself became an important stopoff point on the main Kraków to Vilnius road. The solid, imposing Baroque **Collegiate Church** with adjoining belltower stands as a reminder of better days.

For a bite **to eat**, there's the *Janowianka* on pl. Partyzantów, the main square, while for **accommodation** the *Dom Wycieczkowy*, (☎080/225; ②) at ul. 1 Maja 1, is the only presentable option. Janów is a thirty-minute bus ride from Biała Podlaska, with the possibility of connecting buses on to Białystok (2hr), Lublin and Terespol (border).

East of Lublin

East of Lublin stretches an expanse of the sparsely populated agricultural lowland characteristic of Poland's eastern borders. In the midst of the region lies the recently established **Polesie National Park**, a scenic area of marshy swamps and ancient, largely untouched peat bogs, and the most westerly part of a huge expanse of similar terrain stretching far beyond the border into Ukraine and Belarus, known collectively as Polesie before World War II, when the majority of the region was still within Polish territory.

For those interested in the religious and cultural mix of Poles, Ukrainians and Jews historically associated with southeastern Poland, **Chełm**, the regional capital and the border town of **Włodawa** offer the prospect of an appealing if low key diversion. Although both are well off the beaten track, a combined visit to both merits the backroads detour required.

Chełm

Sixty-five kilometres east of Lublin is the town of **CHEŁM**, a tranquil rural centre with a typically timeless eastern Polish feel to it. Like much of the surrounding area the town centre sits on a deep-running bedrock of **chalk**, providing Chełm with its best known export and with a local landmark hill characteristically formed by limestone deposits. Rudely shunted into rural borderside oblivion by the postwar shifts in the country's frontiers, Chełm is currently experiencing something of a revival thanks to the growth in local cross-border traffic with neighbouring Ukraine, resulting from the opening of an international border crossing at Dorohusk, 30km east of town on the main Kowel-Kiev road.

Historically Chełm is one of eastern Poland's oldest urban settlements. Established in the early tenth century to protect the eastern borders of the nascent Piast-ruled domains, from the start Chełm was embroiled in a protracted contest for domination of the surrounding region between the Duchy of Kiev, the forerunner of Muscovy, and the Polish Piast monarchs. Control passed decisively to the Polish crown in 1387, soon after which the town was granted its charter by Ladislaus (Władysław) II Jagiełło. Formerly home to one of the oldest **Jewish communities** in Poland (Jews arrived here in the 1440s and possibly even earlier), Jews constituted roughly half of the town's population right up till 1939, enjoying legendary status in Jewish folklore as original simpletons and as such the butt of many a popular joke.

Following the local Orthodox acceptance of Rome's jurisdiction sealed in the 1596 Union of Brest (see "History", p.610), Chełm also emerged as a stronghold of **Uniate** (Greek Catholic) devotion, a position it retained until the suppression of the local Uniates and their enforced reconversion to Russian Orthodoxy ordered by the tsarist authorities in the 1870s. After the town's liberation by the Red Army in summer 1944, Chełm briefly enjoyed the dubious honour of being the first base of the Soviet appointed Polish Committee of National Liberation (PKWN) sent into Poland by Stalin to establish a new communist-led government.

The Old Town

Everything worth seeing is concentrated within the relatively tight confines of the Old Town centre. Starting from pl. Luczowskiego, a brisk climb along the path up **Góra Zamkowa**, the hill overlooking the town from the east and the site of the original fortified settlement brings you to the **former Uniate Cathedral complex**, a grandiose set of buildings including the Greek Catholic cathedral turned Roman Catholic church, an imposing twin-towered Baroque structure from the 1740s with a fine high facade, the Uniate bishop's former residence and a seventeenth-century Basilian monastery. Back out of the complex it's worth climbing the fifteen-metre-high mound, the only remains of the original Slavic settlement, rising from the northern side of the hill, for the grandstand views over the town. A short walk northwest down the slopes of Góra Zamkowa brings you to another erstwhile Uniate complex, this time comprising a former seminary and the early eighteenth-century Baroque **St Nicholas's Church**, these days the home of a minor local **museum** (Tues–Sat 10am–3pm).

Back towards the centre along ul. Młodowskiej is the **Orthodox Church**, a white brick nineteenth-century *cerkiew* with an impressive iconostasis. As usual though, the place is generally locked except when there's a service going on, so at any other time you'll have to persuade the priest, who lives close by, or one of his acolytes to open up and let you look inside. South down ul. Kopernika, at the corner with ul. Krzywa, stands the former **Synagogue**, the only one of several that remains. Today it's a bank and there's nothing to inform you of the place's onetime function, though, if you're at all attuned to local synagogue architecture, its outward appearance is an immediate giveaway.

West along ul. Krzywa brings you to the **Town Museum** (Tues–Fri 10am–3pm, Sat & Sun 11am–3pm). The ground floor displays focus on the history of the town, notably the Partition-era Russian occupation, while the upstairs floor houses a collection of local wildlife as well as an extraordinary, and presumably less local selection of a wide variety of molluscs. East along ul. Lubelska stands the **Parish Church**, a Piarist foundation from the 1750s, designed by Italian architect Paolo Antonio Fontana. An extravagant piece of Baroque exuberance, the walls and vaults of the interior boast a fine series of *trompe l'oeil* paintings and frescoes by Joseph Mayer, similar in style to the ones that adorn Lublin Cathedral, this time illustrating scenes from the Life of the Virgin, and in the side chapels, the exploits of St Joseph Calasanza, founder of the Piarist order.

THE CHALK CELLARS

Immediately west of the parish church on ul. Lubelska is the entrance to the town's major curiosity, a labyrinthine network of **underground tunnels** (daily 10am–6pm; tours arranged at the ticket office; English or German guide available by advance appointment ☎ 082/65 25 30) hewn out of the chalk bedrock – the only one of its kind in Europe. The unusual purity of the local chalk, combined with a growing appreciation of its commercial building value, resulted in the development of an amateur chalk-mining industry here as far back as the fifteenth century. Little if any control was exercised over the pattern of the mining, the result being a seemingly unco-ordinated maze of tunnels and mine shafts hacked out by succeeding generations of local entrepreneurs. Eventually, however, much of the several kilometre network of passageways – the deepest going down fifteen metres – fell into neglect and disuse. In the 1960s, in an effort to halt the rot, the deepest sections were silted up and a two-kilometre section of tunnels twelve metres deep was cleaned up and opened to tourists.

These days the standard **tour** lasts about thirty minutes, more than enough for most people, given the cold. The insulating properties of chalk are such that the tunnels maintain a temperature of exactly 9°C regardless of the season, so you'll need to bring a jacket or sweater with you for the tour. As you would expect, there's a stock of historical anecdotes as well as legends of spirits and demons, all of which the torchlight-bearing guide will dutifully provide on demand.

Practicalities

The main stations lie on opposite sides of the Old Town centre. The **bus station** is on ul. Lwowska, a five-minute walk south of pl. Luczowskiego, the central square, and ul. Lubelska, the main thoroughfare bisecting it. The main **train station**, Chełm Główny, is a lot further out, some twenty minutes' walk northeast of the centre off ul. Kolejowa. Virtually all buses from outside the station will take you into the centre.

Transport connections to and from Chełm are relatively sparse, though gradually improving thanks to the opening up of the Dorohusk border crossing. Getting here or heading almost anywhere else involves going via Lublin. Trains to Lublin (1hr–1hr 30min) run relatively infrequently, buses being the more reliable bet. Local buses and trains also run to and from Włodawa (1hr) and Zamość (1hr 30min), and again in both instances the bus is the more regular option.

The **tourist information office**, centrally located at ul. Lubelska 20 (☎082/536 67) is well stocked with maps and other information, including a number of English-language brochures.

Chełm doesn't go overboard on **places to stay** either in number or quality. The only real hotel is the *Kamena*, ul. Armii Krajowej 50 (☎082/65 64 01; ⑤), a decent-quality overnighter with a similarly passable restaurant and café. Other more basic options are the *Domont*, ul. 1 Pułku Szwoleżerów 15 (082/65 68 26; ③), halfway between the train station and town centre, and the **youth hostel** at ul. Czarneckiego 8 (082/65 38 85), handily located close to the centre and also offering a few double rooms (②). For food, your best bet is the *Kamena* hotel **restaurant**, with the *Lotos*, al. Piłsudskiego 14, being the best of the more down-at-heel alternatives.

Włodawa

Hard up by the Belarussian border, 50km north of Chełm, sits the sleepy little town of **WŁODAWA**. Situated on top of a low hill overlooking the banks of the River Bug which here, as for about 100km in either direction, forms the national border established in 1945, Włodawa gets its as yet underdeveloped tourist stars from the presence of one of the best preserved synagogues in the country. As with many towns in this region, Jews formed a clear majority of the town population up till World War II, when virtually all of them perished in the concentration camp at Sobibór, established by the Nazis in May 1942, 12km south of town.

Built in the 1760s on the site of an earlier wooden structure, the main **Synagogue**, one of the many onetime Jewish buildings dotted around the centre, is a typically solid-looking late Baroque construction with a palatial main facade dominated by a high central section and topped by some typically Polish mansard roofing. Despite severe damage by the Nazis, and postwar conversion into a warehouse, the synagogue was thoroughly, and well-restored in the 1960s, since when it's functioned as a local **museum** (Tues–Sun 10am–3pm). In the main interior room, the prayer hall, four pillars supporting the barrel-cross vaulting indicate the spot where the *bimah* once stood. The major surviving original feature is the restored **Aron ha Kodesh**, a colourful, triple-tiered neo-Gothic structure raised in the 1930s and covered with elaborate stucco decoration. Ranged round the walls is a photo exhibition of life in the wartime Warsaw Ghetto, while the upstairs gallery of the synagogue holds a separate display of local ethnography – folk costumes, ploughs and the like (same opening hours) – that seems a little out of keeping with the rest of the building. Across the courtyard from the main synagogue is another smaller house of worship from the mid-nineteenth century, currently under reconstruction, which has preserved sections of the original polychromy as well as its Aron ha Kodesh. Plans are afoot eventually to integrate it and the main synagogue into a more comprehensive museum of local Jewish culture. For the moment, only the ticket office is located here.

If you've the inclination for a stroll around the rest of town, there are a couple of other buildings worth looking in on: **the Parish Church**, a curiously squat-looking late Baroque building designed like its counterparts in Lubartów (see p.285) and Chełm (see p.291) by Paolo Antonio Fontana in the mid-1700s, with some rich Rococo interior polychromy; and across the opposite side of the main square, the Neoclassical Orthodox Church, built in 1842 with funds from the Zamoyski family. Here, as ever, the building's kept locked except for services, so you'll need to rouse the priest, who lives next door, if you want to get in to look at the building.

In the unlikely event of getting stranded here and needing **accommodation**, the only option is the basic *Dom Wycieczkowy*, ul. Szkolna 4 (☎082/72 25 84; ②), where there's also a camping site. For something **to eat**, head for the *Bilard* café on the main square, or one of the snack bars on ul. Czerwonego Krzyża, the street leading off from the square up towards the synagogue.

West to Kazimierz

The Lublin–Warsaw route has a major attraction in the town of **Kazimierz Dolny**, an ancient and highly picturesque grain town set above the Wisła. To reach it on public transport, the easiest approach from Warsaw is to go by train to **Puławy** and catch a connecting bus from there; from Lublin there are direct buses via the old spa town of **Nałęczów**.

Nałęczów

Twenty-five kilometres west of Lublin (regular buses: destination Puławy and/or Kazimierz Dolny), **NAŁĘCZÓW** saw its heyday at the end of the last century, when Polish writers and artists, including the popular novelists Bolesław Prus and Stefan Żeromski and pianist-prime minister Ignacy Paderewski, came here, the quality of the local air and water helping establish it as one of the country's most popular holiday spa towns.

Even today the **spa** is still renowned for its therapeutic waters, heart specialists and generally medicinal climate, and the town retains much of its old-time appearance and atmosphere. A leisurely stroll through the attractively landscaped spa park brings you to the Neoclassical **Małachowski Palace**, an elegant Rococo structure from the 1770s, which is part health centre and part **museum** (Tues–Sun 10am–3pm), devoted to Prus and the "Positivist" literary movement he promoted in reaction to traditional insurrectionary Romanticism. Particularly impressive is the palace ball room, which boasts some exquisite period stucco decoration. Nearby is the **Sanatorium**, fronted by a monument to **Żeromski**, and the neo-Gothic **English Pavilion** (Pavilion Angielski), now the spa office building. For an instant iron-deficiency remedy, you can taste the **local waters** in the pavilion, next to a duck-filled lake in the middle of the park. Back out through the main gate, opposite the bus stop on ul. Ponatowskiego, a short way up Żeromskiego is the **Żeromski Villa**, the writer's Podhale-style residence built at the turn of the century, and now housing a small museum (Tues–Sun 10am–3pm) devoted to the man's life and works.

There are two **hotels** in town, the *Przepiórecka*, at ul. 1 Maja 6 (☎081/129; ③), which provides the bare essentials, restaurant included (it might also be able to arrange **private rooms**), and the even more basic *Batorówka*, ul. Paderewskiego 1 (☎081/11 43 56; ②). Additionally, there is a range of **pensjonat** aimed at people here on rest cures – though you don't have to be enrolled in one to stay. Two good options are the *Jana*, ul. Partyzantów 6 (☎081/11 45 72; ③) and the unnamed *pensjon* at ul. Lipowa 16 (☎081/11 40 76; ④).

Anyone seriously taken by the idea of a therapeutic spa should contact the **main sanitorium** (Uzdrowisko Nałęczów), al. Malachowskiego 5 (☎081/11 43 56, fax 11 46 08) for details of current offers. Many cure-seekers stay in the sanitorium itself.

Puławy

Sprawling over the eastern banks of the Wisła, 20km west from Nałęczów, is **PUŁAWY**, a grubby, medium-sized industrial centre with seemingly little going for it. However, in Polish consciousness, the place is indelibly associated with the Czartoryski family, the noted aristocratic dynasty who moved to the town in the 1730s and made it their base. Best known in the line of residents are **Prince Adam Czartoryski** and his wife **Izabella**, passionate devotees of the arts who, by the end of the eighteenth century, had succeeded in transforming the palace here into one of the country's most dynamic cultural and intellectual centres, accumulating a huge library and noted art collection in the process. Despite the advent of the Partitions and the imposition of Russian rule, the family stuck determinedly to its guns throughout the early 1800s, Izabella founding a national museum – the first of its kind in Poland – and continuing to patronize and cultivate the arts. This was not, however, to last. The failure of the 1830 Uprising (see "History", p.613) and the Czartoryski's involvement in its planning, resulted in the confiscation of the entire family estate, the enraged tsarist authorities even going as far as to rename the town "New Alexandria". The Czartoryskis fled into exile in Paris and their huge art collection was spirited away secretly along with them, where it remained until its return to the family palace in Kraków, where it forms the core of today's museum there (see p.375).

The Czartoryski Palace and Park

The only thing really worth making the effort to seek out, in an otherwise undistinguished town, is the **Palace**, approached from a large pond-filled courtyard off the intersection of al. Królewska and ul. Czartoryskich – a twenty-minute walk south from the main bus station. Built in the 1670s by the veteran Warsaw architect Tylman of Gameren, the main building subsequently underwent a number of remodellings (and significant damage during World War II), the result being the curiously leaden Neoclassical pile you see today. Converted into a scientific research institute in the postwar years, nobody seems to object to you strolling in for a look around the place during regular office hours. Through the main entrance and up the grand cast-iron staircase, the majestically arcaded **Gothic Hall and Music Hall** offer hints of the former grandeur of the place. An elegant statuetted marble balcony offers an enjoyable view over the palace park, and beyond it the Wisła river.

Designed and developed by the industrious Izabella Czartoryska over a twenty-year period (1790–1810), the meandering **palace park** is quintessentially Romantic in feel and conception. A large expanse filled with a widely-variegated collection of trees, both Polish and foreign, the walkways are dotted with the hotchpotch of "historical" buildings and monuments, many of them in the classical mode, popular with the Polish aristocracy of the period (see for example Arkadia, p.128). Southeast of the palace down a treelined avenue, the **Gothic House** (Dom Gotycki), a square, two-storey building with a graceful portico, originally part of the Czartoryski museum, now houses a small exhibition (May–Nov Tues–Sun 10am–4pm) devoted to the family, including a changing selection of exhibits from the family museum in Kraków. Opposite is the **Temple of Sibyl** (Świątynia Sybilli), consciously echoing the temple of the same name in Tivoli, near Rome, and containing another small exhibition (same opening hours), this time devoted to national historical themes along the lines of the museum initiated by Izabella, including the 1830 and 1863 Uprisings.

If you feel like strolling further afield, there are a number of follies and other assorted buildings to detain you on the way along the edge of the park lake, including a Chinese pavilion, Roman gate, the marble Czartoryski family sarcophagus and assorted imitation classical statuary.

Practicalities

Getting here is easy – Puławy is on a major train line from Warsaw (2hr) and has regular bus connections with Lublin (1hr). You're unlikely to want to stay in Puławy, though the proximity to Kazimierz Dolny (see below) can make it a good proposition if accommodation is tight there. Of the various options, the central *Izabella*, ul. Lubelska 1 (☎0831/3041; ⑥), a faded upmarket tourist haunt that's seen better days, has a reasonable restaurant and houses the main **tourist information point**. The *Dom Nauczyciela*, ul. Kołłątaja 1 (☎0831/4277; ②) is a good budget bet, as is the marginally more expensive *Wisła*, ul. Wróbleskiego 1 (☎0831/2737; ③). Other cheaper alternatives are the **PTTK hostel** at ul. Rybacka 7 (☎0831/3048; ②), west of the palace, near the river, and an all-year **youth hostel** at ul. Włostowicka 27 (☎0831/3367), 2km south of the centre on the Kazimierz road.

Hotel **restaurants** aside, there are a number of other undistinguished restaurants and cafés on and around the central ul. Piłsudskiego. *Dom Chemika*, ul. Wojska Polskiego 4, is a nice *kawiarnia* with live jazz several weekends a month.

Kazimierz Dolny and around

Don't be surprised if your first impression of **KAZIMIERZ DOLNY** is one of *déjà vu*: recognizing celluloid potential when they see it, numerous film directors – and not just Polish ones – have used the scenic backdrop of this well-preserved town for historical thrillers and tragic romances. Artists, too, have long been drawn to Kazimierz's effervescent light and ancient buildings. These days the town is unquestionably established as a major tourist venue, a fact reflected in the wealth of hotels and restaurants continuing to spring up. Poles as well as foreign tourists are drawn by the town's memorable combination of historic architecture, riverside setting and scenic surrounding – definitely not one to miss.

Historically, the place is closely associated with its royal namesake, Kazimierz the Great (1333–70), who rescued Poland from dynastic and economic chaos and transformed the country's landscape in the process. It is said of him that he "found a wooden Poland and left a Poland of stone", and Kazimierz Dolny (Lower Kazimierz) is perhaps the best remaining example of his ambitious town-building programme. Thanks to the king's promotion of the Wisła grain and timber trade, a minor village was transformed into a **prosperous mercantile town** by the end of the fourteenth century, gaining the nickname "little Danzig" in the process, on account of the goods' ultimate destination. Much of the money that poured in was used to build the ornate burghers' houses that are today's prime tourist attraction.

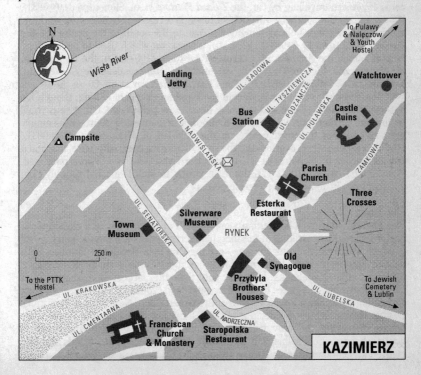

It was during this period, too, that **Jews** began to settle in Kazimierz and other neighbouring towns, grateful for the legal protection proclaimed for them throughout Poland by King Kazimierz. Dynamic Jewish communities of traders and shopkeepers were integral to the character of towns like Kazimierz for over five hundred years: at one time eighty percent of the inhabitants of Kazimierz were Jewish. The soul of the town, you feel, died in the death camps.

Arrival, information and accommodation

Unless you have access to a car, the only way to get to Kazimierz Dolny is by **bus** from Puławy, 15km to the north. From either Puławy's bus or train station, take suburban bus #12 or one of the hourly *PKS* services. The Kazimierz bus station – really just a drop-off point – is on ul. Podzamcze, within spitting distance of the Rynek.

There's a helpful **PTTK office** at no. 27 on the Rynek (☎0831/10046) which can sort out private accommodation. An alternative for **private rooms** (③) is the *Tour Club* office, Rynek 2 (☎/fax 0831/10555). The latter also organizes English-language guided tours of the town and surrounding region. If you're taken by the idea of exploring the charming surrounding countryside, **bike rental** is available at ul. Sadowa 2/4.

Kazimierz's **accommodation** situation has improved rapidly as a result of the new entrepreneurially oriented economic order. Best of the newer places is the *Łaznia*, ul. Senatorska 21 (☎0831/10298; ⑤), between the museum and the river bank. If you are travelling by car, the *Zajazd Piastowski*, ul. Słoneczna 31 (☎0831/10351; ④), on the southern outskirts of town, is a reasonably priced ex-workers' hotel that also offers holiday bungalows. Also to the south of the centre are the *Karlik*, ul. Filtrowa 11 (☎0831/10294; ③), a *pensjonat* which used to be a miners' holiday home; the *Arkadia*, ul. Czerniawy 1 (☎0831/10074; ③); the *Rzemieślnik*, ul. Nadrzeczna 48c (☎0831/10595; ④) and the *górale* chalet-style *Góralski*, ul. Krakowska 47 (☎0831/10263; ③). The *Dom Architectowy* at no. 20 on the Rynek (☎0831/10544; ③) offers beds, decent food and an excellent setting, though it's not a regular tourist place and you may need to be persuasive. Otherwise, you'll be forced further out to the **PTTK hostel**, a converted fourteenth-century granary south of the town centre on the cobbled ul. Krakowska 59 (☎0831/10036), with fine views overlooking the river. There's a **campsite** here, too, and a noisier one at ul. Senatorska 24, nearer the river. The *Pod Wianuszkami*, ul. Puławska 64 (☎0831/10 32 77), the main **youth hostel**, is located roughly 2km north of town in another old riverside granary.

The Town

The **Rynek**, with its solid-looking wooden well at the centre, is a classic *Orbis* poster image. Most striking of the merchants' residences around the square – all of which were restored after the war – are the **Przybyła Brothers' Houses**, both on the southern edge. Built in 1615, they bear some striking Renaissance sculpture; the guidebooks will tell you that the largest one shows Saint Christopher, but his tree trunk of a staff and zodiacal entourage suggest something more like a Polish version of the Green Giant. Next door is the former **Lustig House** – once home to a notable local Jewish mercantile dynasty, its beams displaying the only surviving original Hebrew inscription in town, a quotation from the Psalms. On the south side of the square, stands the late eighteenth-century **Gdańsk House** (Kamienica Gdańska), a sumptuous Baroque mansion originally owned by grain merchants. Immediately west is the **Silverware Museum** (May–Sept Tues–Sun 10am–4pm; Oct–April Tues–Sun 10am–3pm), which contains a highly impressive collection of ornamental silverwork and other decorative metal pieces dating back to the seventeenth century – a must if you are even remotely interested in this craft. A notable feature is the collection of Jewish ritual objects and vessels, many from the town itself. Several floors of the building also house temporary summer exhibitions aimed at the seasonal tourist population.

Other houses still carrying their Renaissance decorations can be seen on ul. Senatorska, which runs alongside the stream south of the square. Of these, the **Celejowski House** (no.17), has a fabulous high attic storey, a balustrade filled with the carved figures of saints and an assortment of imaginary creatures, richly ornamented windows and a fine entrance portal and hallway. It houses the **Town Museum** (same hours as Silverware Museum), which along with paintings of Kazimierz and its surroundings, documents – albeit sketchily – the history of the town's Jewish community. The nineteenth-century paintings in the collection focus partly on the Jews – a kind of Orientalist fascination seems to have gripped the predominantly Gentile Polish artists – and evoke an almost palpable atmosphere.

On the streets of the town, specifically Jewish buildings are scarce. The old **Synagogue** is sited off ul. Lubelska, to the east of the Rynek; constructed in King Kazimierz's reign, it was once a fine building. Following wartime destruction by the Nazis, it was rebuilt in the 1950s and converted into a cinema. Of the decoration only the octagonal wooden dome, characteristic of many Polish synagogues, and the women's gallery have been reconstructed.

Crossing the stream and following ul. Cmentarna up the hill brings you to the late sixteenth-century **Reformed Franciscan Church and Monastery**, from where there's a nice view back down over the winding streets and tiled rooftops. Up the hill on the other side of the square is the **Parish Church**, remodelled impressively in the early seventeenth century. The interior boasts a magnificent organ, Renaissance font and fine stuccoed vaulting.

Further up, there's an excellent view from the ruins of the fourteenth-century **Castle**, built by King Kazimierz and destroyed by the marauding Swedish forces during the ferocious invasion of the country in the mid-1650s. The panorama from the top of the **watchtower** above the castle is even better, taking in the Wisła and the full sweep of the countryside. Another popular alternative is the vantage point from the top of **Three Crosses Hill** (Góra Trzech Krzyży). A steepish climb fifteen minutes east of the square (there's also a path leading directly here fron the castle), the crosses were raised in memory of the early eighteenth-centuy plague that wiped out a large part of the local population.

On the southern side of town, a two-kilometre walk along ul. Czerniawa brings you to the **Czerniawa Gorge**, the site of the main **Jewish Cemetery**. First mentioned in 1568, the cemetery was destroyed by the Nazis, who ripped up the tombstones and used them to pave the courtyard of their headquarters in town. In the 1980s the tombstones scattered around the area were collected here and assembled into a wailing wall-like monument – six hundred fragments in all – to moving and dramatic effect. A jagged split down the middle symbolizes the dismemberment of the local Jewish population, making this one of the most powerful Jewish memorials in the country. Wander up the hill behind the monument and you'll find decaying remnants of the former cemetery sprouting up from among the trees.

Eating, drinking and entertainment

The town's food situation has also improved of late. All the hotels and former workers' holiday homes now have decent **restaurants**, notably the *Zajazd Piastowski* – well worth the journey if you've got transport available – and the *Dom Prasy*.

Other options include the upmarket *Staropolska*, ul. Nadrzeczna 14, which has a good line in traditional Polish cuisine; the *Club II*, ul. Krakowska 11; the *Esterka*, Rynek 13; and the teetotal *Amfibar*, ul. Sadowa 18, down by the waterfront. Otherwise, the *kawiarnia* (notably the *U Rabka*) and fast-food joints on the square offer snacks, and you can get chips and (sporadically) fish or chicken at a makeshift takeaway stand just off the south end of the square.

For sampling the joys of Polish folk music, Kazimierz is the place to be in summer: the annual **Folk Groups and Singers Festival**, a wildly popular national event, takes place here in late June or early July. Unless you have a tent, expect to rough it if you're in town then, as the meagre accommodation is snapped up instantly. Now into its thirtieth year, the festival is undoubtedly the country's premier folk music event – and the only one to which perfomers from all over the country regularly come. Everyone's welcome to play, usually amounting to six or seven hundred performers over the week. Of late, the festival has been spearheading something of a revival of interest in Polish roots music, particularly in regional styles and songs that only a decade ago seemed on the verge of extinction. Highlight of the week are the rural dance parties held on the main square. Awards are presented at the festival, with the winners featuring on CDs put out by Polskie Radio 2 – well worth picking up.

Into the countryside

There's some good **walking** territory around Kazimierz. If you really want to get the feel of the town's gentle surroundings, follow one of the marked paths from the town centre: either the five-kilometre green path which takes you southwest past the *PTTK* hostel and along the river cliff to **Mecmierz**; or the four-kilometre red path that heads northeast to the ruined **Castle of Bochotnica**. King Kazimierz is said to have built the castle here for one of his favourite mistresses, a Jewess called Esterka, with a secret tunnel connecting the fortresses in Kazimierz and Bochotnica.

Another option is to take the **ferry** (summer only) to the ruins of the sixteenth-century **Firlej family Castle** at Janowiec, also situated in attractive countryside. There's an equally improbable tunnel story connected with this castle as well, namely that the well doubled as the entrance to a passage joining this fortress to that of Kazimierz.

Sandomierz and beyond

SANDOMIERZ, 80km south of Kazimierz along the Wisła, is another of those small towns described as "quaint" or "picturesque" in the brochures. Its hilltop location certainly fits the bill, though the charm is dented by the evil stench rising from the polluted Wisła. However, a visit is definitely worthwhile, and access is straightforward, with regular train services from Warsaw and buses from Lublin. The one problem is accommodation: the town gets a lot of summer tourists and rooms in season can be very tricky to find; if you're energetic, it's a conceivable day trip from Lublin.

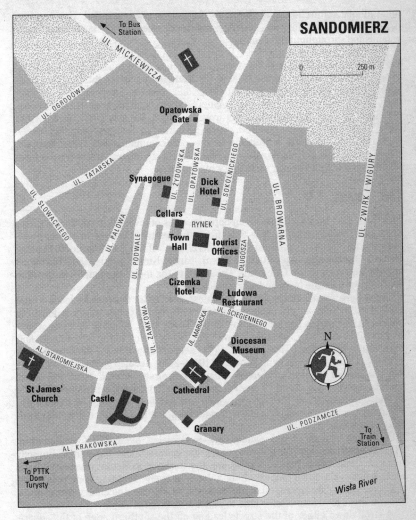

Like other towns in the southeast, Sandomierz rose to prominence through its position on the **medieval trade route** running from the Middle East, through southern Russia and the Ukraine, into central Europe. The town was sacked by the Tartars (twice) and the Lithuanians, in the thirteenth and fourteenth centuries respectively, then completely rebuilt by **Kazimierz the Great**, who gave it a castle, defensive walls, cathedral and town plan – still visible in the Old Town. Subsequently, Sandomierz flourished on the timber and corn trade, with its links along the Wisła to the Baltic ports. It was also the scene of one of the key religious events in Polish history. In 1570, while Catholics and Protestants were slitting each other's throats in the rest of Europe, members of Poland's non-Catholic churches met here to formulate the so-called **Sandomierz Agreement**, basis for the legally enshrined freedom of conscience later established throughout the country.

Physically, Sandomierz suffered badly at the hands of the Swedes, who blew up the town castle in 1656, and it was only thanks to a minor miracle that it survived World War II intact. In August 1944, as the **Red Army** pushed the Germans back across Poland, the front line moved closer and closer to Sandomierz. A popular story in the town relates how one Colonel Skopenko, an admirer of Sandomierz, managed to steer the fighting away from the town. He was later killed further west: his last wish, duly honoured, was to be buried in the town cemetery. Sadly, the anti-Soviet/Russian sentiments of the post-communist era mean that the man's memory is no longer safe – in 1994 there were moves to remove the town statue erected after the war in memory of Skopenko.

The Town

The **train and bus stations** are on opposite sides of town (3km south and 1.5km northwest respectively), a bus ride from the centre. Coming in through the nondescript slabs of modern Sandomierz, get off at the fourteenth-century **Brama Opatowska** (daily 10am–5.30pm), part of King Kazimierz's fortifications and the entrance to the Old Town. The climb to the top of the gate is worthwhile for the view over the town and surrounding area.

From here on it's alleyways and cobblestones, as ul. Opatowska leads to the delightful **Rynek**, an atmospheric square with plenty of places for a leisurely coffee. At its heart is the fourteenth-century **Town Hall**, a Gothic building which had its decorative attic, hexagonal tower and belfry added in the seventeenth and eighteenth centuries. The ground floor section contains a small **museum** (Tues–Fri 9am–4pm, Sat 9am–3pm, Sun 10am–2pm) devoted to the history of the town. Many of the well-preserved **burghers' houses** around positively shout their prosperity: nos. 5 and 10 are particularly fine Renaissance examples. There's a Tuesday market on the square, which, on the first Tuesday of the month, regularly becomes a major rural event, with livestock and produce driven in from the countryside.

A hidden aspect of old Sandomierz is revealed by a *PTTK* guided tour (Tues–Sun 10am–5pm) of the wine and grain **cellars** under the Rynek. Entered from ul. Olesnickich, just off the square, the thirty or so Renaissance-era cellars extend under the town hall, reaching a depth of twelve metres at one point. The registrar's office on nearby ul. Żydowska was an eighteenth-century **synagogue**, though there is – as so often – little to indicate its origins.

A stroll down either of the streets leading off the southern edge of the square will bring you to the murky **Cathedral**, constructed around 1360 on the site of an earlier Romanesque church, though now with substantial Baroque additions. It's worth a look within for the early fifteenth-century **murals** in the presbytery, probably by the same artist who painted the Holy Trinity Chapel in Lublin (see p.277), and a gruesome series of eighteenth-century paintings in the nave, showing the Tartars enjoying a massacre of the populace in 1259, and the Swedes blowing up the castle four centuries later.

Set back from the cathedral, the **Diocesan Museum** (April–Oct Tues–Sun 9am–5pm; Nov–March Tues–Sat 9am–noon, Sun 1–3pm) was the home of Jan Długosz (1415–80), author of one of the first histories of Poland. The building is filled to bursting with religious art, ceramics, glass and other curios, including a collection of Renaissance locks and keys, and a wonderful old pipe supposed to have belonged to Mickiewicz. Among the best works are a twelfth-century stone *Madonna and Child*, a *John the Baptist* by Caravaggio and a fifteenth-century *Three Saints* triptych from Kraków.

Downhill from the cathedral is the **Castle**, currently being restored; it is used occasionally for concerts and plays but otherwise has little going for it. Towards the river stands a medieval **granary**; others are to be found north along the river. Aleja Staromeijska runs from in front of the castle to the **Church of St James** (Kościół Św. Jakuba), a lime-shaded late-Romanesque building that's thought to be the first brick basilica in Poland – its restored entrance portal is particularly striking. Inside, the **Martyrs' Chapel** has a vivid painting of the martyrdom of local Dominicans by the Tartars in 1260, while in the northern nave, there are glass cases said to contain the bones of the murdered monks. The area around the church was the site of the original town, destroyed by the Tartars; recent archeological digs in the area uncovered a twelfth-century chess set, the oldest in Europe. Since the 1960s, this whole southern district has had to be shored up, owing to subsidence caused by the network of tunnels and cellars dug for grain storage and running for hundreds of metres through the soft undersoil.

Head back down the path in front of St James and you re-enter the town walls through the **Ucho Igielne**, a small entrance shaped like the eye of a needle.

Practicalities

The town has two **tourist offices**, sited next door to each other in a corner of the Rynek; *Orbis*, at no. 24, deals with ticket bookings, *PTTK*, at no. 25/26 (☎015/32 23 05), with maps and other local information, including accommodation.

Accommodation is in extremely short supply. The *Hotel Ciżemką*, Rynek 27 (☎015/32 36 68; ③), is ideally situated, but has just fifteen rooms. The *Dick*, a *pensjonat* off the square at ul. Gen. Sokolnickiego 3 (☎015/32 31 30; ②), is also small and only has shared bathrooms. The only other options are the very basic *PTTK Dom Wycieczkowy* at ul. Stefana Zeromskiego 10 (☎015/23088; ②), on the way into town from the bus station; the more pleasant *Dom Turysty PTTK*, ul. Krakowska 34 (☎015/22284; ③), which has a restaurant but is further out of town, a fifteen-minute walk from the Rynek down to the river; and the **youth hostel** on ul. Krępianki, well out of the centre (☎015/2563). There's also a **camp-site** on ul. Podzamcze, right by the river.

The best **restaurants** are in the hotels. The *Ciżemką* does an excellent *krupnik* soup but otherwise predictable food; its basement bar is popular with tourists and the local drinking crowd. The other main alternative in the town centre, the *Winnica*, ul. Mały Rynek 2, offers a reasonable-quality mix of Polish and international food. The restaurant in the *Dom Turysty* is only worth visiting if you're staying there. The *Dick* doesn't do meals, but has a friendly **bar**. Catering to the day-tripper crowd, ice cream and coffee bars are open all over the town centre in summer.

South from Sandomierz

South of Sandomierz along the Wisła basin you soon find yourself heading into the gritty landscape of **TARNOBRZEG**, a major industrial centre with similarly dim surroundings. Although it was previously a poor and neglected rural backwater, since World War II the region has been transformed by the growth of the mining industry built up as a result of the large sulphur deposits discovered around the town.

The sulphur may have done wonders for the local economy, but its exploitation has had serious effects on the environment; travelling through you can see and smell the stuff everywhere. Similar comments apply to **STALOWA WOLA**, 30km east of Tarnobrzeg, another major industrial city created round a burgeoning steel and metal industry in the late 1930s. The castle at **Baranów Sandomierski**, significantly affected by the pollution, will be most people's main reason for visiting the area.

Baranów Sandomierski

Fifteen kilometres south of Tarnobrzeg on the eastern bank of the Wisła, **BARANÓW SANDOMIERSKI**'s chief claim to fame is the spectacular castle located at the edge of the town.

Erected on the site of a fortified medieval structure owned by the Baranów family, the exquisitely formed and well-preserved Renaissance **Castle** (Tues–Sat 9am–2.30pm, Sun 9am–3pm) is as fine a period piece as you'll come across anywhere, well worth the out-of-the-way-trek needed to get here. The epithet "castle" is actually a bit of a misnomer – behind an elegant Italianate facade the rectangular building is really a glorified palace with some fortifications added on to the front for appearance's sake. The place's sumptuously palatial feel is confirmed, too, by a wander through the carefully manicured gardens on the south side of the building. Built in the 1590s for the wealthy Leszczyński family, the castle is constructed on a rectangular plan with an inner courtyard, corner towers and a gateway. The facade is crowned by an attic with a cheerful frieze decoration. In through the gateway you find yourself in a delicately cool, animated Italianate courtyard surrounded on three sides by two tiers of sinuously arcaded passageways, their ceilings decorated with a wealth of family emblems. To reach the upper level you climb the sweeping outer staircase – a later addition – on the southern side of the courtyard. Before doing that it's worth studying the entertaining collection of face-pulling grotesques, many of them animal figures, that decorate the base of the rosette-topped pillars ranged around the courtyard. Inside the building, the ground floor houses a **museum** displaying exhibits relating to the local sulphur industry – hardly surprising, since the castle is owned by one of the major Tarnobrzeg industrial sulphur concerns.

The lavishly decorated rooms of the upper floors of the castle are occupied by a luxury **hotel** (☎015/55 48 76 or 55 48 77; ⑦) with a high-quality **restaurant** used for banquets. Though fairly expensive, the place is understandably popular, so particularly in summer you'd be well advised to book ahead. A cheaper and perfectly acceptable alternative is the *Zamek* hotel housed in a modern building just west of the castle (☎015/11 80 39; ③). There's also the *Zajazd Wisła*, about 1km out of town, on ul. Dąbrowskiego (☎015/11 81 95; ③), with its own restaurant.

Unless you've your own transport the only way to **get to the castle** is by bus: local services run fairly regularly from Tarnobrzeg (30 min) or Sandomierz (1hr 30min, change at Tarnobrzeg) to the bus stop beyond the castle entrance gates or the main bus terminal on the Rynek, a ten-minute walk from the castle.

Zamość and around

The old towns and palaces of southeast Poland often have a Latin feel to them, and none more so than **ZAMOŚĆ**, 96km southeast of Lublin. The brainchild of the dynamic sixteenth-century chancellor Jan Zamoyski, the town is a remarkable demonstration of the way the Polish intelligentsia and ruling class looked towards Italy for ideas, despite the proximity of Russia. Zamoyski, in many ways the archetypal Polish Renaissance man, built this model town to his own ideological specifications close to his childhood village, commissioning the design from Bernardo Morando of Padua – the city where he had earlier studied. Morando produced a beautiful Italianate period piece, with a wide piazza, grid-plan streets,

ZAMOŚĆ

an academy and defensive bastions. These fortifications were obviously well thought out, as Zamość was one of the few places to withstand the seventeenth-century "Swedish Deluge" that flattened so many other Polish towns. Strategically located on the major medieval trading routes linking Kraków and Kiev from west to east, Lublin and Lwów from north to south, the town attracted an international array of merchants from early on, notably Jews, Armenians, Greeks, Scots, Hungarians and Italians, whose presence remains embedded in the diverse architecture of the city.

War returned to Zamość early this century, when the area was the scene of an important battle during the Polish–Russian war of 1919–20. The Red Army, which only weeks before had looked set to take Warsaw, was beaten decisively near the town, forcing Lenin to sue for peace with his newly independent neighbours. Somehow, Zamość managed also to get through World War II unscathed, so what you see today is one of Europe's best-preserved Renaissance town centres, classified by UNESCO as an outstanding historical monument. Chiefly due to its off-the-beaten-track location, the town hasn't yet assumed the prominence it deserves on the tourist trail, though will no doubt change in response to the increasing hype being created by tourist authorities in Poland and abroad.

The Old Town

Regulation-issue urban development surrounds Zamość's historic core, and both **bus** and **train stations** are sited some way from the centre. It's worth taking a bus or taxi to the edge of **plac Wolności**, bordering the Rynek. Once there, you should have no problem finding your way around the Renaissance grid.

The Rynek

The **Rynek**, also known as plac Mickiewicza, is a couple of blocks in from plac Wolności and the partly preserved circuit of walls. Ringed by a low arcade and the decorative former homes of the Zamość mercantile bourgeoisie, the geometrically designed **square** – exactly 100 metres in both width and length – is a superb example of Renaissance town architecture, a wide open space whose columned arcades, decorated **facades** and breezy **walkways** exude an upliftingly light, airy warmth. Dominating the ensemble from the north side of the square is the **Town Hall**, a soaring showstopper that's among the most photographed buildings in the country. A solid, three-storey structure topped by a tall clocktower and spire, the original, lower construction designed by Morando acquired its present Mannerist modelling in the 1640s, the sweeping, fan-shaped double stairway jutting out from the entrance being added in the following century. Successive renovations have kept the building in pretty good shape, though the peeling plasterwork on the staircase could do with some attention. The floodlighting used at night in summer heightens the power of the building, combining with the visual backdrop of the square to undeniably impressive effect. Occupied by local government offices, the town hall doesn't offer much to see inside; even the room commemorating the pivotal socialist-feminist theorist Rosa Luxemburg, born east of the square at ul. Staszica 37, is now under threat of removal.

The Wilczek House and Town Museum

From the town hall the vaulted arcade stretching east along ul. Ormiańska features several of the finest houses on the square. Once inhabited by the

Armenian merchants who moved here under special privilege in 1585, the houses
are fronted by facades that are a whirl of rich, decorative ornamentation, with a
noticeable intermesh of oriental motifs. First along is the splendid **Wilczek
House**, built by an early professor at the Zamość Academy, with some fine decorated bas-reliefs of Christ, Mary and the Apostles gracing the upper storey of the
facade. Number 26 sports similarly exuberant decoration, this time using animal
themes, lions and dragons included. It and the adjoining mansions house the
Town Museum (Tues–Sun 10am–3.30pm): inevitably, the exhibitions focus on
the Zamoyskis, with plenty of portraits of the town's founder and other assorted
family memorabilia. An additional plus is the interior, with much of the original
decoration, wooden ceilings, carved portals and fresco decoration well restored
and preserved. Back out of the museum the sumptuous facades continue, no. 24
(part of the museum) featuring a prim-looking Renaissance couple peering down
from between the windows, and no. 22 next door, bearing a relief of a beatific
Mary trampling a fierce-looking dragon underfoot.

The Morando Tenement House

The **east side** of the square, once another haunt of Armenian merchants and
teachers at the Academy, is similarly enjoyable: here as all around the square it's
well worth wandering along the vaulted passageways and in through the
doorways (many are now shops and several of them beautifully decorated)
notably at no. 6, a bookshop, and no. 2, a 350-year-old apothecary. The **southern
side** of the square contains some of the oldest and most obviously
Italian-influenced mansions, two-storey buildings with regularly proportioned
facades, several designed by Morando himself.

The **Morando Tenement House** at no. 25, where the great architect himself
used to live, boasts an impressive facade with exuberant Mannerist friezes, while
the *PTTK* office at no. 31, in the corner of the square, features some fine stucco
work in the vestibule and another beautifully decorated portal and surrounding
vault.

West of the square

Moving west of the square, first port of call is the towering **Collegiate Church**,
recently upgraded to a cathedral, a magnificent Mannerist basilica designed by
Morando to Zamoyski's exacting instructions. A three-aisled structure with
numerous side chapels, thin, delicate pillars reaching up to the ceiling and a fine
vaulted presbytery, the whole interior is marked by a strong sense of visual and
architectural harmony, a powerful expression of the self-confidence of the Polish
Counter-Reformation.

The **presbytery** houses a finely wrought eighteenth-century Rococo silver
tabernacle, as well as a series of paintings of scenes from the life of Saint Thomas
attributed to Domenico Tintoretto. The **Zamoyski family chapel**, the grandest
in the building, contains the marble tomb of Chancellor Jan topped by some
elegant Baroque stucco work by the Italian architect, J.B. Falconi. Adjoining the
main building is a high **belltower**, the oldest and biggest of its bells – known as
Jan after its benefactor – over three hundred years old. As with the town hall the
whole site is floodlit in summer, creating another impressive ensemble.

West across the main road, ul. Academicka, are two buildings that played a key
role in the historic life of the town. As its name implies the **Arsenal**, built by
Morando in the 1580s, is where the town's ample stock of weaponry used to be

kept alongside Zamoyski spoils of war. These days it houses a small military museum (Tues–Sun 10am–4pm).

The massive **Zamoyski Palace** beyond the arsenal is a shadow of its former self, the original Morando-designed building having undergone substantial modification after the Zamoyskis abandoned the place in the early nineteenth century, when it was taken over by the army and later became a hospital. The shabby old palace courtyard at the back of the building hints at former glories, but otherwise it's a rather mournful, run-down looking place, currently occupied by the town court.

Around the former Jewish quarter

Continuing north along ul. Academicka, west of the main street is the **Old Lublin Gate**, oldest of the entranceways dotted around the Old Town fortifications, and long since bricked up. These days the gate is stranded on the edge of school playing fields, the bas-relief uncovered during renovation earlier this century providing a glimpse of earlier glories.

The impressive-looking former **Zamoyski Academy** across the street, built in the 1630s and an important Polish centre of learning until its enforced closure at the start of the Partitions era, is now a school, albeit on a humbler scale than originally. Beyond it, much of the northern section of the Old Town belongs to the former **Jewish quarter**, centred around ul. Zamenhofa and Rynek Solny. As in so many other eastern towns, Jews made up a significant portion of the population of Zamość – some 45 percent on the eve of World War II. The first Sephardic Jews from L'viv arrived here in the 1580s, their numbers subsequently swelled by kindred settlers from Turkey, Italy and Holland, to be displaced subsequently by the powerful local Askenazi community. With much of eastern Polish Jewry in the grip of the mystical Hasidic revival, uniquely in the Lublin region Zamość developed as a centre for the progressive *Haskalah*, an Enlightenment-inspired movement originating in Germany that advocated social emancipation, the acceptance of "European" culture and scientific and educational progress within the Jewish community. Among its products were **Itzak Peretz** (1851–1915), a notable nineteenth-century Yiddish novelist born here, and **Rosa Luxemburg**, though it's as a radical communist theorist and activist rather than Jewish progressive that she's primarily known.

Most of the buildings in the old Jewish quarter are currently being renovated – another *remont* that looks set to run and run – but from the edge of the building site you can still peer through at some of the old Jewish merchants' houses ranged around the small square. The most impressive Jewish monument, however, is the former **Synagogue**, now a public library, a fine early seventeenth-century structure built as part of Zamoyski's original town scheme. Following wartime devastation by the Nazis, who used the building as a carpentry shop, the synagogue was carefully renovated in the 1960s, and its exterior elevations reconstructed. Traces of the dazzling original decoration have survived too, notably the rich polychromy that once filled the interior, sections of which are still visible behind the stacks of library books filling the main body of the building, the ceiling vaulting and the stone **Aron ha Kodesh**.

The fortifications

East across ul. Łukasińskiego takes you over onto the former town **fortifications**. Designed by Morando, the original Italian-inspired fortifications consisted of a set of seven bastions interspersed with three main gates with wide moats and artificial lakes blocking the approaches to the town on every side. After holding out so impressively against the Cossacks and the Swedes, the whole defensive system went under in 1866, when the Russians ordered the upper set of battlements to be blown up and the town fortress liquidated. A park area covers much of the battlements now, leaving you free to wander along the tops and see for yourself why the marauding Swedes drew a blank at Zamość. The ornamental **Old Lvov Gate**, another Morando construction, bricked up in the 1820s, and the **New Lvov Gate**, added at the same time, complete the surviving elements of the fortifications.

Across pl. Wolności the former **Franciscan Church**, part of an old monastic complex and now an art school, is only half the building it used to be, having lost its Baroque towers in the 1870s. Into the southern section of the Old Town the former Orthodox **Church of St Nicholas**, at the bottom of ul. Bazylianska, a small domed building originally used by the town's many Eastern merchants, still has some of its fine original Renaissance stucco, uncovered during recent renovations of the interior.

The Rotunda

The Nazis spared the buildings of Zamość, but not its people. In the **Rotunda**, a nineteenth-century arsenal south of the Old Town on ul. Wyspiańskiego, over eight thousand local people were executed by the Germans; a simple museum housed in its tiny cells (May–Sept Tues–Sun 9am–6pm; Oct–April Tues–Sun 10am–5pm) tells the story of the town's wartime trauma. In addition, three cells have recently been dedicated to documenting the Soviet-instigated wartime massacre of Polish army officers at Katyń. In fact, Zamość (preposterously renamed "Himmlerstadt") and the surrounding area were the target of a brutal "relocation" scheme of the kind already carried out by the Nazis in Western Prussia. From 1942 to 1943 nearly three hundred villages were cleared of their Polish inhabitants and their houses taken by German settlers – all part of Hitler's plan to create an Aryan eastern bulwark of the Third Reich. The remaining villages were apparently left alone only because the SS didn't have enough forces to clear them out.

Practicalities

Zamość is easiest approached by bus from Lublin; trains take a very roundabout route. The main **bus station** is roughly 2km east of the town centre (buses #10, 22 or 59 will take you into the centre); for details of departures, check at the **tourist office** at Rynek 13, underneath the town hall (Mon–Fri 8am–5pm, Sat & Sun 9am–4pm). The nearby *Orbis* office at ul. Grodzka 13 deals with advance bus and train tickets. Both offices can help with **private accommodation**.

The best **hotel** option is the ugly and characterless *Renesans*, behind the tourist office on ul. Grecka 6 (☎084/2001; ③); it's moderately priced and conveniently close to the Old Town, but very full in summer. A cheap, central alternative is the basic *Hotel Marta*, ul. Zamenhofa 11 (☎084/2639; ②), next to the synagogue, though it is again extremely busy in season. The *Hotel Jubilat* at al. Wyszńskiego 52 (☎084/6400; ⑤) is noisy, more expensive and a fair walk from the Old Town. The **youth hostel**, ul. Sikorskiego 6 (☎084/6615; June–Aug), is better placed, between the bus station and Old Town. An especially cheap alternative is the *Sportowy*, ul. Królowej Jadwigi 14 (☎084/6011; ②), a hotel with its own restaurant, located in a sports complex, 500m west of the centre on the way to the train station. The *PTTK* **campsite** on ul. Królowej Jadwigi is some way to the west of the town centre.

Eating and drinking

Under the influences of privatization and a growing tourist trade, **restaurant** and **bar** life in the Old Town is gradually picking up. Outside the summer season, though, most places shut early in the evening, and anytime after about 8pm you may be hard-pressed to get a meal. In the Old Town the *Royal Kadex*, ul. Żeromskiego 22, is a passable restaurant-cum-disco, as are the established *Staromiejska*, ul. Pereca 12, and *Centralka*, ul. Żeromskiego 3, which provides the usual soup-and-pork-chop menu. The *bar mleczny* at ul. Staszica 10 is exacly what you'd expect of an old-time milk bar, good for a cheap, straightforward daytime fill-up. Of the hotels, the café in the *Renesans*, when not being repaired (which seems to be quite often), serves up standard breakfasts of eggs, cheese and coffee, as well as basic daytime fare. Like the hotel itself, the restaurant in the *Jubilat* hotel is a touch more upmarket, though the menu is fairly limited.

In summer, the square is lined with **outdoor cafés** and ice cream stalls. The appropriately named *Café Padua*, Rynek 23, with a wonderful original ceiling, does a respectable coffee. The slick *Ratuszowa*, strategically placed under the town hall, is top of the new-look Zamość cafés: as well as decent cappuccinos and cakes they do meals during the daytime. For **drinking** the *Piwnica Pod Arkadami*, Rynek 25, is a basement beer dive, another beery option being the bar round the back of the *Renesans* hotel.

Entertainment

If you happen to be in town at the right time there are several annual cultural happenings worth checking out. The Zamość **Jazz Festival**, usually held in the last week of May, is popular with Polish and other Slav jazzers, as is the **International Meeting of Jazz Vocalists** in the last week of September. **Theatrical Summer**, a drama festival held in the latter part of June and early July, features some excellent theatre groups from all over the country, many of whom perform on the stairway in front of the town hall.

At other times of the year, there's not much action. The *Jazz Club Kosz* at ul. Zamenhofa 5 (entrance through the rear courtyard) has a disco (Fri & Sat nights) and occasional live jazz and blues bands on Friday nights.

The Roztoczański National Park

Twenty kilometres southwest of Zamość, the wild expanses of the **Roztoczański National Park** are a must for both walkers and naturalists. Part of the huge former Zamoyski family estates that used to cover much of the Zamość region, the park, created in 1974, occupies a central section of the Roztocze district, a picturesque region of undulating, forest-covered hills, rising to 390m at their highest point, with a varied and colourful flora and fauna, including over 160 different species of birds.

Cutting across the heart of the park is the beautiful and largely uncontaminated River Wieprz, which has its source just east of the park. Most of the park consists of forest and woodland, with pine, fir and pockets of towering beeches (up to 50m high) the commonest trees. Grey stalks, cranes, lizards, wild horses, a wealth of butterflies and, along the banks of the Wieprz, beavers, are among the creatures populating the area.

Frequent local bus and train connections from Zamość to **ZWIERZYNIEC**, at the western edge of the park, make a day trip a feasible prospect. One popular trail is the marked path running south from Zwierzyniec to the edge of the forest in the direction of the village of Sochy, with fine scenic views along the way. Maps and further detailed information about hiking routes in the park are available from the director's office, ul. Plażowa 2, Zwierzyniec (☎084/10 81 26).

Rzeszów

RZESZÓW was essentially a postwar attempt to revive the southeast, providing industry and an administrative centre for an area that had seen the previous half-dozen decades' heaviest emigration. The city's population of over 100,000 is evidence of some sort of success, even if this rapid expansion has produced a soulless urban sprawl. Yet the hinterland still consists of the small villages characteristic of this corner of Poland for centuries, which explains why in 1980 Rzeszów became a nucleus of Rural Solidarity, the independent farmers' and peasants' union formed in the wake of its better-known urban counterpart. If the above suggests you might not want to spend Christmas in Rzeszów, there's little that a visit will do to persuade you otherwise: essentially this is a city to see in transit.

The Old Town

Everything worth seeing is located within the compact confines of the Old Town area, south of the main stations across al. Piłsudskiego. First stop are the two former **synagogues** facing each other along ul. Bożnica at the edge of pl. Ofiara Getta, the heart of the old ghetto area and all that remains of the town's formerly sizeable Jewish population. The **New Synagogue**, a large seventeenth-century brick building designed by Italian architect Giovanni Bellotti, is now an artists' centre: wander up to the *kawiarnia* on the first floor and you'll probably find someone able to point out the surviving features of the original synagogue. The **Old Synagogue**, over a century older and gutted by the Nazis, houses the town archives as well as a recently formed research institute devoted to the history of the Rzeszów Jewry.

A short walk south brings you to the Rynek, a bustling, chaotic place still in the throes of major restoration: if work ever finally finishes it will be a fine location. Plumped in the square centre, as ever, is the **Town Hall**, also in the process of receiving a facelift, a squat sixteenth-century edifice remodelled in the nineteenth with a fine Renaissance facade. The **Ethnographic Museum** (Tues–Thurs 9am–2pm, Fri 9am–5pm) in one of the older burghers' houses on the south side of the square contains a small but well-presented collection of local ethnography. Exhibits include a fine set of the colourful Eastern-influenced traditional local costumes and some good examples of the naive folk art of the region, as well as a couple of complete wayside shrines of the kind you find dotting local highways and byways. The statue of Kosciuszko on the square, removed by the Germans in 1940, was finally replaced in 1980, thanks to the efforts of the local Solidarity committee.

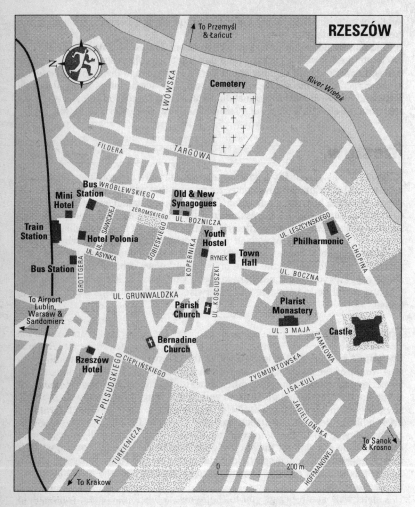

Directly west of the Rynek is the main **Parish Church**, a Gothic structure which was given its current Baroque overlay in the eighteenth century, notable exceptions being the fine Renaissance decoration in the vaulted nave ceiling and a number of early tombstone tablets up by the altar. On south down ul. 3 Maja, the main shopping thoroughfare, brings you to a former Piarist monastery complex, home of the well-stocked **Town Museum** (Tues & Fri 10am–5pm, Wed–Thurs 10am–3pm, Sat & Sun 9am–2pm) ranged around the monastery courtyard. As well as Polish and European painting, the collection includes the frescoes that once decorated the former cloister arcade and a revealing set of exhibits detailing the mass emigrations from the region in the late nineteenth century. Inevitably, the exhibition finishes with details of both local resistance and Nazi atrocities against the town's Jewish population during World War II.

The **Monastery Church** next door has a typically elegant Baroque facade fashioned by Tylman of Gameren in the early 1700s, and a small but well-proportioned interior.

On to the bottom of ul. 3 Maja, past the post office, takes you past the **Lubomirski Palace**, another early eighteenth-century Tylman of Gameren creation set in a small, quiet park away from the town bustle. An elegant-looking palace originally owned by one of the country's most powerful aristocratic clans, it's now occupied by the local music academy. From here it's a short way further south to the walls of the **Old Town Castle**, currently under renovation (*remont*), a huge seventeenth-century edifice also once owned by the Lubomirskis. The castle was converted into a prison by the Austrian rulers of Galicia – of which Rzeszów was a part – at the turn of the century and is now the law courts.

Finally, back up in the northwest corner of the Old Town is the **Bernardine Church**, another sumptuous early seventeenth-century structure considerably more attractive than the nearby Monument to the Revolutionary Movement, a typically ugly, grey communist-era offering that has thankfully now finally been removed from the front of local tourist brochures.

Practicalities

The **bus and train stations** are adjacent to each other, a short walk north from the centre. The city also has an **airport** (11km out), which could provide a useful route into the region from Warsaw, Gdańsk or Szczecin; there is a *LOT* office at pl. Zwycięstwa 6 (☎017/33234 or 33550). **Tourist information** is available from the main tourist office at ul. Żeromskiego 2 (☎017/38264), between the stations and the Old Town, and from *Orbis*, Rynek 7 (☎017/34366). The *PTTK* office, Rynek 22 (☎017/33338), is particularly useful if you're travelling on south to the Bieszczady Mountains. All offices are open Monday to Friday 9am to 5pm.

All the **hotels** are reasonably close to the stations. The *Rzeszów*, al. Cieplińskiego 2 (☎017/37441; ④), is reasonable in the drab, unexciting way of many communist-era Polish hotels. The newly renovated *Polonia*, ul. Grottgera 16 (☎017/32061; ③), is cheaper and very close to the stations. The *Sportowy*, ul. Jałowego 23a (☎017/34077; ②), is a cheap, no-frills-attached sports hotel and slightly further out. Right by the station at plac Kilińskiego 6 is the *MINI Hotel* (☎017/35676; ②), a typical *PTTK* place – cheap, basic, but all right. The all-year **youth hostel** (☎017/34430) is well situated bang in the square at Rynek 25, the major disadvantage being the non-stop noise from the pizzeria and all-night bar occupying the ground floor. The plushest option in town is the *Budimex*, ul. Podwisłocze 48 (☎017/62 68 35, fax 62 77 41; ⑦), a recently completed, luxury four-star joint south of the river.

Among **restaurants**, the *Rzeszów* hotel is the business types' hang-out, offering local specialities including duck, goose and wonderful *Lezajsk* beer from the nearby town of the same name. Ethnic variety is provided by the *Hungaria* at ul. Dąbrowskiego 33, a good Hungarian restaurant south of the Old Town centre, and the *Ha-Long* off the Rynek at ul. Matejki 2, an upmarket Chinese place aimed at businesspeople and tourists. The *Alko*, on the north side of the Rynek, is a pizza place with accompanying disco. Alternatives are the *Rarytas* at ul. Marszałkowska 15 and the *Rzeszówska* at ul. Kościuszki 9, both within walking distance of the centre. If you prefer **milk bars**, there's the *Centralny* at ul. 3 Maja 8, or the downstairs bar of the *PTTK* hostel. **Cafés** are one of the city's growth industries, with both the Rynek and bustling ul. 3 Maja, the main shopping street, already boasting a number of bright new Western-style hang-outs. *Club No. 1*, ul. Hetmańska 20, south of the Old Town, is a modernist café-restaurant popular with the local trendies.

Appropriately enough for a town with such a long history of emigration, the **Festival of Polonia Music and Dance Ensembles** takes place in Rzeszów in June and July every third year (next one is in 1998). It's a riotous assembly of groups from *emigracja* communities all over the world, including Britain, France, USA, Argentina and Australia.

Tarnów

First impressions of **TARNÓW** are less than promising. A major regional centre with a population close on 100,000, much of the city is decidedly lacking in character. At the heart of Tarnów, though, is a medieval Old Town area that more than makes up for the rest in interest. As you'd expect, the background story here is essentially commercial. Founded in the 1330s, like several towns in the southeast of the country, Tarnów rapidly grew fat on the back of the lucrative trade routes running east from Kraków down into Hungary and east on into the Ukraine. Long the seat of the wealthy local Tarnowski family, it remained a privately owned town right up to the end of the eighteenth century. Under their patronage it grew to become an important Renaissance-era centre of learning within the Polish Commonwealth, a branch of the Jagiellonian University in Kraków being set up here in the mid-1500s.

Later centuries of wars and partition brought the inevitable decline, and in this century, Tarnów's significant and long-standing Jewish population was a particular target for the Nazis. Today, the city's notable scattering of surviving Jewish monuments combine with the historic Old Town centre to provide an enjoyable short visit, with enough here to detain you for a good day's sightseeing.

The Old Town

The well-preserved central Old Town area, only a small part of modern Tarnów, retains all the essentials of its original medieval layout. A chequerboard network of angular streets, cobbled alleyways and open squares, the oval-shaped Old Town is ringed by the roads built over the ruins of the sturdy defensive walls, pulled down by the Austrians in the late nineteenth century. Within the area, the compact medieval ensemble retains its original two-tier layout, stone stairways connecting the lower and upper sections of the area.

The Rynek

Approached from the south side of town the steps up from the lower level lead on to the **Rynek**. Overall there's an enjoyably relaxed feel to the place, with arcaded Renaissance burghers' mansions occupying sections of the square, notably the trio of parapeted houses on the **north** side, the facades adorned with their colourful original friezes. The central building of the three (no. 21) is the entrance to an extension of the Town Museum (same opening times as below) displaying varying exhibitions of works by contemporary local and national artists: an additional plus here are the number of wood-beamed rooms retaining their Renaissance

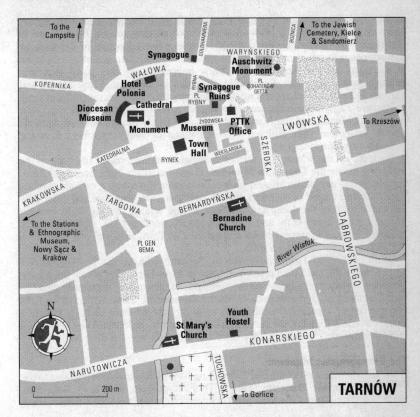

To the
Campsite

KOPERNIKA

WAŁOWA

Synagogue

WARYŃSKIEGO

Auschwitz
Monument

To the Jewish
Cemetery, Kielce
& Sandomierz

BOŻNICA

GOŁDHAMMERA

Hotel
Polonia

RYBNA

Synagogue
Ruins

PL
RYBNY

PL
BOHATERÓW
GETTA

Diocesan
Museum

Cathedral

Monument

Museum

ZYDOWSKA

PTTK
Office

LWOWSKA

To Rzeszów

KATEDRALNA

RYNEK

Town
Hall

WEKSLARSKA

SZEROKA

KRAKOWSKA

TARGOWA

BERNARDYŃSKA

Bernadine
Church

To the Stations
& Ethnographic
Museum,
Nowy Sącz &
Kraków

PL GEN
BEMA

River Wisłok

DĄBROWSKIEGO

N

Youth
Hostel

St Mary's
Church

KONARSKIEGO

NARUTOWICZA

TUCHOWSKA

0   200 m

To Gorlice

TARNÓW

fresco decoration. Centrepiece of the square, though, is the fifteenth-century
Town Hall, a chunky, single-storey building with a roofed circular tower and an
arched Renaissance brick parapet topped by a series of sculpted animal figures, a
device reminiscent of the Sukiennice in the town's former trading rival, Kraków.
The attractive Renaissance portal on the south side of the building takes you
through into the main **Town Museum** (Tues & Thurs 10am–5pm, Wed & Fri
9am–3pm, Sat & Sun 10am–2pm) housed within. Several rooms here also have
their original polychrome decoration, notably the long central room which
displays a typical set of Polish seventeenth- and eighteenth-century portraits,
members of the wealthy local Rzewuski and Sanguszko families sporting Eastern-
influenced period Sarmatian dress being well to the fore. In addition there's a
wealth of exhibits relating to local hero Józef Bem (see box p.316.) and his military wanderings, other rooms containing a largish assortment of European furniture, porcelain, art and sculpture of the same era.

The Cathedral, Diocesan Museum and around
West of the Rynek on pl. Katedralny stands the Gothic **Cathedral**, a cheerful-
looking statue of the Pope greeting you near the entrance. Though much rebuilt
in subsequent centuries, the rather gloomy interior still has a fair bit of its early

Gothic and Renaissance decoration. As well as the early sixteenth-century entrance portal (featuring some fine stone polychromy topped by a figure of Christ and the Madonna), the cathedral boasts a fine collection of Renaissance tombstones, a number executed by the group of noted Italian sculptors employed at the royal court in Kraków. Particularly impressive are the grand sixteenth-century memorial to **Jan Tarnowski**, designed by Giovanni Maria Mosca and surrounded with friezes representing his military triumphs; the magnificent tomb of Barbara Tarnowska in the nave, the slender relief by Bartolomeo Berecci with a frame by Mosca; and the Mannerist Ostrogski family monument, a sumptuous marble ensemble with sculpted representations of family members kneeling beneath a crucifix at the centre.

Back out on the square, the former collegiate buildings round the back of the cathedral house the **Diocesan Museum** (Tues–Sat 10am–3pm, Sun 9am–2pm), the oldest and one of the biggest such collections in the country; notable exhibits here include a couple of roomfuls of Gothic religious art, sculpture and other arte-facts chiefly from the local Kraków–Sącz artistic school, the highlight being a graceful set of fourteenth- and fifteenth-century wooden *pietà*. Out behind the museum, here as at several points around the Old Town area, you can see surviv-ing sections of the Old Town walls.

South of the Old Town and across ul. Bernardyńska, on the bustling market square below the main road is the birthplace of **Józef Bem**, after whom the square is named, a plaque on a house on the north side of the square commemorating the fact. East along ul. Bernardyńska stands the **Bernardine Church**, part of the forti-fied monastery complex established here in the late fifteenth century: clearly a grand place in its heyday, the surviving remnants of the original building decoration include some attractive and richly sculpted Renaissance wooden choir stalls.

The Ethnographic Museum

A ten-minute walk west of the Old Town along busy ul. Krakowski brings you to the local **Ethnographic Museum** (Tues & Thurs 10am–5pm, Wed & Fri 9am–3pm, Sat & Sun 10am–2pm). The focal point of interest here is the set of exhibits relating

---

JÓZEF BEM

Born in Tarnów in the early Partition years, General **Józef Bem** (1794–1850) was a leading figure in the failed 1830–31 Uprising against Poland's tsarist rulers, a role for which he soon became widely celebrated. A prototype of the dashing military figures beloved of the Polish Romantic tradition, the swashbuckling general is almost equally renowned in Hungary for his heroic part in the 1848 rising in Vienna, immediately after which he joined the leadership of the anti-Habsburg forces in Hungary. Heroic adventurer to the core, following the failure of the Hungarian revolt Bem travelled east to join Turkish forces in their struggle with Russia, assuming the name Murat following a rapid (and doubtless tactically appro-priate) conversion to Islam. However, before having the chance to do much militar-ily for the Turks he died, in Aleppo, Syria, his cult status among resistance-minded Poles already safely assured. One of many "oppositional" figures from Polish history the country's former communist rulers were anxious to play down, in recent years Bem has been the subject of a welter of monuments that have gone up around his home town, the most recent addition being a statue of the man on the eastern edge of the Old Town raised by the Polish–Hungarian Friendship Society, a move illustrative of the historic sense of communality between the two countries.

to the local **Roma** (gypsy) population and more generally to the history of the Roma in Poland. Although Roma arrived in Poland at an early stage historically, they have never settled in the country in the same way, for example, as they have in the neighbouring Czech and Slovak republics. From a pre-World War II population estimated at 50,000, their numbers declined at the hands of the Nazis, with up to 35,000 perishing in the concentration camps. Into the 1990s, the population has been swelled by influxes from nearby countries, notably Romania. The Tarnów region has long been a centre for Roma in Poland, and it's this that explains the documentary exhibition, including an absorbing collection of photographs, relating to their culture. In addition, there are a group of four traditional Roma caravans displayed in the yard at the back of the museum. In summer, a traditional Roma camp is recreated in the yard, accompanied by occasional folklore shows.

Jewish Tarnów

East of the Rynek takes you into what used to be the **Jewish-inhabited section** of the town, a fact recalled in the names of streets such as ul. Żydowska and Wekslarska ("money-lenders"). Jews have a long history in Tarnów: the first settlers arrived here in the mid-fifteenth century, and right into the pre-World War II era Jews constituted roughly forty percent of the town's population. The town also became an important centre of Hasidism during the nineteenth century. Following their capture of the town in 1939 the Nazis rapidly established a ghetto area to the east of the Old Town, filling it with all local Jews as well as many transported in from other parts of the country. At its height the population of the massively overcrowded ghetto area rose to 40,000. Between June 1942 and September 1943, virtually the entire ghetto population was either shot or deported to the death camps, principally Auschwitz, and most of the area itself was destroyed. A few Jewish monuments, however, remain in and around the Old Town area.

Architecturally the moody, narrow streets around ul. Żydowska, all of which escaped wartime destruction, are essentially as they were before the war, with traces of the characteristic *mezuza* boxes visible in a couple of doorways. The battered *bimah* covered by a four brick pillared ceiling that stands forlornly in the middle of a small empty square north of ul. Żydowska is what remains of the magnificent sixteenth-century **synagogue** that stood here until the Nazis gutted it in November 1939. Over ul. Wałowa into ul. Goldhammer, named after a prominent local politician from the turn of the century, no. 1 houses the town's only remaining **functioning synagogue** (Sun 1–3pm), while no. 5, a classicist building from the 1890s, is the former home of the local Jewish Credit Company. Turning east into ul. Waryńskiego, past the corner with ul. Kupiecka, where the gate to the Nazi ghetto area stood, the corner of ul. Nowa is the former site of the **New Synagogue**, the biggest and most ornate in the town. Also known as the "Jubilee of Franz Joseph Synagogue" (it was consecrated on the emperor's birthday in 1908), the place burned for three days in 1939 before the Nazis finally resorted to blowing up the remains. The bottom of ul. Nowa leads onto pl. Bohaterów Getta. Across the square is the Moorish-looking **ritual bathhouse**, currently being renovated and converted into an office building: it was from here that a group of 728 local Jews was transported to Auschwitz in June 1940, the first inmates of the camp, a fact commemorated by the monument off the square on ul. Dębowa.

Final stop is the **Jewish Cemetery**, a fifteen-minute walk north along ul. Nowodąbrowska. One of the largest and oldest Jewish graveyards in Poland, the cemetery was established as early as the 1580s, though the oldest surviving gravestone dates from considerably later. Surprisingly untouched by the Nazis, and still in pretty good shape, the overgrown cemetery contains a large number of tombstones, the emphasis being on the traditional type of tablet in which biblical and other illustrative reliefs are used only sparingly. Next to the entrance way on ul. Słoneczna (the cemetery's original gates are now in the Holocaust Museum in New York), stands a monument to the Jews of Tarnów incorporating a column from the devastated New Synagogue.

Practicalities

The main **bus and train stations** are situated next to each other on the southwest side of town, a twenty-minute walk from the Old Town centre – bus #41 drops you on the edge of pl. Katedralna at the southern side of the Old Town. For **tourist information**, the *PTTK* office is at ul. Żydowska 20 (☎014/22 22 00), with the office in the *Hotel Tarnovia* (see below) a useful alternative.

Tarnów's top **hotel** is the *Tarnovia*, ul. Kościuszki 10 (☎014/21 26 71, fax 21 27 44; ⑥), near the train station, a reasonably upmarket place. Other alternatives are the serviceable *Polonia*, ul. Wałowa 21 (☎014/21 33 36; ③), strategically located on the northern rim of the Old Town, the small and lower-grade *PTTK*-run *Pod Murami*, ul. Żydowska 16 (☎014/21 62 29; ③), the only advantage here being the central location, and the better-quality *Pod Dębem*, ul. Heleny Marusarz 9 (☎014/ 21 00 20; ④), well east of town to the north of the main Rzeszów road. The all-year **youth hostel** at ul. Konarskiego 17 (☎014/21 69 16) is a short walk south of the Old Town area and has its own restaurant; buses #1, 8 or 25 from the stations pass close by. You can **camp** at the site at ul. Piłsudskiego 4 (☎014/21 51 24) on the northern side of town – bus #30 from the train station will take you there.

Tarnów doesn't exactly bristle with good **restaurants**, a notable exception being the *Kemora*, ul. Żydowska 13, which boasts of being the only Roma-run restaurant in the country, and worth trying for that reason alone. Unless you want snack food – plentifully available at the fast-food joints springing up all over the town – the hotels, notably the *Tarnovia* and *Pod Dębem*, are the best alternatives, followed by the *Hong Kong*, ul. Dąbrowskiego, a passable and cheap Chinese place.

East from Rzeszów

From Rzeszów the main road and rail line head towards the Ukrainian borderlands. A characteristic eastern mix of villages, farmsteads and wayside shrines is the region's main feature, along with a smattering of historic towns and aristocratic palaces, notably at **Łańcut**, **Leżajsk** and **Jarosław**. All are within an easy travelling distance of Rzeszów, a mix of local bus and train providing the main means of **transport** around the area.

Łańcut

First impressions of the **Castle** that dominates the centre of **ŁAŃCUT** (pronounced "Winesoot"), 17km east of Rzeszów, suggest that it must have seen rather more high-society engagements than military ones. The first building on the site, constructed by the Pilecki family in the second half of the fourteenth century, was, however, burnt down in 1608 when royal troops ambushed its robber-baron owner Stanisław Stadnicki, known by his contemporaries as "The Devil of Łańcut" (see box p.320). The estate was then bought by Stanisław Lubomirski, who set about building the sturdier construction that forms the basis of today's castle. Following contemporary military theory, the four-sided castle was surrounded by a pentagonal outer defence of moat and ramparts, the outlines of which remain.

The fortifications were dismantled in 1760 by Izabella Czartoryska (see "Puławy", p.295), wife of the last Lubomirski owner, who turned Łańcut into one of her artistic salons, laid out the surrounding park and built a theatre in the castle. Louis XIII of France was among those entertained at Łańcut during this period, and the next owners, the Potocki family, carried on in pretty much the same style, Kaiser Franz Josef being one of their guests. Count Alfred Potocki, the last private owner, abandoned the place in the summer of 1944 as Soviet troops advanced across Poland. Having dispatched six hundred crates of the castle's most precious objects to liberated Vienna, Potocki himself then departed, ordering a Russian sign reading "Polish National Museum" to be posted on the gates. The Soviets left the castle untouched, and it was opened as a museum later the same year.

The Castle

Forty or so of the **Castle's** hundreds of rooms are open to the public (mid-April to mid-Oct Tues–Sat 9am–2.30pm, Sun 9am–4pm; mid-Jan to mid-April & mid-Oct to end Nov Tues–Sun 10am–2.30pm; closed Dec–Jan 15; last entry 1hr before closing), and in summer they are crammed with organized tour groups. Ask at the ticket office if one of the two English-speaking guides can take you round – they're worth it for the anecdotes. If you're really lucky your guide might be the highly knowledgeable museum curator.

Most of the interesting rooms are on the **first floor** (though not all of them are always kept open), reached by a staircase close to the entrance hall, which is large enough to allow horse-drawn carriages to drop off their passengers. The **corridors** are an art show in themselves: family portraits and busts, paintings by seventeenth-century Italian, Dutch and Flemish artists, and eighteenth-century classical copies commissioned by Izabella. Some of the nearby bedrooms have beautiful inlaid wooden floors, while the bathrooms have giant old-fashioned bath-tubs and enormous taps.

Moving through the **Chinese apartments**, remodelled by Izabella at the height of the vogue for chinoiserie, and through the **ballroom** and **dining room**, you reach the **old study**, decorated in frilliest Rococo style – all mirrors and gilding – and with a fine set of eighteenth-century French furniture. In the west corner of this floor, the domed ceiling of the **Zodiac Room** still has its Italian seventeenth-century stucco decorations. Beyond is the old **library**, where among the leather tomes you'll find bound sets of English magazines like *Country Life* and *Punch* from the 1870s – which only goes to show how the old European aristocracy stuck together.

On the **ground floor**, the **Turkish apartments** contain a turbaned portrait of Izabella and a suite of English eighteenth-century furniture. Don't miss the extraordinary eighty-seater **Łańcut theatre** commissioned by Izabella: as well as the ornate gallery and stalls, the romantic scenic backdrops are still there, as is the stage machinery to crank them up and down.

THE DEVIL OF ŁAŃCUT

In an era replete with tales of rapacious brigands and swashbuckling freedom-loving heroes, the figure of **Stanisław Stadnicki** (c.1560–1616) stands out from the crowd. Brought up in a remote Carpathian outpost by independent-minded parents – his father, after whom Stanisław was named, was a staunch Arian (see p.436) eventually excommunicated for his religious incalcitrance, while his mother came from the Zborowskis. After his parents' early deaths, the young Stadnicki, together with his six brothers, inherited the family's properties. A sign of things to come was provided by his adoption of the motto *Aspettate e odiate* ("Wait and hate").

After several years participating in military expeditions in Hungary and Muscovy, acquiring a commendation for conspicuous bravery in the field, Stadnicki returned to Poland. Angered by lack of payment for his services Stadnicki seized the estate at **Łańcut**, which became the base for his life of audacious banditry. Nothing was spared his vicious attentions: passing travellers were attacked, properties inexplicably razed to the ground, and local traders and markets systematically terrorized and eventually forced to operate to his benefit through the unlicensed fair he started at nearby Rzeszów. With the help of a motley assortment of spies, torturers, thugs and mercenaries, he extended his grip on the terrorized local populace. Inevitably, Stadnicki's illicit activities eventually caught the attention of the authorities and in 1600 he was sued at the Crown Tribunal in Lublin by another local magnate over his illegal operations at the Rzeszów fair, to which Stadnicki responded by leading an armed raid on his opponent's nearby estate. The conflicts surrounding Stadnicki multiplied. An active participant in the noble *Rakosz* (rebellion) against Zygmunt III in 1605, his public denunciations of the king as a "perjurer, sodomite and card-sharper" can hardly have endeared him to the authorities.

One of Stadnicki's favourite ways of goading his opponents was to circulate libellous verses about them. Eventually, this proved too much for one of his intended victims. In 1608 the nobleman **Łucasz Opaliński**, the subject of a withering Stadnicki broadside entitled "A Gallows for my Guest", retaliated by storming the castle at Łańcut, where prodigious quantities of loot were discovered in the cellars, and massacring everyone there – except Stadnicki, who in characteristic fashion just managed to escape in time. Bloodied, but unbowed, Stadnicki eventually returned to to the area in a bid to pick up his malevolent career once more. Things were never the same again, however: pursued relentlessly by Opaliński's Cossack guard and eventually given away in the hills by his personal servant, a mortally wounded Stadnicki was finally beheaded with his own sword. Symptomatically for a country where the "Golden Freedom" was cherished so highly among the nobility, the references to Stadnicki from his contemporaries suggest that the man's claimed independence and Wild West-style championing of the spirit of liberty were at least as significant for many as his vindictive destructiveness.

The **Carriage Museum** (same hours as the castle) in the old coach house is a treat, including horse-drawn vehicles for every conceivable purpose, from state ceremonies to delivering the mail. Next door, the **old stables** house a large and fabulous collection of Ruthenian **icons**, so numerous that they are hung from the walls in huge racks. More storeroom than real exhibition, it's nevertheless possible to view a portion of the collection – the majority of it taken from the Uniate and Orthodox churches of the surrounding region.

The Town

Łańcut town has a couple of other main points of interest: the old **Synagogue**, close to the castle, just off the main square on ul. Zamkowa, and a newly renovated **Jewish Museum** (June–Sept Tues–Sun 10am–4pm; at other times by request). A simple cream-coloured structure built in the 1760s on the site of an earlier wooden synagogue, the interior survived the Nazi era relatively intact, preserving an authentic and virtually unique taste of what scores of similar such synagogues throughout Poland would have looked like in the pre-World War II era. The walls and ceiling are a mass of rich, colourful polychrome decoration including stucco bas-reliefs, frescoes, illustrated Hebrew wall prayers, zodiacal signs and false marble ornamentation. In the centre of the building stands the *bimah*, its cupola decorated with some striking frescoes of biblical tales and a memorable depiction of a leviathan consuming its own tail – a symbol for the coming of the Messiah – adorning the inner canopy.

The Hasidic movement that swept through Eastern Europe in the nineteenth century took strong hold among the Jews of Łańcut. The **Jewish Cemetery**, ten minutes south of the town centre off ul. Bohaterow Westerplatte, houses the *ohel* (tomb) of **Reb Horovitz**, a noted nineteenth-century *tzaddik* whose grave remains a place of Hasidic pilgrimage.

Practicalities

Łańcut's **train station** is a taxi ride or fifteen-minute walk north from the centre; the **bus station**, however, is only five minutes' walk from the castle. If you're planning to stay overnight, first choice is the wonderful *Zamkowy* hotel (☎017/25 26 71 or 25 26 72; ③), a period piece occupying the south wing of the castle, with a good **restaurant** just opposite. This small hotel is predictably popular, and in the summer you won't get in unless you've booked months in advance. The only other option is the **PTTK hostel** in the former Dominican monastery at ul. Dominikańska 1 (☎017/25 25 12; ②), just north of the Rynek, which offers five-person dorms only. There's also a restaurant, as well as a *PTTK* **tourist office** here. As an alternative, the *Zamkowy* hotel staff can sometimes help with fixing **private rooms** in town.

Every May, Łańcut Castle hosts the **Łańcut Music Festival** (now into its 35th year), an increasingly prestigious event on the international circuit, with a focus on chamber music. In the summer there are international master classes for aspiring young instrumentalists.

Leżajsk

Thirty kilometres north of Rzeszów on the verges of the River San, **LEŻAJSK** is at first sight a typical bustling market town with a main square, a church and precious little else to show for itself. For many, though, the town's name at least will be familiar thanks to the local brewery, long-established producer of one of the country's leading – and best – range of beers. For Catholic pilgrims, and lovers of organ music, the monastery church in the north of town makes the place the subject of a special journey.

Leżajsk's main attraction is some way north of the town centre: arriving by bus or train at the combined central station it's a two-kilometre walk or bus ride north to the vast **Bernardine Church and Monastery**. Built in the late 1670s inside a fortress-like defensive structure, the vast Baroque basilica is an established and important centre of pilgrimage thanks to an icon of the Madonna and Child placed here, venerated for centuries by Catholics as a miracle-worker. On religious holidays, notably the **Feast of the Assumption** (August 15), the church draws huge crowds. At just about any time of year you're likely to find buses full of school children or OAPs doing the rounds of the church and stations of the cross situated in the woods behind the building. The cavernous church interior is a mass of Baroque decoration, with numerous side altars, religious paintings, some finely carved wooden choir stalls and a huge gilded main altarpiece.

Pride of place, however, goes to the monster Baroque **organ** filling the back of the nave, one of the finest – and certainly one of the most famous – in Poland. With nearly six thousand pipes, four manuals and over seventy different registers, the exquisitely decorated instrument produces a stunning sound more than capable of filling the building. That said, it's badly in need of some restoration work – all profits from the 1995 organ festival (see below) went towards the cost of some essential repairs on the organ.

Services apart, you can also get to hear the organ at the concerts held regularly in summer – check with the tourist offices in Rzeszów for details. The **International Organ Festival** held here every May is a mecca for fellow players and a major musical event well worth coinciding with.

Just south of the monastery gates over ul. Klasztorna is the **Leżajsk Brewery**. You can try the draught version of the tasty local brew at the roadside bar along with the hardened local consumers, or stock up on cans of the stuff at the shop next door. Back into the town centre, the late Renaissance **Parish Church**, east of the square, is worth a quick look, featuring some fine early fresco-work in the nave.

Practicalities

For **accommodation**, the hotel options are the *Pilawa*, Rynek 5 (☎0195/20476; ③), which also has a **restaurant** of sorts, and the *Podmiejski*, ul. Studzienna 2 (☎0195/20154; ③). There's also a **youth hostel** (summer only) near the stations. Virtually every bar or takeaway joint in town serves at least one of the excellent beers produced by the Leżajsk brewery.

Local **buses** run to and from Rzeszów (50mins), Łańcut, Przemyśl, via Jarosław (1hr 30 min), while the train station is on the cross-country line from Sandomierz to Przemyśl.

Jarosław

Nestled at the foot of the San River valley on the main road east to the Ukrainian border, the town of **JAROSŁAW** is one of the oldest in the country. An urban settlement is known to have been established here by the mid-twelfth century, on the site of a stronghold raised by a Ruthenian prince known as Jarosław the Wise some two centuries earlier. The town's strategic location at the nexus of major medieval international trade routes led to its rapid development as a commercial settlement.

In their medieval heyday the fairs held in Jarosław were second only to those of Frankfurt in size, drawing merchants from all over the continent. The most tangible reminder of the mercantile glory days is the **old market complex** at the centre of town, which has preserved the essentials of its medieval layout. Like many towns in the region, Jarosław's large and dynamic local **Jewish population** suffered badly at the hands of the Nazis. Jews established themselves here early on, and the importance of the town fairs to Jewish commercial life throughout Poland was such that the **Council of the Four Lands** (see Lublin, p.282) met regularly here during its seventeenth- and eighteenth-century heyday.

The Town

Focal point of the medieval town centre is the breezy, open central square where the fairs used to be held. Filling the centre is the Gothic **Town Hall**, a smart-looking building topped by a tall spire that was burnt down, like much of the town centre, in 1625 and subsequently remodelled in Baroque and later in neo-Renaissance style, when the raised balcony was added. On several sides the square is lined with the arcaded merchants' houses: while not as grand as those in Zamość, some of the houses are impressive nonetheless, most notably the Renaissance **Orsseti Mansion** on the south side. Built in the 1670s by a wealthy family of Italian merchants, the building has a beautifully decorated upper attic and a typically open, airy arcade. It's also the home of the **Town Museum** (Tues–Thurs, Sat & Sun 10am–2pm, Fri 10am–6pm), which contains an enjoyably offbeat collection of portraits of local priests of all denominations and the local aristocratic Potocki dynasty, period furniture and a brilliant collection of early typewriters, gramophones and polyphones. Looking round also gives you a chance to admire the fine original polychromy decorating several of the grand, wooden-beamed rooms.

The clearest evidence of the town's mercantile past comes from the honeycomb of **cellars** stretching beneath the town square. Originally built as storage space for the merchants trading on the square above, the network of cellars served as an effective hide-out for local people during successive assaults on the town, most notably the Tartar raids of the fourteenth century. The cellars were gradually abandoned during later centuries, but a 150-metre-long section of the (by then) flooded cellars was cleared out by miners in the early 1960s and opened to visitors a decade later.

Subject to demand, **tours** through the cellars are conducted by one of the members of staff at the museum ticket office (same opening hours as the town museum). The entrance is through one of the merchants' houses on the eastern side of the square: from here you descend into the brick-walled passageways – many of the walls are original – and wind your way through the gloom down to a depth of twenty metres at the lowest point, eventually re-emerging where you started. The chill down below is explained by the ingeniously constructed and still functioning ventilation system, good enough to allow meat to be kept here.

North of the square, a short walk along the bumpy, cobbled streets is the **Parish Church**, an imposing late sixteenth-century complex surrounded by the town walls. If you are here when it's open, the *cerkiew* down the hill east of the square, a colourful eighteenth-century construction now in use again by its former Uniate occupants, is also worth a look. Completing the tour of religious architecture the former **Synagogue** northwest of the square on the corner of ul. Opolska, built in 1810, now a school building, is one of several that served the town's once thriving Jewish population. Despite the signs warding them off, the **covered market** (Wiała Targowa) on ul. Grodzka, leading west of the square, is popular with Ukrainian and Russian traders from across the border, who've set up an improvised marketplace of their own out on the south side of the building.

Practicalities

The **bus and train station**, at the bottom of ul. Słowackiego, is a fifteen-minute walk southwest of the Old Town. As yet there's no proper tourist information office, about the best you can find being the *Turysta* office at no. 25 on the north side of the square. The *PTTK* hotel at Rynek 13 (☎0194/2298; ②) is the main **accommodation** option in the town centre, the others being the *Turkus*, ul. Sikorskiego 5a (☎0194/2640; ③), and the basic *City*, ul. Grunwaldzka 1 (☎0194/3515; ③). All three also have **restaurants**: otherwise there's a scattering of cafés and snack bars in the Old Town area. For a taste of local nightlife the *Joker* on ul. Grodzka, open till midnight, is the main diversion.

Przemyśl and around

Overlooking the River San, just 10km from the Ukrainian border, with the foot-hills of the Carpathians in the distance, the grubby but haunting border town of **PRZEMYŚL** has plenty of potential. Climbing the winding streets of the old quarter is like walking back through history to some far-flung corner of the Habsburg empire. As yet, it's very little visited and even by normal Polish standards has a serious dearth of accommodation, restaurants or entertainment. Access is straightforward though, with both trains and buses from Rzeszów and Łańcut.

Founded in the eighth century, Przemyśl is the oldest town in southern Poland after Kraków, and for its first few centuries its location on the borders between Poland and Ruthenia made it a constant bone of contention. Only under Kazimierz the Great did Poles establish final control of the town, developing it as a link in the trade routes across the Ukraine. Przemyśl maintained a commercial pre-eminence for several centuries, despite frequent invasions (notably by the Tartars), but as with many Polish towns, economic decline came in the seventeenth century, particularly after Swedish assaults in the 1650s. Much of the town's character derives from the period after the First Partition, when Przemyśl was annexed to the Austrian empire. In 1873 the Austrians added a huge castle to the town's defences, creating the most important fortress in the eastern Austro-Hungarian Empire. During World War I this region was the scene of some of the fiercest fighting between the Austrians and Russians: throughout the winter of 1914 Russian forces besieged the town, finally starving the city into surrender in March 1915, then losing it again only two months later. The devastation of both town and surrounding region was even more intense then than during the Nazi onslaught 25 years later; the castle was totally destroyed and only small sections of the sturdy fortifications survived the siege, though the old town centre escaped, mercifully unscathed by the intense bombardments.

The Town

The main **train station** (Przemyśl Główny) is within walking distance of the centre. The opening up of the borders to the east of Przemyśl has turned the station area into a sort of mass cultural bazaar-cum-transit camp: at almost any time of day or night the station entrance hall is filled with former Soviet citizens – Ukrainians, Georgians and Armenians as well as Kazakhs and other Central Asian peoples – camped out on the way to or from their homelands. Exotic though the sight may appear, this isn't the place to hang around at night, especially if carrying luggage: as with most of the mainline eastern border transit points along the former Soviet border, mafia-type gangs are already well established in the station area. Similar warnings apply to the **bus station**, just behind on ul. Czarneckiego.

Fragments of the **Austrian fortifications** can be seen on the approach to the Old Town, opposite the Reformed Franciscan Church on the corner of ul. Mickiewicza. Ul. Franciszkańska brings you to the **Rynek**, where the mid-eighteenth-century **Franciscan Church** offers a demonstration of unbridled Baroque, including a wealth of sumptuous interior decoration and a fine columned facade. The same goes for the **Cathedral**, further up the cobbled streets leading up to the castle – its 71-metre belltower points the way. Remnants of the first twelfth-century rotunda can be seen in the crypt, and there's a fine Renaissance alabaster *Pietà* on the main altar, but Baroque dominates the interior, most notably in the Fredro family chapel. The fourteenth-century **Castle**, home to the town theatre and currently under restoration, isn't much to look at, but the view from the ramparts makes the climb worthwhile.

Of the other churches in the Old Town, the seventeenth-century **Jesuit Church** contains an extraordinary pulpit shaped like a ship, complete with rigging. Partisans of Catholic religious paraphernalia can visit the **Diocesan Museum** in the adjacent Jesuit college (Tues–Sun 10am–4pm), which nuns take you round. The seventeenth-century **Carmelite Church** functioned as the Uniate (Greek Catholic) cathedral until 1945, when it was handed over to the Roman

Catholics. The church become the focus of national attention in 1991, following the Polish-Catholic hierarchy's decision to hand the building over to the sizeable local Greek Catholic (Uniate) population, hitherto deprived of their own place of worship. The move sparked a wave of local protest, with parishioners blockading the church and refusing to hand it over. Catholic defiance was quickly met with equally spirited opposition, and for a while, the situation looked as if it might develop into a serious confrontation, with disturbing ethnic undertones and old Ukrainian–Polish scores and prejudices coming to the fore. After several weeks of tense negotiations, the Catholics finally gave in and agreed to give the local Uniates free use of the building, a fact reflected in the makeshift iconostasis now in place in front of the altar.

The old wooden iconostasis from the Carmelite Church is on display in the local **Museum** (Tues–Sun 10am–2pm) housed inside the grand old Uniate bishop's palace, opposite the church. The second floor heralds the museum's main attraction, an excellent collection of icons from the Uniate churches of the surrounding region. The influence of Catholic art and theology on these essentially Orthodox-derived pieces is most evident in the Madonna and Child icons, the Christ Pantocrator figures also being decidedly Roman in feel. Highlights include a mystical early eighteenth-century *Assumption of Elijah* and a fabulously earthy *Day of Judgement* from the same era, which has a team of prancing black devils facing off against a beatific angelic host.

Fifty years ago Przemyśl had much greater ethnic diversity than today: old guidebooks indicate that the area around the Carmelite Church was the **Ruthenian district**. There are two **Orthodox churches** still functioning in the east of the town, both of them nineteenth-century constructions. The **Jewish quarter** was more to the north of the old centre. Numbers 33 and 45 in ul. Jagiellońska were both synagogues before World War II, and there was another across the river – off to the left from ul. 3 Maja, now part of a garage workshop.

The decaying **Jewish Cemetery**, well south of the centre off ul. Słowackiego, still contains a couple of hundred tombs and gravestones.

Practicalities

The well-organized *San* **tourist office**, across the square from the train station at ul. Sowińskiego 4 (☎010/78 56 15), is both an information centre and ticket office. The *Orbis* office next door is another useful resource (☎010/78 33 66).

The best **place to stay** in town – which isn't saying much – is the privately run *Pod Białym Orłem* at ul. Sanocka 13 (☎010/78 61 07; ③); it's twenty minutes' walk west along the river from the station, or take bus #10 or #10A. Inexpensive and peacefully located on the edge of a wood, the hotel has a restaurant serving home-cooked specialities. The *Przemysław* (☎010/78 40 32 or 78 40 33; ②), which is next to the tourist centre at ul. Sowińskiego, 4, is a basic bed-and-breakfast place, popular with the Ukrainian "trade tourist" brigade and generally full in season. The *Hala* at ul. Mickiewicza 30 (☎010/78 38 49), ten minutes' walk east from the station, is of similar quality but is less likely to be full. The teachers' union hostel (*Dom Nauczycielskie NZP*), close to the castle at ul. Chopina 1 (☎010/78 27 68; ③), is more expensive though better quality than the nearby *Podzamcze PTTK* at ul. Waygarta 5 (☎010/78 53 74; ②). Przemyśl's **youth hostel** at ul. Lelewela 6 (☎010/78 61 45) stays open throughout the year, while the *Zamek* **campsite** at ul. Piłsudskiego 8a (May–Sept ☎010/78 56 42), about half a mile west of the old town, has bungalows as well as spaces for tents. If you're in a

ON TO L'VIV

There's no better illustration of the current revival of cross-border ties in Poland than the growing tourist influx to **L'VIV**, 60km across the Ukrainian border. Alongside its cultural cousin, Vilnius, L'viv (Lwów to Poles) was long one of the main eastern centres of Poland: like the Lithuanian capital, too, traditionally this was a city characterized by a diverse, **multicultural population** – three cathedrals, Armenian, Orthodox and Catholic, are still there today. In Polish terms, the city's greatest ascendancy was during the Partitions era, when it became at least as important a centre as Kraków: during the interwar years, too, Polish culture flourished in the city. The postwar loss of the city to the Soviet Union was a cruel blow to Poles – L'viv still has a significant Polish-speaking population – who've always remained strongly attached to the place, as evidenced by the scores of old photo albums and prewar guidebooks you can find in the bookshops these days. The liberalization of border controls in the early 1990s has let in a large influx of Polish visitors, thankfully unaccompanied by demands for the "return" to Polish control of a city that was at the forefront of the recent Ukrainian struggle for independence.

The short hop from Przemyśl makes **a day trip to L'viv** a plausible option. With travel costs minimal, the biggest outlay here is on the **visa** (currently £30/$45 a shot) still required by the Ukrainian authorities – though reports suggest they may yet abolish this, or at least considerably reduce the price. Obtaining a visa in Przemyśl is no problem: they can be bought either at the bus station or from one of the tourist offices grouped off the square in front of the train station. (For once things are easier for Poles, for whom regular cross-border travel is now greatly facilitated by a straightforward voucher system.)

The best cross-border travel option is the **bus service**. Starting from around 6am *PKS* buses depart up to ten times a day for L'viv from Przemyśl bus station – a two-hour journey, border formalities included. Return buses from L'viv run till the early evening, leaving you with a good half day to explore the city. Especially in summer when demand is high it's best to book your bus seat in advance. As an alternative to queuing up at the ticket counters in the bus station itself, several local **travel agencies** will make the bookings for you for a minimal fee, notably the *San* bureau, ul. Sowińskiego 4 and the *Orbis* office next door, visas included. The main disadvantage with regular **train** services that also run regularly across the border is the crowds cramming most of them, the fight to get on and off at both ends ranking with the worst Indian-style scrums. In a bid to help the beleaguered customs officials cope with the cross-border influx, the main L'viv train station is now divided into two sections, one for domestic lines, the other for international trains. As well as long tail-backs at the main international **road** border-crossing point at **Medyka**, 9km east of Przemyśl, continuing reports of armed gangs stopping and robbing foreign vehicles along the highway on the Ukrainian side of the border mean that a **car** trip to L'viv is only for the really adventurous.

car, it's worth considering the *U Medarda pensionat* (☎010/71 84 24; ③), with its own restaurant, in **Dybawka**, about 6km west of Przemyśl on the Krasiczyn road.

The *Białym Orłem* also comes first in the restaurant recommendations, followed by *Pizzeria Margherita*, Rynek 4, a cheap, but good pizza joint. If you want to eat late, there's the *Karpacka* at ul. Kościuszki 5, though you may be subjected to a local "dancing band". In the town centre the *Polonia* at ul. Franciszańska 35, the *Bałtycka* in ul. Dąbrowskiego and the *Kmiecianka* at ul. Wieniawskiego 2 will at least fill you up, while for **milk bar** fans the *Expres*, opposite the station, does the honours. If you have a car you could try the good-quality Hungarian *Eger* at ul. Grunwaldzka 134, some way out on the Rzeszów road, or the *Troika*, ul. Lwowska 18, on the border road – both are bar-restaurants. Polish-style **fast food** is picking up in town, notably in the cafés and bars on and around Franciszkańska, a racy local pool hall on ul. Kazimiera Wielkiego included.

Around Przemyśl

For an excellent view, especially towards the Carpathians, the **Kopiec Tartarski** (Tartar Monument) on the southern outskirts of town is worth a trip: buses #28 and #28A deposit you at the bottom of the hill. Legend says the monument at the top marks the burial place of a sixteenth-century Tartar khan who is reputed to have died nearby.

For a slightly longer excursion from Przemyśl, the obvious destination is **Krasiczyn Castle**, a ten-kilometre ride west of town by bus #5. Built in the late sixteenth century for the Krasicki family by Italian architect Gallazzo Appiani, the castle is a fine example of Polish Renaissance architecture. Extensive restoration is in progress, but you can still see round most of the building, including the courtyard. The wooded **park** that shelters the castle makes a cool, relaxing spot for a stroll. When the Austrian-funded restoration is finally completed (on current form this could well take some time yet), Krasiczyn Castle is supposed to be converted into a conference centre and hotel; till then the place will probably remain out of action – check out the Przemyśl tourist office for the latest details. If you're tempted by the location, there's a pleasant enough hotel next to the castle (☎010/18316; ③) with its own restaurant.

The Sanok region

There are two good routes south from Przemyśl towards the **Bieszczady Mountains**, one direct, the other more circuitous. The first involves a two-hour train journey into and out of the **Ukraine**, ending up in **Ustrzyki Dolne** (see p.333), in the foothills of the Bieszczady. If nothing else, it's a chance to travel into former Soviet territory without a visa. Trains leave once a day – currently 4.35pm – passing through several Ukrainian towns and villages without stopping. Soldiers still ride on board to ensure no-one tries any funny business. Controls used to be rigorous: in the early 1980s some Solidarity activists flushed leaflets in Russian down the toilets on the Soviet side; the train stopped and didn't move until the soldiers had recovered every single one. Nowadays the reduced troop contingent keeps a pretty low profile, but taking photos on the Ukrainian side is still not a very good idea, however innocuous you may find snapshots of passing fields and trees.

The alternative option is to go by bus through **Sanok**, sixty-odd kilometres and a two-hour ride southwest from Przemyśl. The advantage of this route is the journey through the foothills: in spring and autumn the mountains are at their most alluring, the sun intensifying the green, brown and golden hues of the beech forests. If you've the time to spare, consider stopping off at picturesque little towns such as **Bircza** or **Tyrawa Wołoska** to soak up the atmosphere; a number of villages with wooden *cerkwi* are tucked away in easy walking distance of Tyrawa.

Further east through the foothills, the village at **Arłamów**, close to the Ukrainian border, is the site of the decommissioned army HQ where ex-president/former

Solidarity leader Lech Wałęsa was imprisoned during the early days of martial law. A luxury palatial-looking complex that used to double as a Party members' **hunting lodge** is now open to the public. Soldiers still guard the entrance, though you get the feeling that they really don't know who the place belongs to these days. The hunting facilities are currently utilized by classier holiday groups.

Sanok

Perched up on a hilltop above the San valley, **SANOK** looks a sleepy sort of place. Best known within Poland for its rubber and bus factories, whose *AutoSan* vehicles can be seen all over the country, of late the town has begun to pick up economically, largely on the back of increased cross-border trade flowing into the surrounding region. For the southbound traveller, though, the important thing about Sanok is that it's the last real town before the Bieszczady Mountains, which loom through the mists on the horizon.

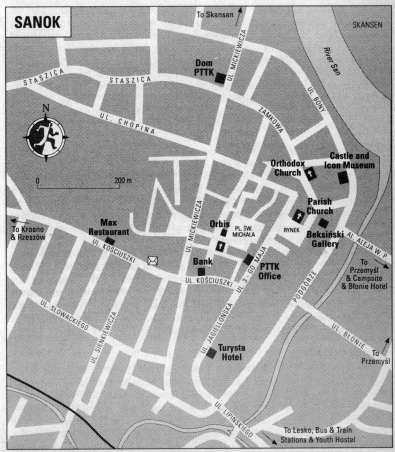

The Town

A number of things in and around the town make it a place worth visiting in its own right, too. The reconstructed fourteenth-century **Parish Church** on the edge of the Rynek hosted the wedding of King Władysław Jagiełło in 1417. Nearby stand the remnants of the sixteenth-century **castle**, built on the site of the original twelfth-century fortress that guarded the main highway running through the town from the southern Carpathians on into the Baltic. Much of the castle is given over to a **Town Museum** (Tues–Sun 10am–4pm), and contains a collection of modern art from all over the region. Across the street from the castle is the **Beksiński Gallery** (Tues–Sun 9am–3pm), devoted to the work of Zdzisław Beksiński, the noted modern Polish artist born in and long-time resident of Sanok. An intriguing selection of his vivid, imaginative canvasses is on display here, though many of the best have long since been bought up by museums abroad.

THE ICON MUSEUM

The main building to head for is the one overlooking the valley, looking like the ancestral pile of some Scottish laird. Two rooms house the fabulous Sanok **Icon Museum** (April 15–Oct 15 Tues 9am–3pm, Wed–Sun 9am–5pm), the largest collection of Ruthenian icons in the world after the one in Moscow. Though most of the pieces on display date from the sixteenth and seventeenth centuries, the oldest comes from the mid-1300s, so the collection gives a clear impression of the development of the **Ukrainian school** of painting, which evolved in tandem with an autonomous and assertive local church.

Unlike Russian and Greek Orthodox iconography, however, much of the work on display here is still pretty unknown to anyone but art historians and specialists, despite its quality. The best of the early icons have both the serenity and severity of Andrei Rublev's greatest works. In contrast, later icons manifest the increasing influence of Western Catholicism – which culminated in the formation of the Uniate Church in 1595 (see box on p.338) – both in their style and subject matter, with an encroaching Renaissance approach to the portraiture. In a few cases, the figures show strong Tartar influences too. Look out too for a large *Icon of Hell*, an icon of a type traditionally housed in the women's section of Orthodox churches: such lurid depictions of the torments of the underworld must have kept a few people in check.

As with all such collections, the presence of these icons is related to postwar "resettlements". With many local villages deserted in the aftermath of "Operation Vistula" (see box on p.338), their wooden *cerkwi* neglected and falling apart, the oldest and most important icons were removed to museums. Genuine artistic concern prompted their removal, but now that local people are returning to the villages and using the churches again, it's high time for the authorities to consider handing at least some of the icons back.

THE SKANSEN

Also worth a visit is the **skansen** in the Biała Góra district, 2km north of the centre (mid-April to mid-Oct Tues–Sun 8am–5pm, mid-Oct to mid-April Tues–Sun 9am–2pm); if you don't want to walk, take a bus north along ul. Mickiewicza to the bridge over the river – the *skansen* is on the other side, spread along the river bank. This open-air museum, one of the best in the country, brings together examples of the different styles of all the region's main ethnic groups – Boyks, Lemks, Dolinianie ("Inhabitants of the Valley") and Pogorzanie. (If you want detailed ethnography, an English guidebook is available at the entrance.) Specimens of every kind of country building have been carefully moved and reassembled here: smithies, inns, granaries, windmills, pigsties and churches. Up on the hillside, a couple of graceful eighteenth-century *cerkwi* nestle in the shade of the trees. In the nineteenth-century school building, you'll find some amazing old textbooks: note too the carefully preserved maps of pre-1914 Poland, showing this area as a region of the Austro-Hungarian province of Galicia – hence the portrait of Kaiser Franz Josef behind the teacher's desk.

Practicalities

The **bus station** is close to the **train station**, about fifteen minutes' walk southeast of the town centre; most buses from here will take you up to the main square. Of the **tourist offices**, the most helpful are the *Turysta* bureau in the hotel of the same name at ul. Jagiellońska 13 (Mon–Sat 9am–5pm), and the *PTTK* office a little further up the road at ul. 3-go Maja 18 (Mon–Fri 8am–4pm; ☎137/32512); if any office has maps and general information, including for the Bieszczady Mountains, the latter will. The *Orbis* office, at ul. Grzegorza 2, deals with tickets.

For an **overnight stay**, the best place in town is the *Turysta* (see above; ☎137/30664; ⑤); it is modern, soulless and quite expensive but worth the price if you can get a top-floor view over the San valley, and the downstairs bar is a weekend hang-out for the Sanok smart set. Other options are the rundown *Dom PTTK* at ul. Mickiewicza 29 (☎137/31439; ③), some way west from the main square, which has its own modest restaurant, and the *Błonie* in the sports centre further on at al. Wojska Polskiego (☎137/30257; ③), on the banks of the River San, with a summer-only *Autocamping* site. The extremely basic **youth hostel** (July–Aug) is at ul. Lipińskiego 34 (☎137/31980), the easterly continuation of the Lesko road. You can **camp** either in Biała Góra, near the *skansen*, or at the *AutoCamping* on al. Wojska Polskiego, situated to the east on the town side of the river.

The privately run *Bartlek* at ul. Padlewskiego 11, a side street on the way to the *skansen* (ask locals for directions), is a reasonable **restaurant**, but open erratically. The *Turysta* apart, there's also *Max*, ul. Kościuszki 24, a little way out of the centre, and a decent pizzeria halfway down central ul. 3-go Maja. Out of town there's the *Adria*, ul. Lipińskiego 58, and the *Dąbrowianka* on ul. Krakowska, the Krosno road. Unless beer rather than food is your main interest, avoid eating at the *Karpacka*, ul. Jagiellońska 24, a grim dive of a place.

Wooden churches around Sanok

If you have your own transport the **wooden church** (*cerkiew*) in ULUCZ, a tiny village 20km north of Sanok on the River San, is worth seeking out. Built in 1510, it's the oldest, and among the finest, of the Boyk *cerkwi* located within Polish territory (others of a similar vintage are all in the Ukraine). A graceful, well proportioned building poised on a hilltop, it boasts a large bulbous dome, fine Baroque iconostasis (though sadly several icons including the entire middle row are now missing following a robbery a few years back) and mural paintings of the Passion and Crucifixion. The key is kept in a house marked by a sign at the village entrance.

At **CZERTEŻ**, immediately north of the main Krosno road, 6km west of Sanok, there's another beautiful Boyk *cerkiew* from 1742, hidden in a clump of trees up above the village. It houses another fine iconostasis, although Roman Catholics have now taken over the church as a place of worship.

Lesko and the foothills

East from Sanok the southbound road passes through Zagórz, the hub of local rail connections, and continues a further 6km to **LESKO**, a tranquil and long-established foothills town that seems to be doing increasingly well out of its strategic tourist location. South off the approach road from Sanok is what remains of the old sixteenth-century town **Castle**, occupied by a fairly posh, but extremely reasonably priced, former miners' holiday centre (☎0137/6268; ②); theoretically at least the place is now open to anybody, though, typically, no one's actually yet got round to advertising the fact. If you fancy staying in what's likely to become a regular hotel, the best thing is just to turn up and ask about rooms: if the conferences the centre now hosts regularly aren't occupying the whole place, they'll happily oblige.

Lesko's other attractions relate to the town's one-time **Jewish community.** Just east off the square stands the former **Synagogue**, a solid-looking Renaissance structure, originally part of the town's defensive system, with a finely sculptured facade reconstructed, like the rest of the building, after World War II, and now home to a local art gallery. Down the hill behind the building and across a stream brings you to the foot of the **Jewish Cemetery**, one of the most beautiful and evocative in the whole country. Hidden from a distance by the trees covering the hillside cemetery, the steps up from the roadside – the Star of David on the gate tells you you're at the right entrance – take you up through a tangled knot of twisted tree trunks and sprawling undergrowth to the peaceful hilltop cemetery site, around which are scattered two thousand-odd gravestones, the oldest dating back to the early 1500s. As in other major surviving cemeteries there's a wealth of architectural styles in evidence, notably a number of ornately decorated Baroque tablets with characteristic seven branched candelabra, recurring animal motifs and often a pair of hands reaching up in prayer towards the heavens from the top of the stone. It's the setting as much as the stones that makes this cemetery so memorable, a powerful testimony to centuries of rural Jewish presence.

Castle apart, the **accommodation** options are the motel at ul. Bieszczadzka 4 (☎137/8081; ③), 500m north on the Sanok road, and the hard-to-find youth hostel (with its own restaurant), 1.5km out on the northern outskirts of town, at al. Jana Pawła II 18 (☎137/6269). There's also a camping site here, nicely situated on the banks of the Sen, with tent space and some bungalows. If you're stopping off between journeys at the bus station on the square in front of the parish church, the *Gyros*, a kebab takeaway on the main square, will keep the wolf from the door. The *piwiarnia Alf* just off the square serves the honeyed *Leżajsk* brew. The best **places to eat** are *Koliba*, Ryek 8, or the castle hotel café.

South from here the bus continues through **UHERCE**, where many Polish tourists veer off towards **Jezioro Solińskie**, a fjord-like artificial lake created in the 1970s for hydroelectric power and watersports purposes. The custom-built lakeside villages of **SOLINA, POLAŃCZYK** and **MYCZKÓW** have more restaurants than anywhere else in the area, but there's little else to recommend them apart from their access to the water. In all three your best bets for **accommodation** now are the numerous workers' holiday houses and camping sites ranged across the water's edge. Yacht and kayak rental can be arranged with the *Bieszczady* tourist office in Solina.

Ustrzyki Dolne

Back on the main road, **USTRZYKI DOLNE**, 25km east of Lesko, is the main base for the mountains, swarming in summer with backpacking students and youth groups, many of them fresh off the afternoon train formerly known as the "Soviet Express" from Przemyśl (see p.324). Otherwise this is a small agricultural town with just a scattering of minor monuments: a synagogue (now a library), a *cerkiew* – both nineteenth century – and several memorials connected with the Ukrainian resistance (see box on p.338).

Accommodation can be very hard to find in the summer hiking season, and completely deserted or closed at any other time of year. Best bets are the *Laworta* at ul. Zielona 1 (☎0137/364; ②), the biggest place in town and so most likely to have a room, the smaller *Strwiąz* off the main square at ul. Sikorskiego 1 (☎0137/303; ③), the *Pensjonat Otryt* at ul. Rzeczna 26 (☎0137/519; ②), and the cheap *ZHP*, ul. Korczaka 11 (☎0137/143; ②), a short walk southwest of the Rynek. Other options worth trying (though again, often full in season) are the *Hotel Bieszczadzka*, on the western edge of the Rynek (☎0137/102; ③), also with its own restaurant. The **PTTK bureau**, at Rynek 14 (☎0137/247), doubles up as a hostel in season (ask about private rooms here also), as does the *Bieszczady* office on the same street. There's plenty of **camping** space, both at the official site on ul. PCK and in the fields around the edge of town. The *Bieszczadzka* hotel **restaurant** aside, the *Pizzeria Romana*, just off the square, is better than most of the other places in town and is the place local youth aims to be seen in.

Getting in and out of town is a taxing business and going anywhere north by train means travelling via Przemyśl. Queues for **buses into the mountains** form early at the stops on the road down from the train station, and everyone has to shove their way on board. Before leaving, stock up in the shops around the station area; supplies of anything edible are unpredictable beyond here.

Krościenko

Nine kilometres north of Ustrzyki Dolne is the village of **KROŚCIENKO**, last train stop before the Soviet border (local buses run here too). The Bieszczady region is full of surprises, and this is one of them. Following the outbreak of civil war in Greece, a small community of Greek partisans and their families escaped to Poland in 1946 and settled in this area. The monument in the village centre is to **Nikos Balojannis**, a Greek resistance hero executed by the generals in Athens soon after his return in 1949. Not expecting to stay long they never made much effort to do up their houses, hence the shabby look of the place. Only a few Greeks remain these days, the younger generation having mostly elected to return to their home country. There's a fine eighteenth-century **cerkiew** in the village too, and another older one a little further north in the Wolica district.

The Bieszczady Mountains

The valleys and slopes of the **Bieszczady Mountains** were cleared of their populations – over eighty percent Boyks – in "Operation Vistula", following the last war (see box, p.338), the majority of the native population being forcibly displaced into the Ukraine. Today, these original inhabitants and their descen-

BIESZCZADY REGION

dants are coming back, but the region remains sparsely populated and is largely protected as national park or nature reserves. The majority of the area is part of the East Carpathian Biosphere Reserve which was established in 1991 with support from the World Bank, which also incorporates similar territory across the border in Slovakia and Ukraine. The reserves are carefully controlled to protect the wildlife, but are open to the public – quite a change from a decade ago, when the Communist Party elite still maintained various sections for its own high-security hunting lodges. Ecologically, the area is of great importance, with its high grasslands and ancient forests of oak, fir and, less frequently, beech. Among the rarer species of fauna inhabiting the area you may be lucky enough to sight **eagles**, **bears**, **wolves**, **lynx** and even **bison**, introduced to the Bieszczady in the 1960s. Even the highest peaks in the region, around 1300m, won't present many **hiking** problems, as long as you're properly kitted out. Like all mountain regions, however, the **climate** is highly changeable throughout the year: on the passes over the *połonina* (meadows) for example, the wind and rain can get very strong. The best time to visit is late autumn: here, as in the Tatras, Poles savour the delights of the "Golden October". Mountain temperatures drop sharply in winter, bringing excellent skiing conditions.

Ustrzyki Dolne to Ustrzyki Górne

The main road out of **Ustrzyki Dolne** winds south through the mountain valleys towards **Ustrzyki Górne**, a ninety-minute journey by bus. If you've developed an enthusiasm for the wooden churches of this area, you've time to spare, and have your own transport, you could consider a diversion a few kilometres east off the road to the border villages of **Jałowe**, **Równia** and **Moczary** (the first is also reachable by bus) to see the fine examples of Boyk architecture there. Back on the main road, you'll also find Boyk churches at **Hoszów**, **Czarna Górna**, **Smolnik** (one of the few remaining remaining Orthodox places of worship in the region), and – on a road off to the east – at **Bystre** (now disused) and **Michniowiec** (bus from Czarna Górna).

Coming over the hill into **LUTOWISKA** you'll see makeshift barracks and drilling rigs, signs of the oil industry that has developed here sporadically since the last century. Locals insist that the Soviets for years blocked full development of the region's resources, fearing Polish economic independence. Even in these remote parts, Jews constituted over half the local population, up until 1939. The abandoned Jewish cemetery contains several hundred tombstones, most from the nineteenth and twentieth centuries, while, near the village church, there's a collective monument to the 650 or so local Jews shot here by the Nazis in June 1942. The grubby roadside restaurant in the village caters mainly for the oil workers.

Ustrzyki Górne

Spread out along the bottom of a peaceful river valley and surrounded by the peaks of the Bieszczady, **USTRZYKI GÓRNE** has a wild, end-of-the-world feel to it. The holiday development at the north end of the village may change things in time, but for the moment Ustrzyki is little more than a few houses, a shop and a clutch of takeaway stands. The main **accommodation** is provided by the *Kremaros*, a *PTTK* hostel (☎105; ①) open all year round, at the southern end of the village; like most others in the region, it is pretty basic but it guarantees to find you at least some floor space, however crowded it gets. The basic hotel (☎104; ①) run by the National Park office, a few hundred yards beyond the *PTTK*, is a similar setup. *PTTK* has also recently opened a slightly better-quality hostel, the *Górnik* (②), with its own restaurant, at the north end of the village. The most comfortable alternative is to ask around for **private rooms** in the houses up the hill on the other side of the road from the *Kremaros*.

For **campers** there's no problem putting up your tent next to the *Kremaros* hostel, or even elsewhere in the valley, as long as you don't make a mess. Nearby, a *baza studentowa* (student camp) operates in the summer months: you can probably get a mattress in a tent here.

Besides the smoky dive of a **restaurant** across from the *Kremaros* hostel, and the one in the *Górnik*, the only other food options in Ustrzyki are a couple of stand-up places by the main road. The wooden hut just up from the *PTTK*, on the same side of the road, has very rudimentary food but plentiful supplies of *Leżajsk* beer: a small but devoted band of locals seem to spend most of their time camped round the bar, joined in the early evening by hard cases off the Ustrzyki Dolne bus, which draws up here. Anglers might note that the stream running through Ustrzyki is prime trout-fishing territory – not that it's seen on local menus; signs on the river banks warn that fishing rights are controlled by the angling club, but permission should be easy to get – ask at the National Park office.

THE BIESZCZADY BY HORSE – OR BIKE

Walking and wintertime skiing aside, there are now (at least) two other ways of exploring the wilder parts of the Bieszczady region. Traditionally the plateaux and high paths of the region have been the natural habitat of *hucule*, an ancient breed of **wild horses** found throughout the Carpathians and named after the equally temperamental people of the eastern stretches of the mountains. Up above the village of **POLANA,** a few kilometres off the main road west of Czarna Górna, a couple of dedicated local enthusiasts have set up a *hucule* stable, currently boasting a stock of around fifty pure-bred horses. In recent summers they've begun offering **riding holidays** in the mountains, mostly in the beautiful **Otryt range** stretching south of the village. If the idea of riding bareback through the mountains appeals, this is the one to go for – first-hand reports suggest it's an exhilarating experience. The stable's proving a success, so anyone seriously interested should write in advance to: *Stadnina Koni Huculskich "Tabun"*, 38-709 Polana, Poland. Otherwise, if you have your own transport you could try turning up for a day or two's riding on the off chance there's a horse free. Finding your way here is impossible without help, so ask anyone in the village for the way and they'll point you in the right direction. If you do come for a while, the owners will also be able to help you find **private accommodation** in the village. Alongside the wooden *cerkiew* now used by Catholics, an additional curio in Polana is *U Żyda* – literally "At the Jew's place" – the local **pub**, which has a painting of a Jew outside, a reminder of the fact that this, like many country inns in Poland, was run by Jews up until World War II.

The other less conventional but equally exciting way of exploring the tops is on **mountain bikes** (*rowerów górskich*). In **DWENICZEK**, a little hamlet off the main road past Smolnik at the southern end of the Otryt range, a local couple have bought up thirty good-quality mountain cycles and set themselves up as a small guest house. They can be contacted via the main Sanok *PTTK* office (☎0137/30113 or 30123), or directly: *BIES Mountain Biking Adventures*, Dwerniczek 9 38715 Dwernik (☎12).

Hiking in the Bieszczady

Walking and winter skiing are the main reasons for coming to the Bieszczady region. From Ustrzyki there are a number of **hiking options**, all of them attractive and accessible for anyone reasonably fit; times given below are reckoned for an average walker's speed, including regular stops. **Skiers** will need to bring along all equipment and be prepared for minimum facilities: there are lifts at just three villages: Ustrzyki Górne, Cisna and Polańczyk. The best **map** is the *Bieszczady Mapa Turystczyna* (1:75,000).

The remoteness and rapid changes of weather that characterize the Bieszczady region make it more than usually essential for hikers to equip themselves well, particularly when planning more extended hikes. At any time of year, you should carry waterproof clothing and rucksack; a reasonable quantity of basic food supplies; a detailed map; compass; and warm clothing. As far as weather conditions go, outside of the summer months (and even, sometimes including them), it is important to keep a check on things: particularly up on the *połonina*, terrific storms often appear seemingly from nowhere. Generally, locals advise you not to set out alone on extended hikes, as the area's overall remoteness means the chances of your being spotted if you have an accident are slim in many places.

East to Tarnica and the Ukrainian border

There are two initial routes east from Ustrzyki, both leading to the high Tarnica valley (1275m). The easier is to follow the road to the hamlet of **Wołosate** (there's a **campsite** just beyond at Beskid, right on the border) then walk up via the peak of Hudow Wierszek (973m) – about four hours all in. Shorter but more strenuous is to go cross-country via the peak of Szeroki Wierch (1268m), a three-hour hike. **Tarnica peak** (1346m) is a further half-hour hike south of the valley.

From Tarnica valley you can continue east, with a stiff up-and-down hike via **Krzemien** (1335m), **Kopa Bukowska** (1312m) and **Halicz** (1333m; 3hr) to **Rozsypaniec** (1273m), the last stretch taking you over the highest pass in the range. This would be a feasible day's hike from the Beskid campsite; the really fit could do an outing from Ustrzyki to Krzemien and back in a day.

Adventurous walkers could consider trekking into the region to the north of Tarnica valley in search of the **abandoned Ukrainian villages** and tumbled-down *cerkwi* scattered along the border (delineated by the River San). Some, like Bukowiec and Tarnawa Wyznia, are marked on the map, but others aren't, so you have to keep your eyes peeled. Many villages were razed to the ground, the only sign of their presence being their orchards. The Polish **border police** who shuttle around the area in jeeps are nothing to worry about as long as you're carrying your passport, and have a plausible explanation of what you're up to. The Ukrainians who watch this area are a different proposition, though, so don't on any account wander into Ukrainian territory – police detention of hikers in L'viv has been known.

A couple of kilometres west of Tarnawa Niżna, on the narrow road back to Ustrzyki Górne at **Muczne**, is another abandoned site, this time of a secret hunting hotel that used to be used by the Communist Party leadership and international guests including French president, Giscard d'Estang and Romanian leader, Nicolae Ceausescu.

West to the Slovak border

There are some easy walks west to the peak of **Wielka Rawka** (1307m), flanked by woods on the Slovak border. One option is to go along the Cisna road and then left up the marked path to the summit (3hr). Another is to head south to the bridge over the Wołosate river, turn right along a track, then follow signs to the peak of Mała Szemenowa (1071m), from where you turn right along the border to the peaks of Wielka Szemenowa (1091m) and Wielka Rawka (4hr).

Northwest of Ustrzyki

The best-known walking areas of the Bieszczady are the **połonina** or mountain meadows. These desolate places are notoriously subject to sudden changes of weather: one moment you can be basking in autumn sunshine, the next the wind is howling to the accompaniment of a downpour. The landscape, too, is full of contrasts: there's something of the Scottish highlands in the wildness of the passes, but wading through the tall rustling grasses of the hillsides in summer you might imagine yourself in the African savannah. Walking the heights of the passes you can also begin to understand how Ukrainian partisans managed to hold out for so long up here; even for the most battle-hardened Polish and Soviet troops, flushing partisan bands out from this remote and inhospitable landscape must have been an onerous task.

BOYKS, LEMKS AND UNIATES

Up until World War II, a large part of the population of southeast Poland was classified officially as **Ukrainian**. For the provinces of L'viv, Tarnopol and Volhynia, in the eastern part of the region (all in the Ukraine today), this was accurate. However, for the western part, now Polish border country, it was seriously misrepresentative, as this region was in fact inhabited by **Boyks** (Boykowie) and **Lemks** (Lemkowie). These people, often collectively called "Rusini" in Polish, are historically close to the Ukrainians but have their own distinct identities, both groups being descendants of the nomadic shepherds who settled in the **Bieszczady** and **Beskid Niski** regions between the thirteenth and fifteenth centuries. Geographically speaking, the Boyks populated the region east of Cisna, while the Lemks inhabited the western part of the Bieszczady, the Beskid Niski and part of the Beskid Sądecki.

For centuries these farming people lived as peacefully as successive wars and border changes allowed. Their real troubles began at the end of World War II, when groups of every political complexion were roaming around the ruins of Poland, all determined to influence the shape of the postwar order. One such movement was the **Ukrainian Resistance Army (UPA)**, a group fighting against all odds for the independence of their perennially subjugated country. Initially attracted by Hitler's promises of an autonomous state in the eastern territories of the Third Reich, by 1945 the UPA were fighting under the slogan "Neither Hitler nor Stalin", and had been encircled by the Polish, Czech and Soviet armies in this corner of Poland. For almost two years small bands of partisans, using carefully concealed mountain hideouts, held out against the Polish army, even killing the regional commander of the Polish army, General Karol Swierczewski, at Jabłonki in March 1947.

This is where the story gets complicated. According to the official account, UPA forces were fed by a local population more than happy to help the "Ukrainian fascists". The locals give a different account, claiming they weren't involved with the UPA, except when forced to provide them with supplies at gunpoint. The Polish authorities were in no mood for fine distinctions. In April 1947 they evacuated the entire population of the Bieszczady and Beskid Niski regions in a notorious operation code-named **"Operation Vistula"** (Akcja Wisła). Inhabitants were given two hours to pack and leave with whatever they could carry, then were "resettled" either to the former German territories of the north and west in the case of many Lemks, or to the Soviet Union with most of the Boyks.

From the Gorlice region of the Beskids, a traditional Lemk stronghold, an estimated 120,000–150,000 were deported to the Soviet Union and a further 80,000 were scattered around Poland, of whom about 20,000 have now returned. The first arrived in 1957, in the wake of Prime Minister Gomułka's liberalization of previ-

Note that you can save walking time in this region by taking a **bus** from Ustrzyki Górne though Wetlina, Dołzyca and Cisna. If you've only got a very short time, you could take just a brief detour off the road north from Ustrzyki Górne to Ustrzyki Dolne. Take the bus a couple of kilometres west to the **Przelec Wyzniańska** pass, the first stop, from where a marked path leads up through the woods on the right-hand side of the road to the **Połonina Caryńska** (1107m) – a steep climb of roughly 45 minutes. You'll have time to walk along the pass a short way to get a feel for the landscape, and then get back down to catch the next bus on.

For a more extended trip from Ustrzyki Górne, take the steep trail marked in red and green north through the woods up to the eastern edge of the **Połonina**

ously hard-line policy. (Rumour has it that this was Gomułka's way of thanking the Lemks who had helped him personally during the war.) The trickle of returnees in the 1960s and 1970s has, since the demise of communist rule, become a flow, with Lemks and a few Boyks reclaiming the farms that belonged to their parents and grandparents. This return to the homeland is bringing a new level of political and cultural self-assertion. In the June 1989 elections, Stanisław Mokry, a Solidarity candidate from near Gorlice, openly declared himself a Lemk representative. In tandem with the country's sizeable **Ukrainian minority** likewise dispersed to the north and west in the postwar period, the Lemks have begun to call for some form of redress for historical injustices. In tandem with the Union of Polish Ukrainians, Boyks and Lemks have pressed for, among other things, official condemnation of the postwar deportations – a demand partially met by the Senate in August 1990 when it passed a resolution condemning "Operation Vistula", though the Sejm failed to follow suit – material compensation for property confiscated in the 1940s and 1950s, the return of some currently state-owned property, particularly the communal woodlands seized in 1949, and the passing of a national minorities law. Like other minorities in Poland, Lemks and Boyks want their own schools, language teaching and the right to develop their own culture.

But the question of self-identity is entangled by the religious divisions within the community. Like their Ukrainian neighbours, in the seventeenth century many previously Orthodox Boyks and Lemks joined the **Uniate Church**, which was created in 1595 following the Act of Union between local Orthodox metropolitans and Catholic bishops. The new church came under papal jurisdiction, but retained Orthodox rites and traditions – including, for example, the right of priests to marry. Today the majority of Lemks in the Bieszczady and Beskid Niski classify themselves as Uniate (or "Greek Catholic", as Poles know them). Encouraged both by the pope's appointment of a Polish Uniate bishop and political changes in the Ukraine, where Uniates are finally coming into the open after years of persecution, Lemk Uniates are tentatively beginning to adopt a higher religious profile.

The Uniates' revival in Poland is still hampered, however, by the vexed question of restitution of property confiscated in the wake of "Operation Vistula", in particular the 250-odd churches in the region taken away from the Uniates and mostly given to the Roman Catholics and Orthodox. The dispute over the Carmelite Cathedral in Przemyśl that broke out in spring 1991 was resolved only after a nasty local dispute with distinctly anti-Ukrainian undertones, and a row that temporarily threatened to jeopardize newly developing Polish–Ukrainian political relations. The Uniates have still not recovered most of their former church property. A further twist is added in the case of Orthodox-occupied buildings – the church in Rzepedź (see p.341) is a good example – since like Ukrainians the Lemk and Boyk communities are divided between the two faiths.

Caryńska, and walk over the top to the western edge (1297m; 2hr 30min). Continue down the hill to the village of Brzegi Górne where there's a **campsite** near the road. From here you can either take a bus to Ustrzyki Górne (or on to Sanok), or take the red-marked path which takes you up the wooded hill to the right to the all-year *PTTK* **hostel** on the eastern edge of the **Połonina Wetlińska** (1228m; 1hr 30min from Brzegi) – the views from this windswept corner are spectacular. Sleeping arrangements are basic and comprise mattresses in ten-person rooms; theoretically you should bring your own food, but the young couple who run the place will probably be happy to feed you from the communal pot.

Beyond the hostel there's an excellent walk over the Połonina Wetlińska to **Przelec Orłowicza** (1075m), where the path divides in three. A sharp left takes you down the hill to **WETLINA** (2hr 30min from the hostel), a scenic and popular holiday centre where **accommodation** is easy to find. As well as plenty of private rooms (③), there's a good *PTTK* hostel and campsite (☎01376/6415; ②), open all year and run by an extremely friendly Pole; the *Leśny Dwór* (☎01376/6454; ③ breakfast and evening meal included), an excellent family-run *pensjonat*; and the *Górski* (☎01376/6434; ③), a *PTTK*-run hotel on the outskirts of the village, with a passable restaurant.

Buses from here take you north to Sanok or south to Ustrzyki Górne. The middle path goes to **Smerek** (1222m) and down through the woods to the bus stop in Smerek village (2hr). The right-hand path is for the long-distance hike via Wysokie Berdo (940m), Krysowa, Jaworzec, Kiczera, Przerenina and Fałówa to Dołzyca (7hr; *PTTK* hostel), or even further on to the villages of Jabłonki and Baligród (see below).

West of Dołzyca: the forest rail line

Continuing west from Dołzyca brings you to **CISNA**, a smallish village that saw some bitter fighting during the 1945–47 civil war, when the UPA (see box, p.338) had one of their main bases nearby, a struggle commemorated by the statue in the middle of the village. The village and surrounding area were ruthlessly emptied during "Operation Vistula" (see above); today's population of a couple of thousand is only a fraction of the 60,000 or so who lived here before 1939. There's a reasonable supply of **accommodation**, including the *Motel Cisna* (☎11; ③), a *PTTK* mountain refuge up above the village, a (summer only) youth hostel and a couple of old workers' holiday homes. A kilometre to the southwest is **MAJDAN**, little more than a group of houses and the main boarding point for the **narrow-gauge rail line** running west through the forests along the Slovak border.

A product of the days when the Bieszczady region was little more than a backwoods of the Austro-Hungarian empire, the 25-kilometre long forest rail line between Majdan and **Rzepedz**, with a short additional connecting track to **Nowy Łupków**, was built in the 1890s as part of a scheme to connect the Austrian army regional headquarters in Majdan with the main Przemyśl–Budapest rail line. In addition to carrying passengers, these days the line forms part of a network of tracks through the forest which are used by the local forestry industry for wood transportation. The economics of the line, with dependency on hefty local subsidies, are not secure, and its future looks uncertain, with summertime tourist runs guaranteed for 1996, but not beyond.

The diesel-powered train leaves Majdan daily at 6.30am on weekdays, arriving in Rzepedz around 11am: at midday it sets off on the downhill return run, arriving at 2.50pm. At weekends it departs Majdan 9.30am, arriving around 12.30: departing again at 1.00pm, arriving around 4.20pm. Though these timetables are pretty established, you'd be advised to check them beforehand – they're posted at both end-stations. Alternatively the forest rail line (*Osródek Transportu Leśnego*) head office is in Komańcza (☎33). If you're only making the northward leg of the journey, buses and PKP trains take you the twenty-odd kilometres onward to Zagórz and Sanok.

The majority of this memorable and out-of-the-way route passes through uninhabited hillside forests filled with a gloriously rich and diverse flora, the beautiful views over the valleys adding a touch of mountain thrill to the experience. The train crawls along at a snail's pace for much of the journey, which is all it can manage on the steep hills it has to negotiate at regular intervals. You can pick the train up at several points along the way, and the driver can usually be persuaded to stop for a while *en route* if anyone wants to take a longer look at the scenery. At weekends the train is liable to be joined by contingents of local drinkers who spend the journey getting absolutely plastered, in many cases falling off the train at regular intervals and clambering drunkenly back on again.

A more salubrious highlight are the gleaming natural **forest lakes**, which local legends hold were created by the Devil when he crashed to the ground on a ball of fire: scientists say it's quite possible they were created by meteorites. If you're lucky you may also catch sight of rare black storks along the stretch of track up near the Slovak border.

Roughly halfway along the journey an additional stretch of track branches off to **NOWY ŁUPKÓW**, a tiny place whose name is familiar to Poles for the nearby internment camp, to which many prominent Solidarity leaders were consigned during martial law. If you have access to transport, there's an interesting Uniate *cerkiew*, now a Roman Catholic church, which is worth a visit at the village of Smolnik, just to the east.

Out of the mountains

There is a choice of routes out of the western Bieszczady back to Sanok. The main one runs **from Nowy Łupków through Komańcza** and a series of tiny Uniate villages such as **Rzepedź**. The other is a more obscure, winding road north from **Cisna**, via **Jabłonki** and **Baligród**. Buses run along both roads, while trains serve only the main route.

Komańcza and Rzepedź

North from Nowy Łupków, buses and *PKP* trains take you north to the village of **KOMAŃCZA**, whose two churches illustrate graphically the religious tensions of the region. Near the main road is a modern building recently constructed by the majority **Uniate** population, while hidden away in the woods on the edge of the hill is a beautiful early nineteenth-century *cerkiew*, used by the tiny local **Orthodox** community. In 1980 the Uniates – Lemks who avoided removal during "Operation Vistula" – petitioned the local authorities for their own place of worship but the *cerkiew* was given instead to the Orthodox worshippers – a good example of the divide and rule tactics used to manipulate the smaller religious groupings. At the other end of the village, uphill to the left, the **Nazarene Sisters' Convent** is something of a shrine for Polish tourists: it was here that Cardinal Wyszyński, the redoubtable ex-primate of Poland, was kept under house arrest in the mid-1950s during the Stalinist campaign to destroy the independence of the Catholic Church. The **PTTK hostel** (☎13; ①) down the hill will put you up for the night, as can the convent (☎56), though the number of pilgrims that flock here, particularly in summer, means it's advisable to book in advance.

You could have a fascinating time searching the Komańcza area for *cerkwi*: modern maps of the region mark them clearly. (Uniate buildings are identified in the key as "churches in ancient orthodox churches".) There's a particularly fine and typically **Lemk Uniate Church** from the 1820s just beyond at **RZEPEDŹ**, roughly fifteen minutes on foot from the train station. Nestled away on a hillside surrounded by tranquil clusters of trees, the church merges into the landscape – a common quality in *cerkwi* that may explain how they escaped the destruction of Bieszczady villages in the wake of "Operation Vistula" (see p.338). Surprisingly, this one only closed down for ten years after World War II, reopening for Uniate worship in 1956. The interior of the church gives a sense of the twin strands of Uniate worship: on the one hand Western Madonnas and insipid oil paintings; on the other the Eastern iconostasis, the absence of an organ (in the Orthodox tradition the choir provides all the music), the pale blue Ukrainian saints, and Ukrainian-script wall inscriptions. If you're planning on staying here, the *Bieszczady Hotel* is at hand in the village.

THE WOODEN CHURCHES OF THE POLISH CARPATHIANS

Despite a modern history characterized by destruction and neglect, both the Bieszczady and neighbouring Beskid Niski regions still have a significant number of villages that boast the wooden Uniate churches – *cerkiew* (plural, *cerkwi*) as they and Orthodox places of worship are known in Polish – traditional to this part of Europe.

Some of the most remarkable date from the eighteenth century, when the influence of Baroque was beginning to make itself felt, even among the carpenter architects of the Carpathians. The simpler constructions with a threesome of shingled onion domes also encountered in the Bieszczady region – a structure common to most Uniate churches – have their origin in the later, **Boyk**-derived architectural styles. Finally in the Lemk-inhabited districts of the Beskid Niski you'll often encounter grander, showier structures wth a marked Ukrainian influence, built in the 1920s and 1930s at the height of Ukrainian self-assertion within Poland.

Without your own transport, the possibility of reaching many of the churches in situ is limited, though several of the small towns mentioned in this chapter have *cerkwi* within reasonable walking distance. The easiest way of having a close look is to visit the *skansens* at Sanok or Nowy Sącz, both of which contain complete churches. If, on the other hand, you do make it out to some of the more remote villages you'll need to ask around for the key (*klucz*), which is more likely than not to be in the hands of the local priest (*ksiądz*) or the person living nearest the building.

The dark and intimate **interior** of a Uniate church is divided into three sections from west to east: the narthex or entrance porch, the main nave and the naos or sanctuary. Even the smallest of the Uniate churches will boast a rich iconostasis all but cutting off the sanctuary, which will contain the familiar icons of (working from left to right) Saint Nicholas, the Madonna and Child, Christ Pantocrator and, lastly, the saint to whom the church has been dedicated. Above the central door of the iconostasis (through which only the priest may pass) is the representation of the Last Supper, while to the left are busy scenes from the great festivals of the church calendar – the Annunciation, the Assumption and so on. The top tier of icons features the Apostles (with Saint Paul taking the place of Judas). Typically, the Last Judgement covers the wall of the narthex, usually the most gruesome of all the depictions, with the damned being burned, boiled and decapitated with macabre abandon.

Locations of a number of *cerkwi* are indicated throughout the chapter. The current pattern of ownership varies: following the expulsions of "Operation Visula", many buildings were taken over by Roman Catholics and some by Orthodox worshippers. Despite the recent upsurge in Uniate activity, Catholics still retain many of these buildings. Some have been returned – grudgingly you feel – to the Uniates, others are shared by both branches of Catholicism, while a good many still remain abandoned.

North from Cisna

From **Cisna**, buses head to Lesko and Sanok, through a region which was the scene of some of the heaviest fighting between the Polish Army and the Ukrainian resistance. At **JABŁONKI** there's a monument to **General Karol Swierczewski**, the veteran Spanish Civil War commander killed here in March 1947 and an all year round **youth hostel**, while further north at the larger village of **BALIGRÓD** a monument commemorates the Polish soldiers who fell – but not, as yet, the Ukrainians. This was the headquarters of the Polish Army during the conflict, and if you root around in the hills, you'll see fortifications and the sites of various villages cleared in 1947.

The Beskid Niski

West from Sanok the main road, closely tracked by the slow rail line, heads towards Gorlice through the Wisłok valley, a pleasant pastoral route, with a succession of wooden villages set back in the hills of the **Beskid Niski** to the south. There's not a great deal to detain you, though, until you get west of Krosno, to the medieval town of **Biecz** and on to **Gorlice**, the centre for Beskid Niski hikes.

Also covered in this section is **Dukla**, an isolated old town that has long controlled the Przelec Dukielska pass into Slovakia – the most important crossing point in the east of the country.

Krosno and around

At the heart of the country's richest oil reserves, **KROSNO**, the regional capital, is also the petroleum centre of Poland, but for the moment the resource is under-exploited, and the town seems more rooted in the past than expectant of future riches. Prior to the discovery of oil, which helped the town grow fairly wealthy in the late 1800s, Krosno had quite a record of mercantile prosperity. In particular, the town's favourable position on the medieval trade routes east meant it rapidly became one of the wealthiest Renaissance-era towns in the country, as evidenced by the plush burghers' mansions lining the square. If you're heading west towards Kraków, then this bustling, pleasantly situated town is worth the stopoff.

The Town

At the core of the busy modern town is the hilltop Old Town centre, a sizeable and reasonably well-preserved area with an attractive, compact-looking **Rynek** at its centre. Ranged round it are the Italianate merchants' houses fronted by arcaded passages – reconstructed in the nineteenth century in this case – characteristic of several towns in the southeast. Notable among these is the early sixteenth-century **Wojtówska Mansion** (no. 12) on the southwest side of the square, which boasts a finely decorated Renaissance portal, underscoring the town's mercantile Italian connections. South of the Rynek on ul. Franciszkańska is the brick-facaded late Gothic **Franciscan Church**, notable features being some Renaissance tombstones of various local dignitaries, and on the left of the building the Baroque **Oświęcim family chapel**, a sumptuously ornate piece designed by Italian architect Falconi.

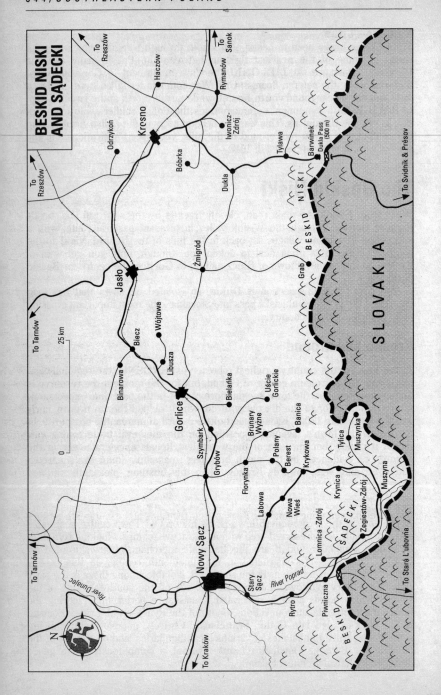

BESKID NISKI AND SĄDECKI

South from the Rynek along ul. Sienkiewicza, a statue on pl. Konstytucji 3 Maja commemorates **Ignacy Łukasiewicz**, the local boy who sunk what's claimed to be the world's first oil well in 1854 in the village of **Bóbrka**, 10km south of town – the pioneering Pole's drilling derrick and oil shaft are in an open-air museum there, twenty minutes away by local bus. North of the square along ul. Piłsudskiego, the main shopping street, is the **Parish Church**, a large Gothic structure with an overlay combining Renaissance and Baroque decoration to impressive effect, including a notable set of richly carved choir stalls and some fine polychromy above the nave. Unsurprisingly the **Regional Museum** (Tues–Sun 10am–3pm), in the sixteenth-century former bishops' palace at the top of the street, is mostly devoted to the local oil-mining trade, the highlight being a lovingly polished collection of early kerosene lamps, the revolutionary device of which Łukasiewicz was the inventor.

The town had a thriving **Jewish community** (Jews first arrived here in the fifteenth century) up until the outbreak of World War II. Most of them perished in the Bełzec concentration camp during 1942. The Jewish Cemetery, northwest of the Old Town, across the River Wistok on ul. Okerzej, still contains a hundred or so gravestones and a monument to those murdered by the Nazis.

Practicalities

The main **bus and train stations** are next to each other, ten minutes' walk northwest of the Old Town. For **tourist information** visit the *PTTK* office at ul. Krakowska 9 (☎0131/21175) or *Orbis* at ul. Blich 1.

Accommodation options include two modest hotels: the *Polonia*, near the centre at ul. Piłsudskiego 18 (☎0131/22034; ③), 1km east of the centre, and the seasonal *Bliźniak*, ul. Czajkowskiego 43 (☎0131/21879; ②). There's also the *Krosno-Nafta*, ul. Lwowska 21 (☎0131/22011; ④) and, for anyone with a car, the *Motel Moderówka* (☎0131/1796; ③) at Moderówka, 8km west on the Gorlice road. Krosno also has a **youth hostel** (☎0131/21 00 09; July & Aug), 2km north of the centre at ul. Konopnickiej 5, and the *PTTK* tourist office may also be able to help fix up **private rooms**.

Best of the **restaurants** is the *Stylowa*, in the *Krosno-Nafta* hotel. On the main square, the *Wojtowska* at Rynek 12 is a decent eatery and *piwnica* with a nice squareside location. Basic cafés are located on ul. Sienkiewicza and Franciszkańska, just off the main square.

Around Krosno

If you feel like venturing round the Krosno area, the ruins of the fourteenth-century **Castle Kamieniec**, one of the oldest fortresses in the Carpathian Mountains, can be seen at **ODRZYKOŃ**, 8km north (occasional buses).

At **HACZÓW**, 12km east (again occasional buses), a medieval town settled by Swedes and Germans in the fourteenth century, there's a beautiful mid-fifteenth-century **cerkiew**, the oldest wooden church in the country, with a fine sequence of scenes of the Passion of Christ and the lives of the Virgin Mary and the saints, arranged in several layers, illuminating the walls of the nave.

IWONICZ-ZDRÓJ, 11km southeast of Krosno (occasional buses) off the main Sanok road, is one of the most agreeable of a succession of pleasant little spa towns nestled in the valleys coursed by tributaries of the Wisłok River. The town's strategic setting also makes it a good base for **walks** in the scenic surrounding *beskidy* (hills), with a couple of good hilltop routes leading westwards to Dukla (see below), some 6km away from town.

The main town thoroughfare leading off from the only road into town is a genteel promenade filled in season by crowds of holidaymakers, many of them staying in the plentiful *pensjonat* available for takers of the supposedly healthy local waters. The **tourist office** at the north end of the promenade will help you with finding accommodation, which given the wealth of options even in season shouldn't pose too much of a problem.

Dukla

DUKLA, 24km south of Krosno, was for centuries the main mountain crossing point on the trade route from the Baltic to Hungary and central Europe. The location has also ensured an often bloody history, the worst episode occurring in the last war, when more than 60,000 Red Army soldiers and 6500 Czechs and Slovaks died in an attempt to capture the valley from the Germans.

Today, rebuilt after comprehensive damage in the fighting, Dukla is a windy, quiet and rather bleak place – every bit the frontier town with its eerie, stage-set main square. There are no real sights, save for a Rococo Parish Church and a local **Museum** (Tues–Sun 10am–4pm), housed in the surviving parts of the former Mniszech family palace, which gives chilling details of the wartime fighting in the "Valley of Death" to the south.

For an overnight **stay** it's a choice between the *PTTK* **hostel** at no. 25 on the main square (☎0131/46; ②), the **youth hostel** at Trakt Węgierski 14 (☎0131/28; July–Aug only), or **private rooms** (ask at the *PTTK* hostel). For food and drink, check out the *Basztowa*, opposite the squat town hall in the main square, or the slightly better *Granicze* round the corner on ul. Kościuszki.

West of Dukla, one or two buses a day cover the backwoods route **to Gorlice**, taking you along the edge of the hills. If you have transport, or have time to hike, the tiny roads leading south into the Beskid Niski are well worth exploring.

Biecz and around

BIECZ is one of the oldest towns in Poland and was the conduit for nearly all the wine exported north from Hungary in medieval times. This thriving trade continued until the middle of the seventeenth century, when the "Swedish Deluge" flattened the economy – but fortunately not the town.

Trains and buses both stop near the centre, with the Old Town a short walk up on the top of the hill. The **Rynek** here is dominated by the fifty-metre tower of the late Renaissance **Town Hall**. Nearby, the large **Parish Church**, complete with a forty-metre-high fortified belltower, contains Renaissance and Gothic pews, as well as a fine seventeenth-century pulpit decorated with musicians. Over the road on ul. Kromera, the local **Museum** (May–Sept Tues–Sun 9am–4pm; Oct–April closes 3pm), housed in a burgher's home that used to be part of the fortifications, has an intriguing collection of artefacts, featuring Baroque musical instruments, carpenters' tools and the entire contents of the old pharmacy – sixteenth-century medical books, herbs and prescriptions included. For the record, guides inform you that Biecz once had a school of public executioners. They were kept busy: in 1614, for example, 120 public executions took place in the square.

For an overnight stay there are two options: the *Adrianka* **hotel**, ul. Świerczewskiego 35 (☎018/51 21 57; ②), close to the train station and formerly a synagogue, and the **youth hostel**, with its own restaurant, at ul. Parkowa 1 (☎018/51214), further along the Krosno road from the hotel. About the only places to eat are the *Max* **restaurant** and a *kawiarnia*, both on the edge of the main square.

Churches around Biecz

Several villages in the vicinity of Biecz have beautiful **wooden churches**. Sadly the beautiful sixteenth-century chapel at Libusza, 9km south of town, was burnt to the ground in a fire a few years ago. If you've got time for only one sortie, go to **BINAROWA**, 5km north of Biecz (local bus or taxi). Constructed around 1500, the timber **Church** here has an exquisitely painted interior, rivalling the better-known one at Dębno in the Podhale (see p.463); the polychromy is part original, part eighteenth-century additions, and all meriting close attention. Notably the marvellous pictures near the altar of devils with huge eyes and long noses cowering in the background at Christ's Resurrection, and the Last Judgement scenes, again populated by fearsome devilish creatures on the north wall. If you can find him around, and you can speak Polish, you should try to get a tour with the local priest, an entertaining commentator who declares that King Kazimierz the Great, who was very fond of visiting Biecz, often stopped off at the Binarowa church on his way home.

Gorlice

GORLICE is a curious base for the **Beskid Niski**, the westerly extension of the Bieszczady: you'll know when you're approaching the town by the suddenly foul air. Like Krosno, the town has for a century been associated with the oil industry, Ignacy Łukasiewicz having set up the world's first refinery here in 1853. If you want further doses of petroleum history, the local **Museum** on ul. Wąska (Tues–Sun 10am–4pm) is devoted to Łukasiewicz and the oil industry generally. That aside, there's not a lot to be said – Gorlice is not the most beautiful of towns.

The **bus and train stations** are both close to the centre on the northern side of town. The train station is the terminus of the Krosno line – trains to Tarnów and on to Kraków leave from Gorlice Zagorzany, 2km up the line (frequent train and bus connections). **Tourist information** is available at the *PTTK* office, ul. Tysiąclecia 3, and the IT bureau in the *Wiktoria*, a rudimentary but centrally located hotel, at ul. 3 Maja 1b (☎20644; ②). Other **accommodation** options include the *Parkowa* hotel (☎21460; ②) in the Park Miejski, the *Dom Nauczyciela* teachers' hostel at ul. Wróblewskiego 10 (☎20231; ②), and the **youth hostel** at ul. Michałusa 16 (☎22558; July & Aug), on the outskirts of town. For **food** try the *Magura*, ul. Waryńskiego 16 (closes 8pm), or the *Gorlicka*, ul. Słoneczna 6. For a snack, there's the *kawiarnia* in the town hall basement.

South of Gorlice: walks in the Beskids

The **Beskid Niski** are a hilly rather than mountainous range, less dramatic than the Bieszczady, but nevertheless excellent walking country. The people – predominantly **Lemks** (see box p.338) – provide a warm welcome to the few hikers who do get to this area, and many of their settlements have fine examples of the region's characteristic **wooden churches**. As a rule you'll find these deliberately tucked away amid the trees, their rounded forms and rustic exteriors seeming almost organic to the landscape. The earliest date from the fifteenth century, most from the eighteenth and beyond. In the Gorlice area, a noticeable feature of most church **cemeteries** is the international collection of names on the tombstones, a legacy of an Austro-Hungarian battle against the Russians in 1915, which left 20,000 dead.

Details of all hill walks are given in the **PTSM youth hostel handbook** (see *Basics*), and should be provided by the tourist offices in towns such as Krosno and Gorlice. A good local map will greatly increase your enjoyment of this region, though the best one, *Beskid Niski i Pogorze* (1:125,000), is often out of print; you might find one in a shop or tourist office. The most ambitious **route**, marked in blue on the *Beskid Niski i Pogorze* map, runs some 80km from Grybow, 12km west of Gorlice, along the Czech border to Komańcza (see "The Bieszczady Mountains", p.333). **Youth hostels** (July & Aug) are strategically placed at twenty- or thirty-kilometre intervals at Uscie Gorlickie and Hańczowa (day 1), Grab (day 2), Barwinek (day 3) and Rzepedz (day 4), all with bus stops nearby.

Bielanka

The physical return of the Lemk and Boyk minorities to their roots has been accompanied by a revival of interest in their cultural and linguistic traditions. **BIELANKA**, 10km southwest of Gorlice, is the base of the **Lemkyownya Music and Dance Ensemble**, which has already toured the Ukraine, Canada and the USA. Though less active of late, you can occasionally catch them rehearsing in the village hall at the weekends. Another route into the intriguing folk music of the region is provided by the annual **Lemk and Ukrainian Festival** held every July in **ZYDNIA**, a remote village, 15km southeast of Bielanka, near the Slovak border – a showcase for music from all over the Carpathian region, Ukraine and Slovakia included.

The Beskid Sądecki

West from Gorlice the hills continue through a range known as the **Beskid Sądecki**, another low-lying stretch of border slopes sheltering a sizeable and expanding Lemk population. **Nowy Sącz**, the regional capital, is the obvious base for the area, which otherwise comprises very small market towns, scattered villlages and traditional peasant farms.

Nowy Sącz

NOWY SĄCZ, the main market town of the Beskid Sądecki, nestles on the banks of the River Dunajec, an out-of-the-way place these days and ideal as a base for exploring the hills. It was once better known, having been a royal residence from the fourteenth to the seventeenth centuries, and in the fifteenth century having seen the birth of the **Kraków-Sącz school** of painters, the first recognized Polish "school".

The Town

The centre of the spacious **Rynek**, in the Old Town, is occupied by the incongruous neo-Gothic **Town Hall**, which hosts occasional chamber music concerts as well as council meetings. The Gothic parish church of **St Margaret**

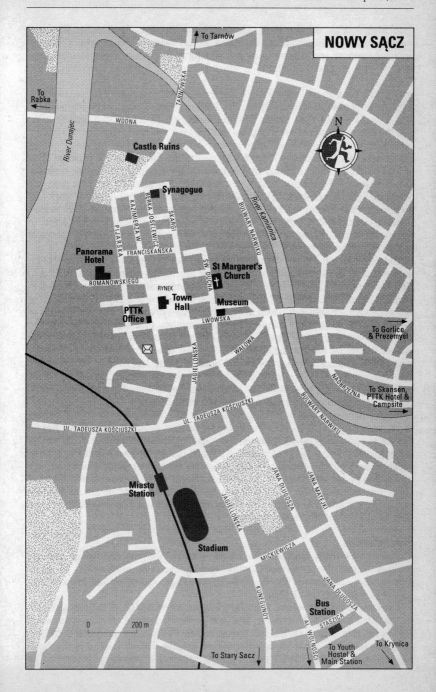

NOWY SĄCZ

To Tarnów

To Rabka

River Dunajec

WODNA

TARNOWSKA

N

Castle Ruins

Synagogue

BERKA JOSELEWICZA

SKARGI

KAZIMIERZA W.

PIJARSKA

River Kamienica

BULWARY NARWIKU

Panorama Hotel

FRANCISKAŃSKA

ROMANOWSKIEGO

RYNEK

ŚW. DUCHA

St Margaret's Church

Town Hall

Museum

PTTK Office

LWOWSKA

To Gorlice & Przemyśl

JAGIELLOŃSKA

WAŁOWA

NADBRZEŻNA

To Skansen, PTTK Hotel & Campsite

BULWARY NARWIKU

UL. TADEUSZA KOŚCIUSZKI

UL. TADEUSZA KOŚCIUSZKI

Miasto Station

JAGIELLOŃSKA

JANA DŁUGOSZA

JANA MATEJKI

Stadium

MICKIEWICZA

KUNEGUNDY

JANA DŁUGOSZA

Bus Station

STASZICA

0   200 m

AL. WOLNOŚCI

To Stary Sacz

To Youth Hostel & Main Station

To Krynica

(Św. Małgorzata), off the east side of the square, has the familiar Baroque overlay, two Renaissance altars excepted. It and many of the burghers' houses lining the square are looking a lot less shabby as a result of the systematic and extensive programme of restoration which is currently being pursued around the Old Town.

Over the road on ul. Lwowska, the sixteenth-century Canonical House contains the **Town Museum** (Tues–Thurs, Sat & Sun 10am–2.30pm, Fri 10am–6pm), which displays those few pieces from the Kraków-Sącz school that haven't been taken off to the national museums in Kraków and Warsaw. Other rooms hold a collection of icons gathered from *cerkwi* in the surrounding region – not as extensive as that in Sanok but amply demonstrating the distinctive regional style of icon painting. There's plenty of folk art on show too, including some typically Polish *Christus Frasobliwy* sculptures, showing a seated Christ propping his mournful face on one hand. Finally there's an interesting collection of works by the Lemk artist Nikifors (1895–1968), known locally as the "Matejko of Krynica". Bearing inscriptions in spidery, childlike handwriting (Nikifors didn't learn to write until late in life), several of the pictures are reminiscent of Lowry's scenes of industrial northern England.

The seventeenth-century **Synagogue** on ul. Berka Joselewicza, in the ghetto area north of the Rynek, where the popular nineteenth-century Tzaddik Chaim Ben Halberstam had his base, houses a contemporary art gallery (Wed–Sun 10am–2.30pm); the building has been so well modernized that there's nothing visibly Jewish left. Further up on the northern edge of the Old Town, the ruins of the **Castle**, built during Kazimierz the Great's reign, give a good view over the valley below. After being used for mass executions of local civilians, the castle was blown up by the Germans in 1945. For the adventurous shopper the daily **Russian Market**, known locally as Red Square, across the river on ul. Lwowska, is worth a look. There are some permanent kiosk-type setups, but the real deals can be found on the long tables or plastic dropcloths spread out on the ground. Keep an eye on your wallet and you may find some bargains.

A few kilometres east of town by bus #14 or #15 from the train or bus station, the **skansen** (May–Sept Tues–Fri 9.30am–4pm, Sat & Sun 9.30am–5pm) has an extensive and still growing collection of regional peasant architecture. If you've already visited the *skansen* at Sanok, the buildings in the Lemk and Pogorzanie sections here will be familiar. What you won't have seen before, however, are buildings like the fragments of a Carpathian Roma hamlet – realistically situated some distance from the main village – and the assortment of manor houses, including a graceful seventeenth-century specimen from Małopolska, complete with its original interior wall paintings.

Practicalities

There are two **train stations**: the Miasto station, near the Old Town, handles Kraków trains; the Dworzec Główny station, 2km south of town, all other destinations. Local buses shuttle between the Dworzec Główny and town centre, via the **bus station** on ul. Staszica.

The central **tourist office**, at ul. Jagiellonska 46 (☎018/42 37 24) has a decent supply of maps and brochures, and are generally helpful, though you won't always be able to find an English speaker. The *PTTK* office at Rynek 9 (☎018/ 12429) is useful for local hiking information, and the *Poprad* bureau in the *Hotel Panorama* will be able to fill you in on festivals and summertime events in the town. The *European Cultural Centre*, ul. Szwedska 2 (☎018/2324), is also worth checking out for local events and contacts with the town's growing community of US and European students.

The choice of **accommodation** is improving. The *Panorama* at ul. Romanowskiego 4a (☎018/42 18 78; ④) is the preferable hotel, central, cheaper and more congenial than the *Orbis Beskid Hotel* near the main station at ul. Limanowskiego 1 (☎018/42 07 70, fax 42 21 44; ⑥). Other options are the small *Zajazd Sądecki* hostel, ul. Król. Jadwigi 67 (☎018/42 67 17; ③), a standard *PTTK* hostel at ul. Jamnicka 2 (☎018/42 27 23; ③), east of the old town on the banks of the river, and the **youth hostel** on ul. Batorego 72 (☎018/42 32 41; July & Aug; buses #14 and #15 stop outside), close to the main train station. For **camping**, there's tent space near the *PTTK* hostel in summer. Ask at the *PTTK* office for **private rooms**: when demand is high the *Poprad* bureau (see above) doles out sleeping places around the town.

Restaurants, though, are pretty good. The cookery-school-assisted *Bona*, on the east edge of the main square in ul. Kościelna, serves an appetizing range of local specialities such as *płacek* (potato pancakes), though it's only open till 9pm. Other reasonable places are the *Panorama* and *Beskid* hotel restaurants, the *Imperial* and the *Stylowa*, both south of the main square on ul. Jagiellońska. **Milk bars**, *kawiarnia* and assorted drinking dives are all over town, especially in the busy shopping area around the Rynek. Try the Cechowa, Rynek 11, a favourite with young locals.

A loop around the Beskid Sądecki

The **Poprad River** – which feeds the Dunajec just south of Nowy Sącz – creates the broadest and most beautiful of the **Beskid Sądecki valleys**. A minor road runs its length to the Slovak border, which it then proceeds to trail for the best part of 25km. Meandering along this route is as good an experience of rural Poland as you could hope for, through fields where farmers still scythe the grass, with forests covering the hills above. Tracks lead off to remote hamlets, ripe for a couple of hours' church-hunting, while along the main body of the valley you can boost your constitution at Habsburg-looking spa towns like **Krynica**. North of Krynica, the road follows another valley to Nowy Sącz, making a satisfying circuit.

Stary Sącz

Nowy Sącz's smaller cousin town of **STARY SĄCZ**, 10km south (buses #8, #9, #10, #21 or #24; or train on the Krynica line), was first recorded in 1163 and is the oldest urban centre of the region. It's situated on a hill between the Dunajec and Poprad rivers, whose confluence you pass soon after leaving Nowy Sącz.

Like its modernized neighbour, the town's cobbled **Rynek** has an expansive feeling to it, the main difference being in the height of the buildings – none of the eighteenth-century houses round the Stary Sącz square has more than two storeys. Even in a town this small, though, you still find two thirteenth-century churches: a fortified Gothic **Parish Church** south of the square, and the convent **Church of the Poor Clares**, to the east, its nave decorated by sixteenth-century murals depicting the life of the Blessed Kinga, widow of King Bolesław Chobry (the Chaste), who founded the convent in 1280. The eccentrically cobbled together **Town Museum** on the square (Tues–Sun 10am–1pm) will kill half an hour.

Accommodation is limited to basic rooms at the *Szalas* (☎018/60077; ②), 1.5km north of the centre on the Nowy Sącz road, the **youth hostel** (July & Aug) at ul. Kazimierza Wielkiego 14 and the *Poprad* **campsite** on ul. Bylych Wiezniow Politycznych, behind the *Szalas*, which also has a few bungalows. The *Poprad* tourist office in Nowy Sącz may also be able to find **private rooms** in or around town. The only real **restaurant** is the *Staromeijska* on the Rynek (closes 9pm), while the tallest of the Rynek's houses has a good *kawiarnia* upstairs, the *Maryszenka*. **Tourist information** is available from the **Kinga** bureau on the Rynek.

The Poprad valley

By local train or bus it's a scenic two-hour ride along the deep, winding Poprad valley from Stary Sącz to Krynica, and if you're not in too much of a hurry, there are one or two places worth breaking your journey at before you reach the terminus.

At **RYTRO**, 16km down the line, there are ruins of a thirteenth-century castle, and lots of hiking trails up through the woods into the mountains; there's a hotel here too. Radziejowa summit (1262m), which is reached by following a ridge path to the southwest, is one of the more popular destinations, about two hours' walk from the village. The stretch of the river after nearby **PIWNICZNA** forms the border between Poland and Slovakia, and is one of the most attractive parts of the valley, with trout-filled water of crystalline clarity. If you're not hoping to catch the fish yourself, call in at the *Poprad* restaurant in **ZEGESTIÓW-ZDRÓJ**, a lovely spa town further down the valley, for excellent poached trout. The old village, some distance uphill from the station, makes for an enjoyable, leisurely post-lunch stroll.

MUSZYNA, next along the valley, has sixteen mineral springs, spa buildings, and the ruins of a thirteenth-century castle, just north of the train station. The Town Museum (Wed–Sun 9.30am–3pm), installed in a seventeenth-century tavern, focuses on local woodwork, agricultural implements in particular. From Muszyna the Poprad runs south and the railway heads off to the north towards Krynica, passing through the village of **Powroznik**, with its fine seventeenth-century *cerkiew*.

Krynica

If you only ever make it to one spa town in Poland, **KRYNICA** should be it. Redolent of *fin-de-siècle* central Europe, its combination of woodland setting, rich mineral springs and moderate altitude (600m) have made it a popular resort for over two centuries. In winter the hills (and a large skating rink) keep the holiday trade coming in.

At the northern end of the promenade, past a statue of Mickiewicz, a **funicular train** (summer daily 9am–midnight) ascends a 741-metre hill for an overview of town. Ranged below you is a fine array of **sanatoria**, including an old-fashioned pump room, assorted "therapeutic centres", and mud-bath houses.

The **pump room** is the place to try the local waters. Rent or buy a tankard from the desk here before heading for the taps, where the regulars will urge you to try the purply-brown *Zuber*. Named after the professor who discovered it in 1914, it is reckoned to be the most concentrated mineral water in Europe – certainly it's the worst-smelling. *Zdroj Główny*, a mixture of three or four different waters, is one of the more palatable brews.

Krynica hasn't yet worked out how to deal with foreigners. **Accommodation** is difficult to track down, and the singularly unhelpful *PTTK* tourist office at ul. Kraszewskiego 6, off the southern end of the promenade, seems to have little interest in revealing what is available.

In fact, *PTTK* not only offer **private rooms**, but also run the *Rzymianka* **hostel** at ul. Dąbrowskiego 15 (☎0187/12227; ②). Otherwise there's the *Belweder* **hotel** at ul. Kraszewskiego 14 (☎0187/15540; ③); it's run by the *Jaworzyna* tourist bureau on ul. Pułaskiego, who also deal with private rooms, and a succession of former state-enterprise holiday *pensjonat*, including the *Lilliana*, ul. Piłsudskiego 11 (☎0187/12234; ③), the adjoining *Stephania* (same phone number; ③), the *Zbyszko*, ul. Kościuszki 18 (☎0187/5604; ②), the *Mewa*, Bulwary Dietla 5 (☎0187/12051; ③) and *Józefa*, ul. Cicha 10 (☎0187/15420; ③), all located in the central spa area. There's a seasonal **youth hostel** at ul. Kraszewskiego 158 (☎0187/1442), and a **campsite** some way out from the centre on ul. Czarny Potok.

Restaurants are less of a struggle to track down. The *Havana* on ul. Piłsudskiego (the Nowy Sącz road) and the *Roma* at ul. Puławskiego 93 are both reasonable – though bedevilled by the usual "dancing bands". *Czarny Kot*, ul. Stara Droga, a bit out of the centre, is a good-quality joint worth the effort of seeking out. More basic are the *Dworcowa* on ul. Waryńskiego, the *Hokejowa* on ul. Sportowa, the *Cichy Kącik* at ul. Nowasadecka 100, and the *Krynicka* milk bar, ul. Dietla 15.

East from Krynica

The region **east from Krynica** is particularly rich in attractive villages and *cerkwi*, including some of the oldest in the country. Villages such as **Wojkowa**, **Ttlicz** and **Muszynka**, up in the hills by the Slovak border, have fine seventeenth-century examples. Local buses run occasionally from Krynica, or you could take a taxi – it won't break the bank.

North from Krynica

North from Krynica buses run to Nowy Sącz and Grybów, to the west of Gorlice. For the first 6km both routes follow the main road to Krzykowa, where the road divides. For Nowy Sącz you continue through the wooded groves of the Sącz Beskids, via villages such as Nowa Wieś and Łabowa.

The **Grybów road** is an even more attractive backroads route, due north through open countryside. The village of **BEREST**, 5km north of the main Nowy Sącz road, is a real treat. Set back from the road in pastoral surroundings, it has an eighteenth-century *cerkiew*, an archetype of the harmonious beauty of this region's wooden churches. The doors, opened by a huge metal key that's kept by an ancient peasant caretaker, creak open to release a damp draft from inside; muted scufflings from the priest's small herd of goats will probably be the only sounds to break the silence. Just a couple of kilometres up the road is **POLANY**, where a contemporary icon painter named Eugeniusz Forycki has a workshop in an old Lemk house; in summer you can visit his workshop – a sort of private *skansen*. From here to Grybów the valley is a gorgeous riverside route; if you have a car, a brief detour south to Brunary-Wyzne, then on to the border villages of Banica and Izby, is worthwhile, as all three have magnificent wooden *cerkwi*. From **GRYBÓW**, you have the choice of frequent buses and trains west to Nowy Sącz or east to Gorlice, or trains north to Tuchow and Tarnów.

travel details

Trains

Lublin to: Białystok (1 daily; 9hr); Gdańsk (2 daily, including 1 overnight with sleepers; 8hr); Katowice (4 daily; 6–7hr); Kielce (8 daily; 3–4hr); Kraków (4 daily including 1 overnight with couchettes; 6–8hr); Przemyśl (1 daily; 6hr); Warsaw (11 daily; 2–3hr); Zamość (4 daily; 3–4hr).

Łańcut to: Przemyśl (15 daily; 1–2hr); Jarosław (15 daily; 1hr); Rzeszów (15 daily; 30min).

Nowy Sącz to: Kraków (6 daily; 2–3hr); Krynica (hourly; 2hr); Tarnów (7 daily; 1hr 30min–2hr).

Przemyśl to: Kraków (15 daily; 3–6hr); Lublin (1 daily; 4hr 30min); Opole (5 daily; 7–9hr); Rzeszów (20 daily; 1–2hr); Tarnów (15 daily; 4–6hr); Warsaw (5 daily; 7–8hr); Zamość (frequent local trains to Jarosław then bus; 3–4hr). Also overnight couchettes to Wrocław and Szczecin and international trains to L'viv, Bucharest and Sofia.

Rzeszów to: Gdańsk (2 daily; 11hr); Kraków (20 daily; 2–4hr); Krosno (2 daily; 3hr); Przemyśl (hourly; 1–2hr); Tarnów (20 daily; 1–2hr); Warsaw (4 daily; 5–7hr).

Sandomierz to: Kielce (3 daily; 2–3hr); Rzeszów (4 daily; 1hr 30min–2hr); Warsaw (4 daily; 4–6hr); Zamość (1 daily; 2 hr 30min–3hr).

Sanok to: Kraków (2 daily; 7hr); Krosno (hourly; 2hr); Lublin (1 daily; 8hr); Przemyśl (2 daily; 3–4hr); Rzeszów (2 daily; 3–5hr); Tarnów (2 daily; 3–

5hr); Warsaw (2 daily, including one sleeper; 10hr).

Tarnów to: Kraków (8 daily; 1hr 30min–2hr); Nowy Sącz (5 daily; 2hr); Rzeszów (7 daily; 1hr 30min–2hr); Zamość (3 daily; 5–7hr).

Zamość to: Kraków (6 daily; 6–10 hr); Lublin (4 daily; 2–4hr); Rzeszów (1 daily; 6hr); Tarnów (3 daily; 4–8 hr); Warsaw (4 daily; 5–7hr).

Buses

Gorlice to: Kraków and Nowy Sącz.

Krynica to: Gorlice and Nowy Sącz.

Lublin to: Kazimierz Dolny, Kraków, Nałęczów, Sandomierz and Zamość.

Łańcut to: Przemyśl and Rzeszów..

Nowy Sącz to: Kraków, Rzeszów, Tarnów, Warsaw and Zakopane.

Przemyśl to: Rzeszów, Sanok, Ustrzyki Dolne, Zamość and international buses to L'viv.

Sandomierz to: Tarnobrzeg, Tarnów, Uzad, Warsaw and Zamość.

Sanok to: Kraków, Przemyśl, Rzeszów and Ustrzyki Dolne and into the Bieszczady Mountains.

Tarnów to: Jasło, Kraków, Krosno, Sandomierz and Zamość.

Zamość to: Chełm, Kraków, Lublin, Przemyśl, Rzeszów, Sandomierz and Warsaw.

CHAPTER FOUR

KRAKÓW, MAŁOPOLSKA AND THE TATRAS

T he Kraków region attracts more visitors – Polish and foreign – than any other in the country, and the attractions are clear enough from just a glance at the map. The **Tatra Mountains**, which form the border with Slovakia, are Poland's grandest and most beautiful, snowcapped for much of the year and markedly alpine in feel. Along with their foothills, the **Podhale**, and the neighbouring, more modest peaks of the **Pieniny**, they have been an established centre for hikers for the best part of a century. And with much justice, for there are few ranges in northern Europe where you can get so authentic a mountain experience without having to be a committed climber. The region as a whole is perfect for low-key rambling, mixing with holidaying Poles, and getting an insight into the culture of the indigenous *górale*, as the highlanders are known. Other outdoor activities are well catered for, too, with raft rides down the Dunajec Gorge in summer and some fine winter skiing on the higher Tatra slopes.

With a population of just under one million, **Kraków** itself is equally impressive: a city that ranks with Prague and Vienna as one of the architectural gems of central Europe, with an Old Town which retains an atmosphere of *fin-de-siècle* stateliness. A longtime university centre, its streets are a cavalcade of churches and aristocratic palaces, while at its heart is one of the grandest of European squares, the Rynek Główny. The city's significance for Poles goes well beyond the aesthetic though, for this was the country's ancient royal capital, and has been home to many of the nation's greatest writers, artists and thinkers, a tradition retained in the thriving cultural life. The Catholic Church in Poland has often looked to Kraków for guidance, and its influence in this sphere has never been greater – Pope John Paul II was Archbishop of Kraków until his election in 1978. Equally important are the city's **Jewish roots**. Until the last war, this was one of the great Jewish centres in Europe, a past whose fabric remains clear in the old ghetto area of Kazimierz, and whose culmination is starkly enshrined at the death camps of **Auschwitz-Birkenau**, west of Kraków.

This chapter also takes in an area which loosely corresponds to **Małopolska** – a region with no precise boundaries, but which by any definition includes some of the historic heartlands of the Polish state. Highlights here, in countryside characterized by rolling, open landscape, market towns and farming villages, include **Kielce**, springboard for hikes into the **Świętokrzyskie Mountains**, the magnificent ruins of **Krzyżtopór Castle** and the pilgrim centre of **Częstochowa**, home of the Black Madonna, the country's principal religious symbol.

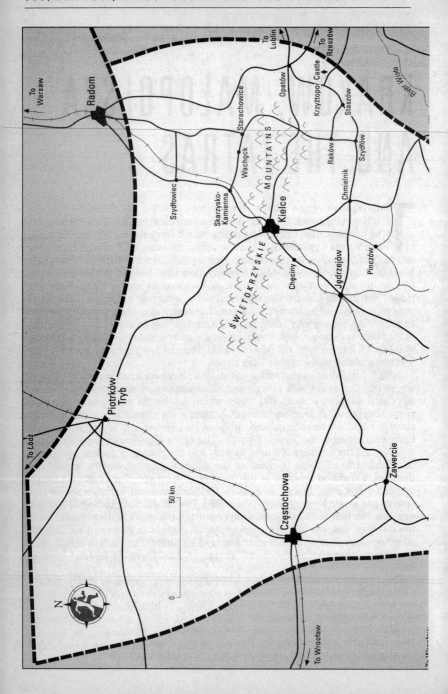

To Warsaw
To Łódź
To Wrocław
To Lublin
To Rzeszów

Radom
Szydłowiec
Skarżysko-Kamienna
Wąchock
Starachowice
Opatów
Krzyżtopór Castle
Staszów
Raków
Szydłów
Chmielnik
Kielce
Chęciny
Jędrzejów
Pińczów
Piotrków Tryb
Częstochowa
Zawiercie

MOUNTAINS
ŚWIĘTOKRZYSKIE

River Wisła

N

50 km

0

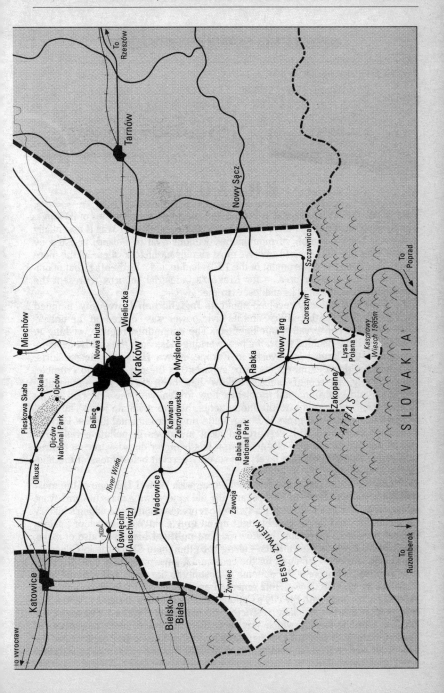

KRAKÓW

KRAKÓW, the ancient capital of Poland and residence for centuries of its kings, was the only major city in the country to come through World War II essentially undamaged. Its assembly of monuments, without rival in Poland, is listed by UNESCO as one of the world's twelve most significant historic sites. All the more ironic, then, that the government of the 1970s had to add a further tag, that of official "ecological disaster area" – for Kraków's industrial suburbs represent the communist experiment at its saddest extreme.

Until the war, the city revolved about its **Jagiellonian University**, founded back in the fourteenth century, and its civic power was centred on the university's Catholic, conservative intelligentsia. The communist regime, wishing to break their hold, decided to graft a new working class onto the city by developing one of the largest steelworks in Europe, **Nowa Huta**, on the outskirts. Within a few decades its effects were apparent as the city began to crumble. Consequently, in recent times, Kraków has been faced with intractable economic and environmental problems: how to deal with the acid rain of the steelworks, how to renovate the monuments, how to maintain jobs. The good news is that steady progress is being made on environmental issues. Foreign assistance combined with resourceful local initiatives in pollution reduction means that Kraków is now cleaner than it has been for decades, recent figures suggesting that air pollution levels are seventy percent below those of the mid-1980s.

What's more, the city remains a visual treat, with **Wawel Hill** one of the most striking royal residences in Europe, and the old inner town a mass of flamboyant monuments. For Poles, these are a symbolic representation of the nation's historical continuity, and for visitors brought up on grey Cold War images of Eastern Europe they are a revelation. Kraków's recent **political history** is also of major importance. It was at Nowa Huta – along with the Lenin Shipyards in Gdańsk – that things started to fall apart for the communist government. By the 1970s, the steelworkers had become the epitome of hostility to the state, and with the birth of Solidarity in 1980, Nowa Huta emerged as a centre of trade union agitation. Working-class unity with the city's Catholic elite was demonstrated by Solidarity's call to increase the officially restricted circulation of *Tygodnik Powszechny*, a Kraków Catholic weekly which was then the only independent newspaper in Eastern Europe. It was in Kraków, as much as anywhere in the country, that the new order was created, and today, it is in Kraków that the economic fruits of that order are most visible.

A brief history

The origins of Kraków are obscure. An enduring legend has it that the city was founded by the mythical ruler **Krak** on Wawel Hill, above a cave occupied by a ravenous dragon. Krak disposed of the beast by offering it animal skins stuffed with tar and sulphur, which it duly and fatally devoured. In reality, traces of human habitation from prehistoric times have been found in the city area, while the first historical records are of **Slavic peoples** settling along the banks of the Wisła here in the eighth century.

Kraków's position at the junction of several important east–west trade routes, including the long haul to Kiev and the Black Sea, facilitated commercial development. By the end of the tenth century, it was a major market centre and had been incorporated into the emerging **Polish state**, whose early **Piast** rulers made Wawel Hill the seat of a new bishopric and eventually, in 1038, the capital of the country. Subsequent development, however, was rudely halted in the mid-thirteenth century, when the Tartars left the city in ruins. But the urban layout established by **Prince Bolesław the Shy** in the wake of the Tartar invasions, a geometric pattern emanating from the market square, remains to this day.

Kraków's importance was greatly enhanced during the reign of **King Kazimierz**. In addition to founding a **university** here in 1364 – the oldest in central Europe after Prague – Kazimierz rebuilt extensive areas of the city and, by giving Jews right of abode in Poland, paved the way for a thriving **Jewish community** here. The advent of the Renaissance heralded Kraków's emergence as an important European centre of learning, its most famous student (at least, according to local claims) being the young **Nicolaus Copernicus**. Part and parcel of this was a reputation for religious tolerance at odds with the sectarian fanaticism then stalking sixteenth-century Europe. It was from Kraków, for example, that King Sigismund August assured his subjects that he was not king of their consciences – bold words in an age of despotism and bloody wars of religion.

King Sigismund III Waza's decision to **move the capital to Warsaw** in 1596, following the Union of Poland and Lithuania, was a major blow. The fact that royal coronations (and burials) continued to take place on Wawel for some time after was little compensation for a major loss of status. Kraków began to decline, a process accelerated by the pillaging of the city during the Swedish invasion of 1655–57.

Following the **Partitions**, and a brief period as capital of a tiny, notionally autonomous republic, the Free City of Kraków (1815–46), the city was incorporated into the **Austro-Hungarian** province of Galicia. The least repressive of the occupying powers, the emperor granted Galicia autonomy within the empire in 1868, the prelude to a major revival. The relatively liberal political climate allowed Kraków to become the focus of all kinds of underground political groupings. **Józef Piłsudski** began recruiting his legendary Polish legions here prior to World War I, and from 1912 to 1914 Kraków was **Lenin**'s base for directing the international communist movement and the production of *Pravda*. **Artists and writers** attracted by the new liberalism gathered here too. Painter Jan Matejko produced many of his stirring paeans to Polishness during his residency as art professor at the Jagiellonian University, and the city was centre of Wyspiański and Malczewski's **Młoda Polska** (Young Poland) movement.

The brief interlude of independence following World War I ended for Kraków in September 1939 when the **Nazis** entered the city. Kraków was soon designated

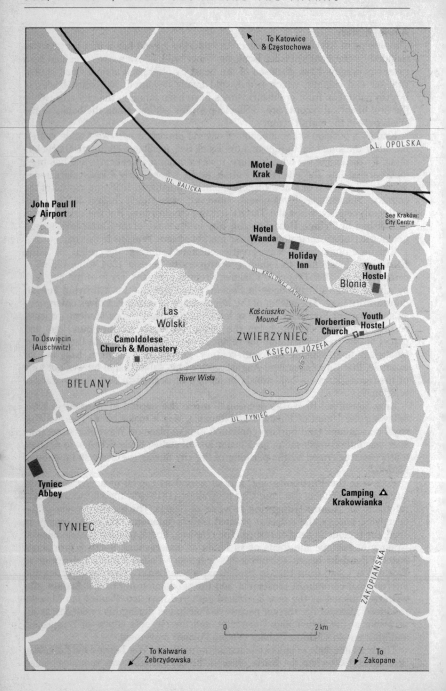

To Katowice
& Częstochowa

AL. OPOLSKA

Motel
Krak

UL. BALICKA

John Paul II
Airport

See Kraków:
City Centre

Hotel
Wanda

Holiday
Inn

Youth
Hostel

UL. KRÓLOWEJ JADWIGI

Blonia

Las
Wolski

Kościuszko
Mound

Norbertine
Church

Youth
Hostel

ZWIERZYNIEC

To Oświęcin
(Auschwitz)

Camoldolese
Church & Monastery

UL. KSIĘCIA JÓZEFA

BIELANY

River Wisła

UL. TYNIEC

Tyniec
Abbey

Camping △
Krakowianka

TYNIEC

ZAKOPIAŃSKA

0   2 km

To Kalwaria
Zebrzydowska

To
Zakopane

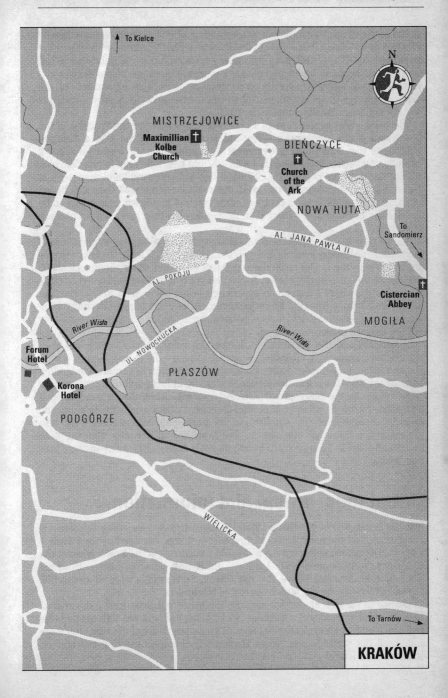

To Kielce

N

MISTRZEJOWICE

Maximillian
Kolbe
Church

BIEŃCZYCE

Church
of the
Ark

NOWA HUTA

To
Sandomierz

AL. JANA PAWŁA II

AL. POKOJU

Cistercian
Abbey

MOGIŁA

River Wisła

River Wisła

UL. NOWOCHUCKA

Forum
Hotel

PŁASZÓW

Korona
Hotel

PODGÓRZE

WIELICKA

To Tarnów

KRAKÓW

capital of the Central Government, incorporating all Polish territories not directly annexed to the Reich. Hans Frank, the notorious Nazi governor, moved into the royal castle on Wawel Hill, from where he exercised a reign of unbridled terror, presaged by the arrest and deportation to concentration camps of many professors from the Jagiellonian University in November 1939. The elimination of the **Kraków ghetto**, most of whose inhabitants were sent to nearby Auschwitz (Oświęcim), was virtually complete by 1943.

The main event of the immediate postwar years was the construction of the vast **Nowa Huta steelworks** a few miles to the east of the city, a daunting symbol of the communist government's determination to replace Kraków's Catholic, intellectually oriented past with a bright new industrial future. The plan did not succeed: the peasant population pulled in to construct and then work in the steel mills never became the loyal, anti-religious proletariat the Party hoped for. Kraków's reputation as a centre of conservative Catholicism was enhanced by the election of **Pope John Paul II** in 1978, who until then had been Archbishop of Kraków.

An unforeseen consequence of the postwar industrial development is one of the highest **pollution** levels in Europe. Dangerously high toxic levels are wreaking havoc with the health of the local population, as well as causing incalculable damage to the ancient city centre. If you find yourself feeling exhausted or dizzy after a few days here – a common experience – then blame it on Nowa Huta, and the fumes blown in from the Katowice region. After years of prevarication, cleaning up the city is now a major local political issue, and in 1989 Kraków actually elected a Green mayor for a period.

Since 1989 and the transition to democratic rule, the city centre has been rapidly transformed by an influx of private capital – local and foreign – with Western-style shops, cafés and restaurants springing up in abundance, lending parts of the Old Town a cosmopolitan, decidedly affluent feel that confirms the city's return to the place proud Kraków residents have always maintained it belonged, in the heartlands of central Europe. Pollution notwithstanding, the historic ensemble of the square and its immediate surroundings are also undergoing a thorough clean-up for the first time in decades, allowing both locals and tourists to appreciate buildings such as the Sukiennice in their pristine beauty.

Orientation, arrival and information

Kraków is bisected by the **River Wisła**, though virtually everything of interest is concentrated on the north bank. At the heart of things, enclosed by the **Planty** – a green belt following the course of the old ramparts – is the **Stare Miasto**, the Old Town, with its great central square, the **Rynek Główny**. Just south of the Stare Miasto, looming above the river bank, is **Wawel**, the royal castle hill, beyond which lies the old Jewish quarter of **Kazimierz**.

Thanks to the lack of wartime damage, the **inner suburbs** have more character than usual, the modern apartment blocks being interspersed with the odd villa and nineteenth-century residential area. If you come in from the east, you'll see and smell the steelworks at **Nowa Huta**, their chimneys working overtime on acid rain production.

Arrival

The recently renovated and expanded **Balice airport**, 11km west of the city, handles both domestic and international flights. Buses #158 and #208 connect it with the main bus station in the city centre (30min). Taxis are always available, too, and pretty reasonable at 20–30zł, although you'll need to bargain.

Kraków Główny, the central **train station**, served by all principal lines and currently the subject of a major overhaul, is within walking distance of the Stare Miasto. The left luggage office at the station is open twenty-four hours a day. Some trains (overnight services particularly) arrive at the southern **Płaszów** station: to get to the city centre from here, catch either a local commuter train or tram #3 #6, #9, #13 or #24. **Dworzec PKS**, the main **bus station**, is sited opposite the central train station.

Arriving by car, major roads from all directions are well signposted, though once in the centre, you'll need to cope with trams, narrow streets, heavy daytime traffic, and in much of the centre, heavily enforced parking restrictions, including wheel clamps on illegally parked vehicles. There are official guarded car parks on plac Św. Ducha and plac Szczepański, although it's often hard to get a space. Although they are technically for hotel guests only, you could also try the *Cracovia*, *Holiday Inn* and *Wanda* hotels (see below).

> The **telephone code** for Kraków is ☎012

Getting around

The central area of Kraków is compact enough to get around on foot; recently introduced restrictions mean that much of the **Stare Miasto** – including the Rynek – is car-free.

Exploring further afield, **trams** are pientiful, start early and run till late at night. Tram routes radiate out from the Planty to the suburbs, and useful services are detailed in the text. **Buses**, which complement the trams and keep similarly long hours (with night buses taking over from around 11pm to 5am), provide the main links with outer suburbs such as Tyniec and Nowa Huta, and local towns such as Wieliczka. Tickets are purchased at kiosks and shops displaying the *MPK* symbol. Current prices are 0.80zł for any daytime journey; 2zł for night buses and 1.2zł for express line buses. Remember to punch your ticket at both ends on entering the bus or tram. Students with ID travel half price in Kraków. If you're caught without a valid ticket, you'll be fined 30zł on the spot. **Local train** services can be handy for trips out of the city centre, such as to Płaszów.

Taxis are still affordable for visitors, though as elsewhere in the country they are highly priced for the local economy. Remember to make sure the driver turns on the meter. Daytime rates are currently one thousand times the price shown on the meter. From 11pm–5am, the multiple goes up by half. There are ranks around the centre of town at plac Św. Ducha, Mały Rynek, plac Dominikański, plac Szczepański, plac. Wszysłkich Świętych, ul. Sienna (by the main post office) and at the main train station. Calling a radio taxi, such as *Krak Taxi* (☎67 67 67 or 66 69 99) can work out significantly cheaper.

Information and maps

Possibly in response to the sheer volume of visitors, Kraków's city **tourist office** is far and away the best organized of any Polish city. The main office, run by *Wawel Tourist*, is just down from the station at ul. Pawia 8 (Mon–Fri 8am–4pm, Sat 8am–noon; ☎22 60 91), with all the maps and brochures you could want. There have been budget cuts, however, and the service has declined of late. Useful alternatives are the *Jordan* bureau, ul. Floriańska 37 (Mon–Sat 9am–5pm; ☎21 77 64), just off Rynek Główny, and *Dexter*, Rynek Główny 1/3 (Mon–Sat 9am–5pm; ☎21 77 06 or 21 30 51) inside the Sukiennice (the former cloth hall), the latter offering a range of local excursions, flight booking facilities and guides for hire. The **Almatur** office at Rynek Główny 7/8 (Mon–Fri 9am–5pm; ☎22 59 42), handles student accommodation and is good for advice on nightlife and alternative events. As usual, **Orbis** also have information points in their hotels as well as a central office at Rynek Główny 41. They organize city tours and day excursions to Tyniec, Wieliczka, Ojców Park and Pieskowa Skała Castle, Oświęcim (Auschwitz), Zakopane and the Dunajec Gorge; details from the main office or the information points in the *Cracovia* or *Holiday Inn* hotels.

There are two glossy English-language monthly **magazines** available from the tourist office, *Orbis* hotels and certain bookstores, *Welcome to Krakow* and *Kraków: What, Where, When*, providing a useful source of up-to-date information and current **listings**, for concerts, theatre and so on. Additionally, *Inside Kraków*, an English-language bi-monthly produced by an expat American Pole has city listings and plenty of insider's tips and information. Availability is a bit unpredictable, but you can generally find it in the major hotels and tourist offices. For comprehensive listings, consult the weekly *Tydzień w Krakowie*, available from all *Ruch* kiosks, or the weekend section of the Kraków edition of *Gazeta Wyborcza* newspaper, or the local *Gazeta Krakowska*.

If you plan a longer stay, or are staying out in the suburbs, it might be worth investing in the fold-out **plan miasta** – available at the tourist offices, the *Ruch*, bookstores or street vendors.

Accommodation

Kraków is becoming one of Europe's prime city destinations – so you should book hotels ahead in summer. **Prices** for hotels are higher than in most Polish cities, but still slightly less than Warsaw's. During office hours any of the tourist offices will help you book a room; otherwise you can call hotels direct. The office next door to the main tourist information, at ul. Pawia 6 (Mon–Fri 8am–9pm, Sat 10am–3pm; ☎22 19 21, fax 22 16 40) organizes **private rooms**, which can be a good bet during the summer. Ask carefully about addresses, as many tend to be a long way out.

Hotels

Many **hotels** are located in and around the Old Town area, with a cluster within striking distance of the train station. Generally speaking, the closer you get to the Rynek, the pricier and noisier it gets, although the really upmarket places tend to be on quieter sidestreets or around courtyards.

The Old Town

Chałupnik, ul. Kochanowskiego 12 (☎33 47 21). Cheap, smallish, privately run overnighter in reasonable walking distance west of the Old Town. ②.

Cracovia, al. Puszkina 1 (☎22 86 66, fax 21 95 86). Oldest and best-located of the *Orbis* hotels, a tram ride (#15 or #18) west of the centre. ⑧.

Elektor, ul. Szpitalna 28 (☎21 80 25, fax 21 86 89). The latest addition to the city's growing stock of smart hotels. Fine central location, swish rooms, upmarket bar and restaurant, all with prices to match; from $170. ⑨.

Europejski, ul. Lubicz 5 (☎22 09 11, fax 23 25 29). Undistinguished place close to the train station. ⑤.

Francuski, ul. Pijarska 13 (☎22 51 22, fax 22 52 70). Elegant old hotel, recently renovated. A long-established favourite with upmarket travellers. ⑨.

Grand, ul. Sławkowska 5–7 (☎21 72 55, fax 21 72 55). Luxury hotel in a good central location. Run by *Orbis*. ⑨.

Logos, ul. Szujskiego 5 (☎22 54 04, fax 22 42 10). Upmarket new hotel, aimed at business people and wealthier tourists alike. An easy walk west of the old town area. ⑦.

PTTK Dom Turysty, ul. Westerplatte 15/16 (☎22 95 66, fax 21 27 26). Large, popular student venue, near the station and nearly always crowded in season. Lots of small but decent double rooms, a few singles, as well as eight-person dormitories. Recently renovated restaurant and bar. ⑤.

Pod Różą, ul. Floriańska 14 (☎22 93 99, fax 21 75 13). Venerable place, now taken over by the crowd using its much-advertised casino. Simple decent-quality rooms, though the street below can be noisy at night. ⑦.

Pollera, ul. Szpitalna 30 (☎22 10 44, fax 22 13 89). Recently renovated and under new (private) management; central location and increasingly popular, though still a bit chaotic at times. ⑥.

Polonia, ul. Basztowa 25 (☎22 12 33, fax 22 16 21). Best of the hotels close to the train station, but not a particularly quiet location. ⑤.

Polski, ul. Pijarska 17 (☎22 11 44, fax 22 14 26). A very central and quiet location, though rather marred by a shabby selection of rooms. ⑦.

Saski, ul. Sławkowska 3 (☎21 42 22, fax 21 48 30). Useful central location and again popular with students – Polish and foreign. ⑤.

University Guest House, ul. Floriańska 49 (☎21 12 25). Good value *pensjonat* in excellent central location. Theoretically it's only open to visiting academics, but you may be able to get a room if you book in advance. ③.

Warszawski, ul. Pawia 6 (☎22 06 22, fax 44 53 06). Good but noisy location close to the train station – ask for a room at the back. ⑤.

Around Wawel Hill

Forum, ul. Konopnickiej 28 (☎66 95 00, fax 66 58 27). Luxury Western-style business travellers' haunt, a block south of Wawel near the river. Much used by tour groups. ⑧.

Garnizonowy, ul. Św. Gertrudy 29 (☎21 35 00). The cheaper part of a former military hotel, next to the *Royal*. ⑥.

Monopol, ul. Św. Gertrudy 6 (☎22 76 66). Good quality rooms in a good central location. ⑨.

Royal, ul. Św. Gertrudy 26 (☎21 35 50 or 21 33 69, fax 21 58 57). Smart, newly renovated former officers' hotel close to Wawel. Popular with small tour groups. ⑧.

The suburbs

Continental, ul. Armii Krajowej 11 (☎37 50 44, fax 37 59 38). Luxury hotel favoured by the tourist jet set, well out of the city centre on the main Balice–Katowice road. ⑧.

Demel, ul. Głowackiego 22 (☎36 16 00, fax 36 45 43). Private hotel with all the facilities but well out of the centre. ⑧.

IBIS, ul Przy Rondzie 2 (☎21 81 88, fax 22 98 58). Newly built motel-style place, located by a main roundabout, a short way east of the main station. ⑦.

Korona, ul. Kalwaryiska 9/15 (☎66 65 11, fax 56 46 66). Located out in the southern Podgorze district, on the edge of the wartime ghetto area, this is a cheap, lesser-known sports hotel. Tram #10. ④.

Krakowianka, ul. Zywiecka (☎66 41 91). A last resort – well south of the centre. Also has bungalows and a campsite. Triple rooms only. ③.

Motel Krak, ul. Radzikowskiego 99 (☎37 21 22, fax 37 25 32). Well outside the city – see "Campsites", below, for transport details. Its advantages are a swimming pool and bungalows. ⑥.

Piast, ul. Radzikowskiego 109 (☎36 46 00, fax 36 47 74). Newish privately run hotel with lots of rooms, 5km northwest of town, beyond the *Motel Krak*. ⑦.

Pod Kopcem, al. Waszyngtona (☎23 03 55). Housed in an old fortress on a hill well west of the centre, this is a delightfully peaceful hotel – well worth the higher than average prices. Increasingly popular, not least for the view over the city. However, it is currently closed for a complete refit, planned reopening in 1997; phone for details. ⑦.

Tramp, ul. Koszykarska 33 (☎56 02 29). Large hostel-type place well east of town in Płaszów district. Bus #108 passes close by. ③.

Wanda, ul. Armii Krajowej 9 (☎37 16 77, fax 37 85 18). Not quite up to the mark of its neighbour, the *Continental*. ⑦.

Wisła, ul. Reymonta 22 (☎33 49 22). Another sports hotel, set in a pleasant park in the western Czarna Wieś district, next to the main football stadium. Bus #144 (from the main bus station) passes close by. Doubles only. ③.

Student hotels and youth hostels

Student hotels run throughout the summer months (June–Sept). Details of locations (which change each year) are available from the *Almatur* office on the main square, as well as the main tourist office.

Letni, ul. Jana Pawła 82 (☎48 20 27). A fairly dependable student hostel, quite a distance east of town on the edge of Nowa Huta. Twin-bedded rooms as well as dormitories. Take bus A or trams #4, #5, #10, or #44 from the central station, direction Nowa Huta. July–Sept. ③.

Merkur, al. 29 Listopada 48a (☎11 82 44). Cheap student dorm a short bus ride north of the main station. Buses #105, 129 pass close by, then follow the signs. Own café/bar. Open June–Sept. ②.

Piast, ul. Piastowska 47 (☎37 49 33). A large, central student dormitory popular with foreigners on summer language courses. ①.

Wawel Tourist Hostel, ul. Poselska 22 (☎22 67 65). A basic, well-run new place in a good central location south of the Rynek. ②.

Zaczek, al. 3 Maja 5 (☎33 54 77). University students' accommodation. May–Sept. ②.

Youth hostels

Ul. Oleandry 4 (☎33 89 20 or 33 88 22). The main hostel is a huge concrete construction behind the *Cracovia* hotel, usually full up during the summer (tram #18 from the train station). Open all year.

Ul. Kościuszki 88 (☎22 19 51). A smaller place, housed in a former convent overlooking the river, 1km southwest of the centre (trams #1, #2, #6, #21). Open all year.

Ul. Szablowskiego 1 (☎37 24 41). Four kilometres west of the centre (tram #4). Open July–Aug.

Ul. Złotej Kielni 1 (☎37 24 41). Open July & Aug only.

Campsites

Krak Camping, ul. Radzikowskiego 99 (☎37 21 22). Near the motel of the same name (see "Hotels", above), 5km northwest of the centre on the Katowice road, and with its own restaurant. The most popular camping site in Kraków. Buses #118, #173, #208, # 218 and #223 pass the motel. May–Sept.

Krakowianka, ul. Żywiecka Boczna (☎66 41 91). Part of the *Krakowianka* hotel complex usefully located on the Zakopane road. Includes bungalows and a restaurant. Bus #119.

Ogrodowy, ul Królowej Jadwigi 223 (☎22 20 11 ext. 67). Decent privately run campsite 5km west of the centre on the road to Balice airport. Buses #B, #102, #134.

Smok, ul. Kamedulska 18 (☎21 02 55). Another privately run site to the west of town on the Oświęcim road. Bus #109, #229 and all lines west towards Bielany run close by.

The City

The heart of the city centre is the **Stare Miasto**, the Old Town, bordered by the greenery of the **Planty**. The **Rynek Główny** is the focal point, with almost everything within half an hour's walk of it. A broad network of streets stretches south from here to the edge of **Wawel Hill**, with its royal residence, and beyond to the Jewish quarter of **Kazimierz**. Across the river, on the edge of the **Podgórze** suburb, is the old wartime ghetto. And finally, a little further out to the west, **Kościuszko's Mound** offers an attractive stretch of woods and countryside, just a ten-minute bus ride from the centre.

Rynek Główny

The **Rynek Główny** was the largest square of medieval Europe – a huge expanse of flagstones, ringed by magnificent houses and towering spires. Long the marketplace and commercial hub of the city, it's an immediate introduction to Kraków's grandeur and stateliness. By day things can get obscured by the crowds, but venture into the square late at night and you can immerse yourself in the aura of the city in its *fin-de-siècle* heyday and the memories of the great events played out here, such as the rallying call to national independence made by revolutionary leader Tadeusz Kościuszko (see box p.402) in 1794. Equally it's worth exploring the network of passageways and atmospheric, often recently restored, Italianate courtyards leading off from the front of the square, many of them enlivened by cafés and restaurants that have colonized the area in the past few years.

The square is more open today than it used to be. Until the last century, much of it was occupied by market stalls, a tradition maintained by the flower sellers and ice cream vendors, and by the stalls in the **Sukiennice**, the medieval cloth hall at the heart of the square dividing it into west and east sections, the latter of which is dominated by the **Mariacki Church**.

Around the square

In the east section, the focus is a statue of the romantic poet **Mickiewicz** (see box p.80), a facsimile of an earlier work destroyed by the Nazis, and a favourite meeting point. To its south, the copper-domed **St Adalbert's** (Św. Wojchecha), is the oldest building in the square and the first church to be founded in Kraków. The saint was a Slav bishop, reputed to have preached here around 995 AD before heading north to convert the Prussians, at whose hands he was martyred. In the basement (reconstructed in the eighteenth century), you can see the foundations of the original tenth-century Romanesque building. Traces of an even earlier wooden building, possibly a pre-Christian temple, and an assortment of archeological finds are also on display.

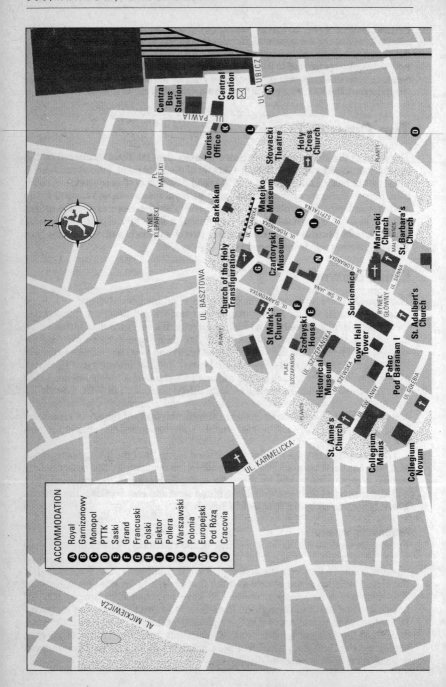

ACCOMMODATION

- **A** Royal
- **B** Garnizonowy
- **C** Monopol
- **D** PTTK
- **E** Saski
- **F** Grand
- **G** Francuski
- **H** Polski
- **I** Elektor
- **J** Pollera
- **K** Warszawski
- **L** Polonia
- **M** Europejski
- **N** Pod Róża
- **O** Cracovia

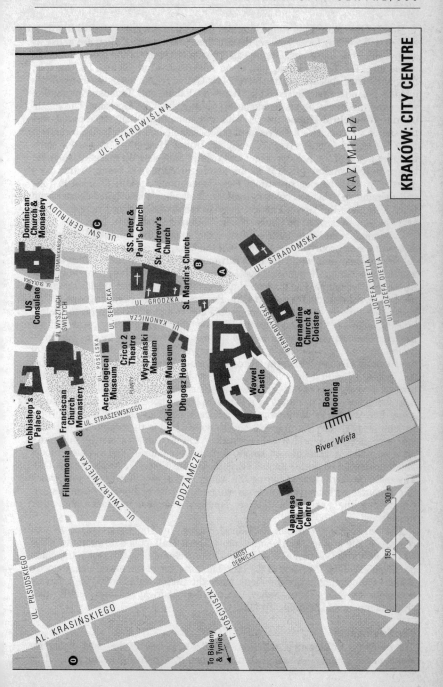

KRAKÓW: CITY CENTRE

KAZIMIERZ

UL. STAROWIŚLNA

UL. ŚW. GERTRUDY

Dominican Church & Monastery

UL. DOMINIKAŃSKA

US Consulate

UL. STOLARSKA

SS. Peter & Paul's Church

St. Andrew's Church

St. Martin's Church

UL. STRADOMSKA

Bernadine Church & Cloister

UL. BERNADYŃSKA

UL. JÓZEFA DIETLA

UL. JÓZEFA DIETLA

PL. WSZYTKICH ŚWIĘTYCH

UL. SENACKA

UL. GRODZKA

Archbishop's Palace

Franciscan Church & Monastery

Archeological Museum

UL. POSELSKA

PLANTY

Cricot 2 Theatre

Wyspiański Museum

UL. KANONICZA

Archdiocesan Museum

Długosz House

Wawel Castle

Filharmonia

UL. STRASZEWSKIEGO

Boat Mooring

UL. ZWIERZYNIECKA

PODZAMCZE

River Wisła

Japanese Cultural Centre

300 m

150

0

UL. PIŁSUDSKIEGO

MOST DĘBNICKI

T. KOŚCIUSZKI

AL. KRASIŃSKIEGO

To Bielany & Tyniec

Many of the **mansions** ranged around the square are associated with artists, writers and wealthy local families, though these days most of them are in use as shops, offices or museums. On the eastern side are some of the oldest buildings in the city. The **Grey House** (no. 6) on the corner of ul. Sienna, for example, despite its later appearance, has many of its Gothic rooms intact; its ex-residents include Poland's first elected king, Henri de Valois, and Tadeusz Kościuszko, who used the house as his headquarters during the 1794 Uprising. The neighbouring **Montelupi House** (no. 7), with a monumental Renaissance portal, was the site of the country's first-ever post office, established by its Italian owners in King Sigismund August's reign. The Gothic **Boner House** (no. 9) was for some time the home of the Kraków writer and painter Stanisław Wyspiański, while the **Wierzynek Mansion** (no. 15) in the southeast corner, is home to the city's oldest and most famous restaurant (see "Restaurants", p.410) founded in 1364 and claiming an unbroken culinary tradition. It also holds its original charter from King Kazimierz the Great. Political heavyweights who've dined here in recent years include presidents de Gaulle, Nixon, Mitterrand and Bush.

Continuing round the south section of the square, the **Potocki Palace** (no. 20), with a small courtyard with loggias at the back, is a good example of a classical Kraków mansion, while the **Pod Baranami** (no. 27), on the western side, is another aristocratic home, constructed from four adjacent burghers' houses in the sixteenth century. The nucleus of nineteenth-century social life, it's nowadays used as a cultural centre (see p.412). Further along the western edge of the square, an orderly collection of shopfronts and restaurants added on to the old houses, ends at the **Krzysztofory Palace** (no. 35) on the corner of ul. Szczepańska, another well-preserved mansion created by fusing burghers' houses into a single building with a fine courtyard at the back. Today it's part of the **Kraków History Museum** (Wed–Sun 9am–3.30pm, closed first Sat & Sun of the month). The first floor houses a large and varied collection relating to the historic development of the city. Interspersed among the historical exhibits is an interesting spread of paintings by artists with connections with the city, including some fine works by Witkiewicz and Małczewski. The section on Piłsudski's legions (see "History" in *Contexts*) and Kraków's role in the promotion of Polish independence post-World War I is revealing. On the top floor are the museum's prize exhibits, a collection of *szopki*, amazingly colourful and detailed model buildings produced for the annual Christmas contest (see "Festivals" box, p.413). The main display is staged during the winter, but at any time of the year, you'll find a couple of examples, generally winners of past competitions, on display. Completing the exhibits is a large, jumbled collection of clocks and other timepieces.

The tall **tower** (Wed–Sun 9am–3pm), facing the Pod Baranami, is all that remains of the original, fourteenth-century **Town Hall**, pulled down in the 1820s by the authorities as part of a misguided improvement plan. It's worth the climb up for an excellent overview of the city. The top floor of the tower features occasionally illuminating local exhibitions, while the Gothic vaults below are currently occupied by the *Teatr Satyry*, a popular satirical cabaret outfit (see "Entertainment and Nightlife", p.412).

The Sukiennice

The medieval **Sukiennice**, rebuilt in the 1550s, is one of the most distinctive sights in the country – a vast cloth hall, topped by a sixteenth-century attic dripping with gargoyles. Its commercial traditions are perpetuated by a **covered market**, which bustles with tourists and street sellers at almost any time of year. Inside, the stalls of the darkened central arcade display a hotch-potch collection of junk and genuine craft items from the Podhale region. Popular buys include amber jewellery, painted boxes in every shape and size and thick woollen sweaters from the mountains. Prices are inevitably inflated, so if you're travelling on to the south, it's better to wait until you get to the market at Nowy Targ (see p.450). The **terrace cafés** on either side of the hall are classic Kraków haunts, although the locals who used to idle away the afternoon over tea and *sernik* have been almost totally replaced by tourists.

The **Art Gallery** on the upper floor of the Sukiennice (Mon 10am–4pm, Thurs noon–6pm, Fri–Sun 10am–4pm) is worth a visit for its collection of works by nineteenth-century Polish artists, among them Matejko, Malczewski, Gierymski and Chełmonski. The Matejkos here include two political heavyweights, the *Homage of Prussia* and the stirring *Kościuszko at Racławice*. As usual with Matejko, the impact is heightened if you appreciate the historical reference points, in this case the homage of the Teutonic Knights in 1525 (see Malbork, p.188) and the Polish peasant army's victory over the Russians in 1794.

Mariacki Church and Square

Mariacki Church (St Mary's) was founded in 1222 and destroyed during the mid-century Tartar invasions. The current building, begun in 1355 and completed fifty years later, is one of the finest Gothic structures in the country. The taller of its towers, a late fifteenth-century addition, is topped by an amazing ensemble of spires, elaborated with a crown and helmet. Legend has it that during one of the early Tartar raids the watchman positioned at the top of this tower saw the invaders approaching and took up his trumpet to raise the alarm; his warning was cut short by a Tartar arrow through the throat. The legend lives on, and every hour on the hour a lone **trumpeter** plays the sombre *hejnał* melody, halting abruptly at the precise point the watchman was supposed to have been hit. The national radio station broadcasts the *hejnał* live at noon every day and Polish writers are still apt to wax lyrical on the symbolism of the trumpet's warning.

First impressions of the **church** are of a cavernous, somewhat gloomy expanse. What little light there is comes from the high windows at each end, the ancient altar window facing the stained glass of the west end, an Art Nouveau extravaganza by Kraków artist Stanisław Wyspiański. Walking down the nave, you'll have to pick your way past devotees kneeling in front of the fifteenth-century **Chapel of Our Lady of Częstochowa**, with its copy of the venerated image of the Black Madonna. Locals claim that this is actually older than the original.

Continuing down the high Gothic nave, under arched stone vaulting enhanced in blue and gold, the walls, like those surrounding the high altar, are decorated with **Matejko friezes**. Separating the nave from the aisles are a succession of buttressed pillars fronted by Baroque marble altars. The aisles themselves lead off to a number of lavishly ornamented chapels, fifteenth-century additions to the main body of the building. Focal point of the nave is the huge stone **crucifix** attributed to Veit Stoss (see box on p.373), hanging in the archway to the presbytery.

The biggest crowds are drawn by the majestic **high altar** at the far east end. Carved by the Nuremberg master craftsman Veit Stoss (Wit Stwosz, as he's known in Poland) between 1477 and 1489, the huge limewood polyptych is one of the finest examples of late Gothic art in Europe. The outer sides of the folded polyptych feature illustrations from the life of the Holy Family executed in gilded polychromy. At noon (Sundays and saints' days excluded) the altar is opened to reveal the inner panels, with their reliefs of the Annunciation, Nativity, Adoration of the Magi, Resurrection, Ascension and Pentecost; for a good view, arrive at least a quarter of an hour before the opening. These six superb scenes are a fitting backdrop to the central panel – an exquisite **Dormition of the Virgin** in which the graceful figure of Mary is shown reclining into her final sleep in the arms of the watchful Apostles. Like most of the figures, the Apostles, several of them well over life-size, are thought to be based on Stoss's contemporaries in Kraków. Certainly there's an uncanny mastery of human detail that leaves you feeling you'd recognize their human counterparts if you met them in the street. Other features of note in the chancel are the Gothic stained-glass windows, the Renaissance tabernacle designed by Giovanni Maria Mosca, and the exuberant early Baroque stalls.

ST BARBARA'S CHURCH AND MARIACKI SQUARE

The side door on the south side of the chancel brings you into **Mariacki Square**, a small courtyard replacing the old church cemetery closed down by the Austrians in the last century. On the far side of the courtyard stands the fourteenth-century **St Barbara's Church** (rarely open except during services), among its contents a remarkable late Gothic *pietà* group, sculpted in stone and attributed to the anonymous local artist known as "Master of the Beautiful Madonnas". During the Partitions, the ruling Austrians took over the Mariacki, so the locals were forced to use this tiny place for services in Polish. The back of the church looks onto the tranquil **Mały Rynek**, whose terrace cafés make an enjoyable venue for postcard sessions or a quiet beer.

From Mały Rynek, the narrow **ul. Sienna** offers an alternative route back to the main square. On the street outside no. 5 there's normally a bunch of students touting political books and badges, alternately amusing, informative or impenetrable to the foreigner. The first floor of the building houses the local branch of the **Catholic Intellectuals Club** (KIK), an organization that's more approachable than it sounds. Founded in the wake of the post-Stalinist political thaw of the 1950s, the KIK was for over thirty years one of the few officially sanctioned independent structures in the country, and its national network played an important part in the last decade's political events. It was to the KIK offices in Kraków, for example, that local steelworkers and farmers came for help when setting up the first Solidarity organizations in 1980. Today, a number of KIK people are now prominent politicians, ex-prime minister Tadeusz Mazowiecki included.

Around the Stare Miasto

Like the Rynek, the streets of the Stare Miasto still follow the medieval plan, while their **architecture** presents a rich central European ensemble of Gothic, Renaissance and Baroque. They are a hive of commercial activity, too, with boutiques, fast-food joints and other new privately owned shops replacing the old state enterprise outlets, and a mass of **street traders**, ranging from young Poles touting Western cassettes to Russian peasants holding up gold trinkets. West of the Rynek, the atmosphere is generated by the academic buildings and student haunts of the **university district**.

VEIT STOSS

As with Copernicus, the issue of the nationality of the man who carved the Mariacki altar – unquestionably the greatest work of art ever created in Poland – was long the source of a rather sterile dispute between Polish and German protagonists. Although his early career remains something of a mystery, it now seems indisputable that the sculptor's original name was **Veit Stoss**, and that he was born between 1440 and 1450 in Horb at the edge of the Black Forest, settling later in Nuremberg, where a few early works by him have been identified. He **came to Kraków** in 1477, perhaps at the invitation of the royal court (the Polish queen was an Austrian princess), though more likely at the behest of the German merchant community, a sizeable but declining minority in the city, who worshipped in the Mariacki and paid for its new altar by subscription.

Despite being his first major commission, the **Mariacki altarpiece** is Stoss' masterpiece. It triumphantly displays every facet of late Gothic sculpture: the architectural setting, complete with its changing lights, is put to full dramatic effect; there is mastery over every possible scale, from the huge figures in the central shrine to the tiny figurines and decoration in the borders; subtle use is made of a whole gamut of technical devices, from three different depths of relief to a graded degree of gilding according to the importance of the scene; and the whole layout is based on a scheme of elaborate theological complexity that would nevertheless be bound to make an impression on the many unlettered worshippers who viewed it. It would seem that it is mostly Stoss' own work: gilders and joiners were certainly employed, but otherwise he was probably only helped by one assistant and one apprentice.

While engaged on the altarpiece, Stoss carved the relief of *Christ in the Garden of Gethsemane*, now in the City Art Museum. Made of sandstone, a material he later used for the Mariacki *Crucifix*, it is indicative of his exceptional **versatility with materials**. This is further apparent in consideration of the works he created after finishing the altarpiece: the tomb of King Kazimierz the Jagiellonian in the Wawel Cathedral is of Salzburg marble, the epitaph to Philippus Buonaccorsi in the Dominican Church is of bronze, while his two other key Polish commissions – the episcopal monuments in the cathedrals of Gniezno and Włocławek – are both of Hungarian marble. These sculptures made Stoss a great Polish celebrity, and he rose far above his artisan status to engage in extensive commercial activities, and to dabble in both architecture and engineering. The forms of the Mariacki altarpiece and his monuments were widely imitated throughout Poland, and continued to be so for the next half century.

It therefore seems all the more curious that he **returned to Nuremberg** in 1496, remaining there until his death in 1533. His homecoming was a traumatic experience: Nuremberg was well endowed with specialist craftsmen, and Stoss was forced to follow suit, concentrating on producing single, unpainted wooden figures. Attempts to maintain his previous well-to-do lifestyle led him into disastrous business dealings, which culminated in his forging a document, as a result of which he was branded on both cheeks and forbidden to venture beyond the city. He never really came to terms with the ideals of the Italian Renaissance, which took strong root in Nuremberg, nor did he show any enthusiasm for the Protestant Reformation, which was supported by nearly all the great German artists of the day, most notably his fellow townsman, Albrecht Dürer. Yet, even if Stoss never repeated the success of his Kraków years, he continued to produce memorable and highly individualistic sculptures, above all the spectacular garlanded *Annunciation* suspended from the ceiling of the city's church of St Lorenz.

South of the main square, the busy **ul. Grodzka** leads down towards **plac Dominikański**, one of the pivotal points of the Old Town, and on to Wawel Hill. The historic streets combine the increasingly fast-paced bustle of the city's commercial life with the tranquillity and splendour of a myriad ancient churches, palaces and mansions. Additionally, there's a brace of museums worth exploring.

Ulica Floriańska

Of the three streets leading north off the Rynek, the easternmost, **ul. Floriańska** is the busiest and most striking. In among the myriad shops, cafés and restaurants are some attractive fragments of medieval and Renaissance architecture. At no. 5, for example, a beautiful early Renaissance stone figure of the *Madonna and Child* sits in a niche on the facade of the **Floriańska Gate**. At no. 14, **Pod Różą**, the oldest hotel in Kraków, has a Renaissance doorway inscribed in Latin, "May this house stand until an ant drinks the oceans and a tortoise circles the world" – it doesn't seem to get much attention from the moneyed revellers who flock to the hotel's reopened casino. Famous hotel guests of the past include Franz Liszt, Balzac and the occasional tsar.

Further up the street, at no. 41, is the sixteenth-century **Matejko House**, home of painter Jan Matejko until his death in 1893. An opulent, slighly gloomy three-storey mansion of the type favoured by the wealthy turn-of-the-century Kraków bourgeoisie, it houses a museum (Tues, Wed & Fri–Sun 10am–3.30pm, Thurs noon–6pm) with a range of Matejko family memorabilia, parts of the man's extensive personal art collection and a number of his own paintings and assorted other artistic outpourings.

The first-floor parlour and a couple of other rooms remain pretty much as the Matejko family kept them, attractive old fireplaces included. The second and third floors house Matejko's private art gallery, notably a number of Renaissance pictures and triptychs. The rest of the exhibition is mostly Matejko's own work, including the sketches of the windows he designed for the Mariacki Church. There's also a collection of old costumes and armour that he used as inspiration for several of his more famous pictures, notably *Sobieski at Vienna*. Not a wildly exciting museum, it's a popular enough place with Matejko freaks, of whom there still seem to be plenty in the country.

Further along, Western fast-food culture has come to town in the form of the McDonald's at no. 55, more or less welcomed by local residents, depending on who you speak to, though plans to build another restaurant right on the revered main square are proving a good deal more controversial.

Floriańska Gate, at the end of the street, marks the edge of the Old Town proper. A square, robust fourteenth-century structure, it's part of a small section of fortifications saved when the old defensive walls were pulled down in the early nineteenth century. The walls lead east to the fifteenth-century Haberdashers' (Pasamoników) Tower and west to the Joiners' (Stolarska) Gate, which is separated from the even older Carpenters' (Cieśli) Gate by the Arsenal. The original fortifications must have been an impressive sight – three kilometres of wall ten metres high and nearly three metres thick, interspersed with 47 towers and bastions. The strongest-looking defensive remnant is the **Barbakan**, just beyond Floriańska Gate. A bulbous, spiky fort, added in 1498, it's unusual in being based on the Arab as opposed to European defensive architecture of the time. The covered passage linking the fort to the walls has disappeared, as has the original moat – all of which leaves the bastion looking a little stranded.

Ulica Szpitalna and around

Immediately east of ul. Floriańska is **ul. Szpitalna**, another mansion-lined thoroughfare. At no. 24, the city's **Orthodox Church** is housed upstairs in a building that used to serve as a synagogue. As usual, the icon-filled church is only open during services, but there's an interesting display of Orthodox-inspired religious art in the entry lobby and ground-floor art gallery, featuring works by the contemporary Polish artist Jerzy Nowoselski.

Further up the street, across plac Św. Ducha is the **Church of the Holy Cross** (Kościół Św. Krzyża) a fabulous building that's unfortunately just as hard to get into and see properly – only open during services. The most impressive feature is the beautifully decorated Gothic vaulting, supported by a single exquisite palm-like central pillar, an extremely unusual architectural phenomenon, built at the time of the reconstruction of the original fourteenth-century Gothic edifice in the 1520s. The graceful fifteenth- and sixteenth-century murals decorating the nave and choir were restored at the turn of the century by Wyspiański among others, who was passionately devoted to the building, regarding it as of the city's finest Gothic churches. When the church is closed, you can catch a glimpse of the palm vaulting through the iron grille, but it's definitely worth the effort of coming back when it's open. Service times are posted on the board outside.

Immediately before the church is the **Słowacki Theatre**, built in 1893 on the site of the ancient Church of the Holy Ghost complex demolished amid loud protests from Matejko and other local luminaries. Modelled on the Paris Opéra, the richly ornate theatre, named after the much-loved Romantic poet and playwright Julius Słowacki, established itself as one of Kraków's premier theatres, a position it still enjoys (see "Entertainment", p.412).

The Czartoryski Palace and Szołayski House museums

Back to Floriańska Gate and past the reproduction Pop Art collections displayed on the old walls, a left turn down the narrow **ul. Pijarska** brings you to the corner of ul. Św. Jana and back down to the main square. On the way, on your right, is the Baroque **Monastery and Church of the Holy Transfiguration**, originally the home of the Piarist order, with a facade modelled on the Gesù Church in Rome; on your left, linked to the church by an overhead passage, is the Czartoryski Palace.

THE CZARTORYSKI PALACE

A branch of the National Museum, the **Czartoryski Palace** houses Kraków's finest art collection (Tues–Thurs & Sun 10am–3.30pm, Fri 10am–6pm, but hours do vary). Its core was established by Izabella Czartoryska at the family palace in Puławy (see p.295) and was then moved to Kraków following the confiscation of the Puławy estate after the 1831 Insurrection, in which the family was deeply implicated. The family were legendary collectors, particularly from the Paris salons of the seventeenth and eighteenth centuries, and it shows, despite the Nazis' removal, and subsequent loss, of many precious items, including Raphael's famous *Portrait of a Young Man*, which has never been recovered.

The **ancient art** collection alone contains over a thousand exhibits, from sites in Mesopotamia, Etruria, Greece and Egypt. Another intriguing highlight is the collection of **trophies from the Battle of Vienna** (1683), which includes sumptuous Turkish carpets, scimitars, tents and other Oriental finery.

The **picture galleries** contain a rich display of art and sculpture ranging from thirteenth- to eighteenth-century works, the most famous being Rembrandt's brooding *Landscape Before a Storm* and Leonardo da Vinci's *Lady with an Ermine*. A double pun identifies the rodent-handler as Cecilia Gallerani, the mistress of Leonardo's patron, Lodovico il Moro: the Greek word for this animal is *galé* – a play on the woman's name – and Lodovico's nickname was "Ermelino", meaning ermine. There is also a large collection of Dutch canvases and an outstanding array of fourteenth-century Sienese primitives, the whole thing arranged following nineteenth-century tradition to form distinct artistic and decorative groupings. As in all Polish museums, you may find several galleries closed off (often the best ones), ostensibly for lack of staff; passing yourself off as an art student or amateur enthusiast may gain you admission.

THE SZOŁAYSKI HOUSE MUSEUM

On down ul. Św. Jana towards the Rynek, there are more wealthy Old Town residences, such as the Neoclassical Lubomirski Palace at no. 15 and the eighteenth-century Kołłątaj House at no. 20, once a meeting place for the cultured elite. Back onto the square and west along ul. Szczepańska, the modest **Szołayski House**, on the eastern edge of plac Szczepański, houses a small but important section of the city **art museum** (Tues 10am–6pm, Wed–Sun 10am–3.30pm), featuring a significant collection of Gothic and Renaissance Polish art and sculpture, much of it taken from churches in the Małopolska region. The best-known exhibit here is the fourteenth-century *Madonna of Krużlowa*, an exquisite Gothic sculpture of the "Beautiful Madonna" school. Unearthed in a local village church attic, this wonderful piece depicts a typically dreamy Mary with a cheerful-looking Christ perched on her shoulder. Other pieces here include a beautiful figure of Christ riding on a donkey from 1470, used in Palm Sunday processions, an expressive cycle of late fifteenth-century altarpieces from the local Augustine and Dominican churches, and a powerful *Christ in the Garden of Gethsemane*, a sandstone relief carved by Veit Stoss for the cemetery beside the Mariacki Church, as well as a small wooden *Crucifixion* attributed to his workshop. The works by Nicholas Haberchrack, a lesser-known local artist are likewise impressive, notably a fine *Christ Washing the Disciples' Feet* and *Adoration of the Magi*. After the joys of this superb selection of Gothic sculpture the later-era art housed on the second floor is a bit of an anticlimax, though the portraits of kings Jan Sobieski and Sigismund August will be familiar enough to anyone who's already trailed round the Wawel collections. It's interesting too to note the distinctive icon-like Uniate influences in many of the pieces gathered from churches in eastern Małopolska, including the triptychs from places such as Dębno (see p.463).

Also on this square are two impressive turn-of-the-century buildings in the Viennese Secessionist style: the decorative **Stary Teatr** to the south, and the **Palace of Arts** to the west, a stately structure with reliefs by Małczewski and niches filled with busts of Matejko, Witkiewicz and other local artists. The latter, adorned with a mosaic frieze, features exhibitions of contemporary art.

The university district

Head west from the Rynek on any of the three main thoroughfares – ul. Szczepańska, ul. Szewska or ul. Św. Anny – and you're into the **university area**. The main body of buildings is south of ul. Św. Anny, the principal Jewish area of the city until the early 1400s, when the university bought up many of the properties and the Jews moved out to the Kazimierz district.

The Gothic **Collegium Maius** building, at the intersection of ul. Św. Anny with ul. Jagiellońska, is the historic heart of the university complex. The university got off to something of a false start after its foundation by King Kazimierz in 1364, foundering badly after his death six years later, until it was revived by King Władysław Jagiełło in the early fifteenth century, when the university authorities began transforming these buildings into a new academic centre.

Through the passageway from ul. Jagiellońska you find yourself in a quiet, arcaded **courtyard** with a marble fountain playing in the centre, an ensemble that, during the early 1960s, was stripped of neo-Gothic accretions and restored to something approaching its original form. The cloistered atmosphere of ancient academia makes an enjoyable break from the city in itself, though actually getting into the building is not so easy. Now renamed and known as the **University Museum**, the Collegium is open to guided tours only (Mon–Sat noon–2pm), for which you need to book places at least a day in advance (☎22 05 49). If you just turn up without having booked, you might be able to talk your way onto a tour, but in summer they're usually full. The shop in the courtyard arcade has caught onto the logo craze, selling mugs, pens, sweatshirts and other items sporting the Jagiellonian University crest.

Inside, **tours** proceed through the ground-floor rooms, which retain the mathematical and geographical murals once used for teaching. The **Alchemy Room**, with its skulls and other wizard's accoutrements, was used according to legend by the fabled magician Doctor Faustus. Stairs leading up from the courtyard bring you to an elaborately decorated set of **reception rooms**. The principal assembly hall has a Renaissance ceiling adorned with carved rosettes and portraits of Polish royalty, benefactors and professors; its Renaissance portal carries the Latin inscription *Plus Ratio Quam Vis* – "Wisdom rather than Strength". The professors' common room, which also served as their dining hall, boasts an ornate Baroque spiral staircase and a Gothic bay window with a replica statuette of King Kazimierz. In the **Treasury**, the most valued possession is the copper Jagiellonian globe, constructed around 1510 as the centrepiece of a clock mechanism and featuring the earliest known illustration of America – labelled "a newly discovered land". If you find old scientific instruments interesting, ask the guide if you can see the other old laboratories and globe rooms.

Several other old buildings are dotted round this area. The university **Church of St Anne**, on ul. Św. Anny, was designed by the ubiquitous Tylman of Gameren. A monumental Baroque extravaganza, built on a Latin cross plan with a high central dome, it's widely regarded as Gameren's most mature work, the classicism of his design neatly counterpoised by rich stucco decoration added by the Italian sculptor Baldaggare Fontana. The **Collegium Minus**, just round the corner on ul. Gołębia, is the fifteenth-century arts faculty, rebuilt two centuries later; Jan Matejko studied and later taught here. On the corner of the same street stands the outsize **Collegium Novum**, the neo-Gothic university administrative headquarters, with an interior modelled on the Collegium Maius. The **Copernicus statue**, in front of the Collegium Novum, on the edge of the Planty, commemorates the university's most famous supposed student – some local historians doubt that he really did study here.

In term time, the university district's **cafés** and **restaurants** are usually lively (see "Eating, drinking and entertainment", p.407), while the graffiti-sprayed southern section of **ul. Jagiellońska** and adjoining **ul. Gołębia** are invariably lined with students hawking books, posters and, of course, Solidarity badges – though that's mainly for the tourists these days. Student artwork, however, remains a fount of political comment, and ex-president Lech Wałęsa and the other opposition veterans are now as much the butt of jokes as their communist predecessors used to be.

The Nowy Gmach Modern Art Museum

For anyone interested in the development of modern Polish art, there's a further section of the city **art museum** worth exploring. Housed in a large concrete block on the corner of al. 3 Maja, a couple of bus stops west of the university district along ul. Piłsudskiego, just beyond the *Cracovia* hotel, the **Nowy Gmach gallery** (Tues–Sat 10am–6pm, Sun 10am–3.30pm) features permanent exhibitions of a wide selection of painting and sculpture from the 1890s and beyond. The turn-of-the-century Młoda Polska movement is particularly well represented here, with a number of notable works by Wyspiański, including the designs for his windows in Wawel Cathedral, as well as a number of other major Polish artists including Mehoffer, Witkiewicz and Ślewiński. The museum also presents a diverse range of roving exhibitions, some of them, like the large "Jews of Poland" exhibition, major national cultural events, so it's always worth checking what's on in the local listings.

The Dominican Church

Ulica Grodzka stretches south of the Rynek, crossing the tram lines circling the city centre at plac Dominikański. East across the square stands the large brickwork basilica of the thirteenth-century **Dominican Church and Monastery**. Constructed on the site of an earlier church, following its destruction during the fearsome Tartar raid of 1241, the modest original Gothic brick church grew to become one the Kraków's grandest churches. Much of the accumulated splendour, however, was wiped out during a fire in 1850, which seriously devastated the church and much of the surrounding quarter, the Franciscan Church included (see below).

Today, the dominant atmosphere of the building is one of uncluttered, tranquil contemplation – like most Polish churches, the main purpose of the building is worship, not display, a fact attested to by the continual stream of services held here on almost any day of the week. However, there is a wealth of architectural detail to appreciate in the church. Adjoining the main nave, redecorated in an airy Neo-Gothic style, are a succession of chapels, many of which survived the 1850 fire in better shape than the rest of the building. Oldest of them all, up a flight of steps at the end of the north aisle, is **St Hyacinth's chapel** (Kaplica Św. Jakuba), dedicated to the joint founder and first abbot of the monastery. Based on the design of the Sigismund Chapel in Wawel Cathedral, the chapel boasts some rich stucco work on the dome above the free-standing tomb, both by Baldassare Fontana. The other notable feature is a sequence of paintings portraying the life of the saint by Thomas Dolabella. The Baroque **Myszkowski family chapel** in the southern isle is a fine creation from the workshop of Santa Gucci (see box p.385), the exuberantly ornamented exterior contrasting with the austere, marble faced interior, with busts of the Myszkowski family lining the chapel dome. Similarly noteworthy is the **Rosary chapel**, built as a thanks-offering for Sobieski's victory over the Turks at Vienna in 1683, and housing a supposedly miracle-producing image of Our Lady of the Rosary. A fine series of **tombstones** survives in the chancel, notably those of the early thirteenth-century Prince of Kraków Leszek Czarny (the Black), and an impressive bronze tablet of the Italian Renaissance scholar Filippo Buonaccorsi, built to a design by Veit Stoss and cast at the Nuremberg Vischer works.

Through the Renaissance doorway, underneath the stairs leading up to St Hyacinth's chapel, are the tranquil Gothic **cloisters**, whose walls are lined with memorials to the great and good of Kraków, leading in the north wing to a fine Romanesque refectory with a vaulted crypt. The Dominicans have a long tradition of involvement with the city's student population, and during the 1980s, the cloisters were a focus of independent cultural and political activism, notably exhibitions of art frowned upon or banned by the authorities.

The Franciscan Church

On the west side of plac Dominikański is the **Franciscan Church and Monastery**, home to the Dominican's long-standing rivals in the tussle for the city's religious affections. Built soon after Franciscan friars first arrived from Prague in 1237, the church was completed some thirty years later. As one of Kraków's major churches it has witnessed some important events in the nation's history, notably the baptism in 1385 of the pagan Grand Duke of Lithuania Prince Jagiełło, prior to (and as a condition of) his assumption of the Polish throne. A plain high brick building, the church's somewhat murky, brooding atmosphere forms a stark contrast to its Dominican neighbour. The most striking feature is the celebrated series of Art Nouveau **murals** and **stained-glass windows** designed and executed by Stanisław Wyspiański in 1900, following the gutting of the church in the fire fifty years earlier (see above). An exuberant outburst of floral and geometric mural motifs extol the naturalist creed of St Francis, culminating in the magnificent stained-glass depiction of **God the Creator** in the large west window, the elements of the scene seemingly merging into each other in a hazy, abstract swirl of colour. By contrast, the floral motif depiction of St Francis and the Blessed Salomea in the window behind the altar conjures up an altogether more restrained, meditative atmosphere, while the **north chapel** contains a flowing set of Stations of the Cross by another Młoda Polska adherent, Jacek Mehoffer. The **south chapel** contains a fine early fifteenth-century image of the Madonna of Mercy, a popular local figure. The Gothic **cloisters**, reached from the southern side of the church are worth a visit for the series of **portraits** of the bishops of Kraków dating back to the mid-fifteenth century and continuing up to the present day, notably the portrait of Bishop Piotr Tomicki from the early 1500s. To complete the ecclesiastical picture, the **Archbishop of Kraków's residence**, not long ago inhabited by Karol Wojtyła, stands across from the Franciscan Church.

South from Plac Dominikański

On down ul. Grodzka, past the gilded stone lion above the **Podelwie House** (no. 32), the oldest such stone emblem in the city, turn right into ul. Poselska to find the house, at no. 12, where novelist **Joseph Conrad** spent his childhood: a commemorative plaque in the corner carries a quotation from his work.

Further down ul. Poselska, through the garden entrance at no. 3 and past the top of ul. Senacka, is the **Archeological Museum** (Mon 9am–4pm, Tues, Thurs & Sat 1pm–5pm, Fri 10am–2pm, Sun 11am–2pm). Housed in a building with a chequered history – it was originally an early medieval stronghold, then successively a palace, monastery and Habsburg-era prison, before becoming a museum – the collections feature an array of Egyptian, Greek and Roman objects alongside a large group of local finds, including an extensive set of Neolithic painted ceramics considered to be among the best in Europe. Even if you're not totally sold on hoards of old coins and pottery there's one totally unmissable object here, the famed figure of a pagan Slavonic god, known as **Światowit**, the only image of a Slav pagan deity ever discovered. An extraordinary carved stone idol standing 2.5m high and sporting what looks like a top hat, its crude decoration, includes a face on each side (one for each of the winds, it is thought).

The route south continues down ul. Grodzka, past another run of churches before ending up at the busy crossroads in the shadow of Wawel. The first, the austere twin-domed **Basilica of SS. Peter and Paul**, a little way back from the street, is fronted by imposing statues of the two Apostles, actually copies of the pollution-scarred originals, now kept elsewhere for preservation's sake. The church's exterior recently received a thorough clean-up, the much reduced pollution levels in the inner city meaning that the distinctive statues should be able to keep their current shine for a while to come. Modelled on the Gesù in Rome, it's the earliest Baroque building in the city, commissioned by the Jesuits when they came to Kraków in the 1580s to quell Protestant agitation. A notable feature here is the crypt of Piotr Skarga (Mon–Fri 9am–5pm) down the steps in front of the altar, where there are piles of slips of paper filled with the prayers of the devout. A noted Jesuit preacher and Polish champion of the Counter-Reformation, Skarga was for some time linked with the church. Fine stucco work by Giovanni Falconi in the chapels on either side of the nave helps to relieve the severity of the place.

Next comes the Romanesque **St Andrew's**, remodelled in familiar Polish Baroque style, where the local people are reputed to have holed themselves up and successfully fought off marauding Tartars during the invasion of 1241; it looks just about strong enough for the purpose. The early thirteenth-century mosaic icon of the Virgin from Constantinople stored in the Treasury is credited with having helped out. A little further on, **St Martin's**, built in the seventeenth century on the site of a Romanesque foundation, now belongs to Kraków's small Lutheran community.

The route to Wawel Hill

The traditional route used by Polish monarchs when entering the city took them through the Floriańska Gate, down ul. Floriańska to the Rynek, then south down ul. Grodzka – part of the old trade route up through Kraków from Hungary – to the foot of Wawel Hill. The alternative route for the last leg of the walk to Wawel Hill leads off ul. Grodzka via ul. Senacka and down **ul. Kanonicza**, a quiet, dusty cobbled back street, unquestionably one of the most atmospheric in the city. Restoration work on the string of neglected-looking Gothic mansions lining the street lurches forward unevenly, but there's little doubt that, if and when the rebuilding is completed, the street will become a prime tourist attraction.

First of the street's pair of museums, two doors down from the legendary Tadeusz Kantor's **Cricot 2 Theatre** at no. 5 (see p.412), is the **Wyspiański Museum** (Tues & Thurs–Sun 10am–3.30pm, Fri 10am–6pm) devoted to the life and works of the brilliant writer/artist and long-time Kraków resident. The ground floor fills you in on the man's background and early development (there's a helpful set of English-language guide sheets you can borrow from the ticket office), and on the staircase there's an arresting set of **photos** of the Kazimierz district, a number taken by Wyspiański himself around the turn of the century, offering a view of life in the ghetto as seen by a Gentile outsider. The second floor houses a collection of paintings by Wyspiański and Młoda Polska movement contemporaries such as Malczewski and Tetmajer. Other notable exhibits here are the models that formed the basis of Wyspiański's plan to refashion and enlarge the Wawel complex as a Polish Acropolis – a bizarre, haunting vision given full reign in his play of the same name. In addition there are sketches from the conservation work carried out on the Church of the Holy Cross (see p.375) by Wyspiański in the 1890s, then in a very dilapidated state, and some fine examples of the **stained-glass windows** he produced for the Dominican Church on plac Dominikański.

Almost at the bottom of the street, housed in an impressive pair of recently renovated mansions from the late 1300s, belonging to the archbishop of Kraków (nos. 19/21), is the **Archdiocesan Museum** (Tues–Sun 10am–3pm), an engaging newcomer to the city's already extensive set of museums. Like the Szołayski House, the wealth of religious art displayed here comes from the churches of the surrounding Małopolska region, much of it never previously put on public show. As well as the permanent collections, the museum is planning to hold a regular series of temporary exhibitions of further treasures from the obviously vast local ecclesiastical collection.

Highlight of the collection in the first gallery is a set of **Gothic sculptures**, including a wonderful early fifteenth-century *Madonna and Child* in the "Beautiful Madonna" style, from the Orawa region, a powerful late Gothic *Martyrdom of St Stephen*, from the Kraków school of the early 1500s and an exquisite relief of the *Adoration of the Magi* dating from the 1460s taken from the Mariacki Church. As with the best of Veit Stoss' work, what's most striking here is the human realism of the figures, the gentle, expressive faces reaching out across the centuries.

The second hall features a notable cycle of pictures by Hans Suess of Kulmbach, illustrating the legend of St Kathryn of Alexandria, executed in 1514 for the Boner family chapel in Mariacki and a notable *Annunciation* by Jakob Mertens from 1580, alongside a wealth of assorted religious artefacts. On into the third gallery there's yet more Gothic art from the region, including a fine early sixteenth-century pentaptych from the St Nicholas Church in Kraków. Rounding off the exhibitions is a room dedicated to Karol Woytyła, its one-time resident in his days as a humble priest in Kraków. As usual with Polish exhibitions devoted to the man, there's a string of papal memorabilia, much of it donated by the pope himself, including sets of his old vestments and to round it all off, a pair of pre-papal shoes.

Back out on the street, the **Ukrainian bookstore** (no. 20) is worth a look for the occasional displays of contemporary Orthodox and Uniate art. At the very end of the street, the fifteenth-century **Długosz House** (Dom Długosza) at no. 25, named after an early resident, the historian Jan Długosz, originally served as the royal bathhouse. Local legend has it that in preparation for her marriage to Lithuanian Grand Duke Ladisław Jagiełło, the future Queen Jadwiga sent one of her most trusted servants to attend the duke during his ablutions and report back over rumours of the grotesque genital proportions of the pagan Lithuanians. Exactly what the servant told her is not revealed, but at any rate the queen went ahead and married the man.

At this point, most people head straight up to the Wawel by the obvious route across the road. If you can't face the crowds swarming up this path in summer, a

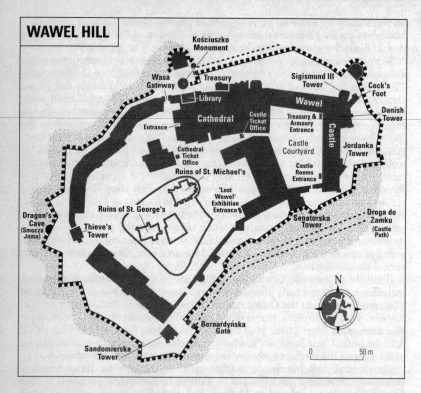

WAWEL HILL

Kościuszko Monument

Wasa Gateway

Treasury

Library

Sigismund III Tower

Cock's Foot

Wawel

Danish Tower

Cathedral

Castle Ticket Office

Entrance

Treasury & Armoury Entrance

Castle

Castle Courtyard

Cathedral Ticket Office

Jordanka Tower

Ruins of St. Michael's

Castle Rooms Entrance

'Lost Wawel' Exhibition Entrance

Ruins of St. George's

Droga do Zamku (Castle Path)

Dragon's Cave (Smocza Jama)

Thieve's Tower

Senatorska Tower

Bernardyńska Gate

N

Sandomierska Tower

0   50 m

quieter (though considerably longer) alternative route is to continue round the southern edge of the complex, and turn either up the castle approach to the right or along ul. Bernardyńska, both of which lead you to the entrance to the complex at the **Bernardine Gate** (Brama Bernardyńska). The absence of tourist-trinket hawkers aside, the advantage of these routes, particularly the latter, is the fine **view** back onto Wawel Cathedral. At the foot of Wawel, along ul. Bernardyńska, in the square of the same name is the **Bernardine Church**, a Baroque basilica built on the site of an earlier Gothic church containing a wealth of lavish period furnishings, notably a graphic depiction of the *Dance of Death* in the main aisle, a well-known local favourite, and a fine sculpture of St Anne with the Virgin and Child attributed to the workshop of Veit Stoss in one of the side chapels.

Wawel Hill: the castle and cathedral

For over five hundred years, the country's rulers lived and governed on **Wawel Hill**, whose main buildings stand pretty much as they have done for centuries. Even after the capital moved to Warsaw, Polish monarchs continued to be buried in the cathedral, and it's at Wawel that many of the nation's venerated poets and heroes lie in state with a set of buildings that serve as a virtual textbook of Polish history. As such, Wawel represents a potent source of national and spiritual pride, and unusually in Kraków, there are always far greater crowds of Poles than foreigners looking around, many of them in large organized groups making a near-obligatory pilgrimage to the fount of national memory.

The cobbled path up Wawel negotiates lines of souvenir touts, silhouette artists and horoscope sellers. At the top, a typically dramatic statue of Tadeusz Kościuszko – a copy of the one destroyed by the Nazis – stands before the sixteenth-century Waza Gate. As you emerge, the cathedral rears up to the left, with the castle and its outbuildings and courtyards beyond. Directly ahead is a huge, open square, once the site of a Wawel township, but cleared by the Austrians in the early nineteenth century to create a parade ground.

The cathedral and castle have separate official opening hours, but times do vary, so it's a good idea to check beforehand at one of the tourist offices or in the local listings newspapers and magazines (see p.364). Keep in mind, too, that Wawel is extremely popular at all times of year – for any chance of avoiding the summer crowds, you'll need to get there well before opening time and queue up for your tickets. **Tickets** for the cathedral and castle chambers are bought separately at the respective entry points. English-speaking **guides** for small groups are available for hire from the *PTTK* office near the entrance to the complex; *Orbis* also arranges **tours** of the Stare Miasto, castle and cathedral, complete with tickets, as do a number of other local tourist offices. If there's one place where it would be worth coughing up for your own guide, this is it. With so much to see, and the crowds to navigate your way through, a reliable local hand can definitely ease the experience.

The Cathedral

"The sanctuary of the nation . . . cannot be entered without an inner trembling, without an awe, for here – as in few cathedrals of the world – is contained a vast greatness which speaks to us of the history of Poland, of all our past." So was **Wawel Cathedral** (May–Sept Tues–Sat 9.30am–5.30pm, Sun 12.15–5.30pm; Oct–April Tues–Sat 9am–3pm, Sun noon–3pm) evoked by former Archbishop Karol Wojtyła of Kraków. As with Westminster Abbey or St Peter's, the moment you enter Wawel, you know you're in a place overloaded with history.

The first cathedral was built here around 1020 when King Bolesław the Brave established the Kraków bishopric. Fragments of this building can still be seen in the west wing of the castle and the courtyard between the castle and the cathedral, while the St Leonard's crypt survives from a second Romanesque structure. The present brick and sandstone basilica is essentially Gothic, dating from the reigns of Władysław the Short (1306–33) and Kazimierz the Great (1333–70), and adorned with a mass of side chapels, endowed by just about every subsequent Polish monarch and a fair number of aristocratic families too.

As you enter the cathedral, look out for the bizarre collection of **prehistoric animal bones**, supposedly the remains of the Krak dragon (see p.359), but actually a mammoth's shinbone, a whale's rib and the skull of a hairy rhinoceros, in a passage near the main entrance. As long as they remain, so legend maintains, the cathedral will too.

The view down the nave of the cathedral, with its arched Gothic vaulting, is blocked by the **shrine of St Stanisław**, an overwrought seventeenth-century silver sarcophagus by the Gdańsk smith Peter van der Rennen commemorating the bishop who is supposed to have been murdered by King Bolesław at Skałka in Kazimierz (see p.399) in 1079 for his opposition to royal ambitions. The remains of the bishop-saint, who was canonized in 1253, were moved to Wawel the following year, and his shrine became a place of pilgrimage. Below the shrine, on the right, is the **tomb of King Ladislaw Jagieło** (Sarkofeg Władystawa Jagiełło), a beautiful marble creation from the mid-1400s with a fine Renaissance canopy added on by the king's grandson, Sigismund the Old (Zygmunt I Stary) a century later. Beyond stands the Baroque **high altar** and choir stalls. However, most people are drawn immediately to the outstanding array of side chapels which punctuate the entire length of the building.

THE CHAPELS

All bar four of Poland's 45 monarchs are buried in the cathedral, and their tombs and side chapels are a directory of central European architecture, art and sculpture of the last six centuries.

Beginning from the right of the entrance, the Gothic **Holy Cross chapel** (Kaplica Świętokrzyska) is the burial chamber of King Kazimierz IV Jagieło (1447–92). The boldly coloured Byzantine-looking paintings on the walls and ceiling were completed by artists from Novgorod, one of a small group of such murals in Poland, while the king's red marble tomb is the characteristically expressive work of Veit Stoss, of Mariacki fame. Two carved Gothic altars and a beautiful triptych of the Holy Trinity in the side panels round off a sumptuously elegant masterpiece.

Moving down the aisle, the next two chapels celebrate aristocratic families rather than kings: the **Potocki** (a Neoclassical creation) and **Szafraniec** (a Baroque ensemble at the foot of the Silver Bells tower). They are followed by the majestic, if gloomy, **Waza chapel**, a Baroque mausoleum to the seventeenth-century royal dynasty whose design is based on the Sigismund chapel (see below). Protecting the chapel are some elaborately worked bronze **doors** displaying the dynastic coats of arms along with those of all their territories. The **Sigismund chapel** (Kaplica Zygmuntowska), whose shining gilded cupola – its exterior regularly replated owing to the corrosive effects of pollution – dominates the courtyard outside. Designed for King Sigismund the Old (1506–48) by the Italian architect Bartolomeo Berrecci and completed in 1533, it's an astonishing piece of Renaissance design and ornamentation, widely regarded as one of the artistic gems of the period, with intricate sandstone and marble carvings, and superb sculpted figures above the sarcophagi of the king, his son Sigismund August and his wife Queen Anna. The two altarpieces are spectacular, too: the silver *Altar of the Virgin* was designed by craftsmen from Nuremberg and includes Passion paintings by George Pencz, a pupil of Dürer. Opposite the chapel is the modern **tomb of Queen Jadwiga**, wife of King Jagieło and one of the country's most loved monarchs – in reality, her remains are buried nearby beneath her own favourite crucifix.

Venerable fourteenth-century bishops occupy several subsequent chapels, while the Gothic red Hungarian marble **tomb of King Kazimierz the Great**, immediately to the right of the high altar, is a dignified tribute in marble and sandstone to the revered monarch, during whose reign the cathedral was actually consecrated. The fourteenth-century **St Mary's chapel**, directly behind the altar and connected to the castle by a passage, was remodelled in the 1590s by Santi Gucci to accommodate the austere black marble and sandstone tomb of King Stefan Batory (1576–86). The **tomb of King Władysław the Short** (1306–33), on the left-hand side of the altar, is the oldest in the cathedral, completed soon

THE ITALIAN RENAISSANCE IN KRAKÓW

Poland's long history of contacts with Italy was particularly fruitful in the artistic sphere, and an amazingly high proportion of the country's principal monuments were created by Italians who were enticed there by lucrative commissions offered by the royal court and the great rural magnates. One consequence of this is that Poland, and Kraków in particular, possesses some of the finest Renaissance architecture to be found outside Italy itself. Although the architects remained true to the movement's original classical ideals, they nonetheless modified their approach to suit the local climate and tradition. The result is a distinctive national Renaissance style which is purer than the derivatives found anywhere else north of the Alps.

The Renaissance was introduced to Poland as a direct result of the Jagiellonians' short-lived dynastic union with Hungary. **Franciscus Italus** (d.1516, and tentatively identifed as Francesco della Lora), who had been employed at the Hungarian court since the 1480s, was summoned to Kraków to reconstruct the royal palace which had been badly damaged by fire in 1499. Work on this occupied him until his death, but it was far from complete by then, as King Sigismund subsequently decided on a complete rebuild.

The present appearance of the complex is due mainly to Franciscus' fellow Florentine and successor as the royal architect, **Bartolomeo Berrecci** (c.1480–1537), who seems to have invented the highly original form of the courtyard. Its first two storeys are reminiscent of the celebrated Palazzo Strozzi in Florence, but the third tier is at twice the normal height, with the columns, which are moulded into bulbous shapes at the normal position of the capital, rising straight to the huge overhanging wooden roof, omitting the usual entablature in between. In his other key commission, the Sigismund chapel in the Wawel Cathedral, Berrecci showed similar ingenuity. The basic shape he chose – a cube divided internally by paired pilasters, and surmounted by a dome, octagonal outside and cylindrical inside, with eight circular windows – represents the Italian ideal. Yet the overall appearance, with its profuse furnishings in a wide range of materials and elaborate surface decoration filling every available space on the walls, is totally unlike anything to be found in Italy. Berrecci built nothing else of significance, as his life was cut short by an assassin's knife.

Many other Italian craftsmen worked on the interior of the Sigismund chapel, the most prominent being **Giovanni Maria Mosca** (c.1495–1573), generally known as "Il Padovano" on account of having been born in Padua. The recruitment of Mosca was seen as a major artistic coup, as he had already established a formidable reputation for himself in his native city and in Venice. Primarily a sculptor, it is probable that he was entrusted with carving the effigy of Sigismund himself; he also made the two memorials to bishops in the chantry chapels of the east end. In addition, he struck four royal medals, carved the tabernacle in the Mariacki, and made many other funerary monuments in Kraków and elsewhere, notably those of the Tarnowskis in Tarnów Cathedral. As an architect, his main work was the addition of the attic and parapet to the medieval Sukiennice, giving it a pronounced Renaissance appearance in a transformation reminiscent of that wrought by Palladio on the Basilica in Vicenza just a few years before.

The outsized savage masks on the Sukiennice were carved by the Florentine **Santi Gucci** (c.1530–1600), who was also responsible for some of the tombs in the Sigismund chapel. Gucci subsequently came to prominence in his own right as court artist to Stefan Batory, adapting the Wawel's Lady chapel into a lavish chantry in his honour. He also seems to have built a number of country houses; not all of those documented have survived, but he is thought to have been responsible for the most spectacular one remaining intact, at Baranów Sandomierski. By the time of his death, Italian Renaissance architects had been dominant in Kraków for exactly a century. The style was to remain popular elsewhere in Poland for a considerable time yet, but in Kraków it was supplanted by the Baroque — introduced, once again, by Italians.

after his death; the reclining, coronation-robed figure lies on a white sandstone tomb edged with expressive mourning figures.

THE TREASURY, TOWER AND CRYPTS
The highlights of the cathedral **Treasury** (in the northeast corner, behind the sacristy) include a collection of illuminated texts and some odd items of Polish royal and ecclesiastical history – Saint Maurice's spear (a present to King Bolesław the Brave from Emperor Otto III when they met at Gniezno in 1000 AD), an eighth-century miniature of the four Evangelists, and King Kazimierz the Great's crown. An ascent of the fourteenth-century **Sigismund Tower** (Wieża Zygmuntowska), access again from the sacristy, gives a far-reaching panorama over the city and close-up views of the five medieval bells. The largest, an eight-tonne monster known as "Zygmunt", cast in 1520, is two and a half metres in diameter, eight in circumference, and famed for its deep, sonorous tone, which according to local legend, scatters rain clouds and brings out the sun. These days it doesn't get too many chances to perform, as it's only rung on Easter Sunday, Christmas Eve and New Year's Eve.

Back in the cathedral, the **crypt** (in the left aisle) houses the remains of numerous Polish kings and queens, many encased in pewter sarcophagi, notably the Sigismunds and Stefan Batory. Also buried here are the poets **Adam Mickiewicz** and **Juliusz Słowacki**, while the early twelfth-century **St Leonard's crypt**, part of a long network of vaults reached from near the main entrance, contains the tombs of national heroes Prince Józef Poniatowski and Tadeusz Kościuszko. The equally sanctified prewar independence leader Józef Piłsudski lies in a separate vault nearby. Standing with the crowds filing past this pantheon, you catch the passionate intensity of Polish attachment to everything connected with past resistance and independent nationhood. The exit from the crypt takes you back out of the building and onto the main Wawel courtyard.

The Castle
Entering the tiered courtyard of **Wawel Castle** (Tues, Thurs, Sat & Sun 10am–3pm, Wed & Fri noon–4pm), you might imagine that you'd stumbled on an opulent Italian palazzo. This is exactly the effect Sigismund the Old intended when he entrusted the conversion of King Kazimierz's Gothic castle to a Florentine architect in the early 1500s. The major difference from its Italian models lies in the response to climate: the window openings are enlarged to maximize the available light, while the roof is sturdier to withstand snow. A spate of fires, and more recently the corrosive effects of Kraków's atmosphere, have taken their toll on the building, but it still exudes a palatial bravura.

After the capital moved to Warsaw, the palace started to deteriorate, and was already in a dilapidated state when the Austrians pillaged and turned it into barracks. Reconstruction began in earnest in 1880, following Emperor Franz Josef's removal of the troops, and continued throughout the interwar years. Wawel's nadir came during World War II, when Governor Hans Frank transformed the castle into his private quarters, adding insult to injury by turning the royal apartments over to his Nazi henchmen. Luckily, many of the most valuable castle contents were spirited out of the country at the outbreak of war, eventually being returned to Wawel from Canada in 1961, after years of wrangling. Alongside many pieces donated by individual Poles at home and abroad – some of these, incidentally, items plundered by the Nazis but subsequently spotted at art auctions – they make up the core of today's ample and well-restored collection.

The **castle** is divided into three main sections: the state rooms, crown treasury and a separate exhibition of Oriental art. The state rooms are the section to focus on if time is limited, their art collections accumulated by the Jagiellonian and Waza dynasties.

THE STATE ROOMS AND ART COLLECTIONS

The centrepiece of the art collections is King Sigismund August's splendid assembly of **Flanders tapestries**, scattered throughout the first and second floors. The 136 pieces – about a third of the original collection – are what remains from the depredations of tsarist, Austrian and Nazi armies. Outstanding are three series from the Brussels workshops of the "Flemish Raphael", Michel Coxie, the first and most impressive of which is a group of eighteen huge Old Testament scenes, featuring a lyrical evocation of Paradise and a wonderfully detailed tapestry of Noah and family in the aftermath of the Flood. The oldest tapestry in the castle is the mid-fifteenth-century French *Story of the Swan Knight* displayed in Sigismund the Old's first-floor bedroom.

In the northwest corner of the first floor is a remnant of the original Gothic castle, a tiny two-roomed watchtower named the **Hen's Foot Tower**. In contrast to other parts of the castle, the rooms of the north wing are in early Baroque style, the result of remodelling following a major fire in 1595. Of the luxurious apartments in this section, the **Silver Hall**, redesigned in 1786 by Domenico Merlini (of Warsaw's Łazienki Park fame), achieves a particularly harmonious blending of the old architecture with period classicism.

The **state rooms** on the top floor are among the finest in the building, particularly those in the **east wing** where the original wooden ceilings and wall paintings are still visible. A glance upwards at the carved ceiling of the **Audience Hall** at the southern end of the wing will tell you why it's nicknamed the "Heads Room". Created for King Sigismund in the 1530s by Sebastian Tauerbach of Wrocław and Jan Snycerz, only thirty of its original array of nearly two hundred heads remain, but it's enough to give you a feeling for the contemporary characters, from all strata of society, on which they were based. The frieze by Hans Dürer, brother of the famous Albrecht, illustrates *The Life of Man*, a sixteenth-century retelling of an ancient Greek legend, while the magnificent tapestries of biblical stories – the Garden of Eden, Noah and the Tower of Babel – are again from the Coxie workshop.

Back down the corridor is the **Zodiac Room**, ornamented by an astrological frieze, an ingenious 1920s reconstruction of a sixteenth-century fresco, as well as another series of biblical tapestries. The northeast corner towers contain the private royal apartments. The **chapel**, rebuilt in 1602, looks onto the king's bedchamber, while the walls of the **study**, with its fine floor and stucco decorations, are a mini-art gallery in themselves, crammed with works by Dutch and Flemish artists, among them a Rubens sketch and a painting by the younger Brueghel. The seventeenth-century **Bird Room**, named after the wooden birds that used to hang from the ceiling, leads on to the **Eagle Room**, the old court of justice, with a Rubens portrait of Prince Władysław Waza. Last comes the large **Senators' Hall**, originally used for formal meetings of the Senate in the days when Kraków was still the capital, which houses a collection of tapestries illustrating the story of Noah and the Ark, another impressive coffered ceiling and a sixteenth-century minstrel's gallery still used for the occasional concert.

THE TREASURY AND ARMOURY

If you've got the stamina, the next thing to head for is the **Royal Treasury and Armoury** in the northeast corner of the castle (entrance on the ground floor). The paucity of crown jewels on display, however, is testimony to the ravages of the past. Much of the treasury's contents had been sold off by the time of the Partitions to pay off marriage dowries and debts of state. The Prussians did most of the rest of the damage, purloining the coronation insignia in 1795, then melting down the crown and selling off its jewels. The vaulted Gothic **Kazimierz Room** contains the finest items from a haphazard display of lesser royal possessions including rings, crosses and the coronation shoes and burial crown of Sigismund August. The oldest exhibit is a fifth-century ring inscribed with the name "MARTINVS", found near Kraków.

The prize exhibit in the next-door **Jadwiga and Jagiełło Room** is the solemnly displayed *Szczerbiec*, a thirteenth-century copy of the weapon used by Bolesław the Brave during his triumphal capture of Kiev in 1018, used from then on in the coronation of Polish monarchs. Like other valuable items in the collection here, the sword was taken to Canada during World War II for safekeeping. The other two exhibits here are an early sixteenth-century sword belonging to Sigismund the Old and the oldest surviving royal banner, made in 1533 for the coronation of Sigismund August's third wife, Catherine von Habsburg. In the following room are a variety of items connected with **Jan Sobieski**, most notably the regalia of the Knights of the Order of the Holy Ghost sent to him by the pope as thanks for defeating the Turks at Vienna in 1683. Things get more military from here on. The next barrel-vaulted room contains a host of finely crafted display weapons, shields and helmets, while the final **Armoury Room** is dedicated to serious warfare, with weapons captured over five centuries from Poland's host of foreign invaders, including copies of the banners seized during the epic Battle of Grunwald (1410), a fearsome selection of huge double-handed swords and a forbidding array of spears with weird and wonderful spikes on top.

THE ORIENT OF THE WAWEL, LOST WAWEL AND THE CAVE

The **Orient of the Wawel** exhibition, housed in the older west wing of the castle, focuses on Oriental influences in Polish culture. The first floor has an interesting section on early contacts with Armenia, Iran, Turkey, China and Japan, but the main "influences" displayed here seem to be war loot from the seventeenth-century campaigns against the Turks. The centrepiece is a collection of **Turkish tents and armour** captured after the Battle of Vienna, with a prize bust of Sobieski swathed in emperor-like laurels in attendance. Other second-floor rooms display an equally sumptuous assortment of Turkish and Iranian carpets, banners and weaponry seized during the fighting – the sixteenth-century **Paradise carpet** must have gone very nicely in the royal front room.

The **Lost Wawel** exhibition (currently closed), beneath the old kitchens, south of the cathedral, takes you past the excavated remains of the hill's most ancient buildings, including the foundations of the tenth-century **Rotunda of SS. Felix and Adauctus**, the oldest known church in Poland. A diverse collection of medieval archeological finds is displayed in the old coach house.

Back out through the castle entrance and into the main square, the western section contains a set of foundations, all that remains of two Gothic churches (St Michael's and St George's) raised in the fourteenth century, but demolished by the Austrians in the early 1800s, along with the surrounding buildings. Beyond the ruins, it's worth taking in the view over the river from the terrace at the western edge of the hill. If you're feeling energetic, you could, instead of returning directly to town, clamber down the steps to the **Dragon's Cave** at the foot of the hill – the legendary haunt of Krak (see p.359) and the medieval site of a fishermen's tavern, now guarded by an aggressive-looking bronze dragon that belches a brief blast of fire every couple of minutes – very popular with the school parties that descend here in droves from the castle, snapping up trinkets from the massed ranks of souvenir sellers. From the Dragon's Cave, a walk west along the bend of the river towards the **Dębnicki Bridge** is rewarded by an excellent view back over the castle. Alternatively, if you fancy a longer walk, stroll south along the river bank a kilometre or so to Piłsudski Bridge and on into Kazimierz (see below). Clearly visible across the other side of the river is the newly built Japanese Cultural Centre initiated by, among others, film-maker Andrej Wajda, and opened amid much public fanfare in November 1994. A large, elegant building designed by Aratolsozaki of the Los Angeles Art Gallery and Barcelona Olympic Stadium fame, the centre houses the extensive collection of Japanese art amassed by Feliks Jasieński (aka Manggha), Poland's leading Japanologist and art collector, notably a valuable collection of woodcuts. Downstairs, there's a large performance hall used mainly for concerts, that looks set to become a leading new cultural attraction in the city.

Finally, if the idea of a boat trip appeals, the **barge** moored by the riverbank, a little way south of the dragon, offers hour-long trips along the river throughout the day (May–Sept; last departure 5.30pm), and there are also trips to Bielany (see p.402). Moored next to the barge is a floating **restaurant and bar**.

Kazimierz, the ghettoes and Płaszów

> *(The) Jews are gone. One can only try to preserve, maintain and fix the memory of them – not only of their struggle and death (as in Warsaw and Auschwitz), but of their life, of the values that guided their yearnings, of the international life and their unique culture. Cracow was one of the places where that life was most rich, most beautiful, most varied, and the most evidence of it has survived here.*
>
> Henryk Halkowski, a surviving Kraków Jew. Extracted from *Upon the Doorposts of Thy House* by Ruth Ellen Gruber (Wiley).

South from Wawel Hill lies the **Kazimierz** district, originally a distinct town named after King Kazimierz, who granted the founding charter in 1335. Thanks to the acquisition of royal privileges, the settlement developed rapidly, trade centring around a market square almost equal in size to Kraków's. The main influence on the character of Kazimierz, however, was King Jan Olbracht's decision to move Kraków's already significant **Jewish population** into the area from the ul. Św. Anny district in 1495.

In tandem with Warsaw, where a **ghetto** was created around the same time, Kazimierz grew to become one of the main cultural centres of Polish Jewry. Jews were initially limited to an area around modern-day ul. Szeroka and Miodowa, and it was only in the nineteenth century that they began to spread into other parts of Kazimierz. By this time there were ghettoes all over the country, but descriptions of Kazimierz in Polish art and literature make it clear that there was something special about the exotic atmosphere of this place.

The soul of the area was to perish in the gas chambers of nearby Auschwitz, but many of the buildings, synagogues included, have survived. Walking round

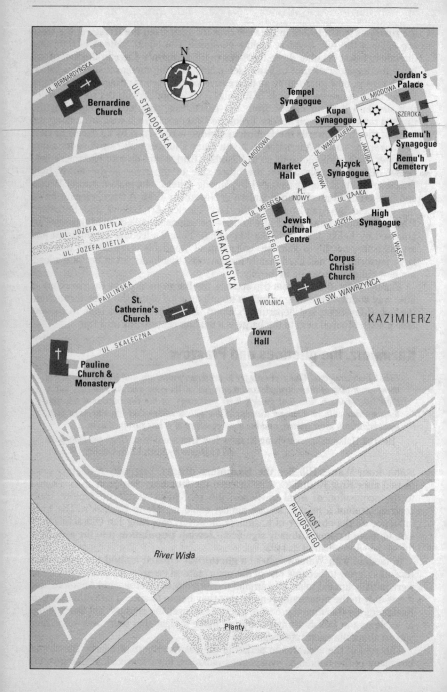

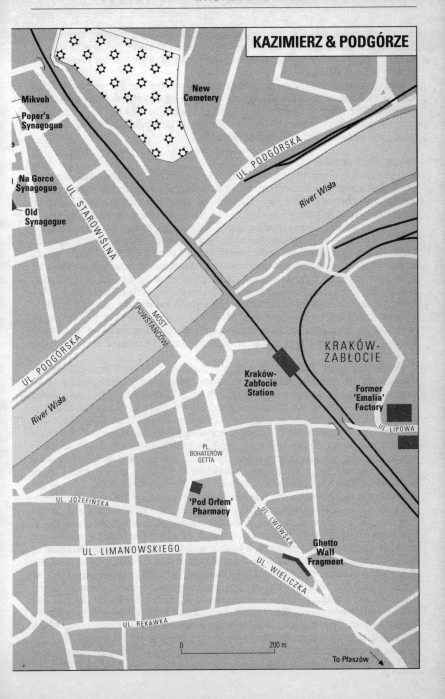

KAZIMIERZ & PODGÓRZE

Mikveh

Poper's
Synagogue

New
Cemetery

UL. PODGÓRSKA

River Wisła

Na Gorce
Synagogue

Old
Synagogue

UL. STAROWIŚLNA

UL. PODGÓRSKA

MOST POWSTAŃCÓW

River Wisła

KRAKÓW-
ZABŁOCIE

Kraków-
Zabłocie
Station

Former
'Emalia'
Factory

UL. LIPOWA

PL.
BOHATERÓW
GETTA

UL. JÓZEFIŃSKA

'Pod Orłem'
Pharmacy

UL. LWOWSKA

Ghetto
Wall
Fragment

UL. LIMANOWSKIEGO

UL. WIELICZKA

UL. RĘKAWKA

0   200 m

To Płaszów

the streets today, you feel the weight of an absent culture. Yiddish inscriptions fronting the doorways, an old pharmacy, a ruined theatre: the details make it easier to picture what has gone than do the drab housing estates covering the former Warsaw Ghetto.

Recent years have seen a marked revival of Jewish life and activity in Kazimierz. Long-neglected buildings are finally being renovated, many with financial assistance from the worldwide community, and the area has seen a marked increase in visitors thanks to Steven Spielberg's film *Schindler's List*, much of which was filmed in and around Kazimierz.

Along Ulica Józefa

If you're coming from the centre of town take a tram (#3, #9, #11 or #13) down ul. Stradomska and its continuation, ul. Krakówska, which formerly separated the ghetto from the rest of the city. The obvious route into the ghetto is along ul. Józefa, so named following Emperor Joseph II's visit to the area during his tour of the regions of Poland annexed by the Habsburgs following the First Partition (1772). Walking along Józefa towards the heart of the ghetto proper, you pass no. 11, the former parish school of the nearby Corpus Christi (Bożego Ciała) church, whose students used to supplement the school income by extorting a transit fee from Jews travelling into the city centre. Here, as elsewhere in the area, wandering into the often dilapidated **courtyards** leading off the main street gives you a feeling of the atmosphere of the vanished ghetto. A memorable example of this is the **courtyard** linking Józefa with ul. Meiselsa, used by Spielberg for the scenes depicting the expulsion of Jews from the ghetto in *Schindler's List*, the whitewashed walls, cobblestones and arcaded wooden attics lending a Mediterranean aura to the place.

Continuing along Józefa, turn left into ul. Kupa and you'll find the **Ajzyck Synagogue**, a graceful Baroque structure named after the wealthy local merchant, Isaac Jakubowicz (in Yiddish, reb Ajzyk) who financed its construction in the 1630s. Getting the building started proved more of a handful than the merchant anticipated: despite securing permission directly from King Władysław IV, Jakubowicz's plans were forcefully opposed by the parish priest of Corpus Christi, who wrote to the Bishop of Kraków protesting that it would result in priests carrying the sacraments having to pass in front of, and thus, presumably be contaminated by, a synagogue. Thankfully the bishop proved rather more enlightened than his ecclesiastical inferior, and building went ahead. Like all the Kazimierz synagogues, Ajzyk's was looted and destroyed by the Nazis, the surviving hull of the building being partially restored in the 1950s when it was turned into an artist's workshop. A more thorough renovation, started in the mid-1980s, is almost complete now, though the final use to which the building will be put remains unclear; for the moment, a Jewish sculptor's workshop occupies part of the upper storey. Unless you're on a pre-arranged tour or visit, getting in to see the building is a somewhat hit and miss business. Set back from the street behind a walled gate, the relatively modest and sedate exterior focuses around a raised twin staircase leading up to the main entrance. If you ring the bell at the gate and ask to see the synagogue, the resident sculptor will generally let you in to have a look if he's in a good mood. Notable features of the synagogue interior, which you're likely to view from the upper women's gallery, are the fabulous stuccoed **ceiling decoration**, most probably from the workshop of Giovanni Falconi, and the reconstructed *Aron Ha Kodesh*.

Continuing along ul. Józefa, the intersection with ul. Jakuba marks the spot where the guarded main gateway to the ghetto stood for centuries. Immediately beyond, at no. 38, is the buttressed **High (Wysoka) Synagogue**, built in the late 1550s, and so named because the synagogue was located on the first floor of the building, the ground floor being occupied by shops, replaced today by store rooms. Devastated by the Nazis, the building was renovated in the 1960s and turned into a conservation workshop, a function it still retains, though there's talk of the Jewish community reclaiming use of the building. The entrance to the building is from a staircase next door (no. 40). Inside the synagogue (again, access is dependent on someone being around to let you in), there's precious little of the original decoration left – the sumptuous stuccoed Renaissance vaulting of the building was completely destroyed by the Nazis – the *Aron Ha Kodesh* still there in wall near the entrance being one of the very few exceptions.

Around Ulica Szeroka

Further east along ul. Józefa brings you out onto ul. Szeroka (Wide Street), a broad open space whose numerous synagogues constituted the focus of religious life in the ghetto. On the southern side of this truncated square stands the **Old Synagogue** (Stara Synagoga), the grandest of all the Kazimierz synagogues and the earliest surviving Jewish religious building in Poland. Modelled on the great European synagogues of Worms, Prague and Regensburg, the present Renaissance building was completed by Mateo Gucci in the 1570s, replacing an earlier brick building destroyed, like much of the surrounding area, by a fire in 1557. The synagogue's story is closely entwined with the country's history. It was here, for example, that Kościuszko came to rally the Jews in 1794, a precedent followed by the Kazimierz rabbi Ber Meissels during the uprisings of 1831 and 1863. President Ignacy Mościcki made a symbolically important state visit to the synagogue in 1931, a move designed to demonstrate official amity with the country's Jewish population. Predictably, the Nazis did a thorough job of destroying the place. Following the war, the painstaking process of refashioning the building on the lines of Gucci's graceful original structure was initiated. The rebuilt synagogue was subsequently converted into a **museum** of the history and culture of Kraków Jewry (Wed & Thurs 9am–3.30pm, Fri 11am–6pm, Sat & Sun 9am–3pm; closed first Sat & Sun of the month when it opens Mon & Tues 9am–3.30pm instead). Nazi destruction was thorough, so the museum's collection of art, books, manuscripts and religious objects has a slightly cobbled-together feel to it, though there's an interesting and evocative set of photos of life in the ghetto before World War II. The wrought-iron *bimah* in the centre of the main prayer hall is original, the masterful product of a sixteenth-century Kraków workshop. In tandem with the general revival of interest in Jewish Kraków, the synagogue now plays host to an increasing number of temporary exhibitions relating to the history and culture of Polish Jewry, as well as providing one of the central locations for the annul summer **Jewish Cultural Festival** (see below).

On the east side of Szeroka, no. 22 formerly housed the **Na Górce Synagogue**, associated with Rabbi Nathan Spira, a celebrated seventeenth-century cabbalist scholar, the tercentenary of whose death was the occasion for a major commemoration in Kazimierz in 1933. This and the surrounding houses were originally owned by the Jekeles family, one of the wealthiest merchant dynasties in Kazimierz and founders of the Ajzyk Synagogue (see above). At nos. 17 and 18 are a pair of well-heeled cafe-restaurants both called *Ariel*. Styling them-

THE JEWS OF KRAKÓW

One of the major Jewish communities in Poland for much of the last six centuries, the **Jews of Kraków** occupy a significant place in the history of the city. The **first Jews** settled in Kraków in the second half of the thirteenth century, a small community establishing itself on ul. Św. Anny, then known as Żydowska (Jewish) street, in today's university district, with a synagogue, baths and cemetery beyond the city walls. A century later, the community still numbered no more than a couple of hundred people. Resentment at the Jewish presence was already growing among the local Gentile population, however, and following a serious fire in the city in 1495, for which Jews were blamed, the majority of the community was forced to moved out to **Kazimierz**, where a number of Jews had already established themselves, with their own ritual baths, market place and a synagogue, the predecessor of the **Old (Stara) Synagogue** which you can still see standing today. The ranks of the community were swelled considerably in the first half of the fifteenth century by an influx of Jews from all over Europe, notably Bohemia, Germany, Italy and Spain, fleeing growing persecution and discrimination in their home lands. The arrival of both **Ashkenazim** and **Sephardic Jews**, with their differing cultural and social traditions, may go some way towards explaining the building of a number of new synagogues during this period. Economically, the Reformation era was a time of significant growth for the city, a development in which Jews participated actively, as goldsmiths, publishers, furriers and butchers especially. Culturally the sixteenth century was also something of a golden age for **Jewish culture** in Kraków, with local talmudic scholars and the books produced on the printing presses of **Menachim Meisler** and others, enjoying high international prestige. As a mark of their growing authority, rabbis and elders of the Kraków community were chosen to represent Małopolska on the **Council of the Four Lands** (see p.282) when it met for the first time in Lublin in 1581. The ghetto area was expanded in 1583, and again in 1603, attaining a considerable size which it retained for the next two centuries, with a fence and stone wall along ul. Józefa separating it from the rest of Kazimierz.

Economically, the community's heyday came to a end with the **Swedish invasions** (known popularly as the "Swedish Deluge") of the mid-1650s, when Charles X's troops occupied the city and systematically destroyed large parts of it. By 1657, the ghetto population of around 4500 had declined by two-thirds, many Jews having emigrated to other parts of the country, notably the new capital Warsaw, in search of better times. Throughout the eighteenth century, the age-old struggle for economic ascendancy between Jewish and Gentile merchants and craftspeople continued apace, as elsewhere, culminating in the issue of an edict severely curtailing Jews' economic freedoms and even, in 1776, an order for them to leave Kazimierz altogether. The **Austrian occupation** of Kraków in 1776 in the wake of the First Partition temporarily put a lid on local squabbling. The Austrians' initial move was to incorporate the whole of Kraków directly into Austrian territory, abolishing the separate judicial status of Kazimierz and all other outlying districts in the process.

Under the terms of a statute promulgated in the wake of the establishment of the Free City of Kraków (1815–46), the **ghetto was officially liquidated** and the walls separating it torn down, with a direct view to encouraging assimilation among the Jewish population. Jews were now permitted to live anywhere in Kazimierz, and with special permits, duly granted to merchants and craftsmen, to reside throughout the city area. It was another almost fifty years, however, before they were granted the **right to vote** in elections to the Austro-Hungarian Diet, eventually also benefiting from the Habsburg declaration of equal rights for all Jewish subjects of the empire.

The latter part of the nineteenth century was marked by a fierce struggle for influence among rival sections of the Jewish community in Kraków. On one side stood the **assimilationists,** favouring progressive integration of Jews, cultural, and in some radical instances, even religious, into mainstream Catholic society, often accompanied by a noticeable hint of Polish nationalism. On the other stood the ranks of **conservative Orthodox Jewry,** zealously committed to the preservation of a radically distinct way of life. In Kraków, as elsewhere, the European-wide upsurge in **anti-Semitism** in the closing years of the century led to a marked dampening of support for the assimilationist programme, a trend exacerbated by intensifying **economic competition** between Gentiles and Jews in which the latter generally appeared to come out best. The early 1900s were also a period of growing political activity, with the formation of several **Jewish political parties,** notably the first **Zionist groupings**.

The period following the end of World War I and the regaining of national independence was one of intense **population growth** in Jewish Kraków, the community rising from 45,000 people in 1921 to nearly 57,000 a decade later, and over 64,000 on the eve of the Nazi invasion of Poland. Most, but by no means all, of Kraków's Jews lived in Kazimierz. The inward-looking and mostly poor **Hasidim** dominated the synagogues, prayer houses and talmudic schools of the quarter, while the more integrated, upwardly mobile sections of the community moved out into other city districts, the Old Town included, and increasingly adopted the manners and educational habits of their Gentile neighbours. This was a period of rich cultural activity, notably in the **Jewish Theatre,** established in 1926 in southern Kazimierz, the biggest star being the legendary **Ida Kamińska,** still remembered today as one of the great prewar Polish actresses. Contemporary accounts make it clear that Kazimierz possessed a memorable and unique atmosphere, the predominantly poor, but intensely vibrant, Jewish community carrying on unchanged the traditions of its forebears, seemingly oblivious to the increasingly menacing world outside it.

Following the **Nazi invasion** of Poland, Kraków was occupied by Wehrmacht units on September 6, 1939, and within days the Nazi Security Police issued an order directing all Jewish-owned commercial enterprises to be **daubed with a Star of David**. A month later, the General Government was established with its capital in Kraków, and the new Nazi governor Hans Frank arrived to take over. A series of increasingly restrictive laws began to affect Jews. From the end of November, 1939, all Jews were required to wear notorious blue and white armbands, and in May 1940, Frank embarked on a drive to enforce this which continued through the winter.

From here on the situation deteriorated. In March 1941, an **official ghetto area** was established. Located in the **Podgórze district,** south of Kazimierz across the river, the ghetto was surrounded and effectively sealed off by two-metre-high walls. Through the rest of the year an increasingly ruthless schema developed. Jews from the area surrounding Kraków were herded into the cramped and insanitary ghetto area, and from June 1942 onwards, fearsome and bloody **mass deportations** from the ghetto to Bełzec concentration camp and eventually Auschwitz-Birkenau, began. Compounding the torture and destruction, a new forced labour camp was set up in November 1942 at **Płaszów,** just south of the ghetto (see p.400).

In a final determined drive, a major **SS** operation on March 14, 1943 removed or murdered the remains of the ghetto population. Those not killed in cold blood on the streets were either marched out to Płaszów or transported to the gas chambers of Auschwitz. Thus was nearly seven hundred years of Jewish presence in Kraków uprooted and effectively destroyed. Under the ruthless rule of its notorious commander **Amon Goeth,** Płaszów was transformed into a murderous work camp

Contd. overleaf

where those who didn't die from hunger, disease and exhaustion were regularly finished off at whim by the twisted Goeth himself, who was later caught, tried and eventually executed in Kraków in September 1946. In January 1945, with Soviet forces rapidly advancing west, many of the surviving camp inmates were moved to Auschwitz (the workers at Oskar Schindler's factory excepted), and the site dynamited by the camp guards.

In many ways, the **postwar history** of Kraków's Jews parallels that of other Polish cities with notable prewar Jewish communities. By the end of 1945, roughly 6000 survivors had returned to the city, about a third of whom had lived there before the war. Subsequent waves of **emigration** to Israel and the USA went in step with the ups and downs of domestic and international politics, the largest occurring in the wake of the post-Stalinist "thaw" (1957), the Six Day War and the semi-official **anti-Semitic campaigns** subsequently unleashed in Poland in 1968–69, leaving an increasingly introverted and elderly community hanging on by the 1980s, mostly in Kazimierz. Developments since the communist demise of 1989 have been marked by a notable **upsurge** in interest in the city's Jewish past, symbolized by the increasingly popular annual summer **Jewish Festival** (June/July) held in Kazimierz, now into its sixth year, and a determined drive to renovate and rebuild the fading architectural glories of the quarter. The city's Jewish population can never be fully reconstituted, but the effort to ensure that their culture and memory receive due recognition today continues.

selves as "authentic" Jewish eateries, both are unashamedly aimed at Western tourists, competing for the gastronomic attentions of the visiting crowds: no. 17 has the edge in entertainment, offering schmaltzy evening concerts of Jewish, Russian and Gypsy music, while no. 18 has the better quality (if stupendously slowly delivered) food, including a decent selection of kosher items. Set back from the square, behind a gated yard, at no. 16 is the former **Poper** or **Stork's Synagogue**, a typical brick structure raised in the 1620s by another wealthy local merchant family. These days it houses a cultural centre, open unpredictably, every trace of its original purpose having been erased by the Nazis. On the far northern corner of the square, stands the old community bath-house and *mikveh*, now a building restoration workshop.

Straddling the intersection with ul. Miodowa at the top of the square, is an old merchant's house known as **Jordan's Palace** (Pałac Jordanów). The building now houses the *Jordan* (Mon–Sat 10am–6pm, Sun 10am–4pm), a cultural centre-cum-bookstore recently established by an enterprising local resident, an exemplary model of sensitivity and commitment to reviving interest in Jewish Kazimierz. As well as a good range of publications relating to Jewish life in Kraków and Poland generally, and a pleasant, animated café, the centre offers guided walking tours (groups and individuals) round the area, including a "Schindler's List Tour", its popularity matched by what some will regard as the exploitative morality of such an enterprise. All the guides speak English and generally know their stuff pretty well, and you can take things as fast or as slowly as you like. You need to book at least a day in advance for the tours (☎ 21 71 66).

Moving round the top of the square, the tiny **Remu'h Synagogue** at ul. Szeroka 40, is one of two still functioning in the quarter. Built in 1557 on the site of an earlier wooden synagogue, it was ransacked by the Nazis and restored after the war. It's named after Moses Isserles, also known as Rabbi Remu'h, an eminent Polish writer and philosopher and the son of the synagogue's founder. On Fridays and Saturdays, the small local congregation is regularly swelled by the increasing number of Jews visiting Poland these days. Behind the synagogue is the **Remu'h Cemetery**, established twenty or so years earlier, and in use till the end of the eighteenth century, after which it was supplanted by the New Cemetery (see below). Many of the gravestones were unearthed in the 1950s having been covered with a layer of earth in the interwar years – a saving grace, as the rest of the cemetery was smashed up by the Nazis during the occupation. One of the finest is that of Rabbi Remu'h, its stele luxuriously ornamented with plant motifs. Just inside the entrance, tombstones torn up by the Nazis have been collaged together to form a high, powerful Wailing Wall.

Around Ulica Miodowa

West of Szeroka, along ul. Miodowa, on the corner of ul. Podbrzezie, is the **Templ Synagogue**, a magnificent, Neo-Renaissance construction founded in the 1869s by the local Association of Progressive Jews, with whose modernist, reforming theology it was long identified. This is the second of the two synagogues in Kazimierz still used for worship today. Opening hours are unpredictable – foreign Jewish guided tours (of which there are plenty in season) often visit the place, but unless you happen to coincide with one, or chance upon one of the growing number of classical concerts held here, it's pure luck whether you'll be able to get in and see the place. The synagogue interior is a grand affair, the large central hall surrounded by the women's gallery, erected on decorated iron supports, and graced by ornate wall decorations and some lavish stucco work in the ceiling. In the centre sits the *bimah*, and beyond it the white marble altar, separated from the main body of the interior by a decorated screen wall. Illuminating the whole building is a glowing set of 36 stained-glass windows restored in the 1970s, and visible only from the inside, featuring geometrical motifs alongside characteristic floral and plant designs.

Southeast of here, ul. Warszauera brings you to the **Kupa Synagogue**, built in the 1640s with funds collected from the local community. The first of the synagogues to be reopened as a functioning religious building after World War II, it's again not easy to get in to see this one without prior arrangement. If the caretaker is around to let you in, the renovated interior shows few traces of its former character, the only surviving decoration being the zodiacal paintings covering the ceiling and beams of the gallery, and a seventeenth-century stone plaque below one of the windows. The exterior of the building stands flush against the old defensive walls of the area which you can see from around the corner on ul. Kupa.

Continuing west along ul. Warsauera brings you to plac Nowy, the **fomer Jewish market place** and still referred to popularly as such. In the middle of the bustling square, stands the old round covered market hall, little changed in appearance from its previous Jewish incarnation, when the building housed its own ritual slaughterhouse.

West of the square along ul. Meiselsa, is the sparkling new **Jewish Cultural Centre** at no. 17 (☎22 55 87 or 22 55 95), a clear expression of the current revival of interest in Kazimierz. Located on the site of a fomer prayer house, the smart new centre was opened in November 1993, complete with plush conference rooms, library and other support facilities. The place doesn't seem to have completely found its feet yet – conferences and exhibitions are still sporadic, though it's always worth looking in to see what's going on, especially if it's hot, when the soothing air-conditioning and genteel café-bar provide a welcome respite from the rigours of the city. Overall there's no doubting the serious intentions of the organizers, however, who describe their central aim as being to "ensure that the experience of Kazimierz is an encounter with the presence of Jewish culture". If future plans to develop a kosher restaurant, offices and eventually a hotel materialize, the centre looks set to become a major fixture in the district.

Finally, through the tunnel underneath the rail track at the far eastern end of ul. Miodowa lies the **New Cemetery** (Mon–Fri, Sun 9am–6pm & Jewish holidays; entrance through no. 55), a little-visited site that succeeded the Remu'h as the main Jewish burial site in the early 1800s. The contrast between the two places is striking. A quiet, brooding place of leafy, overgrown walkways and crumbling clusters of ornately carved monuments and tombstones, the cemetery is among the most powerful testaments to Jewish life in the district. In among the mausolems of the great and good of Habsburg-era Kazimierz, for example, you'll find memorials erected after World War II by relatives of those who perished in the concentration camps, many of them simple tablets recording the names and dates of murdered family members. To the right of the entrance gate stands a memorial to local victims of the Holocaust.

Western Kazimierz

As the presence of several churches indicates, the western part of Kazimierz was the part where non-Jews tended to live. Despite its Baroque overlay, which includes some ornately carved choir stalls and a boat-shaped pulpit complete with rigging, the interior of the Gothic **Church of Corpus Christi**, on the corner of ul. Bożego Ciała, retains early features including stained-glass windows installed around 1420, and tranquil cloisters surrounding the building. The Swedish king Charles Gustaf is supposed to have used the building as his operational base during the mid-seventeenth-century siege of the city. The high church looks onto **plac Wolnica**, the old market square of Kazimierz, now much smaller than it used to be, thanks to the houses built along the old trade route through it in the nineteenth century. The fourteenth-century **Town Hall**, later rebuilt, stands in what used to be the middle of the square, its southern extension an overambitious nineteenth-century addition. It now houses the largest **Ethnographic Museum** in the country (Mon 10am–6pm, Wed–Sun 10am–3pm). The collection focuses on Polish folk traditions, although there's also a selection of artefacts from Siberia, Africa, Latin America and various Slav countries. A detailed survey of life in rural Poland includes an intriguing section devoted to ancient folk customs and an impressive collection of costumes, painting, woodcarving, fabrics and pottery – an excellent introduction to the fascinating and often bizarre world of Polish folk culture.

Two more churches west of the square are worth looking in on. On ul. Skałeczna stands fourteenth-century **St Catherine's**, founded by King Kazimierz for Augustine monks imported from Prague. The large basilican structure is a typical example of Kraków Gothic, though the bare interior has suffered everything from earthquakes to the installation of an Austrian arsenal. The Gothic vestibule on the southern side of the church features some delicate carved stonework. Further down the road is the **Pauline Church and Monastery**, perched on a small hill known as Skałka (the Rock). Tradition connects the church with Saint Stanisław, the bishop of Kraków, whose martyrdom by King Bolesław the Generous in 1079 is supposed to have happened here. Conscious of the symbolic position the canonized martyr grew to assume in the medieval tussle for power between Church and State, later kings made a point of doing ritual penance at the site following their coronation. An altar to the popular saint stands in the left aisle of the remodelled Baroque church, and underneath you can see the block on which he's supposed to have been beheaded. Underneath the church is a **crypt** cut into the rock of the hill, which was turned into a mausoleum for famous Poles in the late nineteenth century. Eminent artists, writers and composers buried here include Kraków's own Stanisław Wyspiański, composer Karol Szymanowski and the medieval historian Jan Długosz.

The wartime ghetto

Following an edict from Hans Frank, in March 1941 the entire Jewish population of the city was crammed into a tiny **ghetto** over the river, south of Kazimierz, in the area around modern-day plac Bohaterów Getta. It was sealed off by high walls and anyone caught entering or leaving unofficially was summarily executed. After waves of deportations to the concentration camps, the ghetto was finally liqui- dated in March 1943, thus ending seven centuries of Jewish life in Kraków.

The story of the wartime ghetto shot to prominence in 1994 due to Steven Spielberg's film *Schindler's List*, based on Thomas Keneally's prize-winning book recounting the wartime exploits of Oskar Schindler, a German industrialist who saved the lives of hundreds of ghetto inhabitants. In search of authenticity, Spielberg shot the majority of the film in and around the area, sometimes using the original, surviving buildings, as in the case of the old Emalia factory, and in other cases, recreating from scratch, for example the Płaszów camp, built in an old quarry in the south of the area. Inevitably, the success of Spielberg's film has spawned a crop of enterprises bent on exploiting the attendant tourist potential. While some may question the ethics of tourist exploitation of Holocaust memory, this needs to be balanced aginst the undoubted and welcome interest in Jewish culture and history that the film has generated.

It's relatively easy to detect signs of past Jewish presence in what is now a quiet, rather run-down suburban district, and there is no shortage of local guides on hand to help. The most obvious is the **Apteka Pod Orłem** (the old ghetto pharmacy) on the southwest corner of plac Bohaterów, now a museum (Tues–Fri 10am–4pm, Sat 10am–2pm) containing a photographic and documentary record of life (and death) in the wartime ghetto and Płaszów camp. Its wartime proprietor Dr Pankiewicz was the only non-Jewish Pole permitted to live in the ghetto, and the exhibition touches on the sensitive question of Polish wartime aid to Jews, notably the role of Pankiewicz himself in assisting the ghetto population, as testified to in letters from the Yad Vashem Centre in Jerusalem displayed among the exhibits. The building at no. 6, on the other side of the square, was the headquarters of the **Jewish Combat Organization** (ŻOB) which continued operating until the ghetto's liquidation. Jews were regularly deported en masse from the square to the extermination camps of Treblinka and Auschwitz-Birkenau.

At the bottom of ul. Lwówska, which runs southeast of the square, there's a short fragment of the **ghetto wall**. West of the square on ul. Węgierska is the burnt-out shell of the old Jewish theatre, while around the corner on ul. Jozefinska, today's state mint turns out to be the former **Jewish bank**. Casting further out in the district, the **Emalia enamel factory** run by Oskar Schindler, these days producing electronic component parts, still stands on ul. Lipowa (no. 4), east of the rail track. If you want to, you can look around the factory (with permission from the caretaker), many of whose features you'll recognize if you've seen the film. There's also a small exhibition displayed just inside the entrance to the building.

Płaszów concentration camp

As well as imprisoning people in the ghetto, the Nazis also relocated many Jews to the **concentration camp at Płaszów**, built near an old Austrian hill fort a couple of kilometres south of Kazimierz. Levelled after the war, the camp's desolate hilltop site is now enclosed by fields and concrete residential blocks. Although none of the local guidebooks mention the site, it is marked on the large *Kraków: plan miasta* city map by two "Pomnik Martyrologii" symbols, just above the junction of ul. Kamienskiego and ul. Wielicka.

To get here, take a local train (Tarnów direction) to Płaszów station or walk from Podgórze (20min), down to ul. Wieliczka and cross over the road. The mortuary that served the Jewish cemetery before the war used to stand on the corner of ul. Jerozolimska. Scramble about in the undergrowth just beyond this and you'll find the remains of the camp gate, blown up by the retreating Nazis in January 1945, and the remains of quarries dug by camp inmates. The villa occupied by camp commander Amon Goeth still stands on ul. Jerozolimska, now occupied by a local resident. From here it's a ten-minute walk along paths through the overgrown surroundings to the brow of the hill and the large **monument** to the victims of the camp erected in the 1960s, clearly visible from the road below. Close to it stands a smaller memorial plaque encased in a stone obelisk put up by the city's Jewish community. Unlike its officially sanctioned neighbour, the plaque dedication recalls the fact that the majority of those who were incarcerated and died in Płaszów were Jewish.

Like all concentration camps, the site has an eerie, wilderness atmosphere, all the more so for the lack of buildings. Scratch beneath the surface of the grass-covered mounds and you'll find shards of pottery, scraps of metal and cutlery – telltale evidence of its wartime use.

Zwierzyniec and beyond

Moving west of Wawel along the loop of the river, you soon enter the Zwierzyniec district, one of the city's oldest suburbs and the home of several Kraków traditions, notably the custom of constructing *szopki* (creches) at Christmas and the Lajkonik ceremony (see Festivals box, p.413).

Perched at the edge of the river, the **Norbertine Church and Monastery Complex** (Kóscióì i Klasztor Norbertanek) is a fortified thirteenth-century structure, with a fine Romanesque portal (all that remains of the original building) and a restful Neoclassical interior. Used by the nuns living in the complex, it's a good spot for a quiet moment away from the city bustle. The church isn't often open, though, so it's best to visit around the time of services – 5pm is generally a good bet. The annual Lajkonik pageant, believed to have been initiated by the nuns, starts from outside the complex.

Just up the hill from here is the Church of the Saviour (Kóscióì Salvatora), one of the oldest in the city. Built on the site of a pagan Slav temple, excavations have revealed three earlier Romanesque churches, the oldest dating back to around 1000 AD. Continue up the hill and after fifteen minutes you'll reach the edge of **Błonia**, the largest green expanse in the city. Originally a marshy bog, the area was subsequently drained and has served all manner of uses, from medieval football field to the site of the huge open-air Masses during the pope's politically charged visits to Poland in 1979, 1983 and 1987, each of which attracted as many as two million people.

The Kościuszko Mound and the Wolski Forest

A three-hundred-metre-high hill stands roughly 3km west of the city centre, capped by a memorial mound erected in the 1820s in honour of Poland's greatest revolutionary hero, **Tadeusz Kościuszko**. A veteran of the American War of Independence, Kościuszko returned to Poland to lead the 1794 insurrection against the Partitions. For Poles he is the personification of the popular insurrectionary tradition that involved peasants as well as intellectuals (see box below).

The **mound** itself is a latterday example of a peculiar Kraków phenomenon – a series of cone-shaped hills built by local people probably for pagan rituals, the oldest dating back to the seventh century. This mound was added onto the hill by the citizenry of Kraków in the 1820s, using earth from Kościuszko's battle sites, both from Poland and (reputedly) from the United States. Access to this section of the hill is only possible via an effusive **museum** of Kościuszko memorabilia (Tues–Sat 10am–4pm). It's worth the few złotys' admission for the view alone. Lower down the hill, the deer roaming about the hillside are a surprising sight so close to a city centre, but the polluted grass can't do them much good. There's also a nineteenth-century Austrian **fort** and an upmarket **hotel and restaurant**, the *Pod Kopcem* (currently undergoing renovation see p.366 and p.409).

From the city centre (plac Matejki) bus #100 runs to the hotel, but if you feel like a walk out of town you can cross the **Błonia** and then, crossing a couple of roads, follow one of the overgrown pathways up the slopes.

For a more extended bout of countryside, you could take an hour's walk west from the mound to the wonderful stretch of woodland known as **Las Wolski**, a popular area for picnics and day outings with city residents. There's a small **zoological gardens** and hearty **restaurant** at the centre. A little further on through the woods, 500m to the north, stands another mound, this one erected, in emulation of Kościuszko's, to the 1920s ruler Józef Piłsudski. Bus #134 runs from the city centre to the mound.

The university conference centre

East of the edge of Las Wolski, about 5km west of the centre along ul. Księcia Józefa, up ul. Jodłowa and a steep climb of the hill north through the woods takes you up to the main **university conference centre**. The first building you encounter is the elegant palatial structure that the city's Nazi wartime ruler Hans Frank planned to convert into his personal residence. Round the back of the main building there's a bar-restaurant, *U Ziyada* (☎21 98 31 or 22 49 94), that's understandably popular among students as a summer evening drinking spot. The main balcony offers a superb vantage point from which to take in the tranquil rural surroundings over a beer or two. In good weather, the views south are fantastic, with the Tatras visible in the distance on a really clear summer's day, and it's hard to believe you're still relatively close to the city centre. Unless you

TADEUSZ KOŚCIUSZKO (1746-1817)

What Adam Mickiewicz is to the Polish literary Romantic tradition, **Tadeusz Kościuszko** is to its heroic military counterpart. Swashbuckling leader of armed national resistance in the early Partition years, Kościuszko was also a noted radical whose espousal of the republican ideals of the French Revolution did little to endear him to fellow aristocrats, but everything to win over the hearts and minds of the oppressed Polish peasantry. As the US towns and streets named after him testify, Kościuszko is also almost as well known in the **USA** as within Poland itself on account of his major role in the **American War of Independence**, in thanks for which he was made both an honorary American citizen and brigadier general in the US Army.

The bare bones of Kościuszko's life story revolve round a fabulously contorted series of battles, insurrections, revolutions and impossible love affairs. An outstanding student from the start, he fled to Paris in 1776 to escape from the general whose daughter he tried to elope with, continuing on to America, where he joined up with the **independence forces** fighting the **British**. In the following five years he was right in the thick of things, helping to bring about the capitulation of the British forces under General Burgoyne at Saratoga (October 1778), and involved in both the important Battle of the Ninety-Six and the lengthy blockade of Charleston (1781).

Returning to Poland in 1784, he finally gained military office in 1789 after a lengthy period out in the political cold, simultaneously failing (again) to win the consent of a general whose eighteen-year-old daughter he had fallen in love with. Kościuszko's finest hour, though, came in 1792 with the tsarist army's invasion of Poland following the enactment of internal reforms intended to free the country from Russian influence. After the bloody **Battle of Dubienka** (July 1792), Kościuszko was promoted to general by King Stanisław Poniatowski, also receiving honorary French citizenship from the newly established revolutionary government in Paris. From enforced exile in Saxony, Kościuszko soon returned to Poland at the request of the expectant insurrectionary army, swearing his famous **Oath of**

have your own transport, you'll have to rely on a taxi to get here – if the driver doesn't know the way, "Instytut Badań Polonijnych" should do the trick; the cost of the journey (approximately 25zł each way at current rates) is more than justified by the experience.

Bielany

A couple of kilometres further west of the city brings you to the Bielany district. Perched high up on the southwest edge of the Las Wolski, overlooking the river, is the monumental **Camadulensian Church and Monastery Complex** (8am–6pm). The only way to get here if you don't have your own transport is to take a bus (#109, 209, 229 or 239) from Zwierzyniec (the tram terminal) and get off at Srebrna Góra, from where it's a fifteen-minute walk up the hill to the church complex. It's a popular place for outings, so follow the crowds if in doubt.

A walled walkway brings you to the entrance to the complex, through which you're confronted by the huge, crumbling facade of the monastery church, the high central section flanked by a pair of equally imposing square towers. The spacious interior of the church consists of a soaring barrel-vaulted nave lined by

National Uprising before a huge crowd assembled on the Rynek Główny in Kraków in March 1794.

The immediate results of Kościuszko's assumption of leadership were spectacular. A disciplined army largely comprising scythe-bearing peasants won a famous victory over Russian forces at the **Battle of Racławice** (April 1794). In a bid to gain more volunteer peasant recruits, Kościuszko issued the **Połaniec Manifesto** (May 1794), offering amongst other things to abolish serfdom, a radical move resisted by aristocratic supporters. Retreating to Warsaw, the embattled Polish forces held out for two months against the combined might of the Prussian and Russian armies, Kościuszko himself leading the bayonet charges at a couple of critical junctures. After inciting an insurrection in the Wielkopolska region that forced Prussian forces to retreat temporarily, Kościuszko was finally beaten and taken prisoner by the Russians at Maciejowice, an event that led to the collapse of the national uprising.

Imprisoned in St Petersburg and by now seriously ill, Kościuszko was freed in 1796 and returned to the USA to an enthusiastic reception in Philadelphia, soon striking up what proved to be a lasting friendship with Thomas Jefferson. The last decades of Kościuszko's life were marked by a series of further disappointments. He revisited France in 1798 in the hope that Napoleon's rise might presage a revival of Polish hopes, but refused to participate in Napoleon's plans, having failed to gain specific political commitments from Bonaparte with regard to Poland's future. Remaining studiously aloof from French advances, Kościuszko was again approached for support after Bonaparte's fall in 1814, this time from the unlikely quarter of the Russian Emperor Alexander I, who atttempted to gain his approval for the new Russian-ruled **Congress Kingdom** established at the Congress of Vienna (1815). Uncompromising republican to the last, the radical conditions he put forward met with no response. Embittered, Kościuszko retired to Switzerland, where he died in 1817. Two years later the legendary warrior's remains were brought to Kraków and buried among the monarchs in the vaults of Wawel – reviving a pagan Polish burial custom, the people of the city raised a **memorial mound** to him.

a series of ornate chapels, the most notable of which, **St Benedict and St Romuald's chapels**, feature a lavish series of paintings by the artist Tommaso Dolabella depicting the lives of the saints. A little behind the entrance is the tomb of the church's founder, Mikołaj Wolski, crown marshal of Poland in the early 1600s, placed here, it is said, so that churchgoers will walk over it – a stirring example of the humility the Camadolese aim to inculcate among their members.

The monks follow a strict routine of prayer and worship, so the chances are you'll catch them intoning plainsong from the raised, partially hidden gallery behind the altar. With the monks chanting in the background, a visit down into the **crypt**, where the bodies of deceased hermits are stored in coffinless niches, sealed and then exhumed eighty years later for their skeletons to be displayed, is an eerie, not to say chilling experience. Bear in mind, too, that the church complex is supposedly only open to men, except during Sunday Mass and on religious holidays, although this doesn't seem to deter the unisex crowd of visitors, mostly Poles, you'll find trekking around the place throughout the summer. Despite its relative proximity to the city, the Bielany complex feels light years away from the world at large.

THE CAMADOLESE ORDER

Of all the monastic orders present in Poland today, few could claim, or wish, to match the **Camadolese Order** for asceticism. Founded in Italy in the second century AD by **Saint Romuald** (c.950–1027), the ultra-ascetic practices of the Camadolese, which include minimal contact between the monks, who live in their own separate hermitages, a vegetarian diet and little connection with the outside world, attracted Polish champions of the Counter Reformation, who invited them to settle in Poland, notably at **Bielany**. This they did, starting in the early 1600s, and they still retain a presence in the country, with two communities continuing to function. Well-known in Polish Catholic circles for their grim motto, "Memento Mori" ("Remember that you must die"), the hermits don't actually sleep in wooden coffins, as popular rumour has it, though they do preserve the skulls of their long-deceased brethren, as proudly displayed in the crypt at Bielany. However, the order's appeal seems to be on the wane. Apart from the two houses in Poland, there are known to be only six other Camadolese hermitages left worldwide, four in Italy and two, somewhat improbably, in Columbia.

The outskirts

If Wawel Hill and the main square are quintessential old Kraków, the steel mills, smokestacks and grimy housing blocks of **Nowa Huta**, 10km to the east of the city centre, are the embodiment of the postwar communist dream, and any Cracovian will want to show them to you.

South of the city, a fifteen-kilometre bus ride offers a glimpse of an earlier industrial past in the form of the medieval **Wieliczka salt mine**, a beautiful, UNESCO-listed site that demands a visit. **Tyniec**, 15km southwest of the city, out along the river, is a fine Benedictine abbey, which holds organ recitals during the summer.

Nowa Huta and Mogiła

Raised from scratch in the late 1940s on the site of an old village, the vast industrial complex of **Nowa Huta** now has a population of over 200,000, making it by far the biggest suburb, while the vast steelworks accounts for more than fifty percent of the country's production. It's worth visiting for the insights it offers into the working-class culture of postwar Poland and the immense ecological problems facing the country.

From Kraków city centre, it's a forty-minute tram journey (#4, #9, #15 or #22) to **plac Centralny**, the main square, now bereft of its statue of Lenin, which was replaced in 1990 by a small replica of the Gdańsk Crosses (see p.167). From here, seemingly endless streets of residential blocks stretch out in all directions. East along the main road are the mills known until recently as the **Lenin Steelworks**, now renamed the Sendzimir Works, but still belching out the thick smoke that covers the whole area with layers of filth. What to do with this vast monster of an industrial complex is something of a political hot potato for the Kraków city authorities. While it's clear that the place can't keep going indefinitely on its current heavily state-subsidized footing, shutting down all or even parts of the plant –"restructuring" is the latest buzzword – would mean major losses for a local economy already badly hit by the austerity measures of the post-communist era. On a more upbeat note, a new industrial management body jointly financed by the French and Polish governments has recently been set up in Kraków to examine this and other industrial issues. A series of new anti-pollution measures such as fitting filters on the main chimneys has resulted in significant reductions in the steelworks' hazardous emission levels.

In keeping with the anti-religious policies of the postwar government, churches were not included in the original construction plans for Nowa Huta. After years of intensive lobbying, however, the ardently Catholic population eventually got permission to build one in the 1970s. The **Church of the Ark**, in the northern Bienczyce district, is the result – an amazing ark-like concrete structure encrusted with mountain pebbles. Go there any Sunday and you'll find it packed with steel workers and their families decked out in their best, a powerful testament to the seemingly unbreakable Catholicism of the Polish working class. The other local church, the large **Maximilian Kolbe Church** in the Mistrzejowice district, was consecrated by Pope John Paul II in 1983, a sign of the importance the Catholic hierarchy attaches to the loyalty of Nowa Huta. Kolbe, canonized in 1982, was a priest sent to Auschwitz for giving refuge to Jews; in the camp, he took the place of a Jewish inmate in the gas chambers. Trams #1, #16 and #20 from plac Centralny all pass by the building.

In total contrast to these recent constructions, a mile east of plac Centralny off al. Jan Pawła II stands the **Cistercian Monastery of Mogiła**, a world away from the bustle of Nowa Huta. Bus #153 passes right by. Built around 1260 on the regular Cistercian plan of a triple-aisled basilica with series of chapels in the transepts, the Abbey Church, one of the finest examples of Early Gothic in the region, is a tranquil, meditative spot, the airy interior graced with a fine series of Renaissance murals. What you won't find any longer is the late medieval paper mill built by the Order on the banks of the nearby River Dłubnia, which exported its products all the way into Russia. Across the road is the Church of St Bartholomew, one of the oldest wooden churches in the country, with an elaboratley carved doorway from 1466 and a Baroque belfry.

Tyniec

Within easy striking distance of the city centre, 15km west along the river, is the village of **TYNIEC**. City bus #112 takes you here, as do excursion boats from below Wawel in summer (see p.389), a nice trip provided you don't inspect the water too carefully.

The main attraction is **Tyniec Abbey**, an eleventh-century foundation that was the Benedictines' first base in Poland. Perched on a white limestone cliff on the edge of the village, the abbey makes an impressive sight from the riverbank paths. The farm plots and traditional wooden cottages dotted around the village lend the place a rural feel at odds with its location so close to the city centre, and it's a popular place for a Sunday afternoon stroll.

The original Romanesque abbey was rebuilt after the Tartars destroyed it during the 1240 invasion, and then completely remodelled in Gothic style in the fifteenth century, when the defensive walls were also added. The interior of the church subsequently endured the familiar Baroque treatment, but bits of the Gothic structure are left near the altar and in the adjoining (but usually off-limits) cloisters. From June to August the church holds a series of high-quality **organ concerts** during which the cloisters are opened.

In the village, the *Srebrna Góra* on ul. Benedyktyńska is a famed and moderately priced fish **restaurant** that Cracovians drive out to in droves.

Wieliczka

Fifteen kilometres southeast of Kraków is the **salt mine** at **WIELICZKA** (Kopalnia Soli "Wieliczka"), a unique phenomenon described by one eighteenth-century visitor as being "as remarkable as the Pyramids and more useful". Today it's listed among UNESCO's World Cultural Heritage monuments. Salt deposits were discovered here as far back as the eleventh century, and from King Kazimierz's time onwards, local mining rights, and hence income, were strictly controlled by the Crown. As mining intensified over the centuries, a huge network of pitfaces, rooms and tunnels proliferated – nine levels in all, extending to a depth of 327m with approximately 300km of tunnels stretching over an area some 10km wide. Scaled-down mining continues today, and there's a sanatorium 200m down, to exploit the supposedly healthy saline atmosphere. The mines are popular with Polish and foreign tourists, so be prepared for crowds in summer.

To get to Wieliczka take a local **train** from the central train station – there are plenty of them – or bus #FB from the main Kraków-Płaszów station. Both drop you off a little way from the mine, but it isn't difficult to locate the pit's solitary chimney and squeaky conveyor belt; follow the "Muzeum" signs. There's also a privately run daily bus service from the central bus station (*PKS*) which leaves roughly every thirty minutes for Wieliczka.

DOWN THE MINE

Entrance to the mine (Mid-April to mid-Oct Tues–Sun 8am–6pm; rest of the year Tues–Sun 8am–4pm) is by guided tour only, in groups of thirty or so. In summer there are also some French-, German- and English-speaking guides around (15zł), probably worth booking in advance (☎78 26 53). *Orbis* currently charges around 21zł for the round trip there and back including the standard guided tour; buses leave at 3pm from plac Szczepański. Alternatively, there's an English-language guide book available at the ticket office. Be prepared for a bit of a walk – the tour takes two hours, through nearly two miles of tunnels.

A clanking lift takes you down in complete darkness to the first of the three levels included in the **tour**, at a depth of 65m (if you're unlucky, you may have to

---

THE FLOODING OF THE MINE

The future of the **Wieliczka salt mine** became uncertain following a serious bout of **flooding** in September 1992, when a huge river of salty water began pouring into the complex through an abandoned mine passageway some 170m underground – too much for the mine pumps to handle. So far none of the decorated chambers have been damaged, but the mine authorities have warned that some may be in danger from the floods. The town of Wieliczka, much of which is built over the mines, was also badly affected: walls collapsed, cracks appeared in the fabric of the local monastery, and the train tracks running through the centre of town shifted and twisted, causing all train services to be suspended. The EC subsequently provided an emergency grant towards the cost of shoring up what's recognized as a unique medieval treasure. It's not the first time there's been a shutdown – major flooding also occurred in the early 1970s, and miners are aware of scores of other small leaks in the passageways. The mine has now been cleared and reopened to visitors, although mine officials fear that something similar could happen again, the threat of ground-water leaks remaining the key worry.

walk the whole way down to the bottom level and up again). The rooms and passageways here were hewn between the seventeenth and nineteenth centuries, and whereas the lower sections are mechanized, horses are still partly used to pull things around on the top three levels. Many of the first-level chambers are pure green salt, including one dedicated to Copernicus, which he is supposed to have visited.

The further you descend, the more spectacular and weird the chambers get. As well as underground lakes, carved chapels and rooms full of eerie crystalline shapes, the second level features a chamber full of jolly salt gnomes carved in the 1960s by the mineworkers. The star attraction, **Blessed Kinga's Chapel**, completed in the early part of the nineteenth century, comes on the bottom level, 135m down: everything in the ornate fifty-metre-long chapel is carved from salt, including the stairs, bannisters, altar and chandeliers. The chapel's acoustic properties – every word uttered near the altar is audible from the gallery – has led to its use as a concert venue, and even, of late, as a banquet hall, ex-US president Bush being one of the first to be feted with a feast in his honour in 1995, a token of thanks for his support for anti-pollution measures in the city. Recent events have included performances of Zbigniew Preisner's film scores for Kieślowski's internationally renowned *Red*, *White* and *Blue* trilogy. A **museum**, also down at the lowest level, documents the history of the mine, local geological formations, and famous visitors such as Goethe, Balzac and the Emperor Franz Josef.

Eating, drinking and entertainment

Kraków's tourist status has given rise to a decent selection of **restaurants**, with new places springing up every week. For the moment, however, keep in mind that demand is also high, and for the better places, booking is essential. In general, you'll need to turn up early, too; this is not a late-night city, its life instead revolving around a central European café culture of afternoon and early evening socializing. There is, however, a good deal happening on the cultural front, with one of the best **theatre** groups in Europe, a long-established **cabaret** tradition and numerous **student events**. The compact size of Kraków's city centre and the presence of the university gives a general buzz that's largely absent in other large Polish cities, Warsaw included.

For local **listings** and general information, the weekly magazine *Tydzień w Krakowie* is invaluable, as is the newspaper *Gazeta Krakowska*. The English-language tourist magazines are also helpful, but less comprehensive.

The **telephone code** for Kraków is ☎012

Restaurants and snack bars

Kraków's Jewish past seems to have rubbed off on some of the better restaurants, with dishes like jellied carp and various versions of *gefillte fisch* appearing on menus. Otherwise it's pretty much a case of traditional Polish fare tempered by splashes of European cuisine – Western and Eastern – plus the new (for Poland) phenomenon of fast food and snacks.

Milk bars, snacks and fast food

You'll have no trouble picking up a hamburger or snack in the city centre – Western-style **fast-food joints** (including a number of big-league franchises, McDonald's included) have moved in on the Old Town area in a major way. In among the new-look Western setups there are a number of places specializing in more traditional Polish dishes, notably *pierogi*, and generally worth hunting out. There's an increasing selection of ethnic, notably Arab places.

Auropolis, ul. Grodzka 9. Passable Greek takeaway and sit-down place, offering filling portions.

Beirut, ul. Floriańska 1. Top corner of the street. Popular takeaway joint, decent falafels and kebabs.

Bistro Pronto, pl. Dominikański 2. Terrace bistro on this busy square. Good lunchtime place.

Chimera, ul. Św. Anny 3. Deservedly popular cellar salad/snack bar in university district. Occasional live music. Open till 10pm.

Da Luigi, Rynek Główny 44. Decent Polish-style pizza – generous portions.

Grace Pizzeria, ul. Św. Anny 7. One of the best of the new pizzeria joints (also takeaways), with prices to match. Open till 10pm.

Grill Hogar, ul. Paderewskiego 4. Good-quality Algerian takeaway serving kebabs, *merguez*, and other favourites.

Kabul, ul. Karmelicka 45a. Afghan-influenced snacks – kebabs, "Afghan" *pierogi* and the like.

Kuchcik, ul. Jagiellońska 12. Good-quality Polish snack bar offering the basics.

Na Rogu, ul. Karmelicka 17. Old-style milk bar with good selection of *pierogi*, takeaway included.

Monika, Rynek Główny 33. Snack bar in passageway just off main square. Good place for a quick lunch.

Pani Stasia's, ul. Mikołajska 18. A small, privately owned fast-food joint, east of the Rynek. Popular with students and offering home cooking including great *pierogi* (cabbage pancakes). It's hidden from the street, but the queues are conspicuous. Lunchtime only.

Piccolo Pizza, ul. Szewska 14a. Useful and popular pizza parlour, again in the university district.

Pod Basztą, ul. Floriańska 55. Reliable snack bar in a street (just north of the Rynek) offering plenty of cheap places to eat.

Pod Żegarem, ul. Basztowa 12. Regular lunchtime milk bar on the northern edge of the Planty.

Różowy Słoń, ul. Straszewskiego. Salad-based snack bar with humorous comic-book decor.

Svensson, ul. Długa 12. Swedish-owned takeaway, good for a lunchtime Scandinavian *pierog* or salad.

Taco Mexicano, ul. Poselska 20. Passable Mexican takeaway. Open till late.

Złoty Smok, ul. Sienna 1. Café-type snack bar, also does breakfast.

Restaurants

The choice of restaurants has broadened considerably during the early 1990s. Places at the lower end of the scale are still generally a bargain, while, at the top, you can expect to pay at least as much as equivalents back home. Encouragingly, there's a growing selection of ethnic restaurants to choose from, not yet the equivalent of Warsaw, but certainly a big improvement on even a couple of years ago.

A Dong, ul. Brodzińskiego 3 (☎56 48 72). New Vietnamese venture stuck out in Pedgórze, but worth seeking out for currently the city's best Asian food. Open till 11pm.

Almayer, Rynek Główny 30 (☎22 32 24). Smartish Chinese restaurant in a courtyard. Reservations advisable in summer. Open till 11pm, also a night bar (till 4am).

Andaluous, pl. Dominikański 6 (☎22 52 27). Good quality Tunisian-run place; try the couscous specialities. Open till 11pm.

Balaton, ul. Grodzka 37. Good, but cramped, Hungarian restaurant; be prepared for a wait, especially in summer.

Cantina Los Sombreros, ul. Czarnowiejska 55 (☎33 15 88). Another Kraków first, a perfectly respectable Mexican joint run by a Mexican family. Open till the last person leaves.

Cechowa, ul. Jagiellońska 11. Handy if you're in the university area, with excellent pancakes and a fast lunchtime service.

Cracovia, al. Puszkina 1 (☎22 86 66). A pricey but good hotel restaurant in striking distance of the centre, with a resident dance band. Reservations advisable, especially at weekends. Open till midnight.

Da Pietro, Rynek Główny 17. Best of the new Italian restaurants in town, in a medieval cellar below a courtyard off the main square. Reasonably priced pasta and salads. Open till midnight.

Dniepr, ul. 18 Stycznia 55. Big modern place near *Pewex*. Ukrainian specialities – and dancing.

Elector, ul. Szpitalna 28 (☎21 80 25). Swish new hotel restaurant offering a mix of Polish and French dishes. Live classical music. Booking recommended in summer. Open till midnight.

Floriańska, Floriańska 43 (1st floor). Excellent restaurant serving traditional Polish food in demure surroundings. Open till 11pm.

Grand, ul. Sławkowska 19. An excellent, if rather pricey, restaurant in the city's newest luxury hotel.

Grodzka, pl. Dominikański 6. Frequented by tourist groups, but still worth a visit for dishes like *sztuka mięsa chrzanowy* (beef with horseradish sauce). Live music in the evenings; speedy lunchtime service.

Hawelka, Rynek Główny 34 (☎22 47 53). Reopened after a complete overhaul and now transformed into a pretentious first-floor restaurant, *Tetmajerowska*, complete with *fin-de-siecle* interior decoration by the artist of same name; with attached café, bar and self-service cafeteria on the ground floor. Restaurant booking advisable in summer.

Kuchcik, Jagiellońska 12. Down-to-earth, good-quality Polish cuisine (the *bigos* and *pierogi* are recommended) in an enjoyable centre-of-town location. Closes at 6pm.

Kurza Stopka, pl. Wiosny Ludów. Cheap and clean with a good reputation among local residents.

Leonard's, Rynek Główny 25. Smart new French cellar restaurant clearly aimed at the wealthy. If you want to blow money, for atmosphere you're better off at *Wierzynek*.

Orbit, ul. Wrocławska 78A. Traditional Polish cuisine, large portions at moderate prices. The *barszcz* is excellent. Open till 10pm (midnight on Sat).

PTTK Hostel, ul. Westerplatte 15–16. Recently tarted-up restaurant offering large portions of solid, no-nonsense meat and veg. Near the train station.

Paese, ul. Poselska 24. Tastefully decorated Corsican place popular with the city smart set and marred by indifferent-quality food. Open till midnight.

Pod Gruszka. ul. Szczepański 1. Upstairs restaurant with a traditional feel to it, a good choice of Polish dishes and very reasonable prices.

Pod Kopcem, al. Waszyngtona (☎22 03 11 or 22 03 55). Restaurant of the elegant hotel below the Kościuszko Mound, specializing in fish from the Tatras. Reservations essential in season. Closed until hotel reopens, hopefully by 1997.

Pod Różą, ul. Floriańska 14. Good-quality hotel restaurant serving standard Polish fare.

Polski, ul. Pijarska 17. Cheap and basic hotel restaurant (pork with sauerkraut and the like), close to the city centre. Live music in the evenings.

Staropolska, ul. Sienna 4 (☎22 58 21). Deservedly popular Old Town venue, with an emphasis on traditional pork and poultry dishes. Booking essential in the evening.

Vega, ul. Św. Gertrudy 7. One of the city's tiny set of vegetarian restaurants, with a growing reputation. Open till 9pm.

Vil-tera, ul. Św. Krzyża 1. Lithuanian restaurant with small but good selection of national specialities. Open till 10pm.

Wierzynek, Rynek Główny 15 (☎22 10 35). This stately place is Kraków's most famous restaurant. On a good night it's one of the best in the country with specialities like mountain trout and the house *wierzynek* dish. For visitors, prices remain very reasonable at around 60zł a head; to have any chance of a table, booking is essential. Open till 11pm.

Żywiec, ul. Floriańska 19. Revamped old snack bar now a brash new restaurant (Polish food).

Cafés and bars

Cafés proliferate on and around the city centre, almost all those on the square adding on an impromptu outdoor terrace section in summer (regulation-issue plastic chairs and Western-brand name sunshades in all but the older-established places). Especially in the evenings, these make nice places in which to soak up the atmosphere, with the additional distraction of the assortment of roving buskers vying for the tourist złoty. An additional recent development are the myriad standup **bars**, mostly of the youthful, trendier variety now making major inroads in the Old Town area. Some of the nicest are tucked away in courtyards off the Rynek Główny. You can always get a drink at one of the larger hotels until around midnight, while a growing number of nightclubs keep going through to around 3 or 4am (see p.413).

Cafés

Alvorada, Rynek Główny 30 (opposite the State Bank). Mouthwatering cakes at this café on the main square, once the centre for black-market moneychangers and invaded by Western beers.

Ariel, ul. Szeroka 18. Fancy café-cum-restaurant in the heart of the Kazimierz district. Live music most evenings.

Behemot, ul. Bracka 4. Smart café with a good line in cakes and gateaux in a pleasant courtyard off the main square; popular with foreigners. Open late.

Europejska, Rynek Główny 36. Smart modern café, indifferent service; its main plus is the terrace views onto the square.

Hetmański, Rynek Główny 17. One of the nicest cafés on the south side of the Old Town.

Jama Michalika, ul. Floriańska 45. Famous and atmospheric old café-cum-cabaret, opened in 1895 – worth dropping in at for the furnishings alone (see also "Theatre and cabaret", p.412).

Krzysztofory, ul. Szczepańska 2. Bohemian combined art gallery, café and bar in the palace of the same name.

Malma, Rynek Główny 25. Swish squareside café, with a good line in espresso and some excellent cakes. Recommended.

Mozaika, ul. Gołębia 5. Small pleasant café with art exhibitions by local artists.

No. 1, ul. Św. Tomasza 7. Large selection of teas; also good for breakfast. Open till midnight.

Pasięka, Mały Rynek. Nice place to sit out and enjoy the relative quiet of the square.

Pod Baranami, Rynek Główny 27. Terrace café in front of the city's cultural centre.

Pod Białym Orłem, Rynek Główny 45. Another café with fine views over the square. Close to the Mariacki Church.

Redolfo, Rynek Główny 37/39 (near the corner with ul. Sławkowska). A cosy haunt with a splendid Art Nouveau interior; the coffee's better than usual too.

Rio, ul. Floriańska 45. Standup café-bar with excellent coffee, frequented by actors and literary types.

Sava, ul. Meiselsa 17. Inside the Jewish Cultural Centre in Kazimierz. Good coffees and snacks.

Staromiejska, Mały Rynek. Nice place to sit out and enjoy the atmosphere of this attractive square. The *Pasieka* next door is rather grander.

U Pugetów, ul. Starowiślna 13. Excellent little café off the southern side of the Old Town. **U Zalipianek**, ul. Szewska 24. Traditionally decorated, serving a range of herbal teas to a trendy crowd.

Vis-a-vis, Rynek Główny 29. Comfy café-bar on the main square.

Zigi, ul. Grodzka 6. One of the more stylish standup coffee bars. *Pod Pawiem*, situated on the same street, is a good second if the *Zigi* is full.

Bars

Bacchus, ul. Św. Marka 21. Cosy, popular little bar to the north of the square. Open until 1am.

Basket, ul. Tomasza 11. Trendy basketball-theme joint with disco and pool table, ideal for late-night drinkers – open till 7am.

Black Gallery, ul. Mikotajska 24. Cellar bar with a good line in alternative/funk sounds. Mixed crowd of drinkers, Open till 4am.

Feniks, ul. Jama 2. Traditional drinking bar, open till late.

Free Pub, ul. Sławkowska 4. Smoky dive popular with seasoned local drinkers. Open till 5am.

Harris, Rynek Główny 28. Upmarket Western-style piano bar popular with Kraków yuppies. Lush decor, Foster's on tap. Open till 1am.

Irish Pub, ul. Św. Jama. Cavernous cellar bar, less tacky than its name suggests. Good pool table. Open till 1am.

JTS Stagger Bar, Mikołajska 6. Cellar bar with a range of beers (Polish and foreign) on tap. Open to 2am.

Maxime, ul. Floriańska 32. Old established bar, again open late.

Ogródek Muzyczny, ul. Jagiellońska 6. Popular university-district bar with outdoor courtyard – strictly piped muzak, though. Open till 2am.

Pod Baranami, Rynek Główny 27. Cellar bar inside the cultural centre (see p.412).

Pod Beczkami, ul. Dietla 46. South of Wawel in the Stradom district. Standing-room only (there are no seats) in Kraków's first beer hall, already a well-established haunt with local swillers. Huge selection of beers, Polish and imported. Open till 9pm.

Pod Papugami, ul. Św. Jama 18. Kraków's response to the Euro-Irish pub craze. Not a bad one either, with occasional live Irish folk, pricey Guinness on tap. Open till 2am weekdays, 4am weekend.

Pod Strzelnicą, ul. Królowej Jadwigi 184. Small, private *kneipe;* snacks, beer and vodka.

Windsor Pub, Rynek Główny 25. Pricey bar on the main square. Open till 3am.

Słanczyck Pub, Rynek Główny. Cellar bar in the Clock Tower. Good vibes, live jazz (Fri & Sat) and a theatre. Open till 1am.

U Słarego, ul. Jagiellońska 5. Housed in the Stary Teatr, a popular local hangout.

ZPAF Photographers' Club, ul. Św. Anny 3. The gallery has a basement dive across the courtyard at the back – a trendy student hangout.

Gay Kraków

The local chapter of the national gay organization *Lambda* is the central contact point: write to them (there's no openly available phone number) at *Lambda Kraków*, PO Box 249, 30-960 Kraków 1. A couple of places in town worth cruising are the *Club 91* bar, pl. Szczepański 7 (closes early), the *Café Club*, pl. Mariacki 7 (open till 10pm) and the *Jama Michalika* café (see listings).

Entertainment and nightlife

Even if you don't speak the language, some of Kraków's **theatrical events** are
well worth catching. In addition to consulting the city's listings magazines (see
"Information" p.364), look in at the Cultural Information Centre at ul. Św. Jama
(Mon–Sat 10am–7pm; ☎21 77 87), which, as well as making bookings, produces a
monthly calendar with comprehensive listings of events. It's as well to bear in
mind that during the summer months everything sells out fast. For **rock** or
vaguely alternative events, check the listings magazines or consult the *Almatur*
office on the Rynek.

Theatre and cabaret

Ever since Stanisław Wyspiański and friends made Kraków the centre of the
Młoda Polska movement at the beginning of this century, many of Poland's
greatest actors and directors have been closely identified with the city. Until his
death in December 1990, the most influential figure on the scene was avant-garde
director **Tadeusz Kantor**, who used the *Cricot 2* theatre at ul. Kanonicza 5, as
the base for his visionary productions.

The *Stary Teatr* currently performs at three different sites: a main stage at ul.
Jagiellońska 1 (☎22 85 66), and studio stages located in a basement at ul.
Sławkowska 14 and Starowiślna 21. They place a strong emphasis on visual aspects,
making the productions that they offer (mostly reinterpretations of Polish and
foreign classics) unusually accessible. The company has built up an international
following from appearances at the Edinburgh Festival and other prestigious events.

Of the city's other fifteen or so **theatres**, the splendid *Teatr im J. Słowackiego* on
plac Św. Ducha, modelled on the Paris Opéra, is the biggest and one of the best-
known, with a regular diet of classical Polish drama and ballet, plus occasional opera.
Check too, for the latest productions at places like the *Miniatura*, pl. Św. Ducha; the
STU, al. Krasińskiego 18; and the *Bagatela*, ul. Karmelicka 6. Ewa Demarczyk, "the
Polish Edith Piaf", has her own theatre at ul. Floriańska 55 – definitely worth a look.

Cabaret is also an established feature of Kraków. Two of the best-known venues
are the *Jama Michalika* café on ul. Floriańska (an old Młoda Polska haunt), and the
popular *Teatr Satyry*, beneath the town hall tower on the Rynek. The *Pod Baranami*,
at Rynek Główny 27, also has a cabaret venue – considered the best in Poland – in its
cellar.

Classical music

For **classical concerts**, the *Filharmonia Szymanowskiego*, ul. Zwierzyniecka 1, is
home of the **Kraków Philharmonic**, one of Poland's most highly regarded orchestras. Following a major fire in December 1991, which gutted the building, destroying
the main concert hall and its valuable organ in the process, the building has been
totally renovated and the orchestra is back in business, offering a regular service of
high-quality concerts (box office Mon–Sat 9am–noon & 5–7pm; ☎22 94 77).

The **Capella Cracoviensis**, the city's best-known choir, gives fairly regular
concert performances at churches and other venues around the city – check the
local listings for details.

Jazz and student clubs

The city's growing nightlife scene is well represented in the host of **student
clubs** operating around the city – unpredictable, not always easy to find but

generally worth the effort. Apart from the regular selection of live events and performances, they offer the additional bonus of some of the cheapest **drinking** in town, and the cover charge is generally minimal around 5zł. Listed below is a selection of the best ones around: a couple of nights in town hanging out in any of these places and you'll pick up on which ones are currently buzzing. Additionally, there's a small but widening choice of other club venues, many still weighted towards the traditional disco formula, although many are more alternative

Café Maraska, ul. Na Błoniach 7, on the edge of Błonia Park. Popular dance place, not student-oriented, but always lively. Open till 2am.

Karlik, ul. Reymonta 17B. Hidden away in downtown student dormitory land west of town – definitely the hardest to find. Largish dance floor, weekend discos (till midnight) and an alternative music night – live bands and assorted happenings every Friday, till 2am.

Pod Jaszczurami, Rynek Główny 7/8 (☎22 09 02 for concert/event information). Large, famously smoky club, inevitably the most popular in town on account of its main square location. Regular discos are usually packed out with a combination of locals and foreign students in the summer months. Live jazz every Tuesday night (check local listings for details). Vodka and orange juice all round is the standard order in the downstairs bar. Open 8pm–3am.

Pod Przewiązka, ul. Bydgozka 19B (☎37 45 02). Popular student hangout, well west of the centre – trams #4, #8, #12, #13 or #44 pass close by. Discos till midnight Fri, Sat & Sun, with a small cover charge. Live jazz every Wed, rock bands on Thurs, as well as other occasional live acts and a CD club. They don't always publish the programme in advance, so it's best just to turn up.

Radio Zet Club, ul. Bracka 4. Newish bar/club sponsored by the national radio station of the same name. Live jazz on Sat.

Ritmo Latino, pl. Szczepański. The beginnings of a world music scene – Kraków's first Latin/salsa disco. Open till 6am.

FESTIVALS

June is the busiest month for festivities, with four major events: the **Kraków Days** (a showcase for a range of concerts, plays and other performances), the **Jewish Cultural Festival**, the **Folk Art Fair** and the **Lajkonik Pageant**. The last, based on a story about a raftsman who defeated the Tartars and made off with the khan's clothes, features a brightly dressed Tartar figure leading a procession from the Norbertine Church in the western district of Zwierzyniec to the Rynek. The costume used in the ceremony was created by Stanisław Wyspiański (see p.380), the original of which is displayed in the City Historical Museum.

Over the **Christmas** period, a Kraków speciality is the construction of intricately designed Nativity scenes or *szopki*. Unlike traditional cribs elsewhere, these amazing architectural constructions are usually in the form of a church (often based upon Mariacki), built with astounding attention to detail from everyday materials – coloured tin foil, cardboard and wood. A special exhibition of the best prize-winning works are displayed at the Historical Museum on Rynek Główny, which lasts until the end of January. Some of the best examples from recent years are kept in the permanent exhibitions on the upper floor of the museum (see p.370), while older *szopki* can be seen in the Ethnographic Museum (see p.398). You can see some of the oldest fourteenth-century *szopki* all year round in St Andrew's Church.

On the cultural front, there are **organ concerts** at Tyniec (see p.405) from June to August, and at various of the city's churches in April. The **Graphic Art Festival**, held from May to September in even-numbered years, is a crowd-puller, too. And finally, on a rather smaller scale, there's an annual **International Short Film Festival** (May–June).

Rotunda, ul. Oleandry 1 (☎33 35 38). Next to a student dormitory, a short hop west of the centre, not far north of the *Cracovia* hotel. Popular student club, particularly for its weekend discos which run until 2am on Sat (midnight on other nights of the week). There's also a film club and occasional live acts. Minimal cover charge.

Shakesbeer, ul. Gotębia 5. Popular cellar bar-cum-club with live DJs. Wed–Sun till 5am.

U Muniaka, ul. Floriańska 3 (☎23 12 05). New jazz club in city centre cellars. Variable quality live music (Thurs–Sat from 9.30pm). Serves food. Open till 2am.

Żelazna, ul. Joselewicza 21. Currently the city's premier heavy rock/alternative venue. Go prepared for sonic assault. Closes when the last person leaves.

Shopping

The city centre's inexorable return to the moneyed heart of central Europe is eloquently expressed in the range of **shops** in the centre, with several commerce-oriented streets, notably ul. Floriańska, gradually acquiring the affluent-looking boutiques and other consumerist hallmarks of the average western European city. Ulica Szewska is also a good street for boutiques as well as more traditional Polish clothes shops. Even by Polish standards, though, **opening hours** are a bit eccentric. Most places don't open till 10 or 11am, closing around 7pm (bakeries are usually an exception), so if you're planning shopping tours, check the opening times first.

Kraków has plenty of useful **bookstores**. Ones to look out for include *Garmond*, ul. Stolarska 1; the *PTTK* shop, ul Jagiellońska 4, which has a good selection of photo albums and postcards, with the additional plus of a bar in the back on a courtyard; *Hetmańska*, Rynek Główny 17, a large shop with a fair number of English books, that stays open late; *Pod Wierchami*, ul. Jagiellońska 6, with a good selection of map and guides; and *Znak*, ul. Sławkowska 1, with some interesting titles in among the theology. *Antykwariat* (old book shops) worth exploring are at ul. Szpitalna 19, ul. Szewska 25 and ul. Sławkowska 10. The best places for **records and CDs** are *Murzyczna*, Rynek Główny 36; *Kompakt*, ul. Jagiellońska 6A; and *Salon CD*, ul. Senacka 6.

For a taste of a more customary postwar Polish style of shopping, the street trader's **market**, it's worth making your way into the **Kleparz** district fifteen minutes' walk north of the Rynek Główny. Rynek Kleparski, just across ul. Basztowa, offers a mixed jumble of Poles and former Soviet citizens touting an imaginative variety of wares, anything from home-picked fruit and veg to books, bootleg cassettes, Soviet army uniforms, moonshine and dubiously antique bric-a-brac. Heading towards the north along shop-lined ul. Długa brings you to the larger plac Nowy Kleparz, surrounded by an array of cheap second-hand and cut-price shops.

Finally, if you need a **late-night store**, most of the following are open 24 hours a day: *Amara* Szewska 15 (spirits and beers); *Cymes*, ul. Szewska 10 (delicatessen); *Delicje*, ul. Basztowa 12; *Monopolowy*, ul. Kalwaryjska 26; *Jubilat*, ul. Krasińskiego 1; *U Francuza*, ul. Mazowiecka 24.

Listings

Airlines *LOT*, ul. Basztowa 15 (Mon–Fri 8am–7pm; ☎22 50 76 or 22 70 78).
Airport information ☎11 67 00 or 11 33 27.
American Express c/o *Orbis*, *Cracovia* hotel, al. Puszkina 1.

Billiards The latest local pastime. If you fancy hitting the tables try *Billiards*, Rynek Główny 9 (pasaż Bielaka); *Billiard*, ul. Karmelicka 10; *Pasaż*, Rynek Główny 9; or *Daddy's Billiards*, ul. Krowoderska 28.

Bus tickets are available in advance from *Orbis* at ul. Św. Marka 25. Buying international tickets in summer can involve hours of queueing. For international routes, try any of the major travel agents: *Jordan*, *Dexter* (see p.364), or *Akcja*, ul. Grodzka 4.

Car rental *Hertz*, ul. Armii Krajowej 15 (☎37 11 20). Airport delivery on request; *Orbis*, ul. Koniewa 9, by the *Continental*; *Budget*, ul. Radzikowskiego 99, inside *Hotel Krak* (☎37 00 89).

Car repairs *Polmozbyt* offices are at al. Pokoju 81 (Mon–Fri 6am–10pm, Sat & Sun 10am–6pm; ☎48 00 34); on ul. Kawiory (daily 7am–10pm; ☎37 55 75); and al. 29 Listopada 90 (daily 6am–10pm; ☎11 60 44). There are now plenty of private places too – ask at the tourist offices, hotels, cafés or the big garages themselves.

Cinemas Check local listings for details of current programmes. A selection of the more important cinemas includes the *Apollo*, ul. Św. Tomasza 11; *Kijów*, al. Krasińskiego 3; *Mikro*, pl. Invalidów; *Rotunda* ul. Oleandry and *Wanda*, ul. Św. Gertrudy 5.

Consulates *France*, ul. Stolarska 15 (☎22 18 64); *Russia*, ul. Westerplatte 11 (☎22 83 88); *USA*, ul. Stolarska 9 (☎22 12 94); *Germany*, ul. Stolarska 7 (☎21 84 73). There is no UK representation.

Crime On the increase. Avoid the mostly unlit eastern section of the Planty at night.

Exchange National Bank (*Bank Narodowy*), ul. Basztowa 20; *PeKaO*, Rynek Główny. 31. Travellers' cheques can be changed at both, but it can be a very slow process. *Orbis*, Rynek Główny 41, also changes cheques but charges a hefty commission. Cash transactions get a lower rate of exchange.

Football Wisła Kraków are one of the oldest clubs in the country, six times league champions, but these days in and out of the First Division. They play out at the Wisła Stadium, ul. Reymonta, in the western Czarna Wieś district (bus #144 passes close by).

Fuel stations 24hr stations (some with unleaded fuel): ul. Wielicka; ul. Podgórska; ul. Jasnogórska; ul. Kamienna; ul. Powst. Wielkopolskich os. Strusia; ul. Zakopiańska; and ul. Kazimierza Wielkiego.

Galleries Among the numerous Stare Miasto galleries, you might check out: *Sztuka Polska*, ul. Floriańska 34; *Krzysztofory*, ul. Szczepańska 2; *Desa*, ul. Św. Jana 3; and the exhibitions in the *Pod Baranami* on the Rynek.

Optician *Foight*, ul. Floriańska.

Parking There are several guarded car parks in the central city area including: pl. Św. Ducha, ul. Karmelicka, ul. Królewska, ul. Powiśle, pl. Szczepański.

Pharmacies ul. Starowiślna 77, ul. Floriańska 15, Rynek Główny 13, 42 & 45, ul. Grodzka 15, ul. Karmelicka 23.

Post office Main office is at ul. Wielopole 2, including poste restante and 24hr phone services. For express mail and parcels go to the post office opposite the main train station.

Radio The local RMF station (70,06FM), eastern Europe's first independently owned radio setup, based inside the *Pod Kopcem* hotel, broadcasts throughout southern Poland. English-language news bulletins five times a day from Monday to Saturday (8.30am, 10.30am, 3.30pm, 5.30pm and 9pm), with BBC news at 9pm on Sundays.

Swimming pool The *Forum* and *Continental* hotels (see p.365) both have indoor pools, open to non-residents for a small fee, as do the *Korona*, ul. Kalwarysk 9 and *Wisła*, ul. Reymonte 22.

Taxis *Wawel taxi*, ☎66 66 66; *Radio Taxi*, ☎44 55 55 or *Tele Taxi*, ☎36 52 52.

Tours *Universal* (☎22 13 44) offers city tours, also Wieliczka, Auschwitz; *Intercrac* Rynek Główny 14 (☎21 98 58) does the same destinations, but in minibuses instead of ordinary buses; *Point*, inside the *Continental* hotel (☎37 50 44), local excursions.

Train tickets are available from the *Orbis* office at Rynek Główny 41 and in the train station. Expect queues at the international ticket desk.

MAŁOPOLSKA

The name **Małopolska** – literally "Little Poland" – in fact applies to a large swathe of the country, for the most part a rolling landscape of traditionally culti-vated fields and quiet villages. It's an ancient region, forming, with Wielkopolska, the early medieval Polish state, though its geographical divisions, particularly from neighbouring Silesia, are a bit nebulous. The bulk of Małopolska proper sits north of Kraków, bounded by the Świętokrzyskie Mountains to the north and the broad range of hills stretching down from Częstochowa to Kraków – the so-called Eagles' Nests trail – to the west.

North of Kraków, into the Małopolska heartlands, towns such as **Pinczów**, **Szydłów** and **Jędrzejów** offer rewarding insights into the Jewish-tinged history of the region, while **Kielce**, a largish industrial centre and the regional capital, provides a good stepping-off point for forays into the **Świętokrzyskie Mountains**, really no more than high hills but enjoyable walking territory. The ruins of the once grand Krzyżtopor Castle, near Opatów, are among the best and most memorable in the country. **Częstochowa**, the only other city of the region, is famous as the home of the Black Madonna, which draws huge crowds for the major religious festivals and annual summer pilgrimages from all over the coun-try. Pope John Paul II is a native of the region, too, and his birthplace at **Wadowice** has become something of a national shrine, while the Catholic trail continues to the west at **Kalwaria Zebrzydowska**, another pilgrimage site.

Due west of Kraków at **Oświęcim** is the **Auschwitz-Birkenau** concentration camp, preserved more or less as the Nazis left it.

Oświęcim: Auschwitz-Birkenau

When you go in there's a sign in five languages that says, 'There were four million'.

I broke down about halfway round Auschwitz, walking away from the wall against which 20,000 people were shot. There's a shrine there now; schoolgirls were laying flowers and lighting candles.

But it wasn't that particular detail that got to me. And it wasn't the stark physical evidence in earlier blocks of the conditions in which people had lived, sleeping seven or nine together on straw in three-high tiers the size of double beds.

It wasn't the enormous glass-fronted displays in which, on angled boards sometimes dozens of feet long, lay great piles of wretchedly battered old boots, or children's shoes. It wasn't the bank of suitcases, their owners' names clumsily written on them in faded paint, or the heaps of broken spectacles, of shaving brushes and hairbrushes.

It wasn't the case the length of a barrack room in the block whose subject was the 'Exploitation of Corpses', the case filled with a bank of human hair, or the small case to one side of that, showing the tailor's lining that was made from it.

It wasn't the relentless documentary evidence, the methodical, systematic, compulsive bureaucracy of mass murder.

And it wasn't the block beside the yard in which the shrine now stands, in whose basement are the 'standing cells' used to punish prisoners, measuring ninety by ninety centimetres. People were wedged together into these bare brick cubicles, and left to starve or suffocate pinned helplessly upright. In other cells in the same basement, the first experiments with Zyklon B as a means of mass extermination were conducted.

It was all these things cumulatively crushing you, a seeping of evil from every wall and corner of the place, from every brick of every block, until you reach your limit and it overwhelms you. For a short while I found myself crying, leaning against the wire. Like they tell you — the birds don't sing.

From Pete Davies *All Played Out* (Heinemann).

Seventy kilometres west of Kraków, **OŚWIĘCIM** would in normal circumstances be a nondescript industrial town – a place to send visitors on their way without a moment's thought. The circumstances, however, are anything but normal here. Despite the best efforts of the local authorities to cultivate and develop a new identity, the town is indissolubly linked with the name the Nazi occupiers of Poland gave the place – Auschwitz.

Some history

Following the Nazi invasion of Poland in September 1939, Oświęcim and its surrounding region were incorporated into the domains of the Third Reich and the town's name changed to **Auschwitz**. The idea of setting up a concentration camp in the area was mooted a few months later by the Breslau (Wrocław) division of the SS, the official explanation being the overcrowding in existing prisons in Silesia combined with the political desirability of a campaign of mass-arrests throughout German-occupied Poland to round up all potentially "troublesome" Poles. After surveying the region, the final choice of location fell on an abandoned Polish army barracks in Oświęcim, then an insignificant rural town well away from major urban settlements – and prying eyes – on the borders of Silesia and Małopolska. As Himmler himself was later to explain, Auschwitz was chosen on the clinically prosaic grounds that it was a "convenient location as regards communication, and because the area can be easily sealed off".

Orders to begin work on the camp were finally given in April 1940, the fearsome **Rudolf Hoess** was appointed its commander, and in June of that year, the Gestapo sent the first contingent of around seven hundred prisoners, mainly Jews, to the new camp from nearby Tarnów. As the number of inmates swelled rapidly, so too did the physical size of the camp, as Auschwitz was gradually, but methodically, transformed from a detention centre into a full-scale **death camp**. The momentum of destruction was given its decisive twist by Himmler's decision in 1941 to make Auschwitz the centrepiece of Nazi plans for the "**Final Solution**", the Nazis' attempt to effect the elimination of European Jewry by systematically rounding up, transporting and murdering all the Jews in Reich territories. To this end a second camp, **Birkenau**, was set up a couple of kilometres from the main site, with its own set of gas chambers, crematoria and eventually even its own railway terminal to permit the "efficient" dispatch of new arrivals to the waiting gas chambers.

By the end of 1942, **Jews** were beginning to be transported to Auschwitz from all over Europe, many fully believing Nazi propaganda that they were on their way to a new life of work in German factories or farms – the main reason, it appears, that so many brought their personal valuables with them. The reality, of course, couldn't have been more different. After a train journey of anything up to ten days in sealed goods wagons and cattle trucks, the dazed survivors were herded up the station ramp, whereupon they were promptly lined up for inspection and divided into two categories by the SS: those deemed "fit" or "unfit" for work. People placed in the latter category, up to 75 percent of all new arrivals, according to Hess' testimony at the Nuremberg trials, were told they would be permitted to have a bath.

They were then ordered to undress, marched into the "shower room" and gassed with **Zyklon B** cyanide gas sprinkled through special ceiling attachments. In this way, up to two thousand people were killed at a time (the process took 15–20 minutes), a murderously efficient method of dispatching people that continued

CONCENTRATION CAMPS IN POLAND

Following the country's conquest in 1939, many of the largest and most murderous of the **Nazis' concentration camps** were established in Poland. The camps described in detail in the *Guide* – Auschwitz, Majdanek and Stutthof – are easily accessible to travellers visiting Kraków, Lublin and Gdańsk. Others, with no less hideous a history, are more difficult to get to. For those wanting to visit them, the other major camps are:

Bełzec Close to the Ukrainian border, some 40km southeast of Zamość. The death camp at Bełzec, a small country town with its own Jewish population, was established in January–February 1942 as an extension of a labour camp opened in May 1940. The camp rapidly began its murderous and clinically planned business, using six gas ovens to dispense its victims at the rate of 4500 a time. By the time the Nazis began liquidating the camp in December 1942, a process completed in spring 1943 (when the whole site had been obliterated and reforested), it is estimated that some 600,000 Roma and Jews, principally from the Lublin region, Lwów (L'viv), Kraków, Germany, Austria, Hungary, Romania and Czechoslovakia, had been murdered. The monument to the Jews murdered here was built in the 1960s on the former site of the camp.

Chełmno Nad Nerem (Cumhof). Established in December 1941 on the banks of the River Ner, 50km northwest of Łódź, this was the first death camp built by the Nazis in Poland, and was liberated in 1945. An estimated 340,000 were murdered here, the majority Polish Jews. Traces of the camp remain alongside an official monument to its victims. The camp was a key subject of Claude Lanzemann's controversial documentary *Shoah*.

Rogoźnica (Gross-Rosen). On the road between Legnica and Swidnica in Silesia this was one of the earliest forced labour/concentration camps, established in August 1940, and liquidated in March 1945. A monument now stands to the 40,000 people who perished here.

Sobibór Seventy kilometres east of Lublin, right up by the Belarus border, this death camp was set up in March 1942 as part of the increasingly desperate Nazi drive towards the Final Solution. It was dismantled by the Nazis in October 1943, following an inmates' revolt led by a Soviet Jewish POW officer (about 300 escaped), by which time an estimated 250,000 inmates – mostly Jews from Poland, Ukraine, Holland, France and Austria – had been murdered, most of them in the camp's gas chambers. A commemorative monument as well as a mound of ashes made from burnt corpses has been erected on the former camp site.

Treblinka Roughly 100km northeast of Warsaw on the eastern edges of Mazovia, the camps (known simply as Treblinka "I" and "II") were built along the borderline agreed between Germany and the Soviet Union prior to their joint invasion of Poland in September 1939. Treblinka was shut down by the Nazis in late 1943, by which time an estimated 800,000 people – Jews, Roma, Poles and and many others – had perished in its gas chambers. A Museum of Remembrance was established in the early 1960s, with a large monument commemorating the inmates' uprising of August 1943.

relentlessly throughout the rest of the war. The greatest massacres occurred from 1944 onwards, after the special railway terminal had been installed at Birkenau to permit speedier "processing" of the victims to the gas chambers and crematoria. Compounding the hideousness of the operation, SS guards removed gold fillings, earrings, finger rings and even hair –subsequently used, amongst other things, for mattresses – from the mass of bodies, before incinerating them. The cloth from their clothes was processed into material for army uniforms, their watches given to troops in recognition of special achievements or bravery.

The precise **numbers** of people murdered in Auschwitz-Birkenau between the camp's construction in 1940 and final liberation by Soviet forces in spring 1945 has long been a subject of dispute, often for reasons less to do with a concern with factual accuracy than "revisionist" neo-Nazi attempts to deny the historical reality of the Holocaust. Though the exact figure will never be known, in reputable historical circles it's now generally believed that somewhere between one and a half and two million people died in the camp, the vast majority (85–90 percent) of whom were Jews, along with sizeable contingents of Romanies (Gypsies), Poles, Soviet POWs and a host of other European nationalities.

The physical scale of the Auschwitz-Birkenau camp is a shock in itself. Most visitors, though – whose numbers, as at all the concentration camps, have dropped significantly in recent years, due largely to the demise of officially sponsored group visits from the ex-communist world – see only the main Auschwitz section of the complex. This, however, was only one component of the hideous network of barracks, compounds, factories and extermination areas. It is only in visiting Birkenau, roughly 3km down the road from Auschwitz, that you begin to grasp the full enormity of the Nazi death machine.

Practicalities

To get to Auschwitz-Birkenau from Kraków by **train**, services to Oświęcim are fairly frequent (six daily from Kraków central station; twelve from Płaszów station), but return services are inconvenient, making an early start essential. It's advisable to check current timetables before setting out. **Buses** run less frequently and several terminate some way from the centre of Oświęcim. Either way, it's a ninety-minute journey.

From Oświęcim station, it's a short bus ride, or twenty-minute walk to the gates of Auschwitz; bus #19 runs to Birkenau, and taxis are also available. If you decide to make the journey on foot, the route to Birkenau, some 3km on from Auschwitz, adds significantly to the walking distance. Rather grotesquely, there's now a **hotel** and a large **cafeteria** inside the Auschwitz camp.

The trip back to Kraków can be awkward as, currently, no trains run to the city between 2pm and 8pm. Your best bet is to return by bus from the main terminal opposite the train station in Oświęcim, but even the last of these leaves at 3.30pm.

Auschwitz-Birkenau is unfathomably shocking. If you want all the specifics on the camp, you can pick up a detailed **guidebook** (in English and other languages) with maps, photos and a horrendous array of statistics. Alternatively, you can join a free **guided group**, often led by former inmates. It's perhaps best to go with friends rather than alone – mutual support and emotional back-up is extremely helpful. Although the ban on children under thirteen entering the complex has been lifted – even school parties visit Auschwitz now – you'd be well advised to consider seriously before exposing young people to such a potentially traumatizing experience.

AUSCHWITZ-BIRKENAU IN POSTWAR POLAND

To describe **Auschwitz-Birkenau** as a "museum" seems morally shocking: strictly speaking, however, the description is correct, if a museum is understood to be a place where objects are chosen, arranged and displayed with a purpose. In the first place, what the visitor to Auschwitz-Birkenau sees today does not reflect the way the camp developed under the Nazis, or the camp that the Soviet liberators found in January 1945. Many important sections of the site, for example, have been altered, destroyed or allowed to fall into ruin. Some cases in point are the entrance kiosk of today's parking lot, originally the site of the main entrance to the camp – not as is commonly assumed, the gate bearing the notorious "*Arbeit Macht Frei*" inscription; the visitor's complex next to the parking lot, originally the reception centre for camp inmates including a series of clothing incinerators; and, most importantly, the crematorium just outside the fence of the main Auschwitz site – a reconstructed replica of the ruined crematoria in Birkenau, though the failure to mention this in the official guidebooks means many visitors form the impression that they are at the site where mass gassing took place.

Secondly, although it is Auschwitz that official tours and guidebooks focus on, it was in Birkenau that the vast majority of the killing (mostly of Jews) occurred – a result, some would argue, of the postwar "museum" planners, focus on presenting and preserving sites connected with Polish martyrdom, and a phenomenon perpetuated to this day in the relatively small proportion of visitors who make it to Birkenau. Thirdly, and most shamefully, until relatively recently officially produced information about the camps downplayed, or to be more accurate, perhaps, omitted to make adequate mention of, the specifically Jewish-related aspects of the genocide enacted in the camp.

The immediate context for the glaring **omission of the Jewish perspective** in official communist-era Polish guidebooks and tours of the concentration camps was straightforwardly political. For Poland's postwar communist regime, like those in other East European countries, the horrors of World War II were a constant and central reference point. Following the official Soviet line, the emphasis was on the war as an anti-fascist struggle, in which good (communism and the Soviet Union, represented by the new postwar governments) had finally triumphed over evil (fascism and Nazi Germany).

This interpretation provided an important legitimizing prop for the new regimes. The Soviet Union, aided by loyal national communists, were the people who had liberated Europe from Hitler, and as inheritors of their anti-fascist mantle, the newly installed communist governments sought to portray themselves as heirs to all that was noble and good. In this schematic view of the war, there was no room for details of the racial aspects of Nazi ideology. People were massacred in the camps because fascists were butchers, not because the victims were Jews or Poles or Romanies. Hence the camps were opened up first and foremost as political monuments to the victims of fascism rather than to the Holocaust. The official decree establishing the museum in 1947 captures the ideological leavening succinctly: "On the site of the former Nazi concentration camp, a monument to the martyrdom of the Polish nation and of other nations is to be erected for all time to come."

Recognizing the sensitivities that continue to surround these issues, Poland's post-communist authorities have shown a greater willingness than their predecessors to acknowledge the specifically anti-Semitic dimensions of Nazi devastation. Along with "revised" figures for the numbers of deaths at Auschwitz and Birkenau, official guidebooks to the camp, for the first time, now state clearly that the vast majority of the victims were Jews, and many of the new signs erected give greater prominence to the specifically Jewish aspects of the genocide practised here.

In the broader sweep of **Polish–Jewish relations**, the biggest running sore of recent years in relation to Auschwitz-Birkenau has been the controversy over the **Carmelite Convent** established in 1984, flush against the walls of Auschwitz, in a building once used by the Nazis as a storehouse for Zyklon B gas crystals. In 1987, following sustained protests from the World Jewish Congress and other concerned organizations over what was viewed as a misconceived and offensive attempt to "baptize" and appropriate the Holocaust for religious ends, the Roman Catholic hierarchy caved in and consented to the removal of the convent. Following the nuns' failure to meet the agreed deadline, the dispute flared up in the summer of 1989. Jewish activists from the USA and Israel staged a series of protests at the site under an international media spotlight. Local residents reacted furiously (and on occasions, violently) to what were interpreted as hostile foreign intrusions into church life. Cardinal Glemp suggested in response that a world Jewish media conspiracy was being directed against the Church, a remark that provoked several noted Polish-Catholic intellectuals to censure him publicly. In turn, it could be argued that Jewish reactions showed little sympathy for or understanding of the widespread Polish perception of Auschwitz as a symbol of national suffering, at Auschwitz, in particular, and under the Nazis in general, and of the more than three million Gentile Poles killed during the Nazi occupation.

All in all, the dispute over the convent provoked much sadness and bitterness, needlessly retarding the slow and often painful process of promoting and reordering Polish–Jewish relations. The collective sigh of relief when the nuns finally moved to the new site designated for them in summer 1993 was audible, not least as their continuing failure to budge had for a while threatened to result in a Jewish boycott of official ceremonies marking the fiftieth anniversary of the 1943 Warsaw Ghetto Uprising. The convent is now located next to the new **Centre for Information, Dialogue and Prayer** at ul. Św. M. Kolbego 1 (☎381/31000). Established in 1992, on a site 1km southwest of the camp, the centre aims to provide a place of reflection and discussion on the meaning and legacy of the Holocaust, in particular a place of encounter between locals and Jewish visitors to the camps. Basic accommodation is available in five-bed dormitories.

The latest twist to the camp's history came during the ceremonies held to mark the **fiftieth anniversary of the liberation of Auschwitz-Birkenau** in January 1995. Once again, an event intended to demonstrate memory and unity threatened to be overshadowed by disputes. Angered by what they saw as a failure to accord Jewish sufferings in Auschwitz their proper place in the two-day commemorations, Jewish participants organized their own emotionally charged act of remembrance at the camp the day before the official ceremony. In his speech at the ceremony the next day, attended by a host of world political and religious leaders President Lech Wałęsa, stung by the perceived slight, deviated from his prepared text to acknowledge the unique and specific suffering of Jews – the first time he had ever done so in public. For all these bickerings, however, the main purpose of the commemorations, to honour the memory and sufferings of all the camp's inmates, Jew or Gentile, and reflect on the contemporary meaning and significance of the Holocaust was achieved. As such, it perhaps provides a model for future approaches to the often difficult and emotionally charged issue of Polish–Jewish relations.

Auschwitz

Most of the Auschwitz camp buildings, the barbed-wire fences, watchtowers, and the entrance gate inscribed "*Arbeit Macht Frei*" ("Work Makes Free") have been preserved as the **Museum of Martyrdom** (daily Jan, Feb & late Dec 8am–3pm; March & Nov–Dec 15 8am–4pm; April & Oct 8am–5pm; May–Sept 8am–6pm). What you won't find here any longer, though, are the memorial stone and succession of plaques placed in front of and around the camp by the postwar communist authorities claiming that four million people died in a place officially described as an "International Monument to Victims of Fascism". In a symbolic intellectual clean-up, the inflated numerical estimates were removed and the lack of references to the central place of **Jews** in the genocide carried out in Auschwitz-Birkenau were remedied in 1990 at the orders of the International Committee set up to oversee the running of the site.

The **cinema** is a sobering starting point. The film shown was taken by the Soviet troops who liberated the camp in May 1945 – its harrowing images of the survivors and the dead aimed at confirming for future generations what really happened. The board outside lists timings for showings in different languages, although you can pay for a special showing of the English-language version (12zł). The bulk of the **camp** consists of the prison cell blocks, the first section being given over to "exhibits" found in the camp after liberation. Despite last-minute destruction of many of the **storehouses** used for the possessions of murdered inmates (there were 35 of them in all), there are rooms full of clothes and suitcases, toothbrushes, dentures, glasses, a huge collection of shoes and a huge mound of women's hair – 70 tonnes of it. It's difficult to relate to the scale of what's shown.

Block 11, further on, is where the first experiments with Zyklon B gas were carried out on Soviet POWs and other inmates in 1941. Between two of the blocks stands the flower-strewn **Death Wall**, where thousands of prisoners were summarily executed with a bullet in the back of the head. As in the other concentration camps, the Auschwitz victims included people from all over Europe – over twenty nationalities in all. Many of the camp barracks are given over to **national memorials**, moving testimonies to the sufferings of inmates of the different countries – Poles, Russians, Czechs, Slovaks, Norwegians, Turks, French, Italians and more. This section is closed October to April, except for those on guided tours.

Another, larger barrack, no. 27 (open year round), is labelled simply "**Jews**". The atmosphere here is one of poignant, quiet reverence, in which the evils of Auschwitz are felt and remembered rather than detailed or observed. On the second floor, there's a section devoted to Jewish resistance both inside and outside the camp, some of which was organized in tandem with the Polish AK (Armia Krajowa) or Home Army, some entirely autonomously.

Despite the strength and power of this memorial, some still find it disconcerting to find it lumped in among the others, as if Jews were just another "nationality" among many to suffer at the hands of the Nazis. Despite other recent changes in the way events in Auschwitz are officially presented, this is one aspect of the old-style presentation of the Jewish dimension of the camp that you may feel has still not been fully addressed.

The prison blocks terminate by the **gas chambers** and the ovens where the bodies were incinerated. "No more poetry after Auschwitz", in the words of the German philosopher Theodor Adorno.

Birkenau

The **Birkenau camp** (same hours) is much less visited than Auschwitz, though it was here that the majority of captives lived and died. Covering some 170 hectares, the Birkenau camp, at its height, comprised over three hundred buildings, of which over sixty brick and wood constructions remain; the rest were either burnt down or demolished at the end of the war, though in most instances you can still see their traces on the ground. Walking through the site, rows of barracks – mostly built without foundations onto the notoriously swampy local terrain – stretch into the distance, barracks in which tens of thousands (over 100,000 at the camp's peak in August 1944) lived in unimaginably appalling conditions. Not that most prisoners lived long. Killing was the main goal of Birkenau, most of it carried out in the huge **gas chambers** at the back of the camp, damaged but not destroyed by the fleeing Nazis in 1945. At the height of the killing, this clinically conceived machinery of destruction gassed and cremated sixty thousand people a day.

Most of the victims arrived in closed **trains**, mostly cattle trucks, to be driven directly from the rail ramp into the gas chambers. Rail line, ramp and sidings are all still there, just as the Nazis left them. In the dark, creaking huts the pitiful bare bunks would have had six or more shivering bodies crammed into each level. Wander round the barracks and you soon begin to imagine the absolute terror and degradation of the place. A monument to the dead, inscribed in ten languages, stares out over the camp from between the chambers.

Kalwaria Zebrzydowska and Wadowice

Southwest of Kraków are two places of great religious significance to Poles: **Kalwaria Zebrzydowska**, a centre of pilgrimage second only to Częstochowa, and **Wadowice**, birthplace of Karol Wojtyła, now Pope John Paul II. From Kraków, buses run daily to both destinations; local trains are slower.

Kalwaria Zebrzydowska

The object of pilgrims' devotions is perched on the hill overlooking the town of **KALWARIA ZEBRZYDOWSKA**: a large complex containing a Bernardine monastery, Church of the Virgin and a Via Dolorosa built by the Zebrzydowski family in the early seventeenth century, following a vision of three crosses here on the family estate. Miracles followed and the country's first and best-known Calvary grew to become one of its most popular sites of pilgrimage.

Before construction began, the Zebrzydowskis sent an envoy to Jerusalem for drawings and models of the holy places. Thus many of the **chapels** built across the nearby hills are modelled on buildings in the holy city. In addition to the main Via Dolorosa, a sequence of Marian Stations was added in the 1630s, including a "House of Mary", the **Church of the Tomb of Mary**, housing a tomb of the Virgin built in the form of a large domed sarcophagus, and a string of other chapels and buildings. The main **church** is a familiar Baroque effusion, with a silver-plated Italian figure of the Virgin standing over the high altar. The object that inspires the greatest devotion, however, is the **painting of the Virgin and Child** in the Zebrzydowski chapel, said to have been shedding tears at regular intervals since the 1640s. The pope is a firm devotee of the place, making regular pilgrimages here ever since his early days in Kraków.

The site always has its crowds, but they are at their most intense during **August**, the traditional time of pilgrimage throughout the country, particularly during the **Festival of the Assumption** (August 15) and at **Easter**, when the Passion Plays are performed here on Maundy Thursday and Good Friday, with the vast accompanying crowds processing solemnly around the sequence of chapels in which the events of Holy Week are fervently re-enacted. The heady atmosphere of collective catharsis accompanying these events offers an insight into the inner workings of Polish Catholicism. To anyone from more sober northern climes, the realism (figures are tied on crosses, while spectators are dressed as Romans) can all be very perplexing, even frightening; however, gruesome enactments of the Crucifixion are an established feature of peasant Catholic festivals throughout Europe.

Despite the place's popularity, **accommodation** is surprisingly thin on the ground, the only options being the *Stadion*, ul. Mickiewicka 16 (☎0387/6492; ④), in the town centre, and the more basic *Indra*, ul. Zebrzydowice 10 (☎0387/254; ③), on the main Kraków road.

Wadowice

Fourteen kilometres further west is the little town of **WADOWICE**, whose rural obscurity was shattered by the election of local boy **Karol Wojtyła** to the papacy in October 1978. Almost instantly the town became a place of pilgrimage, with the souvenir industry quick to seize the opportunities.

The **pope's birthplace** at ul. Kościelna 7, off the market square, has been turned into a shrine-like **Museum** (Tues–Sun 9am–noon & 2–5pm), while the nearby **Parish Church** displays the record of its most famous baptism, in 1920. For the truly devout, the local **football pitch**, where young Karol kept goal with some success, could be an additional point of pilgrimage.

For a **place to stay**, your best bets are the *Beskid* hotel, ul. Lwowska 14 (☎0387/34127; ③) or the *Podhalanik*, ul. Wojske Polskiego 29 (☎0387/33818; ②).

Babia Góra National Park and beyond

The southwesternmost part of Małopolska forms part of the Beskid mountain chain, with by far the most notable part being the **Babia Góra** massif. It's the second smallest of Poland's national parks, though arguably the one most prized by naturalists, being of sufficient importance to be included on UNESCO's World Biosphere list. Much loved by Poles, who visit the area in droves, it's still relatively undiscovered by foreigners. A specific characteristic of the region is the way that the vegetation forms distinct vertical bands. Up to a height of 1150m, it's thickly wooded, particularly with beech, fir and spruce trees which then give way to spruce and rowans. There follows a sector of dwarf mountain pines, while the highest areas have only grasses, mosses and lichen among the loose boulders. Hundreds of different plant species grow in the massif, which is also inhabited by 115 different kinds of bird and a number of wild animals, including lynxes, wolves and brown bears.

West of the park area, on the border with Silesia, **Żywiec**, famous for its beer, is a pleasant place to while away a few hours, benefiting from a favourable location in a broad valley at the foot of three mountain chains, the Beskid Mały to the northeast, the Beskid Śląski to the north and west, and the Beskid Żywiecki to the south.

Zawoja and around

The gateway to the National Park is **ZAWOJA**, a straggling community situated on the banks of the River Skamica, around 65km from Kraków. Its residents claim that it stretches 12km from end to end, making it the longest village in Poland, and perhaps even in Europe. There's no rail line, but direct buses run from Kraków, Katowice and Bielsko–Biała, as well as from Wadowice, 70km to the north.

As a tourist resort, Zawoja has still to develop its potential – apart from private rooms, the accommodation options in and around the village include a pair of **hotels**, the *Sokolica* at Zawoja-Widly (☎031226/151; ③), and the more basic *PTTK*-run *Hanka*, Zawoja–Składy 2 (☎031226/148; ②). There are also a couple of **youth hostels** some way south of the "centre", at Zawoja–Wilczne (☎031226/106) and Zawoja-Smyraki (☎031226/752), on the red and white marked trails up to Babia Góra. Zawoja has several **restaurants and snack bars**, all of which are stuck in a pre-market era time-warp.

Walking in the National Park

If you're driving, the easiest approach to Babia Góra is to go all the way to the end of Zawoja village, then continue up the twisty road beyond, until you reach the car park at the easternmost end of the National Park. On foot, it can be reached by the **blue trail**, leading gently upwards from the village through the woods to the *Markowe Szczawiny* **refuge** (☎105), which serves hot meals and has dormitory accommodation. If time is limited, it's best to switch here to the **yellow trail**, which takes you directly up to **Diablak** (1725m), the highest peak in the range, enabling you to see a good cross-section of scenery en route – beware that there's one place on this route where you have to make a fixed ladder ascent. From the top, which forms part of the international boundary with Slovakia, there's a sweeping panoramic view which stretches on (the regrettably few) clear days as far as the Tatras. It's then a comfortable descent back to the car park by the **red trail**; this offers the best views of the main peak, and should be used in both directions if you're at all wary of sheer drops. If you have more time at your disposal, you can see the whole massif in one long day by continuing west from the summit of Diablak along the green trail, switching to the red to go back to the refuge, then returning to Zawoja by the black trail.

Zubrzyca Górna

It's also worth making a detour to the village of **ZUBRZYCA GÓRNA**, about 4km south of the car park, and also accessible along the green trail. At the northernmost fringe of the village is the **Ethnographical Park** (April 15 to Sept 15 Tues–Sun 9am–3.30pm; Sept 16 to April 14 Tues–Sun 9am–2.30pm), an impressive open-air museum of the region's traditional local architecture.

Żywiec

About 50km west of Zawoja by road – though less than half that as the crow flies – is ŻYWIEC, which is also readily accessible by train from any of the major cities in this corner of Poland. The town enjoys a certain international fame courtesy of its **brewery**, which annually produces thirty million litres of what's generally agreed to be the best **beer** in Poland. There are two main varieties, *Tatra Pils* and *Full Light*, the latter of which confusingly appears under a bewildering variety of colourful labels. Until the end of the communist era, you were far more likely to find Żywiec beer on the shelves of a British or American supermarket than you were anywhere in Poland, most of it being exported in order to obtain desperately needed hard currency. It's now widely available throughout the country. Beer aside, Żywiec is an attractive place to break your journey – you'll get a good **view** of the surrounding mountains from the shore of the often dried-up reservoir at the northern end of town.

The Town

Both the **train** and **bus stations** are located on the opposite side of the River Soła from the town centre, which is a ten-minute walk away along ul. Marchewskiego. Żywiec's **Castle** (Tues, Wed, Fri & Sat 10am–2.30pm, Sun noon–3.30pm) was founded by the Dukes of Oświęcim in the fifteenth century, gaining a handsome arcaded courtyard in the Renaissance period. In the nineteenth century, it was heavily restored by the Habsburgs, who also built the pristine white **palace** opposite, currently the object of a restoration programme. The huge park to the south is well worth a stroll and includes a whimsical eighteenth-century **Chinese tea house**.

Just to the east of the palace is the parish church of **St Mary**, which would be an unremarkable Gothic building with standard Baroque furnishings were it not for the imperious galleried Renaissance tower, which provides a landmark from all over town. On the main street, ul. Kościuszki, immediately north of the church, is the local **museum** (Tues–Sat 10am–2.30pm, Sun noon–3.30pm), housed in a Baroque mansion, while a little further on is one of the towers from the fortification system. The only other sight worth mentioning is the rustic wooden church of the **Holy Cross** on ul. Świętokryska, just off the western end of ul. Kościuszki

Practicalities

Hotel options in town include the *Polonia*, centrally located at ul. Kościuszki 42 (☎030/61 54 51; ④), and the *Luks*, ul. Leśnianka 24 (☎030/61 56 53; ③), a few minutes' walk from the train station. The **youth hostel** is right next to the station at ul. Ks. Słonki 4 (☎030/61 26 39), while the **campsite** *Dębina* is well to the south of town, at ul. Kopernika 4 (☎030/4888), near the Sporysz train station.

There are several decent **restaurants** along the main drag, ul. Kościuszki, and another good one, *Ratuszowa*, at ul. Mickiewicza 1, on the corner of the market square. Every August, there's a **festival** of local folklore when you'll see colourful traditional costumes being worn, the women's outfits especially rich in lace and embroidery. **Christmas** celebrations in Żywiec are among the most characterful in Poland.

The Ojców Valley and the Eagles' Nests

To the northwest of Kraków, the **Ojców Valley** offers an easy respite from the rigours of the city. This deep limestone gorge of the River Prądnik has a unique microclimate and an astonishingly rich variety of plants and wildlife, virtually all of it now protected by the **Ojców National Park**. It's a beautiful area for a day's trekking, particularly in September and October, when the rich colours of the Polish autumn are at their finest.

The valley also gives access to the most southerly of the **castles** built by King Kazimierz to defend the southwestern reaches, and most importantly, the trade routes, of the country from the Bohemian rulers of Silesia. Known as the **Eagles' Nest Trail**, these fortresses are strung along the hilly ridge extending westwards from Ojców towards Częstochowa.

Ojców and into the valley

Access to the gorge is via **OJCÓW**, the National Park's only village, 25km from Kraków; take any bus bound for Olkusz. Unremarkable in itself, its wooden houses straggling along the slope above the valley of the River Prądnik, the village is capped by a fine, ruined **Castle**, the southern extremity of the Eagles' Nest Trail and an evocative place in the twilight hours, circled by squadrons of bats. There's not much of the castle left, apart from two of the original fourteenth-century towers, the main gate entrance and the walls of the castle chapel. The main reason for scrambling up here is for the excellent views over the winding valley. Just below the castle ruins, a long building houses a small **Museum** devoted to the valley's flora and fauna (April 15 to Oct 31 Tues–Sun 9am–4pm). Immediately beyond is another minor museum (same hours) covering the history of the area. If you want to stay, it's usually fairly easy to rent a room in someone's house in the village by asking around, though things get pretty full up in the summer season. The only other option is the basic *Zosia* (②) in Złota Góra, a kilometre west of the castle.

From the village, you can walk down to the valley along marked trails from the bus stop. A notable feature of the gorge is its strange assortment of **caves** and other geological formations, in several of which traces of prehistoric human habitation have been discovered. The best known is **Łokietka Cave** (daily 9am–4pm; Mar–Oct guided visits only), thirty minutes' walk south along the black trail, the largest of a sequence of chambers burrowing into the cliffs outside Ojców. According to legend it was here that King Władysław the Short was hidden and protected by loyal local peasants following King Wenceslas of Bohemia's invasion in the early fourteenth century. Around 250m long, the rather featureless illuminated cave is a bit of a letdown if you've come expecting spectacular stone and ice formations.

A few hundred metres north up the valley from Ojców Castle is the curious spectacle of a **wooden chapel** straddling the river on brick piles. This odd site neatly circumvented a nineteenth-century tsarist edict forbidding religious structures to be built "on solid ground", part of a strategy to subdue the intransigently nationalist Catholic Church. These days, it's only open for visits between Masses on Sunday.

Pieskowa Skała

If the weather's fine and you're up for walking the nine-kilometre road and footpath from Ojców, **PIESKOWA SKAŁA**, home of the region's best-known and best-preserved **Castle**, is an enjoyable and trouble-free piece of hiking. Direct buses also run from Kraków (45min)via Ojców. Arrival is signalled by an eighteen-metre-high limestone pillar known locally as Hercules' Club (Maczuga Herkulesa) rearing up in front of you, beyond which you can see the castle. The castle, long the possession of the Szafraniec family is in pretty good shape following extensive recent renovation, the fourteenth-century original having been rebuilt in the 1580s as an elegant Renaissance residence. As in Wawel Castle, the most impressive period feature is the delicately arcaded castle courtyard, a photogenic construction that's a regular feature in travel brochures. The castle **Museum** (Tues–Sun 10am–4pm) is divided into two main exhibitions, one covering the history of the building, the other illustrating the development of European art from the Middle Ages to the nineteenth century, drawing extensively on the Wawel National Museum's collection. The roomful of Gothic pieces includes some fine carved wooden statues of the saints by unknown local artists, a fifteenth-century tapestry from Tournai and some sturdy chests from the mid-1400s. The second-floor Baroque rooms continue the period furniture theme, sumptuously decorated Flemish and Dutch tapestries lining the walls, the most notable among them depicting a series of heroic scenes from the life of Alexander the Great. To finish off a visit, head for the excellent **restaurant** at the top of one of the fortified towers. In summer they put tables out on the roof terrace, from where you can enjoy a fine view over the valley, and, if you're lucky, some excellent local trout.

The end of the trail

The remaining castles of the Eagles' Nest Trail are very ruined, but dramatic, seeming to spring straight out of the Jurassic rock formations. You really need your own vehicle to follow the whole route as, although all the castles are accessible by bus, you'll experience long waits and frequent detours, and it's unlikely you'd be able to find anywhere to stay. However, the most impressive of the other castles are also the easiest to get to. At **OGRODZIENIEC**, some 35km north of Pieskowa Skała on the main road to Olkusz (served by bus from Kraków), the ruin you see today was built during Kazimierz the Great's reign and remodelled into a magnificent Renaissance residence reputedly the equal of Wawel, before being ravaged by the Swedes in 1655. **ZAWIERCIE** preserves only the substantial shell of a frontier fortress

Even more accessible is **OLSZTYN**, just a few kilometres outside the city boundaries of Częstochowa, to which it's linked by several buses an hour. The **Castle** here is the one generally used to promote the route on tourist brochures and posters. Unusually, it's laid out in two parts, with a round watchtower crowning one outcrop of rock, and a keep on top of another; from each there's a superb view over the whole upland region.

Note that if you're travelling between Ogrodzieniec and Olsztyn by car or bike, there are other castles to see at Mirów, Bobolice and Ostrężnik.

Częstochowa

To get an understanding of the central role that Catholicism still holds in contemporary Poland, a visit to **CZĘSTOCHOWA** is essential and, for many people, quite extraordinary. The hilltop **Monastery of Jasna Góra** (Bright Mountain) is one of the world's greatest places of pilgrimage, and its famous icon, **the Black**

Madonna, has drawn the faithful here over the past six centuries – reproductions exist in almost every Polish church.

The special position that Jasna Góra and its icon hold in the hearts and minds of the majority of Poles is due to a rich web of history and myth. It's not a place you can react to dispassionately, indeed it's hard not to be moved as you overhear troupes of pilgrims breaking into hymn as they shuffle between the Stations of the Cross, or watch peasants praying mutely before the icon they've waited a lifetime to see. One thing that will strike you here, as the crowds swell towards an approaching festival, is the number of excited teenagers in attendance, all treating the event with the expectation you'd find at an international rock concert.

Central to this nationwide veneration is the tenuous position Poland has held on the map of Europe; at various times the Swedes, the Russians and the Germans have sought to annihilate it as a nation. Each of these traditional and non-Catholic enemies has laid siege to Jasna Góra, yet failed to destroy it, so adding to the icon's reputation as a miracle-worker and the guarantor of Poland's very existence.

Transport is easy with direct **trains** from Wrocław and Warsaw via Łódź, and from Kraków via Katowice. **Buses** also run daily from Katowice, Kraków, Łódź and Warsaw.

A brief history

The hill known as Jasna Góra was probably used as part of the same defensive system as the castles along the Eagles' Nest Trail. In the fourteenth century, it came under the control of **Ladislaus II**, whose main possession was the independent duchy of Opole on the other side of the Silesian frontier. In 1382, he founded

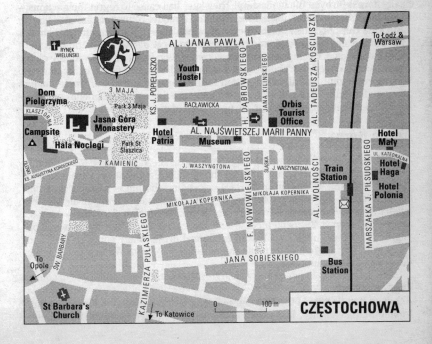

the monastery here, donating the miraculous icon a couple of years later. Ladislaus spent his final years imprisoned in his own castle, having fallen into disgrace for trying to prevent the union with Lithuania. Nevertheless, the monastery quickly attracted pilgrims from a host of nations and was granted the special protection of the Jagiellonian and Waza dynasties, though it was not until the fifteenth century that a shrine of stone and brick was built.

In the first half of the seventeenth century, the monastery was enclosed by a modern **fortification system** as a bulwark of Poland's frontiers – and its Catholic faith – at a time of Europe-wide political and religious conflicts. Its worth was proved in the six-week-long **siege of 1655** by the Swedes, who failed to capture it in spite of having superior weapons and almost 4000 troops ranged against just 250 defenders. This sparked off an amazing national fightback against the enemy, who had occupied the rest of the country against little resistance, and ushered in Poland's short period as a European power of the first rank.

In 1717 the Black Madonna was crowned **Queen of Poland** in an attempt by the clergy to whip up patriotism and fill the political void created by the Russian-sponsored "Silent Sejm", which had reduced the nation to a puppet state. Jasna Góra was the scene of another heroic defence in 1770, when it was held by the Confederates of Bar against greater Russian forces, and retained by them until after the formal partitioning of Poland two years later. Częstochowa was initially annexed by Prussia, but after a few years as part of Napoleon's Duchy of Warsaw, it served as a frontier fortress of the Russian Empire for more than a century. It was incorporated into the new Polish state after World War I, when the icon's royal title was reaffirmed.

In 1945, Soviet troops defused bombs left by the retreating Nazis which might finally have destroyed the monastery. They later had cause to regret their actions, as although Częstochowa itself developed into a model communist industrialized city, Jasna Góra became a major **focus of opposition** to the communist regime. The Church skilfully promoted the pilgrimage as a display of patriotism and passive resistance, a campaign which received a huge boost in 1978 with the election of **Karol Wojtyła**, Archbishop of Kraków and a central figure in its conception, as Pope John Paul II. His devotion to this shrine ensured worldwide media attention for Poland's plight; as a consequence, praying at Jasna Góra has become an essential photo-opportunity for the new breed of democratic politicians.

Jasna Góra

A dead straight three-kilometre-long boulevard, al. Najświętszej Marii Panny (abbreviated as al. NMP), cuts through the heart of Częstochowa, terminating at the foot of **Jasna Góra**. On most days, ascending the hill is no different from taking a walk in any other public park, but the huge podium for open-air Masses gives a clue to the atmosphere here on the major **Marian festivals** – May 3, August 15, August 26, September 8 and December 8 – when up to a million pilgrims converge, often in colourful traditional dress. Many come on foot, and every year, tens of thousands make the nine-day walk from Warsaw to celebrate the Feast of the Assumption.

The Monastery

Although there's little of the souvenir-peddling tackiness found in Europe's other leading Marian shrines, Jasna Góra could hardly be called beautiful: its architecture is generally austere, while the defensive walls give the hill something of a fortress-like feel. Entry is still via four successive **gateways**, each one of which presented a formidable obstacle to any attacker. As you wander around the complex you'll notice two key components of the pilgrimage experience, redemption and commerce. At every turn you'll find **confessionals** at which the faithful eagerly queue, while numerous **offering boxes** outside key doorways and dedicated to one saint or another, comfortably finance the upkeep of the spectacle.

The best way to begin an exploration is by ascending the 100-metre-high **tower** (Mon–Sat 8am–4pm, Sun 8am–10.30am & 1–5pm), a pastiche of its eighteenth-century predecessor, which was destroyed in one of the many fires which have plagued the monastery. An earlier victim was the monastic **church**, which has been transformed from a Gothic hall into a restrained Baroque basilica, now without pews, to make room for more pilgrims. Not that it's without its exuberant features, notably the colossal high altar in honour of the Virgin and the two sumptuous family chapels off the southern aisle, which parody and update their royal counterparts in the Wawel Cathedral in Kraków.

Understandably, the **Chapel of the Blessed Virgin**, a separate church in its own right, is the focal point of the monastery. It's also the only part to retain much of the original Gothic architecture, though its walls are so encrusted with votive offerings and discarded crutches and leg-braces that this is no longer obvious. Masses are said here almost constantly but you'll have to time it right if you want a view of the **Black Madonna** (see box p.433), a sight that should not be missed. Part of the time the icon is shrouded by a screen, each raising and lowering of which presumably exists to add a certain dramatic tension and is accompanied by a solemn fanfare. When it's on view (6am–noon, 3.30–4.40pm, 6.30–7.30pm & 8.30–9.15pm) you only get to see the faces and hands of the actual painting (the Virgin's countenance being famously dour) as the figures of the Madonna and Child are always "dressed" in varying sets of jewel-encrusted robes which glitter all the more impressively against the black walls. Whatever your views on the validity of pilgrimages, veneration of a miraculous wonder or Church-engineered money-making device, you cannot fail to be impressed by the sheer devotion which the icon inspires in the hearts and minds of most Poles.

Other sites in the complex fail to hold the resonance of the chapel, although between them they help to flesh out the site's history. To the north of the chapel, a monumental stairway leads to the **Knights' Hall**, the principal reception room, adorned with flags and paintings illustrating the history of the monastery. There are other opulent Baroque interiors, notably the **refectory**, whose vault is a real tour-de-force, and the **library**. However, you'll have to enquire at the information office by the main gateway for permission to see them, as they are normally closed to the public.

The museums

Jasna Góra's treasures are kept in three separate buildings. The most valuable liturgical items can be seen in the **Treasury** above the sacristy, entered from the southeastern corner of the ramparts (Mon–Fri 9–11.30am & 3.30–4.30pm, Sat & Sun 8am–12.30pm & 3.30–5pm). There's usually a long queue for entry, so be there well before it opens.

At the southwestern end of the monastery is the **Arsenal** (Mon–Fri 9am–noon & 3–5pm, Sat & Sun 9am–noon & 2–5pm), devoted to the military history of the fortress and containing a superb array of weapons, including Turkish war loot donated by King Jan Sobieski. Alongside is the **Museum** (daily 11am–4.30pm), which tells the monastery's story from a religious standpoint. Exhibits include the seventeenth-century backing of the Black Madonna, which illustrates the history of the picture, and votive offerings from famous Poles, prominent among which is Lech Wałęsa's 1983 Nobel Peace Prize.

Elsewhere in town

Other than Jasna Góra, Częstochowa has very few sights, although the broad tree-lined boulevards at least give the heart of the city an agreeably spacious, almost Parisian feel. On pl. Biegańskiego, just off al. NMP, is the district **museum** (Tues–Sun 11am–6pm), which has a decent archeology section plus the usual local history displays. If you want to continue with the ecclesiastical theme, visit the small Baroque church of **St Barbara** to the south of Jasna Góra, allegedly the place where the Black Madonna was slashed (see box).

Near the suburban station of Raków, reached by any southbound tram, is an important **Archeology Reserve** (Tues–Sat 9am–3pm, but subject to random closures), with 21 excavated graves from the Lusatian culture of the sixth and seventh centuries BC.

Practicalities

The well-stocked **tourist information centre** is at al. NMP 65 (Mon–Sat 9am–6pm, Sun 10am–4pm; ☎034/24 13 60 or 24 34 12), with **Orbis** at al. NMP 40/42 (☎24 20 56 or 24 79 87). The regular influx of pilgrims to Częstochowa means that you might have problems finding somewhere to stay. It's worth booking in advance, or even visiting on a day trip from Kraków or Opole.

The most convenient **hotels**, all within twenty minutes' walk of the monastery, are those beside the train station: the basic *Miły* and *Igmar* at ul. Katedralna 18 (☎034/24 33 91 or 24 66 60; ②) and the similar *Ha Ga* down the road at number 9 (☎034/24 61 73; ②); or *Polonia* at ul. Piłsudskiego 9 (☎034/24 40 67; ④). At the foot of Jasna Góra you'll find the luxurious *Orbis* hotel, *Patria*, ul. J. Popieluszki 2 (☎034/24 70 01; ⑨). There are also four **motels** on the eastern outskirts of town – *PZMot*, al. Wojska Polskiego 181 (☎034/63 26 28; ③); *Korona*, ul. Makuszyńskiego 58 (☎034/25 22 38; ④); *Hotel Vegas* ul. Rocha 224 (☎034/25 32 30; ④); *Orbis*, al. Wojska Polskiego 281/285 (☎034/25 72 00; ⑤).

As you'd expect, there's a fair choice of **hostel** accommodation, including two outfits geared specifically to pilgrims – the huge and well-organized *Dom Pielgrzyma* at ul. Wyszyńskiego 1 (☎034/24 33 02; ②), found north of the car park on the west side of the monastery, and the much less convenient *Dom Wycieczkowye* "Budex" at ul. Poselska 12/32 (☎034/63 32 43; ②), 4km south of the centre. There's also an inexpensive *Hala Noclegi* right beneath the monastery's southwest corner, offering basic rooms with basins. Of the two seasonal **youth hostels**, much the more convenient is on Jasnogórska 84/90 (☎034/24 31 21); the other is southwest of town at ul. Powstańców Warszawy 144 (☎034/79 229), reached on bus route #23. There's a **campsite**, *Camping Oleńka*, with a few chalets and rooms in an ideal spot on the west side of the monastery's car park at ul. Oleńki 10/30 (☎034/24 74 95). If you're driving, it's well signposted on the town approaches, until you get to the crucial last turning, between apartment buildings, into ul. Oleńki. Check the map on p.429.

THE BLACK MADONNA

According to tradition, the **Black Madonna** was painted from life by **Saint Luke** on a beam from the Holy Family's house in Nazareth. This explanation is accepted without question by most believers, though the official view is kept deliberately ambiguous. Scientific tests have proved the icon cannot have been executed before the sixth century, and it may even have been quite new at the time of its arrival at the monastery. Probably Italian in origin, it's a fine example of the hierarchical **Byzantine** style, which hardly changed or developed down the centuries. Incidentally, the "black" refers to the heavy shading characteristic of this style, subsequently darkened by age and exposure to incense.

What can be seen today may well be only a copy made following the picture's first great "miracle" in 1430, on the occasion of its theft. According to the official line, this was the work of followers of the Czech reformer Jan Hus, but it's more likely that political opponents of the monastery's protector, King Władysław Jagiełło, were responsible. The **legend** maintains that the picture increased in weight so much that the thieves were unable to carry it. In frustration, they slashed the Virgin's face, which immediately started shedding blood. The icon was taken to Kraków to be restored, but in memory of the miracle, two wounds (still visible today) were scratched into the left cheek of the Madonna.

Sceptics have pointed out that during the Swedish siege, usually cited as the supreme example of the Black Madonna's miracle-working powers, the icon had been moved to neutral Silesia for safekeeping. Yet, such was its hold over the Polish imagination, that its future seemed to occasion more anguished discussion at the time of the Partitions than any other topic. In the present day, the **pope's devotion to the image** has helped to focus the world's attention on Poland, while at the same time approving the country's archaic and nationalistic Catholicism.

For **eating** and **drinking**, there's a large choice of places along al. NMP and near the station, best of which include the restaurant at the *Polonia*, *La Bussola*, 10 al. NMP, *The Alamo* a couple of doors up at no. 14 and *Vecchio Milan* at no. 59. There's a ghastly neon-lit burger joint a few doors up from the *Vecchio* which at least is open late, as are the numerous snack bars and kiosks around the station.

North from Kraków

Travelling north from Kraków on the road to Kielce and Warsaw, you soon find yourself in the heartlands of Małopolska, dominated by sleepy rural towns and a colourful patchwork quilt of traditional strip-farmed fields. The towns of **Jędrzejów**, **Pińczów** and **Szydłów** all offer a characteristic rural Polish combination of historic curiosity and comparative contemporary anonymity. If you've no need to hurry your journey north, they make an enjoyable diversion, with transport connections, chiefly by bus, relatively problem-free.

Jędrzejów

Forty kilometres north of Kraków, **JĘDRZEJÓW** is, in most respects, another sleepy provincial outpost of Małopolska, a two-bit town used as a convenient stopping-off point on the main Kraków–Kielce road which bisects it.

The reason most visitors, mainly Polish, come here is for the **Sundial Museum** (Muzeum Żegarów Słonecznych; Tues–Sun 9am–4pm: compulsory guided tours on the hour every hour), an eccentric setup housing one of the top three gnomical collections in the world (the other two are in Chicago and Oxford), based on the notable collection of three hundred or so sundials amassed by local enthusiast Dr. Tadeusz Przypkowski and left to the museum established in his house after his death in 1962.

What sounds like a potentially less than thrilling proposal turns out to be well worth a visit. Dials of every shape, size and construction are gathered here, the oldest dating back to the early 1500s. Highlights of the collection include a group of attractive sixteenth- and seventeenth-century ivory pocket sundials, a set of Asian instruments and an eccentric piece from the mid-1700s that comes complete with a small cannon tuned to fire on the hour at one o'clock every afternoon. The rest of the museum is taken up with Przypkowski's more rambling collections of stuffy old furniture, books, art, clocks, watches and old bottles.

The other object of note in town is the impressive **Cistercian Abbey** (Opactwo Cystersów) some way west of the centre along ul. 11 Listopada. One of the group of Cistercian foundations established in the region in the early 1200s, the imposing twin-towered Romanesque basilica was remodelled a number of times over the centuries, the final product being the largely late-Baroque interior of today, featuring some ornate wall and altar paintings and lavishly carved choir stalls. Virtually the only feature reminding you of the church's architectural origins is the distinctive cross-ribbed vaulting developed by the Cistercians. Very little of the original monastic buildings survives, the main exception being sections of the cloisters, which the resident parish priest will show you on request.

Praticalities

Jędrzejów's location on the main Kraków–Kielce road means that getting in and out of the place is relatively easy: buses and trains run to both destinations at fairly frequent intervals. The **bus and train stations** are next to each other roughly 2km west of the main square along ul. Przypkowskiego. For **information** there's a *PTTK* office at ul. 11 Listopada 13.

In the unlikely event of you wanting to stay here, the **accommodation** options are the *Hotel PUSB* (☎0498/61825; ③) on al. J. Piłsudskiego, west of the main square and the *Dom PTTK*, ul. 3 Maja 134 (☎0498/61565; ②). Additionally, there's a youth hostel at ul. Przypkowskiego 12 (July & Aug only). The only **restaurant** worth venturing into is the *Zodiak*, at ul. Partyzantów 3, just south of the square.

Pinczów

Southeast of Jędrzejów, 28km along the quiet back roads of Małopolska, the contemporary rural anonymity of **PINCZÓW** belies the town's notable historical role. The old limestone quarries in evidence around the town were long an important source of stone for church building throughout the country. Along with nearby Raków (see p.436), Pinczów rose to prominence during the latter half of the sixteenth century as one of the chief centres of Protestant agitation in Reformation-era Poland, a group of Calvinist divines establishing an academy and a printing press responsible, among other things, for publication of the first Polish grammar in 1568. The town and surrounding region's resistance-minded

streak surfaced again during the latter stages of World War II, when local partisan units were so successful at clearing Nazi troops out of the area that the town
gained the nickname "The Republic of Pinczów", though not surprisingly they
were unable to prevent the wholesale removal of the substantial Jewish population that had lived here for centuries.

Most of the town's collection of historic monuments are ranged on or around
the Rynek, the usual small town square with all main roads leading onto it. On
the west side of the Rynek stands the **Parish Church**, started in the 1430s but
only completed two centuries later. While elements of the original Gothic design
survive in the exterior of the church, the interior is the standard ornate Baroque
including an array of sumptuous side altars, carved choir stalls and an overpower-
ing high altar. The adjoining building, the former Pauline monastery, houses the
local **Museum** (Tues–Fri 10am–5pm, Sat & Sun 10am–3pm), a ramshackle
collection of historical exhibits and local archeological finds enlivened by a small
but interesting set of exhibits relating to the history of the town's Jewish
population.

A few minutes' walk from the square down ul. Klasztorna, is the former
Synagogue, a large cube-shaped brick structure built in the late 1600s and set
back from the street. Despite being looted and damaged by the Nazis during
World War II, the empty remaining shell of the building is nevertheless in better
condition than many others, mainly thanks to the restoration work that seems to
have been carried out intermittently. If the funds ever materialize, there are plans
to turn the place into a museum. A plaque on one of the outside walls commemorates the town's Jewish community – still a rarer occurrence than it ought to be in
Poland. The wall separating the synagogue from the street contains pieced-
together fragments of tombstones from the local Jewish cemetery.

If you don't mind an uphill scramble, the **Chapel of St Anne**, clearly visible on
a hillside overlooking the Rynek, is a fine Renaissance structure, probably
designed by Santa Gucci, and one of the few examples of a free-standing chapel in
the country. The chapel isn't often open, however, which means you may have to
content yourself with admiring the twin-domed structure from the outside, along
with the views over the surrounding countryside.

Practicalities

The bus station is five minutes' walk south of the Rynek on ul. Partyzantów, with
frequent servies to Kielce and less frequently to Jędrzejów. The only places **to
stay** in town are the *Hotel MOSIR*, ul. Pałęcki 26 (☎041/72044; ③) ten minutes'
walk south of the Rynek, and the camping site close by on the edge of the lake
(☎041/2920). For a bite **to eat**, the options are even more limited – a couple of
basic restaurants on the Rynek, including the smoky *Uśmiech,* will serve you up a
regular *kotlet schabowy.*

Szydłów

First impressions of **SZYDŁÓW**, 50km east of Jędrzejów, are less than promising. Perched atop a hill amid undulating Małopolska farmlands, this half-deserted
rural backwater is certainly not the place to head for in search of action. What
makes a visit here worthwhile, however, are the remnants of the fortified Gothic
architectural complex built by King Kazimierz the Great in the mid-fourteenth
century.

THE POLISH BRETHREN (ARIANS)

Among the sects that emerged in Reformation-era Poland to challenge Catholic dominance of religious sympathies the **Polish Brethren** occupy a notable place. Also known by a cluster of other names – Arians, Racovians and Socinians being the commonest variants – this loose cluster of like-minded radically dissenting thinkers crystallized into a distinctive group following the establishment of an **academy** in 1570 at **Raków**, a minor provincial centre 12km north of Szydłow, under the protection of Michał Sienicki, an aristocratic patron and early disciple.

Theologically speaking, what marked the Brethren out from the Calvinists and other Protestant schools developing in Poland at the time was their decisive rejection of the traditional Orthodox doctrines of the Trinity and the divinity of Christ. A leading figure in the development of the Brethren's doctrines was **Fausto Sozzini** (Socinius) who settled in Raków in 1579. Socinius was particularly successful in the spreading of Arian doctrines among the Polish aristocracy. These doctrines were collected in the **Racovian Catechism**, published in Polish in 1605, and subsequently translated into Latin, German and eventually English (1652). Such was the notoriety (and popularity) of the catechism by this stage, that Oliver Cromwell ordered local sheriffs to confiscate the entire print run of the first English edition and burn it as soon as arrived from the continent.

In practical terms, the Brethren espoused a religiously-based **communism** of the kind advocated by the Diggers and other radical sects a century later in Cromwellian-era England. The structure of the settlement at Raków was determined by a thorough-going pacifism, shared manual labour, the complete abolition of social hierarchy and the denial of the authority of the state. From simple beginnings, the Raków Academy grew into a centre of international repute, with over 1000 students by the beginning of the seventeenth century, and its printing presses churning out a steady stream of tracts and catechisms. The model of the academy proved attractive to many and was duplicated elsewhere in the territories of the Polish-Lithuaniuan Commonwealth, most notably at **Nowogródek** in Lithuania.

For all the religious tolerance exhibited in Poland during the Reformation era – "the land without bonfires" as it was popularly known – the Arians were regarded as having gone a theological and political step too far by many. As the one sect explicitly excluded from the provisions of the **Confederation of Warsaw** (1573) regarding religious tolerance in the Commonwealth, they remained constantly open to the threat of persecution, though instances of martyrdom actually proved remarkably few and far between. In the end, though, under pressure from all sides, the state authorities decided to act, closing first the academy at Nowogródek in 1618 and then the centre at Raków in 1638, following a vote in the Sejm occasioned by news that students had destroyed a roadside crucifix. Deprived of their bases, the Brethren retreated into the countryside, continuing their activities, but never fully regaining the heights of influence and renown they had previously enjoyed.

Though Arianism eventually faded as a religious force in Poland, its ideas continued to find resonance in later centuries. In particular, the Polish Brethren are often regarded as precursors of the **Unitarianism** that flourished (often, but not always, minus the social egalitarianism) among the Presbyterians and other non-conformist churches in England and the United States in the nineteenth century, crystallizing in the formation and development of the modern **Unitarian Church**.

As to **modern Raków**, there's little left by way of traces of the Brethren or their academy except a couple of distinctively shaped whitewashed houses built as living quarters for students at the academy. The owner of the *Myśliwska*, the murky bar-restaurant on the square, knows a fair bit about the history of the town, and if your Polish is up to it, can fill you in on the details.

Though the road takes you up around the top of the town, the principal entrance to the old town is through the **Kraków Gate** (Brama Krakowska), a towering structure enhanced by the attic added in the late 1500s. Despite wartime devastation of the town, substantial sections of the fortifications, notably the walls, have survived essentially intact. Clambering around the chunky stone battlements, you sense that King Kazimierz, an indefatigable builder of castles, was a man who put security first. Certainly, the defences he raised here were enough to see Szydłów through the depredations and invasions that ruined many neighbouring towns in later centuries. A fair bit of the castle itself survives, too, notably a solid-looking tower that's now the town **museum** (Tues–Sun 10am–4pm), housing a low-key collection of local artefacts and historical finds.

West across the wide, open square, stuck out on the far edge of the medieval complex is the **Synagogue**, a large structure surrounded by heavy stone buttresses. One of the oldest synagogues in the country and built, according to local legend, at the instigation of Esterka, King Kazimierz's fabled Jewish mistress, the building is currently closed up and empty, waiting for someone to stump up the money to do something with it.

Despite being torched by the Nazis in 1944, the Gothic **Parish Church**, north of the Rynek, retains a few elements of its original decoration, notably the tryptych on the main altar. **All Saints Church** (Wszystkich Świętych), marooned outside the main city walls across the road from the Kraków Gate, fared little better, though you can still see sections of the original Gothic polychromy on the walls.

Buses serving Kielce and Jędrzejów run from the stop on the main square. The only **accommodation** option is the rudimentary *Turstyczny*, ul. Kielecka 8 (☎041/155; ②), just off the Rynek, while there's no real restaurant to speak of, the choice being confined to a couple of basic places on the square.

Kielce and northern Małopolska

Most people see nothing more of the northern reaches of Małopolska than the glimpses snatched from the window of a Warsaw–Kraków express train – a pity, because the gentle hills, lush valleys, strip-farmed fields and tatty villages that characterize the region are quintessential rural Poland. The main town is **Kielce**, roughly halfway between Warsaw and Kraków, but the real attraction for visitors lies in rambling about in the **Świętokrzyskie Mountains** – in reality more of a hill-walkers' range. Lovers of castles will not want to miss the magnificent ruins at **Krzyżtopor**, while south of Kielce, the **Raj Cave**, **Chęciny** and the *skansen* at **Tokarnia** make enjoyable excursions, the latter being one of the best of the country's numerous open-air folk architecture museums. They're all in relatively easy striking distance of the city, making it feasible, given an early start, to combine all three in a day's outing.

Heading north along the main road to Warsaw, through the attractive Małopolska countryside, there are a couple of minor stops worth considering: the Cistercian abbey at **Wąchock** and the old *shtetl* of **Szydłowiec**, which has one of the largest remaining Jewish cemeteries in the country.

Kielce

KIELCE, the regional capital, is nothing much to look at, having undergone the standard postwar development, but it has a relaxed, down-at-heel, rural atmos-

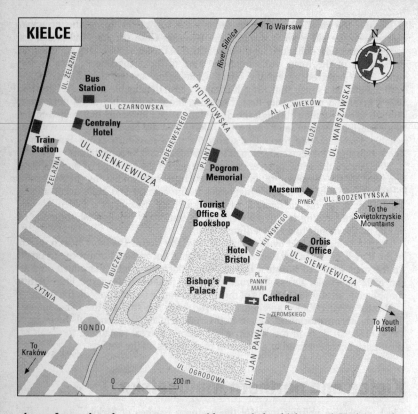

phere. Long the chosen summer residence of the bishops of Kraków, who furnished the city with its main architectural attractions, Kielce registers in the postwar record as the site of the infamous **July 1946 pogrom** when over forty Jewish survivors of the Nazi terror were murdered by elements of a local populace inflamed by wild rumours of ritual murders of Gentile Polish children. A defining moment in the development of postwar Polish–Jewish relations, the pogrom long constituted a blank spot in local memory, a fact remedied in the commemorative plaque to the victims raised in the city in recent years. Economically, the transformations of the post-communist era are gradually beginning to show through, notably in the increasing tally of Western-style shops, cafés and restaurants in evidence in the city centre.

The city centre

All the monuments worth seeing are concentrated around a relatively small central area, bisected by ul. Sienkiewicza, the main city street. North of Sienkiewicza is the pleasant main **Rynek**, lined with crumbling eighteenth- and nineteenth-century mansions, one of which (no. 3/5) houses the **Regional Museum** (Wed–Sun 9am–4pm), with a fairly forgettable collection of local archeological finds and ethnographic exhibits. More diverting are the occasional exhibitions of contemporary Polish art that visit the museum throughout the year, generally in summer.

South of Sienkiewicza, on another square, plac Zamkowy, you'll find the **Cathedral** – Romanesque, lost in the later Baroque reconstruction – highlights of the murky interior being a fine Renaissance monument in red marble to a female member of the local Zebrzydowski family, sculpted by Il Padovano, a sumptuous early Baroque high altarpiece from the workshops of Kraków, and some elaborate Rococo decorative carvings in the choir stalls. During major **religious festivals**, the square east of the cathedral gets packed with smartly dressed locals, many in regional folk costume, processing solemnly around the square. Opposite the cathedral is the early Baroque **palace** built for the bishops of Kraków, the town's owners in the mid-seventeenth century. Now a **Museum of Polish Art** (Tues–Sat 10am–4pm), the building's outstanding features are its period interiors, designed in the 1640s – in particular, the main Portrait Room which boasts a superb larchwood ceiling and a wealth of colourful polychromy.

A short way west of the cathedral is the **Kraków Bishop's Palace**, an impressive early Baroque complex, built on a closed axial plan mimicking the layout of a period north Italian villa supplemented, as in Wawel Castle, by features such as a sturdy-looking roof adjusted to the demands of a northern climate. Constructed in the late 1630s as a residence for the bishops of Kraków, under whose ecclesiastical jurisdiction the city and surroundings fell, up until the late eighteenth century, the palace now houses one of the country's weightier **Regional Museums** (Wed–Sun 9am–4pm; May–June & Sept–Oct also open Tues).

The **ground-floor rooms** are largely taken up with an extensive collection of Polish art from the seventeenth century onwards. As often in such museums, the early works are effectively an extended portrait gallery of the Polish aristocracy alongside the usual selection of patriotic favourites such as Kościuszko and Prince Józef Poniatowski. The nineteenth- and twentieth-century rooms contain a notable selection of Młoda Polska movement era art, including works by Wyspiański, some typically distorted, dreamlike Witkiewicz compositions and a diverting group of self-portraits by Malczewski. On a military note, the museum's collection of swords and other weapons of war from across the centuries culminates in the Piłsudski sanctuary, established in the venerated prewar leader's honour, a few years after his death in 1935, and kept pretty much the same ever since.

The rooms of the **upper floor** comprise the former bishop's apartments, adorned with a sumptious array of period furnishings, several of them still retaining their original decoration. The most notable feature here are the decorated high ceilings with intricately painted larch beams and elaborate friezes running around the tops of the walls. The finest example of this effect is in the **Great Dining Hall**, the frieze here consisting of a mammoth twin-level series of portraits of Kraków bishops and Polish monarchs. A number of apartments display some striking ceiling paintings from the workshop of Thomas Dolabella, notably the **Senatorial Hall** in the west wing, featuring the ominous *Judgement of the Polish Brethren* (see box p.436), with a grand, sweeping depiction of scenes from the Polish–Swedish and Polish–Muscovite wars of the seventeenth century in the adjoining room.

While memories of the notorious **Kielce Pogrom** may have weighed heavily in wider post-war Polish–Jewish relations, the same could not be said in the city itself, where for many years there was no effective recognition of the event in the form of an official monument or commemoration. This has now been rectified – albeit at the instigation of a private Jewish foundation, rather than the city authorities. The house where the pogrom occurred, at no. 7/8 Planty, is a short walk short walk west of the square on the edge of the canal which cuts across ul. Sienkiewicza. It displays a recently erected commemorative plaque in Polish, Hebrew and English "to the 42 Jews murdered . . . during anti-Semitic riots" – a commendably honest description of an event of which some in Poland would prefer not to be reminded. Other sites of historic Jewish interest are the former synagogue on the corner of al. IX Wieków Kielc, now an archive building, and the crumbling **Cemetery** some way south of the centre in the Pakosz district (bus #4 passes fairly close by – get off on ul. Pakosz), where around a hundred gravestones are still standing, along with a dignified monument to local victims of the Holocaust.

Practicalities

The town's **train and bus stations** are close by each other on the west side of town, a ten-minute walk down ul. Sienkiewicza into the town centre. There's no real **information** office to speak of, your best bet being either *Orbis*, ul. Sienkiewicza 12, *PTTK* at pl. Zamkowa 4 or the hotel reception in the *Bristo* hotel. However, the **bookstore** at ul. Sienkiewicza 34 is well stocked with local regional maps and guides.

For **accommodation**, the dingy *Hotel Centralny* at ul. Sienkiewicza 78 (☎041/66 25 11; ④), opposite the train station, is cheap and reasonably clean, though its restaurant is a pretty seedy venue. The central *Hotel Bristol*, ul. Sienkiewicza 21 (☎041/66 30 65; ⑤), is marginally nicer, with a smaller and better restaurant. The reception at the *Bristol* can also arrange **private rooms**, and there is a year-round **youth hostel** at ul. Szymanowskiego 5 (☎041/23735). Another alternative is the *Exbud* hotel, ul. Manifestu Lipcowego 34 (☎041/32 63 93; ④), 2km east of the centre on the Warsaw road.

Hotel **restaurants** apart, the deservedly popular *Winnica*, ul. Kryniczna 4, has some good traditional Ukrainian dishes; the *Promont*, ul. Sienkiewicza 59, is a reasonable local version of a pizzeria; and the *Prezydencka*, Rynek 14, serves a good line in the ubiquitous *kotlet schwabowy*. The big Western chains are getting in on the act now too, with *Pizza Hut* and *Burger King* outlets on ul. Sienkiewicza already established as firm local favourites, the former offering an exceptional spread of salads, by normal Polish standards.

The Raj Cave

Ten kilometres south of Kielce, and roughly 1km west of the main Kraków road, is the **Raj Cave** (April–Nov Tues–Sun 9am–5pm, compulsory guided tours in Polish only), one of the myriad undergound formations dotted around southern Poland, principally in central-northern Małopolska and the Tatra Mountains. Ony discovered in 1964, the "Paradise Cave" (Jaskinia Raj) as it's popularly known, rapidly established itself as a local favourite, and particularly in summer, droves of school buses and day-trippers descend on the place. If you want to avoid the crowds, you'd be well advised to get there early. The **bus** (#31 from Kielce) drops you on the main road, from where you walk to the main car park and on along a wooded path to the ticket office-cum-café/museum at the cave entrance.

Only a stretch of 150 metres inside the caves is open to visitors, but it's a spectacular enough experience comprising a series of **chambers** filled with a seemingly endless array of stalagmites, stalactites and other dreamlike dripstone formations. It's now been established that Neanderthals inhabited the caves as long as 50,000 years ago – these days the wintertime occupants are mainly bats – and scientific research carried out here continues to unearth archeologically significant finds such as a recently discovered stockade constructed from reindeer antlers. Some of the finds are on display in the small museum attached to the ticket office at the cave entrance. If you want to stop over, there's a basic **hotel**, the *Zajazd Raj* (☎041/66 70 27; ③) close to the car park.

Chęciny

Five kilometres further south along the Kraków road (same bus as for the Raj Cave), the little town of **CHĘCINY** makes for an interesting historical diversion. A sleepy provincial town nestled peacefully at the foot of the overlooking hill, and focused around a characteristic open square, the town looks and feels like the kind of place where nothing much has or is ever going to happen. Though there's not a great deal to see, as often an awareness of historical context lends places like this their peculiar aura of poignancy mingled with charm. For centuries Chęciny, like many towns in the surrounding area, was a typical Polish *shtetl*, with Jews making up more than half the population. The Jews are gone now, but the buildings they created remain – synagogue, merchant houses, cemetery – in silent testimony to their age-long presence. Look carefully at some of the houses on and around the square, for example, and you can still see the spot on the doorpost where the *mezuzah* ripped out by the Nazis once sat.

On one side of the square stands the **Parish Church of St Joseph**, an unremarkable place notable mainly for its organ, built in the 1680s and still functioning with the help of its intricate original mechanical action. A short walk along ul. Długa is the former **Synagogue**, a characteristically solid brick structure with a two-tiered roof built in the early seventeenth century. Like many former synagogues this is now a cultural centre, but as with all too many other former Jewish places of worship, a few decorative features apart there's been little attempt to preserve anything of the original features of the building here, the main prayer hall now functioning as a weekend disco complete with glittering lights illuminating the empty frame of the *Aron Ha Kodesh*.

If you're feeling reasonably fit it's worth scrambling up the hill behind the square to the imposing **castle ruins** perched at the top (Tues–Sun 9am–6pm). Completed in the 1310s for King Władysław I and remodelled three centuries later, following major destruction by the Swedes, this strategically significant outpost was eventually allowed to slide into ruin. All that remains today is the polygonal plan of the outer wall, the main gate and a couple of towers, which you can wander around freely. What really makes the trek up worthwhile are the excellent views over the surrounding countryside, with Kielce, and on a clear day, the Świętokrzyskie Mountains visible in the distance. Scrambling down the hill right of the castle brings you to the evocative **Jewish Cemetery**, crumbling and overgrown, but with a fair number of carved tombstones still in evidence.

For an **overnight stay** the choice is between the basic *Dom Wycieczkowy Chęciny*, ul. 1-go Maja 10 (☎041/48921; ③), or the even more rudimentary youth hostel at ul. Białego Zagłębia 1 (☎041/15 10 68). For a bite to eat, your best bet is the *Niemcówka*, ul. Małgosia 5, operating in the same premises as an old sixteenth-century inn.

The Tokarnia skansen

A further 7km south from Chęciny is the outstanding **Museum of Folk Architecture** or *skansen* (April–Oct Tues–Sun 10am–5pm; Nov–March Mon–Fri & Sun 9am–2pm) at **TOKARNIA**. The open-air museum is visible from the road, up on the hillside, though signposting is almost non-existent: if you're travelling by bus (from Kielce, take buses heading for Jędrzejow via Chęciny) ask the driver for the *skansen* and you'll be dropped close by.

The main idea of a **skansen** is to provide a showcase for rural architecture and customs, in many cases all but disappeared now, and on this score the Tokarnia site succeeds admirably. Established in the 1970s, and still adding to its collection of buildings, the *skansen* is one of the largest and best in the country. Well laid out, with all the buildings grouped according to surrounding regions of Małopolska, this museum provides an enjoyable survey of local architectural traditions. Helpfully, there's a brief guide in each building in English, French and German outlining its traditional use, and, if your Polish is up to it, a devoted contingent of women from local villages there to fill you in on all the details. They're clearly (and rightly) proud of their particular building, and in customary rural fashion, in no hurry to see you move on, so be prepared to spend at least a couple of minutes paying each structure the required respect.

The thatched and shingle-roofed buildings assembled here encompass the full range of rural life, with an emphasis on traditional farmsteads, from relatively prosperous setups – the more religious pictures on display the wealthier the family – to the dwellings of the poorest subsistence farmers. Great care and attention has been paid to re-creating the interiors as they would have been in the early part of the century and beyond, with many of the houses containing an amazing array of old wooden farm implements, kitchen utensils and tools used in traditional crafts such as ostlery, shingling, brewing, wood carving, herbal medicinal preparations and candle making. Additionally, there are a number of other buildings such as a wonderful old windmill, a pharmacy and a fine mid-nineteenth-century *dwór* of the kind inhabited by relatively well-off *szchlachta* families from Chopin's generation and beyond up until World War II. The contrast between its size and opulence compared with the other dwellings on display is striking, reflecting the grinding poverty and endemic inequalities of rural Polish society that were a major factor in the successive waves of emigration to the New World from the latter part of the last century on into the 1930s.

The Świętokrzyskie Mountains and beyond

In this low-lying region, the **Świętokrzyskie Mountains**, only 600m at maximum, appear surprisingly tall. Running east from Kielce, their long ridges and valleys, interspersed with isolated villages, are a popular and rugged hiking territory. During World War II, the area was a centre of armed resistance to the Nazis: a grim, essentially factual account of life in the resistance here is given in Primo Levi's book *If Not Now, When?*, in which he refers to the area as the Holy Cross Mountains, a literal translation of their name.

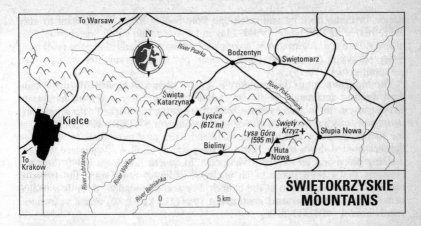

The Łysogóry

The fifteen-kilometre-long **Łysogóry** range is the most popular destination in the Świętokrzyskie. The place to head for is **ŚWIĘTY KRZYŻ**, one hour by bus from the main Kielce station (5 departures daily, from 7am). The journey takes you along the edge of the range and eventually up a lovely mountainside road to the edge of the **Świętokrzyskie National Park**, stopping at a car park near the foot of Łysa Gora (Bald Mountain; 595m).

The bus continues through the park (the only vehicle allowed to do so), but you're better off walking from here, through the protected woodland habitat of a range of birds and animals, including a colony of eagles. The marked path leads to a clearing – from where you can pick up the road again – then past a huge TV mast to the **Święty Krzyż Abbey** (30min), established up here by Italian Benedictines in the early twelfth century. The buildings have changed beyond recognition, about the only remnant of the original foundation being the abbey church's Romanesque doorway. The isolated mountain site, however, maintains an ancient feel; the abbey itself replaced an earlier pagan temple, traces of which were discovered nearby some years ago. On a more sombre note, the abbey buildings were turned into a prison following the enforced dissolution of the Benedictine order in 1825, and it remained so up until 1945, having been used by the Nazis as a concentration camp for Soviet POWs. Just how appalling conditions were then is indicated by photographs in the old monastery building of camp signs (in Russian and German) forbidding cannibalism.

The abbey **Museum** (April–Oct Tues–Sun 10am–4pm; Nov–Mar 9am–3pm) houses one of the country's best natural history collections, covering every aspect of the area's wildlife, with exhibits ranging from butterflies and snakes to huge deer and elks. There's a good view down into the valley below the edge of the abbey, and you can also see some of the large tracts of broken stones that are a distinctive glaciated feature of the hilltops.

The path due east down the mountain leads 2km to the village of **NOWA SŁUPIA** with its **Museum of Ancient Metallurgy** (Tues–Sun 10am–4pm), located on the site of iron ore mines and smelting furnaces developed here as early as the second century AD. For nearly a thousand years, this was one of Europe's biggest ironworks. From Nowa Słupia you can take a bus back to

Kielce, or climb back up and catch one from Święty Krzyż. If you want **to stay** over, there's a *PTTK* hostel (☎041/144) and a year-round youth hostel (☎041/16) in the village too. Alternatively, a couple of kilometres back along the road from Święty Krzyż is the *Jodłowy Dwór*, a clean but basic overnighter with its own restaurant (☎041/28; ③).

The highest point of the Łysogóry is a point known as **Łysica** (611m), a standard walking destination at the far end of the range. If you set out for Święty Krzyż early in the morning you can walk there along the marked path in one day. Otherwise, catch a bus from Kielce to the village of **ŚWIĘTA KATARZYNA**, at the foot of the hills, and take the woodland path, past memorials to resistance fighters hunted down by the Nazis, to the summit (1hr) – a legendary witches' meeting place and an excellent viewpoint. In Święta Katarzyna itself, there's a **convent** that's been home to an enclosed order of nuns since the fifteenth century – you can peer in at the church. For accommodation, there is a choice between a *PTTK* **hotel and restaurant** (☎041/11 21 11; ②) and a year-round **youth hostel** (☎041/11 22 06).

Opatów

Some 60km east of Kielce on the Lublin road, beyond the outer reaches of the Świętokrzyskie Mountains, the little town of **OPATÓW** is as somnolent a place as you would expect in these parts. Yet the town has known better days, originally developing out of its position on one of the major medieval trading routes east into Russia. Badly mauled during the Tartar raids of Poland (1500–1502), the town was purchased and subsequently fortified by Chancellor Krzysztof Szydłowiecki (see p.447). The Old Town complex grouped around the long square at the top of the hill and surrounded by walls is what remains of the chancellor's development of the place.

As often, the most notable building is the **Parish Church** on the main square, dedicated to St Martin, a towering three-aisled Romanesque basilica raised in the mid-twelfth century and remodelled in later centuries. A few features of the original Romanesque decoration survive, notably the main doorway, the dual windows in the south tower and some frieze decoration on the facade. These aside, the thing to look out for is the group of **Szydłowiecki family tombs**, especially that of Chancellor Krzysztof. Executed, like the others in the group, in the 1530s by a duo of Italian architects from the court at Wawel, the tomb has a powerful bronze bas-relief of the citizens of Opatów mourning the chancellor's death – a moving tribute to a man whose family name had died out by the end of the century owing to a persistent failure to produce male heirs.

One section of the square is criss-crossed by a honeycomb of **underground tunnels** and **cellars**, a throwback to the town's merchant past, originally used for storing goods sold in the local market. It's now possible to visit the cellars – ask at the *PTTK* office on the square, which organizes guided visits underground when demand is sufficient. Ten minutes' walk away, back down the hill, through the **Warsaw Gate** (Brama Warszawska) and across the River Opatówka, is the **Bernardine Church**, an ornate late Baroque structure with a fine high altarpiece that replaced the earlier fifteenth-century church destroyed by Swedish troops during the invasions of the mid-1650s.

The **bus station**, in the centre of town, has good connections to nearby Sandomierz and reasonable ones to Kielce. The only **accommodation** option to speak of is the basic *Dom Wycieczkowy*, at ul. 1 Maja 4 (☎041/314; ②), while for simple **meals** there are a couple of restaurants on the main square.

Krzyżtopór

Despite its dilapidated state the **Krzyżtopór Castle**, near the village of Ujazd, 15km southwest of Opatów on the road to Staszów, is one of the most spectacular ruins in Poland (buses from Opatów cover the route). Nothing in the surrounding landscape prepares you for the mammoth building that suddenly rears up over the skyline. Even then, it's not until you actually enter the castle compound (Tues–Sun 10am–4pm, often longer during summer months) that you really begin to get a handle on the scale of the place, a magnificent ruin still bearing many hallmarks of the considerable architectural ingenuity that went into designing and constructing the complex.

The history of the castle is a textbook case of grand aristocratic folly. Built at enormous expense for Krzysztof Ossoliński, the governor of Sandomierz province, by Italian architect Lorenzo Muretto, and completed in 1644, only a year before Ossoliński's death, the castle was thoroughly ransacked by the Swedes only a decade later, a blow from which it never really recovered, despite being inhabited by the Ossoliński family up until the 1770s. Plans to resurrect the castle have come and gone over time, the latest initiative being a somewhat uncertain bid to revive the place as a tourist attraction.

The basic **layout** of the castle comprises a star-shaped set of fortifications surrounding a large inner courtyard, and within this, a smaller elliptical inner area. The original architectural conception mimicked the **calendar** at every level: thus there were 4 towers, representing the seasons, 12 main walls for the months, 52 rooms for the weeks, 365 windows for the days, and even an additional window for leap years, kept bricked up when out of sync with the calendar. Ossoliński's passion for horses was accommodated by the network of stables, some 370 in all, built underneath the castle, each equipped with its own mirror and marble manger. While remnants of the stables survive, the same can't be said for the fabled dining hall in the octagonal entrance tower, originally dominated by an aquarium built into the ceiling.

Carved on the entrance tower before the black marble portal are a large cross (*krzyż*) and an axe (*topór*), a punning reference to the castle's name, the former a symbol of the Catholic Counter-Reformation, of which Ossoliński was a firm supporter, the latter part of the family coat of arms. Inside the complex, you're inevitably drawn to wandering around the rather unstable nooks and crannies of the place. The longer you stay, the more the sheer audacity and expanse of the place hits home, in particular, the murky ruins of the cellars, which seem to go on for ever. With the high inner walls towering above as you descend into the bowels of the building, it's easy to understand why the castle has generated its fair share of legends, notably that of the lady and knight said to prowl the ramparts by moonlight, the knight being Krzysztof Baldwin, the second lord of the castle killed by a Tartar archer.

Most people move straight on after visiting, though such is the magic of the place, that don't be surprised if you end up spending longer here than you planned. If you want **to stay the night**, the building in front of the castle entrance offers basic overnight accommodation and snacks (☎041/54; ②), and there's the additional option of camping in the castle grounds.

Wąchock

The only reason for going to **WĄCHOCK**, 44km north of Kielce (and getting there certainly constitutes something of a detour from the main Radom–Warsaw road) is to visit the town's **Cistercian Abbey Complex**. One of the major Cistercian centres in Poland, the monastery is widely regarded as one of the finest, and best preserved, monuments of Romanesque architecture in the country. Built by the group of Burgundian monks who settled here in 1179 at the invitation of Gedko, Bishop of Kraków, the complex was completed in 1239, probably by Italian masons whose leader, Maestro Simon, carved his name on the facade of the church. The monks of the Cistercian community give guided tours round the abbey, mostly to pre-arranged tourist groups, which you are welcome to tag along with: otherwise the brothers are happy to let people come in and look around the church and main sections of the cloister during specified hours (Mon–Sat 9am–noon & 2pm–5pm, Sun 2pm–5pm).

Just five minutes' walk from the main square, entrance to the complex is through the main abbey door, where you'll need to make yourself known at the reception desk. Opposite is a small **museum** devoted to the history of the place, including its role in the exploits of the Polish insurgents who fought the tsarist forces from their bases in the surrounding hills during the failed 1863 Uprising. The original Romanesque interior design of the basilica-shaped **abbey church**, topped with a high tower, has largely been submerged under a mass of florid Baroque ornamentation, though the cross-ribbed vaulting characteristic of Cistercian architecture is still in evidence. On into the adjoining monastic complex, the most notable features are two well-preserved original Romanesque sections of the **cloisters**, much of which was remodelled in the sixteenth and seventeenth centuries. The **chapter house**, in the eastern section, is the real showstopper, the exquisitely proportioned cross-ribbed vaulting divided into nine sections with a sequence of arches supported by four columns, whose capitals are ornamented with intricately carved floral decoration, also gracing the surrounding walls. On the south side of the cloister, the **refectory** also features more soothing cross-ribbed vaulting and decorative carved stone work, the atmosphere of the place conjuring up visions of the calming rhythms of the monastic life practised here for centuries.

For places to stay, the only current option in town is a summer-only **youth hostel**, ul. Kościelna 10, while for a bite to eat, there are a couple of basic **restaurant/cafés** on and around the Rynek, none of them memorable. There's a reasonably frequent though slow-paced service to and from Kielce, terminating at Wąchock's Rynek.

Szydłowiec

Forty-five kilometres north of Kielce, **SZYDŁOWIEC** is exactly the kind dusty old town most people whizz through on the way to and from Kraków, but there's enough worth seeing in its small, but nonetheless enjoyable, set of historical monuments to justify a brief stopover.

A placid central Rynek provides the focal point of the town, dominated by a fine **Town Hall**, substantially renovated since the late 1980s, a robust early seventeenth-century construction topped with a high tower, the attic's arcaded decorative frieze emphasizing the influence of Kraków's Sukiennice on the style of construction. There's a pleasant café in the cellars underneath the building that also holds occasional concerts and other cultural events. Off the southern side of the Rynek, stands the late Gothic **Parish Church of St Sigismund**, with accompanying belfry, completed in the early 1500s, and mercifully spared the usual later Baroque accretions. Notable features of the largely well-preserved original interior include the sumptuous early seventeenth-century **high altar**, a fine carved **Coronation of the Virgin** from 1531 and most striking of all, the Late Gothic polyptych housed in the presbytery, produced by one of the prolific Kraków workshops of the period, the central panel illustrating the Assumption of the Virgin, with the twelve Apostles gathered round the empty tomb of the resurrected Christ. Below them kneel the figures of the Szydłowiec family, the town founders and financial patrons of the church. Mikołaj Szydłowiecki, royal chancellor until his death in 1532, is commemorated in a fine marble tablet executed by Bartolomeo Berecci of Wawel Cathedral fame.

Half a kilometre west of the Rynek is the town **Castle**, a dilapidated old pile surrounded by a stagnant moat, built for Chancellor Szydłowiecki in the 1510s, overhauled a century later and, by the look of things, allowed to sink gracefully into decline ever since. Much of the castle is closed to visitors, the major exceptions being the cobbled inner courtyard and a **Museum of Folk instruments** (Tues–Fri 9am–3.30pm, Sat 10am–5.30pm; entrance from the south side of the building), which houses an enjoyable selection of musical accoutrements ranging from fiddles, accordions, hurdy-gurdys and bagpipes, to more exotic creations such as animal-shaped whistles and percussion instruments.

Jews formed a sizeable percentage of the town population up until the liquidation of the Nazi-established ghetto here in January 1943, when they were deported en masse to Treblinka. Echoes of their presence revolve around the former **synagogue**, now a library, on ul. Grabarskiej, near the old Jewish-run brewery on ul. Sowińskiego, and most powerfully of all in the **Cemetery**, out at the end of ul. Wschodnia, on the edge of town near the Radom road. One of the largest and most impressive such sites left in Poland, a walk through the walled, overgrown burial ground, where over 3000 tombstones are still standing, the oldest dating back to the late eighteenth century, uncovers numerous examples of the elaborately carved floral and symbolic motifs typical of Jewish *matzevot* in Poland and elsewhere in East-Central Europe. A memorial near the main cemetery gate commemorates the 16,000 Jews deported from the town in 1943.

Practicalities

The **bus station** is a short walk north of the Rynek, on the main Radom road, with regular services to and from Radom and less frequent connections with Kielce. Buses also run to Skarżysko-Kamienna where you can change for the better service to Kielce. Unless you're really desperate, you won't want to stay here for the night: the **accommodation** options are a basic *Dom Wycieczkowy*, the *Pod Dębem*, on the Rynek (☎041/11164; ③), and a youth hostel, ul. Kilińskiego 2 (☎041/17 13 74) with its own makeshift restaurant, near the bus station. The only **restaurants** worth speaking of, the *Ratuszowa* on the Rynek and the *Biesiadia* on the way to the Jewish cemetery, are extremely simple.

PODHALE AND THE TATRA MOUNTAINS

Ask Poles to define their country's natural attractions and they often come up with the following simple definition: The Lakes, The Sea and The Mountains. "The Mountains" consist of an almost unbroken chain of ridges extending the whole length of the southern border, of which the highest, most spectacular and most revered are the **Tatras** – or *Tatry* as they're known in Polish. Eighty kilometres long, with peaks rising to over 2500m, the Polish Tatras are actually a relatively small part of the range, most of which rises across the border in Slovakia. As the estimated three million annual tourists show, however, the Polish section has enough to keep most people happy: high peaks for dedicated mountaineers, excellent trails for hikers, cable cars and creature comforts for day-trippers, and ski slopes in winter. What used to be a prime Eastern bloc holiday region is now being transformed into something of a Western tourist enclave, the legions of East Europeans that used to descend on Zakopane rapidly being replaced by new hordes of Italians, French – and increasingly English – taking advantage of the low cost of holidaying in the Polish mountains.

Podhale – the Tatra foothills, beginning to the south of Nowy Targ – is a sparsely populated region of lush meadows, winding valleys and old wooden villages. The inhabitants of Podhale, the **górale**, are fiercely independent mountain farmers, known throughout Poland for their folk traditions. The region was "discovered" by the Polish intelligentsia in the late nineteenth century and the *górale* rapidly emerged as symbols of the struggle for independence, the links forged between intellectuals and local peasants presaging the anticipated national unity of the post-independence era. As in other neglected areas of the country, the poverty of rural life led thousands of *górale* to emigrate to the United States in the 1920s and 1930s. The departures continue today, with at least one member of most households spending a year or two in Chicago, New York or other US Polish émigré centres, returning with money to support the family and, most importantly, build a house.

Since the demise of communism, the traditional bonds between Podhale and the rest of the country have been shaken by what many locals see as central government's insensitivity to their specific concerns. Tensions surfaced following Solidarity's refusal to adopt a popular *górale* community leader as their main candidate in the elections of summer 1989, choosing instead a union loyalist. Subsequent governments have shown somewhat more concern for regional sensitivities, encouraged, no doubt, by the economic benefits to be reaped from its burgeoning tourist development.

Despite the influx of holidaymakers, the *górale* retain a straight-talking and highly hospitable attitude to outsiders. If you're willing to venture off the beaten track, away from the regular tourist attractions around Zakopane, there's a chance of real and rewarding contacts in the remoter towns and villages.

South to Zakopane

From Kraków, the main road south heads through the foothills towards **Zakopane**, the main base for the Tatras. Approaching the mountains the road runs through a memorable landscape of gentle valleys, undulating slopes and

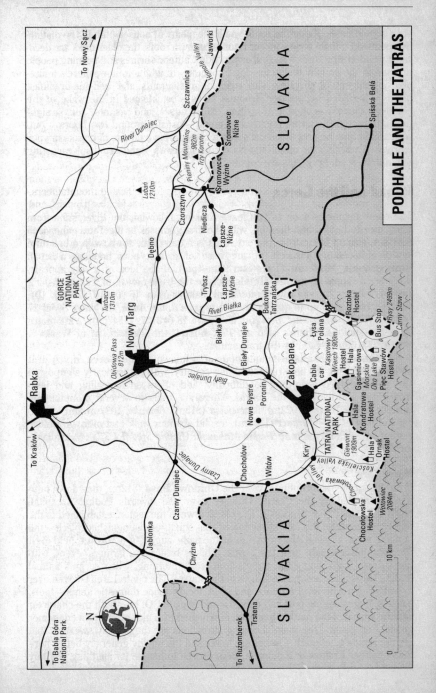

PODHALE AND THE TATRAS

strip-farmed fields. Along the route you'll see plenty of houses built in the distinctive pointed Podhale style – newer houses have tin roofs, the older ones are decorated wooden structures – as well as wayside Catholic shrines and farming people dressed in the equally distinctive local costume. In addition, now, there's a sizeable contingent of privately run roadside restaurants and bed-and-breakfast places – heralded by "*noclegi*" (rooms) signs – established in the wake of the country's current economic transition. Most buses, and visitors, run straight through, though it can be pretty slow going – usually around two hours – but, with a little time on your hands, it's worth considering a couple of breaks in your journey. A warning for motorists: watch out for cows – and drunks – careering out into the road. Accidents are common.

Rabka and the Gorce

The climb begins as soon as you leave Kraków, following the River Raba from Myślenice to Lubień and then on, with the first glimpses of the Tatras ahead, to **RABKA**, around 60km from the city. This is a quiet little town, with a beautiful seventeenth-century **church** at the base of a hill, now housing a small **Ethnographic Museum** (Tues–Sun 9am–4pm). If the idea of a stay appeals, there are a couple of options. **Hotels** include the basic *Sława*, ul. Zakopiańska 2 (☎0187/76120; ②) and the *Janosik*, ul Zakopiańska 16 (☎0187/76980; ②). Smaller, but a step up in quality are two *pensjonat*, the *Anna*, ul. Nowy Świat 27 (☎0187/77477; ③) and the *Manusia*, ul. Bystra 18 (☎0187/77547; ②), a kilometre from the stations. There's also a *PTTK* **hostel**, the *Turbacz*, at ul Wąska 1 (☎0187/77160; ①), right by the train station.

Surrounding Rabka is a mountainous area known as the **Gorce**, much of it national parkland. It's fine, rugged hiking country, with paths clearly signposted and colour-graded according to difficulty, and offers an appealing and less-frequented alternative to the Tatras. There are trails to several mountain-top hostels: *Luboń Wielki* (1022m), *Maciejowa* (815m), *Groniki* (1027m) and – highest and best of all – *Turbacz* (1310m), a solid six-hour walk east of town. Before setting out, pick up the **map** *Beskid Makowski* (*Beskid Średni 1:75,000*) available locally.

Nowy Targ

From Rabka the road continues over the **Obidowa Pass** (812m), then down onto a plain crossed by the Czarny Dunajec river and towards Podhale's capital, **NOWY TARG** ("New Market"). The oldest town in the region, established in the thirteenth century, the key attraction of this squat, undistinguished place – the home of many a Polish American – is, as the name suggests, a **Market**, held each Thursday on a square near the centre. This is basically a farmers' event, with horse-drawn carts lining the streets from early morning, when serious animal trading takes place around the edges of the square. The central area is given over to stalls laden with local produce and solid, locally made domestic items – tools, baskets, huge cooking pots and carved wooden plates. Of late, both the character and the appeal of the market has been diminished by a glut of Western consumer goods. For visitors, the main shopping attractions are the chunky sweaters that are the region's hallmark – prices are lower and the quality generally better here than in either Kraków or Zakopane. Be prepared to haggle for anything you buy (wool and crafts especially), and arrive early if you want to get any sense of the real atmosphere. The market has also been invaded by droves of Russians, Ukrainians and Slovaks, the latter turning up weekly by the busload to benefit from the relatively cheaper prices in Poland, their booty duly wafted through the laxly policed crossings along the Slovak border. By 10am or so, with business done, most of the farmers retreat to local cafés for a hearty bout of eating and, especially, drinking.

As far as sights go, the town centre offers **St Catherine's Church**, which has a Gothic presbytery, and there's an attractive larchwood chapel across the river. The unofficial Podhale **Lenin Trail** begins at the town, too: the old prison beyond the southeast corner of the main square is where he was held in 1914 on suspicion of spying – by then he'd been living in the area for nearly two years. A further Soviet connection is revealed in the local cemetery: a fierce battle for the town during the Red Army's advance in early 1945 left over a thousand Soviet soldiers dead.

Accommodation options are limited. Of the **hotels**, the *Janosik*, ul. Sokoła 8 (☎0187/67064; ③) is pretty grim and the *Gorce*, al. Tysiąlecia 74 (☎0187/62661; ②), south of the centre, isn't much better. As in Rabka and other towns in the region, *pensjonat* are a safer bet. The best choice here is the *Na Kawancu*, ul. Oś. Gazdy 44 (☎0187/68031; ③), a short way out of the centre. There's also a **PTTK hostel**, the *Turbacz* (☎0187/63246), and a **youth hostel** at Dzielnica Nowa, 4km north of town, on the road to Kraków (☎0187/2522; July & Aug only). **Private rooms** can be arranged through the **Podhale Information Office** on plac Pokoju. For **food**, there's little to choose between the *Podhalanka* and the *Dunajec*, both on plac Pokoju, and the *Tatry* at ul. Kopernika 12.

Zakopane and around

South of Nowy Targ, the road continues another 20km along the course of the Biały Dunajec before reaching the edges of **ZAKOPANE**, a major mountain resort, crowded with visitors throughout its summer hiking and winter skiing seasons. It has been an established attraction for Poles since the 1870s, when the purity of the mountain air began to attract the attention of doctors and their consumptive city patients. Within a few years, this inaccessible mountain village of sheep farmers was transformed, as the medics were followed by Kraków artists and intellectuals, who established a fashionable colony in the final decades of Austro-Hungarian rule. A popular holiday centre ever since, Poles began discovering the place en masse in the 1920s and 1930s, and in the postwar era, the town grew to become one of the country's prime tourist hot-spots. In step with the growing influx of foreigners, drawn by the lure of the mountains (and what remain by Western standards bargain prices), Zakopane has of late begun to acquire the hollow, overdeveloped feel of a major European tourist trap. It's a must for the wonderful setting and access to the peaks, but the distinctive traditional *górale* architecture of much of the town is being increasingly submerged in the welter of commercial developments.

The Zakopane area **telephone code** is ☎0165

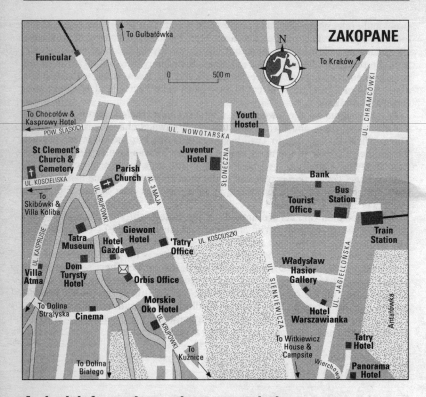

Arrival, information and accommodation

The **bus** and **train stations** are both a ten-minute walk east of the main street, ul. Krupówki. Zakopane has several **tourist offices**. The office at ul. Kościuszki 23 (☎12211), close to both stations, is the main information centre for the whole area; *Orbis* at ul. Krupówki 22 (☎12238) helps with hotels, train and bus bookings and local trips; *Trip*, ul. Zamoyskiego 1 (☎15947), is the most useful and best organized of the new breed of privately owned tourist offices, offering similar services but more attuned to Westerners' demands. Opening hours for the tourist offices are generally Monday to Friday 8am to 6pm, Saturdays 8am to noon. The *PTTK* office, ul. Krupówki 12 (☎12429), and the *CPT* bureau at ul. Calubińskiego 42 (☎63799) are useful if you want to hire a local guide for hiking trips into the Tatras.

Note that **parking** can be a bit of a problem for motorists these days in the increasingly congested town centre. Your best bets are the couple of parking lots on al. 3 Maja, directly east of ul. Krupówki.

Accommodation

All the tourist offices have rooms on offer, many in *pensjonat*, whose stock has greatly increased following the privatization of many workers' holiday homes in town. *Orbis* runs several **pensjonat**, bookable – along with other accommodation – through the reception desk at the *Hotel Giewont*. *Tatry* operates accommodation services for groups at their main office and for individuals (mainly rooms in houses) at ul. Kościuszki 23a. Although privatizations have relieved the town's perennial accommodation problems, it's still worth booking rooms well in advance in midsummer or during the skiing season. Particularly during *ferie*, the traditional two-week break for schoolchilden (usually the last week in January and first week in February), everything on offer is booked solid.

Private rooms are a popular and widespread alternative to the hotels and *pensjonat*; most buses are met by local people offering rooms in their houses – expect to pay 20–40zł per person. Zakopane's basic **youth hostel**, open all year, is at ul. Nowotarska 45 (☎66203). For **campers** there are two sites: *Camping Pod Krokwią*, ul. Żeromskiego, across from the bottom of the ski jump on the east side of town; and *Za Strugiem*, ul. Za Strugiem, a thirty-minute walk west of the centre.

The hotels and *pensjonat* listed below can be subject to huge price hikes during high season:

Dom Turysty, ul. Zaruskiego 5 (☎63281). Cheap hotel popular with Polish students; laundry and showers on the second floor are handy. ③.

Gazda, Zaruskiego 2 (☎15011, fax 15330); Mid-range, central hotel with decent-quality rooms and a reasonable restaurant. ⑤.

Giewont, Kościuszki 1 (☎2011). The town's smartest hotel, right in the centre; chances of getting a room if you haven't booked are virtually zero. ④.

Imperial, ul. Balzera 1 (☎14021). Mid-range hotel with reasonable rooms, southeast of the town centre. ③.

Juventur, ul. Stołeczna 2a (☎66253). Tour-group hotel, although many rooms are without private bathrooms. ④.

Kasprowy, Polana Szymoszkowa (☎14011, fax 15272). Luxury hotel west of town, looking onto the mountains. ⑨.

Morskie Oko, Krupówki 30 (☎15076); Mid-range, central hotel. ④.

Panorama, ul. Wierchowa 6. Another decent pension, next to the *Tatry*. ③.

Sośnica, ul. Modrzejewskiej 7 (☎66796). Reasonably upmarket ex-workers' pension in southern part of town with its own swimming pool, sauna and snooker room. ④.

Tatry, ul. Wierchowa 4 (☎66040). Quiet former workers' holiday home, ideally located for the bus station and town centre. Excellent views over town and mountains. ③.

Warszawianka, Jagiellońska 7 (☎63261). Cheap central hotel close to the stations. ③.

The Town

Zakopane's main street, **ul. Krupówki**, is a bustling pedestrian precinct given over to the traditional assortment of restaurants, cafés and souvenir shops, now spiced by the newly acquired collection of Western-style takeaway joints, delis, billiard halls and sex shops. Uphill, the street merges into **ul. Zamoyskiego**, which runs on out of town past the fashionable *fin-de-siècle* wooden villas of the outskirts, while in the other direction, it follows a rushing stream down towards Gubałówka Hill (see p.458).

The **Tatra Museum** (Tues–Sun 9am–3.30pm), near the centre of ul. Krupówki, covers local wildlife, ethnography and history, including a section on the wartime experiences of the *górale*, who were brutally punished by the Nazis for their involvement with the Polish resistance and cross-mountain contacts with

KAROL SZYMANOWSKI

After Chopin, **Karol Szymanowski** (1882–1937) is Poland's greatest composer, forging his own distinctive style in an exotic and highly-charged mix of orientalism, opulance and native folk music. He was always striving to find a national voice, but feared provincialism. "Poland's national music should not be the stiffened ghost of the polonaise or mazurka . . . Let our music be national in its Polish characteristics but not falter in striving to attain universality."

From the 1920s Szymanowski spent much time in **Zakopane** and became a key member of a group of intellectuals (including the artist and playwright Witkacy) who were **enthused by the folklore of the Tatras** and dubbed themselves "the emergency rescue service of Tatra culture". Among Szymanowski's works that show a direct influence of Tatra music are the song cycle *Seopiewnie* (1921), the *Mazurkas* for piano (1924-5) and, above all, the ballet *Harnasie* (1931) which is stuffed full of outlaws, features a spectacular highland wedding and boasts genuine *górale* melodies in orchestral garb.

Alongside two violin concertos and his Symphony *Song of the Night*, Szymanowski's greatest work is the **Stabat Mater** (1926), which draws on the traditions of old Polish church music and is a stunning choral work of great economy and austere beauty. After many years of ill health, Szymanowski died of tuberculosis in 1937 and received an illustrious state funeral with the Obrochta family, one of the leading *górale* bands, playing around his tomb in the Skałka Church in Kraków.

the Allied intelligence. The museum is dedicated to T. Chałubinski, the doctor who "discovered" Zakopane in the 1870s. Of the number of art galleries sprouting up around town, the **Hasior Gallery** (Wed–Sat 11–6pm, Sun 9–3pm), housed in a wooden building on ul. Jagiellońska, south of the stations, is one of the most interesting, presenting the quirky but nevertheless enjoyable works of the contemporary artist Władysław Hasior.

In the cemetery of the **wooden church** on ul. Kościeliska, you'll find the graves of many of the town's best-known writers and artists, among them that of Stanisław Witkiewicz (1851–1915) who developed the distinctive "Zakopane" architectural style based on traditional wooden building forms. There's also a commemorative tablet to his equally famous son, **Witkacy** (see box), standing by his mother's grave. Alongside the famous are the graves of old *górale* families, including well-known local figures such as the skier Helena Marusarzówna, executed by the Nazis for her part in the resistance. West of the main street is **Willa Atma**, a traditional-style villa and longtime home of composer Karol Szymanowski (see box), now a museum dedicated to its former resident (Tues–Sun 10am–4pm).

Witkiewicz's first architectural experiment, is the **Willa Koliba**, ten minutes' walk west from the centre along ul. Kościeliska, while 1.5km further east, on the road to Morskie Oko, the **wooden chapel** at JASZCZURÓWKA is widely regarded as one of his finest creations. (Two further Witkiewicz buildings can be visited just east of Zakopane: the **Willa Pod Jodłami** at BYSTRE and a wooden **chapel** at CHŁABÓWKA; both are on the Morskie Oko bus route.)

Górale woodcraft is famous throughout Poland, and nowhere is this skill more convincingly demonstrated than in the brace of wooden churches and chapels that can be seen in and around the town area. Two particularly worth visiting are the **Sanctuary of Our Lady of Fatima** (Sanktuarium Matki Bożej Fatimskiej) at

SWIBÓWKI, a thirty-minute walk west of town along ul. Kościeliska, which also has a remarkable chapel at the rear of the main church complex, and the new church on ul. Zamoyskiego, the southern continuation of ul. Krupówki, a ten-minute walk from the town centre.

WITKACY

Stanisław Ignacy Witkiewicz (1885–1939) – **Witkacy** as he's commonly known – is the most famous of the painters, writers and other artists associated with Zakopane. Born in Warsaw, the son of **Stanisław Witkiewicz**, the eminent painter and art critic who created the so-called **"Zakopane Style"** of primitivist wooden architecture, it was in the artistic ferment of turn-of-the-century Zakopane that Witkacy spent much of his early life. After quitting Zakopane following his fiancée's suicide, in 1914, Witkacy joined an expedition to New Guinea and Australia led by a family friend, the celebrated anthropologist Bronisław Malinowski, and returned to a Europe on the verge of war. With the outbreak of World War I, the reluctant Witkacy, a Russian passport-holder, was compelled to travel to St Petersburg to train as an infantry officer. In the event, Witkacy's time in Russia proved influential to his artistic development. As well as experimenting with hallucinogenic drugs he began studying philosophy, a pursuit which strongly influenced the subsequent development of his work and art.

After surviving the war physically, if not mentally, unscathed, Witkacy re-established himself in Zakopane in 1918. From then on he developed his bubbling artistic talents in a host of directions, the most significant being art, philosophy, drama and novel writing. During the following fifteen years or so, Witkacy produced over twenty **plays**, many of which were premiered in Zakopane by his own theatre company, formed in 1925, with several productions being staged in the epic surroundings of Morskie Oko Lake. An exponent of an avant-gardist theory of drama that extolled the virtues of "pure form" over content, Witkacy wrote dramas that are generally bizarre, almost surrealist-pieces spiced up with large dollops of sex and murder. Cold-shouldered by uncomprehending 1920s Polish audiences, the Witkacy dramatic *oeuvre* was rediscovered – and banned for some time by communist authorities – in the 1950s, since when it's consistently ranked among the most popular in the country.

Artistically, Witkacy's main interests revolved around the famous **studio** he set up in Zakopane, where he churned out hundreds of portraits, many commissioned, of his friends and acquaintances from the contemporary artistic world. A dedicated drug-experimenter, Witkacy habitually noted, in the corner of the canvas, which drug he had been taking when painting; the self-portraits in particular reveal a disturbed, restless aesthetic sensibility. Witkacy's **novels** – by common consent almost untranslatable – are similarly fantastic doom-laden excursions into the wilder shores of the writer's consciousness, a graphic example being *Nienasycenie* ("Insatiability", 1930), which revolves around an epic futuristic struggle between a Poland ruled by the dictator Kocmołuchowicz ("Slovenly") and communist hordes from China hell-bent on invading Europe from the east.

In a sense, reality fulfilled Witkacy's worst apocalyptic nightmares. Following the Nazi invasion of Poland in 1939, the artist fled east. On learning that the Soviets were also advancing into Poland in the pincer movement agreed under the terms of the notorious Molotov-Ribbentrop Pact, a devastated Witkacy committed suicide, a legendary act that ensured his place in the pantheon of noble patriots, as well as that of great artists, in the eyes of the nation.

Eating, drinking and entertainment

Eating is never a problem in Zakopane. If you want a fast snack there are plenty of cafés, fast-food joints and streetside *zapiekanki* merchants to choose from. **Restaurants** are plentiful, too, with very good ones in the hotels *Gazda* and *Giewont*, and a very upmarket one, aimed at tourists, at the *Kasprowy*. A local product worth trying at least once are the bun-shaped **sheep's milk cheeses** you see on sale all over town: don't be put off by the strong smell – they're very tasty. **Bars and nightlife** are a growing feature of the town centre, though many of the venues are pretty tacky. Out of season, everything is quiet by 10pm.

Restaurants

Chata Zbójnicka, ul. Jagiellónska. One of the best of the new places, specializing in regional cuisine.

Czardasz, ul. Nowotarska. Hungarian restaurant with a good line in spicy goulashes, but the wine is overpriced.

Empire, ul. Krupówki. A newish and vaguely upmarket Chinese restaurant. Open till midnight.

Giewont, ul. Kościuszki 1 (☎12011). Restaurant in the hotel of the same name. Standard international cuisine plus a number of regional specialities – the dishes with goat's cheese are worth a try. Reservations advisable.

Karczma Redykołka, at the corner of ul. Krupówki and Kościeliska. A touristy traditional-style inn with waitresses dressed in local costume.

Obrochtówka, ul. Kraszewskiego 10a. Reasonably priced and easily the best of the traditional-style restaurants – the *placki* (potato pancakes) in particular are excellent. Folk music Thursday evenings.

Robber's Hut, ul. Jagiellońska. Restaurant decked out as a mock mountain-smuggler's den, serving traditional *górale* fare.

Śwarna, ul. Kościeliska 4. A no-nonsense traditionally oriented restaurant.

U Wnuka, ul. Kościeliska 8. Wooden building housing another restaurant focusing on regional dishes, but tends to be less crowded than a lot of the others.

Venecjia, ul. Krupówki. Passable Italian restaurant. Open late.

Watra, ul. Zamoyskiego 2. Often has live music at night.

Entertainment

Entertainment varies according to season. Founded in memory of the man who staged many of his own plays here, the **Teatr im. Stanisława Witkiewicza**, at ul. Chramcówki 15, north of the train station, stages a regular variety of performances (serious and not so serious) throughout the year – check with the tourist offices for current details. The biggest cultural event, however, is the annual **International Festival of Mountain Folklore** held since the late 1960s, and now occupying the prime tourist season mid-August spot. A week-long extravaganza of concerts, music competitions and street parades, alongside the sizeable contingent of local *górale* ensembles, the festival draws highlander groups from a dozen or so European countries. The timing means hefty crowds are guaranteed, and there's enough going on to keep most people happy. Along with the summer musical events in the Pieniny region further east (see p.465) you won't get a better chance to sample the tub-thumping exuberance of a *górale* choir dressed to the nines, whooping their way through a string of joyous mountain melodies. Other local cultural events of note are the **Karol Szymanowski Music Days** held every July, featuring classical concerts by Polish and guest foreign artists in and around the town, and an **Art Film Festival**, held every other March.

ADVENTURE SPORTS

Poles have been enjoying the winter **ski** slopes in Zakopane for as long as there's been a resort, and in the case of the *górale*, for a good deal longer. The **winter season** traditionally runs from December to March, though the snow has been very unpredictable in recent years. **Slopes** in the area vary greatly in difficulty and quality. In accordance with international standards, they are graded black, red, blue and green in order of difficulty, with the cross-country routes marked in orange. Many otherwise closed areas of the National Park are open to skiers once the snows have set in, but you must remember to avoid the avalanche (*lawina*) areas marked on signs and maps, and check conditions before leaving the marked routes.

The most popular runs are on **Kasprowy Wierch**, mostly off-piste. This route is serviced by the main cable car and a couple of pretty decrepit old chair lifts (supposedly in line for replacement soon). There are a fair number of shorter routes in easy striking distance of the town itself: from the Gubałówka funicular (get there early to avoid the worst of the queues), on Antałówka hill, in Bystre (ski jumps, slalom and racing slopes) and immediately above the train station. One of the best slopes around is at **Bukowina Tatrzańska**, a few kilometres east of Zakopane and served by local bus. All of these are serviced by chair lifts: passes for each lift are bought at the hut next to the ski-tow (around 5zł per day). If you haven't brought your own gear with you, you can **rent skis** and other equipment at a number of sports shops in town such as *Alpin Sport,* on ul. Granwaldzka (ski rental around 20zł per day).

Mountain-biking has now established itself as a wildly popular summertime pursuit, with legions of enthusiastic young bikers heading for the slopes. After an initial flush of enthusiasm, the National Park authorities have woken up to the environmental threats posed by unregulated biking access to the slopes. There are now five designated **cycle routes** within the park area: around Morskie Oko; up to Hala Gąsienicowa: to Kałatówki; along the Kościeliska and Chocołowska valleys; and up to Droga pod Reglami. In addition, there are a number of cycle routes in the hills north of Zakopane – some 650km of them in total. You can **rent mountain bikes** at a number of places around town, including *Bzyck*, ul. Krupówki 37 (☎14707), *Rent a Bike*, ul. Sienkiewicza 37 (☎64266) and the *Pod Krokwią* camping site. Bike rental costs around 30zł a day.

Paragliding, a relatively recent arrival on the local scene, is already proving very popular, though it's confined to areas outside the National Park, including the Nosal slope, Gubałówka and Wałowa Góra. If you've never tried it before, there are several instructors in town who also rent all the necessary gear (around 100zł a day). Try the *Fly Centre*, ul. Krupówki 12 (☎63859), or the sports shop-cum-flying school at ul. Kościuszki 15 (☎63365).

The latest addition to the adventure sports league is a **metal slide** (*rynna*) set up in 1994 on the Gubałówka slope. You shoot down the 750-metre-long slide in a special sledge, reaching speeds of up to 40km/h. The ride (around 20zł a time) is already a confirmed favourite.

Listings

American Express c/o *Orbis*, ul. Krupówki 22 (Mon–Fri 8am–6pm, Sat 8am–noon).

Banks *PKO Bank*, ul. Gimnazjalna 1 (Mon–Fri 10.15am–2.30pm), and *Pekao*, ul. Gimnazjalna 1, both accept travellers' cheques.

Bike rental ul. Sienkiewicka 37 (daily 9am–6pm; ☎4266).

Bus information ☎14603 (9am–6pm).

Car repairs ul. Nowsterska 35.

Hospital ul. Kamieniec 10 (☎62021).

Pharmacy ul. Krupówki 37 & 39; ul. Witkiewicza 3.

Post office ul. Krupówki.

Police ul. Jagiellońska 12.

Night shops *Baca*, ul. Krupówki 32 (daily 2.30pm–7am); *Rarytas*, ul. Chramcówki, 3 (daily 4pm–6am).

Swimming pools *Hotel Sport*, ul. Czecha, and *Hotel Kasprowy*, Polana Szymoszkowa; both have indoor pools which can be used by non-residents for a small fee. In addition, there are hot springs at ul. Jagiellońska on the Antatówka slope.

Taxi *Radio Taxi* ☎14232.

Telephone Phone centre on the corner of Kósciuszki and Krupówki (Mon–Fri 7am–9pm, Sat 8am–9pm, Sun 8am–noon). There are plenty of blue phone-card booths around town also.

Train information ☎14504 (9am–6pm).

Around Zakopane

If hiking in the Tatras proper sounds too energetic, there are a number of easy and enjoyable walks in the foothills and valleys surrounding Zakopane. A useful **map** to look out for is *Tatry i Podhale* (1:75,000).

Gubałówka Hill

There's an excellent view of the Tatras from the top of **Gubałówka Hill** (1120m) to the west of town (follow ul. Krupówki out from the centre). However, it's very popular, as you'll see from the long queues for the **funicular** (July & Aug 7.30am–9pm, Sept–June 8am–5pm). Walking up is possible, though strenuous (1hr). From the summit, a good day reveals the high peaks to the south in sharp relief against clear blue mountain skies. Most people linger a while over the view, browse in the souvenir shops and head back down again, but the long wooded hill ridge is the starting point of several excellent **hikes**, taking you through characteristic Podhale landscape.

To the **west**, from the top of the funicular, past the refreshment stop, the trails begin as a single path, which soon divides. Continue south along the ridge and you gradually descend to the Czarny Dunajec valley (black route), ending up at the village of **WITÓW**, around two hours' walking in all; buses back to Zakopane take fifteen minutes. Alternatively, take the north fork and it's a four-hour hike to the village of **CHOCHOŁÓW**, with its fine wooden houses and church; you can get here by two routes, either following the track (which soon becomes a road) through the village of Dzianisz, or taking the cross-country route marked *Szlak im. Powstania Chochołowskiego* on the *Tatry i Podhale* map.

East of the funicular, the main path leads to **PORONIN**, on the Zakopane–Kraków road, a sleepy village distinguished by a statue of Lenin. The great man spent nearly two years here (1913–14), which used to be commemorated in a small Lenin museum, closed for the new political era. **Places to stay** include the *Maria*, ul. Za Torem 42a (③), the *Matuska*, ul. Tatrzańska 36 (☎74207; ③), the *Paryżanka*, ul. Stasikowka 1 (③) and *Pawilkowski*, ul. Kasprowicza 1 (☎74412; ④). A steep climb up the marked path east of the village takes you to a hilltop area with wonderful views. Continue east from here and you come to **BUKOWINA**

TATRZAŃSKA, a largish village with buses back to Zakopane (15min). An established holiday base, **accommodation** options have increased of late, fuelled by the privatization of workers' holiday centres. The *Tęcza*, ul. Słoneczna 10 (☎2763; ③), *Warta*, ul. Bundowy Wierch 47 (☎7203; ③), *Śnieżka*, ul. Tatrzańska 15 (☎7205; ③) and *Szatas*, ul. Długa 150 (☎77566; ③), are all reasonable. There's also a private accommodation office at ul. Słoneczna 17 (9am–5pm; ☎7293) and a **restaurant**.

Dolina Białego and Dolina Strążyska

For some easy and accessible valley hiking, Dolina Białego and Dolina Strążyska each provide a relaxed long afternoon's walk from Zakopane; taken together they would make an enjoyable and not over-strenuous day's outing.

Leaving Zakopane to the south, along ul. Strążyska, you reach **Dolina Strążyska** after around an hour's walk. At the end of the valley (3hr) you can climb to the **Hala Strążyska**, a beautiful high mountain pasture (1303m); the **Siklawica waterfall**, on the way, makes an enjoyable rest point, a stream coursing down from the direction of Giewont. The views are excellent too, with Mount Giewont (1694m) rearing up to the south, and to the north a wonderful panorama of Zakopane and the surrounding countryside. Walk east along the meadow to the top of **Dolina Białego** and you can descend the deep, stream-crossed valley, one of the gentlest and most beautiful in the region, continuing back to the outskirts of Zakopane (6–7hr in total).

Dolina Chochołowska and Dolina Kościeliska

Two of the loveliest valleys of the area are Dolina Chochołowska and Dolina Kościeliska, both a bus ride west of town and offering an immensely enjoyable and rewarding full day's hiking excursion. It would also be possible to combine the two, staying at the *Chochołowska* hostel (see below) or one of the mountain/shepherds' huts along the way, some of which are marked on the map. For the latter, the *Halit* inn (☎70353) in Kiry (see below) makes an excellent overnight base.

Dolina Chochołowska, the longest valley in the region, follows the course of a stream deep into the hills. From Zakopane, take a bus toward Polana Huciska, a couple of kilometres into the valley. From the car park at the head of the valley, it's a good hour's walk to the *Chochołowska* hostel, beautifully situated overlooking the meadows, with the high western Tatras and the Czech border behind. A clandestine meeting between the pope and Lech Wałęsa took place here in 1983 and is commemorated by a tableau on the wall. The steep paths up the eastern side lead to ridges that separate the valley from Dolina Kościeliska – one path, from a little way beyond the car park, connects the two valleys, making the cross trip possible.

Dolina Kościeliska is a classic beauty spot, much in evidence on postcards of the region. To get here, take the bus to the hamlet of **KIRY** and set off down the stone valley track ahead. For around 40zł a horse-drawn cart will run you down the first section of the valley to a point known as Polana Pisana, but from here on it's walkers only. A distinctive feature of Kościeliska is the **caves** in the limestone cliffs – once the haunts of robbers and bandits, legend has it. Take a detour off to the left from Polana Pisana – marked *jaskinia* (caves) – and you can visit various examples, including **Jaskinia Mroźna**, where the walls are permanently encased in ice.

Beyond Polana Pisana, the narrow upper valley is a beautiful stretch of crags, gushing water, caves and greenery reminiscent of the English Lake District, leading to the *Hala Ornak* **hostel**, a popular overnight stop with a restaurant. Day walkers return back down the valley to take the bus back to Zakopane, but if you want to continue, two marked paths lead beyond the hostel: the eastern route takes you the short distance to **Smreczyński Staw** (1226m), a tiny mountain lake surrounded by forest; the western route follows a high ridge over to Dolina Chochołowska – a demanding walk only for the fit.

The Tatras

Poles are serious mountaineers, with an established network of climbing clubs, and it's in the **Tatras** that everyone starts and the big names train. Most of the peaks are in the 2000–2500m range, but these unimpressive statistics belie their status, and their appearance. For these are real mountains, snowbound on their heights for most of the year and supporting a good skiing season in December and January. They are as beautiful as any mountain landscape in northern Europe, the ascents taking you on boulder-strewn paths alongside woods and streams up to the ridges, where grand, windswept peaks rise in the brilliant alpine sunshine. Wildlife thrives here: the whole area was turned into a National Park in the 1950s and supports rare species such as lynx, golden eagles and brown bear, and there's a good chance of glimpsing them.

The steadily increasing volume of climbers, walkers and skiers using the slopes is having its effect on the area though, and in a bid to generate funds for local environmental protection, the park authorities have now imposed a (nominal) entry charge on all visitors entering the park area, collected at booths at the main access points to the mountains. Groups of ten people or more must have an official guide, arranged, unless you're part of a pre-booked touring group, through the park offices in Zakopane (ul. Chałubińskiego 10; ☎63203). Tussles between the conservationist-minded park authorities and local tourism developers are also holding back **skiers**, in an attempt to protect the rich flora of the slopes, and the authorities have steadfastly refused to countenance the building of any further facilities, such as new ski-lifts, within the territory of the park.

Though many of the peak and ridge climbs are for experienced climbers only, much is accessible to regular walkers, with waymarked paths which give you the top-of-the-world exhilaration of bagging a peak. For skiers, despite the relative paucity of lifts and hi-tech facilities, there are some high-quality pistes, including a dry slope running down from peaks such as **Kasprowy Wierch** and Nosal.

Afraid of their citizens catching "the Polish disease" (Solidarity), the Czechs virtually closed this part of the border in 1980, and for the next ten years, hikers were confronted with the somewhat comical sight of uniformed police sweating it out over the mountain passes. Things have eased up these days, with the current editions of the *Tatry i Podhale* map showing cross-border walks in great detail, though the border police are still in evidence and a number of official crossing points remain mysteriously closed to foreigners (see *Basics*, p.7 for details). Where crossing is permitted, most foreigners just need a passport stamp, however, and the new political climate means that exploration of the whole Tatra region is possible for the first time since the war.

Practicalities

A decent **map** of the mountains is indispensable. The best is the *Tatrzański Park Narodowy* (1:30,000), which has all the paths accurately marked and colour-coded. The often hard to obtain *Polskie Tatry* **guidebook** is likewise invaluable, giving all the main walking routes in several languages, though the English version is still awaiting a long overdue reprint. Alternatively, you could consider picking up a copy of *The High Tatras* (Cicerone Press) written jointly by an Englishman and Slovak woman, an authentic guide to hikes in the mountains aimed at the serious enthusiast.

Overnighting in the *PTTK*-run **huts** dotted across the mountains is an experience in itself. There are seven of them in all, clearly marked on the *Tatrzański Park Narodowy* map (for up-to-date information on openings, check at tourist offices in Zakopane). In summer, the huts are packed with student backpackers from all over the country, and are an ideal place to mix in, preferably over a bottle of vodka. As they generally can't afford the beds, they kip down on the floor, and if it's really crowded you'll probably be joining them. **Food** is basic, but pricey for Poles, and most bring their own. Even if you don't want to lug large weights around the mountain tops, a supply of basic rations is a good idea. **Camping** isn't allowed in the National Park area, and rock-climbing only with a permit – ask at the park offices (see above) for details. For anyone attempting more than a quick saunter, the right **footwear and clothing** are, of course, essential.

Walks in the Tatras

The easiest way up to the peaks is by **cable car** (July & Aug 7.30am–8pm, Sept–June 8am–5pm; 10zł return) from the hamlet of **KUŹNICE**, a three-kilometre walk or bus journey south from Zakopane along the Dolina Bystrego. In summer, the cable car is a sell-out, making advance booking at the *Orbis* office a virtual necessity, unless you're prepared to turn up before 8am; the only way round this – and it doesn't always work – is to buy your ticket for ten times the normal price from the touts lurking near the entrance. For the journey down, priority is always given to people who've already got tickets, however, return tickets only allow you two hours at the top – this is fine if you only want to get up to Kasprowy Wierch (see below), but no good if you're planning more extended hiking. One way of avoiding the biggest queues is to make the ascent on Sunday mornings when the majority of Poles are likely to be at Mass.

Kasprowy Wierch – and descents to Kuźnice

The cable car ends near the summit of **Kasprowy Wierch** (1985m), where weather-beaten signs indicate the border with Slovakia. From here, many day-trippers simply walk back down to Kuźnice through the Hala Gąsienicowa (1hr). An equally popular option is to walk up and return by cable car (2hr 30min). A rather longer alternative is to strike west to the cross-topped summit of **Giewont** (1894m), the "Sleeping Knight" that overlooks Zakopane. Watch out if it's been raining, however, as the paths here get pretty slippery and are very worn in places. The final bit of the ascent is rocky with secured chains to aid your scramble to the top. From the summit, topped with a tall cross, the views can be spectacular on a good day. For the return, head down to Kuźnice through the

---

HIKING IN THE TATRAS

It is as well to remember that the Tatras are an alpine range and as such demand some respect and preparation. The most important rule is to stick to the marked paths, and to arm yourself in advance with a decent **map**. Take a whistle (blow six times every minute if you need help) and a flask of water.

The **weather** is always changeable, and you should not venture out without waterproofs and sturdy boots: most rain falls in the summer, when there may also be thunderstorms and even hail- and snow-showers. Even on a warm summer's day in the valleys, it can be below freezing at the peaks. Set out **early** (the weather is always better in the morning), and tell someone when and where you're going. Don't leave the tree line (about 2000m) unless visibility is good, and when the clouds close in, start descending immediately.

In addition, respect the National Park rules: don't leave any rubbish, keep to the marked paths and don't pick flowers or disturb the wild animals.

Dolina Kondratowa past the *Hala Kondratowa* hostel. This is fairly easy going and quite feasible in a day if you start out early.

East: the Eagles' Path and Morskie Oko Lake

East of Kasprowy Wierch, the walking gets tougher. From **Świnica** (2300m), a strenuous ninety-minute walk, experienced hikers continue along the **Orła Perć** (Eagles' Path), a challenging, exposed ridge with spectacular views. The *Pięc Stawów* **hostel**, in the high valley of the same name, provides overnight shelter at the end (4hr).

From the hostel you can hike back down Dolina Roztoki to **Łysa Polana**, a border crossing point in the valley (2hr), and get a bus back to Zakopane. An alternative is to continue east to the **Morskie Oko Lake** (1399m; 1hr 30min). Encircled by spectacular sheer cliff faces and alpine forest, this large glacial lake is one of the Tatras' big attractions, most frequently approached on the winding forest road from the border crossing at Łysa Polana, some 11km away. During the summer, the paths round the lake are packed with visitors out for the day from Zakopane. Crumbling roads mean there's currently no bus service direct to **Morskie Oko** from Zakopane, the nearest bus stopping at Polana Palenica, east of the resort. If you don't feel like walking much, you can rent a horse-drawn buggy to take you to Włosienica from Polana Palenica, in striking distance of the lake: at a current cost of around 25zł for the round trip it's a fair bargain. The journey takes under an hour each way.

The *Morskie Oko* **hostel**, situated by the side of the lake, provides a convenient base for the ascent of **Rysy** (2499m), the highest peak in the Polish Tatras. Closer to hand, on the same red-marked route is **Czarny Staw** (1580m), a lake which if anything, appears even chillier than Morskie Oko.

East to the Pieniny

East of the Tatras, the mountains scale down to a succession of lower ranges – *beskidy* as they're known in Polish – stretching along the Slovak border. The walking here is less dramatic than in the Tatras, but excellent nonetheless, and the locals are a good bunch too, including *górale* and a long-established Slovak minority. The highlights of the region are the **Pieniny Mountains**, hard by the Slovak border, and a raft run through the **Dunajec Gorge**, far below.

Transport in this little-known region can be a bit of a struggle, away from the immedate vicinity of **Szczawnica**, a spa town that makes the best base for exploring the Pieniny.

The Spisz region

The road east from Nowy Targ to Szczawnica is one of the most attractive in the country, following the broad valley of the Dunajec through the **Spisz**, a backwoods region whose villages are renowned for their wooden houses, churches and folk art. Annexed by Poland from the newly created Czechoslovak state in 1920, for centuries it was part of the semi-autonomous province of Spis (Slovak)/Spisz (Polish)/Zips (German) that formed part of the Hungarian kingdom. The old aura of a quiet rural backwater remains, the region's Slovak minority bearing testimony to its historic borderland position. Buses cover the route four or five times a day.

DĘBNO, 14km from Nowy Targ, boasts one of the best-known **wooden churches** in the country, a shingled, steep-roofed larch building, put together without using nails and surrounded by a charming wicket fence, with a profile vaguely reminiscent of a snail. Inside, the full length of walls and ceiling is covered with exuberant, brilliantly preserved fifteenth-century polychromy and wood **carving**. Their subjects are an enchanting mix of folk, national and religious motifs, including some fine hunting scenes and curiously Islamic-looking geometric patterns. In the centre of the building, fragments survive of the original roodscreen, supporting a tree-like cross, while the original fifteenth-century altarpiece triptych features an unusually militant-looking Saint Catherine. In addition, there's a fine carved statue of Saint Nicholas, a medieval wooden tabernacle and some banners reputedly left by Jan Sobieski on his return from defeating the Turks in Vienna in 1683. The local priest, a fervent enthusiast of his church, is often on hand to show people around (8am–noon & 2–5pm). If he's not there and the church is shut, you can usually find him in his house, just over the road. For an overnight stay, there's a **youth hostel** (July–Aug) in the village.

Just to the south of the road, 12km on from Dębno, is **CZORSZTYN**, a small village with a memorable, if very ruined, **Castle**. From its heights you get a sweeping view over the valley and to the castle of Niedzica (see below) across the mouth of the Dunajec Gorge. The valley itself is the subject of a controversial hydroelectric **dam project**, whose initial stages are already disfiguring the land below Czorsztyn. Environmentalists fear that the flooding of the Czorsztyn area will transform the Spisz into mosquito-ridden marshland, but despite strong protests and considerable technical problems, the project is inching ahead, supported by the heavy industry lobby – though the government has recently promised a review of the whole project.

Niedzica and west along the Slovak border
NIEDZICA lies just across the gorge from Czorsztyn, a thirty-minute walk heading south and over a pedestrian bridge or, more circuitously, by road to the west of Czorsztyn; some of the Nowy Targ–Szczawnica buses take a detour here en route.

The village occupies a strategic position at a major confluence of the Dunajec, with a large tributary plunging down from Slovakia. Control of this valley and the border territory explains the presence of the **castle**, perched above the river. Originally raised in the fourteenth century as a stronghold on the Hungarian border, it was reconstructed in its current Renaissance style in the early 1600s, and today lies under threat from the hydroelectric scheme, which some experts believe will erode its rock foundations. It today houses a **Museum of Spisz Folk Art** (Tues–Sun 9am–5pm) and an artists' retreat. A Tintin-like folk tale associates the castle with the Incas. The wife of the last descendant of the Inca rulers allegedly lived here in the late eighteenth century, and left a hidden document detailing the legendary Inca treasure buried in Lake Titicaca in Peru – a document supposedly discovered in 1946. There's a basic **hotel** here (②), currently the only place to stay in the surroundings.

To the **west of Niedzica**, a little-frequented backroad winds its way towards Nowy Targ and Zakopane through the heart of the Spisz. Most villages here were effectively cut off from the outside world well into the nineteenth century, and serfdom was only abolished here in 1931. It still feels like another world, particularly in villages like **TRYBSZ** and **ŁAPSZE** which have Slovak populations. If you get the chance, visit on a Sunday morning, when you may catch the music of the excellent local choirs. The churches in both villages are equally enjoyable, the one in Trybsz, a wooden construction whose interior is lined with a fine sequence of mid-seventeenth-century frescoes illustrating biblical scenes and the lives of the saints in colourful, naive relief.

Szczawnica and around

East of the Tatras, there's a plethora of spa towns amid the river gorges and steep valleys of the border area. **SZCZAWNICA**, one-time haunt of Nobel Prize-winning novelist Henryk Sienkiewicz, is a highly picturesque example, sited on the edge of the sparkling River Dunajec below the peaks of the Pieniny. It is also by far the most visited town in the region, crowded through the summer with all types of mountain holidaymakers: canoeists setting off down the gorge, hikers heading off to the hills, industrial workers recuperating in the sanatoria.

Buses run here from both Nowy Targ (40km) and, on a slightly roundabout route, from Zakopane (50km), dropping you in the centre of town, by the river. From here it's a short walk up to the bustling square, and the staid health establishments of the **upper town**. In the communist era, Szczawnica's alkaline spring water was consumed by miners and steelworkers, now replaced by the regular brand of health-seeking tourists, Polish and foreign; casual visitors are free to wander in and sample the waters. There's little else to see in town, unless you happen to be around during *górale* folk events. The attraction for most foreign visitors lies in getting out to explore the Pieniny and the Dunajec Gorge.

There are no real hotels, but **accommodation** isn't a problem: in season half the town population rent out rooms in their homes for next to nothing and there's the usual full range of former workers' holiday *pensjonaty*, notably the *Jakubówka*, ul. Jana Wiktora 17 (☎01872/22239; ③); *Palma*, ul. Park Górny 14 (☎01872/22324; ③); *Pod 9*, ul. Manifestu Lipcowego 9 (☎01872/22676; ③); and, next door, *Wiktorialis* (☎01872/22325; ③). You can arrange lodgings through the *PTTK* office at ul. Manifestu Lipcowego 2a, the Pieniny bureau, ul. Wygon 4a, or at *Orbis*, on the main square at plac Dietla 7. More spartan alternatives are the *Orlica* **PTTK hostel** at ul. Pienińska 12 (☎01872/22248; ②), right on the edge of the gorge, a kilometre south along the river, and the *Pod Bereśnikem* hostel, ul. Języki 22, also well out of the centre.

Krościenko

The small town of **KROŚCIENKO**, a ten-minute bus ride north of Szczawnica, is an alternative base for the Pieniny, located right at the edge of the mountains and the starting point for hikes to the Trzy Korony (see below). It again has the possibility of **private rooms**, arranged through the **PTTK office** at ul. Jagiellońska 28 (☎01872/3059), and an undistinguished collection of restaurants.

Dolina Homole

A short local excursion worth considering is to the **Dolina Homole**, 8km east of Szczawnica. This is a peaceful valley of wooded glades and streams, and you can walk up to the surrounding hilltops in less than two hours. There's a *PTTK* **campsite** up here too.

From Szczawnica, it's a fifteen-minute bus ride east to the village of **JAWORKI**, starting point for the walk and an interesting example of the ethnic and religious twists characterizing the eastern hill country. At first sight, the late eighteenth-century **church**, a cavernous construction with an elaborately decorated balcony, looks like a regular Catholic building, but a glance at the iconostasis behind the altar indicates a different history. Although now Roman Catholic, it was originally a Uniate *cerkiew*, in what was the westernmost point of Lemk settlement in Poland (see p.338). Today only a couple of Lemk families remain. If you find the church closed, ask for the key from the house next door. A basic **bar/restaurant** (closed Mon) in the village serves fine fish dishes and *Okocim* beer.

The Pieniny

A short range of Jurassic limestone peaks, rearing above the spectacular Dunajec Gorge, the **Pieniny** offer some stiff hill walking, but require no serious climbing to reach the 1000-metre summits. Jagged outcrops are set off by abundant greenery, the often humid mountain microclimate supporting a rich and varied flora. Like the Tatras, the Pieniny are an officially designated National Park and have a network of controlled paths. The detailed *Pieniński Park Narodowy* (1:22,500) **map** is useful and is available in most tourist offices and bookstores.

Trzy Korony

The main range, a ten-kilometre stretch between Czorsztyn and Szczawnica, is the most popular hiking territory, with the peaks of **Trzy Korony** (Three Crowns; 982m) the big target.

There are several routes up, the best-known leading from **Krościenko**. From the bus stop here you can follow the signs – and in summer the packs of hikers – south on the yellow route. The path soon begins to climb through the mountainside woods, with plenty of meadows and lush clearings on the way. Around two hours from Krościenko, you'll reach **Okrąglica**, the highest peak of the Trzy

---

PIENINY GORALE: MUSIC EVENTS

Like the Podhale, the Pieniny region is populated by **górale highlanders** who for much of the century have been migrating to the United States in great numbers; it's not uncommon to come across broad Chicago accents in the villages. To the outsider, the main distinction between the Podhale and Pieniny clans is the colours of their **costumes** – the reds, browns and blacks of the western Podhale giving way to the purple-blues of the Pieniny decorated jackets. Like their Podhale neighbours, the *górale* of the Pieniny dress up traditionally on Sundays and for other major community events – weddings, festivals and the like. The men's costume consists of tight-fitting woollen trousers decorated with coloured strips of embroidery (*parzenice*), high leather cummerbund-type bands round the waist, decorated jackets and waistcoats and a feather-topped hat. The women wear thin woollen blouses, thickly pleated skirts festooned with flowers and brightly coloured headscarves. The men also go in for thick embossed leather shoes (*kierpce*) of the type you can pick up in the tourist shops. Besides costume, the clans have their own distinct **dialects**, and even Polish speakers find it hard to follow a Pieniński in full swing.

Music is the most accessible aspect of their culture. In summer, you may well catch vocal ensembles at open-air folk evenings held in Szczawnica or Krościenko – a good excuse for everyone to dress up and sing their hearts out. While the harmonies and vocal style are similar in both *górale* regions, the Pieniński make more use of instruments – violins and a thumping bass in particular – to create a sound that has marked similarities to Slovak and Hungarian country styles. The visiting crowds are overwhelmingly Polish at these traditional old-time romps, and for the atmosphere alone it's well worth joining them.

Korony, via some chain-bannistered steps. On a clear day there's an excellent view over the whole area: the high Tatras off to the west, the slopes of Slovakia to the south, and the Dunajec Gorge far below.

Many hikers take the same route back, but two alternatives are worth considering. One is to walk to Szczawnica, a two- or three-hour trip. Head back along the route you came as far as Bajków Groń (679m), about three-quarters of the way down, and from there follow the blue path across the mountains south to Sokolica and down to the river, where you can get a boat across to the *Orlica* hostel. The other, if you want to combine the walk with the Dunajec Gorge, is to descend the mountain south to Sromowce Niżne (2hr), one of the two starting points for the raft trip upriver (see below).

The Dunajec Gorge

Below the heights of the Pieniny the fast-moving Dunajec twists and turns below great limestone rockfaces and craggy peaks. The river is a magnet for **canoeists**, who shoot fearlessly through the often powerful rapids; for the less intrepid, the two- to three-hour **raft trip** provides a gentler though thoroughly enjoyable version of the experience. Tourists have been rafting down these waters since the 1830s, a tradition derived in turn from the ancient practice of floating logs down river to the mills and ports. Contrary to what the tourist brochures lead you to believe, this is not exactly white water rafting – the journey is smooth-going, giving you the chance to appreciate the scenic surroundings of forest, fields and sheer limestone crags – the real plusses of the experience.

The most popular **starting point** for this trip is **KĄTY**, a few hundred metres east of Sromowce Wyżne; regular buses run to Kąty from Szczawnica and Nowy Targ. There's a second landing stage further downriver at **SROMOWCE NIŻNE**, easier to reach if you've been hiking in the Pieniny; this village has a large *PTTK* hostel and lies across the river from the Slovak settlement and monastery of **ČERVENY KLÁŠTOR**, the main Slovakian starting point for raft trips.

Weather permitting, the rafting season runs from early May to late October, operating 8am to 4pm between May and August; finishing at 1pm in the last two months. In season, rafts leave as soon as they're full, and the earlier you get here the less likely it is you'll have to queue up. If you want to be really sure, advance bookings can be made through local *Orbis* offices, regional hotels (in Kraków and Zakopane for example), and tourist offices, including *Tatry* and *Związek Podhalański* bureaux.

The rafts are sturdy log constructions, made of five pontoons held together with rope and carrying up to ten passengers, plus two navigators in traditional Pieniny costume. Here, as further east, the river forms the border with Slovakia, and at several points, Slovak villages face their Polish counterparts across the banks, with their own rafters and canoeists hugging the southern side of the river. After plenty of sharp twists and spectacular cliffs, the rafts end up at Szczawnica, from where buses return to Kąty until 4pm, from a stop a few minutes' walk from the landing stage.

travel details

Trains

Częstochowa to: Katowice (hourly; 1–2hr); Kielce (10 daily; 2hr); Kraków (11 daily; 2–3hr); Łódź (15 daily; 2–3hr); Warsaw (14 daily; 3–4hr).

Kielce to: Częstochowa (10 daily; 2hr); Kraków (8 daily; 2–3hr); Łódź (1 daily; 4hr); Warsaw (12 daily; 3–4hr).

Kraków to: Białystok (1 daily; 10hr); Bydgoszcz (3 daily; 7–9hr); Częstochowa (10 daily; 2–4hr); Gdańsk (3 daily; 5–11hr); Katowice (26 daily; 1hr 30min–2hr); Kielce (11 daily; 2–3hr); Krynica (8 daily; 5–6hr); Lublin (3 daily; 5–7hr); Nowy Sącz (11 daily; 3–4hr; 1 express); Poznań (7 daily; 7–8hr); Przemyśl (12 daily; 3–5hr; 1 express); Rzeszów (20 daily; 2–3hr); Szczecin (5 daily; 12–14hr); Warsaw (19 daily; 2hr 30min–6hr; expresses every hour from 6.15am–12.15pm, every 2 hrs 2.15–6.15pm); Wrocław (15 daily; 4–6hr); Zakopane (15 daily; 2–5hr; 1 express).

Zakopane to: Częstochowa (3 daily; 7–8hr; sleepers); Gdańsk (1 daily; 12hr; sleeper); Katowice (2–4 daily; 4–6hr); Kraków (15 daily; 3–5hr); Warsaw (2 daily; 5–12hr).

Buses

Kraków to: Gieszyn (7 daily; 3hr); Nowy Targ (12 daily; 1–2hr); Sandomierz (2 daily; 4–5hr); Oświęcim (9 daily; 1hr 30min); Tarnów (15 daily; 1–1hr 30min); Zamość (2 daily; 6–8hr); Zakopane (8–10 daily; 2hr 30min–3hr).

Zakopane to: Bielsko-Biała (3 daily; 2hr 30min–4 hr); Katowice (2 daily; 4hr); Kraków (regular throughout the day; 2hr 30min–3hr); Lublin (1 daily; 8hr); Nowy Sącz (3 daily; 1–2hr); Nowy Targ (hourly; 30min); Reszów 1 daily; 3– 4hr); Szczawnica (5 daily; 1hr); Warsaw (1 daily; 8–9hr).

Planes

Kraków Gdańsk (1 daily July & Aug; 2hr); Warsaw (1–3 daily May–Oct; 1hr).

CHAPTER FIVE

SILESIA

I n Poland it's known as *Śląsk*, in the Czech Republic as *Slezsko*, in Germany as *Schlesien*: all three countries hold part of the frequently disputed province that's called in English **Silesia**. Since 1945, Poland has had the best of the argument, holding all of it except for a few of the westernmost tracts, a dominance gained as compensation for the Eastern Territories, which were incorporated into the USSR in 1939 and never returned.

Silesia presents a strange dichotomy. On the one hand there's its notorious heavy industry, especially in the huge **Katowice** conurbation, but also spread all over the region right down to the smallest village. Similar problems, as well as the countrywide legacy of wartime ruin, also affect the province's chief city, **Wrocław**, holding back its potential to become a rival to Kraków, Prague and Budapest as one of central Europe's most enticing cosmopolitan centres.

Silesia's other face is its role as a regional playground, the Sudeten mountain chain at its western extremity containing the most popular recreation areas in this corner of the country. Of these, the **Karkonosze National Park** is most visited, although the **Kłodzko region**'s outlying massifs provide some of Poland's best hiking country, along with a series of resorts offering everything from spa treatments to winter sports.

None of the other old ducal capitals, such as **Legnica**, **Świdnica**, **Brzeg**, **Opole** and **Cieszyn**, is developed to anything like the same extent as Wrocław; some possess an attractively small-town air while others seem indifferent to their historical heritage. Many of the province's finest surviving monuments are to be found in these towns; other slightly less accessible sights are the medieval fortifications of **Paczków** and the Baroque monasteries of **Legnickie Pole** (close to Legnica) and outstanding **Krzeszów**

Along with Wielkopolska and Małopolska, Silesia was a key component of the early Polish nation. Following the collapse of the country's monarchical system, the Duke of Silesia, a member of the Piast dynasty, sometimes served as Poland's uncrowned king. However, this system fell by the wayside in the wake of the Tartar invasions in the thirteenth century, and the duchy was divided into **Lower** and **Upper Silesia**, the northwestern and southeastern parts of the province respectively. As the succeeding dukes divided their territory among their sons, Silesia became splintered into eighteen principalities: hence what you see today is the legacy of a series of pint-sized former capitals, each with its fair share of churches and other religious institutions as well as a few surviving castles and palaces.

As each line died out, its land was incorporated into **Bohemia**, which eventually took over the entire province when the Piasts were extinguished in 1675 – by which time it had itself become part of the Austrian-dominated **Habsburg Empire**. In 1740, Frederick the Great, king of the militaristic state of **Prussia**, launched an all-out war on Austria, his pretext being a dubious claim his ancestors had once had to one of the Silesian principalities. After changing hands

several times, all but the southern part of the province was taken over by the
Prussians in 1763, becoming part of Bismarck's Germany in 1871.

In 1921 a plebiscite resulted in the industrial heartlands of the eastern province
becoming part of the recently resurrected Polish state. A further 860,000
Silesians opted for Polish rather than German nationality when given the choice
in 1945, and displaced Poles from the Eastern Territories were brought in to
replace the Germans who were now evacuated from the region. Yet, although
postwar Silesia has developed a strongly Polish character, people are often
bilingual and consider their prime loyalty to lie with Silesia rather than Poland. It
was only as a result of international pressure that the German government
decided not to stake a claim to Silesia as part of the unification talks;
notwithstanding the November 1990 treaty confirming the borders, the issue will
probably only be buried completely when Poland manages to close the gap in
living standards between the two countries.

Wrocław

Lower Silesia's historic capital, **WROCŁAW**, is the fourth largest city in Poland
with a population of 650,000. There's an exhilarating big city feel to it, yet behind
this animated appearance lies an extraordinary story of emergence from the
verge of ruin. Its special nature comes from the fact that it contains the souls of
two great cities. One of these is the city that has long stood on this spot, Slav by
origin but for centuries German (who knew it as Breslau). The other is **Lwów**
(now L'viv), capital of the Polish Ukraine, which was annexed by the Soviets in
1939 and retained by them in 1945. After the war, its displaced population was
encouraged to take over the severely depopulated Breslau, which had been
confiscated from Germany and offered them a ready-made home.

Part re-creation of Lwów, part continuation of the tradition of Breslau, postwar
Wrocław has a predominantly industrial character. However, there's ample
compensation for this in the old city's core. The multinational influences which
shaped it are graphically reflected in its architecture: the huge Germanic **brick
Gothic churches** which dominate the Od Town centre are intermingled with
Flemish-style Renaissance mansions, palaces and chapels of Viennese Baroque,
and boldly utilitarian public buildings from the early years of this century. The
tranquillity of the parks, gardens and rivers – which are crossed by over eighty
bridges – offer a ready escape from the urban bustle, while the city has a vibrant
cultural scene, its **theatre** tradition enjoying worldwide renown.

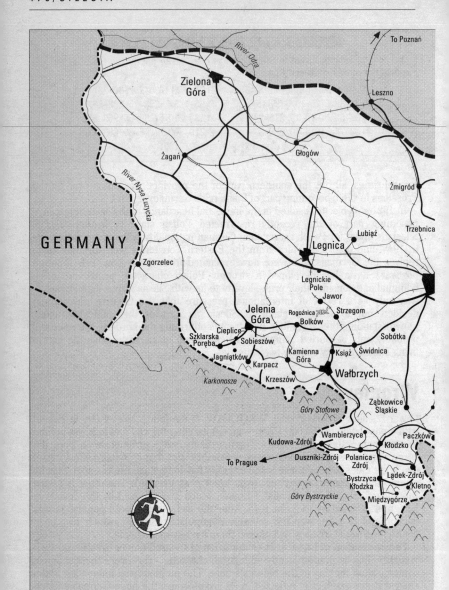

To Poznań

Leszno

River Odra

Zielona Góra

Żagań

Głogów

Żmigród

River Nysa Łużycka

GERMANY

Zgorzelec

Trzebnica

Lubiąż

Legnica

Legnickie Pole

Jawor

Jelenia Góra

Rogoźnica

Strzegom

Cieplice

Bolków

Szklarska Poręba

Sobieszów

Sobótka

Jagniątków

Kamienna Góra

Książ

Świdnica

Karpacz

Karkonosze

Krzeszów

Wałbrzych

Góry Stołowe

Ząbkowice Śląskie

Wambierzyce

Paczków

Kudowa-Zdrój

Kłodzko

To Prague

Duszniki-Zdrój

Polanica-Zdrój

Lądek-Zdrój

Bystrzyca Kłodzka

Kletno

Góry Bystrzyckie

Międzygórze

N

CZECH REPUBLIC

0   25 km

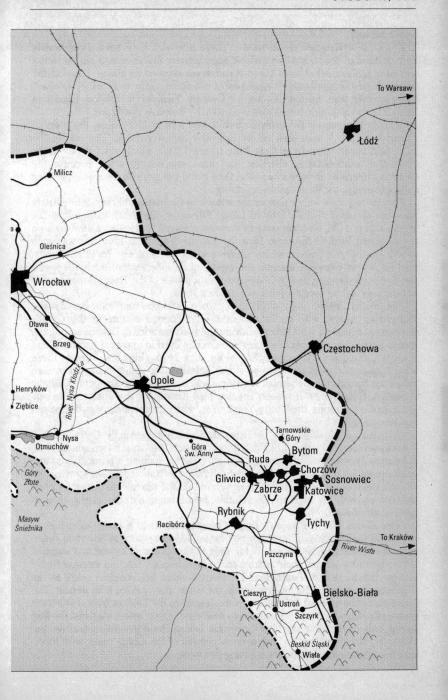

Some history

The origins of Wrocław are unknown. There may well have been a community here in Roman times, but the earliest documentary evidence is a ninth-century record of a Slav market town called **Wratislavia** situated on a large island at the point where the sand-banked shallows of the River Odra were easily crossed. Subsequently, this became known as **Ostrów Tumski** (Cathedral Island) in honour of the bishopric founded here in 1000 by Bolesław the Brave.

German designs on Wratislavia came to the fore in 1109, when the army of Emperor Henry V was seen off by Bolesław the Wrymouth. The site of the battlefield became known as **Psie Pole** (Dogs' Field), which today is one of the city's five administrative districts; the name supposedly arose because the Germans retreated in such chaos that they could not retrieve their dead, leaving the carcasses to the local canine population.

This proved to be only a temporary setback to German ambitions. Immediately after the creation of the duchy of Lower Silesia on the death of Bolesław the Wrymouth in 1138, German settlers were encouraged to develop a new town on the southern bank of the river. Destroyed by the Tartars in 1241, this was soon rebuilt on the grid pattern which survives to the present day. In 1259 the city, now known as **Breslau**, became the capital of an independent duchy. It joined the Hanseatic League, and its bishop became a prince of the Holy Roman Empire of Germany, ruling over a territory centred on Nysa.

The duchy lasted only until 1335, when Breslau was annexed by the **Bohemian kings**, who had sufficient clout to rebuff Kazimierz the Great's attempts to reunite it with Poland. During the two centuries of Bohemian rule the mixed population of Germans, Poles and Czechs lived in apparent harmony, and the city carried out the construction of its huge brick churches. Most of these were transferred to Protestant use at the Reformation, which managed to take root even though the Bohemian crown passed in 1526 to the staunchly Catholic **Austrian Habsburgs**. However, Breslau paid heavily for the duality of its religious make-up during the Thirty Years' War, when its economy was devastated and its population halved.

The years of Austrian rule saw Breslau become increasingly Germanized, a process accelerated when it finally fell to Frederick the Great's **Prussia** in 1763. It became Prussia's most important city after Berlin, gaining a reputation as one of the most loyal lynchpins of the state during the Napoleonic wars, when the French twice occupied it, only to be driven out. In the nineteenth century it grew enormously with the Industrial Revolution, becoming one of the largest cities of the German nation.

After World War I, Breslau's **Polish community** held a series of strikes in protest at their exclusion from the plebiscite held elsewhere in Silesia to determine the boundaries of Poland. Being only tweny thousand strong and outnumbered by thirty to one, their actions made little impact. Nor did Breslau figure among the targets of Polish leaders when looking for possible gains at the expense of a defeated Nazi Germany. In the event, they gained it by default. The Nazis made the suicidal decision, on retreating from the Eastern front, to turn the entire city into a fortress. It managed to hold out for four months against the Red Army, only capitulating on May 6, the day before the unconditional surrender. However, street fighting had left seventy percent of the city in ruins, with three-quarters of the civilian population having fled west.

The subsequent **return to Poland** of this huge city, rechristened with the modern Polish version of its original name, shocked the Germans more than any other of their many territorial losses. Its second transformation occurred much faster than that of seven centuries earlier: over the next few years, most of the remaining German citizens were shunted westward, while the inhabitants of Lwów were transferred here across Poland, bringing many of their institutions with them.

A relatively modest amount of government aid was made available for the **restoration of the city**, much of which remained in ruins for decades. Nonetheless, a distinctive and thoroughly Polish city has gradually emerged, one whose revival finally seemed complete in the 1980s when its population level surpassed the prewar figure of 625,000.

The **telephone code** for Wrocław is ☎071

Arrival, information and getting around

The main **train station**, Wrocław Główny – itself one of the city's sights – faces the broad boulevard of ul. Marz. Józefa Piłsudskiego, about fifteen minutes' walk south of the centre. All international and most major domestic services stop here, but there are two other stations you may find yourself using. **Wrocław Świebodzki**, another fine structure from the nineteenth-century rail heyday, located close to the inner ring road on pl. Sergiusza Kirowa, is used by most trains between Wrocław and Jelenia Góra, plus some of those to and from Legnica and Głogów. On pl. Staszica, well to the north of Ostrów Tumski and connected to the centre by trams #0 and #1, is **Wrocław Nadodrze**, for trains to and from Łódź and Trzebnica.

The main **bus station** is on ul. Sucha, at the back of the train station, the terminal also used by international services. The small bus stations beside each of the other train stations are only for destinations within the Wrocław district. Bus #106 runs between Wrocław Świebodzki and the **airport**, which lies in the suburb of Strachowice, 10km west of the centre.

The main organization for local tourism, **Odra-Tourist**, is at ul. Piłsudskiego 98 (Mon–Fri 8.30am–5pm, first Sat in month 8.30am–2pm; ☎44 41 01). For maps and leaflets, it's better to go to the small **tourist information office** at ul. Kazimierza Wielkiego 39 (Mon–Sat 10am–4pm; ☎44 31 11). The main **Orbis** offices, including car rental, are at Rynek 29 (Mon–Fri 9am–5pm, Sat 10am–2pm; ☎32665 or 33371), or try the *CIT* office situated in the southwest corner of the Rynek (Mon–Fri 9am–5pm, Sat 10am–4pm; ☎44 77 51). Similar services are available at several new private agencies mushrooming all over town, but these are mostly geared up for the lucrative international travel market. The English-speaking **Welcome-Tourist** on the first floor of the *Hotel Saigon*, ul. Wita Stwosza 22/23 (☎44 28 85) is also worth a try. Information about what's on is in the monthly *Informator Wrocławski*, available at news-stands.

Trams cover almost the entire built-up area of Wrocław; the #0, a circular route round the central area, makes an easy introduction to the city. A pair of historic trams, known as *Jaś i Małgosia* (Hänsel and Gretel) run throughout the summer.

Accommodation

Wrocław has **accommodation** to suit every taste and pocket, with prices within each category a good bit lower than in Warsaw, a touch lower than in Poznań and roughly comparable to Kraków's. There is no especially busy time of year. Rooms in **private houses** can be booked at the *Biuro Zakwaterowania* at ul. Piłsudskiego 98 (☎44 41 01).

Around the train station

Europejski, ul. Piłsudskiego 88 (☎31071). Good quality hotel close to the station, with recently refurbished and well-equipped rooms. ⑦.

Grand, ul. Piłsudskiego 100 (☎36071). This doesn't quite live up to its name with rooms decidedly modest in size, but it's the most enticing of this group of hotels. ⑤.

Piast I, ul. Piłsudskiego 98 (☎30033). A step down in class from the neighbouring *Grand*, a fact reflected in the lower prices. ③–④.

Polonia, ul. Piłsudskiego 66 (☎31021). A lively place to stay, thanks in part to its casino. ⑥.

Wrocław, ul. Powstańców Śląskich 7 (☎61 46 51). The most prestigious of the *Orbis* group, popular with visiting bus parties and located a short distance southwest of the main train station. ⑧.

Old Town centre

Bacardi Club, ul. Kazimierza Wielkiego 45 (☎44 43 84). The only inexpensive hotel in the city centre, housed on the upper floors of a night club. There are no single rooms and bathrooms are shared. ③.

Dwór Wazów, ul. Kiełbaśnicza 2 (☎72 34 19). The city's classiest and most expensive hotel, a small establishment offering quality service and twenty well-equipped double rooms or suites. ⑨.

Monopol, ul. Modrzejewskiej 2 (☎37041). Least expensive of Wrocław's *Orbis* hotels, an externally good looking *fin-de-siècle* establishment that despite its attractive exterior is actually well past its prime. ⑦.

Panorama, pl. Dominikański 8 (☎44 36 81). Typical "four-star" *Orbis*–run concrete box, conveniently located on the eastern side of the Old Town centre. ⑧.

Saigon, ul. Wita Stwosza 22/23 (☎44 28 81). Great value Vietnamese-owned establishment right in the centre of the Old Town. ⑤.

Out of the centre

Irys, ul. Irysowa 1 (☎25 32 78). Newish establishment located 5km to the northwest of the city and reached by bus #108. ④.

Orka, ul. Międzyleska 2 (☎67 60 51 ext. 47). Run by the same management as *Irys* and located just beyond the terminus of trams #2, #15 and #22, 4km southeast of the main train station. ④.

Śląsk, ul. Oporowska (☎61 16 11). Sports hotel in a park 3km southwest of the main train station and served by trams #4, #5, #1, #13, #16, #18 and #20. ③.

Żeglarz, ul. Władysława Reymonta 4 (☎21 29 96). Four kilometres northwest of the Rynek near Nadodrze station and on route of tram #14. ③.

Hostels and campsites

The *PTTK* **tourist hostel** has an excellent location at ul. Szajnochy 11 (reception open 5–9pm; ☎44 30 73; ②), just off pl. Solny, and has rooms with six to eighteen beds. The most central **youth hostel** is a couple of minutes' walk north of the main station at ul. Hugona Kołłątaja 20 (☎38856). It's a rather soulless place, offering mixed six-bed rooms or twenty-bed dorms, but it's equipped with clean showers and toilets. There's a **campsite** with chalets to rent on the east side of town near the Olympic Stadium at al. Ignacego Padarewskiego 35 (☎48 46 51) – trams #9, #12, #17 and #32 pass just to the south of the site.

The City

Wrocław's **central area**, laid out in the usual grid pattern, is delineated by the **River Odra** to the north and by the bow-shaped **ul. Podwale** to the south – the latter following the former fortifications whose defensive moat, now bordered by a shady park, still largely survives. The main concentration of shops and places of entertainment is found at the southern end of the centre and in the streets leading south to the train station. Immediately bordering the Odra at the northern fringe of the centre is the **university quarter**. Beyond are a number of peaceful traffic-free islets, formerly sandbanks where the shallow river was once forded, and now linked to each other and to the mainland by graceful little bridges which add a great deal to the city's appeal. The southern part of the much larger island of **Ostrów Tumski**, further east, is the city's ecclesiastical heart, with half a dozen churches and its own distinctive hubbub. Further north is an area of solidly nineteenth-century tenements, while the city's main green belt lies off the eastern side of the island.

The Rynek

Fittingly, the core of the Old Town's grid is occupied by the vast space of the **Rynek**, its centre taken up by the superb edifice of the town hall and surrounded for the most part by the equally grandly renovated facades of former town houses. No longer a place of commerce, it's now a tourist and leisure-oriented zone, given over mainly to museums, restaurants, *al fresco* cafés, bookshops and, a telling new development, antique shops.

THE TOWN HALL

The magnificent **Town Hall**, symbol of the city for the last seven centuries, was originally a modest one-storey structure erected in the wake of the ruinous Tartar sacking and progressively expanded down the years. Its present appearance dates largely from the fifteenth-century high point of local prosperity, when the south aisle was added and the whole decorated in an elaborate Late Gothic style. The international mix of stylistic influences reflects the city's status as a major European trading centre, creating one of the city's finest and most venerable buildings.

The **east facade** is the one which catches the eye and figures in all Wrocław's promotion material. It features an astronomical clock from 1580 and an elaborate central gable decorated with intricate terracotta patterns and exquisite pinnacles. In contrast, the west facade (the main entrance) is relatively plain, save for the octagonal Gothic belfry with its tapering Renaissance lantern. The intricate carvings embellishing the **south facade** are worthy of more protracted scrutiny, lined up between the huge Renaissance windows crowned with their spire-like roofs. Along its length are filigree friezes of animals and foliage as well as effigies of saints and knights, mostly nineteenth-century pastiches, overshadowed by an old crone and a yokel. This pair appear above the doorway leading to the vaulted cellars of the *Piwnica Świdnicka*, a tavern since the thirteenth century, named after Świdnica's famous brew.

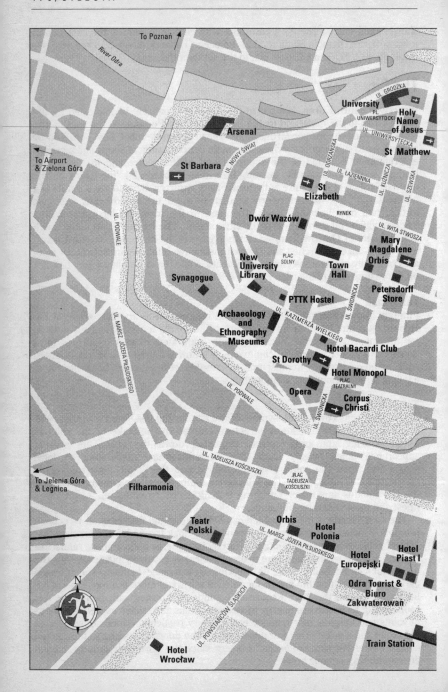

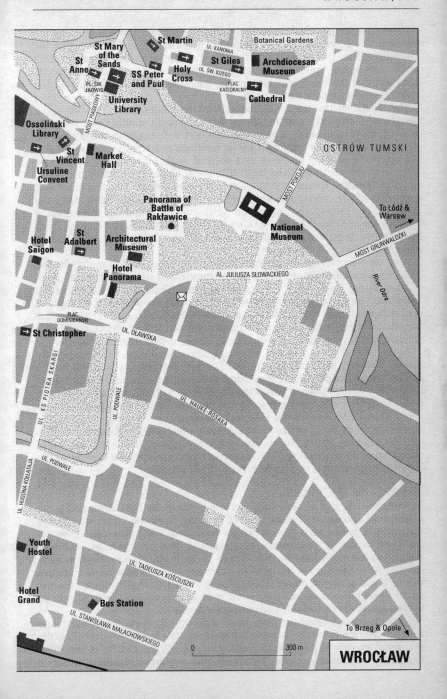

St Martin

St Mary
of the
Sands

UL. KANONIA

Botanical Gardens

St Anne

SS Peter
and Paul

Holy
Cross

St Giles

Archdiocesan
Museum

PL. ŚW.
JADWIGI

UL. ŚW. IDZEGO

University
Library

PLAC
KATEDRALNY

Cathedral

Ossoliński
Library

MOST PIASKOWY

OSTRÓW TUMSKI

St
Vincent

Market
Hall

Ursuline
Convent

Panorama of
Battle of
Racławice

MOST POKOJU

To Łódź &
Warsaw

Hotel
Saigon

St
Adalbert

Architectural
Museum

National
Museum

MOST GRUNWALDZKI

Hotel
Panorama

AL. JULIUSZA SŁOWACKIEGO

River Odra

PLAC
DOMINIKAŃSKI

St Christopher

UL. OŁAWSKA

UL. KS PIOTRA SKARGI

UL. PODWALE

UL. HAUKE-BOSAKA

UL. HUGONA KOŁŁĄTAJA

UL. PODWALE

Youth
Hostel

UL. TADEUSZA KOŚCIUSZKI

Hotel
Grand

Bus Station

UL. STANISŁAWA MAŁACHOWSKIEGO

To Brzeg & Opole

0   300 m

WROCŁAW

Relieved of its municipal duties by the adjoining nineteenth-century offices, the town hall now serves as the city's **Historical Museum** (Wed–Fri 10am–4pm, Sat 11am–5pm, Sun 10am–6pm), although it's the largely unaltered interior itself which constitutes the main attraction. If you've an interest in the precise chronology of the building's components, check out the colour-coded plan just inside the main doorway on the right.

The kernel of the town hall, dating back to the 1270s, is the twin-aisled **Burghers' Hall** situated on the ground floor, just past the rather cute sculpture of a bagpipe-playing bear – a representation from a seventeenth-century legend. Not only the venue for important public meetings and receptions, the hall also did service throughout the week as a covered market, functioning as such for 450 years. The next part to be built, at the very end of the thirteenth century, was the **Bailiff's Room** immediately to the east, which was the office and courtroom of the official who governed the city in the duke's name. Over the centuries, it gained an extravagant vault and a couple of doorways in Renaissance and Neoclassical styles, one of which leads to a small meeting room fitted with a huge ceramic-tiled heater and adorned with portraits of former majors and other civic dignitaries.

A tasteless nineteenth-century marble staircase decorated with an illuminating 1927 reproduction map of the fifteenth-century island town of "Breslau" leads upstairs to the resplendent three-aisled **Knights' Hall**. The keystones of the hall's vault are highly inventive, some of them character studies of all strata of society, while heavy oak wardrobes and chests from subsequent centuries line the otherwise empty hall. Even more richly decorated is the coffer-ceilinged oriel window, which gives a Renaissance flourish to the otherwise Gothic character.

At the far end of the hall are two stone portals, the one on the right (usually closed) adorned with hairy wild men. The left doorway gives access to the **Princes' Room**, a pure example of fourteenth-century Gothic with a vault resting on a single central pillar. It was originally built as a chapel, but takes its name from its later use as a meeting place for the rulers of Silesia's principalities. Today it's a repository for various municiple treasures of religious and secular silverware. From here you can visit the warmly wood-panelled Alderman's Office and the adjacent Strong Room, with displays of ancient coins and the heavy stamps used to make them. The actual treasury was securely located in the adjoining oriel which protrudes from the building's corner.

THE REST OF THE RYNEK

Among the cluster of modern buildings to the rear of the New Town Hall is the celebrated **Laboratory Theatre** founded by **Jerzy Grotowski**. For two decades this was one of the most famous centres for experimental drama in the world. Dissolved following Grotowski's emigration to Italy in 1982, its successor founded by his pupils has also been wound up. In its place is a research institute devoted to Grotowski's work, and you can see an exhibition on the original theatre if you ask at the offices down the alley to the left. The tiny studio theatre, on the second floor of the building, is still used for experimental performances by visiting actors: check the billboard outside for details.

Of the mansions lining the main sides of the Rynek, those on the south and western sides are the most distinguished and colourful. Among several built in the self-confident style of the Flemish Renaissance, no. 2, the **Griffin House** (Pod Gryfami), is particularly notable. Number 5, with a reserved Mannerist facade, is known as the **Waza Court** (Dwór Wazów), in honour of the tradition that it was the place where King Zygmunt Waza stayed during secret negotiations for his marriage to Anna von Habsburg. The mansion's cellars have been converted into one of Wrocław's best gourmet restaurants (see "Restaurants", p.486).

Next door, at no. 6, is the **House of the Golden Sun** (Pod Złotym Słońcem), behind whose Baroque frontage is a suite of Renaissance rooms containing the **Museum of the Art of Medal Making** (Tues–Sun 10am–6pm); its shop sells examples of the craft. The last striking house in the block is no. 8, again Baroque but preserving parts of its thirteenth-century predecessor; it's known as the **House of the Seven Electors** (Pod Siedmioma Elektorami), a reference to the seven grandees superbly depicted on the facade who elected the Holy Roman Emperor, Leopold I. A black Habsburg eagle cowers menacingly over the building's doorway.

West of the Rynek

The southwest corner of the Rynek leads to a second, much smaller square, **plac Solny**. Its traditional function as a market has been recently revived, with the salt after which the market takes its name now replaced by flowers. Most of the buildings offer substantially less sensory delight, dating back no further than the early nineteenth century, with pride of place taken by the Neoclassical **Old Stock Exchange**, which occupies most of the southern side of the square.

Just off the northwest corner of the Rynek are two curious Baroque houses known as **Jaś i Małgosia**, linked by a gateway giving access to the **Church of St Elizabeth**. Proving that brick need not be an inherently dull material, this is the most impressive of Wrocław's churches. Since the mid-fifteenth century its huge ninety-metre **tower**, under construction for 150 years, has been the city's most prominent landmark. Originally a lead-sheeted spire added another 36m to the steeple's height, but this overambitious pinnacle was blown down by storms a year after completion and never rebuilt. Ill fortune has continued to dog the church, which was burnt out under suspicious circumstances in 1976; restoration work looks like it might be completed by 1996, adding possibly the finest and certainly the oldest church to Wrocław's already generous collection.

Facing the inner ring road just west of here is the only other block of old **burghers' houses** surviving in the city. Across the road and down ul. Antoniego Cieszyńskiego is the **Arsenal**, originally sixteenth-century but considerably altered by the Prussians a couple of hundred years later. Most of it is dilapidated, but a restored section houses a splendidly fusty branch of the **Historical Museum** (Tues, Thurs & Fri 10am–4pm, Sat 11am–5pm, Sun 10am–6pm).

On the next street to the south, ul. Mikołaja, stands the Gothic **Church of St Barbara**, which has been given to Russian Orthodox exiles from Lwów. If you come here on Saturday evening or on Sunday morning you can hear their gravely beautiful sung services, which last for well over two hours. At other times, only the chapel entered from the cemetery on the north side of the church is open.

Two streets further to the south is the plain Baroque **Church of St Anthony**, immediately to the east of which is the maze-like former **Jewish quarter**, whose inhabitants fled or were driven from their tenements during the Third Reich, never to return. It seems that the postwar authorities have always been unsure as to how to react to this embarrassing legacy of the city's German past: a recent Polish guidebook to Wrocław makes no mention of the quarter's existence nor of the city's Ukrainian connection. The Neoclassical **Synagogue**, tucked away on a tiny square halfway down an alley, must once have been a handsome building, for all its shocking dereliction. (Another poignant reminder of the Judaic heritage is the **Jewish Cemetery**, south of the main train station at ul. Ślęża 113, on the route of trams #9 and #19. However, although this is now officially recognized as a historical site of considerable significance, access is possible only at weekends.)

South of the Rynek

Immediately to the east of the Jewish quarter lies a part of the city built in obvious imitation of the chilly classical grandeur of the Prussian capital, Berlin. Indeed it was Carl Gotthard Langhans, designer of the Brandenburg Gate, who built the Neoclassical palace on the northern side of ul. Kazimierza Wielkiego, now the **New University Library**. He also had a hand in the monumental **Royal Palace** on the opposite side of the street. The central block of this now houses the **Archeology Museum** (Wed & Fri 10am–4pm, Thurs 9am–4pm, Sat & Sun 10am–5pm), a dry survey of the region's prehistory. Rather more fun is the **Ethnographical Museum** (Tues, Wed, Fri–Sun 10am–4pm, Thurs 9am–4pm;) in the southern wing, a good place to visit if you're with children.

The royal flavour of this quarter continues in a different vein with the lofty Gothic **Church of St Dorothy**, also known as the "Church of Reconciliation". This was founded in 1351 by Charles IV, King of Bohemia and the future Holy Roman Emperor, in thanks for the conclusion of his negotiations with Kazimierz the Great, which secured Bohemia's rule over Silesia in return for a renunciation of its claim to Poland. Unlike most of Wrocław's other brick churches, this stayed in Catholic hands following the Reformation, becoming a Franciscan monastery. Its interior was whitewashed and littered with gigantic altars in the Baroque period, giving it a relatively opulent appearance in comparison to its neighbours which still bear the hallmarks of four centuries of Protestant sobriety. It underlines the fact that if you're looking for lavish Baroque church interiors, Wrocław is not the place.

Behind St Dorothy's stands the **Opera House**, built by Carl Ferdinand Langhans in a faithful continuation of his father's Neoclassical style. Facing it is another example of fourteenth-century Gothic, **Corpus Christi** (Kościół Bożego Ciała), distinguished by the delicate brickwork of its facade, porch and gable, and by the elaborate interior vaulting.

East of the Rynek

Returning to ul. Kazimierza Wielkiego and proceeding east, you come to the part-Gothic, part-Renaissance **Church of St Christopher**, used by the small minority of German-speaking Protestants who remain here. Behind it stretches the vast esplanade of **pl. Dominikański**. Until 1945 there was a heavily built-up quarter on this spot, but this was so badly damaged in the street fighting that it was completely razed. There's some compensation for this loss in the unusually wide **view** of the old city which has been opened up as a result. Between here and the Rynek, at the junction of ul. Oławkska and ul. Szewska, is a classic of twentieth-century design, the former **Petersdorff store** by Erich Mendelssohn. Built in 1927 and used for retail purposes ever since, it's the only one of several stores by the great German Expressionist architect to have survived, its counterparts all having fallen victim to modernization. The concrete and glass building relies for its effect on the interplay between the bold horizontals of the main street fronts and the dramatically projecting cylinder on the corner.

The twin-towered **St Mary Magdalene**, a block north of here, is another illustration of the seemingly inexhaustible diversity of Wrocław's brick churches: this fourteenth-century example is unusual in having flying buttresses, giving it a French feel. Like St Elizabeth's Church, two slender spires originally capped the towers, but were dismantled and replaced with Baroque domes to escape their neighbour's fate. A bevy of funeral plaques and epitaphs from the fifteenth to eighteenth centuries lines its exterior, though the most striking adornment is the twelfth-century stone **portal** on the south side. This masterpiece of Romanesque carving dating from 1180 (and whose tympanum has been moved for conservation to the National Museum) came from the demolished Abbey of Ołbin in the north of the city which was dissolved in 1546 to strengthen the city's defences. The church is also notable as being the site of the first Protestant sermon to be held in Wrocław in 1523 during the earliest days of the Reformation.

At the northern end of pl. Dominikański are the buildings of the **Dominican Monastery** centred on the thirteenth-century **Church of St Adalbert** (Św. Wojciecha), which is embellished with a fine brickwork gable and several lavish Gothic and Baroque chapels. A couple of blocks east, the gargantuan former **Bernardine Monastery** stands in splendid isolation; there's a particularly fine view of its barn-like church from the park beyond. The last important example of Gothic brickwork in the city, the monastery was begun in the mid-fifteenth century and finished only a few years before the Reformation, whereupon it was dissolved and the church used as a Protestant parish church. Severely damaged during the war, the church and cloisters have been painstakingly reconstructed to house the somewhat misleadingly named **Museum of Architecture** (Tues, Thurs & Fri 10am–3.30pm, Wed 10am–4pm, Sat 10am–4pm, Sun 10am–5pm). In fact, this is a fascinating documentary record, using sculptural fragments and old photos, of the many historic buildings in the city which perished in the war and is well worth a visit.

THE RACŁAWICE PANORAMA

Wrocław's best-loved sight, the **Panorama of the Battle of Racławice** (Tues–Sun 9am–6pm, ticket office 9am–4pm), is housed in a specially designed rotunda in the park by the Bernardine Monastery. This gigantic painting, 120m long and 15m high, was commissioned in 1894 to celebrate the centenary of the defeat of the Russian army by the people's militia of Tadeusz Kościuszko near the village of Racławice, between Kraków and Kielce. Ultimately this triumph was in vain: the third and final Partition of Poland, which wiped it off the map altogether, occurred the following year. Nonetheless, it was viewed a century later by patriots of the still subdued nation as a supreme example of national will and self-sacrifice, which deserved a fitting memorial.

For a few decades, panorama painting created a sensation throughout Europe and North America, only to die abruptly with the advent of the cinema. In purely artistic terms, most surviving examples are of poor quality, but this one is an exception, due largely to the participation of **Wojciech Kossak**, one of the most accomplished painters Poland has produced. Amazingly, he and his co-worker, **Jan Styka**, completed the project in just nine months. Seven other painters were hired for the execution of details, but the vast majority of the canvas is the work of these two men.

The subsequent **history of the painting** is a remarkable saga which tells a great deal about the political situation of Poland. Despite an attempt by Polish-Americans to buy it and have it shipped across the Atlantic, it was placed on public view in Lwów, which was then part of Austria – the only one of the Partitioning powers which would have tolerated such nationalist propaganda. It remained there until 1944, when it was substantially damaged by a bomb. Although allocated to Wrocław, as the cultural heir of Lwów, it was then put into storage – officially because there were no specialists to restore it and no money to build the special structure the painting would need. The truth was that it was politically unacceptable to allow Poles to glory in their ancestors' slaughter of Russians.

That all changed with the events of 1980. Within five years the painting had been immaculately restored and was on display in a snazzy new building, with much attention being paid to a natural foreground of soil, stones and shrubs, which greatly adds to the uncanny appearance of depth. Not only is it one of Poland's most hi-tech tourist attractions, it's also one of the most popular, an icon second only in national affection to the Black Madonna of Jasna Góra. Poles flock here in their droves, and you may have to book several hours in advance for a showing which lasts for thirty minutes: ask for the **English-language commentary** which explains all the details of the painting. Be warned that everyone is marched out of the forty-person auditorium as soon as the show's over; you can, however, study the scale model of the battlefield downstairs at leisure.

THE NATIONAL MUSEUM

At the opposite end of the park is the ponderously Prussian neo-Renaissance home of the **National Museum** (Tues, Wed, Fri 10am–4pm, Thurs 9am–5pm, Sat 11am–5pm, Sun 10am–3pm), which unites the collections of Breslau and Lwów. One of the most important sections of **medieval stone sculpture** is housed in the hall around the café including the delicately linear carving of *The Dormition of the Virgin* which formed the tympanum of the portal of St Mary Magdalene. The other major highlight is the poignant early fourteenth-century **tomb of Henryk the Righteous**, one of the earliest funerary monuments to incorporate the subsequently popular motif of a group of weeping mourners.

On the first floor, one wing is devoted to an impressive display of Silesian **polychrome wood sculptures**. The most eye-catching exhibits are the colossal late fourteenth-century statues of saints from St Mary Magdalene, their raw power compensating for a lack of sophistication. More pleasing are the many examples of the "Beautiful Madonnas" which were for long a favourite subject in central European sculpture: a particularly fine example is the one made in the early fifteenth century for the cathedral.

The **foreign paintings** in the opposite wing include few worth seeking out. Among these are Cranach's *Eve*, originally part of a scene showing her temptation of Adam which was cut up and repainted as two portraits of a burgher couple in the seventeenth century. *The Baptism of Christ* is a fine example of the art of Bartholomeus Spranger, the leading exponent of the erotic style favoured at the imperial court in Prague at the turn of the seventeenth century.

One of the star pieces in the comprehensive collection of **Polish paintings** on the top floor is the amazingly detailed *Entry of Chancellor Jerzy Ossoliński into Rome in 1633* by Bernardo Bellotto, best known for his documentary record of eighteenth-century Warsaw (see p.78). The other leading exhibit here is an unfinished blockbuster by Matejko, *Vows of King Jan Kazimierz Waza*. Set in Lwów Cathedral, it illustrates the monarch's pledge to improve the lot of the peasants at the end of the war against his invading Swedish kinsmen. Other works to look out for are Piotr Michałowski's *Napoleon on Horseback*, the *Fatherland Triptych* by Jacek Malczewski, and some mountainscapes by Wojciech Gerson. A number of galleries are devoted to **contemporary arts and crafts**, much of it surprisingly daring for work executed under communist rule.

The university quarter

Wrocław's academic quarter can be reached in just a few minutes from the Rynek by ul. Kuźnicza, but the most atmospheric approach is to walk there from the National Museum along the south bank of the Odra, for a series of delightful **views** of the ecclesiastical quarter opposite.

Overlooking the Piaskowski Bridge is the **Market Hall** (Hala Targowa), a preformed concrete update of the brick church idiom built in 1908. Most days it's piled with irresistible food and other commodities, and boasts that it was equally replete even during martial law. From this point, the triangular-shaped university quarter, jam-packed with historic buildings, is clearly defined by two streets, ul. Uniwersytecka to the south and ul. Grodzka, which follows the Odra.

Along the northern side of the former are three religious houses. First is **St Vincent**, founded as a Franciscan monastery by Henryk the Pious not long before his death at the Battle of Legnica (see p.490). One of the grandest of the city's churches, it was severely damaged in the war and rebuilt in 1991. Inside, several altarpieces by the renowned Silesian artist, Michael Willmann have been returned to their former glory, while its Baroque monastic buildings overlooking the Odra are now used by the university. Henryk also founded the **Ursuline Convent** alongside, which served as the mausoleum of the Piasts, who ruled the city during its period as an independent duchy.

Last in the row is the fourteenth-century **Church of St Matthew** (Św. Macieja), containing the tomb and memorial portrait of the city's most famous literary figure, the seventeenth-century mystic poet Johann Scheffler – better known as **Angelus Silesius** ("the Silesian Angel"), the pseudonym he adopted after his conversion to Catholicism. Facing the south side of the church is the Renaissance Palace of the Piasts of Opole, while across ul. Szewska is the Baroque residence of their cousins from Brzeg-Legnica; both are now used by the university.

Behind St Matthew's stands one of Wrocław's most distinguished buildings, the domed **Ossoliński Library**. Originally a hospital, it was erected in the last quarter of the seventeenth century and designed by the Burgundian architect Jean Baptiste Mathey. The library collections are another legacy from Lwów, where they were assembled by the family whose name they still bear. Among the many precious manuscripts is the original of the Polish national epic, Mickiewicz's *Pan Tadeusz*. Check on the boards outside for details of special exhibitions.

The elongated pl. Uniwersytecki begins on the southern side with a dignified eighteenth-century palace, **Dom Steffensa**, again owned by the university. Facing it is one of the most obviously Austrian features of the city, the **Church of the Blessed Name of Jesus**, built in the Jesuit style at the end of the seventeenth century, one of the rash of Counter-Reformation religious buildings in the Habsburg lands. Its most arresting feature is the huge allegorical ceiling fresco by the most celebrated Austrian decorative painter of the day, Johann Michael Rottmayr.

Adjoining the church is the 171-metre-long facade of the Collegium Maximum of the **University**, founded in 1702 by Emperor Leopold I who is depicted on the front of the House of the Seven Electors on the Rynek's west side. The wide entrance portal bears a balcony adorned with statues symbolizing various academic disciplines and attributes; more can be seen high above on the graceful little tower.

A frescoed staircase leads up to the main assembly hall or **Aula** (open daily 9am–3.30pm, but frequently closed). The only historic room which remains in the huge building, it's one of the greatest secular interiors of the Baroque age, fusing the elements of architecture, painting, sculpture and ornament into one bravura whole. Lording it from above the dais is a statue of the founder, armed, bejewelled and crowned with a laurel. The huge illusionistic **ceiling frescoes** by Christoph Handke show the *Apotheosis of Divine and Worldly Wisdom* above the gallery and auditorium, while the scene above the dais depicts the university being entrusted to the care of Christ and the Virgin Mary. On the wall spaces between the windows are richly framed oval portraits of the leading founders of the university, while the jambs are frescoed with *trompe l'oeil* likenesses of the great scholars of classical antiquity and the Middle Ages.

Wyspa Piasek, Ostrów Tumski and beyond

From the Market Hall, the Piaskowski Bridge leads you out to the sandbank of **Wyspa Piasek**, with a cluster of historic buildings crammed together in the centre. The first you come to on the right-hand side is the **University Library**, installed in an Augustinian monastery which was used as the Nazi military headquarters. Beside it is the fourteenth-century hall **Church of St Mary on the Sands** (Kościół NMP na Piasku), dull on the outside, majestically vaulted inside. The aisles have an asymmetrical tripartite rib design known as the Piast vault, which is peculiar to this region. In the south aisle is the Romanesque tympanum from the previous church on the site, illustrating the dedication by its donor, Maria Włast. Across the road stands the Baroque **Church of St Anne**, now used by a Ukranian Orthodox (Uniate) community from Lwów (see p.338), while at the far end of the islet are two old **mills**, known as *Maria i Feliks*.

OSTRÓW TUMSKI

The two elegant little painted bridges of Most Młyński and Most Tumski connect Wyspa Piasek with Ostrów Tumski. For those not already sated by medieval churches, there's a concentration of five more here, beginning just beyond Most Tumski with the fifteenth-century **SS Peter and Paul**, behind which is the squat hexagonal **St Martin** of a couple of centuries earlier.

Far more prepossessing than these is the imperious **Holy Cross and St Bartholomew**, which, with its massive bulk, giant buttresses and pair of dissimilar towers, looks like some great fortified monastery of definitive Silesian Gothic. In fact, it's really two churches, one on top of the other. The lower, originally dedicated to St Bartholomew, is more spacious and extensive than an ordinary crypt, but lacks the exhilarating loftiness of its partner upstairs. The complex was founded in 1288 by Duke Henryk the Righteous as his own mausoleum, but his tomb has now been removed to the National Museum. A highly elaborate Baroque **monument to St Jan Nepomuk** stands in the square outside; his life is illustrated in the column bas-reliefs and like St Anne's is used by the Uniate community.

Ulica Katedralna leads past several Baroque palaces (among which priests, monks and nuns are constantly scuttling) to the slender twin-towered **Cathedral of St John the Baptist**. Grievously damaged in 1945, this has been fully restored to its thirteenth-century form – it was Poland's first cathedral built in the

Gothic style, completed in 1272 – but is not one of the more attractive of Wrocław's churches. The one exterior feature of note is the elaborate **porch**, though its sculptures, with the exception of two delicate reliefs, are mostly replicas from the last century. Three chapels behind the high altar make a visit to the dank and gloomy interior worthwhile, reminiscent of the relatively unadorned English equivalents from the same era. On the southern side, **St Elizabeth's chapel** dates from the last two decades of the seventeenth century, its integrated architecture, frescoes and sculptures created by Italian followers of Bernini. Next comes the Gothic **lady chapel**, with the masterly Renaissance funerary plaque of Bishop Jan Roth by Peter Vischer of Nuremberg. Last in line is the **Corpus Christi chapel**, a perfectly proportioned and subtly decorated Baroque gem, begun in 1716 by the Viennese court architect Fischer von Erlach. To see the chapels, you'll probably have to ask at the sacristy, or tag onto one of the organized groups passing through.

Opposite the northern side of the cathedral is the tiny thirteenth-century **Church of St Giles** (Św. Idziego), the only one in the city to have escaped destruction by the Tartars, and preserving some finely patterned brickwork. Down ul. Kanonia, the **Archdiocesan Museum** (Tues–Sun 10am–3pm) has a sizeable and ramshackle collection of sacred artefacts. By now you'll be craving for some relief from cultural indigestion; escape from the same street into the **Botanical Gardens** (Mon–Fri 8am–6pm or dusk), established in the Odra's former river bed at the beginning of the last century when a municiple ornamentation programme of the city was undertaken.

Ulica Szczytnicka leads east to the elongated avenue of pl. Grunwaldzki, which gained notoriety in 1945 when it was flattened into an airstrip to allow the defeated Nazi leaders to escape. At its southern end is the most famous of the city's bridges, **Most Grundwaldzki**, built in 1910.

EAST OF OSTRÓW TUMSKI

Wrocław's most enticing stretch of greenery is the **Park Szczytnicki**, east of Ostrów Tumski, on the route of trams #1, #2, #4, #10 and #12. Its focal point is the **Hala Ludowa**, a huge hall built in 1913 to celebrate the centenary of the liberation of the city from Napoleon. Designed by the innovative Max Berg, it combines traditional Prussian solidity with a modernistic dash – the unsupported 130-metre-wide dome is an audacious piece of engineering even by present-day standards. The hall is still used for exhibitions, sporting events and other spectaculars, but even if there's nothing on you can ask at the porter's desk to see inside. Around the Hala Ludowa are a number of striking colonnaded pavilions; these were built a few years earlier by Berg's teacher Hans Poelzig, who was responsible for making the city a leading centre of the *Deutscher Werkbund*, the German equivalent of the English Arts and Crafts Movement.

In the same park is a work by a yet more famous architect: the box-like **Kindergarten** with peeling whitewash is Eastern Europe's only building by Le Corbusier. Along with the huge steel needle beside the hall, this is a legacy of the Exhibition of the Regained Territories, held here in 1948. Other delights in the park include an amphitheatre, a Japanese garden and pagoda, an artificial lake and hundreds of different trees and shrubs – including oaks that are more than six hundred years old. Best of all is a sixteenth-century **wooden church**, brought here from Kędzierzyn in Upper Silesia. Its tower is particularly striking, especially the lower storey with its highly distinctive log construction, a form normally associated with the Ukraine. Across the road lie the **Zoological Gardens** (summer 9am–7pm, winter 9am–5pm), with the largest collection of formerly wild animals in Poland.

Eating, drinking and entertainment

Wrocław has a good selection of places to **eat and drink**, most of which are within the old central area – the episcopal and university quarters are noticeably barren. All the *Orbis* hotels, plus some of those around the main station, have both a restaurant and a café, but although these are all safe bets, Wrocław is one city where you can eat as well elsewhere. **Nightlife** isn't exactly a Wrocław strong point, but the city's theatre is maintaining its high reputation. Note that addresses below with "Rynek-Ratusz" denote the central buildings of the market square, while those with "Rynek" refer to the periphery.

Restaurants

Bel Epoque, south side of the Rynek. New French restaurant with the distinct advantage of Polish prices.

Dwór Wazów, Rynek 5 (☎44 16 33). The "King's Restaurant" of this complex is the best and most expensive in town, specializing in regal banquets with flambé meat dishes. Reservations recommended.

Dwór Wazów, ul. Kiełbaśnicza 6/7. The "Burghers' Restaurant", entered from the first street west of the Rynek, is just as recommendable as its prestigious stablemate, yet its prices are only marginally higher than those of other restaurants.

Grunwaldzka, pl. Grunwaldzki 6. Pick of the few restaurants on Ostrów Tumski.

KDM, pl. Tadeusza Kościuszki 5/6. Much the best choice for inexpensive but hearty traditional dishes. Polish drinks only and dancing in the evenings.

Krawczyck, pl. Solny 5. Traditional Polish restaurant on the first floor with the *Irish Pub* (serving Guinness) below.

Medalion, 26 ul. Świdnicka. Friendly bistro right opposite St Dorothy's Church.

Piwnica Świdnicka, Rynek-Ratusz. This famous old restaurant under the town hall is a city institution, but beware of outrageously marked-up imported drinks which can easily double the price of a meal. Dancing in the evenings.

Saigon, ul. Wita Stwosza 22/23. The hotel's restaurant appropriately specializes in Vietnamese food, expertly prepared in the traditional way.

Spiż, Rynek-Ratusz 2. Highly regarded restaurant incorporating Poland's first boutique brewery, with a strong dark beer, a light Pils and a tangy wheat beer all brewed on the premises.

Vega, 7–8 Rynek Ratusz. A rare treat for vegetarians and located just to the right of the town hall's famous facade.

Zorba, Rynek-Ratusz. Tiny authentic Greek restaurant hidden away in the alley behind the new town hall.

Snack bars and cafés

Cocktail Bar, ul. Komandorska 4a. Close to the station, with the best ice creams and milk shakes in town.

Dwór Wazów, Rynek 5. Situated above the restaurant, with a real palm-court atmosphere. There's also a courtyard at the back if you don't fancy sitting out front.

Małgosia, corner of Rynek and ul. Odrzańska. Relaxed basement café in one of Wrocław's most famous houses.

Mały, corner of ul. Tadeusza Kościuszki and ul. Hugona Kołłątaja. Handy snack bar close to the youth hostel.

Miś, Kuźnicza 48. Milk bar close to the university quarter.

Monopol, ul. Modrzejewskiej 2. The hotel's *kawiarnia*, with its perfectly preserved Jugendstil wall paintings, carved wood and plaster mouldings, is an ideal place for a spot of relaxation.

Pod Kalamburem, ul. Kuźnicza 29a. Beautiful Jugendstil decor with very low prices.

Prospera, Rynek 28. Another first-floor café, with a predominantly young clientele.

Saba, ul. Św. Jadwigi. Housed in a splendid Baroque palace on Wyspa Piasek; one of the few refreshment spots in the episcopal quarter.

Tutti Frutti, pl. Tadeusza Kościuszki 1. Probably the most popular rendezvous point, and frequently packed.

Uni-café, pl. Uniwersytecki 11. Popular student hang-out in the shadow of the great University facade.

Zak, Rynek-Ratusz 7. Has a tempting array of high-calorie desserts.

Entertainment and festivals

Outside the big hotels, lively **nightspots** in Wrocław are thin on the ground. The most obvious place to drink and dance the night away is *Winiarnia Bacchus* at no. 16 on the Rynek, which is open from 10pm to 5am. There's live music every evening at the *Rura* jazz club, ul. Łazienna 4, while the main student club, *Pałaczyk*, ul. Tadeusza Kościuszki 34, has discos each Saturday with plenty more nightclubs popping up all around the town.

Despite the demise of Grotowski's famous studio, Wrocław remains a major **theatre** centre. Henryk Tomaszewski, a former associate of Grotowski, has built up an international reputation for his pantomime company, which performs in alternation with classic drama at the *Teatr Polski*, ul. Gabrieli Zapolskiej 3 (☎38653). *Teatr Kameralny*, ul. Świdnicka 28 (☎44 63 01), is the other main venue for straight plays, while the experimental mantle has been taken up by *Kalambur*, ul. Kuźnicza 29a (☎44 54 11). *Jedliniok*, a student song-and-dance ensemble decked out in colourful traditional costumes, perform at the *Teatr Gest*, pl. Grunwaldzki 63 (☎21 00 14). *Teatr Lalek*, right opposite the Opera on pl. Teatralny 4 (☎44 12 17), is a celebrated puppet theatre: book well in advance for its regular weekend shows, which are invariably sold out. The city's annual **drama festivals** include one devoted to monologues in January, and a contemporary Polish play season in May and June.

There's a similarly wide choice in classical **music**. Both the *Opera*, ul. Świdnicka 35 (☎38641), and the *Operetka Wrocławska*, ul. Piłsudskiego 67 (☎44 49 16), maintain high standards: tickets are easy to obtain and absurdly cheap by Western standards. Orchestral concerts and recitals take place regularly at the *Filharmonia*, ul. Piłsudskiego 19 (☎44 20 01).

Wrocław hosts two contrasting **international music festivals** each year: the renowned Jazz on the Odra in May, and Wratislavia Cantans, devoted to oratorios and cantatas, in September. There's also a festival of early music at the beginning of December.

The Wrocław district

The administrative **district of Wrocław** – covering a roughly circular area, with the city itself at the centre – is predominantly rural, with the River Odra and its tributaries draining some of the most productive agricultural land in the country. The scenery doesn't offer any surprises, being at its best around the isolated massif to the southwest with some forests and a chain of small lakes in the north-west. Due to the extensive **public transport** network, Wrocław itself makes a perfectly adequate touring base, though there's plenty of **accommodation** else-where should you prefer to stay in a more tranquil location.

Ślęża and Sobótka

The flatness of the plain south of the Odra is abruptly broken some 30km from Wrocław by an isolated outcrop of rocks with two peaks, the higher of which is known as **Ślęża** (718m). One of the most enigmatic sites in Poland, Ślęża was used for pagan worship in Celtic times, and was later settled by the Slav tribe after whom the mountain – and Silesia itself – are named.

Ślęża is normally approached from **SOBÓTKA**, which is on the rail line and some bus routes to Świdnica. Between the bus terminal and the train station is the Gothic Parish Church, outside which stands the first of several curious ancient **sculptures** to be seen in the area – consisting of one stone placed across another, it's nicknamed *The Mushroom*. On the slopes of Ślęża, there's a large and voluptuous statue of a woman with a fish, while the summit has a carved lion on it. Exactly what these carvings symbolize is not known: some certainly postdate the Christianization of the area, but that hasn't prevented their association with pagan rites. Even though the site hasn't achieved cult status, it's not exactly a place to look for quiet mystery, being enormously popular with day-trippers and often teeming with busloads of schoolkids.

Five separate **hiking trails** traverse the hillsides, some of them stony, so it's wise to wear sturdy shoes. More than an hour is necessary for the busiest stretch, the direct ascent from Sobótka to the top of Ślęża by the route indicated by yellow signs. The summit is spoiled by a number of ugly buildings including the inevitable television tower, while the neo-Gothic chapel is a poor substitute for the castle and Augustinian monastery which once stood here. Recompense is provided in the form of an extensive panoramic view including, on a clear day, the Karkonosze and Kłodzko highlands to the south and west.

Should you wish to stay, there are a couple of **tourist hostels** in Sobótka: *Pod Misiem*, ul. Mickiewicza 7 (☎071/199; ①), and *Pod Wieżycą*, ul. Żymierskiego 13 (☎071/147; ②). At Sulistrowice, 2km to the south, there's a **campsite** (☎071/604) with chalets. On Sobótka's main square you'll find a couple of snack bars.

Trzebnica

TRZEBNICA, 24km north of Wrocław, has a long and distinguished history, having been granted a charter in 1250 by Duke Henryk III, so making it one of Silesia's oldest recorded towns. It was his marriage to the German princess Saint Hedwig (known in Poland as Jadwiga) which was largely responsible for shifting Silesia towards a predominantly German culture, setting the trend for the next six centuries.

The couple established a **Cistercian Convent** in the town in 1202, the sole monument of note. Built in the plain style favoured by this order – still Romanesque in shape and feel, but already with the Gothic pointed arch and ribbed vault – it was progressively remodelled and now has a predominantly Baroque appearance evident in its main feature, the **Basilica of St Jadwiga**. A survival from the original building is the **portal**, which was found during excavation work and re-erected, half-hidden, to the left of the porch. Its sculptures, showing King David playing the harp to Bathsheba attended by a maidservant, are notably refined thirteenth-century carvings. The northern doorway also survives, but is of a lower standard of workmanship.

Inside the church, every column features a sumptuous Baroque altarpiece, while, to the right of the choir, the **St Hedwig's chapel's** resplendent gilt and silver altar almost outshines the main item. The princess, who spent her widowhood in the convent, was canonized in 1267, just 24 years after her death, whereupon this chapel was immediately built in her memory. In 1680, her simple marble and alabaster sepulchral slab was incorporated into a grandiose tomb, whose sides are lined with sacred statuary while Jadwiga clutches a model of the basilica. At the same time, a considerably less ostentatious memorial to her husband was placed in the choir, its entrance guarded by statues of Saint Hedwig and her even more celebrated niece, Saint Elizabeth of Hungary.

To stay overnight in Trzebnica try the *Hotel Pod Płatanem*, ul. Pilsuckiego 8 (☎12 09 80; ③) or the *OSiR* campsite (☎12 07 47) which also has chalets, a restaurant and a pool; it's signposted east of the basilica on the Wrocław road. There's another **restaurant** right opposite the convent, the *Kasztelańska*, and the *Ratuszowa* in the town square.

The Żmigród and Milicz lake district

North of Trzebnica lies a lake district with several nature reserves, centred on the small towns of **ŻMIGRÓD** and **MILICZ**, which both lie in the valley of the Barycza, a tributary of the Odra. The former is on the main rail line to Leszno and Poznań, the latter on a different northbound route.

Between Milicz and Sulmierzyce, just over the Wielkopolska border, is one of Poland's most important **bird reserves**. Over 170 different water and moorland species breed in the area, while an even larger number use it as a stopoff point on their migration. Black and white storks, swans, herons, seagulls, cranes, cormorants and great crested grebes are among the species most likely to be seen, apart from the inevitable ducks and geese. If you're lucky, you might even be able to spot sea eagles, who spend the winter here. Autumn, as the birds prepare to leave, is the best season for a visit: they are less timid at this time and more likely to be seen in groups in the open countryside. There are marked trails throughout the area, and an observation tower at the Wzgórze Joanny (Joanna Hill) south of Milicz. Other parts of this lake district are designated **forest reserves**, in some of which wild boar and both red and fallow deer roam freely. Be warned, however, that the marshy soil often means that stretches of this countryside are impassable.

Accommodation options are limited: Żmigród has a tourist hostel, *Żmigrodzianka*, at ul. Wojska Polskiego 5 (☎3738; ②), or alternatively, a campsite with chalets can be found at ul. Poprzeczna 13 (☎41215) in Karłowo, just south of Milicz.

Lubiąż

Set close to the north bank of the Odra, 51km west of Wrocław (regular daily buses) and signposted off the Wrocław–Zielona Góra road, the quiet village of **LUBIĄŻ** stands in the shadow of a **Cistercian Abbey** which ranks as one of the largest and most impressive former monastic complexes in central Europe. Originally founded by the Benedictines in the first half of the twelfth century, it was taken over by the Cistercians a generation later.

Although resting on medieval foundations, the appearance of the complex – laid out in the ground plan of a squared-off figure 6 – is one of sober Baroque: the community flourished in the aftermath of the disastrous Thirty Years' War, and was able to build itself palatial new headquarters, with over three hundred halls and chambers. Silesia's greatest painter, **Michael Willmann** (see p.504), lived here for over four decades, carrying out a multiplicity of commissions for the province's religious houses, and was interred in the church's crypt. However, prosperity was short-lived: decline began in 1740, when Silesia came under the uncompromisingly Protestant rule of Frederick the Great's Prussia, and continued until the monastery was dissolved in 1810. Since then, the complex has served as a mental hospital, stud farm, munitions factory, labour camp and storehouse, in the process drifting into a state of semi-dereliction. After the fall of communism, the Lubiąż Fund was established to attract foreign capital to renovate the site and presently the Polish state and private German investment are slowly financing the gargantuan task of restoring the massive complex. During the summer of 1995 reroofing was nearly complete, leaving only the vast interior to be overhauled – a task that is likely to take at least another couple of years.

In the meantime, what has undoubtedly the potential to become one of Poland's leading tourist attractions has the merest trickle of visitors. At present the main reason for making a visit is to appreciate the colossal exterior – something that would stand out in any capital city let alone lost here in the Silesian countryside. Most impressive, and readily accessible by walking through the gatehouse, is the 223-metre-long **facade**, whose austere economy of ornament is interrupted only by the twin towers of the church at the point where the figure 6 plan joins back onto itself. Unfortunately, the latter's interior (currently out of bounds) was stripped of most of its rich furnishings during World War II, and a few small frescoes on the cupola of scenes from the lives of saints Benedict and Bernard are all that remain of Willmann's extensive decorative scheme. The rest of the abbey is similarly inaccessible, but nevertheless a visit to this huge relic of the country's grand past still makes an evocative excursion.

Legnica and Legnickie Pole

In 1241 the Tartar hordes – having ridden five thousand miles from their Mongolian homelands and ravaged everything in their path – won a titanic battle 60km west of Wrocław against a combined army of Poles and Silesians, killing its commander, Duke Henryk the Pious. Silesia's subsequent division among Henryk's descendants into three separate duchies began a process of dismemberment which was thereafter to dog its history. One of the new capitals was **LEGNICA**, a fortified town a few kilometres from the battlefield, one of the few in the area to have escaped destruction. It remained a ducal seat until the last of the Piasts died in 1675, but by then its role as their main residence had been taken over by Brzeg.

Although often ravaged by fires and badly damaged in World War II, Legnica has maintained its role as one of Silesia's most important cities, and is nowadays a busy regional centre preserving a wide variety of monuments. The most interesting of these relics, a castle and three churches, are set at the cardinal points around the city centre, now comprising undeveloped open spaces and residential concrete blocks – the legacy of Legnica's wartime ruin.

The Town

If you're arriving at the **train station** to the northeast of the old city centre, or the **bus station** just over the road, the main sights can be covered by a circular walk in an anticlockwise direction. Following ul. Dworcowa (between the stations) to the right, you shortly come to the wide pl. Zamkowy, with the early fifteenth-century **Głogów Gate** (one of only two surviving parts of the city wall) standing in isolation and the enormous **Castle** behind.

The latter is a bit of a mish-mash and now houses administrative offices, with no worthwhile interiors open to inspection, apart from the chapel. Nonetheless, it has some interesting features, particularly the **gateway** in the form of a triumphal arch, the only surviving part of the Renaissance palace built here. All that remains of the earlier defensive castle, long since replaced by a Romantic pseudo-fortress designed by the great Berlin architect Karl Friedrich Schinkel, are two heavily restored towers; the higher octagonal, the lower cylindrical and ringed by a crenellated balcony capped by an octagonal tower.

Continuing down ul. Nowa, which offers the best overall view of the castle, you arrive at ul. Pantyzanow, the axis of a well-preserved Baroque quarter. On the right are the Jesuit buildings including the **Church of St John's** massive facade, appearing all the more impressive for being confined to a narrow street. Protruding from the eastern side of the church, its orientation and brick Gothic architecture looking wholly out of place, is the presbytery of the thirteenth-century Franciscan Monastery which formerly occupied the spot. It owes its survival to its function as the Piast mausoleum: if you can get inside you'll see several sarcophagi, plus Baroque frescoes illustrating the history of Poland and Silesia under the dynasty. Appropriately enough, *Piast* beer, popular throughout the province, is brewed in town.

Across the road stands the **Regional Museum** (Wed–Sun 11am–5pm), its garden featuring a display of sections of architectural masonry from the Gothic period onwards. Another fine palace of the same epoch, the **Rycerska Academy**, can be found in ul. Chojnowska, the street immediately behind. Here also is the late fourteenth-century **Chojnow Tower** plus a small section of the medieval wall.

This same street runs into the elongated **Rynek**, which has lost much of its character: the two rows of historic buildings placed back-to-back along the central part of the square are now set off by functional modern dwellings which have transformed the Rynek into an undistinguished public space. Eight arcaded Renaissance houses, all brightly coloured and a couple decorated with reliefs, have managed to preserve a little old-time character. At the end of this block is the **Old Town Hall**, a restrained Baroque construction, while behind stands the **theatre**, built in the first half of the nineteenth century in a style reminiscent of a Florentine palazzo. There's also a fine eighteenth-century fountain dedicated to Neptune.

From this point, and probably long before, you can't miss the huge twin-towered **Cathedral of SS Peter and Paul**, with its rich red brick neo-Gothic exterior, stylistically matched by the arcaded turn-of-the-century buildings facing it on the corner of the Rynek. Two lovely fourteenth-century portals have survived: the northern one, featuring a tympanum of *The Adoration of the Magi* flanked by statues of the church's two patrons, overshadows the more prominent facade doorway with its *Madonna and Child*. The furnishings of the interior, which largely retains its original form, range from a late thirteenth-century font with bronze bas-reliefs to an elaborately carved Renaissance pulpit and a typically theatrical Baroque high altar.

Ulica Piotra i Pawła leads back to the train station via pl. Mariacki, with the brick Gothic **Church of Our Lady**, whose gaunt exterior brings to mind military rather than ecclesiastical architecture. Notwithstanding its dedication, it's still the place of worship of the remnant of the Protestant community, who were in a majority here until 1945.

Practicalities

The only **hotel** is the four-star *Cuprum* (☎076/28544; ③) on ul. Skarbowa, 7, right by the castle; it may look like the usual overpriced *Orbis* joint, but it's actually pretty good value although the restaurant is much less impressive. The other accommodation possibility is the **youth hostel** at ul. Jordana 17 (☎076/25412), a ten-minute walk east of pl. Mariacki down ul. Wrocławska.

To **eat** and **drink** try the popular *Adria Café*, Rynek 27, *Tivoli* **restaurant**, ul. Złotoryjska 31, southwest of the Rynek and *Hortex*, ul. NMP 11. The best place is the pricier than average *Astron* on ul. Jaworzyńska 246, the road out of town towards the A4 motorway. The deep-fried camembert, goulash soup and house special, "three little beef steaks", are all recommended. For some liquid refreshment, you'll find Guinness on tap at the *Green Island* at Złotoryjska 250, under the *Club Legmet* working-men's club.

Legnickie Pole

LEGNICKIE POLE, 11km southeast of Legnica, stands on the site of the great battleground; it can be reached by any bus going to Jawor, or by the municipal services #9, #16, #17 and #20. Extensive repair work was carried out in 1991 on the village's principle buildings in conjunction with the 750th anniversary of the battle.

A church was erected on the spot where Henryk the Pious' body was found (according to tradition, his mother, later Saint Jadwiga of Trzebnica, was only able to identify the headless corpse from his six-toed foot), and in time this became a Benedictine monastery – said to be the stone chapel facing the abbey complex. A Protestant parish for four centuries, the church now houses the **Museum of the Battle of Legnica** (Wed–Sun 11am–4.30pm), which includes diagrams and mock-ups of the conflict and a copy of Henryk's tomb (the original is in Wrocław's National Museum). Outside the museum are several large wooden carvings commissioned for the 750th anniversary, including depictions of a wily Tartar archer and Henryk's severed head.

The Benedictines, who were evicted during the Reformation, returned to Legnickie Pole in the early eighteenth century and constructed the large **Church of St Jadwiga** directly facing the museum. It was built by **Kilian Ignaz Dientzenhofer**, the creator of much of Prague's magnificent Baroque architecture. His characteristic use of varied geometric shapes and the interplay of concave and convex surfaces is well illustrated here. The interior of the church (entry only with a museum visit) features an oval nave plus an elongated apse and is exceptionally bright, an effect achieved by the combination of white walls and very large windows. Complementing the architecture are the bravura **frescoes** covering the vault by the Bavarian **Cosmos Damian Asam**. Look out for the scene over the organ gallery, which shows the Tartars hoisting Henryk's head on a stake and celebrating their victory, while the duke's mother and wife mourn over his body.

Since the second dissolution of the monastery in 1810, the **monastic buildings** (currently a women's hospice) have been put to a variety of uses. For nearly a century they served as a Prussian military academy; its star graduate was Paul von Hindenburg, German commander-in-chief during World War I and president from 1925 until his death in 1934.

Legnickie Pole has little in the way of facilities. You'll find an officially designated **restaurant**, *Rycerska*, on the main square, but don't expect too much. At the edge of the village is the only **campsite** (☎076/82397) in the Legnica area; it also has chalets for rent.

Northwestern Silesia

Northwestern Silesia is a little-visited region containing still less in the way of tourist attractions. However, if you're coming or going from Poland through this area you might like to check out a few old towns which are, for different reasons, worth a passing look.

Głogów

GŁOGÓW, 60km north of Legnica, is a name which crops up often in history books. The capital of one of the many Piast duchies, it has produced a remarkable number of influential citizens for a place whose population has never numbered more than a few thousand. These include Jan of Głogów, teacher of Copernicus; Andreas Gryphius, the greatest German poet and dramatist of the seventeenth century; and Arnold Zweig, the Jewish novelist who became a leading intellectual figure in Israel and then in the German Democratic Republic. The town was also the scene of one of E.T.A. Hoffmann's chilling fantasies on the theme of schizophrenia, *The Jesuit Chapel at G*. More tangibly, Głogów is an auspicious example of how a once eminent town ruined by the war and neglected during the communist era is reshaping itself to face an optimistic future.

In the final months World War II Głogów was turned into a fortress by the retreating Nazis and, in the process, completely destroyed. Visiting the Old Town, ten minutes' walk to the left of the station just past the box girder bridge, was until recently a shocking experience. The historic centre was abandoned as a pile of rubble in an increasingly overgrown wasteland while the new town sprang up to the west. However, since the early 1990s, the Old Town site has been undergoing gradual **redevelopment**, with building following a tasteful reintepretation of Głogów's former heyday. The Renaissance-style town hall, still bearing its fifty-year-old shrapnel scars, is soon set to match the fully renovated Baroque church which has given the town a new focal point. Even the ruined shell of the Gothic brick church nearby, as well as the less damaged spired example over the river, are receiving attention from the builders, hopefully returning some character and municipal pride to the town.

This is a cycle that several prominent towns in Poland have been through many times; a prosperous building boom following the reversals of war or other upheavals. It's all documented in the **Museum** (Wed–Sun 10am–5pm), housed in the old castle by the box girder bridge between the Old Town and the station. Still retaining the rotund tower of its Piastic origins, the castle also houses a gruesome collection of medieval instruments of torture and execution.

Should you find yourself wanting **to stay** overnight, the rather pricey *Hotel Kasztelanski*, at the Old Town end of al. Wolności (☎076/33 22 16; ⑤), is your only choice at present, with its *Salome* restaurant, or the *Piastowska/Zamkowa* alternative in the basement of the castle, being the best bets for a decent meal.

Zielona Góra

The wartime experience of **ZIELONA GÓRA,** 60km northwest of Głogów, was very different. Hardly damaged at all, it has grown to become an important centre for the machine and textile industries since passing into Polish hands, and now has a population numbering some 100,000. It also has a somewhat esoteric claim to fame, being the only place in Poland where wine is produced. Although it lacks any outstanding sights, Zielona Góra may be your first taste of a sizeable Polish town if driving through from eastern Germany.

The whole central area of Zielona Góra has a certain novelty value, full of examples of the sorts of buildings which in most other central European towns tended to fall to the bulldozers if they hadn't already been destroyed in the war. It's a patchwork of the architectural styles practised in turn-of-the-century Germany, with the solidly historicist Wilhelmine rubbing shoulders with the experimental forms of Jugendstil. There are also a few older landmarks in the midst of these, including a couple of towers surviving from the fifteenth-century ramparts, the Gothic Church of St Hedwig and the much-remodelled Renaissance Town Hall in the centre of the Rynek. Most imposing of all is the **Church of Our Lady of Częstochowa**, an eighteenth-century example of the Silesian penchant for half-timbered ecclesiastical buildings.

Orbis obviously think well of Zielona Góra, as they have an expensive **hotel**, the *Polan*, a couple of blocks east of the station at ul. Staszica 9a (☎076/27 00 91; ⑥). Alternatively, there's a less expensive hotel, *Śródmiejski*, right in the town centre at ul. Żeromskiego 23 (☎076/25 44 71; ④) and a **youth hostel**, open all year with **camping** allowed, just to the southeast of the station at ul. Wyspiańskiego 58 (☎076/27 08 40). To get to the hostel from the train station, turn left and walk under the flyover, take the first right up the hill and, passing the *Polan*, turn left at the lights into ul. Wyspiańskiego – altogether about a twenty-minute walk.

The *Orbis* **travel bureau** is at ul. Kupiecka 23 (Mon–Fri 9am–4.45pm, Sat 9am–2pm; ☎076/27 17 11), while *Lubtour* is on ul. Sikorskiego 4 (☎076/27 27 00). Pick of the many **restaurants** in the town are *Topaz* on ul. Boharetów Westerplatte, the main road where you'll also find the **post office**, or *Thang Long*, a Chinese-Vietnamese establishment on ul. Chopina.

Żagań

Some 40km west of Głogów, 50km southwest of Zielona Góra, and reachable from either by train, is the old ducal capital of **ŻAGAŃ**. Like Głogów it suffered badly in World War II, when it gained international notoriety as the site of the Nazi prisoner-of-war camp, Stalag VIIIC. Although it has been partially restored, it stands very much in the shadow of what was an exceptionally illustrious past for such a small town: the duchy was once conferred on Albrecht von Waldstein (aka Wallenstein), the military genius who had commanded the imperial forces in the Thirty Years' War; the astronomer Johannes Kepler passed the last two years of his life there, as Wallenstein's guest; while the great French novelist Stendhal was a later resident.

Starting at the western end of the compact centre, you first see the finest of the half-dozen historic churches, **St Mary**, formerly part of an Augustinian monastery. Originally a high gabled Gothic hall church from the fourteenth century, its interior, which boasts a beautiful Renaissance altar dedicated to the Holy Trinity, was completely remodelled in the Baroque epoch. Further east is the first of two large market squares, the Old Rynek, lined with a number of sixteenth- and seventeenth-century burghers' mansions, and the Gothic **Town Hall**, to which a Florentine-style loggia was appended last century. Beyond is the larger New Rynek, with the Jesuit Church on the north side. Set in a park just to the south is the **Palace**, begun in the Renaissance period by order of Wallenstein, but mostly built in an Italianate Baroque style later in the seventeenth century. It was badly desecrated during World War II, when its rich interiors were destroyed; it's now used as a cultural centre.

On ul. Ilwianska in the suburb of Stary Żagan is the site of Stalag VIIIC, today designated the **Museum of Martyrology** (daily 10am–5pm). Some 200,000 prisoners from all over the world, most of them officers, were incarcerated here, and the film *The Great Escape* is based on a true episode in its history. A monument commemorates those who were killed, while a special room displays prisoners' beds along with samples of their hair, glasses, clothes and documents, plus photographs and a plastic model of how the camp once looked.

Practicalities

Żagań has three **hotels**, of which the best value is the parkside *Mylnowka*, ul. Żelazna 2a (☎068/77 30 74; ③), a black and white building situated in the park behind the palace. Alternatives are the more upmarket *Nadbrodzański*, ul. Kilińskiego 1 (☎068/77 34 47; ④), just over the river, and the basic *Dom Turysty* (☎068/77 34 67; ②), a gloomy proposition set in the courtyard of pl. Klasztorny bordered by the brooding hulk of St Mary's Church.

The best place to **eat** is the *Nadbrodzański*'s restaurant; otherwise try *Staromiejska* pizzeria on the Rynek or the *Tropic* on the opposite side of the square. Each May, the Crystal Room of the Palace is put to appropriate use as the venue for the main local **festival**, the All-Polish Dance Competition.

Jelenia Góra and around

JELENIA GÓRA, which lies 60km southwest of Legnica and some 110km from Wrocław, is the gateway to one of Poland's most popular holiday and recreation areas, the Karkonosze National Park. Its name means "Deer Mountain", but the rusticity this implies is scarcely reflected in the town itself which has been a manufacturing centre for the past five centuries. Founded as a fortress in 1108 by King Bolesław the Wrymouth, Jelenia Góra came to prominence in the Middle Ages through glass and iron production, with high-quality textiles taking over as the cornerstone of its economy in the seventeenth century. With this solid base, it was hardly surprising that, after it came under Prussian control, the town was at the forefront of the German Industrial Revolution.

The Town

Thankfully Jelenia Góra's present-day factories have been confined to the peripheries, leaving the traffic-free historic centre remarkably well preserved. Even in a country with plenty of prepossessing central squares, the **plac Ratuszowy** is an impressive sight. Not the least of its attractions is that it's neither a museum piece nor the main commercial centre: most of the businesses are restaurants and cafés, while the tall mansions are now subdivided into flats. Although their architectural styles range from the late Renaissance via Baroque to Neoclassical, the houses form an unusually coherent group, all having pastel-toned facades reaching down to arcaded fronts at street level. The latter feature is an attractive characteristic of several Polish town squares. Occupying the familiar central position is the large mid-eighteenth-century **Town Hall**, its unpainted stonework providing an apposite foil to the colourful houses.

To the northeast of pl. Ratuszowy rises the slender belfry of the Gothic **Parish Church of SS Erasmus and Pancras**. Epitaphs to leading local families adorn the outer walls, while the inside is chock-full of Renaissance and Baroque furnishings. Yet another eye-catching tower can be seen just to the east, at the point where the main shopping thoroughfare, ul. Marii Konopnickiej, changes its name to ul. 1 Maja. Originally part of the sixteenth-century fortifications, it was taken over a couple of centuries later to serve as the belfry of **St Anne's Chapel**. The only other survivor of the town wall is the tower off ul. Jasna, the street which forms a westward continuation of pl. Ratuszowy.

Continuing down ul. 1 Maja, you come in a couple of minutes to the Baroque **Chapel of Our Lady**; it's normally kept locked, but if you happen to be here on a Sunday morning you can drop in to hear the fervent singing of its Russian Orthodox congregation. At the end of the street, enclosed in a walled park-like cemetery, is another Baroque church, **Holy Cross**, built in the early eighteenth century by a Swedish architect, Martin Franze, on the model of St Catherine's in Stockholm. Though sober from the outside, the double-galleried interior is richly decorated with *trompe l'oeil* frescoes.

From the bustling ul. Bankowa which skirts the Old Town to the south, ul. Jana Matejki leads to the **District Museum** (Tues, Thurs & Fri 9am–3.30pm, Wed, Sat & Sun 9am–4.30pm) at its far end, just below the wooded Kościuszki Hill. Apart from temporary exhibitions, the display space here is given over to the history of **glass** from antiquity to the present day, with due emphasis on local examples and a particularly impressive twentieth-century section.

For the best **viewpoint** in town, head west from pl. Ratuszowy along ul. Jasna, then cross ul. Podwale and continue down ul. Obrońców Pokoju into the woods and over the bridge. Several paths lead up the hill, which is crowned with an outlook tower that's permanently open. From the top there's a sweeping view of Jelenia Góra and the surrounding countryside.

Practicalities

The main **train station** is about fifteen minutes' walk from the centre, at the east end of ul. 1 Maja. Local buses plus a few services to nearby towns leave from the bays in front, but the **bus station** for all inter-city departures is at the opposite end of town off ul. Obrońców Pokoju.

English is spoken at the **Orbis** office, ul. 1 Maja 1 (Mon–Fri 9am–5pm, Sat 10am–1pm; ☎075/26206); ask here if you want a room in a **private house** in Jelenia Góra or one of the nearby resorts. Other services available here include mountain guides and flights by hang-glider or helicopter (not outrageously expensive if you're in a large enough group). If you need more help try the *Mouflon Central Tourist Information* office on the south side of pl. Ratuszowy (Mon–Fri 9am–5pm, Sat 9am–1pm).

There's yet another *Orbis* agency in the luxury **hotel**, *Jelenia Góra* (☎075/24081; ⑧), located at ul. Sudecka 63, about a mile from the centre on the main southeastern road to Kowary and Karpacz. The considerably less expensive alternatives are the *Camp*, just down the road from the *Jelenia Góra* on ul. Sudecka 42 (☎075/26942; ②) where, as the name suggests, you can also **camp**, or the ideally central *Europa* on ul. Maja 16(☎075/23221; ③). There's also a small and friendly **youth hostel**, *Bartek*, quietly but conveniently situated in ul. Bartka Zwycięzcy 10 (☎075/25746), while the **PTTK hostel** nearby on ul. 1 Maja 88 (☎075/23059) may now have reopened following a long overdue renovation.

On the western side of pl. Ratuszowy are three **restaurants**, *Pokusa*, *Retro* and *Smok*, all with outside tables. The last-named, specializing in flambé dishes, is the pick of the trio. Fiery Hungarian-style dishes are served at *Tokaj* on ul. Pocztowa, just round the corner from the *Pizza Hut Polska*, a safe if predictable choice located next to the *Orbis* office on ul. 1 Maja. There are plenty of **snack bars** and **cafés** in the centre, among which *Hortus* on pl. Ratuszowy is popular.

Cultural life centres on the Secessionist-style **Cyprian Norwid Theatre** at al. Wojska Polskiego 38 (☎075/23274), whose main season is in the autumn. Jelenia Góra hosts concerts of chamber and organ music in July, while early to mid-August sees a **festival** of street theatre, and there's also a **cinema** on ul. 1 Maja, showing the latest releases with Polish subtitles.

Cieplice Śląskie-Zdrój

The municipal boundaries of Jelenia Góra have been extended to incorporate a number of communities to the south, nearest of which is the old spa town of **CIEPLICE ŚLĄSKIE-ZDRÓJ**, 8km away. Local bus #9 passes through the centre of Cieplice; #7, #8 and #15 stop on the western side of town, enabling you to connect with buses and trains to Szklarska Poręba (see "The Karkonosze Mountains", p.499), while #4, #13 and #14 stop on the eastern side, with bus connections to the other main resort in the range, Karpacz.

Although it has a number of modern sanatoria, along with concrete apartment blocks in the suburbs, Cieplice still manages to bask in the aura of an altogether less pressurized age. To catch this atmosphere at its most potent, attend one of the regular concerts of **Viennese music** in the spa park's delightful Neoclassical **theatre**.

The broad main street of Cieplice is designated as a square – plac Piastowski. Its main building is the large eighteenth-century **Schaffgotsch Palace**, named after the German grandees who formerly owned much of the town. There are also a couple of Baroque **parish churches** – the one for the Catholics stands in a close at the western end of the street and is generally open, whereas its Protestant counterpart to the east of the palace is locked except on Sunday mornings. Next to the Catholic church is a curious carved wooden fountain with three giant chicks guzzling at the plumes of 50°C spring water, their refreshment occasionally interrupted by a bottle-bearing *zdrójnik*.

A walk south through the Park Norweski, which continues the spa park on the southern side of the River Podgórna, brings you to the small **Ornithological Museum** (Tue 9am–2pm, Wed–Fri 9am–6pm, Sat & Sun 9am–5pm) housed in the so-called Nordic Pavilion. Inside the wooden building, erected here earlier this century, you'll find cases of butterflies as well as the stuffed avians in which the museum specializes.

Practicalities

At the western edge of the spa park is the **hotel** *Cieplice*, ul. Cervi 11 (☎58560; ⑥), which caters for the elderly German bus parties who mill around town. There's also the much less expensive *Sigon* next to the *Cieplice* on ul. Zamoskiego 3 (☎50222; ②), but it reeks too much of a sanatorium rather than a hotel. The cheaper still **tourist hostel**, *Pod Różami*, at pl. Piastowski 26 (☎51454; ②) is the best choice for budget lodgings, although facilities here are shared. The **campsite**, *Rataja* (☎52566), is near the Orłe train station southwest of town, on the routes of buses #7 and #15.

In the assembly rooms beside the spa theatre there's a good **café** with a cold buffet service and dancing in the evenings. The hostel has a **restaurant** with the *Mafioso* pizzeria next door and there's a decent **milk bar** at the western end of pl. Piastowski.

Sobieszów

Buses #7, #9 and #15 all continue the few kilometres south to **SOBIESZÓW**. Once again, there are two Baroque **parish churches**, both located off the main ul. Cieplicka: the Protestant one is appropriately plain, while the Catholic is exuberantly decorated. In an isolated location on the southeastern outskirts is the **Regional Museum** (Tues–Sun 9am–4pm), with displays on the local geology, flora and fauna.

From here, red and black trails offer a choice of ascents to **Chojnik Castle** (Tues–Sun 9am–4pm), which sits resplendently astride the wooded hill of the same name. It's actually much further from town than it appears – allow about an hour for the ascent. Founded in the mid-fourteenth century, the castle is celebrated in legend as the home of a beautiful man-hating princess who insisted that any suitor had to travel through a treacherous ravine in order to win her hand. Many perished in the attempt: when one finally succeeded, the princess chose to jump into the ravine herself in preference to marriage. The castle was badly damaged in 1675, not long after the addition of its drawbridge and the Renaissance ornamentation on top of the walls. Yet, despite its ruined state, enough remains to give a good illustration of the layout of the medieval feudal stronghold it once was, with the added bonus of a magnificent **view** from the round tower.

The castle houses a restaurant and **tourist hostel** (☎53535; ②), though its isolated position makes the novelty value the sole reason for staying. Sobieszów itself has another hostel, *Nad Wrzosówką*, at ul. Cieplicka 213 (☎53627; ②), along with a **campsite**, *Łazienkowska*, at the northern edge of the town centre on ul. Łazienkowska. Also on ul. Cieplicka are a **restaurant**, *Ostoja*, and a couple of snack bars.

Jagniątków

At the very edge of the Karkonosze, just south of Sobieszów but beyond the municipal boundaries of Jelenia Góra, is the village of **JAGNIĄTKÓW**, once home of the
German novelist and playwright **Gerhart Hauptmann**, winner of the 1912 Nobel
Prize for Literature. Having fallen foul of the Nazis he formerly supported,
Hauptmann spent his last years in this isolated corner of his native province, staying on even when it came under Polish rule in 1945. The psychological novels he
wrote here have worn less well than his earlier naturalistic works, notably his
drama of Silesian industrial life, *The Weavers*. **Hauptmann's house** (daily 10am–
noon or later in summer) is an impressive Jugendstil mansion, now a convalescent
home for young victims of industrial pollution from the Katowice conurbation. Its
Great Hall, decorated with giant murals with a ceiling depicting the firmament, is
the most outstanding feature, although you can visit the Memorial Room, with its
first editions of his major works. The path leading to the house (as well as many
other tourist traps in the mountain resort areas) is lined with stalls selling
engraved crystalware, a definitive souvenir of Silesia's highland regions.

There's a new **youth hostel** in the nearby village of Michałowice, a couple of
kilometres to the west (☎53344) which makes a lovely quiet spot to rest up away
from the busy resorts to the east and west.

The Karkonosze Mountains

The **Karkonosze** are the highest and best-known part of the chain known as the
Sudety Mountains, which stretch 300km northwest from the smaller Beskid
range, forming a natural border between Silesia and Bohemia. Known for its raw
climate, the predominantly granite Karkonosze range rises abruptly on the Polish
side, and its lower slopes are heavily forested with fir, beech, birch and pine,
though these are suffering badly from the acid rain endemic in central Europe. At
around 1100m, these trees give way to dwarf mountain pines and alpine plants,
some of them exotic to the region.

Primarily renowned as **hiking** country, these moody, mist-shrouded mountains
strongly stirred the German Romantic imagination and were hauntingly depicted
by the greatest artist of the movement, Caspar David Friedrich. From the amount
of German you hear spoken in the resorts, it's clear that the region offers a popular and inexpensive vacation for its former occupants – and the Polish tourist
authorities certainly aren't complaining.

The two main sprawling resorts of **Szklarska Poręba** and **Karpacz** lying just
outside the park's boundaries have expanded over recent years to meet this need,
with the worldwide craze of **mountain biking** adding a new lease of life to
summertime activities. Indeed, if you decide to stay you might find it preferable
to secure lodgings in the surrounding smaller villages, away from the high-
summer bustle of the two resorts. As the area is relatively compact – the total
length of the Karkanosze is no more than 37km – and the public transport system
good (if circuitous), there's no need to use more than one base. The upper
reaches of the Karkonosze have been designated a **National Park** (entry 5zł per
day), but as elsewhere, this label does not guarantee an unequivocal vision of
natural splendour. If you're not into extended walking or off-road biking, a **chair
lift** ascent up to the summits will make an enjoyable day's excursion.

The 1:30,000 **map** of the National Park, available from kiosks and travel offices, shows all the paths and viewpoints and is a must if you intend doing any serious walking. Like all mountain areas, the range is notorious for its changeable weather; take warm clothing even on a sunny summer's day. **Mist** hangs around on about three hundred days in the year, so always stick to the marked paths and don't expect to see much.

Szklarska Poręba

SZKLARSKA PORĘBA lies 18km southwest of Jelenia Góra and just to the west of a major international road crossing into the Czech Republic. It can be reached from Jelenia Góra either by train, depositing you at the station on the northern heights of the town, or by bus, whose terminus is at the eastern entrance to the resort.

You might prefer to walk the last few kilometres of the bus route from Piechowice (which also has a train station); although not actually in the National Park, this offers some fine scenery. The road closely follows the course of the **Kamienna**, one of the main streams rising in the mountains, which is joined along this short stretch by several tributaries, in a landscape reminiscent of the less wild parts of the Scottish highlands. Much the best vistas are to be had from the road itself, which has an intermittent lane set aside for walkers; the views from the hiking trails are obscured by trees most of the time. However, you do need to make a detour down one of the paths in order to see the **waterfall** formed by the Szklarska about a kilometre after the *Hotel Las*; the point to turn off is easy to find being usually thronged with souvenir sellers.

The Kamienna slices Szklarska Poręba in two, with the main streets in the valley and the rest of the town rising high into the hills on each side. It's well worth following the stream all the way through the built-up part of the resort, as there follows another extremely picturesque stretch, with some striking rock formations (the **Kruce Skalny**) towering above the southern bank. Beyond, at the extreme western edge of town, is the celebrated **Huta Julia glassworks**, source of the region's lead crystal and whose nineteenth-century core can be visited by guided tour on weekday mornings.

From the busy town the quickest way up to the summits is by **chair lift**, which goes up in two stages and terminates a short walk from the summit of **Szrenica** (1362m). Its departure point is at the southern end of town: from the bus station, follow ul. 1 Maja, then turn right into ul. Turystyczna, continuing along all the way to the end, following green then black markers. Despite its rickety appearance, the chair lift, which generally operates between 9am and 5pm, is quite secure. Having effortlessly attained height you can now walk back down or, more ambitiously, follow the ridge east to the sister peak of Snieżka and the resort of Karpacz beneath it (see below), a good day's walking.

Practicalities

As you'd expect, Szklarska Poręba has a great variety of accommodation. Of the **hotels**, the best value is *Piechowice*, ul. Turystyczna 8 (☎075/17 36 93; ④); others include the upmarket *Sudety*, right in the heart of the resort at ul. Krasickiego 10 (☎075/17 22 25; ⑧), and the aforementioned *Hotel Las* (☎075/17 29 11; ⑥–⑦), on the Piechowice road about 2km east of town. It's been done up into a smart new alpine-style hotel, although it's most handy if you've got your own transport.

The *Biuro Zakwaterowania* across from the bus station at ul. Maja 4 (☎17 23 93) can arrange stays in **private rooms**, while the tourist information centre at ul. Jedności Narodowej 3 (☎075/17 24 94) has access to **pensions** offering good-value, all-in deals; there are at least thirty pensions (③) offering half-board accommodation. The **Altur** office opposite (☎075/17 21 23) offers a similar service.

There are also **tourist hostels** at ul. Sportowy 6 (☎075/17 22 37; ②) and ul. 1 Maja 16 (☎075/17 27 09; ②) and the Kochanówka *PTTK* hut by the Szklarska waterfall (☎075/17 24 00; ②) on the road east. The **youth hostel** is a less enticing option, a long way out at ul. Piastowska 1 (☎075/17 21 41), on the wrong side of town for the best walks, and there's a **campsite** off ul 1 Maja by the bridge or the equally crowded *Weneda* about a kilometre east of town on the Piechowice road (☎075/17 32 87).

Ulica Jedności Narodowej offers the main concentration of places to **eat** and **drink**, with *Polonia* at no. 5 being the most recommendable; several alternatives can be found on uls. Turystyczna and 1 Maja.

Karpacz and around

KARPACZ, 15km south of Jelenia Góra and linked to it by three trains and at least twenty buses a day, is an even more scattered community than Szklarska Poręba, occupying an enormous area for a place with only a few thousand permanent inhabitants. Much of it is built along the main road, ul. 1 Maja, which stretches and curves 3km uphill to the *Hotel Biały Jar*. The hotel marks the convergence of four hiking trails and the terminus for some buses; others continue up the road to Karpacz Górny (at least 1hr).

In the centre of Karpacz Górny is the most famous, not to say curious, building in the Karkonosze – the **Wang Chapel**. This twelfth-century wooden church with Romanesque touches boasts some wonderfully refined carving on its portals and capitals as well as an exterior of tiny wooden tiles giving it a scaly, reptilian quality. It stood for nearly six hundred years in a village in southern Norway, but by 1840, it had fallen into such a state of disrepair that the parishioners sought a buyer for it. Having failed to interest any Norwegians, they sold it to the most powerful architectural conservationist of the day, King Friedrich Wilhelm IV of Prussia. He had the church dismantled and shipped to this isolated spot, where it was meticulously reassembled over a period of two years. The stone tower added at the beginning of the present century is the only feature which is not original and looks conspicuously inappropriate. In deference to Friedrich Wilhelm's wishes, the chapel is still used on Sunday mornings for Protestant worship; there are also organ recitals on alternate Sundays in summer. There are twenty-minute **guided tours** of the inside of the church (8am–4pm); the commentary is usually in Polish or German, but English cassettes are also available.

Next to the Wang Chapel is one of the entry points to the National Park from where the blue hiking trail goes up into the hills. More fun, if less worthy, you can take a ride on the **chair lift** (8am–5pm) which is situated midway between here and the *Biały Jar* and terminates at Kopa, just twenty minutes from the Karkanosz's high point of **Śnieżka** (see below).

A short distance west of the chair lift, is the upper of two **waterfalls** on the Łomnica river, which rises high in the mountains and flows all the way through Karpacz, defining much of the northern boundary of the town, as well as the course of ul. Konstitucji 3 Maja, which follows a largely parallel line. The second waterfall, below *Biały Jar* on a path waymarked in red, is less idyllic, having been altered to form a dam. However, on its northern bank there's the attraction of the pleasantly secluded wooded heights of Karpatka and a café on the waterfront.

The only other sightseeing attraction in Karpacz itself is the small **Museum of Sport and Tourism** (Tues, Wed, Fri–Sun 9am–4pm, Thurs 11am–6pm), housed in an alpine chalet on ul. Kopernika. Inside you'll find a selection of archaic bobsleighs and crampons and upstairs, a lovely room full of lace, carved furniture and traditional dress, as well as a model of Chojnik Castle. Below the museum is the valley of the Dolna, which offers a superb **view** over the National Park.

Hikes from Karpacz

Before undertaking any day walks in this area it's worth getting yourself a copy of the 1:30,000 *Karpacz i Okolice* **map**, if you haven't already got the National Park map mentioned earlier. It includes a plan of the town and is sold at the tourist office on ul Konstitucji 3 Maja 52a. The following descriptions will be all the clearer with a copy of this inexpensive map.

The most popular goal for most walks is the summit of **Śnieżka**, at 1602m the highest peak in the range and sometimes covered with snow for up to six months of the year. Lying almost due south of Karpacz, it can be reached by the **black trail** in about three hours from the *Biały Jar*, or in about forty minutes if you pick up the trail at the top of the Kopa chair lift. From the chair lift you pass through the Kocioł Łomniczki, whose abundant vegetation includes Carpathian birch, cloves, alpine roses and monk's hood. Access to the actual summit is by either the steep and stony "Zigzag Way" (the red trail) which ascends by the most direct method, or the easier "Jubilee Way" (the blue route), which goes round the northern and eastern sides of the summit. At the top is a large modern weather station-cum-snack bar, where you can get cheap hot meals; refreshments are also available in the refuges on Kopa and Pod Śnieżka, and at the junction of the two trails.

The **red path** also serves the summit. From Biały Jar it follows the stream to the chair lift terminal and then forks right near the *Orlinek* hotel onto an unmade track which climbs steadily for forty minutes to a junction with a yellow path and a refuge. The path continues above the tree line and after some steeper zigzags reaches the Pod Snieżka refuge, another forty minutes later: the refuge is less than fifteen minutes above the Kopa chair lift terminal, following the black waymarkers. From here the side-trip east to the summit of Śnieżka takes twenty minutes by the "Zigzag Way". On a clear day, the **view** from Śnieżka stretches for 80km, embracing not only other parts of the Sudety chain in Poland and the Czech Republic, but also the Lausitz Mountains in Germany.

Once at the summit, it's worth following the red trail immediately to the west above two glacial **lakes**, Mały Staw and Wielki Staw just above the tree line. Assuming you don't want to continue on to Szklarska Poręba, you can then descend by the black trail and switch to the blue, which brings you out at Karpacz Górny. If you're feeling energetic you might like to go a bit further along the red trail and check out the Słonecznik and the Pielgrzymy **rock formations** thereafter descending by the yellow and later blue trails back to Karpacz Górny. If the above routes seem too strenuous, a satisfyingly easy alternative is to take the blue trail from the Karpacz Górny to the Samotnia refuge on the shore of Mały Staw, a round trip taking about three hours.

Practicalities

In the Dolna valley, below the museum at ul. Obrońców 5, is the Karkonosze's leading **hotel**, the luxurious and ultra-modern *Skalny* (☎075/19721; ⑦). The alternatives are the aforementioned *Biały Jar*, ul. 1 Maja 79 (☎075/19319; ②), and *Bacowki*, ul. Obrońców 6b (☎075/19764; rooms ②, six-berth chalets with kitchenette ⑤), just opposite the Skalny. There's a **tourist hostel** in the town centre at ul. Waryńskiego 6 (☎075/19513; ②), and a **campsite** at the swimming pool. The *Liczyrzepa* **youth hostel** is at ul. Gimnazjalna 9 (☎075/19290) on the corner of ul. Żeromskiego, most easily reached by following the green waymarkers downhill from *Biały Jar*. Near the northern entry to Karpacz are the train station and the main **campsite** (☎075/19316), both at the top end of ul. Konstitucji 3 Maja 8. Information about **pensions** offering full and half board is available from **Karpacz tourist information** at no. 52a on the same street in the main part of town (☎075/19547). Several places to **eat** and **drink** can also be found around here.

From the Karkonosze to the Kłodzko Region

In the stretch of land between the Karkonosze Mountains and Silesia's other main recreation area – the Kłodzko valley to the southeast – lie several historic towns, most of them connected with the former **Duchy of Świdnica**, which lasted only from 1290 to 1392 but exerted a profound influence on Silesian culture. The places mentioned are best visited in passing from the one holiday district to the other, or on day trips from Wrocław or the resorts themselves. Accommodation is limited, and there's not likely to be a reason for wanting to spend the night anyway.

Krzeszów

The village of **KRZESZÓW**, 46km southeast of Jelenia Góra via Kamienna Góra (a grubby textile town useful only for the regular bus service to the village), lies in the shade of a huge **Abbey** complex which ranks, historically and certainly artistically, among the most exceptional monuments in Silesia. If you're anywhere near the area you won't regret making the effort to visit the place. It was first settled in 1242 by Benedictines at the instigation of Anne, widow of Henryk the Pious. However, they stayed for less than half a century; the land was bought back by Anne's grandson, Bolko I of Świdnica, who granted it to the Cistercians and made their church his family's mausoleum. Despite being devastated by the Hussites and again in the Thirty Years' War, the abbey flourished, eventually owning nearly 300 square kilometres of land, including two towns and forty villages. This economic base funded the complete rebuilding in the Baroque period, but not long afterwards the community went into irreversible decline as the result of the confiscation of its lands during the Silesian Wars.

For over a century the buildings lay abandoned, but in a nicely symmetrical turn of events they were reoccupied by Benedictine monks from Prague in 1919, with a contingent of nuns joining them after World War II. Restoration work commenced a few years ago and should be completed during 1996, with both the main churches returned to an outstanding condition. That you should find such an architecturally impressive institution dominating this tiny Silesian village only adds to its splendour.

The two churches are very different in size and feel. The smaller and relatively plainer exterior of the two, **St Joseph's**, was built in the 1690s for parish use. In replacing the medieval church, its dedication was changed to reflect the Counter-Reformation cult of the Virgin Mary's husband, designed to stress a family image which was overlooked in earlier Catholic theology. Inside, the blue-veined marble and high windows give a bright impression with the newly renovated altar resplendent in the typically Baroque style. The magnificent **fresco cycle** in which Joseph – previously depicted by artists as a shambling old man – appears to be little older than his wife and is similarily transported to heaven, is a prime artistic expression of this short-lived cult. Executed with bold brushwork and warm colours, it is the masterpiece of **Michael Willmann**, an East Prussian who converted to Catholicism and spent the rest of his life carrying out commissions from Silesian religious houses. On the ceiling, Willmann continued the family theme with various Biblical genealogies.

The **Monastic Church** built in the grand Baroque style, was begun in 1728 and finished in just seven years – hence its great unity of design, relying for effect on a combination of monumentality and elaborate decoration. Its most striking feature is undoubtably its imposing **facade**, with gravity-defying statues of various religious figures filling the space between the two domed towers. Inside, the three altarpieces in the transept are all Willmann's work, but the most notable painting is a Byzantine icon which has been at Krzeszów since the fourteenth century. The nave ceiling frescoes illustrate the life of the Virgin, and thus form a sort of counterpoint to those in the parish church; that in the south transept shows the Hussites martyring the monks.

From the south transept you pass into the **Piast Mausoleum** behind the high altar. This is kept open when tourist groups are around (which is quite frequently in summer); at other times you'll have to persuade a monk or nun to open it up. Focal point of the chapel is the grandiose coloured marble monument to Bernard of Świdnica, to each side of which are more modest Gothic sarcophagi of Bolko I and II. The history of the abbey is told in the frescoes on the two domes.

Other buildings in the close include the monastic quarters adjoining the church, the now derelict hostelry beside St Joseph's, a shrine which is part of a series of wayside chapels continued outside the precincts, and the former estate management offices fronting the entrance gateway. There's a snack bar in the car park opposite the abbey's entrance.

For an **overnight stay** the *Bethlehem* pension (☎12324; ⑥ including full board), signposted 2km south of town, makes an idyllic retreat: a *dzewnianka* (wooden chalet) situated in the woods, which you'll find hard to leave. Adjacent to the building is the little-known *Pawilion na Wodzie* (Water Pavilion), a former summer house for Krzeszów's bishops. Set in its own moat, the interior was decorated in the Willmann school at the end of the seventeenth century with key scenes from the Old Testament. If you want to have a look for yourself, the owners of the house (who speak some English and German between them) will show you around for a small fee. A less memorable night can be spent at Kamienna Góra's *Pan Tadeusz* **hotel**, ul. Legnicka 2e (☎5227; ③); little more than a converted modern house signposted close to the traffic lights on the Bolków road out of town.

Bolków, Jawor and Strzegom

The very name of **BOLKÓW**, 35km east of Jelenia Góra and 19km north of Kamienna Góra, proclaims its foundation by the first duke of Świdnica, Bolko I. Although a ruin, his **Castle** (Tues–Fri 9am–3pm, Sat 8am–3pm, Sun 9am–4pm) is still an impressive sight, rising imperiously above the little town. Later converted into a Renaissance palace, it passed into the control of the monks of Krzeszów, and was finally abandoned after their Napoleonic suppression. A section of the buildings has been restored to house a small museum on the history of the town, and you can ascend the tower for a fine panoramic view. Below it is the old well, now a wish-fulfilling repository for near worthless old złoty notes.

There's little to see in the lower town, though the gaudily painted Gothic Parish Church and the sloping Rynek have a certain charm. On the square you'll find the *Astra* pizzeria. The town has one **hotel**, *Bolków*, ul. Sienkiewicza 17 (☎1341; ⑥), with an excellent **restaurant** and offers a ten percent discount to readers of this book. Various special interest **excursions** such as heraldic tournaments in early July, rides on the old Jaworzyna Śląska–Bolków–Marciszów rail line and barbecue evenings in the castle are also operated from here.

Jawor

Some 20km north, about halfway towards Legnica, lies the somewhat larger town of **JAWOR**, which was formerly the capital of one of the independent Silesian duchies. It preserves a fair number of colourful Renaissance and Baroque town houses, many of them on the small arcaded Rynek from which erupts the neo-Renaissance bulk of the **Town Hall** nicely complementing its tower, retained from its fourteenth-centruy Gothic predecessor. A somewhat later Gothic style is evident in the **Church of St Martin**, a fine hall design, with varied furnishings including Renaissance choir stalls and a Baroque high altar. Behind the church, a hole in the epitaph-laden brick wall leads to some even older, rubbish-strewn ruins.

From the Rynek, ul. Grundwalska heads northwest through pl. Wolności. On the far side, a gate leads to the town's most historically if not necessarily visually intriguing monument, the barn-like, timber-framed **Church of Peace** (Kościół Pokoju). Its name derives from the Peace of Westphalia of 1648, which brought to an end the morass of religious and dynastic conflicts known as the Thirty Years' War, though the name could equally well apply to the tranquil setting outside the old town walls. The church was one of three (two of which survive) that Silesia's Protestant minority were allowed to build following the cessation of hostilities, and both the material used – wood and clay only, no stone or brick – and the location outside the town centre were among the conditions laid down by the ruling Habsburg emperor. Designed by an engineer, Albrecht von Säbisch, the church was cleverly laid out in such a way that an enormous congregation could be packed into a relatively modest space, an effect illustrated even more clearly in its more charismatic counterpart in Świdnica (see below).

Strzegom

STRZEGOM, 15km southeast of Jawor and 20km east of Bolków on the road and train routes to Wrocław, is regarded by some as Silesia's oldest town, and might be among the oldest in Poland. A long-established source of granite extracted from nearby quarries, it nevertheless preserves few suggestions of its antiquity. Approaching from afar you can't miss the huge Gothic bulk of its **Basilica of SS**

Peter and Paul, built from the local rock with more readily workable sandstone typanums illustrating *The Last Judgement* (with what seems like an excess of Apocalyptic Horsemen) and on the southern porch, *The Dormition of the Virgin.*

Continuing onwards from Strzegom by rail, you shortly come to the junction of Jaworzyna Śląska, where the lines to Wrocław and Świdnica split. Train enthusiasts should make a point of alighting here: steam engines are still in operation, and a number of historic locomotives have been parked as static displays. Excursions services also run west via Bolków to Marciszów: check locally for the latest situation.

Książ

One of the best-preserved castles in Silesia – and the largest hilltop fortress in the country – is to be found in **KSIĄŻ**, southeast of Jelenia Góra. By public tranport your best bet is to approach from the dreary mining and industrial town of Wałbrzych, a couple of kilometres south, from where bus #8 commutes regularly and delivers you right at the foot of your destination. By car you'll have to walk the last half-kilometre or so through the thick woodland which gives Książ the appearance of being in deep countryside.

Before you the majestic **Castle** (May–Sept Mon–Fri 10am–5pm, Sat & Sun 10am–6pm; Oct & April Mon–Fri 10am–4pm, Sat & Sun 10am–5pm; Nov–March Mon–Fri 10am–3pm, Sat & Sun 10am–4pm) sits on a rocky promontory surrounded from three sides by the Pełcznica river's ravine. Despite a disparity of styles taking in practically everything from the thirteenth-century Romanesque of Duke Bolko I's original fortress to idealized twentieth-century extensions, it makes as impressive a sight as you'll get in Silesia's war- and industry-ravaged environs. Partially transformed into a bomb-proof bunker for Hitler during the war, the castle was subsequently occupied by the Soviet army and what they and the Germans hadn't pillaged was picked away by nearby residents until the local authorities took it upon themselves to restore the site. At present, the condition of the four hundred room castle might be described as "stabilized", undertaking a variety of roles including bar, restaurant, art gallery, hotel and historic tourist attraction. However this lack of identity, added to the freedom to wander around the deserted corridors (possibly a result of contradictory signposting) makes for an agreeable if not quite fascinating visit.

If you do decide to visit, make sure you splash out for the escorted ascent of the main **tower** (minimum 2 maximum 6 people) which takes about 25 minutes. Built over the original core of Bolko's citadel, ascending the ever-diminishing staircase to the Baroque lantern is like climbing through centuries of Książ's past. On the way the guide will point out salient details which include Gothic elements and graffiti from the wartime and Soviet occupants. From the top, the view across the terracotta-tiled roofs and forest to the surrounding hills will absorb you while you catch your breath with the guide pointing out distant hills from where V2 rockets were fired on England fifty years ago.

Back at ground level are some rather staid exhibitions of contorted glass at which the Poles excel, along with the customary collection of historical artefacts. By far the finest interior is the **Maximilian Hall**, a piece of palatial Baroque complete with carved chimneypieces, gilded chandeliers, a fresco of Mount Parnassus and colourful marble panelling. Either side of the hall are salons which continue the ornamentation with colour-themed decor.

The basement houses an inexpensive **restaurant**, while on the other side is an authentically cramped beer cellar which leads onto an attractive terrace. This western side of the castle, clad in thick ivy, but not even a century old, overlooks the small French ornamental gardens and the entrance to what are presumably the vestiges of Hitler's bunker – a few poorly lit concrete-lined corridors leading nowhere. Close to the entrance gate the *Hotel Książ* (☎43 27 98; ②) has been extracted from some outbuildings to make an inexpensive and unusual place to spend the night.

Świdnica

Although visible as a collection of ever-familiar smoke stacks when approached by road, **ŚWIDNICA**, 16km northeast of Wałbrzych and for centuries Silesia's second most important city, is blessed by the fact that it suffered little damage in World War II. Today the town still manages to preserve some of the grandeur of a former princely capital resulting in an attractive Silesian town with a tangible self-confidence.

Although Świdnica's period of independent glory – coming soon after its twelfth-century foundation – was short-lived, the town continued to flourish under Bohemian rule. Not only was it an important centre of trade and commerce, it ranked as one of Europe's most renowned brewing centres, with its famous *Schwarze Schöps* forming the staple fare of Wrocław's best-known tavern and exported as far afield as Italy and Russia.

A couple of minutes' walk east from the **train** and **bus stations**, the lively **Rynek** is predominantly Baroque, though the core of many of the houses is often much older. Two particularly notable facades are at no. 7, known as **The Golden Cross**, and no. 8, **The Gilded Man**. In the central area of the square are two fine fountains and the handsome early eighteenth-century **Town Hall**, which preserves the tower and an elegant star-vaulted chamber from its Gothic predecessor.

SS Stanislaw and Wenceslas

Off the southwestern corner of the Rynek, the main street, ul. Długa, curves gently downhill. The view ahead stretches past a number of Baroque mansions to the majestic **belfry** – at 103m the second highest in Poland – of the Gothic **Parish Church of SS Stanislaw and Wenceslas**. Intended as one of a pair, the tower was so long under construction that its final stages were finished in 1613, long after the Reformation. This incomplete nature is visible from the strikingly unsymmetrical facade where the matching right side is conspicuous by its absence. Nevertheless, the extant facade, in front of which stands a Baroque statue of Saint Jan Nepomuk, is impressive enough, featuring a sublime Late Gothic relief of *St Anne, the Virgin and Child*. Around the early fifteenth-century portals, the two patrons occupy a privileged position in the group of Apostles framing the Madonna – notice also the relief to the right of a man being thrown from a bridge for some arcane felony.

During the Thirty Years' War, the church was returned to Catholic use and shortly afterwards given to the Jesuits, who subsequently erected the large college building on the south side which actually appears much younger. They also carried out a Baroque transformation of the **interior**, respecting the original architecture while embellishing it to give a richer surface effect. A massive high altar with statues of the order's favourite saints dominates the east end; the organ with its carvings of the heavenly choir provides a similar focus to the west, while the lofty walls were embellished with huge Counter-Reformation altarpieces, some of them by Willmann.

The Church of Peace

Set in a quiet walled close ten minutes' walk north of the Rynek, the **Church of Peace** (Kościół Pokoju) was built in the 1650s for the displaced Protestant congregation of SS Stanislaw and Wenceslas, according to the conditions on construction applied at Jawor (see p.505) a few years before and to plans drawn up by the same engineer. Although the smaller of the two, it is the more accomplished: indeed, it's considered by some to be the greatest timber-framed church ever built. At first sight, the rusticity of the scene, with its shady graveyard, seems to be mirrored in the architecture, but it's actually a highly sophisticated piece of design. Over 3500 worshippers could be seated inside, thanks to the double two-tiered galleries: all would be able to hear the preacher, and most could see him.

The whole appearance of the church was sharply modified in the eighteenth century, as the Protestant community increased in size and influence after Silesia came under the rule of Prussia. A domed vestibule using the hitherto banned materials was added to the west end, a baptistery to the east, while a picturesque group of **chapels and porches** was tagged on to the two long sides of the building. The latter, recognizable today by their red doorways, served as the entrances to the private boxes of the most eminent citizens whose funerary monuments are slowly crumbling away on the exterior walls. At the same time, the church was beautified inside by the addition of a rich set of furnishings – pulpit, font, reredos and the large and small organs.

Practicalities

Świdnica's main **hotel**, the *Piast*, situated just west of the Rynek at ul. Kotwarska 11 (☎074/52 34 77; ⑤) is as plush an establishment as you're likely to find in the region and includes the excellent *Piast Roman* **restaurant**. The only other choice is the adequate *Sportowy*, south of the centre at ul. Śląska 37 (☎074/22536; ②); from the train station walk south a bit and follow ul. Pionierów for about a kilometre. As for food, on the Rynek the *Kupiecki* at no. 18 is the dirt-cheap antithesis of the *Piast Roman*, while the *Casanova Café*, on the Rynek's south side, falls somewhere between the two. At no. 31 on the square you'll find the **Orbis** office (☎074/22674).

Henryków

If you're travelling between Wrocław and Kłodzko by either road or rail, it's worth considering a stop at **HENRYKÓW**, although be warned that the train station is more than 2km from the village. In 1220, the first **Cistercian Abbey** in Silesia was founded here by Duke Henryk the Bearded, who immodestly named it after himself. Half a century later, the abbot, a man named Piotr, compiled a chronicle in which appears the earliest written sentence in the Polish language – a fact which has bestowed on Henryków a special place in the national consciousness.

In the late seventeenth and early eighteenth centuries, the monastery was greatly expanded in the monumental Baroque style then in vogue. These buildings still dominate the village, which, since the monastery's suppression, has been left with the problem of how to make full use of them. The architecture of the church, whose plain Gothic style reflects the Cistercians' ascetic principles, has survived largely intact, though its interior is swamped with Baroque furnishings, including much fine woodwork and several altarpieces by the ubiquitous Michael Willmann. The church is normally kept locked, so you may have to search out a priest to show you round.

The Kłodzko region

Due south of Wrocław is a rural area of wooded hills, gentle valleys and curative springs that provides a timely antidote to the heavy industry which blights so much of Silesia. Known as the **Kłodzko region** after its largest town, it's surrounded on three sides by the Czech Republic along which the Sudety mountains form a natural frontier.

A popular holiday area for insolvent Silesians looking for a break from the industrial conurbations, you won't find many of the five **spa resorts** (identified by the suffix *-Zdrój*) as appealing as they may sound. The gracious prewar days when "taking the waters" was a fashionable indulgence are long gone and today the resorts are shadows of their former selves. Nevertheless, if you're heading for the Czech Republic then a visit to one or two and a quick swig of the effervescent local tonic won't ruin your day.

In the hills above these resorts are some fine **hiking routes** passing through landscapes dotted with sometimes bizarre rock outcrops. A network of marked paths covers the entire region, in which there are several separate ranges; the best are found in the southeast of the area, taken up by the **Masyw Śnieżnika**. This specific area is as yet little touched by the more rapacious tourist development elsewhere and is a worthwhile destination for spending a few quiet days in the hills. The red and yellow 1:90,000 *Ziemia Kłodzka* **map**, easily available from local bookshops, is an essential companion.

Accommodation throughout the Kłodzko region is plentiful, although the bigger resorts tend to fill up with partying youngsters in high summer. Nevertheless it's possible to stay here very cheaply, with the custom-built **pensions** offering particularly good value. For **getting around**, buses, which eventually get to even the smallest villages, or hitching are your best bets; picturesque rail lines hug the valleys, but train stations are usually on the outskirts of the towns.

Kłodzko

Spread out beneath the ramparts of a stolid Prussian fortress, the thousand-year-old town of **KŁODZKO** was for centuries a place of strategic importance and today its Old Town still retains some of the charm of its medieval origins – a rarity in Silesia which makes a stopover here rewarding. Situated on the main trade route between Bohemia and Poland, until the eighteenth-century Prussian take-over, Kłodzko's ownership fluctuated between the adjacent nations. Indeed at one point the town once belonged to the father of Adalbert, the Czech saint who was to have a crucial impact on the development of the early Polish nation (see p.562).

From the main train and bus stations situated side by side in the centre of town, the best way to enjoy an exploration of the attractive **Old Town** is to cross the steel girder bridge beside the prominent *Hotel Astoria* which brings you into ul. Grottgera. At the end of this street you'll find the main survivor of the town's medieval fortifications, the **Gothic bridge**, adorned in the Baroque period by a collection of sacred statues who still manage to look pleadingly heavenward despite centuries of weathering.

On the opposite bank, grand nineteenth-century mansions rise high above the river. Passing them, you ascend to the sloping Rynek (known as plac Bolesława Chrobrego) which has a number of fine old houses from various periods, an undistinguished nineteeth-century Town Hall and an ornate Baroque fountain which looks up to the fortress's walls. Greatly extended by the Prussians in the eighteenth century from earlier defensive structures built on the rocky knoll, the squat **Fortress'** (Tues–Sun 9am–5pm) impregnability was successfully tested during a siege in 1807 by the all-conquering army of Napoleon. As with other historical monuments which have suffered the vagaries of several disparate owners, the fortress nowadays has become a repository for a variety of objects and activities from old fire engines to contemporary local glassware, and you can even learn to abseil in one of the courtyards. However, most visitors come here for the stronghold's extensive network of **tunnels** (guided tours) which were excavated by prisoners of war during the Prussian era, and today still entail a fair amount of crawling around in semi-darkness while the guide rattles through his spiel.

During the last war the fortress was used as a prison camp and in one of the many galleries you'll find a memorial to the thousands of prisoners who perished here. Near the uppermost terrace a small chamber also houses a genuinely chilling sculpture which further commemorates the wartime dead. Nearby is the **viewpoint** over the town's roofscapes to the hills beyond; it bears a striking resemblance to the comparable, if somewhat grander, panorama from Grenoble's similar fort in southeastern France.

By the entrance of the fortress is the northern aperture of yet another **underground passage** (daily 9am–5pm), this 600-metre example making an unusual and blissfully cool way of passing under the Old Town on a hot summer's day. There's little to see along the way, bar bricked-up passages and the odd half-hearted attempt at evoking a dungeon, but the exit brings you out just below a small square in which stands one of the finest Baroque church interiors in Poland. Kłodzko's **Parish Church of Our Lady** really should not be missed and will have avid church-spotters drooling in the aisles. Outside, the Gothic building's shell remains remarkably well preserved, but inside, two and a half centuries of Baroque ornamentation were undertaken with such zeal that you hardly know where to rest your eyes. Barely a surface is left without some kind of embellishment in gold, marble or paint, giving a busy impression that either fills you with awe or gives you a headache. One of the many things to look out for is the fourteenth-century tomb of the founder, Bishop Ernst of Pordolice, which somehow managed to survive the desecrations of the Hussites five centuries ago.

Leaving the church square to the west and following ul. Łukasiewicza, brings you to the **Kłodzko Regional Museum** (Tues 10am–3pm, Wed–Fri 10am–5pm, Sat & Sun 11am–5pm) whose sole redeeming feature, apart from the occasional concert recitals in the adjacent hall, is the exhaustive assembly of over four hundred clocks located on the top floor. The collection is based on the fruits of the Świedbodzia and Srebrna Góra clock factories and displays everything from ancient astronomical devices, working grandfather and irritating cuckoo clocks, to porcelain-backed kitchen clocks. One small dark room features a mirrored floor reflecting a ceiling covered in still more clocks.

Practicalities

Kłodzko Miasto **train station**, which is beside the **bus station**, is only a few minutes' walk from the centre; this station is also the best place to catch trains heading south, and to the two spa valleys to the east and west. The main station, Kłodzko Główny, is over 2km north and only worth using if you're heading to Wrocław or Jelenia Góra.

The **Orbis** office, located just beside the Gothic bridge at ul. Grottgera 1 (Mon–Fri 10am–5pm, Sat 10am–2pm; ☎074/3978), may be of some help although their prime concern these days is selling package holidays to Rome or the Grand Canyon. A more useful source of information is the **regional tourist office** just off the southeast corner of the Rynek on ul. Wita Stwosza (Mon–Thur 8am–4pm, Fri 8am–6pm, Sat 9am–1pm), which leads up from the old bridge. You'll also find a helpful *PTTK* office next door advocating the wonders of the Kłodzko region and providing good local maps.

Kłodzko venerability makes it a much more appealing touring base than the nearby spas, but the town has a fairly brief selection of accommodation options. Of the **hotels**, *Astoria* on pl. Jedności (☎074/3035; ④) is easy to find, being right opposite the bus and train stations. Alternatives include the *Nad Młynówką* at ul. Daszyńskiego 16 (☎074/2563; ④), five minutes' walk west of the bus station just over the modern bridge and on the right, or the *Motel Zosia* about 3km south of town at Noworudska 1 (☎074/3737; ③), although this place is usually full of semi-permanent guests who hoard the few self-contained rooms. For the cheapest bed, try the chalets at the **campsite**, immediately north of the fortress on ul. Nowy Świat (☎074/3031).

Away from the hotels, the best of the few **restaurants** are on ul. Grottgera, where you'll find the *Wilcza Jama* along with the *Czardasz* across the road, the latter specializing in Hungarian dishes. Other than that there's the pleasant *Ratuszowa* in the town hall on the Rynek or the inevitable *Pizza Romano*, ul. Armii Krajowej 1. The handiest **snack bar** is the good old-fashioned *Małgosia*, to the rear of the Miasto station at ul. Połabska 2 – walk under the rail bridge and you'll see it on the left.

Wambierzyce

Heading west from Kłodzko on the main road to Prague are a string of **spa towns**. The first of these, **Polanica-Zdrój**, is not worth the detour in its own right, but a right turn at the west end of town leads 9km to the village of **WAMBIERZYCE** (buses from Polanica-Zdrój or Kłodzko), another tiny rural settlement set out of all proportion to the huge religious institution found there.

The Baroque **Basilica**, perched above a broad flight of steps above the village square has been the site of pilgrimages since 1218, when a blind man regained his sight by praying at a statue of the Virgin Mary enshrined in a lime tree. Pilgrimages ensued over the following centuries with the shrine growing ever bigger on the donations of its visitors. The impressive monumental facade of the basilica is all that remains of the third shrine built here at the end of the seventeenth century, the main body of the building collapsing soon after completion, at which point it was rebuilt with the interior you see today. The basilica is circumvented by a broad ambulatory with a variety of chapels and grottoes representing the Stations of the Cross. The small nave of the basilica is a fairly reserved octagon hung with altarpieces by Michael Willmann, while the all-important pulpit gets the usual excess of ornamentation. On the ceiling is a fresco depicting an angel passing the design for the basilica to the local people, its anticipated form appearing as a ghostly image on the hill behind them. The oval chancel has a cupola illustrating the fifteen Mysteries of the Rosary with a magnificent silver tabernacle from Venice bearing the miraculous image, accompanied by a profusion of votive offerings encased to its side.

Found all around the town are nearly one hundred **shrines** depicting further scenes from the Passion, culminating appropriately at **Calvary**, the wooded hill facing the basilica up which lead a long series of steps lined by still more shrines. Halfway up on the left is the **Szopka** (daily 10am–1pm & 2–4pm), a large mechanical contraption from the early nineteenth century that presents biblical and everyday local scenes, laid out like miniature theatre sets.

Wambierzyce has only one basic **restaurant**, *Turystyczny*, on the square below the basilica. The restaurant may also have **rooms** to let; otherwise see if Pan Gancarski's rooms are available, he lives at ul. Wiejska 52 (☎074/284; ②), the road leading off to the left of the restaurant.

Duszniki-Zdrój

Back on the main Prague road, continuing 10km west of Polanica-Zdrój brings you to the much older spa resort of **DUSZNIKI-ZDRÓJ**, which has a little more going for it than the younger Polanica. The town is best known for its **Chopin Musical Festival** held here in the first half of August each year, an event which commemorates the concerts given by the sixteen-year-old composer during a convalescence in 1826. This, and the unusual industrial museum (see below), are the only bright aspects to this rather weary and neglected spa town.

Duszniki is divided by the Wrocław–Prague road with the **train station** to the north and the Old Town and spa quarter located on the south side. On the **Rynek**, Renaissance and Baroque styles are mingled with less edifying postwar additions, with one of the old town houses bearing a plaque recording Chopin's stay. Leaving the market square to the east down ul. Kłodzko, you pass the **Parish Church of SS Peter and Paul**, an externally bland example of early eighteenth-century Baroque with two unusually ornate pulpits inside. One is shaped like a whale, with the creature's gaping maw forming a preaching platform – a zany stylistic reference to the Jonah story which is occasionally found in other Polish churches.

At the bottom of the same street is the **Museum of the Paper Industry** (Tues–Fri 9am–5pm, Sat & Sun 9am–3pm), which occupies a large paper mill dating from the early seventeenth century and constitutes the town's chief curiosity. One of Poland's most precious industrial buildings, its fine half-timbering, sweeping mansard roof, novel domed entrance turret and crude gable end add up to an eye-catching if understated piece of Baroque architecture.

Practicalities

The **PTTK** office, at no. 14 on the Rynek (☎074/540), operates a room-finding service and runs its own **tourist hostel**, the *Pod Muflonem* (☎074/339; ②), signposted just off pl. Warszawy. Other options include the rather forlorn *Hotel*

Miejski, just off the Rynek at ul. Karola Świerczewskiego 2 (☎074/504; ②); don't worry if it looks closed, they're just saving electricity. There's also a **campsite**, close to the station at Dworcowa 6 (☎074/489). Besides the hotel's equally gloomy **restaurant** there are a couple of lacklustre **snack bars** dotted around town; try the *Bar Jędruś*, ul. Klodzka 36, but don't expect much.

West to Kudowa-Zdrój and the Góry Stołowe

Leaving Duszn
iki and heading towards the Czech frontier, you pass through the village of **SZCZYTNA** with its glass factory producing more of Silesia's famous crystal and pollution. You might be intrigued by the impressive **neo-Gothic Castle** situated near the summit of **Szczytnik** (589m), south of town, but it's actually some kind of children's home and not open to visitors. However, a winding road leads up the hill to a fine viewpoint over the valley below.

KUDOWA-ZDRÓJ lies at the foot of the Góry Stołowe and Wzgórza Lewińskie, 16km west of Duszniki and a couple of kilometres before the crossing into the Czech Republic. Its **springs** were discovered in 1580, and two centuries later, the first spa building was erected so creating the beginnings of today's resort. More than any of the other resorts, Kudowa preserves the feel of the bygone days when it was patronized by the internationally rich and famous, and today it continues to prosper albeit on a more prosaic level.

Grand old villas set in their own grounds give Kudowa its erstwhile aristocratic air, yet it has no obvious centre other than the **spa park**. Here the huge domed **Pijalnina** (pump room) houses the venerated marble fountain from which issue hot and cold springs. Nearby a stall cashes in on visitors' sentimentality, selling the pipe-like *kóbki*, small flattened jugs with swan-necked spouts, from which the surprisingly refreshing water – slightly sweet and carbonated – is traditionally imbibed. Adjacent to the pump room is a concert hall where a festival celebrating the music of Stanisław Moniuszko takes place each July. Sharing the nationalist outlook of Chopin, his compatriot and contemporary, Moniuszko's music has never caught on abroad to anything like the same extent, although you'll see a few bars of his music set into the amusingly kitschy "sheet music" railings installed around town. The spacious spa park's appeal continues with well-kept flower beds and over three hundred different species of tree and shrub.

Practicalities

Orbis and **PTTK** both have offices on ul. Zdrojowa – at no. 47 (☎074/66 12 66) and no. 42a (☎074/66 11 62) respectively. The main room-finding agency, however, is in the resort's leading **hotel**, *Kosmos* at ul. Mariana Buczka 8a (☎074/66 15 11; ⑤). A kilometre from the town centre, just off the the main road leading to the border, is the *Hotel OSiR* (☎074/66 16 27; ③) and the **tourist hostel**, *Pod Strzechą* (☎074/66 12 62; ②), which between them offer a mixture of rooms, pokey chalets and dorms plus a **campsite**. There are also plenty of **pensions** on offer including *Gwarek*, ul. Juliusza Słowackiego 10 (☎074/66 16 61; ②), and the *Dunajec*, ul. Słoneczna 14 (☎074/66 14 48; ②).

Kudowa has a decent variety of places to **eat** and **drink**, with the *Jagodalnia Kosmiczna* opposite the *Orbis* office being especially good and cheap and a Greek restaurant, the *Amfora*, on ul. 1 Maja, the continuation of ul. Zdrojowa. Down on the main road, on the way to the *OSiR* complex, the *Zodiak* restaurant has a pleasant alpine-style interior and all the popular permutations of Polish cuisine on the menu.

Into the Góry Stołowe

Rising above 900m and almost as flat as their name suggests, the **Góry Stołowe** (Table Mountains) are not the most enticing range in the Kłodzko Region, but do have some extraordinary rock formations which can be appreciated in a full day's walk from Kudowa. **Karłów**, 11km east of Kudowa via the so-called "road of a hundred bends", is nearer but there's only a campsite (plus a restaurant and a couple of bars), leaving Kudowa itself as the main alternative if you don't have a tent with you.

From Kudowa, the green trail leads north to the outlying hamlet of **Czermna**, only thirty minutes from town, where the **Chapel of Skulls** (daily 10am–1pm & 2pm–5pm) contains a macabre scene which threatens to undo the curative effects of Kudowa's springs. Its walls and ceiling are decorated with over three thousand skulls and crossed bones from the dead of various wars and epidemics. The project was the morbid obsession of the chapel's priest who, with the help of his devoted grave-digger, amassed the gruesome collection during the last decades of the eighteenth century. Their own remains are set in a glass case by the altar and thousands more skulls are stashed in the crypt.

The trail then goes northeast to the first of several fantastic rock formations in the range, the **Błędne Skały** (Erratic Boulders; entrance fee in summer), where it twists and turns, squirming through narrow gaps between gigantic rocks. It then continues via Pasterka (basic *PTTK* **hostel** open all year; ☎219) to Karłów, from where a climb of nearly seven hundred steps leads to the **Szczeliniec Wielki**, the highest point in the range at 919m. Here the rocks have been weathered into a series of irregular shapes nicknamed "the camel", "the elephant", "the hen", and so on. There's a small entrance fee once you get to the top where a *PTTK*-run café offers refreshments, then you follow the trail which goes down through a deep chasm, on to a viewpoint and back by a different route.

From Błędne Skały the **red trail** leads directly to Karłów continuing east 5km to the largest and most scattered group of rocks in the area, the **Skalne Grzyby** (Petrified Mushrooms), rocks whose bases were worn away by uneven erosion producing the top-heavy appearance their name suggests.

Bystrzyca Kłodzka

Midway down the valley south of Kłodzko, some 15km away, is **BYSTRZYCA KŁODZKA**, its peeling medieval core reminiscent of a charismatically decayed Mediterranean town. This impression is particularly strong if you cross over the river to get a magnificent full-frontal view of the town's tier-like layout, which on a sunny day looks more like southern France than Poland. There's little to see in town, but it's the feel of the place rather than its heritage rating which warrants a brief visit. In summer, people slump on their windowsills, idly surveying the activity below, or snooze on shady benches, giving the town a decidedly laid-back air.

Substantial sections of the **walls** survive, including the Kłodzko and Water barbicans and the Knights' Tower. The tower later became a belfry for the Protestant Church, which is set off the edge of the smaller of the two central squares, the Mały Rynek. Now it houses what must be one of the dullest exhibitions in the land; the **Museum of Fire-Making** (Tues–Sun 9.30am–3pm but usually closed); ask at the *Muzelska Café* opposite or the *Modano* next door if you'd like to survey the matchbox label collection, the museum's *pièce de résistance*. In the middle of the main square, pl. Wolności, is the **Town Hall**, which has a nineteenth-century body tacked onto an octagonal Renaissance tower.

Bystrzyca's train station is conveniently situated right in the centre of town. The only **hotel** is the *Piast* at ul. Okrzei 26 (☎072/11 03 22; ②), inexpensive enough to warrant a night stopover. There are a couple of **restaurants** on pl. Wolności; try the *Regionalna*. Tourist queries are dealt with at the *Bis* **tourist information centre**, ul. Okrzei 16 (☎072/11 27 42), just off the main square.

Międzygórze and the Masyw Śnieżnika

At the southeastern corner of the Kłodzko region is the enticing **Masyw Śnieżnika**, the best of whose scenery can be seen in a good day's walk and which unlike the overrun Karkonosze to the west, seems to be pleasingly ignored by the crowds. The main jumping-off point is the charming hill resort of **MIĘDZYGÓRZE** ("Among the Hills"), a dead end 13km southeast of Bystrzyca and well served by buses which terminate in the village centre. The village itself is lightly commercialized while lacking the accompanying sloth of the spa resorts, and is one of the quieter, more pleasant corners of the Kłodzko region with enough facilities and recreative potential to warrant a couple of days' stay. Despite what some maps show, the sealed road ends at Międzygórze, but on foot or by bike you can easily make the connection to Kletno where the road resumes – a distance of about 10km.

In the village, ul. Sanatoryjna has some lovely wooden villas dating from the turn of the century. With carved balustrades and equally attractive interiors, many are now being done up into holiday homes, a trend that is evident throughout the Kłodzko region. These timber dwellings, known as "*dzewnianki*" and only found in the country's highland areas, are the most evocative expression of the otherwise drab rural domestic architecture found on the plains. On the western outskirts, by the *Hotel Nad Wodospadem* (see below), the 27-metre **waterfall** is the village's most popular attraction.

Międzygórze has several central **bars and cafés** (many of which offer **pension** accommodation), or there's the **hotel**, *Hotel Nad Wodospadem* (☎072/ 13 51 20; ②), out by the waterfall. In addition, an unofficial, but prettily situated **campground**, lies a kilometre east of town, by the river.

Walks in the Masyw Śnieżnika

At the main junction on ul. Sanatoryjna, there's a **signpost** bristling with boards indicating the many waymarked tracks in the area. One particularly good walk follows the **red waymarked trail**, which rises steeply through lovely wooded countryside for about three hours, leading to the *Na Śnieżniku* **refuge** (☎072/13 51 30). Set in total isolation at over 1200m, it offers dormitory accommodation and also serves inexpensive homely meals. From here it's then a much gentler ascent to the flat summit of **Śnieżnik** (1425m), the highest point in the Kłodzko Region, set right on the Czech border.

From the summit it's worth descending north by the yellow trail towards Kletno, which will bring you in about an hour to the **Bear's Cave** (Jaskinia

Niedźwiedzia; Feb–Nov daily 10am–5pm except Mon & Thurs). Discovered in 1966 during quarrying, the cave takes its name from the bear fossils discovered there. Bats still inhabit the cave which boasts the usual anthropomorphically wondrous stalactites and stalagmites. Visits are by guided tour only with group numbers limited to fifteen people. You can also get to the cave directly from Międzygórze, without scaling any mountains, in about two hours.

From the cave, another kilometre's walk brings you to the village of **KLETNO**, which has only a couple of snack bars, a youth hostel 3km down the road and a bus service to Kłodzko via Stronie Śląskie and Lądek Zdrój.

Through the hills to Lądek-Zdrój and beyond

Returning to Bystrzyca Kłodzka, a scenic drive winds back up into the hills directly east of town. Climbing up through forested slopes and emerging from the trees, the narrow road reaches a **pass** where it's worth stopping to appreciate the superb panorama around you. Descending down the other side, the valley unfolds revealing an isolated Lutheran chapel near the village of Sienna, and brings you to the pleasant town of **Stronie Śląskie** (terminus of the rail line from Kłodzko) whose *Sudety* glass works have managed not to turn the place into the usual eyesore.

Eight kilometres further north is the spa resort of **LĄDEK-ZDRÓJ**, where, according to tradition, the waters were known for their healing properties as early as the thirteenth century, when the bathing installations were allegedly destroyed by the Tartars. They've certainly been exploited since the late fifteenth century, and in later years attracted visitors as august as Goethe and Turgenev. Today the town, strung out along the river Biała Lądecka, retains a charm that the more popular western spa resorts cannot match.

Centrepiece of the grandiose Neoclassical **spa buildings** at the east end of town is the main sanatorium, a handsome domed building evoking the heyday of the spa, and hereabouts you'll find the odd villa still surviving from that era. In the older part of town, about a kilometre to the west, a mid-sixteenth-century stone **bridge** can still be seen, decorated with statues of religious figures. The town's spacious **Rynek** features some Baroque-fronted houses, all facing the octagonal tower of the Town Hall.

PTTK have an office at ul. Kościuszki 36 (☎255), near the spa quarter with **Orbis** a couple of doors down at no. 44 (☎273). The only two **restaurants**, *Pod Filarami* and *Ratuszowa*, are both to be found on the Rynek. Oddly enough Lądek has no proper hotels but the *PTTK* can help you secure rooms at a number of **pensions**. There's also a **youth hostel** (☎540) in the outlying hamlet of Stójków to the south.

Immediately to the east of the town, the **Góry Złote** (Golden Mountains) offer some good hiking routes. Check out the blue trail which leads southeast of the town, ascending within an hour to a ruined medieval castle near the summit of **Karpień** (776m), via a series of strangely weathered rocks so often found throughout the region.

Leaving Lądek and heading north, the road continues winding through the forests where you'll encounter soot-spewing trucks transporting rubble from the region's quarries to the processing plants. Soon the road decends swiftly to the town of **Złoty Stok**, sat on edge of the interminable plain which stretches, with only modest variations in elevation, all the way to the Baltic.

Paczków to Nysa

Heading east from the Kłodzko region, you traverse the undulating plateau of Upper Silesia, which stretches down to the Beskid Mountains. The route runs through a string of small fortified towns associated for most of their history with the bishops of Wrocław, who ruled an independent principality here from 1195 until its dissolution by Prussia in 1810. Covering this stretch by public transport, buses have the edge on trains for both convenience and frequency of service.

Paczków

In contrast to its neighbours, the quiet little market town of **PACZKÓW**, 30km east of Kłodzko, has managed to preserve its medieval fortifications almost intact – hence its designation as "Poland's Carcassonne". In reality, Paczków is hardly in that league, but has the advantage of being untouched by the hands of Romantically inclined nineteenth-century restorers, as well as being generally overlooked by crowds of tourists.

Nowadays, the mid-fourteenth-century **ramparts** form a shady promenade around the centre of the Old Town; their visual impact is diminished by the enveloping later buildings, though it's a wonder that the town managed to grow so much without their demolition. As it is, nineteen of the twenty-four towers survive, as does nearly all of the original 1350 metres of wall, pierced by three barbicans: the square Wrocław Gate of 1462 and the cylindrical Ząbkow and Kłodzkego gates from around 1550.

The area within the walls, spread across a gentle slope, consists of just a handful of streets, but is centred on a large **Rynek**. In the familiar off-centre position is the **Town Hall**, so comprehensively rebuilt last century that only the belfry of its Renaissance predecessor is left; ask inside for permission to ascend for the best view of the town.

Rearing up behind the Rynek stands the dull brick edifice of **St John's Church**, a strongly fortified part of the town's defences. Begun soon after the completion of the walls, it was under construction for a century, with the crenel-lated attic not added until the Renaissance period. A section was lopped off the tower in the early eighteenth century, and a bell-like Baroque helmet put in its place in 1557. Inside, the box-like geometry of the design is particularly evident, with the chancel the same length as the main nave.

Practicalities

Paczków's has two **hotels**. The refurbished and renamed *Karan*, ul. Wojska Polskiego 31 (☎077/31 62 77; ②), lies outside the ramparts on a street leading directly off the east side of the Rynek. Out of town on the Nysa road, the *Energopol 7*, ul. Chrobrego 2 (☎077/31 62 98; ②), is a former workers' hostel which makes up for its undistinguished prefabs with friendly service and good value. There's also a **campsite** near here at ul. Jagiellońska 5 (☎077/31 65 09). As for food, there's very little other than the **hotel restaurants**. On the Rynek, the *Kawiarnia Carcassonne* can only offer you *pierogi* and *barsccz*, albeit in a mock Gothic interior, or there's a small pizzeria by the town hall.

Otmuchów

OTMUCHÓW, 14km east of Paczków, was the original capital of the prince-bishopric. In the centre of town is the **Castle**, originally twelfth-century Romanesque, which guarded an extensive fortification system now all but vanished. It was transformed into a palace in the sixteenth century, and in 1820 was sold to Wilhelm von Humboldt, founder of the University of Berlin and architect of Prussia's educational system. He lived here in retirement, the liberal views he had championed having fallen from official favour. Nowadays, it's a great value **hotel** (☎31 51 48; ②), although the grandeur ends in the cobbled courtyard and bathroom facilities are shared.

On the Rynek is the Renaissance **Town Hall**, adorned with a beautifully elaborate sundial. The square slopes upwards to a well-kept floral garden and the **Parish Church**, a very central European-looking Baroque construction with a customary twin-towered facade. Recently renovated to perfection by German capital (a practice now occurring throughout the former German territories of post-communist Poland), its ample interior is richly decorated with stucco work by Italian craftsmen and large painted altarpieces, including several by Michael Willmann.

Other than the castle, the only **places to stay** are the campsites to the west of town, the nearer being at Ścibórz (☎077/31 53 93), the other a few kilometres on at Sarnowice (☎077/31 52 25). To **eat** in Otmuchów, there are the café-restaurants *Zamkowa* and *Eva*, both on the Rynek.

Nysa

The name of **NYSA**, 12km east of Otmuchów, has become synonymous with the trucks made here for export all over Eastern Europe. Yet industry is a relative newcomer to this town which, in spite of the devastation of 1945, still preserves memories of the days when it basked in the fanciful title of "the Silesian Rome", a reference to its numerous religious houses and reputation as a centre of Catholic education. It came to the fore when the adoption of the Reformation in Wrocław forced the bishops to reside outside the city; they then built up Nysa, the capital of their principality for the previous couple of centuries, as their power base.

The Town

Both the **bus** and **train stations** are at the eastern side of the town; from there, bear right along the edge of the park, then turn left into ul. Kolejowa which leads in a straight line towards the centre. On the way, you pass the fourteenth-century **Wrocław Gate**, an unusually graceful piece of military architecture with wrought iron dragons' heads acting as gutter flues, left stranded by the demolition of the ramparts. It's a tantalizing reminder of Nysa's long role as a border fortress: first fortified in the twelfth century by Bolesław the Wrymouth in his struggles against his Bohemian-backed brother Zbigniew. The only other remnant of the fortifications is the **Ziębicka Gate** on ul. Krzywoustego, further down to the right, a plain brick tower similarily isolated from its walls and now marking a roundabout. You can climb up its 150 steps for a couple of złoty.

Having lost its Town Hall and all but four of its old houses during the war, Nysa's vast **Rynek** is nevertheless not as bad as you might expect, with a few flowerbeds and benches on which repose the town's idle, weary and inebriate.

Only the jolly seventeenth-century **Weigh House**, which looks as if it belongs somewhere in the Low Countries, has been rebuilt.

Off the northeastern side of the Rynek is the **Cathedral of St Jacob** (Św. Jakuba) which long served the exiled bishops. Put up in just six years in the 1420s, it's a fine example of the hall church style, with nave and aisles of equal height – a design much favoured in Germany but rare in Poland. Although it was rebuilt from a ruin after the war, it's also unusual for this part of the world in having been very little altered, the only modifications being the reconstruction in Renaissance or Baroque style of three of the chapels and a postwar revision of the brick facade. Entering through the graceful double portal, it's the spareness of the lofty thirty-metre interior which makes the strongest impression. So crushing is the weight of the vault that many of the uncomfortably slender octagonal brick pillars visibly bow under the strain. The chapels provide the only intimate note: fenced off by wrought iron grilles, they feature funerary plaques and monuments to the bishops and local notables. The tomb of St Jacob rests to the right of the altar. His flattened effigy carved in orange marble is accompanied by the portentious depictions of hour glass and skull commonly found on medieval tombs throughout Christian Europe. Outside, the church's detached stone **belfry** was abandoned after fifty years' work and further damaged during the war, after which it seems to have been left to its own devices.

South of St James' lies the well-preserved if generally deserted Baroque episcopal quarter. The **Bishops' Palace**, reached down ul. Jarosławka, is now fitted out as a surprisingly good local **museum** (Tues–Sun 10am–3pm), with well-documented exhibits on the history of Nysa. Inside you'll find spacious displays of sixteenth- to eighteenth-century engravings, several pictures of Nysa's postwar ruin, including a shrapnel-damaged 1574 weather vane, as well as fragments from irreparable buildings. There's also a model of the town as it was three hundred years ago, various secular and religious treasures and perhaps best of all, some wonderfully chunky carved and inlaid Baroque furniture, including a few huge wardrobes it would take a crane to shift and on which you could justifiably observe "they don't make them like that anymore".

At the end of the street in ul. Grodzka is the **Bishops' Residence**, which was built right up against the ramparts but now stands seemingly neglected, concealing some light industrial activities. Turning right here you reach the complex of **Jesuit buildings** in pl. Solny, which have survived in better shape. The white-walled Church of Our Lady (usually locked) is in the plain style, though its austerity is softened by some recently discovered ceiling frescoes and a beautiful eighteenth-century silver tabernacle at the high altar. Adjoining it is the famous **Carolinum College**, whose luminaries included the Polish kings Michał Korybut Wiśniowiecki and Jan Sobieski.

South of the Rynek, the only other reminder of "the Silesian Rome" is the **Monastery of the Hospitallers of the Holy Sepulchre** (Klasztor Bożogrobców). This order moved to Nysa from the Holy Land at the end of the twelfth century, but the huge complex you see today dates from the early eighteenth century. It's now a seminary, and you have to ask at the reception on ul. Św. Pawła to get into the magnificent Baroque **Church of SS Peter and Paul** on the parallel ul. Bracka. Passing a rather creepy Eye of Providence looking down on you in the courtyard, you'll soon have your efforts rewarded. The resplendent interior features gilt capitals, a multi-coloured marble altar that's one of the best for miles, and a reproduction of the Holy Sepulchre in Jerusalem.

There's also a cycle of highly theatrical frescoes by the brothers Christoph Thomas and Felix Anton Scheffler.

Practicalities

Nysa has only one central **hotel**, the rather pricey *Piast* right by the Ziębicka Gate at ul. Krzywoustego 14 (☎077/40 84 80; ⑥). Otherwise, there's the *Lazorowy* **motel** on the outskirts of town heading west (☎077/4077; ⑤) – only practicable if you've got a car, although bus #2 goes there too – and a **youth hostel** close to the station at ul. Bohaterów Warszawy 7 (☎077/3731).

The best **restaurants** are the snazzy *Capri* and *Kama*, close to each other on the Rynek near *Orbis*, the *Warszawianka* near the hotel at ul. Krzywoustego 25 and the uninspiring *Pod Starą Wagą* also on the Rynek. For a lighter meal, try the *Bar Tiffany* by the Wrocław Gate on ul. Wrocławska. **Orbis**, for what they're worth, are at the market end of the same street (☎077/33 27 82).

Brzeg

A worthwhile stopover for a few hours between Wrocław and Opole is the old ducal seat of **BRZEG**, an easily manageable and agreeable market town with an impressive array of monuments. Originally a fishing village on the bank (*brzeg*) of the Odra, Brzeg was documented in the early thirteenth century as having a castle associated with the Piast dynasty. In 1311 it became a regional capital in the continuing subdivision of Silesia, and ousted Legnica as the main residence of the court. The Piasts remained there until 1675 when the family, a prominent dynasty throughout the recorded history of Poland, finally died out.

The Palace

Brzeg's most historic area lies by the park a few minutes northwest of the town centre, close to the river. Seen from its spacious square, the **Palace** (Tues, Thurs–Sat 10am–4pm, Wed 10am–6pm) is a bit of an anticlimax: predominantly Renaissance, with the Gothic presbytery of St Hedwig's (the mausoleum of the Piasts), plus various misjudged additions which have all but ruined any visual integrity. Badly damaged by Frederick the Great's troops in 1741, the palace was relegated for the next century and a half to the status of an arsenal. Only in the last decade has restoration returned parts of the structure to something like their former glory, which, in the case of the interior Renaissance sections, is something special. Built in the 1530s by a team of Italian masons, Brzeg became the prototype for a whole series of palaces in Poland, Bohemia, northern Germany and Sweden.

The extravagantly rich **gateway** is perhaps the finest Renaissance feature, modelled on Dürer's woodcut of a triumphal arch in honour of Emperor Maximilian. Above, in a shameless piece of self-glorification, are portrait figures of Duke George II and his wife, Barbara von Brandenburg. At the same level are pairs of knights whose coats of arms include those of Brzeg, Legnica and the Jagiellonian monarchs of Poland – the last, given that Silesia had not been a part of Poland for the past three centuries, being an expression of unrequited loyalty. Two tiers of busts above the windows trace the duke's genealogy, beginning with what appears as a rather regal interpretation of the peasant Piast at the upper left-hand corner. On the left rises the Lwów Tower, a survival of the medieval castle, along with part of its fortifications.

To some extent, the three-storey **courtyard** resembles the much larger Wawel palace in Kraków, above all in the lofty arcades. However, its carved decoration ultimately gives it a different character, with the heraldic motif continued on the more modest interior gate and antique-style medallions to the sides of the arcades.

The halls of the second floor have been adapted to house the **Silesian Piast Museum.** At the time of writing, exhibits from the National Museum in Wrocław were on view here, including an impressive array of devotional sculptures and a magnificent group of canvases, including a hauntingly powerful series of *The Four Doctors of the Church* by Michael Willmann.

The rest of the town

Next to the castle is the superbly renovated Jesuit **Church of the Holy Cross**, which dates back to the turn of the eighteenth century. Sober enough from the outside, its single interior space is encrusted with Rococo decorations with an illusionist altar replacing the usual epic construction. Across from the palace stands the **Piast College**, which was built some thirty years later. It has suffered even more from the vagaries of time and now houses a police academy.

Back towards the centre is the **Town Hall**, which belongs to the same architectural school as the palace, and again is an adaptation of an older structure, from which the tall belfry survives. It consists of two long parallel buildings, each terminating in a tower crowned by a bulbous Baroque steeple, joined together by the triple gabled facade, although this all makes it sound much more impressive than it actually is. Further on towards the bus and train stations is the market square, centred on the fourteenth-century **Church of St Nicholas** (Św. Mikołaja), its twin towers rebuilt last century and linked by an unusual arched bridge. The interior is startlingly spacious and boasts a varied collection of finely carved memorial plaques of prominent families. To the left of the altar is a carved wooden **triptych** presenting mysterious medieval interpretations of various Biblical events, while the opposite side offers a rather wily depiction of the Matka Boska Częstochowska; certainly an improvement on the po-faced original venerated in Częstochowa (see p.431).

Practicalities

The train and bus stations are both just a few minutes' walk south of the town centre. Brzeg has only one **hotel**, the *Piast*, situated near the station on the way to the town centre at ul. Piastowska 14 (☎077/2027; ③), though there's also a motel, *U Rybiorza*, on ul. Obwodnica (☎077/3473; ③), at the edge of town on the way to Opole.

The classiest **restaurant** by far is the *Ratuszowa* in the town hall cellars, which is excellent and inexpensive. Alternatively try the popular *Ambrozja* near St Nicholas'. In late May, Brzeg's castle, town hall and churches are put to impressive use for a four-day-long international **festival** of classical music.

Opole

If you're planning on spending a fair amount of time in Silesia, chances are you'll end up in **OPOLE** sooner or later. Situated in the very heart of the province, midway down the train line between Wrocław and Katowice, and within easy reach of Nysa, the Kłodzko Region and Częstochowa, the city makes a convenient touring base. Though ravaged by scores of fires throughout its history, the centre presents a well-balanced spread of old and new, ringed by a green belt and with the unsightly industrial installations banished to the outskirts.

One of Opole's main assets is its setting on the banks of the Odra. The river divides to form an island, the **Wyspa Pasieka**, which was inhabited in the ninth century by a Slavic tribe called the Opolanes. Bolesław the Brave established the island as a fortress, but subsequently became divorced from its mother country, serving as the capital of a Piast principality from 1202 until this particular line died out in 1532.

The city and the highly productive agricultural land around were understandably coveted by the Polish state after World War I, but Opole voted to remain part of Germany in the plebiscite of 1921, subsequently becoming the capital of the German province of Upper Silesia. In contrast to most other places ceded to Poland after World War II, the Opole region retained a sizeable **German minority**, and is the prime focus of German political troublemakers.

The City

The hub of Opole has long moved from the Wyspa Pasieka to the right bank of the Odra, where the central area is laid out on a grid-iron pattern. Nonetheless, the island in many ways makes a chronologically correct place to begin an exploration.

The island

Of the four **bridges** crossing the arm of the river, look out for the second, one of several structures in Opole built around 1910 in the Secessionist style. Arched like a bridge in a Japanese garden, this steel construction was made so cheaply that it was once known as the Groschen Bridge after the smallest coin then in circulation. It bears the curious coat of arms of the city, showing half an eagle and half a cross: the local Piasts allowed one side of the family's traditional blazon to be replaced by a symbol of the city's acquisition of a relic of the True Cross. Halfway across the bridge, take a glance in either direction; the thick lining of willow trees along the bank give an uncannily rural impression light years away from its urban location.

The medieval Piast **Castle** certainly hasn't been done any favours by the city planners, its surviving **round tower** now partly hidden behind ugly 1930s council offices which were built over the ruins. In summer you can climb to the top of the tower for a view of the city. The castles's grounds have been converted into a park with a large artificial lake and an open-air amphitheatre, the setting for a **Festival of Polish Song** held each June. Continuing north along ul. Piastowska, you get a good view of the Old Town on the opposite bank, lined with a jumble of riverside buildings.

The city centre

Returning across the Odra by ul. Zamkowa, you soon arrive at the **Franciscan Church**, a much-altered Gothic construction chiefly remarkable for the richly decorated Chapel of St Anne, erected in 1309, off the southern side of the nave. Endowed by the local Piasts to serve as their **mausoleum**, it has an exquisite star vault including keystones of the family eagle and painted with floral and heraldic motifs. The two magnificent double tombs were carved around 1380 by a member of the celebrated Parler family. Although he was still alive, an effigy of

Duke Bolko III was made to accompany that of his recently deceased wife, with a similar monument created in belated memory of his two ancestral namesakes. The retable is from a century later, and shows Bolko I offering a model of this monastery to Saint Anne and the Virgin, while Ladislaus II presents her with a model of the great church of Jasna Góra in Częstochowa. If you get to the **Franciscan Monastery**, just around the corner on pl. Wolności, 2, at 2pm and ring the bell at the little window, a monk will lead you on a 45-minute tour of the **catacombs**, which contain the unadorned coffins of other members of the dynasty and a number of fourteenth-century frescoes, notably a faded but tragically powerful *Crucifixion*.

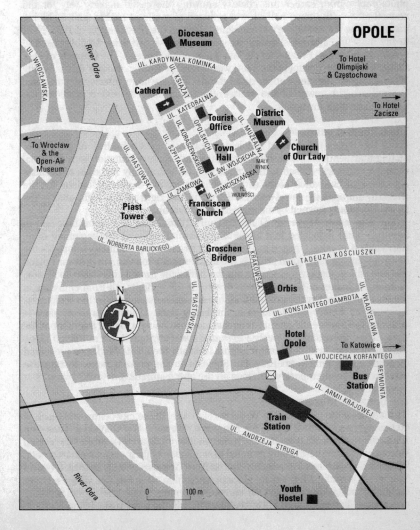

Immediately beyond the Franciscan monastery is the **Rynek**, some of whose cheerful mansions were badly damaged in World War II, but which have been deftly restored. A **Town Hall** has stood on the square since 1308, but the fine tower you see today – a pastiche of the Palazzo Vecchio in Florence – originates from an early nineteenth-century neo-Renaissance design, being rebuilt true to form in the mid-1930s when it unexpectedly collapsed during repairs.

Housed in the former Jesuit College on ul. Św. Wojciecha just off the Rynek is the **District Museum** (Tues–Fri 9am–5pm, Sat 10am–3pm, Sun noon–5pm), whose main strength is the archeology section, with exhibits from prehistoric to early medieval times. Also worth looking out for are some attractive tinted photographs from earlier this century showing the castle making way for the council offices, the town hall's tower reduced to a pile of rubble, and a chilling monochrome shot of Opole's synagogue ablaze on the *Kristallnacht* of 1938. Next to the museum, a broad stairway ascends to a hill where Saint Adalbert used to preach as bishop of Prague, Opole being part of his diocese. The **Church of Our Lady**, which now occupies the spot, was originally Gothic, though this is hardly apparent from the neo-Romanesque facade and Baroque interior decorations. Beyond are the tower of the fourteenth-century fortress and remains of the sixteenth-century town wall.

The cathedral quarter

From the Rynek, ul. Książąt Opolskich leads to the **Cathedral of St Jacob**, mixing fourteenth-century Gothic and nineteenth-century imitation with the usual Baroque excesses. Raised to the status of a cathedral only a couple of decades ago, the church, which soars with Gothic verticality, is chiefly famous for the allegedly miraculous, jewel-encrusted icon to the right of the main altar – the *Opole Madonna* crowned by a gaggle of gaily cavorting cherubs.

The **Diocesan Museum** (Tues & Thurs 10am–noon & 2–5pm, first Sun in month 2–5pm) is located in a block of modern buildings at the beginning of ul. Kardynała Kominka. Opened in 1987 largely as a result of voluntary effort, it's the object of considerable local pride as the first non-state museum in postwar Poland and one whose display techniques put the nationally owned collections to shame. Ask for the leaflet in English which describes the exhibits, all from churches in the Opole region. On the ground floor are several outstanding Gothic sculptures, including an *Enthroned Madonna* in the Parler style. Upstairs, pride of place is taken by the fourteenth-century reliquary made to house Opole's fragment of the True Cross; there's also a lovely *Virgin and Child* attributed to Fra Filippo Lippi. The small room next door features gifts to adorn the *Opole Madonna* presented by worthies ranging from King Jan Sobieski to the present pope. Imaginative exhibitions of contemporary religious art are also featured.

The Open-Air Museum

By the side of the main road to Wrocław, 8km west of the city centre and reached by bus #5 is an excellent **Open-Air Museum** (Muzeum Wsi Opolskiej; Tues–Sun 10am–5pm). Some sixty examples of the wooden rural architecture of the region have been erected here, many grouped in simulation of their original environment. Particularly notable is the wooden church from Gręboszów built in 1613, a typical example of what is still the main place of worship in a few Silesian villages. Other highlights are a windmill and an eighteenth-century water mill in full working order, as well as an orchard full of bee hives built in the same rustic idiom.

Practicalities

Opole's main **train** and **bus** stations are at the southern end of town a few minutes along ul. Wojciecha Korfantego from the Wyspa Pasieka.

The best **accommodation** bets include the *Zacisze*, just east of the historic quarters at Grundwaldzka 28 (☎077/53 95 33; ③), with the city's leading hotel being the *Opole*, across from the station at ul. Krakowska 59 (☎077/53 86 51; ⑥). Better value is the motel *Olimpijska*, not far from the northern suburban station of Opole-Wschodnie at ul. Oleska 86 (☎077/52 63 51; ④); from the centre take bus #3, #11, #C, #D or #N. The **youth hostel** is to the rear of the main train station at ul. Struga 16 (July & Aug; ☎077/53 33 52). Opole has no camping facilities.

Prices in the *Hotel Opole*'s **restaurant**, the *Hotelowa*, are great value in comparison with the accommodation. Alternative choices for a full meal are *Europa*, pl. Wolności 1, and *Festiwalowa*, ul. Kościuszki 3. More adventurous menus are on offer at *Skorpion*, ul. Książąt Opolskich 6, and the Hungarian *Casino*, to the east of the centre at ul. Katowicka 63, which has dancing in the evenings. At the tip of Wyspa Pasieska on ul. Ostrowek you'll find the *Pub pod Smokiem* a pleasant spot in summer.

If you're after something less fancy, there's the *Ambrozja* on ul. 1 Maja, a **milk bar**, the *Starowiejska*, on ul. Krakowska 11, the *Rybny* fish bar on ul. Władysława Reymonta 9 and crepes at the popular *Naleśniki Francuski* on pl. Wolności. Among the many **cafés** are two on the Rynek, *Pod Arkadami*, and a couple more on ul. Krakowska, *Ptyś* and *Teatralna*, right next to the *Orbis* office.

As for **night life**, there's a disco worth checking out, *Romans* on ul. Wrocławska, and two **cinemas**: the *Odra* on ul. Ozimska and the *Kraków* on ul. Katowicka.

Góra Świętej Anny

Forty kilometres southeast of Opole, conspicuous on its 410-metre-hill, is the village of **GÓRA ŚWIĘTEJ ANNY**. Associated with the cult of Saint Anne, mother of the Virgin Mary, it's one of the most popular places of **pilgrimage** in Poland and is the scene of colourful processions on July 26 each year. Outside major church festivals, however, it's a moribund little place, the antithesis of the relentlessly busy Jasna Góra and not really worth the detour unless you've your own transport. Getting here by public transport is a long-winded process best done by taking a train from Opole to the hideously industrialized Zdzieszowice and then covering the remaining 6km on foot or by bus.

Although the cult of Saint Anne is long established in Silesia, Góra Świętej Anny's status as a major pilgrimage shrine dates back only to the mid-seventeenth century, when a **Franciscan Monastery** was built to replace a modest Gothic votive chapel. As is the case with Jasna Góra, its popularity is intimately associated with Polish nationalism, fanned by the fact that the monks have been expelled three times (as a result of the policies of Napoleon, Bismarck and Hitler). For five days in May 1921, the village was the scene of bitter fighting following the Upper Silesia plebiscite, which left it in German hands. Ill-feeling has persisted: it was only in 1989 that the outlawing of Masses in German, introduced when the monks returned in 1945 in retaliation for previous bans on Polish services, was rescinded.

The church, decorated in a restrained Baroque style, houses the source of the pilgrimage, a tiny miraculous statue of *St Anne with the Virgin and Child*, high above the main altar. An unassuming piece of folksy Gothic carving, it's usually decked out in gorgeous clothes. Below the monastery buildings is the mid-eighteenth century **Calvary**, an elaborate processional way with 33 chapels and shrines telling the story of the Passion. A large and less tasteful **Lourdes grotto** was added as the centrepiece in 1912.

You'll find a small shop in the town square below the church and the pricey but tidy *Pensionat Anna* on the main road a short distance away (③). Half a kilometre southeast of town on a bend, the *Zakład* roadhouse provides a **restaurant**, bar and possibly some rooms by 1996.

Katowice and around

Poland's main industrial area consists of an almost continuously built-up conurbation of about a dozen towns, beginning around 65km southeast of Opole. Two million inhabitants make this the most densely populated part of the country, with 400,000 in the largest city, **KATOWICE**, home to the Silesian Philharmonic and the successful football team, GKS Katowice.

Since the beginning of the *glasnost* era, the region has attracted worldwide attention because of the horrendous **pollution** produced by its outdated factories. It's even classified as an environmental disaster area by the Polish Academy of Sciences and many of its inhabitants are constantly subjected to severe health hazards, as the large number of disease-ridden children testifies.

The region's rich mineral seams have been extensively mined since the Middle Ages – nearly a tenth of the world's known coal exists here, but it wasn't until the

---

THE UPPER SILESIA DISPUTE OF 1918–22

In the aftermath of World War I, the dispute between Poland and Germany over the ownership of Upper Silesia represented the first reasonably successful attempt by the international community at providing an enduring, if not permanent, solution to a potentially explosive problem by means of mediation rather than through military force.

Following Germany's wartime defeat, the Allies at first intended to transfer the whole of Upper Silesia to the newly resurrected Poland, which would otherwise have been a poor agricultural country with no industrial base. Polish spokesmen stressed their **historical claim** on the territory and on its **demographic make-up**, although the latter couldn't be quantified exactly. Strongly partisan support for the transferral of sovereignty came from France, which wished to weaken Germany as much as possible and establish a strong ally to its east. This rather unnerved the British, ever anxious about the balance of power in Europe and concerned at the potential danger of French hegemony. They gradually came to back the ferocious German backlash against the proposed change in ownership, believing that it was in Europe's best interests for industries to be left in the hands of the nation that had developed them, rather than being handed over to a new country with no business experience: Prime Minister Lloyd George went so far as to suggest that allocating Upper Silesia to Poland was like giving a clock to a monkey.

As the Allies dragged their feet on the issue, Upper Silesia remained the one unresolved question on the now much-changed map of Europe. Frustrated at the

nineteenth-century **Industrial Revolution** that the area became heavily urbanized. In 1800, Katowice had just 500 inhabitants. Fifty years later, its population was a still modest 4000 before Upper Silesia mushroomed into the powerhouse of the Prussian state, in tandem with the broadly similar Ruhr at the opposite end of the country.

With a population composed almost equally of Germans and Poles (and with many of mixed blood), the fate of the area became a hot political issue after World War I – and one that was to be of far more than local significance (see box below for the full story). In the communist period, the conurbation maintained its high-profile position, thanks to the ideological stress placed on heavy industry. Workers here enjoyed a privileged position; mining wages, for example, were three times the national average income. However, the failure to modernize plant and machinery is now taking its toll; on top of health and environmental problems many enterprises have been shut down in the past couple of years, resulting in high unemployment and a very uncertain future for the region.

By now you've probably guessed that Katowice and the surrrounding mire may be crucial to the Polish economy, but have little of real interest to the overseas visitor; do yourself and your health a favour by avoiding the place altogether.

Practicalities

Should you find yourself having to make an overnight stay in town, there are three inexpensive **hotels** conveniently close to the train station. A couple of minutes' walk west, at ul. Dworcowa 9, is the *Centralny* (☎032/53 90 41; ③) and a few minutes further on, the *Śląski* at ul. Mariacka 15 (☎032/53 70 11; ②). Just behind the station you'll also find the *Polonia* at ul. Kochanowskiego 3 (☎032/51 40 51; ②). A slightly plusher establishment is the *Katowice* at ul. Korfantego 35

lack of progress, the Poles staged **insurrections** in 1919 and 1920. Eventually, the Allies decided to test popular feelings by means of a **plebiscite**, which was held in March 1921. This was won by the Germans by 707,000 votes to 479,000, but the result was discredited by the fact that a large number (thought to be around 182,000) of former citizens were temporarily shipped back from their new homes elsewhere in Germany. Support for continued German sovereignty was strongest in the industrial communities closest to Poland, making the solution of partition seemingly intractable, particularly as it was taken for granted that the conurbation could not be divided satisfactorily .

In May 1921, a third insurrection led to the occupation of the territory by the Polish army. Realizing the need for a quick solution, the Allies referred the matter to the **League of Nations**, the body newly established to promote world peace. The neutral observers who were assigned to the task decided that partition was the only fair solution, and used the plebiscite returns as the basis for determining the respective shares of the carve-up. By the **Geneva Convention on Upper Silesia** of 1922, which ran to 606 articles, the Germans retained two-thirds of the land and three-fifths of the population, but an international boundary was cut through the industrial conurbation, a somewhat over-pragmatic Solomonic solution which left Poland with the vast majority of the coal mines and blast furnaces. However, in what was itself a radical and previously untried experiment, the area was kept as an economic unit, with guarantees on the movement of goods, material and labour, the provision of public services and the rights of individuals who found themselves living under an alien flag.

(☎032/59 80 21; ③), just north of the *Centralny*. Top of the range are the two overpriced *Orbis* offerings: the *Silesia*, right in the heart of the shopping district at ul. Piotra Skargi 2 (☎032/59 62 11; ⑤) and the *Warszawa*, east of the Rondo at ul. Rożdzieńskiego 16 (☎032/58 70 81; ⑥). Katowice's all-year **youth hostel** is about fifteen minutes' walk west of the station at ul. Graniczna 27a (☎032/51 94 57; trams #7, #15 or 40#). **Camping** in Katowice might sound paradoxical, but die-hards will find a campsite southwest of the city centre by a lake at ul. Adamieckiego 6 (☎032/51 87 84) and reached by buses #4, #673 or #E1.

As usual the best **restaurants** are in the hotels, notably *Polonia* and both *Orbis* establishments, although these are the usual soulless places. *Kaczma Słupska*, ul. Mariacki 1, offers traditional Polish food and on ul. Stawowa, the pedestrian precinct opposite the station, you'll find two popular places: the *Restauracja Chińska*, and the fast-food *Best*. *Kryształowa*, a real old-world central European **café** at ul. Warszawska 5, is the best choice for coffee, cakes or ice cream.

If you need any further **information** about the city, there's a municipal tourist office right beside the train station at ul. Młyńska 11 (☎032/53 95 66) and an *Almatur* bureau nearby at ul. Maja 7 (☎032/59 64 18).

Tarnowskie Góry

From a tourist point of view, the only worthwhile town in the area is **TARNOWSKIE GÓRY**, at the far northern end of the conurbation, and even then it's not worth going too far out of your way to get there. The town is reached from Katowice in about an hour by train with the station located a couple of minutes' walk east of the central Rynek. It's a place with a far more venerable history: silver and lead deposits were discovered in the thirteenth century and it was given an urban charter and mining rights in the sixteenth by the dukes of Opole. Some idea of its underground wealth is given in a document dated 1632, listing twenty thousand places where minerals could be exploited.

The principle reason for coming here is to undertake two historic mining tours, one of which, while not quite matching the famous salt mines of Wieliczka (see p.406), makes an amusing excursion underground. On arrival it's worth checking the frequency and times of these **guided tours** from the office of the *Friends of Tarnowskie Góry Association* (*FTGA*) at ul. Gliwicka 2 (☎03/185 49 96); from the Rynek follow the yellow colonnade to the southwest and the office is over the road. Both sites are a walkable couple of kilometres south and southwest of the town centre; an inexpensive map from the *PTTK* office (see below) will make things clear, although some street names have since been changed.

The mine sites

The first of the sites, the **Staszica Mine and Museum** (Tue–Sun 9am–2pm), is the more educational, but less interesting of the two. To get here, leave town on the main Gliwice road, go through the lights and take the second left into ul. Jedności Robotniczej and you'll find the mine a little further on on the left – altogether about thirty minutes' walk. Dating back to medieval times, the mine was formerly worked for silver, lead and copper, and in the small museum you'll see the old equipment, plus models of how the mine was operated and water levels controlled. The highlight, though, is a motorboat trip along the flooded drainage tunnels which were excavated as needs arose; dozens of kilometres of passageways undermine the entire area.

A large wall map explains the connection between the mine and the **Sztolina Czarnego Pstąga** (Black Trout Shaft), 3km away. It takes its name from the eponymous fish which occasionally get into the tunnels from the rivers into which they drain. If coming from the town centre, walk west past the park along ul. Kard. S. Wyszyńskiego, cross the lights and continue down the hill. You'll see the signs to the left before a Lutheran chapel. If you have a car, leave it at the edge of the woods and walk down to the nearest of the two entrances; "Szyb Sylvester". Outside, a blackboard will indicate the times of the half-hourly excursions to the other entrance, "Szyb Ewa", 600m away through the woods. Once inside, you descend down a vertical shaft and make a spooky journey by boat along one of the former drainage channels. Typically in midsummer there are departures from "Sylvester" at 1 and 3pm and from "Ewa" at 2pm.

Perhaps the best thing about the tour is the utterly convincing optical illusion that's played on you as you approach your steel canoe. As soon as the boat gets underway the guide rattles affably through his routine, barely pausing for breath, while heaving the entourage of up to eight vessels along the walls with his arms. Passing through rock-hewn "gates", associated legends are recounted; at one point any woman wanting to find a husband within the year is invited to rap on the wall.

Practicalities

If you want to spend the night in town the *FTGA* offer a few inexpensive beds in dormitory-style **accommodation** at the back of their office. Other than that there's the *Hotel Gwarek* on ul. Kard. S.Wyszyńskiego (☎03/185 38 91; ②–⑤) or the sports hotel, *Śląsk* at ul. Korczaka 23 (☎03/185 54 24; ③)The **PTTK office** is in ul. Górnicza 7 (☎03/185 29 81), just south of the pleasant Rynek, which preserves a few old buildings and where you'll find a couple of **restaurants and snack bars**.

South of Katowice

Directly south of Katowice, the outstanding castle museum in the otherwise unremarkable town of **Pszczyna** makes an unmissable stopover on the way to the hills of the **Beskid Śląski**, just south of the mildly absorbing twin towns of **Bielsko-Biała**. Although lacking the grandeur of the nearby Tatra Mountains, the region's highlands are worth investigating on your way to the Czech Republic, not least for the chance to experience the undeveloped charm of the border-divided town of **Cieszyn**. There are regular bus and train services from Katowice to Bielsko-Biała from where the Beskid resort of **Szczyrk** and Cieszyn are easily accessible, although the latter town is more easily reached directly from Katowice.

Pszczyna

About forty minutes from Katowice by train, or the same number of kilometres by road is the small town of **PSZCZYNA**, a world away from the conurbation's industrial squalor. If Nysa is the "Polish Rome" and Paczców "Poland's Carcassonne" then the **Castle** (May–Oct Tues–Thurs 9am–3pm, Fri & Sat 10am–3pm, Sun 10am–4pm; Feb–April & Nov Wed 9am–4pm, Thurs & Fri

9am–3pm, Sat 10am–3pm, Sun 10am–4pm), just off the town's market square, might with the same inflated logic elevate Pszczyna to "Silesia's Versailles".

Originating as a Piast hunting lodge in the twelfth century, it was successively expanded and rebuilt in the Gothic and Renaissance styles before gaining its largely Baroque appearance following a fire, with other features added in the nineteenth century. In 1946, it was opened as a museum of some of Poland's finest historical artefacts, many rescued from Silesian stately homes ruined by the war. These are set among tasteful period furnishings in a slowly growing number of rooms refurbished to the stunning level of detail of their eighteenth-century heyday.

The collection starts off on the ground floor with an array of hunting trophies including a wild boar leaping out of the wall and a rather more docile European bison (ask at the town tourist office about the **bison reserve** – *reservevat żubrów* – nearby), while neatly arranged expositions of European and Oriental armour fill the adjacent rooms. The works of obscure German and Flemish painters are found in the recently completed **Great Hall** which offers a fine display of Baroque and Regency furniture under a superbly gilded stucco ceiling. Ascending the aptly named Grand Staircase bordered by its stone balustrade and early seventeenth-century tapestry, you come to the museum's finest room, the stunning **Chamber of Mirrors**. At each end of the hall, huge mirrors in gilded brass frames create an impression of a much larger room, embellished by crystal chandeliers hung from a ceiling depicting a swirling sky. Splendidly ornate balconies look down onto the chamber from the second floor, while murals depicting the four seasons and the signs of the zodiac are squeezed in between the gilded stucco decoration. The rows of period chairs filling the chamber are used during the monthly chamber music recitals held here.

Subsequent rooms nearby and on the second floor are rather anticlimactic by comparison, none presently matching the lavish decor of the rooms preceding them. The final point of interest inside is the **Hunting Room**'s barrel vaulting which hints at the castle's origins and is hung with still more antlers. Outside though, the English-style **park** is kept in a condition befitting its reputation, featuring a lake with water lilies and a wooden bridge.

The handsome late eighteenth-century **Rynek** in front of the palace is lined with fine mansions and a bright white Baroque-fronted Protestant Church with an incompatibly plain, bright interior. On ul. Parkowa, a block north of ul. Dworcowa, the road between the town centre and the station, is the only other attraction worth mentioning, a small **skansen** (Wed–Sun 10am–3pm) of reassembled rural buildings.

Practicalities

You'll find the **train** and **bus stations** located a kilometre east of the town's market square. The only places to **stay the night** are the rather stuffy and over-priced *Hotel Retro* on ul. Warowna (✆03/110 22 45; ④), off the south side of the Rynek, and the *PTTK* **tourist hostel**, located at ul. Bogedania a kilometre south of the Rynek (✆03/110 38 33; ③). The *PTTK* also have a helpful office on the Rynek at at no. 3 (✆03/110 35 30).

Pszczyna has plenty of **cafés** and **bars** in which to eat and drink on ul. Piastowska, the pedestrianized street leading off the Rynek's northeast corner: try the *Pizzeria Primavera* at no. 14, the *Restauracja Kasztelanska* round the corner on ul. Bendarska and the *Old Smuggler's Pub* just over the road. Finally, the *Czartak Bookshop* on ul. Pistowska 1 has an especially good selection of national and **local maps** as well as the full range of trusty *Rough Guides* – in Polish.

Bielsko–Biała

A further 25km south of Pszczyna, at the foot of the Beskid Śląski ranges, lies **BIELSKO–BIAŁA**, two formerly separate towns, united in 1951. Now forming one seamless whole around the River Biała which formerly divided them, the two towns spent most of their history in different countries – Bielsko belonged to the duchy of Cieszyn, which in due course became part of Bohemia, whereas Biała was part of the Oświęcim duchy, which fell to the Polish crown in the fifteenth century.

Both towns flourished in the late-nineteenth century, thanks to their high-quality textile products, and the cityscape today, like its northern English counterparts, is dominated by the imposing buildings of that period, as well as many mansions in the more refined Viennese Secessionist style. The city's present-day prosperity derives from its car plants, and the main thoroughfares are lined with parts suppliers and accessory manufacurers associated with that industry. In the early 1970s the centre of the old town was cleared with such vigour that it earned the mayor of the time the nickname "Anton Burzyciel" or Antony the Destroyer. For the culture-hungry visitor, little historical evidence survives from before the the conurbation's industrial expansion, but should you find yourself changing trains on the way to the hills or needing an urban service, a couple of hours can be adequately filled wandering around.

The town centres

Arriving at the main **bus or train stations** in the northern part of **Bielsko**, it's a fifteen-minute walk to its centre down ul. 3 Maja, a broad boulevard lined with the turn-of-the century tenements so characteristic of the city. It ends at the busy pl. Bolesława Chrobrego, above which stands the entirely underwhelming edifice of the **Castle** (Tues, Wed & Fri 10am–3pm, Thurs 10am–6pm, Sat 9am–3pm, Sun 9am–2pm), an architecturally confused building containing a small **museum** whose historical displays are barely worth the paltry entry fee.

Instead, head west of the castle into the network of hilly, twisting streets and alleys which define Bielsko's Old Town centre and now has an appealing down-at-heel feel. A couple of blocks south of the small Rynek, on ul. Schodowa, is the unusual **St Nicholas' Cathedral**, dating from early this century. The tall belfry, flanked by two smaller towers, could be described as an Escheresque vision of the Italian Renaissance and provides the city with its most visually striking landmark. The interior is less enthralling, featuring a number of impressive Secessionist stained-glass windows. North of the Rynek is a quiet district where you'll come across the occasional turn-of-the-century mansion decorated with floral window boxes and, in **plac Luthra**, underlining the historical strength of Protestantism in these parts, the country's only statue of **Martin Luther**. Behind him stands a typically angular Evangelical Church dating from 1782, with its traditionally light but spartan interior ending in an altar so underplayed it might not be there.

Just east of pl. Chrobrego **Biała's centre** features a neo-Renaissance Town Hall whose most outstanding feature is its small basement restaurant, the *Ratuszowa*. From here, walk north to pl. Wojska Polskiego, a pleasant broad square on whose northeastern corner stand two of the town's best-preserved Secessionist buildings side by side. The **House of Frogs** (Pod Żabami) is so named because of the amusing reliefs seen round the corner, dating from the late eighteenth century. Over the doorway repose two smartly-dressed and rather self-satisfied frogs puffing on a pipe and strumming a mandolin while two beetles scurry across the wall.

At the extreme southeastern edge of the urban area, reached by bus #2, #5 or #55, you'll find the formerly separate village of **Mikusowice** whose **wooden Church of St Barbara** is the finest example of this highly distinctive form of vernacular architecture to be found in the region and rarely found in an urban setting. Built at the end of the seventeenth century, the church is strikingly geometric, with a square tower and nave and a hexagonal chancel, while its skyline, with bulbous bell turrets and steeply pitched shingle roofs, is aggressively picturesque. The interior was adorned a generation after its construction with a series of naive wall paintings illustrating the legend of its patron saint. There's also a lovely fifteenth-century carving of the Madonna and Child in the left aisle.

Practicalities

The **tourist office** for the Beskid Śląski area, **In-Tour**, is across from the station at ul. Piastowska 2 (☎030/22406). **Orbis** are at ul. 3 Maja 9 (☎030/27906) and **PTTK** at ul. Wzgórze 7 (☎030/23648).

Bielsko-Biała hardly warrants a voluntary overnight stay but if you need **accommodation** the venerable *Prezydent*, ul. 3 Maja 12 (☎030/27211; ⑦), is the city's top hotel, with the two-star *Pod Pocztą*, ul. 1 Maja 4a (☎030/26037; ⑤), just off pl. Chrobrego, performing the same function with less luxury and at half the price. There's also a motel, *Ondraszek*, to the north of Bielsko, at ul. Warszawska 185 (☎030/22037; ⑤), reached by bus #58. The **PTTK hostel** on ul Krasinskiego 38 (☎030/23018; ②) is three blocks west of the bus station, while cheapest of all is the **youth hostel**, handily located in the northern part of central Biała at ul. Komorowicka 25 (☎030/27466).

Among the places to **eat and drink**, check out the *Ratuszowa* in Biała's town hall (see above). Another good choice for traditional Polish fare is *Teatralna*, ul. 1 Maja 4. There's also the *Pizzeria Capri*, ul. 3 Maja 13 and a popular bistro, *Starówka*, ul. Smolki 5, which has Italian, Chinese and Polish dishes on the menu. For an evening's entertainment, it's worth seeing what's on at the two **theatres** – *Teatr Polski*, ul. 1 Maja 1 (☎030/2851), and *Banialuka*, ul. Mickiewicza 20 (☎030/21046). The latter is the national puppet theatre, and in May during even-numbered years a world **festival** is held here.

Szczyrk and the Beskid Śląski

Immediately south of Bielsko–Biała lies the small Silesian section of the **Beskid Mountains**, an archetypal central European landscape characterized by fir-clad slopes reaching up towards bald summits. Within Poland, it's a popular holiday area with **SZCZYRK**, the main resort 15km southwest of Bielsko–Biała (frequent bus connections), offering an an ever-widening range of places to stay but not so much to do. Things liven up in winter when the combination of guaranteed snowfall and steep slopes provides the country's most demanding **downhill skiing**, considered superior, though less varied, to its Tatran equivalents. Unfortunately the same acute contours and uninspiring summit vistas make summertime hiking rather effortful and dull, although if you're heading for the hills by foot or mountain bike, the locally available *Beskid Śląski i Żywiecki* (1:75,000) map will come in very handy.

If you're not skiing or walking, the town, stretched out along one main road, has only one thing to offer: the all-year-round two-stage **chair lift** which runs from the west end of town to the summit of **Skrzyczne** (1245m), the highest peak in the range. In summertime it's used by bucket-swinging bilberry pickers who comb the slopes and sell their produce by the roadsides on either side of town. From the summit you'll face the 1117m peak of Klinczok with the conurbation of Bielsko–Biała beyond. There's also the usual refuge and restaurant up here. The energetic alternative is to slog up either the blue or the green trail for a couple of hours from Szczyrk. The latter continues south to Barania Góra (1220m), the source of the **River Wisła**, Poland's greatest waterway which winds a serpentine 1090km course through Kraków, Warsaw and Toruń before disgorging itself into the Baltic near Gdańsk.

Szczyrk's many **accommodation** options include the monolithic *Orle Gniazdo* hotel 3km up on the town's northern slopes at ul. Wrzosowa 28a (☎030/17 82 99; ③), great value in the summer and with good views all year round. Back in town, there's the *CoS* sports hotel signposted off the main road (☎030/17 84 41; ③) or, just west of the shopping centre, the *Hotel Ewa* at ul. Beskidska 4 (☎030/17 85 85; ②). There's also a a *Dom Turysty* **PTTK hostel**, ul. Górska 7 (☎030/17 85 78; ②), a **youth hostel**, ul. Sportowa 2 (☎030/17 89 33) and the large *Skalisty* **campsite**, at the east end of town (☎030/17 87 60).

Plenty of snack bars line the main road; besides the hotel **restaurants** try out the *Gopiania* near the trail signpost close to the *Hotel Ewa*.

Wisła and around

From Barania Góra, there's a choice of marked descents to the town of **WISŁA**, which can also be reached by bus from Szczyrk via the spectacular main road which makes a looping circuit through the valleys and passes of the range. There's an even more circuitous rail link with Bielsko–Biała, the latter stages of which closely hug the banks of the Wisła, which has already metamorphosed from a mountain stream to a significant river. The best **hike** from here is southwest via the blue then the yellow trail to **Stożek** (978m), a fine vantage point which forms part of the border with the Czech Republic. Among the **places to stay** in Wisła are two cheap hotels, *Piast*, ul. 1 Maja 47 (☎3578; ②), and *Centrum*, ul. 1 Maja 57 (☎3577; ②); the *Nad Zaporą PTTK* hostel, ul. Czare 3 (☎2411; ②); and the *Jonidło* campsite on ul. Wyzwolenie (☎2820).

Ustroń and Brenna

USTROŃ, a few kilometres downstream from Wisła and likewise on the rail line to Bielsko–Biała, stands just to the west of one of the most popular peaks in the Beskids, **Równica** (884m). This can be reached by the red trail, but it's more fun to ascend by car or bus via a tortuous mountain road. A second recommended hike in the area is southwest from Ustroń by the blue route to **Czantoria** (995m), another summit right on the Czech frontier. Accommodation possibilities in Ustroń include a basic **hotel**, *Równica*, ul. 22 Lipca 63 (☎2427; ②); the *Motel*, ul. Baranowa (☎2546; ③), and *Czantoria*, ul. 1 Maja 99 (☎3468; ③), both in the outlying village of **Polana**; and a **youth hostel** (☎3501) in the hamlet of **Jaszoiwec** below Równica.

On the eastern side of Równica, on the bank of the River Brennica, lies **BRENNA**, the most secluded resort in the range. The course of the river has been terraced here, and there are good opportunities for bathing; there's also an open-air theatre which is used for regional song and dance events on weekends throughout the summer. Accommodation includes a simple **hotel**, the *Beskid*, at no. 760 (☎553; ②).

Cieszyn

Straddling the Czech frontier 35km west of Bielsko–Biała, the divided town of **CIESZYN** somehow managed to escape wartime ruin and today retains a charming old centre of somewhat faded old buildings. It's one of the region's most attractive old towns and is well worth a visit if coming from or going to the Czech Republic. The ancient town, established nearly twelve centuries ago, was claimed by both Czechoslovakia and Poland following the break-up of the Habsburg Empire after World War I. In 1920 the Conference of Ambassadors decided on using the River Olza as the new frontier, making the eastern part of the town Polish and the opposite side (known as Český Těšín) Czech. Ignoring the fact that people of mixed ethnicity were living all over town, no attempt was made to rationalize the nationality problem, and until recently, special passes were used to allow estranged nationals to visit their former homeland. The exception was All Saints' Day, when the border was thrown open. Nowadays the frontier at the town centre bridge flows freely in both directions.

The central Rynek, with the eighteenth-century Town Hall, stands at the highest point of the central area. Just off the southwest corner of the square is the Gothic **Church of St Mary Magdalene**, containing a mausoleum of yet more Piast dukes who established an independent principality here in 1290.

The main street, ul. Głęboka, lined with some of the most imposing mansions, sweeps downhill from the Rynek towards the river. If you take ul. Sejmowa to the left and then the first turning right, you'll find yourself on ul. Trzech Braci ("Street of the Three Brothers"). Here stands the **well** associated with the legend of the town's foundation. In the year 810, the three sons of King Leszko III met up at this spring after a long spell wandering the country. They were so delighted to see each other again that they founded a town named "I'm happy" (*cieszym się*). From the foot of ul. Głęboka, it's only a few paces along ul. Zamkowa to the Most Przyjazni, the **frontier post** for the one-way crossing over to the Czech part of town, although most cars use the viaduct to the north for speedier transit avoiding the town centre. The pedestrian crossing from the Czech Republic back to Poland is about 700m upstream across Most Wolności.

On the west side of ul. Zamkowa rises a hill crowned by a fourteenth-century Gothic **tower** (daily April–Oct 9.30am–5pm, Nov–March 9.30am–3pm), the only surviving part of the Piast Palace. From the top, there's a superb view over both sides of the town and the Beskidy beyond. Alongside stands one of the oldest surviving buildings in Silesia, the **Chapel of St Nicholas**, a handsome Romanesque rotunda dating back to the eleventh century, with the vestiges of a contemporaneous well in front of it. Also on the hill are a Neoclassical hunting palace and a "ruined" Romantic folly among the trees. Other than that, idle ambling might lead you to the Baroque-towered Protestant **Church of Jesus**, visible on the hill just east of the centre. Inside, its statues of the four Evangelists crowd over the altar and liven up the otherwise plain interior.

Practicalities

Cieszyn's **bus and train stations** are centrally located about ten minutes' walk east of the Rynek. The best accommodation bet is the attractive **hotel** *Rafael*, just off the Rynek at ul. Szersznika 3 (☎033/52 43 57; ④). *Orbis* also has a four-star **motel** about 2km north of the town centre at ul. Motelowa 93 (☎033/20451; ⑤). The **campsite**, the *Olza*, is a few blocks south of the Rynek at al. Jana Łyska 13 (☎033/20833).

For a good feed try the Zamkowa **restaurant** which overlooks the frontier post at the bottom of ul Gleboka, or you could always try something over the border in Český Těšín. There's a **PTTK tourist office** at ul. Głębocka 56 (☎033/2186), while the **Orbis** office is at Rynek 19 (☎033/21240). If you need a **Czech visa** you've left it a bit late; the nearest consulate is in Katowice at ul. Pawła Stelmacha 21 (☎033/51 85 76).

travel details

Trains

Jelenia Góra to Bydgoszcz (1 daily; 8hr; couchettes); Częstochowa (2 daily; 6hr); Gdańsk (1 daily; 10hr; couchettes); Kalisz (4 daily; 5–6hr 30min); Katowice (6 daily; 6hr 30min–8hr); Kielce (1 daily; 8hr; couchettes); Kłodzko (4 daily; 2hr); Kraków (2 daily; 9–10hr; couchettes); Leszno (3 daily; 4–5hr); Lublin (1 daily; 11hr 30min; couchettes); Łódź (4 daily; 6hr 30min–9hr); Opole (4 daily; 4hr–4hr 30min); Poznań (4 daily; 5hr–6hr 30min); Szczecin (1 daily; 9hr; couchettes); Wałbrzych (23 daily; 1hr); Warsaw (4 daily; 8hr 30min–9hr 30min); Wrocław (18 daily; 2hr 30min–3hr); Zielona Góra (2 daily; 4hr 30min–5hr 30min).

Katowice to Białystok (2 daily; 6–8hr; couchettes); Bydgoszcz (6 daily; 5–7hr; couchettes); Częstochowa (34 daily; 1hr 30min–2hr); Gdańsk (8 daily; 6hr 30min–9hr; couchettes); Jelenia Góra (3 daily; 7hr); Kielce (11 daily; 2hr 30min–3hr 30min); Kołobrzeg (2 daily; 10hr 30min–1hr 30min; couchettes); Kraków (40 daily; 1hr 30min–2hr); Legnica (7 daily; 4–7hr); Leszno (7 daily; 4hr 30min–5hr); Lublin (5 daily; 6–7hr); Łódź ((8 daily; 3hr 30min–5hr); Olsztyn (2 daily; 8hr 30min–11hr); Opole (23 daily; 2hr); Poznań (15 daily; 5–7hr); Przemyśl (7 daily; 5hr 30min); Rzeszów (8 daily; 4–5hr); Słupsk (2 daily; 10–13hr; couchettes); Szczecin (7 daily; 9–10hr); Świnoujście (3 daily; 10hr–1hr 30min); Wałbrzych (3 daily; 6hr); Warsaw (17 daily; 3hr 30min–5hr); Wrocław (23 daily; 3–4hr); Zakopane (3 daily; 5–7hr; couchettes); Zamość (2 daily; 8–10hr); Zielona Góra (4 daily; 5–6hr).

Wrocław to: Białystok (2 daily; 10hr 30min–13hr; couchettes); Bydgoszcz (6 daily; 4–5hr); Częstochowa (6 daily; 3–4hr); Gdańsk (7 daily; 6hr–7hr 30min; couchettes); Jelenia Góra (18 daily; 2hr 30min–3hr); Kalisz (3 daily; 2hr–2hr 30min); Katowice (21 daily; 3–4hr); Kielce (3 daily; 5hr–6hr 30min; couchettes); Kłodzko (7 daily; 2hr 30min); Kołobrzeg ((3 daily; 8–10hr); Kraków (17 daily; 4–6hr); Legnica (22 daily; 1hr); Leszno (27 daily; 1hr–1hr 30min); Lublin (3 daily; 8hr 30min–9hr 30min; couchettes); Łódź (14 daily; 4–6hr); Olsztyn (2 daily; 7hr 30min–10hr; couchettes); Opole (42 daily; 1hr–1hr 30min); Poznań (26 daily; 2hr–3hr 30min); Przemyśl (5 daily; 8hr 30min; couchettes); Rzeszów (6 daily; 7hr; couchettes); Słupsk (2 daily; 9–10hr); Szczecin (11 daily; 6hr–7hr 30min; couchettes); Świnoujście (3 daily; 7–8hr); Wałbrzych (20 daily; 1hr 30min); Warsaw (16 daily; 6–7hr; couchettes); Zakopane (1 daily; 8hr 30min; couchettes); Zielona Góra (10 daily; 2–3hr). Also **international connections** to Görlitz, Dresden and Prague.

Buses

Wrocław to Kłodzko, Legnica, Oleśnica, Sobótka, Świdnica, Trzebnica.

Jelenia Góra to Bolków, Kamienna Góra, Karpacz, Kłodzko, Legnica, Szklarska Poręba.

Kłodzko to Kudowa-Zdrój, Lądek-Zdrój, Międzygórze, Paczków, Otmuchów, Nysa, Opole.

Katowice to Cieszyn, Pszczyna. Bielsko-Biała, Opole.

CHAPTER SIX

WIELKOPOLSKA AND POMERANIA

Wielkopolska and **Pomerania**, the two northwest regions of the country, constitute a large swathe of modern Poland. Despite their proximity, however, the feel and history of each is highly distinct. Wielkopolska formed the core of the original Polish nation and has remained identifiably Polish through subsequent centuries; Pomerania, by contrast, bears the imprint of the Prussians, who ruled this area from the early eighteenth century through to 1945 – the province only became Polish after 1945, and "Lower Pomerania", to the west of Świnoujście, remains German territory.

In **Wielkopolska** the chief interest is supplied by the regional capital **Poznań**, an attractive city famed within Poland for the 1956 riots which were the first major revolt against communism. **Gniezno**, the ancient capital of the first Piast monarchs and the normal seat of the primate of Poland, is a big church centre, full of seminaries and trainee priests. Appropriately it's the central point on the **Szlak Piastowski** or "Piast Route" which follows a 240km waymarked figure-of-eight to the northeast of Poznań, visiting a dozen or so sites associated with the dynasty. A short detour off the route leads to the reconstructed Iron Age village of **Biskupin**, Poland's most ancient preserved settlement, while the **Wielkopolska National Park** just south of Poznań offers a rare chance to explore a region of wilderness in this heavily agricultural belt.

Bordering the Baltic, **Pomerania**'s ports such as **Szczecin** still play a crucial role in the country's economy – the Polish merchant navy remains a viable earner in the face of Far Eastern competition. The **Baltic** may not be quite the Med, but a string of seaside resorts pulls in large numbers of Polish and neighbouring tourists with **beaches** sweeping away far enough to escape the crowds. Among the towns, the architectural high points are **Stargard Szczeciński**, with some of the finest examples of the brick Gothic buildings so typical of the Baltic lands,

---

ACCOMMODATION PRICE CODES

The accommodation listed in this book has been given one of the following price codes. For more details see p.34.

① under 20zł (under £5/$7.5)   ⑤ 75–95zł (£20–25/$30–38)
② 20–38zł (£5–10/$7.5–15)   ⑥ 95–135zł (£25–35/$38–53)
③ 38–58zł (£10–15/$15–23)   ⑦ 135–210zł (£35–55/$53–83)
④ 58–75zł (£15–20/$23–30)   ⑧ 210–300zł (£55–80/$83–120)
⑨ over 300zł (over £80/$120)

and **Kamień Pomorski**, an old lagoon settlement with a wonderful cathedral. The region has wildlife appeal, too, with a rich variety of animal and bird life in the **Słowiński National Park** and a European bison reserve in the forested **Woliński National Park**. Inland, the Pomeranian **lakeland** is less known than its counterpart in Mazury, but offers a few low-key lakeside resorts as well as enjoyable recreation for cyclists and hikers.

WIELKOPOLSKA

The undulating landscape of **Wielkopolska** may not offer much drama, but its human story is an altogether different matter, as its name – "Greater Poland" – implies. This area has been inhabited continuously since prehistoric times, and it was here that the Polish nation first took shape. The names of the province and of Poland itself derive from a Slav tribe called the **Polonians**, whose leaders – the **Piast** family – were to rule the country for five centuries. Their embryonic state emerged under Mieszko I in the mid-tenth century, but the significant breakthrough was achieved under his son, Bolesław the Brave, who gained control over an area similar to that of present-day Poland, and made it independent from the German-dominated Holy Roman Empire. Though relegated to the status of a border province by the mid-eleventh century, Wielkopolska remained one of the indisputably Polish parts of Poland, fighting the Germanization which swamped the nation's other western territories.

The major survival from the early Piast period is at **Lake Lednica**, located on the Piast Route just west of **Gniezno**, the first city to achieve dominance before decline brought about the consolation role of Poland's ecclesiastical capital. It was quickly supplanted as the regional centre by nearby **Poznań**, which has retained its position as one of Poland's leading commercial cities.

Even older than either of these is **Kalisz**, which dates back at least as far as Roman times, while the region's prehistoric past is vividly represented at the Iron Age village of **Biskupin**, a halfway point on the **narrow-gauge rail line** which rattles along between the town of **Żnin** and the village of Gąsawa. Another town in the province which has played an important part in Polish culture, albeit at a later date, is **Leszno**, once a major Protestant centre. Yet this is predominantly a rural province, and perhaps its most typical natural attraction is the **Wielkopolska National Park**, epitomizing the region's glaciated landscape. On the eastern border of Wielkopolska lies the minute ancient province of **Kujawy**; it has a few fairly interesting towns, notably the historic capital of **Włocławek**.

As elsewhere in Poland, there are plentiful trains and buses, even to the smallest outpost, with the former usually having the edge in terms of speed and convenience.

Poznań

Thanks to its position on the Paris–Berlin–Moscow rail line, and as the one place where all international trains stop between the German border and Warsaw, **POZNAŃ** is many visitors' first taste of Poland. In many ways it's the ideal introduction, as no other city is more closely identified with Polish nationhood. *Posnania elegans Poloniae civitas* (Poznań, a beautiful city in Poland), the

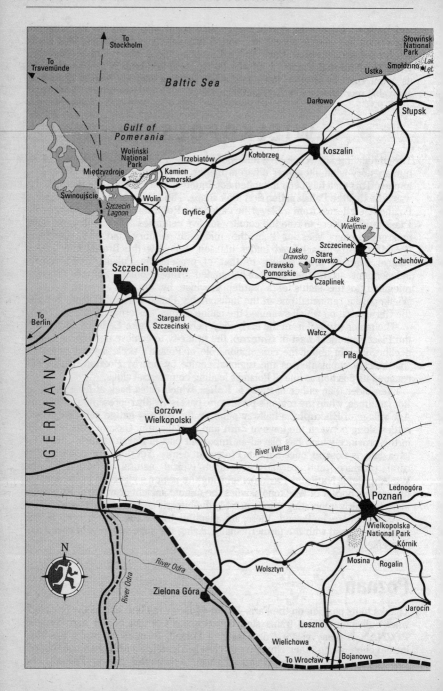

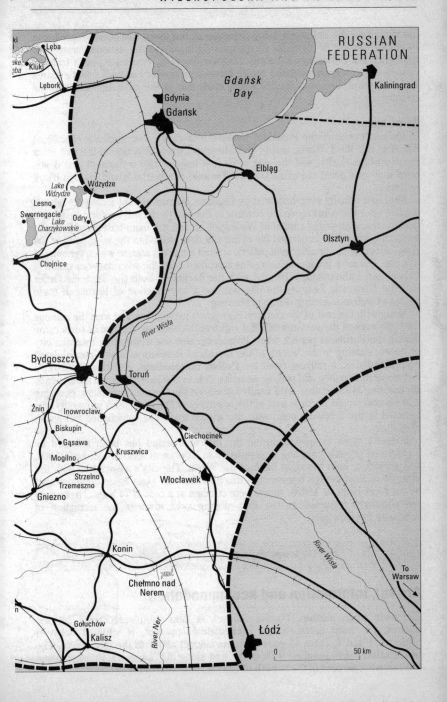

inscription on the oldest surviving depiction of the town, has been adopted as a local catchphrase to highlight its unswerving loyalty to the national cause over the centuries. Nowadays it's a city of great diversity, encompassing a tranquil cathedral quarter, an animated centre focused on one of Europe's finest squares and a dynamic business district whose trade fair is the most important in the country.

Some history

In the ninth century the Polonians founded a castle on a strategically significant island in the River Warta, and in 968 Mieszko I made this one of the two main centres of his duchy, and the seat of its first bishop. The settlement that developed here was given the name **Ostrów Tumski** (Cathedral Island), which it still retains.

Although initially overshadowed by Gniezno, Poznań did not follow the latter's decline after the court moved to Kraków in the mid-thirteenth century. Instead, it became the undisputed capital of Wielkopolska and the main bastion of Poland's western border. The economic life of the city then shifted to the west bank of the river, adopting the familiar grid pattern around a market square which remains to this day. Poznań's prosperity soared as it profited from the advantageous union of Poland and Lithuania in 1569, and with the decline of both the Teutonic Order and the Hanseatic League, the city became a key junction of European trade routes as well as a leading centre of learning.

Along with the rest of the country, regression inevitably set in with the ruinous Swedish wars of the seventeenth and eighteenth centuries. Revival of sorts came during the Partitions period, when Poznań became the thoroughly Prussian city of Posen; sharing in the wealth of the Industrial Revolution, it also consolidated its reputation as a rallying point for **Polish nationalism**, resisting Bismarck's Germanization policy and playing an active role in the independence movements. An uprising in December 1918 finally forced out the German occupiers, ensuring that Poznań would become part of the resurrected Polish state. A university was founded in the following year, with the annual trade fair established two years after that.

Poznań's rapid expansion during the interwar period has been followed by accelerated growth, doubling in population to its present level of almost 600,000, and spreading onto the right bank of the Warta. The city's association with the struggle against foreign hegemony – this time Russian – was again demonstrated by the **food riots of 1956**, which were crushed at a cost of 74 lives. These riots are popularly regarded as the first staging post towards the formation of Solidarity 24 years later.

The **telephone code** for Poznań is ☎061

Arrival, information and accommodation

The main **train station**, Poznań Główny, is 2km southwest of the historic quarter; the front entrance, not immediately apparent, is situated between platforms 1 and 4. Tram #5 goes from the viaduct above to the city centre. The **bus station** is five minutes' walk to the east along ul. Towarowa. Buses #59 and #78 serve the **airport** in the suburb of Ławica, 5km west of the centre.

As elsewhere in the country, **tourist offices** are sprouting like mushrooms; for information try the *PTTK* bureau at Stary Rynek 90 (Mon–Fri 9am–5pm, Sat 10am–2pm; ☎52 37 56) or the *Almatur* office at al. Aleksandra Fredry 7 (☎52 36 45). International rail tickets can be purchased from the *Orbis* office at al. Karola Marcinkowskiego 21 (☎53 20 52).

Accommodation
Because of its trade fair, Poznań has plenty of accommodation, but **hotel** prices consequently tend to be on the high side. Staying here on a tight budget shouldn't present any real problems, however, if you use the city's inexpensive **hostels**.

CENTRAL HOTELS
Dom Turysty, Stary Rynek 91 (☎52 88 93). About as central as they get, this former *PTTK* hostel has shrewdly hiked up its prices, but it's still essentially a hostel, albeit a touch grander than most, offering shared facilities. ⑥.

Ikar, ul. Kościuszki 118 (☎57 67 05). A rather soulless-looking building but with well-equipped rooms. ⑥.

Lech, ul. Św. Marcin 74 (☎53 01 51). One of a pair of long-established "three-star" hotels right in the heart of the commercial district. ⑥.

Royal, ul Św. Marcin 71 (☎53 78 84). A welcoming, clean and tidy option squeezing in between the *Lech* and *Wielkopolska* and undercutting them both. ③.

Rzymski, al. Karola Marcinkowskiego 22 (☎52 81 21). Spruced-up hotel with a good restaurant and just a couple of minutes' walk from the Stary Rynek. ⑥.

Wielkopolska, ul. Św. Marcin 67 (☎52 76 31). Good location directly across the street from *Lech*, but a bit cheaper and also with a good-value restaurant. ⑤.

OUT OF THE CENTRE
Naramowice, ul. Naramowicka 150 (☎20 27 81). Two-star hotel 3km north of the Rynek, reached by bus #51, # 67 or # 90. ③.

Olimp, ul. Warmińska 1 (☎41 50 41). Sports hotel by a stadium 3km northwest of the train station and reached by tram #9 or #11. ②.

Meridian, ul. Litewska (☎41 12 01). Expensive privately run hotel in a tranquil setting by a lake in Park Sołacki, 2km northwest of the centre. Half-price weekend deals. ⑧.

Merkury, ul. Franklina Roosevelta 20 (☎55 80 00). Typical *Orbis* joint close to the train station and trade fair buildings. ⑦.

Novotel, ul. Warszawska 64/66 (☎77 00 11). Plush *Orbis* motel situated by a park 2km from the centre, off the main Warsaw road. ⑦.

Park, ul. Majakowskiego 77 (☎79 40 81). German-owned hotel on the southern bank of Lake Maltańskie 2km east of the city centre. Prices for rooms and food are comparable with its *Orbis* rivals, but it surpasses them in quality; higher price for lakeside rooms. ⑧.

Polonez, al. Niepodległości 36 (☎36 12 57). Another *Orbis* establishment; located to the north of the centre, it's quieter and less expensive than its counterparts. ⑥.

Poznań, pl. Gen. Henryka Dąbrowskiego 1 (☎33 20 81). Located just 1km south of the city centre, this high-rise building is the flagship of *Orbis*'s concrete fleet. Even if you're not staying here it's a useful place to know about, as services include the main *Orbis* travel bureau as well as a car rental office. As with all these top-notch hotels, English is spoken. ⑧.

HOSTELS AND CAMPSITE
The handiest **hostel** is at ul. Berwinskiego 2/3 (☎66 36 80; ②), five minutes' walk west of the train station, but it's only open during school terms. Most useful and open all year is the hostel at al. Niepodległości 34 (☎53 22 51; ②), about ten

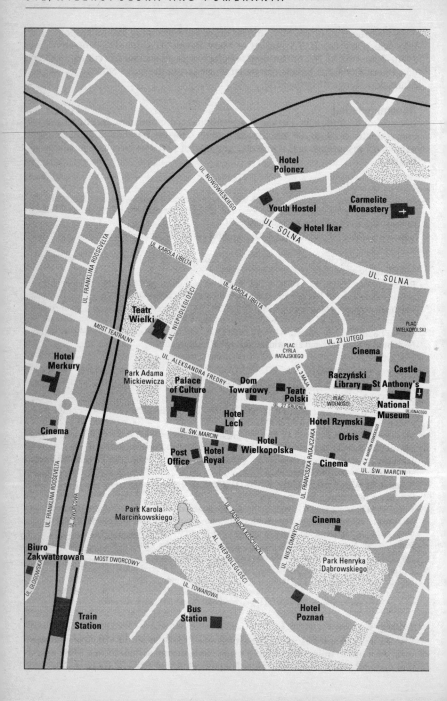

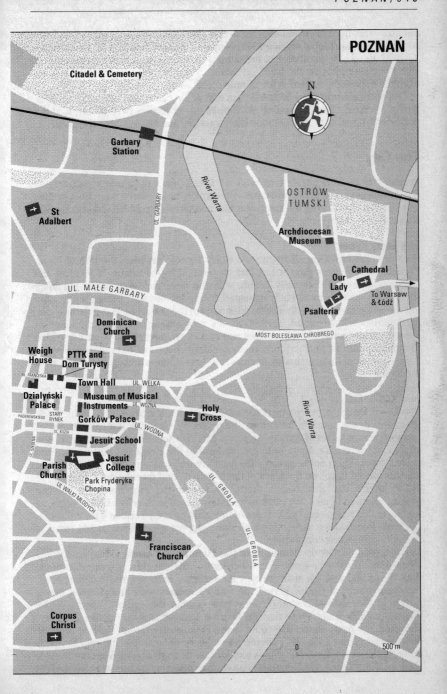

POZNAŃ

Citadel & Cemetery

Garbary
Station

N

OSTRÓW
TUMSKI

River Warta

UL GARBARY

St
Adalbert

Archdiocesan
Museum

Cathedral

Our
Lady

To Warsaw
& Łódź

Psalteria

UL. MAŁE GARBARY

Dominican
Church

MOST BOLESŁAWA CHROBREGO

Weigh
House

PTTK and
Dom Turysty

UL FRANCESKA

Town Hall

UL. WELKA

Dzialyński
Palace

Museum of Musical
Instruments

UL. WOZNA

Holy
Cross

PADEREWSKIEGO

STARY
RYNEK

Gorków Palace

UL. WODNA

River Warta

UL. KOZIA

Jesuit School

UL. SZOLNA

Parish
Church

Jesuit
College

Park Fryderyka
Chopina

UL GROBLA

UL WALKI MLODYCH

Franciscan
Church

UL. GROBLA

Corpus
Christi

0   500 m

minutes' walk from town and offering decent twin rooms but less salubrious bath-rooms. If you don't mind staying a long way out, the new hostel at ul. Biskupińska 27 (☎22 10 63; ②), 5km west in the suburb of Strzeszyn, is well recommended. Bus #95 goes right past the front, or Poznań Strzeszyn train station (one stop up from the main train station) is ten minutes' walk away.

The nearest **campsite** is situated 2km east of the centre and offers the consola-tion of a relaxing lakeside setting. *Maltańska*, ul. Krańcowa (☎76 60 11), is at the northeastern end of the eponymous lake; trams #6 and #8 pass by to the north.

The City

Poznań may be a big city, but, as is often the case, most of its primary attractions are grouped in a central, walkable core which is in places free from traffic. Outside the central area the rattle of trams and tyres on cobbled streets makes it a pretty noisy place.

The Stary Rynek

For seven centuries the distinguished **Stary Rynek** has been the hub of life in Poznań, even if these days it has lost its position as the centre of political and economic power. Archetypally Polish, with the most important public buildings sited in the middle, it was badly damaged during the last war, subsequently gain-ing the sometimes overenthusiastic attentions of the restorers. However only die-hard purists will be upset by this, as it's now among the most attractive of Poland's rejuvenated old city centres and makes you appreciate what a fine idea the town square is. Furthermore, many buildings have had bas-reliefs applied to them – not all of them orthodox designs, but nevertheless adding to the charm of the Rynek.

THE TOWN HALL

The **Town Hall** is in every way predominant. Originally a two-storey Gothic brick structure, it was radically rebuilt in the 1550s by Giovanni Battista Quadro of Lugano, whose turreted facade gives it a Moorish feel. Every day at noon, the effigies of two rams emerge onto the platform of the **clock** and butt their heads twelve times. This commemorates the best-known local legend in which the two animals locked horns on the steps of the town hall, and thereby drew attention to a fire which had just begun there, so saving the city from yet another conflagration. In thanks, the rams were immortalized in the city's coat of arms, as well as in this timepiece. Other sides of the building are inscribed with the words of Polish Renaissance sages, to which the restorers were forced to add extracts from the communist constitution.

The interior is now the **Museum of the History of Poznań** (Mon, Tues & Fri 10am–4pm, Wed noon–6pm, Sun 10am–3pm), though this is less educational than it sounds, and the main reason for entering is to see the building itself. Surviving from the Gothic period the vaulted **cellars** were transformed into a prison in the sixteenth century; they now contain the earliest objects in the display, notably items excavated on Ostrów Tumski and the medieval pillory. However, the most impressive room is the Renaissance **Great Hall** on the first floor, dating from 1555. Its coffered vault bears polychrome bas-reliefs which embody the exemplary civic duties and virtues through scenes from the lives of Samson, King David and Hercules. The southern section by the staircase depicts

HENRYK SIENKIEWICZ (1846–1916)

Outside Poland, **Henryk Sienkiewicz**'s reputation has rested largely on *Quo Vadis?*, an epic on the early Christians in the decadent days of the Roman Empire, which won him the 1905 **Nobel Prize for Literature** and quickly became a favourite subject for movie moguls. Yet the huge popular success of this led, after the author's death, to the almost total international neglect of the remainder of his colossal oeuvre, which, even in hopelessly inadequate translations, had marked him out as Poland's answer to Charles Dickens. The sudden interest in all things Polish which followed the collapse of communism has already spawned new English translations of several of his other books, which should help to restore his literary status to its rightful place.

Born in the Podlasie region to a minor aristocratic family of Tartar origin, Sienkiewicz began his career as a **journalist** and **short story writer**, the culmination of which was a trip to the United States in 1876–77, where he worked in a short-lived Polish agricultural commune in California. Here he wrote *Letters from America* (containing vivid descriptions of such diverse subjects as New York City and the Indian campaigns), and the burlesque novella *Charcoal Sketches*, a satire on rural life in Russian Poland. On his return home, he drew on his experiences of émigré life in *American Stories*, which includes his one work in this genre which frequently turns up in literary anthologies, *The Lighthouse Keeper*. These were followed by the despairing novella *Bartek the Conqueror*, the finest of a number of works set in the Poznań region – which, being under Prussian control, made a safer medium for the nationalist message of an author subject to Russian censors.

Thereafter, Sienkiewicz changed tack, reviving what was then regarded as the outmoded form of the **historical epic**. His vast trilogy *With Fire and Sword*, *The Deluge* and *Fire in the Steppe* is set against the heroic backdrop of Poland's seventeenth-century wars with the Cossacks, Swedes and Turks. It is remarkable for its sure sense of structure, employing a permanent set of characters – whose language is skilfully differentiated according to their class and culture – with plentiful genealogical digressions and romantic interludes to break the unfolding of the main plot. Historical realism, however, was sacrificed in favour of Sienkiewicz's own Catholic, nationalist, chivalrous and anti-intellectual outlook. *Quo Vadis?*, which followed the trilogy, is his only novel without a Polish setting, although it has always been regarded as a fable about the country's oppression under the Partitions, emphasized by the fact that two of the leading characters are Lygians – inhabitants of what subsequently became the heartlands of Poland. Ironically, it is really one of Sienkiewicz's weaker works, irredeemably marred by its maudlin sentimentality, for all its mastery of narrative, description and characterization. He showed a greater concern for historical accuracy in his final epic, *The Teutonic Knights*, in which Poland's plight was reflected in the clearest and most relevant parallel from the past.

Sienkiewicz also produced a couple of novels with contemporary settings, *Without Dogma* and *The Połaniecki Family*. These helped increased his cult status in **nationalist circles**, and political activity, boosted by the international celebrity status bestowed by *Quo Vadis?*, became increasingly important to him after the turn of the century. At the same time, his creative powers began to wane: he abandoned a planned trilogy on the life and times of King Jan Sobieski, though the excellent children's novel, *In Desert and Wilderness*, showed his continuing versatility. On the outbreak of World War I Sienkiewicz moved to Switzerland where, along with the pianist Ignacy Jan Paderewski, he was instrumental in setting up the **Polish National Committee**, which in due course came to be recognized by the Western allies as a provisional government. However, he did not live to play the direct political role that might otherwise have fallen to him when Poland was resurrected at the end of the war.

astrological and bestial figures (including a rather fantastical rhino), while the marble busts of Roman emperors around the walls are reminders of the weighty tradition of municipal leadership. The top floor continues with a relatively dull display of local treasures, portraits and old postcards.

AROUND THE STARY RYNEK

Outside the Town Hall stands a fine Rococo **fountain**, alongside a copy of the **pillory** in its traditional location. Further to the south are the colourful **Houses of the Keepers**, once home of the market traders, many of whom sold their wares in their arcaded passageway. The present structures, each varying in height from its neighbour by a few inches, date from the sixteenth century and are thus the oldest in the square.

Behind a fountain of a water-bearing maiden is the **Weigh House** (Waga Miejska), now a restaurant but once the most important public building in this great trading centre; what you see today is a reproduction of the original, again the work of Quadro. Round the corner from here is the sternly Neoclassical **Guardhouse** (Odwach), built for the "defence and decoration" of the city in the 1780s – just before the whole Polish state crumbled. In recent years, a **museum** of the history of the working-class movement has been housed here; lately they've been celebrating the Poznań riots of 1956. Between here and the Houses of the Keepers are two ugly structures which add the only discordant notes to the square – communist legacies which should be disowned even more urgently. One of them is now the **Wielkopolska Museum of Arms** (Tues noon–6pm, Wed & Fri 10am–4pm, Thurs 9am–3pm, Sat 9am–4pm, Sun noon–3pm), a dreary display of weaponry in the province, from the Middle Ages onwards.

Many a medieval and Renaissance interior lurks behind the Baroque facades of the **gabled houses** lining the outer sides of the Stary Rynek, most of them shops, restaurants, cafés or banks and more recently, antique shops. On the eastern side, at no. 45 is the **Museum of Musical Instruments** (Tues 11am–5pm, Wed & Fri 10am–4pm, Sat 10am–5pm, Sun 10am–3pm), the only collection of its kind in Poland. Its exhibits range from folk instruments from all over the world, through Chopin memorabilia to a vast array of violins. The last is a reminder that every five years the city hosts the Wieniawski International Violin Competition, one of the most prestigious events for young virtuosi (next in November 1996).

The western side of the square is almost equally imposing, above all because of the massive green and white **Działyński Palace** at no. 78, which was one of the headquarters of the nineteenth-century struggles to keep Polish culture alive. The houses at the extreme ends of this side were the homes of prominent Poznań personalities. Number 71 belonged to Jan Chróściejewski, twice the mayor of the city around 1600 and the author of the first book on children's diseases. Giovanni Battista Quadro lived in no. 84, whose facade has been painted with scenes narrating his life. Its interior houses the **Henryk Sienkiewicz Literature Museum** (Mon–Fri 10am–5pm). Although Poland's most celebrated novelist (see box on p.545) had only a rather tenuous connection with Poznań, this is the most important museum dedicated to his life and works.

West of the Stary Rynek

Just to the west of the Stary Rynek stands a hill with remnants of the inner circle of the medieval walls. This particular section guarded what was once the **castle** (Zamek Przemysława), seat of the rulers of Wielkopolska. Modified down the centuries and almost completely destroyed in 1945, a part has been restored to house the **Museum of Decorative Arts** (Tues, Wed, Fri & Sat 10am–4pm, Sun 10am–3pm). This features an enjoyable collection from medieval times to the present day, while the Gothic cellars are used for changing displays of posters, an art form taken very seriously in Poland.

Below the hill is the Baroque **Church of St Anthony**, its transepts formed by sumptuous chapels dedicated to the Virgin and Saint Francis. Its decoration, including the ornate stalls and high altar, was executed by the Franciscan brothers Adam and Antonin Swach, the former a painter, the latter a sculptor and stuccoist. On the interior of the west wall you can see examples of a uniquely Polish art: portraits of nobles painted on sheet metal, which were placed on the deceased's coffin.

From here it's only a short walk round the corner to the vast elongated space of **plac Wolności**, which formerly bore the name of Napoleon, then Kaiser Wilhelm, only gaining its present designation – Freedom Square – after the Wielkopolska uprising in 1918. Here stands another seminal centre of the fight to preserve Polish culture, the **Raczyński Library**. Architecturally, it's one of the most distinguished buildings in the city, erected in the 1820s in the grand style of the Louvre.

THE NATIONAL MUSEUM

Directly facing the Raczyński Library is the ill-named **National Museum** (Tues noon–6pm, Thurs 10am–5pm, Wed, Fri and Sat 10am–4pm, Sun 10am–3pm). At present it's more of a gallery, with one of the few important displays of old master paintings in Poland, located on the first floor. The **Italian** section begins with panels from Gothic altarpieces by artists such as Bernardo Daddi and Lorenzo Monaco, and continues with Renaissance pieces such as Bellini's *Madonna and Child with Donor* and Bassano's *At Vulcan's Forge*.

Prize exhibit of the gallery's small but choice **Spanish** section is Zurbarán's *Madonna of the Rosary*. This Counter-Reformation masterpiece was part of a cycle for the Carthusian monastery at Jerez, and features actual portraits of the silent monks. By the same artist is *Christ at the Column*, a sharply edged work from the very end of his career, and there are also a couple of notable works by his contemporary Ribera. In the extensive display of the **Low Countries**, highlights are an affectionate *Madonna and Child* attributed to Massys and the regal *Adoration of the Magi* by Joos van Cleve.

The **Polish** canvases are an anticlimax, but look out for the room dedicated to the inconsistent Jacek Malczewski, the historical scenes by Jan Matejko, the landscapes of Wojciech Gerson and the subdued portraits of Olga Boznańska.

BEYOND PLAC WOLNOŚCI

Moving into the business and shopping thoroughfares which branch out west from pl. Wolności, you shortly come to the **Theatr Polski** on ul. 27 Grudnia. Erected in the 1870s by voluntary contributions, this was yet another major cultural institution during the Partitions period: the uphill nature of this struggle is reflected in the inscription on the facade – "The Nation by Itself". Overlooking the busy junction at the end of the street is the city's most distinguished postwar building, the **Dom Tomarowy** department store. Built in the mid-1950s, it's an imposing ten-storey cylinder constructed round a hollow core in which unfolds a spiral staircase – Poznań's version of Harrods or Bloomingdales.

An insight into the curious dichotomy of life during the Partitions is provided by the large buildings standing further to the west, which reflect the self-confidence of the German occupiers in the first decade of this century. Ironically, many of these cultural establishments and administration offices were taken over just a few years after they were built by an institution with very different values, the new University of Poznań. The most imposing of the group, the huge neo-Romanesque **Kaiserhaus**, had an even more dramatic change of role. Built in imitation of the style favoured by the Hohenstaufen emperors of early medieval Germany, it was intended to accommodate the Kaiser whenever he happened to be in town. Instead, it has become a Palace of Culture with a distinctively populist stamp. In the park beyond are two huge crucifixes bound together with heavy rope, forming a **monument** to the victims of the Poznań food riots and also celebrating the birth of Solidarity. It was put up on the 25th anniversary of the former event in 1981 – during martial law.

South and east of the Stary Rynek
Returning to the Stary Rynek and continuing along ul. Wodna brings you to the **Górków Palace**, which still preserves its intricate Renaissance portico and sober inner courtyard. The mansion now houses the **Archeology Museum** (Tues–Fri 10am–4pm, Sat 10am–6pm, Sun 10am–3pm), where the displays are short on aesthetic appeal but commendably thorough. They trace the history of the region from the time of the nomadic hunters who lived here between 15,000 and 8000 BC, all the way to the early feudal society of the seventh century AD.

Ulica Świętosławska ends in a cluster of former Jesuit buildings, the finest examples of Baroque architecture in the city. The end of this street is closed by the facade of what's understatedly known as the **Parish Church** (Kościół Frany), completed just forty years before the expulsion of the Jesuits in 1773. Its magnificently sombre interior is all fluted columns with gilded capitals, monumental sculptures, large altarpieces framed by twisted columns and rich stuccowork, in the full-blown Roman manner. Over the high altar is a painting illustrating a legendary episode from the life of Saint Stanisław. Then a bishop, he was accused by King Bolesław the Generous of not having paid for a village he had incorporated into his territories. In order to prove his innocence, the saint resurrected the deceased former owner of the land to testify on his behalf. It's the one church in town worth seeing and makes a fitting place in which to enjoy the daily **organ recitals** which usually commence at noon.

Across the road is the **Jesuit School**, now one of Poland's main ballet academies; take a peek at its miniature patio, an architectural gem. To the east of the church is the front section of the **Jesuit College**, currently the seat of the city council. The Jesuits have returned to Poznań, though they were unable to reclaim the buildings they created. Instead, they now occupy the oldest left-bank building, the **Dominican Church** to the northeast of the Stary Rynek. Despite a Baroque recasing, this still preserves original Romanesque and Gothic features, as well as a stellar-vaulted Rosary chapel.

The late Baroque **Church of the Holy Cross** (Kościół Wszystkich Świętych), almost due east of the Stary Rynek, is the epitome of a Lutheran church, with its democratic central plan layout and overall plainness. Yet although it survives as an almost complete period piece, the exodus of virtually all the Protestants this century means that it's now used for Catholic worship, as is evidenced by the jarring high altar.

At no. 25 on the adjacent ul. Grobla is the former lodge of the freemasons, now the **Ethnographical Museum** (Tues, Wed, Fri and Sat 10am–4pm, Sun 10am–3pm). Further south you'll see the twin-towered Baroque church of the **Franciscan Monastery**, which has been gleamingly restored by the monks who repossessed it following its wartime use as a warehouse. Built in 1473 and destroyed by the Swedes two hundred years later, photographs in the vestibule show the church before, during and after the war when the Franciscans completed their masterful repair. What you see now is a gleaming bright interior of white and gold with shades of ochre and Rococo flourishes. At the southern extremity of the old town is **Corpus Christi** (Kościół Bożego Ciała), a forlorn fifteenth-century Gothic church that once belonged to a Carmelite monastery, but now seems ignored and is usually locked.

North of the Stary Rynek

The northern quarters are best approached from plac Wielkopolski, a large square now used for markets. From here ul. Działowa passes two churches facing each other on the brow of the hill. To the right is the Gothic **St Adalbert** (Św. Wojciecha), chiefly remarkable for its little seventeenth-century wooden belfry which somehow got left on the ground in front of the brick facade. Opposite, the handsome Baroque facade of the **Carmelite Monastery** reflects a more complete image. Further uphill are the most exclusive cemeteries in Poznań, reserved for people deemed to have made a valuable contribution to the life of Wielkopolska, as well as a monument to the defenders of the city in 1939.

Beyond, al. Niepodległości ascends to the vast former **Citadel**. This Prussian fortress was levelled after the war to make a public park, albeit one whose main appeal is to necrophiles. There's a cemetery for the six thousand Russians and Poles who lost their lives in the month-long siege which led to its capture, while to the east are the graves of British and Commonwealth soldiers.

Ostrów Tumski and the right bank

From the left bank the Bolesława the Great Bridge (Most Bolestawa Chrobrego) crosses to the holy island of **Ostrów Tumski**, a world away in spirit, if not in distance, from the hustle of the city. (Trams #1, #4, #8 go over the bridge.) Only a small portion of the island is built upon, and a few priests and monks comprise its entire population. Lack of parishioners means that there's not the usual need for evening Masses, and after 5pm the island is a ghost town.

The first building you see is the late Gothic **Psalteria**, characterized by its elaborate stepped gable. It was erected in the early sixteenth century as a residence for the cathedral choir. Immediately behind is an earlier brick structure, the **Church of Our Lady** (Kościół Panny Marii). This seemingly unfinished and unbalanced small church was given supposedly controversial stained glass and murals after the war. A couple of minutes' walk north of the cathedral is the **Archdiocesan Museum** (Mon–Fri 9am–3pm, Sat & Sun 1–3pm), with a spread of sculptures, treasure and some rather fine religious art that ought to be on show somewhere more prominent.

THE BASILICA OF SS PETER AND PAUL

The streets of the island are lined with handsome eighteenth-century houses, all very much in the shadow of the **Basilica of SS Peter and Paul**, Poland's first and foremost cathedral. Over the centuries the brickwork exterior succumbed to Baroque and Neoclassical remodellings but when much of this was stripped by wartime devastation, it was decided to restore as much of the Gothic original as possible. Unfortunately, the lack of documentary evidence for the eastern chapels meant that their successors had to be retained. The Baroque spires on the two facade towers and the three lanterns around the ambulatory, which give a vaguely Eastern touch, were also reconstructed. Indeed it is the view onto this end of the building which offers it's most impressive, if misleading aspect.

Inside, the basilica is impressive, but not outstanding as befits its pre-eminent status among the nation's places of worship. The **crypt**, entered from below the northern tower, has been extensively excavated, uncovering the thousand-year-old foundations of the pre-Romanesque and Romanesque cathedrals which stood on the site – two models depict their probable appearance. Also extant, though isolated by grilles as if they were the Crown Jewels, are parts of the sarcophagi of the first two Polish kings, Mieszko I and Bolesław the Brave. Their remains currently rest in the **Golden chapel** behind the altar. Miraculously unscathed during the war, this hyper-ornate creation, representing the diverse if dubious tastes of the 1830s, is the antithesis of the plain architecture all around it. Its decoration is a curious co-operation between mosaic artists from Venice (who created the patterned floor and the copy of Titian's *Assumption*) and a painter and a sculptor from the very different Neoclassical traditions of Berlin, although the untutored eye is unlikely to spot any stylistic discord.

Of the many other **funerary monuments** which form one of the key features of the cathedral, that of Bishop Benedykt Izdbieński, just to the left of the Golden chapel is notable. This was carved by Jan Michałowicz, the one native Polish artist of the Renaissance period who was the equal of the many Italians who settled here. The other outstanding tomb is that of the Górka family, in the Holy Sacrament chapel at the northern end of the nave, sculpted just a few years later by one of these itinerant craftsmen, Hieronimo Canavesi. Other **works of art** to look out for are the Late Gothic carved and gilded high altar triptych from Silesia, the choir stalls from the same period and fragments of sixteenth-century frescoes, notably a cycle of the Apostles on the south side of the ambulatory.

ŚRÓDKA

Crossing Most Mieska I brings you to the right-bank suburb of **Śródka**, the second oldest part of the city, whose name derives from the word for Wednesday – market day here in medieval times. Though there's nothing special to see, something of the atmosphere of an ancient market quarter survives. Just beyond is another distinct settlement, known as **Komandoria** after the commanders of the Knights of Saint John of Jerusalem, who settled here towards the end of the twelfth century. The late Romanesque church of this community, **St John's**, survives with Gothic and Baroque additions and now stands in splendid isolation by a busy roundabout.

Just south of here is the western end of **Lake Maltańskie**, the city's most popular playground. This artificial stretch of water, more than 2km in length, has watersports facilities, along with restaurants, a campsite and top-class hotels. Beyond its eastern edge is a wooded park with a cluster of small lakes, crisscrossed by marked walking trails. Here also is the **Zoo** (daily 9am–dusk), which is connected to St John's by a **narrow-gauge rail line** (hourly services, May–Sept only) specially designed for children.

Eating, drinking and entertainment

In choosing somewhere to eat and drink, the luxury **hotels** (see p.541) should always be borne in mind. Each establishment has a restaurant and café with prices which compare well with elsewhere in town. Otherwise, the gastronomic situation is in more of a state of flux with a number of Chinese and Italian-style eateries, plus a host of Westernized fast-food joints and trendy café-bars emerging. Understandably the Poles are enjoying the change but you might be rather disappointed. Note that Poznań is a major brewing centre, and that its **beers**, *Ratusz* and (especially) *Lech*, are not the inferior products their price tags would suggest.

Restaurants and snack bars

Adria, ul. Głogowska 14. Just across from the station, and with its own nightclub.

Arezzo, 49 Stary Rynek. One of several Italian restaurants on the square, with outdoor seating on warm days.

Avanti, Stary Rynek 76. Ever-popular spaghetti house and snack bar that continues to offer good value.

Azalia, ul. Św Marcin 34. Undistinguished Chinese dishes and, if you're unlucky, someone karaokeing.

Bambou, 64/5 Stary Rynek. Probably the best Chinese restaurant in town, but not cheap.

Club Elite, Stary Rynek 2. A good place to sample traditional Polish cuisine, but as the name suggests, it's twice the price of elsewhere.

Pizzeria Apollo, pas. Apollo. Huge selection of pizzas as well as other Italian favourites; the delicious *calzone* is big enough to get into.

Pizzeria Capriccio, Stary Rynek 95. Unusual in Poland in serving genuine pizza, as opposed to the imitations which have become such a national craze.

Pod Arkadami, pl. Cyryla Ratajskiego 10. This Poznań institution is the only milk bar surviving in the central area and offers lashings of cheap wholesome Polish food.

Tivoli, ul. Wroniecka 13. Decent and inexpensive trattoria just north of the Rynek.

U Dylla, Stary Rynek 37. Serves good and reasonably priced food in an ideal setting, with a choice of Western and Polish drinks.

W-Z, ul. Aleksandra Fredry 12. An old favourite with long opening hours on account of the nightly dances, for which there's a surcharge.

Cafés and café-bars

Ali Baba, corner of ul. 3 Maja and pl. Cyryla Ratajskiego. 24-hour bar.

Green Pub, 26 ul. Piekary. Neo-Irish-style pub serving Guinness; every emerging Polish city has one.

Sukiennicza, Stary Rynek 98. Superb coffee, cakes and ice cream dishes in an unhurried setting, complete with resident pianist, reminiscent of central Europe's pre-communist days.

U Rajców, Stary Rynek 93. Tea house, with a sideline in mead.

Winiarnia Ratuszowa, Stary Rynek 55. An expensive "Gothic-ized" restaurant at ground-floor level, with a wonderfully atmospheric wine bar in the genuinely medieval cellars.

Nightlife and culture

Nightspots in Poznań are rare, unless you count the cabaret scene in the fancy hotels and the restaurants around the station. Best chance of some action is to ask around the university buildings about **student clubs**: the largest, *Odnowa*, is at ul. Św. Marcin 80/82. The lively *Bratniak* peace and environmentalist group meets in building B on ul. Dożynkowa to the north of the centre, reached by tram #4 or #16.

There's a far better choice if you want highbrow **culture** in the evening, something Poles do far better than their crass disco efforts. The *Teatr Polski*, ul. 27 Grudnia 8/10 (☎52 05 41), presents classic plays, while the *Teatr Muski*, al. Niepodlegości 26 (☎52 60 76), specializes in modern fare. **Opera** is performed at the *Teatr Wielki*, ul. Aleksandra Fredry 9 (☎52 82 91), and the *Polski Teatr Tańca*, ul. Kozia 4 (☎52 42 41), is the home of the Balet Poznański and offers varied **dance** programmes. **Classical concerts** are held at the *Filharmonia Państwowa*, ul. Św. Marcin 81 (☎52 47 48). **Musicals** are put on at the *Teatr Muzuczny*, ul. Niezłomnych 1a (☎52-17-86), while **puppet shows** are among the attractions at the *Teatr Animacji* in the *Pałac Kultury* at the corner of ul. Św. Marcin and al. Niepodległości (☎52 88 16).

There are a dozen **cinemas** in town, most showing the latest releases with Polish subtitles, so you can enjoy the film and learn a few Polish expletives on the way. The most central theatres are: the *Apollo* down pas. Apollo; the *Muza* nearby on ul. Św. Marcin 30; the *Gwiazda* just to the north on al. K. Marcinkowskiego 28 and the *Bałtyk* near the main train station on ul F. D. Roosevelta 22.

Listings

Airlines *LOT*, ul. Św. Marcin 69 (☎52 28 47); *British Airways*, ul. Dąbrowskiego 5 (☎48 88 88).

British Council Ul. Franciszka Ratajczaka at the corner with ul. 27 Grudnia.

Car rental Office in *Hotel Poznań*, pl. Gen. Henryka Dąbrowskiego 1 (☎33 20 81).

Festivals The main folklore event is the *Jarmarkt Świętojański* (St John's Market) held during the International Trade Fair in the second week of June. There's a festival of boys' choirs every February, and the Wieniawski International Violin Competition will next be staged in November 1996.

Football Lech Poznań, currently among Poland's best teams, play at the *Lech* stadium, west of the city centre on ul. Grunwaldzki, reached by tram #13.

Post offices Head office is at ul. Kosciuśki 77.

What's on A free monthly programme in Polish and an English abridgement, both known as *iks*, are available from tourist information points.

Around Poznań

It's simple to escape from the big-city feel of Poznań, as its outskirts soon give way to peaceful agricultural villages set in a lake-strewn landscape. Within a 25-kilometre radius of the city is some of the finest scenery in Wielkopolska, along with two of Poland's most famous **castles**, which, with your own transport, combine to make a full day's excursion.

Kórnik

KÓRNIK, site of one of the great castles of Wielkopolska, is 22km southeast of Poznań on the east bank of lakes Skrzynki and Kónickie, the first two in a long chain of six. There are regular services from the main bus station and from the terminus at Rondo Rataje; don't go by train, as the station is 4km from the village.

Kórnik has an appealing rural feel, consisting essentially of one long main street, ul. Poznańska (along which you'll find a few restaurants and snack bars).

This street culminates in a market square by the red-brick **Parish Church** which contains tombs of the Górka family, the first owners of the town.

The Górkas built their **Castle** at the extreme southern edge of the village in the fourteenth century. A fragment of the original survives, as does the medieval layout with its moat, but the castle was rebuilt in neo-Gothic style last century by Italian and German craftsmen including Karl Friedrich Schinkel, best known for his Neoclassical public buildings in Berlin. However, his designs were considerably modified, and credit for the final shape of the castle is due to the owner, Tytus Działyński, whose aim was as much to show off his collection of arms and armour, books and *objets d'art* as to provide a luxurious home for himself.

In contrast to the affected grandeur of the exterior, with its mock defensive towers and Moorish battlements (most evident on the south side, opposite the entrance) the **interior** (daily 9am–5.30pm) is rather more intimate. Ask to borrow the cumbersome English-language folder which describes the exhibits room by room, or you can buy the much handier guide version for 4zł. Most of the rooms feature decorative parquet flooring, honed to a fine polish by the over-slippers you are required to wear. On the ground floor especially it's the flooring and some examples of Regency and older furniture which catch the eye. The **Drawing Room** with its superb gilded ceiling and huge carved wooden portal bears Działyński's coat of arms, with none other than Chopin having once run his fingers across the keyboard of the nearby grand piano.The spacious **Black Hall**, with its slender white vaulting, gives a hint of the Moorish excesses upstairs, while next door, the **Dining Room** returns to a medieval European theme with its wooden coffered ceiling displaying heralds of almost the entire fifteenth-century Polish nobility. On the first floor is the one really theatrical gesture, the **Moorish Hall**, which attempts to mimic Granada's Alhambra. Here Działyński displayed his collection of antique Polish armour and weapons including an impressive feather-peaked suit once worn by a hussar and a cannon bearing the pretentious inscription: *ultima ratio regis* (a king's last resort). Other objects to look out for include a chest with a phenomenally complex locking mechanism in its lid, as well as porcelain vases, a three-hundred-year-old silver triptych and hefty carved and inlaid wardrobes also from that era.

To see all sides of the castle's exterior, you have to visit the **arboretum** (May–Oct daily 9am–6pm). Originally in the formal French style, this was transformed in the seemingly arbitrary manner of a *jardin anglais*. There are over two thousand species of trees and shrubs, from all corners of the world as well as a Gothic-Moorish view of the castle's south facade. The lakeside offers an even more pleasant stroll, particularly the western bank with its fine distant views.

Rogalin

With your own transport, it's easy to combine a visit to Kórnik with the castle near the hamlet of **ROGALIN**, 10km to the west on the road to Mosina. Unfortunately, only three buses pass this way in each direction, and the time-tables don't work out for seeing both monuments on the same day, unless you're prepared to take a chance on hitching, which is feasible.

The **Palace** (Wed–Sun 10am–4pm, last admission 3.30pm; May–Sept open until 6pm on Sat) was the seat of many Polish nobles from the eminent Poznań family, the Raczyńskis. In contrast to Kórnik, Rogalin is one of Poland's finest mansions, a truly palatial residence forming the axis of a careful layout of buildings and gardens. Built in a style which shows the earlier Baroque tastefully blending with the prevailing Neoclassical, the gleaming middle block centring the facade still remains closed pending renovation of the interior. In the meantime, you can visit the restored rooms in the two **bowed wings** which feature some fine furniture including a lovely lyre cabinet as well as portraits of illustrious Raczyńskis, most notably a sinister depiction of Roger who's buried in the chapel (see below) and a far more agreeable looking Anna Raczyńska. Best of all is the **art gallery** off the southern side; its primarily nineteenth-century examples of Polish and German works adding up to a better – and better laid–out – collection than you'll find in Poznań's disappointing National Museum. Jacek Malczewski was a frequent guest at Rogalin and his works are well represented here as are those of Jan Matejko, his epic *Virgin of Orleans* taking up an entire wall.

Fronting the palace courtyard is a long forecourt, to the sides of which are the stables and **coach house**, the latter now a repository of carriages once used by owners of this estate, along with the last horse-drawn cab to operate in Poznań. Passing outside the gates, a five-minute walk brings you to the unusual **chapel** which undertakes the duties of a parish church and mausoleum of the now defunct Raczyńskis. Set peacefully at the side of the road, it's a copy of one of Europe's best-preserved Roman monuments, the Maison Carrée in Nîmes, but built in a startlingly pink sandstone.

At the back of the main palace is an enclosed and rather neglected *jardin français*. More enticing is the English-style park beyond, laid out on the site of a primeval forest. This is chiefly remarkable for its **oak trees**, three of the most ancient of which have been fenced off for protection. Among the most celebrated natural wonders of Poland, they are at least one thousand years old – and thus of a similar vintage to the Polish nation itself. Following World War II they became popularly known as Lech, Czech and Rus, after the three mythical brothers who founded the Polish, Czech and Russian nations; with all due modesty, the largest is designated as Rus.

There's a **restaurant** and bar by the road, opposite the entrance to the palace, and a new upmarket **hotel** (☎061/13 80 30) is under construction in the palace grounds.

The Wielkopolska National Park

The only area of protected landscape in the province, the **Wielkopolska National Park** occupies an area of some 100 square kilometres to the south of Poznań. Formed in geologically recent times, it's a post-glacial landscape of low moraines, gentle ridges and lakes. Half the park is taken up by forest, predominantly pine and birch planted as replacements for the original hardwoods.

Although the scenery in the park is hardly dramatic, it's unspoiled by any kind of development and warrants a visit if you're passing, or fancy a day out from Poznań. By public transport the main point of access to Poznań is **MOSINA**, a small town on the Poznań–Wrocław rail line. The sole **hotel** and restaurant is *Morena* (☎13 27 46; ②) on ul. Konopnickiej, close to the park on the main road to **STĘSZEW**. The latter, 13km to the west on a regular bus route, and on the rail line between Poznań and Wolsztyn, is the other possible base if you want to stay in the area, as it has a **campsite** (☎13 40 61), set on the banks of Lake Lipno just

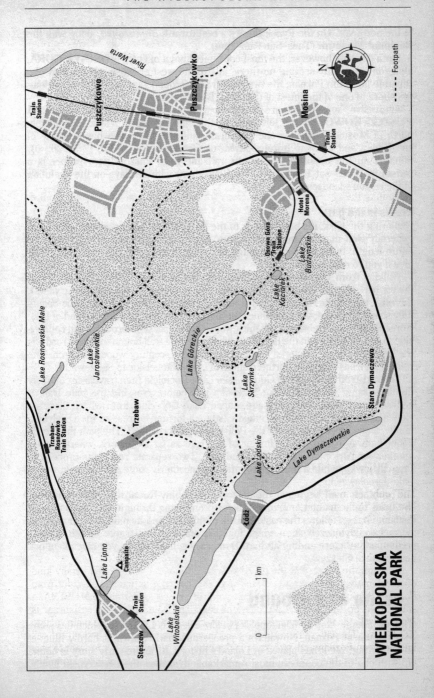

WIELKOPOLSKA NATIONAL PARK

to the northeast. On the Rynek there's a **restaurant**, *Broniszanka*, along with the **Regional Museum** (Tues–Sun 9am–1pm).

For a day trip, however, the most convenient point of entry is OSOWA GÓRA, a station apparently serving nowhere, just to the west of Mosina at the end of a separate line from Poznań; the two daily trains (around 7am and 2pm) pass along the shore of one of the finest of the lakes, Budzyńskie.

Alternative approaches are the twin villages of PUSZCZYKÓWKO and PUSZCZYKOWO, on the left bank of the snaking River Warta immediately north of Mosina. Each has one restaurant, and the latter also has a couple of snack bars and a cheap **hotel**, *Sadyba*, ul. Brzozowa 15a (☎061/13 31 28; ②). Situated on the opposite side of the rail line from Puszczykowo proper is a **museum** (Tues–Sat 10am–3pm, Sun 10am–4pm) with displays on the evolution of the region's landscape.

Walks in the park

Exploring the park, it's best to stick to the three official **hiking paths**, which are generally well marked and unstrenuous. Each takes several hours to cover its entire length, though it's easy enough to switch from one to the other – the best idea if you're restricted for time.

Walking **from Osowa Góra** gets you into the best of the terrain quickly. From the car park above the station (which offers one of the park's few panoramic views), the **blue trail** leads round the small heart-shaped Lake Kociołek, which is beautifully shaded by trees, then continues through the forest to the southern end of Lake Góreckie. It then climbs through thick woods before passing through open countryside to Lake Łódzkie, on the far side of which – off the trail but on the main road – is the hamlet of Łódź, clustered around a seventeenth-century wooden church. The route then leads along the northern shore of Lake Witobelskie to Stęszew.

The **red trail** from Osowa Góra passes Lake Kociołek, then travels circuitously uphill, skirting the small Lake Skrzynka just before crossing the blue trail. It arrives at the bend in the sausage-shaped Lake Góreckie, from where there's a view across to an islet with a ruined castle – a former fortress of the Działyński family, and a meeting point for the Polish insurgents of 1863. The path then leads about halfway round the perimeter of the lake as far as Jeziory, where there's another car park plus a restaurant and café. Two separate red paths proceed to Puszczykówko, while a third follows the long northerly route to Puszczykowo via Lake Jarosławieckie.

The **black trail** begins at the station of **Trzebaw-Rosnówko**, then traverses the fields to the hamlet of Trzebaw, before continuing through the woods to Lake Łódzkie. It then follows the eastern bank of this lake and its much longer continuation, Lake Dymaczewskie – which together make up the largest stretch of water in the park – before ending at Stare Dymaczewo, from where you can take a bus to Mosina or Steszew.

Leszno and around

The last notable stop in Wielkopolska before Silesia is **LESZNO**, which lies some 90km south of Poznań. Nowadays a prosperous market town, it hardly hints at the glittering role it has played in Poland's history. Its entire early story is bound up with one of the country's most remarkable dynasties, the Leszczyński family, who founded Leszno in the late fourteenth century. The last of the male line, **Stanisław Leszczyński**, deposed the hated Augustus the Strong of Saxony to become King of Poland in 1704, only to be overthrown by the same rival six years later. He briefly regained the throne in 1733, but met with far more success in exile in France, marrying his daughter to Louis XV, and himself becoming Duke of Lorraine and gaining a reputation as a patron of the arts.

The Town

The **train station** is less than a kilometre west of the town centre: from the station go over the level crossing (or use the underpass) and cross the road which brings you to Leszno's main street, ul. Słowiańska. Just to the left from here is the **bus station**.

Continuing straight ahead brings you to the pedestrianized section of ul. Słowiańska and ultimately the **Rynek**, a handsome cobbled square. It's ringed by predominantly Neoclassical buildings with the odd Baroque facade surviving the Swedish Wars which left Leszno in ruins. The colourist approach favoured by the architects – prominent among whom was the Italian Pompeo Ferrari – is shown to best effect in the white and ochre tones of the **Town Hall**, which has just been spruced up and now makes a friendly rather than imposing municipal landmark.

Just south of the Rynek, the exterior of the twin-towered church of **St Nicholas** (Św. Mikołaja) strikes a more typically sombre note. Its interior, on the other hand, displays a good example of Rococo ornamentation – the florid style of Late Baroque's death throes. On each side of the altar are the huge, seemingly unpainted monuments to the Leszczyńskis. A fascinating contrast with this richness is provided by the clean, sober lines of the **Holy Cross** (Św. Kryża), a couple of minutes' walk to the southwest on pl. Metziga. The church is surrounded by the ornate remains of crumbling epitaphs set in its perimeter walls, while a collection of small memorial obelisks from the late-eighteenth century further commemorate the passing of Leszno's prominent families. Inside the vestibule a life size angel bears a huge shell; an unusual vessel for holy water.

THE BOHEMIAN BRETHREN

Along with many other Polish grandees, the Leszczyńskis enthusiastically adopted the Reformation, though Stanisław, like Augustus the Strong, was forced to convert to Catholicism in order to launch his bid for the crown. In the first half of the seventeenth century Leszno became a refuge for the **Bohemian Brethren**, Czech Protestants who were forced to flee their homeland by the religious intolerance of the Thirty Years' War. The Academy these exiles founded in Leszno developed into one of Europe's great centres of learning, thanks to the leadership of Jan Amos Komeński, known as **Comenius**. Creator of the first illustrated textbook, he was called to put his educational theories into practice in England, Sweden, Hungary and Holland, and even received invitations from the Protestant-loathing Cardinal Richelieu in France and from Harvard University, which wanted him as its president. Though Comenius and his colleagues were eventually forced to leave Leszno by the Swedish Wars of the 1650s, the town remained a major educational centre into the last century. The Brethren were later transformed into the **Moravian Church**, a body which continues to have an influence out of all proportion to its size, particularly in the USA.

NARROW-GAUGE RAIL LINES IN WIELKOPOLSKA

The best-known **narrow-gauge line** in Wielkopolska, the Biskupin Railway between Gąsawa and Żnin, is described on p.567. However, this is essentially a tourist facility, as opposed to other such lines in the province which still serve the needs of local communities.

A highly recommended example of these runs from Stare Bojanowo, 18km south of Leszno on the main line to Wrocław, to Wielichowa, 15km to the northwest. The poor state of repair of the tracks suggest that closure may be imminent, but modern, immaculately maintained little diesels are in operation. Strung out along the route are a number of small communities, many of which have hardly changed in centuries, while a few others have been transformed by recent political and economic reforms – as the new German cars parked beside some of the farms testify.

Another line worth sampling starts at Środa Wielkopolska, 30km southeast of Poznań, and runs southwest through 12km of pleasant pastoral scenery to its terminus at Zaniemyśl.

On the same square, shaded by a huge oak tree. is the **Museum** (Tues & Thurs 2–7pm, Wed & Fri 9am–2pm, Sat & Sun 10am–2pm), a miscellaneous local collection, featuring a room devoted to Comenius of the Bohemian Brethren. A few streets east of here, off ul. Bolesława Chrobrego, is the brick **Church of St John**, aesthetically unremarkable but semi-interesting as the place where the Bohemian Brethren held their services.

Practicalities

The least expensive **hotel** in town is on ul. Słowiańska 30, the aptly named *Centralny* (☎065/20 31 61; ③). There's also a brand new and expensive hotel, the *Akwawit* on ul. Sw Josefa 5 (☎065/20 97 81; ⑥), visible just west of the flyover on the west side of town, next door to an aquatic centre. You'll find a **hostel** in the **campsite**, 2km from the centre on the very western edge of town, near the airfield. If you want an overnight stay with some panache, you could head for the palace designed by Pompeo Ferrari for the Sułkowski family – who bought Leszno from the Leszczyńskis – at **Rydzyna**, 9km to the southeast and reached by regular buses; it has been coverted into a **hotel** and restaurant (☎065/20 58 47; ⑤).

There's a surprisingly good variety of places to **eat and drink** in town. For a Polish meal try the *Leszno*, ul. Słowiańska 11, otherwise there's the *El Greco* opposite, a *Pizza Hut* a few doors down and a Chinese restaurant, the *Tien Cin*, at no. 31. The **Orbis** office is at ul. Słowiańska 61 (Mon–Fri 9am–5pm, Sat 9am–1pm; ☎065/20 15 65).

Wolsztyn

Those with a nostalgia for the days of steam should make tracks for the little lakeside town of **WOLSZTYN**, 60km northwest from Leszno, where live steam engines operate passenger services to Poznań, Leszno and Zbąszynek. If you happen to go via the town of Wschowa, you'll spot a couple of delapidated **wooden windmills** in the villages just to the north of that town. Each mill is set on a huge oak tree trunk still rooted to the ground to give the structure the required support when the sails were spinning. The northernmost example – on the east side of the road – is just about hanging on to its tattered wooden sails.

The town centre has a few fine buildings, notably a Neoclassical palace and a Baroque church with an impressive frescoed vault. At the end of the main street, ul. 5 Stycznia, is the **Marcin Rożek Museum** (Tues–Fri 9am–4pm, Sat & Sun 10am–2pm), occupying the home of this artist, one of the best Poland ever produced, who died in Auschwitz. It's his sculptures which stand out, notably the large reliefs on the rear of the house and the classically inspired portrait busts in the garden (just about visible from the back when the museum is closed) – mostly replicas of works destroyed by the Nazis.

Leaving the museum through the garden brings you to the shore of Lake Wolsztyn. If you follow its perimeter back towards the rail line, then continue north of town, you shortly come to a *skansen* or **open-air museum** of traditional farm buildings; it's always accessible through an unlocked gate.

For **accommodation** there's an *OSiR* sports hotel and **campsite** just over the road from the *skansen*, but much more convenient and impressive is the former workers' holiday home, the Neoclassical *Dom Turysty* set in the lakeside park off ul. Drzymały (☎3375; ②) just north of the town centre on the Poznań road. The former palace has a **restaurant** and bar, and there are sailing boats and other watercraft available for rent by the small beach. A more conventional alternative is the clean and modern *Hotel Maria* on ul Spokojna 23 (☎3303; ③), the road opposite the vehicular entrance to the park.

Kalisz and around

At the extreme southeastern corner of Wielkopolska, 130km from Poznań and 115km west of the city of Łódź, lies the town of **KALISZ**. Almost universally held to be Poland's oldest recorded city, it was referred to as Calissia by Pliny in the first century and was described in the second century as a trading settlement on the "amber route" between the Baltic and Adriatic. Though apparently inhabited without interruption ever since, it failed to develop into a major city. Despite its long history, Kalisz is not worth a special journey, but it makes a convenient stopover if you're passing this way, and is on the way to the palace at **Gołuchów**.

The Town

Both the **train** and **bus** stations are to be found 8km from the centre at the southwestern end of the city. To reach the centre, take bus #19, #101 or #102: no buses run within the **old quarter**, which is situated between the rivers Prosna and Bernardynka. On the way down ul. Górnośląska and ul. Śródmiejska you'll pass two space-age churches which shoot up from parallel boulevards – contemporary symbols of the key role of Catholicism in modern Poland. A couple of stops before the bridge into the old quarter you can turn left down ul. Kościuszki to check out the **Museum** at no. 12 (Tues, Thurs, Sat & Sun 10am–2.30pm, Wed & Fri noon–5.30pm), which displays locally excavated Roman and Neolithic artefacts rarely seen elsewhere in Poland.

Ulica Śródmiejska terminates at the attractive Rynek, with its large Neoclassical Town Hall. Down ul. Kanonicka at the northwestern end of the square is the brick Gothic **Church of St Nicholas** (Św. Mikołaja), which has been subject to a fair amount of neo-Gothic tinkering (and has recently gone through a further renovation), though for once this is not entirely to its disadvantage. Inside, the prize item is the altarpiece of *The Descent from the Cross*, brought here from Rubens' workshop in Antwerp. Located just off the southeastern corner of the Rynek is a smaller square which lies in front of the **Franciscan Church**, an older and simpler example of Gothic brickwork, but with generous Baroque interior decorations – unfortunately it's usually locked.

From here, it's just a short walk to ul. Kolegialna, which defines the eastern perimeter of the Old Town. Along it you'll pass the long facade of the **Jesuit College**, a severe Neoclassical composition incorporating a finely carved Renaissance portal. The only part of the building that visitors are allowed to enter is the church, which follows the plain Mannerist style of the Jesuits' most important church, the Gesù in Rome. Immediately beyond the college, standing beside the surviving fragment of the city's ramparts, is the single-towered **Collegiate Church**, a more adventurous example of late eighteenth-century Baroque which includes parts of its Gothic predecessor. The interior bristles with works of art, the most notable of which is a Silesian polyptych from around 1500 – but unfortunately again, only the vestibule is normally kept open.

Practicalities

For **information** you'll find the *Orbis* office at ul. Śródmiejska 1 (☎062/73816). Kalisz is reckoned prestigious enough to warrant its own luxury *Orbis* **hotel**, *Prosna*, ul. Górnośląska 53/55 (☎062/64 49 74; ⑥), about a third of the way down the road from the bus station to the town. A much less expensive and more central option is the ageing and somewhat gloomy *Europa*, by the river at al. Wolności 5 (☎062/72031; ③–④). There's also a **youth hostel** in a small park east of the *Europa*, with the reception nearby at ul. Częstochowska 17 (☎062/72636).

For **eating** and **drinking** away from the hotels' restaurants, try the *Paradise*, ul. Piekarska 13, east of the Rynek, *U Barbary i Bogumiła*, at ul. Górnośląska 69, just up from the bus station, the little *Pięterko* restaurant at ul. Zamkowa 12 or the *Restauracja Kalmar*, ul. Śródmiejska 26.

Gołuchów

Twenty kilometres from Kalisz on the main road to Poznań, and reached by frequent intercity buses or by local bus #A, lies the village of **GOŁUCHÓW**, a place you'd whizz through were it not for its **Palace**, the one outstanding monument in the Kalisz area.

It began as a small defensive castle, built for Rafał Leszczyński of the famous Leszno family in 1560. Early the following century, his son Wacław completely transformed it into a palatial residence worthy of a man who had risen to be royal chancellor. Like the Polish state itself, it gradually fell into ruin. In 1853 it was bought by Tytus Działyński, the owner of Kórnik (see p.552), as a present for his son Jan, who married Izabella, daughter of the formidable Adam Czartoryski. While her husband languished in exile for his part in the 1863 Uprising, Izabella devoted herself to re-creating the glory of the castle, eventually opening it as one of Poland's first museums. Rather than revert to the Italianate form of the original, she opted for a distinctively French touch – with its steeply pitched roofs, prominent chimneys, pointed towers and graceful arcaded terrace, the palace looks like a passable pastiche of something you might find in the Loire Valley.

The small **apartments** (tours Tues–Sun 10am–4pm, last admission 3.15pm; leaflet in English available) are crammed with paintings and *objets d'art*. Highlight of the display are some magnificent antique vases – just part of an assembly whose other items are now kept in the National Museum in Warsaw. After the guided tour you can wander off to the two rooms under the stairway, in which changing exhibitions from the castle's collection of engravings are held.

The landscaped **park** surrounding the palace looks in need of a trim, and contains a **Museum of Forestry** (Tues–Sat 10am–3pm, Sun 10am–4pm) – near here you'll also come across Izabella's neo-Baroque funerary chapel. For refreshments, there's a **café** in the park and a **restaurant** in the village.

If you want to stay, the sole possibility is the **campsite**, which is well signposted from the main road.

Gniezno and around

Despite the competing claims of Poznań, Kruszwica and Lednica, **GNIEZNO** 50km east of Poznań, is generally credited as the first capital of Poland, a title based on the dense web of myth and chronicled fact which constitute the story of the nation's earliest years. Nevertheless Poland's current ecclesiastical capital

has an oddly undistinguished and neglected feel; cars tear round the cobbled Rynek which barely suggests its leading role in the country's history.

Gniezno lies at the cross-over of the "figure-of-eight" **Piast Route** (Szlak Piatowski), a tourist trail between Poznań and Inowrocław which highlights salient locations associated with the Piast dynasty. The first major sight east of Poznań is **Lake Lednica**, which is most easily reached from Gniezno and has therefore been included in this section.

Gniezno's history

Lech, the legendary founder of Poland, supposedly came across the nest (*gniazdo*) of a white eagle here; he founded a town on the spot, and made the bird the emblem of his people, a role it still maintains. Less fancifully, it's known for sure that Mieszko I had established a court here in the late tenth century, and that in the year 1000 it was the scene of one of the landmarks in the country's history.

The catalyst for this, ironically enough, was a Czech, **Saint Adalbert** (Wojciech), the first bishop of Prague. Unable to cope with the political demands of his office, he retired to a monastery, but later bowed to pressure from Rome to take up missionary work. In 997 he set out from Gniezno to evangelize the Prussians, a fierce Baltic tribe who lived on Poland's eastern borders – and who quickly dispatched him to a martyr's death. In order to recover the body, Mieszko I's son, **Bolesław the Brave**, was forced to pay Adalbert's weight in gold, an astute investment as it turned out. At the pope's instigation, Emperor Otto III made a pilgrimage to Gniezno, bringing relics with him which would add to the site's holiness. Received in great splendour, he crowned Bolesław with his own crown, confirming Poland as a fully fledged kingdom and one which was independent of the German-dominated Holy Roman Empire. Furthermore, Gniezno was made the seat of Poland's first archbishopric; Adalbert's brother was the first to be appointed to the post.

Gniezno was soon replaced as capital by the more secure town of Kraków, and although it made a partial recovery in the Middle Ages, it never grew very big. Nevertheless, it has always been important as the official **seat of the primate of Poland**. Throughout the period of elected kings, the holder of this office functioned as head of state during each interregnum, and it is still one of the most prestigious positions in the land. In recent times, the Gniezno archbishopric has been coupled to that of Warsaw, with the primate tending, for obvious reasons, to spend far more time in the capital. The pressures this caused led in 1992 to Gniezno losing its historic role as the primate's seat in return for its own full-time archbishop, though it will permanently regain the honour on the retirement or death of the present incumbent, Cardinal Glemp.

The City

The compactness of Gniezno is immediately evident: arriving at either the **train** or **bus station**, side by side about a kilometre south of the centre, it's only a few minutes' walk straight down ul. Lecha to ul. Bolesława Chrobrego, the quiet end of Gniezno's main thoroughfare. In ten minutes you pass into the pedestrianized section of this street which terminates at the **Rynek**. Normally the showpiece of a Polish city, this one remains open to traffic and is hardly restful; a test pad of squeeling rubber and raucous exhausts.

There are, however, three Gothic churches worth a quick look. Just off the southern side of the Rynek is the **Holy Trinity** (Św. Trójcy), partly rebuilt in the Baroque style following a fire, beside which stand the only surviving remains of the city walls. Off the opposite side of the Rynek towers the **Franciscan Church**, while further to the north is **St John's**. The latter, a foundation of the Knights Templar, preserves fourteenth-century frescoes in its chancel and has carved bosses and corbels depicting virtues and vices.

The Cathedral

Northwest from the Rynek down ul. Tumska lies Gniezno's episcopal quarter, and protruding fittingly above it is the **Cathedral** in whose forecourt stands a statue of Bolesław the Brave. Reminiscent of Poznań Cathedral, the basic brick structure was built in the fourteenth century in the severest Gothic style, but was enlivened in the Baroque period by a ring of stone chapels and by the addition of steeples to the twin facade towers. Entering the cathedral to the right of the memorial bell and following the ambulatory in an anticlockwise direction, you soon come to the high altar and the silver **shrine of Saint Adalbert,** the martyr seen here reclining on his sarcophagus. The work of Gdańsk craftsman, Peter van Rennen, the shrine is surrounded by figures representing the different social classes, along with depictions of the chief events of Saint Adalbert's life. The shrine itself is housed in a huge and recently re-gilded frame flanked by arches of black and white marble. Other monuments to prominent local clerics and laymen can be seen throughout the cathedral. One which may catch your attention is that to **Primate Stefan Wyszyński**, in the north side of the ambulatory (see box, p.564).

Just past the primate's tomb is another porch which leads to the **archive** (9am–2pm) where several of Poland's earliest manuscripts are kept. The most beautiful of these is the eleventh-century *Golden Codex*, made for Gniezno at Reichenau in southwestern Germany, the most inventive centre of European book illumination at the time. A far simpler gospel book from a couple of centuries earlier has annotations by Irish missionaries, which has prompted the suggestion that it was the Irish who converted the Polish tribes. Although not formally open to the public, objects including illuminated manuscripts are occasionally exhibited at the information kiosk on the opposite side of the nave. Near here is the entrance to the newly restored **crypt**, final resting place of former primates with evidence of the Romanesque foundations as well as some relics pre-dating that time. Other valuable treasures are kept in the **Archdiocesan Museum** (Tues–Sat 9am–4pm), housed in one of the cluster of buildings on the north of the cathedral, the star item being a chalice said to have belonged to Saint Adalbert.

The cathedral's monumental highlight is the magnificent pair of **bronze doors** located at the entrance to the southern aisle. Hung around 1175 and an inevitable influence on van Rennen, these are among the finest surviving examples of Romanesque decorative art, and are unique in Poland. Adalbert's life from the cradle to beyond the grave is illustrated in eighteen scenes, going up the right-hand door and then down the left, all set within a rich decorative border. Quite apart from their artistic quality, the doors are remarkable as a documentary record: even the faces of the villainous Prussians are based on accurate observation. Unfortunately, until the things are properly lit, the detail described above is difficult to distinguish, although buying the colour guide (see below) certainly helps. Passing through the doorway reveals the intricate **portal** on the other side. Though its tympanum of *Christ in Majesty* is orthodox enough, the carvings of griffins and the prominent mask heads give it a highly idiosyncratic flavour.

At the kiosk on the south aisle you can buy a glossy if rather skimpy trilingual **guide** (including English) on the cathedral as well as a much better example describing the bronze doors in detail.

Lake Jelonek

Just west of the cathedral is Lake Jelonek, a peaceful spot with a wonderful view of the town. Overlooking its far bank, but more easily approached via the main road, is a large modern building containing a college and the **Museum of the Origins of the Polish State** (Tues–Sun 10am–5pm). This contains some immensely dull archeological finds from various Wielkopolska sites on the entrance floor, along with changing art exhibitions upstairs. Much more worthwhile is the absorbing display of artefacts and thirty-minute **audio-visual** presentation downstairs (English commentary available on request) which elaborates on the the development of medieval life in Wielopolska and the significance of the Piast dynasty. You'll also find a replica of the cathedral's bronze doors which you can study closely.

CARDINAL STEFAN WYSZYŃSKI 1901–81

In the history of communist Europe, there is nothing remotely comparable to the career of Stefan Wyszyński, who adapted the traditional powers of the primate of Poland to act as spokesman and regent of his people in a strikingly novel way. Not only did he function as a permanent and high-profile opposition leader to the communist regime; he was also seen as a powerful and influential figure in his own right.

Wyszyński's early ministry was centred in Włocławek, where he was ordained in 1924, quickly establishing a reputation in the social field. He spent the war years in the **underground resistance movement**, having been saved from the German concentration camps, which accounted for most of his colleagues in Włocławek, through the prompt action of his bishop, who had ordered him to leave the town. He returned as head of the Włocławek Seminary in 1945, and then had a meteoric rise, being appointed Bishop of Lublin the following year, before his elevation to the archdiocese of Gniezno and the title of **Primate of Poland**, in 1948.

The elimination of Poland's formerly substantial Jewish, Orthodox and Protestant minorities as a result of World War II and its aftermath meant that **nearly 98 percent of the population professed Catholicism**, as opposed to the prewar figure of 75 percent. At the same time, however, organized religion came under threat from the atheist communist regime which was imposed on the country. Matters came to a head with the Vatican's worldwide decree of 1949, which ordered the withholding of sacraments to all communist functionaries and sympathizers: this caused particular tensions in Poland, where the new administration, particularly in rural areas, was dependent on practising Catholics. Wyszyński reached a **compromise agreement** with the government the following year whereby the affairs of church and state were clearly demarcated.

This cosy relationship did not last long: a wave of **Stalinist repression** in 1952–3 led to the end of religious instruction in schools, the usurpation of most of the Church's charitable activities, and to the imprisonment and harassment of thousands of priests. As a culmination, the Bishop of Kielce was sentenced to

Practicalities

There's little evidence to show that Gniezno is expecting foreign tourists. Both **Orbis** and **PTTK** have offices on the Rynek, but neither has any tourist information.

There are three **hotels** in town; two good ones and one basic. Top of the range is the *Mieszko*, beside the sports stadium above Lake Jelonek (☎061/26 46 25; ④). A similar but more expensive pre-fab also with sporty connections is the *Hotel Lech*, in ul. Jolenty 5 (☎061/26 23 85; ⑤), a kilometre northeast of the centre. Last and least is the *Orle Gniazdo* situated right next to a speedway oval at ul. Wrzesinska 25 (☎061/26 34 64; ③), 1.5km south of the centre, although with the right room on the right night you'll get a free view of the races. The **youth hostel** is conveniently close to the stations at ul. Pocztowa 11 on the top floor (☎061/26 13 23); for once they've done a good job here, making it a welcoming place with no rough edges.

There's a cluster of pleasant **restaurants** with outdoor seating in the centre of town on the pedestrianized section of ul. Bolesława Chrobrego. The *Teatralna, Królowska* and *Molca* are all popular or you could try the more utilitarian *Robotnicza* at the corner of uls. Mieszka I and Dąbrówki.

twelve years' imprisonment on charges of espionage. Wyszyński's protests led to his own **arrest**, and he was confined to the Monastery of Komańcza in the remote Bieszczady Mountains. The detention of a man widely regarded as possessing saintly qualities had the effect of alienating the regime even further from the bulk of the populace, and Wyszyński acted as the symbolic figurehead of the unrest which reached crisis proportions in 1956.

Wyszyński was **released** later that year as part of the package – which also included the return of Gomułka to power – forestalling the Soviet invasion which would almost certainly have ensued had a political breakdown occurred. From then on, the communists were forced to accept the **special status** of the Catholic Church in Polish society, and they were never afterwards able to suppress it: in 1957, Wyszyński was allowed to travel to Rome to receive the cardinal's hat he had been awarded five years previously. Under his leadership – which, from a theological point of view, was extremely conservative – Poland came to be regarded as **the most fervently Catholic nation in the world**, with the Jasna Góra pilgrimage (see p.428) promoted as the central feature of national consciousness. Wyszynski's sermons, often relayed from every pulpit in the country, became increasingly fearless and notable for such pronouncements as his celebrated claim that "Polish citizens are slaves in their own country".

Although Wyszyński did not live to see the collapse of the communist regime against which he had fought so doggedly, his last years were ones of unbridled triumph. The standing to which he had raised Poland within the Roman Catholic faith was given due reward in 1978, when his right-hand man, Karol Wojtyła – once courted by the communists as a potentially more malleable future primate – leapfrogged over him to become the first-ever Polish pope. Then, at the very end of his life, the government was forced to yield to him as a powerbroker at the heart of the **Solidarity crisis**. When Wyszyński died, he was rewarded with a **funeral** matched in postwar Europe only by those of the victorious war leaders, Churchill and de Gaulle; the country came to a standstill as even his communist opponents were prominent in paying their last respects.

Lake Lednica

One of the key places in the early life of Poland is the slender **Lake Lednica**, 18km west of Gniezno and easily reached by bus. The place to get off is across from the entrance to the **Wielkopolska Ethnographic Park** after the turnoff to Dziekanowice (mid-April to Oct Tues–Sun 9am–5pm, Nov to mid-April 9am–3pm). Driving from Poznan it's the second turn left after the three roadside windmills. Laid out in an exhilarating location by the side of the lake, this open-air museum, or *skansen*, consists of about fifty traditional rural buildings from the last 250 years or so, mostly originals – including windmills, a Baroque cemetery chapel with all its furnishings, and several farmsteads.

From here, continue through the village of Siemanowo to the disparate tourist complex known as the **Museum of the First Piasts at Lednica** (same hours as the *skansen*). Entered through an impressive wooden gateway, whose upper storey turns out to be a snack bar, this features a craft shop, yet another windmill and a small collection of archeological finds. More significantly, it's the departure point for **Ostrów Lednicki**, the largest of the three tiny islands in Lake Lednica, which can easily be reached in a couple of minutes by the chained **ferry** (daily 9am–5pm, every 30min).

This unlikely site, uninhabited for the last six centuries, was once a royal seat equal to Poznań and Gniezno in importance – Bolesław the Brave was born here, and it may also have been where his coronation by Emperor Otto III took place, rather than in Gniezno. It began life in the ninth century as a fortified town covering about a third of the island and linked to the mainland by a jetty. In the following century, a modest **palace** was constructed, along with a church: the excavated remains only hint at its former grandeur, but the presence of stairways prove it was probably at least two storeys high. By the landing jetty a model of the former settlement gives an idea of how it may have looked, surrounded by the still extant earth ramparts from which now flutters a Polish flag. The buildings were destroyed in 1038 by the Czech Prince Brzetysław, but the church was rebuilt soon afterwards, only gradually to fall into disuse, along with the town itself. For centuries the island served as a cemetery, only to be lulled out of its sleep by tourism.

Żnin and Biskupin

Forty kilometres north of Gniezno on the Bydgoszcz road the small town of **Żnin** would be ordinarily unremarkable were it not for the ageing narrow-gauge rail line which meanders for 12km through the pastures and along the lakes south of town to the village of Gąsawa. It's an ideal and idle way of visiting the famous reconstructed Iron Age settlement of **Biskupin**, situated between the rail line's termini, but also accessible by road. If you've an aversion to rickety trains, the ancient site is also accessible by walking from the bus terminal at Gąsawa.

Żnin

Set between two lakes is the small town and rail junction of **ŻNIN**. In the centre of its Rynek stands the octagonal brick **tower** of the demolished fifteenth-century

Town Hall, whose interior has been fitted out as the local **museum** (Tues–Fri 9am–4pm, Sat 9am–3pm, Sun 10am–3pm).

There are a couple of **restaurants** in town, and some uninspiring **accommodation** options: the *Hotel Brda* on ul. 700 Lecia 1 (☎0534/207; ③) looks like it's going bust and the *Hotel Heva* (☎0534/22531; ②), the only building, other than factories, at the end of ul. Fabryczna, 3km north of the town centre on the Bydgoszcz road. There's also a **campsite** (☎0534/76) by Lake Mały Żnin, 1km south of the centre on ul. Szkolna.

The narrow-gauge rail line

An enjoyable and popular way of visiting Biskupin is on the narrow-gauge rail line which has been running from the train station south of Żnin for over a century. The narrow-gauge terminus is just over the road from the main line Żnin Waży station on the south side of town. There are departures from Żnin between April and September at 9am, 10.10am, 11.25am, 12.40pm and 2pm with return runs from Gąsawa at 10.10am, 11.25am, 12.40pm, 2pm and 3.40pm. The train journey costs 2zł each way and takes fifty minutes between Żnin and Biskupin, with returns from Biskupin to Żnin about ten minutes after departures from Gąsawa.

The train rattles noisily through hay fields and vegetable patches, its second stop, **WENECJA**, being the halfway point. This hamlet's name is the Polish word for Venice, fancifully justified by the fact that it is almost surrounded by water, lying as it does between two lakes. To the left of the station are the remains of the fourteenth-century **Castle** of Mikołaj Nałęcz, a notoriously cruel figure known as the "Devil of Wenecja". Only the lower parts of the walls survive. On the opposite side of the tracks is the open-air **Museum of Narrow-Gauge Railways** (daily 9am–5pm), exhibiting a motley collection of undersized engines and rolling stock which once served the area.

From Wenecja the train continues along the edge of Lake Biskupin and stops right outside the entrance to the settlement a few minutes later.

Biskupin

The Iron Age village of **BISKUPIN**, 30km north of Gniezno, is one of the most evocative and exciting archeological sites in Europe. Discovered in 1933, when a a wayward schoolmaster banished to a local school noticed some hand-worked stakes standing in the reeds at the lakeside, excavations commenced the following year until experts fromm Warsaw soon pronounced that the site had been a **fortified village** of the Lusatian culture, founded around 550 BC and destroyed in tribal warfare some 150 years later. The subsequent uncovering of the settlement has thrown fresh light on the tribal life of the period, enabling the solution of many previously unresolved questions.

The site

In contrast to the overcautious approach which makes so many famous archeological sites disappointing to non-specialists, it was decided to take a guess and reconstruct the palisade, ramparts and part of the village. The price to be paid for this approach is evident at the entrance to the **Archeological Park** (daily mid-April to end Sept 8am–7pm; Oct 8am–6pm subject to weather), with souvenir and snack bars lining the car park on the other side of the tracks. An excellent handbook and less detailed pamphlet in English are for sale at the gate. Polish-speaking tour guides, distinguishable by their period attire, are also available.

From the entrance, it's best to go straight ahead past a re-erected eighteenth-century cottage and get the obligatory visit to the **museum** over with. Inside you'll find all manner of objects dug up here – tools, household utensils, weapons, jewellery, ornaments and objects for worship, some thought to be ten thousand years old. Unfortunately they're displayed in a manner that fails to encourage prolonged scrutiny. Piecing together the evidence, archeologists have been able to draw a picture of a society in which hunting had been largely superseded by arable farming and livestock breeding. Their trade patterns were surprisingly extensive – their iron seems to have come from Transylvania, and there's an intriguing group of exhibits imported from even further afield, the most exotic being some Egyptian beads. Most remarkable of all was the tribe's prowess in building, as can be seen in the model reconstruction of the entire village. Beyond the museum buildings is an enclosure for tarpans, miniature working horses which have evolved very little since the time of the settlement.

Backtracking to the cottage and turning right, it's only a couple of minutes' walk down the path to the **reconstructed site**. The foreground consists of the uncovered foundations of various buildings, some from as late as the thirteenth century; of more interest are re-creations of the Iron Age buildings – although only a section of each has been built, and not exactly on their former site, it requires little imagination to picture what the whole must have looked like. Close by the *Diabeł Wenecki* offers thirty-minute cruises on the lake (Tues–Sat 9am–5pm, Sun 9am–4pm), allowing you to view the site from the water.

The **palisade** was particularly ingenious: it originally consisted of 35,000 stakes grouped in rows up to nine deep and driven into the bed of the lake at an angle of 45 degrees. It acted both as a breakwater and as the first line of the fortifications. Immediately behind was a circular **wall** of oak logs guarded by a tall watchtower: the latter is the most conjectural part of the whole restoration project. Inside the defences were a ring road plus eleven symmetrical streets, again made of logs and filled in with earth, sand and clay; the **houses** were grouped in thirteen terraces ranged from east to west to catch the sun. An entire extended family would live in each house, so the population of the settlement probably numbered over a thousand. As you can see from the example open for inspection, each house had two chambers: pigs and cattle – the most important privately owned objects – were kept in the lobby, while the main room, where the family slept in a single bed, was also equipped with a loft for the storage of food and fuel.

Trzemeszno to Inowrocław

Sixteen kilometres east of Gniezno, the Piast Route winds through **TRZEMESZNO**, now a lightly industrialized town that was founded, according to tradition, by Saint Adalbert. It can be reached either by bus or Baltic-bound train – the latter involving a 3km walk south to the town.

The ancient church which Adalbert is said to have established was succeeded by a Romanesque structure, parts of which are incorporated in the town's main sight, the Baroque **Basilica**. From the outside it appears merely pleasingly rotund, but once inside you'll find a revelation of light and colour that – if you've developed a taste for Baroque church interiors – is well worth the break in your journey. In this instance it's the **superb paintings** in the dome and along the transept that for once take the attention away from the central altar, under which an effigy of Adalbert reposes. The ceiling frescoes vividly depict three crucial scenes from the saint's life and death: his vicious slaying by the Prussian pagans; the retrieval of his remains for their weight in gold, with Adalbert now just a few body parts on a scale, and his eventual entombment in the basilica.

In the main square is a monument to the local hero, the shoemaker Jan Kiliński, who played a leading role in the 1794 Insurrection (see p.87). Right opposite the church is the **hotel** *Czeremcha* (☎0533/54386; ①), which has surprisingly inexpensive rooms and a restaurant.

Mogilno

A further 16km northeast, 8km north of the main road, is **MOGILNO**, again set on the east bank of a lake. Mogilno is a pleasant enough place and its excuse for being a stop on the Piast Route is a couple of churches, the Gothic **St James** and the eclectic **St John the Evangelist**, both by the lakeside on the south side of town. The latter has just been renovated and preserves its Romanesque crypt and apse (this, clearly visible from the outside), complete with carved frieze, though the building was heavily transformed in both the Gothic and Baroque epochs.

The town has a smart, new **guest house** the *Gozdawa* in a quiet rural location 3km southwest of town; follow the signs down the narrow country lane near the petrol station and turn left at the shrine (☎52416; ④ for half board). Alternatively there's a smaller **hotel** in the centre of town on ul. Halesa 8a (☎0533; ②).

Strzelno

More of the Piast Route's artistic treasures are found 17km east of Mogilno in the sleepy town of **STRZELNO**. Both the **bus and train stations** lie at the southwestern fringe of town; from there, walk straight ahead, turning left up ul. Ducha to reach the rather unprepossessing main square. Continuing down to the right brings you to two outstanding Romanesque buildings.

The **Monastery of the Holy Trinity** is a typically Polish accretion: brick Gothic gables and a monumental Baroque facade sprout from a late twelfth-century Romanesque shell. After the war, some of the interior plasterwork was removed to reveal, in well-nigh perfect condition, three original nave **pillars**. Two of these, adorned with figurative carvings are crafted with a delicacy found in few other European sculptures of the period; a third is quite plain. Another slimmer column of almost equal quality forms the sole support of the vault of the somewhat neglected chapel of St Barbara, to the right of the altar over which hangs a huge crown.

Beside the monastery church stands the slightly older little red sandstone **Chapel of St Procopius**. In contrast to its neighbour, this has preserved the purity of its original form, its half-round tower perfectly offset against the protruding rotund apses to a most pleasing effect. It's kept locked, but you could ask in the Holy Trinity or the buildings alongside for a look inside. Incidentally, the churches are not the earliest evidence of worship on this site: the large stone boulder in front of them is thought to have been used for pagan rites.

Kruszwica

The Piast Route moves on to **KRUSZWICA**, a town surrounded by grain silos and ugly factories about 16km northeast of Strzelno. Standing at the head of the pencil-slim **Lake Gopło**, the largest of all western Poland's lakes, Kruszwica is enshrined in Polish folklore as the cradle of the Piast dynasty.

Both the **bus** and **train stations** are located at the northwestern fringe of the town. From here, walk ahead to the main street, ul. Niepodległości, where you'll find the only **restaurant** worth mentioning, the inevitably named *Piatowska*. Continuing down the street, you come to the spacious but unremarkable Rynek, just east of which is a bridge over the lake.

The shady tree-lined peninsula immediately to the south of this is a popular tourist spot, as evidenced by the presence of a *PTTK* information point and a number of snack stands. It's dominated by a brick octagon known as the **Mouse Tower** (Mysia Wieża). Allegedly, this was where the rodent feast took place (see box below); in fact, ironically enough, it was part of a castle built by the last of the Piast dynasty, Kazimierz the Great. During the summer season, you can climb to the top for a sweeping view down the length of Lake Gopło, on which hour-long **cruises** operate aboard the *Rusałka* (daily 9.30, 11am, 12.30pm, 2.30pm, 4pm and 5pm).

Kruszwica's only other historic monument is the early twelfth-century **Collegiate Church**, situated on the eastern shore of the tip of the lake which lies north of the bridge – coming from town take the first left after the bridge and continue for a kilometre. A grim granite basilica with three apses, it has been stripped of most of its later accretions, except for the brick Gothic tower, and gives a good impression of what an early Christian church may have once looked like. Supposedly occupying the miraculous site of Piast's cottage, it served as a cathedral for the first half-century of its life, before being supplanted by Włocławek.

THE LEGEND OF THE FOUNDATION OF THE PIAST DYNASTY

The legend goes that the **descendants of Lech** were ousted as the nation's rulers by the evil Popiel family. To ensure there was no competition for his succession, the last King Popiel killed all his male kin except his own children, then established himself at a castle in Kruszwica, where he subjected his people to a reign of terror. One day, saints John and Paul came in the guise of poor travellers, but the king refused them hospitality and they were forced to lodge with a peasant named **Piast**. They baptized him and his family, and predicted that he would be first in a long line of monarchs, whereupon they vanished. Shortly afterwards, the Poles rose up against their evil ruler. He took refuge in his castle tower, where he was eventually devoured by rats. The people then chose the worthy Piast as his successor.

Inowrocław

The easternmost extent of the Piast Route comes 15km north of Kruszwica at **INOWROCŁAW**. Here the main monument is the **Church of the Assumption**, a contemporary of the Romanesque basilicas in Strzelno and Kruszwica, albeit one heavily altered. A Romantic spire was added last century along with an attractive, if less accomplished, interior paint job to Włocławek's St John's Church (see below). It occupies a pleasantly landscaped position in a park, a few minutes' walk east of the big roundabout which lies between the compact commercial centre and the bus and train stations, respectively ten and fifteen minutes' walk to the north.

In the heart of the Old Town, just south of the Rynek down ul. Paderewskiego and then right, is **St Nicholas** (Św. Mikołaja), a Gothic parish church with Renaissance and Baroque additions. Coming this way you'll catch the church's mellifluous arch styles jumbled and mixed in an evocative manner. Inside the vault's ribs lead down to murals depicting key events from the bible – starting with Adam and a shame-faced Eve's explusion from the Garden. Behind the church is the less imposing twin-towered **Church of Our Lady** – far less altered and better demonstrating its Romanesque origins. Clearly evident are the various rebuilds of the brick towers onto the church's granite body, while near the north porch a devout mason bravely attempted to sculpt two distinctly demonic faces into the rock.

Around the time St Nicholas' was being built in the fifteenth century, underground salt springs were discovered in the area, but it was not until the 1870s that Inowrocław became a popular **spa**, with thermal establishments built to the west of the Old Town. The prosperity this brought is reflected in the grand turn-of-the-century buildings erected along the town's main axis, ul. Królowej Jadwigi, which are now re-emerging from decades of neglect in their full colourful pomp. Unfortunately, although the baths are still in use, the modern town has harnessed the waters as the basis of a chemical industry which has led to heavy pollution and the mushroom growth of concrete suburbs whose only saving grace is the fact that they're spread out with plenty of greenery.

Given the current appearance of Inowrocław, it's not likely to rate as an overnight stop. If you do want to use it as a touring base, there's a **hotel** on ul. Królowej Jadwigi: the *Bast* at no. 35 (☎0536/72888 or 72024; ④). For a meal, the **restaurant**, *Pod Lwem* near the Rynek at no. 1, provides a cheaper alternative to the *Bast*, with both offering the usual inexpensive prices and uncannily speedy service. When you're ready to move on, Inowrocław offers a wide choice of connections onwards to Toruń and Bydgoszcz, or else back to Gniezno either directly or via Żnin.

Włocławek and Ciechocinek

The only other places of interest nearby lie to the east, on or near the River Wisła – the province's historic but now grittily industrialized capital, **Włocławek**, and the distinctive spa town of **Ciechocinek**. If you're travelling along the Piast Route, it's best to head for these places by bus; otherwise they are readily accessible by train from either Płock (see p.138) or Toruń (see p.195).

Włocławek

Some 60km southeast of Inowrocław, **WŁOCŁAWEK** is nowadays an ugly industrial town, with a huge paper mill fed by the neighbouring forests, though it's best known for its production of one of Poland's favourite tourist souvenirs – glazed earthenware, hand-painted with brown floral motifs. Włocławek's early development owed much to its strategic position on the River Wisła; it has been the seat of a bishop since the mid-twelfth century, and it remains an important episcopal centre – the formidable Stefan Wzyszyński (see box on p.564), scourge of successive communist governments, spent most of his early priesthood here. For long the town operated a rigid anti-Semitic policy, with Jews prohibited from settling until the eighteenth century.

The Town

Arriving at either the **bus** or **train station**, situated together at the southwestern end of the centre, ul. Kościuszki leads to pl. Wolności, a characterless large square forming the hub of the modern business district, which has migrated here from its original position overlooking the Wisła. The Stary Rynek (Old Market), is in a run down area several blocks north along ul. 3 Maja. Nowadays it has a certain dilapidated charm, looking more like the centrepiece of a rural village than of a sizeable town. Its decrepit houses range in date from the seventeenth to the nineteenth centuries with a better maintained Baroque example on the east side now containing the **District Museum** (Tues 10am–6pm, Wed, Fri & Sat 10am–3pm, Thurs 10am–noon & 3–6pm, Sun 10am–2pm), with displays on the archeology, history, art and folklore of the Kujawy region. On the north side of the square, nearest the river, is the squat Parish Church of **St John**, originally Gothic but heavily remodelled in the Baroque period. An effective mosaic of Matka Boska Chestochowska in azure and gold glitters at you as you approach. Inside the low ceiling gives a cosy feeling, offset by the wobbly lines of the brick vaulting hanging over the customary Baroque exuberance.

Visible a short distance to the west is the brick Gothic **Cathedral**, which was begun in 1340, a few years after a fire which completely destroyed its predecessor along with much of the rest of the town. At the end of last century, it was restored and embellished – notably by the addition of the fantastical spires. Just as the silhouette now has a predominantly Romantic flavour, so too does the interior, which was treated to a beautiful painted decoration. Blue walls with gold outlining embrace columns painted in earthy tones decorated with birds and floral motifs. It all adds up to a stunning effect and proves that neo-Gothic alterations were no less valid than the varied modifications of the preceding centuries. Traditionalists can recover by peering into the poorly lit and locked chapels, particularly that dedicated to Saint Joseph on the north side, with the **tomb** of Bishop Piotr Moszyński, carved in Hungarian marble by Veit Stoss (see "Kraków", p.373). The tomb adopts a highly individual but subsequently much imitated arrangement, featuring a full-length relief carving of the deceased seemingly sliding off the sloping lid of the sarcophagus. Also of note is the late Renaissance **mausoleum of the Tarnowski family**, its coloured marble exterior adorned with a golden sundial, its interior richly furnished with statues and busts.

Practicalities

Orbis have an office just off the eastern side of pl. Wolności at ul. Zduńska 8 (☎054/25228 or 23021). Accommodation includes two mid-range **hotels**, of which the old coaching inn *Zajazd Polski*, pl. Wolności 5 (☎054/31 18 51; ④), scores in atmosphere over the functional modern *Kujawy* on ul. Kościuszki 18/20 (☎054/32 68 00; ④), right by the station. The seasonal **youth hostel** is a few blocks east of pl. Wolności at ul. Chmielna 24 (☎054/27363). For **eating** and **drinking**, the hotels are just about the only options in the centre, except for the uninspiring snack bars in the vicinity of the station.

Ciechocinek

CIECHOCINEK, a town with its own microclimate, and with rather more life about it than the normal run of spas, lies slightly back from the Wisła, about half-way between Włocławek and Toruń. It can be reached directly from either city by bus; if travelling by train, alight at Aleksandrów Kujawy, from where there are fairly regular services down a seven-kilometre-long branch line terminating at what must be a strong contender for the title of Poland's most salubrious train station.

Straight ahead from here is the **Park Zdrojowy**, with floral gardens, tree-lined avenues and the usual spa buildings – pump room, concert hall and bandstand. Far more intriguing, however, is the **Park Tężniówy** on the opposite side of the tracks from the town. Here, in three separate sections stretching for over 1.5km, is the mass of wooden poles and twigs which make up the **saltworks**, begun in 1824 but not completed until several decades later. It's an extraordinary sight and is all the more remarkable in that it can still be seen functioning as originally intended. The technology behind it is very simple: water from the town's saline springs is pumped to the top of the structure, from where it trickles back down through the twigs. This not only concentrates the salt, it also creates a reputedly recuperative atmosphere in the covered space below. Formerly, patients would walk through the saltworks, breathing in deeply as they went, but, for conservation reasons, this is unfortunately no longer permitted.

For somewhere **to stay** try the modern *Hotel Restaurant Amazonka* at the end of ul. Traugatta (☎054/4271; ④–⑤). There are a few other restaurants in the town centre, plus several cafés here and in the parks.

POMERANIA (POMORZE)

Pomerania's long, sandy coastline is its major attraction, and a couple of days holed up on the Baltic here is one of the most pleasant ways of unwinding that the country can offer. Less known but equally appealing, especially travelling by bike, is the inland forested lake district, with its Prussian peasant villages and conspicuous absence of heavy industry.

Bydgoszcz, a major industrial city with a small historic centre, serves as the gateway to the **lakes** to the north, but it's a typically hideous place good for nothing but changing trains or buses. A good base in the lake district is **Czaplinek**, on the shores of Lake Drawsko, or **Chojnice**, close to the network of eastern lakes and forest. On the coast there are plenty of resorts to choose from: **Łeba** combines beaches with the **Słowiński National Park**; the old port of **Darłowo** preserves a distinctively Pomeranian character; while to the west many of the finest beaches are found around **Kołobrzeg** and on the islands of **Wolin** and **Uznam**. Just inland, **Kamień Pomorski** warrants a visit, whether for its cathedral or the summer music festival. All places are readily accessible from the great port of **Szczecin**, Pomerania's largest city and historic capital, while nearby **Stargard Szczeciński** offers several of the province's architectural highpoints.

Transport links within Pomerania are good: there's a reasonable train service that runs parallel to the coast on the Gdańsk–Szczecin line, with local connections up to the coastal resorts and buses for excursions inland into the countryside.

A BRIEF HISTORY OF POMERANIA

In prehistoric times the southern Baltic coast was inhabited by the Celts, who were later displaced by a succession of Germanic tribes. By the end of the fifth century they too had been ousted by Slav people known as the **Pomorzanie**, relics of whose settlements are preserved on Wolin island, in the west of the region. The lands of the Pomorzanie were in turn conquered by the Piast **King Mieszko I**, who took Szczecin in 979 – a campaign which is cited by the Poles in support of their claim to ownership of this often disputed territory. Thereafter the picture gets more complicated. Throughout the medieval era, Pomerania evolved as an essentially independent dukedom ruled by a local Slav dynasty commonly called the **Pomeranian princes**, who nonetheless owed loyalty to the Polish monarch. Eastern Pomerania was conquered by the Teutonic Knights in 1308, and was later known as Royal Prussia; this part of the region returned to the Polish sphere of influence under the terms of the 1466 Treaty of Toruń (see p.196).

The ethnic mix of the region played a dominant part in governing its allegiances. While a Slav majority retained its hold on the countryside, heavy German colonization of the towns inexorably tilted the balance of power to the territorially ambitious Brandenburg margraviate. In line with the westward drift, the Pomeranian princes finally transferred formal allegiance to the Holy Roman Empire in 1521, and the inroads of the Reformation further weakened the region's ties with Catholic Poland, which anyway was more interested in its eastern borderlands than its western terrains. In 1532, the ruling Gryfit dynasty divided into two lines, and their territory was partitioned along a line west of the Odra delta: the larger eastern duchy was henceforth known as Hinter Pomerania; the small one to the west as Lower or Hither Pomerania. None of the latter's territory has ever subsequently formed part of Poland.

Control of the region was fiercely disputed during the **Thirty Years' War**, with the Swedes taking over all of Lower Pomerania, plus some of the coastline of Hinter Pomerania. The Treaty of Westphalia of 1648 formalized the division of the latter, whose capital, Szczecin/Stettin, thereby became part of Sweden. Following the departure of the Swedes in the 1720s, **the Prussians** reunited Lower and Hinter Pomerania into a single administrative province, and during the Partitions were able to join it up with their territories to the east by the annexation of Royal Prussia. Their control over the region was undisturbed until after the Versailles Treaty of 1919, when a strip of Pomerania's eastern fringe was ceded to Poland, some of it forming part of the notorious "Polish Corridor". Nearly all of the territory of the old duchy of Hinter Pomerania was **allocated to Poland** in 1945, as part of the compensation deal for loss of the Eastern Territories to the Soviet Union. Mass emigration of the area's German population, which started during the final months of the war, gathered apace after the transfer of sovereignty; in their place came displaced Polish settlers, mostly from the east.

Bydgoszcz

BYDGOSZCZ is a sprawling industrial city, developed around a fortified medieval settlement strategically located on the River Brda, shortly before its confluence with the Wisła. Its growth towards its present size began at the end of the eighteenth century when, as the Prussian town of Bromberg, it became the hub of an important waterway system due to the construction of a canal linking the Wisła to the Odra via the rivers Brda, Noteć and Warta. Unlike much of the region to the north, it has been Polish since 1920, when it was ceded by Germany and incorporated into the province of Poznań. During World War II, the city suffered particularly badly at the hands of the Nazis: mass executions of civilians followed its fall, and by the end of the war over fifty thousand people – a quarter of the population – had been murdered, with many of the rest deported to labour and concentration camps.

In addition to this miserable recent history, it has to be said that there's nothing of special interest to see here. Unless you've a specific reason for visiting the city, you're much better off avoiding the place or shooting straight through – something easier said than done as the network of trunk roads and junctions will soon confuse unfamiliar drivers.

The City

As ever, the focal point of the medieval centre is the Rynek, on which stands a typical communist-style **monument** to the victims of Nazism. There are also a few Baroque and Neoclassical mansions, notably no. 24, which contains the municipal library. These are rather overshadowed by the vast bulk of the **Jesuit College**, which closes the west side of the square, with another fine frontage along ul. Jeznicka. Begun at the end of the seventeenth century, this was for long the town's leading educational establishment, now used as municipal offices.

In a secluded corner just to the north is the redbrick fifteenth-century **Parish Church** (Kościół Farny). This has recently been raised to the status of a co-cathedral, though its dimensions and appearance are more modest than those of many a village church. Nonetheless, its exterior is graced by a fine Gothic gable, while inside, among the usual Baroque ornamentation, is the sixteenth-century high altar of *The Madonna with the Rose*. The church overlooks what is fancifully styled the "Bydgoszcz Venice", the banks on either side of the island formed by two arms of the Brda. On the peninsula at the edge of this island are an old **granary** and **mill**; the latter is designated as a museum.

The south side of the main **waterfront** is dominated by two, much larger half-timbered granaries from the eighteenth century. One of these contains the **Historical Museum** (Tues–Sun 10am–4pm), with displays on the history of the town, including archive material on the Nazi atrocities.

Crossing over to the northern bank, you come to the former **Convent Church of the Poor Clares** (Kościół Klarysek), a curious amalgam of late Gothic and Renaissance, with later alterations. Its conventual buildings now contain the **District Museum** (Tues–Sun 10am–4pm), which is mostly given over to the work of the eclectic local artist Leon Wyczółkowski.

Five blocks east of here is a historical curiosity which rewards the short detour – the **Basilica of St Vincent de Paul**, a vast circular brick church self-consciously modelled on the Pantheon in Rome and capable of accommodating twelve thousand worshippers. Its construction was a direct result of the town's change in ownership from Protestant Prussia to Catholic Poland, which necessitated a much larger space for the main feast days than the small existing churches were able to provide. Passing through the brick-columned portico into the basilica the vast space beneth the dome momentarily distracts you, but after a while the lack of a focal point makes itself felt, and it dawns that the circular design is better used in stadiums, not churches. One thing the basilica has got going for it is a rather snazzy collection of Deco-esque pine confessionals.

Practicalities

Both the **bus** and **train stations** are located to the northwest of the city centre: a fifteen-minute walk straight down ul. Dworcowa brings you out at al. 1 Maja, or take tram #1, #2, #4 or #8. There's a **tourist office** (Mon–Sat 7am–3pm; ☎052/22 53 50) just across from the station at ul. Zygmunta Augusta 10.

For an **overnight stay**, the *Orbis*-run *Pod Orlem*, al 1 Maja 14 (☎052/22 18 61; ⑦)), relives its *fin-de-siècle* elegance, with the gleaming new *City Hotel*, ul. 3 Maja 6 (☎052/22 88 41; ⑧), being a smart, modern and astonishingly expensive alternative. For those not on expense accounts, the slightly run-down *Centralny*, ul. Dworcowa 85 (☎052/22 88 76; ③), is worth considering, as is the sporty *Hotel Esperanto*, 2km east of the centre at ul. M. Sklodowskiej 10a (☎052/41 51 15; ③). The **youth hostel** is also handily placed, just a couple of minutes' walk from the station at ul. Józefa Sowińskiego 5 (☎052/22 75 70).

Each of the first three hotels listed has a good **restaurant**; other options include *Śródmiejska*, ul. Dworcowa 19, *Rybna*, al. 1 Maja 22, and *Kaczma Słupska*, al. 1 Maja 28. A few decent **milk bars** still survive, such as *Dworcowy*, ul. Dworcowa 75, and *Ratuszowy*, ul. Długa 27.

For an evening's entertainment, the *Filharmonia Pomorska*, just east of ul. 1 Maja at ul. Karola Libelta 16, is the main **musical** venue; as well as regular concerts, it features a fortnight-long classical festival each September. The main **theatre** is the nearby *Teatr Polski*, al. Mickiewicza 2.

The Pomeranian Lakeland

The **Pomeranian Lakeland** lies over to the northwest of Bydgoszcz, centred on the resort town of **Szczecinek**. An area of low undulating hills smothered by bygone glaciers, patches of pine and birch forest and quiet, tree-lined roads linking small market towns separated by over a thousand lakes. Tourist infrastructure seems to have dwindled from a high point as a workers' holiday retreat about twenty years ago, although as elsewhere in the country, there's newer evidence of entrepreneurial speculation in the form of the odd refurbished holiday *dacha*.

Most Poles who come here are merely content to park up at the few **lakeside resorts** (sometimes little more than camping parks) where the accommodation tends to be concentrated and idle away a couple of weeks. While this may be alright for some, the region's gentle gradients, quiet villages and lack of heavy traffic make a lovely if undemanding location for a **cycling tour**, although even fat-tyred mountain bikes might find some of the sandy forest tracks hard work.

Two good **maps** cover the entire area in detail: the green *PPWK 1:300,000* "*Kaszuby, Kujawy, Wielopolska*" sheet #2 covers the eastern lake district from Poznań to Gdańsk, and the same scale "*Pomorze, Wielopolska*" sheet #1 takes you west to Szczecin and the German border.

Chojnice and the Eastern Lake District

Some 50km north of Bydgoszcz, near Lake Charzykowskie, lies **CHOJNICE**, a quiet, unpretentious place with a dusty, open square – the setting for its main bit of animation, a weekly market, when the streets are filled with traders.

Architecturally, the town has a few reminders of its past as the last Polish stronghold of the Teutonic Knights, although Chojnice also bears the ignominious distinction of being the first town to be attacked by the Nazis on September 1, 1939. The most impressive old building is the **Town Hall** whose stepped gable looks down on the Rynek. Sections of the town **walls** have also survived the battering of the centuries, most notably the five-storey **Czucholow Gate** (Brama Czuchołowoska), off the western edge of the Rynek, which houses a **museum** displaying an unexceptional array of historical items.

At present there are just two unsophisticated options should you need **to stay** – the *Olimp*, ul. Kościerska 9 (☎0531/73629; ②), and the *Turystyczny*, ul. Myśliboja 5 (☎0531/75185; ②), right on the Rynek, which can get rather noisy at night. There's a basic **café** on ul. Kościuszki just past the church and a plusher **restaurant** on ul. Staroszkolna, just south of the Rynek.

You'll find an *Orbis* **tourist information office** at Stary Rynek 5 (☎0531/73146). The **bus** and **train stations** are both next to each other just over 1km southeast of the town centre – buses #1, #6 and #LN go to the town centre.

Lake Charzykowskie and the Zaborski Conservation Park

Northwest of Chojnice, a series of lakes and waterways extends for an unbroken 60km towards the edges of Kashubia (see p.184). There's little of interest here, but the relaxed rural pace encourages a gentle exploration of a couple of days. Equipped with your own tent and a modicum of discretion you can pretty much camp for free (bearing in mind the usual precautions for fire).

From Chojnice, the place to head for is **Lake Charzykowskie**, at whose southern end is the village of **CHARZYKOW**, a five-kilometre bus ride from Chojnice. It's nothing special, a low-key resort with a couple of hotels and restaurants and a campsite by the lake. Driving up through scented forests of pine and beech, the road crosses an isthmus separating Lake Charzykowskie from Lake Karsińskie, at whose northern end is the pleasant resort village **SWORNEGACIE**. Once the site of a twelfth-century Augustinian and later Cistercian monastery, these days the devotion leans firmly towards waterborne recreation – watercraft can be rented near the bridge (an Omega-class dinghy costs just 24zł a day). Opposite the eighty-year-old neo-Baroque church you'll find the *Wagant* **restaurant** with the well-equipped *JÓSK* **holiday resort** up the small hill offering self-contained chalets (☎81337; ④) and boat rental.

From Swornegacie you can wind your way along a variety of routes to the small working village of **LEŚNO**, with its seventeenth-century church shell disclosing some modest Baroque details. There's an archeological site here, dating back through the medieval era to the Iron Age of the fourth century BC, which includes a stone circle similar to that at Odry (see below). Unfortunately it's not signposted, and you'll have to get directions from someone in the village.

Odry and around

Just outside the village of **ODRY**, 20km northeast of Chojnice (served by sporadic buses), a wooded nature reserve hides a well-preserved megalithic site. A sequence of irregular **stone circles** and overgrown burial mounds, it covers an area about half the size of a football pitch. It has been dated to the first or second century, though little is known of its origins. To find the clearing in which it stands isn't easy, adding to the enjoyment of the site when you finally arrive; before setting out from the village ask directions for the *Kręgi Kamieniece*.

A short distance north of Odry is **Lake Wdzydze** surrounded by the Wdzydzki Conservation Park. The main, indeed only, resort here is the village of **WDZYDZE**, which is tucked in above the lake's northeastern arm and boasts a campsite, a couple of shops and the new *Hotel Neidźniadek,* which has great views over the lake from its restaurant (☎80 60 80; ④).

The Western Lake District: Szczecinek and Czaplinek

One of the most popular lakeland bases is the town of **SZCZECINEK,** in the relatively more visited western lake district. A modern and rather over-functional holiday centre on the Koszalin–Poznan road, it stands by **Lake Wielimie,** where formerly grand mansions hint at the town's bygone heyday. **Szczecinek** is a handy way of getting into the area, but not a place you'd want to linger as the unblemished countryside around has more to offer.

Accommodation in town is provided by the central *Hotel Pojezierzei,* ul. Wyszyńskiego 69a (☎0966/43341; ③), the town's main road, and the *Garnizonowy,* pl. Wolności 6 (☎0966/40172; ③), close to the lake, but past its prime. There's also the *Motel Merkury,* ul. Cieślaka 11 (☎0966/43525; ③), the main highway bypassing the town, and a **camping site,** the *Leśny,* at ul. Kościuszki 76 (☎0966/40102).

Czaplinek and Lake Drawsko

The best-known lake area is the Drawskie region, 40km west of Szczecinek. **Lake Drawsko,** the centre of the district, is one of the largest Pomeranian lakes, a tranquil expanse of deep, clear water some 10km in length. In summer you'll find groups of Polish canoeists powering their way through the area: if you feel like joining them, there are rental facilities in town. Walking is wonderful, too, with paths rambling off through the lakeside woods for miles in all directions.

On the banks of Drawsko is **CZAPLINEK,** an early Slav stronghold eventually wrested into the Brandenburg domains from the Teutons. The town has a drowsy charm about it and tourism doesn't seem to have much affected the easy-going life of the place. Despite the popularity of the lake, **accommodation** is limited to the *Hotel Pomorski,* ul. Jagiellońska 11 (☎55444; ④), and the new *Paradise Motel/ Restauracja,* (☎55402; ③), just a minute south of pl. 3 Marca. There's also a lovely lakeside **campsite** 1km north of town, with a small beach and a jetty. The **bus station** with connections to Szczecinek and other towns in the region is in pl. 3 Marca, while the **train station** is about 3km south of the village. The small *Sandal* **tourist information centre** on ul. Watecka 3 by the main square (Mon– Fri 10am–6pm, Sat 10am–5pm; ☎54577), can provide a few ageing maps and brochures on the area (some in English).

Stary Drawsko

Heading up the east side of Lake Drawsko you can meander at will through the back roads and woodland trails of the **Drawski Park Narodowy,** ringed from all but its eastern side by a convenient rail line. Seven kilometres north of Czaplinek **STARY DRAWSKO** straddles a bridge of land between Drawsko and the lesser Lake Żerdno. Once a small medieval settlement on the coast-bound Salt Route, only the rubbish-strewn ruins of a fourteenth-century **castle** next to the church recall that era. Excavations on the site during the sixties discovered five hundred counterfeit coins from what was thought to have been a illicit minting operation dating from the fourteenth century. The town today comprises another secluded lakeside campsite and a couple of restaurants and kiosks to cater for the visitors.

Łeba and around

For a taste of a traditional, thriving Polish seaside resort, visit ŁEBA, an attractive old fishing village which has spawned a bustling holiday centre at the mouth of the river of the same name. It's 90km from Gdańsk with reasonable train and bus connections via Lebork – which is also the route taken by trains from Słupsk, Koszalin (see p.583) and points west. Buses from Gdańsk take the main roads; if you're coming by car, a more appealing approach is on the backroads, taking you through the tiny hamlets and along the delightful tree-lined avenues that characterize this part of the country. The PPWK "Pomorze, Wielopolska" #1 map covers the area in deatail.

The **town** itself is set a kilometre back from the sea: dunes and beaches cover the original site of the village, which was forced to move inland in the late sixteenth century because of shifting sands and erosion. Both buses and trains drop you just off ul. Kościuszki, the main street running down the middle of the resort, which bridges a canalized branch of the river where trawlers and pleasure boats moor. The street bustles in summer with cheerful holidaymakers engaged in tacky consumption or heading for the unbroken sandy **beaches** which are widely regarded as among the cleanest on the Baltic coast. Poles aren't the only people who have enjoyed the bracing location: wandering through the park that provides the main approach to the beaches, you'll pass the summer house used by Nazi propaganda chief Josef Goebbels. Closer to the sea, along ul. Tyrystyczna to the west of town, are the ruins of **St Nicholas' Church**, a lone reminder of the village's former location.

Even in season, **accommodation** shouldn't be too much of a problem here: the town is crammed with signs to one establishment or another. There's a welter of former workers' holiday homes on or around ul. Nadmorska, the main route east of the town, and in striking distance of the sea: the Przymorze **tourist office**, ul. Tyrystyczna 3 (☎059/66 13 60), or the PTTK bureau at ul. 1 Maja 6 (on the corner of ul. Kościuszki, two streets down from the bridge) can help. In town, the options include the Morski, ul. Morska (☎059/66 14 68; ④), close to the seafront but overpriced for what you get; the Pensjonat Angela, pl. Dworcowy 2a (☎059/66 26 47; ②), a stone's throw from the central bus and train stations; the Wodnik, ul. Nadmorska 10 (☎059/66 13 66; ④), and the inexpensive and therefore popular PTTK hostel at ul. 1 Maja 6 (☎059/66 13 24; ②). For **campers** – and there are plenty of them in summer – there are several sites along ul. Turstyczna and ul. Nadmorska, all close to the beaches, a number of them rent chalets too. There's a surfeit of inexpensive **snack bars** selling locally caught fried fish (smarzona ryba) but the only half-decent **restaurant** is the Karczma Słowińska on ul. Kościuszki 28.

If you fancy exploring the area on two wheels, you'll find a bike shop just south of the bridge **renting bicycles**; they can also be rented at **Rabka** if you're heading for the coastal dunes (see below). Less strenuous is a **boat cruise** out across Lake Łabsko (see below): expect to shell out around 6zł for an hour on the water.

The Słowiński National Park

West of Łeba is Lake Łabsko, separated from the sea by mobile sand dunes and comprising the **Słowiński National Park**, one of the country's most memorable natural attractions, special enough to be included in UNESCO's list of world Biosphere Reserves. The park gets its name from the **Slovincians**, a small ethnic group of Slav origin who, like their neighbours the Kashubians, have retained a distinctive identity despite centuries of Germanization.

This area is an ornithologist's paradise, with over 250 **bird** species either permanently inhabiting the park or using it as a migratory habitat. Geomorphically speaking this is an unusual region: the shallow lagoons covering the central part of the park once formed a gulf, which the deposition of sand eventually isolated from the sea. Between them a narrow spit of land emerged roughly two thousand years ago, whose dense original covering of oak and beech forests was gradually eroded by intensive animal grazing and tree felling, the forests disappearing under the dunes that overran the thirty-kilometre spit. Abandoned to the elements by its few original human inhabitants, during World War II the expanse of shifting, undulating sand provided an ideal training ground for units of Afrika Korps, who drilled here in preparation for the rigours of Rommel's North African campaigns. In the latter stages of the war the park was turned into one of several launch sites for the fearsome V1 and V2 rockets that bombarded London – you can still see the remains of some of the rocket installations a couple of kilometres west of Łeba.

Access to the east of the park is from **RĄBKA**, a small holiday village on the shores of **Jezioro Łebsko**, the largest and best-known of the lagoons, a bus ride or twenty-minute walk west of Łeba. The shores are covered with thick reeds, making access to the water difficult, but providing ideal cover for the birds: sanctuaries at several points protect the main breeding sites. Though it's possible to skirt some of the southern edge, most visitors continue along the **northern** side, on a road into the dune territory that is the park's distinguishing feature. From July to August tourist buses from Łeba and Rąbka run west to the edge of the sands; at other times you'll have to walk.

Most people are content to venture a kilometre or so beyond where the electric -powered bus stops, returning either by bus or along a parallel path running beside the coast. If you're feeling up to a sterner challenge you could walk on to the village of Smołdzino (see below), 12km from the bus stop, returning to Łeba

---

FAUNA IN THE PARK

Birds in the park are classified into three main groups: nesting, migratory and wintering species. Nesters include such rare species as the white-tailed eagle, black stork (you're bound to encounter the site of a stork nesting atop a telegraph pole before long), crane, ruff and eagle-owl. During the late autumn migration period you'll see large flocks of wild geese winging over the lakes, and in winter you'll find ducks and other fowl from the far north of Europe sheltering here on the warmer southern shores of the Baltic – velvet scoters, mergansers, auks and whooper swans included. **Mammals** are numerous too, the shores of the lakes harbouring deer and boar, with elks, racoons and badgers in the surrounding woods.

by a roundabout bus route in the evening, or even staying overnight. Alternatively, ask at the *Rybak* cinema on ul. Morska in Łeba (☎059/66 14 43) about the **cruiser** which undertakes regular crossings of the lake to the village of Kluki on its southwestern shore. A handy way of heading west from Łeba, it leaves at 11.30am daily and costs around 6zł, but it's best to confirm these details in town.

Even a brief hike will give you the flavour of the terrain, though. A short distance out of the lakeside woods, huge dunes are piled up to 40m high; dried by the sun and propelled by the wind, they migrate over 10m per year on average, leaving behind the broken tree stumps you see along the path. Out in the middle of the dune area, there's a desert-like feeling of desolation with the sands rippling in the wind giving an eerie sense of fluidity.

Smołdzino

SMOŁDZINO is the site of the park's **Natural History Museum** (daily 9am–5pm), which contains an extensive display of the park's flora and fauna; the park offices here can provide you with detailed information about the area, including advice on bird-watching around the lake. Just to the west of the village is the 115-metre-high **Rowokół Hill**, whose observation tower at the top affords a panoramic view over the entire park area. There's a summer **youth hostel** and a farm hostel in the village as well.

Kluki

Five kilometres east of Smołdzino, on the western edge of Lake Łebsko and at the end of a minor road, is the little Slovincian village of **KLUKI**, which is served by occasional buses from Smołdzino and more frequent ones from Słupsk. Entirely surrounded by woods, Kluki has a *skansen* of Slovincian timber-framed architecture (May–Sept Tues–Fri 10am–5pm, Sat & Sun noon–6pm); you'll see similar, if more delapidated, buildings still in use in several villages all over the region.

Słupsk and the central coast

Continuing west through lush farming country along the sub-coastal back road, the next place of any significance is **SŁUPSK**, 20km beyond the former Teutonic but otherwise nondescript town of Lębork. An early Slav settlement, ruled by Pomeranian princes and Brandenburg margraves for much of its history, Słupsk was completely wrecked in 1945, and faceless postwar development has even spoiled the usually sacrosanct Stary Rynek which now boasts a cinema where the town hall stood. Best known in Poland for its annual **Piano Festival**, held in September, Słupsk is not a place to detain you, although it can be useful as a base for exploring the Słowiński National Park, to which the **Orbis** office at ul. Wojska Polskiego 1 (☎23614) organizes summer excursions.

What little there is worth seeing in the town centre can be covered in an hour or two. On the banks of the river, the Renaissance castle houses a **Regional Museum** (Tues 10am–5pm, Wed–Sun 10am–4pm). Alongside displays of local ethnography, there's a large collection of modern Polish art, most notably a series of distorted caricatures and self-portraits by Stanisław Ignacy Witkiewicz who commited suicide soon after the start of World War II. The old castle **mill** opposite is one of the earliest specimens of its kind in the country, packed with more folksy exhibits, while the reconstructed Gothic **Dominican Church** has a fine Renaissance altarpiece and the tombs of the last Pomeranian princes.

This scattering of historic sites aside, the town's main attractions are two highly reputable **restaurants**, the *Karczma Słupska* at ul. Wojska Polskiego 11 and the *Pod Kluką* at ul. Kaszubska 22 – both in the centre and offering a spread of traditional Polish cuisine with a sprinkling of regional specialities. For a quick and inexpensive snack, check out *Bar Malgosia* on ul. Bema, just north of the Rynek.

Accommodation is provided by the passable *Przymorze* **motel**, ul. Szwedka 41 (☎059/43 08 53; ④), the *Piast* **hotel**, ul. Jednosci Narodowej 2 (☎059/2586; ⑤), and the *Zamkowy* hotel, ul. Dominikańska 9 (☎059/25294; ④), near the castle. There's a summer-only **youth hostel** at ul. Deotymy 15a (☎059/24632), a short distance southwest of the Stary Rynek, with the nearest **campsite** on ul. Rybacka (☎059/24419). The **train station**, with the **bus station** just opposite, is at the west end of ul. Wojska Polskiego, the kilometre-long boulevard leading to the centre.

Ustka

Twenty kilometres northwest of Słupsk (and accessible by bus or local train) is **USTKA**, one-time member of the Hanseatic League that's become an established member of the bucket-and-spade league for well over a century. Its a big resort and getting bigger, with its beaches, as good as any on the Baltic coast, especially those east of town, stretching along towards the Słowiński National Park. If the idea of a seaside stopover here appeals, there is plenty of **accommodation** in and around the town including the *Bałtycki*, ul. Przewłoka (☎059/14 47 57; ④), east of town, and right in the town centre, the *Dom Rybaka*, ul. Marynarki Polskiej 31 (☎059/14 57 55; ④), on the same street as the train station. For **campers** there's a good site at ul. Armii Krajowej, a couple of kilometres southeast of town. The best **restaurant** is the *Messa,* close to the beach at the top of ul. Żeromskiego.

Darłowo and beyond

A more attractive proposition than Ustka is **DARŁOWO**, 40km further west and a couple of kilometres inland on the River Wieprza, though here the drawback is the difficulty of public transport – trains from Słupsk involve a change at Sławno, and buses take nearly two hours.

The beaches north of the town, around the resort of Darłówko, are as popular as any, but what makes Darłowo special are the buildings of the old Hanseatic fishing centre. The **Rynek**, still a marketplace, is the site of a gracefully reconstructed Town Hall, complete with its Renaissance doorway and a rather cleverly designed fountain. On one side of the Rynek sits the Gothic **St Mary's Church**, an attractive brick building with a relatively restrained Baroque interior overlay; in among a clutch of royal tombs is that of the notorious Scandinavian ruler King Erik VII (1397–1459), a relative of King Kazimierz the Great, who was deposed in 1439 and lived out the last years of his life in exile here. Further out from the centre you'll find parts of the fifteenth-century walls, including the **town gate** visible in the Rynek's northeast corner. Half a mile away is the extraordinary white-walled **St Gertrude's Chapel**, with its roof of slender wooden slats draped over the unusual twelve-sided ambulatory. On the other side of town, just before the river on the right, the well-preserved fourteenth-century castle of the Pomeranian princes now houses an interesting **Regional Museum** (Tues–Sun 10am–4pm) which focuses on the town's Hanseatic past.

The well-meaning but ultimately ineffective **information office**, left of the town gate at 3a ul. Zielona, might be able to sort out private rooms, but they're more likely to direct you to the *Hotel Irena* over the river at ul. Wojska Polskioego 64 (☎094/14 36 92; ③), or the *Kubuś* (☎094/2392; ③) right next door. Both places are a short walk from the **train** and **bus stations**, situated at the end of ul. Bogusława X. For food, try the *Paloma* **restaurant** on the Rynek.

West from Darłowo

If you've a car it's worth taking the backroads west from Darłowo, which pass through an attractive open landscape of fields, woods and quiet old Pomeranian villages. The sagging timber-framed farm buildings are still just about standing, as in several cases are the similarly aged brick churches. A charming example is at **IWIĘCINO**, a tiny village halfway between Darłowo and Koszalin. The fourteenth-century structure features a faintly painted wooden ceiling and sixteenth-century pews, a delicate Renaissance altarpiece and a splendid Late Baroque organ.

Koszalin and around

As even the determinedly upbeat tourist brochures tacitly admit, **KOSZALIN**, the bustling provincial capital 25km west of Darłowo, isn't the sort of place that gets the crowds shouting. The one-time seat of a local line of Pomeranian prince-bishops, who were eventually replaced in the mid-seventeenth century by Pomerania's Brandenburg rulers, like so many towns in this region, the Old Town was badly damaged during 1945, and hurried postwar reconstruction of the newly vacated German city was more about residential building and intensive industrial development than aesthetic statements. That said, the town's historic core has at least retained the basics of its regular medieval layout, including the rectangular central **Rynek**, a large area effectively built from scratch after World War II. Just south of the square is **St Mary's Cathedral**, an imposing, oft-remodelled Gothic structure with a few pieces of original decoration, notably a large fourteenth-century crucifix and a scattering of Gothic statuary, originally from the main altarpiece and now incorporated into the stalls, pulpit and organ loft. The nineteenth-century water mill facing the Old Town walls from the corner of ul. Młyńska houses the **Regional Museum** (Tues–Sun 10am–4pm) with a varied collection of folk art, archeological finds and other regional miscellany. The most interesting part is the mini-*skansen* next to the building, which contains a number of examples of the sturdy peasant architecture characteristic of the Pomeranian coastal region. Back into the centre is the old sixteenth-century **Town Executioner's House** on ul. Grodzka, rebuilt to serve as a local theatre, while a short walk south of the cathedral stands the octagonal **St Gertrude's Chapel**, just next to another theatre and the town's main surviving Gothic structure.

Practicalities

For **information** the local tourist office at ul. Dworcowa 10, just across from the bus and train stations, and the next-door *Orbis* bureau ought to provide everything you need to know. The few **accommodation** options are the plush

Arka, ul. Zwycięstwa 20/24 (☎42 79 11; ⑦), next to *Orbis*, a Western holidaymakers' favourite; the *Turystyczny*, ul Głoowackiego 7 (☎42 30 01; ③), a more reasonably priced establishment north of the centre; the *Za Lasem*, ul. Morska 152 (☎42 34 26; ④) on the main Kołobrzeg road north of town; and an all-year **youth hostel**, ul. Gwiaździsta 3 (☎42 60 68), south of town. Best of the town's **restaurants** are the *Balaton*, in the *Arka* hotel, the nearby *Bałtyk*, ul. Zwycięstwa 28, for Polish staples, and the slightly pricier *Ratuszowa* at Rynek 11.

North of Koszalin

For Polish holidaymakers, Koszalin is mainly known as a convenient access point for the spread of beaches along the coast to the north of town. The most popular resort is **MIELNO**, a thirty-minute bus ride (#1 from the main bus station) some 12km northwest of town. Local trains also run from Koszalin during the summer season. The town was an early Slav stronghold and fishing settlement, formerly the main port for Koszalin. If you feel like mingling with the holiday crowds you could do worse than stop off at this small coastal resort for a relaxing night or two.

Places to stay range from the upmarket *Motel Mister*, ul. Lechitów 22 (☎094/18 99 20; ④), to the **campsite** at ul. Orła Białego 9 (☎094/18 95 75) near the main beach. Alternatively there's **UNIEŚCIE**, a newer resort a couple of kilometres' bus ride west of Mielno with a wide sandy beach from which fishing boats push off into the sea each morning. There are half a dozen inexpensive **places to stay** here including the *Agawa*, ul. Róży Wiatrów 38 (☎094/18 96 78; ③), and the larger *Hotel Adrianna*, ul. Teligi 1 (☎094/18 94 21; ③). There are a couple of **campsites** here too.

Kołobrzeg

Beyond Darłowo the next coastal town of any size is **KOŁOBRZEG**, a large seaside resort clumped around the mouth of the River Parsęta, a forty-kilometre bus or train ride west of Koszalin. With one and a half million visitors annually, it's one of the country's busiest seaside resorts, with a decent collection of holiday-oriented amenities concentrated within a kilometre of the train station.

The paucity of ancient buildings belies the town's history. One of the oldest Pomeranian settlements, it grew on the economic foundations of the **salt works** established here in the seventh century. By the mid-800s a decent-sized fortified town had developed, and in 1000 Bolesław the Brave founded one of the early Piast bishoprics in what was becoming a significant port. A steady influx of German merchants and sailors eventually led to its incorporation into the Hanseatic League in the mid-thirteenth century. Badly hit by the Thirty Years' War, it passed into the control of the Brandenburg margraves in 1655, and a fortress was established here. A change of emphasis came two centuries later when a new spa resort began to develop, attracting crowds from all over the Baltic region. The Germans defended the town to the last in 1945, leaving the place a ruin by the time the Polish and Russian armies arrived in March. A band of patriots gathered on the beach to swear an oath that this ancient Piast town would thenceforth be Polish forever, sealing the vow in suitably dramatic style by hurling a wedding ring into the sea – "Poland's Reunion with the Sea", as the event came to be known.

The Old Town and the beach

If you've come here in search of historic buildings, the only remotely interesting bit of Kołobrzeg is the **Old Town**, situated ten minutes' walk southeast of the bus and train stations. The **Collegiate Church of St Mary** was originally built as a simple Gothic hall, but was extended in the fifteenth century with the addition of star-vaulted aisles, adding to the impression of depth and spaciousness. A particularly striking effect was achieved with the facade, whose twin towers were moulded together into one vast solid mass of brick. Many of the furnishings perished in the war, but some significant items remain, notably several Gothic triptychs and a fourteenth-century bronze font. To the north stands the other key public building, the **Town Hall**. A castellated Romantic creation incorporating some of its fifteenth-century predecessor, it was built from designs provided by the great Berlin architect Karl Friedrich Schinkel. In the surrounding streets you'll find a number of Gothic burghers' houses – look out in particular for the Dom Schlieffenów on ul. Gierczak.

It's the beachlife that the visitors come for, and throughout the summer you'll find throngs of Polish holidaymakers soaking up the sun on the main strand, a short walk north of the station behind a line of coastal trees. The **beach** has a typically congested feel, with wicker cots for rent and few people bothering to spread out onto the unpopulated stretches to the east. There's plenty of scope for a decent stroll, with a concrete jetty (8am–8pm) and a seafront parade edging an attractive park. Beyond the jetty at the western end stands a tall brick lighthouse and a stone monument marking the spot where Kołobrzeg married the ocean.

Practicalities

The main **information** office is the *Orbis* bureau at ul. Dworcowa 4, in the centre of town. Expensive **accommodation** options include the upmarket *Skanpol*, ul. Dworcowa 10 (☎0965/28211; ⑦), and *Orbis' Hotel Solny*, ul. Fredry 4 (☎0965/22401; ⑦). Better value is the huge *Bałtyk* right by the sea (☎0965/24841; ③) or the *PTTK Hotel Turów* on ul. Portowa 17 (☎0965/24071; ③). There is, in addition, a summer **youth hostel** at ul. Łopuskiego 13 (☎0965/22131) with the town **campsite**, the *Bałtywia*, at ul. Wojska Polskiego 1 (☎0965/24569).

As you might expect, the best **restaurants** in town are those in the *Solny* and *Skanpol* hotels, otherwise the choice is pretty uninspiring, with the bar in the train station a good place for an inexpensive feed.

Along the Hanseatic Route

Moving on from Kołobrzeg, the choice is between continuing west along the coastal area by bus, or heading southwest towards Szczecin, a journey more conveniently made by train. The former is the more obviously attractive option, but if heading for Szczecin you have a chance to see the towns of **Trzebiatów**, **Gryfice** and **Goleniów**, all once prominent members of the Hanseatic League. For all their former prosperity however, their churches and fortifications offer the only tangible reminder of their heyday; all three towns are now in varying stages of neglect.

Trzebiatów

By far the most attractive of the trio (and that's not saying much) is **TRZEBIATÓW**, which lies on the banks of the Baltic-bound River Rega, just under 30km from Kołobrzeg. It's a place where time seems to have gone backwards, transforming a well-heeled trading town into a straggling agricultural village with a pronounced rural air. A good deal of imagination is required to visualize this sleepy Polish backwater as it was four hundred years ago when it played a key role in the Reformation. Johannes Bugenhagen, who spent nearly two decades as rector of its Latin School, became one of Luther's leading lieutenants, returning in 1534 to persuade the Pomeranian Assembly which had specially convened here to adopt the new faith throughout the province.

Trzebiatów's skyline is dominated by the magnificent tower of **St Mary**, one of the most accomplished Gothic churches in the region, crowned with the unusual combination of a brick octagon and a lead spire. In it hang two historic bells – one, named Gabriel, is from the late fourteenth century; the other, known as Mary, dates from the early sixteenth century. The building's interior is chiefly notable for its clear architectural lines and uncluttered appearance which, like the German epitaphs on the walls, are evidence of the four centuries it spent in Protestant hands.

Close to the church is the Rynek, in the centre of which stands the recently renovated **Town Hall**, constructed in the sober Baroque style favoured in northern German lands. One or two Gothic houses line the square, their appearance heightened by the presence of so many undistinguished newer buildings. Just off the southern side is the abandoned **Chapel of the Holy Ghost**, the setting for the Assembly which decided to introduce the Reformation into Pomerania. At the end of the street you can see the rotund **Kaszana** bastion and **town walls**, one of a few other points of interest indicated by historical plaques strategically dotted around town. Among them are the **stone bridge** and **palace** you'll pass on the way to the station.

Both the **bus** and **train stations** are located outside the built-up part of town, about ten minutes' walk to the east. The only place to stay in town is the summer-only **youth hostel** located opposite the church entrance (☎092/72355) and the only **place to eat** is the first-floor *Ratuszowa* restaurant next to the bar on the opposite corner of the Rynek.

Gryfice

About 20km up the Rega from Trzebiatów is **GRYFICE**, a slightly larger town with a decidedly more urban feel to it. German commentators on Pomerania are readily stirred to anger at the mere mention of its name: the town was taken undamaged by the Red Army in 1945, only to be set ablaze soon afterwards, and was later used as the site of a penal camp in which a large number of civilians were detained.

The Gothic **Church of St Mary** is a copybook example of the Baltic style, notable chiefly for its sturdy single western tower and its finely detailed portals, many of which have since been bricked up. Inside you'll find some good Baroque furnishings, in particular the pulpit and the high altar. The surviving parts of the **fortifications** – the Stone Gate, the High Gate and the Powder Tower – can be seen towards the river to the east.

Gryfice has a **hotel**, the *Cukronica*, a couple of minutes east of the Rynek (☎2051; ②). The only obvious place to **eat** is *Gryfiszanka*, just by the church at pl. Zwycięstwa 10.

Goleniów

The largest and liveliest town of the group is **GOLENIÓW**, 55km southwest of Gryfice. It's an important rail junction, the meeting point of the line between Kołobrzeg and Szczecin with those to Kamień Pomorski and Świnoujście. Among its few assets is its situation in the middle of the **Puszca Goleniowska**, a vast forested area which stretches almost all the way up to Wolin – a particularly scenic journey by train.

Goleniów's main church, **St Catherine**, is imposing largely owing to extensive remodelling last century when the tower was added – today its brick columns bow visibly under the strain. Nearby are the **town walls**, whose surviving towers and gateways make a nicely varied group, with the showpiece being the **Wolin Gate**, an elaborate building in its own right now housing a cultural centre. Also worth a look is the timber-framed **granary** standing all alone on the banks of the River Ina.

Again, there's just the one **hotel**, *Słowianin*, ul. Jedności Narodowej 34 (☎091/2201; ②), and for a meal, the *Restauracja Ina*, ul. Jedności Narodowej 4, opposite the post office.

Kamień Pomorski

Some 60km west of Kołobrzeg lies the quiet little waterside town of **KAMIEŃ POMORSKI**, an atmospheric Pomeranian centre which demands a visit for its fine cathedral and agreeable setting. For public transport from Trzebiatów you'll have to rely on buses to take you across country; there are no train connections along this bit of the coast, only north from Szczecin. Travelling on the main routes it's easy to miss this town, since it's not on the major coastal road to Świnoujście, and getting there by any means of transport involves a detour.

The town's history began in the ninth century, when a port was established here on the River Dziwna, a short stretch of water connecting the huge Szczecin Lagoon (Zalew Szczeciński) with the smaller Kamień Lagoon (Zalew Kamieński) – all of which are part of the delta formed by the Odra as it nears its mouth at the Gulf of Pomerania. By the late twelfth century, Kamień was significant enough to be appointed as the seat of the bishopric of West Pomerania, a position it kept for nearly four hundred years, while by the late 1300s it felt rich enough to join the Hanseatic League. The Swedes seized the town during the Thirty Years' War, but by the late seventeenth century it had been appropriated by the Brandenburg rulers, not coming under Polish control until after World War II. Despite extensive wartime damage, Kamień Pomorski seems to have come out better than most towns in the area: concrete buildings fill in the huge gaps between the occasional burghers' mansions, yet there's enough of the older architecture to retain a sense of times past.

The Town

All Kamień's sights are some way north of the bus and train stations, on and around the **Rynek** whose north edge looks out onto the lagoon. The fifteenth-

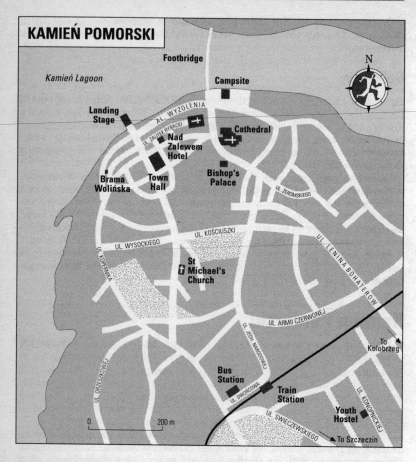

century **Town Hall**, in the middle, is a careful reconstruction, its brick archways rising to a stepped and curvilinear Baroque gable at each end – a rarely seen combination. Parts of the walls ringing the Old Town have survived, notably the **Brama Wolińska** west of the square, an imposing Gothic gateway, surrounded by apartment buildings.

East of the square stands the **Cathedral**, retaining its Romanesque features at ground level, but otherwise the customary mass of brickwork is in the Gothic idiom. Construction of the brick and granite basilica began in the 1170s, following the creation of the Kamień bishopric, with many subsequent additions over the following centuries. Inside the cathedral, you're enveloped by majestic Gothic vaulted arches; the presbytery is older, and covered with flowing early thirteenth-century decoration. Other sections of the earliest polychromy are tucked away in corners around the transept, including a stern *Christ Pantocrator* and a fine *Crucifixion* that was uncovered in the 1940s. The focus of attention, though, is the superb fifteenth-century triptych gracing the altar, the most outstanding of many such Gothic pieces in the building – the rest are in the **Sacristy Museum**. A central *Coronation of Mary* is surrounded by scenes from the lives of the saints, most notably John Chrysostom, to whom the building is dedicated. To the right of the altar is another finely sculpted Romanesque portal, leading to the sacristy.

The cathedral's most famous feature, however, is its massive **Baroque organ**, at the back of the building, its forest of silver pipes and exuberant detail crowned by a procession of dreamy gilded saints. As you approach from the nave, a portrait of the instrument's creator, a local bishop by the name of Bogusław de Croy i Archot, stares down on the congregation from a cherub-encircled frame. From June to August the cathedral hosts an International Organ and Chamber Music Festival, with concerts every Friday – details from the *Biuro Katedralny* opposite. To complete the ensemble, across pl. Katedralny is the **Bishop's Palace**, a stately, Late Gothic structure with a finely carved attic.

Practicalities

In summer the tourist **information point** on plac Katedralny dispenses maps and information; otherwise try the *Orbis* office on the Rynek. The best **accommodation** option is the timber-framed *Pod Murzami*, on the northeast corner of the Rynek (☎0928/22240; ④), just off the Rynek with a view of the lagoon. Otherwise there's the plainer but less expensive *Nad Zalewem* next door (☎0928/28817; ③), a summer **youth hostel** at ul. Konopnickiej 19 (☎20784), and a **campsite** by the lagoon on ul. Wyzwolenia (☎0928/21280).

A decent selection of **restaurants** include the one in *Pod Muzami* on the Rynek, the *Ratuszowa* by the town hall, and the *U Klecia* set off the esplanade in the town walls below the white Baroque church.

Wolin

Across the water from Kamień Pomorski is **WOLIN**, the first of two large, heavily indented islands which separate the Szczecin Lagoon from the Gulf of Pomerania. The gap dividing Wolin from the mainland is at times so narrow that it's often described as a peninsula rather than an island; indeed, roads are built directly over the River Dziwna in two places – near its mouth at Dzwinów, some 12km from Kamień, and at **Wolin town** towards the island's southern extremity, where it is also forded by the rail line between Szczecin and the border town of **Świnoujście**, at the western extremity of Wolin. From Kamień, you can choose to approach by either of these two roads, the only ones of significance on the island. They converge at the seaside resort of **Międzyzdroje**, before continuing onwards to Świnoujście.

Wolin, which is 35km long and between 8km and 20km across, offers a wonderfully contrasted landscape of sand dunes, lakes, forest, meadows and moors. Part of its dramatic **coastline** – undoubtedly its most memorable feature – has attracted crowds of holidaymakers since last century; it is likely to be heavily developed in the future, but in the meantime it remains relatively unspoilt. A sizeable portion of the island is under protection as a national park, and you really need to take time to hike if you want to appreciate it to the full.

Wolin Town

The town of **WOLIN** occupies the site of one of the oldest Slav settlements in the country. According to early chronicles, a pagan tribe known as the Wolinians established themselves here in the eighth century, developing one of the most important early Baltic ports. A temple to Trzygłów and to Światowid, a triple-headed Slav deity (the only extant image of which sits in the Kraków Archeological Museum, p.379), existed here until the early twelfth century, and was presumably destroyed by the Christian Poles only when they captured the stronghold.

Echoes of the town's pagan past are present in the totem-like reconstructed wooden figures dotted around close to the water, all depicting Slav gods. The rebuilding of the once desolate ruins of a medieval church just up from the main square should be complete by now. Recent excavations have uncovered plentiful evidence of the Wolinian settlement: you can see their discoveries in the local **Museum** (Tues–Sun 10am–4pm) on the main road at the eastern end of town.

For an overnight stay there's one **hotel**, the *Wineta* on the main road (☎0936/61884; ③), a summer **youth hostel** at ul. Mickiewicza, and a **camping** space right by the water's edge, popular with anglers and sailors.

Międzyzdroje

By far the best base for exploring the island is **MIĘDZYZDROJE**, which offers easy access to the best hiking trails in addition to a long sandy beach. A favourite Baltic resort with the prewar German middle class, it went downmarket with its transferral to Poland but is now the west Baltic's busiest resort. In a swift about-turn since the fall of communism, Międzyzdroje has embraced western consumerism and new hotels are springing up all around town, popularily visited by German and Scandinavian holidaymakers getting a seaside vacation at a fraction of their countries' cost. The tatty trade-union holiday homes and flats which make up the rest of the resort's accommodation are also being swiftly converted to further capitalize on the resort's booming trade.

Międzyzdroje's **promenade** stretches for all of 4km, the focal point being the pier, beside which is a bandstand. If you want to find out more about the island's flora and fauna, visit the **National Park Museum** (Tues–Sun 10am–3pm) at ul. Niepodległości 3 in the town centre.

Practicalities

The **train station** is at the southeastern fringe of town, fifteen minutes' walk from the beach, while the **bus station** is closer to the centre, on ul. Niepodległości – what would be the town's square if it had one.

If you want to stay in unbridled comfort, the **hotel** *Amber Baltic*, ul. Bohaterów Warszawy 26a (☎0936/80800; ⑥–⑧), charges standard international prices for its facilities, which include golf, bowling, tennis and surfing, plus an outdoor swimming pool. Other places to stay include the smaller *Nautilus*, ul. Bohaterów Warszawy 25 (☎0936/51093; ⑦), right opposite the *Amber Baltic*, with an unnamed *noclegi* next door and the *Bursztynek*, Niepodległości 4 (☎0936/80649; ④). Another moderately expensive beachside choice is the *Merlin*, ul. Bohaterów Warszawy 37 (☎0936/80728; ⑥), with the *Pensionat Amandea* at ul. Gryfa Pomorskiego 2 (☎0936/81018; ⑤) being the best choice in this category. The **PTTK hostel** in the town centre at ul. Kolejowa 2 (☎0936/80382; ④) is no longer a bargain, although there's a seasonal **youth hostel** at ul. Leśna 17 (☎0936/80611), and two **campsites** on the west side of town at ul. Polna 10a (☎0936/80275). For more information, contact the **tourist office**, ul. Światowida 19 (☎0936/80770) or **Orbis**, ul. Kolejowa 20 (☎0936/80015).

Eating outside the hotels is also diverse and getting better. Along with a string of snack bars and cafés all over town try the *Atlantis* pizzeria next to the *Hotel Nautilus* on ul. Bohaterów Warszawy which offers three dozen different toppings or the cheaper *Marina* pizzeria opposite the *Pensionat Amandea*.

The Woliński National Park

The **Woliński National Park** is an area of outstanding natural interest: apart from its richly varied landscapes, it is the habitat of over two hundred different types of bird – the sea eagle is its emblem – and numerous animals such as red and fallow deer, wild boar, badgers, foxes and squirrels. It would take several days to cover all its many delights, but a good cross-section can be seen without venturing too far from Międzyzdroje. Alternatively, take a bus or train going in the direction of Wolin town, or a bus going towards Kamień or Kołobrzeg, and alight at any stop: you'll soon find signs enabling you to pick up one of the colour-coded trails. A good aid to walking in this region is the 1:75,000 *Zalew Szczeciński* map which has all the paths clearly marked; it's readily available from kiosks and bookstores throughout Pomerania.

The trails

Some of the most impressive scenery in the park can be seen by following the **red trail** along its eastward stretch from Międzyzdroje, which passes for a while directly along the beach. You soon come to some awesome-looking tree-crowned **dunes**, where the sand has been swept up into cliff-like formations up to 95m in height – the highest to be seen anywhere on the Baltic. Quite apart from its visual impact, much of this secluded stretch is ideal for a spot of swimming or sunbathing away from the crowds. After a few kilometres, the markers point the way upwards into the forest, and you follow a path which skirts the tiny Lake Gardno before arriving at the village of **WISEŁKA**, whose setting has the best of both worlds, being by its eponymous lake, and above a popular stretch of beach. Here there's a restaurant, snack bars, an excellent ice cream kiosk and several shops. The trail continues east through the woods and past more small lakes to its terminus at **KOŁCZEWO**, set at the head of its own lake, and the only other place along the entire route with refreshment facilities. From either here or Misełka, you can pick up a bus back to Międzyzdroje.

Also terminating at Kołczewo is the **green trail**: if you're prepared to devote a very long day to it, you could combine this with the red trail in one circular trip. You pick up the path near Międzyzdroje's train station, then ascend gently through the woods to a small **European bison reserve** (Tue–Sun 10am–6pm), set up a couple of decades ago to reintroduce the animals to this habitat. Few realize that these extraordinary beasts, which closely resemble their better-known North American counterparts, even exist. At the end of the war only twenty or so examples of this unique animal remained, but conservation has increased this figure to a much healthier 3300. The reserve is also home to a few wild deer, some eagles and a clutch of amusing wild boars who loll about in the mud, twitching their prodigious snouts. The trail continues its forest course, emerging at a group of glaciary lakes around the village of Warnowo (which can also be reached directly by train), where there's another reserve, this time for mute swans. Five lakeshores are then skirted en route to Kołczewo.

The third route, the **blue trail**, follows a southerly course from Międzyzdroje's train station, again passing through wooded countryside before arriving at the northern shore of the Szczecin Lagoon. Following this to the east, you traverse the heights of the Mokrzyckie Góry, then descend to the town of Wolin.

Finally, the western section of the **red trail** follows the coast for a couple of kilometres, then cuts straight down the narrow peninsula at the end of the island to the shore of the islet-strewn Lake Wicko Wielkie, before cutting inland to Świnoujście.

Świnoujście

The bustling fishing port, naval base and frontier post of **ŚWINOUJŚCIE** is a popular entry point into Poland, thanks to the passenger ships which sail here from Sweden, Denmark and Germany. Its international **ferry terminal**, together with both the **bus and train stations** (of which the latter is a dead end), are stranded at the end of the island of Wolin. The town centre, reached by regular car ferries on which pedestrians travel free, lies on a quite separate island across the River Świna, another part of the Odra delta, just before it opens out into the Gulf of Pomerania.

In 1945 the victorious Allies decided to allocate all of Świnoujście to Poland, rather than use the more obvious river boundary, with the result that the town was left as a tiny enclave at the end of an otherwise German island. Świnoujście is almost entirely devoid of sights: the town was very badly damaged in the war and now has a nondescript commercial centre which is nonetheless noticeably more prosperous-looking than the Polish norm. Beyond it lies the spacious **spa park**, which stretches all the way up to the one big attraction, the lovely white sandy **beach**. Nevertheless, if you're departing Poland this way (there being no other reason to come here) it makes a fittingly lively place in which to fritter away your last złotys.

Practicalities

Overlooking the harbour at ul. Armii Krajowej 5 (☎0936/2391; ③) is the **hotel** *Bałtyk*, with the basic *Bryza*, ul. Gdyńska 28 (☎0936/2491; ②), being right next to the **youth hostel** at number 26 (☎0936/5961). The **campsite**, *Relax*, is a few blocks further east at ul. Słowackiego 1 (☎0936/3912). There's little to get excited about in the way of places to **eat** and **drink**: it's best to stick to the hotels or try the *Restauracja Jantor* on ul. Slowianska 5.

The main **Orbis** office is at ul. Świerczewskiego 24 (☎0936/4411). In summer **ferries** operate along the coast to Kołobrzeg, Darłowo, Ustka and other ports: details and bookings from the Wasów marine terminal (☎0936/3006) or the *Orbis* office. Also a **hydrofoil service** runs across the lagoon to Szczecin. For services to Scandinavia, ask at the international terminal, or contact the *Polferries* office in Szczecin at ul. Kardynała Wyszyńskiego 28 (Mon–Sat 11am–4.30pm; ☎0936/34238 or 35945).

Szczecin

The largest city in northwestern Poland, with 400,000 inhabitants, **SZCZECIN** sprawls around the banks of the Odra in a tangle of bridges, cranes and dockside machinery: a city with a long maritime and shipbuilding heritage.

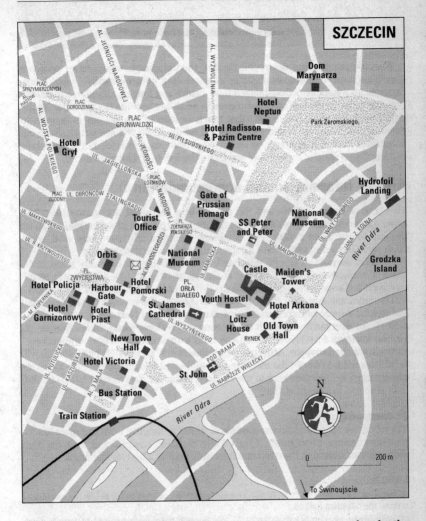

SZCZECIN

Dom Marynarza

Hotel Neptun

Park Żeromskiego

Hotel Radisson & Pazim Centre

Hotel Gryf

PLAC SPRZYMIERZONYCH

AL. PIASTÓW

AL. WOJSKA POLSKIEGO

AL. JEDNOŚCI NARODOWEJ

AL. WYZWOLENIA

PLAC ODRODZENIA

PLAC GRUNWALDZKI

UL. PIŁSUDSKIEGO

UL. JAGIELLOŃSKA

AL. JEDNOŚCI NARODOWEJ

PLAC LOTNIKÓW

UL. OBROŃCÓW STALINGRADU

PLAC ZGODNY

UL. MAKKOWSKIEGO

UL. B. KRZYWOUSTEGO

Gate of Prussian Homage

Tourist Office

PL. ŻOŁNIERZA POLSKIEGO

SS Peter and Peter

National Museum

Hydrofoil Landing

UL. WAŁY CHROBREGO

River Odra

UL. JANA Z KOLNA

Grodzka Island

Orbis

AL. NIEPODLEGŁOŚCI

National Museum

UL. MARIACKA

UL. MAŁOPOLSKA

PL. ZWYCIĘSTWA

Hotel Policja

Harbour Gate

Hotel Pomorski

PL. ORLA BIAŁEGO

Castle

Maiden's Tower

Youth Hostel

UL. M. KOPERNIKA

Hotel Garnizonowy

Hotel Piast

St. James Cathedral

UL. WYSZYŃSKIEGO

Loitz House

Hotel Arkona

Old Town Hall

RYNEK

POD BRAMĄ

New Town Hall

Hotel Victoria

UL. POTULICKA

UL. KASZUBSKA

AL. 3 MAJA

St John

UL. NABRZEŻE WIELECKI

Bus Station

Train Station

River Odra

N

0   200 m

To Świnoujście

The Slav stronghold established here in the eighth century was taken by the first Piast monarch, Mieszko I, in 967 – a point much emphasized in Polish histories. From the early twelfth century, Szczecin became the residence of a local branch of Piast princes, rulers of Western Pomerania, but German colonists were already present in force by the time the city joined the Hanseatic League in the mid-thirteenth century. The next key event was the port's capture by the Swedes in 1630, after which it was held by them for nearly a century. Sold to the Prussians in 1720, it remained under Prussian rule until 1945, when it became an outpost on Poland's newly established western frontier. With the border just west of the city limits and Berlin – for which Stettin/Szczecin used to be the port – only a couple of hours away by car or train, the German presence is still palpable.

> The **telephone code** for Szczecin is ☎091

Wartime pummelling destroyed most of the old centre, which never received quite the same restorative attention as some less controversially Polish cities. There is no Rynek or pedestrianized town centre any longer, although a distinctly Parisian radial pattern of streets survives in what has become the main part of the city. Despite it's size, there isn't that much to take in – a full day is enough to cover all the main sights and even this will hardly leave you awestruck. Szczecin is worth a visit if it happens to be on your route into Poland, but it preserves comparatively little of its heritage and lacks the feel of a rejuvenated city.

Arrival, information and accommodation

The central **train station** and the nearby **bus terminal** are located near the water's edge, from where it's a fifteen-minute walk (or a quick tram ride) north up the hill to the town centre. For details of the comprehensive **bus and tram** routes you'll need to get hold of a copy of the red Szczecin town **map**.

Szczecin **airport** – chiefly dedicated to internal flights but with some international services – is in fact located at Goleniów (☎18 28 64), 45km north of the city, with bus services to and from the *LOT* office at al. Wyzwolenia 17 (☎33 99 26).

The municipal **tourist office**, *Szczecinska Agencja Turystyczna* (*SAT*), is a small but helpful source of information located at al. Jedności Narodowej 1 (☎39253 or 42581). An alternative source of information is the **Pomerania** tourist bureau, pl. Brama Portowa 4 (☎34561), which can help with accommodation arrangements throughout the province. **Almatur**, ul. Bohaterów Warszawy 83 (☎84 40 97), will be able to tell you where the international student hotels are operating – locations are changeable. As elsewhere in the country, **Orbis**, pl. Zwycięstwa 1 (☎34 31 06), is of little use to foreign visitors.

Accommodation

There's a fair spread of **accommodation** in town, ranging from the most luxurious international-class hotels to a couple of basic hostels, and even in high summer you shouldn't have too much trouble finding a bed for the night.

CENTRAL

Arkona, ul. Panieńska 10 (☎88 02 61). Overpriced *Orbis* concrete block below the castle, just behind the old town hall. ⑦.

Garnizonowy, ul. Potulicka 1/3 (☎79 26 85). Former barracks privatized to form a good-value hotel right in the heart of town. All rooms have TVs, but showers and toilets are shared. Unguarded parking in the courtyard. ③.

Gryf, al. Wojska Polskiego 49 (☎33 45 66). Nicest of the mid-range bunch, with colourfully furnished rooms, most with private bathrooms. ⑤.

Piast, pl. Zywcięstwa 3 (☎33 66 62). Unspectacular rooms in busy central location. ⑤.

Policja, corner of pl. Zwycięstwa and ul. Potulicka (☎33 77 45). Excellent location and seemingly part of the *Garnizonowy*, but cheaper still and with a couple of self-contained rooms on offer. ③.

Pomorski, pl. Brama Portowa 4 (☎43507). Grubby-looking but ideally central. ③.

Neptun, ul. Matejki 18 (☎88 38 83). Luxury *Orbis* joint on the west side of Park Żeromskiego. ⑧.

Radisson, pl. Rodła 10 (☎59 55 95). Gleaming custom-built luxury hotel with its own casino, nightclub, fitness centre and swimming pool along with all the other upmarket facilities expected by its largely expense-account clientele. ⑨.

Victoria, pl. Batorego 2 (☎34 38 55). New upmarket hotel with neo-English decor, a restaurant and a nightclub. Rooms come with satellite TV. ⑦.

Wodojewódzkiego Domu Sportu (*WDS*), ul. Unisławy 29 (☎22 28 56). Sports hotel five minutes' walk north of pl. Grundwaldzki. ③.

OUT OF THE CENTRE

Dom Marynarza, ul. Malczewskiego 10 (☎24 00 01). Moderatly priced but well-equipped hotel just to the north of Park Żeromskiego, about 2km from the centre. ⑤.

Kolarski, al. Wojska Polskiego 246 (☎79 26 85). Sports hotel on the edge of town, 5km northwest of centre on the route of trams #1 and #9. ③.

Pensionat FRDL, ul. Marii Sklodowskiej-Curie 4 (☎70472). Just off al. Wojska Polskiego about 4km northwest of the centre, this large guest house makes a friendly alternative to a hotel. Tram #9. ③.

Reda, ul. Cukrowa 2 (☎82 24 61). The third *Orbis* hotel, situated 2km southwest of the centre. ⑦.

Szmaragd, ul. Kopalniana (☎60 81 32). The hotel to go for if you want to stay somewhere more reminiscent of the countryside than the city: it's right by a lake in the suburb of Zdroje, 9km southeast of the centre, and a one-kilometre walk southwest of the suburban station of that name. ⑤.

HOSTELS AND CAMPSITES

Ul. Unisławy 26 (☎23 25 66). Main hostel, on the top floor of a school building; open all year. Take tram #2 or #3 to pl. Kilińskiego, north of the centre.

Pl. Monte Cassino 19a (☎22 47 61). Comfortable and friendly summer-only hostel situated just southwest of the centre, past the south end of ul. M. Koperika.

PTTK Camping, ul. Przestrzenna 24 (☎61 32 64). In Dąbie, 3km east of town – take the local train to Szczecin-Dąbie station. Open May–Sept; tent space and chalets available.

The City

The medieval **Old Town**, laid out on a slope on the left bank of the Odra, was heavily bombed in the last war. Restoration work on the showpiece buildings went on until the 1980s, with the gaps either left vacant or filled by drab modern housing. While you're walking around you'll notice very few people and a distinct lack of shops in this area; commercial life shifted west a kilometre to a part of town which survived in better shape. This was laid out towards the end of last century in the Parisian manner, with broad boulevards radiating out from pl. Grunwaldzki, the vicarious heart of Szczecin.

The commercial centre

Ascending ul. Dworcowa from the train station, you soon see some of the massive late nineteenth- and early twentieth-century Prussian buildings so characteristic of the heart of the city. Commanding the heights is the bulky red brick frame of the neo-Gothic **New Town Hall**, now the seat of the maritime authorities. In the square below is a fountain in the form of an anchor, symbolizing Szczecin's indebtedness to the sea; you'll see plenty more real anchors as well as the odd propeller scattered around town commemorating the town's seafaring past. Across the street, steps lead up to the former **Savings Bank**, a Jugendstil fantasy whose slender tower and decorative facades seem to echo the faintly oriental gothic flavour of that architectural style.

At the top of ul. Dworcowa is the traffic-engulfed square named after the **Harbour Gate** (Brama Portowa), not so much a gate as two ornate Baroque gables linked by a long hall, built by the Prussians in 1725 to mark their purchase of the city. Immediately to the west of the gateway is the largest and busiest of the squares, pl. Zwycięstwa, on which stand a couple of turn-of-the-century churches which have successively served the local garrison. Leading off to the north is al. Niepodległości, the city's main thoroughfare, on whose western side stand two more of the big Prussian public buildings – the Post Office, still fulfilling its original function, and the administration building of the Pomeranian district, which has been taken over by the displaced Savings Bank.

On pl. Rodła, an intersection on al. Wyzwolenia, the northern continuation of al. Niepodległości, the **Pazim Centre**, a hotel, shopping, banking and business complex of steel-framed, blue glass buildings, has been thrown up since the fall of communism. So far no other modern development has matched the clutch of glass rotundas and blocks giving the centre a rather showy but anachronistic look, like a piece of downtown Chicago dropped into town.

The Cathedral and around

Heading east from the Harbour Gate to the river, ul. Kardynała Wyszyńskiego brings you to the **Cathedral of St James** (Św. Jakuba), a massive Gothic church grievously damaged in 1945, and the subject of over-expedient restoration (including some concrete windows) which was only completed in 1982, an event celebrated by its elevation to the seat of a bishop the following year. The oldest parts of the church date back to the fourteenth century and are the work of Hinrich Brunsberg, the finest of the specialist brickwork architects of the Baltic lands. The hall design he used here is notable for its consummate simplicity. In the middle of the following century, the single **tower** was constructed to replace the previous pair; this is now only half of its prewar height of 120m, having been rebuilt minus the spire and further trivialized with the addition of a clock. Its five-and-a-half-tonne bell now hangs in a frame outside, as does a memorial to Carl Loewe, one of the great ballad composers and singers of last century, who was for several decades the church's organist and music director. Today the building's profile is rather plain, with it's bulky exterior best appreciated coming up ul. Kardynała Wyszyńskiego from the river, although to the rear of the church you'll find a pretty little Gothic rectory.

On pl. Orła Białego, the square on the north side of the cathedral, is the Baroque **Pod Globusem Palace**, originally built for the ruler of the Prussian province of Pomerania and now used as the medical academy. Across from it, part obscured by a willow tree, stands an intriguing **fountain** adorned with the eponymous white eagle (*biały orzeł*) overlooking a group of satyrs who gurgle stoically into an enormous clam. Hidden among the trees at the cathedral end of the square is another piece of Baroque frippery, a statue of the goddess Flora.

The lower town

Down ul. Wyszyńskiego towards the river, you come on the right-hand side to the oldest surviving building in Szczecin, the Franciscan **Monastery of St John** (Św. Jana), part of which dates back to the thirteenth century. It's distinctive feature is its geometric inconsistency showing that medieval builders could and did get their calculations wrong. The chancel is an irregular decagon, yet has a seven-part vault, while the later nave adjoins at an oblique angle, its off-centre vaulting a vain attempt to align the bays with the aisle windows. It's a rare example of a building that was never rebuilt properly but never quite collapsed: looking inside you can see the alarmingly warped columns braced by a network of steel girders.

Far more distinguished though equally skewed, is the attractively gabled **Old Town Hall**, now rather lost in the concrete blocks and vacant lots of the Stary Rynek. It's an artful reconstruction of the fourteenth-century original, probably designed by Hinrich Brunsberg, which was flattened in the war. The restorers opted to return it to something like its original appearance, preserving only one Baroque gable while presumably managing to artfully incorporate the lopsidedness of an aged building. These days the building serves as a small **Museum of Local History** (Wed & Fri 9am–3.30pm, Tues & Thur 10am–5pm, Sat & Sun 10am–4pm), a lacklustre and generally ignored collection of relics where somnolent attendants illuminate the rooms as you go.

The only burgher's mansion still standing in Szczecin is the mid-sixteenth-century **Loitz House**, just uphill at the corner of ul. Kurkowa, a tower-type residence of a prominent local banking and trading dynasty. Further down the same street are two other rare medieval survivors, a grange and the municipal weigh house. Of the once formidable fifteenth-century fortification system, almost nothing remains save the appropriately graceful **Maiden's Tower**, now stranded between the castle and a network of interchanges funnelling the city's traffic over the river.

The Castle

By now you'll have spotted the **Castle** of the Pomeranian princes commanding the river from its hillside perch. A Slav fortified settlement on this spot was replaced in the mid-fourteenth century by a stone structure, the oldest section of the current building. The whole thing was given a Renaissance enlargement in the late sixteenth century, and again remodelled in the 1720s. Princes and dukes aside, the building has been used as a brewery, office block, barracks and anti-aircraft emplacement – the last function being the direct cause of its flattening in an air raid in 1944. Reconstruction continued into the 1980s, since when it's been turned into a museum and cultural centre. Much of the building is closed to the public, the **museum** (Tues–Sun 10am–4pm) occupying two vaults, displaying a few repaired sarcophagi as well as photographs of the castle's restoration from postwar ruin.The chapel on the ground floor of the north wing is now a concert hall. In the east wing, much of the exterior decoration has been reworked with the addition of a few more *faux* concrete windows and the castle's distinctive clock; most of this section is now occupied by a cinema and other cultural facilities. If you're here in summer, you might get to hear an open-air concert in the castle courtyard.

After a visit to the castle **café** – a popular rendezvous point – it's worth climbing the two hundred or so steps up the **belltower** for the view over the city, port and surroundings.You'll notice a striking absence of industrial chimneys; instead church spires and dockside cranes pierce the skyline.

The rest of the centre

Immediately to the west of the castle is ul. Farna, where the residence of the commandant formerly stood. This was the birthplace in 1729 of Sophie von

Anhalt-Zerbst, a princess of a very minor German aristocratic line who has gone down in history as **Empress Catherine the Great of Russia**. A character of extreme ruthlessness – she deposed her own husband, and was probably behind his subsequent murder – her reputation has always been a matter of controversy. Among her "achievements" was a considerable imperialistic expansion, one manifestation of which was a leading role in the three Partitions which wiped Poland off the map. That her native city is now Polish is a truly delicious irony.

A couple of blocks further west is ul. Staromłyńska, at the corner of which rises an elegant Baroque palace, formerly the Pomeranian parliament and now home of a section of the **National Museum** (Tues & Thurs 10am–5pm, Wed & Fri 9am–3.30pm, Sat & Sun 10am–4pm). The ground floor features several important Polish artists, most notably Waliszewski, Zofia Stryjenska and the broodingly introspective Jacek Malczewski. Upstairs there's an even mushier collection of paintings by local artists on sea-based themes, although the fine Baroque-era furniture is worth an admiring look. Older works are displayed in the annexe across the street. On the ground floor here is an impressive display of medieval Pomeranian **sculpture**. Highlights include the thirteenth-century columns, topped with delicately carved capitals, from the monastery of Kołbacz; a monumental wooden sacromenteum of the same period from Wolin, and several expressively carved and painted mid-fifteenth century triptychs from Pomerania. Upstairs, later sections emphasize Polish painters, with a token German work occasionally thrown in.

Across the broad open space of pl. Żołnierza Polskiego is the Baroque **Gate of Prussian Homage** (or Royal Gate), whose design, with reliefs of military trophies, echo those of the Harbour Gate. Its interior is now used for changing exhibitions of the work of contemporary painters and photographers. Facing it to the east is the beguiling fourteenth-century **SS Peter and Paul**, a Gothic church built on the site of one established by Polish missionaries in the early twelfth century. In a rich ensemble of original ornamental detail the most striking elements are the seventeenth-century memorial tablets, the German inscriptions reminding you of the city's Teutonic heritage, and the unusual wooden vaulting.

On the north side of the church, ul. Małopolska leads to **Wały Chrobrego**, a showpiece boulevard lined with towering prewar German public buildings. One of these houses a branch of the **National Museum** (same hours). As soon as you step in you know it's a much livelier exhibition than that at the museum in ul. Staromłyńska. Here they've gone to town on the seafaring Slavs and Celts, with graphic displays from the Stone, Iron and Bronze Ages. Huge arrow-covered maps delineate bygone migrations, while upstairs a gallery is obediently devoted to the objects from classical antiquity. However, most impressive and unexpected is an inspired ethnographic exhibition with detailed dioramas of a Dogon village in Mali, a shoreside equivalent from the Ivory Coast and, in the next room, some creepy West African statues, fetishes and carved masks. On the next floor, a Papuan village gets the same treatment, although the budget or the enthusiasm seems to have waned at the rather feeble rendition of a Buddhist temple.

A block to the north of the museum lies the **Park Żeromskiego**, the only significant stretch of park in the centre.

The harbour

Szczecin is one of the largest ports on the Baltic, with a highly developed shipping industry, and you'll appreciate the essence of the city more fully if you take a **boat trip** round the port and harbour. Excursions, lasting just over an hour, leave from the **Dworzec Morski** terminal, northeast of Wały Chrobrego. Ask here about the boat and hydrofoil services across the vast Szczecin Lagoon to Świnoujście. The border with Germany cuts across the middle of the lagoon, but the demise of the GDR means this is no longer a source of tension for local sailing enthusiasts. It's also worth crossing the Odra to **Łasztownia**, a free port constructed at the end of last century, which still preserves many grand buildings of that epoch.

The outskirts

Despite the patchily built-up character of its centre, Szczecin has plenty of stretches of greenery, which are ideal for a quick break from the urban bustle, particularly on summer evenings. Just to the north of the centre is the **Park Kasprowicza**, which can be reached by tram #1 or #9. It's best known for the huge triple eagle monument made to commemorate the fortieth anniversary of the outbreak of World War II, symbolizing the three generations of Poles who lost their lives. Across the narrow Lake Rusałka is the **Dendrological Garden**, which contains over two hundred species of trees and shrubs, including a host of exotic varieties. Continuing on either of the same trams to the terminus, you arrive at **Park Głębokie**, centred on the sausage-shaped lake of the same name, a small part of which is developed, the rest preserved in rustic tranquillity.

The most distinctive park in the city is that in the eastern suburb of **Zdroje**, reached either by a slow train, or buses #A or #B. Here you'll find a number of hiking trails, a couple of restaurants, and the **Emerald Lake** (Jezioro Szmaragdowe), which was created in the 1920s by flooding a former quarry; you can go for a swim here, or simply admire the play of light on its deep green waters.

One train stop further east is **DĄBIE**, for centuries a separate town, and one formerly prosperous enough to have been a member of the Hanseatic League. It's set at the mouth of the River Regalica, part of the Odra's delta, at the head of the Dąbie Lagoon, a miniature version of the Szczecin Lagoon immediately to the north. The attractive waterfront is a popular sailing area, while the town centre boasts the Gothic Church of St Mary, an archetypal example of Baltic brickwork, and the Renaissance Princes' Palace.

Eating, drinking and entertainment

The gastronomic situation in Szczecin has improved enormously since the fall of communism. At least for the time being, the city has the best of both worlds, as some good old-fashioned **milk bars, snack bars and restaurants** have managed to survive alongside a host of new ventures (not all of which can be expected to last), including a number of ethnic places plus the ubiquitous Westernized **fast-food joints**. There's certainly no longer the old problem about eating late, as many places stay open until midnight. If you discount the ghastly hotel nightspots, **bars** are in shorter supply, but the students in town provide some term-time action.

Restaurants

Argentyna, al. Wojska Polskiego 39. Plush new establishment specializing in huge grilled steaks, Argentine-style.

Balaton, pl. Lotników 3. Respectable and reasonably priced offerings of Hungarian food and wine.

Bajka, ul. Niepodległości 30. Upmarket restaurant/bar offering cordial service in the hunting lodge-style restaurant and awful live music nightly.

Bistro 2000, al. Wojska Polskiego 21. Extremely popular bistro with a varied and esoteric menu featuring French, Italian and Chinese dishes, plus delicious desserts.

Café Castellari, 43/1 al. Jedności Narodowej. Vinyl and chrome coffee bar popular with young trendies into good cappuccinos and ice cream.

Chief, pl. Grunwaldzki (☎34-37-65). Probably the single most recommendable restaurant in Szczecin, with tasteful decoration, a good ambience, and a wide selection of sea and river fish specialities, plus a limited choice of other fare.

Gryf, al. Wojska Polskiego 49. Better than average hotel restaurant.

Hai-Phong, ul. Szarotki 16. Vietnamese restaurant at the far northeastern corner of Park Żeromskiego, just a couple of minutes' walk from the ferry terminal.

King, Małkowskiego 27. Elegant and centrally located restaurant with dishes from 12zł upwards.

Pod Muzami, pl. Żołnierza Polskiego 2. Long-established restaurant in in the quiet old part of town.

Riga, al. Piastów 16. Latvian restaurant, with traditional Polish and Lithuanian dishes also on offer, on the main boulevard west of the centre.

Snack bars

Jedyna, al. Jedności Narodowej 42. Decent and very cheap milk bar.

Rendy, Bolesława Krzywoustego 71. *Bas cuisine* cafeteria knocking out all your favourite Polish food at minimal prices.

Rybarex, ul. Obrońców Stalingradu 5a. Fish bar with a wide and adventurous selection of dishes: ideal for fast lunchtime service.

Turysta, ul. Obrońców Stalingradu 6. Milk bar with a large menu of classic homely Polish food.

Bars and cafés

Duet, ul. ks. Bogusława 1/2. Relaxing café with a wide choice of teas, cakes and ice creams.

U Wyszaka, Stary Rynek. Trendy upmarket hang-out in the old town hall cellars.

Royal Pub, pl. Żołnierza Polskiego 66. Something of a rarity in Poland: a self-conscious imitation of a London tavern.

Zamkowa, ul. Rycerska. *Kawiarnia* inside the castle.

Nightlife

There are a number of **student clubs**, the top venues being the *Pod Wieża* at ul. Rybacka 1, and the *Kontrasty* at ul. Wawrzyniaka 7; details of where the current action is can be had from the *Almatur* office. The trendiest **disco** is the perversely named *Miami Nice*, ul. Bohaterów Warszawy 35.

The *Filharmonia Szczecińska*, pl. Armii Krajowey 1 (☎22 12 52), has a regular programme of **classical music** concerts, while operas and operettas are sometimes performed in the castle (☎88802 for information). Szczecin's main **theatre** is the *Teatr Polski*, ul. Swarożyca 5 (☎22 16 21), while puppet shows are held at the *Teatr Lalek Pieciuga*, ul. Kaszubska 9 (☎45274). You'll find a cluster of multiplex **cinemas** around the south end of al. Wojska Polskiego.

Stargard Szczeciński

Some 35km southeast of Szczecin, on the Bydgoszcz road, lies **STARGARD SZCZECIŃSKI**, the town which replaced Szczecin as capital of Pomerania for the duration of the Swedish occupation of the western part of the province. Situated on the River Ina, a tributary of the Odra, Stargard owed its early development to its position on the old trade routes to and from the Baltic. Nowadays primarily an industrial centre, it suffered severe damage in World War II, but most of the principal monuments of the medieval Old Town survived. Carefully restored, they give ample evidence of a prosperous past, and are of sufficient interest to warrant a visit, despite being surrounded by a depressing number of modern concrete buildings.

The Old Town

Arriving at the train station, or the bus station to its rear, it's just a few minutes' walk east down ul. Kardynała Wyszyńskiego to the **Old Town**. This nestles behind fifteenth-century brick walls some four metres thick, of which substantial sections remain, including five towers and four gateways. The shady **Park Chrobrego** has been laid out as a promenade along the western side, containing the longest surviving portion of the ramparts. One standing tower in unusually good condition is in fact a nineteenth-century water tower mimicking the Gothic vernacular, with the similarly styled **Church of SS Peter and Paul** cowering nearby among the trees. Another uninterrupted stretch can be seen round to the north, at the back of the genuine Gothic **Church of St Joseph**, whose ninety-metre tower is now the highest in Pomerania, given the reduced height of St James' Cathedral in Szczecin. Following ul. Chrobrego downhill from here, you come to the River Ina, where down to the left stands the most impressive survivor of the fortification system, the **Mill Gate** (Brama Młyńska). This is a covered bridge under which boats could pass, protected by a mighty pair of battlemented octagonal towers topped with sharply pointed steeples.

The **Rynek**, which occupies an unusually off-centre location towards the south-eastern end of the Old Town, about five minutes' walk from the Mill Gate, has a number of impressive reconstructed burghers' houses. At the corner stands the renovated **Town Hall**, a plain Renaissance structure featuring a superbly curvaceous gable adorned with colourful terracotta tracery. Next to it is the **Guard House**, whose open arcades and loggia suggest the Mediterranean rather than the Baltic. Together with the **Weigh House** next door, it houses the local **museum** (Tues–Sun 10am–4pm, May–Sept Tues and weekends till 5pm).

Next to the town hall stands the magnificent **Church of Our Lady**, one of the most original and decorative examples of the brickwork Gothic style found in the Baltic lands, probably the work of Hinrich Brunsberg and commissioned around 1400. The two towers, with their glazed green and white ceramics, can be seen from all over the town: the southern one, topped with a fancy gable and flanked by a luscious coat of ivy, resembles a great tower-house; its higher northern counterpart is a truly bravura creation, topped by four chimney-like turrets and a great central octagon, itself crowned in the Baroque era with a two-storey copper lantern. As a fittingly small-scale contrast, the east end and the protruding octagonal chapel dedicated to the Virgin show off the decorative potential of carved brick. The interior was impressively repainted in the nineteenth century and features an earlier and quite over-the-top illusionist altarpiece.

Practicalities

For **tourist information**, try the *Orbis* office on the main square, Rynek Staromeijski 5 (☎092/77 26 45). **Accommodation** options are limited to the

PTTK **hostel** at ul. Kuśnierzy 5 (☎092/77 31 91; ②–③) and the *Hotel Staromiejski*, a converted apartment building by the Mill Gate on ul Spiichrzowa 2 (☎092/77 22 23; ③). Places to **eat** and **drink** are more prolific in the central area – try *Basztowa*, ul. Chrobrego 7a, the *Ratuszowa* in the Rynek's shopping centre or the *Pasadena* pub-café in the town hall's basement. There's also a Vietnamese restaurant, the *Huong Nam* on ul. Chrobrego.

travel details

Trains

Bydgoszcz to Częstochowa (5 daily; 5hr); Gdańsk (hourly; 2hr); Kołobrzeg (8 daily; 4hr 30min); Kraków (3 daily; 7–8hr); Łódź Kaliska (11 daily; 3–4hr); Poznań (11 daily; 2–4hr); Szczecin (2–3 daily; 4–6hr); Toruń (hourly; 40min); Warsaw (6 daily; 4–5hr).

Kalisz to Białystok (1 daily; 8hr); Jelenia Góra (4 daily; 5–6hr 30min); Legnica (5 daily; 4hr–5hr); Leszno (3 daily; 2hr 30 min); Lublin (3 daily; 7hr); Łódź (half-hourly; 1hr 30min–2hr); Poznań (6 daily; 3hr); Szczecin (2 daily; 6hr); Warsaw (11 daily; 3hr–4hr 30min); Wrocław (14 daily; 2hr–3hr 30min); Zielona Góra (3 daily; 4–5hr).

Kamień Pomorski to Szczecin (3 daily; 2hr 30min).

Kołobrzeg to Bydgoszcz (6 daily; 5hr); Gdańsk (4 daily; 4–5hr); Koszalin (9 daily; 1hr); Szczecin (4 daily; 4–5hr); Warsaw (8 daily; 8–10hr).

Leszno to Białystok (1 daily; 12hr); Bydgoszcz (5 daily; 3hr 30min–4hr 30min); Gdańsk (6 daily; 5hr 30min–6hr 30min); Jelenia Góra (4 daily; 4hr–4hr 30min); Kalisz (3 daily; 2hr 30min); Katowice (6 daily; 4hr–5hr); Kraków (4 daily; 6hr 30min); Łódź (3 daily; 4hr); Olsztyn (3 daily 6–8hr; couchettes); Opole (9 daily; 2hr 30min–3hr 30min); Poznań (half-hourly; 1hr–1hr 30min); Przemyśl (1 daily; 10hr 30min; couchettes); Rzeszów (1 daily; 9hr; couchettes); Słupsk (2 daily; 7hr 30min–8hr 30min; couchettes); Szczecin (7 daily; 5–6hr); Świnoujście (1 daily; 6hr); Toruń (2 daily; 3–4hr); Wałbrzych (4 daily; 3–4hr); Warsaw (2 daily; 6hr); Wrocław (26 daily; 1hr 30min–2hr); Zakopane (1 daily; 10hr; couchettes); Zielona Góra (2 daily; 2hr).

Poznań to Białystok (1 daily; 10hr 30min; couchettes); Bydgoszcz (12 daily; 2hr–2hr 30 min); Częstochowa (8 daily; 4hr); Gdańsk (8 daily; 4hr); Gniezno (hourly; 55min); Inowrocław (12 daily; 1hr 50min); Jelenia Góra (5 daily; 5–6hr); Kalisz (6 daily; 3hr); Katowice (15 daily; 5–6hr); Kołobrzeg (5 daily; 5hr); Kraków (8 daily; 6hr 35min); Leszno (half-hourly, 1hr–1hr 30min); Łódź (7 daily; 4–5hr); Olsztyn (4 daily; 4hr 30min–6hr); Opole (9 daily; 3hr 30min–4hr 30min); Przemyśl (3 daily; 11–13hr; couchettes); Rzeszów (3 daily; 10–11hr; couchettes); Słupsk (5 daily; 5–6hr); Szczecin (18 daily; 3–4hr); Świnoujście (7 daily; 4–5hr); Toruń (8 daily; 2hr 30min–3hr); Warsaw (20 daily; 4–5hr); Wrocław (26 daily; 2hr–3hr 30min); Zakopane (2 daily; 11–13hr; couchettes); Zielona Góra (6 daily; 2hr 30min–3hr). Also **international connections** to Berlin, Moscow, Riga and St Petersburg.

Słupsk to Gdańsk (12 daily; 2–3hr); Kołobrzeg (4 daily; 2–2hr 30min); Koszalin (hourly; 1hr); Szczecin (9 daily; 3–4hr); local trains to Ustka (via Sławno) and Darłowo.

Świnoujście (all via Szczecin) to Kraków (2 daily; 12–13hr; couchettes); Poznań (7 daily; 4–5hr); Szczecin (18 daily; 2–2hr 30min); Warsaw (3 daily; 8–10hr; couchettes).

Szczecin to Bydgoszcz (3 daily; 4–5hr); Gdańsk (7 daily; 5–6hr); Kołobrzeg (6 daily; 3–4hr); Kraków (6 daily; 10–11hr); Łódź (4 daily; 6–7hr); Poznań (20 daily; 3–4hr); Słupsk (9 daily; 3–4hr); Świnoujście (20 daily; 2hr–2hr 30min); Warsaw (7 daily; 5–8hr; couchettes).

Szczecinek to Czaplinek (8 daily; 1hr); Kołobrzeg (4 daily; 2hr–2hr 30min).

Buses

Bydgoszcz to Toruń, Chojnice and Szczecinek.

Gniezno to Gąsawa and Żnin (for Biskupin), Mogilno, Żnin/Bydgoszcz.

Kamień Pomorski to Świnoujście, Wolin, Szczecin and Kołobrzeg.

Kołobrzeg to the coast (Sarbinowo, Mielno), Kamień Pomorski and Świnoujście.

Leszno to Gołuchów/Kalisz.

Łeba to Słupsk and Gdańsk.

Poznań to Kórnik/Rogalin/Mosina, Gniezno and Kalisz.

Słupsk to Darłowo, Ustka and Koszalin.
Szczecin to Stargard Szczeciński, Wolin and Świnoujście.

Szczecinek to Czaplinek, Słupsk and Szczecin.
Świnoujście to Wolin, Międzyzdroje, Szczecin, Kołobrzeg and Trzebiatów.

PART THREE

THE

CONTEXTS

THE
HISTORICAL
FRAMEWORK

No other European country has had so chequered a history as Poland. At its mightiest, it has been a huge commonwealth stretching deep into what is now the CIS; at its nadir, it has been a nation that existed only as an ideal, its neighbours having on two occasions conspired to wipe it off the map. Yet, for all this, a distinctive Polish culture has survived and developed without interruption for more than a millennium.

THE BEGINNINGS

The great plain that is present-day Poland, stretching from the River Odra (or Oder) in the west all the way to the Russian steppes, has been inhabited since the Stone Age. For thousands of years it was home to numerous tribes – some nomadic, others settlers – whose traces have made Poland a particularly fruitful land for archeologists. Lying beyond the frontiers of the Roman Empire, it did not sustain anything more socially advanced than a tribal culture until a relatively late date.

The exact period when this plain was first settled by **Slav** tribes is uncertain, but it may have been as late as the eighth century. Although diffuse, the various Slav groups shared a common culture – certainly to a far

greater extent than is true of the Germanic tribes to the west – and the Polish language can be said to have existed before the Polish state.

It was the **Polonians** (the "people of the open fields"), based on the banks of the River Warta between Poznań and Gniezno, who were ultimately responsible for the forging of a recognizable nation, which thereafter bore their name. From the early ninth century, they were ruled by the **Piast dynasty**, whose early history is shrouded in legend but emerges into something more substantial with the beginnings of recorded history in the second half of the tenth century.

In 965, the Piast **Mieszko I** married the sister of the Duke of Bohemia and underwent public baptism, thus placing himself under the protection of the papacy. Mieszko's motives appear to have been political: Otto the Great, the Holy Roman Emperor, had extended Germany's border to the Odra and would have had little difficulty in justifying a push east against a pagan state. By 990, Mieszko had succeeded in uniting his tribal area, henceforth known as Wielkopolska (Great Poland), with that of the Vistulanian tribe, which took the name of Małopolska (Little Poland). Silesia, settled by yet another Slav tribe, became the third component of this embryonic Polish state.

Mieszko's policies were carried to their logical conclusion by his warrior son **Bolesław the Brave**. In 1000, the Emperor Otto III was despatched by the pope to pay tribute to the relics of the Czech saint, Adalbert, which Bolesław had acquired. During his stay, the emperor crowned Bolesław with his own crown, thus renouncing German designs on Polish territory. Subsequently, Bolesław established control over Pomerania, Kujawy and Mazovia; he also gained and lost Bohemia and began Poland's own easterly drive, pushing as far as Kiev. The name "Poland" now came into general use, and its status as a fully fledged kingdom was underlined by Bolesław's decision to undergo a second coronation in 1022.

PIAST POLAND

By the middle of the eleventh century, Małopolska had become the centre of the nation's affairs and Kraków had replaced Gniezno as capital, owing to Wielkopolska's vulnerability to the expansionist Czechs and Germans. Political authority was in any case overshadowed by the **power of the Church**: when Bishop Stanisław of Kraków was murdered in 1079 on the orders of Bolesław the Generous, the clergy not only gained a national saint whose cult quickly spread, but also succeeded in dethroning the king.

In the early twelfth century, centralized monarchical power made a comeback under **Bolesław the Wrymouth**, who regained Pomerania – which had become an independent duchy – and repulsed German designs on Silesia. However, he undid his lifetime's work by his decision to divide his kingdom among his sons: for the rest of the century and beyond, Poland lacked central authority and was riven by feuds as successive members of the Piast dynasty jostled for control over the key provinces. Pomerania fell to Denmark, while Silesia began a long process of fragmentation, becoming increasingly Germanic.

In 1225 Duke Konrad of Mazovia, under threat from the heathen Prussians, Jacwingians and Lithuanians on his eastern border, invited the **Teutonic Knights**, a quasi-monastic German military order, to help him secure his frontiers. The Knights duly based themselves in Chełmno, and by 1283 they had effectively eradicated the Prussians. Emerging as the principal military power in mainland Europe, the Knights built up a theocratic state defended by some of the most awesome castles ever built, ruthlessly turning on their former hosts in the process. They captured the great port of Gdańsk in 1308, renaming it Danzig and developing it into one of Europe's richest mercantile cities. At the same time, German peasants were encouraged to settle on the fertile agricultural land all along the Baltic. Poland was left cut off from the sea, with its trading routes severely weakened as a result.

If the Teutonic Knights brought nothing but disaster to the Polish nation, the effects of the **Tartar invasions** of 1241–42 were more mixed. Although the Poles were decisively defeated at the Battle of Legnica, the Tartars' crushing of the Kiev-based Russian empire paved the way for Polish expansion east into White and Red Ruthenia (the forerunners of Belarus and Ukraine), whose principalities were often linked to Poland by dynastic marriages. On the down side, the defeat spelt the beginning of the end for Silesia as part of Poland. It gradually split into eighteen tiny duchies under the control of Bohemia, then the most powerful part of the Holy Roman Empire.

KAZIMIERZ THE GREAT

It was only under the last Piast king, **Kazimierz the Great** (1333–70), that central political authority was firmly re-established in Poland. Kraków took on some aspects of its present appearance during his reign, being embellished with a series of magnificent buildings to substantiate its claim to be a great European capital. It was also made the seat of a university, the first in the country and before long one of the most prestigious on the continent. Kazimierz's achievements in **domestic policy** went far beyond the symbolic: he codified Poland's laws, created a unified administrative structure with a governor responsible for each province, and introduced a new silver currency.

With regard to **Poland's frontiers**, Kazimierz was a supreme pragmatist. He secured his borders with a line of stone castles and formally recognized Bohemia's control over Silesia in return for a renunciation of its claim to the Polish crown. More reluctantly, he accepted the existence of the independent state of the Teutonic Knights, even though that meant Poland was now landlocked. To compensate, he extended his territories east into Red Ruthenia and Podolia, which meant that, although the Catholic Church retained its prominent role, the country now had sizeable Eastern Orthodox and Armenian minorities.

Even more significant was Kazimierz's encouragement of **Jews**, who had been the victims of pogroms all over Europe, often being held responsible for the Black Death. A law of 1346 specifically protected them against persecution in Poland and was a major factor in Poland's centuries-long position as the home of the largest community of world Jewry.

THE JAGIELLONIANS

On Kazimierz's death, the crown passed to his nephew Louis of Anjou, King of Hungary, but this royal union was short-lived, as the Poles chose Louis' younger daughter **Jadwiga** to succeed him in 1384, whereas her sister ascended the Hungarian throne. This event was important for two reasons. First, it was an assertion of power on the part of the aristocracy and the beginnings of the move towards an elected monarchy. Second, it led soon afterwards to the most important and enduring alliance in Polish history – with **Lithuania**, whose Grand Duke, **Jagiełło**, married Jadwiga in 1386. Europe's last pagan nation, Lithuania, had resisted the Teutonic Knights and developed into an expansionist state which now stretched from its Baltic homeland all the way to the Crimea.

After Jadwiga's death in 1399, Jagiełło ruled the two nations alone for the next 45 years, founding the **Jagiellonian dynasty** – which was to remain in power until 1572 – with the offspring of his subsequent marriage. One of the first benefits of the union between the two countries was a military strength capable of taking the offensive against the Teutonic Knights, and at the **Battle of Grunwald** in 1410, the Order was defeated, beginning its long and slow decline. A more decisive breakthrough came as a result of the **Thirteen Years' War** of 1454–66. By the Treaty of Toruń, the Knights' territory was partitioned: Danzig became an independent city-state, run by a merchant class of predominantly German, Dutch and Flemish origins, but accepting the Polish king as its nominal overlord; the remainder of the Knights' heartlands around the Wisła (Vistula) became subject to Poland under the name of Royal Prussia; and the Order was left only with the eastern territory thereafter known as Ducal Prussia or East Prussia, where it established its new headquarters in the city of Königsberg.

Towards the end of the fifteenth century, Poland and Lithuania began to face new dangers from the east. First to threaten were the Crimean Tartars, whose menace prompted the creation of the first Polish standing army. A far more serious threat – one which endured for several hundred years – came from the **Muscovite tsars**, the self-styled protectors of the Orthodox faith who aimed to "liberate" the Ruthenian principalities and rebuild the Russian empire which had been destroyed by the Mongol Tartars. The Jagiellonians countered by building up their power in the west. The Bohemian crown was acquired by clever politicking in 1479 after the religious struggles of the Hussite Wars; that of Hungary followed in 1491. However, neither of these unions managed to last.

THE RENAISSANCE AND REFORMATION

The spread of **Renaissance** ideas in Poland – greatly facilitated by the country's Church connections with Italy – was most visibly manifested in the large number of Italianate buildings constructed throughout the country, but science and learning also prospered under native Polish practitioners such as Nicolaus Copernicus.

This period saw a collective muscle-flexing exercise by the Polish nobility (*szlachta*). In 1493, the parliament or **Sejm** was established, gaining the sole right to enact legislation in 1505 and gradually making itself an important check on monarchical power.

The **Reformation** had a far greater impact on Poland than is often admitted by Catholic patriots. Its most telling manifestation came in 1525, with the final collapse of the Teutonic Order when the Grand Master, Albrecht von Hohenzollern, decided to accept the new Lutheran doctrines. Their state was converted into a secular duchy under the Polish crown but with full internal autonomy – an arrangement that was to be disastrous for Poland in the long term, but which removed any lingering military strength from the Order. Lutheranism also took a strong hold in Danzig and the German-dominated cities of Royal Prussia, while the more radical Calvinism won many converts among the Lithuanian nobility. Poland also became home for a number of refugee sects: along with the acceptance already extended to the Jewish and Orthodox faiths, this added up to a degree of religious tolerance unparalleled elsewhere in Europe.

THE REPUBLIC OF NOBLES

Lacking an heir, the last of the Jagiellonians, **Sigismund August**, spent his final years trying to forge an alliance strong enough to withstand the ever-growing might of Moscow. The result of his negotiations was the 1569 **Union of Lublin**, whereby Poland, Royal Prussia, Livonia (subsequently part of Latvia) and Lithuania were formally merged into a commonwealth. In the same year the Sejm moved to Warsaw, a more central location for the capital of this new agglomeration; its capital status became official in 1596.

On the death of Sigismund August in 1572, the Royal Chancellor, Jan Zamoyski, presided over negotiations which led to the creation of the so-called **Republic of Nobles** – thenceforth kings were to be elected by an assembly of the entire nobility, from the great magnates down to holders of tiny impoverished estates. On the one hand this was a major democratic advance, in that it enfranchised about ten percent of the population, by far the largest proportion of voters in any European country; but on the other hand it marked a strengthening of a **feudalistic social system**. Capitalism, then developing in other European countries, evolved only in those cities with a strong German or Jewish burgher class (predominantly in Royal Prussia), which remained isolated from the main power structures of Polish society.

In 1573, the Frenchman Henri Valois was chosen as the first elected monarch, and, as was the case with all his successors, was forced to sign a document which reduced him to a managerial servant of the nobility. The nobles also insisted on their **Right of Resistance** – a licence to overthrow a king who had fallen from favour. The Sejm had to be convened at two-yearly intervals, while all royal taxes, declarations of war and foreign treaties were subject to ratification by the nobles.

Although candidates for the monarchy had to subscribe to Catholicism, the religious freedom which already existed was underpinned by the **Compact of Warsaw** of 1573, guaranteeing the constitutional equality of all religions. However, the Counter-Reformation left only a few Protestant strongholds in Poland: a large section of the aristocracy was re-converted, while others who had recently switched from Orthodoxy to Calvinism were persuaded to change allegiance once more. The Orthodox Church was further weakened by the schism of 1596, leading to the creation of the Uniate Church, which recognized the authority of Rome. Thus Poland gradually became a fervently Catholic nation once more.

The Republic of Nobles achieved some of its most spectacular successes early on, particularly under the second elected king, the Transylvanian prince **Stefan Bathory**. Having carried out a thorough reform of the army, he waged a brilliant campaign against the Russians in 1579–82, neutralizing this particu-

lar threat to Poland's eastern borders for some time to come.

THE WAZA DYNASTY AND ITS AFTERMATH

The foreign policy of the next three elected monarchs, all members of the Swedish **Waza** dynasty, was less fortunate. Sigismund August Waza, the first of the trio, was a Catholic bigot who soon came into conflict with the almost exclusively Protestant population of his native land and was deposed in 1604. Though his hamfistedness meant that Poland now had a new (and increasingly powerful) enemy, he continued as the Polish king for the next 28 years, having fought off a three-year-long internal rebellion.

In 1618, Poland's situation became even more precarious, as John Sigismund von Hohenzollern inherited Ducal Prussia as well as the Electorate of Brandenburg. A couple of decades later, the Hohenzollerns inherited much of Pomerania as well, with another section being acquired by Sweden. Poland managed to remain neutral in the calamitous series of religious and dynastic conflicts known as the **Thirty Years' War**, from which Sweden emerged as Europe's leading military power.

The reign of the third of the Wazas, **Jan Kazimierz**, saw Poland's fortunes plummet. In 1648, the year of his election, the Cossacks revolted in the Ukraine, eventually allying themselves with the Russian army, which conquered eastern Poland as far as Lwów. This diversion inspired the Swedes to launch an invasion of their own, known in Polish history as the "Swedish Deluge", and they soon took control of the remainder of the country. A heroic fightback was mounted, ending in stalemate in 1660 with the Treaty of Oliwa, in which Poland recovered its former territories except for Livonia. Three years earlier, the Hohenzollerns had wrested Ducal Prussia from the last vestiges of Polish control, merging it with their other territories to form the state of Brandenburg-Prussia (later shortened to Prussia).

As well as the territorial losses suffered, these wars had seen Poland's population reduced to four million, less than half its previous total. A further crucial development of this period had been the first use in 1652 of the *liberum veto*, whereby a single vote against a measure was enough to cancel it. In principle, the nobility governed the republic as a sort of collective conscience in a wholly disinterested manner – and thus would be expected to act with unanimity. The first time someone objected to a measure, there was some debate as to whether its veto was sufficient to override the will of the majority: once it had been ruled that indeed it was, the practice soon became widespread in the protection of petty interests, and Poland found itself on the slippery slope towards ungovernability. This process was hastened when it was discovered that one dissenter was constitutionally empowered to object not only to any particular measure, but to dissolve the Sejm itself – and in the process repeal all the legislation it had passed. Meanwhile, the minor aristocracy gradually found themselves squeezed out of power, as a group of a hundred or so great **magnates** gradually established a stranglehold.

JAN SOBIESKI

Before repeated use of the *liberum veto* led to the final collapse of political authority, Poland had what was arguably its greatest moment of glory in international power politics – a consequence of the **Ottoman Turks'** overrunning of the Balkans. They were eventually beaten back by the Poles, under the command of **Jan Sobieski**, at the Battle of Chocim in 1673 – as a reward for which Sobieski was elected king the following year. In 1683 he was responsible for the successful **defence of Vienna**, which marked the final repulse of the Turks from Western Europe.

However, Poland was to pay a heavy price for the heroism of Sobieski, who had concentrated on the Turkish campaign to the exclusion of all other issues at home and abroad. His relief of Vienna exhausted Poland's military capacity while enabling Austria to recover as an imperial power; it also greatly helped the rise of the predatory state of Prussia, which he had intended to keep firmly in check. His neglect of domestic policy led to the *liberum veto* being used with impunity, while Poland and Lithuania grew apart as the nobility of the latter engaged in a civil war.

THE DECLINE OF POLAND

Known as "Augustus the Strong" owing to his fathering of over 300 children, Sobieski's successor, **Augustus Wettin**, was in fact a weak ruler, unable to shake off his debts to the Russians who had secured his election. In 1701, Friedrich III of Brandenburg-Prussia openly defied him by declaring Ducal Prussia's right to be regarded as a kingdom, having himself crowned in Königsberg. From then on, the Hohenzollerns plotted to link their territories by ousting Poland from the Baltic; in this they were aided by the acquisition of most of the rest of Pomerania in 1720. Augustus's lack of talent for power politics was even more evident in his dealings with Sweden, against whom he launched a war for control of Livonia. The conflict showed the calamitous decline of Poland's military standing, and the victorious Swedes deposed Augustus in 1704, securing the election of their own favoured candidate, **Stanisław Leszczyński**, in his place.

Augustus was reinstated in 1710, courtesy of the Russians, who effectively reduced Poland to the role of a **client state** in the process. The "Silent Sejm" of 1717, which guaranteed the existing constitution, marked the end of effective parliamentary life. The Russians never hesitated to impose their authority, cynically upholding the Republic of Nobles as a means of ensuring that the liberal ideals of the Age of Reason could never take root in Poland and that the country remained a buffer against the great powers of western Europe. When Leszczyński won the election to succeed Augustus the Strong in 1733, they intervened almost immediately to have him replaced by the deceased king's son, who proved to be an even more inept custodian of Polish interests than his father. Leszczyński was forced into exile, spending the last thirty years of his life as the Duke of Lorraine.

In 1740, Frederick the Great launched the **Silesian Wars**, which ended in 1763 with Prussia in control of all but a small part of the province. As a result, Prussia gained control over such parts of Poland's foreign trade as were not subject to Russia. The long-cherished ambition to acquire Royal Prussia and thus achieve uninterrupted control over the southern coast of the Baltic was Frederick's next objective.

When the younger Augustus Wettin died in 1763, the Russians again intervened to ensure the election of **Stanisław-August Poniatowski**, the former lover of their empress, Catherine the Great. However, Poniatowski proved an unwilling stooge, even espousing the cause of reform. Russian support of the Orthodox minority in Poland led to a growth of Catholic-inspired nationalism, and by obstructing the most moderately liberal measures, Russian policy led to an outbreak of revolts. By sending armies to crush these, they endangered the delicate balance of power in Eastern Europe.

THE PARTITIONS

Russia's Polish policy was finally rendered impotent by the revolt of the **Confederacy of Bar** in 1768–72. A heavy-handed crackdown on these reformers would certainly have led to war with Prussia, probably in alliance with Austria; doing nothing would have allowed the Poles to reassert their national independence. As a compromise, the Russians decided to support a Prussian plan for the **Partition of Poland**. By a treaty of 1772, Poland lost almost thirty percent of its territory. White Ruthenia's eastern sectors were ceded to Russia, while Austria received Red Ruthenia plus Małopolska south of the Wisła – a province subsequently rechristened Galicia. The Prussians gained the smallest share of the carve-up in the form of most of Royal Prussia, but this was strategically and economically the most significant.

Stung by this, the Poles embarked on a radical programme of reform, including the partial emancipation of serfs and the encouragement of immigration from the three empires which had undertaken the Partition. In 1791, Poland was given the first **codified constitution** in Europe since classical antiquity and the second in the modern world, after the United States. It introduced the concept of a people's sovereignty, this time including the bourgeoisie, and adopted a separation of powers between executive, legislature and judiciary, with government by a cabinet responsible to the Sejm.

This was all too much for the Russians, who, buying off the Prussians with the promise of Danzig, invaded Poland. Despite a tenacious resistance under **Tadeusz Kościuszko**, erstwhile hero of the American War of Independence, the Poles were defeated the following year. By the **Second Partition** of 1793, the constitution was annulled; the Russians annexed the remaining parts of White

and Red Ruthenia, with the Prussians gaining Wielkopolska, parts of Mazuria and Toruń in addition to the star prize of Danzig. This time the Austrians held back and missed out on the spoils.

In 1794, Kościuszko launched a national **insurrection**, achieving a stunning victory over the Russians at the Battle of Racławice with a militia largely composed of peasants armed with scythes. However, the rebellion was put down, Poniatowski forced to abdicate, and Poland wiped off the map by the **Third Partition** of 1795. This gave all lands east of the Bug and Niemen rivers to Russia, the remainder of Małopolska to Austria and the rest of the country, including Warsaw, to Prussia. By an additional treaty of 1797, the partitioning powers agreed to abolish the very name of Poland.

NAPOLEON AND THE CONGRESS OF VIENNA

Revolutionary France was naturally the country that Polish patriots looked to in their struggle to regain national independence, and Paris became the headquarters for a series of exiles and conspiratorial groups. Hopes eventually crystallized around **Napoleon Bonaparte**, who assumed power in 1799, but when three Polish legions were raised as part of the French army, Kościuszko declined to command them, regarding Napoleon as a megalomaniac who would use the Poles for his own ends.

Initially, these fears seemed unfounded: French victories over Prussia led to the creation of the **Duchy of Warsaw** in 1807 out of Polish territory annexed by the Prussians. Although no more than a buffer state, this seemed an important first step in the re-creation of Poland and encouraged the hitherto uncommitted **Józef Poniatowski**, nephew of the last king and one of the most brilliant military commanders of the day, to throw in his lot with the French dictator. As a result of his successes in Napoleon's Austrian campaign of 1809, part of Galicia was ceded to the Duchy of Warsaw.

Poniatowski again played a key role in the events of 1812, which Napoleon dubbed his "Polish War" and which restored the historic border of Poland-Lithuania with Russia. The failure of the advance on Moscow, leading to a humiliating retreat, was thus as disastrous for

Poland as for France. Cornered by the Prussians and Russians near Leipzig, Poniatowski refused to surrender, preferring to lead his troops to a heroic, suicidal defeat. The choice faced by Poniatowski encapsulated the nation's hopeless plight, and his act of self-sacrifice was to serve as a potent symbol to Polish patriots for the rest of the century.

The **Congress of Vienna** of 1814–15, set up to organize post-Napoleonic Europe, decided against the re-establishment of an independent Poland, mainly because this was opposed by the Russians. Instead, the main part of the Duchy of Warsaw was renamed the **Congress Kingdom** and placed under the dominion of the Russian tsar. The Poznań area was detached to form the **Grand Duchy of Posen**, in reality no more than a dependency of Prussia. Austria was allowed to keep most of Galicia, which was governed from Lwów (renamed Lemberg). After much deliberation, it was decided to make Kraków a city-state and "symbolic capital" of the vanished nation.

THE ARMED STRUGGLE AGAINST THE PARTITIONS

The most liberal part of the Russian Empire, the Congress Kingdom enjoyed a period of relative prosperity under the governorship of **Adam Czartoryski**, preserving its own parliament, administration, educational system and army. However, this cosy arrangement was disrupted by the arch-autocrat Nicholas I, who became tsar in 1825 and quickly imposed his policies on Poland. An attempted **insurrection** in **November 1830**, centred on a botched assassination of the tsar's brother, provoked a Russian invasion. Initially, the Polish army fared well, but it was handicapped by political divisions (notably over whether the serfs should be emancipated) and lack of foreign support, despite the supposed guarantees provided by the Vienna settlement. By the end of the following year, the Poles had been defeated; their constitution was suspended and a reign of repression began. These events led many to abandon all nationalist hopes: the first great wave of Polish **emigration**, principally to America, began soon after.

An attempted insurrection against the Austrians in 1846 also backfired, leading to the end of Kraków's independence with its re-incorporation into Galicia. This setback was a factor in Poland's failure to play an active role in the European-wide revolutions of 1848–49, though by this time the country's plight had attracted the sympathy of the emergent socialist movements. Karl Marx and Friedrich Engels went so far as to declare that Polish liberation should be the single most important immediate objective of the workers' movement. The last major uprising, against the Russians in 1863–64, attracted the support of Lithuanians and Galicians but was hopelessly limited by Poland's lack of a regular army. Its failure led to the abolition of the Congress Kingdom and its formal incorporation into Russia as the province of "Vistulaland". However, it was immediately followed by the **emancipation of the serfs**, granted on more favourable terms than in any other part of the tsarist empire – in order to cause maximum ill-feeling between the Polish nobility and peasantry.

CULTURAL AND POLITICAL RESISTANCE

Following the crushing of the 1863–64 rebellion, the Russian sector of Poland entered a period of quiet stability, with the abolition of internal tariffs opening up the vast Russian market to Polish goods. For the next half-century, Polish patriots, wherever they lived, were concerned less with trying to win independence than with keeping a distinctive **culture** alive. In this they were handicapped by the fact that this was an era of great empires, each with many subjugated minorities whose interests often conflicted: Poles found themselves variously up against the aspirations of Lithuanians, Ukrainians and Czechs. They had the greatest success in Galicia, because they were the second largest ethnic group in the Habsburg Empire, and because the Habsburgs had a more lax attitude towards the diversity of their subjects. The province was given powers of self-government and, although economically backward and ruled by a reactionary upper class, flourished once more as a centre of learning and the arts.

Altogether different was the situation in Prussia, the most efficiently repressive of the three partitioning powers. It had closely followed the British lead in forging a modern industrial society, and Poles made up a large percentage of the workforce in some of its technologically most advanced areas, notably the rich minefields of Upper Silesia. The Prussians, having ousted the Austrians from their centuries-long domination of German affairs, proceeded to exclude their rivals altogether from the **united Germany** they created by 1871, which they attempted to mould in their own Protestant and militaristic tradition.

For the Poles living under the Prussian yoke, the price to be paid for their relative prosperity was a severe clampdown on their culture, seen at its most extreme in the **Kulturkampf**, whose main aim was to crush the power of the Catholic Church, with a secondary intention of establishing the unchallenged supremacy of the German language in the new nation's educational system. It misfired badly in Poland, giving the clergy the opportunity to whip up support for their own fervently nationalistic brand of Catholicism.

Meanwhile, an upturn in political life came with the establishment, in response to internal pressure, of representative assemblies in Berlin, Vienna and St Petersburg. Towards the end of the century, this led to the formation of various new Polish **political parties and movements**, the most important of which were: the Polish Socialist Party (PPS), active mainly in the cities of Russian Poland; the Nationalist League, whose power base was in the peripheral provinces; the Peasant Movement of Galicia; and the Christian Democrats, a dominant force among the Silesian Catholics.

THE RESURRECTION OF POLAND

World War I smashed the might of the Russian, German and Austrian empires and allowed Poland to rise from the dead. Desperate to rally Poles to their cause, both alliances in the conflict made increasingly tempting offers: as early as August 1914 the Russians proposed a Poland with full rights of self-government, including language, religion and government, albeit one still ultimately subject to the tsar.

When the German and Austrian armies overran Russian-occupied Poland in 1916, they felt obliged to trump this offer, promising to set up a **Polish kingdom** once the war was over. The

foundations of this were laid immediately, with the institution of an interim administration – known as the Regency Council – and the official restoration of the Polish language. Even though carried out for cynical reasons, these initial steps were of crucial importance to the re-launch of a fully independent Poland, a notion which had soon gained the support of the US President Woodrow Wilson and of the new Bolshevik government in Moscow.

Meanwhile two bitter rivals had emerged as the leading contenders for leadership of the Polish nation. **Józef Piłsudski**, an impoverished noble from Lithuania and founding member of the PPS, had long championed a military solution to Poland's problems. During the war, his legions fought on behalf of the Germans, assuming that the defeat of the Russians would allow him to create the new Polish state on his own terms. In this, he favoured a return to the great tradition of ethnic and religious diversity of centuries past. **Roman Dmowski**, leader of the Nationalist League, represented the ambitions of the new middle class and had a vision of a purely Polish and staunchly Catholic future, in which the Jews would, as far as possible, be excluded. He opted to work for independence by exclusively political means, in the hope that victory over Germany would lead the Western allies to set up a Polish state under his leadership.

In the event, Piłsudski came out on top: the Germans, having held him in internment for well over a year, released him the day before the **armistice of November 11, 1918**, allowing him to take command of the Regency Council. He was sworn in as head of state three days later. Dmowski had to accept the consolation prize of head delegate to the Paris Peace Conference, though his associate, the concert pianist Ignacy Jan Paderewski, became the country's first prime minister.

POLAND REDEFINED

The new Poland lacked a defined territory. Initially, it consisted of the German and Austrian zones of occupation, centred on Warsaw and Lublin, plus Western Galicia. Wielkopolska was added a month later, following a revolt against the German garrison in Poznań, but the precise frontiers were only established during the following three years on an *ad hoc* basis. Yet, though the Paris Conference played only a minor role in all this, it did take the key decision to give the country access to the sea by means of the **Polish Corridor**, a strip of land cut through the old Royal Prussia, which meant that East Prussia was left cut off from the rest of Germany. Despite intense lobbying, it was decided to exclude Danzig from the corridor, on the grounds that its population was overwhelmingly German; instead, it reverted to its former tradition as a city-state – an unsatisfactory compromise which was later to have tragic consequences.

The **Polish-Soviet War** of 1919–20 was the most significant of the conflicts that crucially determined the country's borders. Realizing that the Bolsheviks would want to spread their revolution to Poland and then to the industrialized West, Piłsudski aimed to create a grouping of independent nation-states stretching from Finland to Georgia to halt this new expansionist Russian empire. Taking advantage of the civil war between the Soviet "Reds" and the counter-revolutionary "Whites", his army marched deep into Belarus and the Ukraine. He was subsequently beaten back to Warsaw, but skilfully regrouped his forces to pull off a crushing victory and pursue the Russians eastwards, regaining a sizeable chunk of the old Polish-Lithuanian Commonwealth's eastern territories in the process, an acquisition confirmed by the Treaty of Riga in 1921.

At the very end of the war, Piłsudski seized his home city of Wilno (Vilnius), which had a predominantly Polish population but was wanted by the Lithuanians – who had opted for independence rather than a revival of the union. The grudge borne by Lithuania over this proved costly to them, as they became dependent on, and were later annexed by, the Soviet Union. Other border issues were settled by **plebiscites** organized by the League of Nations, the new international body set up to resolve such matters. In the most significant of these, Germany and Poland competed for Upper Silesia. The Germans won, but the margin was so narrow that the League felt that the distribution of votes justified the partition of the province. Poland gained most of the

Katowice conurbation, thus ensuring that the country gained a solid industrial base.

THE INTER-WAR YEARS

Although the Polish state managed to develop coherent political, economic and educational institutions, plus a transport and communications network, all were essentially fragile creations, as became obvious when Piłsudski refused to stand in the **1922 presidential elections** on the grounds that the office was insufficiently powerful. Worse, the victor, Gabriel Narutowicz, was hounded by the Nationalists for having won as a result of votes cast by "non-Poles", and was assassinated soon afterwards. For the next few years, Poland was governed by a series of weak governments presiding over hyper-inflation, feeble attempts at agrarian reform and a contemptuous army officer class.

In May 1926, Piłsudski staged a military coup, ushering in the so-called **Sanacja** regime, named after a slogan proposing a return to political "health". Piłsudski functioned as the state's commander-in-chief until his death in 1935, though he held no formal office after an initial two-year stint as prime minister. Parliamentary life continued, but opposition was emasculated by the creation of the so-called Non-Party Bloc for Co-operation with the Government, and disaffected groups were brought to heel by force if necessary.

Having a country led by Stalin on one frontier was bad enough; when Hitler seized power in Germany in 1933, Poland was a sitting target for two ruthless dictators, despite managing to sign ten-year non-aggression pacts with each. Hitler had always been open about his ambition of wiping Poland off the map again, regarding the Slavs as a race who were fit for no higher role than to be slaves of the Aryans. His foreign policy objectives were quickly put into effect by his annexation of Austria in 1937 and of parts of Czechoslovakia – with British and French connivance – in 1938. As Hitler's attentions turned towards Poland, his foreign minister Joachim von Ribbentrop and his Soviet counterpart Vyacheslav Molotov concluded the notorious **Nazi-Soviet Pact** in August 1939, which allowed either side to pursue any aggressive designs without the interference of the other. It also included a secret clause

POLAND 1938

LITHUANIA

• Königsberg

Danzig
(Gdańsk)

GERMANY
(EAST PRUSSIA)

• Wilno
(Vilnius)

Stettin
(Szczecin) •

GERMANY

• Berlin

Wisła

Oder

Niesse

• Poznań

• Warsaw

• Łódź

• Lublin

Breslau •
(Wrocław)
SILESIA

C Z E C H O S L O V A K I A

• Kraków

• Lwów
(Lvov)

U

S

S

R

N

0   100 km

POLAND 1945

• Kaliningrad (Königsberg)

Gdańsk
(Danzig)

• Vilnius

E
A
S
T

Szczecin
(Stettin) •

Berlin
•

G
E
R
M
A
N
Y

Oder

Niesse

• Poznań

Wisła

• Warsaw

U   S   S   R

Wrocław
(Breslau) •

• Łódź

• Lublin

C Z E C H O S L O V A K I A

• Kraków

• Lvov

N

0   100 km

which agreed on a full partition of Poland along the lines of the Narew, Wisła and San rivers.

WORLD WAR II

On September 1, 1939, Hitler **invaded Poland**, beginning by annexing the free city of Danzig, thereby precipitating World War II. The Poles fought with great courage, inflicting heavy casualties, but were numerically and technologically in a hopeless position. On September 17, the Soviets invaded the eastern part of the country, claiming the share-out agreed by the Nazi-Soviet Pact. The Allies, who had guaranteed to come to Poland's defence, initially failed to do so, and by the end of the first week in October the country had capitulated. A government-in-exile was established in London under **Władysław Sikorski**.

Millions of civilians – including virtually every Jew in Poland – were to be slaughtered in the Nazi **concentration camps** that were soon being set up in the occupied territory. And as this was going on, Soviet prisoners were being transported east to the **Gulag**, while wholesale murders of the potentially troublesome elements in Polish society were being carried out, such as the massacre of Katyn, where 4500 officers were shot.

With the Nazi disavowal of the 1939 Pact and the invasion of the Soviet Union in June 1941, the Polish resistance, led by the **Home Army** (AK), no longer had to fight on two fronts, as it prompted Stalin to make an alliance with Sikorski. The Soviet victory at Stalingrad in 1943 marked the beginning of the end for the Nazis, but it enabled Stalin to renege on his agreement with the government-in-exile. At the **Tehran Conference** in November, he came to an arrangement with Britain and America with regard to future spheres of influence in Europe, making it almost inevitable that postwar Poland would be forced into the Soviet camp. He also insisted that the Soviet Union would retain the territories it had annexed in 1939. Allied support for this was obtained by reference to the current border's virtual coincidence with the so-called "Curzon Line", which had been drawn up by a former British Foreign Secretary in 1920 in an unsuccessful attempt at mediation in the Polish-Soviet War.

During the **liberation of Poland** in 1944, any possibility of reasserting genuine Polish control depended on the outcome of the **uprising in Warsaw** against the Nazi occupiers. On July 31, with the Soviets poised on the outskirts of the city, the Home Army was forced to act. The Red Army lay in wait during the ensuing bloodbath. When the insurgents were finally defeated at the beginning of October, Hitler ordered that the city be razed before leaving the ruins to the Red Army. In early 1945, as the Soviets pushed on through Poland, the Nazis set up last-ditch strongholds in Silesia, but these were overrun by the time of the final armistice in April.

No country suffered so much from World War II as Poland. In all, around 25 percent of the population died, and the whole country lay devastated. Moreover, although the Allies had originally gone to war on its behalf, it found itself **reduced in size** and **shifted west** across the map of Europe by some 200 kilometres, with its western frontier fixed at the lines of the Odra and Nysa rivers. Stalin had in effect achieved his twin aims of moving his frontiers and his sphere of influence well to the west.

The losses in the east – including Lwów and Wilno, both great centres of Polish culture – were painful, and involved the transfer of millions of people across the country in the following two years. There were compensations, however: Pomerania and the industrially valuable Silesia were restored after a gap of some seven centuries; and the much-coveted city of Danzig, which had been detached since its seizure by the Teutonic Knights, was also returned – and as Gdańsk, it was later to play a major role in the formation of postwar Poland.

THE RISE OF POLISH COMMUNISM

The Polish communists took power, not through popular revolution – as their Soviet counterparts had – nor even with significant public support – as the Czech communists had – but through the military and political dictate of an occupying force. Control was seized by the **ZPP** (Union of Polish Patriots), an organization formed by Stalin in 1943 from Polish exiles and Russian placemen with polonized names. As the Red Army drove the Germans west, the ZPP established a Committee for National Liberation in Lublin, under the leadership of **Bolesław Bierut**. This was to form the core of the Polish government over the next few years.

Political opposition was fragmented and ineffectual. From the government in exile, only a single prominent figure returned to Poland after 1945 – Stanislaw Mikolajczyk, leader of the prewar Peasants' Party. He was to leave again in 1947, narrowly avoiding imprisonment.

The Polish communists and socialists who had remained in Poland during the war now regrouped. The communists, though suspicious of Moscow, joined the ZPP to form the Polish Workers' Party under general secretary **Władysław Gomułka**, as the socialists attempted to establish a separate party. Meanwhile, the Soviets ran the country as an outlying province, stripping factories of plant and materials, intimidating political opponents, and orchestrating the brutal suppression of a nationalist uprising in the Western Ukraine by the Polish army, in what is referred to as the **Civil War** (1945–47).

The economic and political framework of Poland was sealed by the elections of 1947. The communists and socialists, allied as the **Democratic Bloc**, won a decisive victory over their remaining opponents through an extended campaign of political harassment and manipulation. After the forcible merger of the socialists and communists in 1948 as the **PZPR** (Polish United Workers' Party), it only remained for the external pressures of the emerging Cold War to lock Poland completely into the Soviet sphere of influence and the Soviet model of economic and political development.

THE TRANSFORMATION OF POLAND

Polish history from 1947 to 1955 must be understood against the backdrop of an emergent Cold War. After the Berlin Blockade (1948), the formation of NATO (1949) and the rearmament of the German Federal Republic, the Soviet Union regarded a stable, communist Poland as an essential component of its defence. The realpolitik of Soviet foreign policy was not lost on the Polish communists, who, though subordinate in many areas, retained a degree of independence from Moscow. Thus, while foreign policy was determined by Moscow, and Poland joined the Warsaw Pact on its formation in 1955, some

leeway remained in domestic policy. For example, First Secretary Gomułka, although deposed and arrested in 1951, was not executed, unlike other disgraced leaders in Eastern Europe. Nor were the purges of the Party and the suppression of civil opposition as savage as elsewhere.

Nonetheless, the new constitution of 1952 enshrined the leading role of the PZPR in every aspect of Polish society, designating the country as the **Polish People's Republic (PPR)**. Further, while the trappings of elections and a two-house parliament were retained, the other parties – the Democratic Party (SD) and the reconstituted Peasants' Party (ZSL) – were under the effective political control of the PZPR. Real power lay with the Politburo, Central Committee and the newly formed economic and administrative bureaucracies. Only the Catholic Church, although harassed and extensively monitored by the authorities, retained a degree of independent political and cultural organization – a defiance characterized by the Primate, **Cardinal Wyszyński**, arrested in 1953 for "anti-state" activities and imprisoned for three years.

Nationalization continued throughout this period, accelerated through the first **Three Year Plan** (1947–50) and the first **Six Year Plan** (1950–1956). Although the former retained some emphasis on the role of private ownership, the thrust of both was towards the collectivization of agriculture and the creation of a heavy industrial base. Collectivization proved impossible in the absence of the sort of force used by Stalin against the Kulaks: the programme slowed in the mid-Fifties and was tacitly abandoned thereafter. Industrially the plans proved more successful: major iron and steel industries were established, mining extensively exploited in Silesia and an entire shipbuilding industry developed along the Baltic coast – most notably in Gdańsk. There were, inevitably, costs: standards of living remained almost static, food was scarce, work was long, hard and often dangerous, and unrestrained industrialization resulted in terrible pollution and despoilation of the land. Perhaps the most significant achievement of the period was the creation of an **urban industrial working class** for the first time in Polish history. Paradoxically, these very people proved to be the backbone of almost every political struggle against the Party in the following decades.

1956 – THE POLISH OCTOBER

In Poland, as in Hungary, **1956** saw the first major political crisis of the communist era. Faction and dissension were already rife, with intellectuals calling for fundamental changes, splits within the Party leadership and increasing popular disenchantment with the excesses of Stalinism. In February 1956 **Khrushchev** made his famous "secret" speech to the Twentieth Congress of the Soviet Communist Party, denouncing Stalin and his crimes: for Bolesław Bierut, President and First Secretary of the PZPR, as for other Eastern European leaders, the speech was a bombshell, unmasking the lie of the absolute correctness of Stalin's every act. Reform-minded members of the Party in Poland were the first to make copies available in the West, but for Bierut and the hardline leadership it was the end: Bierut died directly after the congress, many suspecting that he had committed suicide.

Then in June, workers in Poznań took to the streets over working conditions and wages. The protest rapidly developed into a major confrontation with the authorities, and in the ensuing street battles with the army and security police up to eighty people were killed and many hundreds of others wounded. Initial government insistence that "imperialist agents" had instigated the troubles gave way to an admission that some of the workers' grievances were justified and that the Party would try to remedy them.

The Poznań riots further divided an alarmed and weakened Party. Hardliners pushed for defence minister General Rokossowski to take over the leadership, but it was Gomułka, with his earnest promises of reform, who carried the day. In October, the Party plenum elected Gomułka as the new leader, without consulting Moscow. An enraged Khrushchev flew to Warsaw to demand an explanation of this unprecedented flouting of Moscow. East German, Czech and Soviet troops were mobilized along Poland's borders, in response to which Polish security forces prepared to defend the capital. Poland held its breath as Gomułka and Khrushchev engaged in heated debate over

the crisis. In the end, Gomułka assured Khrushchev that Poland would remain a loyal ally and maintain the essentials of communist rule. Khrushchev returned to Moscow, Soviet troops withdrew, and four days later Gomułka addressed a huge crowd in Warsaw as a national hero. The Soviet invasion of Hungary to crush the national uprising there in early November 1956 provided a clear reminder to Poles of how close they had come to disaster.

The **Polish October**, as it came to be known, raised high hopes of a new order, and initially those hopes seemed justified. Censorship was relaxed, Cardinal Wyszyński was released and state harassment of the Church and control over the economy eased. But the impetus for reform quickly faded, and the 1960s saw a progressive return to centralized planning, a stagnant economy and steadily increasing levels of political control.

1970–79: FROM GOMULKA TO GIEREK

The final days of the Gomułka years were marked by a contrast between triumph in foreign policy and the harsh imposition of economic constraint. Pursuing his policy of Östpolitik, Willy Brandt – SPD Chancellor of the German Federal Republic – visited Poland in December 1970 and laid to rest some of the perennial concerns of postwar Polish foreign policy. In signing the Warsaw Treaty, West Germany recognized Poland's current borders and opened full diplomatic relations. And in an emphatic symbolic gesture, Brandt knelt in penance at the monument to those killed in the Warsaw Uprising.

A few days later, on December 12, huge food price rises were announced, provoking a simmering discontent that was to break out in strikes and demonstrations along the Baltic coast, centring on Gdańsk. When troops fired on demonstrators, killing many, the protests spread like wildfire, to the point of open insurrection. A traumatized Central Committee met five days before Christmas, hurriedly bundling the moribund Gomułka into retirement and replacing him as First Secretary with **Edward Gierek**, a member of the Party's reformist faction in the 1960s. Price rises were frozen and wage increases promised, but despite a Christmas calm, strikes broke out throughout

January 1971, with demands for free trade unions and a free press accompanying the more usual economic demands. Peace was only restored when Gierek and the Minister of Defence, General **Wojciech Jaruzelski**, went to the Gdańsk shipyards by taxi to argue their case and admit their errors to the strikers.

The Gierek period marked out an alternative route to social stability. Given access to Western financial markets by Brandt's reconciliation, the Gierek government borrowed heavily throughout the early Seventies. Food became cheaper and more plentiful as internal subsidies were matched by purchases from the West and the Soviet Union. Standards of living rose and a wider range of consumer goods became more freely available. However, the international economic recession and oil crises of the mid-Seventies destroyed the Polish boom at a stroke. Debts became impossible to service, new loans harder to obtain, and it became apparent that earlier borrowing had been squandered in unsustainable rises in consumption or wasted in large-scale projects of limited economic value.

By 1976 the wheel had turned full circle with remarkable rapidity. The government announced food price rises of almost treble the magnitude of those proposed in the early Seventies. This time the ensuing strikes were firmly repressed and many activists imprisoned, and it is from this point that one can chart the emergence of the complex **alliance between Polish workers, intellectuals and the Catholic Church**. In response to the imprisonment of strikers, the KOR (Committee for the Defence of Workers) was formed. Comprising dissident intellectuals, it was to provide not only valuable publicity and support for the opposition through Western contacts, but also new channels of political communication through underground *samizdat* publications, plus a degree of strategic sophistication that the spontaneous uprisings had so far lacked.

But perhaps even more decisive was the election of **Karol Wojtyła**, Archbishop of Kraków, as **Pope John Paul II** in 1978. A fierce opponent of the communist regime, he visited Poland in 1979 and was met by the greatest public gatherings that Poland had ever

seen. For the Polish people he became a symbol of Polish cultural identity and international influence, and his visit provided a public demonstration of their potential power.

1980–89: SOLIDARITY

Gierek's announcement of 100 percent price rises on foodstuffs in July 1980 led to more strikes, centring on the **Gdańsk shipyards**. Attempts by the authorities to have a crane operator, Anna Walentynowicz, dismissed for political agitation intensified the unrest. Led by a shipyard electrician, **Lech Wałęsa**, the strikers occupied the yards and were joined by a hastily convened group of opposition intellectuals and activists, including future prime minister Tadeuz Mazowiecki. Together they formulated a series of demands – the so-called **Twenty-one Points** – that were to serve not only as the principal political concerns of the Polish opposition, but to provide an intellectual template for every other oppositional movement in Eastern Europe.

Demands for popular consultation over the economic crisis, the freeing of political prisoners, freedom of the press, the right to strike, free trade unions and televised Catholic Mass were drawn up along with demands for higher wages and an end to party privileges. Yet the lessons of Hungary in 1956 and Czechoslovakia in 1968 had been learnt, and the opposition was careful to reiterate that they "intended neither to threaten the foundations of the Socialist Republic in our country, nor its position in international relations".

The Party caved in, after protracted negotiations, signing the historic **Gdańsk Agreements** in August 1980, after which free trade unions, covering over 75 percent of Poland's 12.5 million workforce, were formed across the country, under the name *Solidarność* – **Solidarity**. Gierek and his supporters were swept from office by the Party in September 1980, but the limits of Solidarity's power were signalled by an unscheduled Warsaw Pact meeting later in the year. Other Eastern European communist leaders perceptively argued that Solidarity's success would threaten not only their Polish counterparts' political futures, but their own as well. Accordingly, Soviet and Warsaw Pact units were mobilized along Poland's borders. The Poles closed ranks:

the Party reaffirmed its Leninist purity, while Solidarity and the Church publicly emphasized their moderation.

Throughout 1981 deadlock ensued, while the economic crisis gathered pace. Solidarity, lacking any positive control over the economy, was only capable of bringing it to a halt, and repeatedly showed itself able to do so. General Jaruzelski took control of the Party in July 1981 and, in the face of threats of a general strike, continued to negotiate with Solidarity leaders, but refused to relinquish any power. A wave of strikes in late October 1981 were met by the imposition of **martial law** on December 12, 1981: occupations and strikes were broken up by troops, Solidarity was banned, civil liberties suspended and union leaders arrested. However, these measures solved nothing fundamental, and after a second visit by Pope John Paul II in 1983, martial law was lifted.

The period 1984 to 1988 was marked by a final attempt by the Jaruzelski government to dig Poland out of its economic crisis. The country's debt had risen to an astronomical $39 billion, wages had slumped, and production was hampered by endemic labour unrest. In 1987, Jaruzelski submitted the government's programme of price rises and promised democratization to a referendum. The government lost, the real message of the vote being a rejection not merely of the programme but of the notion that the Party could lead Poland out of its crisis. As the Party's route lay blocked by popular disenchantment, the opposition's opened up after major strikes in May 1988.

Jaruzelski finally acknowledged defeat after a devastating second wave of strikes in August of that year and called for a "courageous turnaround" by the Party, accepting the need for talks with Solidarity and the prospect of real power sharing – an option of political capitulation probably only made possible by the accession of Gorbachev to the Kremlin.

1989–90: THE NEW POLAND

The **round-table talks** ran from February to April 1989, the key demands being the absolute acceptance of the legal status of Solidarity, the establishment of an independent press and the promise of what were termed semi-free elections. Legalization of Solidarity was duly agreed, opposition newspapers were to be allowed to publish freely and all 100 seats of a reconstituted upper chamber, the Senate, were to be freely contested. In the lower house of parliament, the Sejm, 65 percent of seats were to be reserved for the PZPR and its allied parties, with the rest openly contested.

The communists suffered a humiliating and decisive defeat in the consequent **elections** held in **July 1989**, whereas Solidarity won almost every seat it contested. Thus while the numerical balance of the lower chamber remained with the PZPR, the unthinkable became possible – a Solidarity-led government. In the end, the parties which had previously been allied to the PZPR broke with their communist overlords and voted to establish the journalist **Tadeusz Mazowiecki** as prime minister in August 1989, installing the first non-communist government in Eastern Europe since World War II. Subsequently the PZPR rapidly disintegrated, voting to dissolve itself in January 1990 and then splitting into two notionally social democratic currents.

The tasks facing Poland's new government were formidable: economic dislocation, political volatility and a rapidly changing foreign scene in the rest of Eastern Europe. For the most part, the government retained a high degree of support in the face of an **austerity programme** far stiffer than anything proposed under the communist regime.

PRESIDENT WAŁĘSA AND THE FIRST FREE ELECTIONS

Lech Wałęsa, long out of the main political arena, forced the pace in the **presidential election of 1990**, calling for the removal of Jaruzelski, a faster pace of reform and a concerted effort to remove the accumulated privileges of the senior Party men. Against him stood Prime Minister Mazowiecki and the previously unknown Jan Tymiński, a Canadian-Polish businessman employing free-market rhetoric and Western-style campaigning techniques. Although clearly in the lead in the first round of voting in December 1990, Wałęsa was required to face a second round against Tymiński. Mazowiecki, having finished a disappointing third, then resigned as prime minister, taking the whole government with him. Wałęsa won the second round comfortably.

In January 1991 Wałęsa appointed as prime minister Jan Krzysztof Bielecki, a leading intellectual force within Solidarity. This appointment was symptomatic of the country's changing political and social climate: a business-oriented liberal from Gdańsk (as opposed to the hitherto dominant school of Warsaw intellectuals), Bielecki represented the new technocratic elite already making rapid headway in the "new Poland". Significantly, Bielecki retained the services of Leszek Balcerowicz as finance minister (and deputy prime minister), a move indicative of the new government's commitment to continuing along the path of economic reform that had been followed by the Mazowiecki administration.

Throughout 1991 the **economy** – specifically the government's commitment to persevering with a tough **austerity programme** – continued to dominate the national agenda, with steadily rising prices, rocketing unemployment (up to 11 percent by November 1991) and continued government spending cuts making heavy inroads into the pockets and lives of ordinary Poles. Internationally, however, Balcerowicz's tough policies gained the support of the Western financial institutions, a fact that found practical expression in a landmark agreement with the Paris club of the International Monetary Fund (IMF) on a fifty-percent reduction of Poland's estimated 33 billion dollars of official debt (providing the country continued to pursue IMF-approved economic policies, including keeping the budget deficit at under five percent of GDP).

Elections – the first fully free ones since World War II – were planned for the spring of 1991, but eventually postponed until October; preparations were hampered by continuing rows over the precise form of electoral system to be used. The election campaign itself was a fairly tame affair, the most notable feature being the spectacular array of parties (nearly seventy in total) taking part, including everyone from national minorities like the Silesian Germans to the joke "Beer Lovers' Party" as well as a bewildering array of old-time opposition factions, religiously based parties, nationalists and one-off independents.

The "**hyper proportional**" **system** (with no percentage entry hurdles) finally agreed for the elections during the autumn, however, was a recipe for political factionalism and fragmentation in the time-honoured Polish mould: 29 parties entered the new Sejm, the highest

scorer, the Democratic Union (UD), gaining a meagre 14 percent of the alarmingly low (43 percent) turnout. Bielecki resigned, and a two-month period of confusion followed during which he tried in vain to cobble together a new and workable governing coalition. In the end, Wałęsa ended the disarray by inviting **Jan Olszewski**, a lawyer and prominent former dissident, to form a new coalition government.

One issue that remained unresolved at the end of 1991 was the vexed question of **withdrawing Soviet troops.** Deadlocked negotiations and strong resistance from the Soviet and subsequently Russian authorities meant that unlike Czechoslovakia and Hungary, Poland still had no firm timetable for the removal of the fifty thousand or so combat troops stationed in the country over two years on from the demise of communist authority. The decisive breakthrough came during Wałęsa's high-profile official visit to Moscow in May 1992, when the Polish president signed a treaty with his Russian counterpart, Boris Yeltsin, confirming that all Russian troops were to be withdrawn by end of 1993. Troop withdrawals proceeded apace, and in October 1992 the last Soviet combat forces pulled out of Poland, leaving behind just a few support units.

Abandoning Bielecki's emphasis on economic reform, the new centre-right coalition government put together by Olszewski adopted an aggressively confrontational emphasis on those elements of political reform – notably the highly-charged issue of "**decommunization**" – which it believed the previous two administrations had ignored. The most explosive of these proved to be a government-sponsored parliamentary motion in May 1992 envisaging the production of a list of public figures suspected of having collaborated with the security services during the communist era. A political crisis blew up rapidly over what became known as the **lustration** issue. A no-confidence vote in the Sejm at the beginning of June 1992 led to Olszewski's enforced ousting as prime minister. Despite Wałęsa's best efforts, the president's initial candidate to assume the premiership, the youthful Waldemar Pawłak of the Peasants' Party (PSL), failed to muster the necessary parliamentary support. After some ten weeks of bargaining, **Halina Suchocka** of the Democratic Union was nominated as Poland's **first woman**

prime minister. Her new cabinet embraced everyone from the Catholic rightists of the Christian National Association (ZChN) to members of her own left-liberal-inclined UD, a consummate piece of political bargaining and compromise that surprised many observers accustomed to the infighting and posturing that at times still appears to be endemic to Polish political life.

THE SUCHOCKA GOVERNMENT

In many respects, the Suchocka government proved surprisingly successful and cohesive. Domestically its most important achievement was a **social pact** over wage increases, concluded between government and trade unions (the remnants of declining Solidarity included) in autumn 1992 after a major wave of strikes – a temporary resolution, at least, of an issue which has regularly threatened to derail Poland's post-communist reform project. On the darker side, the increasingly powerful role of **the Church** in Poland's political and social life came well to the fore, above all in the heated national debate sparked by government moves to **criminalize abortion**, a move supported strongly by the Catholic Church but opposed by many within the country, as well as by Western institutions like the Council of Europe. Internationally, the most significant long-term development under the Suchocka government was the **EC Association Agreement** signed in January 1992 and formally ratified by the Sejm in the autumn, amid loud accusations of a sell-out to the West from conservative, nationalistically minded forces fearful of the tacit acceptance of liberal secularism they saw implied by European integration.

In early 1993 the question of large-scale **privatization** emerged as a contentious political hot potato. In contrast to the country's ailing, debt-ridden state industries the flourishing private sector, already reckoned to account for almost fifty percent of national output, appeared to be doing well, providing the basis for the economic upturn. In March, the Sejm threw out a bill designed to privatize over six hundred major state enterprises, with members of government coalition parties voting against Suchocka in a characteristically defiant display of Polish independent-mindedness.

Shrugging off this setback, the government immediately put forward an amended set of privatization proposals, which were duly passed by the Sejm in April and by the Senate a month later. Just as things appeared to be calming down, however, a motion of "no confidence" in the government, specifically its handling of the economy tabled by the malcontent Solidarity opposition faction, was passed by an agonizing one vote majority in the Sejm. Rejecting Suchocka's subsequent offer of resignation, President Wałęsa dissolved the Sejm and called for fresh elections to both houses in the middle of September 1993. In the mean time, changes to the "hyper-proportional" **electoral system** were passed by the Sejm in late May, the main aim being to cut down the number of parties represented in parliament and thus promote greater national political stability. Under the new electoral law, parties needed to pass a threshold of five per cent of the vote (eight per cent in the case of party alliances) to win seats in the Sejm.

The **September elections** resulted in victory for the post-communist Democratic Left Alliance (SLD)-PSL electoral coalition, which won nearly 36 percent of the vote, way ahead of its nearest rival, Suchocka's Democratic Union (UD), which scored a miserable 10.6 percent. Due to the new electoral system, scores of parties failed to make it into parliament, despite receiving a total of nearly 35 percent of the vote between them, a result perceived by some as equally unacceptable as the proliferation of parliamentary parties produced by the previous system. While the scale of the SLD-PSL victory surprised many both inside and outside the country, few doubted that, as in several other post-communist countries, discontent with the decline in popular living standards stemming from the economic reform programmes lay behind the election of a post-communist-led government.

THE CONFLICT WITH WAŁĘSA

In the event, after protracted negotiations PSL leader and ex-prime minister **Waldemar Pawłak** announced the formation of a new coalition government in October, comprising PSL and SLD nominees plus a number of independent ministers. In line with the public mood that had produced his party's electoral successes, Pawłak affirmed his commitment to continuing along the path of market reform, but at the same time pledged to do more to address its negative social effects.

From early on, Pawlak's administration was embroiled in a succession of constitutional and political tussles. Tensions within the new government coalition surfaced in early 1994 following Pawlak's dismissal of the deputy finance minister, an SLD appointee, over the alleged undervaluing of Bank Śląski in the run up to its privatization. As a result, Deputy Prime Minister and Finance Minister Marek Borowski (also of the SLD) tendered his resignation, protesting that coalition terms had been violated by Pawlak. A new wave of public-sector strikes initiated by a revived Solidarity hit the country in the early spring. Direct union–government negotiations made little headway, and with Solidarity calling for a general strike in May, things looked ugly. In the event, the strike plan was called off, Silesian coal workers returning to work after being awarded major pay increases.

Ultimately, however, the conflict that most undermined Pawlak's government was a prolonged **tussle with President Lech Wałęsa**. Frustrated by the left's electoral success and what he (correctly) perceived to be his own increasing political marginalization, Lech Wałęsa engaged the government in a fierce tussle over proposed constitutional amendments that aimed to transfer responsibility for ratifying government appointments from the President to the Sejm. Wałęsa got his way for the time being, personally nominating Grzegorz Kołodzko as Marek Borowski's replacement in April. Things blew up again later in the year when Wałęsa demanded the resignation of Defence Minister Admiral Piotr Kołodziejcyk for his supposed failure to carry out reforms of the military. Pawlak caved in and dismissed Kołodziejcyk, though for the next two months the two were unable to agree on who should succeed the Admiral.

Seemingly intent on confrontation, in January 1995 Wałęsa attacked new government legislation raising personal income tax levels and urged a campaign of **popular tax refusal**. In the end it was left to a constitutional tribunal to rule that the president had acted unconstitutionally, and Wałęsa was compelled to approve the new tax law. The showdown came in February, when Wałęsa **demanded Pawlak's resignation** and threat-

ened to dissolve parliament if he was not replaced immediately. Incensed by this blatant display of presidential arrogance, the Sejm voted to initiate **impeachment proceedings** against Wałęsa should he make good his threats. A full-scale crisis was prevented by Pawlak's eventual decision to quit, to be replaced in early March by the SLD's **Józef Oleksy**, speaker of the Sejm, who proceeded to form a new government based on the same coalition of the SLD, PSL and independents.

THE 1995 PRESIDENTIAL ELECTIONS

As the year progressed, the focus of domestic political attention shifted towards the November **presidential elections**, the first since Wałęsa assumed office in 1990. Early opinion polls pointed to Wałęsa's deep unpopularity among an electorate weary of his constant manoeuvring and seemingly unquenchable appetite for political intrigue. Of the wealth of candidates opposing Wałęsa early evidence suggested the SLD's **Aleksander Kwaśniewski** was going to be the key challenger. A polished, smooth-talking character who knew how to win over audiences potentially alienated by his ex-communist political record, Kwaśniewski cut a strikingly contrasting figure to Wałęsa. Throughout a hard-fought election campaign, Kwaśniewski proved adept at neutralizing the effect of Wałęsa's increasingly bitter and personalized attacks on him, focusing instead on projecting a modernizing, future-oriented image that particularly appealed to younger people and the emergent, increasingly prosperous middle classes. Despite Wałęsa's unquestioned national standing as a key architect of the overthrow of communism, it became increasingly apparent as the election campaign gathered pace that trying to discredit his chief opponent by focusing on the sins of the communist past was not going to be enough to carry the electorate.

As anticipated, the **first round of elections**, held at the beginning of November 1995, saw off all the other contenders including Freedom Union (UW) candidate and veteran opponent Jacek Kuroń, former prime ministers Jan Olszewski and Waldemar Pawlak and Hanna Gronkiewicz-Waltz, president of the

National Bank and a former Wałęsa protégé. Kwaśniewski topped the field by two points, but with a number of opinion polls suggesting that Wałęsa would pick up strongly on the anti-communist vote in the second round, the stage was set for a tight result. In the event that was exactly what it proved to be. Following a final campaign marked by some pretty gruesome mudslinging, including accusations of serious financial impropriety on both sides, **Kwaśniewski carried the second round** by a slim margin of 52 percent to Wałęsa's 48, on a 68 percent voter turnout. A chastened Wałęsa made little effort to hide his anger at the result, and the final weeks of his presidency were marked by further characteristically intemperate outbursts, notably his refusal to attend Kwaśniewski's swearing-in ceremony just before Christmas.

There was one final act of vengeance left, however. Days before stepping down from office, minister of internal affairs, Andrzej Milczanowski, a Wałęsa appointee, released documents reportedly suggesting that prime minister Józef Oleksy was suspected of having **collaborated** with the KGB and the Russian intelligence agency. An enquiry into the claims, centring around Oleksy's connection with a known KGB agent and former staff member of the Soviet embassy in Warsaw was duly launched, and despite Oleksy's persistent denial of the charges, the political pressure on him to resign rapidly mounted. Following the announcement that the state prosecutor's office was to start an official investigation into the issue, Oleksy threw in the towel in late January, still defiantly protesting his innocence. After a further fortnight of intense political horse trading, the SLD's **Włodzimierz Cimoszewicz** was nominated to the post. A lawyer and former justice minister, Cimoszewicz's reputation as one of the most outspoken and independent-minded of the ex-communist political coterie – he stood as the most credible (or any rate, least despised) available PZPR candidate in the 1990 presidential elections – made him an obvious candidate for restoring credibility to the government's badly shaken position. The team of ministers appointed by Cimoszewicz in early February retained essential continuity with Oleksy's administration. Into early 1996, it looked as if the major storms had subsided. How long this situation will hold is an open question. Much of the opposition is deeply unhappy with the effective monopoly of state power now exercised by the post-communists, and if the centre-right parties manage to keep their perennial tendency towards factional infighting in check and unite against the "red threat" persistently trumpeted by Wałęsa, there may yet be a few surprises in store.

POLAND IN EUROPE

Whatever the potential for political turbulence, **economically**, Poland entered 1996 on a tide of mounting optimism, a result of a combination of continuing growth in GDP – once again projected at over five percent – expanding foreign investment, decreasing inflation and steadily (though slowly) declining unemployment. In **foreign policy**, the twin goals of **membership of NATO and the European Union** remain the principal preoccupation. The association agreement with the EU signed in January 1992 became fully effective in February 1994. Two months later, Poland lodged a formal application for EU membership, and, along with other central European countries, an official Polish delegation attended the annual EU summit for the first time, in Essen in December 1994, though it was apparent that membership applications would not be considered formally until after the crucial 1996 Maastricht review conference. The **December 1995 EU summit** in Madrid gave qualified endorsement to a strong push by Germany's Chancellor Kohl to establish a clear timetable for the central European countries' membership negotiations, the most optimistic scenario being final negotiations beginning in 1998 with the prospect of entering the Union in the year 2000.

In the **security** domain, the situation is currently even more ambiguous. Despite openly grumbling about the continuing lack of a clear timetable for membership of NATO, Poland signed up to the **Partnership for Peace Agreement** in January 1994. For the moment, NATO remains extremely cautious about making any further formal overtures towards the central European countries, Poland included, the crucial complicating factor being Russia's oftstated and increasingly fierce opposition to ex-Warsaw Pact countries' membership of NATO.

MONUMENTAL CHRONOLOGY

1500 BC	Iron Age tribes of Lusatian culture.	Fortified settlement of **Biskupin**.
10C	Creation of Polish state.	Ruins of palace at **Ostrów Lednicki**, St Mary on the Wawel, **Kraków**.
11–12C	Poland under the early Piasts.	**Romanesque** architecture – cathedrals of **Gniezno** (bronze doors only survive) and **Kraków** (crypt); Collegiate church, **Kruszwica**; Premonstratensian monastery, **Strzelno**.
Early 13C	Monasticism spreads to Poland; Teutonic Knights invited into the country.	**Transitional** style introduced by Cistercians – monasteries at **Trzebnica** and **Henryków**. Fully fledged **Gothic** first appears in Dominican and Franciscan churches in **Kraków**. First Teutonic buildings – castle of **Kwidzyn**, beginning of construction of fortress at **Malbork**.
14C	Teutonic Knights establish a Baltic state; reign of Kazimierz the Great (1333–70); Bohemian control of Silesia recognized.	Great century of Gothic building, particularly in brick, in the Teutonic territories. Middle Castle, **Malbork**; castle at **Lidzbark Warmiński**; town hall and churches of St Mary and St John, **Toruń**; town hall, Great Mill, St Mary, **Gdańsk**; cathedral, **Frombork**. **Kraków** adorned with Gothic buildings – Sukiennice (cloth hall), churches of Corpus Christi and St Catherine, suburb of Kazimierz. Laying out of new town of **Kazimierz Dolny**; stone castles of the **Eagles' Nest Trail**; cathedrals of **Gniezno** and **Poznań** rebuilt. Series of brick churches in **Wrocław** (Breslau) – cathedral, Holy Cross, St Mary of the Sands; fortifications of **Paczków**.
Late 14C, 15C	Poland under the Jagiellonians; Silesia officially part of Bohemia.	**Late Gothic** buildings – university and town gates, **Kraków**; town hall and further brick churches, **Wrocław**; St James, **Nysa**.
16C	Last of Jagiellonian dynasty; creation of Republic of Nobles (1572).	Italian architects bring **Renaissance** to Poland, introduced at Wawel Castle, **Kraków**. In same city, Zygmuntowska Chapel in Wawel Cathedral, rebuild of Sukiennice, Old Synagogue. Palaces at **Brzeg** and at **Krasiczyn**; rebuild of town hall at **Poznań**. **Late Renaissance** and **Mannerist** styles practised from 1570s until around 1610. Layout of planned town of **Zamość**, including town hall, collegiate church and synagogue, by Bartolomeo Morandi. Beginning of construction of Royal Palace, **Warsaw**. Armoury and Golden House, **Gdańsk**; other town mansions in **Kraków**, **Kazimierz Dolny**, **Sandomierz** and **Wrocław**.

1587–1668	The Waza dynasty.	Early **Baroque** style of the Jesuits introduced with SS Peter and Paul, **Kraków**. Rebuilding of monastery of Jasna Góra, **Częstochowa** and palace of **Łańcut**. Waza Chapel in Wawel Cathedral, **Kraków**, marks Polish debut of full-blooded Baroque.
Late 17C	Turkish Wars; Poland at height of its international prestige.	Extensive building in **Warsaw**, including palace of Wilanów, the more restrained Krasiński and Radziwiłł palaces and Church of Holy Sacrament. All except the first designed by Tylman of Gameren, architect also of St Anne, **Kraków**, and the palace of **Nieborów**.
Late 17C, early 18C	Poland under the Saxon kings; Silesia part of Habsburg Empire.	Italianate Baroque in parish church, **Poznań**; town hall and churches, **Leszno**. Additions to Royal Palace, **Warsaw**. Buildings by Baroque architects from Vienna and Prague in Silesia: Ossoliński Library, Elector's Chapel in cathedral, Church of Holy Name and university, **Wrocław**; St Joseph and Monastery Church, **Krzeszów**; monastery of **Legnickie Pole**.
1764–1795	Reign of Stanisław-August Poniatowski; Silesia under Prussian rule.	**Neoclassicism** appears in additions to Royal Palace and in Łazienki Palace, **Warsaw**. Period of great country houses, including **Arcadia** and **Rogalin**. More severe version of Neoclassical style is adopted in Silesia – university library and royal palace, **Wrocław**; fortress at **Kłodzko**.
1795–1914	Poland under Partition.	Late Neoclassical buildings include Raczyński Library, **Poznań**, and theatre, **Wrocław**. Neo-Gothic of Berlin architect Karl Friedrich Schinkel in palace of **Kórnik** and castle of **Legnica**; castle in **Lublin** is in similar vein. Grandiose, derivative styles characteristic of the nineteenth century best illustrated in Polish Bank and Grand Theatre in **Warsaw** and in factories and houses of **Łódź**. In early twentieth century, notable public works in **Wrocław** – Grunwaldzki Bridge and Max Berg's Hala Ludowa. Also **Jugendstil** and **Secessionist** styles in then German cities such as Zielona Góra and Opole.
1918–present	Resurrection of Polish state; World War II; Poland under communism; democracy restored.	**Nazi** architecture in German lands, notably Wolf's Lair, **Gierłoz**. Postwar concentration on factories and housing estates, with occasional showpieces, such as Palace of Culture, **Warsaw**. After an initial ban, spectacular modern churches built: two of the finest are in Kraków suburb of **Nowa Huta**.

POLAND'S ENVIRONMENT

The following piece, which examines the current state of the Polish environment in the aftermath of the heavy-industry oriented communist era, is by David Goldblatt, a political analyst and researcher with the Open University who has recently completed a PhD on the history and politics of the environment movement in Britain. Thanks are also due to Iza Kruszewska of Greenpeace and the Environmental Service Agency, Warsaw, for some of the background material to the article.

THE COMMUNIST LEGACY

Perhaps, of all the heavy legacies that 45 years of state socialism have left the Polish people, the environmental legacy is the most onerous. Capitalist societies, as we know, have hardly proved environmentally benign. However, few societies have matched the environmental devastation wrought by Polish communism. The path of economic modernization pursued after World War II, when combined with the institutional failures of a centrally planned economy and an authoritarian polity, has yielded an almost unparalleled record of environmental degradation. It seems that only parts of the ex-Soviet Union – where the same conditions operated in an even more extreme fashion – can match this.

The heart of the problem has been the peculiarly lopsided structure of the Polish economy. Pursuing an inappropriate Soviet model of economic development after World War II, Poland embarked on the **rapid expansion** of its energy and heavy industries: coal mining, electricity production, steel, concrete, shipbuilding. The country is still dependent on domestically produced coal, especially the brown coal lignite, which has created a particularly damaging mix of energy and industry. These facts alone would have ensured rising levels of atmospheric, aquatic and soil **pollution**. However, the institutional structures of state socialism made matters considerably worse. The **inefficiency of the Polish economy** meant that older and more polluting plant was kept running for longer and in worse condition; investment in new technologies was blocked by a desperate lack of foreign exchange; and pollution regulations were rarely enforced – all in a political climate where any threat of local or national protest was repressed. The only saving grace of technological lag and the scarcity of capital is that Poland has never seriously embarked upon a nuclear programme, although both the communists and the post-communist governments have contemplated it.

THE STATE OF POLISH CITIES

The environmental consequences of state socialism have fallen most heavily upon some of Poland's cities, the most seriously affected area being Upper Silesia in the southwest corner of the country. At its heart is the sprawling industrial conurbation of **Katowice**, the industries and households of which consume a vast quantity of locally mined coal for production and heating. In addition, zinc and lead ores are mined and smelted, and the region receives significant atmospheric pollution from Northern Bohemia in the Czech Republic and Saxony in eastern Germany. Together these areas form "**The Black Triangle**", producing a phenomenal cocktail of sulphur dioxide, nitrogen oxides, dust and particulates, smog and ozone. Twenty-five percent of total atmospheric emissions are generated in this two percent of the country, and that's not including the range of carcinogenic chemicals produced and released by factories into local communities and water courses. The mining industry has left widespread subsidence and discharges untreated saline waste into the Odra (Oder) and Wista (Vistula) rivers.

The consequences of these emissions are predictable, if no less horrific for that. People are ill more often and more seriously, and die in greater numbers after shorter lives; **life expectancy** for adults in the region is three years less than the Polish average. Infant mortality is running at the rate of twenty deaths per thousand births, which is around double the Western European average. In the Bytom area it is almost three times that rate. The number of children born with **congenital defects** is sixty percent higher than Poland as a whole, child leukaemia rates are double an already high national average and bronchial illness and circulatory problems are widespread.

To the east of Katowice, and downwind of much of its atmospheric pollution, lies Kraków. Here the story is just as grim: on top of imported pollution, the city houses the infamous **Nowa Huta steelworks**, still the largest factory in Poland and already out of date by the time it went into operation in the 1940s. Designed in the previous decade, Nowa Huta was based on a steel plant in Pittsburgh, the plan of which was stolen from the Americans by the Soviets, who passed it on to the Poles. Producing steel at a price that almost no one will buy, the plant consumes vast amounts of coal, electricity and iron ore with the result that iron dust, cadmium, zinc and lead deposits envelop the city in a stationary cloud of smog for over a hundred days a year. Not surprisingly, adults in Kraków have four times as many colds as other Poles and three times as much asthma; lung cancer and degenerative bone diseases are also widespread. Also, the sulphur dioxide emitted from both Nowa Huta and the power stations that supply it are rapidly eating away at the very stone fabric of both old and new parts of the city; the faces have been wiped from statues; stained glass is destroyed. It is proving easier to raise international funding to save the buildings of Kraków – a United Nations' world heritage site – than to ease the plight of its inhabitants.

AGRICULTURE AND THE COUNTRYSIDE

Outside of the cities, in Poland's extensive rural areas, the situation is bad but less serious. **Agriculture** is a major contributor to both water and soil pollution. Compared to Western farming methods, Poland uses significantly less fertilizer and pesticide, but poor techniques and antiquated chemicals mean that more of these substances are leached into the environment with more **toxic effects**. In addition, ill-conceived, large-scale drainage programmes orchestrated by the communists have caused the loss of valuable wetlands.

More significantly, pollution from Poland's industrial cities has seeped into the countryside. It is estimated that nearly eighty percent of the land has **acidic soils**, while those areas near non-ferrous metal-smelting industries have recorded extremely dangerous levels of **heavy-metal contamination**. These heavy metals find their way into vegetables and cereals, leading people in the worst-affected areas to turn to their own allotments and gardens.

At the same time, however, Poland has some of the most untouched and unique landscapes in the whole of Europe: the pristine primeval forest of Białowieża on the Belarus border; the mountain forests of Carpathia; the untouched bogs and peatlands of the Biebrza swamps that teem with birdlife; the southeastern steppe lands. The result is an abundance of rare fauna, including bears, lynx, wildcats and golden eagles, though – along with 25 percent of all Polish vertebrates and 28 percent of flowering plants – these are sadly in **danger of extinction**.

In 1989 the United Nations Environment Programme estimated that between five and ten percent of Poland's forests were damaged. More accurate unofficial estimates suggest a figure nearer 75 percent. The **Sudetan Mountains** in the south are especially threatened. In many areas only blackened tree stumps remain, the result of destruction by acid rain blown north over the border from the Czech Republic and south from Silesia. Not only are the trees dying, but the remaining acidified soil is being washed into the Odra River basin, nowadays threatened with regular flooding.

Most under-reported of Poland's rural environmental problems is the quiet crisis of **rural sanitation and health**. If a partially organic agriculture and extensive wilderness are the environmental benefits of underdevelopment, then its underside is the minimal provision for sewerage, clean water and safe disposal of waste that Poland's rural population continues to endure. Over half of community and privately owned wells have water unfit for human consumption. Few villages have any collective facilities for the collection and disposal of waste, so that ditches and forests all over the countryside are littered by thousands of untreated and unregulated dumps.

POLAND'S RIVERS AND THE BALTIC SEA

Poland's rivers and lakes are in no better state than its land. According to the government's own system of classification, less than twenty percent of rivers are fit for consumption and two-thirds are already so badly polluted that they are unsuitable to receive industrial wastes.

Most of the effluents are carried by the **Wisła and the Odra rivers**. Both flow north from Upper Silesia, adding its pollution to that of western and eastern Poland, and then into the **Baltic**. According to the Polish Ministry of the Environment, the Baltic is now the **most polluted sea in Europe**, although the Poles have been generously helped in making it so by the twelve other nations with Baltic coastlines.

The Baltic Sea is a particularly fragile ecosystem because it is so shallow and so little of its polluted waters can escape into the North Sea. Many of Poland's Baltic beaches have been closed to the public owing to health risks, the coastlines around Gdańsk and Szczecin being worst affected. In addition, the leaching of nitrogen and phosphorus compounds from agriculture to rivers and then to the sea is causing an excessive growth of **algae** in the Baltic. The dead algae accumulate on the sea floor, concentrating pollutants and creating large areas of dead sea without oxygen – approximately 260,000 square kilometres to date.

ENVIRONMENTAL POLITICS AND POLICIES

Despite the widespread abuse of civil liberties under the communists and their draconian repression of all dissident political activity, a small **environmental movement** did emerge to challenge the wave of environmental degradation engulfing Poland in the late 1970s and early 1980s. This included groups like the National Conservation League (LOP) and Polski Klub Ekologiczny (PKE) founded in Kraków in 1980. In the early 1980s, the movement, in close cooperation with Solidarity, forced the publication of secret government reports acknowledging the catastrophic state of the Polish environment and the cosmetic nature of environmental policy and legislation, plus the closure of the heavily polluting Skawina aluminium plant.

Since 1989, environmental pressure groups and research institutes have proliferated in Poland and a **Green party** has been formed, although it failed to win any seats at the parliamentary election in December 1991. While post-communist governments have proved more receptive to environmental issues and a great deal more open about the state of the Polish environment, there have been considerable conflicts.

Current government policy is addressing itself to global and national environmental problems, the establishment of strict environmental standards and the creation of adequate enforcement agencies. However, as the Polish Green movement has sharply pointed out, **capitalist democracy** is not, as yet, proving to be that much more effective at curbing environmental degradation than its socialist predecessor. The social costs of environmentally restructuring Polish industry are enormous. There is little chance of domestic lignite being replaced by imported fuels. Clean technologies are available but expensive. Above all, the market is proving as environmentally problematic as central planning. The arrival of capitalism has brought the familiar detritus of Western economic growth: the rise of the car and the demise of public transport, the proliferation of unrecyclable and wasteful packaging. However, these developments have not as yet got out of control. It is not inconceivable that with a degree of foresight and international assistance and finance, the Poles may both deal with the legacy that state socialism has left them and circumvent some of the worst aspects of the West's poor environmental record. If they are able to do so it will be an achievement every bit as great as the peaceful revolution of 1989.

WOMEN IN POLAND

In 1990–91 Małgorzata Tarasiewicz worked as Women's Officer for Solidarity, a position from which she eventually resigned following disagreements with the trade-union leadership over the controversial issue of abortion and the question of democracy within the movement. A former president of the Polish section of Amnesty International and active in grassroots organizations, for many years she was a leading member of Wolność i Pokój (Freedom and Peace), an oppositional movement with close connections with Western peace groups such as European Nuclear Disarmament (END). The following article, which offers a personal perspective on the issues facing women in post-communist Poland, was originally published in *Feminist Review* (no. 39), winter 1991.

WOMEN IN POLAND: CHOICES TO BE MADE

Some people say: let us first establish our democracies and then we can work out the details (meaning the rights of women). But if these two things do not go hand in hand, not only will women remain second-class citizens but also our societies will remain backward civilizations, limiting themselves only to talk about democracy. Without the participation of women in changes in Poland and without their being involved in political, social and economic life, democracy will never be achieved. The new situation creates new conditions in all spheres of life. Economic competition and new routes to political posts mean new opportunities for women, opportunities to take positions in which they will have a chance to influence the society they live in.

Eastern Europe is in a **transitional period**. This period is marked by a struggle of ideas, which is especially important since whichever ideas emerge as dominant are going to influence the lives of more than one generation.

Some years ago, an unofficial organization in Poland received a letter from somebody who had a paint sprayer and wanted to write slogans on walls but did not know what to write, so asked for advice. It is a present-day reality in Poland that where government positions are at stake, the only groups that can make any gains are those that are well organized and experienced in using **political pressure**. Women are definitely not such a group. They are like the person with the paint sprayer; their problem is how to exert their rights.

Over the past forty years women's organizations were treated instrumentally, and though the legal system could have been considered pro-feminine, in Poland, as in other eastern European countries, there was a great discrepancy between the legal system and social reality. "Front" women's organizations, with a conformist membership, have created a destructive and demoralizing image of what a women's organization is like. The stereotype that originated in this way is now very much predominant within the society. So new attempts to establish a women's group are often discredited as the second Women's League, as the communist organization was named. Moreover, issues like **abortion** are used instrumentally during political turning points like the parliamentary elections in the spring of 1989 or the presidential elections in the autumn of 1990. All the major political forces are playing on the issue of abortion for their own ends. Catholic fundamentalists reject any kind of discussion of the topic and support the criminalization of abortion. Ex-communists, surrounded by some remnants of the Women's League, advocate the right to choose. The alliance with the Church makes it rather awkward for other major forces to speak up about this issue. Because of this, popular consciousness identifies pro-choice attitudes with the corruption of the past 45 years. The strong influence of the Catholic Church makes society stick to the traditional vision of the female role, limited to a wife and mother stereotype.

The political climate is dominated by traditional values. With the growth of unemployment, there are government plans to send women home from their jobs in order to improve the situation on the labour market. The only point of reference for Poland is the prewar period, which is the only model of the social organization of an independent Polish nation. It is viewed with nostalgia and among other things it provides the image of what a family should be like and what the feminine role is. Polish prewar society, dominated by Catholic ideals, definitely cannot be a model for a completely different post-totalitarian country aspiring to a free market economy, with all the setbacks and benefits that such a situation brings about. The most visible advantage consists in transforming the image of work. In the communist period, work was not considered to be a source of independence. **Low wages** became a kind of substitute for social welfare. In the new situation women will probably develop a new attitude towards gaining professional skills. The most common danger that women, like the rest of society, will have to face is unemployment.

By the end of October 1990, women formed 51 percent of the one million unemployed. It's important to stress that among young people more women than men remained unemployed. By the end of October 1990 there were 37.3 percent **unemployed women** for one vacancy compared with 9.5 percent men. In six regional districts there were over a hundred women for one job vacancy (and in one district as many as 1,398). For 97.3 percent of registered unemployed women there was no offer of a job at all. Women, because of their double duties, cannot compete with men on the labour market. Women's situation will get even worse with time and advances of restructuring in those branches of industry – like the textile industry – that employ mainly women. At the moment, employment in some textile enterprises is kept stable but, in order to avoid mass redundancies, women are sent on unpaid leave or work only two days a week, earning 500,000zł, which is well below the poverty level.

Economic recession and the urge to cut costs has led to degradation of the value of women's work. According to data from 1988, almost two-thirds of Polish women worked outside the home. However, the motivation for most of them was not the hope of fulfilling career ambitions or the intentions of being financially independent but a much more mundane need to make ends meet. This situation led to mass participation of women in the labour market. Since all consumer goods were scarce in eastern Europe, women had a second full-time job running the household. The difficulty of obtaining goods forced many women to take part-time jobs. Now it is often this kind of a job that disappears first. Polish women are also less qualified than men and as such are easier to dismiss. Another reason for dismissing women is a **cultural** one: it seems to be generally accepted in Poland that a man needs a job more than a woman.

In an opinion poll carried out at the end of 1990, 45 percent of working women's husbands thought that women should not work outside their homes. The same opinion was shared by 53 percent of men whose wives did not work professionally, by 35 percent of working women and by 47 percent of housewives.

It was a common belief that as soon as we got rid of communist rule the aid and investment would start pouring in from the Western countries. This turned out not to be true. The majority of Western businessmen interested in eastern Europe are interested in quick profits only. They do create some jobs, but on their own conditions: **no trade unions**, no complaints about work conditions, low wages. That is why few men want to work there; women have no choice no matter how big the **health hazards** are. Women's cooperatives and the training of women managers are discussed both in the Ministry of Labour and the trade unions, but as funding is insufficient and women are not adequately organized, it only remains in the domain of wishful thinking. The conditions of work that are offered to unskilled workers are often unacceptable and the pay too low for men.

A woman's position on the labour market is perceived as more flexible due to the predominant image of woman as wife and mother whose main life goal is to support the family. Escaping the social pressure to become a mother of the traditional type and "**finding alternative forms of female identity**" are among the most important women's issues in Poland. This adds to the problem of unemployment. The traditional role models determine women's position in public life, resulting in male domination in all spheres of social and political activity. Women's internalized negative view of themselves leads many women to reject institutions aimed against existing inequalities. Recently, hearing about the possibility of creating a **Ministry of Women's Affairs**, one woman was shocked and said she felt human first and foremost so why should such an institution be needed at all?

Besides an internalized negative view of themselves, there is another factor responsible for women's denial of the existence of discrimination in our society. This other factor is pride in being a Polish mother and in preserving the **patriotic values** of the Polish nation. That is why women's problems are crucial in the transition period in Poland and eastern Europe. George Konrad, a writer from Hungary, in his book *Anti-Politics* explains how, during the last forty years, the private sphere was the only place where people could retain their soul and resist the intrusiveness of the state. The importance of the **private sphere** which was mainly women's domain made the role essential to all forms of resistance to the communist system. Now the uniqueness of the private sphere is much diminished as the civil

society establishes itself. When men join public life women are left in a less valued sphere of life. Long associated with the home, women are simply not seen as part of the new civil society.

In the immediate future, the main things to be achieved for women's benefit will lie in two spheres. The first is concerned with the better circulation of information between eastern bloc countries, so that particular solutions can be found together. The experience of Western countries is equally valued, as it can be applied to Polish conditions so that we do not have to break through an open door. The information should cover such questions as ways of retraining women, of creating new jobs and legislative problems. The other sphere of activity consists of what may seem to be more abstract, that is, changing the stereotype of a woman. This would involve a broad range of activities including work with the mass media and revision of educational systems. In this respect, too, we will need extensive support from our more experienced peers.

REFERENCES

Małgorzata Dobraczynska *Dilemmas of Polish Women — Let's Work?* Paper given at CSCE Women's Conference, Berlin, November 1990.

Ruth Rosen "Women and Democracy in Czechoslovakia — an interview with Jirina Siklova" in *Peace and Democracy News* (Campaign for Peace and Democracy, New York), Fall 1990.

GAYS AND LESBIANS IN POLAND

In a country where official Catholic attitudes to gender, morality and sex continue to exercise a powerful influence on national life, social attitudes to gays and lesbians are imbued with a specific complex of prejudices and dilemmas. The following article by Lucy Kimbell, a US citizen living and working in Poland, provides an insight into the situation of gays and lesbians in contemporary Poland. The article originally appeared in 1991 in *The Warsaw Voice*, to which thanks are due for permission to reproduce it.

NOT SO ROSY

We meet in a trendy bar in the centre of Warsaw. We talk in English and, although it is unlikely that many of the people around us will understand what we are saying, we keep our voices low. Piotr (not his real name), a teacher aged 28, tells me his story concisely over a dish of cream and fruit. He is happy to talk to someone – it gives some perspective – but he is not optimistic about what the future holds for him and many others. When one of us mentions the h-word (homosexual), we automatically flinch as if someone at another table has overheard.

Poland has relatively liberal laws regulating sexual behaviour in comparison with, for example, the United Kingdom. The Criminal Code of 1963 does not even mention, let alone criminalize, homosexual activity and the **age of consent** for sex is fifteen across the board, without specifying whether heterosexual or homosexual. Gays and lesbians have more legislative freedom in Catholic post-communist Poland than in that bastion of freedom, the United States, where in some states homosexual relations are banned, or in Britain, where the age of consent for men is 21.

But in North America – and nearer to this Warsaw bar – in Germany or Britain, while there may be legislative restrictions through which the state polices sexual behaviour, there is such a thing as a lesbian and gay subculture,

even a **"pink" counter-culture**. There are lesbian and gay studies programmes at universities, there are TV programmes catering for the lesbian and gay audience. There is certainly lesbian and gay politics.

Gays and lesbians in Poland, like any other minority group, are sensitive about the language used to describe what defines their difference. Piotr corrects himself when he says "homosexual" when he means "gay". The word "homosexual" was originally a nineteenth-century medical category which sought to identify – and treat – a pathology. The h-word differs from "gay" or "lesbian" in the assumptions behind it. Homosexuality is almost a condition: being lesbian or gay is just one of those things.

The words are pretty much the same in many languages. Slang varies, of course, expressing on a more fundamental level each society's attitudes. Polish slang for gay or queer is *pedał*, literally a pedal, but close to *pederasta*, with all the condemnation invested in it.

In the West, lesbian and gay activists have been reclaiming the g-word since the beginning of **Gay Liberation** in the early 1970s, a movement which learned its lessons from the Civil Rights Movement. During the last twenty years in the West, despite legislative and organization difficulties in some countries, a distinct culture of liberation has developed – liberation and celebration, evidenced in the annual June Gay Pride marches in cities throughout the world. In Poland we keep our voices low and Piotr asks me not to use his real name in the article.

Lesbian and gay activists say that it is important to draw a distinction between a gay (as opposed to gay and lesbian) community that is literally **underground** – men meeting in stations, hotel bars and public toilets – and a community of lesbian and gay activists. The history of lesbian and gay activism in Poland is brief.

After the defeat of communism in Poland, it seemed that many minority groups would be able to develop their communities without the hindrances the former authorities put in their way. Democracy is supposed to recognize difference. But the spark that was lit in the Polish gay scene never became the roaring, warming fire that it might have. "People are not interested in gays at all here," Piotr says. He doesn't look so interested himself. His bowl of cream glows a sickly yellow in the artificial light.

Poland's first gay **magazine**, *Filo*, published in Gdańsk by a nucleus of activists who later became the city's **Lambda group**, started publishing six years ago when the communist authorities were still in power. That it was allowed to publish is significant, as is the fact that its circulation was restricted to a hundred copies. The first Polish lesbian and gay organization, Polish Lambda, was not allowed to register formally until February 1990 after several attempts.

Lambda groups were set up around the country in all the major cities, and more magazines were founded by private companies. The Lambda groups had dozens of members – some actively campaigning, others just there to meet people. At its high point, the Warsaw Lambda group had over 200 members.

Warsaw's first openly **gay disco** with a capacity of 500, *Café Fiolka*, opened in September 1990, linked with Poland's first lesbian and gay information agency, **Pink Service**. A British TV company came to make a documentary about the lesbian and gay scene in Poland for Channel 4. The Warsaw Lambda group got coverage in the national press and radio, and with the help of this publicity more people got in touch through the box number.

A community of activists began developing and adopted the slogans of pride and liberation and personal identity politics from the West. The Warsaw Lambda group set up an informal café staffed by volunteers, providing somewhere to meet and information about safer sex and the dangers of **HIV and AIDS**. It was possible to meet people elsewhere than in public toilets or at stations – if you knew the right people and got to hear about what was happening.

As with the gay movements elsewhere in the world, more men than women were involved. No one is able to offer a simple explanation as to why **lesbians** are more invisible than gay men in Poland. Ania who is nineteen and still at school is reluctant to explain her opinion. "We go to meetings but the men talk about things that don't really interest us. We want to set up a group for lesbians in Warsaw." I ask the question that is begging to

be asked: Where can a young lesbian or gay man have sex since most young people live with their parents into their twenties or older?

Ania shrugs: "I am lucky because my mother knows about me, and she lets my girlfriend come and stay at our flat. But for most people it is impossible. . . . You have to stay with friends, wait for your parents to go out. . . . I don't know anyone whose mother is as understanding."

However, despite the burgeoning gay activism, during the **presidential election campaign** last autumn [1990] – an ideal time for all minority groups to draw attention to themselves – the subject of sexuality remained closed. The newsletter *Warsaw Gay News*, printed in English by Pink Service, undertook a survey of the candidates' opinions about homosexuality and homosexuals. The conversations with the various candidates or their spokespeople provide an interesting perspective on what for most Poles seems to be barely an issue.

Former prime minister Tadeusz Mazowiecki's spokesman said, "It would be wiser not to touch the subject." Sexual politics often confuses the traditional alignments across the political spectrum. Leszek Moczulski of the **Confederation for an Independent Poland** claimed that "the question of sexuality is a very individual issue. Everyone has a right to choose how, where, and with whom. . . . We have to protect one's privacy. The legal system should be focused on this issue."

Jan Tymiński's assistant fell in with more predictable attitudes when he said that "this problem is not a good one to discuss during his campaign. . . . We are not interested in minorities." **Lech Wałęsa**'s press office was also reluctant to discuss it, declaring that he was not interested in this issue. In answer to the question as to how, if he became president, he would treat the minority, he said: "I don't know yet whether I will treat them as outcasts of society. It is hard for me to answer this question now. We'll see after the elections. . ."

The staunchly Catholic Wałęsa had been the focus of foreign interest earlier in the year when it was reported at the **International Lesbian and Gay Association** (ILGA) conference in Stockholm that he had said that drug users and homosexuals should be eliminated. Western journalists – in particular the **gay press** – were quick to pick up on the story.

However, the apparent source of the alleged comments, the editor of *Filo* magazine, said that he had not heard the statement himself. There were no records of any statement on the subject in the minutes of Solidarity's second conference at which the comments were alleged to have been made.

Wałęsa's press spokesman, Andrzej Drzycimski, said that they had received a lot of letters about the alleged comments. He suggested that for the Polish gay activists it was a way to get attention from the international gay community and general public opinion.

The altercations around Wałęsa's alleged comments, and the initial enthusiasm displayed by (admittedly mostly young, mostly well-educated) urban lesbians and gays, could have provided a sound basis for a movement similar to, and linked by ILGA with, lesbian and gay liberation movements elsewhere in the world. *Café Fiolka* was busy every Friday night and Pink Service was making money. Poland even had a publicly gay man, **Sławek Starosta**, pop star and director of Pink Service, who refused to compromise and keep his sexual orientation secret.

In April 1991 there was a **big meeting** of all the Polish lesbian and gay groups, new businesses and publications held over a weekend at *Café Fiolka*. But somehow, the initial post-communist euphoria had gone. The energy for organizing, for activism along the lines common in the West, dissipated.

Activists began slipping away. The 24-year-old chairman of the Warsaw Lambda group died tragically of a heart attack and the vice-chairman assumed his responsibilities without an election. The group lost its office at the university, and without this focus, lost much of its energy. Some of the new magazines went out of business after only a few issues. Even after the long summer break during which one expects activity to quieten down, things did not pick up. **The spark really had gone out**. What happened to the energy?

Irek Krzemiński, assistant professor of sociology at Warsaw University and a former Solidarity activist, makes reference to ideas of democracy in his analysis of what put out the spark. His was the **generation of '68** which experienced the transition from traditional Polish patterns to the idea that individuality –

including sexual individuality – was connected with freedom. "In the 1970s, Polish society was changing in this direction – openness toward sex in general and accepting all minorities. Now it is quite different. . . . Society is changing in an unpleasant direction. It is paradoxical that at the beginning of the 1990s we have in some senses more of a closed mind, a **more traditional**, more collectivist attitude than we had during the last ten years of communism in Europe."

To develop a campaign, a movement needs more than enthusiasm. It needs to be able to organize and it needs money, and above all it needs to come from within a community. According to Sławek Starosta of Pink Service, those involved in setting up Lambda made a lot of mistakes. "We were really isolated from the existing gay community. We looked around and we didn't see it. We were young and inexperienced and the people from the gay community didn't want any kind of group set up so they didn't help."

According to Krzemiński, another factor in the dampening of activism is the **Church**, which always plays a special role in Poland. "The Church had a big, big role in the defeat of Communism. . . . In contrast to the soldiers on the streets, there was the visible freedom of the Church. But now the Church has the idea of continuing to have a political role in the state."

The Church is traditionally antagonistic to sexual freedom of any kind. As Polish society continues to negotiate the major readjustments of the last two years, the Church carries on clinging onto the fiercely traditional values which are being undermined. Krzemiński sums them up: "Women should be at home, men should be out working hard for their families, gays are dreadful. . ."

The Church's attitude toward lesbians and gays, and particularly to lesbian and gay organizing, is one element of a general **hostility** to "other", to the very concept of strangers. According to Krzemiński, as Poland continues down the path of reform and transformation, political, economic and social, the kinds of frustrations that people are experiencing are the ideal vehicle for developing hostility to "other". The racism and xenophobia now rampant in Germany provide a **warning** of how the energies unleashed by the post-communist changes can be channelled. "It's only during the past few years that I have begun to feel in personal danger because of my sexuality," he adds, somewhat ominously.

In Starosta's opinion, there is little sign that the current trend in Polish lesbian and gay activism will reverse. "People are now very much involved in their lives – trying to survive – and they don't have the time or the money to do things for other people. I don't see any signs of change."

Café Fiolka may have to close in the spring [see p.114] since although it is busy every Friday night, no one goes the other nights it is open and it is losing money. Pink Service is still expanding and the newly founded erotic gay men's magazine it publishes, *Men*, is doing well, but other magazines have closed.

While the Church continues to have a prominent role in society and people are not prepared to put energy into organizing, things are unlikely to change. In those quiet conversations in trendy Warsaw bars, it is the h-word that you will hear, not the word "gay". It is desperation you will sense, not celebration.

Attitudes in Poland are likely to remain distinct from those experienced by gays and lesbians elsewhere in Europe or in the United States. Levels of "queerbashing" have forced gay groups to organize **protection** for visitors to bars and clubs and to protect the community since the police often won't.

In Poland, while there is always the possibility of violence, for example from the gangs who occasionally lie in wait outside *Fiolka*, it is an indifferent hostility. It is not the sort that makes you feel the attackers wish you weren't there, but the sort that says you really don't matter.

CONTEMPORARY POLITICS

Poland's modern political transformation can be attributed to many factors, first and foremost the concerted efforts of the oppositional triad – unique in East-Central Europe – of Church, workers (Solidarity) and intellectuals. In the following excerpt from her book, *Poles Apart* (see "Books", p.660), Irish journalist Jaqueline Hayden, a seasoned visitor to Poland, profiles Janek and Krystyna Lityńska, a couple whose lives exemplify in many respects the struggles that have given birth to a new political order in the country.

RELUCTANT HEROISM

Krystyna Litynska is always quick to point out that she was interned for ten weeks after martial law while many of her friends served much lengthier sentences. But though the duration was shorter the long-term effects of that two-and-a-half month incarceration have remained with her to this day. The 13th of December 1981 was bitterly cold, like any other winter night in Warsaw. It was not a night to huddle in a freezing cold barracks with no blankets, running water, light or heating. Unwilling to glorify her experience, Krystyna is almost matter-of-fact in her description of the tuberculosis she contracted as a result of her period in Olszynka women's prison. Perhaps one side-effect of the mass communication of the horrors of war and torture is to lessen the impact of the withdrawal of basic human rights, wrongful imprisonment and non-violent inhuman treatment. It appears to make even the victims unwilling to complain lest it appear that they seek to compare their treatment with that meted out by more gruesome or brutal regimes.

The night of 13 December is in the same category as the day of the assassination of President John F. Kennedy for most Poles. Everyone remembers where they were and what they were doing. Rumours of a possible Soviet intervention or military clamp-down had been circulating on and off since the strikes began in July and August 1980. Tensions rose and eased, hopes ran high, and then low. But in a country where people had grown used to living on a knife edge and where people had begun to regard Solidarity's power as real rather than symbolic the coup d'etat in the end came as a surprise.

By the autumn of 1981 Krystyna and Jan had moved from his mother's apartment into a rented flat in a housing scheme, built for army and police families, on the outskirts of Warsaw. Given their political activity, the occupation of most of their neighbours was a bit unfortunate. The couple's relations with the secret policeman who lived opposite were not good. They had deteriorated rapidly after he stuffed their keyhole with a sealing agent in protest at the caterwauling of their dog, Pilsudski (named after Marshall Josef Pilsudski, because of the dog's likeness to the controversial dictator).

In recalling the events of 13 December, Krystyna remembers hurling abuse at the secret policeman as she was led past him on her way to the police car. In retrospect she felt she had been unfair because he had had the courage to confront the arresting officers. Neighbours told her that he had called after them: "So now you're taking women." Later she found out that his son-in-law, like many other sons and daughters, was active in Solidarity.

The first inkling Krystyna and Jan had that something was wrong was when they tried to telephone a cab for a friend who was about to leave their flat. It is not unusual, even today, to have difficulty phoning from one side of Warsaw to another. So, when neither his own nor a neighbour's phone upstairs worked, Jan left the building and went to another block in the hope that he could make the connection through a different exchange network. By the time it dawned on him that the phones were not working anywhere, the police were already knocking on their door. When Krystyna opened it, she was grabbed by the throat and inside. In the struggle that ensued, she asked for a search warrant. "This time," the secret policeman told her politely, "we will not be searching your flat. Pack your bags, Pani Krystyna and wear something warm. It is very cold out tonight." It was only when he entered the hallway of his own apartment block that Jan saw what was happening. He ran upstairs to a third-floor flat where some friends lived, but before he was able to jump out of the window the door was bashed in by a crowbar and he was nabbed before he could escape. Hearing the shouting upstairs, Krystyna ran up to find Jan being pulled downstairs by the police, who were so angry about their near miss that they were going to take him away wearing only his shirt and slippers. In the mêlée that followed Krystyna remembers being pulled off Jan by a huge Ubek (policeman) with flat eyes. It was then that she broke her golden rule of not reacting or showing emotion in the presence of "them". So, as she shouted to all around her that they were "sons of bitches" she was nearly strangled by the furious Ubek with the funny eyes.

Eventually they packed their bags in peace. The police tried to remain polite and kept a decent distance while the neighbours hung around the landings so as to get a good view of the goings on. Both remember being more worried about what would happen to their dog than about what the night held in store for them. In a country where queueing for food was the most important daily chore, Jan remembers how awful it was to have to leave behind them a five-pound tin of ham which he had been given as a present. There was no bread in the house so they couldn't even make sandwiches.

Krystyna remembers how strange the atmosphere was when they arrived at Wilcza Street police station. The place was packed with all their friends who were greeting each other. "The whole thing was very dramatic but in a serious way." The first group she saw included a famous theatre director who was handcuffed to his son. At about five in the morning the first transport of women left the station en route to the women's prison. Looking out of the window of the police van, Krystyna saw a huge phalanx of ZOMO (riot police) guarding Solidarity headquarters in the centre of Warsaw. It is an image that is indelibly printed on her memory. Later, as the van moved towards the outskirts of the city, she watched as column after column of tanks slowly lumbered snake-like towards Warsaw, intent on strangling Solidarity's newly won freedom.

When her group reached the prison, it was obvious that the women guards did not know how to act towards the rather cosmopolitan and unusual batch of newly arrived prisoners.

For a start they seemed unsure about how they should address them. "Pani" is a term of politeness not normally afforded the criminal community in Poland, so the guards avoided direct references altogether at first. The scene degenerated into complete farce when it was realized that one of Poland's most famous stage and film actresses, Halina Mikolajska, was about to be incarcerated in a barracks with no heat, window panes, water, blankets or light. As the revered actress was being led down to her new accommodation, an enthralled warder urged her to mind the icy steps as well as enthusiastically telling Ms Mikolajska how delighted she was to meet her and how much she admired her work. In fact the actress was made of stern stuff. Since she had first became involved in KOR [Workers Defence Committee – opposition group formed in 1976 to defend striking workers that grew to become the intellectual nucleus for Solidarity] in 1977, she had grown used to being the victim of the secret police's dirty tricks department. She often found the keyholes in her apartment blocked with glue or her car sprayed with noxious chemicals. And of course she had suffered the hardest cut of all; she had on occasion been banned from working. Krystyna remembers her with great affection as a "real", as opposed to a political, Catholic. She was a believer in the fullest sense.

Olszynka prison had until the previous March been used as a barracks. Since then it had been vacant and ready but without running water, heating or light. When the women arrived, there was dust and dirt everywhere. There were seven bunk beds in their room. There was no blankets despite the freezing weather, so on that first night the women huddled under filthy mattresses to try and keep warm. It took three days for the prison authorities to organize a water supply. While Krystyna and her thirteen companions waited for the authorities to get organized, they gathered snow to flush the toilet which was behind a screen in the corner of the room. Slowly over the following days, lights and blankets began to appear...

Krystyna refers to Olszynka prison as the "health farm". When she was released, having been diagnosed as suffering from tuberculosis, she weighed forty-five kilos. "There was no temptation to eat. Breakfast and supper were the same, with bread, margarine and fifth-grade jam which came off a block. Dinner or lunch was either pea, cabbage or Scotch broth. Sometimes the barley stew had fragments of bacon in it with tufts of hair stuck to it. You can imagine the effect on our stomachs."

Given the nature of the women involved it is not surprising that many ex-internees shrug off the experience. Krystyna's cell adopted a non-conformist approach to dealing with the prison authorities. "If you rebel, you automatically acknowledge their power and authority. If you ignore them you win." So, roll-call, where the warders tried to impose some sort of military regime, became hysterical, with women shouting out that nobody had escaped that night. Like many other women who were interned or jailed, Krystyna's memories are of the camaraderie and spirit that developed between them. Perhaps it was fortuitous that Christmas followed less than two weeks after the mass arrests.

The Christmas holiday is celebrated with particular emphasis on tradition in Poland. After the fast on Christmas Eve, families start their festivities when the first star appears in the sky with a meal that has come from the sea, the woods, the mountains and the fields. Presents are then exchanged after midnight Mass. But on Christmas Eve 1981, Krystyna and her cell mates had what she describes as "a very elegant supper" of boiled eggs. Because it is regarded as a potential narcotic, prisoners are not normally allowed tea, but Regina Litynska, Krystyna's mother-in-law, had sent in a parcel with tea, sardines and a jumper. So, that night, the women celebrated by drinking, what the authorities judged to be a terribly dangerous brew.

Behaving and acting normally was the essence of the KOR philosophy of opposition. Celebrating Christmas as best they could, was much more than an attempt to keep their spirits high: the women were defying, by ignoring it, the attempt to crush their spirit of opposition. They even managed to adorn their quarters with a symbolic Christmas tree. On one of the daily walks around the quadrangle one of the women found a spiky twig which she brought back with her. And with great ingenuity they used the cotton wool from some Red Cross sanitary towels and some silver paper from their cigarette allowance to decorate their little bare twig. Then by "recycling" the packaging and the tinsel paper from their *Cosmos* cigarettes, Krystyna's adept colleagues made themselves a set of playing cards using the rocket on the back as the standard image and drawing the faces of the cards on the front: "We drew our King to look like Jaruzelski. I remember that we played a lot of Patience."

On New Year's Eve, they were allowed a great privilege. The lights, which normally went out at nine o'clock were left on until ten. Krystyna remembers it as being a funny night: "We had three liqueur chocolates between seven of us. The next day was my birthday. I actually got presents. A Solidarity badge and ring were smuggled into the prison. I was delighted."

*

Coming out of jail or any confinement can be a frightening experience. It was doubly so in Krystyna's case. Her husband was still interned as were many of her friends. She knew she was blacklisted and would be unable to get a job. She was not even sure where she could stay: "Inside the rules were clear cut. Outside there was a world without a future for me." Because she was ill, the authorities decided not to transfer Krystyna to Rakowiecka Street prison....

For at least a year after her release, Krystyna had a large shadow on her lung and was registering a high temperature every day. She was receiving treatment for tuberculosis but nothing improved her condition. When after three months in Warsaw's respiratory hospital the doctors decided to operate for suspected cancer, Krystyna thought better of it and signed herself out. She is convinced that she took the right decision.

Krystyna Litynska is an able and talented psychologist. Now that Poland is free, she is much sought after and was at one point running two separate psychiatric facilities. But from the time of her association with Jan in 1975, she was blacklisted and found it very difficult to get work officially after the middle of 1976. Following her release in March 1982 it took her over a year to find what she calls a "real" job.

While she was imprisoned Krystyna received just two letters from Jan. One had been brought to her by a priest, while his mother brought another during a visit. Like so many other men grabbed in the Warsaw region that apocryphal night Jan was taken to Bialolenka internment camp just outside Warsaw. It was there that Krystyna headed as soon as she was able after her own release. "It was a Garden of Eden," Jan recalls, by comparison with the conditions he experienced later in Warsaw's main prison on Rakowiecka Street. There is almost a nostalgia in his tone when he describes life at Bialolenka. Because it was an internment camp the Bialolenka regime was less harsh and provided reasonable library facilities for the inmates. Jan also remembers that the company was good. After all he was among friends. However, once he was served with a warrant charging him with treason in September 1982, Jan was moved to Rakowiecka Street, where life became much tougher on every level: "It was far worse to be taken from Bialolenka to Rakowiecka than to be taken there from freedom." For the first three months he was allowed no visits at all and received post only after seven weeks. Krystyna describes that period as "very nasty: the minimum sentence he faced was five years and because he was charged with treason, the possibility of a death sentence was on our minds all of the time."

For Krystyna, this period was one of constant organizing: "It takes so much time when a person is in jail. First, letters have to be written to arrange visits and parcels. In the political cases the letters have to go to the censor so that takes even more time. Then, because he was trying to study, I had to ask the prosecutor for permission to get certain books in for him. The men were allowed a three-kilo parcel per month, so I had to try and get the best, the most nutritious food, into the parcels. That was not easy with all the shortages at the time. He was having a lot of problems with his teeth so I wanted to get him vitamins."

With so many people interned or imprisoned, lots of families found themselves involved in organizing visits, petitions and food parcels. In fact it had the opposite effect to the one desired by the government. People who were not overtly political became part of a network of support activity which by its very nature had political overtones. So, while a clandestine underground was slowly establishing itself furtively, on the surface of Polish society,

old ladies, brothers and sisters, fathers and mothers crossed backwards and forwards over cities and countryside carrying food parcels for the "boys" (and girls). In their attempt to destroy Solidarity, the government gave the union what it needed to become invincible. It gave Solidarity a common mythology.

But, of course, while history tends to look at the political dimension of important events, for those involved there is also the very human reality of their experience. "Jail cemented our relationship. It was Janek's fourth time inside. I felt he really needed me. I felt very responsible. When you're on the outside, you feel obliged to carry on no matter what's going on inside oneself. You've got to provide comfort. Letters become very important for both people. I wrote a sort of diary for Janek. Love returns when people are in jail. During the Solidarity period (before martial law) we were ships in the night. Then there was a terrible longing."

In June 1983, Jan's mother Regina went to see the Interior Minister, General Czeslaw Kiszczak, and asked him to allow her son to attend the First Holy Communion of his daughter, Basha: "Basically the cops just arrived at the door and there was Janek. There were guests everywhere. All those people, it was quite frightening for someone who had been locked up for so long in a tiny cell. I hardly got a chance to talk to him." Krystyna remembers that many of their friends were saying they would try and get him taken into hospital so that he would not have to go back to Rakowiecka. "But in the end Janek said that it was up to me to decide whether he should go underground or not."

When Jan disappeared there was a national alert and because his photograph was posted everywhere he had to change his appearance rapidly. That was actually quite difficult in his case. Jan Litynski is a slight man with very distinct mannerisms. When he speaks, the thoughts and words shoot like bullets from a rapid fire machine gun. He never sits still. And in those rare moments when he does he is either chain smoking or repeatedly wrapping a lock of hair around his finger. He is just like a sprint athlete straining on the blocks in the excruciating moment before the starter pistol relieves the tension.

But with the aid of a beard, new glasses and a suit, something he was not used to, Jan took on a new persona. He was one of the most successful members of Solidarity's underground. He was never re-arrested and remained in hiding until September 1986, when after a general amnesty for political prisoners, he came out, along with the other last remaining underground activist, to a joint press conference of both groups. Nearly five years of his life had passed by since martial law.

The underground period has had important political ramifications. By its very existence it maintained a beacon of hope but, more importantly, its existence eventually forced the one-party state into a position where it tacitly accepted the reality of an opposition.

For Krystyna Litynska it was not a very happy time: "I very rarely met Janek. It was too dangerous. I was watched all of the time. The arrangements to go and see him were incredible. I only saw him once or twice every three months or so. Before he came out I hadn't seen him for six months – that was from March to September. That was too long. Jail is much better for a relationship than being underground. When one's husband is in jail, you still get to see him, even if it is through a glass window. But then you feel useful. You're participating and involved. The underground had a bad effect on marriages. One learns to live independently. One develops one's own life, has one's own responsibilities. If a person didn't detach a little they'd become psychologically unwell."

Though Jan Litynski was a leader among activists, his road to internment and arrest after martial law mirrored that of many others of his generation. After he went to Warsaw University in 1983 to study mathematics he became involved in the numerous political discussion clubs that were springing up all over the place in those years. One of the most famous groups was organized by Adam Michnik (later an MP and editor of *Gazeta Wyborcza*). Its title translates into "the club of the searchers for diversity". Like Litynski, Michnik came from both a communist and Jewish background and was later to become one of the most important interpreters of modern Polish history. Ludka Wujec, now a prominent member of the Democratic Union, has known Jan since he was five: "I suppose up to about 1968, perhaps it was earlier, Janek wanted to fix socialism. The word 'reformer' is

a difficult one here, but basically most of the people involved in those discussion groups were moving in the direction of rejecting the system. But at the time they perceived themselves as operating from within it." The authorities dubbed them the "March Commandos" and the name stuck.

Essentially the groups were made up in the main of young Marxist intellectuals who were struggling to find socialism in the so called socialist state in which they lived. Jan says that he was influenced by the thinking of October '56 when for a brief period it looked as if a brand of liberal communism was about to sweep through Poland. That short flirtation with workers' councils and talk of liberal economics ended with the rehabilitation of Gomulka, though it took a little while for Poles to realize that Wladyslaw Gomulka was not some great reforming knight in shining armour: "I felt that there had never been real socialism in Poland because socialism was based on a combination of workers ruling and democracy. During 1964 and 1965 both Jacek Kuron and Karol Modzelewski had been jailed for their writing. We were studying their texts and believed in a society based on a series of links between worker self governing enterprises and democracy. The problem was that we had no contact with the workers but we certainly had a lot of contact with the lack of democracy. It was a long process, but the more we read and the more we analyzed Marxism, the more we questioned why democracy had to be limited to the proletariat. When you're young and you've read right through Marxist literature and you've worked out that it doesn't hold water you try and work out where the mistake happened. Then eventually you realize that the big mistake was at the beginning."

Jan was twenty-two when he was arrested following the student protests after the closure of the play *Forefather's Eve* [performed in May 1968]. Sentenced to two and a half years for supposedly setting up an illegal organization, Jan ended up serving a year and a half in Rakowiecka Street prison. The jailings and persecution of both the Jews and the intelligentsia in 1968 galvanized a whole network of people, including lecturers and students, into an opposition stance. It also provided those who were jailed with credibility in the eyes of people who might otherwise have been dismissive of the activities of young hothead students. It would, however, be difficult to be dismissive of one-, two- and three-year jail sentences.

Jan is quite philosophical about his experience of imprisonment: "It either breaks you and your character is gone for the rest of your life or else you stick it out. I had known that I had taken a certain course in life. I knew what the risks were. I thought I was doing what was right and just. If your attitude is that going to jail is the end of your life, that you are losing today, tomorrow and the future, then you'll break down." Jan quotes the robust and colourful Jacek Kuron, who was no stranger to Polish jails: "When you get involved you have to measure your arse up to the accused's bench. If you think it fits, continue."

From that point on, there was no doubt that Jan Litynski's posterior measured up. "It is important to understand that what the government engaged in during 1968 was one of the nastiest campaigns against the Jews and against the intelligentsia in the history of Poland." As someone who was a member of both groups, Jan was now clearly identified as being opposed to "them". Because he had been kicked out of the university in March, Jan had been unable to sit the exams in June. When he was released in 1969 he found work as a barman and as a metal grinder as well as working at a shoe factory. Eventually he was able to get a job more commensurate with his skills at a computer centre where he worked as a programmer.

Jan never thought of leaving Poland, but many others did. Those who stayed found that the base of opposition within which they operated was broadening. From the outside it looked as if two extremes had joined forces. In reality as long as there was just one foe there was little to separate the aims of the Catholic intellectuals who began to cooperate with the Marxist and former Marxist dissidents whose characters had been moulded by the '68 experience. It would, however, be the late seventies before this new rainbow coalition of thinkers was able to put its theories of worker support and stimulation into practice. In the meantime the martyred workers in Gdansk, bloodied but victorious after their opposition to the Christmas 1970 food price increases, were creating their own mythology of heroic resis-

tance. And though the intellectuals played no role in Gdansk, it was, combined with the events of '68, the end for many of any residual belief that the system was reformable.

Looking back at the sequence of events one could be forgiven for thinking that the Party almost connived in the making of the opposition. In its proposed changes to the Constitution in 1975, the Party attempted to have its leading role and the special relationship with the Soviet Union formally enshrined. The move resulted in a series of protests against the changes... And so when, in June 1976, Edward Gierek decided that the Polish economy could not sustain the food pricefreeze any longer, the workers once again resisted. This time however they did not have to fight alone.

Krystyna remembers the night the massive food hikes were announced very clearly. "It was hot and Midsummer's Eve and ... many people were having parties. The windows were open, so we could hear all the radios. The prime minister was making a speech announcing the huge increases. It was very dramatic because they'd been frozen for so long. There had been gossip, but it was a shock. The next day the protests began at the Ursus factory. A big crowd marched off to the nearby railway lines and dug up the sleepers. It stopped the Paris–Moscow express. A wave of strikes followed. At Radom workers set fire to the local party headquarters. After that it spread all over the country. The government reacted with incredible brutality. There were murders and terrible beatings. Workers were literally terrified. Many were made to run through a 'path of good health'. That was two lines of truncheon-wielding cops. In Radom it was particularly bad. There was incredible terror there. People were being thrown out of their jobs under paragraph 52, which allowed the authorities to sack a worker who was absent without leave." What would later be known as an intervention committee then became active on an *ad hoc* basis. In the beginning its activities were unstructured: "It was all very spontaneous. It was an effort to help those who'd been imprisoned. Their families were normally very afraid and didn't know what to do. Often they were even afraid to come forward when help was offered. Basically we started going to the places where there'd been trouble, to places where people had been sacked or beaten up and we tried to help. Janek went to Radom very early on. He gathered information about what was going on and tried to help get people out of jail. Then after there was a series of suspicious deaths at militia stations, he began writing articles based on the information he had gathered." Ludka Wujec was with a group of intellectuals who attended the trials of those charged with offences after Ursus: "When we saw how helpless the families were, how frightened they were, we just spontaneously approached them and raised money, there and then in the corridor at the court. There were no leaders at Ursus. These people had been picked out of the crowd for punishment. They were entitled to a state appointed defence lawyer, but we got our own lawyers to help on a voluntary basis. It was the beginning of an organized network of help. We learned a lot from the workers we met. We heard a lot about arrests, sackings and all kinds of illegal procedures."

Very shortly after the protests Jan, along with several other activists, began publishing an information bulletin detailing what was happening, where, and to whom. That "Information Bulletin" was probably the first of the literally hundreds of dirty grey sheets that would play a vital role in counteracting the government's disinformation activities. That the pen is mightier than the sword is a truism but if it had ever required verification the period following Radom and Ursus which culminated in Solidarity's victory in August 1980 would surely be proof enough.

As the contacts were made and the truth was outed it became clear that spontaneous help was not enough. It needed an umbrella under which to operate. And so, in September, a diverse group of intellectuals got together calling themselvs, at first the Workers' Defence Committee (later, the Social Self-Defence Committee). Well known and respected economists, writers, lecturers, former communists and former pre-war socialists headed the list of KOR's members in the hope that they would afford protection to the less well known activists who were working at the grassroots level to help the workers. However, it would soon become clear that no amount of moral authority would keep Adam Michnik, Jacek Kuron, Jan Litynski or indeed many other young KOR activists out of jail.

Krystyna remembers 1977 as a tragic year but Jan points out that it was also the year of KOR's first success: "First of all Janek was sacked from his job at the computer centre in February. So from then on, I was trying to earn a living for both of us. It was not easy because I was blacklisted as well. On 12 March my mother died. On 14 May a student activist, Stanislaw Pyjas, was killed in a militia station in Cracow. They said he fell down the stairs, but they killed him. Then on the 19th, Janek was arrested. I think about fourteen other KOR members were arrested at the same time. From then on the searches at the flat were regular. They (the secret police) would often follow me. They'd walk just a couple of metres behind me." But as Jan emphasizes, the year was not all bleak. On 22 July, Independence Day, the government announced an amnesty and thus avoided the embarrassment of a series of trials of martyrs.

Within a month of his release Jan was busy establishing *Robotnik* which played a key role in fostering self-organization among workers. Over the next few years he travelled all over Poland gathering information, giving information and forging contacts between the intellectuals and the rank-and-file factory workers. He was particularly involved in the mining towns of Silesia and was later to be one of Walbrzych's first freely elected members of parliament.

*

Meeting Jan and Krystyna Litynski was a milestone in my life. The meeting made me do what young people often don't have time to do. It made me stop and think. I had arrived at Warsaw's somewhat undistinguished airport on an afternoon in late July 1980. In my notebook I had what turned out to be a fairly comprehensive list of KOR's most famous members. That, as I remember, was about the height of my organization. Having got through the agony and fear of being identified as a journalist travelling on a visitor's visa, I was delighted at having crossed the first hurdle. Being a bit of a prude I was somewhat put out when I was informed at the student hostel where I was to stay that because they were full I would have to share the room with three men. There were not even curtains between the beds. In my confused expectations of the trip I had anticipated all sorts of cloak and dagger scenarios straight out of Freddie Forsyth. But none of his anti-heroes had to undress underneath a blanket. Having mumbled my goodbyes to my new Swedish room-mates I set off to find the great and famous Jacek Kuron. Needless to say KOR's ebullient guru was not at home. In his place I found an intense young German who announced himself to be in the middle of a major thesis on Polish dissidence. This young man, sensing that I was in a bit of a muddle, suggested that I go over and see Jan Litynski. More importantly, he added that I should meet his wife Krystyna, who spoke English...

That first evening, I sat on the bed-cum-settee in the corner of the sitting room on Wyzwolenia Street, sipping lemon tea and explaining who I was, and why I had come. Amid the constant interruption of the telephone and door bell I listened as Krystyna told me about the series of strikes which were breaking out all over Poland. As the hours passed I listened as she both received and passed on information about strikes, plans and meetings. By the time Jan returned to the flat, she had already promised me that I could travel with him wherever he went. What is more, she would not hear of me staying at the hostel. The offer of a corner on her floor was more wonderful than the promise of a four-poster bed. I was bowled over by their kindness. Over the next couple of weeks I travelled with Janek to the mining towns of Silesia for meetings with workers who were trying to set up alternative trade union structures, and to places like Cracow for secret meetings between intellectual activists and workers from the Nowa Huta steel works which is nearby. In Warsaw I was secretly introduced to worker leader Zbigniew Bujak in a safe flat. He was constantly on the move that July and August as the arrest and harassment of activists increased and the tension heightened. On and off over the period I became conscious of the presence of shadows when I moved around with Jan. In the days immediately before and of course after the Gdansk strike the secret police presence became frightening. For the Litynskis, it was part of their normal life experience. I am not ashamed to say that I was terrified...

What impressed me about Jan and Krystyna was the knowledge that they had never

thought of leaving Poland. In a Western country this couple would have had a secure income and a good lifestyle. In Poland they lived with Jan's mother in a cramped flat. Though enormously talented they had difficulty getting suitable work because of their politics. When Krystyna did get a job, it was at a clinic two hours away from her home. And after all of that travelling she had to queue for basic food stuffs like countless other Polish women. Both were regularly harassed and intimidated. Their home was repeatedly searched. Jan, was, by then very familiar with conditions in Polish jails. But never once had I heard them proffer information about their personal troubles and hardships. They certainly never moaned. Talking to them I realized that they were firmly focused on their political goals. Years later, when I talked to them about martial law, about jail and about the underground years, their attitude was still the same. Incredibly they simply weren't bitter.

Jan's attitude to "them" (the Party) has more than likely kept him sane through many difficult experiences: "I don't feel any bitterness. Why should I? All my life I've been a vulture on them. As a totality I can't tolerate them but I've rarely had a personal feeling of hate to any individual." Jan explains that there was not any big decision to become political: "Being a dissident is about the choice of a certain style of life. It does require courage but that was not a problem for me."

Krystyna was twenty-five when she met Janek in 1974: "I was bookish, but not sheltered. My family was too big and too poor for any of us to be sheltered. My sisters, my brothers, we saw how hard our parents worked. They fought hard for our existence. I met Janek at an important time in my life when I was deciding what I should do with myself I was working out what I wanted from life. He stepped out of a different world. All his friends had been together since '68. I began to hear about anti-Semitism, about people who were leaving the country or had left. I began to meet people who were names from another world. I began to open my eyes and see and understand things completely differently."

I remember being struck by how difficult it was to categorize Jan and Krystyna's politics. And, as I've mentioned earlier, that was a problem the whole world faced when Solidarity failed to fit into a neatly defined pigeonhole. In *The Captive Mind*, Czeslaw Milosz highlights the unreality of many western Marxists who refused, even at the height of Stalinism, to acknowledge that in practice the Marxist model was not working out in Eastern Europe. Jan and Krystyna were well used to meeting ardent young communists from the United States, Germany or Britain who had to perform mental cart-wheels in order to retain their belief following a visit to Poland.

Unlike many people in the west who took a political stand on places like Poland, Cambodia or Angola, politics was not an abstract, idealistic or doctrinaire thing for them. They were living the reality of Utopian socialism but were far too intelligent to think that its political opposite alone was the cure for Poland's ills. In a sense then it was impossible to politically define Jan and Krystyna and many people like them, because politics, as defined in terms of right and left did not come into the frame in pre-1989 Poland. For Krystyna, like Janek, the dissident road is a question of choice: "f you looked at Radom, at Ursus and at what happened to people there. If you looked at their suffering and at how people lived, if you come from a poor family yourself and know how difficult life can be, and then if you look at 'them', at the secret police and think of the obscenities they whisper in your ear, you have to turn. It is not a political thing, it is basically about human sensitivity. Things are either right or wrong. It starts as a moral thing but then one's actions become political. You've no choice."

By 1978, Krystyna was well and truly aware of the consequences of her choice. She remembers that in one week their flat was searched twice: "There was one day – a very important day for me. In many ways it was a milestone. The police arrived at about five-thirty or six in the morning. I was on the afternoon shift at the clinic which was outside of Warsaw. The job was very important to me, I really wanted to get there. Normally the men who searched were very polite. There were four or five of them this time. They searched our tiny flat for hours. I had just had a tooth removed and I was still bleeding. The police were drunk and unpleasant. I was nervous and upset. The older man, the one in charge of the search, agreed in the end to let me go to work. So he drove me to where I got the works' bus and waited until I'd

got on. It is very hard to explain how I felt. Nobody would have understood my feelings. What could I have said had I not been able to get to work. With the secret police shadowing me, I felt as if I was in a ghetto. I was alone. It was so different after the strikes, after Solidarity and martial law. In 1982 people would have understood if I'd explained what had happened. But in 1978, if I'd said anything, people would have been too frightened to help me."

While it might have been the Pope who began the breakdown of the sense of individual isolation in Polish society, and though it was Solidarnosc that gave birth to the individual's sense of power within a mass movement, it was "they", the Party, with the introduction of martial law, who generalized the dissident experience. It was not a simple case of creating martyrs and heroes. Solidarity at its height had ten million members. That was nearly a third of the total population. By resorting to martial law in order to deal with a situation it felt it could no longer control, the Party declared war on a huge section of Polish society. In doing so it turned dissidence into a mass movement. Jan Litynski sees 13 December as "a farce. Everything had been said and done, everything had changed and they were returning to their old ways." And what for? Over the next five years the Polish economy continued to deteriorate while the Party exercised power for power's sake. Eventually with the threat of economic collapse looming, the Party chose to recognize the existence of an opposition, by offering to share responsibility if not power. Jaruzelski's *coup d'etat* was eventually brought down by the sterility of the power it sought to maintain.

In "the new reality", as Krystyna likes to call post-communist Poland she has been busy working both in the field of psychiatric care as well as working for various academic institutions. Jan is an MP and chaired the important Parliamentary Commission on Social Policy until the return of the post-communist coalition government in September 1983. Both are acutely aware of the range of complex problems Poland now faces: "In socialist countries in the past, there was secret police and harassment but there was also a funny sense of safety. Big Daddy was always there to look after you. With no official unemployment, people were always sure of being paid. Now everyone has to be his own Big Daddy. Today the enemy is gone and people aren't sure who the new enemy is. As a nation we're having to learn how to deal with different political views and to learn political language. People are having to learn how to relate to people that they disagree with politically. There are so many new questions and problems. In the past there was just one ideology. One was either for it or against it. Now we're trying to find out what we meant when we said that we wanted a 'civil society'. What does it mean? It is not just the economy that has to be built. We have to establish new health, education and social security structures. We have to decide what kind of political model we want to operate in Poland. Should we have a strong President? Should parliament play the role it has been playing since the first elections?"

But whatever the problems, Krystyna is sure that she now lives in a real world where people are responsible for themselves: "Life is much safer in one way, but in another way people here are very afraid of the future. Now everything depends on oneself. For me personally things are better. We have more money. It is good to have a husband who is bringing in a salary. I'm not the only one responsible anymore. We have our own flat. It is not big, but we're not living with my mother-in-law. But the best thing of all is the knowledge that I can walk down the street and not be afraid of the secret police. I'm not afraid of searches anymore and of course it is like being in paradise to read a free press."

In 1991 President Lech Walesa gave a speech to the European Parliament in which he virtually told the West that it had a moral obligation to financially support Poland because it had rid itself of its communist manacles. So what?, was the response from Western business interests who would have preferred to hear what Walesa had to say about the progress the country was making in completing the transformation of the economy. Jan Litynski feels that people find it difficult to move on and respond to the rapidly changing world in which the whole of Eastern Europe finds itself: "People here saw communism as a sort of cancer. They thought that if you operated and removed it, that afterwards, everything would be okay." Lech Walesa knows full well that the

battle was only beginning when the communists fell, but in continuing the rhetoric, albeit abroad, of looking for adulation and support simply for removing communism, he is copperfastening a false expectation that the changes will be rapid and painless. Another side effect of seeing the future through the eyes of the past is to inhibit political development and growth.

Jan is no longer comfortable being described as a dissident. He wants to leave that old battle behind him and start building "the new reality". For him that means many things, including the view that anticommunist witch-hunting is divisive, and a diversion from real political progress. But it is not just the communist past that should be jettisoned according to this view. Jan knows that hankering after Solidarity's halcyon days is perverting the development of parliamentary democracy: "Of course we all grew out of a movement of protest. But things are more complex now and some of us have moved on." The split within Solidarity was a painful one. Jan now acknowledges that thinking that the union would remain undivided was probably naive. He now thinks that it was also wishful thinking to hope that post-communist political activity would develop through a social movement. He is critical of the role of the various Solidarity offshoots which entered parliament: "In the past the workers and of course, Solidarity, were to the forefront in the call for change. Now they're a very conservative force. They're now the biggest obstacle on the road to change." At the heart of what Jan is saying is the view that the political game must be played within parliament, that the players must move in from the streets. "It is more pleasant to be in a mass movement, to be without responsibility, than to have to deal with reality. Fighting for power isn't nice but it is real."

It is somewhat ironic that the political party which is loudest in its opposition to what it regards as the diversionary rhetoric of decomrnunization is the one whose most prominent members were almost martyred by the Party. Jan Litynski belongs to the secular and liberal end of the Democratic Union, born out of the grouping which supported Poland's first noncommunist premier, Tadeusz Mazowiecki, when he ran against Lech Walesa for the Presidency. In crude terms, that battle was waged between populist and sober politics: "The party was created, it evolved around the defence of the liberal changes that were introduced by Tadeusz Mazowiecki's first government. In simple terms we backed Balcerowicz [Leszek Balcerowicz, deputy premier and architect of the first economic reform plan]. The best way to characterize the Democratic Union is to say that it has a sober way of thinking. We're not populist. We believe in a step by step evolutionary approach to the economy. We don't believe in short cuts or miracles. There is no getting away from hardship during the short term. We believe that the flow of money within the economy has to be strictly controlled. Otherwise inflation is inevitable. On the other hand, many of us would be Keynesian if the conditions existed." In other words Jan's wing of the party believes in a capitalist market economy with a "human face".

With many of the most famous names from KOR and the Young Poland Movement now involved in UD, it is largely a party of the intelligentsia. It is going after the middle class voter, a category that up until recently did not exist in Poland. The old school of secular dissidents generally looked West rather than East for inspiration. Today UD supports membership of the European Community and shies away from nationalist or xenophobic rhetoric.

*

I visited Poland during the first, partially free, elections in 1989. This was how I began one newspaper article: "There are two gold leaf invitations pinned to the kitchen door of the Litynski flat on Filtrowa Street. One invites 'Mr Jan Litynski MP and Mrs Litynski' to meet the American Ambassador, while the other is from the Indian Embassy. This would not be unusual were it not for the fact that, as a dissident and founder of Solidarity, Jan Litynski spent the years between 1981 and 1986 either in jail or in hiding." The invitation contrasted starkly with the dark days of martial law when Krystyna had fashioned a Christmas tree from a fallen twig and the cotton wool from a sanitary towel. The Litynskis had come in from the cold.

"Reluctant Heroism" is reprinted by permission of Irish Academic Press, Dublin.

POLISH FOLK MUSIC

For anyone with an interest in traditional music, Poland boasts some of the most distinctive sounds in Europe, and the experience of a *górale* (highland) wedding – fired by furious fiddling, grounded by a sawing cello and super-charged with vodka – is unforgettable. As everywhere, outside festivals, this music is a disappearing phenomenon and can take some hunting down, but it's a good way to meet people and, armed with the information below, you might be able to make sense of what you hear.

ROOTS AND DEVELOPMENT

All the countries of eastern Europe – predominantly agrarian and undeveloped compared to western Europe – entered the twentieth century with rich traditions of **indigenous folk music** and many of them can still be heard into the late 1990s. In Poland, as elsewhere in eastern Europe, an interest in folklore emerged in the nineteenth century allied to aspirations for national independence – folk music and politics in the region often have symbiotic links. The pioneering collector of songs and dances from all over the country was **Oskar Kolberg** (1814–90). From the early years of this century gramophone recordings were made, and by 1939, substantial archives had been amassed in Poznań and Warsaw. Both collections were

completely destroyed during **World War II** and scholarly collecting had to begin anew in 1945. The wartime anhillilation and shifting of ethnic minorities in Poland also severely disrupted the continuity of folk traditions. The postwar **communist regimes**, throughout eastern Europe, endorsed folk culture as far as it could be portrayed as a cheerful espousal of healthy peasant labour, but each regime adopted a different approach. What survives today is sometimes in spite of, but largely a result of those policies. At one extreme, Bulgaria strongly encouraged amateur grass-roots music; on the other, Czechoslovakia effectively sanitized its folk music to irrelevance. Poland took something close to the Czech approach, but with slack enough for a few local bands to keep some genuine traditions going.

The official face of Poland's folk culture was presented by professional folk troupes – most famously the **Mazowsze** and **Śląsk** ensembles – who gave highly arranged and polished virtuoso performances; middle-of-the-road massed strings and highly choreographed twirls, whoops and foot stamping. The repertoire was basically core Polish with, perhaps, a slight regional emphasis (the Mazowsze territory is around Warsaw, the Śląsk around Wrocław), but the overall effect was homogenization rather than local identity. The groups were regularly featured on radio and TV and they had their audience. Smaller, more specialized groups, like **Słowianki** in Kraków, were also supported and kept closer to the roots, but for the most part the real stuff withered away as the image of folk music was tarnished, for many, by the bland official ensembles.

POLISH DANCES

Thanks to Chopin, the **mazurka** and **polonaise** (*polonez*) of central Poland are probably the best-known dance forms and form the core of the folk repertoire. Both are in triple time with the polonaise generally slower and more stately than the mazurka. In fact there are really three types of mazurka, the slower *kujawiak*, medium tempo *mazur* and faster *oberek*. The polonaise is particularly associated with the more ceremonial and solemn moments of a wedding party. It was taken up by the aristocracy from a slow walking dance (*chodzony*), given a French name identifying it as a dance of Polish origin and then filtered back down to the lower classes. In addition to the triple-time dances of central Poland, there are also some characteristic five-beat dances in the north-eastern areas of Mazury, Kurpie and Podlasie. As you move south, somewhere between Warsaw and Kraków, there is a transitional area where the triple-time dances of central Poland (the mazurka and polonaise) give way to the duple-time dances of the south like the **krakowiak** and **polka**. Generally speaking the music of central Poland is more restrained and sentimental than that of the south, which is wilder and more full-blooded. The krakowiak is named after the city of Kraków and the polka is claimed by both the Poles and the Bohemians as their own, although it was in Bohemia that it became most widely known. Of course, all these dances are not confined to their native areas, but many have become staples across the country and abroad. **Weddings** are the main occasion for traditional music, but in an agrarian country where barely eight percent of the land was collectivized, important annual events like the harvest festival (*dozynki*) have persisted as well.

FESTIVALS AND REGIONAL BANDS

Today, with the notable exception of the Tatra region and a few other pockets, traditional music has virtually ceased to function as a living tradition and has been banished to **regional folk festivals**. Several of these are

very good indeed, with the **Kazimierz Festival** in June foremost amongst them (see box). But the best way to hear this music is at the sort of occasion it was designed for – a wedding (*wesele*), for instance, where lively tunes are punched out by ad hoc groups comprising (nowadays) clarinet, saxophone, accordion, keyboard and drums. At country weddings there is often a set of traditional dances played for the older peole, even when the rest of the music is modern. In the rural areas people tend to be hospitable and welcoming and, once you've shown a keen interest, an invitation is often extended. Among the best regional bands still active are: the Franciszek Gola Band in **Kadzidło** (Kurpie), the Kazimierz Meto Band in **Glina** and the Tadeusz Jedynak Band in **Przystałowice Małe** (Mazowsze), the Edward Markocki Band in **Zmysłówka-Podlesie** and the Stachy Band in **Haczów nad Wisłokiem** (Rzeszów region), the Kazimierz Kantor Band in **Głowaczowa** (Tarnów region), the Swarni Band in **Nowy Targ**, the Ludwik Młynarczyk Band in **Lipnica**, the Trebunia Family Band in **Poronin** and the Gienek Wilczek Band in **Bukowina** (Podhale). Typically, the areas where the music has survived tend to be the remoter regions on the fringes – **Kurpie** and **Podlasie** in the northeast, around **Rzeszów** in the southeast (where the *cimbaly* – like the Hungarian cimbalom – is popular in the local bands), and the **Podhale** and highland regions in the Tatras along the southern border. But this isn't the whole story.

FESTIVALS

Kazimierz Dolny Festival of Folk Bands and Singers (June) ☎0831/24927.

Kraków Festival of Jewish Music & Culture (June/July) ☎012/214294.

Rzeszów World Festival of Polonia Folklore (every 3 years, next in July 1998) ☎022/635 04 40; fax 022/26 87 40; Folk Dance Festival (Oct) ☎017/35257.

Sejny Borderlands Cultural Festival (April) ☎189/200.

Toruń International Meeting of Folk Bands (May).

Zakopane International Festival of Highland Folklore (late Aug) ☎0165/66950.

Zielona Góra International Festival of Folk Ensembles (Aug).

Zydnia Festival of Łemk/Ukrainian Culture (July).

Zyndranowa Festival of the Łemk Tradition (June) ☎038454/12 or 057/435061.

Żywiec International Folk Meetings (July/Aug) ☎033/125276.

For more details on these festivals see the relevant accounts. General information should be available from the Ministry of Culture and Art, 00-071 Warszawa, ul. Krakowskie Przedmieście 15/17 (fax 022/ 26 19 22).

PODHALE MUSIC

Podhale, the district around Zakopane, which probably has the most thriving musical tradition in the country, has been one of Poland's most popular resorts for years and is in no way remote or isolated. The Podhale musicians are familiar with music from all over the country and beyond, but choose to play in their own way. This sophisticated approach is part of a pride in Podhale **identity** which probably dates from the late nineteenth century when several notable artists and intellectuals (including the composer **Szymanowski**, see p.454) settled in Zakopane and enthused about the music and culture. Music, fiddlers and dancing brigands are as essential to the image of Podhale life as the **traditional costumes** of tight felt trousers, broad leather belts with ornate metal clasps and studs, embroidered jackets and black hats decorated with cowrie shells. This music has more in common with the peasant cultures along the Carpathians in Ukraine and Transylvania than the rest of Poland.

The typical **Podhale ensemble** is a string band (the clarinets, saxophones, accordions and drums that have crept in elsewhere in Poland are much rarer here) of a lead violin (*prym*), a couple of second violins (*sekund*) playing accompanying chords and a three-stringed cello (*bazy*). The music is immediately identifiable by its melodies and playing style. The tunes tend to be short-winded, angular melodies in an unusual scale with a sharpened fourth. This is known to musicians as the Lydian mode and gives rise to the Polish word *lidyzowanie* to describe the manner of singing this augmented interval. The **fiddlers** typically play these melodies with a "straight" bowing technique – giving the music a stiff, angular character as opposed to the swing and flexibility of the more usual "double" bowing technique

A PODHALE WEDDING

Believe it or not, *górale* **weddings** are often held in the local fire station. There's room enough for feasting and dancing and it provides useful extra income for the fire brigade. It was here that the family members assembled and the couple were lectured by the leader of the band on the importance of the step they were taking – an indication of how integral the band is to the event. Then came the departure for the church in a string of horse-drawn carriages – the band in one, the bride in another and the groom following in one behind. At the front, the *pytacy*, a pair of outriders on horseback, were shouting rhymes to all and sundry.

The band played the couple into the wooden church and, unusually, played *Krywan* from the gallery inside the church while communion was taking place. Then it was back to the fire station for the party. The incredible thing was the way the band kept going for hours, substituting different players from time to time to give themselves a short break. Quite unexpected until you get used to it is the way the *górale* **dances and songs are superimposed**, often with no relation to each other. A fast up-tempo dance will be in progress when suddenly a group of women will launch into a slow song seemingly oblivious to the other music. I was putting it down to the vast quantities of vodka consumed or perhaps a serious underlying quarrel between family groups who wanted different sorts of music. But no, it is typical of the way music is performed in these circumstances and, when you get used to it, the tensions between the instrumental music and song are obviously calculated and fascinating. Among the **dances** the local *ozwodne* and *krzesane* figure highly, begun by one of the men strutting over to the band and launching into the high straining vocals that cue the tune. The man then draws a girl onto the floor, dances a few steps with her before handing her over to the man on whose behalf he originally selected her. All this is part of a carefully structured form which culminates late in the evening with the ritual of the *cepiny* (or *cepowiny* as it's known in Podhale), the "capping ceremony". This is one of those peasant rites of passage, which happens all over Poland, when the bride has a scarf tied round her head symbolizing her passage from the status of a single to a married woman.

The music whirls on throughout the night and extends well beyond the Podhale repertoire. There are romantic waltzes and mazurkas, fiery polkas and *czardasz* – tunes that you might hear in northern Poland, Slovakia, Hungary or Romania, but always given a particular Podhale accent. The *górale* people are famed for keeping themselves to themselves and mistrusting outsiders, but there's no blinkered puritanism. They take and enjoy what they want from outside, confident and proud of the strength of what they have.

common in eastern Europe and typified by Gypsy fiddlers. The straining high **male vocals** which kick off a dance tune are also typical. At the heart of the repertoire are the *ozwodna* and *krzesany* couple **dances**, both in duple time. The first has an unusual five-bar melodic structure and the second is faster and more energetic. Then there are the showy Brigand's Dances (*zbójnicki*) which are the popular face of Podhale culture – central to festivals and demonstrations of the music. Danced in a circle by men wielding small metal axes (sometimes hit together fiercely enough to strike sparks), they are a celebration of the *górale* traditions of brigandage, with colourful robberies, daring escapes, festivities and death on the gallows for anti-feudal heroes. "To hang on the gibbet is an honourable thing!" said the nineteenth-century *górale* musician Sabała; "They don't hang just anybody, but real men!"

The **songs** you are most likely to hear as a visitor to Zakopane are those about the most famous brigand of them all, **Janosik** (1688–1713). Musically they are not Podhale in style, but are lyrical ballads with a Slovakian feel, and countless tales of the region's most famous character are sung on both sides of the border. The most played songs are *Idzie Janko* and *Krywan* - and the tune for the former seems to be used for many other Janosik songs as well. The latter is not actually about the brigand, but one of the Tatra's most celebrated mountains.

The mountain regions **around Podhale** also have their own, if less celebrated, musical cultures. To the west there is **Orawa**, straddling the Polish/Slovak border and the Beskid Żywieckie to its north, with an annual festival in the town of **Żywiec** itself. To the east of Zakopane, the music of the **Spisz** region has more Slovak bounce than the Podhale style and boasts an excellent fiddle-maker and musician in **Woytek Łukasz**. Even if you don't make it to a highland wedding, music is relatively accessible in Zakopane. Many of the restaurants have good bands that play certain nights of the week, there are occasional stage shows and there's the Festival of Highland Folklore in August.

ETHNIC MINORITIES

Since the political changes of the 1980s, there's been something of a revival in the music of some of the **national minorities** living in Poland. First, there's a more liberal climate in which to express national differences and travel is easier across the borders between related groups in Lithuania, Belarus and Ukraine. Poland's Boyks and Lemks are ethnically and culturally linked to Ukranians and the Rusyns of Slovakia, and their music betrays its eastern Slavonic leanings in its choral and polyphonic songs. Recently some fascinating work has been done by the **Kresy Foundation** based in Lublin, who have gathered diverse groups of musicians from several territories to play together and compare their music in informal gatherings. These "symposiums" are perhaps academic in intent, but practical and enjoyable in their approach – trying to escape the formalized stages, microphones and performances of festivals. The work they are doing is unquestionably successful in revealing the diversity of musical cultures in eastern Poland and the neighbouring countries and is hopefully raising its profile at the grass roots. Otherwise, Boyk and Ukrainian groups are now a regular feature of the Kazimierz Festival.

World War II saw the effective extermination of **Jewish** life and culture in Poland along with the exuberant and melancholy *klezmer* music for weddings and festivals that was part of it. The music had its distinctive Jewish elements, but drew heavily on local Polish and Ukranian styles. Thanks to emigration and revival, the music now flourishes principally in the USA and is barely heard in Poland except at the annual Festival of Jewish Culture in Kraków. The city is, though, home to its own Polish *klezmer* band, *Kroke*, who, one suspects, are catering for the same market as the *Schindler's List* location tours.

REVIVAL AND NEW MUSIC

It is perhaps not over-optimistic to sense a slight picking up of interest in Polish traditional music as the exhortations of the sanitized troupes slip further into the distance. In the western region of Wielkopolska there's been something of a revival in **bagpipe** (*kozioł* – literally "goat") playing, a tradition reaching back to the Middle Ages in Eastern Europe. And in the last few years a few good **contemporary folk groups** have emerged on the scene. Not surprisingly, some of the most interesting developments have come out of Podhale and in particular the **Trebunia** family band of Poronin. Here the stern fiddler Władiław Trebunia and his son Krzysztof are both preservers of and experimenters with the tradition, as well as being leaders of one of the very best wedding bands around. In 1991 they joined up with reggae musician Norman "Twinkle" Grant to produce two albums of **Podhale reggae**, or perhaps more accurately, reggae in a Polish style. Surprising as it might seem, once you get used to the rigid beat imposed on the more flexible Polish material, the marriage works rather well and there are interesting parallels between Rasta and Podhale concerns. In 1994, the Trebunias teamed up on another project with one of Poland's leading **jazz** musicians, saxophonist Zbigniew Namysłowski. Here the usual *górale* ensemble meets saxophone, piano, bass

and drums in an inventive romp through classic Podhale hits such as *Zbójnicki* tunes, *Krywan* and *Idzie Janko*.

Elsewhere, contemporary folk bands to look out for are **Rawianie** and, particularly, the **Kwartet Jorgi**. Although based in Poznań, the group takes its music from all round Poland and beyond with many of the tunes coming from the nineteenth-century collections of Oskar Kolberg. The group's leader, Maciej Rychły, plays an amazing range of ancient Polish bagpipes, whistles and flutes which are sensitively combined with guitars, cello and drums. The music isn't purist, but is inventive and fun and shows how contemporary Polish folk music can escape the legacy of sanitized communist fakelore.

Simon Broughton
(with thanks to Krzysztof Cwizewicz)

DISCOGRAPHY

TRADITIONAL

Gienek Wilczek 's Bukowina Band *Music of the Tatra Mountains* (Nimbus, UK). Gienek is an eccentric peasant genius taught by Dziadonka, a notorious female brigand of Podhale who had learned from Bartus Obrochta, the favoured *górale* fiddler of Szymanowski. His playing is eccentric with a richly ornamented, raw but inspirational sound.

Sowa Family Band *Songs and Music from Rzeszów Region* (Polskie Nagrania, Poland). A wonderful disc of authentic village dances from a family band with over 150 years of recorded history. The 1970s recordings are rather harsh, but splendid all the same. Sadly, the band is no longer playing.

Trebunia Family Band *Music of the Tatra Mountains* (Nimbus, UK). A great sample of *górale* music recorded not in a cold studio session, but at an informal party to bring that special sense of spontaneity and fun. Wild playing from one of the region's best bands and well recorded. The first in Nimbus's series of traditional Tatra music.

Trebunia Family *Polish Highlanders Music* (Folk, Poland). This is the Trebunia's own label version of their *górale* music. There's terrific repertoire and playing, but it suffers from a touch too much reverb and not enough of the fun that makes the Nimbus recording so good.

Various *Poland: Folk Songs and Dances* (VDE, Switzerland). Another good selection

compiled by Anna Czekanowska and released by the Archives Internationales de Musique Populaire in Geneva. Includes some recent recordings of music by ethnic minorities.

Various *Polish Folk Music* (Polskie Nagrania, Poland). A good cross-section of songs and music from all over the country – an enticing glimpse of the material that must be available in Polish archives.

CONTEMPORARY

Kwartet Jorgi *Jam* (Jam, Poland). The quartet's first release from 1990 is the best, featuring lots of old tunes collected by Kolberg. The Jewish-sounding Ubinie tune seems to tie in with the Chagall picture on the cover.

Kwartet Jorgi *Kwartet Jorgi* (Polskie Nagrania, Poland). Their second CD is a release of older material recorded in 1988. It ventures more widely in repertoire with Irish and Balkan tunes as well as excursions into what sounds like medieval jazz.

Namysłowski Jazz Quartet & Kapela Góralska (ZAIKS/BIEM, Poland). This Trebunia jazz collaboration is well worth hearing. If you are in Zakopane be sure to pick up a cassette.

Twinkle Brothers and Trebunia Family *Higher Heights* and *Comeback Twinkle 2* (Ryszard Music, Poland). The intriguing sounds of "góralstafarianism".

WALKING IN THE TATRAS

The pine-forested slopes and glacier-carved ridges of the Polish Tatra Mountains are by far the most spectacular and challenging mountain walking area in the country. Travel writer and enthusiastic hiker, Chris Scott, visited the region twice in 1991. The following piece is an account of his contrasting experiences in summer and on his return in winter.

The area within the Tatrzański Park Narodowy (Tatras National Park or TPN) encompasses peaks in the 1800–2100m range from the less visited western frontier ridge past the cable car station at **Kasprowy Wierch** (1985m), midway along the park's southern flank. East of Kasprowy, the park's most frequently visited summit, are the Wysokie or **High Tatras**, including the demanding Orła Perch and inaccessible Liptowskie Mury ridges; the latter end at the 2499m peak of **Rysy**, the highest in Poland. Best of all, the small park provides seven hostels ranging from diminutive "Hansel and Gretel" cabins to grand interwar lodges in the main valleys leading north from the border, and comes complete with a well-developed network of clearly waymarked tracks criss-crossing the entire area.

The colours of the tracks detailed below refer to their corresponding waymarks on trees and signposts in the Tatras National Park and on the yellow 1:30,000 tourist map which covers the park.

*

A few years ago I visited the Tatras, having taken the bus from Dover to Kraków, a surprisingly effortless thirty-hour journey. Once in Kraków, a week's wages converted into what was then two and a half million złotys, a huge wad of low-value notes which the recent currency revisions have thankfully eliminated. First impressions of the country contradicted the drab visions of austerity then associated with Poland. Although poverty was still endemic, the commerce – or "*handel*", for which the Poles are well known – thrived in all forms, with shops replete with an unexpected variety of food at prices around a quarter of those in England.

Just a dollar's worth of złotys secured a seat on the next bus leaving for **Zakopane** from where next morning, loaded with sausage and bread, I set off south to **Kuźnice** and the start of the **black trail** which winds west through the forested foothills to the beautiful valley, **Dolina Chochołowska**. Mistakenly presuming I'd chosen a moderate introduction for my first hill walking in ten years, I in fact found myself panting and sweating in the 30°C heat. Closer scrutiny of the excellent TPN tourist map available in Zakopane revealed that far from being a "low-level introductory route", the black track labouriously climbed and descended successive spurs between the valleys running north off the main ridge, rather than simply slowly gaining height and maintaining it. This, combined with a hot summer's day and full camping gear saw me relish the refreshment at each valley-bed stream before commencing yet another slog up into the woods and over the next spur. The plunge pool at the **Wodospad Siklawica** (Siklawica Waterfall) was thronged with sunbathers and their gambolling children, while all along the way, similarly casually attired Poles bade me "*Cześć*", the customary salute meted out to passing walkers. Indeed, it soon became clear that an unusually broad cross-section of society was on the march in the Tatras. Most prolific were keen school-aged kids sporting ex-army rucksacks and clumpy boots, oblivious to the wonders of modern lightweight gear but enjoying themselves none the less.

By the time I reached the **Dolina Kościeliska**, the contour-mashing trudge had worn me out and so I decided to investigate the promising-sounding **Jaskina Mrozna** (Frozen Cave) a short distance up the valley. On the way *górale* (pronounced "gouraleh"), the indigenous mountain folk of the Tatras, dressed traditionally in their white felt outfits, ferried tourists up and down the valley in horse-drawn carts. A popular Polish folk song relates the pitiful plight of the proud and distinctive *górale*, forced to seek work in the despised factories of the lowlands, their days of shepherding and guiding in the hills having come to an end.

Dumping my overloaded pack in some ferns, I skipped weightlessly up to the cave entrance and enjoyed a blissfully refrigerated grope through the dimly lit tunnel that was only truly appreciated once I emerged back into the late afternoon heat. Deciding I'd had enough for one day, I made one final climb up the **blue track** to the clearing on top of **Polana Stoły** where I flopped down exhaustedly on the grass.

By late next afternoon I found myself camped above the tree line on a spur beneath **Wołowiec**, the 2063m peak on the frontier ridge in the park's southwestern corner. Perplexed at the lack of fellow campers, I later realized that the practice is forbidden in the park and anyway, the hostels (*skroniska*) or basic refuges (*szałasy*) are much more enjoyable places to spend the night. Nevertheless, my borrowed tent successfully beat off a convoy of ensuing thunderstorms and by nine next morning I'd passed over the summit of Wołowiec, decending to the Jamnickie Stawy (lakes) on the Czech side of the frontier; an infringement of cross-border etiquette, but the only source of water nearby. Wisps of the previous night's storm trailed from the surrounding peaks as I washed and fed myself, while *świstaki* — beaver-like rodents similar to Alpine marmots — scurried from burrow to burrow. Once I was back on the main frontier ridge, it was a straightforward walk west along the **red track** over a succession of 2000m summits to **Starorobociański Wierch** (2176m) at which point the next 10km of the frontier ridge remain out of bounds to all except the wildlife. Instead, the path turns north along the Ornak ridge, for me an excruciatingly protracted and waterless six-kilometre slog down to the Ornaczańska hostel. Set at the head of the Dolina Koqcieliska, whose lower reaches I'd crossed a couple of days ago, the large timber cabin was packed to the gills with hard-up but cheerful teenagers making their own sandwiches and tea in an attempt to save what was to me, the negligible expense of a cooked meal. Kids sat around on tables singing along to a strumming guitar, or repairing ageing equipment until lights-out came, and those who could not afford bunks unrolled their sleeping bags on the tables and benches.

Next morning I decided that hostels were far preferable to further illicit camping, so I returned to Zakopane, diverting to make a torchlit crawl through the unmarked interior of **Jaskina Mylna** about which I'd been told the

night before. Back in town a cheap guest house performed the role of a left luggage office while I headed back to Kuźnice and up the **yellow track** to the ample Murowana hostel, ideally placed for excursions into the High Tatras visible to the southeast. Again I met up with gregarious Polish youths who quizzed me about life in England and explained their frustration with the government austerity measures distancing them further from the increasing range of imported commodities.

Next morning I and a small group of disparate hikers headed up the **blue track**, passing Czarny Staw (Black Lake) before the steep ascent up to the **Orla Perch**, a dramatic ridge of jagged 2300m peaks that requires a steady head for heights and includes several exposed sections safeguarded by chains and rails. Indeed, even getting onto the ridge required occasional clambering hand over hand up fixed chains until we reached the saddle. From here a wonderful panorama spread out east down the upper reaches of the **Dolina Pięciu Stawów Polskich** (Valley of the Five Polish Lakes), wrapped in a horseshoe of 2000m high ridges. A hard-earned four-kilometre descent brought us to the isolated cabin situated by the lowest lake where some of the group continued on down the Dolina Roztoki and the bus to Zakopane. If the other hostels had been crowded, this one was positively sinking into its foundations with the weight of its guests. Dinners were passed over the heads jammed along the benches and by night-time every body-sized flat surface was covered in recumbent figures.

The next afternoon was spent basking by the lakeside of **Morskie Oko** (Eye of the Sea), one of the Tatra's most famous landmarks, chatting with a couple of Danes I'd met a few days earlier. Situated below the towering walls of the Liptowskie Mury ridge, which defines the Czech border, the lake is dominated by the bare slopes of **Rysy**, Poland's highest peak. Its summit was my destination the following day, and following a frosty night bivouacked by the shores of a higher lake, a clear dawn start saw the arduous scramble up the peak completed by 8am. Sitting with satisfaction on the cemented **summit** block inscribed with "P"on one side and "CH" on the other, I looked out over the distant farmlands of the Czech and Polish republics which surrounded me. Over the

Liptowskie Mury, a helicopter was performing a recovery exercise or possibly an early rescue, and clambering down from the summit block I was dismayed to encounter three smartly uniformed soldiers, armed with heavy rifles and radios. A short chat with them revealed that the ascent of Rysy was a tiresome but regular task undertaken for the security of the forthcoming weekend's hikers.

Back in Zakopane, I became the victim of a bizarrely pre-meditated overnight robbery by the over-friendly weirdo with whom I shared my room – an instance of Poland's opportunistic crime epidemic to which foreign visitors are especially vulnerable. Fortunately, the landlady was so distraught by this event that she gave me the fare back to Kraków where I picked up my bus home.

*

Four months later, on Christmas Eve, a friend and I tramped by torchlight through the snow to the grand alpine hostel at the head of the Dolina Chochołowska, arriving just as the festive feast laid on for the guests was being cleared away.

With borrowed or homemade ice axes and crampons, and inexpensive Polish down jackets, we were hoping to repeat my west–east traverse of the previous summer, conditions permitting. However, next day an attempt to get up to **Wołowiec** was soon aborted when, exhausted by repeated falls through deep snow, we were beaten back by the biting winds once out on the bare slopes. Acknowledging that the short winter days made a walk along the exposed frontier ridge too risky, we instead walked back down the valley and took the **yellow track** east through the thick forests leading up to the **Iwaniacka Pass** and down to the Ornaczańska hostel into which I'd stumbled exhausted a few months earlier in T-shirt and shorts. One thing all of the Tatra's hostels share in common is a robust central heating system that's more than capable of putting up with the severest Polish winter and, following a typically crowded but affable evening, we walked back down the Kościeliska, passing the Mrozna Cave, and turned east along the black and yellow tracks. These led us close to the 1909m summit of **Giewont**, whose twenty-metre high steel crucifix is visible from all over Zakopane. From Giewont we slid semi-controllably down into the **Dolina Kondratowa**, using our ice axes as brakes, and were soon stamping the snow off our boots outside the idyllically situated Kondratowa hostel, a small log cabin only a couple of kilometres beneath the Czerwone Wierchy (Red Peaks) on the frontier ridge, which was at this point again open to walkers. With an eye out for the weather, we pre-cooked some food for tomorrow's anticipated walk along the ridge to Kasprowy Wierch, and squeezed two-to-a-bunk, ready for an early start. Next day dawned clear and so we set off up the **Dolina Sucha Kondracka**, occasionally sinking through the soft snow up to our chests, although as the slope steepened conditions improved and we doggedly kicked our way up to **Suchy Wierch Kondracki** (1890m) where a furious wind all but blew us back down. Crawling along the knife-edge ridge with thought-provoking drops down into the Czech valleys was a little more difficult than we had planned, as we occasionally lost the track and clambered around the ice-clad precipices of the Suche Chuby. Any intentions we may have had about undertaking the difficult traverse of the Orła Perch were soon brought into perspective as we completed the broad climb up to **Kasprowy Wierch**, site of a cable-car station adjacent to a huge mountain-top restaurant. Unfortunately for those who had struggled up here along the paths from Zakopane, this was closed, but the hall provided welcome shelter from the storm building up outside. Groups of cheerful but under-dressed Poles huddled together, stamping their numbed feet and re-wrapping sodden scarves around their heads. One of them begged to buy one of our sandwiches, before we all set off down the valley into the fading light and a lull in the blizzard. If most mountain accidents occur during final descents then here were several waiting to happen, as the frozen but happy daytrippers slithered down the slopes hand in hand, laughing uproariously and singing refrains from their favourite ballads. By now our home-welded ironware was beginning to show its limitations and when Bob's ice axe pick separated from its shaft while breaking a controlled slide, we accepted the limitations of our homemade gear and said goodbye to the snowbound Tatras.

Chris Scott

BOOKS

A vast amount of writing both from and about Poland is available in English, and the quantity looks set to increase at an accelerated pace with the advent of the post-communist regime.

Most of the books listed below are in print, and those that aren't should be easy enough to track down in second-hand bookstores; where two publishers are given, the first is British, the second US. In the UK, the best source for Polish books is the Polish-run *Orbis Books*, 66 Kenway Rd, London SW5 ORD (☎0171 370-2210), which also stocks a large selection of photo albums (many out of print) from Poland itself.

TRAVEL WRITING AND GUIDEBOOKS

Anne Applebaum *Betwen East and West* (Papermac). Well-informed, vividly written account of British-based US journalist's travels through the eastern Polish borderlands. Starting from Kaliningrad and moving down through Lithuania, Belarus, Ukraine and Moldava, Applebaum's broad-ranging cultural-historical frame of reference means the book suffers less than others from being too close to immediate events.

Karl Baedeker *Northern Germany, Southern Germany and Austria, Russia* (all o/p, but staple finds in second-hand shops). The old nineteenth- and early twentieth-century Baedekers are always fascinating, but never more so than in the case of Poland, which was then under Partition. A strong German bias is evident in the first two books, with Polish elements often ignored or glossed over; even in the later editions there's not the slightest anticipation of Poland's possible re-emergence as a nation.

Hilaire Belloc *Return to the Baltic* (Constable, o/p). Whimsical account of Belloc's travels through Denmark, Sweden and Poland – he clearly felt more at home among his fellow-Catholics in Warsaw and Kraków than in Lutheran Scandinavia.

Tim Burford *Hiking Guide to Poland and Ukraine* (Bradt Publications). Thoroughly researched guide to hiking in the region.

Alfred Döblin *Journey to Poland* (I.B. Tauris/ Paragon House). Döblin, best known for his weighty Expressionist novels, visited the newly resurrected Polish state in 1923, primarily to seek out his Jewish roots, though he himself was non-practising, and was later to convert to Catholicism. The result is a classic of travel literature, full of trenchant analysis and unnervingly prophetic predictions about the country's future, interspersed with buttonholing passages of vivid descriptive prose (see p.142).

Ruth E. Gruber *Jewish Heritage Travel: A Guide to East-Central Europe* and *Upon the Doorposts of Thy House: Jewish Life in East-Central Europe Yesterday and Today* (both Wiley). The first title is a useful country-by-country guide to Jewish culture and monuments of the region. The practical information tends to be basic, verging on the hieroglyphic, so will need supplementing for the serious searcher. The more discursive *Upon the Doorposts of Thy House* gives Gruber the space she needs to stretch out and really get into her subject. The sections on Auschwitz and Kraków's Kazimierz district, are masterly, thought-provoking essays.

Jim Haynes *Poland: People to People* (Zephyr/ Handshake). One of an imaginative, if eccentric series of guides to East-Central Europe. The author, an itinerant Paris-based American, has essentially compiled directories of hundreds of people from around the country interested in making contact with travellers from the West.

Eva Hoffman *Exit into History: A Journey through the New Eastern Europe* (Viking Penguin). US journalist of Polish Jewish origin returns to her roots on a journey through the early 90s post-communist landscape. Inevitably already dated, but the sections on Poland stand out for their combination of shrewd political insight and human warmth.

Joram Kagan *Poland's Jewish Heritage* (Hippocrene). A useful summary of the Jewish sites of Poland, along with an outline history.

Rory McLean *Stalin's Nose* (Flamingo). One of the best of the flurry of accounts of "epic" journeys across post-communist East-Central Europe. The author's quirky brand of surrealist humour enlivens the trip, which takes in obvious Polish stopoffs, Auschwitz and Kraków, en route for Moscow.

Philip Marsden *The Bronski House: A Return to the Borderlands* (HarperCollins). Sensitively written account of the author's journey to the Polish/Belarussian borderlands in the company of Zofia Ilińska, an aristocratic former resident returning for the first time in fifty years.

Colin Saunders and Renata Narozna *The High Tatras* (Cicerone). Detailed and comprehensive recent guide to the ins and outs of scaling the Tatras. For dedicated hikers and climbers.

HISTORY

Chimen Abramsky, Maciej Jachimczyk and Antony Polonsky (eds) *The Jews in Poland* (Basil Blackwell). Historical survey of what was for centuries the largest community of world Jewry.

Neal Ascherson *The Struggles for Poland* (Pan/Random). Ascherson's book was designed to accompany the Channel 4 TV series and its focus is squarely on the twentieth century, with just a thirty-page chapter on the previous thousand years. For most general readers, though, this is the best possible introduction to modern Polish history and politics.

Norman Davies *The Heart of Europe: A Short History of Poland* (OUP). A brilliantly original treatment of modern Polish history, beginning with the events of 1945 but looking backwards over the past millennium to illustrate the author's ideas. Scrupulously gives all points of view in disentangling the complex web of Polish history.

Norman Davies *God's Playground* (2 vols; OUP/Columbia UP). A masterpiece of erudition, entertainingly written and pretty much definitive for the pre-Solidarity period.

Norman Davies *White Eagle, Red Star: The Polish Soviet War, 1919–20* (Orbis Books/Hippocrene). Fascinating account of a little-known but critically important episode of European history, at a time when Lenin appeared ready to export the Soviet Revolution into Europe.

Norman Davies and **A. Polonsky** (eds) *Jews in Eastern Poland and the USSR 1939–49* (Macmillan). Meticulously researched and well-written account of the fate of eastern Europe's largest Jewish population in time of war.

Wacław Jedrzejewicz *Piłsudski – a Life for Poland* (Hippocrene). Comprehensive biography of the enigmatic military strongman.

Paul Latawski (ed.) *The Reconstruction of Poland 1914–23* (Macmillan). Useful set of essays on the run up to and early period of interwar Polish independence. Good on the nationalist leader Roman Dmowski and the minorities issue.

Czesław Miłosz *The History of Polish Literature* (California UP). Written in the mid-1960s, it is however still the standard English-language work on the subject, informed by the author's consummate grasp of the furthest nooks and crannies of Polish literature.

Krystyna Olzer (ed.) *For Your Freedom and Ours* (F. Ungar). Anthology of Polish political writings over the centuries with an emphasis on progressive traditions. Some stirring pieces from Kosciusko ("The Polanic Manifesto"), Piłsudski and the World War II Polish resistance among others. A useful reference book.

Bianka Pietrow-Ennker *Women in Polish Society* (Columbia UP). Intriguing collection of academic essays on the prominent but under-recognized role of women in Partitions-era Poland. Radical feminist its perspective isn't, however.

Józef Piłsudski *Memoirs of a Polish Revolutionary and Soldier* (Faber & Faber, o/p/ AMS Press). Lively stuff from Lech Wałęsa's hero, who – after a dashing wartime career – was Poland's leader from 1926 to 1934.

Iwo Pogonowski *Jews in Poland: A Documentary History* (Hippocrene). Thorough if idiosyncratically presented account of Polish Jewry from the earliest times up until the present day – not too many axes to grind either. Contains an intriguing selection of old prints from everyday life in the ghettos, *shtetls* and synagogues.

Antony Polonsky (ed.) *The Jews in Old Poland 1700–1795* (I.B. Tauris); *Studies From Polin: From Shtetl to Socialism* (Littman). The first is an informative, wide-ranging set of historical essays by a combined team of Polish and Israeli scholars covering Jewish life in Poland from earliest times up to the end of the Partitions era. The second, a collection of essays drawn from the learned journal of the Oxford Institute for Polish-Jewish Studies, covers diverse aspects of Polish Jewish history, politics, literature and culture. Doesn't shrink from the more controversial and sensitive topics either.

Adam Zamoyski *The Polish Way* (John Murray/ Watts). The most accessible history of Poland, going right up to the 1989 elections. Zamoyski is an American émigré Pole, and his sympathies – as you would expect in a member of one of Poland's foremost aristocratic families – are those of a blue-blooded nationalist.

WORLD WAR II AND THE HOLOCAUST

Alan Adelson and Robert Lapides *The Łódź Ghetto – Inside a Community under Siege* (Penguin). Scrupulously detailed narrative of the 200,000-strong ghetto, with numerous personal memoirs and photographs.

Janina Bauman *Winter in the Morning* (Pan/ Free Press); *A Dream of Belonging* (Virago/ Trafalgar Square). Bauman and her family survived the Warsaw Ghetto, eventually leaving the country following the anti-Semitic backlash of 1968. *Winter* is a delicate and moving account of life and death in the ghetto. Less dramatic but equally interesting, *Belonging*, the second volume of her autobiography, tells of life in the Communist Party and disillusionment in the early postwar years.

Jan Ciechanowski *The Warsaw Uprising of 1944* (CUP). Compelling, day-by-day account – the best of many on this subject.

Martin Gilbert *The Holocaust* (Fontana). The standard work, providing a trustworthy overview on the slaughter of European Jewry – and the crucial role of Poland, where most Nazi concentration camps were sited.

Geoffrey Hartman (ed.) *Holocaust Remembrance: the shapes of memory* (Blackwell). Wide-ranging collection of essays by artists, scholars and writers on diverse aspects of contemporary remembrance of the Holocaust. A number of chapters on Polish themes, including useful pieces on Lanzemann's *Shoah*, Auschwitz and the construction of the Jewish memorials in Poland.

Gustaw Herling *A World Apart* (OUP/Arbor House, o/p). Account of deportation to a Soviet labour camp, based on the author's own experiences.

Rudolf Höss *Kommandant at Auschwitz* (o/p). Perhaps the most chilling record of the barbarity: a remorseless autobiography of the Auschwitz camp commandant, written in the days between his death sentence and execution at Nürnberg.

Stefan Korbonski *The Polish Underground State* (Hippocrene). Detailed account of the history and inner workings of the many-faceted Polish wartime resistance by a leading figure of the time. Korbonski has produced a number of other books on related themes, notably *Fighting Warsaw*, an account of the 1944 Warsaw Uprising drawing on his own experience.

Dan Kurzman *The Bravest Battle* (Pinnacle, o/p/ Putnam, o/p). Detailed account of the 1943 Warsaw Ghetto Uprising, conveying the incredible courage of the Jewish combatants.

Primo Levi *If This is a Man* and *The Truce*; *Moments of Reprieve*; *The Drowned and the Saved*; *The Periodic Table*; *If Not Now, When?* (all Abacus). An Italian Jew, Levi survived Auschwitz because the Nazis made use of his training as a chemist in the death-camp factories. Most of his books, which became ever bleaker towards the end of his life, concentrate on his experiences during and soon after his incarceration in Auschwitz, analysing the psychology of survivor and torturer with extraordinary clarity. *If Not Now, When?* is the story of a group of Jewish partisans in occupied Russia and Poland: giving plenty of insights into Eastern European anti-Semitism, it's a good corrective to the mythology of Jews as passive victims.

Betty Jean Lifton *Janusz Korczak: The King of the Children* (Chatto/Farrar, Srauss & Giroux). Biography of the Jewish doctor who died in Treblinka with the orphans for whom he cared. He was the eponymous subject of an Andrzej Wajda film.

Richard C. Lukas *The Forgotten Holocaust* (Hippocrene). Detailed study of Nazi atrocities against Polish Gentiles which, in the author's view, were every bit as barbaric as against their Jewish counterparts.

Jan Nowak *Courier for Warsaw* (Collins Harvill). Racily written memoir of the Polish underground resistance.

Emmanuel Ringelblum *Polish-Jewish Relations during the Second World War* (Northwestern UP). Penetrating history of the Warsaw Ghetto focusing on the vexed issue of Polish–Jewish wartime relations. Written from the inside by the prominent prewar Jewish historian – history recorded as it was occurring. Tragically, only a portion of Ringelblum's own writings and the extensive ghetto archives he put together were recovered after 1945.

Saul Rubinek *So Many Miracles* (Penguin, UK). Rubinek's interviews with his parents about their early life in Poland and survival under Nazi occupation make a compelling piece of oral history, and one that paints a blacker than usual picture of Polish–Jewish relations.

Art Spiegelman *Maus* (Penguin/Pantheon). Spiegelman, editor of the cartoon magazine *Raw*, is the son of Auschwitz survivors. *Maus* is a brilliant comic-strip exploration of the ghetto and concentration camp experiences of his father, recounted in flashbacks. The story runs through to Art's father's imprisonment at Auschwitz; subsequent chapters of the sequel – covering Auschwitz itself – have been printed in recent editions of *Raw*, now available as a separate book, *Maus II* (André Deutsch).

Carl Tighe *Gdańsk: National Identity in the German-Polish Border Lands* (Pluto). Alternatively titled "Gdańsk: the Unauthorised Biography", an apt description of a fascinating history of a city that Poles and Germans have tussled over for centuries. Studiously avoiding the pro- or anti-Polish/German dichotomy that bedevils many interpretations, the author sets out to capture the unique story of the Gdańsk/Danzig citizenry, arguing that claims of real Polish or German identity tell us more about the needs of latterday nationalists than the cultural complexities of the past.

The Warsaw Ghetto (Interpress, Warsaw). Official state publication, issued in several languages, that documents the destruction of the capital's Jewish population.

Harold Werner, *Fighting Back: A Memoir of Jewish Resistance in World War II* (Columbia UP). Gripping, straightforwardly written account of the author's experiences as a member of a Jewish partisan unit fighting against the Nazis in wartime Poland.

POLITICS AND SOCIETY

Mark Frankland *The Patriots' Revolution* (Sinclair Stevenson). After Tim Garton Ash, the best of the snap reports on the eastern European revolutions.

Timothy Garton Ash *The Polish Revolution: Solidarity 1980–82* (Cape/Random); *The Uses of Adversity* (Granta/Penguin/Random); *We The People: The Revolution of 89* (Granta/Penguin/Random). Garton Ash has been the most consistent and involved Western reporter on Poland in the Solidarity era, displaying an intuitive grasp of the Polish mentality. His *Polish Revolution* is a vivid record of events from the birth of Solidarity – a story extended in the climactic events of 1989, documented as an eyewitness in Warsaw, Budapest, Berlin and Prague.

Misha Glenny *The Rebirth of History: Eastern Europe in the Age of Democracy* (Penguin). One chapter deals with Poland, homing in on the economic and political difficulties of post-communist reconstruction.

Grupa Publikacyjna Forum *Forum Polek: Polish Women's Forum* (available from POSK, 238–246 King St, London W6 0RF). Highly worthwhile anthology – in English and Polish – of essays, memoirs, fiction and poetry by London-based émigré (and second-generation émigré) writers.

Jaqueline Hayden *Poles Apart: Solidarity and the New Poland* (Irish Academic Press). Personal account of political developments in Poland from August 1980 up to the election of the SLD-led government in 1993 by an Irish journalist who visited the country throughout the period. The format – a series of extended interviews with key opposition figures, tracing their lives and political development – offers an interesting overview that combines the personal with the political. See pp.638–48 for an extract from the book.

Paul Latwski (ed.) T*he Reconstruction of Poland 1914–23* (Macmillan). Wide-ranging set of academic essays focusing on the lead-up to the country's (re)achievement of independence, and subsequent struggles with newfound statehood, particularly the sensitive question of minorities. Useful annex of period documents.

Jan Josef Lipski *A History of KOR – The Committee for Workers' Self-Defence* (University of California Press). Detailed history of key 1970s opposition movement that is regarded as one of Solidarity's main inspirations. A resistance veteran and leading light in KOR, Lipski shows how it developed ideas and strategies of non-violence and an "independent civil society" as a response to totalitarianism. A demanding but worthwhile read.

Grazyna Sikorska *Jerzy Popiełuszko, a Martyr for Truth* (Fount/Eerdmans, o/p). Hagiographic biography of the murdered Catholic priest and national hero.

Stewart Steven *The Poles* (Collins Harvill/Macmillan, o/p). Excellent journalistic account of all aspects of society in early 1980s Poland.

ESSAYS AND MEMOIRS

Kazimierz Brandys *Warsaw Diary 1977–81* (Chatto/Random, o/p); *Paris/New York: 1982–84* (Faras Straus Giroux). The *Warsaw Diary* by this major Polish journalist and novelist brilliantly captures the atmosphere of the time, and especially the effect of John Paul II's first papal visit in 1979. During martial law, possession of this book carried an automatic ten-year sentence. *Paris/New York* powerfully traces his early life in imposed exile while continually reflecting on developments at home.

Adam Czerniawski *Scenes from a Disturbed Childhood* (Serpent's Tail). Uplifting, entertainingly written account of a childhood spent escaping the traumas of World War II – to Turkey and an Arab school in Palestine, before ending up with his impoverished upper-class family in southeast England. A welcome addition to wartime émigré memoir literature.

Hans Magnus Enzensberger *Europe, Europe* (Picador/Pantheon). A tour de force from the German anarchist, delving outside the mainstream to answer the question "What is Europe?" The section on Poland is a wonderfully observant roam around the main cities in 1986.

Granta 30: New Europe! (Penguin, UK). Published at the beginning of 1990, this state-of-the-continent anthology includes Neil Ascherson on the eastern Polish borderlands and a series of brief reactions to events from a dozen or so European intellectuals.

Zbigniew Herbert *Barbarian in the Garden* (Harvest/HBJ). Stirring, lyrical set of essays on Mediterranean themes by a noted contemporary Polish poet, with 1960s post-Stalinist era Poland – the period when they were written – a recurring background presence.

Eva Hoffman *Lost in Translation* (Minerva). Wise, sparklingly written autobiography of a Polish Jew centring, as the title suggests, around her experience of emigration from Kraków to North America in the 1960s. Plenty of insights into the postwar Jewish/Eastern Europe émigré experience.

Lynne Jones *States of Change – A Central European Diary* (Merlin, UK). Highly personal account, wandering mainly through Poland and paying special attention to the alternative scene of punks, greens, anarchists, peaceniks, etc.

Ryszard Kapuscínski *The Soccer War* (Granta, UK). For many years Kapuscínski was the only full-time Polish foreign correspondent, and he's best known for his trilogy on the dictators of Iran, Angola and Ethiopia. His latest book, a collection of sketches of Third World politics, offers many wry insights into his native land.

Adam Michnik *Letters From Prison* (University of California Press). Collection of writings by prominent opposition intellectual and editor of the *Gazeta Wyborcza*, once Solidarity's house newspaper, now critical of (and disowned by) Wałęsa. The essay "A New Evolutionism" is a seminal piece of new political writing, and the more historical pieces are fascinating, too.

Czesław Miłosz *The Captive Mind* (Penguin/Random); *Native Realm* (Penguin/University of California Press); *Beginning with my Story* (I. B. Tauris). The first is a penetrating analysis of the reasons so many Polish artists and intellectuals sold out to communism after 1945, with four case-studies supplementing a confession of personal guilt. *Native Realm*, the unorthodox autobiography of the years before Miłosz defected to the West, is especially illuminating on the Polish–Lithuanian relationship. The last is a wide-ranging collection of essays by the Nobel Prize-winning author, including an envigorating set of pieces revolving around Wilno (Vilnius), the author's boyhood home and spiritual mentor in later life.

Toby Nobel Fluek *Memoirs of my Life in a Polish Village 1930–39* (Hamish Hamilton). Touching memoir of a young Jewish girl growing up in a village near Lwów in the 1930s. Plenty of insights into the traditional prewar Polish rural way of life, enhanced by the author's simple but evocative illustrations.

Barbara Porajska *From the Steppes to the Savannah* (Ham). Simply written yet informative memoir of one of the hundreds of Poles deported to Kazakhstan and other parts of Soviet Asia following the Soviet annexation to eastern Poland in 1939. Like many others, too, the author finally made it to Britain, via adventures in Iran and East Africa.

Tim Sebastian *Nice Promises* (Chatto). Former Warsaw BBC correspondent's reflections on the early 1980s in Poland. Chatty, anecdotal stuff, but plenty of insights into the politics and spirit of the times.

Teresa Torańska *Oni: Poland's Stalinists Cross-Examined* (Collins Harvill/Harper Collins). Interviews with Polish communists and Party leaders from the Stalinist era carried out during the Solidarity era by investigative journalist Torańska. The result is a fascinating insight into how Stalin established Soviet control over Eastern Europe, and Poland in particular.

Lech Wałęsa *An Autobiography: A Path of Hope* (Pan/H. Holt). Ghostwritten, it would seem, by a Solidarity committee, in the years before Lech split the party and created his own role as "axe-wielding" president.

CULTURE, ART AND ARCHITECTURE

F. C. Anstrutter *Old Polish Legends* (Hippocrene). Entertaining retellings of some of the best-known traditional Polish tales and legends, including the legends of Krakus, Wanda and most famously, the story of the trumpeter of Kraków *hejnał* fame.

Adam Bujak *Kraków* (Sport y Turystyka). Beautiful collection of photographs of the city and its surroundings by one of Poland's premier contemporary photographers.

David Buxton *The Wooden Churches of Eastern Europe* (CUP). Wonderful illustrations of Poland's most compelling architectural style. Well worth hunting out in libraries: it will make you want to traipse around Silesia, the Bieszczady Mountains and Czech borderlands.

Huit Siecles d'Eglises Polonaises: le Cas du Ermland (Romain Pages Editions). Beautifully photographed French album of the distinctive church architecture of the Warmia region of northeast Poland, including useful background text. An English-language edition is supposed to be due out soon, which you should be able to pick up in the area.

Les Icones de Pologne (Editions de Cerf/ Arkadia, o/p). Good reproductions of most of the major icons from Poland's regional museums. Scour the *antiquariats* of the big cities for a copy.

Sophie Knab *Polish Customs, Traditions & Folklore* (Hippocrene). Compendium of Polish folklore grouped according to months of the year and central rites of passage. A delight for anthropologists as much as anyone interested in delving into what lies behind ethnographic exhibits on show in regional museums throughout the country.

Jan Kott (ed.) *Four Decades of Polish Essays* (Northwestern University Press). Culture-based anthology – on art, literature, drama, plus politics – that features most of the major intellectual names of postwar Poland.

Anna Nietksza *Impresje Polskie* (Fundacja Buchnera). Excellent set of photographic portraits of contemporary Poland, taking in everything from rural life and industrial landscapes to the face of the emerging postcommunist social order. Accompanying booklet with summary captions in English and German. Widely available in Poland.

The Polish Jewry: History and Culture (Interpress, Warsaw). Wide-ranging collection of essays and photographs on all aspects of culture – from customs and family life to theatre, music and painting. A beautiful production.

Polish Realities *The Arts in Poland 1908–89* (Third Eye Centre, Glasgow). Excellent anthology of essays on all aspects of cultural life in Poland in the 1980s – architecture and youth culture alongside the obvious pieces on film, literature and theatre – which accompanied a major season of events in Glasgow under the same title. A testimony to the city's special links with Poland.

Reise nach Masuren (Rautenberg Verlage). One of the large series of photo albums based on East Prussian memorabilia, produced by the German Rautenberg publishing house. Despite some dubious *alte Heimat* politics that occasionally steer dangerously close to straightforward revanchism, these volumes are nevertheless infused with a clear love of the old East Prussian territories, and the photographs of the region are some of the best around.

Roman Vishniac *Polish Jews – A Pictorial Record* (Schocken Books). Haunting selection of pictures by the legendary photographer, evoking Jewish life in the *shtetls* and ghettoes of Poland immediately before the outbreak of World War II. A good introduction to the great man's work if you can't get hold of *A Vanished World* (Penguin, o/p), the acclaimed album that brings together most of the 2000 or so photos from Vishniac's travels through Jewish Poland.

Tomasz Wiśniewski *Synagogues and Jewish Communities in the Białystok Region: Jewish Life in Eastern Europe before 1939* (David). Encyclopedic survey of the wealth of pre-Jewish architecture in the eastern borderlands, much of it destroyed but with a significant number of buildings still surviving. Only available in Poland so far – a useful companion to any trip through the region.

POLISH FICTION

Shmuel Yozef Agnon *A Simple Story* (Schocken); *Dwelling Place of My People* (Scottish Academic Press). Agnon, Polish-born Nobel Prize-winner and father-figure of modern Hebrew literature, sets *A Simple Story* in the Jewish communities of the Polish Ukraine, belying its title by weaving an unexpected variation on the traditional Romeo-and-Juliet-type tale of crossed lovers. In *Dwelling Place* he recalls his childhood in Poland, in a series of highly refined stories and prose poems.

Jerzy Andrzejewski *Ashes and Diamonds* (o/p in UK/Northwestern). Spring 1945: resistance fighters, communist ideologues and black marketeers battle it out in small-town Poland. A gripping account of the tensions and forces that shaped postwar Poland, and the basis for Andrzej Wajda's film of the same title.

Asher Barash *Pictures from a Brewery* (Peter Owen). Depiction of Jewish life in Galicia, told in a style very different from the mythic, romantic approach favoured by Agnon.

Tadeusz Borowski *This Way for the Gas, Ladies and Gentlemen* (Penguin). These short stories based on his Auschwitz experiences marked Borowski out as the great literary hope of communist Poland, but he committed suicide soon after their publication, at the age of 29.

Joseph Conrad *A Personal Record* (with *The Mirror of the Sea*, OUP). An entertaining, ironic piece of "faction" about Conrad's family and his early life in the Russian part of Partition Poland, addressing the painful subjects of his loss of his own country and language.

Ida Fink *A Scrap of Time* (Penguin/Schocken). Haunting vignettes of Jews striving to escape the concentration camps – and of the unsung Polish Gentiles who sheltered them.

Adam Gillon (ed.) *Introduction to Modern Polish Literature* (Orbis/Hippocrene). An excellent anthology of short stories and extracts from novels, many of them (eg Reymont's *The Peasants*) out of print in English.

Witold Gombrowicz *Ferdydurke* (Penguin); *Pornografia* (Penguin); *The Possessed* (Boyars). The first two experimentalist novels concentrate on humanity's infantile and juvenile obsessions, and on the tensions between urban life and the traditional ways of the countryside. *The Possessed* explores the same themes within the more easily digestible format of a Gothic thriller.

Pawel Huelle *Who Was David Weiser?*; *Moving House* (both Bloomsbury). The first is the well-translated first novel by a young Gdańsk-born writer, centring on an enigmatic young Jewish boy idolized by his youthful contemporaries: author's themes and style show an obvious debt to fellow Danziger Günter Grass. Huelle's magic realist propensities are further developed in *Moving House*, his latest work to be translated, a marvellous collection of short stories, with the intersecting worlds of Polish and German/Prussian culture again providing the primary frame of reference.

Marek Hłasko *The Eighth Day of the Week*; *Killing the Second Dog* (single Minerva paperback in UK; Greenwood Press and Cane Hill Press respectively); *Next Stop – Paradise & the Graveyard* (Heinemann). Poland's "Angry Young Man", Hłasko articulated the general disaffection of those who grew up after World War II, his bleak themes mirrored in a spare, taut prose style.

Henia Karmel-Wolfe *The Baders of Jacob Street* (Lippincott, o/p). Kraków-set tale of the impact of Nazi occupation on a Jewish family.

Tadeusz Konwicki *A Minor Apocalypse* (Faber/Random); *A Dreambook for our Time* (Penguin, o/p); *The Polish Complex* (Farrar, Strauss & Giroux). A convinced Party member in the Fifties, Konwicki eventually made the break with Stalinism; since then a series of highly respected novels, films and screenplays have established him as one of Poland's foremost writers. Describing a single day's events, *A Minor Apocalypse* is narrated by a character who constantly vacillates over his promise to set fire to himself in front of the Party headquarters. *Dreambook* is a hard-hitting wartime tale, while *The Polish Complex* is a fascinating, often elusive exploration of contemporary life in Poland. Like Miłosz and many others who grew up in Wilno, now the capital of Lithuania, Konwicki betrays a yearning for a mystic homeland.

Janusz Korczak *King Matty the First* (Hippocrene). Written by the famous Jewish doctor who died, along with his orphans, at Treblinka, this long children's novel, regarded as the Polish counterpart of *Alice in Wonderland*, appeals also to adults through its underlying sense of tragedy and gravitas.

Stanisław Lem *Return from the Stars*; *Tales of Pirx the Pilot*; *His Master's Voice* (Mandarin/Harcourt Brace). The only recent Polish writing to have achieved a worldwide mass-market readership, Lem's science fiction focuses on the human and social predicament in the light of technological change.

Czeslaw Miłosz *The Seizure of Power* (Faber/Farrar, Strauss & Giroux); *The Issa Valley* (Carcanet). *The Seizure of Power*, the first book by this Nobel Prize-winning writer, is a wartime novel, while the semi-autobiographical *Issa Valley* is a wonderfully lyrical account of a boy growing up in the Lithuanian countryside.

Jan Potocki *Tales from the Saragossa Manuscript: Ten Days in the Life of Alphonse von Worden* (Dedalus/Hippocrene). A self-contained section of a huge unfinished Gothic novel written at the beginning of the nineteenth century by a Polish nobleman: a rich brew of picaresque adventures, dreams, hallucinations, eroticism, philosophical discourses and exotic tales.

Bolesław Prus *Pharaoh* (Polonia); *The Doll* (Hippocrene). The first, a late nineteenth-century epic, set in ancient Egypt, offers a trenchant examination of the nature of power in a society which was of more than passing relevance to Partition-era Poland. *The Doll* is a recent reissue after several years out of print of probably the most famous of the "Polish Tolstoy's" lengthier works: widely regarded as one of the great nineteenth-century social novels, this is a story of obsessive love against the backdrop of a crisis-ridden *fin-de-siècle* Warsaw.

R. Pynsent and S. Kanikova (eds) *The Everyman Companion to East European Literature* (Dent). The Polish section combines thoughtful introductory essays on the place of literature and writers in the national consciousness. Includes short extracts from works by major artists (Prus, Witkiewicz, Mickiewicz), a literary itinerary through the country and a brief authors' A–Z.

Władysław Reymont *The Peasants*; *The Promised Land* (both o/p). Reymont won the Nobel Prize for *The Peasants*, a tetralogy about village life (one for each season of the year), but its vast length has led to its neglect outside Poland. *The Promised Land*, which was filmed by Wajda, offers a comparably unromanticized view of industrial life in Łódź.

Bruno Schulz *Street of Crocodiles* & *Sanatorium under the Sign of the Hourglass* (Picador/Viking Penguin). These kaleidoscopic, dream-like fictions, vividly evoking life in the small town of Drohobycz in the Polish Ukraine, constitute the entire literary output of their author, who was murdered by the SS.

Isaac Bashevis Singer *The Magician of Lublin* (Penguin/Fawcett); *The Family Moskat* (Penguin/Farrar, Strauss & Giroux); *Collected Stories* (Penguin/Farrar, Strauss & Giroux); *The Slave* (Penguin/Avon); *Satan in Goray* (Penguin/Fawcett); *The King of the Fields* (Penguin/NAL Dutton). Singer, who emigrated from Poland to the USA in the 1930s, writes in Yiddish, so his reputation rests largely on the translations of his novels and short stories. Only a selection of his vast output is mentioned here. *The Magician of Lublin* and *The Family Moskat*, both novels set in the ghettoes of early twentieth-century Poland, are masterly evocations of life in vanished Jewish communities. *The Slave* is a gentle yet tragic love story set in the seventeenth century, while *Satan in Goray* is a blazing evocation of religious hysteria in the same period. His penultimate work, *The*

King of the Fields, re-creates the early life of the Polish state, and is his only novel without a Jewish emphasis.

Henryk Sienkiewicz *Quo Vadis?* (Alan Sutton/Hippocrene); *Charcoal Sketches and Other Tales* (Angel/Dufour); *With Fire and Sword*; *The Deluge*; and *Fire in the Steppe* (all Copernicus/Hippocrene). Sienkiewicz's reputation outside Poland largely rests on *Quo Vadis?* (which won him the Nobel Prize), treating the early Christians in Nero's Rome as an allegory of Poland's plight under the Partitions. Until recently, Sienkiewicz's other blockbusters existed only in inadequate and long out-of-print translations, but the Polish-American novelist W.S. Kuniczak has recently rendered the great trilogy about Poland's seventeenth-century wars with the Swedes, Prussians, Germans and Turks into English in a manner which at last does justice to the richly crafted prose of the originals. If the sheer size of these is too daunting, a more than adequate taste of the author's style can be had from the three novellas in the *Charcoal Sketches* collection, which focus on the different classes of nineteenth-century Polish rural society with a wry wit and a sense of pathos.

Andrzej Szczypiorski *The Beautiful Mrs Seidemann* (Abacus). Best-selling novel by prominent contemporary Polish writer who survived both the Warsaw Uprising and subsequently the concentration camps. The story centres around a Jewish woman who uses her wits – and beauty – to survive the Nazis. Stirringly written, though the fatalistic historical musings (he's obviously got a foreign audience in mind) become increasingly oppressive as the book progresses.

Stanisław Ignacy Witkiewicz *Insatiability* (Quartet/Salem House). Explicit depiction of artistic, intellectual, religious and sexual decadence against the background of a Chinese invasion of Europe. The enormous vocabulary, complicated syntax and philosophical diversions don't make an easy read, but this is unquestionably one of the most distinctive works of twentieth-century literature.

POLISH POETRY

S. Barańczak and C. Cavanagh (eds) *Spoiling Cannibal's Fun: Polish Poetry of the Last Two Decades of Communist Rule* (Northwestern University Press). Representative anthology of recent Polish poetry with informative introductory essay by co-editor and translator Stanisław Barańczak, one of the country's pre-eminent émigré literary figures whose poems are also featured in this volume.

Susan Bassnett and Piotr Kuhiwczak (eds) *Ariadne's Thread: Polish Women Poets* (Forest Books/Three Continents). Poems by eight distinctive contemporaries, ranging from re-interpretations of classical myth to the horrors of torture.

Adam Czerniawski (ed.) *The Burning Forest* (Bloodaxe/Dufour). Selected by one of Poland's leading contemporary poets, this anthology covers Polish poetry from the laconic nineteenth-century verses of Cyprian Norwid, through examples of Herbert, Różewicz and the editor, up to young writers of the present day.

Zbigniew Herbert *Selected Poems* (Carcanet/ Ecco Press); *Report from the Besieged City* (OUP/Ecco Press). Another fine contemporary poet, with a strong line in poignant observation; intensely political but never dogmatic.

Adam Mickiewicz *Pan Tadeusz* (Everyman, o/p; parallel text published by the Polish Cultural Foundation/Hippocrene); *Konrad Wallenrod* & *Grażyna* (University Press of America). Poland's national epic, set among the gentry of Lithuania at the time of the Napoleonic invasion, is here given a highly effective verse translation. In contrast to the self-delusion about Polish independence shown by the characters in *Pan Tadeusz*, *Konrad Wallenrod* demonstrates how that end can be achieved by stealth and cunning; like *Grażyna*, its setting is Poland-Lithuania's struggle with the Teutonic Knights.

Czesław Miłosz *Collected Poems* (Penguin/ Ecco Press); *Polish Postwar Poetry* (California UP). A writer of massive integrity, Miłosz in all his works wrestles with the issues of spiritual and political commitment; this collection encompasses all his poetic phases, from the surrealist of the 1930s to the émigré sage of San Francisco.

Czesław Miłosz (ed.) Useful anthology selected and mostly translated by Miłosz, with an emphasis on poetry written after the thaw of 1956. The closer you get to the 1980s the grittier and more acerbic they become, as befits the politics of the era.

Tadeusz Rożewicz *Conversations with the Prince* (Anvil Press, UK). These uncompromising verses, rooted in everyday speech, are among the most accessible examples of modern Polish poetry.

Anna Swir *Fat Like the Sun* (Women's Press). Selection from a leading feminist poet.

Wisława Szymborska *People on the Bridge* (Forest). Recent volume of poems by one of the country's most distinctive modern (female) voices, translated by fellow poet, Adam Czerniawski.

Aleksander Wat *Selected Poems* (Penguin). Dating from Wat's middle and later years, these wide-ranging poems, with their predominant tone of despair at the century's excesses, make a fascinating contrast to the Futurist short-story fantasies he wrote in the interwar period.

Karol Wojtyła *Easter Vigil and Other Poems* (Hutchinson/Random, o/p). Pope John Paul II followed a sideline career in poetry throughout his priesthood. This selection casts light on the complex private personality of a very public figure.

POLISH DRAMA

Solomon Anski *The Dybbuk* (in *Three Great Jewish Plays*, Applause). Written by a prominent member of the Jewish socialist movement, this drama of divine justice is the masterpiece of Yiddish theatre. Also included in the anthology is a work on a similar theme, *God of Vengeance* by Scholem Asch

Daniel Gerould (ed.) *The Witkiewicz Reader* (Quartet). Painstakingly compiled and well-translated anthology of writings by the great artist/philosopher/dramatist covering the various stages of Witkiewicz's development, from the early plays via explicitly drug-induced musings through to later philosophical and literary critical pieces.

Witold Gombrowicz *The Marriage; Operetta; Princess Ivona* (all Boyars/Northwestern University Press). Three plays exploring similar themes to those found in Gombrowicz's novels.

Tadeusz Kantor *Wielopole/Wielopole* (Boyars). One of the most successful products of Poland's experimental theatre scene, complete with a lavish record of its production plus the author/director's rehearsal notes.

Sławomir Mrożek *Tango* (Cape, o/p); *Vatzlav* (Applause/Grove Weidenfeld); *Striptease, Repeat Performance* & *The Prophets* (Applause, UK). Mrożek is the sharpest and subtlest satirist Poland has produced, employing nonsensical situations to probe serious political issues.

Tadeusz Rożewicz *The Card Index; The Interrupted Act* & *Gone Out; Marriage Blanc* & *The Hunger Artist Departs* (all Boyars). The best works by an unremittingly inventive experimentalist.

Juliusz Słowacki *Mary Stuart* (Greenwood Press). Słowacki ranks second only to Mickiewicz in Polish esteem, but his reputation hasn't travelled. Nonetheless, this is a fine example of Romantic drama, set against the backdrop of the murders of David Rizzio and Mary's husband, Henry Darnley.

Stanisław Ignacy Witkiewicz *The Madman and the Nun, The Water Hen* & *The Crazy Locomotive* (Applause, UK). Witkiewicz created a Theatre of the Absurd twenty years before the term came into common use through the work of Ionesco and Beckett. This volume makes the ideal introduction to the versatile avant-garde painter, novelist and playwright.

LITERATURE BY FOREIGN WRITERS

E. T. A. Hoffmann *The Jesuit Chapel at G___* (in *Six German Romantic Tales*, Angel, UK); *The Artushof* (in *Tales of Hoffmann*, Penguin). Hoffmann began writing his masterly stories of the macabre while a bored civil servant in Prussian Poland; these are two with a specifically Polish setting.

Gerhart Hauptmann *The Weavers* (Eyre Methuen/Ungar). Set against the background of an heroic but inevitably futile mid-nineteenth-century uprising by the Silesian weavers against the mill owners, this intense drama gained its reputation as the first "socialist" play by having a collective rather than a single protagonist.

Isaac Babel *Red Cavalry* (in *Collected Stories*, Penguin/NAL Dutton). A collection of interrelated short stories about the 1919–20 invasion of Poland, narrated by the bizarrely contradictory figure of a Jewish Cossack communist, who naturally finds himself torn by conflicting emotions.

Günter Grass *The Tin Drum* (Picador/Random); *Dog Years* (Picador/Harcourt Brace); *Cat and*

Mouse (Picador/Ameron). These three novels, known as the "Danzig Trilogy", are one of the high points of modern German literature. Set in Danzig/Gdańsk, where the author grew up, they hold up a mirror to the changing German character this century. His latest novel, *The Call of the Toad* (Secker & Warburg/HBJ), provides a satirical commentary on post-communist Polish and German attitudes towards the same city's past.

Leon Uris *Mila 18* (Corgi/Bantam). Stirring tale of the Warsaw Ghetto Uprising – Mila 18 was the address of the Jewish resistance militia's HQ.

James Michener *Poland* (Corgi/Fawcett). Another of Michener's blockbusters, larded with highly symbolic peasants and aristocrats. Characterization is wooden and schematic, but a lot of research went into it, and it's no bad introduction to the intricacies of Polish history.

Thomas Keneally *Schindler's Ark* (Coronet/ Viking Penguin). Based on the life of Oskar Schindler, a German industrialist who used his business operations to shelter thousands of Jews, this powerful novel – the subject of Spielberg's film – won the 1982 Booker Prize.

FILM

Brian McIlroy *World Cinema: Poland* (Flicks Books/H. Holt). In-depth study of the contemporary film scene including interviews, biographies and plenty of black and white stills.

Andrzej Wajda *Double Vision: My Life in Film* (Faber, UK). Autobiography of Poland's most famous director; rather more rewarding than some of his recent celluloid creations.

Krzysztof Kieślowski and Krysztof Piesiewicz *Decalogue* (Faber, UK). Transcripts of the internationally acclaimed series of fims, set in a Warsaw housing estate, featuring tales of breaches of the Ten Commandments.

LANGUAGE

Polish is one of the more difficult European languages for English speakers to learn. Even so, it is well worth acquiring the basics: not only is Polish beautiful and melodious, but a few words will go a long way. This is especially true away from the major cities where you won't find a lot of English spoken. (Knowledge of German, however, is quite widespread.)

The following features provide an indication of the problems of Polish grammar. There are three genders (masculine, feminine and neuter) and no word for "the". Prepositions (words like "to", "with", "in" etc) take different cases, and the case changes the form of the noun. Thus, "miasto" is the Polish for "town", but "to the town" is "do miasta" and "in the town" is "w mieście". You don't have to learn this sort of thing off by heart, but it can be useful to be able to recognize it.

Such grammatical complexity is a product of Polish history. During the periods when Poland didn't even exist as a nation, Polish was taught as virtually a foreign language, and the teachers were determined that nothing should be lost. Hence the "conservative" retention of so many archaic features.

Finally, a brief word on how to address people. The familiar form used among friends, relations and young people is "ty", like French "tu" or German "du". However, the polite form which you will usually require is "Pan" when addressing a man and "Pani" for a woman (literally "Sir" and "Madam"). ALWAYS use this form with people obviously older than yourself, and with officials.

PRONUNCIATION

While Polish may look daunting at first, with its apparently unrelieved rows of consonants, the good news is that it's a phonetic language – ie it's pronounced exactly as spelt. So once you've learnt the rules and have a little experience you'll always know how to pronounce a word correctly.

Stress:
Usually on the penultimate syllable, eg Warsz**a**wa, przyj**a**ciel, m**a**tka.

Vowels:
a: as "u" in "run".
e: "e" in "neck".
i: "i" in "Mick", never as in "I".
o: "o" in "lot", never as in "no" or "move".
u: "oo" in "look".
y: unknown in Standard English; cross between "e" and Polish "i", eg the "y" in the Yorkshire pronunciation of "Billy".

Three **specifically Polish** vowels:
ą: nasalized – like "ong" in "long" or French "on".
ę: nasalized – like French "un" (eg Lech Wałęsa).
ó: same sound as Polish "u".

Vowel combinations:
ie: pronounced y-e, eg "nie wiem" (I don't know): ny-e vy-em (not nee-veem).
eu: each letter pronounced separately as above, eg "E-u-ropa" (Europe).
ia: rather like "yah", eg "historia" (history): histor-i-yah.

Consonants:
Those which look the same as English but are different:
w: as "v" in "vine", eg "wino" pronounced "vino" (wine).
r: trilled (as in Scottish pronunciation of English r).
h: like the "ch" in Scottish "loch".
Some consonants are pronounced differently at **the end of a word** or syllable: b sounds like p, d like t, g like k, w like f.

Specifically Polish consonants:
ć = ci: "ch" as in "church".
ł: "dark l" sounding rather like a "w".
ń = ni: "soft n", sounding like "n-ye", eg "koń" (horse): kon-ye.

ś = si: "sh" as in "ship".
ź = zi: like the "j" of French "journal".
ż = rz: as in French "g" in "gendarme". (Note that the dot over the z is sometimes replaced by a bar through the letter's diagonal.)

Consonantal Pairs:
cz: "ch" (slightly harder than "ć" and "ci").
sz: "sh" (ditto "ś", "si").

dz: "d" as in "day" rapidly followed by "z" as in "zoo", eg "dzwon" (bell): d-zvon. At the end of a word is pronounced like "ts" as in "cats".
dż: "d-sh", eg "dżungla" (jungle): d-shun-gla.
dź: sharper than the above; at the end of a word is pronounced like "ć" (ch).
szcz: this fearsome-looking cluster is easy to pronounce – "sh-ch" as in "pushchair", eg "szczur" (rat): sh-choor.

A POLISH LANGUAGE GUIDE

BASIC WORDS

Tak	Yes	Teraz	Now	Więcej	More
Nie	No/not	Później	Later	Mniej	Less
Proszę	Please/you're welcome	Otwarty	Open	Mało	A little
		Zamknięty	Closed/shut	Duzo	A lot
Proszę bardzo	More emphatic than "proszę"	Wcześniej	Earlier	Tani	Cheap
		Dosyć	Enough	Drogi	Expensive
Dziękuję; dziekuję bardzo	Thank you	Tam	Over there	Dobry	Good
		Ten/ta/to	This one (masc/ fem/neuter)	Zły/niedobry	Bad
Gdzie	Where			Gorący	Hot
Kiedy	When	Tamten/ tamta/tamto	That one	Zimny	Cold
Dlaczego	Why			Z	With
Ile	How much	Wielki	Large	Bez	Without
Tu; tam	Here; there	Mały	Small	W	In
				Dla	For

BASIC PHRASES

Dzień dobry	Good day; hello	Co to znaczy po polsku?	What's the Polish for that?
Dobry wieczór	Good evening		
Dobra noc	Good night	Jestem tu na urlopie	I'm here on holiday
Cześć!	"Hi!" or "'Bye" (like Italian "ciao")	Jestem Brytyjczykiem/ Brytyjka	I'm British (male/ female)
Do widzenia	Goodbye	Irlandczykiem/Irlandką	Irish
Przepraszam	Excuse me (apology)	Mieszkam w . . .	I live in . . .
Proszę Pana/Pani	(ditto) requesting information	Dzisiaj	Today
		Jutro	Tomorrow
Jak się masz?	How are you? (informal)	Pojutrze	Day after tomorrow
Jak się Pan/Pani ma?	(ditto: formal male/female)	Wczoraj	Yesterday
		Chwileczkę	Moment! Wait a moment
Dobrze	Fine		
Czy Pan/Pani mówi po angielsku?	Do you speak English?	Rano	In the morning
		Po południu	In the afternoon
Rozumiem	I understand	Wieczorem	In the evening
Nie rozumiem	I don't understand	Gdzie jest . . .	Where is . . . ?
Nie wiem	I don't know	Jak dojechać do . . . ?	How do I get to . . . ?
Proszę mówić trochę wolniej	Please speak a bit more slowly	Która (jest) godzina?	What time is it?
Nie mówię dobrze po polsku	I don't speak Polish very well	Jak daleko jest do . . . ?	How far is it to . . . ?

ACCOMMODATION

Hotel	Hotel	*To drogo*	That's expensive
Noclegi	Lodgings	*To za drogo*	That's too expensive
Czy jest gdzieś tutaj hotel?	Is there a hotel nearby?	*Czy to obejmuje śniadanie?*	Does that include breakfast?
Czy Pan/Pani ma pokój?	Do you have a room?	*Czy nie ma tańszego?*	Do you have anything cheaper?
Pojedynczy pokój	Single room		
Podwójny pokój	Double room	*Czy mogę zobaczyć pokój?*	Can I see the room?
Będziemy jedną dobę	For one night (doba: 24 hours)	*Dobrze, wezmę*	Good, I'll take it
Dwie noce	Two nights	*Mam rezerwację*	I have a booking
Trzy noce	Three nights	*Czy możemy tu rozbić namioddy?*	Can we camp here?
Tydzień	A week		
Dwa tygodnie	Two weeks	*Czy jest gdzieś tutaj camping?*	Is there a campsite nearby?
Pokój z łazienką	With a bath		
Z prysznicem	With a shower	*Namiot*	Tent
Z balkonem	With a balcony	*Schronisko*	Cabin
Z ciepłą wodą	Hot water	*Schronisko młodzieżowe*	Youth hostel
Z bieżącą wodą	Running water	*Proszę o jadłospis*	The menu, please
Ile kosztuje?	How much is it?	*Proszę o rachunek*	The bill, please

TRAVELLING

Auto	Car	*W jedną stronę*	Single
Samolot	Aircraft	*Proszę z miejscówką*	I'd like a seat reservation
Rower	Bicycle	*Kiedy odjeżdża pociąg do Warszawy?*	When does the Warsaw train leave?
Autobus	Bus		
Prom	Ferry	*Czy muszę się przesiadać?*	Do I have to change?
Pociąg	Train		
Dworzec, samochód, stacja	Train station	*Z jakiego peronu odjedzie pociąg?*	Which platform does the train leave from?
Autobusowy	Bus station	*Ile to jest kilometrów?*	How many kilometres is it?
Taksówka	Taxi	*Ile czasu trwa podróż?*	How long does the journey last?
Autostop	Hitchhiking		
Piechotą	On foot	*Jakim autobusem do ... ?*	Which bus is it to ...?
Prosze bilet do ...	A ticket to ..., please	*Gdzie jest droga do ...?*	Where is the road to ...?
Bilet powrotny	Return	*Następny przystanek, proszę*	Next stop, please

SOME SIGNS

Wejście; wyjście	Entrance; exit/way out	*Peron*	Platform
Wstęp wzbroniony	No entrance	*Kasa*	Cash desk
Toaleta	Toilet	*Stop*	Stop
Dla panów; męski	Men	*Granica międzynarodowa*	Polish state frontier
Dla pan; damski	Women	*Rzeczpospolita Polska*	Republic of Poland
Zajęty	Occupied	*Uwaga; baczność*	Beware, caution
Wolny	Free, vacant	*Uwaga; niebezpieczeństwo*	Danger
Przyjazd; odjazd	Arrival; departure (train, bus)	*Policja (formerly: milicja)*	Police
Przylot; odlot	(ditto for aircraft)	*Informacja*	Information
Remont	Closed for renovation/ stocktaking	*Nie palić; palenie wzbronione*	No smoking
Ciągnąć; pchać	Pull; push	*Nie dotykać*	Do not touch
Nieczynny	Out of order; closed (ticket counters, etc)		

DRIVING

Samochód, auto	Car	Benzyna	Petrol/gas
Na lewo	Left	Stacja benzynowa	Petrol/gas station
Na prawo	Right	Olej	Oil
Prosto	Straight ahead	Woda	Water
Parking	Parking	Naprawić	To repair
Objazd	Detour	Wypadek	Accident
Koniec	End (showing when a previ-	Awaria	Breakdown
	ous sign ceases to be valid)	Ograniczenie	Speed limit
Zakaz wyprzedzania	No overtaking	prędkości	

DAYS, MONTHS AND DATES

Poniedziałek	Monday	Kwiecień	April	Poniedziałek, pierwzy	Monday, 1st
Wtorek	Tuesday	Maj	May	Kwiecień	April
Środa	Wednesday	Czerwiec	June	. . . drugi Kwiecień	. . . 2nd April
Czwartek	Thursday	Lipiec	July	. . . trzeci Kwiecień	. . . 3rd April
Piątek	Friday	Sierpień	August	Wiosna	spring
Sobota	Saturday	Wrzesien	September	Lato	summer
Niedziela	Sunday	Październik	October	Jesień	autumn
Styczeń	January	Listopad	November	Zima	winter
Luty	February	Grudzień	December	Wakacje	holidays
Marzec	March			Święto	bank holiday

NUMBERS

Jeden	1	Jedenaście	11	Trzydzieści	30	Czterysta	400
Dwa	2	Dwanaście	12	Czterdzieści	40	Pięćset	500
Trzy	3	Trzynaście	13	Pięćdziesiąt	50	Sześćset	600
Cztery	4	Czternaście	14	Sześćdziesiąt	60	Siedemset	700
Pięć	5	Piętaście	15	Siedemdziesiąt	70	Osiemset	800
Sześć	6	Szesnaście	16	Osiemdziesiąt	80	Dziewięćset	900
Siedem	7	Siedemnaście	17	Dziewięćdziesiąt	90	Tysiąc	1 000
Osiem	8	Osiemnaście	18	Sto	100	Milion	1 000 000
Dziewięć	9	Dziewietnaście	19	Dwieście	200		
Dziesięć	10	Dwadzieścia	20	Trzysta	300		

Dwadzieścia pięć	25
Sześćset dziewięćdziesiąt cztery	694
Trzy tysiące dwieściesiedemdziesiąt osiem	3278

GLOSSARIES

GENERAL TERMS

ALEJA Avenue (abbreviation al.).

BESKIDY Range of hills, eg Beskid Niski.

BIURO ZAKWATEROWAŃIA
Accommodation office.

BRAMA Gate.

CERKIEW (pl. CERKWIE) Orthodox church, or a church belonging to the Uniates, a church loyal to Rome but following Orthodox rites.

CMENTARZ Cemetery.

DOLINA Valley.

DOM House.

DOM KULTURY Community arts and social centre, literally a "Cultural House".

DOM WYCIECZKOWY Cheap, basic type of hotel.

DROGA Road.

DWÓR Country house traditionally owned by member of the *szchlachta* class.

DWORZEC Station.

GŁÓWNY Main – as in Rynek Główny, main square.

GÓRA (pl. GÓRY) Mountain.

GRANICA Border.

JEŻIORO Lake.

KANTOR Exchange office.

KAPLICA Chapel.

KAWIARNIA Café.

KATEDRA Cathedral.

KLASZTOR Monastery.

KOŚCIÓŁ Church.

KSIĄDZ Priest.

KSIĄŻĘ Prince, duke.

KSIĘGARNIA Bookshop.

KRAJ Country.

LAS Wood, forest.

MASYW Massif.

MIASTO Town. (Stare Miasto – old town; Nowe Miasto – new town.)

MOST Bridge.

NARÓD Nation, people.

NYSA River Neisse.

ODRA River Oder.

OGRÓD Gardens.

PAŁAC Palace.

PIWNICA Pub.

PLAC Square.

PLAŻA Beach.

POCZTA Post office.

POGOTOWIE Emergency.

POKÓJ (pl. Pokóje) Room.

POLE Field.

PROM Ferry.

PRZEDMIEŚCIE Suburb.

PRZYSTANEK Bus stop.

PUSZCZA Ancient forest.

RATUSZ Town Hall.

RESTAURACJA Restaurant.

RUCH Kiosk.

RYNEK Marketplace, commonly the main square in a town.

RZEKA River.

SEJM Parliament.

SHTETL Yiddish name for a rural town, usually with a significant Jewish population.

SKAŁA Rock, cliff.

SKANSEN Open-air museum with reconstructed folk architecture and art.

STOCZNIA Shipyards.

ŚWIĘTY Saint (abbreviation św.).

STAROWIERCY (Old Believers) Traditionalist Russian Orthodox sect, small communities of which survive in east Poland.

STARY Old.

SZLACHTA Term for the traditional gentry class, inheritors of status and land.

ULICA Street (abbeviation ul.).

WOJEWÓDZTWO Administrative district.

WIEŚ (pl. WSIE) Village.

WIEŻA Tower.

WINIARNIA Wine cellar.

WISŁA River Vistula.

WODOSPAD Waterfall.

WZGÓRZE Hill.

ZAMEK Castle.

ZDRÓJ Spa.

ZIEMIA Region.

ART/ARCHITECTURAL TERMS

AISLE Part of church to the side of the nave.

AMBULATORY Passage round the back of the altar, in continuation of the aisles.

APSE Vaulted termination of the altar end of a church.

ARON HA KODESH Place in synagogue for keeping the scrolls of the Torah (law), conventionally in the form of a niche in the eastern wall.

BAROQUE Exuberant architectural style of the seventeenth and early eighteenth centuries, characterized by ornate decoration, complex spatial arrangement and grand vistas. The term is also applied to the sumptuous style of painting of the same period.

BASILICA Church in which nave is higher than the aisles.

BIMAH Raised central platform in a synogogue containing the pulpit from which the Torah is read.

BLACK MADONNA National icon, an image of the Virgin and Child housed in the Jasna Góra monastery in Częstochowa.

CAPITAL Top of a column, usually sculpted.

CHANCEL Section of the church where the altar is situated, usually the east end.

CHOIR Part of church in which service is sung, usually beside the altar.

CRYPT Underground part of a church.

FRESCO Mural painting applied to wet plaster, so that colours immediately soak into the wall.

GOTHIC Architectural style with an emphasis on verticality, characterized by pointed arch and ribbed vault: introduced to Poland in the thirteenth century, surviving in an increasingly decorative form until well into the sixteenth century. The term is also used of paintings and sculpture of the period.

HALL CHURCH Church design in which all vaults are of approximately equal height.

ICONOSTASIS Screen with a triple door separating the sanctuary from the nave in Uniate and Eastern Orthodox churches.

JUGENDSTIL German version (encountered in western Poland) of Art Nouveau, a sinuous, highly decorative style of architecture and design from the period 1900–15.

MANNERISM Deliberately over-sophisticated style of late Renaissance art and architecture.

MANSARD Curb roof in which each face has two slopes, with the lower one steeper than the upper.

MATZEVAH An upright traditional Jewish tombstone adorned with inscriptions and symbolic ornamentation.

MEZUZAH Scroll containing handwritten parchment scrolls of the scriptures, traditionally placed in a small case and fixed on the righthand doorpost of a Jewish house.

MŁODA POLSKA (Young Poland) Turn-of-the-century cultural movement centred on Kraków.

NAVE Main body of the church, generally forming the western part.

NEOCLASSICAL Late eighteenth- and early nineteenth-century style of art and architecture returning to classical models as a reaction against Baroque and Rococo excesses.

POLYPTYCH Painting or carving on several hinged panels.

RENAISSANCE Italian-originated movement in art and architecture, inspired by the rediscovery of classical ideals.

ROCOCO Highly florid, light and graceful style of architecture, painting and interior design, forming the last phase of Baroque.

ROMANESQUE Solid architectural style of the late tenth to mid-thirteenth centuries, characterized by round-headed arches and geometrical precision. The term is also used for paintings of the same period.

ROMANTICISM Late eighteenth- and nineteenth-century movement, rooted in adulation of natural world and rediscovery of the country's rich historic heritage, strongly linked in Poland to the cause of national independence.

SECESSIONIST Style of early twentieth-century art and architecture, based in Germany and Austria, which reacted against academic establishments.

STUCCO Plaster used for decorative effects.

TRANSEPT Arms of a cross-shaped church, placed at ninety degrees to nave and chancel.

TRANSITIONAL Architectural style between Romanesque and Gothic.

TRIPTYCH Carved or painted altarpiece on three panels.

TROMPE L'OEIL Painting designed to fool the onlooker into believing that it's actually three-dimensional.

HISTORICAL AND POLITICAL GLOSSARY

ARIANS Radical Protestant grouping that gained a strong footing in the Reformation-era Polish-Lithuanian Commonweatlh.

ASTRO-HUNGARIAN EMPIRE Vast Habsburg-ruled domain incorporating most of Central Europe, enlarged to include Polish province of Galicia during the Partition period.

BALCEROWICZ, LESZEK Finance minister following the 1989 elections; responsible for introducing the post-communist programme of radical, free-market economic reform.

BIELECKI, JAN Solidarity adviser and young technocrat, based in Gdańsk; was prime minister from December 1990 to November 1991.

CENTRE AGREEMENT Political grouping formed by Lech Wałęsa in 1990, and subsequently estranged from him, critical of the supposedly slow pace of government reforms.

CHRISTIAN NATIONAL UNION (ZChN) Most important of the Catholic-based political parties formed in the early post-communist era.

CITIZENS MOVEMENT-DEMOCRATIC ACTION (ROAD) Coalition of intellectuals and former Solidarity activists formed to oppose Wałęsa's Centre Agreement. Key figures included the then prime minister Mazowiecki, Adam Michnik, Zbigniew Bujak and Bronisław Geremek. Became *Democratic Union* in 1991.

COMMONWEALTH Union of Poland, Lithuania, Royal Prussia and Livonia (Latvia); formed by Lublin Union (1569), it lasted until the Third Partition of 1795.

CONGRESS KINGDOM OF POLAND Russian-ruled province of Poland established in 1815, following the Congress of Vienna.

DEMOCRATIC LEFT ALLIANCE (SLD) Alliance of SDRP (Social Democracy of the Republic of Poland) and other post-communist forces. Effectively successor to the now defunct communist party (PZRP), from whose ranks both the current prime minister, Włodzimierz Cimoszewicz, and the president, Aleksander Kwaśniewski, are drawn.

DEMOCRATIC UNION (UD) Centrist political party which attracted strong support among former Solidarity intellectuals, now merged in the Freedom Union.

DUCAL PRUSSIA (East Prussia) The eastern half of the territory of the Teutonic Knights, converted into a secular duchy in 1525 and divided in 1945 between Poland and the Soviet Union.

EMIGRACJA Commonly used Polish term for the worldwide Polish community living outside the country.

FREEDOM UNION (UW) *Unia Wolności* Main centrist/liberal party founded as a successor to the UD when it merged with a smaller liberal party in 1994. Currently headed by Tadeusz Mazowiecki and a coterie of heavyweight former dissidents including Leszek Balcerowicz and 1995 presidential candidate manqué Jacek Kuroń.

GALICIA Southern province of Poland including Kraków incorporated into Austro-Hungarian Empire during the Partition period, granted autonomy in latter half of nineteenth century.

GEREMEK, BRONISŁAW Medieval historian at Warsaw University who acted as adviser to Wałęsa and the Solidarity movement. Elected leader of the Solidarity group in parliament after the June 1989 elections but resigned in November 1990. Now a key figure in the Freedom Union.

GIEREK, EDWARD Leader of the Communist Party in the 1970s, until removed following the strikes of summer 1980.

HABSBURG The most powerful imperial family in medieval Germany, operating from a power base in Austria.

HANSEATIC LEAGUE Medieval trading alliance of Baltic and Rhineland cities, numbering about a hundred at its fifteenth-century peak. Slowly died out in seventeenth century with competition from the Baltic nation-states and rise of Brandenburg-Prussia.

HASIDISM Mystical religious and social movement founded by Israel ben Elizer (1700–1760) known as *Baal Schem Tov*. Hasidism opposed rabbinical Judaism and preached joy in life through religious ecstasy, dance and song.

HETMAN Military commander; a state officer in the Polish-Lithuanian commonwealth era.

HOLY ROMAN EMPIRE Name of the loose confederation of German states (many now part of Poland) which lasted from 800 until 1806.

JAGIELLONIAN Dynasty of Lithuanian origin which ruled Poland-Lithuania from 1386 to 1572.

JARUZELSKI, WOJCIECH General of the armed forces, called in by the Party in 1981 to institute martial law and suppress Solidarity. His subsequent flexibility and negotiating skill helped to usher in democracy and he became president after the June 1989 elections, until the election of Wałęsa in December 1990.

KULTURKAMPF Campaign launched by German Chancellor Bismarck in the 1870s, aimed at suppressing Catholic culture (including the Polish language) inside German territories.

KUROŃ, JACEK Veteran opposition activist and key figure in Solidarity movement; served as minister of labour in the Mazowiecki government returning to the same position in the Suchocka administration. Stood as the Freedom Union's official candidate in the 1995 presidential elections.

KWAŚNIEWSKI, ALEKSANDER Former communist government minister in the 1980s elected as president in November 1995. Cuts a confident eloquent figure, though given political divisions over his communist background, it remains to be seen whether he can act as "president of the whole nation".

LUSTRATION Vexed controversy during the Olszewski premiership surrounding the question of prominent politicians supposed to have collaborated with the communist-era security services.

MARTIAL LAW Military crackdown instigated by General Jaruzelski in December 1981 and remaining in effect until summer 1983.

MAZOWIECKI, TADEUSZ Catholic lawyer and journalist and longtime adviser to Solidarity. Country's first post-communist prime minister who ran unsuccessfully for president against Wałęsa in December 1990. Currently leads the Freedom Union.

MICHNIK, ADAM Warsaw academic and leading Solidarity theoretician and activist. Currently chief editor of the independent daily *Gazeta Wyborcza*.

NAZI–SOVIET PACT (or MOLOTOV–RIBBENTROP PACT) 1939 agreement between Nazi Germany and the Soviet Union, which contained a secret clause to eliminate Poland from the map.

ODER-NEISSE LINE Western limit of Polish territory set by Yalta Agreement, 1945.

OLEKSY, JÓZEF Former communist who became prime minister in March 1995 following the resignation of Waldemar Pawłak, only to be forced out of office under a year later as a result of a spying scandel.

OLSZEWSKI, JAN Combative former dissident and lawyer who become prime minister at the end of 1991, his leadership floundering six months later (June 1992) over the **lustration** issue (see above).

PARTITION PERIOD Era from 1772 to 1918, during which Poland was on three occasions divided into Prussian, Russian and Austrian territories.

PAWŁAK, WALDEMAR Youthful Peasant Party (PSL) leader and prime minister from October 1993 to February 1995. Taciturn figure who found it hard to develop his popular appeal.

PIASTS Royal dynasty which forged the Polish state in the tenth century and ruled it until 1370; branches of the family continued to hold principalities, notably in Silesia, until 1675.

POLISH UNITED WORKERS PARTY (PZPR) Former communist party who disbanded themselves in January 1990, the majority forming a new Social Democratic Party.

POLONIANS Slav tribe which formed the embryonic Polish nation.

PRUSSIA Originally a Slavic Eastern Baltic territory, now divided between Poland and the Russian Federation. It was conquered by the Teutonic Knights in the thirteenth century and acquired in 1525 by the Hohenzollerns, who merged it with their own German possessions to form Brandenburg-Prussia (later shortened to Prussia).

ROUND TABLE AGREEMENT Pathbreaking bi-partisan agreement between Jaruzelski's communist government and the Solidarity opposition in spring 1989, leading to the elections in June of that year.

ROYAL PRUSSIA (or WEST PRUSSIA) Territory centred on the Wisła delta, originally the easternmost sector of Pomerania, renamed after its capture from the Teutonic Knights in 1466.

RUTHENIA A loose grouping of principalities, part of which formed Poland's former Eastern Territories.

SARMATISM Seventeenth-century Polish aristocratic cult based on the notion of their ancient Eastern ("Sarmatian") origins.

SOLIDARITY (Solidarność) The eastern bloc's first independent trade union, led by Lech Wałęsa, suppressed under martial law and relegalized in 1989, before forming the core of the new democratic government. Subsequently irrevocably split into pro- and anti-Wałęsa factions, it enjoyed something of a renaissance in the mid-1990s.

SUCHOCKA, HALINA Lawyer from Poznań chosen as Poland's first ever woman prime minister in summer 1992. A popular, if somewhat aloof figure.

TARTARS Mongol tribe who invaded Poland in the thirteenth century, some of them settling subsequently.

TEUTONIC KNIGHTS Quasi-monastic German military order who conquered parts of the eastern Baltic, establishing their own independent state 1226–1525.

TZADDIK Charismatic Hasidic religious teacher and leader belonging to hereditary dynasty.

UNIATES (also known as Greek Catholics) Eastern-rite Christians who, following the Union of Brest (1595), formally accepted the pope's authority, though they retained many Orthodox rites. Within modern Poland, Uniates comprise a mixture of Ukrainians, Lemks and Boyks.

WAŁĘSA, LECH Shipyard electrician who led strikes in the Gdańsk shipyards in 1980, leading to the establishment of the independent trade union, Solidarity, of which he became chairman. In this role, he opposed the communist government throughout the 1980s, and led negotiations in the Round Table Agreement of 1989. Following the June 1989 elections, he parted company with many of his former Solidarity allies, forcing a presidential contest, which he won in December 1990. Defeated in the next presidential elections (Nov 1995). Awarded the Nobel Peace Prize in 1983.

WAZA (Vasa) Swedish royal dynasty which ruled Poland 1587–1668.

WORKERS' DEFENCE COMMITTEE (KOR) Oppositional group formed in the mid-1970s, regarded by many as a precursor to Solidarity.

YALTA AGREEMENT 1945 agreement between the victorious powers which established Poland's (and Europe's) postwar borders.

AN A–Z OF STREET NAMES

The stars from the pantheon of Polish communist iconography after whom many streets were named after World War II have now largely disappeared. Since the Solidarity election victory of 1989 a systematic renaming of streets has been carried out, though in classic Polish style it took local authorities a lot longer to agree on new names than in, say, neighbouring Czech and Slovak republics, the whole process being held up by interminable local infighting. It's not the first time such a process has occurred either: nineteenth-century Russian and German street names were replaced by Polish ones after World War I, which themselves came down following the Nazi wartime occupation. Many older streets have simply reverted to their prewar names, the new ones showing a marked preference for Catholic identification. Remember that street names always appear in their genitive or adjectival form, eg Franciscan Street is Franciszkańska, Piłsudski Street is Piłsudskiego and Mickiewicz Street Mickiewicza.

General Władysław Anders (1892–1970) Renowned military figure who led the Polish troops was exiled to Siberia at the start of World War II and later returned to fight on the Allied side in the Middle East, then in Europe.

Józef Bem (1794–1850) Swashbuckling military figure who participated in the 1848 "Springtime of the Nations" in both Austria and Hungary.

General Zygmunt Berling (1896–1980) First commander-in-chief of communist-sponsored Polish forces in the Soviet Union

Bohaterów Getta Literally "Heroes of the Ghetto", in memory of the April 1943 Warsaw Ghetto Uprising against the Nazis.

Władysław Broniewski (1897–1962) Early socialist adherent of Piłsudski's World War I

Legions, revolutionary poet and famously unreformed drunkard.

Fryderyk Chopin (1810–49) (also sometimes spelt "Szopen" in Polish). Celebrated Romantic-era composer and pianist, long a national icon (see p.102).

Chrobrego Refers to Bolesław the Great, first king of Poland and the man who established the country as a definite independent state.

Maria Dąbrowska (1889–1965) Fine modern Polish writer best known for her epic novels.

Aleksander Fredro (1793–1876) Popular dramatist, especially of comedies.

Grunwald Landmark medieval battle (1410) where combined Polish-Lithuanian forces thrashed the Teutonic Knights.

Jan Kasprowicz (1860–1926) Popular peasant-born Neo-Romantic poet and voluminous translator of Western classics into Polish.

Jan Kochanowski (1530–84) Renaissance-era poet, the father of the modern Polish literary canon.

Maksymilian Kolbe (1894–1941) Catholic priest martyred in Auschwitz, canonized by Pope John Paul II.

Tadeusz Bór-Komorowski (1895–1966) Commander of AK (Home Army) forces during the 1944 Warsaw Uprising.

Maria Konopnicka (1842–1910) Children's story writer of the nineteenth century, adherent of the "Positivist" School which developed in reaction to the traditional national preference for Romanticism.

Mikołaj Kopernik (1473–1543) Indigenous name of the great astronomer known elsewhere as Copernicus, who spent much of his life in the Baltic town of Frombork.

Tadeusz Kościuszko. (1746–1817) Dashing veteran of the American War of Independence and leader of the 1794 Insurrection in Poland (see p.331).

Armii Krajowej (AK) The Home Army, forces of the wartime Polish resistance.

Józef Ignacy Krasicki (1735–1801) Enlightenment-era poet-bishop of Warmia, dubbed the "Polish Lafontaine".

Zygmunt Krasiński (1812–59) Author of *Nieboska Komedia*, one of the trio of Polish Romantic messianic greats.

Józef Kraszewski (1812–87) Hugely popular historical novelist. His novels (over 200 of them) cover everything from the early Piasts to the Partition era.

6 Kwietnia Battle of Racławice (1794) where Kościuszko's largely peasant army defeated the tsarist forces.

11 Listopada (11 November) Symbolically important post-World War I Polish Independence Day.

29 Listopada Start of (failed) November 1830 Uprising against the Russians.

1 Maja Labour Day.

3 Maja Famous democratic Constitution of 1791.

9 Maja Polish "V" Day – the Russian-declared end of World War II – one day after Britain and other western European countries.

Jan Matejko (1838–93) Patriotic *fin-de-siècle* painter closely associated with Kraków, where he lived most of his life.

Adam Mickiewicz (1798–1855) *The* Romantic Polish poet, a national figure considered kosher by just about everyone, former communist leaders included (see p.80).

Stanisław Moniuszko (1819–72) Romantic composer, popular in Poland but little known elsewhere.

Gabriel Narutowicz (1865–1922) First president of the Second Polish Republic, assassinated a few days after his nomination.

Ignacy Paderewski (1860–1941) Noted pianist and composer who became the country's first prime minister post-World War I and the country's regaining of independence.

Jan Paweł II. The incumbent Catholic pontiff and Polish national hero. Many streets are now renamed after Pope John Paul.

Józef Piłsudski (1867–1935) One of the country's most venerated military-political figures, key architect of the regaining of independence after World War I, and national leader in the late 1920s and early 1930s.

Józef Poniatowski (1767–1813) Nephew of the last Polish king who fought in numerous Polish and Napoleonic campaigns: an archetypal Polish military-Romantic hero.

Jerzy Popiełuszko Radical Solidarity-supporting priest murdered by the Security Forces in 1984, and since elevated to the ranks of national martyrs.

Bolesław Prus (1847–1912) Positivist writer, best known for quasi-historical novels such as *Pharaoh* and *Lalka* (The Doll).

Kazimierz Pułaski (1747–79) Polish-American hero of the US War of Independence.

Mikołaj Rej (1505–69) So-called "Father of Polish Literature", one of the first to write in the language.

Władysław Reymont (1867–1925) Nobel Prize-winning author of *The Peasants* and *The Promised Land*.

Władysław Sikorski (1881–1943). Prewar Polish prime minister and wartime commander-in-chief of Polish forces in the West.

Marie Skłodowska-Curie (1867–1934) Nobel Prize-winning scientist and discoverer of the radioactive elements radium and polonium.

Juliusz Słowacki (1809–49) Noted playwright and poet, one of the three Polish Romantic greats.

Henryk Sienkiewicz (1846–1916) Stirring historical novelist who won the Nobel Prize for his epic *Quo Vadis?*

Jan Sobieski (1635–96) Quintessentially Polish king famous for his celebrated rescue of Vienna (1683) from the Ottoman Turks.

15 Sierpnia Date of the battle of Warsaw (August 1920) that halted the Soviet offensive against Poland, popularly known as the "miracle on the Vistula".

Bohaterów Stalingradu "Heroes of Stalingrad", a reference to the turning point in the defeat of Nazi Germany; less common than it was, but one of the few communist names to survive.

22 Stycznia Date of the start of January Uprising of 1863 against the Russians.

Karol Świerczewski (1897–1947) One of the few commmunist figures to survive the post-1989 street name clearout (not everywhere though), a fact probably explained by his role in the controversial 1947 "Operation Vistula" (see p.338).

Świętego Ducha Literally "Holy Spirit", generally used in square names.

Świętej Trójcy Holy Trinity – another self-explanatory Catholic favourite.

Karol Szymanowski (1882–1937) Noted modern Polish classical composer, a long-time Zakopane resident.

Kazimierz (Przerwa) Tetmajer (1865–1940) Turn-of-the-century Neo-Romantic poet, part of the Kraków-based Młoda Polska school.

Westerplatte The Polish garrison the attack on whom by the Nazis in September 1939 signalled the start of World War II.

Wszystkich Świętych Literally "All Saints" – a popular Catholic festival.

Stanisław Ignacy Witkiewicz (1885–1939) Maverick modernist artist and writer whose plays anticipated postwar Theatre of the Absurd.

Stanisław Wyspiański (1867–1907) Renowned *Młoda Polska* era poet, playwright and painter best known for his plays *Wesele* (The Wedding) and *Wyzwolenie* (Liberation).

Wilsona After US President Woodrow Wilson, who supported the cause of Polish independence at the Versailles Conference (1919).

1 Września Start of World War II – the September 1939 Nazi invasion of Poland.

Kardynał Stefan Wyszyński (1901–81) Tenacious postwar Catholic primate of Poland, figurehead of popular resistance to communism.

Stefan Żeromski (1864–1925) One of the most renowned Polish novelists, a Neo-Romantic writer best known for his historical novel *Popioły* (The Ashes).

TOWN NAMES

Because Poland's borders have changed so often, many of its towns, including virtually all which were formerly German, have gone under more than one name. What follows is a checklist of names most of which can now be regarded as historical. The letters in parenthesis identity the language of the non-Polish form: G=German, OS=Old Slav, C=Czech, R=Russian, U=Ukrainian, L=Lithuanian, E=English.

Barczewo Wartenburg (G)
Biała Biala (G)
Bielsko Bielitz (G)
Bierutowice Brückenberg (G)
Bolków Bolkenhain (G)
Braniewo Braunsberg (G)
Brzeg Brieg (G)
Brześć Brest (E), Briest (R)
Brzezinka Birkenau (G)

Bydgoszcz Bromberg (G)
Bystrzyca Kłodzka Habelschwerdt (G)

Chełmno Kulm (G)
Chmielno Ludwigsdorf (G)
Chojnice Kornitz (G)
Cieplice Śląskie-Zdrój Bad Warmbrunn (G)
Cieszyn Teschen (G)
Czaplinek Tempelburg (G)

Daręóko Rügenwaldermünde (G)
Darłowko Rügenwalde (G)
Dąbie Altdamm (G)
Dobre Miasto Guttstadt (G)
Duszniki-Zdrój Bad Reinerz (G)

Elbląg Elbing (G)
Ełk Lyck (G)

Frombork Frauenburg (G)

Gdańsk Gyddanyzc (OS), Danczik, Dantzig,
   Danzig (G), Dantsic (E)
Gdynia Gdingen (OS), Gottenhafen (G)
Gierłoż Görlitz (G)
Giżycko Lötzen (G)
Głogów Glogau (G)
Gniezno Gnesen (G)
Goleniów Gollnow (G)
Góra Świętej Anny Sankt Annaberg (G)
Grudzidz Graudenz (G)
Grunwald Tannenberg (G)
Gryfice Greifenberg (G)

Hel Hela (G)
Henryków Heinrichau (G)

Inowrocław Hohensalza (G)
Iwięcino Eventin (G)

Jagniątków Agnetendorf (G)
Jawor Jauer (G)
Jelenia Góra Hirschberg (G)

Kadyny Cadinen (G)
Kamienna Góra Landeshut (G)
Kamień Pomorski Cammin (G)
Karłów Karlsberg (G)
Karpacz Krummhübel (G)
Kartuzy Karthaus (G)
Katowice Kattowitz (G)
Kętrzyn Rastenburg (G)
Kluki Klucken (G)
Kłodzko Glatz (G)

Kołczewo Kolzow (G)
Kołobrzeg Kolberg (G)
Koszalin Kösel (G)
Kraków Cracow (E), Krakau (G)
Kruszwica Kruschwitz (G)
Krzeszów Grüssau (G)
Książ Fürstenstein (G)
Kudowa-Zdrój Bad Kudowa (G)
Kwidzyn Marienwerder (G)

Lądek-Zdrój Bad Landeck (G)
Legnica Liegnitz (G)
Legnickie Pole Wahlstatt (G)
Leszno Lissa (G)
Lidzbark Warmiński Heilsberg (G)
Lubiąż Leubus (G)
Lwów Lemberg (G), Lvov (R), Ł'viv (U)
Łeba Leba (G)
Łódź Litzmannstadt, Lodsch (G)

Malbork Marienburg (G)
Międzygórze Wölfesgrund (G)
Międzyzdroje Misdroy (G)
Mikołajki Nikolaiken (G)
Milicz Militsch (G)
Morąg Mohrungen (G)
Mrągowo Sensburg (G)

Nysa Neisse (G)

Oleśnica Oels (G)
Oliwa Oliva (G)
Olsztyn Allenstein (G)
Olsztynek Hohenstein (G)
Opole Oppeln (G)
Orneta Wormditt (G)
Oświęcim Auschwitz (G)
Otmuchów Ottmachau (G)

Paczków Patschkau (G)
Pasłęk Preussisch Holland (G)
Polanica-Zdrój Bad Altheide (G)
Poznań Posen (G)
Pszczyna Pless (G)

Reszel Rössel (G)
Ruciane Nida Niedersee (G)

Słupsk Stolp (G)
Smołdzino Schmolsin (G)
Sobieszów Hermsdorf (G)
Sobótka Zobten (G)
Sopot Zoppot (G)

Sorkwity Sorquitten (G)
Stargard Szczeciński Stargard (G)
Strzegom Striegau (G)
Strzelno Strelno (G)
Szczecin Stettin (G)
Szczecinek Neustettin (G)
Szklarska Poręba Schreiberhau (G)
Sztutowo Stutthof (G)
Świdnica Swidnitz, Schweidnitz (G)
Święta Lipka Heiligelinde (G)
Świnoujście Swinemünde (G)

Tarnowskie Góry Tarnowitz (G)
Toruń Thorn (G)
Trzebiatów Treptow (G)
Trzebnica Trebnitz (G)
Trzemeszno Tremessen (G)

Ustka Stolpmünde (G)

Wałbrzych Waldenburg (G)
Wambierzyce Albendorf (G)
Warszawa Warsaw (E), Warschau (G)
Węgorzewo Angerburg (G)
Wilkasy Wolfsee (G)
Wilno Vilnius (L), Vilna (R)
Wiselka Neuendorf (G)
Wisła Weichsel (G)
Włocławek Leslau (G)
Wolin Wollin (G)
Wrocław Breslau (G), Wratislavia (OS),
  Vratislav (C)

Ząbkowice Śląskie Frankenstein (G)
Zielona Góra Grünberg (G)
Ziębice Münsterberg (G)
Żagań Sagan (G)
Żmigród Trachenberg (G)
Żukowo Zuchau (G)
Żywiec Saybusch (G)

ACRONYMS AND ORGANIZATIONS

ALMATUR Official student organization and travel office.
IT (Informator Turystyczny) Tourist information office.
NBP (Narodowy Bank Polski) Polish National Bank.
ORBIS State travel agency; abroad, Orbis offices are called POLORBIS.
PKO (Polska Kasa Oszczędności) State savings bank.
PKP (Polskie Koleje Państwowe) State railways.
PKS (Polska Kommunikacja Samochodowa) State bus company.
PTTK (Polskie Towarzystwo Turystyczno-Krajoznawcze) Tourist agency – literally Polish Tourism and Nature Lovers' Association.
PZMot (Polski Związek Motorowy) National motorists' association.
PZPR (Polska Zjednoczona Partia Robotnicza) Polish Communist Party – now defunct.

INDEX

Amsterdam	1-85828-086-9	£7.99	US$13.95	CAN$16.99
Andalucia	1-85828-094-X	8.99	14.95	18.99
Australia	1-85828-141-5	12.99	19.95	25.99
Bali	1-85828-134-2	8.99	14.95	19.99
Barcelona	1-85828-221-7	8.99	14.95	19.99
Berlin	1-85828-129-6	8.99	14.95	19.99
Brazil	1-85828-102-4	9.99	15.95	19.99
Britain	1-85828-208-X	12.99	19.95	25.99
Brittany & Normandy	1-85828-224-1	9.99	16.95	22.99
Bulgaria	1-85828-183-0	9.99	16.95	22.99
California	1-85828-181-4	10.99	16.95	22.99
Canada	1-85828-130-X	10.99	14.95	19.99
China	1-85828-225-X	15.99	24.95	32.95
Corsica	1-85828-089-3	8.99	14.95	18.99
Costa Rica	1-85828-136-9	9.99	15.95	21.99
Crete	1-85828-132-6	8.99	14.95	18.99
Cyprus	1-85828-182-2	9.99	16.95	22.99
Czech & Slovak Republics	1-85828-121-0	9.99	16.95	22.99
Egypt	1-85828-188-1	10.99	17.95	23.99
Europe	1-85828-159-8	14.99	19.95	25.99
England	1-85828-160-1	10.99	17.95	23.99
First Time Europe	1-85828-270-5	7.99	9.95	12.99
Florida	1-85828-184-4	10.99	16.95	22.99
France	1-85828-124-5	10.99	16.95	21.99
Germany	1-85828-128-8	11.99	17.95	23.99
Goa	1-85828-156-3	8.99	14.95	19.99
Greece	1-85828-131-8	9.99	16.95	20.99
Greek Islands	1-85828-163-6	8.99	14.95	19.99
Guatemala	1-85828-189-X	10.99	16.95	22.99
Hawaii: Big Island	1-85828-158-X	8.99	12.95	16.99
Hawaii	1-85828-206-3	10.99	16.95	22.99
Holland, Belgium & Luxembourg	1-85828-087-7	9.99	15.95	20.99
Hong Kong	1-85828-187-3	8.99	14.95	19.99
Hungary	1-85828-123-7	8.99	14.95	19.99
India	1-85828-200-4	14.99	23.95	31.99
Ireland	1-85828-179-2	10.99	17.95	23.99
Italy	1-85828-167-9	12.99	19.95	25.99
Kenya	1-85828-192-X	11.99	18.95	24.99
London	1-85828-231-4	9.99	15.95	21.99
Mallorca & Menorca	1-85828-165-2	8.99	14.95	19.99
Malaysia, Singapore & Brunei	1-85828-103-2	9.99	16.95	20.99
Mexico	1-85828-044-3	10.99	16.95	22.99
Morocco	1-85828-040-0	9.99	16.95	21.99
Moscow	1-85828-118-0	8.99	14.95	19.99
Nepal	1-85828-190-3	10.99	17.95	23.99
New York	1-85828-171-7	9.99	15.95	21.99
Pacific Northwest	1-85828-092-3	9.99	14.95	19.99

Paris	1-85828-235-7	8.99	14.95	19.99
Poland	1-85828-168-7	10.99	17.95	23.99
Portugal	1-85828-180-6	9.99	16.95	22.99
Prague	1-85828-122-9	8.99	14.95	19.99
Provence	1-85828-127-X	9.99	16.95	22.99
Pyrenees	1-85828-093-1	8.99	15.95	19.99
Rhodes & the Dodecanese	1-85828-120-2	8.99	14.95	19.99
Romania	1-85828-097-4	9.99	15.95	21.99
San Francisco	1-85828-185-7	8.99	14.95	19.99
Scandinavia	1-85828-039-7	10.99	16.99	21.99
Scotland	1-85828-166-0	9.99	16.95	22.99
Sicily	1-85828-178-4	9.99	16.95	22.99
Singapore	1-85828-135-0	8.99	14.95	19.99
Spain	1-85828-240-3	11.99	18.95	24.99
St Petersburg	1-85828-133-4	8.99	14.95	19.99
Thailand	1-85828-140-7	10.99	17.95	24.99
Tunisia	1-85828-139-3	10.99	17.95	24.99
Turkey	1-85828-242-X	12.99	19.95	25.99
Tuscany & Umbria	1-85828-243-8	10.99	17.95	23.99
USA	1-85828-161-X	14.99	19.95	25.99
Venice	1-85828-170-9	8.99	14.95	19.99
Vietnam	1-85828-191-1	9.99	15.95	21.99
Wales	1-85828-245-4	10.99	17.95	23.99
Washington DC	1-85828-246-2	8.99	14.95	19.99
West Africa	1-85828-101-6	15.99	24.95	34.99
More Women Travel	1-85828-098-2	9.99	14.95	19.99
Zimbabwe & Botswana	1-85828-186-5	11.99	18.95	24.99

Phrasebooks

Czech	1-85828-148-2	3.50	5.00	7.00
French	1-85828-144-X	3.50	5.00	7.00
German	1-85828-146-6	3.50	5.00	7.00
Greek	1-85828-145-8	3.50	5.00	7.00
Italian	1-85828-143-1	3.50	5.00	7.00
Mexican	1-85828-176-8	3.50	5.00	7.00
Portuguese	1-85828-175-X	3.50	5.00	7.00
Polish	1-85828-174-1	3.50	5.00	7.00
Spanish	1-85828-147-4	3.50	5.00	7.00
Thai	1-85828-177-6	3.50	5.00	7.00
Turkish	1-85828-173-3	3.50	5.00	7.00
Vietnamese	1-85828-172-5	3.50	5.00	7.00

Reference

Classical Music	1-85828-113-X	12.99	19.95	25.99
Internet	1-85828-198-9	5.00	8.00	10.00
Jazz	1-85828-137-7	16.99	24.95	34.99
Opera	1-85828-138-5	16.99	24.95	34.99
Reggae	1-85828-247-0	12.99	19.95	25.99
Rock	1-85828-201-2	17.99	26.95	35.00
World Music	1-85828-017-6	16.99	22.95	29.99

Good Vibrations!

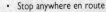

SLEEP EASY
BOOK AHEAD

AUSTRALIA
02 261 1111

CANADA
FREEPHONE 0800 663 5777

DUBLIN
01 301766

LONDON
0171 836 1036

BELFAST
01232 324733

GLASGOW
0141 332 3004

WASHINGTON
0202 783 6161

NEW ZEALAND
09 379 4224

IBN INTERNATIONAL BOOKING NETWORK

Call any of these numbers and your credit card secures a good nights sleep ...

in more than 26 countries

up to six months ahead

with immediate confirmation

HOSTELLING INTERNATIONAL

Budget accommodation you can **Trust**